# PEOPLING INDIANA:
# THE ETHNIC EXPERIENCE

# PEOPLING INDIANA: THE ETHNIC EXPERIENCE

EDITED BY ROBERT M. TAYLOR, JR., AND CONNIE A. McBIRNEY

INTRODUCTION BY JOHN BODNAR

INDIANA HISTORICAL SOCIETY
INDIANAPOLIS 1996

©1996 Indiana Historical Society. All rights reserved

Printed in the United States of America

The paper in this publication meets the minimum requirements of American
National Standard for Information Sciences—Permanence
of Paper for Printed Library Materials, ANSI Z39.48-1984. ∞

Library of Congress Cataloging-in-Publication Data

Peopling Indiana: the ethnic experience / edited by Robert M. Taylor,
  Jr. and Connie A. McBirney; introduction by John Bodnar.
      p.    cm.
    Includes bibliographical references (p.  ) and index.
    ISBN 0-87195-112-6
      1. Ethnology—Indiana—History.  2. Indiana—History.  I. Taylor,
Robert M., 1941-  .  II. McBirney, Connie A., 1954-  .
III. Indiana Historical Society.
F535.A1P46   1996
305.8′009772—dc20                             96-2850
                                                     CIP

# CONTENTS

# PREFACE

This volume is the final and most ambitious product of an ethnic history project launched in 1989 by the Indiana Historical Society. Two years previously, 1987, the Society completed a successful project celebrating the bicentennial of the Northwest Ordinance. Having exposed the public to the significance of the famed document in opening the West for settlement, what better way to proceed, we surmised, than to give an accounting of the peopling of the state in all its ethnic and national variegation. We had an inkling that viewing Indiana through time would reveal it to be more heterogeneous than assumed. Only bits and pieces of the state's rich history of diversity had been unearthed, and no single publication existed that attempted to survey the past and present of the state's ethnic composition. This book, then, fills an important conceptual and informational gap in Indiana's cultural and social history.

After receiving from around the state many positive responses to a questionnaire asking if a project on Indiana's ethnic groups had merit, we planned and carried out a number of activities around this subject. In 1989 the Society embarked on the project by bringing to Indiana the French musical ensemble Lo Jai, then on a nationwide tour, along with Bon Jolais, an Indiana band, which drew attention through song to the French, the earliest known European nationality to explore and inhabit the Indiana territory. In 1990 the Society's calendar featured photographs of Hoosier ethnic groups and individuals. In 1991 the Society's annual photography contest highlighted the ethnic theme. Also in 1991 the staff completed an exhibition entitled *Who Do You Think You Are?* The exhibition, using photographs, maps, statistics, and graphics, examined the definition of ethnicity, reasons for migration, settlement patterns, stereotypes, and family life. After a yearlong circuit to eighteen sites around the state, the exhibition became part of the Society's traveling exhibits program. In the fall of 1992 the Society sponsored a onetime presentation of the play, *The Melting Pot*, performed by the Indianapolis Civic Theatre at the Madame Walker Urban Life Center and Theatre in downtown Indianapolis. The Israel Zangwill classic, first produced in 1908, dramatized his faith in America's ability to forge a new nationality, a new ethnicity, from its different peoples. Before curtain time, playgoers could enjoy a sampling of ethnic cuisine. The topic of ethnicity took center stage at the Society's 1992 annual meeting, which served the double function of allowing us, through authors' presentations, to preview the contents of the forthcoming ethnic history book and to give recognition to the Columbus quincentennial then in progress. During the life of the project the Society's library gathered ethnic materials, while the grant-making apparatus of the institution focused on relevant studies.

Through all the activities supporting the ethnic theme the book remained the major goal. The most daunting of responsibilities in the beginning of the book's life entailed the selection of ethnic groups and the recruitment of authors to write the essays. We had early on through analyses of census records made a list of over eighty races and nationalities that at one time or another set foot in Indiana. Through collapsing nationalities into broad headings, such as Scandinavians, Hispanics, Southeast Asians, Middle Easterners, Baltic States, and so forth, we created twenty-nine chapters, plus one on midwest ethnicity in 1850 and the introduction, and thereby touched on many, but not all, of the past and present ethnic groups that populated the state.

The recruitment of authors presented a greater problem than determining which groups to include in the book. We aimed to find individuals who either had personal knowledge of a particular group or had previously researched and written on it (preferably both), and, in either case, had the seasoning necessary to conduct competent research and to write an essay that met the standards of the educated public as well as the scholar. It took well over a year to match author and subject. The halls of academe yielded a number of specialists in the race or nationality we sought but few had direct knowledge of the Indiana experience. Nevertheless, they enthusiastically signed on to the project and brought a wide historical perspective to the localized subject. Some scholars participated because they belonged to the ethnic group under investigation, though not an expert on that race or nationality. In other cases we relied on talented lay persons, professionals from a variety of fields, whose background linked them with the subject needing attention. All in all, we sought to avoid, on the one hand, the antiquarian or filiopietistic, and, on the other hand, the esoteric or narrow scholastic unable to communicate to a broad audience.

The authors were given fairly wide latitude to structure their own essays. Beside some stylistic directions, they received few initial instructions. Each contributor was given a copy of *They Chose Minnesota: A Survey of the State's Ethnic Groups* (1981), arguably the finest history yet produced of ethnic population in any one state. We requested authors to consider this volume as a model for the quality of essays desired in the Indiana book. In addition, we urged each writer to review the monumental *Harvard Encyclopedia of American Ethnic Groups* (1980) edited by Stephan Thernstrom, and from that work's "Introduction" each author received a copy of the "Checklist Outline for Group Entries." The outline contains chronological and thematic suggestions for organizing an essay. Beyond this, we asked writers to aim at treating each ethnic group in its varied locales throughout Indiana and also chronologically from the beginnings of settlement in the state to the present. In addition, we pressed them to balance the "contributions" or "gifts" narrative of their particular group with an objective assessment of the group's adjustments to life in Indiana. They were asked not to whitewash inter- and intra-cultural conflict. Finally, we wanted them to keep in mind our need for photographs, maps, and other graphics for the publication.

From the start, an occasional newsletter alerted the authors to developments in the project and detailed the range of items mailed to them pertinent to studying ethnicity in Indiana. For example, they received a copy of the *1876 Indiana Atlas,* along with published data for the censuses of 1890 through 1990. We contracted to have compiled data on ethnicity from the 1850 and 1880 manuscript censuses of Indiana. The abstracting and aggregating of foreign birthplace for Indiana residents in 1850 and 1880 turned out to be exceptional outgrowths of the project. On the other hand, the Hoosier ethnic count from the 1860 census was readily available because of a recent Society undertaking to computerize that census's information. Drawing from both in-house-generated and published accounts, we transformed the census data into machine-readable tables, hard copies of which we forwarded

to the authors. Several of these exercises are reproduced here in an appendix. Also to the authors went registers of ethnic organizations in various parts of the state, lists of relevant journals, an alphabetical register by ethnic group of manuscript collections in the Society's library, relevant articles out of books, newspaper items, information on the 1910 Dillingham Report, and so forth.

The different ethnic and academic backgrounds of the authors and the degree of freedom given them to structure their essays contributed to varied results. The symmetry of carefully formulated and rigidly imposed instructions of composition gave way, in this case, to idiomatic styles, some more academic, others more anecdotal, some more based in secondary rather than primary sources, others grounded in interviews or surveys of contemporaries, while still others preferred to give a greater weight to certain aspects of an ethnic group's experience. Thus, the reader should not expect essays that in all particulars are consistent with some orthodox standard of writing history. Occasionally some warmth and devotion, even zeal, shines through and gives the story a personal and human dimension.

Certainly not all ethnic groups or nationalities are represented in this volume. We had to make choices and in a few cases the choices were made for us because of lack of sources, the failure to match author with subject, assigned but incomplete manuscripts at the time of publication, or simply not knowing of the existence in the state of a particular nationality. The editors apologize for falling short or slighting any person or group, and we can only hope that our effort stimulates like efforts until the universe of diversity in the state is rightfully and correctly made public. We do think a beginning is made in this book.

Robert M. Taylor, Jr.
Connie A. McBirney

# ACKNOWLEDGMENTS

A project of this magnitude reaches print and the public only through a massive injection of hard work, good will, and proficiency from many individuals and institutions. Peter T. Harstad, executive director of the IHS, suggested the ethnic theme, and the board of trustees added its all-important approval and has continued to support the project, as has Raymond L. Shoemaker, administrative director. Every division of the Society has contributed. The library, under the direction of Bruce L. Johnson, played a major role in helping the authors locate manuscripts, books, and photographs. Of particular long-term assistance has been Susan S. Sutton, visual collections coordinator, Stephen J. Fletcher, curator of visual collections, Wilma L. Gibbs, a program archivist and editor of *Black History News & Notes,* and Kim Charles Ferrill, photographer for the IHS. Thomas K. Krasean, director of the Community Relations Division, and Ray Boomhower, public relations coordinator, have seen that the project received generous doses of publicity.

The Publications Division, under the leadership of Thomas A. Mason, has been most directly involved. Paula Corpuz, IHS senior editor, has been with the book project from the beginning and has overseen, so capably as always, every aspect of its production. In copyediting the manuscripts and preparing the index Corpuz had able assistance from editor Shirley S. McCord and editorial assistants Kathleen M. Breen and George Hanlin. Jeanette Vanausdall consulted on the style and content of a number of the essays. Elizabeth Van Allen read and helped shape the front matter of the book. We want to thank, also, Margaret Bierlein, secretary of the Education Division, for her indispensable coordination of many of the details associated with the book's development. The Education Division's office also generated the maps for each chapter. These maps reflect 1994 boundaries and may not indicate a nation's or area's boundaries at the time of an individual's immigration.

As the IHS reaches statewide and beyond with its publications and programs it becomes indebted to many persons, and this book is no exception. Some acknowledgments are appended to the individual chapters in the book. Here we want to pay special gratitude to all the libraries, archives, museums, officials, teachers, and others who willingly responded to our call for guidance through the state's mosaic of ethnic literature, personalities, and locales. Our initial exploration into ethnic history, in 1987, led us to the Minnesota Historical Society and to Deborah L. Miller, then research supervisor, who met with us and gave us the benefit of her experience in helping to produce *They Chose Minnesota.* Joel Wurl of the Immigration History Research Center in St. Paul, Minnesota, informed us of Indiana-related items at that important repository.

When we launched the project we turned to persons in the state who we knew had an immediate knowledge of resources. Especially we want to thank Steve McShane, director of the Calumet Regional Archives, a treasure trove of ethnic documents. As well, Theodore Mason and Eileen Cvitkovich of the East Chicago Public Library generously allowed us use of their institution's enviable collection of ethnic materials. We benefited from the discussions of the project with James Lane, Lance Trusty, Jay Dolan, Charles Guthrie, Rebecca Shoemaker, Sylvia Neely, Peter Sehlinger, Sabine Jessner, Thomas Griffin, Irving Katz, John Martin Smith, and June Alexander. Julie Miller and Philip Hartzler carefully compiled statistics from the 1850 and 1880 federal censuses. Ann Leonard Willson, Ken Schoon, and Amy Fletcher helped supply photographs as did many others (check the credit line on the photographs). Michael Hawfield and Walter Font of the Allen County Fort Wayne Historical Society permitted us to explore their archive on alien registrations and settlement houses. Robert Carter of Indiana State University's Cunningham Library fed us information on ethnic documents housed in Special Collections. Mary Renshaw, Northern Indiana Historical Society, Priscilla Felton, La Porte County Historical Society Museum, and Deborah Peters, Lake County Public Library, sent us information on their area's ethnic makeup. Vicki Nelson, of the Indiana University School of Business, worked closely with us to retrieve 1980 census data. Kathleen Van Nuys, columnist for the *Indianapolis News,* not only met with us and wrote about the project, but also gave us free access to her "Weekly Ethnic Series" of 1977–78, brought together in her publication *Indy International.* Ernie Hernandez also permitted us to utilize a series of columns he wrote in 1983–84 for Gary's *Post-Tribune,* which the newspaper in 1984 published under the title *Ethnics in Northwest Indiana.* The Nationalities Council of Indiana, Inc., and its president Dan Anderson, proved a constant source of enlightenment on ethnic matters, and its newsletter *The Ethnic Hoosier* graciously gave space to our project.

To John Bodnar a special word of thanks for his endorsement of the project, his willingness to share with us his vast knowledge of the ethnic experience, and his ready acceptance of an invitation to write the introduction that fittingly leads off this volume. Bodnar begins the process of synthesizing the story of Indiana's ethnic experience, a service we hope others will take up and expand. To the authors another special thank you for lending their time and talents to uncovering lives and events that make up the history of diversity in Indiana.

# CONTRIBUTORS

**James A. Baldwin** is associate librarian, University Libraries, Indiana University-Purdue University at Indianapolis. His degrees include an M.L.S. from Indiana University. He is also a trained geographer with extensive field experience in, and numerous publications on, the islands of the Pacific Ocean and Australia.

**Paulette Pogorzelski Bannec** is a second-generation descendant of Polish immigrants and was raised in a Polish neighborhood in northwest Indiana. She now resides at Fremont in the northeast corner of Indiana, where she substitutes in the local schools. She has an M.A.L.S. from Valparaiso University and has taught at Purdue University Calumet, Calumet College of St. Joseph, and Tri-State University.

**Harbans Singh Bhola** received his Ph.D. in education from Ohio State University. He joined the Indiana University faculty in 1970. Bhola has published widely in the areas of educational innovation and social intervention and evaluation of policy and program impact. Three of his books have been published by UNESCO.

**Carolyn S. Blackwell** is an associate faculty member in the history department of Indiana University-Purdue University at Indianapolis. She received her Ph.D. from Purdue University. A contributor to *The Encyclopedia of Indianapolis*, recently Blackwell has had essays on German Jews published in *German American Emigration and Settlement Patterns of German Communities in North America* (1995).

**Frank W. Blanning** of Indianapolis passed away during this book project. An accomplished educator, he served in the administration at Hanover College and in many distinguished capacities in the Middle East, including Dean of Students for American University in Cairo, Egypt, and adviser to the Saudi Arabian Ministry of Education. He taught at Franklin College and the University of Indianapolis.

**John Bodnar** is professor of history, Indiana University, Bloomington, and directs the Oral History Research Center at that school. The author of numerous books and articles on American ethnic groups, including the highly regarded *The Transplanted*, Bodnar most recently has edited and contributed to *Bonds of Affection: Americans Define Their Patriotism* (1996). He is past president of the Immigration History Society.

**Carl Cafouros**, an Indianapolis attorney, received his Doctor of Jurisprudence degree from Indiana University School of Law. He has an M.A. in history from the University of Illinois at Champaign/Urbana where his thesis focused on the Indianapolis Greek community. He contributed the entry on the Greeks to *The Encyclopedia of Indianapolis*.

**Inta Gale Carpenter** is the assistant research scientist/scholar and associate director, Special Projects, Folklore Institute, Indiana University, Bloomington. Carpenter received her Ph.D. from Indiana University. Active in folklore and ethnic organizations, including the American Association for the Advancement of Baltic Studies, she has published widely in both fields, most recently in a special issue of *Folklore in Use 2/2*.

**Linda Dégh** is retired Distinguished Professor of Folklore, Indiana University, Bloomington. She is past president of the American Folklore Society and edited *Indiana Folklore* for two decades. She has conducted field research on the Hungarian diaspora in North America and has written extensively on ethnic Hungarians.

**James J. Divita** is professor of history at Marian College, Indianapolis. He received his doctorate from the University of Chicago. Divita has written extensively on the Italian and Slovenian communities and Catholicism and was a major contributor on the subjects to *The Encyclopedia of Indianapolis*. In 1995 the Holy Rosary Pastoral Council and the Italian Heritage Society of Indiana published his *L'italia on the White River*.

**William W. Giffin** is professor of history at Indiana State University. A Ph.D. from Ohio State University, Giffin, in a number of published articles and presentations, has illumined the lives of midwestern African Americans, Irish, and Scots. In 1995 he presented a paper on Irish Americans in the twentieth century to the Indiana German Heritage Society. He has served as treasurer of the Indiana Association of Historians since 1983.

**Elizabeth Glenn** teaches anthropology at Ball State University, Muncie, Indiana. An Indiana University Ph.D., she is an expert in the ethnohistory of Native Americans, particularly in Indiana. Glenn has consulted in the field and participated extensively in public and policy matters related to Native Americans. Most recently she contributed to *The Encyclopedia of Indianapolis*.

**Giles R. Hoyt** is professor, Department of German, Indiana University-Purdue University at Indianapolis. He took his Ph.D. at the University of Illinois at Champaign/Urbana. He serves as associate dean of International Programs at IUPUI. A prolific author, he most recently wrote several articles on Germans in Indianapolis for *The Encyclopedia of Indianapolis*. He is a board member of the Society for German-American Studies.

**Lilia Georgiev Judson** received a B.A. degree in political science, with a concentration in East European studies, from Indiana University, Bloomington, and a J.D. from Indiana University School of Law. She has served as the executive secretary of the Indiana Judicial Study Commission and presently directs the Division of State Court Administration.

**Mary Leuca** is outreach coordinator and visiting assistant professor in education at Purdue University Calumet. She has degrees from Northwestern University and Indiana University, and a Ph.D. from Purdue University. As a Fulbright Scholar she conducted research at the University of Cluj, Romania. Her publications and honors in ethnic studies reflect her interest in international education.

**Justin H. Libby** is associate professor of history at Indiana University-Purdue University at Indianapolis. He received his Ph.D. from Michigan State University and took his undergraduate degree in Tokyo from Waseda University. He is the adviser to the Indiana Board of Trade on Japanese Business Policies and is the author of *The Irresolute Years: American Congressional Opinion toward Japan, 1937–1941* (1984).

**Gordon R. Mork** is professor of history at Purdue University with a Ph.D. from the University of Minnesota. His professional expertise lies in twentieth-century German history and the Holocaust, but he is of Scottish descent and is a member of the 42nd Royal Highlanders of Lafayette, Indiana. He recently contributed "Thinking Historically in the Classroom," to *Perspectives: American Historical Association Newsletter* (1995).

**Helen Jean M. Nugent** is professor of history, Franklin College. Her Ph.D. is from Michigan State University. She founded and directed the distinguished Canadian Studies Program at the college at Franklin. In 1996 she assumed the chair of the history department. A recent publication is her contribution on the Canadians to *The Encyclopedia of Indianapolis*.

**Elisabeth E. Orr** is nearing completion of her Ph.D. at Indiana University and is presently living in California where she teaches part-time at Long Beach City College. Her master's thesis looked at Korean immigrants in Indianapolis, and she contributed an entry on the Koreans to *The Encyclopedia of Indianapolis*.

**Cyriac K. Pullapilly** took his Ph.D. at the University of Chicago and presently teaches history at Saint Mary's College, Notre Dame, Indiana, where he directs that school's College Semester around the World Program. He has published recently in *The Encyclopedia of Reformation* and the *Harvard Theological Review*.

**Gregory S. Rose** is associate dean of the Marion campus of Ohio State University and is associate professor in the Geography Department. He received his Ph.D. in geography from Michigan State University. Rose has contributed articles on the distribution of Indiana ethnic groups to *The Encyclopedia of Indianapolis* and to the *Indiana Magazine of History*, among others.

**Stewart Rafert** of Newark, Delaware, graduated from Earlham College and completed his Ph.D. at the University of Delaware. Since 1982 he has worked closely with the Miami Indians of Indiana to restore federal recognition of the tribe. His book *The Miami Indians of Indiana: A Persistent People, 1654–1994* was published by the Indiana Historical Society in 1996.

**Ophelia Georgiev Roop** is associate librarian, University Libraries, Indiana University-Purdue University at Indianapolis. She took her undergraduate degree from Indiana University in Russian Language and Slavic Studies and her M.L.S. from the same institution. She recently contributed the entry "Eastern Orthodox Churches" to *The Encyclopedia of Indianapolis*.

**Leo Schelbert**, a native of Switzerland, is professor of history, University of Illinois at Chicago. He took his Ph.D. from Columbia University. A past president of the Swiss American Historical Society and editor of that organization's publications, Schelbert has authored numerous books and articles on the Swiss, his most recent being *America Experienced: Eighteenth and Nineteenth Century Accounts of Swiss Immigrants* (1995).

**R. Keith Schoppa** is professor of history at Valparaiso University, Valparaiso, Indiana. He received his Ph.D. from the University of Michigan. Widely published in

Chinese history, particularly the twentieth century, his most recent book is *Blood Road: The Mystery of Shen Dingyi in Revolutionary China* (1995). In 1994 he was named Indiana Professor of the Year by the Carnegie Foundation for the Advancement of Teaching.

**Monsignor Joseph Semancik** is a priest of the diocese of Gary, diocesan director of Catholic Charities, and pastor of Sacred Heart (Slovak) Church in East Chicago. His Ph.D. is from the University of Chicago. He helped organize the Indiana Catholic Conference. A major figure in a variety of community endeavors, he has published in the area of Catholic charities and has served on the editorial board of the journal *Social Thought*.

**Samuel Shapiro**, a South Bend resident, is a retired associate professor from the University of Notre Dame. He received his Ph.D. from Columbia University. He is the author of *Invisible Latin America* and editor of *Man and Society in Latin America*. He has contributed over one hundred articles to leading magazines such as *The London Economist*, *The Nation*, and *The New Republic*.

**Robert P. Swierenga** retired this year as professor of history at Kent State University and now is the A. C. Van Raalte Research Professor at Hope College, Holland, Michigan. He received his Ph.D. from the University of Iowa. His ten books and more than eighty articles have focused largely on rural, religious, and Dutch history and historical methods. His most recent book is *The Forerunners: Dutch Jewry in the North American Diaspora* (1994).

**Emma Lou Thornbrough** passed away on 16 December 1994. She received her Ph.D. in history from the University of Michigan and launched a long and productive career teaching at Butler University and researching African Americans in Indiana. Among her many published works are the two classics *The Negro in Indiana before 1900* (1957) and *Indiana in the Civil War Era* (1965).

**William Van Vugt** is professor of history at Calvin College in Grand Rapids, Michigan. He earned his Ph.D. at the London School of Economics and Political Science (University of London). Van Vugt's most recent publication detailed the life of Samuel Fowler Smith, an English shoemaker, which appeared in the *Indiana Magazine of History*. His book on British immigration to the United States in the mid-nineteenth century will be published in 1997.

**Aurele J. Violette** is associate professor of history, Indiana University-Purdue University Fort Wayne. He received his Ph.D. from Ohio State University. Though many of his scholarly publications are in Russian history his background is French Canadian, and he has spent considerable time studying American and Canadian French history. Most recently he has contributed "Doing History on the Internet" in *Internet World*.

**Natalie Vujovich**, a grandchild of Serbian immigrants, grew up in East Chicago, Indiana, and graduated from Washington High School. She did her undergraduate work at Vassar with a major in drama and minors in child study and history and received an M.A. in English at Purdue University Calumet. She taught high school in the Calumet Region, and most recently the Highland, Indiana, resident taught English to refugees from Sarajevo.

**Alan H. Winquist** is professor of history, Taylor University, Upland, Indiana. This New York native did graduate work at the University of Stockholm and received his Ph.D. at New York University. His books include *Scandinavians and South Africa: Their Impact on Cultural, Social and Economic Development before 1900* (1978) and *Swedish- American Landmarks: Where to Go and What to See* (1995).

# INTRODUCTION

## Ethnic History in America and Indiana

JOHN BODNAR

In 1993 *Newsweek* magazine asked a sample of Americans what they thought about immigration. Although most respondents felt immigration was good for the nation in the past, a majority thought it was undesirable in the present.[1] What the modern survey could not convey was that Americans have always been ambivalent about immigration and ethnic diversity. Some have valued the contributions immigrants made to economic growth. It was for this reason that midwestern states attempted to recruit newcomers in the nineteenth century. Others, however, feared for the future of American institutions and imagined that strange newcomers would not exhibit the same devotion to the values of democracy and freedom as the native born. In recent times employers dependent upon immigrant labor, such as agricultural interests in California, have lobbied to sustain the flow of unskilled workers. But many other Americans, often forgetting their own immigrant ancestry, have supported measures restricting immigration or denying newcomers access to various forms of government assistance. Whatever side one takes, the historical study of immigration and ethnic diversity in the United States makes it clear that despite controversy people of varying backgrounds continued to come to the United States and make a place for themselves regardless of whether they were welcome or not.

Both America and Indiana were affected deeply by the continual arrival of people with distinctive cultures. Whether the portal was Plymouth Rock, Ellis Island, or a train station in Hammond, new settlers, often with beliefs or traits vastly different from the majority, entered the nation and its states to play an active role in social and political events. While some fled political turmoil or religious persecution, most were motivated by economic considerations and were seeking places to earn a living. Some came to stay and others intended to return to a homeland. Although immigrants were often at the center of disputes, they invariably played vital historical roles wherever they located.

The volume of immigration to the United States was staggering. From 1820 to 1975 over forty-seven million people came as immigrants. That figure included eight million from the Western Hemisphere, two million from Asia, and nearly thirty-six million from Europe. By the time of the first federal census in 1790 one million African Americans and four million Europeans, mostly English, Welsh, Scotch-Irish, and Germans, already resided in the United States. In the nineteenth century the ethnic structure of the colonial period was quickly transformed. The earlier English, Scotch-Irish, German, and African-American groups expanded, and new clusters of Irish, Italians, Jews, Swedes, Norwegians, Slavs, Hungarians, and Mexicans emerged. Canada also supplied nearly four million newcomers, including many who spoke French.

Immigration to colonial America was based on an acute need for inexpensive labor. Proprietors seeking to develop large colonies and planters, such as those in the Virginia tidewater seeking to grow crops for a world market, needed a constant stream of settlers and workers. Probably over one-half of all white laborers drawn to the colonies before 1776 were indentured servants or poor Englishmen who worked in the colonies for a fixed period of years to pay off their debts and gain their freedom.

Indentured servants either died from poor living conditions or eventually completed their obligations and left their employers. Thus the need for labor was continuous. African labor was one solution that Virginia planters turned to in 1619. Although most African Americans were not legally slaves when they first arrived, a system of slavery was gradually imposed upon these involuntary immigrants by the 1660s.

Impoverished Englishmen and African Americans were quickly joined by Scotch-Irish, Scots, and German settlers. As many as 250,000 Scotch-Irish immigrated to the American colonies before 1776. Although their decision to move was influenced by Protestant ministers in Ulster, they began leaving in 1717 primarily because of a dramatic increase in the rents they were charged as tenant farmers. They were joined by artisans and laborers from the Scottish

Lowlands who faced economic hard times and moved to the tobacco colonies as indentured servants. Germans started to arrive in Philadelphia in 1683, attracted in part by William Penn's promises of religious toleration. By the 1760s over 60 percent of Pennsylvania was German.

Immigrant streams to America often grew as extensions of European population movements. In the century after 1630 rural workers were always moving because of poverty and land shortages. Agents hired by land speculators and proprietors in the colonies could tap into these migratory streams and entice already mobile individuals to move across the ocean. This is essentially what happened between 1630 and 1642 when 21,000 immigrants moved out of the migratory patterns of East Anglia and sailed to Puritan New England.[2]

The modest levels of colonial immigration were dwarfed by the movements of the nineteenth century. From 1815 to the Civil War, five million people immigrated to the United States. About one-half that number came from

*Front and back of a Missler Labor and Travel Agency canvas pouch (4½" x 7¼") used to contain one's passport and important travel documents and provided by the German labor agency for laborers transported to places of employment in the New World.*

England and about 40 percent of the total came from Ireland. Another ten million came between 1865 and 1890, mostly from northwestern Europe. Finally about fifteen million arrived between 1890 and 1914 when the outbreak of war in Europe temporarily arrested the flow. This later group brought many more southern and eastern Europeans—Poles, Jews, Slovaks, Italians, and Greeks—than had ever come before.

The American economy produced a steady demand for unskilled and skilled workers and farmers throughout much of the nineteenth century. After the 1880s, however, this demand was almost exclusively for unskilled workers to fill the growing number of factory jobs. The impact of this growing demand was felt more heavily in areas of Europe that were undergoing substantial economic changes by the 1880s. Dislocated from the land, unsure of whether to remain in the United States, and possessing few skills, southern and eastern Europeans moved into industrial work in pursuit of a livelihood.

Five major factors in nineteenth-century Europe led to increases in immigration: a dramatic population increase, the spread of commercial agriculture, the rise of the factory system, the proliferation of inexpensive means of transportation such as steamships and railroads, and outbreaks of religious intolerance. These factors did not make an impact everywhere at once, but where they did, especially in fertile agricultural regions, immigration to America became a distinct possibility.

Agricultural regions were the crucible in which these forces met. The need of growing cities such as London, Budapest, or Berlin to import food encouraged farmers with means to acquire more land in order to expand production and profits. Commercial rather than subsistence farming stimulated the rise of large estates and increased the overall price of land. Thus, small owners or aspiring owners found it increasingly difficult to acquire sufficient acreage in Europe to support themselves. The problem for these smaller farmers and tenants was compounded by the marked rise in European population rates after the Napoleonic Wars. Food supplies, no longer drained off by war, were now more plentiful, diets improved, and life expectancy increased. Family members lived longer and had more children. A reduction in the amount of land available for farming and an increase in the number of people attempting to live off the land meant that some would have to leave.

Immigrants who were farmers in Europe often attempted to farm in the United States, especially before the 1880s when land was cheap and readily available. Skilled artisans from Europe sought factories and small shops. Immigrants from southern and eastern Europe, especially Jews, Italians, and Slavs, almost invariably settled in cities. Regardless of their point of origin or their destination, they all developed a set of strategies that would facilitate their settlement and adjustment in a new land. Ethnic difference aside, all immigrants were pragmatic people who acquired much information about America before they arrived. Letters from relatives in the United States told them something about land costs, wages, and job openings. Promotional literature from railroads and states unfortunately offered exaggerated descriptions of opportunities.

Because agriculture required much planning and investment, the Swedes, Germans, and Norwegians who settled in regions such as the Midwest seldom decided to return to Europe. Between 1868 and 1873, when crop failures devastated their homeland, over a hundred thousand Swedes crossed the ocean, influenced by news of the Homestead Act and the promise of free land. These immigrants quickly learned what crops would bring market rewards. Thus, Norwegians in Wisconsin planted wheat and Mennonites in Kansas brought hardy wheat strains from Russia that flourished on the plains.

Those moving to cities exhibited a similar degree of knowledge and adaptability. Jews, Italians, Greeks, and Slavs concentrated in industrial cities such as New York, Chicago, Cleveland, Detroit, and Boston, where they knew unskilled jobs and entrepreneurial opportunities were increasing. They moved in intricate networks of family and ethnic contacts that provided them with information on occupations, housing, wages, weather, and transportation. Thus, Italians already knew of the harsh conditions that existed in the meatpacking plants in Chicago and tended to shun them in favor of outdoor construction work. In the same way Irish immigrant families, who needed the income of children as well as adults, tended to settle in areas where child labor was plentiful.

For some the decision to move to America was compulsory. Persecution for religious or political beliefs forced many to flee their homes in search of greater tolerance. In late-nineteenth-century Russia and eastern Europe, Jews were attacked in pogroms, prevented from owning land, and hindered in their pursuit of higher education. In Sweden, prior to 1860, public worship in the country was forbidden outside the Church of Sweden. Many dissenters from the Lutheran establishment left for Illinois between 1846 and 1854. Chicago was the destination of German radicals and socialists in the same period who fled arrest for their political views in their homeland and established organizations in the United States that supported labor and political protest.[3]

American society reacted to the foreign born with a mixture of acceptance and contempt. Settlement house workers such as Jane Addams and Lillian Wald operated centers in urban neighborhoods to teach newcomers domestic and civics lessons and help them adjust. Other Americans were less considerate. Fearing for the future of their jobs or for the strength of American institutions, some citizens sought to end immigration completely. Early in this century the American Federation of Labor supported a bill preventing the entry of newcomers who were unable to read. In 1920 California denied Japanese immigrants the right to own land, and native-born citizens actually beat Italian Americans in Illinois and burned their homes.[4]

Despite the obstacles immigrants made lasting contributions to American society. They gave this country its major religious strains—Protestant, Catholic, and Jewish. British coal miners and German, Italian, and Jewish socialists brought traditions of social justice that resulted in better wages and improved working conditions for millions. Significant American business ventures such as the Bank of America and Steinway pianos were founded by immigrants. Elizabeth Arden founded a business empire based on cosmetic products for women. Major works of literature, often about the immigrant experience, were written by foreign-born writers such as Ole Rölvaag and Mary Antin. Immigrant groups brought such a variety of foods to this country that ethnic restaurants constituted one of the key ways in which newcomers entered the American economy. And the number of immigrants who made major contributions to American life is striking: John Jacob Astor, Alexander Graham Bell, Samuel Gompers, Alexander Hamilton, John Paul Jones, Colin Powell, and Knute Rockne. Irving Berlin wrote "God Bless America." Gerty Cori, who was born in Prague, was the first American woman to win a Nobel Prize for medicine. Mary Anderson, from Sweden, and Angela Bambace, from Italy, became leading labor organizers.

The Johnson-Reed Act of 1924 established annual quotas that favored northern Europeans over southern and eastern Europeans and curtailed the massive flow of immigrants into the country that had started in the nineteenth century. And the Great Depression and World War II kept immigration rates low; some five hundred thousand Mexican workers were actually deported during the early 1930s because it was feared they took jobs away from the native born. In 1948 Congress did pass a Displaced Persons Act that eventually admitted some four hundred thousand Europeans uprooted by war, although refugees from Palestine, China, and India were ignored. But a substantial return of immigrants to America would have to await congressional action in the 1960s.[5]

The Immigration Act of 1965 abolished the discriminatory quotas of the 1920s. In its place it substituted a system based on family preference. Only about 290,000 immigrants would be allowed to enter the country each year, but relatives of newcomers already here would be exempt from such quotas. Thus, once an immigrant became a citizen he could bring relatives here and reconstitute his family. This provision would ultimately result in the arrival of a much larger number of newcomers than legislators had ever imagined. Skilled workers in demand by the American economy and refugees stood in line after kin as categories that could also gain ready admittance.

Congress anticipated that migration streams would continue to emanate primarily from Europe after 1965. But a general improvement in the European economy, worsening conditions in Latin America, a war in Indochina, and the system of family preferences resulted in a complete shift in immigrant origins. Newcomers from Asia and Latin America quickly began to outnumber Europeans. During the 1970s three-quarters of the four million immigrants who came to the United States were from the Third World. In a twelve-year period after 1966 more people came here from Asia than from Europe, and Mexican immigration increased significantly.

Although historic immigrant streams consisted of some people with strong educational and skilled backgrounds, the incidence appeared to be higher after 1965. Arriving in sleek jetliners rather than steamships, many urban professionals now immigrated to the United States. Between 1965 and 1974, seventy-five thousand foreign-born physicians entered the country in response to an increased call for medical services resulting from the initiation of Medicare programs. If the American press gave relatively little attention to the changes enacted in the 1965 legislation, newspapers in countries such as Korea featured discussions of the law and explained its details. Over thirteen thousand Korean medical professionals, a majority of whom were female nurses, entered the United States after 1965. Thousands of additional Koreans entered large cities and opened small businesses that served inner-city residents. These newcomers were doing what immigrants to America had always done: entering niches in the economy left open to them. By 1977 there were over forty-five hundred Korean-American small businessmen in southern California.[6]

Not all contemporary immigrants were skilled professionals or aspiring businessmen. Large numbers of Arabs entered Detroit-area auto plants, and Mexicans in southern California moved primarily into that region's service economy. Haitian immigrants who moved to south Florida in the 1980s encountered problems of adjustment that were exceedingly difficult. Fleeing political repression and one of the poorest economies in the Caribbean, these Haitians, most of whom were under thirty, were treated harshly by Florida officials who feared they would become public charges. The Haitians were kept in government detention centers where they suffered psychological distress. With few relatives or skills to rely on, these arrivals found it difficult to secure work. By 1985 about one-third of the Haitian males in Florida were unemployed. To adjust and survive in a strange land, Haitians were forced to rely heavily on female household members who could earn a minimal wage and some form of public assistance.[7]

Many immigrants after 1965 were refugees. They consisted of people with a wide diversity of skills, educational training, and cultural backgrounds that influenced their adjustment to American society. The major refugee groups included Cubans and Indochinese. About two hundred thousand people, mostly from the middle class, fled Cuba after Fidel Castro's assumption of power in 1959. Subsequent waves consisted mostly of poor, working-class Cubans who often arrived in Florida in boats operated by relatives already living in Florida. By 1980 Cuban Americans dominated the economic and political life of the Miami area.

Indochina was the second major source of refugees after 1965. The United States immediately accepted 130,000 Vietnamese after the fall of Saigon in 1975. As Communist power spread through southeast Asia, an increasing number of ethnic Chinese, Cambodians, and Laotians sought asylum in the United States as well. By 1985 about 700,000 Indochinese had entered the country, many of whom were resettled through churches and other sponsoring agencies rather than through networks of kin and friends. Although large numbers of Vietnamese possessed skills and strong educational backgrounds, many Cambodians and Laotians were peasants who could not enter the economy easily. By 1985 Indochinese refugees were 15 percent less likely to be employed in southern California than the population as a whole and were in need of some form of government aid.

The largest ethnic group to enter the United States after 1965 came from Mexico. By the 1970s over sixty thousand Mexicans were entering the country legally each year, and a far greater number were undocumented aliens moving into manufacturing jobs in Texas and California. By 1980 nearly one million aliens from Mexico were apprehended annually by the Immigration and Naturalization Service. Many, of course, intended to stay in the country only temporarily, and large numbers returned to Mexico, especially each December when they rejoined their families for Christmas. It was because of the strong links between the employers of unskilled Mexicans in agriculture and manufacturing and the aliens themselves that the Immigration Reform Act of 1986 provided amnesty to undocumented aliens who had been in the United States continuously since 1982.

By the 1980s the pattern of immigrant adjustment revealed mixed results. Those with skills, educational training, and extensive family networks did reasonably well. Thus, the median family income of Cubans was nearly 30 percent higher than that of other immigrants of Hispanic origin. Asian immigrants arriving between 1970 and 1980 had mean household incomes that nearly equaled the income of the native born. On the other hand, Mexican Americans forced into unskilled work earned mean family incomes well below the Asians and the native-born whites.

The complex process that shaped the ethnic history of the nation also left its imprint on the state of Indiana, although sometimes to a lesser extent. In the 1860s the United States consul at Glasgow, Scotland, noted that while emigrants leaving the city knew a great deal about Wisconsin, they knew little of Indiana. In part, this was due to a state legislature, unlike the legislature in Wisconsin, that was reluctant to spend much money on promotional literature designed to attract newcomers. As a result of limited advertising and slower economic development in the nineteenth century, Indiana's foreign-born population was less than the other states in the Old Northwest. Even after industrial expansion attracted more newcomers after the 1880s, the 1920 federal census showed that Indiana had the highest proportion of native-born whites of any state in the nation.[8]

But the image of a largely homogenous state is revised considerably in the essays in this book. Once historians decided to investigate more carefully, they found an extensive and rich record not only of ethnic diversity but also of the significant role immigrant and racial groups played. If Indiana did not replicate the extent of ethnic diversity in the rest of the nation, these essays prove that the encounter between people with different cultural and racial backgrounds was still a pivotal theme in its history.

Many writers have noted the popular image of Indiana as a location of prosperous farms and small towns inhabited by "confident, prosperous, neighborly, tolerant, and shrewd" people. Turn-of-the-century Hoosiers lauded James Whitcomb Riley for fostering this image in his poetry, which praised the spirit of friendship and community in the state. The "people's poet," and this celebration of the idea of a rustic and homogenous state devoid of the urban scars and ethnic and racial diversity of the rest of America, was so popular by 1900 that many citizens framed his poems in their homes. Riley's view of Indiana was steeped in the memory of the pioneers who settled the region in the early nineteenth century. Riley referred to modern inventions like the railroads and factories as "foolery" as he sang the praises of an agrarian world.[9]

This book challenges the homespun notion of Indiana. It does not say that neighborliness and a significant level of homogeneity were absent in the state, but it does prove that Indiana was not nearly as provincial as Riley thought and that it experienced ethnic and racial differences to a greater extent than its popular image would suggest. Ironically, as the book explores the state's ethnic diversity, it actually reveals the ability of Hoosiers to be open-minded. Writers such as John Bartlow Martin and John Gunther, who rightly pointed to a pattern of intolerance in the state's history, have tended to ignore the state's capacity to accommodate variety. Ultimately in Indiana, as in America, people with different cultural backgrounds found ways to participate in the common project of building a civil society.[10]

Individuals from all over the world and from throughout the United States were attracted to Indiana for reasons that were more complex than the presumption that it was a special place of neighborliness. This book demonstrates that the goals and aspirations of the people who settled the state were varied. In the nineteenth century the availability of land and opportunity and the launching of vast internal improvement projects attracted newcomers. Pioneer farmers entered Indiana on the National Road or along water routes like the Ohio River and found land in the southern part of the state.[11] Development of the northern part of the state was hastened in the 1830s by the construction of the Wabash and Erie Canal. Boats taking grain to Toledo would return with immigrants. And who could blame them for coming. Land in Lagrange in 1833 was selling for $1.25 an acre.[12] Settlers of Scottish descent arrived from Pennsylvania about 1813 and settled the area around Canaan in Jefferson County. Englishmen from Yorkshire came to Wayne County as early as the first decade of the nineteenth century because they could get land upon which to employ their well-developed agricultural expertise. Most Scandinavians moved into farming in the upper Midwest and avoided Indiana in the last century because they felt the soil was "slack and swampy." But many did settle in Tippecanoe, Fountain, Warren, Benton, Newton, and Jasper counties where some better land existed. In fact, it was at the site of a Scandinavian immigrant's farm that plans were made in 1918 to create the Indiana Farm Bureau. Even Poles came to farm Indiana in the nineteenth century. Although the majority of Poles eventually settled in industrial areas, as early as 1860 Poles from Poznan settled near La Porte and worked on existing farms in order to save money to afford places of their own.

Some early immigrants to the state were simply unusual individuals who saw unique opportunities to pursue highly personal dreams. A few German women probably came to the state because marriage partners were rather easy to find. One immigrant in Indiana wrote to Germany explaining how two females he knew found spouses less than six weeks after arriving in Indianapolis.[13] George Rapp and his followers left Germany and attempted to create a religious enclave in the wilderness. They finally arrived in Indiana in 1814 and established a community based on Christian fellowship. John Rice Jones, born in Wales in 1750, headed west to the Northwest Territory in 1786, moved into the practice of law, and soon became attorney general of the territory he helped to organize. Stephen Theodore Badin, who came to the United States from France in 1792, became the first priest ordained in this nation and until his death in 1853 ministered to the needs of Catholics throughout Kentucky and Indiana.

Canal and railroad construction attracted laborers as well as farmers. By the time the Wabash and Erie Canal was completed in 1853, thousands of Irish settlers, fleeing famine in Ireland, had come into the state to find work. Irish and German laborers worked on building the National Road in the 1830s and often ended up staying in towns such as Indianapolis and Terre Haute. By 1860 the capital city had two German-American newspapers.[14] Eventually railroad construction had the same effect. Thus, French Canadians were drawn to northwest Indiana both to farm and to work on the New York Central rail line.

Industrialization not only created more work opportunities for newcomers to the state but it also created more attempts at the direct recruitment of immigrants. In 1882 thirty-two villagers in Sopron County, Hungary, accepted the offer of steamship agents of the Studebaker wagon works and the Oliver plow plant in South Bend to book passage to the United States. Their intention may have been to return eventually to their native land after increasing their savings, but, of course, thousands did

*Many nationalities gather in front of Gary's Neighborhood House, a settlement house, in 1917.*

stay. In a similar fashion the American glass industry brought skilled Walloon Belgians from the Liege district to the Muncie area. By 1900 nearly fifteen hundred persons of Belgian birth lived in the six-county region around Hartford City. Between 1906 and 1914 the United States Steel Corporation recruited Croats, Slovaks, Lithuanians, and Poles to its Gary works. In Indianapolis a Slovene immigrant by the name of Jurij Lampert recruited workers between 1895 and 1907 for the National Malleable Castings Company from villages in his native land.

Even without direct recruitment the expansion of industrial jobs in the state acted as a magnet to people seeking improvement in their incomes and their lives. The proximity of steel mills in Gary to Chicago's large Scandinavian communities drew many Swedes and Norwegians across the state line. In a similar manner Sicilians, Piedmontese, and Venetians "who had strong backs and were good workers" moved to Vermillion County to mine coal. Additional numbers of Italians settled in Richmond, Logansport, Fort Wayne, and Elkhart to work in the repair shops and yards of the Pennsylvania and New York Central railroads.

African-American migration to the state was stimulated tremendously by occupational opportunities created by wartime. Freedom from slavery caused the first major thrust of blacks into the state once the Civil War had ended. The state's African-American population more than doubled in the decade of the 1860s; Evansville's black population went from 96 in 1860 to 1,408 in 1870. During World War I blacks found many more job openings in Indiana factories. United States Steel in Gary directly recruited black workers from 1914 to 1918, and the *Chicago Defender,* a leading black newspaper, advertised jobs in Indiana. By the war's end, Gary had nearly 5,000 blacks. In World War II a similar pattern was evident. In the first two years of the war the black population of Evansville increased by 2,000 and the overall unemployment rate for African Americans in the entire state declined by over one-half.[15]

Economic forces alone, however, could not explain entirely the pattern of ethnic settlement in Indiana in this century. After World War II many displaced persons, unable to return to their European homelands, were brought to Indiana by the charitable actions of Hoosiers. Latvians and Estonians came to Indianapolis in 1949 and 1950 through the efforts of a Lutheran church that helped them find jobs and homes. To qualify for admittance to the United States under the Displaced Persons Act of 1948, newcomers needed the assurance of sponsors that suitable housing and employment were available. Balts were dispersed throughout the state under this program. In the Calumet Region

Hungarian Americans already here helped refugees from the 1956 Hungarian Revolution. In a display of neighborliness that would have pleased James Whitcomb Riley, women in Indiana Harbor held bake sales and collected clothing and household goods to help the newly arrived refugees. In Gary Polish Americans established a club to help displaced Poles learn to speak, write, and read English. At Richmond, Earlham College brought young Japanese-American students who had been interred in detention camps in the West to Indiana for an education.

In the late twentieth century neither industrial jobs nor charity can fully explain the pattern of immigrant settlement in the state. Highly trained professionals, intent on careers in modern society, have located in the state. These immigrants came more often by plane than boat and were much less likely to settle in ethnic neighborhoods or communities as their predecessors had in the previous century. In the 1950s a closer relationship between the United States and Iran caused many educated Iranians to move to Indiana. Two Iranian engineers started an engineering firm in Lafayette in that decade and invited colleagues from their homeland to join them. Among the earliest known Korean residents in Indianapolis were Han Won Paik and Chinok Chang Paik who moved to Indianapolis in 1962 after completing graduate degrees at Northwestern University. Both eventually became college teachers. As early as 1971 the Indiana-Philippine Medical Association listed 179 members in the state who were practicing in seventy-two different communities. In 1984 an Indiana Chinese Professional Association was organized that included professors and scientists from Purdue and Butler universities.

Variations in ethnic backgrounds and motivations for coming to Indiana did not preclude the existence of distinct similarities in the process of adjustment. In both the nineteenth and twentieth centuries, as this collection of essays makes clear, most newcomers inevitably built a rich communal and institutional life that facilitated their adjustment to a new and often strange environment. The energy they invested in building churches, community centers, and fraternal associations was impressive. If their economic situation was at times precarious, their associational life was vibrant. In these communities they not only found comfort and friendship, but they also blended the old culture with the new.

Organizing was what immigrants and migrants did best. By 1840 African Americans formed Bethel AME Church in Indianapolis, Allen Chapel in Terre Haute, and a Baptist church in Evansville. These early churches helped blacks develop a sense of community while being shunned by whites, and they served as social centers as

well. By 1916 Indianapolis contained sixteen black Baptist churches. In the nineteenth century residents of Fort Wayne were aware that "Irish Town" was located in the southwestern part of the city. In New Albany an Irish settlement known as "Bog Hollow" was located between the Southern Railroad tracks and the Ohio River. The counterpart in Indianapolis to these communities was known as "Irish Hill." In addition to the central role played by the Roman Catholic Church in such neighborhoods, St. John's Church in Indianapolis sponsored lectures, Irish cultural entertainment, card parties, and religious retreats. The Irish newcomers could join a whole host of ethnic organizations including the Knights of Father Matthew and the Catholic Knights of America. Founded in 1851, the Indianapolis Turner Society became the center of German-American political and educational activity. These organizations offered immigrants and migrants a forum to discuss the leading political issues of the times and furthered their adjustment to a new society.

The associational impulse continued unabated in the twentieth century. Italians in Mishawaka formed two neighborhoods: Calabrians settled north of the St. Joseph River while northern Italians lived south of the river. By 1927, ten years after the wartime demand for labor had brought them to the Calumet Region, Mexican Americans had built a church, Our Lady of Guadalupe, opened a grocery, two tailor shops, four barbershops, nine restaurants, and eleven pool halls. Similarly in Whiting Slovaks organized St. John's Church in 1899, created a branch of the First Catholic Slovak Union, and built the Slovak Dom, a home for plays, weddings, dances, and other social activities. In the 1920s in South Bend the names of Belgian organizations revealed how these communities promoted both ethnic and American identities. Belgians could join the Belgian-American Club, the Belgian Bicycle Club, or the Belgian Archery Club. In the Belgian section of the third ward residents not only preserved ethnic identity by continuing to speak Belgian into the 1960s but also fostered Americanization by electing members of their community to the city council. In a similar manner Slovenes in the Haughville neighborhood of Indianapolis supported a church as well as two dozen saloons where they could speak their native language. Slovenes also used their organizational base to ease themselves into the larger society by forming a football team that would play other teams—such as the Fort Harrison Eleven—in the 1930s.

The voluntary imperative to assimilate, a major theme documented in this collection, was clearly evident in the widespread involvement of newcomers in entrepreneurial activities. Both the Indiana and American economies were ultimately open to ethnic newcomers in the nineteenth and twentieth centuries. This collection indicates that the drive for business success marked all groups in both centuries under review. As early as 1799 a Swiss immigrant named Jean Jaques Dufour and his wife were the proprietors of lucrative vineyards and pastures in New Switzerland and had attracted other Swiss families to the site. At New Harmony George Rapp not only sought to build a religious community but also purchased land on the Wabash River to build a brewery, a distillery, and mills, which not only provided for the members' own needs but also allowed them to sell a surplus. By 1819 the Harmonists were making more than twelve thousand dollars annually and had the highest per capita income in the state. The Harmonists were so successful that they eventually organized their own bank. Hoosiers saw Jewish and Syrian peddlers carrying their goods across the state in the last century. In Richmond in the 1850s Germans owned the three largest dry goods stores in the town. In Evansville John A. Reitz, who emigrated from Westphalia in 1836, started a sawmill and became a "lumber king."

The entrepreneurial drive continued in the twentieth century as a means of adjusting. In Indianapolis black businesses dominated the area around Indiana Avenue. Funeral homes, restaurants, and clothing stores were operated by African-American proprietors. Syrians opened at least eleven groceries in Terre Haute, and Slovak immigrants in Whiting bought a bank. In the 1920s East Chicago Poles could get loans to buy homes from a building and loan association established by Joseph Wlekinski and his brother. By 1915 Lithuanians in East Chicago had established taverns, meat stores, a bakery, a tailor shop, restaurants, and a printing house. Today Chinese restaurants, like the one Lee Lai Fong and his family started in Valparaiso in 1976, represent a continuation of the theme of ethnic enterprise.

Indiana not only welcomed the economic assimilation of newcomers but also their political participation. John Badollet, a native of Switzerland, became the land register at Vincennes and in 1816 was a delegate to the Indiana constitutional convention. He joined five other European immigrants at the gathering in Corydon, which included four from Ireland and one from Germany. Edward Hannegan, born in Ohio but proud of his Irish ancestry, was elected to Congress from Indiana in 1832 and was known throughout the state for his oratory and his "Irish wit."[16] The presence of Irish immigrants in the state, in fact, caused the state constitutional convention in 1850–51 to ease voting requirements for immigrants. In the 1850s there were twenty-two natives of Ireland in the General Assembly. Samuel Judah, an early Jewish settler in the state, practiced law in Vincennes, was a

Inland Steel Company employees in East Chicago dressed in native costumes, 1952.

delegate to the Democratic National Convention in 1824 and an outspoken Jacksonian, and was elected to the state assembly five times between 1827 and 1840.

The political participation of various ethnic groups, as this collection suggests, continued in a vigorous fashion into the twentieth century. In 1934 Daniel Perrotta, an Italian American, was elected to the Gary city council, and his attempt to lead a fight against organized crime in the city cost him his life. After World War II African Americans in the state pursued an agenda to ease segregation. Their efforts helped pass a measure abolishing segregation in the public schools in 1949 and the adoption of civil rights laws in Indiana in 1961 and 1963. In 1967 Gary elected a black mayor, Richard Hatcher. Slovak Americans attained political recognition when Robert A. Pastrich was elected mayor of East Chicago and Peter Visclosky was elected to Congress in 1984.

The inclusion of ethnic groups into political life was invariably hastened by the pressures of wartime. These moments allowed newcomers to demonstrate their loyalty to the host nation and gain greater acceptance by joining the armed services. During the Civil War many men from England and Wales in Indiana enlisted in the Union army. One, William Stockdale, lost an eye and a leg but received reassurance from his father in England that he had fought for a good cause. German immigrants in Indianapolis also became active supporters of the abolitionist crusade and the war. The Turner Hall in the city was a center of antislavery activity, and many Germans were attracted to the Union army because military service meant certain citizenship. During World War I Belgians in Mishawaka volunteered to fight with American forces in Europe out of hatred for the German kaiser. When Germany was defeated these same citizens burned the kaiser in effigy and played patriotic tunes. Slovak women in the Calumet Region prepared bandages and performed other tasks useful to the war effort. During World War II all ethnic groups in the state bought war bonds, and families from ethnic communities shared with other Hoosiers the sacrifice of their sons on the battlefield. Louis and Maria Scotece, natives of Italy and residents of Richmond, sent five sons to the military, including one who was lost at the Battle of Midway in 1942. Even during the Cold War ethnic Hoosiers demonstrated their desire to be part of the state and the nation by protesting the visit of Nikita Khrushchev with a parade of five hundred cars near Hammond.

Despite the general thrust toward assimilation and acceptance, Indiana's ethnic history contains episodes of hostility and intolerance. Often bias in Indiana as elsewhere resulted from the fear of losing jobs. Thus, when Irish and German workers came into the state during the building of the canals in the nineteenth century, many citizens joined Know-Nothing organizations that denounced immigrants. Slovenes in Indianapolis were the target of rock-throwing residents who feared their wages would be lowered. In 1907 native-born Hoosiers in Bedford, feeling the impact of layoffs from a recession, set fire to some Italian property and posted handbills urging them to "vacate" the town. In the 1920s the Ku Klux Klan directed its hostile views toward newly arrived ethnic groups. A lady in Clinton recalled how the Klan broke into her house and destroyed the wine her Italian-born father made, and a woman in Logansport claimed the Klan prevented Italians from getting jobs. Mexican Americans in East Chicago still note the fact that many of their relatives were deported in 1932 for fear they were taking jobs away from native-born Hoosiers.

Race, of course, led to conflict in Indiana as it did in every other state. In the early nineteenth century Native-American villages were destroyed, and tribes such as the Miami suffered removal from the state in 1846. In the 1920s the increased movement of blacks into Gary and Indianapolis, initiated by the demand for wartime workers in 1917 and 1918, led to the construction of segregated high schools such as Gary Roosevelt and Crispus Attucks. In Marion in 1930 two young black men were lynched by an angry mob.[17]

One of the most virulent examples of intolerance toward people with distinctive ethnic traits may have taken place during World War I. Incited by national patriotic campaigns, many Hoosiers carried the war against the Germans home to German Americans in their state. In 1869 the Indiana legislature exhibited tolerance by allowing German to be taught as a language in the public schools. By May 1917 public schools in the capital city enrolled nearly ten thousand students in German classes. But during World War I an intense debate took place over whether such instruction was unpatriotic and should be allowed to continue. Critics claimed that the study of the German language would ruin the "moral welfare" of the city's children and thus were able to get German instruction eliminated. The town of Germany, Indiana, actually changed its name to Loyal, and East Germantown became Pershing.[18]

Towns and people altered their names to gain acceptance and overcome prejudice. But ethnic communities and their members generally flourished in the state, and newcomers continually pursued paths into the Indiana economy and political system. In the end the ethnic history of Indiana and America proved immigrants and migrants could be embraced and accommodated despite their unique cultures. The spirit of neighborliness that intrigued James Whitcomb Riley proved equal to the task of confronting bigotry. The essays that follow underscore this process of adjustment. Taken together they convey the rich story of immigrant movement into Indiana throughout its history and contribute to our understanding of a very vital process that continues to affect our lives.

## Notes

1. *Newsweek,* 9 Aug. 1993, p. 19.

2. For the colonial experience in immigration see Bernard Bailyn, *The Peopling of British North America: An Introduction* (New York: Knopf, 1986).

3. Philip Taylor, *The Distant Magnet: European Emigration to the U.S.A.* (New York: Harper, 1971), 58; John Bodnar, *The Transplanted: A History of Immigrants in Urban America* (Bloomington: Indiana University Press, 1985), 86; George M. Stephenson, *The Religious Aspects of Swedish Immigration: A Study of Immigrant Churches* (New York: AMS Press, 1972).

4. See John Higham, *Strangers in the Land: Patterns of American Nativism, 1860–1925* (New Brunswick, N.J.: Rutgers University Press, 1988).

5. See Mark Wyman, *DP: Europe's Displaced Persons, 1945–1951* (Philadelphia: Balch Institute Press, 1989).

6. David Reimers, *Still the Golden Door: The Third World Comes to America* (New York: Columbia University Press, 1985).

7. Alejandro Portes and Alex Stepick, *City on Edge: The Transformation of Miami* (Berkeley: University of California Press, 1993), 38–60.

8. Maurice G. Baxter, "Encouragement of Immigration to the Middle West during the Era of the Civil War," *Indiana Magazine of History* 46 (Mar. 1950): 34–36.

9. See John Bartlow Martin, *Indiana: An Interpretation* (1947; reprint, Bloomington: Indiana University Press, 1992), 105–8. James H. Madison, in the introduction to the 1992 edition of Martin's book, discusses the rural image of the state. See also John Gunther, *Inside U.S.A.* (New York: Harper and Brothers, 1947), 386.

10. Gunther, *Inside U.S.A.,* 386–90.

11. Logan Esarey, *A History of Indiana: From Its Exploration to 1850* (Indianapolis: W. K. Stewart Co., 1915), 239–47, 254–57.

12. *My Town, Your Town, La Grange 1836–1936* (Lagrange, Ind.: Lagrange Sesquicentennial Committee, 1986), 7; John Ankenbruck, *Twentieth Century History of Fort Wayne* (Fort Wayne, Ind.: Twentieth Century Fort Wayne, Inc., 1975), 114.

13. George Theodore Probst, *The Germans in Indianapolis, 1840–1918,* rev. ed. by Eberhard Reichmann (Indianapolis: German-American Center and Indiana German Heritage Society, Inc., 1989), 15.

14. James J. Divita, *Ethnic Settlement Patterns in Indianapolis* (Indianapolis: Indiana Division of Natural Resources, 1988), 14.

15. See Robert A. Lowe, "Racial Segregation in Indiana, 1920–1950" (Ph.D. diss., Ball State University, 1965), 20, 113–14; Darrel E. Bigham, *We Ask Only a Fair Trial: A History of the Black Community of Evansville, Indiana* (Bloomington: Indiana University Press, 1987), 21–23, 226; James B. Lane, *"City of the Century": A History of Gary, Indiana* (Bloomington: Indiana University Press, 1976), 70.

16. Martin, *Indiana,* 44–45.

17. Lowe, "Racial Segregation in Indiana," 57–60.

18. Clark Douglass Kimball, "Patriotism and the Suppression of Dissent in Indiana during the First World War" (Ph.D. diss., Indiana University, 1971), 163–78.

# AFRICAN AMERICANS

EMMA LOU THORNBROUGH

> *But as the twentieth century draws to a close, demographic realities and changing racial attitudes seem to show that the goal of the civil rights years—a truly racially integrated society—has eluded Indiana and the nation as a whole.*

## Before the Civil War

The first people of African origin in the area that became Indiana were slaves of the French who founded Vincennes on the lower Wabash River. The records of St. Francis Xavier, the parish church of that town, which extend back to 1749, include baptisms, marriages, and burials of Negro slaves.

In 1779 George Rogers Clark, in an expedition authorized by the state of Virginia, captured Vincennes from the British, who had acquired the French settlement in the peace settlement of 1763. A Virginia law confirmed the title of the French inhabitants to their possessions, which included their slave property. After Virginia ceded her territorial claims to the United States, the Continental Congress in 1787 adopted the Northwest Ordinance, which included the provision (Article VI): "There shall be neither slavery nor involuntary servitude in the said territory, otherwise than in punishment of crimes, whereof the party shall have been duly convicted." Nevertheless, in spite of this language, the ordinance was interpreted as not being retroactive and not affecting the status of slaves in the territory before 1787. They and their descendants continued to be held in bondage until Indiana became a state.[1]

Most of the Anglo Americans initially in the territory came from the slave states in the upper South. The most influential among them were proslavery men who

petitioned Congress to repeal the section of the Northwest Ordinance that prohibited slavery. When this failed, the territorial legislature in 1805 passed "An Act concerning the introduction of Negroes and Mulattoes into this Territory," which was a brazen attempt to evade the ordinance's provision against involuntary servitude. Under this act slaves could be indentured for an undefined term of years. Most contracts required service for twenty to forty years, but some provided for terms far beyond the life expectancy of the slave. Children of indentured persons were required to serve that person's master; males until age thirty, females until age twenty-five. After Illinois was separated from Indiana Territory the Indiana legislature repealed the indenture law, but repeal did not affect the status of persons already indentured.

During the territorial period the black population was very small. The United States census of 1810 showed a total of 630 Negroes and 23,890 whites in Indiana. Of the Negroes 237 were slaves, 393 "free," a number which included many who were indentured. Most blacks concentrated around Vincennes in Knox County.

A majority of the men who met in 1816 to frame a state constitution opposed the continuation of slavery. The Bill of Rights declared: "There shall be neither slavery nor involuntary servitude in this State, otherwise than for the punishment of crimes, whereof the party shall have been duly convicted, nor shall any indenture of any negro [*sic*] or mulatto hereafter made and executed out of the bounds of this State be of any validity within the State."[2] Although opposed to slavery, many of the men voting for this article wanted to exclude free blacks as well as slaves and to keep Indiana for whites only.

After the adoption of the state constitution the Indiana Supreme Court in a number of freedom suits declared slavery and the system of involuntary indentures null and void. However, in spite of these rulings vestiges of slavery lingered for several years.

African Americans who moved into Indiana before the Civil War fell into three general groups: persons who

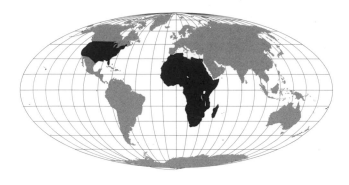

were free in the state where they lived before migrating; recently emancipated slaves who became free when they arrived in Indiana; fugitive slaves—persons who were not legally free and who could be captured and returned to their masters.

A substantial number of free blacks and emancipated slaves came in company with white Quakers who freed their slaves and moved into Indiana because they were opposed to slavery. Many of them came from North Carolina where state law required that manumitted slaves leave the state within ninety days. Once in Indiana, both emancipated slaves and free blacks often settled near Quaker communities. Emancipated slaves were also brought into the state by non-Quakers. In some cases the slaves appear to have been freed by their masters for humanitarian reasons. In other cases, which are difficult to authenticate, masters may have brought aged slaves to Indiana in order to avoid caring for them when they were no longer able to work. Fear of large numbers of these paupers was one excuse for efforts to bar all black migrants from entering the state.

The number of blacks in the state remained relatively small throughout the antebellum period. In 1820 there were 1,420 Negroes and 145,758 whites. In 1860 there were 11,428 Negroes and 1,338,710 whites. Over the forty-year period, white population had increased more than 900 percent, blacks more than 800 percent, but the percentage of blacks to total population declined from 1 percent in 1820 to nine-tenths of 1 percent in 1860.

Blacks concentrated in certain areas. In 1820 they lived around Vincennes and the Ohio River counties, Clark, Floyd, and Jefferson. By 1860 much of the black population remained in these counties, but both black and white settlers had moved northward. The black population like the white remained predominantly rural, but by 1860, 825 blacks resided in Marion County, many of them residents of Indianapolis, the state capital. Many of the others were in counties where there were large numbers of Quakers. Wayne County had the largest African-American population (870), and in neighboring Randolph the number was 825.

Blacks moved into the state in spite of efforts of lawmakers to restrict migration. A law passed in 1831 required persons of color who came into the state to post bond as a guarantee of good behavior and provided that persons who did not comply with the law could be removed from the state by the overseers of the poor. This measure does not appear to have been enforced except in a few cases. Article XIII of the second state constitution, adopted in 1851, went further than the 1831 law. It said: "No negro [sic] or mulatto shall come into or settle in the state, after the adoption of this Constitution" and declared void all contracts made with persons coming into the state in violation of the article and imposed penalties on persons who employed them. This article, submitted to the voters separately, was ratified by a larger margin than the rest of the new constitution.

Article XIII, like the 1831 law, was more symbolic than enforceable, but it reflected the desire of most white Hoosiers to keep the soil of Indiana for whites. That desire was also shown by popular support for the colonization movement, which sought to persuade black residents to leave Indiana and settle in Liberia in Africa, a plan initiated by the American Colonization Society that was supported by many prominent white leaders. The movement met with little success among black residents in Indiana, but it was supported with funds from the state government.

The Fugitive Slave Act of 1793 permitted the seizure and return of runaway slaves who escaped into "free" states like Indiana. As a consequence of the law African Americans who were legally free feared being seized and claimed as fugitive slaves and sold into slavery in the South. Free blacks along the Ohio River lived in constant danger of being kidnapped. After adoption of the Fugitive Slave Act of 1850, which tightened the procedures of the 1793 law, dangers increased for both free blacks and escaped slaves. As a result some of them fled from Indiana to Canada.

African Americans who settled in Indiana were not regarded as citizens and were subject to legal disabilities. Under the state constitution only white males could vote and serve in the militia. Persons with as little as one-fourth of Negro blood (later changed to one-eighth) could not testify in court in any case involving a white person. A law "to prohibit the amalgamation of whites and blacks" prohibited persons with one-eighth or more of Negro blood from intermarriage with a white person. Public tax-supported schools, in their infancy in Indiana before the Civil War, served white pupils only. Black children could not attend even if they paid their own tuition.[3]

Not all white citizens shared the prejudices reflected in these restrictions and disabilities. Members of the Society

*Eli Archey farming at Beech settlement in Rush County, ca. 1910.*

of Friends (Quakers) and some other citizens sought repeal of the restrictive laws and participated in private efforts to aid black settlers. In spite of prejudice and bigotry shown them, blacks who came to the state came with hopes of a better life for themselves and their families.

In spite of limited resources a number of African Americans bought uncleared land from white property owners and established themselves as independent farmers. Others worked as tenant farmers or as hired farm laborers. These blacks had a part in clearing the forests and transforming the wilderness into a prosperous agricultural society. A few families acquired sizable tracts (eighty acres or more) directly from the United States government in sparsely settled counties. Some rural communities took the names of families who acquired large tracts of land— Lyles Station in Gibson County, Roberts settlement in Hamilton County, Weaver settlement in Grant County, and Bassett settlement in Howard County.

In the towns most blacks worked as manual laborers or in domestic service. Among skilled workers listed in the 1850 census barbers were most numerous. Others worked as carpenters, brick masons, plasterers, and whitewashers. There were also blacksmiths, cobblers, and drivers of horses and carriages. A few who owned their own wagons and horses became quite prosperous.[4]

The first blacks who arrived in Indiana communities attended the same churches as whites, sitting in separate sections. As their numbers increased they established their own churches with their own distinctive services. Both African Methodist Episcopal and Baptist churches were founded in the pioneer years in rural communities and in towns. By 1840 Bethel AME Chapel in Indianapolis, Allen Chapel in Terre Haute, and Mount Pleasant AME Church in the Beech settlement in Rush County and similar churches in rural communities had

been founded. By 1850 the AME Church claimed a membership of 1,387 in Indiana—more than one-fifth of the entire African-American population. Blacks founded a Baptist church in Evansville in 1842 and Second Baptist in Indianapolis and another in New Albany in the same year. There were also black Baptist churches in several rural communities.

These early churches were important in developing a sense of community and identity among a group shunned or ignored by most whites. They served as centers of social and cultural as well as religious life. Members looked to their ministers for leadership and guidance in secular as well as religious affairs.

Churches and meetinghouses often served as schools for black children who were excluded from public schools. Members of the Society of Friends and the Anti-Slavery Friends who seceded from the main body in the 1840s actively helped blacks establish schools. By 1855 the Indiana Yearly Meeting reported a total of more than thirty schools under their sponsorship, while the Western Yearly Meeting reported fifteen schools in 1859. The Committees on Persons of Color helped raise funds and recruit teachers for the schools and sometimes furnished books, but Quakers were not solely responsible for the schools. Some schools met in black churches, some in private homes, and some in schoolhouses built on land contributed by blacks. Costs of maintenance came principally from tuition paid by pupils. Pupils received very limited education in these schools. Terms were irregular, often for only two or three months a year. Subjects taught were rudimentary: spelling, reading, writing, arithmetic.

A few fortunate African Americans were able to obtain more education by attending academies, such as the Union Literary Institute in Randolph County. Though chartered in 1848 by a group of Anti-Slavery Friends, blacks and whites from other denominations supported it and served on the board of managers. At first a majority of the students were white, but in later years enrollment was entirely black, and for a few years an African American, Samuel Smothers, served as principal of the school.

In addition to their own churches and schools African Americans formed a number of social and fraternal organizations and celebrated their own particular holiday—Emancipation Day, in observance of the abolition of slavery in the British West Indies. The first black Masonic lodge was organized in Indianapolis in 1842, and a second one in 1849. Blacks organized lodges in Madison and Terre Haute before the Civil War. The most important figures in the Masonic movement in the early period were John G. Britton and James S. Hinton of Indianapolis. The two led the movement for statewide

IHS C4329

*In 1880 James S. Hinton became the first African American to be elected to the Indiana General Assembly.*

conventions of African Americans, a movement which began in Philadelphia. In Indiana, as in other states, the first conventions, called in the 1840s, opposed colonization of black Americans in Liberia. In 1851 a convention protested the new state constitution with its hateful Article XIII and other discriminatory provisions. In following years conventions were held before meetings of the state legislature to petition for repeal of legal disabilities. Years before they received the right to vote some African Americans showed political awareness and organized protests over denial of the rights of citizenship.

### Civil War to First World War

When the Civil War began, northern blacks tried to enlist in the Union cause, and at first the Lincoln administration refused them. After Gov. John Andrews of Massachusetts received authority to raise a regiment of African-American volunteers, about eighty men from Indiana enlisted to serve in the famous Massachusetts Fifty-fourth.

In the early stages of the war white Hoosiers opposed the use of black troops, but attitudes changed as recruitment of volunteers to fill quotas assigned to Indiana

became difficult. Even racially prejudiced whites were willing to avoid the draft by using black volunteers. Most of the Indiana men were enrolled in the Twenty-eighth Regiment United States Colored Troops. It is impossible to determine accurately the number of Indiana blacks who aided the Union cause, but it appears to be a large percentage. The number credited to Indiana was increased by fugitive slaves from Kentucky who risked capture to enlist on Indiana soil. Most of the men from Indiana went to Virginia after a training period. They suffered heavy casualties in the campaign before Petersburg and were among the first to enter Richmond in the closing weeks of the war. At first black soldiers did not receive the same pay as whites but earned only laborers pay. Not until the closing months of the war did Congress expressly provide that they should receive the same uniforms, arms, equipment, rations, and pay as white soldiers. Black units were always commanded by white officers.

As runaway slaves and "contrabands," slaves freed by Union troops, came from Kentucky to Indiana's Ohio River towns, local whites feared that the end of slavery would mean an influx of poverty-stricken freedmen and their families. Racial tensions increased, and violence against the newcomers was common. A full-scale riot in New Albany occurred in 1862, and a lynching, followed by a riot, in Evansville in 1865.

The migration continued throughout the war and postwar years. Many of the newcomers remained in the river settlements, but more and more of them pushed northward. Between 1860 and 1870 the number of African Americans in the state more than doubled and by the end of the century had reached 57,505 out of a total population of 2,516,402, more than five times the number on the eve of the Civil War, but still a small fraction (2.3 percent) of the whole. In the early years of the twentieth century their numbers continued to grow but at a slower rate. Before the World War most of the migrants were from the upper South. In 1910 slightly more than half of the total black population had been born outside the state.

After the Civil War most of the newcomers settled in cities and towns. Older residents also left rural areas and headed for the cities. By 1910, 80 percent of the black population was classified as urban, compared to 42 percent of the total population. By far the largest number of African Americans came to Indianapolis, the state capital and an important railroad center. Black population in that city increased from 498 in 1860 to 15,931 out of a total population of 169,164 in 1900—9.4 percent of the population of the city and 27.7 percent of the entire black population in the state. In Evansville, at that time the second largest city in the state, blacks numbered 7,515 out of a total population of 59,007 or 12.7 percent of the whole. In some smaller towns in the southern counties the percentage of blacks was even higher, but after 1900 these percentages declined as blacks moved to other Indiana cities or left the state. Few blacks went to South Bend or Fort Wayne in northern Indiana, and before the World War only a handful settled in Gary, the steel town founded in 1906.[5]

After the Civil War most legal disabilities of African Americans ceased. The Fourteenth and Fifteenth Amendments to the United States Constitution gave citizenship and political rights to Indiana blacks. In 1866 the Indiana Supreme Court declared Article XIII of the state constitution invalid. The ban on testimony in court was removed by legislative and judicial decisions. In 1869 and 1877 the state legislature passed laws that provided for schools for black children. Thereafter the only remaining racial distinctions in Indiana law prohibited mixed marriages, provided in the state constitution for a militia of white males, and permitted but did not require separate schools for blacks.

As thousands of blacks moved into the state some white leaders, recognizing the dangers of illiterate citizens, urged establishment of tax-supported schools for them. In resolutions adopted at state conventions African Americans also emphasized education. In Indianapolis, before the legislature acted, a number of schools opened through private voluntary efforts of black churches with the cooperation of the Plainfield Quarterly Meeting of Friends. Moses Broyles, minister of Second Baptist Church, and other black ministers taught in several of the schools. Adults as well as children enrolled in some schools. In Evansville and elsewhere similar efforts surfaced.

In 1869 the state legislature finally passed a law requiring school trustees to organize separate elementary schools for black children where there was a large enough group to justify a school. School districts could be consolidated to establish such schools, but if the number of blacks was too small to justify this, trustees could provide "other means of education." In 1877 this inadequate law was replaced by one that remained the state's basic school law until the abolition of segregation in public education in 1949. The measure permitted but did not require school authorities to provide separate schools for black children but said where no separate schools existed "colored children shall be allowed to attend the public schools with white children." The measure further provided that when a pupil had advanced beyond the grades offered in the colored school, he or she should be admitted to the school for whites and that no distinction on account of race or color should be made in that school.[6]

In Indianapolis, which had the largest school population in the state, separate elementary schools had been established under the 1869 law. After the adoption of the 1877 law segregation continued to be the policy for elementary schools, but occasionally a few black pupils enrolled in white schools. African Americans almost always taught in the black schools. Since teaching was one of the few occupations to which educated African Americans could aspire, the schools attracted able men and women who were looked upon as community leaders. Although the condition of school buildings provoked complaints, the course of study and length of terms in the black schools virtually approximated those in the white schools. At the secondary level, no separate high school existed for blacks until the opening of Crispus Attucks High School in 1927. The first African-American student was admitted to Indianapolis High School, which was later renamed Shortridge, in 1872 and graduated in 1876. Black students continued to attend that school and other high schools built later until 1927.[7]

In towns and cities in the northern half of the state where numbers of African Americans were small, schools were not segregated, but in a few places where all the pupils in a school were black as the result of residential patterns, black teachers were employed. Black teachers were never employed in schools with racially mixed enrollments.

In the southern half of the state segregation ruled as education policy. Blacks in Evansville attended elementary schools with grades one through six and Clark School with eight grades and a four-year high school. The black community took pride in Clark School despite its comparatively inferior facilities and equipment. Black teachers, although paid less than whites, remained dedicated and influenced civic and cultural affairs.[8]

Segregated elementary schools prevailed in smaller cities in southern Indiana and some central communities as well. Nearly all communities maintained "high schools" for the few blacks who enrolled in them. These high schools consisted of two or three rooms in the elementary school buildings. Some teachers taught in both the elementary and high schools.

Scattered one-room "colored" schools with one teacher could be found in rural areas throughout the southern and central part of Indiana. As blacks moved northward and to the cities some of these schools were abandoned, but in 1916 the State Superintendent of Public Instruction reported the presence of Negro schools of some sort in at least thirty-one counties.[9]

In 1897 the state legislature passed a law that made school attendance compulsory until age fourteen. Accurate statistics on school attendance are not available, but few blacks remained in school after that age. Many did not graduate from elementary school. Only a few entered high school, and most of them did not graduate. However, graduation from high school came to be regarded as a mark of distinction in the African-American community. The small number who held high school diplomas often found employment opportunities no better than for blacks with less schooling. While this fact may have discouraged some from continuing their education, poverty loomed as a more important reason as it forced young blacks to leave school and seek jobs to help support parents and younger brothers and sisters. But in spite of obstacles most young African Americans obtained the rudiments of an education. By 1900, according to the United States census, only 1.5 percent of black children between the ages of ten and fourteen could not read and write.[10]

Politically, African Americans voted Republican. Democrats consistently opposed any expansion of rights for blacks and continued to play upon racial fears and prejudices. In every political campaign members of the GOP reminded black voters of their debt to the party of Lincoln and their obligation to support its candidates, and for more than half a century after enfranchisement the black vote was nearly always solidly Republican.[11]

In politics as in other aspects of life African Americans looked to their ministers for leadership and guidance, and white politicians tried to reach black voters through their ministers. Moses Broyles of the Second Baptist Church in Indianapolis became one of the most stalwart Republican speakers although he never ran for office. Both Baptist and AME churches sponsored political rallies. Political leaders frequently came from fraternal organizations.

During every political campaign Colored Republican Clubs formed to encourage blacks to vote. White politicians came into black districts to make speeches and rally voters. They promised rewards in patronage, such as janitorial jobs in public buildings, to political workers if Republicans won in local elections. Blacks regarded the patronage rewards as status symbols.

A few blacks, endorsed by white political leaders, gained nomination for public office. The highest position to which an African American could aspire was membership in the lower house of the state legislature. The first such representative was James S. Hinton of Indianapolis, a leader in the black conventions and a prominent Mason, elected in 1880. Between 1880 and 1900 three other African Americans served in the legislature. Two were ministers, James M. Townsend of Richmond, a Civil War veteran and respected AME minister, elected in 1884, and Richard Bassett, a little-known Baptist minister from Howard County, elected in 1892. The third representative was Gabriel Jones, an Indianapolis schoolteacher, elected in 1896. Each man served a single two-year term.

In Indianapolis, where members were elected from wards rather than at large before 1909, three black men held city council seats before 1900: Robert Bagby, John Puryear, and Henry Sweetland. In smaller cities also an occasional black candidate was elected to municipal office.

In 1896 Republicans began a long period of control of state government. In Indiana, as in the rest of the nation, as racism reached its apogee at the turn of the century, "lily white" influence became powerful among Republicans who regarded identification with black voters as a liability. After Gabriel Jones no African American sat in the state legislature until 1932. The only exception to this pattern of exclusion worth mentioning was the election of Dr. Sumner Furniss to the Indianapolis city council in 1918. Although their numbers increased, the political power of black voters reached its lowest depth in the early years of the twentieth century.

Growth of an urbanized society strengthened and expanded existing African-American institutions and led to the beginning of new ones. A middle class of businessmen and professionals rose to meet the needs of the growing black communities. Black-owned businesses tended to be small-scale enterprises that served a black clientele. In Indianapolis, Indiana Avenue and its environs, just northwest of the center of the city, became the hub of business and entertainment. Restaurants, saloons, grocery stores, clothing stores, barbershops, cobblers, realtors' offices, lawyers, physicians, and dentists clustered along the "Avenue." Funeral homes were among the most enduring and prosperous of black-owned businesses in Indianapolis and Evansville. The most widely known and financially successful black business in Indiana was the Madam C. J. Walker Manufacturing Company, a cosmetic firm incorporated in 1911 to market a product discovered by Madam C. J. Walker for straightening hair. Agents sold Walker products throughout the United States, and beauty schools that taught the use of Walker products could be found in several cities.[12]

Some successful businesses also catered to white customers. A few black barbers with their own shops prospered by serving white patrons only. Teamsters, draymen, caterers, blacksmiths, and operators of coal yards who had their own businesses also had white customers.[13]

Black newspapers seldom prospered but they proved to be cohesive forces in the black community. Indianapolis hosted the only newspapers published by African Americans in Indiana before the World War. The Bagby brothers, Robert, Benjamin, and James, all schoolteachers, established in 1879 the *Indianapolis Leader* and published the state's first black newspaper until 1885. In 1882 the *Colored World,* later called the *Indianapolis World,* begun by another teacher, Levi E. Christy, appeared. It continued publication well into the twentieth century under several other owners. In 1892 the *Indianapolis Freeman,* which began publication in 1888, became the property of George L. Knox, the most influential black Republican in the state. It continued publication until after his death in 1927. In 1901 George P. Stewart became sole owner of the *Indianapolis Recorder,* which he had started with Will H. Porter in 1897. The *Recorder,* still published, was owned by the Stewart family until 1988. All these papers except the *World,* which sometimes had ties with Democrats, strongly supported the Republican party and its candidates.[14]

The great majority of African Americans earned a living working for white employers. United States census reports listed most blacks simply as "laborers," working at unskilled manual labor often temporary or seasonal. Many African-American wives with children as well as unmarried women worked as domestics in the homes of whites. Others supplemented family income as laundresses and as cooks in restaurants. Men frequently toiled as janitors, porters, cooks, and waiters. Some worked as common laborers in foundries, but few found skilled factory jobs largely because of policies of employers and trade unions. Unions affiliated with the American Federation of Labor (AFL) barred blacks from apprenticeship training, thus excluding them from work in building trades. Only the Hod Carriers Union had a large black membership. The United Mine Workers had a few black members in the coal mines in the southwestern counties.[15]

As population increased, a growing number of blacks became lawyers, mainly in Indianapolis. James T. V. Hill became the first black man admitted to that bar and the first member of his race to become active in Democratic politics. Black lawyers could not join the professional organizations of white attorneys. Therefore, they formed their own local organizations, which became affiliated with the National Bar Association.[16]

In addition, a growing number of African Americans joined the ranks of physicians and dentists. Like lawyers they actively participated in civic affairs and in politics. Samuel A. Elbert, the first African American to receive the M.D. degree in the state, had a long and successful career as physician and race leader in Indianapolis. One of the most prominent blacks in Evansville was Dr. George Washington Buckner. Although a Republican he received an appointment as minister to Liberia by President Woodrow Wilson.[17]

In Indianapolis physicians organized the Aesculapian Society that became affiliated with the Indiana Association of Negro Physicians, Dentists and Pharmacists. It in turn affiliated with the National Medical Association.

IHS C6274

*George Washington Buckner served as minister to Liberia from 1913 to 1915.*

Black physicians and surgeons could not practice in any of the hospitals in the state. Although Sumner Furniss worked as an intern in the Indianapolis City Hospital in the 1890s, in later years no black interns broke the barrier even though some of them had graduated from the School of Medicine of Indiana University. Black women could not train as nurses at City Hospital. The few qualified black nurses in Indiana received their training in other states.[18]

Administrators at City Hospital, the state's only public hospital and the only one admitting black patients, segregated blacks in "jim crow" wards. The inadequacy of hospital facilities and lack of opportunities for training led to the establishment of several short-lived private hospitals. Lincoln Hospital in Indianapolis, for example, opened in 1909 with a staff of nineteen physicians and five dentists and a training program for nurses but closed after a few years.[19]

African Americans could not go into hospitals, public parks, hotels, restaurants, etc., in spite of a Civil Rights Law adopted in 1885. The Indiana legislature passed the law after the United States Supreme Court declared the federal Civil Rights Act of 1875 unconstitutional because it exceeded the powers of Congress. The Indiana law entitled all persons to equal treatment in places of public accommodation without regard to race. Once adopted the law received little attention. The few blacks who attempted to invoke it learned that, as interpreted by white judges, it had little force. Restaurants and hotels that catered to white patrons openly refused service to blacks, and theaters either barred them completely or seated them in segregated sections. Most African Americans appeared to accept discrimination and segregation as inevitable. In an age when both whites and blacks regarded Booker T. Washington as the leader and spokesman of his race, the black press, political leaders, and ministers articulated his accommodationist philosophy. Few protests against discrimination took place.[20]

Churches continued to be the strongest institutions in black communities. The vast majority of African Americans attended Baptist or Methodist churches, with fewer communicants as Presbyterians, Episcopalians, or Roman Catholics. Baptists, migrating from the South, expanded older congregations and established new churches. By 1900 fifteen black Baptist churches existed in Indianapolis and thirty by 1916. Baptists outnumbered other denominations in Evansville. Every small town with sufficient numbers of blacks contained a Baptist church, and many founded before the Civil War continued to survive. The autonomy of Baptist churches allowed ministers to start their own churches. The size and character of the church often depended upon the minister's personality. Most congregations affiliated with the Indiana Negro Baptist Association.

Although less numerous than Baptist congregations, the African Methodist Episcopal Church exerted important influence. Other blacks belonged to the African Methodist Episcopal Zion Church. Jones Chapel in Indianapolis, founded in 1872, ranked as the largest church of that denomination. A few congregations affiliated with the Colored Methodist Episcopal Church. In Indianapolis, national headquarters of the Christian Church (Disciples of Christ), Second Christian Church had influence in the black community, partly because of its minister, Henry L. Herod, who served from 1898 until his death in 1935.

A significant development, little noticed at the time, was the conversion of African Americans in Indianapolis to a Pentecostal movement led by Garfield Thomas Haywood, a dynamic preacher who attracted whites as well as blacks and became head of the Pentecostal Assemblies of the World.[21]

Next to churches men's fraternal organizations and the women's auxiliaries were the most important and influential organizations in black communities. Much of the social life and recreation of the community, as well as leadership training, centered around the fraternal orders, along with the dozens of social clubs of great variety.[22]

Black women's clubs, which grew rapidly in the early 1900s, helped develop leadership, a feeling of sisterhood,

*The Woman's Improvement Club operated the Oak Hill Convalescent Tuberculosis Camp in the Brightwood area of Indianapolis from 1905 to 1916.*

and an involvement in social issues. The Woman's Improvement Club in Indianapolis soon after its founding shifted from the study of African-American literature to the problem of tuberculosis, a scourge among black city dwellers. For several years the club maintained a fresh-air camp on the outskirts of Indianapolis.

Prominent black women from around the state founded in 1904 the Indiana State Federation of Colored Women's Clubs. The federation grew rapidly. Programs at its annual conventions particularly addressed social and economic problems of black homemakers. Lillian Thomas Fox and Sallie Wyatt Brown played significant roles in the leadership of the federation.[23]

Flanner House, founded in Indianapolis in 1898 and the first settlement house for blacks, supplemented the voluntary efforts of churches, fraternal orders, and women's clubs. Governed by a biracial board and financed largely by white philanthropy, Flanner House reflected the philosophy of Booker T. Washington in its goals, while its program patterned itself on that at Tuskegee Institute. Social workers, doctors, and other volunteers carried out the Flanner House's agenda in the early years. Initially, the most valuable work of Flanner House entailed training and employment activities for women in domestic service and a day nursery for their children. However limited its goals and services, middle-class blacks gave it strong support.[24]

The Indianapolis Colored YMCA, founded at about the same time as Flanner House, began because the Indianapolis Central YMCA (white) refused membership to a young doctor, Henry L. Hummons. He and other young doctors then founded the "Colored Young Men's Prayer Band," which joined the state YMCA in 1902. In 1913 it moved to a large new building financed by a

*Madam C. J. Walker, along with (left to right) George Knox, Freeman B. Ransom, Booker T. Washington, Alexander Manning, Dr. Joseph Ward, R. W. Bullock, and Thomas A. Taylor attended the Senate Avenue Young Men's Christian Association dedication in 1913.*

grant from Julius Rosenwald as well as contributions from local white philanthropists and local blacks. Its location gave it the popular name of the Senate Avenue YMCA. By 1917 the Indianapolis organization had grown to be the largest black YMCA in the United States. Much of the success of the "Y" can be traced to the aggressive efforts of Faburn DeFrantz, who served as executive director from 1915 until 1951. In addition to his adult education, recreation, and sports programs, DeFrantz sponsored the nationally known "Monster Meetings." Begun earlier as evangelical religious lectures, he made them into forums for discussions of social, economic, and political issues.[25]

The Indiana Branch of the National Association for the Advancement of Colored People (NAACP) received its charter in 1913, just three years after the founding of the national organization. Mary Cable, principal of an elementary school and an active club woman, first presided over the Indianapolis branch. Women also comprised the first board but African-American men—civic leaders, lawyers, ministers, physicians, and businessmen—supported the new organization. Lawyer Robert L. Brokenburr succeeded Cable as president in 1914. The NAACP branch attracted little attention at first, but during the 1920s it led the struggle against increasing prejudice and segregation that followed the First World War.[26]

## 1914 to 1945

The "Great Migration" of blacks from the rural South to the cities in the North during the First World War started the most significant change in African-American society since emancipation. In 1910, 89 percent of blacks in the United States lived in the South, and the census classified them as 72.6 percent rural. By 1970 the number of blacks in the North approximately equaled the number in the South, and blacks had become the most urbanized segment of the entire population.

Blacks left the South because of a series of natural disasters that caused a decline in cotton farming, in hopes of bettering their condition, and in response to the cry for workers that attended the demand for products generated by the war. The movement of African Americans into Indiana was less than that moving into neighboring states, but their number almost doubled in the period from 1910 to 1930.[27]

The largest number of migrants came to Indianapolis, where the black population increased from 21,816 in 1910 to 43,967 in 1930, from 9.3 percent to 12.1 percent of the city's total population. A more spectacular increase occurred in the Calumet area where a steel empire burgeoned on the shores of Lake Michigan. By 1930 the population of Gary had increased from 16,802 in 1910 to 100,426. The number of African Americans increased from 383 (2.3 percent) to 17,922 (17.8 percent). By 1930, 92 percent of the black population in Indiana was classified as urban.

In 1930, 67 percent of the African-American population had been born outside of Indiana. Natives of Kentucky were the largest element, but in Gary, where in 1930 more than 86 percent of the blacks had been born outside of Indiana, most newcomers came from the states of the lower South.[28]

The outbreak of war in Europe in 1914 opened new employment possibilities for blacks as immigration of European workers abruptly ended and others left the United States for their native land. After the United States entered the war in 1917, increasing labor shortages created more job opportunities, but war also meant that some African-American men faced military service. The *Indianapolis Freeman,* like black papers elsewhere, predicted that by fighting, African-American soldiers would win recognition of full citizenship rights for all members of the race. At first, volunteers for service were often rejected because of a lack of training facilities for black troops. But once the Selective Service Act began operating, draft boards in Indiana began registration of blacks. Few black soldiers saw combat overseas. A disproportionate number found themselves assigned to labor units. Available records show that few Indiana blacks died in combat and that more died of disease at home and abroad. The most distinguished African-American unit from Indiana comprised a group of Indianapolis professionals, physicians mostly, commissioned after training at a special camp for colored officers at Des Moines, Iowa.[29]

On the home front African Americans enthusiastically supported their troops and the war effort. They planted victory gardens and sacrificed to buy Liberty Bonds. For both newcomers and older residents the war meant some new job opportunities. In Gary blacks found employment in unskilled jobs in steel mills, and their numbers increased during and after the Great Steel Strike of 1918. By 1923 estimates put mill employees as 20 percent black. In Indianapolis, no single industry existed comparable to the steel mills of the Calumet area. Some blacks took jobs in foundries and meatpacking plants, but the percentage of black employees fell below that in Gary.[30]

Hopes that the war would result in recognition of the rights of full citizenship for all African Americans soon dissipated. Instead racial prejudice and discrimination increased in the postwar years. In the larger urban centers of Indiana racial lines stood out more sharply than ever. The increase in bigotry and enforcement of segregation coincided with the period when the Ku Klux Klan wielded political power in Indiana. The Klan supported the supremacy of native-born, white, Protestant Americans.[31]

The Klan domination of the Republican party raised problems for African Americans and for the first time opened the door for Democrats to win their votes. In the 1924 primary elections Klan-backed Republicans won throughout the state. Many Democrats as well as Republicans belonged to the Klan, but the Democratic candidate for governor and other leading Democrats strongly opposed the Klan. After the primary election George L. Knox of the *Indianapolis Freeman* declared, "The Republican party as now constituted is the Ku Klux Klan of Indiana," and called upon African Americans to support the Democrats. The Indianapolis branch of the NAACP organized an Independent Voters League for the purpose of defeating Klan-backed candidates. Leading African-American lawyers toured the state, campaigning for Democrats, and a mass meeting of the Independent Voters League endorsed the entire Democratic ticket.[32]

On election day in Indianapolis predominantly black wards voted Democratic for the first time. In Gary and Evansville, however, most blacks again voted the Republican ticket. Klan-backed candidates won the governorship and other state offices. Klan members or Klan-supported members dominated the new state legislature. However, at its next session legislators introduced no measures harmful to blacks.[33]

In 1925 a Klansman became mayor of Indianapolis. A Klan-backed city council passed a city ordinance intended to prevent African Americans from moving into white neighborhoods.

The influx of blacks into the city during and after the war strained the already inadequate housing available in black neighborhoods. As newcomers arrived they concentrated in established neighborhoods, while older residents who had enough money tried to buy homes in formerly all-white, middle-class areas. White homeowners, fearful of black neighbors and of a decline in real estate values, resorted to a variety of methods to exclude blacks. Members of civic clubs pledged not to sell or rent property to nonwhites. Indianapolis Real Estate Board members refused to show property in white areas to African Americans. When blacks acquired houses, white neighbors sometimes resorted to direct intimidation, such as throwing a hand grenade into a window, or circulating handbills asking, "Do You Want a Nigger for a Neighbor?"

After Klan-backed officials gained control of the city government, civic groups circulated petitions asking for government action. A zoning ordinance became law in 1926. The language applied to both races, but the ordinance was intended to harm only blacks. If a Negro sold property to a white, or vice versa, the buyer could not take possession without obtaining written consent of a majority of persons of the opposite race in the immediate neighborhood.

The mayor signed the measure even though advised of its probable unconstitutionality. Members of the Indianapolis branch of the NAACP, backed by the national office, instituted a suit that resulted in the ordinance being declared unconstitutional. Hopes of white groups for a successful appeal ended when the United States Supreme Court declared a similar ordinance adopted in New Orleans unconstitutional.[34] This legal victory did not end efforts to prevent African Americans from moving into white neighborhoods. In all cities, and even in small towns, blacks were consigned to clearly recognizable neighborhoods.[35]

In Indianapolis and Gary increased black population also led to greater school segregation. As colored elementary schools in Indianapolis became overcrowded, some pupils attended schools in predominantly white districts. Neighborhood groups began to petition the Indianapolis school board to insure a completely segregated system. The board, in 1923, set up new boundaries for fourteen elementary schools for Negroes and required attendance even if it meant traveling long distances. As the result elementary schools were almost completely segregated, and in later years the board continued to redraw school districts to preserve segregation as residential patterns changed.[36]

Meanwhile, numerous influential organizations joined neighborhood civic groups to campaign for a segregated high school, a movement closely related to the movement for a new building in a new location for Shortridge High School, where the largest number of blacks was enrolled. A petition presented to the school board by the Indianapolis Chamber of Commerce in 1922 emphasized the "necessity" for a "separate, modern, completely equipped and adequate high school for colored students." A petition from the Federation of Civic Clubs argued that the presence of blacks at Shortridge menaced the health of white students. The petition alleged that the presence of a large number of cases of incipient tuberculosis among black students, due to the crowded and unsanitary conditions of housing in black neighborhoods, argued for segregation: a remarkable comment from a group dedicated to preventing blacks from moving into better housing in white neighborhoods!

The movement for a segregated high school met with strong and bitter opposition in the African-American community. A delegation led by Robert L. Brokenburr petitioned the school board, declaring the movement for a separate school "unjust, un-American, and against the spirit of democratic ideals." A group of black ministers said that segregation meant inequality of opportunity and was inspired by a desire to keep blacks in a subordinate class.[37]

The school board, in December 1922, voted to authorize the construction of the separate school, saying that the desire of Negroes for an education was "laudable," and that a new, well-equipped high school of their own would provide them a "maximum educational opportunity" and the fullest opportunity to develop qualities needed for "good citizenship."

Before construction began a group of African-American parents recruited by the Indianapolis NAACP brought a suit to enjoin construction on the grounds that the proposed school could not fulfill the "equality" provision of the Fourteenth Amendment of the United States Constitution and that it could not equal the course offerings of the existing high schools. An Indianapolis court refused to issue the injunction. The plaintiffs appealed to the Indiana Supreme Court, which upheld the lower court in 1926, saying that the suit was premature; that if, in operation, the new school denied pupils educational opportunities available in white high schools, proceedings could be undertaken to secure constitutional rights. Meanwhile, in May 1924 the Indianapolis school board had voted to go ahead with construction of the school while the appeal was pending. The school, named after Crispus Attucks, the black hero of the American Revolution, opened in September 1927.[38]

In later years a popular tradition claimed that the Ku Klux Klan was responsible for building a segregated high school. It is true that a Klan-dominated school board and city government won election in November 1925, but members of the "Klan board" did not take office until 1926. The chronology of events shows that the former school board, elected in 1921, voted to build the segregated school in 1922 and authorized continued construction during the appeal to the Indiana Supreme Court. The "Klan board" carried out a program initiated by the previous board.

Another tradition holds that Attucks High School came to be because the black community wanted it. However, school board minutes contain no evidence of any petition from blacks asking for a separate school; they do contain records of petitions by blacks opposing it. After construction began, some African Americans supported it because it would offer opportunities for black teachers. The new school enlisted a highly educated faculty, and once opened the school became a center of cultural activity and an object of pride for the entire black community.[39]

In Gary, where the black population grew at a faster rate than in Indianapolis, William E. Wirt, the powerful school superintendent, sought to "Americanize" children of European immigrants but believed in segregating black children. Segregated elementary schools served most of the burgeoning school population. At the Froebel School, which contained elementary and high school levels, black elementary students studied under black teachers in separate classes. In the high school no separate classes existed, but black students could not join in extracurricular activities and social events.

In September 1927 a racial crisis arose when, as a temporary measure, Superintendent Wirt transferred eighteen African-American students from an overcrowded black school, Virginia Street School, to Emerson High School. About six hundred white students staged a strike and marched through the city carrying placards which said, "We won't go back to Emerson 'til it's white." The strike ended after four days with a promise of no penalties for the strikers, and with an understanding that a new black high school would be built. At midyear nearly all of the African-American students went back to the Virginia Street School. Backed by the NAACP a black family sought a court order to transfer their daughters back to Emerson. Their lawyers argued that the Virginia Street School did not meet the state requirements for a high school. In 1931, after delays, the Indiana Supreme Court upheld a lower court that had rejected the plea.[40]

By 1932 a new black high school had been built and opened. The Roosevelt School, a modern building with facilities equal in every way to the schools for whites in Gary, included kindergarten through high school. Some African Americans deplored the appointment of Frederick C. McFarlane, an outspoken admirer of Marcus Garvey and black separatism, as principal, but they admitted his ability to inspire pride and self-respect in the students. Even opponents of a separate school were proud of Roosevelt, which, like Attucks in Indianapolis, served as a cultural and community center. The student body at Roosevelt was entirely black, but a large number of blacks continued to attend racially mixed Froebel School.[41]

Evansville schools had always been strictly segregated. A new school, Lincoln, opened in 1928 to replace the shabby Clark School. It included classrooms for elementary and high school students and a large combination gymnasium and manual training facility. Although blacks had no voice in planning the school they held it in great esteem, and blacks throughout the state admired the athletic teams of Attucks, Roosevelt, and Lincoln. Teams from these schools could not be part of the Indiana High School Athletic Association and could not play in the state basketball tournament, but they competed with each other and with black schools in neighboring states.[42]

Signs of racial bigotry and segregation multiplied during the 1920s. In addition to school and residential segregation, one could find separate public parks and more signs "For white customers only" in restaurants and other places of public accommodation. However, no riots or serious racial disorders occurred until 1930, when a lynching took place in Marion, a small city northeast of Indianapolis. Two black youths, one eighteen years old, the other nineteen, accused of killing a young white man during a holdup and raping his female companion, were seized from the county jail, beaten to death, and their bodies hung from trees in the courthouse square. An innocent sixteen-year-old boy was accused of complicity in the crime and jailed. He escaped lynching, and at his trial a year later Robert L. Bailey and Robert L. Brokenburr, defending him without pay, saved him from the death sentence sought by the prosecutor. The judge sentenced him to one year at the state reformatory. None of the members of the white lynching mob faced criminal charges.[43]

Although Indiana was not the "promised land" migrants from the South dreamed of, they found life there preferable to the one they had left. Until the Great Depression, that is, which shattered their lives. The depression meant unemployment and hardship for most American workers, but for blacks it proved "a disaster of unparalleled proportions." African-American workers were usually marginal, "the last to be hired, the first to be fired." Accurate figures on the unemployed are unavailable because the government had not begun to compile them, but no doubt the number of unemployed blacks stood disproportionately high. As unemployed whites began displacing blacks in menial jobs, the problem became more acute. Wives of unemployed black men who tried to get work in domestic service found white women preempting jobs held traditionally by black women.

Government agencies could not deal with a problem of such magnitude as the growing unemployment and poverty, and both state and national governments bound themselves to inhibiting philosophies of volunteerism and self-help. In black communities churches and other benevolent organizations with limited resources tried to help. Efforts took place, also largely unsuccessful, to persuade stores in black neighborhoods to hire blacks or face boycotts.[44]

The growing impatience by all segments of the population with the failure of government to deal with the depression resulted in a Democratic landslide in 1932. In 1932 both major parties actively wooed black voters and nominated black candidates for the state legislature and local offices. The Democratic victory brought, for the first time, two African-American Democrats into the legislature: Henry J. Richardson, an Indianapolis lawyer, and Dr. Robert L. Stanton, an East Chicago dentist. The 1932 election and the New Deal marked the beginning of a political revolution among black voters. By 1936 the mass of African Americans in Indiana identified themselves

*Robert L. Brokenburr was the first African American to serve as an Indiana state senator.*

as Democrats. In 1940 Republicans were victorious in both the state and national elections, but the black vote remained solidly Democratic and has remained Democratic, although a few prominent African Americans are Republicans. In 1940 Robert L. Brokenburr, a lifelong Republican, became the first black to be elected a state senator. Black Democratic representatives from cities where Democrats were stronger than in Indianapolis acquired seniority and influence as they won successive terms; for example, J. Chester Allen, a South Bend lawyer; James S. Hunter, an East Chicago labor leader; and Jesse L. Dickinson, a South Bend social worker.[45]

Blacks, because of the disproportionately high rate of unemployment among them, probably benefited more from relief programs than any other segment of the population. In some communities the Works Progress Administration (WPA), which furnished jobs to the unskilled, became the most important employer of black workers.[46]

Black men and women and black communities benefited from the WPA and other New Deal programs, but encountered discrimination in hiring, particularly in construction projects. The largest public housing project in the state, Lockefield Gardens in Indianapolis, involved slum clearance and apartment construction for occupancy by African Americans, who were hired for unskilled jobs. However, they received few opportunities at higher-paying work because of union opposition. In Gary, blacks complained because they had no voice in the construction of Delaney Houses, a public housing project intended for them. But, in spite of complaints about discrimination in hiring, in Indianapolis, Gary, and Evansville's Lincoln Gardens, blacks benefited from the chance to acquire modern low-cost housing.[47]

By 1940 few jobs had opened for blacks, and a disproportionate number remained on relief rolls. However, as Congress began to reduce funds for the WPA, prospects of jobs in defense industries arose as American factories geared up to supply the needs of nations in Europe fighting Nazi Germany in the Second World War. As the United States moved toward active participation in the war, the black press and civic leaders warned that black soldiers would face discrimination and humiliation. Once hostilities began some African-American leaders said the members of their race would be fighting two wars—one against the Axis powers, the other against racism at home.[48]

Segregation in the armed forces did continue throughout the war, but black servicemen experienced generally better conditions than previously. For the first time African Americans could enlist in combat service in the navy and marines. Blacks took particular pride in pilots who were trained for the air corps in a special

school at Tuskegee, Alabama. African-American women were also accepted for service in both the WACs and the WAVES.[49]

Both black and white troops received training at camps in Indiana, always in segregated units. In spite of orders by President Franklin Roosevelt prohibiting discrimination, black servicemen sometimes experienced prejudice in the camps. In one of the most notorious incidents a group of black officers who ventured into a club for white officers at Freemen Field in southern Indiana were arrested and brought before a court-martial. In all the larger cities and in smaller communities near the camps, white citizens eagerly supported USO clubs, but they took for granted their service was for white personnel only. Black soldiers who occasionally ventured into a white club were rejected. With no alternative, blacks who opposed segregation as a matter of principle nevertheless gave support to separate facilities. In Indianapolis a "Colored Citizens Selective Service Steering Committee" helped organize recreation centers. Similar groups organized centers in Gary, Evansville, and smaller communities where enough blacks lived to maintain them. So long as African Americans confined themselves to the facilities of these segregated centers no trouble occurred.[50]

As thousands of young African-American men and a few women entered the armed forces, others, as well as white migrants, flocked into Indiana cities seeking jobs in war industries and creating dramatic demographic and social changes. Between 1940 and 1950 the state's black population jumped 45 percent to 175,712. The largest number came to Indianapolis, but Gary had the greatest rate of increase. In other industrial centers in the northern part of the state—South Bend, Fort Wayne, and East Chicago—sharp increases occurred, and also in smaller cities like Muncie and Anderson. Evansville underwent a relative decline in the postwar years, and the percentage growth of blacks in Terre Haute, about 5 percent, remained unchanged.[51]

The war brought an end to widespread unemployment, and most blacks found some sort of work, often because of government pressures prohibiting racial discrimination in industries with government contracts. President Roosevelt created a Fair Employment Practices Commission to enforce equity in hiring. At the state level Gov. Henry F. Schricker appointed a biracial committee to encourage employment of black workers. J. Chester Allen, the former state legislator, traveled tirelessly over the state as agent of the committee, persuading employers to broaden employment policies. Some employers resisted complying with government policies because they feared that white workers would refuse to work with blacks, and throughout the war years blacks complained that they were not admitted to some of the vocational programs intended to train workers in war industries.

New employment opportunities for blacks came also through the efforts of unions, particularly the Congress of Industrial Organizations (CIO), to open jobs in defense-related industries. The CIO, which opposed discrimination in employment practices, in addition worked for civil rights legislation after the war. Moreover, new employment opportunities opened when white workers left former jobs for better paying jobs in war industries. As a result some businesses and nondefense industries began to hire black workers for the first time. Because of manpower shortages a few black women found work in factories and also filled vacancies when white clerical workers quit for better-paying jobs in war industries.[52]

While economic conditions improved for African Americans, the rapid increase in population and wartime conditions brought acute housing shortages and other social problems. Those who wanted to buy homes met the same obstacles they had encountered before the war, and the influx of white workers exacerbated the problem. White landlords increased already exorbitant rents for substandard houses and apartments. Often several families crowded into a single unit. In some communities the government built a few temporary houses or trailers, but shortages of materials and labor restricted building permanent housing. Evansville, Gary, and other cities applied for Federal Housing Authority funds for public housing for black families, but authorities in Indianapolis adamantly opposed public housing.[53]

Wartime conditions, particularly lack of housing, contributed to an increase in crime, juvenile delinquency, and racial tensions. Resentment that old patterns of racial discrimination persisted at home while African-American men were being drafted and sent overseas to destroy a racist enemy caused some black citizens to become more assertive in demanding their rights to equal treatment. Some thoughtful white citizens also became increasingly aware of the contradiction between segregation and discrimination and the proclaimed war aims. However, fear of race riots, like those in wartime New York and Detroit, probably served as a more compelling reason for white citizens to think seriously about correcting some of the racial wrongs in Indiana. Throughout the state, white churches, civic organizations, and city governments created or revived interracial committees and held conferences and seminars on race relations in the hope of allaying unrest.[54]

## Since 1945

The migration of African Americans from the South to the states of the North and West accelerated in the years following the Second World War, and the rate of urbanization increased. Between 1950 and 1960 Indiana's black population increased an estimated 54.3 percent to 268,358 (5.8 percent) out of a total of 4,662,451. Thirty years later, in 1990, blacks numbered 432,092, or 7.8 percent of the whole and continued to concentrate in urban areas. By 1990 two-thirds of black residents lived in Marion and Lake counties. In Lake County blacks made up 22 percent of the population, and 90 percent of the blacks lived in Gary and East Chicago. In Marion County (Indianapolis) blacks comprised 21 percent; in Allen (Fort Wayne), 10 percent; in St. Joseph (South Bend), 9.7 percent. In sixty-eight of the ninety-two counties of the state blacks totaled less than 1 percent. Thirteen counties had ten or fewer African Americans, and in many townships there was not a single black resident.[55]

In the urban counties with the largest numbers, African Americans were usually concentrated in a single township in the inner city. In Indianapolis in 1950 there were 59,530 blacks in Center Township; in 1960 there were 89,903—an increase of 51 percent in a decade. During the next ten years the total population of the township declined by about 18 percent as more and more whites moved to other parts of the city or to the suburbs, and as a result the percentage of blacks increased. In Gary and other cities there were similar trends, and the 1980 and 1990 censuses showed that the pattern continued.[56]

While demographic changes took place—northward migration and increasing concentration in inner cities—important changes occurred in the legal status of African Americans and in race relations in Indiana and in the nation. Returning black veterans refused to accept the inferior status they held before the war. Black civilians had no intention of losing the economic gains they had won. The war also led many whites to reassess their attitudes on race and race relations. Many viewed the question of racial prejudice and discrimination as a moral and religious issue. Others, reluctant to promote racial equality, nevertheless recognized that in the Cold War era the United States had to change its image if it hoped to win Third World support.

In Indiana a revitalized state conference of the NAACP, particularly its Indianapolis branch, took the lead in the struggle for civil rights. Willard Ransom, five-time state conference president, led the fight. Ransom, the son of Freeman Ransom, business manager for the Madam C. J. Walker Manufacturing Company, earned a law degree at Harvard, where he was the only black member in a class of three hundred. During the war he served as a captain in the department of the Judge Advocate General. Like his father, he was a Democrat. William T. Ray, president of the Indianapolis branch of the NAACP, was the son-in-law of Republican leader Robert L. Brokenburr. Jessie Jacobs, also a Republican, proved an indefatigable ally of Ransom and Ray. Democrat Henry J. Richardson, although not very active in the NAACP at this time, nevertheless gave legal advice and helped frame civil rights legislation.[57]

The Federation of Associated Clubs (FAC), founded by Sterling James, and with a membership numbering in the thousands, supported and strengthened the efforts of the NAACP in Indianapolis after the war.[58] National Urban League affiliates in some northern cities took the lead in programs for civil rights. In Gary, in particular, where the NAACP had become inactive, the local Urban League played an important part in the beginning of school desegregation. Indianapolis, however, had no National Urban League affiliate until 1966.[59]

The NAACP adopted four main legislative goals at state conferences: a law abolishing segregation in public education; an effective Fair Employment Practices Commission (FEPC) law prohibiting discrimination in the workplace; a fair housing law; and a stronger public accommodations law. A law abolishing segregation in public education passed the General Assembly in 1949, but the other laws failed to pass until after 1960.[60]

Meanwhile, activists undertook a nonviolent campaign to gain access to public accommodations and enforcement of the 1885 Civil Rights Law. The movement centered in Indianapolis, but other communities witnessed similar efforts. In Indianapolis a loose coalition of the NAACP, black social and fraternal organizations, the CIO, and white church groups began a campaign to secure service in downtown restaurants and hotels and gain access to public parks and swimming pools. The leaders of the movement made it clear that they were not engaging in "civil disobedience" but asking merely for rights guaranteed by the 1885 law. The usual pattern called for a racially mixed group to seek service in a restaurant. Sometimes proprietors turned them away immediately. Some lunch counters and restaurants closed rather than serve the unwelcome patrons. Sometimes the groups received service immediately without problems; sometimes they found themselves seated in an isolated section. The few attempts to file suits against businesses flouting the law failed because of reluctant prosecution by public officials, who apparently could not be compelled to do so under the 1885 law.[61] Persuasion and peaceful "sit-ins" brought some measure of progress, but widespread desegregation of places of public accommodation did not occur until the adoption of the Indiana Civil Rights Laws of 1961 and 1963 and the federal Civil Rights Law of 1964.[62]

African Americans, as a minority, with few state legislators and limited lobbying influence, had neither the numbers nor political "clout" to pass civil rights measures. Enactment of laws required legislative allies and a coalition of lobbying groups. The NAACP and black fraternal and ministerial groups actively lobbied for the 1949 school law, but support from the CIO, the Federation of Churches, the Indianapolis Community Relations Council, Jewish organizations, the Congress of Parents and Teachers, the League of Women Voters, and other predominantly white organizations probably turned the tide in persuading lawmakers to support the measure.[63]

More Democrats voted for civil rights legislation than did Republicans, but not always. A Democrat and a Republican member frequently cosponsored civil rights bills. During the 1950s, with Republicans usually in a majority in the General Assembly, legislators introduced civil rights bills at every session, but delaying tactics prevented their enactment.[64]

During the 1960s the national civil rights movement as well as changes in Indiana created a climate more favorable to legislation. For the first time a governor, Democrat Matthew E. Welsh, emphasized civil rights in his campaign and in his legislative agenda. The Indiana Conference on Civil Rights, a coalition similar to that which supported the 1949 school law, but larger, lobbied successfully. As the result, the Civil Rights Laws adopted in 1961 and 1963 (before the enactment of the federal Civil Rights Law of 1964) created a Civil Rights Commission with enforcement powers against discrimination in jobs and in access to public accommodations. In 1965 a Fair Housing Law passed giving the Civil Rights Commission authority over real estate transactions and rental property.[65]

The one goal of civil rights groups most easily attained was concerned with access to public accommodations. Harold Hatcher, the first director of the Indiana Civil Rights Commission, had much to do with the commission's early success. Hatcher, a Quaker with long experience in civil rights work, usually succeeded in resolving complaints of discrimination by persuasion and conciliation rather than through administrative orders. Indiana law covered most of the provisions of the Civil Rights Law passed by Congress in 1964, but the federal law helped reinforce the authority of the state laws. Restaurants and taverns in some small towns continued to refuse service to African Americans, but this type of complaint to the Civil Rights Commission declined and surfaced only occasionally by 1967. It became commonplace for blacks and racially mixed groups to be accommodated in bars, restaurants, and hotels and motels, particularly those of national chains. Access to entertainment and recreation, such as private amusement parks and public swimming pools, occurred less often, but in most places the presence of blacks caused no overt comment, and these changes took place relatively calmly.[66]

The NAACP furnished the leadership for enactment of civil rights legislation, and it continued to play an important part in monitoring compliance, particularly school desegregation. It played a less conspicuous role, however, in the turbulent years of the late 1960s and the 1970s. On the national scene more activist groups, inspired by the Reverend Martin Luther King, Jr., led the drive for civil rights in the South. As the civil rights campaign moved northward to the large metropolitan centers other young blacks became predisposed toward the separatist ideas of Malcolm X. Only to a limited extent did Indiana feel these developments. Some young African Americans, inspired by the movement in the South, picketed stores of national chains that student groups happened to be boycotting in southern cities. In Indianapolis a short-lived branch of CORE (Congress on Racial Equality), while sharing the integrationist goals of the NAACP, criticized the older organization for its lack of militancy and carried on demonstrations against continuing segregation in the schools.[67] In Gary and Indianapolis whites viewed with alarm the establishment of mosques by Black Muslims and the organization of Black Panther groups. However, the Black Panthers soon disappeared, and the Black Muslims lived peacefully.[68]

Meanwhile the Indianapolis Urban League organized in 1966, years after similar bodies had been operating in most Indiana cities. It came about through the support of white and black civic leaders, most prominently Henry J. Richardson, an early president. Sam Jones, an experienced social worker, came from Minneapolis to direct it and later serve as its president.[69]

The Southern Christian Leadership Conference (SCLC), founded by Martin Luther King, Jr., with headquarters in Atlanta, also came to Indianapolis. The Reverend Andrew Brown, pastor of St. John's Missionary Baptist Church, presided, and Baptist ministers made up most of the membership, involving themselves in civil rights and urban problems.[70]

The Indianapolis Urban League, while not openly involved in political lobbying, nevertheless influenced the climate of opinion favorable to civil rights. Its work, like that of the National Urban League, concentrated on employment and housing issues. The work of the NAACP, conversely, traditionally centered on the attainment and protection of legal rights. Both organizations included a racially mixed membership and boards of directors. Many people belonged to both organizations. The Indianapolis Urban League and affiliates of the national organization in other Indiana cities received some funding from the United Way or similar organizations as well as private sources. The NAACP, because of its political orientation, was ineligible for such funds. Although rivalry existed

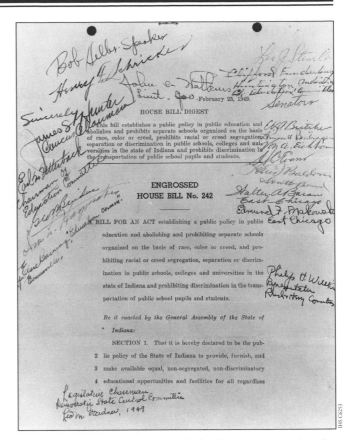

*Indiana House Bill 242 outlawed school segregation within the state in 1949.*

among the three organizations, leaders of the NAACP, the urban leagues, the SCLC, and other black ministers and church groups cooperated with white city officials and civic leaders to control urban tensions that might lead to riots and disorder. As a result, perhaps, no serious riots such as those that erupted in many northern cities in the sixties and seventies occurred in Indiana.[71]

The 1949 law abolishing segregation in public education was the first important civil rights law passed in Indiana, but implementation of the law proved more controversial than any of the other civil rights laws. Prior to this law, northern cities in the state had taken steps to desegregate schools. A statement adopted by the Gary school board in August 1946 declared that students in their districts should not be discriminated against because of race, color, or religion. The school board's action came after a committee appointed by the chamber of commerce drafted a code on race relations which deplored segregation and discrimination. This action followed a strike by white students at Froebel High School demanding the removal of all Negroes. Later the board changed its tactics, demanding that all Gary schools be racially integrated.

Implementation of the school board policy against discrimination began in September 1947 with the redrawing of school districts and assigning of all students to the district where they lived, thus establishing the principle of integration. But enrollment at most schools continued to be predominately white or black because of residential patterns.[72]

No separate schools for blacks existed in nearby East Chicago, but in the racially mixed schools blacks could not participate in extracurricular activities. After Gary announced an end to segregation the East Chicago city council passed a resolution demanding the school board (appointed by the council) end discriminatory practices. In Elkhart segregation ended when the school board closed a black elementary school housed in a substandard building and redrew school districts. Following these actions only Indianapolis and Evansville and small towns in southern counties retained a policy of segregation.[73]

In postwar Indianapolis the NAACP, labor leaders, church leaders, PTAs, the League of Women Voters, Jewish organizations, and others carried on a campaign to end segregated schools, though opposed by school authorities. A 1947 bill to end segregation in Indiana school systems met defeat in the General Assembly largely through the lobbying by the Indianapolis school board.[74]

In 1949 a bill, in great measure a product of NAACP lawyers and supported by an impressive array of civic organizations, passed the General Assembly. Gov. Henry F. Schricker signed the law, which provided for gradual implementation of a public policy to eliminate segregation and discrimination in public education. The law stipulated that children entering kindergarten or the first grade in September 1949 attend the school in the district in which they lived, and that desegregation through high school be completed by 1954. The law also prohibited segregation or color discrimination in higher education and prohibited any public educational institution from employment or on-the-job discrimination.[75]

Some Ohio River communities, such as New Albany, welcomed the 1949 law because it relieved them from financing a dual school system. Evansville school authorities, on the other hand, officially complied but drew school districts to give pupils a choice of attending either of two existing schools—one all-white, one black—a device obviously intended to perpetuate segregation. Although Evansville had a relatively small percentage of African-American students, about 12 percent, they concentrated in a few schools, such as all-black Lincoln Elementary. Litigation over continuing segregation ultimately resulted in some all-black schools closing and students transferring to predominantly white schools, along with two-way busing as a means to integration.[76]

Indianapolis, with the state's largest school population, moved slowly and reluctantly to comply with the 1949 law.

A few black children began to attend previously all-white schools in 1949 following the redrawing of district boundaries for elementary schools. By 1953 about two-thirds of the children in the city attended racially mixed elementary schools although in some "integrated" schools there were only one or two black pupils. Desegregation of high schools moved even more slowly. No white student attended Crispus Attucks High School until 1972. Black enrollment at Shortridge High School grew rapidly, reflecting the changing composition of the school's neighborhood. At other high schools integration moved very slowly, but by 1953 the school board announced desegregation completed—a year before the United States Supreme Court declared school segregation unconstitutional in *Brown* v. *Board of Education*. Delegations from the NAACP and other organizations, both white and African-American, continued to appear before the school board to complain, but progress toward desegregation continued to be slow.[77]

The continued growth of the African-American population and changing residential patterns made desegregation difficult in Indianapolis and Gary. Blacks moved into formerly white neighborhoods and whites moved to the suburbs creating de facto segregation—segregation not caused by statute.

In Gary, by 1961 approximately 97 percent of the 23,055 black pupils went to mostly or all-black schools with nearly all-black teachers and administrators. Most of these schools were seriously overcrowded, and the school board, with limited funds, made frantic efforts to build more classrooms. Nearly all of the new schools went up in predominantly black neighborhoods.[78]

In 1962 the Gary NAACP filed suit in federal district court on behalf of one hundred black plaintiffs, who claimed that school authorities promoted a segregated school system by drawing school boundaries and selecting sites for new schools. However, in *Bell* v. *School City of Gary,* one of the first desegregation suits in a northern city, the judge ruled that no proof existed that the decisions of the school board regarding school districts and locations of new schools had been racially motivated, a decision upheld by the Seventh Circuit Court of Appeals.[79]

In Indianapolis, where authorities faced increasing criticism for not making more positive efforts toward desegregation, the school board welcomed the Gary decision. After the legislature in 1965 passed a law intended to give school authorities added powers to desegregate, the Indiana Civil Rights Commission, the NAACP, and numerous white civic- and church-related organizations continued to criticize the school board for policies that they claimed perpetuated a segregated school system.[80]

Meanwhile the Civil Rights Act of 1964 authorized the attorney general of the United States to act on complaints that a school board denied students equal protection. Consequently, the United States Justice Department, encouraged by the local NAACP to observe the Indianapolis situation, accused school officials of "racial discrimination in the assignment of pupils and faculty members." When the school board failed to respond adequately, the Justice Department filed suit in 1968. The suit boiled down to a body of evidence that showed the Indianapolis public school system (IPS) still segregated de jure long after passage of state desegregation laws and the Supreme Court decision *Brown* v. *Board of Education*.[81]

At the trial, which took place in 1971, lawyers for IPS argued that segregation in the schools was not due to school board policies but simply to residential patterns. Judge S. Hugh Dillin, citing impressive amounts of evidence, found IPS guilty of de jure segregation. Dillin ordered immediate steps to desegregate teaching staffs and Attucks High School students and to make similar changes in some elementary schools. He recognized, however, that because of shifting residential patterns and changes in the city's racial composition, lasting desegregation could not be attained within the existing boundaries of IPS. Therefore, to find a remedy he ordered the Justice Department to add outlying school corporations and the state of Indiana as defendants in the suit.[82]

In 1981, after more trials, appeals, and delaying tactics, the Seventh Circuit Court of Appeals upheld Judge Dillin's earlier decisions that the state of Indiana and IPS perpetuated de jure segregation. The United States Supreme Court refused to review this decision. The Appeals Court also upheld one-way busing of blacks from IPS to the township schools as a remedy for segregation within IPS. Two-way busing of both white and African-American students within the boundaries of IPS had begun earlier.[83] The court justified one-way busing on the grounds that the township school corporations had not been found guilty of de jure segregation. The order, however, aroused bitter criticism among many African Americans and integrationist whites. Nevertheless, busing of about 5,500 black students to township schools in Marion County began peacefully in September 1981 under a plan intended to insure that African Americans made up about 15 percent of the total enrollment in each township.[84]

In Fort Wayne, South Bend, and smaller cities, increases in the number of African Americans and changes in residential patterns resulted in some predominantly black schools. These conditions led to complaints to the Indiana Civil Rights Commission. In most cases school authorities agreed to reduce segregation by drawing new districts and building new schools in locations where enrollments would be racially mixed. In a few cases complainants began court actions that were usually settled by consent decrees.[85]

In Gary and Indianapolis genuine racial integration became impossible with the increase of black students and the continued white flight to the suburbs. By the 1980s African Americans made up more than 80 percent of Gary's students. In Indianapolis enrollments in excess of one hundred thousand in the 1960s had halved by the 1980s with blacks making up about half of the students. In Gary, where the mayor appointed the school board, black members played an important role when the city embarked upon desegregation. In Indianapolis, with elected school board members, the powerful Citizens School Committee for years failed to endorse a single black candidate. In 1976, while the desegregation case was in progress, the influence of blacks increased as the public elected a biracial prointegrationist board. By 1990 the seven-member board contained a majority of African Americans, and for the first time a black school superintendent, Shirl E. Gilbert, administered the school system, which in spite of declining enrollments remained the largest in the state. In the state's school systems with black enrollments the numbers of black teachers and administrators multiplied. African Americans made up more than half of Gary's teacher corps. Indianapolis had a much smaller percentage, partly because fewer qualified persons applied. Some of the suburban school systems in Marion County employed black administrators as well as teachers.[86]

While public schools grappled with integration issues, racial patterns underwent change at colleges and universities in the state. Before 1900 very few African Americans from Indiana graduated from institutions of higher learning. A study made at Atlanta University found only nine graduates, although a greater number undoubtedly attended but did not graduate. The three state institutions (Indiana University, Purdue University, and Terre Haute Normal School) all admitted blacks before 1900, but few graduated. In 1894 the first African American graduated from Purdue, the first from Indiana University the following year. An occasional black attended one of the private colleges, but there is little accurate information about them. Because of its location in Indianapolis probably the largest group attended Butler College, where the first black, Gertrude Mahorney, graduated in 1887.

During the early years of the twentieth century the number of black students increased slowly. In 1928, for example, at Indiana University, only 71 blacks attended out of a total enrollment of 3,493. The number at other institutions was even smaller.

All institutions, public and private, barred African Americans from living in dormitories and participating in college social life. At Indiana University, black male students organized their own fraternity, Kappa Alpha Psi, in 1911. Within a few years chapters had spread across the United States. At Indiana, Samuel Dargan, who received a law degree from the university in 1909 and worked as curator of the law library, served as a kind of unofficial dean of black students. Out of his own funds he built Dargan House, where all black women students had to live unless they lived with relatives. He also owned rooming houses and a house that served as a cafeteria.[87]

Ironically, although excluded from student life generally, African Americans found acceptance as athletes. Preston Eagleson, who later received a Ph.D. from Indiana University, played on the football team in the 1890s. In later years several blacks played football for Indiana, and some Attucks graduates played football at Butler University.[88]

The Second World War brought changes, especially after large numbers of veterans arrived on university campuses as the result of the GI Bill of Rights. Some changes resulted from pressures on administrators by the Indianapolis branch of the NAACP, others through the efforts of student groups. Student branches of the NAACP surfaced on some campuses, usually supported by white students and faculty. Improvements in housing and admission to the state-owned dormitories took priority. In 1944 the Indianapolis NAACP persuaded Indiana University President Herman B Wells to open a dormitory for black women. Later desegregation occurred in all residence halls on the Bloomington campus. Student groups gained access to the Student Union, and with administrative support persuaded most private eating establishments to open to black patrons.[89]

Adoption of the 1949 school law, which prohibited racial discrimination in state universities as well as elementary and secondary schools, gave added impetus to change, but progress came more slowly at Purdue and other state schools than at Bloomington. Black enrollments at private colleges remained small but increased as the result of the GI Bill of Rights.

Change accelerated in the 1960s as the civil rights movement gained momentum. Both public and private institutions made efforts to recruit black students, partly because the Civil Rights Act of 1964 and other federal measures made grants contingent upon proof of elimination of racial discrimination. Nevertheless the percentage of African Americans who went on to colleges and universities remained small. Students who demonstrated academic achievements received scholarships, but poverty as well as lack of preparation prevented many from enrolling. A large percentage of African-American students had to work in order to attend school. For this reason many blacks enrolled part-time at the regional campuses of Indiana and Purdue, while smaller numbers took full loads at Bloomington and West Lafayette. At all campuses a higher proportion of blacks than whites dropped out of school without finishing degrees.

The elimination of barriers to employment of faculty and administrators paralleled attempts to recruit black students. The civil rights revolution also led to curriculum changes as campuses introduced courses in African-American history, literature, and music, as well as African studies.[90]

Following the war, manufacturers lost defense contracts and returning veterans sought jobs, thus temporarily wiping out some of the gains blacks had made in wartime. But by the 1950s the United States entered upon a long period of economic growth and unprecedented prosperity that brought greater economic opportunities for both whites and blacks.

In 1961, after much debate and delay, the state legislature finally passed a Fair Employment Practices Act that made it public policy to encourage all citizens to engage in gainful employment. The Civil Rights Commission, created by the act, had authority to investigate charges of discriminatory practices. By 1963 it had been given the power to issue cease and desist orders against persons practicing discrimination. The amended law included charges of discrimination because of sex. As complaints over discrimination in public accommodations declined, hearings over discrimination in employment became more important in the work of the Civil Rights Commission.[91]

During the turbulent 1960s employers actively sought African Americans, sometimes as a way to attract patronage of a growing body of prosperous black consumers. The chamber of commerce, which persistently opposed FEPC legislation, began programs to encourage training and employment of blacks. Educated blacks gained appointments as minor executives in banks and to corporate boards of directors. Such firms as Eli Lilly and Company of Indianapolis avidly sought the small number of black men and women trained in science.[92]

For the first time opportunities existed for large numbers of blacks in middle-level civil service jobs in federal, state, and municipal offices. Women found work as clerical workers in private businesses and as salespeople in department stores—employment heretofore closed to blacks. As already noted, the demand for teachers and educational administrators was greater than the number of qualified applicants. The numbers of African

Americans trained as lawyers, physicians, surgeons, and nurses increased as educational barriers fell. Blacks gained admittance to hitherto all-white professional organizations.[93]

The unforeseen decline of enterprises catering to black customers, following the end of discrimination in places of public accommodation, gave impetus to efforts to nurture minority-owned businesses. In the 1980s the Indiana General Assembly appropriated three million dollars for an Enterprise Development Fund to aid businesses owned by members of racial minorities. In addition, federal regulations required that a certain percentage of contracts in some government construction projects be allotted to minority businesses. A few black enterprises succeeded, but in an age of ever-increasing consolidation of huge corporations small minority-owned businesses confronted serious obstacles.[94]

In the early postwar years those industries that had hired blacks for only janitorial or custodial jobs began placing qualified blacks in all positions. Racial distinctions ceased in union training programs and leadership positions. However, with the decline of heavy industry jobs and the rise of service employment, large numbers of factory workers lost jobs and unions no longer assured security.[95]

Blacks had made up a disproportionate percentage of persons on relief rolls, and by the 1970s it became evident that all African Americans did not share the same benefits. An expanding gap emerged between the middle-class blacks and the growing "under class." Government statistics showed that many blacks existed below the poverty line. The large number of unemployed black males in inner city communities spoke to the plight of African Americans in modern America. Many of the jobless had not graduated from high school, had never worked for wages, and had no employment prospects. The seeming hopelessness of their condition often led them to crime and drugs.

Census figures showed an increasing number of households headed by single African-American women and a large number of illegitimate births and teenage pregnancies in the inner cities. The high rate of infant mortality due to poverty and lack of prenatal care reflected these discouraging conditions.[96]

As racial barriers began to fall and their incomes increased, some middle-class African Americans moved out of inner-city ghettos. However, in the immediate post-war years the old obstacles to better housing remained. White realtors refused to show houses to blacks; landlords refused to rent to them; and banks refused credit. Many white homeowners would not accept the possibility of black neighbors, and when the first house in a neighborhood sold to an African American or when rumors spread of such sales, panic selling occurred among whites. Exceptions to this pattern existed, particularly in northern sections of Indianapolis where white homeowners formed neighborhood associations that worked to maintain racial balance.

Fair housing legislation constituted a priority for civil rights lobbies, but the state legislature resisted mandating open housing, favoring instead school desegregation laws and measures against discrimination in public accommodations and employment.[97] Finally in 1965 an amended civil rights law gave the Civil Rights Commission authority to hear complaints about housing discrimination, to issue cease and desist orders, and require affirmative action to discharge the aims of the law.

The law acted as an incentive to real estate brokers and homeowners who had been fearful of selling to African Americans because of reprisals from whites. It led to some dispersal from Center Township in Indianapolis to other parts of the city and to outlying townships. Similar trends took place in Gary. Concurrently more and more apartment buildings in the cities accepted black tenants. African Americans, however, labeled the law ineffective and argued that no law could be viable because of subterfuges and other tactics to evade compliance open to realtors and landlords.

Some suburbs featured housing developments open to both whites and blacks, but few whites chose to purchase homes there. Consequently, black families concentrated in these suburban areas, which became predominantly black. Not many neighborhoods could be called racially "integrated."

The building of nearly all public housing projects in the inner cities with the expectation of primarily black residents also contributed to racial concentration. Once built these projects frequently fell into disrepair and were regarded as breeding grounds for crime. Federally subsidized housing projects in the suburbs attracted few black tenants. Long waiting lists and lack of public transportation discouraged some from applying. The shortage of transportation also prevented some blacks from seeking employment in the suburban job market and from utilizing the services of suburban hospitals and other health facilities which moved away from the central cities.[98]

As the number of actual and potential African-American voters increased, white politicians more vigorously wooed them, and the concentration of blacks in central cities in some respects gave blacks more political power. As whites moved away the percentage of blacks rose and their power swelled, but at the same time blacks remained to confront urban problems—declining industries, eroding tax bases, decaying infrastructures, and inflating lawlessness and crime.

In 1967 Gary attracted national attention when it elected Richard Hatcher, an African American, as mayor. By that date blacks made up more than half of the population of the steel city. In every political campaign they worked faithfully for white Democratic candidates, but they received few rewards for their efforts.

Hatcher, a young lawyer deeply involved in the civil rights movement, received the support of the white-dominated Democratic organization when he sought a city council seat. However, racial feelings ran strong in the Calumet area, where a majority of white Democrats voted for George Wallace in the 1964 presidential primary. When Hatcher campaigned for mayor few white precinct committeemen supported him, and many white Democrats voted Republican. Hatcher tried to minimize the race issue, emphasizing the theme, "Let's Get Ourselves Together." Once elected as a reform candidate he found his efforts frustrated by an entrenched bureaucracy. Nevertheless his first term instituted social and urban renewal programs with initial help from federal and foundation grants. Under Hatcher, Gary became known as an "urban laboratory" for President Lyndon Johnson's "Great Society" experiments. During the Nixon years, however, federal funding dried up, and Gary's problems of unemployment and poverty deepened with the decline of the steel industry upon which the economic life of the city had depended. In spite of the dismal prospects Hatcher held the mayoral office for five consecutive terms before losing in 1987 to Thomas Barnes in the Democratic primary. Barnes won in the November election and was reelected in 1991.[99]

In Indianapolis the possibility of the election of a black mayor appeared to be precluded by the adoption of the so-called Uni-Gov law in 1969—a measure which African Americans interpreted as weakening their hard-earned political power. During and following the Second World War a number of able black members served on the city council. During the 1960s civil rights movement, black voter registration increased substantially, as evident in the 1963 election of Rev. James L. Cummings to the city council by a larger margin than the victorious mayoral candidate Democrat John Barton.

Members of the administration of Mayor Richard Lugar (later United States senator), elected mayor of Indianapolis in 1967, framed the Uni-Gov law adopted by a Republican-controlled state legislature. As a product of compromises and concessions to vested political interests the law consolidated some offices and functions of city and county government, but it did not affect such powerful agencies as police and fire departments and did not take in the township school systems. It provided for a mayor elected by the voters of the entire county and a twenty-nine member city-county council, twenty-five from single member districts, and four at-large members. Three incorporated cities or towns—Beech Grove, Lawrence, and Speedway—continued to elect mayors and councils as they had done before Uni-Gov, but their residents could also vote for the Uni-Gov mayor.

Black voters saw Uni-Gov as intended primarily to weaken their power and to create a government dominated by the white suburbs. The Indiana Conference on Civil and Human Rights, the coalition which monitored bills before the legislature, agreed that as the result of the measure political parties would show less concern for the interests of minorities.[100]

That Uni-Gov insured Republican control seems evident. Democrats have not elected a mayor since John Barton's victory in 1963, and Democrats have never elected a majority of the city-county council. The at-large members of the council are almost always Republicans. Black Democrats always win four or five seats in black districts in the inner city, but their influence in decision making is slight in the twenty-nine-member council.

While the African-American vote as a whole remains Democratic, Uni-Gov mayors have tried to win support of black leaders with some success. Mayor William Hudnut III appointed two blacks as deputy mayors—Joseph Slash followed by Paula Parker-Sawyer, previously an at-large member of the city-county council. Hudnut also won praise from blacks by opposing efforts of President Ronald Reagan's administration to weaken affirmative action policies.[101]

The number of African Americans in the state legislature increased as the result of legislative reapportionment in 1972. Nearly all of the black members elected from northern cities were Democrats and served multiple terms, consequently gaining seniority and influence. James S. Hunter of East Chicago, a twenty-five-year legislator (longer than any other black representative), became head of the Democratic caucus and played an important role in enactment of the 1949 school desegregation law. Jesse Dickinson led in the fight for civil rights legislation. After serving several terms as a representative from South Bend he gained a state senate chair. Three women lawmakers from Gary have been among the most able and influential African-American members. After being elected to the lower house in 1974 Katie Hall won two terms in the state senate, from 1977 to 1982, when she resigned in order to fill the term in the United States House of Representatives of Adam Benjamin, who died. She became the first and only African-American member of Congress from Indiana. Carolyn B. Mosby, already a member of the state house of representatives, succeeded Hall in the state senate, where she served until her death in 1990. Earline Rogers, a representative, succeeded her. In recent years another representative from Gary, Charlie Brown, has been one of the most active and influential members, particularly in legislation intended to foster minority businesses.[102]

In Indianapolis, with the exception of Robert L. Brokenburr, no black legislator gained much influence, since prior to legislative reapportionment in 1972 all legislators from Marion County were elected at-large. Because control in Marion County alternated between Democrats and Republicans, lawmakers did not gain seniority. Nevertheless, able black members emerged. Daisy R. Lloyd, a Democrat elected in 1964 and a licensed realtor, held a doctorate from Purdue University and became the first African-American woman to be elected to the General Assembly. Harriet Bailey Conn, a Republican lawyer who served in the lower house from 1967 to 1969, had a notable record in civil rights and civic affairs before her election. In the legislature she sponsored legislation to protect the property rights of married women. Ray Crowe, another Republican, known to the public as the coach of the championship Crispus Attucks High School basketball teams, served five terms in the house of representatives.[103]

The 1972 reapportionment law, which divided most house of representative districts into single member districts, opened the way for the election of black Democrats from the Indianapolis inner city. Julia M. Carson, a strong advocate of civil rights and feminist causes and a member of the staff of United States Representative Andrew Jacobs, Jr., was elected to the lower house in 1972 and to the state senate in 1977, serving until 1990 when she began a term as trustee of Center Township. As a lawmaker she worked for penal and welfare reform. William A. Crawford, elected in 1972, continues in the house of representatives, directs the Indiana Christian Leadership Conference, and helps organize Black Expo as well as serves in such organizations as the Indianapolis Urban League. He has a special interest in the Indianapolis Public Schools and successfully sponsored legislation to make the school board more representative of the city's population. Joseph W. Summers, a businessman, owner of a funeral chapel, and active in the NAACP as well as Democratic politics, held a seat in the house of representatives from 1976 until his death in 1990.[104]

Unlike other blacks in the General Assembly elected from districts with a predominantly black population, Democrat Hurley C. Goodall of Muncie represented all of Delaware County, where blacks are a decided minority. Before his election to the legislature in 1978 he was the first black member of the Muncie school board, a member

of the Human Rights Commission of Muncie, and active in labor organizations.[105]

Black lawmakers showed a special interest in civil rights legislation, but by 1970 the important laws on which they had concentrated their efforts had been adopted. Since then they have turned their attention to other problems of black communities such as penal reforms, public health, and housing, problems not unique to blacks but more widespread and acute for blacks than for whites. They organized a Black Political Caucus in 1979 to bring attention to these problems and to frame laws to alleviate them. The caucus paid particular attention to the 1983 founding of the Minority Business Development Commission and to other measures of aid to minority businesses.[106]

While a small number of blacks gained prestige and influence in the General Assembly, larger numbers held posts in local governments, most often in urban city councils with large black populations. In 1958 Mercer Mance, a graduate of Howard University Law School, made history as the first elected black judge in Indiana when chosen as a superior court judge in Indianapolis. Since that time an increasing number of black judges have been elected or appointed to local judgeships throughout the state.

The number of blacks in public office at the state level remains relatively small. In 1973 Gov. Otis Bowen appointed William T. Ray, a realtor who had served as president of the Indianapolis NAACP, as an administrative assistant, the highest state post held by a black to that time. Bowen also appointed Beatrice Holland, a Richmond schoolteacher, as head of the Indiana Civil Rights Commission—a position held continuously by African-American appointees since then.

In 1990 Gov. Evan Bayh appointed Robert D. Rucker, Jr., as the first African-American member of the Indiana

*African Americans serving in the Indiana General Assembly, ca. 1985.*

Court of Appeals. Rucker, a lawyer from East Chicago, had served earlier as Lake County prosecutor. In 1990 Dwayne M. Brown, a graduate of Columbia University School of Law, became the first African American elected to state office when he became clerk of the Indiana Supreme Court. In 1992 Pamela Carter was elected Indiana's attorney general, becoming the first woman as well as the first African American to hold that office.[107] In 1995 Governor Bayh appointed Myra Selby as the first African American on the Indiana Supreme Court.

The immediate post–Second World War years witnessed the most important changes in the status of African Americans since Reconstruction. Blacks won, in the eyes of the law at least, the full citizenship so long denied them. In Indiana, as noted, the legislature outlawed segregation and racial discrimination before the enactment of federal laws.

The booming economy of these years expedited the acceptance by whites of programs designed to remedy discrimination in the workplace and the classroom. Yet, in spite of progress, racism and injustice had not disappeared. For example, a disproportionate number of blacks, lacking funds for higher education, had to fight in the seemingly futile war in Vietnam.

In the years following the Vietnam War no president except Jimmy Carter attempted to lead an assault against racism. That the long period of unprecedented prosperity appeared to be ending in the late 1980s and early 1990s and the economic security of the middle class seemed threatened gave politicians an opening to capitalize on these fears and prejudices. Across the country and in Indiana white racism surfaced, including revivals of Ku Klux Klan groups and cross burnings. Racial incidents at universities and public schools multiplied.

African Americans reacted variously, but withdrawal and black separatism seemed to be the prominent tendencies. These trends appeared earlier in the civil rights movement when such groups as CORE and SNCC repudiated white leadership and became all-black. By the 1980s separatist doctrines had broader appeal as black youths rejected ideals of racial integration. At universities African Americans deliberately segregated themselves and focused their attention on black student unions. Some blacks as well as whites turned against busing as a remedy for earlier segregation and appeared to accept a "separate but equal" doctrine of education.

The desire to establish a separate identity manifested itself in the interest in African history and culture and the search by African Americans for their "roots." Universities increased courses in African history, literature, art, and music, and black students often insisted that they be taught by blacks. Public schools developed "Afro-Centrist"

curricula that included African-American history. The annual Black Expo in Indianapolis that attracts growing attendance reflects the new pride in racial achievements, as does the observance of Kwanza, the African harvest celebration.

The NAACP, the National Urban League, their local affiliates, and most black political leaders oppose moves that threaten legal and economic gains of the civil rights era, but as the twentieth century draws to a close, demographic realities and changing racial attitudes seem to show that the goal of the civil rights years—a truly racially integrated society—has eluded Indiana and the nation as a whole.

## Notes

1. Emma Lou Thornbrough, *The Negro in Indiana before 1900: A Study of a Minority* (Indianapolis: Indiana Historical Bureau, 1957), 1–5. Unless otherwise noted the material in the first two sections of this essay, covering the period up to World War I, is drawn from the above work.

2. Ibid., 23.

3. Ibid., 121–27, 165–66; *Lewis v. Henley et al.,* 2 Ind. 332 (1850).

4. Thornbrough, *Negro in Indiana,* 133–42; Stephen Vincent, "African-Americans in the Rural Midwest: The Origins and Evolution of Beech and Roberts Settlements, ca. 1760–1900" (Ph.D. diss., Brown University, 1991).

5. Thornbrough, *Negro in Indiana,* 229; U.S. Bureau of the Census, *Negro Population in the United States, 1790–1915* (Washington, D.C.: Government Printing Office, 1918), 67, 91, 92.

6. *Indiana Laws,* 1869 (special session), 41; *Indiana Laws,* 1877, p. 124.

7. Thornbrough, *Negro in Indiana,* 324, 332–35, 340–41.

8. Darrel E. Bigham, *We Ask Only a Fair Trial: A History of the Black Community of Evansville, Indiana* (Bloomington: Indiana University Press, 1987), 40–48, 125–27, and passim.

9. Indiana Department of Public Instruction, *Report of the Superintendent, 1903–1904* (Indianapolis: Wm. B. Burford, 1905), 238–39, 263–67; Emma Lou Thornbrough, *Since Emancipation: A Short History of Indiana Negroes, 1863–1963* (Indianapolis: Indiana Division, American Negro Emancipation Centennial Authority, 1963), 53.

10. Thornbrough, *Negro in Indiana,* 339–40, and *Since Emancipation,* 52.

11. Thornbrough, *Negro in Indiana,* 243, 254, 288–91.

12. Clyde Nickerson Bolden, "Indiana Avenue: Black Entertainment Boulevard" (Master's thesis, University of Cincinnati, 1983), 10; Charles Latham, Jr., "Madam C. J. Walker and Company," *Traces of Indiana and Midwestern History* 1 (Summer 1989): 29–36; A'Lelia Perry Bundles, *Madam C. J. Walker* (New York: Chelsea House Publishers, 1991).

13. Thornbrough, *Negro in Indiana,* 360, and *Since Emancipation,* 73.

14. Thornbrough, *Negro in Indiana,* 384–88; John W. Miller, *Indiana Newspaper Bibliography* (Indianapolis: Indiana Historical Society, 1982), 268, 283, 290; Willard B. Gatewood, ed., *Slave and Freeman: The Autobiography of George L. Knox* (Lexington: University Press of Kentucky, 1979). Knox, born a slave in Tennessee, escaped by accompanying a Union regiment back to Indiana after the Civil War.

Gatewood's book includes Knox's autobiography, ending in 1894, and a lengthy introduction covering Knox's later years.

15. Thornbrough, *Negro in Indiana,* 348–58, and *Since Emancipation,* 71–72.

16. Thornbrough, *Negro in Indiana,* 366. In the early years of the twentieth century three young black lawyers, all southern-born, opened an office in Indianapolis. Robert Lee Bailey, Robert Lee Brokenburr, and Freeman Ransom became recognized leaders in the black community, in politics, and in the NAACP. Bailey became noted for his defense of blacks accused of crime. Brokenburr held the distinction of being the first black elected to the state senate. Ransom as business manager of the Walker Manufacturing Company contributed to its financial success and served as a member of the board of Flanner House and president of the Colored YMCA. Emma Lou Thornbrough, "Blacks in Indiana in the Twentieth Century" (Unfinished manuscript).

17. Thornbrough, *Negro in Indiana,* 363–65.

18. Ibid., 346. An important figure in the Indianapolis community until his death in 1953, Furniss served as president of the board of Lincoln Hospital, the Colored YMCA, the board of Flanner House, and as a member of the Indianapolis city council.

19. Thornbrough, "Blacks in Indiana in the Twentieth Century."

20. *Indiana Laws,* 1885, pp. 76–77; Thornbrough, *Negro in Indiana,* 259–65.

21. Thornbrough, *Negro in Indiana,* 371–72, and "Blacks in Indiana in the Twentieth Century."

22. Thornbrough, "Blacks in Indiana in the Twentieth Century," and *Negro in Indiana,* 375–78.

23. Earline Rae Ferguson, "The Woman's Improvement Club of Indianapolis: Black Women Pioneers in Tuberculosis Work, 1903–1938," *Indiana Magazine of History* 84 (Sept. 1988): 237–61; Darlene Clark Hine, *When the Truth Is Told: A History of Black Women's Culture and Community in Indiana, 1875–1950* (Indianapolis: National Council of Negro Women, Indianapolis Section, 1981), passim; Thornbrough, "Blacks in Indiana in the Twentieth Century."

24. Ruth Hutchinson Crocker, *Social Work and Social Order: The Settlement Movement in Two Industrial Cities, 1889–1930* (Urbana: University of Illinois Press, 1992).

25. Thornbrough, *Negro in Indiana,* 380–81, and "Blacks in Indiana in the Twentieth Century."

26. Thornbrough, "Blacks in Indiana in the Twentieth Century."

27. U.S. Bureau of the Census, *Negroes in the United States, 1920–1932* (Washington, D.C.: Government Printing Office, 1935), 15, 12, 51; David Gerald Jaynes and Robin M. Williams, Jr., eds., *A Common Destiny: Blacks and American Society* (Washington, D.C.: National Academy Press, 1989), 35–37.

28. Emma Lou Thornbrough, "Segregation in Indiana during the Klan Era of the 1920's," *Mississippi Valley Historical Review* 47 (Mar. 1961): 595, and *Since Emancipation,* 16–18.

29. Thornbrough, "Blacks in Indiana in the Twentieth Century"; Elder W. Diggs, "Some Data Bearing upon the Part which the Colored Citizens of Indianapolis and Marion County Took in the World War" (Typed manuscript, Indiana State Library, Indianapolis); Indiana World War Records Commission, *Gold Star Honor Roll: A Record of Indiana Men and Women Who Died in the Service of the United States and the Allied Nations in the World War, 1914–1918,* vol. 6 of *Indiana Historical Collections* (Indianapolis: Indiana Historical Commission, 1921), passim.

30. Thornbrough, *Since Emancipation,* 75.

31. Leonard J. Moore, *Citizen Klansmen: The Ku Klux Klan in Indiana, 1921–1928* (Chapel Hill: University of North Carolina Press, 1991), 56–57 and Chapter 3, passim. This recent scholarship has demonstrated from quantitative analysis of Klan membership lists that the Klan was not a fanatical fringe group, but included a large percentage of native, white Americans, both urban and rural from all occupational levels, including many white Protestant ministers who were attracted to it because it supported Prohibition.

32. Thornbrough, *Since Emancipation,* 31–33, "Segregation during the Klan Era," 613–15, and "Blacks in Indiana in the Twentieth Century"; William W. Giffin, "The Political Realignment of Black Voters in Indianapolis, 1924," *Indiana Magazine of History* 79 (June 1983): passim.

33. Thornbrough, "Segregation during the Klan Era," 615.

34. Ibid., 597–601.

35. Thornbrough, *Since Emancipation,* 24.

36. Thornbrough, "Segregation during the Klan Era," 603.

37. Ibid., 603–4.

38. Ibid., 605; *Greathouse* v. *Board of School Commissioners of City of Indianapolis,* 198 Ind. 95 (1926–27).

39. Thornbrough, "Segregation during the Klan Era," 616–17; Frederick H. Gates, "The First Twenty–Five Years of Crispus Attucks High School, Indianapolis, Indiana, 1927–1952" (Master's thesis, Ball State University, 1955), passim.

40. Thornbrough, "Segregation during the Klan Era," 606–8; Ronald D. Cohen, *Children of the Mill: Schooling and Society in Gary, Indiana, 1906–1960* (Bloomington: Indiana University Press, 1990), 94–99; *State, ex rel. Cheeks* v. *Wirt, Superintendent of Gary Schools et al.* 203 Ind. 121 (1932).

41. Cohen, *Children of the Mill,* 99, 148–53.

42. Bigham, *We Ask Only a Fair Trial,* 143–45.

43. Thornbrough, "Segregation during the Klan Era," 609, *Since Emancipation,* 38, and "Blacks in Indiana in the Twentieth Century."

44. Thornbrough, "Blacks in Indiana in the Twentieth Century," and *Since Emancipation,* 75.

45. Thornbrough, *Since Emancipation,* 34–37; Alan January and Justin E. Walsh, *A Century of Achievement: Black Hoosiers in the General Assembly, 1881–1986* (Indianapolis: The Select Committee on the Centennial History of the General Assembly in Cooperation with the Indiana Historical Bureau, 1986), 23, 24, 26, 28, 29, 30. Henry J. Richardson served in the General Assembly from 1932 to 1936. His defeat in the May primary in 1936 came about probably because he offended conservative white Democrats by his efforts to strengthen the Civil Rights Law of 1885. Richardson helped lead the campaign to desegregate Indianapolis schools and frame and adopt the 1949 school law. A successful civil rights lawyer, he practiced before the United States Supreme Court.

46. Thornbrough, *Since Emancipation,* 76.

47. Thornbrough, "Blacks in Indiana in the Twentieth Century."

48. Ibid.

49. Ibid.

50. Emma Lou Thornbrough, "Breaking Racial Barriers to Public Accommodations in Indiana, 1935–1963," *Indiana Magazine of History* 83 (Dec. 1987): 310; Max Cavnes, *The Hoosier Community at War,* vol. 9 of *Indiana in World War II* (Bloomington: Indiana University Press, 1961), 148–54.

51. Thornbrough, *Since Emancipation,* 19–20.

52. Ibid., 77–79; Cavnes, *Hoosier Community at War,* 111–37.

53. Cavnes, *Hoosier Community at War,* 137–44.

54. Ibid., 174–78; Thornbrough, "Blacks in Indiana in the Twentieth Century."

55. United States Census of Population 1960, *Indiana Detailed Characteristics* (Washington, D.C.: Department of Commerce, 1961),

321, 322; United States Census of Population 1970, *Negro Population* (Washington, D.C.: Department of Commerce, 1973), 10; Morton J. Marcus, "Indiana's Minorities: 1980," *Indiana Business Review* 56 (Apr. 1981): 2–6; 1990 Census of Population and Housing, *Summary Population and Housing Characteristics, Indiana* (Washington. D.C.: Department of Commerce, 1991), 38–74.

56. "Indiana Foreign Born for 1980 by Nationality and County." Source of the original table was U.S. Bureau of Census "1980 Census Summary Tape File 4," Indiana Business Research Center, Graduate School of Business, Indiana University.

57. Thornbrough, "Breaking Racial Barriers," 312. Willard Ransom left the Democratic party briefly in 1948 to support Henry Wallace and the Progressive party, a deviation which aroused criticism among some NAACP members, but it did not prevent his reelection as state president.

58. Ibid., 314.

59. Ronald D. Cohen, "The Dilemma of School Integration in the North: Gary, Indiana, 1945–1960," *Indiana Magazine of History* 82 (June 1986): 167.

60. Thornbrough, "Breaking Racial Barriers," 311.

61. Ibid., 311, 318–24.

62. *Indiana Laws,* 1961, pp. 500–5; *Indiana Laws,* 1963, pp. 216–21.

63. Emma Lou Thornbrough, "The Indianapolis Story: School Segregation and Desegregation in a Northern City" (Unpublished manuscript, Indiana Historical Society Library, Indianapolis), 119–20.

64. Thornbrough, "Breaking Racial Barriers," 327–29.

65. Ibid., 331, 342–43.

66. Ibid., 335, 342–43.

67. Thornbrough, "Indianapolis Story," 175–76. CORE, like SNCC (Student Non-Violent Coordinating Committee), founded on principles of integration, later became an all-black organization.

68. Thornbrough, "Blacks in Indiana in the Twentieth Century." There has been a revival of the Black Panthers since 1990.

69. Thornbrough, "Indianapolis Story," 181–82, and "Blacks in Indiana in the Twentieth Century." For years the board of Flanner House, and particularly its longtime director, Cleo Blackburn, resisted the establishment of an Indianapolis Urban League as unnecessary and an infringement on local autonomy.

70. Thornbrough, "Blacks in Indiana in the Twentieth Century."

71. Ibid.

72. Cohen, "Dilemma of School Integration," 161–71.

73. Thornbrough, "Indianapolis Story," 114–16.

74. Ibid., 91–95, 98–101.

75. Ibid., 117–24; *Indiana Laws,* 1949, pp. 604–7.

76. Thornbrough, *Since Emancipation,* 62; Indiana Department of Public Instruction, *Indiana School Desegregation: A Brief Historical Overview* (Indianapolis, 1979), 3; Thornbrough, "Blacks in Indiana in the Twentieth Century."

77. Thornbrough, "Indianapolis Story," 128–31 and Chapter 4, passim.

78. Cohen, "Dilemma of School Integration," 173, 175, 179.

79. Ibid., 179–82.

80. Thornbrough, "Indianapolis Story," Chapter 5, passim; Emma Lou Thornbrough, "The Indianapolis School Busing Case," in *We the People: Indiana and the United States Constitution—Lectures in Observance of the Bicentennial of the Constitution* (Indianapolis: Indiana Historical Society, 1987), 72–73.

81. Thornbrough, "Indianapolis School Busing Case," 76; *U.S.* v. *Board of School Commissioners, Indianapolis, Indiana,* 332 F Supp 655.

82. Thornbrough, "Indianapolis School Busing Case," 78–80.

83. Ibid., 80–82, 84–85. The measure known as Uni-Gov enacted in 1969 was part of the evidence that the state of Indiana was guilty of perpetuating unlawful segregation and that one-way busing was a legal remedy. See pages 84–85, ibid.

84. Thornbrough, "Indianapolis School Busing Case," 88, and "Indianapolis Story," 480–81.

85. Indiana Department of Public Instruction, *Indiana School Desegregation,* passim.

86. Thornbrough, "Indianapolis Story," Chapter 10, and "Blacks in Indiana in the Twentieth Century."

87. Thornbrough, *Since Emancipation,* 66–68, and "Blacks in Indiana in the Twentieth Century."

88. Thornbrough, "Blacks in Indiana in the Twentieth Century."

89. Ibid.

90. Ibid.

91. *Indiana Laws,* 1961, pp. 500–5; *Indiana Laws,* 1963, pp. 216–21. The 1963 law provided for appeals from the rulings of the Civil Rights Commission to the courts. Earlier, in 1945, the General Assembly passed a much publicized FEPC law. However, in its final form, after numerous amendments, it contained no powers of enforcement and was quite ineffectual. The most persistent and influential opposition to fair employment legislation came from the Indiana Chamber of Commerce.

92. Thornbrough, "Blacks in Indiana in the Twentieth Century."

93. Ibid.

94. January and Walsh, *Black Hoosiers in the Indiana General Assembly,* 14; Thornbrough, "Blacks in Indiana in the Twentieth Century."

95. Thornbrough, "Blacks in Indiana in the Twentieth Century."

96. Ibid.

97. Thornbrough, "Breaking Racial Barriers," 332; *Indiana Laws,* 1965, pp. 484–86. The law provided for appeals of the commission's orders to the courts and also gave the commission the right to obtain court orders to enforce its rulings.

98. Thornbrough, "Blacks in Indiana in the Twentieth Century." Indianapolis, after years of disdaining public housing, revived the Indianapolis Housing Authority in 1964 and began applying for federal aid to subsidize housing projects.

99. James B. Lane, *"City of the Century": A History of Gary, Indiana* (Bloomington: Indiana University Press, 1978), 282–303; William Edward Nelson and Philip J. Meranto, *Electing Black Mayors: Political Action in the Black Community* (Columbus: Ohio State University Press, 1977), 176–84, 197–99, 286, 300; Richard Hatcher, "How It Looks from the Center of the City," in Charles Y. Glock and Ellen Siegelman, eds., *Prejudice U.S.A.* (New York: Praeger, 1969), 184–94; Thornbrough, "Blacks in Indiana in the Twentieth Century."

100. Thornbrough, "Indianapolis Story," 252–55; *Indiana Laws,* 1969, pp. 357–448.

101. Thornbrough, "Blacks in Indiana in the Twentieth Century."

102. January and Walsh, *Black Hoosiers in the Indiana General Assembly,* 50, 54, 56, 58.

103. Ibid., 38, 40, 41.

104. Ibid., 45, 47, 52.

105. Ibid., 53. The only black elected to the General Assembly from the southern part of Indiana was Charles Edward Decker of Evansville, a Republican, a leader of the CIO in Vanderburgh County, and elected to the house of representatives in the Republican landslide of 1946. Ibid., 33.

106. Ibid., 14; Thornbrough, "Blacks in Indiana in the Twentieth Century."

107. Thornbrough, "Blacks in Indiana in the Twentieth Century."

# ASIAN INDIANS

H. S. BHOLA

*Asian Indians have the advantage of an old and resilient culture with a rich collective memory. It is rare to find an Asian Indian who is ashamed of his or her cultural heritage. Indeed they take every possible opportunity to show pride in their traditions.*

To understand the Asian Indians who have made Indiana their home, a broad understanding of the history and culture of India is necessary to see the continuities from the old within the new confluence of cultures emerging in Indiana.[1]

## I

### The Historical Framework

The Indian subcontinent is a mix of races and cultures. The Indus Valley civilization of 3000 B.C.E. is the earliest known civilization in the area. From around 1750 B.C.E. to 3 B.C.E., the Indo-Aryan civilization flourished. During this time the Vedas and the Upanishads were composed.[2] Hinduism built on the Vedantic traditions and evolved during the next two thousand years, overlapping with Buddhism.

The first Arab military incursion in India took place in 712 C.E. Invaders followed from Turkey, Persia, Afghanistan, and other nearby places. The Moguls who came to India in the early 1500s ruled until the British took over from them in the midnineteenth century. The Mogul influence on India perhaps lasted longer than that of any of the Muslim invaders.

Incursions from the sea began in the early 1500s. The British contact with India began in the middle of the sixteenth century with landings on the southern coast of India. However, Western-type industrialization began in India only toward the end of the nineteenth century. Worldwide historical pressures for decolonization, along with the great sacrifices made by Indians during the Indian Independence Movement, forced the British to "quit India" in 1947. Before their departure the British ruled the whole of India as part of the British Empire.

Since independence in 1947 India has been able to build and sustain credible democratic institutions. Its system of higher education has developed the world's third-largest pool of scientists who, ironically, cannot always find suitable jobs in the Indian economy. Educated persons are unemployed and underemployed pervasively. The best-trained specialists find jobs in the international job market. The population explosion at home continues to neutralize most of the development gains as India tries new economic policies and new political coalitions in the aftermath of the Cold War.[3]

### Cultural Roots and Traditions of Asian Indians

India is the home of some of the world's great religious traditions, among them Hinduism, Buddhism, Jainism, and Sikhism. India has been a congenial host to almost all of the world's religious faiths: Judaism, Christianity, Zoroastrianism, Islam, and Bahaism. The "Great Tradition" in the Indian culture during the last two thousand years has been predominantly Hindu in spirit. Buddhism, Jainism, and Sikhism, of course, all resonate more or less to Hindu values, ethos, and social behavior. Even Indian Christians and Muslims have absorbed the Hindu ethos to a large extent. Ironically, the Hindu caste system has permeated Indian Christianity, Islam, and Sikhism—all of which were meant to be casteless religions.

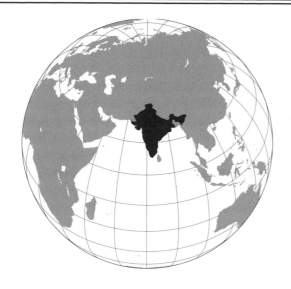

Indian philosophic texts date back as far as three thousand years. One of the old texts, the *Bhagavad-Gita* (which some think might be as recent as 800 C.E.), is considered one of the most important philosophic treatises ever written. *Gita* lives in the thoughts and daily actions of common people even today. As Professor T. N. Madan explains, the main issue discussed in *Gita* is Dharma—what a man ought to do and to be. Dharma, he goes on to say, is a many-layered concept that includes social, legal, ethical, and cosmological principles to sustain an ordered gender and caste universe. While Dharma is relative to the individual and his or her caste, Dharma categorically rejects "untruthfulness, wanton killing, stealing, sexual assault, or self-seeking endeavor" and promotes "forgiveness, work, sincerity, cleanliness and moral watchfulness." A person in an ideal state of Dharma experiences "choiceless awareness" and acquires a "seamless moral sensibility." Karma is action taken in the practice of Dharma. Karma is the "ethics of altruism." One's entitlement is to Karma alone, never to its fruit. Good Karma leads to *Moksha*—release from the cycle of life and death.[4]

Indians believe in the immortality of the soul and its transmigration across the cycles of birth to rebirth. The Indian view is a cosmic view rooted in the unity of origins. This unified sensibility enables Indians to see matter, life, and mind as one. Since the Indians see kinship between mankind and the animal world, many prefer to be vegetarians to avoid eating animal meat. Beef is particularly avoided as the cow is held sacred.

Indians believe in the theory of constant change and perpetual motion, that is, in the flux of all things. There are no discontinuities because time is cyclic. There is the principle of conjunction and reconciliation of opposites; and there is nonsequential—that is dialectical—way of

thinking. This creates the ability to accommodate contradictions, to join intuition with intellect, to practice renunciation and acquisitiveness as part of the same one identity, and to borrow the new and to conserve the old at the same time.

The Indian caste system, a system of culturally (not constitutionally) institutionalized inequality, is based on four varnas (colors): Brahman (priest); Kshatrya (warrior); Vaishya (trader); and Sudra (cultivator). Later in history, the caste of untouchables was appended to the system at the lowest rung of the caste-system hierarchy. Each of these castes is divided into several subcastes. Since most of the last names in India are caste labels, the Indians have in one sense brought their caste system with them to Indiana. It does not, of course, have much, if any, of the ritualistic value of the back-home caste categories, but sometimes defines social groups in the new community.

Family plays an important part in the socialization and support of the Asian Indian. It is the site for character formation, insurance against unemployment and material loss, and an institution for nurturing and nursing in the face of personal defeats and tragedy. Connections with members of the extended family in India are maintained.

Even though "Mother" has a high ritualistic status alongside of God and Teacher, in the context of ordinary realities the boy child is preferred to the girl child in India, and the status of women remains low in relation to the men in the family. There is a strong expectation of virginity before marriage from both females and males, though a double standard in favor of the male prevails. Overt expression of tenderness in public is a taboo, and marriages are arranged. In urbanized metropolitan areas where the old face-to-face communities are breaking down, young people are choosing their own life partners. Divorces are possible today but are relatively rare. There is religious emphasis on asceticism and a puritanical social life, values not necessarily practiced in real life by the well-to-do.

### Immigration from India to America

Asian Indian immigration to the United States has a British connection and two histories: one from 1790 to 1965, and another after 1965.[5]

Tapan Mukherjee and J. John Sunny Wycliff recently wrote that the first "recorded" visit of an Indian in the United States took place on 29 December 1790 when a "Man from Madras" was seen on the streets of Salem, Massachusetts, by Rev. William Bentley, pastor of East Church. Bentley wrote in his diary that he "had the

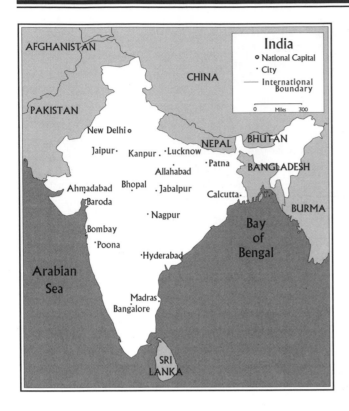

India

o National Capital
· City
—— International Boundary

0   Miles   300

AFGHANISTAN

CHINA

PAKISTAN

New Delhi o

Jaipur·   Kanpur ·  ·Lucknow

NEPAL   BHUTAN

·Patna

BANGLADESH

Allahabad

Ahmadabad   Bhopal   · Jabalpur

Baroda

Calcutta·

· Nagpur

BURMA

Bombay

·Poona

Bay
of
Bengal

·Hyderabad

Arabian
Sea

Madras
Bangalore

SRI
LANKA

## At Home in Indiana:
## A Statistical Profile of Asian Indians

In 1850, 11 of the 60,473 foreign born in Indiana were from Asia, with 10 of the 11 coming from the Indian subcontinent and residing in the five northern counties of Adams, Allen, Carroll, Elkhart, and Lagrange. The 1860 census showed 14 immigrants from India coming to Indiana. The figures reflected widespread settlement of the few Asian Indians in seven counties, including Madison, Marion, Montgomery, Ohio, St. Joseph, Tippecanoe, and Lagrange. Over the next century data on Asian Indians specifically have been difficult to find. In 1908–9 the Indianapolis Public School system reported some 400 foreign-born children in its schools, 4 of whom were from India. These students may not have been the children of Asian Indians but rather English children born in India whose parents had since immigrated to the United States.[9]

The 1960 population census for Indiana recorded a total of 361 Asian Indians in the state with 220 of these foreign born and 141 native born or born of mixed parentage. Twenty years later in 1980 the census showed the breakdown of population in Indiana from East and South Asian countries as follows:

| Country | |
| --- | --- |
| India | .2,510 |
| Pakistan | .390 |
| Bangladesh | .41 |
| Nepal | .0 |
| Bhutan | .31 |
| Tibet | — |
| Sri Lanka | .59 |

Most of the Asian Indians concentrated in the urban areas of Marion, Allen, Tippecanoe, Lake, Vigo, St. Joseph, and Monroe counties.[10] In addition to the usual birthplace questions, the 1980 census asked an open-ended ancestry question based on self-identification. In Indiana 3,419 persons said their ancestors were Asian Indians, with 3,221 of these declaring descent from Asian Indians only, leaving 198 persons reporting a multiple ancestry.

In the latest census count, 1990, the number of Asian Indians in Indiana stood at 7,095. Of Asian nations only the Chinese had more of its stock in the state. Marion County continues to be a prime center of Asian Indian residence followed by Tippecanoe, Lake, Allen, St. Joseph, and Monroe counties. Seventy-nine of the ninety-two counties can count among their inhabitants one or more Asian Indians.[11]

pleasure of seeing for the first time a native of the Indies from Madras." This man arrived in Salem with Captain Gibaut, a local merchant mariner returning from a voyage off the coast of Malabar. While this may be the first recorded visit of an Indian to America, others probably had preceded him.[6]

Joan M. Jensen, writing for the *Harvard Encyclopedia of American Ethnic Groups*, states that "only 700 scattered adventurers, merchants, monks, and professional men—mainly from northern India—came [to America] during the 19th century." Between 1820 and 1965 fewer than 17,000 Indians came and settled. The second phase of Asian Indian immigration began with the 1965 immigration law that eliminated national quotas. The 1970 census counted 76,000 Asian Indians in the United States, and within five years there were another 72,000.[7] In 1980 the federal census counted over 360,000 Asian Indians in the country, while in 1990 some 815,000 persons identified themselves as "Asian Indians." This figure does not include some other Indian Americans, such as those of Indian origin who migrated from Africa, the Caribbean, and Asian countries such as Singapore, Malaysia, and Thailand; and in some cases, second-generation Indian Americans with one non-Indian parent. It is notable that the Asian Indians are more evenly dispersed over the United States than any other ethnic group from Asia.[8]

## II

### Asian Indian Communities in Indiana

As shown by the above statistics, emigration from the Indian subcontinent was a phenomenon of the 1960s. The immigration law of 1965 phased out the quota system and for the first time enabled a large number of East Asians to immigrate to the United States.[12] As Joan Jensen points out, "almost 46,000 engineers, physicians, scientists, professors, teachers, and businessmen entered the United States during the next ten years along with almost 47,000 wives and children. These families became the basis for the new East Indian communities." Some of them, of course, headed toward Indiana.[13]

The Asian Indian immigrants comprised a special group. Unlike many earlier ethnic groups they did not settle on the land or congregate together as one ethnic community in a single neighborhood. The Asian Indian immigrants were a highly trained professional group of doctors, engineers, and academics, noticeably proficient in the English language. They obtained jobs in manufacturing industries, in hospitals, and in universities, and they lived in the suburbs. They created "reference communities" of Asian Indians rather than the traditional ethnic neighborhoods. Their spread over the state (and throughout the United States) forms a pattern similar to the spread of industries, hospitals, and universities.

In the 1980s, as relatives joined the children who had "made it" in America, a new population blend emerged, especially in the big cities. The relatives of doctors, engineers, and academics who now joined them did not necessarily have professional training. Many opened shops and small businesses while others had to find blue-collar jobs in factories.

Both race and culture have set the Asian Indians somewhat apart from their neighbors in Indiana communities and, therefore, their integration into the host communities has been relatively slow. They are of non-European ancestry and are easily distinguishable because of their brown color and East Asian physiognomy. Most of them are non-Christians, thus the sense of community that comes from worshiping the same God and honoring the same prophets has been missed in their cultural encounters. However, the religious barriers did not bring more severe prejudice or discrimination against the Asian Indians; indeed, religious and cultural America of the 1970s and the 1980s proved more tolerant than the America of the 1950s or the 1960s.

Indianapolis may one day become salient in the lives of Asian Indians spread all over the state, but in the 1980s and the mid-1990s Chicago is clearly the "cultural center of gravity" for Asian Indians in Indiana. They travel to Chicago to purchase Indian groceries, clothing, and jewelry; to participate in big ethnic celebrations; to worship at one of the big temples; to spend a weekend at the house of a friend; to enjoy cultural programs on the special Asian Indian radio and television channels; to attend a musical evening or a poetic symposium showcasing actors, actresses, poets, and play back singers of the Indian silver screen; to take their children for lessons in Indian languages, classical or popular music, and dance; to pick up their children from the University of Chicago or Northwestern University campuses; and to board planes for the most convenient connection to India.

The population of greater Indianapolis according to the 1990 census topped one million inhabitants, among which were 1,538 Asian Indians. While relatively slight in numbers, the Asian Indian community plays a significant part in the life of the city. Many health-related professionals and engineers, not to mention several university academics, accountants, architects, and businessmen, contribute to the city's economy and quality of life. This predominantly professional community has been joined by small businessmen, restaurateurs, grocers, and some blue-collar workers.

The Indianapolis community began relatively small and young in age, but acquired a vitality during the decades of the 1970s and 1980s. In fact, the history of the Asian Indians in Indianapolis did not precede the early 1960s. When Kanwal Prakash (K. P.) Singh, a well-known architect-artist of Asian Indian origin, came to Indianapolis on 30 September 1967 to take a job as a senior urban planner with the Department of Metropolitan Development, no more than eight to ten families of Asian Indians resided in the city, in addition to a few bachelor "households" and students. When they celebrated *Diwali*—the Festival of Lights—in October of that year, eighteen to twenty people gathered in a classroom at Indiana University-Purdue University at Indianapolis (IUPUI) on 38th Street across from the fairgrounds. Most were young adults, and several among them bachelors. Perhaps six or seven ladies attended and cooked the food, and two children lit up the gathering. Two years later in 1969 around fifty to sixty people came to the Student Center Building at the Indiana University (IU) Medical Center to celebrate *Diwali*. Significantly, seven or eight among them were invitees—mostly white Americans.[14]

In the late 1970s *Diwali* celebrations attracted four hundred or more people, and festivities took place at such facilities as the Murat Shrine, the Holiday Inn North, the Marriott Inn, and several high schools in Indianapolis. The *Diwali* celebration in 1991 brought together over five hundred people, one-fourth of them non-Asian Indian guests. It was a wonderful opportunity to eat together, to laugh together, to celebrate together, and to deepen personal friendships through joyful immersion in each other's cultures.

In the 1990s the Asian Indians in Indianapolis are a diverse but not a divided group. The largest group is most likely from Gujarat, the province of India where Mahatma Gandhi, the father of the Indian nation, was born. The second largest group consists of peoples from southern India. Punjabis and other north Indians probably make up the third largest group.

The Asian Indian community of Hindus, Jains, Christians, Sikhs, Muslims, and others remains well integrated. The year 1984 presented a tough test to the Sikhs and Hindus in the Indianapolis community. In June of that year Prime Minister Indira Gandhi ordered Indian military armor to roll into the Golden Temple—the holiest shrine of the Sikhs in Amritsar, India—to flush out Sikh separatists.[15] On 31 October 1984 Gandhi was assassinated by her Sikh bodyguards, which led to organized violence by some Hindus against the Sikhs throughout India that took thousands of Sikh lives. The reverberations of this cruel and senseless cycle of violence were felt all over the world—wherever the Asian Indian people had settled. Indianapolis was no exception. For a time Sikhs and Hindus—especially Hindus from north India—drifted away from each other as did "moderates" and "fundamentalists" among both Sikhs and Hindus. Fortunately the anger and resentment was contained to a great degree. Sikhs and Hindus from north India who had been praying together did segregate in special religious gatherings of their own. Fortunately, social intercourse was maintained. Personal griefs and regrets were shared as the violence in India acquired a life of its own, fueled by the politics of cynicism. Old wounds have slowly begun to heal.

## Meeting Needs, Sacred and Secular

During 1968–69 the Asian Indians met in the basements of each other's homes for Sunday worship. In the 1970s a sizable group of Asian Indians arrived in Indianapolis. A Sikh *Satsang* (a congregation of the Sikhs from India) formed in 1970 and started meeting at the International Center on the Butler University campus. A *Gita Mandal* (a group formed to organize Hindu worship and religious celebrations) had been established in 1973, and it started meeting on the second Sunday of the month at the International Center. To fulfill special social and religious needs a Society of Indian-Pakistani-Bangladeshi Muslims in America was founded in 1972.

To meet the more secular social needs of the community an India Association of Indianapolis was chartered in 1971. The India Community Center built on West 56th Street at Guion Road signified the maturity and solidarity of the Asian Indian community in Indianapolis. Ground for the center was broken in the summer of 1984, and by the fall of 1984 the center was ready for use. By 1991 it had already undergone expansion. Presently the India Community Center has two big halls wherein four hundred guests can be seated. The center can serve dinners to two hundred guests at one time. The facility includes a formal stage for presentations and performances, and there are several additional classrooms. The center has indeed become a center of activity for the Indian community that gathers there to celebrate festivals like *Diwali, Lohri,* and Christmas; to solemnize marriages; to organize wedding receptions and graduation parties; to listen to poets and popular and devotional music; and to worship.

## The Asian Indian Community within the Larger Culture

The Asian Indian community in Indianapolis is too small to have an India town or even to have an Indian bazaar. There are, however, more than a couple stores that sell Indian groceries, and three Indian restaurants—India Garden, India Palace, and Star of India—operated in 1992. Although the dependence on Chicago remains, Indianapolis has become a minihub of activity. The Indianapolis Asian Indians can find tutors of Indian music and dance for their children, and the city has become an important way station for poets, artists, and singers from India on their way to or from Chicago.

While politics has not attracted anyone in the Asian Indian community in Indianapolis yet, Asian Indians have made, though hesitatingly, social commitments and connections by contributing to local charities, participating in fund-raising efforts for the larger Indianapolis community, offering food to a few hundred poor families each Thanksgiving Day, and participating in the International Festival. Such activities make the statement that Asian Indians have arrived, feel at home, and are ready to contribute to the Indianapolis community. The mainstream community in Indianapolis welcomes the Asian Indian groups and their culture as evidenced by Indian devotional music and performances aired on radio stations and cable and commercial television channels. The print media also began to show increased interest in the Indian community in Indianapolis and in events on the Indian subcontinent.

All of this occurred within the larger cultural encounter that was inexorably developing a new cultural symbiosis. On the one hand there was resilience in regard to values of family life and obligations to the family in India, of food habits, and dress codes. On the other hand there was resonance to the new American values of individualism, personal independence, gender equality, and the need to achieve. New sexual mores, rejection of arranged marriages, and interracial marriages were becoming a part of the new bicultural identity.

## History through a Biography

The history of the Asian Indian community in Indianapolis during the last twenty-five years has been played out in some significant ways in the biography of K. P. Singh, who has been a resident of Indianapolis since 1967. As an architect trained in India and the United States, he developed sensibilities that enabled him to accommodate two great cultures—Eastern and Western—and many great religious traditions—Hindu, Christian, Islamic, and Sikh. As an artist he created drawings and sketches of Indiana's historic courthouses, homes, landmarks, churches, and monuments and invited Hoosiers to view and cherish their own architectural heritage—to revere the old as they constructed the new. As a preservation artist and activist, he joined with other concerned Indianans in challenging the conscience of the people of Indiana to save the best of their architectural heritage from the wrecker's ball and the bulldozer. Singh's active role in the preservation of Union Station in Indianapolis is universally and gratefully recognized.[16]

Singh is more than an architect-artist with aesthetic sensitivities broad enough to encompass two architectural traditions. He is a humanist, philosopher, and a true cosmopolitan. While he continues to wear a turban, the distinguishing headdress of a person of Sikh faith, he made his personal symbiosis between cultures by marrying Janice Dorothy Bean, a former planner for the Model Cities Program whom he met in the early 1960s during his days in Michigan, and who is now a lecturer in the department of education at IUPUI. While Singh's work adorns public and private collections all over the United States, India, and twenty-five other countries, the place of his aesthetic and social praxis is Indiana, where he has become a cultural ambassador of Asian Indians to Indiana and has been honored as a Sagamore of the Wabash.

## A University Town: Bloomington

Indiana University in Bloomington is one of the Big Ten midwestern universities and attracts students and faculties from not only other states in the Union but also from all over the world.[17] Indiana University first brought foreign faculty members to Bloomington. Chancellor Herman B Wells, in an interview with the author, pointed out that the appointments of foreign academics in Indiana

higher education were post–World War II phenomena. Chancellor Wells recalled that foreign academics were not necessarily welcomed with open arms in Indiana, and, in fact, faculty members in most of the state's institutions of higher education resisted appointments of academics from abroad. Indiana University at Bloomington may have been an exception in the state. As Chancellor Wells remembered it, enrollment had increased at the time, and the various faculties at Indiana University were receptive to the idea of foreign academics, believing cosmopolitanism to be essential to a world-class institution.[18]

Europeans mostly made up the first wave of foreign academics to Indiana. Most of the Asian Indians who are today on the faculties of Indiana's colleges and universities first came as graduate students on Fulbright and Smith-Mundt grants in the late 1950s and early 1960s. Some were encouraged to stay, while many others decided on their own to stay to teach at the universities, to practice medicine, to work as engineers in industries, and to work as middle-level managers in businesses.

Asian Indian doctors came to Bloomington soon after the Asian Indian academics settled in the various departments of Indiana University, particularly mathematics and physics. Later, Otis Elevator hired some Asian Indian engineers, as did General Electric. Small businesses run by Asian Indians came much later and to this day are few in number.

Academic communities in internationally known universities are, by definition, cosmopolitan. As a result, their local roots sometimes can be quite shallow. Academics may buy and bank in their local communities and send their children to local schools, but their "reference groups" are spread all around the globe. This is particularly true in the case of Asian Indian teachers who have to negotiate a racial and cultural divide to become acceptable in the local community. Obligations to the community frequently are met by financial contributions rather than by individual presence and personal service.

If making friends across the racial-cultural divide has been difficult, making friends within the Asian Indian community has not been any easier because Asian Indians can have inner divisions. Fortunately, being a small community the Asian Indian community of Bloomington is a tight-knit group; however, it does not effectively meet all the emotional and social needs of Bloomington families. As a result, the typical Asian Indian home in Bloomington serves as a castle, club, restaurant, pub, and movie theater all rolled into one. Most of the Asian Indians in Bloomington spend the greater part of their time after work at home within the nuclear family. Most of the family resources are spent on the education of their children in prestigious private colleges and universities.

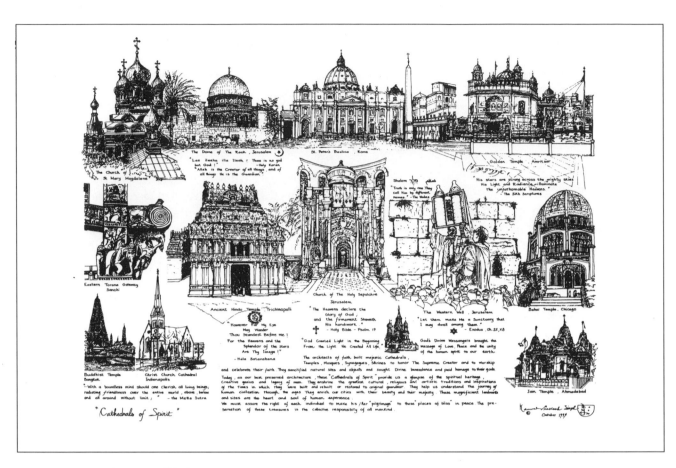

"Cathedrals of Spirit"

K. P. Singh, Indianapolis artist.

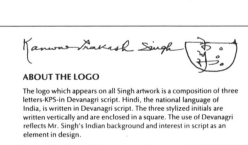

## ABOUT THE LOGO

The logo which appears on all Singh artwork is a composition of three letters-KPS-in Devanagri script. Hindi, the national language of India, is written in Devanagri script. The three stylized initials are written vertically and are enclosed in a square. The use of Devanagri reflects Mr. Singh's Indian background and interest in script as an element in design.

The Indic Society of Bloomington, a nonprofit voluntary organization of Asian Indian women, was established in the mid-1980s to raise funds to support charitable work in Bloomington and in a few selected poor communities in India. The annual dinner, cooked by the Indian women as a fund-raising event, has become a popular tradition and everyone involved—Asian Indian hosts and guests from the community—look forward to the annual feast.

The Asian Indian professors who joined the university in the early 1960s will be retiring in the 1990s. Most of them have come to consider Bloomington as their home and will most likely retire there. However, their sons and daughters have gone to distant places as accountants, managers, lawyers, doctors, computer analysts, and artists. They are unlikely to return to Bloomington except for Thanksgiving dinners or Christmas holidays. Unless new economic opportunities open, the life of the Asian Indian community in Bloomington will depend upon continuing university appointments.

### Northwest Indiana

The Asian Indians in the string of communities of Merrillville, Munster, Hammond, Gary, Griffith, Dyer, Hobart, Sherwood, and Valparaiso speak of being from northwest Indiana. Then they quickly tell the visitor that while they are physically in Indiana they are economically and socially integrated into Chicago. They watch Chicago television stations. For most of them it takes about half an hour to reach downtown Chicago, where they go to shop, to eat, and to be entertained. Many of these people from northwest Indiana are "influentials" within the Chicago community.

Before 1970 there may have been as few as two or three Asian Indians in the area. The mid-1970s saw a sizable influx. All the Asian Indians came to the area from Chicago. The most important reasons for this in-migration were economic. Because of the high malpractice insurance rates in Illinois many of the hospitals and providers of health services, and with them their doctors and health practitioners working in greater Chicago, decided to move to Indiana, where lower insurance rates prevailed. Real estate values were also lower so both homes and offices were moved to Indiana. Engineers and other professionals working for Inland Steel and US Steel also moved their homes to Indiana to enjoy small-city life and to obtain for their children the advantages of some of the better-known school districts in Indiana such as in Munster. Purdue University Calumet proved to be another node of attraction for Asian Indian teachers and researchers.

The Asian Indians of northwest Indiana do not live in clusters that could be called ethnic neighborhoods but are scattered all over and constitute what can be called a "reference community." They reaffirm themselves as a community by joining a variety of secular and cultural-linguistic groups and associations that are interlocking at various levels.

The local leadership within the Indian Medical Association of northwest Indiana, for instance, played an important part in building bridges between the Asian Indian community and the mainstream economy, polity, and culture. In addition to watching out for their professional interests, they facilitated contacts with politicians—mayors, legislators, congressmen, senators, and the governor. Their well-organized annual gala dinner and cultural evening entertained as many as five hundred non-Asian Indian guests and thereby provided opportunities not only for making political acquaintances but also for mutual cultural understanding.

While contacts with politicians and campaign contributions to political campaigns helped the Indian community to collect useful IOUs, the Asian Indians took no direct participation in the political process. No Asian Indian from the area sought political office, and only a few joined the Rotarians or the Lions Club.

Cultural activities abounded, however. Indian festivals and religious holidays were celebrated by various linguistic-cultural groups from India such as the Gujarat Samaj (Society), the North Indian Samaj, and others. The cultural contact provided by such events kept the group integrated and the group's cultural ways and mores in tact. But, to paraphrase Dr. Vijay Dave of Valparaiso: "The daughters were already more Westernized than the mothers and sons more so than their fathers."

Karl Bilimoria, a tenth grader, son of a senior staff engineer at Inland Steel and president of the local chapter of the American Society of Engineers from India, reflected thus: Asian Indian girls were more easily accepted by their peers than boys. Perhaps this is so because boys were expected to be sportsmen or at least sports buffs which Asian Indian boys were often not. Tennis, for some reason, seemed to be the only sport for Asian Indians. Otherwise, Asian Indian boys and girls lived up to the stereotype of being good students, even "super intelligent." Growing up in America need not be as difficult as some parents have made it for their kids. They expect their children to live by the norms of a different time and place that the parents had experienced and the children had only heard about. The burden of transition had fallen on the children. Bilimoria pointed out that only a few of the boys and girls of his age danced the traditional dance on the night of 5 October 1991, when the festival of *Navratari*—the Homecoming of Lord Rama—was being celebrated. Either much older youth or those much younger than he danced. Teenagers like Karl Bilimoria danced to a different drummer!

## India Association of Michiana: The Celebration of *Diwali* in 1991

They call it Michiana: the string of townships along Indiana's northern border with Michigan—South Bend, Notre Dame, Mishawaka, Elkhart, Lagrange, Goshen, and places in between. Some two hundred families of Asian Indians live in the area. They form a relatively stable community with a cultural flavor of Gujarat and southern India. Some 40 percent of the families are associated with universities, and another 40 percent work in business firms such as UniRoyal, Bendix, and Dodge. Some are in business for themselves. Satish Shah of Accrapack Industries, which manufactures aerosol products and employs some two thousand workers, and Jayanti Bhai of Randall Inn are mentioned with pride as successful businessmen. Several others are also in the hotel-motel business. The rest are engaged in a variety of occupations. Academics came to the area initially to work in the cluster of universities that includes Notre Dame and Indiana University's regional campus. Professor Karamjit Singh Rai may have been the first to arrive when he came to teach at Notre Dame in 1962.

As elsewhere in Indiana, Asian Indians do not cluster in small neighborhoods. Michiana is thus a reference community. While the Michigan-Indiana border defines the territoriality of the Asian Indian community, their reference point is Chicago. It is a two-hour drive from Lagrange to downtown Chicago. Indian programs on Chicago television are watched while the "Indian bazaar" on Devon Street, part of which is now renamed Gandhiji Marg, is often visited to buy food and clothing imported from India.

The India Association of Michiana was established in 1990. The *Diwali* function held at Clay High School, St. Joseph County, on 16 November 1991, was its first major function. *Diwali* celebrated the vitality of the Michiana community. It also was meant to be an important "substitute experience" of food, ritual, and fun for the Asian Indian children who had had little real experience with *Diwali* or other festivals in India. How they observe *Diwali* in Michiana speaks volumes about the nature and development of the Asian Indian community not only in Michiana, but also in Indiana and elsewhere in the United States.

*Diwali,* the Festival of Lights, has come to be a truly national festival of India. *Diwali* celebrates the triumph of light over darkness, of good over evil. Around this theme, people from different cultural traditions, regions, and faiths have created legends of their own to celebrate *Diwali.* Hindus of all colors, Sikhs, Jains, and Buddhists have all found legends of their own to join in the celebration.

On the evening of 16 November 1991 Clay High School was transformed from its sparsely lit, lonely emptiness of after-school hours into a place full of men, women, and children from India and their neighbors, friends, and colleagues who came as their guests.

All the faces of India—from north, south, east, and west—could be found among these four hundred people. Most men came dressed in western attire, though some of them donned traditional Indian dress. The women dressed mainly in beautiful saris of silk and brocades embroidered with threads of silver and gold. Most were bedecked in gold jewelry—rings, chains, bracelets, pendants, necklaces, *manglasutras,* wedding bands, and much else. The some twenty or so local women guests wore western dresses. Judy Patel—a local girl married to an Asian Indian—wore a sari and conducted the children's show in the dining hall and organized the raffle.

The sumptuous Indian dinner cost twelve dollars per person and was catered by one of the best-known Indian restaurants in Chicago called the Tandoor. On the menu was the Indian nan (bread), chicken tandoori (chicken roasted in a clay oven), saag paneer (cubes of Indian cheese cooked in spinach sauce), channa masala (chick-peas cooked in curry sauce), urd daal (a favorite legume dish), gobi-alu (curried cauliflower and potatoes), and papar (a crisp relish that comes closest to a potato chip). The sweet dish was the favorite raas malai, Indian cheese patties wrapped and dipped in a thick sauce of milk and flavored with cardamom. The hosts offered pizza to those children who had learned to prefer hamburger and pizza to Indian food. Soft drink fountains dispensed a variety of cold drinks.

At the head table in the dining hall sat the guests of honor: Honorable Tim Roemer, third district congressman; Honorable B. S. Dhir, vice consul, consulate general of India, Chicago office; Dr. R. Nagarajan, Federation of India Associations; and leaders of the India Association of Michiana.

The after-dinner cultural program, with Malini Janakiraman as the master of ceremonies, followed introductions of the guests of honor and other guests. Congressman Roemer, in his short but informative speech, spoke of the historical and ideological affinities between the United States and India—one, the oldest democracy in the world, the other, the most populous. He referred to the improved relationships between the two countries with the lifting of the United States ban on the export of super-computer technology to India, the new trade agreements, and America's central role in the World Bank's giving a line of credit to India. He took note of the many contributions of Asian Indians in the region not only to the economy and education but also to the various communities where the Asian Indian families lived.

Dr. R. Nagarajan invited the India Association of Michiana formally to join the Federation of India Associations that he represented and cautioned against the tendencies among Asian Indians to become fragmented into small provincial and parochial groups. He asked people to enter the local community organizations and government institutions. He also asked them to serve first and ask for recognition later.

The twenty-item cultural program exhibited an amazing array of local talent studded with sculpturesque postures, rhythmic footwork, and gracefully measured hand gestures. Many of the performers were trained in the song and dance schools that sprouted up in the area, and they presented a dizzying variety of art forms: Banniro (a folk dance), Rhas (a stick dance), kathak dance, a prayer dance and dances from the Krishna lore, and a piece of modern dance; devotional songs, Jai Bharathi (a patriotic song), a film song, and a children's song sung by children; violin, tabla, and other instrumental music; and, yes, a jazz dance. The program had an Indian twist; in what could have been mixed dances with males and females, females played both parts. The event ended with the playing of the national anthems of the United States and India. The free distribution materials on the table outside included materials of interest to the tourist and the businessman.

### III

### Integration within the New Society

The pattern of integration of Asian Indians as a new community in Indiana and the pattern of its integration within the mainstream American culture are at the same time similar and different from the experiences of Asian Indians in other states. The most important difference compares the historical experience of Asian Indians in Indiana to that of earlier Asian Indians who went to California and New York. The history of Asian Indians in Indiana is relatively short, beginning with the 1960s, and their incorporation in the new society in Indiana has been relatively painless. This is dramatically different from the trials and tribulations of the Punjabi, predominantly Sikh, agricultural workers who arrived in California during the first four decades of the twentieth century.[19] This difference arises from the fact that the Asian Indians in Indiana are highly qualified professionals, coming to Indiana as part of the "brain gain" from independent India. The pioneers

of yesteryear came as colonized people, physically sturdy, morally strong, but mostly illiterate. They labored on land owned by local farmers, trying hard to save to buy some land of their own to farm for themselves. They met vicious discrimination and frequent violence and fought tough political battles first to survive and then to win civil rights denied them on racial grounds.[20]

In the post-1965 era, however, the experiences of Asian Indians in various states may have been quite similar, with due regard, of course, for differences in place of residence, gender, occupational level, and generation. It is ironic that while the outsider may look at all Asian Indians as one cohesive group, Indiana's Asian Indians themselves do not necessarily have the same feeling of communal solidarity. They are subjected to a whole series of opposite pulls. First, they are divided among a number of religious groups of Hindus, Sikhs, Muslims, and Christians, and not every professionally trained Asian Indian is enough of a cosmopolite to accommodate people of all faiths in his or her circle of solidarity. Both Muslims and Christians have become "invisible" groups in relation to Hindu and Sikh Asian Indians. Hindus and Sikhs are divided among themselves in terms of the gods they worship and the gurus and saints that they adore.

Second, there is the tension between narrow linguistic nationalism and an Indian nationalism in general. Most Indians are prone to think of themselves first as Bengalis, Keralites, Tamils, Maharashtrians, Gujaratis, Rajasthanis, Uttar Pradeshis, Biharis, Oriya, or Punjabi and only secondarily as Indians. Various caste categories among these parochial nationalisms introduce further fragmentations among these linguistically defined provincial groupings.

Finally, there is the cultural push and pull—the desire to stay rooted in the old cultural traditions and the need to incorporate the new values of the American culture. This is reflected in the tension between *sanskritization* and westernization, in this case Americanization.[21] The result is a certain fragmentation of identity and compartmentalization of social existence among the Asian Indians in Indiana as elsewhere in the Asian Indian diaspora. Hardly any city in Indiana boasts of a "Little India" with its predominant Indian population or an Indian bazaar. Not all communities have been able to build community centers or places of worship. Sunday community lunches in homes and functions organized around visiting religious personalities or concert artists in rented halls are looked forward to with great expectation. The local and Indiana branches of a multiplicity of national associations of Asian Indians provide a formal structure for cohesiveness, while cultural consumption made possible by the tape and videocassette imported from India provides further sustenance.

## Economic Integration

The Asian Indian immigrants in America are a cerebral group: two Nobel Laureates, about twenty-five thousand physicians, an EEOC commissioner, several thousand Ph.D.s, engineers, and other professionals in many universities, corporations, and federal, state, and local governments.[22] The Asian Indians in Indiana are also a predominantly professional community—doctors, engineers, managers, and academics. Chancellor Wells, when interviewed, suggested that the presence of Asian Indian workers in the health professions as nurses, lab technicians, and related professions may be more pervasive than imagined. To find jobs these workers move to places where there is a university campus or a concentration of hospitals and manufacturing facilities. Hard work is an important value. To buy a home of one's own is another. Asian Indian owners of large businesses or industrialists are few in Indiana. Even fewer have succeeded in business and manufacturing. More work in retail businesses than in the manufacturing sector. Some Asian Indians have come to Indiana from East Africa as political refugees and have set themselves up in the hotel and motel business.

## Political Integration

In the post-1965 period, Asian Indians in America have been relatively inactive in the political arena. They have been satisfied to establish national-level political associations such as the Indo-American Political Association (IAPA), India-America Political Action Committee (IAPAC), Asian-American Voters Coalition, Asian American National Leadership Conference, and the Indian-American Foundation for Political Education (IAFPE). These organizations protect narrow interests and create "photo opportunities" for community leaders.

At the end of the term of office of the first Asian Indian congressman, Dalip Singh Saund of California from 1956 to 1962, a long dry spell occurred nationally, regionally, and even locally in regard to seeking and winning political office.[23] New names have appeared recently: Peter Matthew, a California legislator, and Kumar Bharve in Maryland's legislature. No Asian Indian has sought or held political office on any level in Indiana. Few, if any, have had critical positions in managing political campaigns in the state. Less than half of the Asian Indians may be voting in general elections.

Asian Indians generally take news from India more seriously than news concerning Indiana. Events such as the assassination of Prime Minister Indira Gandhi by her two Sikh bodyguards, the separatist movement in Kashmir, and the protests and counterprotests regarding the Babri Masjid and Ram Janmabhoomi controversy have fragmented the community of Asian Indians during the 1980s.[24] Asian Indians rely on the ethnic newspapers and magazines in Chicago, among them the *India Tribune* and the *Spotlight*.

## Social and Cultural Integration

Intercultural integration is a door that has to open from both sides. When racial differences are also involved, social and cultural integration becomes even more difficult. Asian Indians in Indiana, as elsewhere in America, are not always accepted as socially or racially equal by whites. But while suffering from discrimination from their white hosts, Asian Indians are themselves what has been called "coconuts"—brown on the outside and white inside. They want to be accepted by whites as equals, but they do not offer equality to blacks. Within Asian Indian families, their own children with comparatively darker skins are likely to suffer subtle and not so subtle discrimination relative to the children who are fair skinned.

The reconciliation of opposites is at work in the Indian family and extended family. Change is taking place, but traditions remain strong. Relatives and visitors from India are entertained for months and years due to obligations generations old. On the other hand, relationships between husbands and wives and between parents and children are changing dramatically. Children born out of wedlock are a rarity, but grown children have started living away from home, sharing apartments with fellow students or workmates of the opposite sex. The family, though, remains the anchor of stability. It is the nursing home, the mental health clinic, the welfare department, and, through the parents, the preserver of the mother tongue.

Asian Indians admire and practice American values at work and in the marketplace, but not in their private lives. That is what creates problems between the sexes and the tension between parents and their children. The gender revolution in process in America has affected the Asian Indian families as well. While most couples are still living up to the traditions, many others are influenced by the new gender values.

As for leisure activity, Asian Indian parents are neither joiners of clubs nor ardent vacationers, though some of the children are developing a wanderlust. Education, however, attracts parental attention to a degree not present in other cultures. Education in America is indeed a surefire way to economic success and upward mobility. This is understood by both the professionally trained parents and their children. Asian Indian parents typically allocate large proportions of their income and their life savings to the education of their children at some of America's most prestigious universities. The Asian Indian lifestyles and family support networks enable children to put in prodigious amounts of time on academic tasks and to compete for places in universities and then in the economy. The stakes are high for the Asian Indian youths. Success in school and university can mean the continuation of what their professional parents have been able to provide. Failure, on the other hand, can mean downward mobility and a life in social settings where they may not be as welcome. While most of the time the results are beneficial for the family, sometimes the parental pressures on children to succeed have led to tragic results such as suicides and family violence.

Like education, Asian Americans take seriously their religious heritage. The *NFIA News* of July–August 1991 reported that there may be 130 temples and *gurudwaras* (the Sikh temples) in the United States, with total assets of two hundred million dollars.[25] The famous Sri Venkateswara Temple of Pittsburgh alone has an annual budget of just under two million dollars. The Sri Venkateswara Swami Temple (called the Balaji Temple) of Greater Chicago, in Aurora, Illinois, is equally spectacular. It serves communities from far and near, and Sunday congregations can total six thousand or more persons. The temple is the center for receptions, cultural activities, and social functions in addition to religious festivals.

Asian Indians in Indiana visit Pittsburgh and Chicago temples on important occasions. Since the Asian Indian community in Indiana is relatively small, no *gurudwaras, mandirs* (the Hindu temples), or mosques (the Muslim place of worship) have been built in Indiana. A North American Islamic Center has been established in Plainfield, and plans are afoot for the construction of a mosque in Indianapolis. In Indianapolis, for the present, the India Community Center serves both sacred and secular purposes.

As Vaidyanathan points out, the *guru-shishya* (teacher-disciple) relationship "infuses all of India's practices—secular and religious, artistic and philosophic, trivial and fantastical, primitive and political."[26] There is a tradition of gurus, saints, sadhus, and yogis coming from India to the United States starting from J. Krishnamurty to Rajneesh. Indiana devotees are seldom able to invite gurus and sadhus from India on their own but do so often in cooperation with groups in Illinois, Ohio, and Michigan.

In smaller communities in Indiana Asian Indians worship inside their homes. The attic, the basement, a small room, or the corner of a larger room is made into an abode for gods. The abode is covered with silk or brocade curtains, with images of gods in gold, silver, or brass, behind the curtains surrounded by flowers, incense, and candles. Tape recorders play the *Arati* (hymns of prayer) or devotional songs from sacred temples and well-known singers of devotional music from India. On Saturdays or Sundays friends and families meet in each other's homes by rotation and worship together. A community lunch, to which all contribute food and service, typically follows the worship service.

Asian Indian immigrants to Indiana often have been invited by local friends to worship with them in churches. Even when they are not of the Christian faith they have willingly gone into local churches. Some have stayed and converted to Christianity.

As part of the enculturation into India's native culture, festivals such as *Diwali, Holi,* and the Muslim *Id-ul-Fitr* are celebrated with enthusiasm. In small towns with few Indian families these festivals have become private celebrations at home. At the same time Asian Indians have joined in on American festivals: Christmas, Thanksgiving, Halloween, and with their Jewish friends at Passover.

## Marriages

Intermarriage is a very significant indicator of the quality of mutual relationships between races. It is significant that intermarriages between Asian Indians and others in Indiana have remained few, but they are by no means rare. When intermarriages have taken place the Asian Indian "coconuts" have married whites, not blacks or Hispanics. In addition, double standards apply to boys and girls. Asian Indian parents who would tolerate a white daughter-in-law would be less tolerant of a white son-in-law.

Racial categories are not the only explanation for this attitude, however. Cultural realities also explain what happens. Marriageable Asian Indians in Indiana have continued to return to India for traditionally arranged marriages. In India, prospective husbands can find wives who do not claim equality with them—at least to begin with! It takes quite a few years for the imported wife to undergo the "second socialization" during which gender equality and individual freedom take place. Indian girls can easily find husbands from India because even the very best doctors and engineers in India are vying for an opportunity to come to the United States to settle.

This pattern of marriage, however, is undergoing alteration. The new Indian woman from cities in India is departing from the old mold of docility. Conversely, the doctor- or engineer-husband imported from India cannot tolerate the independence of his Asian Indian wife who grew up in the United States, which can lead to divorce. Indian women residing in the United States complain about being captives in "the golden cage"—good food and shelter but no freedom to grow. Sons and daughters are moving out. Some daughters are sharing apartments with the opposite sex. While statistics are unavailable, experimentation with sex and drugs is not unknown. The battered woman phenomenon is surfacing.

Accommodation and assimilation is taking place both in life and death. Asian Indian funerals are beginning to look more and more like funerals in Christian America. While Hindus and Sikhs both cremate their dead, they have begun to send their dead to the mortuary first for preparation. Family and friends are allowed to come and take leave of the departed one in the western style. There are eulogies. The religious service, however, remains typically Hindu or Sikh when it comes to reading the scriptures and singing devotional songs.

In the world of sports there are no players with Asian names on Indiana high school or university teams. One reason may be that Asian Indians are not encouraged to be sportsmen and sportswomen. There is also the possibility that few Asian Indians have the physique to compete for spots on football or basketball teams.

### Asian Indians in Music, Art, and Literature

The intermix of American and Asian Indian music, of course, is not contained within Indiana; it is a worldwide phenomenon. American rock music and an Indian version of rock is being heard as film music throughout India, and it is being shipped back to the United States in the form of tapes and videotapes. Chicago has hundreds of shops that sell or rent such materials. Major towns and cities of Indiana have similar shops run by entrepreneurial Indians and Pakistanis.

The encounter between the two "classical" traditions of music is a different story. There is no known systematic effort by Asian Indians in Indiana to practice, promote, or present Indian classical music to others in their communities. The Karnataka Music Society of Indianapolis may be an exception. The world-renowned School of Music at Indiana University in Bloomington does not include Indian music in its curriculum or its schedule of presentations and recitals. As an individual interest and initiative, Professor Lewis Rowell of the Indiana University School of Music is a serious student of Indian music and has brought Indian musicians to the campus off and on as an extracurricular activity. Nivedita Rangnekar offers lessons in Bharat Natyam in Indianapolis as does Rita Ghosh in Terre Haute and G. Jaynagarkar in Fort Wayne. As a result, Indian classical music is kept alive in small performances organized in the homes of connoisseurs in which both Indians and non-Indians participate.

The second generation of Asian Indians has made bold new choices in the performing arts. Meera Popkin, daughter of Prema Popkin, an Indian Christian, and

*Meera Popkin (left), 1985.*

William D. Popkin, a law professor at Indiana University in Bloomington, played the starring role in the hit musical, *Miss Saigon,* at the Drury Lane Theatre in London. During the same period, Meera's brother, Lionel Popkin, after studying the Kathak dance at a dance academy in New Delhi, India, run by the famous Birju Maharaj, probably the best known exponent of the Kathak dance tradition in India, brought the moves and memories of the East to the dance traditions of the West that he was studying at Oberlin College in Ohio.

Across town, again in Bloomington, Joy Basu, son of Ilora Basu, a physiologist and a serious guitarist herself, and Abhijit Basu, a geology professor at Indiana University, went to Hollywood and merged the Indian guitar with American rock. The few thousand other teenagers in Asian Indian families are, of course, not quiet. They are listening and singing. What they choose to sing and listen to is confusing to their parents, sometimes even exasperating. To the children, of course, it is not mere noise and nonsense, but the outlet for their new musical sensibilities.

The contributions of K. P. Singh of Indianapolis to the fine arts in Indiana are well known, as documented above. However, Asian Indian poets and novelists living in Indiana are yet to be heard from.

The most significant changes taking place in the Asian Indian community in Indiana (and America) may be in the areas of language, personal relations, economic transactions, and cultural consumption. The English language is reconstructing the Asian Indian identity. Children return from school with new Anglo-Saxon nicknames given to them by their new friends, such as Nick, Paul, Herb, Buck, Pat, Su, and Mona. While they still understand the remarks addressed to them by their parents in their mother tongue, they cannot always respond in the mother tongue. The loss of the native Indian language disassociates the children from the grandparents visiting from India and from the mythology and the scriptures written in the language of their ancestors. Old sacred words become mere mumbo jumbo devoid of any meaning, and ritual becomes laughable. As larger communities become established in California, New York, Pennsylvania, and Texas attempts are being made to regain both old language and tradition. The battle will not be easily won, and may be futile.

*Indiana University Chancellor Herman B Wells and Abid Hussain, India's ambassador to the United States in Washington, D.C., confer on the occasion of a fund-raiser in Bloomington for the India Studies program at Indiana University, 21 September 1991.*

## Projecting the Indian Heritage: An Endowment for the India Studies Chair at Indiana University

It is finally dawning on the Asian Indians living in various communities in Indiana that it is not enough to be known and liked by one's neighbors at home and one's colleagues at work; it is important to be known more widely by the citizens of the state and the nation. The wider community must know the Asian Indians in terms of their historical and cultural roots and as fruits of that culture. Indeed, it is becoming clear to the Asian Indians that their own children as well need to know about their roots.

This has led to the acceptance of an uncomfortable truth: while Asian Indians have been teaching at the various universities in Indiana for at least thirty to thirty-five years, the academic study of India has been in comparative neglect. There are several scholars with interests in India who can be called friends of India on various university campuses in Indiana, but there are only a few courses, if any, on Indian history, Indian languages, and Indian civilization in any of Indiana's institutions of higher education. In 1989 Professor Patrick Olivelle, a Sri Lankan who is now an American citizen, took the initiative and asked Indiana University to establish a chair of India Studies. The university countered with an offer to establish a chair if the group initiating the idea would raise an initial sum of $250,000. On 21 September 1991 the India Studies group in Bloomington, with assistance from other state groups, organized a fund-raising dinner at the Indianapolis Hilton. The speaker was Professor Abid Hussain, India's ambassador to the United

States in Washington, D.C., and he called on the Asian Indian residents in America and particularly in Indiana to support enthusiastically and generously the establishment of an India Studies program at Indiana University and the appointment of a Rabindranath Tagore professor of Indian Civilization. Fund-raising groups visited several communities in Indiana and tried to get people to contribute to the establishment of this chair. An India Studies chair at Indiana University, Bloomington, is already a reality.

## On the Brink of the Twenty-First Century

The first-generation Asian Indians who came to the United States in the mid-1960s are still culturally and psychologically rooted in the land they left long ago. The second-generation Asian Indians, who were born here or came as children in the mid-1960s with their parents, are today going through a process of bisocialization—one socialization at home and another socialization at school or work. They are straining at the parental leash. Their parents want them to be Indians culturally and successful middle-class Americans socioeconomically.

The Asian Indian immigrants who came in the 1980s and 1990s are yet another group. India of the 1990s is not the India of the 1960s. It is now highly industrialized and westernized. These second-wave Asian Indians are quite sophisticated in the ways of the West and are the beneficiaries of the communal patterns and social structures that have been built by the Asian Indian community here. In interacting with the host culture the inevitable is slowly happening. Asian Indians have the advantage of an old and resilient culture with a rich collective memory. It is rare to find an Asian Indian who is ashamed of his or her cultural heritage. Indeed they take every possible opportunity to show pride in their traditions. On the other hand, the American culture has become much more open and hospitable to different cultures, religions, and views on life. The Hindu and Buddhist views of life and values of austerity and tolerance are indeed being appreciated and integrated by many Americans. Consequently, no dramatic changes are likely to happen in the decade of the 1990s or in the first decade of the twenty-first century in the lives of the peoples from India in Indiana. The Asian Indians living in Indiana probably will continue to live as they have: sending their children to school and going to school themselves; working every day and seldom going on vacations; saving to buy appliances, electronic goods, cars, and homes in pursuit of the American dream; eating, drinking, and viewing Indian films on VCRs at home, not in bars, restaurants, or clubs; worshiping at the little shrines set up at home and sometimes driving three hundred miles to Chicago to worship at the big temple; and being good neighbors, and staying out of trouble and far away from politics.

In personal encounters Asian Indians will continue to make deep friendships with local Hoosiers and establish partnerships with them at work and at leisure. Some Asian Indian children will intermarry within local communities. But the overall racial barrier between the Asian Indian and the white native will not evaporate anytime soon.

With the availability of modern modes of intercontinental travel the first-generation Indians in Indiana will continue to travel home. With the second- and third-generation Indians in Indiana things will be different. They will not only lose touch with the folks in India, but also their connections with people of the Indian subcontinent in Indiana will change. The melting pot will not melt all, but quite a few. Those who are teenagers in the 1990s will be a different breed. They will be bolder in their immersions in the culture of their land of birth—America. Their social and cultural identities will be merging and emerging.

## Notes

1. Asian Indians have been called variously Hindoos, Hindus, East Asians, and Indo-Americans. Presently, the label Asian Indians is in frequent use. However, as Srini Muktevi points out in "The Immigrant Experience: Coming to Terms with a Hyphenated Identity" (*The Indian-American* 2 [Mar. 1992]: 6), the term Asian Indian is beginning to be seen as empty of any American association and identity, thereby rendering Americans of Indian origin forever peripheral in their new

homeland. Indian-American seems to be emerging as the label of preference. British India was partitioned in 1947 into two independent states—India and Pakistan. In 1971 Pakistan was divided into the two sovereign states of Pakistan and Bangladesh. Political divisions did not, of course, create instant cultural divides. A "cultural India" has survived several political divisions throughout its history. Indeed, the cultural India can be seen to include, in addition to the present-day political India, Pakistan, Bangladesh, Nepal, Tibet, Bhutan, and Sri Lanka. While several cultural differentiations unique to each of these groups have emerged over the centuries, the larger, shared Indian ethos has survived. In this essay, the label "India" will be used to refer to both political and cultural India. The boundaries of India, in the case of each usage, will be clarified through the context of its use.

The history of Asian Indians in Indiana essentially begins with the 1960s. The brevity of this historical period required a specific methodological approach in the writing of this essay. First, as compared to the groups of immigrants from Europe, too little is known about the history and culture of the Asian Indian immigrants. What little is known is exotic rather than substantive. This meant that the culture and history of Asian Indians had to be described in some detail to provide a proper context to the experience of Asian Indian immigrants in Indiana. Second, the Asian Indian group in Indiana is relatively small and quite a bit reticent. Little has been written on or by the Asian Indians in Indiana about their experience in the state. Except for some statistical information in the more recent national census and a few journalistic articles, there is no historical documentation. Indeed this essay may be the first such piece of writing on Indiana's Asian Indians. As a result, the author had to depend on the individual experiences and memories of the immigrants who are living in Indiana today. Thus, this history of Asian Indians in Indiana in part became an oral history project. Third, to interpret this oral history material, a rather systematic social-scientific framework had to be built on the basis of the experiences of immigrants to America in general and the experiences of Asian Indians to America in particular. This essay, therefore, has become much more comparative in nature than perhaps it would have been otherwise. The framework of comparative analysis uses the trinity of economy, society, and polity. In each case two related questions are asked: What kind of economy, society, or polity have the Asian Indians created in their new home state? And how is their micro-economy, society, or polity interfacing with the larger state economy, society, and polity?

2. Unless otherwise indicated, facts and interpretations of historical and cultural nature included in this essay have come from Romila Thapar, vol. 1 of *A History of India* (Harmondsworth, Eng.: Penguin Books, 1966) and Richard Lannoy, *The Speaking Tree: A Study of Indian Culture and Society* (New York: Oxford University Press, 1971). Vedas are collections of Indian sacred writings dating from the second millennium B.C.E. that form the Hindu scriptures. Upanishads are philosphical treatises on the nature of man and the universe, ancillary to the Vedas.

3. For some insightful analyses of contemporary Indian politics, economy, society, and culture, see "Another India," *Daedalus* 118 (Fall 1989). For a broader historical perspective on independent India, see Gunnar Myrdal, *Asian Drama: An Inquiry into the Poverty of Nations,* 3 vols. (New York: Pantheon Books, 1968).

4. The material in this section is developed from T. N. Madan, "Religion in India," *Daedalus* 118 (Fall 1989): 115–46. See also Barbara Stoler Miller, trans., *The Bhagavad-Gita: Krishna's Counsel in Time of War* (New York: Bantam Books, 1986).

5. See Arthur W. Helweg and Usha M. Helweg, *An Immigrant Success Story: East Indians in America* (Philadelphia: University of Pennsylvania Press, 1990).

6. Tapan Mukherjee and J. John Sunny Wycliff, "The History of the Early Arrivals of Asian Indians to America," *The Spotlight* (Chicago), 13 Jan. 1990.

7. Joan M. Jensen, "East Asians," in *Harvard Encyclopedia of American Ethnic Groups,* Stephan Thernstrom, ed. (Cambridge, Mass.: The Belknap Press of Harvard University Press, 1980), 296–301. See also Joan M. Jensen, *Passage from India: Asian Indian Immigrants in North America* (New Haven, Conn.: Yale University Press, 1988). Other useful references are: Richard Harvey Brown and George V. Coelho, eds., *Tradition and Transformation: Asian Indians in America,* Studies in Third World Societies, Publication No. 38 (Williamsburg, Va.: Department of Anthropology, College of William and Mary, 1986); S. Chandrasekhar, ed., *From India to America: A Brief History of Immigration, Problems of Discrimination, Admission, and Assimilation* (La Jolla, Calif.: Population Review Publications, 1982); and Helweg and Helweg, *Immigrant Success Story.*

8. See *NFIA News,* vol. 10, no. 4, July–Aug. 1991. *NFIA News* is the bimonthly newsletter of the National Federation of Indian-American Associations.

9. *Indianapolis Public Schools Annual Report of the Secretary, Business Director, Superintendent of Schools and Libraries,* 1908–9; Gregory S. Rose, "The Distribution of Indiana's Ethnic and Racial Minorities in 1850," *Indiana Magazine of History* 87 (Sept. 1991); "1860 Census Foreign–Born for Indiana" (Unpublished manuscript, Indiana Historical Society, Education Division, 1991).

10. Figures in this section are from "Indiana Foreign Born for 1980 by Nationality and County." Source of the original table was U.S. Bureau of Census "1980 Census Summary Tape File 4," Indiana Business Research Center, Graduate School of Business, Indiana University.

11. "1990 Census of Population and Housing Summary Tape File 1A," Indiana Business Research Center, Graduate School of Business, Indiana University.

12. U.S. Congress, Senate Committee on the Judiciary, Subcommittee on Immigration and Naturalization, *Aliens in the United States* (Washington, D.C.: Government Printing Office, 1965).

13. Jensen, "East Asians," 299.

14. K. P. Singh, interview with the author, 19 Oct. 1991.

15. Mark Tully and Satish Jacob, *Amritsar: Mrs. Gandhi's Last Battle* (New Delhi: Rupa and Co./London: Pan Books Ltd., 1985).

16. From materials so kindly provided by K. P. Singh. In 1994 Singh had a twenty-five-year retrospective exhibit of his works at Editions Limited in Indianapolis. Richard G. Lugar, United States senator from Indiana, served as an honorary chairperson for the event.

17. *The University Looks Abroad: Approaches to World Affairs at Six American Universities* [A Report from Education and World Affairs] (New York: Walker and Co., 1965).

18. Herman B Wells, interview with the author, 28 Aug. 1991, and Herman B Wells, *Being Lucky: Reminiscences and Reflections* (Bloomington: Indiana University Press, 1980).

19. Jensen, "East Asians," 296, 298.

20. See Harish K. Puri, *Ghadar Movement: Ideology, Organisation & Strategy* (Amritsar: Guru Nanak Dev University Press, 1983).

21. See M. N. Srinivas, *Social Change in Modern India* (Berkeley: University of California Press, 1969).

22. *NFIA News,* July–Aug. 1991.

23. Jensen, "East Asians," 299.

24. The controversy has arisen from Hindus reclaiming a site that is supposed to be the birthplace of the Hindu God Lord Rama and on which site the Mogul emperor built a mosque in the 1500s. Nearly five hundred years later, the Hindus set the wrong right by demolishing the mosque!

25. See *NFIA News,* July–Aug. 1991.

26. T. G. Vaidyanathan, "Authority and Identity in India," *Daedalus* 118 (Fall 1989): 148.

# BALTIC PEOPLES: LITHUANIANS, LATVIANS, & ESTONIANS

INTA GALE CARPENTER

*When the Lithuanian Socialist Federation, founded in 1907, joined the Socialist party of America in 1916, it was the third largest foreign language section, with 200 chapters and 6,700 members. Acutely ethnocentric, often anticlerical, these socialist-activists challenged established religious, educational, social, and political life.*

## Introduction: Two Waves of Immigration to the United States

Shortly after World War I Jānis Pļavnieks, a young farmer in the Baltic territory of czarist Russia, dreamed of immigrating to America. He was fascinated by machines and thought that in America he would have more opportunity to work with them. "Oh, but my wife," he recalled, "better not even talk about it to her, if you don't want a fight. And so, I said, 'You have a house. You have livestock. I'll go by myself. If all goes well, I'll send for you.'"[1]

Despite such dreams, Pļavnieks remained in Latvia for almost thirty more years, during which time Latvia became an independent nation. Pļavnieks and his wife prospered. They built up the family farm, accumulated livestock, cleared fields, harvested crops, and reared children. Then one day in the fall of 1944, as World War II turned their farm into a war zone, they fled their burning house together with their twenty-four-year-old daughter and infant granddaughter: "My wife is wailing, where will we go? What will we do? No money. No belongings. . . . Houses are burning. Tanks booming. Everywhere there were Russians. . . . We were struggling to live in the basement. A couple of shots even entered and ricocheted off the cement walls, but didn't hurt anybody. Then the flight began. Everyone left."[2] Although he did not know it at the time, Pļavnieks had at last taken his first steps toward America, and toward Indiana.

Individuals who emigrate choose to solve their problems through mobility. From 1880 until the 1920s a number of factors sent about twenty-five million people to America. Pragmatism, the willingness to take all steps necessary to meet changing economic realities, including a trip across the Atlantic, brought craftsmen, artisans, and small farmers to America.[3] States competed among themselves, hiring promotional agents to work in Europe on their behalf and to offer various inducements to immigrants. In addition, informal channels such as letters and oral accounts spurred emigration. As letters passed from hand to hand and as stories about immigrant life circulated by word of mouth America became a household word, even in remote corners of the Baltic. "America" stories encapsulated individual dreams, whetted people's curiosity, and reinforced their resolve to emigrate. Pļavnieks recalled a family story about a relative who sent his old clothes to relations in Latvia. These clothes were

fine and fancy and well-tailored. There was a vest in which the pocket watch had left an impression, marked with sweat or grease, and you could see the impression on the outside. So, he had been walking around [in America] with the watch in that vest for years. I thought a lot about America. Yes, I believed in America.[4]

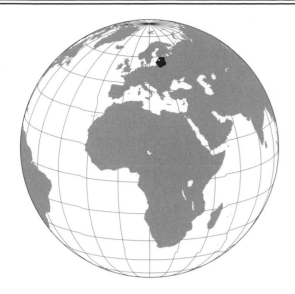

Pļavnieks was enticed by America's promise of self-advancement, but his wife's reluctance as well as their growing prosperity took precedence over his dreams.

The experiences of those who made the trip to "the Promised Land" in the late nineteenth and early twentieth centuries are well documented.[5] In contrast, relatively little has been written about the events that transformed Pļavnieks into a refugee and then brought him to the United States as a political immigrant under the Displaced Persons Act of 1948.[6] Political emigration is a neglected area of study, perhaps, as Robert C. Williams speculates, because historians dislike lost causes.[7] Or perhaps neglect stems from the misconception that only a trickle of immigrants arrived after World War II. In reality, from 1945 to 1962 more than four million immigrants were admitted to the United States.[8] Among them were 495,000 World War II refugees whose refusal to return to communist-occupied or dominated homelands prompted America to liberalize the restrictive immigration policies and quotas legislated in 1924.

The Balts in Indiana reflect these two waves of immigration to America. The Lithuanians arrived first, just after the turn of the century. Latvians and Estonians made their presence felt only after World War II. According to the 1990 United States census, 811,865 individuals claimed Lithuanian ancestry, a figure eight times larger than the 100,331 respondents claiming Latvian ancestry. Estonians, in comparison, comprised a tiny group of 26,672.[9]

### Historic Background of the Baltic Peoples

The origins of the people who came to be called Balts and who had appeared on the eastern shore of the Baltic Sea by 2500–2000 B.C., in the approximate territory now called Estonia, Latvia, and Lithuania, are unknown.

Though often grouped together, the three are ethnically, culturally, and historically distinct. Their territories are small. Latvia and Lithuania are roughly two-thirds the size of Indiana; Estonia, about one-half.[10] Their combined area is approximately that of Missouri, while their total population is slightly higher than New Jersey. In 1993 Estonia had a population of 1,573,000, Latvia, 2,681,000, and Lithuania, 3,690,000.

In a part of Europe that is largely Germanic and Slavic, the Baltic peoples are neither. Latvians and Lithuanians belong to a distinct Baltic branch of the Indo-European family and represent one of the oldest spoken language groups in Europe. The structure of the Lithuanian language resembles the reconstructed Proto-Indo-European language. The Estonians, in contrast, are a mix of East and West. Their Finno-Ugric language suggests links with the Uralic and Paleo-Asiatic peoples but together, with the majority of Latvians, Estonians are Lutherans. Christianity was introduced by conquering Germans between the eleventh and thirteenth centuries. Lithuanians, together with about a quarter of the Latvians, are Roman Catholic, a faith accepted without conquest in the fourteenth century.

All three countries share a complex historical development characterized by war, political union, annexation, foreign domination, brief independence, and contention among themselves. Their location at the crossroads between East and West has proved fortuitous economically but disastrous politically. The Estonians and Latvians view themselves as sharing a six hundred-year history of subjugation by powerful neighbors—Swedes, Poles, Germans, and Russians. Lithuanians, on the other hand, recall that from the late fourteenth to the midfifteenth century the Grand Duchy of Lithuania was united with Poland, forming a multinational military and political confederation that extended eastward from the Baltic Sea to the Black Sea. All three territories were absorbed into the Russian empire in the eighteenth century, although local power remained in the hands of German- or Polish-speaking nobility. Only peasants spoke Estonian, Latvian, or Lithuanian. Reduced to serfdom, barred from political and economic power, the Baltic peoples nurtured language, ancestral culture, and self-identity in social isolation.

Then, in the space of barely two generations, during a remarkable period of Baltic history beginning in the second half of the nineteenth century, three modern nations emerged. Lithuania declared the restoration of its independence on 16 February 1918, after what it viewed as 120 years of Russian domination. In the same year Estonians declared independence on 24 February and Latvians on 18 November. Nationhood, however, proved

Baltic States

- ⊙ National Capital
- ● City
- —— International Boundary

250 Km
250 Mi.

FINLAND

Tallinn
Tartu
ESTONIA

Baltic Sea

Riga
LATVIA

LITHUANIA
Kaunas
Vilnius

RUSSIA

BELARUS

POLAND

UKRAINE

brief. Shortly after Germany and the Soviet Union signed secret protocols as part of the Molotov-Ribbentrop Pact on 23 August 1939, Estonia, Latvia, and Lithuania were occupied by Soviet forces and formally annexed by the Soviet Union in the summer of 1940. Between 1941 and 1944 Germany established its own occupation and made plans for a Baltic "Ostland," but in 1944 the Soviets returned and for the next forty-seven years all three countries were republics of the Soviet Union.

The Baltic nations are more significant than their tiny populations would suggest. Historically, they have held center stage in many dramatic confrontations among the world's powers. Their territory has been coveted by expanding empires, and this desire has given them an international image and profile. The Baltic nations' differential historical development has led to perceived differences in character. For example, Lithuanian defiance of the Soviets in the winter of 1990, when Estonians and Latvians were more cautious but still actively resistant, prompted a Latvian living in Indianapolis to muse that Lithuanians "always were a bit heroic."[11] Recalling their once great empire, more than one Lithuanian concurred. All three countries were in the forefront of the movement to dismantle the USSR. In August 1991 Estonia, Latvia, and Lithuania once again became independent nations.

### Turn-of-the-Century Baltic Immigration to America

Individual Estonians, Latvians, and Lithuanians are known to have arrived in the United States long before any significant group emigration ensued. They came to Colonial America along with early Swedish settlers. Later Balts in the czarist army jumped ship and headed for the gold mines of California and Alaska. Balts also fought (and died) in the Civil War. The first numerically significant

emigration occurred with the arrival of Lithuanians in 1867, then they came in growing numbers between 1899 and 1914. Shenandoah, Pennsylvania, is the oldest Lithuanian community in the United States. The first exclusively Lithuanian organization was founded in 1877; the first Lithuanian newspaper appeared in 1879; and the first parish school was established in 1888. By 1914 a half million Lithuanians lived in the United States.

Estonians and Latvians came later and in far smaller numbers.[12] They established tiny communities in rural Wisconsin, the Dakotas, and the Pacific Northwest. These proved short-lived. In many cases Baltic settlers were undertaking a second emigration from farms in the Crimea and other parts of Russia. Simultaneously, small urban colonies were forming. Estonians founded their largest community in New York City. The earliest Latvian community was established in Boston when Jacob Siebergs (1863–1963), a master carpenter, arrived on Christmas Day 1888 with seven men. In 1900 about 4,000 Latvians, but only a few hundred Estonians, were in the United States. Numerically significant Estonian and Latvian emigration occurred after the 1905 Russian Revolution, bringing socialist-oriented activists to metropolitan areas of the Northeast and Midwest. According to census figures, by 1930 nearly 40,000 Latvians lived in the United States, 20,673 of them foreign born and 17,418 native born. The Estonian population at that time was 30,000.[13]

The same variety of factors that prompted the general turn-of-the-century emigration motivated the first wave of Baltic immigrants. Agrarian reforms facilitated mobility as did the abolishment of serfdom (by 1819 in Estonia and Latvia and 1861 in Lithuania). Severe droughts and famines in the 1860s and 1890s disrupted the peasant economy. Balts joined other Europeans seeking to solidify an economic base and find a more favorable market for their labor. Lithuanian emigration was politically motivated as well. Intensifying Russification policies proscribed the use of indigenous languages in schools, publications, and government offices, made Russian Orthodoxy the ascendant faith and, after 1874, mandated long years of service in the czar's army. Men seeking to avoid military service constituted the largest category of Baltic emigrants.

Early Lithuanian immigrants arrived in a three to one ratio of men to women. Most were single, illiterate peasants.[14] Intellectuals, patriotic nationalists, and priests joined them as Russification fueled a nascent Lithuanian cultural nationalism, leading to rebellions and czarist persecutions. In the United States these political émigrés injected a degree of social stratification into Lithuanian communities and sharpened identity consciousness. They printed tracts and pamphlets to send to Lithuania, helped finance uprisings, and gave refuge to other political activists from the homeland. When the Lithuanian Socialist Federation, founded in 1907, joined the Socialist party of America in 1916, it was the third-largest foreign-language section, with 200 chapters and 6,700 members. Acutely ethnocentric, often anticlerical, these socialist-activists challenged established religious, educational, social, and political life. The outbreak of World War I exacerbated power struggles among nationalists, socialists, and clericals.

After Baltic independence in 1918 nationalism became a new force in the immigrant communities. For Balts, as for many other immigrant groups, internal conflicts rather than friction with mainstream American society tended to be the primary factors generating national and ethnic consciousness.[15] For example, although Estonian Communists controlled community life in New York City between 1922 and 1939, they had vocal opposition. An Estonian-language monthly reported, "A good man could cast a stone from one camp to the other. In one there waved a red banner, and in the other, the blue-black-white flag [of independent Estonia]."[16] Some Balts returned to their homelands (e.g., 20 percent of Latvians, including about four hundred Latvian Communists).

In the long run, however, interest in the homelands flagged following independence. Assimilation accelerated, and emigration from the new Baltic nations all but ceased. The outbreak of World War II briefly revived interest in homeland politics and led to the formation of relief organizations and political lobbies denouncing Soviet occupation, condemning the forcible repatriation of Baltic refugees, and seeking immigration legislation. In the early 1940s the Baltic states emerged as political symbols. New York Gov. Herbert H. Lehman, for example, proclaimed 28 May 1941 as "Baltic States Day" and described the peoples of the three "enslaved nations" as "freedom fighters." The scene was being prepared for the refugee influx.

## Lithuanian Immigrants in Indiana

Lithuanians constituted the first and only Baltic group migration to Indiana until after World War II. By 1890, as Lithuanians began drifting into Indiana, hardly a village in Lithuania had not contributed to the tide of immigration to America. Lithuanian migration to Indiana did not begin in earnest until after 1900, although a Lithuanian from East Prussia might have served as a Moravian missionary in the White River region in 1793.[17] In the late 1800s a visiting priest, Rev. Valentinas Čizauskas, served the few Lithuanian settlers. As a young monk in Lithuania, Čizauskas had taken part in a civil uprising against the

Russians. Arrested and sentenced to hard labor in Siberia, he escaped to the United States in 1870. He was ordained and assigned to South Bend in 1876.[18] In the late 1890s a few Lithuanians entered northern Indiana as part of the large influx into Chicago, which Sinclair Lewis fictionally chronicled in *The Jungle*.

At first, the Calumet Region was a wasteland of shifting sand dunes, swamps, scrub oaks, and fleas. It gradually became an industrial hub, built from the ground up by European laborers. In East Chicago, Inland Steel financed the drainage of a swampland to build its mill in 1902. A few years later US Steel completed Gary, the "miracle City of the Century." Living conditions for workers were harsh. Steelworkers received seventeen cents an hour for a twelve-hour day, seven days a week. Others found jobs in bakeries, shops, taverns, and shipping lines. South Gary was an unplanned slum of shacks and boardinghouses, where men slept in shifts. Steel mill managers and professionals lived in North Gary, where a subsidiary land company of US Steel built rows of neat bungalows. In addition to the steelworkers, a small group of educated Lithuanians lived in East Chicago. One of them owned a loan company (and perhaps also a print shop), was a notary public, and served as a translator in court cases involving Lithuanians. Approximately 50 percent of all immigrant laborers came directly from the homeland. In contrast, 90 percent of the Lithuanians resettled from Chicago, Pittsburgh, and Cleveland, or the mining areas of Pennsylvania, southern Illinois, and West Virginia. The 10 percent arriving directly from Lithuania were mainly blacksmiths and construction workers.

Between 1907 and 1925 Lithuanians developed active colonies in the Calumet Region, especially in Gary and East Chicago. Newcomers arrived in increasing numbers until 1918. However, as Petras Indreika writes in his sixty-one-page mimeographed history, "The East Chicago Lithuanians," a lack of materials obscures their "hardships and struggles" and "time has covered their footsteps with a thick layer of dust."[19]

In 1915 Gary's first known census registered 120 Lithuanian families and about 80 single men, although a quarter of the population may have been overlooked. The community reached its peak population in 1920 with 300 families and 100 individuals. By then Lithuanians in East Chicago had established many businesses:

> There were 11 Lithuanian taverns, B. Jasiulis ran a
> printing house, several restaurants, 3 meat stores and
> other food stores, three shoe stores and shoe repair
> shops, one bakery and one taylor [sic] shop. Besides
> that, Lithuanians had a show that they could call their

own "The Garden"—which was run by J. Pivariūnas from 1922, another VIC theater—which was run by a Lithuanian family, the Auseklis family.[20]

The European atmosphere in the Calumet Region was palpable well into the 1930s:

> Stand half an hour any day at the foreign money order window of the postoffice and watch the American dollars go flitting off to become rubles, marks, pesos, lire, kronen, and all manner of foreign coins. Go to the south side and listen in vain for English speech in the coffee houses, the national centers, the clubs. Attend a few of the innumerable national and racial meetings.[21]

By 1930 Lithuanians were the eighth largest ethnic group in Gary, but they represented only a tiny portion of the Lithuanian population in America: 4,488 of 439,195.[22] In 1930 significant numbers of Lithuanians (foreign born plus native whites of foreign or mixed parentage) lived only in East Chicago (1,374) and Gary (1,215).[23]

Lithuanians in the United States re-created the familiar folk-peasant lifestyle, which was centered on the patriarchal family, the Catholic Church, and the Lithuanian language. Many lived frugally and were undoubtedly among those immigrants whose average savings deposit in 1915 was $194, considerably higher than the native-born American average of $115. In 1911 the Gary postmaster estimated that $5 million was being sent to the homelands.[24]

Interethnic conflicts and jealousies were routine, and ethnic parishes became safe havens where Lithuanians could escape the taunts and snide remarks directed at them by other immigrants, who called them lugens, hunkies, and greenhorns.[25] Animosity between the Irish and the Lithuanians seems to have been sharp, in large part because Lithuanians willingly accepted low-paying jobs.[26]

Following the general pattern of immigrant groups, clusters of laypersons organized community life around mutual aid and benefit societies. These same leaders later took steps to establish Lithuanian parishes. During the early adjustment period mutual aid societies provided social security and insurance, particularly for the sick or widowed. In addition, they fostered cultural, patriotic, and religious activities locally and nationally. In East Chicago the oldest of these societies was established in 1903 as "The Society of the Five Wounds of St. Francis." It was modeled on the St. Francis Order in Lithuania, influential since the thirteenth century in converting the populace to Catholicism and in establishing convents and schools. The society was open to Catholics between eighteen and forty-five who were "in good health" and of upright character. Each member contributed twenty-five cents a month, which guaranteed a weekly allotment of five dollars in the event of illness. Other organizations founded between 1911 and 1942 included charity groups, prayer societies, parish committees, women's guilds, local chapters of men's groups, educational organizations, youth groups, and national organizations such as the Lithuanian Roman Catholic Alliance of America, the Lithuanian Alliance of America, and the United Lithuanian Relief Fund of America.

Most of the early organizations were for adults since there were few young people in the community. One of the earliest activities begun specifically for young people was a choir. Another key organization for young Lithuanians was "Lietuvos Sakalai" (Lithuanian Knights), a national association founded by A. Nork ūnas in 1913 in Massachusetts. The chapters established in 1919 in East Chicago and Gary nurtured many of those who subsequently became leaders in the local Lithuanian community. In 1925 the East Chicago chapter had fifty active members, who presented plays, sponsored sporting events, sang in the choir, and collected money for the homeland.

The first efforts to establish a Lithuanian-language parish took place in East Chicago. For years Lithuanians had worshiped with Poles or in rented space. In 1908 a parish committee was established and soon thereafter four lots in the 138th block of Deodar Street were purchased for the construction of the new church, whose patron saint was to be St. Francis. The church was finally built in 1913 at 390 Fir Street. It had three hundred and fifty members. Although the rapid succession of eight priests during the next decade hampered sustained efforts to improve the property, the congregation grew by some two hundred families. The church closed in 1989 (see below).

Until 1957 all the priests who served St. Francis in East Chicago had been born in Lithuania. Their revolutionary roots and continued commitment to Lithuania are clear from their biographies. Juozapas Jakštys, an early priest, returned to Lithuania, where he died in 1931. Rev. J. Čiuberkis actively promoted the sale of Lithuanian Freedom Bonds during his tenure from 1919 to 1924. The Rev. Pranas Meškauskas, who served the parish briefly in 1925, had been persecuted by czarist authorities and then was imprisoned by the Soviets in 1940 at the age of seventy-one. Msgr. Kazimieras Bičkauskas, who served from 1925 to 1957, had worked with Lithuanian refugees during World War I, organizing a Lithuanian-language school in Siberia. Later the Bolsheviks sentenced Bičkauskas to a work camp, where he performed his priestly duties at night. When he returned to Lithuania in 1922 he received an invitation from the parishioners in East Chicago and was reassigned. He arrived at a crucial time because the congregation of about five hundred was strapped financially and lacked positive leadership. He was responsible for major building projects, including a rectory, a parish hall, a convent, and a school.

In 1910 in Gary laymen also took the first steps toward establishing a Lithuanian parish. But when the priest they hired proved to be an impostor the demoralized congregation lost its initiative. Seven years later, under the leadership of the newly ordained priest, Rev. F. Rusis, the community mobilized to erect St. Casimir's Church, hall, and rectory. It was valued at forty-five thousand dollars. The parish remains active today (see below).

Lithuanians placed a high value on work, perhaps at the expense of education. In 1922, at a time when mandatory schooling was enforced to age fourteen, nearly one in three Lithuanians dropped out of high school, the third highest rate in the Calumet Region. The drop-out rate for native-born whites was 19.8 percent.[27] Only a few immigrant workers sent their children to college. Most offspring followed the footsteps of their fathers and worked in the mills; others left the Region.

A unique opportunity for education developed in the nearby community of Valparaiso. Between 1905 and 1925 about one thousand Lithuanians studied at Valparaiso University (once known nationally as the "poor man's Harvard").[28] They were attracted by the low tuition, the proximity to the large Lithuanian colonies of Chicago, Detroit, and Cleveland, and by the opportunity to earn money by working on the school's farm. According to Indreika, Lithuanian students called Valparaiso University "the potato peeling university."[29] They met to discuss Lithuanian history, geography, language, and literature, established a library of some two thousand volumes, and formed local branches of national Lithuanian organizations. The Lithuanian Literary Society, which they founded in 1905, had one hundred members in 1913. About forty Lithuanians received degrees in medicine, art, engineering, education, and law.[30]

Plans to establish a Lithuanian parish school in Gary began soon after Rev. Joseph Martis took charge in 1920. Lithuanian nuns, however, were not available to serve as teachers so the school's opening was delayed until September 1928. It opened with an enrollment of 115, but by 1931 the Lithuanian population in Gary had dwindled, making it increasingly more difficult to support the school. When it closed in 1966 it had graduated 365 students. In East Chicago St. Francis school opened in 1927 with 85 students, not all of them Lithuanian. The church organist and other "well-read parishioners" took charge of instruction until the arrival of Lithuanian nuns.[31]

In 1968, largely because of financial difficulties, the bishop consolidated the St. Francis school with other parish schools.

Already by the 1920s Lithuanians were homeowners and businesspeople. They were active in well-established ethnic institutions and in local political and social life, despite once being viewed with distaste and suspicion by those bent on Americanizing the "offscourings and unwanted peoples of Europe."[32] Nevertheless, the majority of the first generation failed to establish a secure financial base. Only a minority found employment outside the steel mills.[33]

Local cultural life flourished in the period just after World War I. At one time each local organization sponsored at least two annual events—one for the parish in general, another for itself. According to the descriptions by aged parishioners quoted in Indreika's history, East Chicago was a bustling Lithuanian community, well known for its parish hall (erected in 1929) and active cultural life. Lithuanians gathered for concerts, conferences, holiday programs, picnics, masquerade balls and dances, and memorial days. Audiences reared on farms enjoyed watching theater productions featuring sophisticated city slickers in an idealized Lithuania. A vaudevillian political satire, "Dzimdzi dzimdzi," was particularly popular. Local Lithuanian booksellers sold books following church services, donating all proceeds to local organizations. Choirs, usually organized through the church, continued a tradition popular in Lithuania.

Political and social organizations coalesced around issues of workers' benefits, homeland relief, and general politics. For example, the Gary Workers' Society (founded in 1910) and the East Chicago Lithuanian White Rose Political and Relief Club (founded in 1925) supported the rights and needs of the Lithuanian workers. At one point the White Rose club had 160 active members. It also organized a library, distributed publications, and sought an active voice in local politics. It did not outlast the first generation, however. In 1932 East Chicago Lithuanians established the American Lithuanian Democratic League, gathering delegates from various organizations throughout the area to foster an understanding of the duties of citizenship in America.

Like other immigrants, many first-generation Lithuanians in the United States sustained an interest in the homeland: they followed its fortunes closely, returned to fight its wars, marched in demonstrations, and lobbied for legislation related to independence and to immigration quotas. Through a committee formed in 1919 in New York City to sell bonds issued by the Lithuanian government, Lithuanians in the Calumet Region bought nearly $25,000 in bonds, in addition to donating silver and gold pieces and objects. They also organized relief efforts. In 1939, for example, the Federation of Lithuanian Organizations in East Chicago coordinated assistance to war-torn Lithuania, until Soviet occupation in 1940 stopped all shipments. In September 1943 delegates from sixteen local organizations reorganized the federation into a chapter of the national Lithuanian American Council, which became the chief local organization concerned with the restoration of Lithuanian independence.

Second-generation Lithuanians usually were good parishioners, but most lost interest in the homeland and did not preserve Lithuanian language and culture. Many changed their names, for example, from Vasiliauskas to Wilson or Maskauskas to Mason.[34] Distanced from Lithuanian concerns and identity, they took a less active role in community life, and the social gulf between them and their parents widened.[35] Increasingly secularized, they exited from the family circle and the home community via education, marriage, and occupation. By 1947, on the doorstep of the postwar refugee immigration, the intermarriage rate was 66 percent, and the first Lithuanians in America were largely assimilated.[36] In the Calumet Region, as elsewhere, the influx of Displaced Persons between 1949 and 1954 rejuvenated local social and cultural life. Many first settlers sponsored the refugees, giving them shelter and helping them find jobs. Earlier immigrants watched as the institutions they had founded and nurtured, and which their children had largely abandoned, were shaped by the refugees to suit their particular vision and goals.

**Immigration of Displaced Persons**

Estonians, Latvians, and Lithuanians were among the thirty million refugees who flooded Europe, especially

*Latvian kindergarten class at a refugee camp in Regensburg, Germany, ca. 1949.*

Germany, Austria, and France during and after World War II. They were part of the first organized international resettlement effort. Carried out by the newly formed United Nations Relief and Rehabilitation Administration, popularly called UNRRA, the resettlement of these so-called Displaced Persons represented an unprecedented shift of populations. UNRRA was founded in 1943 on the assumption that "the first impulse of all displaced persons, when enemy control was removed, would be to return to their homes."[37] But this assumption proved erroneous for citizens of countries that the Soviets had occupied or annexed. Most Baltic refugees knew that deportations to Siberia continued, and they were afraid to return. A Latvian woman in Indiana remembers that she and others "absolutely could not understand how the U.S. and England and France could be on the same side as the Russians. It was just something inconceivable."[38]

In the fall of 1945 the Balts were exempted from forcible repatriation because the United States and Britain did not recognize Soviet occupation of their countries. Nevertheless, Balts were called before screening boards, whose mandate was to identify bona fide refugees. A Latvian woman in Indiana remembered, "There were screenings: 'Why don't we go back?' Russians came. They were sent to question everybody, and in some refugee camps people were sent back. And it was a real tragedy. It all depended on how good the commander or the officer in the camp was. Did he have any idea why the people ran away? What, who they are?"[39] Of the estimated 160,000 to 190,000 Balts in Germany only about 2 percent applied for repatriation.[40]

In the spring of 1946 the "last million" refugees remained in Europe. Poles, Balts, Ukrainians, Czechs, Slovaks, Hungarians, and Romanians lived in refugee camps, some for five years and more. Some of the camps housed as many as ten thousand people and essentially were complete communities, with their own police and fire departments, schools and churches, entertainment and sports centers, print media, and medical facilities. An Indiana Latvian woman recalled, "We kept laughing that all the refugees were employed taking care of each other. Some of them became cooks and kitchen workers. Some chopped wood. My mother worked as a doctor. There were nurses, teachers, street sweepers. I mean, they were all doing something, taking care of each other."[41] For the children camp life was relatively normal: "I'm studying. I have friends. I find a boy. I fall in love. You know, all this stuff."[42] But for most adults it was "a helpless, useless kind of living."[43]

Although a small number of refugees lived with German families or in private apartments, most were clustered into enclaves of their own nationality. A Latvian resident of Columbus, Indiana, recalled that living conditions were difficult, "We lived in barracks which the Germans had built for their war prisoners—full of lice, dirty, leaking roofs. We slept there on dirty straw on the floor, with an umbrella over our head."[44] Often the refugees banded together to fix leaking roofs, replace windowpanes, and install heating systems. Typically, several families shared a large room partitioned off with blankets hanging across ropes. A Lithuanian woman in Indianapolis said that she and her family lived "like gypsies with three families in two and three story [bunk] beds." They ate cabbage so their children could have bread.[45] For many the monotonous food is a vivid memory of refugee life: "I was telling my daughters that for a while the meals varied day to day. One day it was noodles; and the next, it was split pea soup. I do not want to see either of them ever again in my life."[46] In over 50 percent of the camp population, mass health checks revealed illnesses or the secondary effects of malnutrition.

The proximity of individuals who shared language, history, and a familiar world view and who had abundant free time and no financial worries facilitated the rapid establishment of diverse cultural and social activities. Camp authorities supported cultural endeavors as morale boosters. The large number of artists, intellectuals, and academics in the camps provided additional stimulus: "We had writers and actors and singers and ballet dancers, and everything, so cultural life didn't stop. Even though there were no pretty dresses and our stomachs were sometimes empty, and the bed was just a bunk bed, but the children didn't stop learning."[47] In the United States, Balts never achieved an equal level of cultural productivity.

The Displaced Persons were not "ordinary immigrants" who had left their homes voluntarily to seek economic well-being. They migrated under compulsion and out of fear. Emigration from the camps began in 1947 and intensified after the United States Congress passed the Displaced Persons Act on 25 June 1948. Destinations were often random and sometimes multiple. A Latvian in Indiana expected to join her relatives in Australia, but when the ship for Australia was delayed she boarded one for America instead. A Lithuanian woman first moved to England, where she met and married a fellow Lithuanian. In 1952 they immigrated to Gary.

Passage of the Displaced Persons Act in the United States was slow and accompanied by much debate since it represented a sharp departure from existing immigration laws. To qualify for admission all refugees had to have assurance of suitable housing and employment. No one was admitted without a "screening report" to certify character, history, and eligibility. Thirty percent of visas were for those with agricultural experience; the rest were

for household, construction, clothing and garment workers, those with special education, scientific, technological, or professional qualifications and, finally, blood relatives of United States citizens.

Between October 1948 and March 1952, 339,520 Displaced Persons were admitted to the United States. It was the largest concentrated immigration to the United States during the twentieth century. Voluntary agencies played a major role in this resettlement, although some individuals also sponsored refugees. The Lutheran World Federation, the National Catholic Welfare Conference, and the Church World Service were the principal sponsors. Their staffs canvassed the United States to identify suitable job and housing assurances, distributed sponsorship applications, and met the newcomers.

Balts arriving in Indiana were dispersed to sponsoring families in hundreds of locations, ranging from Indianapolis to the smallest rural towns. Such dispersion among English-speaking Americans contrasts sharply with the absorption of turn-of-the-century immigrants into ethnic neighborhoods. The sudden immersion into American life was particularly shocking after the years of close—even too intimate—contact with compatriots in the refugee camps. A Latvian woman, who considered herself "a reasonably intelligent human being—with a high school education," remembers feeling "deaf and dumb: you can't speak. I had just a little bit of English in school, but I had much more French, Latin, and German. And you know, you'd say 'Hi' to everybody and you'd smile, but you can't talk. That is probably the biggest adjustment of all of them."[48] Those who lived in the camps as children describe the early months in America as "hell." They remember the friendliness and freedom of the camp years as "paradise." People who flee from homelands generally have more difficulty resettling than those who anticipate change by planning immigration.

After years of deprivation the Baltic refugees sought economic integration and security, but they held onto an ideal of economic integration without cultural assimilation.[49] The camp years provided them an important experience: they had learned how to live in a foreign society without belonging to it. In the fairly stable camp communities they had developed a complex, well-integrated, and differentiated social system which, with the exception of economic institutions, resembled the society and culture of their origin.[50] This social structure was successfully transplanted to a number of large American cities, including Indianapolis. Baltic immigrants who chose to sustain their national identity viewed themselves as exiles, not emigrants. They valued their remembered social and cultural life and consciously held it "in trust" until they or their children could return. Consequently, they sought a dual allegiance—to the United States and to the homeland.

Among the Baltic Displaced Persons a significant number reared offspring who spoke the native language and who actively claimed and developed ethnic identity. For example, a young man born in 1964 in Chicago said, "I am a Latvian born in America." He displayed a "diaspora consciousness," a term that Joshua Fishman uses to describe individuals who view themselves as the only ones at liberty to preserve and perpetuate "true culture" during a period of "foreign" domination.[51] Following the restoration of Baltic independence in 1991, a core group of young Estonians, Latvians, and Lithuanians returned to their parents' homelands, where they launched professional lives in medicine, social work, journalism, law, and technology.

## Lithuanian Displaced Persons in the Calumet Region

The second wave of Lithuanian immigrants to Indiana also settled in northwest Indiana. At the end of World War II about sixty thousand Lithuanians remained in the refugee camps. Approximately half immigrated to the United States, a large majority heading for Chicago, where the largest number of Lithuanians outside of Vilnius live. Few Lithuanian Displaced Persons came to Indiana. Exact figures are hard to determine, but by most accounts about three hundred families moved into Gary and about seven hundred to East Chicago.[52] While Lithuanians live elsewhere in Indiana, including Indianapolis, communities with extensive Lithuanian religious, social, and educational organizations evolved only in East Chicago and Gary.

In contrast to the first Lithuanian immigration in Indiana, which was dominated by single men, the Lithuanian Displaced Persons, or *dipukai,* as they called themselves, came primarily in family units, often including small children and elderly relatives. Most were sponsored by Lithuanian residents in East Chicago and Gary. According to Elena Bradunas,[53] Antanina Neinienė, who had emigrated to Gary from independent Lithuania in 1925, became a bridge between the two groups. She reportedly found hundreds of sponsors. The parishes also were active. St. Francis in East Chicago, for example, accepted responsibility for 125 families. These informal efforts were supplemented later by the United Lithuanian Relief Fund (BALF) organized in East Chicago. To the new arrivals economic prospects in the United States looked promising, especially compared to the dreary conditions in the camps. Concerned for friends and relatives still waiting to emigrate, the Displaced Persons themselves also became sponsors whenever financially possible.

Relations between the early immigrants and the refugee arrivals cooled after the initial warm welcome and helping hand. Rather than finding common cause with their predecessors, the refugees forged their own path, and for most of them it led out of Indiana. The early immigrants had been ordinary workers in czarist Russia, of which Lithuania was but a small part. Indreika reports that many of them "refused to believe that the communistic government had changed the structure of Lithuania's lifestyle that much."[54] One Lithuanian reported that he was accused of telling "lies" when he described life in Soviet Lithuania. Most older immigrants believed that a "workable 'Workers' Regime'" had been established in Lithuania. They could not comprehend why so many had fled "a worker's paradise" and were baffled by the horror stories the Displaced Persons told about communist occupation and deportations. Like most residents in Lake County, the first Lithuanians were loyal Democrats who idolized President Franklin D. Roosevelt. The refugees, on the other hand, were staunch nationalists and anticommunists[55] who charged that Roosevelt had sold the Baltics to the Soviets and who, almost without exception, voted Republican.

For the two groups the motivations for departure from the homeland also differed. Most of the old-timers had left for economic reasons. The refugees had abandoned homes, professions, friends, and families, fully expecting to return after the war. The early Lithuanians underestimated the degree to which the refugees yearned for and expected to return to their homeland. One *dipukai* couple interviewed by Bradunas provides a vivid example. The man had been a teacher in Lithuania and, for a time, an assistant mayor of Kaunas. In Gary he accepted work in a bakery because the steel mills were on strike when he arrived in July 1949. He worked there for twenty-three years, loading the ovens and mixing the bread. His wife, who had been a teaching physician in Lithuania, worked in a hosiery mill. When the couple first arrived they lived for a short time with a Lithuanian woman who had settled in Gary in 1904. One day, the wife recalled, she told her Lithuanian sponsor about something she had seen in a store:

> I said, "Oh, I like that. I'll take it home." Mrs. M [responded], "Where home?" "Oh, to our country, home," [I said]. "All right, go right now today. I'd like to see you buy a ticket." You know, she was very much surprised. But later I saw there was no way [to return]. I thought we had come only for a couple of years.

The couple was active in the Gary Lithuanian community, especially in its Saturday school. In 1992, after the restoration of Lithuania's independence, the man was one of two Lithuanians in the Region who returned to Lithuania after forty-three years in Gary.[56]

After the hardships of war-torn Europe the refugees were impatient to "make up for lost time." They were grateful for jobs since they would not have been able to leave Germany otherwise, and they worked long hours in blue-collar jobs for which few had experience. But they sought to advance themselves as rapidly as possible, by changing jobs, relocating, or seeking further education. Occupational adjustment generally was facilitated by the relatively high standard of living in the United States during the affluent 1950s. On the average the refugees had fewer language problems than their peasant predecessors. Some had learned English in Lithuania or in the refugee camps; others spoke Russian or German. Many had benefited from job retraining programs in the camps. Limited language skills and age usually prevented the grandparents and older relatives from finding jobs, but they provided crucial child care so that both parents could work. The family's pooled energy resulted in faster economic prosperity.

Some old-timers, remembering their early economic hardships as well as the depression years, watched with envy as refugees purchased cars and houses within a year or two of their arrival. The difference in the economic achievement of the two groups is clear. In the 1960s and 1970s, when the first Lithuanians were retiring, "a large number of them were not very secure," writes Indreika, for they lived only "a few thousand dollars" above the poverty line in deteriorating neighborhoods.[57] In 1992 retiring *dipukai* lived relatively comfortably, according to Rev. Ignatius Urbonas, pastor of St. Casimir's parish in Gary since 1966. He remarked with humor that only he and his dog remained in the parish neighborhood, for his parishioners had moved to Beverly Shores, Highland, Hebron, Schererville, and Crown Point. Out of loyalty to tradition they returned to St. Casimir for Mass, baptisms, confirmations, weddings, and funerals. Among the few Lithuanian offspring still in the area, some of whom commuted to Chicago to work, there were civil servants, policemen, teachers, librarians, businessmen, doctors, veterinarians, and professors.

The first-generation *dipukai,* like Baltic refugees in general, lived double lives. During the day most worked as common laborers. With their predecessors they shared the philosophy that "where there's smoke there is work," to quote Albert Vinick, a past president of the Lithuanian American Council in Lake County. They lived in working-class neighborhoods but shared little with their neighbors, most of whom were less educated and less interested in culture. Outside of work, in the company of other Lithuanian Displaced Persons, they recouped "former

*Lithuanian display, International Festival, Gary, ca. 1956–57.*

identities," still addressing each other in conversations as professor or general, lawyer or teacher, doctor, and so on. Homeland status remained credible and influential because its loss had stemmed from a political cause rather than a personal failure.

A number of Lithuanian artists and intellectuals moved to the Calumet Region and, for a time, put their talents to work to support local social and cultural life. Former teachers founded the Lithuanian Saturday schools, organized scouting troops, and coached basketball teams; well-known artists gave concerts and literary readings, directed choirs and folk dance groups, put on exhibits, and planned celebrations and commemorations, especially of Lithuanian independence day on 16 February and of Soviet deportations of Lithuanians on 14 June 1941. In 1950 a group of former actors organized a drama troupe, which, for more than a decade, produced plays in the Region and toured to other Lithuanian communities. They, in turn, hosted Lithuanian artists from Chicago. Five organizations have dominated Lithuanian community life in Indiana: the two parishes of St. Francis and St. Casimir; the American Lithuanian Council of Lake and Porter counties; the American Lithuanian Community, Inc., of East Chicago; and the Hunters and Fishermen Club of East Chicago. The latter sponsored social activities that strengthened friendship ties among widely dispersed Lithuanians. In the late 1970s the Region had a small but vibrant community of young Lithuanians. They toured locally and regionally with a folk dance group. They met friends at a Lithuanian camp near Manchester, Michigan. Occasionally they traveled to distant places such as South America, where hundreds of Lithuanians outside the homeland gathered for youth congresses.

For the first Lithuanian settlers schools were viewed primarily as a means to support Catholicism. The refugees, in contrast, emphasized education as a means to nurture intense national loyalty. Both parishes supported cultural and social life by providing space for diverse activities, most crucially for the Lithuanian Saturday school. Lithuanian parochial schools in the area had closed by the late 1960s, but the Saturday schools remained active. The *dipukai* had launched Saturday schools immediately after their arrival in order to teach their children Lithuanian language, history, geography, literature, music, and dance. The school curriculum followed the remembered homeland model and often was taught by refugees who had been teachers in Lithuania. The East Chicago Saturday school existed for seventeen years and graduated one hundred students, some of whom went on to the Lithuanian high school in Chicago. St. Casimir's Saturday school was started in 1966 on the same day that the parochial school closed. By the mid-1970s, reflecting the rapid language loss among younger Lithuanians, it offered a special class for nonnative speakers. In 1992 St. Casimir's Saturday school had fifteen students and one teacher, a former student who commuted from Chicago.

For a time the refugee newcomers extended the social and cultural life of the Lithuanian colony in the Region. In 1954 one-third of the Lithuanian population in East Chicago was from the Displaced Persons migration (374 of 1,200). When the refugees joined St. Francis parish they doubled its size to 800. But the revival was short-lived. In 1959 only one-fifth of the 500 families in St. Francis were from among the refugees, and as the years passed the percentage of non-Lithuanians in the parish grew. When the parish celebrated its fiftieth anniversary in 1963, membership had dropped to 300 families. The parish school closed in 1968 because of financial difficulties. Between 1959 and 1961 the church income had jumped 25 percent, but by 1971 it had fallen by more than 40 percent and the parish was beginning to experience strained finances and internal crises over identity. In 1989 the local bishop closed St. Francis parish despite the protest of its 165 parishioners. Most transferred to St. Casimir's in Gary.

Historically, homeland politics galvanized both the Lithuanian old-timers and the refugees to united action. When Nikita Khrushchev visited the United States in 1959 Lake County Lithuanians organized a protest march. An estimated five hundred cars moved along the demonstration route from Hammond to Whiting. Lithuanians annually commemorated the Soviet deportations of 1941 with such activities as "genocide exhibits." They lobbied to name a street in East Chicago "Lituanica Avenue." In 1971 they protested the return of seaman Simanas Kudirka to the Soviet Union after he had asked for political asylum in the United States.

In 1990 about thirty Region Lithuanians drove to Indianapolis to join others protesting George Bush's accommodationist policies toward Mikhail Gorbachev.

When the refugees arrived in this country many of the older immigrants still spoke Lithuanian, cooked native foods, remembered old songs, and continued celebratory traditions. But they sustained ethnic identity primarily as familiar custom rather than national cause. Few of their children spoke Lithuanian or practiced the culture because their parents had placed greater value on good jobs and a good Catholic mate (no matter what the ethnic background) than on retention of Lithuanian identity. Refugees, in contrast, consciously practiced Lithuanian culture and commemorated historical events because they sought to transmit a sense of love and duty toward the homeland to their offspring. Refugee homes often resemble miniethnic museums, displaying objects of folk art (such as painted Easter eggs, miniatures of the wooden crosses that dot Lithuania's countryside, and embroidered pillows), national emblems such as flags, maps, coats of arms, wooden plaques inlaid with amber, photos of the old homestead or of Vilnius, the capital, books by Lithuanian exiles, albums and cassettes of Lithuanian music, and videos of Lithuanian events.

Like Balts in other small colonies in the United States, Lithuanians in Indiana were victims of their own success. Viewing education as something no political reversals could destroy, they dedicated themselves to educating their children. Seeking to recoup lost financial status they instilled bourgeois values and material aspirations in their children, leading them to assimilation. Although the 1990 United States census indicates that over eleven thousand residents in Indiana claim Lithuanian ancestry, this large figure does not translate into an active ethnic community anywhere in the state. Individual Lithuanians live in Indianapolis, where they join forces annually for the International Festival. Widely dispersed Lithuanians in northwest Indiana retain friendship ties. In small numbers Lithuanians in Indiana rally for political demonstrations, such as those connected to the 1991 restoration of Lithuanian independence. But those who wished to practice Lithuanian culture more actively have migrated to larger colonies, such as Chicago or Los Angeles, where they and their children can live more fully as Lithuanians in America.

### Latvians and Estonians in Indianapolis

Latvian and Estonian settlement concentrated in Indianapolis. Nearly 40,000 Latvian Displaced Persons entered the United States between 1949 and 1952. Few *veclatviesi* (or old Latvian immigrants) remained to greet

INTA GALE CARPENTER

*Latvian Youth Theatre, Indianapolis, ca. 1960.*

them, only about 20,000 nationally. Among all the Displaced Persons entering the United States, Latvians were the second largest population group (11.6 percent). Their community in Indianapolis began in 1949 with about 70 to 100 people, but by 1960 had grown to 1,526.[58] In 1990 there were 604 foreign-born Latvians and 1,622 residents claiming Latvian ancestry. While the number of foreign-born Latvians had decreased by half since 1960, those claiming Latvian ancestry had increased fivefold.

In the same period, more than 10,000 Estonians entered the United States, 5,422 in 1950 alone, according to Tönu Parming.[59] Fifty percent of them live in the corridor from Washington, D.C., to Boston, but sizable numbers also reside in the Great Lakes states and on the West Coast. According to the 1990 census 315 Estonians lived in Indiana, 50 of them foreign born. Estonian sociologist Ain Haas has produced an uncommonly concrete demographic picture of the Indianapolis Estonians based on his in-depth interviews and examination of membership applications and other documents of the Estonian Society.[60]

The first 30 to 40 Estonians in Indianapolis were sponsored directly from the refugee camps. A second group of less than 20 came from Seabrook Farms in New Jersey, where Estonian Displaced Persons worked in a cannery. A still smaller group arrived somewhat later via Sweden or Australia to join relatives. Most of the Estonians coming to Indianapolis had been urbanites, primarily from Tallinn. They were in their late thirties to early fifties and had typically spent several years in refugee camps in Germany, awaiting permission to relocate to locales where younger and healthier refugees had already been allowed to settle. They had no particular reason to come to Indianapolis but gladly took advantage of the opportunity when it was offered. According to Haas, of the 114 Estonians who entered the Indianapolis area between

1947 and 1959, 36 were still living there in 1991, 31 had died, and 47 had moved out of state.[61] The community did not grow through new migration, although some two dozen Estonians who had already become accustomed to American life elsewhere arrived in the Indianapolis area individually in the 1960s. Seven of them remained in 1991. The core group of Estonians in Indianapolis consisted of about 70, mostly in their late seventies to early nineties, making Estonians in Indiana, to quote Haas, "truly an endangered species."[62]

Individual Estonians and Latvians lived in Indiana before World War II. In doing his research Haas learned of a prominent early Estonian immigrant in Indianapolis named Alexander Sangernebo.[63] An architectural sculptor, Sangernebo was responsible for adornments on such public buildings as the Murat Temple, the Athenaeum, the Columbia Club, Union Station, Ayres and Block's department stores, the Indiana and Lyric movie theaters, and Shortridge High School. He died in 1930 and was unknown among the Estonians who two decades later worked in or helped to restore the buildings for which Sangernebo had sculpted facades.

The only known *veclatvietis* (immigrant settler) in Indianapolis was Georgs Inka, who welcomed the first Latvian refugee family. Inka had emigrated from Latvia in 1915 at the age of seventeen as a ship's hand. He lived in a remodeled garage on the west side, where he ran a gas station. Some Latvian refugees looked upon Inka as a warning to themselves because Inka had married an American and spoke Latvian poorly. For a while Inka took an active interest in the evolving Latvian community. On occasion the newcomers sought his help with jobs, language difficulties, legal matters, meeting room facilities, and so on, but he soon disappeared from active participation.

Like the Lithuanian refugees, the Estonians and Latvians had experienced dramatic, sometimes narrow escapes from the occupying Soviets. As a teenager, an Indianapolis Estonian remembers returning home after an overnight visit to find his house in flames and his family deported. A woman told Haas that she was "held in Tartu Prison for six months during the first Soviet occupation of 1940–41. When taken out to be executed, she and some other captives got a temporary reprieve because the well where bodies were being dumped was filled before their turn came. On the way to another site, she managed to escape distracted guards."[64] A Latvian woman in Columbus, Indiana, speaks for most Balts when she stresses that she left her home seeking temporary safety and somewhat unexpectedly ended up emigrating:

> We did not seek to come to America—we were hard-working people, in a small country, without natural

resources. We had only what our plain soil could give us in crops . . . but we were happy and in our independence time we were really happy. . . . I never would have left my country. Never. My children would have had everything there.[65]

America was a "detour": "Do you know what I felt when I boarded that ship: 'I am still going home, just a long way around.' [America] was my detour, my detour back home."[66] Oral histories of the first years invariably describe "packed suitcases under beds" in preparation for return. Those who struck roots too deeply in American culture were criticized by their peers, but as the decades passed the self-reference "when I go back" shifted to the children— "when you go back."[67]

An article in the *Indianapolis Times,* 5 November 1948, reporting about the experiences of the first family of Displaced Persons to arrive in Indianapolis, presents an archetypical saga of flight, hardship, and rapid adjustment. Georg and Magda Saar, along with his seventy-five-year-old mother and their children, Georg, sixteen, and Eva, ten, are described as having lived in an "ample house with a servant" before being forcibly evacuated by the Germans. In the camps in Germany the Saars lived five to a room and ate "coffee and black bread three times a day with potatoes added at dinner." Six weeks after their arrival in Indianapolis, the article reports, they were self-supporting and well acclimatized. They were living on the near east side in the house of an invalid whom they cared for in exchange for room and board. Mr. Saar was working as an architect at a local firm; his son, a junior at Tech High School, was a Boy Scout "first-class." Daughter Eva had attended her first American birthday party. The parents were learning English in a public school class. Few Balts adjusted as quickly or smoothly as this article would suggest. Its editorial slant seems intended to assuage native fears about the ability of the refugees to adjust to American society.

According to a history of the Indianapolis Latvian community written by Kārlis Vanags, the first Latvian family to arrive in 1948 came under the quota for Russians. They were Arturs and Milda Celmiņš and their two teenaged daughters. After greeting them in New York City, staff from the Church World Service asked them where they would like to settle: "The Americans spread a big map of the U.S. on the table and, hoping for the best, the Celmiņš family pointed to the center of the country, where they thought it would be safest under conditions of war. . . . The CWS officials agreed on Indianapolis."[68]

The Displaced Persons Act of 1948 stipulated that state agencies assist in refugee resettlement. It linked emigration to guaranteed work. To meet these expectations, an advisory committee, called the Indiana Economic Council, was established. Its members, including such early activists as Msgr. H. F. Dugan, Rev. F. M. Hanes (head of the Lutheran Synod), and Rev. Paul E. Huffman (pastor of the First United Lutheran Church), represented churches and welfare organizations. The Church World Service and the Indianapolis Church Federation sought to enlist the support of Protestant churches in the state, but they detected considerable apathy among Indiana natives. Some residents feared economic competition from the refugees, while others, including many ministers, were unwilling to shoulder responsibility for invalids, families with children, or those with elderly relatives. At first the refugees themselves sponsored friends and relatives in the camps, but later officials questioned their suitability, given their precarious financial situation and lack of United States citizenship.

After May 1949 the process of finding sponsors was facilitated by the decision of the Indiana Lutheran Synod to hire recent Displaced Person arrival Anna Blūmkalne as coordinator of settlement efforts. Blūmkalne came to the attention of Hanes, who heard her speak to a church group about the plight of the Latvian refugees. As Blūmkalne herself recalls, on one "lucky" day she identified sponsors for eleven families at South Bend's Holy Trinity Lutheran Church. Blūmkalne worked in the resettlement bureau until 1952, securing sponsors for two hundred families. Blūmkalne and her son and daughter lived in the home of Rev. and Mrs. Huffman for five years.

Most of the Latvians and Estonians arriving in Indianapolis in 1949–50 were sponsored by Huffman's Lutheran church, located at 701 North Pennsylvania Street. Dynamic, goal-oriented, and articulate, Huffman personally signed hundreds of sponsorship affidavits and was wholeheartedly committed to the task of finding jobs and housing. He was new at First Lutheran and perhaps saw the refugee population as a way to enlarge his congregation. Of Dutch descent, Huffman spoke some German but also tried to learn enough Latvian and Estonian to make the Displaced Persons feel welcome. The Huffman home, located in the 3300 block of North Park Avenue, became a way station where "many, many refugees rested up, washed their worn clothes, and familiarized themselves with the local scene." When a former Latvian schoolteacher became bedridden with a malignant tumor, the Huffman family cared for her for three years until her death.[69] Neither Huffman's congregation nor the Lutheran Synod was as enthusiastic about helping the refugees as he was, and they sought unsuccessfully to limit the number of sponsorships he signed. By 1952, by his own account in a newspaper article, Huffman had sponsored four hundred refugees. He proudly credited them with earning over one million dollars a year. When he died in 1966, in fulfillment of his wish, Anna Blūmkalne's son served as pallbearer.

In the late forties and into the fifties there was a severe housing shortage in Indianapolis, especially for families with children. For one group of Latvians Huffman located a house in the 2200 block of Park Avenue, owned by a Jewish couple willing to rent to families with children. The eight or so families who shared the house over a period of four years nicknamed it "the *kolhoz*," meaning collective farm.[70] Most Latvians initially settled on the near north side, in the 1600–2500 blocks to the east and west of Central Avenue. A few lived on the west and south sides. Estonians lived nearby, largely in the Old Northside and the Herron-Morton Place historic districts.

After ten years of displacement, the refugees desired their own homes and pursued a strategy of "sitting tight" in dingy or overcrowded apartments until they had saved enough money for a down payment. In the 1950s, when few Estonians had any resources, they were holding seminars for each other on investment strategies.[71] Local Latvian societies also sponsored *veclatvieši* (immigrant settlers) from nearby Chicago to lecture on the United States tax system and insurance and to answer financial questions. The first Latvian families bought homes in the fall of 1950. They then became a resource to others about banks, mortgages, realtors, and so on. Estonians first bought small "starter" homes, mostly on the near east side of town. In the 1960s they began to spread out, settling into amply furnished suburban homes.[72] Latvians first moved to the far north side, primarily to the Glendale area, then to Carmel and Zionsville in the 1980s and 1990s.

Generally the arriving refugees were not choosy about work. Accountants, theater directors, composers, academics, and civil servants, among others, milked cows, cleaned barns, and tended cornfields. Some of the Latvians who settled in Indianapolis first picked cotton in the Deep South for several months. A government official from Riga arrived in Hagerstown, Indiana, with his wife and three children to work on a chicken farm. He toiled seven days a week for a daily wage of ten dollars and one gallon of milk. Housing, though free, consisted of a lightly constructed one-room summer cottage with one bed for the five people. In the fierce winter of 1950–51 the family woke up to find frost on their quilts and ice in the kitchen sink.[73]

Most refugees responded to the unfamiliar farm responsibilities and unexpected drudgery by resolving to find new employment as quickly as possible. Former draftsmen, engineers, and pharmacists, whose jobs were

*Latvian piano students of V. Melkis, Indianapolis, ca. 1955.*

less language dependent, more easily found jobs in their previous fields than did teachers, doctors, and lawyers. Teaching was the most common former occupation among Estonians in Indianapolis. It became the most popular career among the second generation, followed by engineering (for women as well as men) and accounting.[74] Haas found that in the 1980s more than twice as many Estonians in Indianapolis were in "high white-collar" occupations than the general population (57 percent vs. 25–31 percent).

Those settling in Indianapolis took whatever jobs were available. For example, among the Estonians a former schoolteacher, bank manager, restaurateur, government official, and notary became, respectively, an assembly line worker, janitor, night watchman, slaughterhouse worker, and kitchen helper. Both Estonians and Latvians acquired reputations as quick and accurate workers. Those with good jobs actively campaigned among supervisors to hire friends and relatives. As a result clusters of Balts formed in many workplaces: at Insley, Howe Engineering, Midwest Engineering, Peerless Pump, Western Electric, RCA, Methodist Hospital, Kingan Meat Processing, Kroger, Stark & Wetzel, the U.S. Post Office, the Ford plant, and the Beech Grove railroad yards. Numerous Latvians worked in construction and a few started their own companies, building inexpensive garages to gain experience and then gradually moving into remodeling, development, and commercial construction. In the early years Latvians owned an insurance company, a barbershop, a restaurant, a carpenter shop, a florist shop, and a parcel service. A Latvian neighborhood, in which private businesses might have flourished, never developed. Overall, few showed an interest in entrepreneurship.

Estonian and Latvian women played a vital part in family economic life. Most took jobs they would have deemed beneath them in the homeland, working as housekeepers, cooks, and nannies, even though some had once had their own household help. Others found jobs in fields related to their former professions (physicians became lab technicians, for example) or turned their talents into paying jobs (e.g., becoming seamstresses). Both men and women often studied on the side, earning various certifications and degrees in order to advance themselves.

Relations between sponsors and refugees were complicated. Language barriers hampered their mutual understanding and also underscored the refugees' profound isolation and status loss. A local minister who was "a student of German 'long ago'" was called by a sponsoring family in Zionsville to interpret for its new Estonian housekeeper. In a newspaper account he reports pulling "an awful boner. I got mixed up in my German and instead of telling her not to work so hard I told her not to eat so much. It was hard getting her to believe it was a mistake."[75] American sponsors generally were not well informed about the refugees. A man who had been a schoolteacher in Estonia remembered that his sponsor assumed that because he and his wife were immigrants they were also "peasants." He accused them of putting on airs "when they got tired of margarine and went out and bought their own butter," a staple in dairy-rich Estonia.[76] Friction between sponsors and refugees also stemmed from their diverging expectations of each other and of America. Anticipating experienced farm laborers, most sponsors instead got cultured urbanites. A man who had been a theater professional in Latvia, on the other hand, expressed a common first impression among the refugees: the America they encountered did not correspond to the "beautiful and rich America" envisioned and talked about in the camps.

Latvian Displaced Persons in Indianapolis recall their ambiguous early relationship to American society. On the one hand the press hailed them as "freedom fighters" and absorbed details of their hardships into local and national Cold War rhetoric. Such attention supported Latvian efforts to preserve their culture and identity. But simultaneously the social climate of the 1950s was assimilationist. For example, the American Lutheran Synod stated in a 1950 memo that "the establishment of nationalistic congregations definitely should be discouraged."[77] Refugees were urged to become "new Americans." A Latvian minister recalls a church official asking, "How long are you going to hobble in two directions? This is a melting pot." The Baltic refugees disagreed among themselves about the "proper" relationship to Americans. One faction emphasized gratitude and loyalty and seemed to accept the inevitability of assimilation. Another faction focused on the duty to preserve Latvian identity in the face of Soviet occupation of the homeland.

In Indianapolis these divergent attitudes were sharply and publicly played out in terms of affiliation to the First United Lutheran Church. The church had sponsored two Latvian ministers (Pēteris Nesaule and the late V. Īsaks) as part of a "training pastors" program. While the program temporarily permitted separate Latvian-language services, the expectation was that the Latvian ministers would master English and serve the full congregation. In 1951 tensions arose between the Latvians and Americans when several parents asked that their children's confirmation ceremony be in the Latvian language according to traditional customs. Church officials denied this request, and heated discussions ensued. In the end the disgruntled parents rented facilities in a church where two Latvians worked as janitors, and on 19 August 1951 Nesaule presided over the confirmation of ten Latvian youths.

This conflict triggered a split among the Latvians in the First Lutheran Church. On 7 October 1951, 103 of them met in the YMCA and founded the Indianapolis Latvian Evangelical Lutheran Church, with Nesaule as minister. Within three years the congregation had 300 members. In 1967 they bought a church at 4717 East Michigan Street for thirty-two thousand dollars, with the help of seven thousand dollars from the Lilly Endowment. By 1986, 145 infants had been christened, 203 members confirmed, 120 married, and 198 buried. Nesaule retired in 1988 after thirty-seven years of service.

In 1957 those 200 Latvians who initially chose to remain with the American church also left to form a second Latvian Lutheran congregation in Indianapolis. The group's departure was eased by the general social climate in the late fifties, which viewed independent ethnic congregations more favorably. Despite Huffman's protest, the Lutheran Synod granted permission to found the First Latvian Lutheran Church and agreed to pay Īsaks a salary of fifteen hundred dollars. The initial membership was 241. After Īsaks's untimely death in 1968 the congregation was served by a succession of visiting ministers until the two congregations merged in 1986 as the Latvian Evangelical Lutheran Church of Indianapolis. In 1995 church membership was 300.

In addition to two Lutheran congregations Latvians established a Catholic congregation. Nationally only 10 percent of Latvians are Catholic; in Indianapolis 30 percent are Catholic. During the formative period of the community in the 1950s and 1960s, Indianapolis had a Catholic congregation of 350, the largest of the twelve Latvian Catholic congregations in the United States. Two Masses were held each month at Saints Peter and Paul

Cathedral at 1347 North Meridian Street, with the Very Reverend Monsignor Adolfs Grosbergs presiding. Catholic Latvians have held key leadership positions in the broader Latvian community.

Catholic Latvians formed their own youth groups, choir, and camps; they sponsored sports activities and hosted national culture days (with exhibits, lectures, and poetry readings). In effect, such activities created a familiar religious and social environment for all generations. They also served as rhetorical forums that promoted and expressed the exile goal of return, shared with the Lutheran community of Latvians. As one speaker during the 1958 Culture Days in Indianapolis declared, "If our young people will take back [to Latvia] the knowledge they've gained and if the older generation will take back their accumulated capital, we will raise the well-being of our country."

In the Estonian community disagreement over the formation of separate religious and secular organizations, culminating in the creation of an Estonian Lutheran congregation in 1964 in addition to the extant Estonian Society, caused the only "serious controversy in the four-decade history of the community."[78] Amicable relations were restored, and the Estonians still worship in the First United Lutheran Church. A visiting pastor from Chicago performs three or four Estonian-language services annually in the church. The Estonian Society helps organize pitch-in meals and secular programs following services, such as the visit of Jõuluvana (Santa Claus).[79]

For Estonians and Latvians alike the church supported ethnic identity. The Latvian Lutheran Church remains a conservative institution, whose elderly constituency holds onto familiar worship practices and discourages the introduction of even limited English-language usage. Throughout the years it has provided space for a variety of ethnic events and has fostered the formation of special interest groups, such as women's guilds, a Saturday school, youth groups, Sunday schools, choirs, and summer camps. Regional and national Lutheran and Catholic congresses, board meetings, and youth organizations have brought Latvians and Estonians from all over the United States to Indianapolis.

In contrast to the important role of mutual aid and workers' societies in the old Baltic immigrant colonies, the key organizations in Baltic refugee communities fostered cultural and national-political activities. Partly for their own comfort and partly in hopes of transmitting knowledge to children, the older members sought to re-create the homeland context outside territorial borders. Typically the young people were steered toward the remembered homeland and warned away from the physical one, which was perceived to be "contaminated and dangerous." Beginning in the 1970s many young Balts made pilgrimages to parental homelands, and some reported intense "conversion" experiences.

In the first years Estonian social life in Indianapolis centered on picnics and trips to the Dunes and calendrical festivals such as Midsummer Day, Martinmas, Christmas, and New Year's Eve. For a time there was a local choir. Guest artists from nearby Chicago and Columbus (Ohio) regularly were invited to perform, and Indianapolis Estonians also hosted regional meetings, especially of the midwest Estonian Youth Association. As the original population aged and the younger generation assimilated, earlier activities showed signs of degeneration or vanished altogether. For example, at the Christmas banquet hot dogs and ham became substitutes for the traditional blood/barley sausages that had become too difficult to make.[80] The Estonian Society, founded as an offshoot of the Chicago branch, remains at the center of community life. Displays at the International Festival absorb one-fourth of its budget and have become a focal point for collective life. A number of Indianapolis Estonians achieved prominence on the boards of national Estonian organizations and involved themselves in Estonia's struggle to regain independence, which was achieved in 1991.

Such standard activities of larger Baltic communities as theater troupes, athletic teams, scouts, summer camps, folk art classes, and literary evenings did not develop among the Estonians in Indianapolis given their small and aged population. Language transmission was also problematic. Haas reports that less than a third of the twenty-four second-generation Estonians speaks Estonian. Among them only three are active in community life. Of third-generation Estonians only two youngsters can claim fluency. In contrast, the Indianapolis Latvian society in 1990 had an active base of several hundred.

Indiana University has played a small but significant role in the cultural life of Estonians in Indianapolis. Estonian faculty members lectured on Estonian history, art, and culture. Indiana University's Uralic-Altaic department attracted Estonian students, and some of them became active in the Indianapolis Estonian community.

Estonians of the Indianapolis area organized choirs, youth orchestras, language schools, folk dance troupes, and political groups. Such endeavors were intermittent because they depended upon personal interest and sustained commitment, and the pool of potential participants was very limited due to the small number of Estonians in Indiana.

The Estonian community began with a stable core of middle-aged, practical individuals who were serious about preserving their heritage and keeping the plight of their homeland from being forgotten, writes Haas.[81] Activism in the ethnic sphere partially recouped the self-esteem lost by those elders who had to take low-status jobs in their new country. At a much earlier date than the Indianapolis Latvians, Estonians viewed films, listened to music, read publications, and sponsored touring choirs from Soviet Estonia, perhaps because they realized that such contact was vital for both sides.[82] Except for some rivalry in the first years, the kind of factionalism, petty criticism, competing organizations, and events that characterize larger exile colonies has been rare.[83] In general, Haas notes, Indianapolis Estonians have placed high value on accountability and accessibility, turning out in large numbers for community activities and welcoming new recruits to organizations. In contrast, second-generation Latvians have remarked that elders would rather see the community self-destruct than relinquish authority to offspring. Among the Estonians personal interactions have been informal, with the result that consensus on issues has been easier to reach.

Education for the young was a primary goal of Baltic parents. Many held advance degrees themselves and, despite their own occupational disappointments, valued education as the best insurance for their children's futures. Parents placed emphasis on practical degrees—engineering and pharmacy—rather than on the humanities. While more than one-third of the Estonians arriving in Indianapolis in the 1950s had some higher education, Haas learned that more than two-thirds of their children obtained college degrees. Nearly one in five earned master's degrees. Of those remaining in Indianapolis 38 percent have bachelor degrees. Locally and nationally, Estonian women are particularly high achievers, outstripping Estonian men slightly in the percentage of college graduates. Haas notes that twice as many Estonian men than women arrived with college degrees. The high percentage of college graduates among the young meant that they subsequently tended to be largely professionals. While no hard statistics are available for the Latvian population in Indianapolis, the same trend generally holds true.

The early Indianapolis Latvian colony was described by the national Latvian newspaper as one of the most active in the country. In Germany a number of Indianapolis Latvians had lived in Eslingen, where one of the largest and culturally most active of refugee camps evolved. With the hope of making Indianapolis a center for Latvian culture in America, those from Eslingen actively sponsored Latvian teachers and artists who would contribute to the cultural life of the Indianapolis exile community.

Latvian organizational life was born in the basement of Huffman's First United Lutheran Church, where the first

*Latvian florist at 110 West 38th Street, Indianapolis, 1960, Laimonis Martinsons, owner.*

official social gathering marked Latvian independence day on 18 November 1949. The following month the Latvian Welfare Fund was established. Its goals were to secure jobs and housing for the new arrivals, to assist the needy, to defend Latvia's rights, and to preserve Latvian culture. For the next decade, under the new name, the Latvian Society (Latviešu biedrība), it promoted cultural activities from a house it purchased at 2511 Central Avenue. Larger events were held at the YMCA, the World War Memorial, the Knights of Columbus, or local hotels. The core leadership was concentrated in a few activists. One man reportedly held seven different positions, and another held four, while on the average, individuals juggled two or three posts. The Indianapolis community has sustained perhaps atypical continuity of leadership, and community participation has been relatively high and loyal. A Latvian Community Center was built debt free in 1965 with volunteered labor and donated money at 1004 West 64th Street.

Latvian community life was especially rich and diverse for the first two decades. In June 1950 Latvians in Indianapolis founded one of the first half dozen Latvian choirs in the United States. The choir continues to perform locally and to participate nationally in Latvian song festivals. A drama troupe performed its first play in the fall of 1951 on the YWCA stage. In all 412 plays were produced. Theater activity attracted young Latvians and not only provided an effective medium through which to experience Latvian history, culture, aesthetics, and values but it also provided a time to socialize after rehearsals. In 1952 the Latvian Trio, composed of a Latvian pianist, violinist, and cellist, began touring the United States. A Baltic concert subscription series was coordinated from Indianapolis, and a literary monthly was published. In 1960 Indianapolis Latvians hosted a regional

*Estonians, Latvians, and Lithuanians turned out in force with flags and placards for a demonstration at the City-County Building in Indianapolis on 3 April 1990 to encourage visiting President George Bush to support more actively their countries' efforts to break away from Soviet control. The Baltic republics regained their independence the following year.*

song festival, which realized a profit of $3,200. A music ensemble, Idvasa, was founded in 1971 to bring young Latvians together. Daugavas vanagi, a veterans group founded in the camps, remains a cornerstone organization. In 1990 the Indianapolis Latvian folk dance group Jautrais pāris (the happy couple) celebrated its fortieth anniversary. Reconstituted Latvian academic fraternities and sororities remain vital contexts for identity transmission and socializing. They form a bridge between generations and link Latvians regionally, nationally, and internationally through annual congresses and balls.

In contrast to the Lithuanian children who attended parochial schools for a number of years, Estonian and Latvian children attended public schools. Knowledge of Estonian and Latvian language, culture, and history was transmitted within the family or in Saturday schools. A national network of supplementary Saturday schools evolved seemingly spontaneously in all the larger Baltic colonies soon after 1949 and reached a peak enrollment of 2,200 in sixty-seven schools in 1956.[84] They represent a species of education previously unknown and not foreseen in the camps. The Indianapolis Saturday school also was

born in the basement of the First United Lutheran Church on 31 March 1951 with 21 students. In 1953 the school reached its peak enrollment of 57. Now in its fourth decade the school is largely in the hands of Latvians who came of age in the United States, though some Latvians in their teens and early twenties also assist. It conducts weekly classes at the Latvian Community Center and in 1993 had an enrollment of around 30, two-thirds of whom were under the age of ten.

Young Estonians and Latvians acclimated quickly to American culture because parents urged them to seek university degrees and economic success. A large percentage married outside the Baltic community and moved out of state to follow educational or career paths. American spouses are sometimes drawn into ethnic life: one American wife bakes traditional Latvian bread, which is eagerly purchased by Latvians in the community; an American husband has used his position as principal of an elementary school to arrange teacher exchanges with Latvia; and American spouses join folk dance groups (where instruction remains in Latvian!) and perform at song festivals, including the 1993 song festival in Riga. In the Estonian community, where English usage is more acceptable, non-Estonians fit in more easily.

Both Estonians and Latvians have rallied around political concerns connected to their homelands, focusing intensely on issues of human rights and foreign policy. A national network of Estonian-American Republican Clubs developed, including one in Indiana. Organized support for Democrats is nonexistent among Balts. Political activity has galvanized the young as well. Among the Latvians, for example, teens in the 1950s organized an information bureau to coordinate demonstrations and launched letter-writing campaigns and petition drives. Indiana Balts worked with other groups whose countries were in the Soviet sphere to plan Captive Nations Week activities. In April 1990 about one hundred Latvians, Estonians, and Lithuanians protested President George Bush's policies toward Gorbachev with such posters as "Broccoli no, Lithuania yes," "Forget your broccoli, renew Latvia," "Estonia has been Bushwacked," and "The Evil Empire strikes again." Renewed foreign policy continues to activate Baltic communities now that the three countries have regained their independence.

The older generation sought to create a Latvian *vide* (or context) for its young. While parents could live contently among homeland family and friends, having little contact with American society outside of work and shopping, their children were immersed in American society. Both consciously and unconsciously they sensitized children to their feelings, even into the third generation: "My daughters have absorbed my feelings about Latvia, as I did my mother's. My daughter thinks she's 100 percent Latvian (although her father is an American native)."[85] A young man explained his sense of commitment to Latvia in this way:

> Even though I was born here—their struggle in a sense becomes your struggle. You have the awareness that you are not here of your own will completely, but that your parents were forced out. And in a sense, you're different—and to this day I feel like I don't completely fit into the American mold. . . . It's not so much what they told me as it is a sense of what happened. You kind of get this feeling. I've heard it compared to someone who's been in a big auto crash. You don't remember the details but you get a sense that this really terrible thing happened and it's still happening.[86]

In four decades of social life Latvians projected a vivid folk history, which has given substance to social life and identity to the next generation. This folk history not only appears in verbal and written forms, but it is also acted out nonverbally. The raising of the flag, the singing of the

Estonians and Latvians in traditional folk costumes were among those meeting Gov. Otis Bowen (center) at a reception of the Indiana Republican Heritage Group Council in 1976. The Estonians are Aita Haas (far left) and Elly Haas (far right). The Latvians are Baiba Vanags (second from left), Ruta Sventeckis, and Peter Rekis.

national anthem, and independence day commemorations all depend on an informed audience capable of translating images and sounds into historical facts, associations, and feelings. A middle-aged woman said:

> The most interesting thing is when you go to a song festival and sing in a choir, and look around to see which generation it is that's crying when we sing "Tev mūzam dzīvot, Latvija [May You Live Eternally, Latvia]." It's not just the oldest, but the twenty—thirty-year-olds. It's really funny. I think it's phenomenal. And I don't think they are "brainwashed" or "indoctrinated." I think it's a natural process.[87]

For some young Latvians folk history is not enough. A young woman in Indianapolis felt that the older generation provided her with sufficient reasons "why" she should remain Latvian in America, but they failed to provide her with sufficient guidelines for "how" to do so. Therefore she joined a national revitalization movement called *dievturi,* which turns to Latvian folk religion and folklore as the means for transmitting Latvian identity and for creating a network in which to socialize.

In the long run Indianapolis did not develop into the cultural center the early leaders envisioned. There were few new arrivals, and until 1991 return migration was inconceivable. The community remained stable and relatively vital throughout the years, even though most of those who were active as teenagers moved away. A small group of middle-aged Latvians continues to rear children as Latvians. All generations hook into national and even international networks, but the "global community" works most effectively among the young, for whom address books are their tickets to the world.

## Conclusion

Post–World War II refugees were more urban, literate, and skilled than their earlier counterparts. Many entered the United States having studied English in school or they quickly learned it because of a general facility in languages. Most arrived as extended families, but family members were sometimes separated from one another because of their chaotic departures. Many were educated professionals or prosperous landholders, frustrated that their skills were underutilized in the New World. Consequently, they sought a creative outlet by forming a vital ethnic life, which in turn nurtured the national consciousness so typical of refugee communities. While quick to adapt to new ways, they tended to be ill-suited to assimilation. They had not departed from "the Old Country" but had fled "an occupied country" and thus were homesick for their nation as well as fearful for relatives and friends left behind. Until Stalin's death in 1953 correspondence was cut off, and travel was impossible until well into the 1960s.

In contrast to the interaction of Baltic immigrants with those in the homeland, the refugees cut off all but the most intimate personal contact (and sometimes even that with the homeland). Exile ideology depicted those still in the occupied Baltic republics as "suspects" contaminated by their need to accommodate to Soviet power rather than as "compatriots" separated merely by distance. The job of protesting the status quo devolved on those in the West and led to a diaspora community that formed politically vocal and active national groups that drew young and old into multilevel networks and activities.

Among the Displaced Persons, generally and in Indiana, there is little evidence of the conventional wisdom that in the initiatory stages of adjustment old- and new-country patterns and values clash. There is little evidence of social disorganization, particularly if measured in terms of crime and suicide, although there are reports of alcoholism and depression.[88] Clashes primarily were intraethnic, but even these, in many cases, strengthened and revitalized social life and loyalty to a cause rather than disrupting or terminating it. The observations of a Latvian sociologist thirty years ago remain true for thousands of hard-core activists who maintain a dual identity, "living among Americans geographically, economically, educationally, but living as Latvians socially, aesthetically, personally."[89]

In the summer of 1990 Latvians and Estonians in the homelands sang for their freedom in mass choral festivals that for the first time since the 1940s were free of Soviet

*In the 1980s the International Festival of Indianapolis became an important focal point of local Estonian efforts to preserve and display their culture. Participating in the 1990 festival's Parade of Nations are (from left) Vaike Haas, Aita Haas, and former Estonian Society president Nanny Johanson.*

influence. The Lithuanians canceled a scheduled song festival because of a Soviet economic blockade in retaliation for Lithuania's declaration of independence in May 1990. Just over one year later, following the coup of August 1991 in the Soviet Union, all three Baltic republics rather unexpectedly regained their independence. Atlases throughout the world added these new nations to their pages, and the nearly one million Americans who claim Estonian, Latvian, and Lithuanian descent could now also claim a country.

## Notes

1. Inta Gale Carpenter, *A Latvian Storyteller: The Repertoire of Janis Plavnieks* (New York: Arno Press, 1980), 76–77.

2. Ibid., 96.

3. John Bodnar, *The Transplanted: A History of Immigrants in Urban America* (Bloomington: Indiana University Press, 1985), 56.

4. Carpenter, *Latvian Storyteller,* 33.

5. The bibliography on immigration between 1890 and 1914 is vast. The *Harvard Encyclopedia of American Ethnic Groups,* Stephan Thernstrom, ed. (Cambridge, Mass.: Belknap Press of Harvard University Press, 1980), is probably the most comprehensive resource. Its entries, written by recognized scholars, describe the history and present situation of 106 groups, plus it includes 29 thematic essays.

6. The neglect of political refugees undoubtedly also stems from the inaccessibility and unavailability of primary materials. In the introduction to a special issue of *International Migration Review* (1977) on refugees, Barry M. Stein writes that material on refugees in the files of refugee, governmental, and voluntary agencies "will never find its way into library catalogs or references indices." In writing this essay, the author gleaned materials from private collections, newspaper accounts, and interviews.

7. Robert C. Williams, "European Political Emigration: A Lost Subject," *Comparative Studies in Society and History* 12 (1970): 140–48.

8. Juris Veidemanis, "Neglected Areas in the Sociology of Immigrants and Ethnic Groups in North America," *The Sociological Quarterly* (1963): 325–33.

9. U.S. Bureau of the Census, *1990 Census of Population. Supplementary Reports: Detailed Ancestry Groups for States* (Washington, D.C.: Government Printing Office, 1992), 3.

10. Lithuania, 25,174; Latvia, 24,595; Estonia, 17,413 sq. miles. *Webster's New Geographic Dictionary* (Springfield, Mass.: Merriam Webster, Inc., 1988).

11. Unless otherwise identified, all uncited quotes are from interviews conducted by the author during the course of research with Latvians since 1984.

12. Figures are approximate at best. Until 1899 immigration authorities classified Balts as Russians, Germans, or Poles; some Balts classified themselves as such. Later, immigration figures included Jews, Germans, and Russians living in the Baltic territories. In Lithuania, for example, Jews constituted 13 percent of the country's total population in the 1890s, but 33 to 50 percent of the urban populations from which the heaviest out-migration occurred. See Timo Riippa, "The Baltic Peoples—Estonians, Latvians, and Lithuanians," in June Drenning Holmquist, ed., *They Chose Minnesota: A Survey of the State's Ethnic Groups* [St. Paul: Minnesota Historical Society, 1981], 326. Only in 1920 did census records list Lithuanians separately; in 1930, Latvians and Estonians.

13. Jaan Pennar, comp. and ed., *The Estonians in America, 1627–1975: A Chronology and Fact Book* (Dobbs Ferry, N.Y.: Oceana Publications, Inc., 1975), 20; U.S. Bureau of the Census, *Fifteenth Census of the United States: 1930, Population* (Washington, D.C.: Government Printing Office, 1933), 2:268.

14. As late as 1930 an estimated 24.5 percent of the foreign-born Lithuanians ten years and older were illiterate, a very high rate, reflecting the prohibition by the Russian government of Lithuanian schools and language. Leo J. Alilunas, ed., *Lithuanians in the United States: Selected Studies* (San Francisco: R. & E. Research Associates, 1978), 55; *Fifteenth Census of the United States: 1930*, vol. 2:1315.

15. Victor Greene, *For God and Country: The Rise of the Polish and Lithuanian Ethnic Consciousness in America, 1860–1910* (Madison: Wisconsin State Historical Society, 1975).

16. Pennar, comp. and ed., *Estonians in America*, 83.

17. Algirdas M. Budreckis, comp. and ed., *The Lithuanians in America, 1651–1975* (Dobbs Ferry, N.Y.: Oceana Publications, Inc., 1976), 3.

18. Petras Indreika, "The East Chicago Lithuanians" (Unpublished manuscript, 1972), 18.

19. Ibid., i. Language provides an additional barrier since valuable archival sources, including letters and journals, are in Lithuanian. The author wishes to acknowledge the assistance of Guntis Šmidchens in translating a number of church and school histories, including *St. Casimir Parish, 1916–1976* and *Saint Francis Lithuanian Parish, 1913–1963*.

20. Indreika, "East Chicago Lithuanians," 11.

21. Isaac James Quillen, *Industrial City: A History of Gary, Indiana to 1929* (New York: Garland Publishing, Inc., 1986), 491.

22. Lithuanians in Indiana were fairly evenly divided between foreign and native born. Among Lithuanians in the United States, 193,606 were foreign born and 245,589 native born. Only about one-third (or 156,152) listed Lithuanian as their mother tongue in the 1930 census, reflecting the rapid assimilation of second-generation Lithuanians. *Fifteenth Census of the United States: 1930*, vol. 2:232, 268, 347.

23. Less than 300 resided in Hammond (257) and Indianapolis (210); still fewer in South Bend (192) and Terre Haute (165). Less than 100 lived in La Porte (90), Marion (64), and Michigan City (81) and less than 50 in Whiting (25), Fort Wayne (48), and Mishawaka (30).

24. Powell A. Moore, *The Calumet Region: Indiana's Last Frontier,* vol. 39 of *Indiana Historical Collections* (Indianapolis: Indiana Historical Bureau, 1959), 371.

25. Indreika, "East Chicago Lithuanians," 10.

26. Ibid.

27. Raymond A. Mohl and Neil Betten, *Steel City: Urban and Ethnic Patterns in Gary, Indiana, 1906–1950* (New York: Holmes and Meier, 1986), 153–54, 164.

28. A visit to the Valparaiso University archives in fall 1992 yielded little further information about the Lithuanian student body than is summarized in available English-language sources.

29. Indreika, "East Chicago Lithuanians," 42.

30. Ibid., 37.

31. Ibid., 38.

32. Moore, *Calumet Region,* 357.

33. Indreika, "East Chicago Lithuanians," 11.

34. Ibid.

35. Arūnas Ališauskas, "Lithuanians," in Thernstrom, ed., *Harvard Encyclopedia of American Ethnic Groups,* 673.

36. Alilunas, *Lithuanians in the United States,* 120.

37. G. Woodbridge, *UNRRA: The History of the United Nations Relief and Rehabilitation Administration* (New York: Columbia University Press, 1950), 469.

38. Susan Cooper, Ethnic History Project of the Oral History Research Center, Indiana University [Meijers], 8.

39. Cooper [Asars], 29.

40. Jacques Vernant, *The Refugee in the Post-War World* (New Haven, Conn.: Yale University Press, 1953), 68.

41. Cooper [Meijers], 10.

42. Ibid.

43. Ibid.

44. Ibid. [Asars], 27.

45. *Indianapolis Star,* 16 Sept. 1977.

46. Cooper [Meijers], 3.

47. Ibid. [Asars], 28.

48. Ibid. [Meijers], 14.

49. Liucija Baskauskas, *The Urban Enclave: Lithuanian Refugees in Los Angeles* (New York: AMS Press, 1985).

50. Veidemanis, "Neglected Areas in the Sociology of Immigrants and Ethnic Groups in North America," 332-33.

51. Joshua A. Fishman, *Language Loyalty in the United States: The Maintenance and Perpetuation of Non-English Mother Tongues by American Ethnic and Religious Groups* (The Hague: Mouton, 1966).

52. Rev. Ignatius Urbonas, interview, Gary, Ind., 21 Sept. 1992.

53. The information about Antanina Neinienė is from a 1977 interview of Elena Bradunas by Richard M. Dorson. The spelling of this name may be inaccurate. The interview is Dorson #115 in the Gary Project materials at the Indiana University Archives of Traditional Music. Bradunas interviewed Lithuanians in northwest Indiana during the Gary Project, which was conducted by the Indiana University Folklore Institute between 1975 and 1977. Her tapes, which are mostly in Lithuanian, are also deposited in the Archives of Traditional Music.

54. Indreika, "East Chicago Lithuanians," 48.

55. In one extreme case, an argument over communism resulted in a lawsuit although it is not clear whether the suit was one among the

Displaced Persons or between the two groups. In 1974 the superior court in Lake County settled a charge brought by a couple against two women they accused of slandering them by calling them communists. The defendants agreed to "recognize and declare that they believe the [plaintiffs] are not Communists."

56. Bradunas, taped interviews, Archives of Traditional Music.

57. Indreika, "East Chicago Lithuanians," 12.

58. The first year after immigration some fifty Latvians lived in Anderson where they had obtained jobs with the Pierce Government Metal factory and Delco-Remy. For a short time there was a small but very active group of Latvians in Terre Haute. Others lived with sponsoring families in Fort Wayne, Kokomo, Elwood, Union City, Brazil, Decatur, New Castle, Columbia City, South Bend, Hagerstown, Richmond, Batesville, Carmel, and Zionsville. Within a year most had resettled to Indianapolis. *Detailed Ancestry Groups for States, 1990,* p. 15.

59. Unpublished study of Estonian emigration printed in Karl Aun, *The Political Refugees: A History of Estonians in Canada* (Toronto: McClelland and Stewart, 1985).

60. The material on the Estonians in Indianapolis derives primarily from Ain Haas's 1991 manuscript, an interview with the author on 12 Mar. 1992, and from Indianapolis newspaper accounts. *Detailed Ancestry Groups for States, 1990,* p. 15.

61. Ain Haas, "The Estonian Community of Indianapolis," *FUSAC '91: Proceedings of the Eighth Meeting of the Finno-Ugric Studies Association of Canada,* ed. by Joel Ashmore Nevis and Juta-Kõvamees Kitching.

62. Ibid., 16.

63. Ibid., 1.

64. Ibid.

65. Cooper [Asars], 30–31.

66. Ibid., 30.

67. Haas interview.

68. Kārlis Vanags, *Latviešu pagasts Indianā* [The Latvian Community in Indiana] (Indianapolis: Taurus, 1987), 9–10.

69. Ibid., 16.

70. Since the refugees had lived collectively in barracks in the refugee camps in Germany, they could have drawn upon this experience in selecting the nickname. Instead, they connect figuratively with Latvians in the homeland who at the time were being forcibly gathered into collective farms. It is as if they were saying that in the United States, economic necessity produced effects similar to political ideology in Latvia.

71. Haas interview.

72. Haas, "Estonian Community of Indianapolis," 11.

73. Vanags, *Latviešu pagasts Indianā,* 12.

74. Haas, "Estonian Community of Indianapolis," 6.

75. *Indianapolis News,* 2 Feb. 1949.

76. Haas interview.

77. From an entry on the Latvian Lutheran Church in exile in Edgars Andersons, ed., *Latvju enciklopēdija, 1962–1982, J–L* (Rockville, Md.: American Latvian Association, 1985), 405.

78. Haas, "Estonian Community of Indianapolis," 12.

79. Ibid., 12–13.

80. Ibid., 14.

81. Ibid., 13.

82. Ibid.

83. Ibid.

84. Zinta Sanders, "Latvian Education in the U.S.: Antecedents and Development of Supplementary Schools," *The Journal of Ethnic Studies* 7, no. 1 (1974): 31–42.

85. Interview by the author with Ieva Sijāts Johnson, Apr. 1986.

86. Interview by the author with Aldis Elberts, 1 May 1985. Elberts is currently minister of a Latvian Lutheran church in Australia.

87. Johnson interview.

88. The topic of alcoholism is generally marginalized, and to the author's knowledge no serious research has been undertaken to estimate how widespread it was during the first years among Latvians in the United States. Within the Indianapolis Latvian community the general tendency to criticize the young for drinking points to a source of intergenerational conflict, as reported, for example, in the Latvian youth newsletter *Ausma* in November 1955, p. 4: "But do only the young drink? Absolutely not, the older generation drinks as well and I'd like to bet that proportionately, many more. Precisely those who should be setting the example, do it themselves."

89. Juris Veidemanis, "The New Immigrant: A Challenge to an Older Theory" (Paper read at the Midwest Sociological Society, Des Moines, Iowa, 1962), 13.

# CANADIANS

HELEN JEAN M. NUGENT

*Throughout the history of Indiana Canadians have been a growing part of the immigrant population, albeit largely unnoticed. Because "Canadian" is not easily identifiable as an ethnic group, but shares the same European, Asian, or native ethnicity as many other Hoosiers, Canadians have become the invisible foreigners.*

There is no evidence to indicate that Canadians have ever immigrated to Indiana for different reasons than they have to other states. To understand the background and motivation of these immigrants, a general view of Canadian immigration to the United States is helpful.

Identification of Canadians is complicated by similarities between Canadians and other people: French Canadians and French, English Canadians and English, German Canadians and Germans, etc., as well as the general similarities between Canadians and Americans. Canadian immigrants are not sufficiently different or unique as to be thought of by Americans as "foreigners." Therefore, Canadian immigrants often are not noticed among the foreign-born elements of our nation or state. Canadians are easily assimilated and usually do not feel so threatened by life in the United States that they settle in clustered neighborhoods or form "Canadian" ethnic societies, as other immigrant groups may do. Since Canadians cannot be definitively identified by name or physical features, it may be helpful to construct an illustration of a "typical" Canadian immigrant. Canadian census figures, collected

since 1871, provide material for creating a composite profile of the Canadian character.

In 1871 the Canadian population was 61 percent of British Isles ethnic origin and 31.1 percent of French origin. By 1981 those two "founding" cultures were still dominant at 42.2 percent and 28.1 percent respectively.[1] The likelihood of immigrants being of British or possibly French origin remains strong, but less certain than a century ago.

Canada never had an established tax-supported religion. Roman Catholics have always been the most numerous religious group, including most of the French and Highland Scot descendants. The percentage of Catholics among Canadians rose from 42.9 percent in 1871 to 46.6 percent in 1981. Anglicans, members of the Church of England in Canada, were about equal in numbers with Methodists and Presbyterians until 1925. The United Church of Canada, created in that year through a merger of Congregationalist, Methodist, and most Presbyterian bodies, represented about 20 percent of the Canadian population until declining to 15.6 percent in 1981.[2] Canadian immigrants in any locale are likely to be found in Anglican or Roman Catholic parishes,or, if Protestant, among Methodist, Presbyterian, or Episcopalian congregations.

Like the United States, Canada was created by an immigrant population from Europe. During the late nineteenth and early twentieth centuries, Canadian governments encouraged immigration into a "social mosaic" pattern by a policy that invited newcomers to retain their ethnic heritage in direct contrast to the "melting pot" immigration policy of the United States. The Dominion government attracted immigrants willing to live under a constitutional monarchy, with more government regulation of the economy than in the free enterprise system to the south.

In all Canadian history there never has been religious, political, social, or economic upheaval that forced refugee groups to leave the country. Canadians tend to immigrate for individual reasons rather than in groups driven by

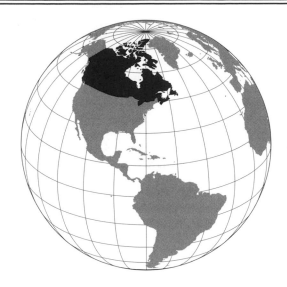

oppression or discrimination. The major recipient of Canadian immigrants has always been the United States, and the major reason for emigrating is because of perceived greater economic opportunity. Since passage of the Free Trade Agreement in 1989 Canadian immigration to the United States has increased. In 1991 Ronald Raby, chief of population estimates with Statistics Canada, confirmed that the major reason for people leaving Canada is for economic opportunity and not for political reasons.[3]

Large numbers of Canadians coming to the United States do not necessarily mean large numbers of Canadians staying in the United States. Unlike most other immigrant populations Canadians easily can return to their home country, and many do so. Permanent immigrants to the United States usually become naturalized citizens within a few years, but in the twentieth century only about 40 percent of Canadian arrivals applied for naturalization.[4] During the 1960s, 68 percent of Canadians immigrating to the United States did not take American citizenship, and more than half of that percentage returned to Canada.[5] Nearly half of the professionals, especially in medicine and education, who came to the United States for greater profit during that period returned to Canada because the profit was not sufficient: "They were better educated than the Canadian and U.S. population in general. Their earnings in the U.S., however, did not reflect the level of education they had attained."[6]

One group of Canadian immigrants that does not match the foregoing composite portrait are Francophone Canadians from Québec. During the past century those immigrants have tended to cluster in mill towns in New England where emigration from French Canada has been significant since the late nineteenth century. As late as 1981 New England population of Québec origin was over 25 percent. These "Little Canadas" in the northeast, designed to protect Québec culture from total assimilation in the

United States, were never present in Indiana, even though the earliest Canadians in Indiana were from Québec.

The first Canadians to arrive in the state came before there was an Indiana and before there was a Canada, but their motivation was definitely economic. *Les Canadiens,* French-Canadian and Métis fur traders whose roots were in New France, were present in many locations in the Old Northwest from the late seventeenth century. Their presence in Indiana is documented by early land boundaries, genealogical studies, and county histories. Land plots similar to the seigneurial system of Québec were evident along waterways in Allen, Blackford, Cass, Daviess, Knox, Miami, Pike, Sullivan, Tippecanoe, Warren, and Whitley counties into the late nineteenth century.[7]

Vincennes, in Knox County, is the best-known early "French" settlement in the state. The city developed around a fur trading post on the Wabash River that was established about 1732. It was eventually named for the Sieur de Vincennes, who was either the great-nephew or the grandson of Francois Bissot, a settler in New France before 1647.[8] Bissot's grant was to the Sieur de la Riviere. His son, Jean Baptiste Bissot, was granted land as the Sieur de Vincennes.[9] Most Indiana historians claim that the title passed to Jean Baptiste Bissot's son Francois Marie Bissot.[10] Vincennes was named for a third-generation Québecois who held title to the Seigneury of Vincennes located on the south bank of the St. Lawrence River near the western tip of Ile d'Orleans.[11]

Many family names in the Vincennes region also can be traced to immigrants from New France. Lists presented to the federal Senate in 1812 as claims for lands in the area, later lists of claims that the Senate confirmed, and still later lists of lands granted by the state of Indiana contain numerous Québec names of derivatives recognized in Thomas J. LaForest's *Our French-Canadian Ancestors.* Names such as Barrois, Bonhomme, Buse and Bouchey (Boucher), Boyer, Cardinal, Cartier, Delisle, Dubois, Dupre, Mieure (Mierre), Racine, Richard, Urno (Renault), and Richardville are found repeatedly on the lists.[12] Michel Brouillet, a French-Canadian fur trader who had been part of George Rogers Clark's entourage, built the now reconstructed French House in Vincennes shortly after 1800. He married Marie-Louise Drouet de Richardville about 1830.[13]

Governmental policies in the French colony of New France, unlike English colonial policy, encouraged intermarriage with natives. The object was to provide a hybrid population that combined Old World culture with the New World strength of the native Indians. In every recorded case the marriages united French men with native women, never the reverse. The hybrid Métis (half-breed in French) provided the largest number of

*Bailly's Trading Post, Porter County, from old postcard.*

fur traders and early settlers in the area that later would become Indiana. A number of well-known Indiana names are included among the Métis population. Some are called "French," others "Indian," but in reality they are the result of a Québec father and Indian mother, perhaps some generations back. The cultural orientation of the individual depended upon whether the French or Indian lineage was most influential. A prime example was Joseph Bailly.

Bailly established a fur trading post known as Baillytown in Porter County in 1822. He was descended from four early Québec settlers: Robert Giffard, Pierre Boucher, Jean Juchereau, and Christophe Crevier.[14] Bailly married twice, both times to Métis women. His daughters were educated in Upper Canada, and a son died while a student at Carey Mission, a school for Indians located in southern Michigan. His third daughter became Mother Cecilia, superior general of the Sisters of Providence at St. Mary-of-the-Woods, 1856–68. His eldest son Alexis left Indiana

to become part of the French-Canadian fur empire in Minnesota.[15] Joseph Bailly, born in Québec in 1774, was six generations removed from his French ancestors. When he died in Indiana in 1835 he was a product of French-Canadian culture.

The Richardville name, found in Knox County and also in northern Indiana, is an interesting example of how Métis were recognized as both Indian and French.[16] Joseph Drouet de Richardville, characterized as "a fur dealer of noble French ancestry,"[17] had a son by Tacumwah, a sister of Miami Chief Little Turtle.[18] The son, Jean Baptiste de Richardville, was born near the present-day city of Fort Wayne in 1761.[19] This renowned Métis was known among the Miami as Peshewa, meaning Wildcat, and Wildcat Creek in Howard County is named in his honor. The town of Russiaville also was named for Richardville, but the name fell victim to an Anglophone recorder.[20] Originally Howard County was organized as Richardville County, but an act of the Indiana legislature in 1847 changed it to honor Tilghman A. Howard, an Indiana congressman.[21] Indian reserves in four counties, Allen, Cass, Miami, and Tippecanoe, bore the name Richardville as late as 1876.[22] Jean Baptiste de Richardville had four sons, all of whom became chiefs among the Miami people. One of them, Chief Kokomo, gave his name to the county seat of Howard County.[23]

In Knox County, land grant lists include Jean Baptiste Richardville, Sr., John Richardville, Jr., and Henry Richardville.[24] These Richardvilles may not be closely related to the Jean Baptiste de Richardville of Allen County, but all descend from Claude Drouet de Richardville of Québec. In 1812 the list of land claims in the district of Vincennes included "Drouet, widow, dit Richardville, present claimant: Antoine Drouet."[25] The entry refers to the widow of a man using his *dit* name Richardville while the present claimant prefers the family name of Drouet.[26]

Another prominent Métis in early Indiana was Francis Godfroy, a Miami war chief, whose "father was a Frenchman who took to wife a Miami maiden."[27] Francis also married an Indian woman, and his son James R. Godfroy is listed (along with J. B. Richardville) among early Catholic settlers in the Fort Wayne area.[28] James, who was born about 1810, married the granddaughter of Jean Baptiste Richardville, who was also the daughter of La Blonde Richardville.[29] The Québec connection of Godfroy is documented in an Allen County history that mentions "a Canadian, of the name of Godfroi (or Godfri), accompanied 'by two other white men.'"[30]

Many other early settlers of "French" ancestry were Métis, of Québec-descended fathers and Indian mothers, whether or not the relationship was a recognized marriage.

These names are especially evident in Allen, Blackford, Cass, Knox, Miami, Porter, Warren, and Whitley counties. The percentage of identifiable French Canadians immigrating into Indiana declined rapidly as the Métis and fur trading population moved west. By midnineteenth century the majority of emigrants from Canada coming to Indiana descended from United Kingdom stock or were returning Americans.

In a study of the distribution of ethnic and racial minorities in Indiana in 1850 Gregory Rose found that the manuscript census indicated more settlers from English-speaking Canada than from French-speaking Canada.[31] British North America at that time contained six English colonies and only one French colony. Rose also found that "none of the three counties that contained early French-Canadian settlements—Allen, Knox, and Tippecanoe—had Lower Canadians in excess of Upper Canadians."[32]

By 1850 the ethnicity of people in Québec was French-Canadian, not French, just as the ethnicity of Indiana residents at that time was American rather than English. By the last half of the nineteenth century there is no reason to believe that Francophone immigrants from Québec would be particularly attracted to the Indiana counties that had been the seats of heaviest fur trade and Métis population. A century had passed since the French empire in North America ended, and all immigrants to the area were aware that the language of Indiana was a variant of English. Most residents of the eastern townships in Québec, south of the St. Lawrence, were descended from Loyalists and therefore English speaking. Québec immigrants seeking an area of their own language and culture were more likely to prefer the "Little Canadas" in New York and New England. Those immigrants coming to Indiana were comfortable in Anglophone society.

The 1860 census of Knox County listed nineteen persons born in Canada. Three were specifically born in Canada West (Ontario), two in Lower Canada (Québec), and two in Nova Scotia (technically a separate British colony until 1867). Those born in Canada East (also Québec) had names that could indicate English derivation (Woodman, Caldwell), while there were five among the unspecified that could indicate French heritage (Goerty, Martin, Prier, Soudriette, and Buling).[33] The vulnerability of French names to the spelling of the census taker makes a definite conclusion difficult.

One of the earliest identifiable immigrants of English-Canadian background came to Lawrence County about 1814. After service in the American forces during the War of 1812, a young naval ensign, Samuel Jackson, Jr., and his wife Hannah, exercised squatters' rights in the area now encompassed by Spring Mill State Park. On 26 October 1816 he received legal patent to a three-quarters section of land.[34] This patent was granted under an act of Congress designed to reward Canadians who had taken the oath of allegiance to the United States. Although Jackson had a gristmill and quarry at the location, he decided to leave Indiana for Pennsylvania. By a deed dated 3 March 1817 Cuthbert and Thomas Bullitt became the owners of Jackson's holdings.[35]

Two Canadians were furniture makers when the 1850 census was taken. Otis Bartlett, born in Canada in 1805, was a cabinetmaker in De Kalb County in Newville Township.[36] By 1860 he was gone from the Indiana census, but Silas H. Bartlett, born in Canada ca. 1825, farmed in Stafford Township.[37] In nearby Noble County Simon Bartlett, born in Canada ca. 1832, was a Methodist clergyman in 1860.[38] A chair maker in Mishawaka, Albert Cap, was born in Canada ca. 1815. His success was such that he had taken on a New York-born apprentice, eighteen-year-old Henry Sherman.[39]

Nineteenth-century Canadian immigration to the United States included a number of immigration patterns: single men; single girls working as domestic help; families with one parent born in Canada and the other elsewhere; families with children born in several locations; families with immigrant parents; and "over-and-back" Americans who went to Canada then returned to the United States. Census schedules since 1850 clearly indicate that Canadians coming to Indiana represented all of these patterns. In many cases the immigrants had lived elsewhere in the United States before arriving in Indiana.

George Riley, in Adams County, is representative of single men coming alone. Sixteen years old and Canadian born, Riley lived as a farm laborer with an elderly couple, aged seventy-two and seventy-six, who were English born.[40]

In Elkhart County the Hitchcocks illustrate a family with one Canadian parent that had lived elsewhere in the United States after leaving Canada. William Hitchcock, a Baptist clergyman, was born in New York, his wife Eliza in New Brunswick. Two children, ages fifteen and thirteen, were born in Canada; two others, ages ten and seven, were born in Michigan; and the two youngest, five and "baby," in Indiana.[41] Since New Brunswick was a separate British colony until 1867, the family seems to have been in Ontario (Canada) until at least 1847, in Michigan from 1850 until at least 1853, and in Indiana after 1855. William Hitchcock is also representative of an "over-and-back" American who had entered Canada, married, and returned to a different sector of his native country.

An example of a family that had immigrant parents from Europe, had lived elsewhere in the United States before arriving in Indiana, and had children born in several locations was the family of Phelix McManomer in Decatur County. Phelix and his wife Bridget were both born in Ireland. A sixteen-year-old daughter Wovery and ten-year-old son John were born in Canada. Another son Michael, age seven, was born in Virginia, and the youngest children, Anna, age four, and Henry, age two, were born in Indiana.[42] The family was resident in Canada from at least 1844 through 1850, in Virginia in 1853, and in Indiana by 1856. The time spent in Canada was certainly too short to leave a lasting impression on family members.

Many families from Europe merely passed through Canada en route to the United States. The 1860 census lists Nicholas Rich, a sixteen-year-old resident of Adams County, as Canadian born. No father is included in the listings. His mother was born in Switzerland as was her eldest son Joseph. Another household member, two years older than Nicholas, was born in France. The surrounding households in Adams County contained many people born in Switzerland and France.[43] It is unlikely that the few years spent in Canada had any lasting effect on the family—even on Nicholas who was Canadian by birth.

The Ontario peninsula was a popular route for New York or Pennsylvania residents to "go west," and it was not unusual for a child or two to be born while families were resident in Canada. An entry from De Kalb County exemplifies American couples who returned to the United States, probably after crossing the fertile Ontario peninsula. Solomon Merrill and his wife Rachel were born, respectively, in New York and Pennsylvania. A son, age nineteen, was born in Canada, while three other children, ages five through fourteen, were born in Indiana.[44] The couple may have married in the United States before immigrating, or in Canada, but they were resident in Canada in 1841. By 1846 they had settled in Indiana.

An unusual variation of immigration is shown by the Rhein family in Allen County. Both parents were born in German provinces. Two older children, ages twenty and eighteen, were born in Ohio, a sixteen year old in Indiana, two, ages fourteen and thirteen, in Canada West, and six additional, from eleven years down to "baby" in Indiana.[45] This very productive couple originally immigrated to the United States at least by 1840, stayed in Ohio until at least 1842, then came to Indiana at least by 1844. By 1846 and until at least 1847 they were in Ontario but returned to Indiana by 1849.

Before Canada achieved Dominion status in 1867, emigration from British North America into the United States was already considerable. An immigration historian lists Canadians as one of the greatest groups of immigrants to the United States during the late nineteenth century.

Soon after 1820, Ireland replaced the United Kingdom as the country providing the largest number of U.S. immigrants. By 1850, Germany was the immigrants' leading country of origin. Other countries of origin were France, Norway, and Sweden. Canadians of English and French ancestry also came to the U.S. Many Americans can trace their ancestors' arrival to one of these great migrations to the United States.[46]

Another writer compared Canadian immigration to Chinese:

The "old immigrants," from northern and western Europe—mostly Irish, Germans, and Scandinavians—arrived before 1800. This first great wave from Europe coincided with two simultaneous 19th century migrations: one from China, the other from Canada.[47]

Indiana has never attracted a significant number of foreign-born immigrants. The percentage of Canadians among the foreign born in Indiana has increased gradually, as the percentage of other foreign born has declined, as Table 1 illustrates.

Table 1. Percentages of Foreign Born in Indiana and Canadian Born among the Foreign Born, 1850–1980

| Census | Percentage of foreign born in Indiana | Percentage of Canadians among foreign born in Indiana |
|---|---|---|
| 1850 | 5.6 | 3.7 |
| 1860 | 8.8 | 2.7 |
| 1870 | 8.4 | 3.4 |
| 1880 | 7.3 | 3.8 |
| 1890 | 6.7 | 3.5 |
| 1900 | 5.7 | 4.2 |
| 1910 | 5.9 | 3.6 |
| 1920 | 5.2 | 3.4 |
| 1930 | 4.2 | 5.0 |
| 1940 | 3.2 | 5.1 |
| 1950 | 2.6 | 6.1 |
| 1960 | 2.0 | 7.0 |
| 1970 | 1.6 | 6.7 |
| 1980 | 1.9 | 6.4 |

Source: Derived from U. S. Census Bureau and Dominion Bureau of Statistics figures for the appropriate year.

Table 1 shows that the percentage of foreign-born residents of Indiana has declined consistently since 1860. The percentage of Canadian born among the foreign-born population increased most dramatically during the 1940s and 1950s.[48] There was no large-scale exodus from Canada during those years to explain the increase and no specific location in Indiana where Canadians arrived in large numbers.

No one county in Indiana has ever monopolized Canadian arrivals, although northern counties have always had more Canadian born than southern Indiana counties. Many of these arrivals came into Indiana from Michigan where they, or their parents, first emigrated from Canada. Census records for counties in the southern half of the state often show no Canadian born and frequently no foreign born. Table 2 illustrates the counties with the highest Canadian-born population and counties with the highest percentage of Canadian born for each year that figures were available from 1850 to 1980.

Table 2. Counties with Significant Canadian Population, 1850–1980

| Census | County with highest number of Canadian born | County with highest percentage of Canadian born among the foreign born |
|---|---|---|
| 1850 | Porter (231) | Porter (55.4) |
| 1860 | Elkhart (383) | Newton (26.7) |
| 1870 | Elkhart (381) | not available |
| 1880 | Porter (416) | Benton (23.8) |
| 1890 | Marion (525) | Benton (14.5) |
| 1910 | Marion (896) | Benton (14.5) |
| 1930 | Lake (1,869) | Morgan (16.7) |
| 1940 | Lake (1,659) | Steuben (31.9) |
| 1950 | Lake (1,625) | Randolph (25.8) |
| 1980 | Marion (910) | Blackford (43.0) |

Source: Derived from U.S. Census Bureau statistics of appropriate year.

Only occasionally in any Indiana county have Canadians been the most numerous foreign-born group. When this phenomena occurred, it was usually because a few Canadians had come into a county that contained few foreign-born residents. In 1850, for example, Canadians were the most numerous foreign-born group in Porter County when 231 Canadians composed 55.4 percent of the foreign-born population. In Jasper County they were also the highest percentage group with 44 percent, but this figure represented 33 Canadians in a total foreign-born population of only 74.

Northern Indiana contained the majority of Canadian-born immigrants during the nineteenth century. In 1850 only five counties had more than one hundred Canadian-born residents: Allen, Elkhart, Lake, La Porte, and Porter. There were no Canadian born in Brown, Dubois, Ohio, or Orange counties. By 1870 every county in Indiana had at least one Canadian-born resident, although Blackford and Union counties had only one. Eleven counties counted more than one hundred Canadian born. By 1880 Vigo County had become the first county south of Marion County to register more than one hundred

Canadian-born residents. In the 1890 census twelve Indiana counties had more than one hundred Canadian-born residents.

Prior to the Second World War Canadian-born Hoosiers remained in higher concentrations in the northern counties. The census of 1950 indicated that Vanderburgh County, in the extreme southwest corner of the state, had more than one hundred Canadian-born residents. Census figures for the postwar years indicate larger numbers of Canadian born in counties with greater urbanization.

Some significant information stands out about the Canadian-born population in various counties of Indiana. Allen County had a large number of Québecois and Métis prior to statehood and has had more than one hundred Canadian-born residents in every census since 1850. Because of the high number of foreign-born residents in that county the percentage of Canadians has been consistently low, ranging from 1.7 percent in 1860 to 8.1 percent in 1980. Although the 1860 number split about evenly between Canada East (Québec) and Canada, there is no evidence that any significant number of Québecois came to Fort Wayne because of its early French connection.

French-language Canadians have not been present in large numbers in Indiana since the days of the fur trade. In 1910 two northern counties bordering Illinois, Newton and Benton, had a significant number of French Canadians. This fact stems from construction on the Big Four Line of the New York Central Railroad that was begun in Kankakee, Illinois, in 1871. A number of Québec immigrants farming in that area were recruited as railroad

Dr. Norman London (left), academic affairs officer at the Canadian Embassy in Washington, D.C., presents one hundred volumes to the Franklin College Library in November 1984. Receiving the gift are Dr. Helen Jean M. Nugent, director of Canadian Studies, and Robert Y. Coward, head librarian.

laborers. They were attracted to the rich soil in Benton County and settled there.[49] The railroad line passed through a small portion of Newton County so the same pattern probably occurred there.[50] Despite the early prominence of Vincennes and Knox County in the French fur trade, that county never contained a significant number or percentage of Canadian-born residents.

Census records indicate that Elkhart County has had the most consistently high Canadian-born population, both in numbers and in percentages of foreign-born residents. In 1850, 185 Canadian born in that county were 30.2 percent of the foreign-born population. In succeeding years the number was never lower than 229 in 1940. In 1980 the 529 Canadian born constituted 17 percent of the foreign-born residents. Other counties along the Michigan border have counted more than 100 Canadian born in each census, but none has had percentages as high as Elkhart. Elkhart is not, however, among the counties of highest foreign-born population.

Counties with no Canadian born among their residents have always been in the southern third of Indiana. Dubois County had no Canadian born among those counted in 1850 or 1860, and the five who were included in the 1870 figures were not present in 1880. Dubois County has never registered more than five Canadian-born residents in any census since 1870. Crawford County counted ten Canadian-born residents in 1850 and 1860 and eleven in 1870. A slow decline began in 1880, and there have been no Canadian-born residents since 1930.

Canadians have come to Indiana as individuals or in family groups. Even in counties with a large number or percentage of Canadian-born residents, there is no evidence that they identified with their fellow Canadians in any obvious fashion. Their choices of religious, social, and political organizations were made by individual preference, not because of their Canadian birth.

Most early Indiana county and community histories contain biographies of men, and occasionally a woman, considered to be distinguished members of their communities. Histories of those counties where Canadian-born populations are most evident contain a sampling of Canadian born or descended who merited inclusion. Several members of early Québec-descended families were included: Richardville (in Knox, Howard, and Allen counties), Godfroy (Allen), Lafontaine (Huntington), Moran (Elkhart), and Peltier (Allen).[51]

The 1860 census figures indicate that there were probably some Canadian born who came to a specific sector in Indiana because their talents were marketable there. Clark and Floyd counties had several Canadian born employed in the boat building industry as steamboat pilot, ship carpenter, steamboat fireman, boat engineer, or

*Mark Lemieux, consul general of the Detroit Consulate, speaks in 1988 at the first Indiana Film Society's Canadian Film Festival held in Indianapolis.*

machinist. In Floyd County twenty of these persons indicated the specific province in which they were born, and fifteen were from the maritime provinces where shipbuilding had just started to decline as the provinces' economic mainstay.[52]

A review of biographical and historical records contained in late-nineteenth-century Indiana histories indicate additional references to Canadian-born residents, mostly of English background. The majority were born in Ontario. Some came to the United States as children, others immigrated as young adults. These residents represent a variety of immigration patterns, including a few who returned to Canada to marry after successful beginnings in Indiana. As one might expect of such "successful" Hoosiers, they left Canada because of perceived greater economic opportunity in the United States. Some made their mark in agriculture, as did J. S. Holton in Lake County: "He came here a poor boy, but now owns 100 acres adjoining the original town site, besides other property—all the result of enterprise and labor."[53] Others, including Holton's younger brother Hiram, were merchants. In southern Indiana, Ohio County listed twenty-three-year-old C. A. McIntyre as a successful jeweler.[54] A number of Canadian-born entries in Lake and Porter counties included William H. Gostlin who had learned distilling in Canada. Gostlin practiced the art in Chicago for fifteen years before migrating to Lake County where his establishment produced thirty barrels of vinegar and ten barrels of corn syrup per day.[55] Porter County's only dental school graduate, Dr. J. H. Edmonds, had immigrated first to Detroit, then to Illinois, studied dentistry in Philadelphia, and settled in Indiana, his wife's home state.[56]

*Participant in the 1978 Indianapolis-Scarborough Peace Games.*

ROBERT MEIER

Nevertheless, Canadian achievement has been at least equivalent with American-born Hoosiers. They have brought to the state, as to the nation, a variant of North American culture. French Canadians, more numerous in the area before Indiana became a state, brought names, architectural styles, and customs unlike any other. English Canadians have contributed political, social, and religious habits compatible with and assimilated by those of other Hoosiers. Both French and English Canadians came for economic reasons, and their enterprise has helped to make Indiana what it is today.

Upon occasion, Canadians may come together for a social purpose. In 1911, for example, a "Canadian Club" existed in Indianapolis and celebrated both Empire Day on 24 May and Dominion Day on 1 July.[60] Currently, Canadian-born residents are strong supporters of the Indiana Film Society's annual Canadian Film Festival and the Indianapolis-Scarborough Peace Games, held alternately in the two cities.

Canadians have in the past assimilated totally into the Indiana lifestyle as they have in most parts of the United States. As Canadian identity becomes more clearly defined in Canada one may expect that Canadians will become more recognizable throughout the world. In the United States, when Canadians make their cultural distinction known, Canadians in Indiana will be no exception.

A twentieth-century publication that claims to list the most meritorious citizens of the state's population contains thirty-five-hundred entries, twenty-four of whom claim Canadian ancestry. Many others list "French" and "Indian" descent, which could well indicate Québec lineage. It is probable that others, especially those claiming English or Scottish ancestry, unwittingly omitted some Canadian residence for an ancestor.[57]

Not all Canadians living in Indiana were totally successful. Like all immigrant groups there were a few criminals and insane. Some were illiterate. In 1860 Clark County census takers found eight Canadian born in the penitentiary for crimes ranging from receiving stolen goods to murder.[58] Throughout the state several other Canadian born were in jail at the time of the census, and three were classified as idiotic. A slightly higher percentage of Canadian born, 6.9 percent, could neither read nor write.[59]

Throughout the history of Indiana Canadians have been a growing part of the immigrant population, albeit largely unnoticed. Because "Canadian" is not easily identifiable as an ethnic group, but shares the same European, Asian, or native ethnicity as many other Hoosiers, Canadians have become the invisible foreigners.

## Notes

1. Canada, Dominion Bureau of Statistics, Census for 1891, Bulletin #11, "Nationalities of the People"; and Census for 1981, Table 92.227, "Ethnicity of the Population."

2. Canada, Dominion Bureau of Statistics, Census for 1961, Table 31, "Numerical and Percentage Distribution of the Population by Religion," 37-1; Census for 1971, "Percentage Distribution of Population by Religious Denomination for Canada: 1921–1971," 9.0; and Census for 1981, Table 5, "Population by Sex, Showing Specific Religions," 5-1.

3. *The London (Ontario) Free Press,* 15 June 1991.

4. Kenneth Lines, *British and Canadian Immigration to the United States since 1920* (San Francisco: R. & E. Research Associates, Inc., 1978), 101.

5. T. J. Samuel, *The Migration of Canadian-Born between Canada and the United States of America, 1959 to 1969* (Ottawa: Research Branch, Program Development Service, Department of Manpower and Immigration, 1969), 39.

6. Ibid., 43.

7. *Illustrated Historical Atlas of the State of Indiana, 1876* (1876; reprint, Indianapolis: Indiana Historical Society, 1968). See maps of counties referenced.

8. Thomas J. LaForest, *Our French-Canadian Ancestors,* 16 vols. (Palm Harbor, Fla.: LISI Press, 1983– ), 1:42.

9. John J. Doyle, *The Catholic Church in Indiana, 1686–1814* (Indianapolis: Criterion Press, 1976), 6.

10. Pierre-Georges Roy, "Sieur de Vincennes Identified," Indiana Historical Society *Publications,* vol. 7, no. 1 (Indianapolis: C. E. Pauley and Co., 1923): 1–130.

11. Marcel Trudel, *An Atlas of New France* (Quebec: Laval University, 1973), 175.

12. *American State Papers: Public Lands,* List E, Claimants which "ought to be confirmed," paper #205, 2:382–88. Margaret R. Waters, *Indiana Land Entries,* 2 vols.; Vincennes District, Part 1, 1807–1877 (Indianapolis, 1949), 2:105–22 passim.

13. Joseph Henry Vanderburgh Somes, *Old Vincennes* (New York: Graphic Books, 1962), 64.

14. Extensive files of correspondence and research into Bailly's lineage by Olga Mae Schieman are contained in St. Mary-of-the-Woods Archives, St. Mary-of-the-Woods, Ind.

15. Sarah P. Rubinstein, "The French Canadians and French," in *They Chose Minnesota,* ed. by June Drenning Holmquist (St. Paul: Minnesota Historical Society Press, 1981), 38.

16. Additional information on the Richardville connection is found in Donald Chaput, "The Family of Drouet de Richerville: Merchants, Soldiers, and Chiefs of Indiana," *Indiana Magazine of History,* 74 (June 1978): 103–16.

17. Mary Elizabeth Wood, *French Imprint on the Heart of America* (Knightstown, Ind.: The Bookmark, 1977), 105. Wood and other historians frequently claim "noble French ancestry" for titled names. Many of these titles (such as Vincennes) relate to North American land grants and do not necessarily indicate nobility.

18. B. J. Griswold, *The Pictorial History of Fort Wayne, Indiana,* 2 vols. (1917; reprint, Evansville, Ind.: Unigraphic, Inc., 1971), 1:48. Also Wood, *French Imprint,* 47.

19. Griswold, *Pictorial History of Fort Wayne,* 1:48; Wood, *French Imprint,* 105.

20. Wood, *French Imprint,* 195.

21. Ibid., 105.

22. *Illustrated Historical Atlas,* county maps as referenced.

23. Wood, *French Imprint,* 105.

24. Waters, *Indiana Land Entries,* 2:104, 106.

25. *American State Papers: Public Lands,* 2:383.

26. *Dit* names are a common problem in French Canadian genealogy. Translated "called," these names probably originated with the military or former military personnel in New France. The percentage of persons using a *dit* name in North America is significantly higher than the 10 percent in France.

27. *Valley of the Upper Maumee River,* 2 vols. in 1 (1889; reprint, Evansville, Ind.: Unigraphic, Inc., 1974), 1:212.

28. John F. Lang, "The Catholic Church in Allen County," in ibid., 2:413.

29. Ibid., 1:212.

30. Wallace A. Brice, *History of Ft. Wayne from the Earliest Known Accounts* (1868; reprint, Evansville, Ind.: Unigraphic, Inc., 1971), 71.

31. Gregory Rose, "The Distribution of Indiana's Ethnic and Racial Minorities in 1850," *Indiana Magazine of History,* 87 (Sept. 1991): 242.

32. Ibid., 243.

33. Manuscript Census for 1860, Knox County, reel 272, pp. 1081–1174, passim.

34. Ralph L. Brooks, *The Village that Slept Awhile* (Indiana Department of Conservation, State Parks Division, 1956), 2–3.

35. Ibid., 3.

36. Betty Lawson Walters, *Furniture Makers of Indiana, 1793–1850* (Indianapolis: Indiana Historical Society, 1972), 46.

37. Manuscript Census for 1860, De Kalb County, reel 254, p. 161.

38. Ibid., Noble County, reel 285, p. 310.

39. Walters, *Furniture Makers of Indiana,* 62, 190.

40. Manuscript Census for 1860, Adams County, reel 242, p. 151.

41. Ibid., Elkhart County, reel 252, p. 24.

42. Ibid., Decatur County, reel 253, p. 684.

43. Ibid., Adams County, reel 242, p. 173.

44. Ibid., De Kalb County, reel 254, p. 145.

45. Ibid., Allen County, reel 243, p. 650.

46. Leon F. Bouvier, *Think about Immigration: Diversity in the United States* (New York: Walker and Co., 1988), 45.

47. David M. Reimers, *The Immigrant Experience* (New York: Chelsea House, 1989), 45.

48. From 1910 to 1940 statistics for Newfoundland were not included in immigration or emigration statistics for Canada. Had they been included statistics for those years might be slightly higher.

49. Wood, *French Imprint,* 73.

50. John Ade, *Newton County, 1853–1911* (Indianapolis: Bobbs-Merrill, 1911), 203.

51. George E. Green, *History of Old Vincennes and Knox County, Indiana,* 2 vols. (Chicago: S. J. Clarke Publishing Co., 1911); Griswold, *Pictorial History of Fort Wayne;* Brice, *History of Ft. Wayne; Valley of the Upper Maumee;* Wood, *French Imprint.* Entries passim in all publications.

52. Manuscript Census for 1860, Floyd County, reel 257, pp. 166–440, passim.

53. *Counties of Porter and Lake Indiana* (Chicago: F. A. Battey and Co., 1882), 615.

54. *History of Dearborn, Ohio, and Switzerland Counties, Indiana* (Chicago: Weakley, Harraman and Co., 1885), 833–34.

55. *Counties of Porter and Lake,* 696.

56. Ibid., 243–44.

57. Hubert Hawkins and Robert R. McClarren, eds., *Indiana Lives* (Hopkinsville, Ky.: Historical Record Association, 1967), passim.

58. Manuscript Census for 1860, Clark County, reel 248, pp. 476, 478, 481, 483, 484.

59. Manuscript Census for 1860, Indiana, passim.

60. *Indianapolis News,* 25 May 1911.

# CHINESE

R. KEITH SCHOPPA

*It was not only the emergence of professional Chinese on the Indianapolis stage that altered Hoosier views of the Chinese, but it was also world events. The efforts of patriotic Chinese to reconstruct their country in the 1930s fell before the onslaught of the Japanese attack first in Manchuria in 1931 and then in a general war in 1937 and after. As Americans were upset by the newsreels that showed the brutality of the Japanese attack against Chinese civilians, the earlier condescension and ignorant bemusement of the Chinese turned to compassion and concern. The Chinese community in Indianapolis, evidencing their patriotism, played a role in sending money to the imperiled Chinese nation.*

An article in the *Indianapolis Star Magazine* in March 1949 called the Chinese the "least known among Indiana's minority groups."[1] Making the Chinese of Indiana and their story known requires an analysis of at least five major components that are part of any immigrant experience: the patterns and timing of the immigration; the native culture of the immigrants; the spatial, social, political, cultural, and economic contexts into which they came; their settlement patterns; and their social outlooks and interactions in their new contexts. These components are not discrete but interact in dynamic fashion continuously over time in a process known as the immigrant experience.

## Laundrymen and Restaurateurs: The First Phase, 1870s–1910s

The first Chinese immigrants came to the United States in the early 1850s, in the wake of the gold rush, to the Frontier West, where they were brought to provide labor in mines, forests, railroads, agriculture, labor-intensive industries, and the "women's work" of cooking and washing.[2] Composed mostly of young male peasants, they came mainly from seven counties in the vicinity of Guangzhou (Canton) in south China; up to 60 percent of them came in fact from one county, Taishan, with a soil that because of its rocks and hills could feed less than half its people even in years of good harvests.[3] Initially, most did not come to be permanent residents, but to work a number of years, send money regularly to their families in China, and eventually return to their homeland in their later years.

Though they were perhaps for many years uprooted from their native culture, most did not sink roots down into American soil. In the midst of the new contexts they maintained their cultural identity as Chinese, holding to those commonalities of culture that had developed over the centuries among both Chinese elites and masses. These included a deep attachment to their native place with all its important "localisms"—traditions, food, and local products—and a central focus on the family unit, based as it was on patriarchal authority and a pragmatic sense that the family's character was "as much an enterprise group" as it was anything else.[4] Though the immigrant was taken from the family circle, he was advancing the "enterprise group" through his actions. During his years in the United States, the immigrant maintained the psychology of the sojourner:

one who clings to [the] cultural heritage of his own ethnic group and tends to live in isolation, hindering

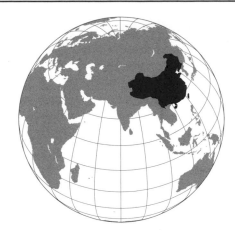

his assimilation in the society in which he resides. . . .
The sojourn is conceived by the sojourner as a "job"
which is to be finished in the shortest possible time. . . .
He is comparable to the "marginal man."[5]

He was, in effect, not an active participant in American culture, for his eyes remained on China where there was home and family: "Consciousness of being a full participant in the total political, cultural, and social arrangements of the Chinese state and Chinese civilization was what being Chinese was all about."[6]

The sense of marginality, of sojourning, was only exacerbated by the increasingly hostile reactions that Chinese laborers began to draw. While American employers saw Chinese workers as a cheap labor force (mostly young men with no families in this country), American workers were infuriated by Chinese who, they alleged, were taking jobs from whites. Economic resentment fueled racial and cultural misunderstandings and fears; in economic hard times, like the Panic of 1873 and its depression aftermath, violence erupted in murders, lynchings, and the destruction of property. Racism created a sameness in some people's minds between blacks and Chinese; and for many in the West the alleged black excesses of Reconstruction in the South stood as a warning about what the "yellow" race might become. This racism and fear became the backdrop for the efforts beginning in the late 1870s to restrict Chinese immigration.[7]

The first Chinese residents in Indiana apparently arrived in the 1870s, for Chinese first appear in the census of 1880. They came at a time that was not very conducive to multiracial harmony and understanding. The state as a whole did not indeed draw many foreign born. In his account of Indiana during the Gilded Age and the Progressive Era, Clifton Phillips notes that "Although Indiana absorbed many thousands of Germans, Irish, and other northern Europeans in the nineteenth century, it remained remarkably homogeneous, with a proportion of foreign-born residents which was extremely small in

comparison with most other industrial states."[8] In 1920 its population was 92.1 percent native-born white—the highest proportion in the United States.[9]

Into this rather intimidating context came the first Chinese immigrants. Though there were only thirteen in the state in 1880, the data on even this small number confirm their similarity to those Chinese of the initial great wave of immigration into the West.[10] All thirteen were males, ranging in age from twenty-one to twenty-eight, and all but one were unmarried—single sojourners coming to make their fortune. The occupation of eleven of the 1880 Chinese was laundryman; one was listed as a "huckster"; and the last resided in the Hospital for the Insane.

Settlement patterns revealed the realities of the Indiana context and of the Chinese response to it. Ten of the thirteen lived in Indianapolis; two resided in Richmond; and one in Crawfordsville. The three urban residence sites lie in the center of the state, with Chinese avoiding both the south, populated by many whose heritage was the pre–Civil War South, and the north as well. Chinese settlement in Indiana was from the beginning basically urban. Rural Chinese were not attracted to rural Indiana. The corn culture of Indiana bore no similarity to the paddy culture and sericulture of Guangdong. In addition, though the state was generally homogeneous, the cities and towns had more diversity than the rural areas. It was easier for queue-wearing Chinese men and foot-bound Chinese women (the few that there were), speaking Cantonese and living according to the tenets of an alien culture, to live in the urban centers than in the more conservative countryside or village.

By 1890 there was a somewhat more dispersed quality to the Chinese settlement. Thirty-five counties reported resident Chinese, though the numbers in all were small. Only Marion County (Indianapolis) and Allen County (Fort Wayne) reported double-digit population—the former, twelve, and the latter, eleven. Eleven of the counties reported only one resident Chinese; twelve reported two; nine reported three; and one reported four.[11] This greater dispersal from 1880 points not to a farmer's life in rural Indiana for these Chinese, but likely underscores the conclusion of a commentator several decades later: "Almost every Indiana city of any size boasts one Chinese restaurant as well as a laundryman or two."[12] It is clear that after 1900 the trend to urban residentiality became even more marked.

Though there were never enough Chinese to make up a "Chinatown" in Indianapolis as in other major cities, Chinese still tended to concentrate their residences in the same general area. In the last years of the nineteenth century, "there was a geographically defined Chinese community along Fort Wayne and Massachusetts avenues, anchored by hand laundries,

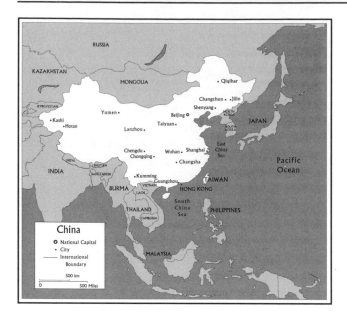

restaurants and discreet social clubs where men wagered on mah-jongg and fan tan games."[13]

The history of Chinese immigration into Indiana has been shaped largely by the immigration policies of the United States government. Reacting to bitter anti-Chinese sentiment on the West Coast, Congress passed the first national law suspending Chinese immigration in 1882. Originally to last for a ten-year period, the exclusion act was extended into the 1920s, when it was made even more stringent, and continued into the 1940s. In the country as a whole, these decades were a period of unremitting hostility to Chinese, a reality that led many to choose to return to China. Discrimination and laws kept Chinese from owning land, from holding certain jobs, from intermarrying, and from voting.[14] It is little wonder that in most areas the Chinese population declined.

In the state the numbers of Chinese inched slowly higher. In 1898, for example, the *Indianapolis News* reported that only one out of 905 steerage passengers bound for Indiana was from China.[15] But beginning with the 1910 census the numbers stagnated until the 1950s.

### Chinese Population in Indiana[16]

| | |
|---|---|
| 1880 | 13 |
| 1890 | 89 |
| 1910 | 273 |
| 1920 | 283 |
| 1930 | 279 |

There is no data indicating that the Chinese in Indiana suffered especially harsh treatment during these years. It is likely that the almost infinitesimally small numbers of Chinese in the state kept them from being seen as a threat as they were in some other regions of the country. The fact

that almost all resided in Indianapolis also lowered their general visibility in the state.

One pattern of the early Chinese immigration into the state seems clear. Indiana was a secondary settlement objective: most Chinese chose to come to Indiana after they had first resided in other states. The seventy-six more Chinese in Indiana in 1890 than in 1880 (entering after the passage of the exclusion act) likely sought residence in the state after an initial residence elsewhere in the country. As a specific example, one of the most well-known Chinese immigrants in the years from the 1880s to 1910 was Moy Kee, who filed for naturalization in New York City in 1880, before the exclusion law was passed. Moy's naturalization was completed and sworn in Indianapolis in the fall of 1888.[17] It is not known why Moy and others chose to come to Indiana. As in traditional Chinese society, it is probable that personal connections—either family or native place ties—to already established Indianapolis residents were the attraction for most.

In the unfamiliar surroundings where new immigrants did not understand the realities of the local situation, much less the language, the emergence of a community patriarch was a logical cultural development. In China a local population normally looked to its elite members for leadership both in daily affairs and in special community needs—whether in charity, public works, or mediation. In the early years of this century Moy Kee had emerged as such a paternalistic figure. He was apparently a very successful businessman. He began with a tea store on Massachusetts Avenue on the block between Pennsylvania and Delaware streets, challenging the business of H. H. Lee, who had monopolized the tea business in the city to that point. Moy's business interests spread first to Oriental wares—porcelains, fans, and lacquerware—and then to a restaurant on East Washington Street.[18] His commercial success brought Moy status in the small Chinese community, and both Chinese and local authorities sought him out as the man to turn to in times of difficulty. A piece in the *Indianapolis Star* noted that "in the Juvenile court, Nazaphor Evans, a colored girl, was arraigned for stealing a watch, a diamond pin, and $120 from Ching Wing, a Maryland St. laundryman. Moy Kee, Chinese Mayor of Indianapolis, acted as interpreter."[19]

Social interactions between natives and immigrants are always problematical; neither understands the cultural approaches and values of the other. Stereotypes of one offer the uncertain other some false certainty through the misrepresentation of reality. In this vein Chinese were crafty, silent and inscrutable, and mysterious. An article in the *Indianapolis Star Magazine* in March 1949 noted the mundane and normal Chinese lives, then continued:

"But in the dim laundries tucked away on side streets, there remains an air of mystery. . . . Here the casual visitor meets blank expressions . . . [and] has little chance of striking up a conversation."[20]

But what happened when a Chinese did not act as expected, when he contravened all stereotypes, when he perhaps went beyond generally accepted American standards of "normal" behavior? There are very few records of Chinese in Indianapolis for the late nineteenth and early twentieth centuries. It is intriguing that of the small handful of Chinese residents there are at least two who were committed to the Central Indiana Hospital for the Insane. One, Yung Lee, was recorded in the 1880 census. Another, Wah Sing, was deported in 1906. To be sure, both men may have indeed been insane. But, as Jonathan Spence has suggested, insanity may be a culture-specific condition; and it may thus be defined differently across cultures.[21] Having roughly 1 percent of the Chinese population committed for insanity during these years (two of roughly two hundred) seems a rather high rate of institutionalization. There is at least the possibility that these men's actions were perceived as unusual enough because of cultural ignorance, fear, or repugnance.

Nothing is known of Yung Lee's situation; it is Wah Sing's case that raises questions. Wah was the nephew of Moy Tom, an established restaurateur in the Indianapolis Chinese community.[22] Initially Wah Sing had been employed as a waiter in the restaurant, a good example of the role of connections in the immigration process. A man of obvious ability, Wah grew prosperous enough to open his own restaurant on North Illinois Street. It was there, according to newspaper reports, that he began to show undisclosed "signs of insanity." He was eventually declared insane and incarcerated, but his unhappiness at being locked up led asylum administrators to contact his friends about taking him back to China. When Moy Tom picked him up at the asylum and was accompanying Wah to the train, Wah "slipped away through the crowd" and ended up at a police station, where he "talked pleasantly with a number of officers before his disappearance was reported." Apparently his insanity was unnoticed by the policemen, and it had not prevented him from finding his way around or experiencing happiness at logical times. In any case, whatever the truth of the situation (and only enough is known to make the case mysterious), Wah Sing left the next day with eight of his fellow sojourners to return to China.[23]

One Chinese social institution that made its way to Indianapolis was the tong, a secret society that functioned in many American Chinatowns as a mutual aid group— "believed to have resulted from the needs of a predominantly male society whose desires for rapid social advancement in America were blocked."[24] In large cities around the country the tong became synonymous with crime, racketeering, prostitution, drug trafficking, and vicious wars with rival tongs. Indianapolis also had its tong in the early years of the century, with at least one opium den fronting as a laundry and with attendant mysterious violence. One laundryman, Lee Sing, "died violently in a struggle with mysterious attackers who slashed his throat and escaped in broad daylight without being seen." The presence of the tong came to light when a police informant on a powerful New York City tong, the Highbinders, was advised by a rival tong to flee to Indianapolis for safety. He was told to meet one E. Lung in Indianapolis, an owner of a chain of Chinese laundries and a man who "appeared to be a quiet, reserved businessman."[25] Lung took the informant under his wing, paternalistically bringing him into his family. When the informant subsequently traveled to New Orleans to realize some greater sense of security, Lung followed to protect him, seen off by a crowd of Chinese at Union Station. Lung never returned; the speculation was that the Highbinders, who were also a significant force in New Orleans, did in both Lung and the informant.

The visit of a Chinese prince to Indianapolis in May 1904 provides interesting glimpses of the views of Indianans to China, Chinese, and the Chinese community in Indianapolis. Prince Pu Lun was a member of the Manchu imperial family, the great-great-great-grandson of the Qianlong Emperor, one of China's most impressive monarchs, who ruled from 1736 to 1795. The prince himself was twice suggested as heir to the throne—in 1875 and 1908; both times the empress dowager, the main power broker in the last decades of Manchu rule, rejected him.[26] Many Indianans who welcomed Pu Lun believed he would one day sit on the Dragon Throne.[27]

Pu Lun came to the United States to attend the Louisiana Purchase Exposition in St. Louis. Wong Kai Kah, Yale University graduate and vice-imperial commissioner from the Chinese government to the exposition, invited Pu Lun to Indianapolis.[28] During his stay in the United States, Wong made Indianapolis his base under the urgings of personal friend William Fortune, newspaperman, civic leader, and onetime president of the State Board of Commerce.[29] There is little doubt that the capital elites saw the ten-day visit as an exceptional opportunity to impress upon the potential future Chinese leader the educational and industrial glories of Indianapolis and the agricultural bounty of the state. Behind every speech and encomium was the alluring vision of the China market. On the prince's arrival, the leader of the State Board of Commerce pointedly noted that there was "not a county seat that did not manufacture some article for which its manufacturers seek a market outside of the

State."[30] H. H. Hanna, the chairman of the state committee on the extension of trade relations, later during the visit conveyed the wish that a Chinese commission be sent to "present to the merchants your claims for the need and desirability to our people of the merchandise and general industrial products of your labor, and at the same time to become informed of what we provide that may be desirable or necessary for the pleasure, comfort, and nourishment of your people, or the construction of the great public works and institutions that seem certain soon to be built in the physical and economic development of China."[31]

In the prince's party (riding from Union Station to the statehouse in a carriage) were Moy Kee and Pang W. Jung, owner of an Oriental goods store and Moy's business partner. It is hard to imagine the awe with which these leaders of the small Chinese community approached the potential Son of Heaven, the focal point of the traditional culture to which they still held allegiance. In the receiving line, "some men carelessly went by with their hats on. The two Indianapolis Chinese who joined the line of handshakers bowed to him elaborately, almost touching the floor with their heads" (in the traditional kowtow). When the prince was seated, Moy and Pang, who sat on the platform, presented two bouquets, one wrapped in celebratory red paper with Moy's name card. The reaction of the nonelite Indianapolis Chinese is not known, but Moy, as their leader, did not forget them at this once-in-a-lifetime event. When Moy and Pang met the prince later at the Claypool Hotel, Moy invited him to his home and restaurant, where "a few of his countrymen in this city" could meet the prince and "have some slight form of refreshment."[32] This took place at a luncheon on 27 May. The Chinese must have marveled: in China, persons of their low social status would never have dreamed of being able to meet, much less eat with, a likely emperor—only as sojourners in Indiana! Moy himself was reportedly "thrown into raptures over such an honor." At his restaurant, "oriental rugs were spread from the street to a teakwood table and intricately inlaid chairs covered with crimson satin draperies. On the carved tables were burning incense, oriental delicacies 'of every kind,' and Chinese wine."[33]

On paper Pu Lun's schedule looks exhausting: a continuous round of visits to schools, industry, and public institutions (prisons, institutes for the blind and for the deaf, and the Central Indiana Hospital for the Insane). His hosts worried over what he should eat; a newspaper marveled over his love of ice cream and noted at one meal that he "ate lightly of American dishes, but . . . drew deep breaths of enjoyment through numerous heavy cigars." Speeches noted the close relationship between China and the United States and praised the prince's insight and his future leadership.[34]

Beneath the surface of the ceremony and the hyperbole of speeches were hints of the less positive views of Chinese and their role in Indiana during the Progressive Era. Newspaper reports reflect many of the ambivalent attitudes to this "strange" culture and its upholders; speeches reveal a mixture of American idealism and paternalism—in the aftermath of the Spanish-American War—to "the little brown brother." These are significant in the study of the Indiana Chinese because they reveal the daily attitudes that the Chinese had to face even if there is no record of outright violence against them in Indianapolis. The discrimination was an ongoing reality.

On the third day of the prince's visit, a newspaper published the following poem, calling for good weather after the clouds and rain of the first two days.[35] Addressed in the poem is the dragon, the symbol of China; the poet notes that on "the Chinese flag is a dragon trying to swallow the sun." The telling point is that the poem is written in black dialect.

*Mr. Dragon, Cough Up Dat Sun*

Oh Mr. Dragon, cough up dat sun.
We need him to shine on good Prince Pu Lun.
Dribe back dem clouds o'er de Prince's train.
He ain't huntin dat kind ob rain.

Dem Chinese umbrellas are built for style,
If you git 'em wet, dey's boun' to spile.
An' all dat yellow's a-gwine to run
If you, Mr. Dragon, don't cough up dat sun.

And dem bright glad rags what de ladies got
If de son don't shine, is boun' to spot
An' git all drabbled like an' shrink
An' dat mud'll make 'em black as ink.

How kin we look our very best
When de blamed ole rain don' take no rest?
What will become of all our fun
If you, Mr. Dragon, don' cough up dat sun?

The racist linkage, at least, in the mind of the poet (and likely the newspaper's readers) between the "colored" cultures of the black and of the Chinese seems clear; it stands in sharp contrast to the civilized, even sophisticated, public treatment of the prince and the Indianapolis Chinese elites.

Another indication of the attitude of the times was the furor that developed among certain Christian ministers when Pu Lun's schedule did not include a Sunday morning church service. Some argued matter-of-factly that it would have been reasonable for the prince, who was seeing many other aspects of Indiana culture, to visit a church. But there was considerable condescension running through the arguments raised by some ministers: "Why did they not take him to church, if for no other purpose than to give him an opportunity to contrast a Christian service with his own joss worship?" The dismissal of Chinese religious practices in this way points to the disgust with the assumed superstitious nature of the "heathen" Chinese. Another, as if to pit the American nation against the Chinese, declared that "The *American* sabbath was outraged in a public way" [emphasis added].[36]

Yet another episode of the prince's visit was the late arrival of Miss Wong Ah Mae to be with Mr. and Mrs. Wong Kai Kah. Miss Wong, a medical student in Toronto, had tried to enter the United States at Detroit but was turned back because of her Chinese identity, despite having all her proper papers and identification. Eventually she entered via upper New York State and arrived at Indianapolis in time to be on the dais at the women's reception for the prince at the Propylaeum.[37] Her difficulty in entering the country became a topic at the German House "smoker" held for the prince. The treatment of Miss Wong was decried in a resolution sent to President Theodore Roosevelt, "declaring against the crude interpretation of the Chinese exclusion act." This act of personal support for an individual Chinese closely related to the Chinese host of the guest of honor was ultimately undercut by the assertion at the smoker that the body was "not questioning the wisdom of the so-called Chinese exclusion act."[38] Individual Chinese with the proper connections were clearly placed in a different category from Chinese en masse.

In the first decade of the century yet one more indication of the attitudes toward Chinese comes from a compilation called "The Life of Our Foreign Population" by John H. Holliday, president of the Immigrants' Aid Society. After a brief listing of the numbers of Chinese in Indianapolis (they appear to be vastly underestimated) and some of their laundries and restaurants, the text calls for "uplifting these strange brethren by all means available."[39] Though the intent of the essay is to include all foreigners, it is the Chinese and Japanese who are mentioned immediately before the society's goals. The organization's aims were clearly assimilation and defensive action "to maintain the standards of American life"; the methods were to be the "protection, enlightenment and evangelization of the immigrant population."[40]

As for enlightenment through education of the Chinese children at this time, records of the Indianapolis Public Schools show that there were only three foreign-born Chinese among the schoolchildren in September 1909.[41] This small number does not include Chinese who were born in Indianapolis. It does, however, underscore the

effects of the exclusion acts on the influx of Chinese into the state. The greater context for this statistic was the general decline in the number of foreign born in Indianapolis and the state as a whole in the first decades of the century. In the capital city the percentages in 1900, 1910, and 1920 were 10.1, 8.5, and 5.4, respectively; while statewide, the percentages in 1910, 1920, 1930, and 1940 were 5.9, 5.1, 4.4, and 3.2, respectively.[42]

## Transition to a New Chinese Identity: 1920s to 1960

United States immigration policies and developments within China joined to give rise to a different type of Chinese immigrant after the first wave of sojourning laborers. The exclusion that was enacted into law in 1882 and extended to 1943 allowed only certain classes of Chinese to enter the country. These included merchants and government officials and their families, teachers, ministers, newspaper editors, students, and tourists. Though these immigrants still might be considered sojourners, the men and women came from higher social classes than the laundrymen and restaurateurs, and they had as their objective not simply making money but learning the secrets of Western modernization and subsequently returning to China to help reconstruct their country. They were ineligible for citizenship. According to the Immigration Act of 1924, only students pursuing master's degrees or doctorates were eligible for immigration; but there were substantial numbers of such students ready to enter.[43]

In 1912 the Manchu regime of which Prince Pu Lun had been a representative was overthrown in a revolution that ushered in a republic; gone were any hopes Hoosiers may have had that their royal treatment of the prince would reap economic benefits for the state. But the Chinese hopes that a new, stronger nation was being constructed, capable of dealing effectively with the West, were also dashed in the four-year presidency of autocratic Yüan Shih-k'ai and in the devastating warlord period that followed his death. From 1916 to 1928 there was no effective central control in the country. The May Fourth Movement, taking its name from a demonstration against decisions at the Versailles Peace Conference in 1919, initiated a revolution against traditional Chinese thoughts and ways. Out of this cultural revolution came the Chinese Communist party (Gongchandang) and a reconstructed Nationalist party (Guomindang) of Sun Yat-sen. In the mid-1920s the Nationalists, overcoming the perceived Communist threat, fought to a military victory over the warlords and reestablished some semblance of order and central control.

The new regime had a definite West-leaning character. Though President Chiang Kai-shek had not been trained in the West, his wife had been graduated from Wellesley College; similarly, many in the top leadership posts had been educated in the United States. Many young Chinese from elite backgrounds, hoping to help reconstruct their nation, came to study in the United States, focusing in the main on science and technology, the disciplines that seemed to be the keys for national development. From the Chinese perspective, it was imperative that these temporary intellectual sojourners return with their expertise. Most did, but there were some who chose to remain for various reasons in the United States.

In Indiana Chen Ko-kuei and his wife Ling Shu-hao epitomize the nature of the new immigration—from elite family background to higher education in the United States to leading professionals in their adopted community. Though Chen's specific social background is not known, Ling's father had been governor of Zhili Province in north China. She remembered years later that they had lived in a government house with sixty rooms and twenty servants.[44] From Chen's educational experiences in China, his social status was surely among the elite. They met at the Peking Union Medical School after he had graduated from Qinghua University (often called China's MIT), and she had attended Beijing University. Chen came to the United States in 1918, attaining a Ph.D. in physiology and pharmacology from Wisconsin in 1923 and, in 1927, his M.D. from the Johns Hopkins School of Medicine. Ling received her M.D. from the (Case) Western Reserve in Cleveland in 1928. The couple was married in 1927.[45]

Chen served as an associate in pharmacology at the Johns Hopkins School of Medicine until 1929 when he joined Eli Lilly and Company in Indianapolis. Though they returned once to China in 1936, they had made the decision to remain permanently in Indiana and to become Americanized. He chose to be known in Western style as K. K. Chen and she, Amy. A 1941 newspaper description notes that their home, "though thoroughly American, retains the atmosphere of quiet dignity, of perfection of detail, which is so typical of their own country."[46] Both Chens were able researchers in the Pharmacology Division, with K. K. serving as director until his retirement in 1963. From various Chinese herbs, Chen developed the cold medicine ephedrine; and with Amy developed various cardiac drugs from research with toads. In addition, K. K. developed "cyanide poison antidotes" and "new synthetic analgesics." He was a member of the Indiana University School of Medicine from 1937 into the late 1960s. In 1965 he was awarded the Remington Medal, which is "awarded each year to an individual who has given outstanding service to American pharmacy."[47]

The point of this biographical information is to underscore the differences between the Chens and the earlier Chinese immigrants. The Chens' elite backgrounds, their advanced education, and their scientific contributions recognized on a national scale separate them by a large gulf from former Indianapolis Chinese elites like Moy Kee or E. Lung, the tong chieftain. Moreover, the reaction of the non-Chinese of Indianapolis to the Americanized professional Chinese was much more supportive. The Chens' lives and contributions were featured in Indianapolis newspapers in 1941 and 1972, with mention in at least one other feature story in 1949. The white establishment saw the Chens as legitimate in their Americanization. One other noteworthy point is that the professional Chinese had children who became as professional and upper middle or upper class as their parents. The Chens' son, Tao-yuan, became a surgeon; and their daughter, Mei, married a professor at the University of Missouri.[48]

It was not only the emergence of professional Chinese on the Indianapolis stage that altered Hoosier views of the Chinese, but it was also world events. The efforts of patriotic Chinese to reconstruct their country in the 1930s fell before the onslaught of the Japanese attack first in Manchuria in 1931 and then in a general war in 1937 and after. As Americans were upset by the newsreels that showed the brutality of the Japanese attack against Chinese civilians, the earlier condescension and ignorant bemusement of the Chinese turned to compassion and concern. The Chinese community in Indianapolis, evidencing their patriotism, played a role in sending money to the imperiled Chinese nation. A report in the *Indianapolis News*, two months after general war erupted, noted that the Indianapolis "Chinatown," composed of "sixty-five men, women, and children have contributed more than $1000 to China." Restaurateur Harry K. Jung reported that nationwide the Chinese had contributed two million dollars for supplies in the Chinese war effort.[49] At the Chinese New Year in 1938, always the chief holiday of the year for Chinese at home or abroad, the main celebration consisted of collecting more contributions for the war effort; Joe Bing, owner of an Indianapolis tea importing business, headed the collections committee.[50]

One important element in the demography of Indiana Chinese that remained little changed in the period until the end of the war was the wide discrepancy in sex ratios. Generally, women had not accompanied the peasants who came in the first wave of Chinese immigration, as they remained home to await the sojourners' return. With the stringent immigration laws in force, the situation could not change much. Only two groups of women could enter the country according to the 1882 statute: students and wives of merchants and government officials. In the nativist

1920s, it became even more difficult for women to enter the country. A 1921 law stated specifically that "an alien-born woman marrying a citizen could no longer automatically assume his citizenship."[51] According to the 1924 law, alien-born women could not even enter the country to join their spouses. Little wonder that the ratio of women to men remained very low. The following table reveals the pattern:

### Chinese Male and Female Population in Indiana, 1910–1950[52]

| Year | Total | Males | Percent | Females | Percent |
|------|-------|-------|---------|---------|---------|
| 1910 | 259 | 251 | 97% | 8 | 3% |
| 1920 | 278 | 272 | 98% | 6 | 2% |
| 1930 | 273 | 242 | 89% | 31 | 11% |
| 1940 | 207 | 169 | 82% | 38 | 18% |
| 1950 | 431 | 324 | 75% | 107 | 25% |

The pattern shows that the percentage of women was slowly increasing. In part this can be explained by the increasing numbers of Indiana-born Chinese women, though those numbers were inching up only slowly. The percentage of Indiana-born Chinese of the total Chinese population in Indiana increased from only 29.3 percent in 1910 to 34.3 percent in 1940. In part the increase in women in 1950 over that of 1940 can be explained by the shift in immigration policy in 1943.

That year, as a result of the wartime alliance into which the attack on Pearl Harbor had thrown the United States and China, the United States government repealed the Exclusion Act of 1882. But the annual quota that was established for the Chinese was not generous; only 105 people of Chinese ancestry were permitted to enter. Chinese, however, could once again become naturalized citizens.[53] K. K. Chen and his wife "were naturalized in 1947, almost as soon as it was legally possible for them to be," after almost thirty years in the country and countless contributions in the field of science.[54] As for the immigration of women from China, in 1946 wives of citizens were allowed to enter "on a non-quota basis." And in mid-1947, the War Brides Act allowed about ten thousand Chinese wives of American GIs to enter the country.[55] These wartime and postwar immigration decisions changed the demographic sex-ratio configuration of resident Chinese in the country and the state of Indiana as much as the earlier restrictions had shifted the social class composition of resident Chinese.

By the end of the 1940s the Indianapolis Chinese community was in its initial stage of becoming a bifurcated society. There were the Chens and a few other professional or quasi-professional Chinese like P. H. Ho, portrait photographer of the political and social leaders of the state.[56] Though it was difficult to tell at the time, the world of the professional would be the trend of the future. This trend was difficult to detect because the majority of the Chinese in Indianapolis and other cities and towns in the state were still predominantly operators of laundries and restaurants. At midcentury there were still unmarried laundrymen and other businessmen in the city. Jim Moy, for example, over seventy years old, had been in Indianapolis since the mid-1920s. A native-born American, he had come to the city from Terre Haute. Though he had gone to China, he returned to establish his career in the United States. Like Hong Sing, another single laundryman, Moy lived in quarters behind the laundry—one room with a bed, stove, and radio. Another example of the older resident type was unmarried Charles Lee, a barber, who had lived in the city since the mid-1920s.

The settlement pattern in Indianapolis seemed changed from that of half a century earlier. In the early century, even without a "Chinatown," there was a distinct locus for Chinese settlement, but by midcentury families lived on the north, south, and west sides of the city. But the community's social and cultural structure looked much like it had fifty years earlier. Laundryman and Oriental gift shop owner Wellise K. Hui had inherited the mantle of Moy Kee as the advisor to many of the city's Chinese on a multitude of business and personal problems. With Harry Jung and Joe Bing, Hui had headed the China Relief Society in the late 1930s. He was married to the daughter of E. Lung, the tong chieftain, or as the 1949 article put it, the "past grand master of the Chinese masons." Mrs. Hui and her brother were the first Chinese born in the city of Indianapolis; she attended DePauw University, an indication that Chinese laundrymen and restaurateurs were intent on having the second generation enjoy more educational opportunities than they had. As an indication of the scarcity of traditional Chinese families (due largely

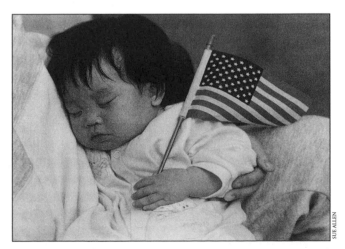

*Heidi Chen falls asleep celebrating being an American citizen, 1991.*

to the paucity of women), the Huis' daughter Cordelia was only the second Chinese girl born in the city—a whole generation after the first! Cordelia Hui's career points once again to the increasing education and professionalization among the Chinese community. A graduate of St. Mary-of-the-Woods College, she entered a law degree program at Indiana University and in 1949 was working on a master's degree at that school.[57] The children of laundryman William Lee followed the same pattern, with one daughter becoming a registered nurse and two sons studying premed at Indiana University. In Gary the son of laundryman Dong Ming Lee was the first Chinese-American graduate of Froebel High School.[58]

Two other patterns of Chinese immigration continued into this period. First, Indiana remained mainly a secondary site for immigrants. An example was newcomer Gene Chinn, a restaurateur who had come to Indianapolis from his original residence in Cleveland in the late 1940s. After his business was established, his cousin, Howard Wee, came with his family to join Chinn in the operation of the restaurant. Illustrative of immigration into Indiana because of family connections, the Wees had come to the United States from Guangzhou (Canton) and settled in New York City before they decided to resettle in Indiana.[59]

A second pattern was that Chinese residential settlement became even more concentrated in urban centers than it had been previously. A county analysis of the 1930 census figures shows a much greater concentration of Chinese in urban areas compared to the more dispersed 1890 population. Chinese in 1930 were residents in only twenty-six counties in the state (as compared to thirty-eight in 1890). Double-digit county population was found only in counties with larger urban centers: Lake (Gary and Hammond), St. Joseph (South Bend and Elkhart), Allen (Fort Wayne), Delaware (Muncie), Madison (Anderson), Wayne (Richmond), Vigo (Terre Haute), and Marion (Indianapolis).[60] A mapping of the counties with Chinese residents shows them as a band of counties on the state's northern border and a concentration, clustering to the northeast of Indianapolis, in the center of the state. Very few Chinese (only eleven) lived in counties to the south and east of Indianapolis.

This increasingly urban-centered nature of Chinese settlement by the early years of the century is striking.

### Urban and Rural Chinese Population, 1910–1940[61]

| Year | Urban | Percentage | Rural | Percentage |
|------|-------|-----------|-------|-----------|
| 1910 | 259 | 93.8 | 17 | 6.2 |
| 1920 | 278 | 98.2 | 5 | 1.8 |
| 1930 | 273 | 97.8 | 6 | 2.2 |
| 1940 | 207 | 99.5 | 1 | 0.5 |

These statistics parallel but are even more overwhelmingly urban than national statistics. In the country as a whole, 66 percent of Chinese in 1920 lived in cities over 25,000; by 1940, 91 percent lived in urban areas. In 1950 that figure had increased to 94 percent and in 1960 to 99 percent.[62] In contrast, the percentage of urban Chinese in Indiana had hovered around that top percentage since 1920. Though population statistics in the available municipal data from the 1950 census are given for only select cities in certain counties, it is clear that the trend continued— about 99 percent of the Chinese resided in urban centers, specifically the cities of Bloomington, East Chicago, Gary, Hammond, Evansville, Fort Wayne, Indianapolis, Muncie, South Bend, Valparaiso, West Lafayette, and nearby centers.[63]

By midcentury the white reaction to the Chinese—not only to the professional Chens but also to the nonprofessional stratum—was to recognize them as either assimilated or assimilable. The *Indianapolis Star Magazine* essay of 20 March 1949 calls the Chinese "more thoroughly American than the Smiths and Joneses." Even recent immigrant Mrs. Howard Wee, who could not speak a word of English, could, the article noted, function effectively in Hoosier society. The Chinese, the article avers, "are a quiet law-respecting group who live anonymously and like it that way." They are later again described as "quiet, church-going and thrifty." The author especially notes that Gene Chinn, restaurateur and recent immigrant, "attends church and Sunday School almost every Sunday" with his family.[64] Gone were the concerns with Chinese "joss worship" enunciated in the press and among Christian ministers forty-five years earlier or of the titillating violence and crime of Chinese tongs.

A crucial decision often facing the American-born Chinese—the second- or third-generation residents— was the choice between becoming Chinese or American; it is said that "most opted for assimilation or Americanization."[65] Certainly there are few on record who favored following their fathers' careers of laundrymen or restaurateurs. The *Star Magazine* essay notes that "the younger element, more used to American ways, are somewhat more independent than their elders."[66] The words of a restaurant owner in 1981 express clearly the dilemma for both older and younger Chinese, whether in the 1940s or the 1980s: "The kids now don't want to be tied down by the restaurant business. They want to get a degree and work for somebody else. My son now, he wants to be a policeman. With what (older brother) Henry and I know about Chinese food stuff, we could make him a millionaire. We could franchise this thing. We'd do it ourselves, but you got to have bodies—somebody to watch the back door while you're watching the front door."[67]

## Political and Social Divisions: A Diversity of Identities, 1970s–1990s

In the 1950s and 1960s immigration patterns once again shifted. From 1947 to 1949 a civil war raged in China between the Communists and Nationalists. After the Communist victory, United States support of the discredited Nationalist forces of Chiang Kai-shek and its opposition to Mao Zedong, coupled with the Chinese government's "leaning to one side" (the Socialist), led to years of implacable hostility. Without diplomatic relations, there was no immigration from the mainland. In addition, many mainlanders in the United States at the time of the break in relations were forced or chose to stay. As year followed year, they dispensed with any pretense that they were sojourners in the traditional sense. Several thousand Chinese were admitted to the United States under refugee acts. Many had strong educational and professional backgrounds, and the Chinese government had sent some to be educated and return as the vanguard for postwar reconstruction. Moreover, in the years after 1949, more liberal United States immigration policies attracted large numbers of students from the Republic of China on Taiwan, Hong Kong, and various countries in Southeast Asia.[68] These male and female immigrants came from a diversity of social class origins; although they were largely an educational elite, they represented a broader range of backgrounds and perhaps interests than either of the first two waves of immigration.

The Chinese civil war and the years of political separation it brought between the People's Republic on the mainland and the Republic of China on Taiwan substantially changed the old cultural identity that had united all Chinese. As the People's Republic strove to dismantle the old culture and as Taiwan began to adopt a modern capitalistic approach, traditional values seemed to be submerged in the quest for modernity. Columbia University Professor Myron Cohen has argued persuasively that in such a situation the "new definition of being Chinese is firmly rooted in nationalism."[69] Since Chinese nationalism developed out of a sense of Chinese inferiority, the new definition was based on negative and defensive views of the fatherland rather than on the old sense of cultural superiority. Such a perception increased the possibility that many Chinese living in the United States would be less likely than earlier immigrants to look to China, given the higher standard of living and the material wealth and power of their adopted country. This greater attachment to the United States did not completely overcome the strong attraction that the home country and its affairs had for many Chinese, but the shift in situation is notable. Such a political definition of identity

meant that political processes and events had the potential to modify and even shift allegiances and identity.

The United States immigration law of 1965 both confirmed and accelerated the trends of the late 1950s and early 1960s. It abolished the old system of racially based quotas with a new system of "preferences for quota immigrants," specifically allowing for the reunification of Chinese families and the entrance of large numbers of top-ranked Chinese students.[70] The 1970s saw the thaw in Cold War Sino-American relations with President Richard Nixon's trip to the People's Republic in February 1972. The Shanghai Communique, signed at the end of the stay, inaugurated cultural and educational exchanges. Seven years later, the Carter administration established diplomatic relations with the People's Republic, stimulating even more exchanges and student admissions. A 1979 amendment to the 1965 immigration law set up yearly quotas of twenty thousand for both Taiwan and the People's Republic. In 1988, in expectation of the 1997 return of Hong Kong to the People's Republic, its annual quota was raised to 5,000 (from 600). In the quarter century after the more liberal law was enacted, there were 460,000 immigrants under Chinese quotas and 150,000 nonquota immigrants from Taiwan and the People's Republic. In addition, the turmoil and instability in Vietnam, Laos, and Cambodia after 1975 gave rise to an exodus of several hundred thousand people who were largely ethnic Chinese. Studies have suggested that many of these former Indochinese nationals are identifying themselves in the 1990s as Chinese.[71]

Given this large increase in Chinese immigration, it is little wonder that Indiana has also seen a meteoric rise in the number of Chinese in the state. Because of the impossibility of determining the exact numbers of ethnic Chinese in the state, the following table should be seen as suggestive of the scope of the increase. While early censuses differentiated between native- and foreign-born Chinese, more recent censuses have not. The 1980 census asked respondents to report their ancestry group, yet the open-endedness of the question makes the validity of the answers difficult to determine. That census listed 2,688 foreign born and 5,212 who identified their only ancestry group as Chinese.[72]

### Chinese Population and Percentage Increase, 1930–1990[73]

| Year | Total | Percentage Increase |
|------|-------|---------------------|
| 1930 | 279   | −    1.4%           |
| 1940 | 208   | −   25.4%           |
| 1950 | 431   | + 107.2%            |
| 1960 | 986   | + 128.7%            |
| 1980 | 5,212 | + 428.6%            |
| 1990 | 7,371 | +   41.4%           |

The continuing strikingly urban nature of Chinese settlement is apparent in township statistics of foreign-born Chinese from the 1980 census.[74] They resided in thirty-eight of the ninety-two Indiana counties. In all but seven of those thirty-eight (Allen, Clay, Hamilton, Kosciusko, Marion, Montgomery, and Morgan), all Chinese population was centered in the township containing the county seat. Only in five counties were there rural or village foreign-born Chinese: Clay, Kosciusko, Montgomery, Morgan, and Ripley. Not only is the urban character of the immigrants noteworthy, but also the township concentration of the immigration suggests the traditional Chinese pattern of concentrated communities.

The census data of 1990 reveal that the Chinese population has not only increased but that it has also dispersed through most of the counties of the state.[75] Seventy-five of the ninety-two counties have Chinese residents. Those areas without Chinese population are a band of counties near the western border (from Benton and Carroll south to Clay), a cluster in the south (Martin, Orange, Crawford, Washington, Harrison, and Jennings), and a cluster in the southeast (Rush, Franklin, and Union). These counties contain no cities or major towns. Despite the more general dispersal of Chinese throughout the state, comparison of the Chinese with other East Asian immigrants (Japanese, Koreans, and Vietnamese) reveals some interesting points. While there are far fewer Japanese and Korean residents in the state (4,715 and 5,475, respectively), they are more widely dispersed than the Chinese. There are Japanese residents in eighty-eight of the ninety-two counties and Korean residents in ninety-one of the counties. These figures seem to suggest that the Chinese, who have a longer history of immigration than the other two groups, still tend to a greater concentration of residentiality. In contrast, the 2,467 Vietnamese residents reside in only sixty-three of the counties. Their pattern seems more like the Chinese; it should be remembered, moreover, that many of the Vietnamese nationals are ethnic Chinese. The reasons for this interesting pattern may be partly occupational (there may be more opportunities for Chinese in certain centers), and they may be partly cultural (various connections, perhaps native place or kin ties, to Chinese already resident in certain areas).

What is the nature of the Indiana Chinese in the period from the 1970s to the present? What has happened to the laundrymen and restaurateurs? And how has the incipient professional class of the war and postwar years fared? While the Chinese hand laundry has disappeared with the appearance of laundromats and residential washers and dryers, the Chinese restaurant has not. Many Indiana Chinese still own, operate, or are employed in such businesses. In 1981 restaurateur Paul Cheung of Indianapolis called the restaurant "the 'bloodline' of the Chinese family and community." For him and for others the restaurant has become not the stereotype of the Chinese American, but the very symbol. He says, "no matter how bad the times, you keep the restaurant open. When there's no business, you just pull the belt tighter. That's the Chinese way. Sell the house, give up all your money, but keep the restaurant open."[76] In 1991 there were at least 171 Chinese restaurants in the state; they were located in fifty-six cities and towns in thirty-nine counties.[77]

In many ways restaurants are indicators of immigration patterns and continuing Chinese cultural patterns. Like Gene Chinn's coming from Cleveland in the late 1940s, Lee Lai Fong and family came to Valparaiso in 1976 from Chicago, where he had been a cook at a major Chinese restaurant, and established the China House in the almost completely white northwest Indiana town.[78] It was another example of Indiana serving as a secondary destination for ethnic Chinese and of the opening up of a community to new ethnic cultures. Restaurants in the larger cities became "landing points" for other immigrants—Chinese and Indochinese in the 1960s, 1970s, and 1980s. Paul Cheung described how restaurateurs "provide[d] them with work in the kitchen and help in finding places to live" when they arrived with no money and no knowledge of English. He also claimed that the restaurants became schools in which cooks and waiters might learn the trade and start off on their own. Like the "insane" Wah Sing who learned the restaurant business in Moy Kee's restaurant in the early days of the century, twenty-five of the owners of Indianapolis's twenty-eight Chinese restaurants, according to Cheung, "worked with his family at one time or another."[79]

In some cases the restaurant culture merged with the increasingly dominant professional culture in these years. A Chinese medical doctor in Valparaiso financed and opened the Jade East restaurant in the 1970s, and a Chinese university professor in Muncie opened Chinese Gourmet and Arts, Inc., in 1973. Such efforts differed from those of the old restaurateurs in that they were not the primary source of livelihood for the owners. The Muncie store of Grace and Teh-kuan Chang featured artwork and furniture as well as food and cookware; they intended it to be "a showroom for their culture."[80] Occasionally the two cultures merged in marriage. Restaurateur Paul Cheung, for example, was married to a pediatrician.[81]

But more often than not the two cultures remained separate as the numbers of professional Chinese far surpassed those in the restaurant world and began in these years to celebrate their identity as Chinese elite professionals and their potential to contribute to American society. In 1984 an Indiana Chinese Professional Association was established. Meeting annually, its objectives are to bring together Chinese-American professionals, to establish networks of talent, and to seek opportunities for cooperation.[82] This organization reaches beyond Indianapolis Chinese; its head in 1990 was Franklin College political science professor Ling Yu-lang, and key participants were professors and scientists from Purdue and Butler universities. A special guest at the 1990 annual meeting was the vice chairman of the Republic of China's Northern United States office in Chicago. In addition to joint sessions and a banquet, the annual meeting's agenda includes discussion sessions divided according to professional interests: life sciences, mathematics and engineering, business, and society and politics. Such an organization enhances the sense of Chinese community and cooperation, as it leads to the possibility of Chinese contributions to issues and problems in the state.

Two important Indianapolis Chinese organizations were formed in these years: the Indianapolis Association of Chinese-Americans (IACA) in 1973 and the Taiwanese American Association (TAA) in the early 1980s. They were both dominated by professionals and their culture. But, more important, they included and emphasized the participation of families, and their agenda went far beyond calling upon professional background and expertise. Lillian Wang, president of the IACA in 1989, indicated in an interview that the restaurant people did not join these organizations because of their different backgrounds, educational levels, and dialect (they spoke Cantonese while IACA and TAA members spoke Mandarin), and because of their lack of time.[83] The following list of presidents of the IACA and their professions indicates clearly the professional base and orientation of this organization and of this significant group of Chinese.[84]

### Presidents of the IACA and Their Professions

| President | Year | Occupation |
| --- | --- | --- |
| David Wang | 1974 | mathematician & statistician, Indiana Bell |
| Peter Ho | 1975 | biochemist, Eli Lilly |
| Pao-Lo Yu | 1976 | genetics professor, Indiana U. Medical School |
| Terrence Yen | 1977 | biochemist, Eli Lilly |
| Eddie Tao | 1978 | biochemist, Eli Lilly |
| Bill Dawn | 1979 | business professor, Butler University |
| Sam Wang | 1980 | biochemist, Dow Chemical |
| Josephine Yu | 1981 | librarian, Belzer Junior High School |
| Clifford Yee | 1982 | engineer |
| Eusebio Young | 1983 | physician |
| Larry Gee | 1984 | engineer, General Motors |
| Kathleen Yee | 1985 | homemaker |
| James Ku | 1986 | sanitary engineer |
| | 1988 | |
| David Wong | 1987 | biochemist, Eli Lilly |
| Lillian Wang | 1989 | biologist, Eli Lilly |
| Hank Wong | 1990 | insurance actuary |
| Feng C. Zhou | 1991 | neurology professor, Indiana U. Medical School |

Like the IACA, the TAA is also primarily composed of professionals: doctors, professors, and research scientists and their families.[85] The immigrants making up both organizations were drawn to Indiana by their jobs.

Lillian Wang and Alfred Tsang, one of the IACA founders still active in the organization in the 1990s, are the epitomes of this stratum of Chinese residents, most of whom are first- and second-generation immigrants. Lillian Wang's parents are much like K. K. and Amy Chen, who came to the United States for an education in the 1920s. Wang's mother came about the same time to study at the University of Denver and Columbia; her father received a degree from the Colorado School of Mines. Like the Chens, Wang's parents remained in the United States. Wang and her husband David both received master's degrees from Purdue University and became Ph.D. candidates.[86] Alfred Tsang, who was born in China, has lived in the United States since he was twelve and in Indianapolis since 1967. "I was an engineer," he says, "when I found myself starting law school at 45. My

*Indianapolis Association of Chinese-Americans picnic.*

daughter has three degrees. My son is a graduate of Purdue and is now in night school studying for an MBA." Tsang, who served as a deputy state attorney general in the 1980s, sees the emphasis on a high level of education as stemming from Chinese traditions. He argues that "the Chinese child is expected to be an 'A' student—nothing less."[87]

The high level of professionalization among this stratum of Chinese and their drive for educational success is evident beyond Indianapolis. In his book, *Ethnics in Northwest Indiana*, Ernie Hernandez (himself part Chinese) notes the academic "high-achievers" from the region's Chinese families: there has been a spate of Chinese valedictorians and salutatorians in area high schools. In many cases, the fathers of these students were leading doctors such as Swei H. Tsung, a pathologist at Methodist Hospital in Gary, and James Dy of Portage. Dr. Wei-Ping Loh and his wife, also a medical doctor, were one of the first Chinese professional families in Gary, arriving about 1949; he was chief pathologist at Methodist Hospital from 1956 to 1981. Their children also excelled academically.[88] This pattern, which often has led the Chinese to be called "the model minority," is evident in Chinese communities around the state.

Alfred Tsang believes that the reputation of Chinese doctors and other professionals has enhanced the Chinese reputation in the eyes of many Hoosiers. He recalls trying a jury case at Princeton, known as the base for a powerful Democrat, when he was working as a state attorney general during a Republican administration. "I got a tremendous verdict. No one else from our office ever had any luck there. And I know why I won. The town had a Chinese physician. He had won their trust, and they transferred that trust to me."[89] Certainly the political opening to the People's Republic in the 1970s and subsequent exchanges have exposed more Hoosiers to Chinese culture and initiated a greater awareness of the Chinese and their contributions. Immediately after President Richard Nixon's 1972 visit restaurants noted an increase in business, with people asking to use chopsticks for the first time. Also, mainline American grocery stores began to offer wider stocks of Oriental vegetables and products.[90] Later in 1972, Indianapolis was one of four American cities to host the Shenyang Acrobatic Troupe.[91] The Changs' Muncie Chinese Gourmet and Arts, Inc., flourished in the beginning due partly to the China opening.[92]

But despite a greater openness, Alfred Tsang also feels that "people in Indiana haven't accepted plurality. There was a [Chinese] engineer here in the highway department who was very competent in a technical sense but had a language problem. He was afraid to be promoted. Felt he would be less secure."[93] Josephine Yu, who served as president of the IACA in 1981, says, "we still have to

educate Americans to be more broad-minded. My Oriental face still makes me the object of curiosity. In bigger cities, people would never stop to think about it. But in Indianapolis, you just don't see that many Chinese people."[94] In looking at life for the Indiana Chinese community, one must add to that acute sense of identity as a minority the difficulties in acculturation to American life. Josephine Yu remembers the difficulties: continuing to think in Chinese long after her arrival, or learning to stomach the idea of drinking cold milk.

In light of these realities, the voluntary Chinese associations dating from the 1970s and 1980s are expressions of the desire for community and mutual support. The rationale for the IACA is stated in the following way:

> The last decade had brought a rapid and steady influx of individuals with Chinese ancestry to the greater Indianapolis area. Chinese-Americans now occupy responsible positions in government, education and industry. Many own thriving businesses and have successful professional practices. As schools in the area gain prominence in higher education, the number of students with Chinese ancestry will increase. Due to the lack of a central organization, newcomers to the area do not have the opportunities that they should have to make acquaintance with other Chinese-Americans in the area. Similarly, many long time Chinese residents have left [sic] the need for a forum where common interests and problems can be shared and resolved.[95]

Similar organizations of Chinese do not exist elsewhere in the state, although informal networks that hold occasional dinners and sponsor holiday gatherings serve the same purpose.[96] The IACA, which has a membership of approximately 300 to 400, has four purposes, one of which is "to improve the overall well-being of Chinese-Americans in Indianapolis."[97] Similarly, the TAA, with 150 to 180 members, serves among other things as a mutual support and mutual help society.[98] But the goals go beyond this inner-directed desire for security and support.

Especially in the IACA there is considerable thrust to the non-Chinese community. Two other key goals are "to foster constructive citizenship on the part of all Chinese-Americans in the greater Indianapolis area" and "to enrich the Indianapolis society with more Chinese-American contributions."[99] With these goals in mind, the association now admits non-Chinese who are interested in China; and the TAA meetings (held about every two months) are open to the public—though they are conducted in Mandarin. The IACA holds symposia on topics such as how to prepare for leadership in American society and on the East-West culture clash. It has raised money for scholarships to high schools and colleges and donated money to the Indiana University Asian Studies program to help in a critical staffing matter.

Finally these organizations celebrate Chinese culture and traditions, though the IACA even tempers this objective with a gesture to their adopted homeland: "to cultivate understanding and appreciation of both American and Chinese cultural heritages."[100] The TAA celebrates key Chinese festivals, the Double Fifth Holiday and the Mid-Autumn Festival. The IACA's initial project after its founding in November 1973 was hosting a Chinese New Year dinner, attended in January 1974 by more than two hundred.[101] Though the 1991 activities of the IACA included a Christmas party and volleyball and ping-pong tournaments, the major activities focused on traditional Chinese holidays. The association also participates in the city's International Festival with culture, food, and merchandise booths.[102] These celebrations of Chinese holidays call to mind that the Chinese Americans still see the differences in themselves and non-Chinese Americans. Alfred Tsang's earlier mention of Chinese academic excellence attests to that. Josephine Yu's child-rearing techniques also point out the desire to retain key Chinese practices: "In China, children are taught to be very polite, not to be outspoken within the family. The American family is more liberal. Here, parents want children to learn from their mistakes. I raised my children the way I was raised, but I kept an open mind, so that they wouldn't get rebellious."[103] As an expression of the role Chinese parents play in regard to their teenagers, parents serve as advisors to the IACA's Youth Council, which organizes its own activities.

Although both the IACA and the TAA call themselves "non-political, non-religious, and non-partisan," there is a political difference reflecting Chinese politics in the home country. Lee Chao-hung, the president of TAA in 1991, suggested that the IACA is composed of those who identify the China of the Communist and Nationalist parties as their native place, while the TAA is made up of those who identify Taiwan as their native place. In the 1980s growing democratic trends in Taiwan had brought into the open long-standing dissatisfaction among some Taiwanese with rule by the Nationalist party. Taiwanese forces advocated a "free Taiwan," controlled neither by the Nationalists nor by the mainland Communists. It is possible to overdraw the differences between the TAA and the IACA, for an estimated one-third of TAA members are also IACA members; but the organization was established by "Taiwanese who want to have an association to belong to and identify themselves with" and "who feel that Taiwan needs its own identity."[104] The

TAA, for example, does not celebrate Double Ten, the commemoration of the overthrow of the Manchu regime in 1912—celebrated as National Day by the Nationalist government on Taiwan. It is notable that political differences over issues related to the homeland have given rise to different organizations in Indiana. Just as Indiana Chinese played roles in supporting China against the onslaught of Japan in World War II, Chinese in the 1980s and 1990s are acutely aware of and even participants in the issues facing China today.

The IACA membership application points to that group's concern about political issues and the role that its members might play in their adopted country.[105] Question 8 asks whether the applicant has citizenship in the United States or permanent residency. Question 9 asks: "Are you a member of any (a) foreign political party; (b) subversive organization; (c) foreign government agency?" Before their signatures, the applicants must agree that "we subscribe to the IACA purposes, *abide by the U. S. Constitution*, and meet the IACA membership qualification" [emphasis added]. New members are added with care by recommendation; their acceptance comes only after recommendations by both the membership committee and the council of the IACA and subsequent approval by the organization's membership at a business meeting.

There is one other significant organization in Indianapolis that has relevance for some Chinese in other parts of the state, the Chinese Community Church. The church was organized in 1974 and met from then until 1982 at the Meridian Street United Methodist Church, with church services conducted in Mandarin and Cantonese with English translation.[106] Though it initially

*Chinese Community Church, Indianapolis, 1995.*

was established to serve the Indianapolis Chinese community, "when we organized here, people started driving from Lafayette, Bloomington, Anderson, [and] Kokomo each Sunday."[107] The appeal of the church to area Chinese came not only from its religious contribution but also its array of social services. Beginning in 1976, semimonthly medical clinics operated at the church following postservice fellowship luncheons. Four physicians gave free medical service to parishioners: Amy Cheung, wife of restaurateur Paul Cheung; her brother-in-law, Abraham Law of Valparaiso; and Joseph Chan and Danny Bao, medical residents at Indianapolis hospitals. By the middle of the 1980s, the clinic was opened on Sundays from 1:00 to 3:00 P.M.[108]

The church also provided educational programs for recent immigrants. In 1978 the Reverend Peter Ying established "language classes after midnight" for restaurant workers whose work did not allow them any other time for language training.[109] This foray into education expanded after the church purchased property at 56th and Broadway in 1982. Under the leadership of Peter Chen, a Taiwan native and graduate of the Anderson, Indiana, School of Theology, the church continued with English classes for immigrants. Also offered were Chinese classes each Sunday from 1:30 to 3:30 for the "new generation of Chinese-Americans" and a Tai-chi program.[110]

## Coming Full Circle: The 1980s and 1990s as Culmination of the Hopes of 1904

Some eighty years after Pu Lun's welcome to Indianapolis and the hopeful speeches about the possibilities of trade and other exchanges with China, Indiana's Gov. Robert Orr put life into those hopes with his own China initiative. The opening up of diplomatic relations between China and the United States in 1979 had roughly corresponded with the adoption of a more pragmatic policy in the People's Republic that called not only for quasi-capitalist economic plans but also a greater opening to the high technology of the West. From the standpoint of Indiana's economic future, the governor contended that domestic markets would not be as available as they had been in the past; therefore, "you have to go to foreign lands to sell our products."[111]

In November 1986 Orr and a delegation of Indiana political and business representatives went to Beijing to meet with Chinese governmental representatives and with United States representatives of Eli Lilly and Company and Cummins Engine Company. They then flew to Hangzhou in Zhejiang Province, "China's leading province in farm productivity," where on 14 November Governors Orr and Ju Xue signed a "memorandum of understanding"

*Pair of lions, gift from Zhejiang Province, Indiana's sister-state province. They are located in front of the Indianapolis Zoo.*

stating their goal of establishing a "sister-state" relationship between Indiana and Zhejiang.[112] A sumptuous banquet that evening at the Huagang Hotel, hosted by the Hoosiers and featuring delicacies such as jellyfish and lotus powder soup with chestnuts, was replicated in April 1987 when a Chinese delegation feasted on bird nest and crabmeat soup and sea slugs and shark fin at the Mark Pi Restaurant in Indianapolis. The sister-state connection was formalized at a signing ceremony and reception at the Governor's Mansion in Indianapolis on 23 July 1987.[113] With each meeting and obligatory banquet, the Hoosiers and the Chinese extended their knowledge of each other, making more likely the possibility of meaningful business and educational exchanges. Such political and social intercourse with delegations traveling frequently from one nation to the other was a mark of how different the situation in Indiana had become for China and the Chinese in the 1980s. The international and state context seemed light years away from 1904 and the Progressive Era.

Organizations to facilitate exchanges with the People's Republic of China had emerged in the 1970s. In 1976, for example, the United States–China People's Friendship Association and the United States–China People to People Committee of Indiana had been formed, the purpose of the latter "to promot[e] understanding of the Chinese people and their heritage and relat[e] to them on the basis of intelligent, informed, and friendly mutuality."[114] But there had been nothing like the possibilities that Governor Orr's initiatives had opened up. There were trade possibilities for the China market of industrial engines and revolving doors as well as agribusiness products like new breeds of soybeans, cattle embryos, and alfalfa cubes.[115] Also, businessmen from both countries have been more likely to travel between the countries to find out about other opportunities.

*Children practicing calligraphy during Chinese New Year celebration at the Chinese School.*

The exchange seems to have been most productive in the educational arena. Visiting scholars from Chinese universities have come to Indiana campuses to study and sometimes to serve even as advisors to Indiana business firms.[116] Chinese graduate students have come to obtain advanced degrees. This has not only been an Indiana phenomenon but also a national one. The International Institute of Education reported in 1987–88 that Taiwan and the People's Republic ranked first and second in the number of students sent to American universities. One writer calls it "the most important immigration of intellectuals to the United States since the prewar influx of Jewish intellectuals."[117] Whereas in 1955 there had been ten thousand students in the United Sates from all Asian countries, by 1987 there were some sixty-seven thousand from the People's Republic, Taiwan, Hong Kong, and Malaysia—20 percent of all the foreign students in the country.[118] The goals expressed by H. H. Hanna in May 1904 at the smoker for Prince Pu Lun seem to have been realized: "We are unable to express the importance we attach to the manifest desire of many young men of China to come into the atmosphere and under the training of our school and university life."[119]

Their presence, if only as sojourners, has an impact on both Chinese and non-Chinese communities, especially in and near university towns. For example, the Indianapolis Association of Chinese-Americans has changed its policies regarding membership qualifications. Whereas at first only citizens and permanent residents were admitted, by 1991 students from the People's Republic of China were accepted as associate nonvoting members.[120] Many Chinese students, however, have attempted to remain in the United States; and a large number have succeeded. In addition, President George Bush's decision to offer protection to the almost thirty thousand students in the United States during the June 1989 massacre of Chinese citizens in Beijing swelled the numbers of Chinese in the country, just as the Communist victory had stranded Chinese in the United States in 1949.[121]

The following tables indicate the great wave of Chinese students at three Indiana universities.

### Chinese Students from People's Republic of China (PRC) and Taiwan at Three Major Indiana Universities[122]

|      | Indiana University | | Purdue University | | Univ. of Notre Dame | |
|------|-----|--------|-----|--------|-----|--------|
|      | PRC | Taiwan | PRC | Taiwan | PRC | Taiwan |
| 1970 | 0   | 66     | —   | —      | 3   | 13     |
| 1980 | 0   | 183    | —   | —      | 0   | 11     |
| 1985 | —   | —      | 149 | 231    | —   | —      |
| 1990 | 251 | 196    | 407 | 345    | —   | —      |
| 1991 | 295 | 206    | 409 | 344    | 113 | 24     |

FRANCES RUSSELL

*Indianapolis Association of Chinese-Americans cultural booth at the International Festival, 1993.*

As Chinese immigration from the beginning has reflected the situation in China, so this new sojourning immigration reveals the priority in China today. Just as in the 1910s, 1920s, and 1930s, Chinese graduate students came to study mainly science and technology in the 1990s; the large numbers at Purdue University reflect that concentration. An analysis of the fields of study of students from the People's Republic at Indiana University in the fall 1991 academic semester reveals the same phenomenon: 59 percent of PRC students at the Bloomington campus study for advanced degrees in mathematics, computer science, the biological and physical sciences, and technology. Forty-seven percent of the Taiwanese students are in these areas of concentration. The numbers of Chinese men (176) and women (177) at Bloomington are almost equal, but those figures mask the reality of the immigration from each: 119 men and 65 women come from the People's Republic of China, while 57 men and 112 women come from Taiwan.

The nature and pace of Chinese immigration in the last century depended largely on United States immigration policy and internal political dynamics in China. For its Chinese immigrants and residents, the Indiana experience has been made up of an array of elements. A feature essay in the *Indianapolis Star* perspicaciously noted some of these, particularly the "parallels between the Chinese-American and Jewish-American experience. Historically, both communities have been noted for scholarship, entrepreneurship, retention of cultural identity, and . . . the suffering of discrimination."[123] Even as the old has continually made way for the new, the restaurant culture of the early immigrants has continued to thrive amid the more numerous highly educated professionals. In the 1980s and 1990s these two strata have been joined by an increasing number of students and intellectuals from East Asia. Though the Chinese residents, even today, have been attuned to developments

across the Pacific, the history of the Chinese in Indiana has been not one primarily of sojourners but of significant contributions to state, society, and academe. The increasing diversity of Chinese immigration and its residential dispersal seems likely to promise continuing and expanding contributions to the state in the years ahead.

The author wishes to thank David and Lillian Wang for the time that they generously gave for interviews and for their insights into the lives of Indianapolis Chinese.

## Notes

1. Carl Lewis, "Chinese Hoosiers," *Indianapolis Star Magazine,* 20 Mar. 1949.

2. Rose Hum Lee, *The Chinese in the United States of America* (Hong Kong: Hong Kong University Press, 1960), 9, 12–13; L. Ling-chi Wang, "Roots and Changing Identity of the Chinese in the United States," *Daedalus* 120, no. 2 (Spring 1991): 185.

3. Betty L. Sung, *The Story of the Chinese in America* (New York: Collier Books, 1967), 11–14 as cited in Sarah R. Mason, "The Chinese," in *They Chose Minnesota: A Survey of the State's Ethnic Groups,* ed. by June Drenning Holmquist (St. Paul: Minnesota Historical Society Press, 1981), 532. See also Wang, "Roots and Changing Identity of the Chinese in the United States," 186.

4. Myron Cohen, "Being Chinese: The Peripheralization of Traditional Identity," *Daedalus* 120, no. 2 (Spring 1991): 116.

5. Paul C. F. Siu, "The Sojourner," *American Journal of Sociology* 58 (July 1952): 34–44, as quoted in Lee, *The Chinese in the United States of America,* 69.

6. Cohen, "Being Chinese," 125.

7. Wang, "Roots and Changing Identity of the Chinese in the United States," 186.

8. Clifton J. Phillips, *Indiana in Transition: The Emergence of an Industrial Commonwealth, 1880–1920* (Indianapolis: Indiana Historical Bureau and Indiana Historical Society, 1968), 368.

9. Ibid., 369.

10. Ruth Slevin, "Index to Blacks, Indians, Chinese, Mulattoes in Indiana, 1880 Census," Genealogy Division, Indiana State Library, Indianapolis. "Group China" sheets, compiled by Indiana Historical Society staff, show twenty-nine Chinese in the state in 1880. Since some of the "Chinese" in the Slevin index were obviously not Chinese (they had English surnames), the author assumes that sixteen of the "Group China's" number were also not ethnically Chinese but were the results of the census taker's error.

11. Table 33: "Foreign Born Population, Distributed According to Country of Birth, by Counties: 1890," based on 1890 Census [Vol. I] *Report on Population of the United States, 1895–97,* pp. 622–23.

12. Lewis, "Chinese Hoosiers."

13. *Indianapolis Star,* 12 July 1981.

14. Wang, "Roots and Changing Identity of the Chinese in the United States," 187.

15. *Indianapolis News,* 26 Nov. 1898.

16. Sources for the 1880 and 1890 figures have been given. For the statistics from 1910, 1920, and 1930 see Table 17: "Indians, Chinese, and Japanese, 1910 to 1930, and Mexicans, 1930, for Counties and for Cities of 25,000 or More," based on 1930 Census, *Composition and Characteristics of the Population,* 720.

17. Jane E. Darlington, comp., *Marion County, Indiana Records Miscellanea* (Indianapolis: Indiana Historical Society, 1986), 2a. Newspaper columnist Anton Scherrer's claim in a 1937 *Indianapolis*

*Star* column that Moy came from California is not borne out by the records. See *Indianapolis Times,* 26 Nov. 1937.

18. *Indianapolis Times,* 26 Nov. 1937 and *Indianapolis Star,* 4 Apr. 1906.

19. *Indianapolis Star,* 16 Nov. 1905. The author wishes to thank Robert M. Taylor, Jr., for bringing this incident to his attention.

20. Lewis, "Chinese Hoosiers."

21. See Jonathan D. Spence, *The Question of Hu* (New York: Knopf, 1988) and "Madness and Culture: Exporting the Cuckoo's Nest," *East-West Perspectives* 1, no. 3 (Summer 1980): 30–36.

22. John H. Holliday, "The Life of Our Foreign Population" (typescript [1907–21?], Indiana Historical Society Library, Indianapolis), 16.

23. *Indianapolis Star,* 4 Apr. 1906.

24. Lee, *The Chinese in the United States of America,* 162.

25. *Indianapolis Star,* 27 Sept. 1953.

26. Arthur W. Hummel, ed., *Eminent Chinese of the Ch'ing Period* (1943; reprint, Taipei: Ch'eng Wen Publishing Co., 1970), 378.

27. *Indianapolis News,* 18 May 1904.

28. The following account is based upon the *Indianapolis News,* 18–21, 23 May 1904. See also Lloyd B. Walton, "The Prince Who Rated Hoosier Cars and Carpets," *Indianapolis Star Magazine,* 25 Nov. 1979.

29. Jacob Piatt Dunn, *Greater Indianapolis,* 2 vols. (Chicago: The Lewis Publishing Co., 1910), 2:685–87.

30. *Indianapolis News,* 18 May 1904. See also the address by Indianapolis Mayor John W. Holtzman, ibid.

31. Ibid., 23 May 1904.

32. Ibid., 19 May 1904.

33. Walton, "The Prince Who Rated Hoosier Cars and Carpets."

34. *Indianapolis News,* 20 May 1904.

35. Ibid., 18 May 1904.

36. Ibid., 23 May 1904.

37. Ibid., 21 and 23 May 1904.

38. Ibid., 23 May 1904.

39. Holliday, "The Life of Our Foreign Population," 16.

40. Ibid., 17.

41. *Indianapolis Public Schools Annual Report of the Secretary, Business Director, Superintendent of Schools and the Librarian,* 1908–9, p. 30.

42. Phillips, *Indiana in Transition,* 370, and James H. Madison, *Indiana through Tradition and Change: A History of the Hoosier State and Its People, 1920–1945* (Indianapolis: Indiana Historical Society, 1982), 13.

43. Lee, *The Chinese in the United States of America,* 14.

44. *Indianapolis News* 23 Feb. 1972.

45. *Indianapolis Star,* 8 June 1941.

46. Ibid.

47. *The Lilly News* 9, no. 11 (29 May 1965), 3. See also Lewis, "Chinese Hoosiers."

48. *Indianapolis News,* 23 Feb. 1972.

49. Ibid., 6 Sept. 1937.

50. *Indianapolis Star,* 25 Jan. 1938.

51. Lee, *The Chinese in the United States of America,* 14.

52. Sources for this table are Table 6: "Minor Races, by Nativity and Sex, for the State, Urban and Rural: 1910 to 1940" in the 1940 Census, *Characteristics of the Population,* 12, and Table 47: "Indians, Japanese, and Chinese, by Sex, for Selected Counties and Cities, 1950" in *General Characteristics of the 1950 Population Census,* 14–129. Note that the latter source is not all-inclusive: statistics are given for "counties and for cities of 10,000 inhabitants or more with 10 or more" Chinese. The author would argue that the figures nevertheless

approximate the actual sex ratios in the Chinese population of 1950.

53. Wang, "Roots and Changing Identity of the Chinese in the United States," 189, and Lee, *The Chinese in the United States of America,* 17.

54. Lewis, "Chinese Hoosiers."

55. Lee, *The Chinese in the United States of America,* 17–18, and Wang, "Roots and Changing Identity of the Chinese in the United States," 189.

56. Lewis, "Chinese Hoosiers."

57. The description of Chinese in Indianapolis in the late 1940s is based upon Lewis, "Chinese Hoosiers."

58. Ernie Hernandez, *Ethnics in Northwest Indiana* (Gary, Ind.: Post-Tribune, 1984), 100.

59. Lewis, "Chinese Hoosiers."

60. See Table 17: "Indians, Chinese, and Japanese, 1910 to 1930, and Mexicans, 1930, for Counties and for Cities of 25,000 or More," 720. A county analysis is possible only for the 1930 figures, for both the 1910 and 1920 statistics include Chinese in the category of "All other counties."

61. Sources for this table are Table 17 of the 1930 census cited above and Table 6 ("Minor Races, by Nativity and Sex") of the 1940 census.

62. Lee, *The Chinese in the United States of America,* 37.

63. See Table 47: "Indians, Japanese, and Chinese, by Sex, for Selected Counties and Cities, 1950," 14–129. The 1950 select listing, which on its face looks to be somewhat lower in percentage, omits urban centers in several counties in which other Chinese in this count almost certainly lived: Hobart, Highland, and Munster in Lake County, Elkhart and Mishawaka in St. Joseph County, and Lafayette in Tippecanoe County.

64. Lewis, "Chinese Hoosiers."

65. Wang, "Roots and Changing Identity of the Chinese in the United States," 188.

66. Lewis, "Chinese Hoosiers."

67. *Indianapolis Star,* 12 July 1981.

68. Wang, "Roots and Changing Identity of the Chinese in the United States," 189–90.

69. Cohen, "Being Chinese," 126.

70. Wang, "Roots and Changing Identity of the Chinese in the United States," 190.

71. Ibid., 190–91.

72. The census data for 1980 are difficult to analyze because of variance in a number of statistics. Table 3: "Asian and Pacific Islander Persons by Nativity: 1980," from the 1980 Population Census, 12, lists the number of foreign-born Chinese in Indiana as 3,107; however, Table A: "Foreign-Born Persons by Country of Birth for Indiana: 1980," Bureau of the Census, 1990, manuscript, lists only 1,260 from China. Yet a third figure comes from the "Group China" table compiled by the Indiana Historical Society staff: there the total for the state is 1,204 Chinese foreign born. Because Table 3 is described as composed of "estimates based on a sample," the author assumes that that figure is least reliable. Table A adds the interesting information of source of origin of the Chinese population. If one adds the totals from China, Taiwan, Hong Kong, and Macao—all ethnically Chinese—the total is 2,688. This figure seems more likely to reflect the foreign-born ethnic Chinese population in the state in 1980.

73. Sources for this table are for 1930 and 1940, Table 6: "Minor Races, by Nativity and Sex," 12; for 1950 "Group China" data; for 1960 Table 99: "Country of Origin of the Foreign Stock, by Nativity, Color, and Sex . . ." from the 1960 Population Census, Indiana, 16–330; and for 1980 *Ancestry of the Population by State* (Indiana) *1980,*

Supplementary Report, Bureau of the Census, unpaginated; and for 1990 "1990 Census STF 1A, File 0, Geography and Tables P1 to P10," photoduplicated, Indiana Historical Society.

74. Table: "Indiana Foreign Born for 1980 by Township within Each County," based upon "1980 Census Summary Tape File 4," Indiana Business Research Center, Graduate School of Business, Indiana University.

75. Generalizations about the 1990 data are based upon "1990 Census STF 1A, File 0, Geography and Tables P1 to P10."

76. *Indianapolis Star,* 12 July 1981.

77. *Indiana Business Directory* (Omaha, 1991), 740–62. As this computation was based upon restaurant names, there may be a slight degree of error.

78. Interview with Lee Lai Fong, 8 Nov. 1991.

79. *Indianapolis Star,* 12 July 1981. For a recent description of Chinese restaurants in Indianapolis see the *Indianapolis Business Journal,* 20-26 Feb. 1995, p. 4A.

80. *Indianapolis News,* 27 Mar. 1974.

81. *Indianapolis Star,* 21 Nov. 1976.

82. "Huaren xushu jiehui zhouliu yantaohui" [Chinese Professional Association's Sixth Annual Meeting], *Shijie ribao* [World Journal], 3 Dec. 1990.

83. Interview with Lillian Wang, 29 June 1991.

84. "Indianapolis Association of Chinese Americans: Membership Directory, 1991," p. 2, and interview with David and Lillian Wang, 29 June 1991.

85. Interview with Lee Chao-hung, president of TAA, 9 June 1991.

86. Interview with Lillian Wang, 29 June 1991.

87. *Indianapolis Star,* 12 July 1981.

88. Hernandez, *Ethnics in Northwest Indiana,* 99–101.

89. *Indianapolis Star,* 12 July 1981.

90. Ibid., 21 Mar. 1972.

91. See "The US-China People to People Committee of Indiana," 27 Apr. 1976, mimeographed sheet, Indiana State Library. Note also the coverage in the *Indianapolis Star,* 14 Nov. and 26 Dec. 1972 and the *Indianapolis News,* 28 Dec. 1972.

92. *Indianapolis News,* 27 Mar. 1974.

93. *Indianapolis Star,* 12 July 1981.

94. Ibid., 3 Feb. 1981.

95. "An Invitation to Join the Indianapolis Association of Chinese-Americans, Inc.," mimeographed sheet provided by David and Lillian Wang, ex-presidents of the association.

96. Conversations with James Tan and Huang Daqing, 1988–91, reflecting the practices of the Chinese community in northwest Indiana.

97. "The Purposes of the Indianapolis Association of Chinese-Americans, Inc." in Indianapolis Association of Chinese-Americans, Membership Directory, 1991, unpaginated.

98. Interview with Lee Chao-hung, 9 June 1991.

99. "The Purposes of the Indianapolis Association of Chinese-Americans, Inc."

100. Ibid.

101. *Indianapolis Star,* 17 Jan. 1974.

102. Data on the IACA and TAA are based on the interviews cited earlier and on the IACA Membership Directory for 1991.

103. *Indianapolis Star,* 3 Feb. 1981.

104. Interview with Lee Chao-hung, 9 June 1991.

105. "Indianapolis Association of Chinese-Americans, Inc. (IACA) Membership Application Form," mimeographed sheet, provided by David and Lillian Wang.

106. *Indianapolis News,* 15 Apr. 1978 and 8 Dec. 1984.

107. *Indianapolis Star,* 21 Nov. 1976.

108. *Indianapolis News,* 8 Dec. 1984.

109. "An International Album," *Indianapolis Star Magazine,* 8 Jan. 1978.

110. *Indianapolis News,* 8 Dec. 1984.

111. Peter Fullam, "Hands Across the Water: Hoosier Delegation Courts Southern Sung Capital," *Indianapolis Business Journal* (1–7 Dec. 1986), 10.

112. Ibid., 11.

113. Unpublished diary entries, R. Keith Schoppa, 14 Nov. 1986, 8 Apr. and 23 July 1987.

114. "The US-China People to People Committee of Indiana."

115. Peter Fullam, "Zhejiang Attorney Helps Local Firm Establish Business Ties in China," *Indianapolis Business Journal* (15–21 June 1987), 9a, 17a. Also unpublished diary entry, R. Keith Schoppa, 14 Nov. 1986.

116. Fullam, "Zhejiang Attorney," 9a.

117. Wang, "Roots and Changing Identity of the Chinese in the United States," 190.

118. Ibid.

119. *Indianapolis News,* 23 May 1904.

120. Interview with Lillian Wang, 29 June 1991.

121. Wang, "Roots and Changing Identity of the Chinese in the United States," 191.

122. For these statistics, the author is grateful to Ruth Miller, associate director of international programs at Indiana University, Bloomington; to June Vore, secretary to the director of international programs at Purdue University; and to Arthur Grubare, director of international studies at the University of Notre Dame.

123. *Indianapolis Star,* 12 July 1981.

# ENGLISH & WELSH

WILLIAM VAN VUGT

*The majority of English and Welsh immigrants were neither the well-to-do nor the very poor, but rather could be described as ambitious people with at least some assets who seized the greater opportunities that Indiana offered them.*

I am happy however to inform you of my increasing satisfaction with this our adopted country. The more I see and know of its government, customs, manners, and people, the more am I convinced that it will one day be (if it is not at present) the most powerful, the most prosperous, and the most happy community in the world. . . . This, in the full sense of the word, is a "young country."[1]

When Cornelius Pering wrote these enthusiastic words about his new home in Indiana it had been only a year since he had emigrated from England. And, though not all of the English and Welsh immigrants in Indiana at this time were as satisfied and optimistic, Pering was in some ways a rather typical English immigrant. Two of his cousins had immigrated before him and paved the way with encouragement and advice. Despite the emotional pain of leaving England, Pering had few regrets because England simply did not offer him the economic opportunities that Indiana did.[2] Indiana never was a major destination for English or Welsh immigrants. Other states of the Old Northwest and the mid-Atlantic regions took the lion's share of these people, and already by 1850 Germans out-numbered Englishmen in Indiana by a ratio of more than six to one.[3] Nevertheless, it is clear that the English and Welsh had an impact on Indiana's history and growth that was far greater than their numbers would

suggest. As people from the world's first industrial nation, and with a language and political and cultural heritage most similar to that of the United States, the English and Welsh (and Scots) were unique among all other immigrant groups in Indiana.

## Background: Immigration before Statehood

The earliest known English and Welsh presence in Indiana dates back to the early eighteenth century, when British and French soldiers and traders jockeyed for power in lands that were already occupied by various Native American peoples. Not until the conclusion of the Seven Years' War in 1763 did this struggle end, and by 1765 Indiana territory was under British rule. Even then the British presence in what would become the state of Indiana consisted largely of troops and traders rather than permanent immigrants, and the Proclamation Line of 1763 was drawn to restrict white settlement in the region. A generation later the British were again fighting for control over Indiana, this time against the rebellious American colonists. The most pivotal event in this conflict as far as the British in Indiana were concerned was George Rogers Clark's daring capture of Fort Sackville (Vincennes) on the Wabash River in 1779, for after this date those English and Welsh who came to settle in Indiana did so as immigrants, as new Americans—not as members of the British empire.[4]

The meager sources of information that do exist for the study of English and Welsh immigration to Indiana during its territorial status indicate that considerable numbers of ambitious, competent, and independent-minded risk takers from England and Wales arrived in Indiana between the 1790s and statehood in 1816. Most had already spent at least a few years in eastern states but saw greater opportunities in Indiana. Some became prominent people and leaders on the frontier or in the growing towns and were later remembered, with some justification, as colorful characters who contributed much to the birth and development of the state. John Rice Jones, for example, was

born in Wales in 1750, immigrated to America shortly after its independence, and headed west to the Northwest Territory in 1786. An accomplished scholar and linguist, Jones was reputedly the first and ablest person to practice law in what became Illinois and was known as a "perfect master of satire and invective." He soon moved his law practice to Vincennes, where he quickly rose to prominence and became attorney general of the territory that he had helped organize and, "being a warm friend" of Gen. William Henry Harrison, in 1805 was appointed by Thomas Jefferson to the Legislative Council of Indiana Territory, in which capacity he did much to revise the territorial laws in 1809.[5] Englishman James Jones, who emigrated from Herefordshire with his parents in 1803, attained another kind of prominence. After a religious conversion at an Ohio camp meeting during the Second Great Awakening, Jones became a leading Methodist preacher at Rising Sun, Dearborn County, and then a circuit rider for the region. He also served in the War of 1812.[6]

Along with political and religious leaders, the earliest English and Welsh immigrants in Indiana included hardy pioneers who moved west with the frontier in pursuit of independence and virgin land. They made several moves and entered Indiana in its early days when they could make profitable land deals in the eastern and southern counties.[7] Some early arrivals came directly to Indiana from Great Britain, as did Yorkshireman Richard Sedgwick in 1806. One of the first settlers in Wayne County, Sedgwick used his English farming experience to become a successful and prominent agriculturalist, and he imported the first Shorthorn bull into the region.[8]

The early English and Welsh immigrants to Indiana also included veterans of the American Revolution—from both sides of the conflict. English immigrant John Vincent eagerly joined the American cause and then after the war became one of the first settlers west of Brookville, Franklin County, where he led his neighbors in armed conflict with the Indians.[9] William Rooker's experience was rather different. The son of a silversmith, Rooker was drafted by British officers while at a party in London and was sent

over to fight against the American rebels. But he quickly deserted, hid in Knoxville, Tennessee, for the remainder of the war, and then came to Morgan County during the territorial days and took up farming.[10]

When Anglo-American relations soured in the decades after American independence, English and Welsh immigrants in the United States had to endure suspicions of disloyalty and discrimination. During the War of 1812, which some Americans called "the second war for independence," English aliens in the United States were treated as potential enemies, and all males more than fourteen years of age were required to register at the nearest United States marshal's office. Waivers were granted to those who before the war had declared their intention of becoming naturalized citizens or had married Americans, and in Indiana very recent immigrant Englishmen fought on the American side, in part, it seems, to prove their loyalty to their adopted country. It is remarkable that people like Samuel Eakright immigrated as late as 1811 and yet served on the American side of the conflict. Eleven Hughes did the same, was captured by his former countrymen, but then managed to escape by "running the gauntlet through the Indian lines." Eventually he settled as a farmer in Clark County.[11] The English and Welsh immigrants during this turbulent period were not just adopting a new country; they were adopting a country at war with their native land.

### Early English Colonies in Indiana

Notwithstanding the periodic Anglo-American tensions, the English in the United States had certain advantages over other immigrants. Because they already shared the language and culture of their newly adopted country, their interaction with American society was more immediate than it was for non-English-speaking groups. They generally did not form separate ethnic communities, nor did they have to establish their own churches, as every English denomination had its American equivalent and every English arrival could worship in his native tongue. Historian Charlotte Erickson has called them "invisible immigrants" because they could blend in with American society, and most native-born Americans seldom thought of them as true foreigners.[12] Yet, the early English immigrants in Indiana did not always fit this pattern. Some settled in clusters or even colonies and were conspicuous as Englishmen, with no intention of blending in with society or setting aside their ethnic identity. This was particularly true in the early days on the lonely and rigorous Indiana frontier, where groups of English immigrants relied on their ethnic ties to cope with their new environment.

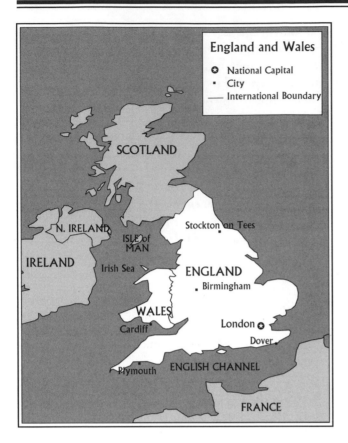

In some cases a successful English immigrant in Indiana became a magnet for additional English families who had known him in England, corresponded with him, and then joined him to form a colony or ethnic cluster. A good example is John Ewbank, a Yorkshireman who married a strict Wesleyan in 1792, converted to her faith, and suffered the consequences when the ninety-nine-year lease on his farm expired in 1805. His landlord refused the customary renewal because of Ewbank's nonconformity. At age fifty-three Ewbank found himself without his farm, with a wife and ten children, and with very little money. So he immigrated alone to New York, where he worked for two years as a farm laborer and farm manager, after which he was able to send for his family that had remained in England. In 1815, after a few years as tenant farmers in New Jersey, the Ewbanks moved to Tanner's Creek, near Guilford, Dearborn County, where they were able to purchase five and a half quarter sections of virgin land. But the Ewbanks were merely the "advanced guard," for within three years many other Yorkshire farmers and their families joined them, apparently after reading encouraging letters from the Ewbanks themselves, and these too attracted still more from Yorkshire. York Township, Yorkville, and other places in the county received their characters as well as their names from these settlers, who were remembered as "thrifty, high-class

citizens." Sixty years later historians recorded that this English colony "was regarded with great favor at the time as it was soon ascertained that they were intelligent men and families of respectability and high standing . . . as a community they have been industrious, law abiding and peaceable citizens."[13]

What happened in Dearborn County was not an isolated case. Similar English colonies were established in the northwest and northeast sections of Whitewater Township in Franklin County during its early days of settlement, New Albany in Floyd County (a colony of mostly Wesleyan Methodists from Lincolnshire), what is now Calumet Township in Lake County during the 1830s, and in Benton County as late as 1850, among other places.[14] For new immigrants such communities lessened the trauma of moving from England to the isolated wilderness of Indiana by providing familiar people, speech patterns, fellowship, and suitable marriage partners.[15]

One particularly well documented English colony in Indiana was that established in Vanderburgh County in 1817 by Saunders Hornbrook, an educated iron founder and woolen mill operator from Devon. Hornbrook originally intended to join the rather grandiose and ill-conceived English colony that Morris Birkbeck and George Flower were trying to establish across the Wabash River in Edwards County, Illinois. However, Hornbrook and soon many other Englishmen heading for the Illinois colony became disenchanted with Flower's and Birkbeck's scheme: each settler was limited to 320 acres of land that would be assigned to them by Flower and Birkbeck. This arrangement was unacceptable to people like Hornbrook, who had immigrated to be independent landowners with the freedom to make their own decisions. Thus Hornbrook and others remained east of the Wabash and settled on cheaper land north of Evansville, at a place they called Saundersville. By the time William Faux visited this English settlement in 1819 it consisted of fifty-three English families owning 12,800 acres of land with a total value of $80,000. The short-lived colony was dominated by businessmen like Hornbrook, professional men, and farmers who had been losing money in England because of high land rents. Most had left England not only out of an anxiety over what the future held for them there, but also because they could purchase land in Indiana for less than the cost of renting it in England. Life was exceedingly difficult in those early days. William Faux was appalled by the shoddy accommodations and lack of comforts. Some of the immigrants regretted their move. However, most would have echoed Mr. Peck, who was "born and bred a laborer," had become a small tenant farmer near Chatteris, Cambridgeshire, and had joined the colony out of frustration in England:

Now . . . I feel I can live, and live well, by working, and without fretting and working, seventeen, out of the twenty-four hours, all the year round, as I used to do at Chatteris. And what is sweeter than all, I feel I am now the owner of 300 acres of land, all paid for, and free from all poor-rates, parsons, and tax-gatherers, and that I shall be able to give and leave each of my children, 100 acres of good land to work upon, instead of the highway, or Chatteris work-house. No fear of their committees now, nor of Ely jail.[16]

Of course the most famous colony established by a Briton in Indiana was that of New Harmony in 1825 by socialist philosopher and reformer Robert Owen. The seventh son of a saddler in Montgomeryshire, South Wales, Robert Owen came to America in 1824 looking for a site on which to build a utopian industrial community even larger and more complete than the one he established in the Scottish mill town of New Lanark.[17] He found the ideal place in what was then called Harmony, along the Wabash River in the extreme southwest corner of the state. Here Owen purchased for $95,000 the land and buildings of German immigrant George Rapp and his Rappite religious community, which was moving on to even more austere surroundings. Owen's total property

consisted of twenty thousand acres of land and the industries left behind by the Rappites—mills, workshops, tanneries, and so on. By 1825 hundreds of people had arrived from diverse parts of the country to help Owen build what he called a "community of equality, based on the principle of common property," where people could be "nearer to a natural order of society." Though perhaps a few English and Welsh participated in the project, most were American born, and in any case the community soon was dissolved by economic problems, personal squabblings, and the other tensions often inherent in such utopian communities. Robert Owen soon returned to Great Britain, but his Scottish-born sons remained in Indiana and became leading citizens in their own right. Robert Dale Owen became a congressman, introduced the bill to found the Smithsonian Institution, and was appointed minister to Naples in 1853.[18]

### The English and Welsh as Pioneers

Throughout most of the nineteenth century Indiana was far less economically developed than Great Britain and generally had lower standards of housing, lower per capita incomes, and inferior public facilities. Particularly during

*Ernst and Caroline Sibley Hohman, Hammond's first permanent settlers. Caroline Hohman was from Wales.*

Indiana's pioneer era, some English and Welsh immigrants found themselves ill-prepared to face the hardships and loneliness that came with life on the frontier. Most eventually succeeded, but they had seriously underestimated the difficulties that they would face.

Some members of the Hornbrook colony in Vanderburgh County were apparently stunned by the realities of the American frontier. They had made the arduous Atlantic voyage in a ship's dark and poorly ventilated steerage compartment, trekked into the interior, and floated down the Ohio River in a "little stinking ark," only to endure a "little log-hole" for a cabin in the Indiana wilderness.[19] Such primitive conditions were traumatic, especially for those English and Welsh people who were at least somewhat refined. Indeed, some were well educated, had artistic sensibilities, and shared a widespread concern "that the frontier would have a barbarizing effect" upon themselves and their children. They tried to combat these tendencies by providing some form of education, as did Jonas Rhodes, who organized spelling bees for his children and taught them to read Shakespeare, Robert Burns, and the Bible.[20] But sheer loneliness continued to be a major problem, especially in some of the more isolated areas. When Samuel and Mary Eakright came to De Kalb County from Ohio in 1836, having emigrated from England in 1811, eighteen months passed before Mary saw another white woman.[21] Other disadvantages were harder to bear. William Faux tells of an English immigrant in Vanderburgh County who broke his leg, had it misset by a quack doctor, and was then crippled for life.[22] More commonly the English and Welsh combated diseases and mosquitoes, and those who found these conditions unbearable headed back to eastern states or Great Britain.

English and Welsh immigrants of educated and affluent backgrounds often stood out for their polished and sometimes eccentric qualities. Physician William Harris, a graduate of Oxford University, arrived in Dearborn County "a gentleman of refined social qualities, great learning" who brought with him a personal library that was then one of the best in the state. Harris was also known for enjoying conversations with Gov. James Whitcomb in several languages.[23] There were other English people with elite backgrounds and educations making their new home in Indiana, but these people were a small minority of the immigrants.[24] For every immigrant of wealth and high social class there were many of lesser means.

### Indiana as a Haven for Troubled Britons

The majority of English and Welsh immigrants were neither the well-to-do nor the very poor, but rather could be described as ambitious people with at least some assets who seized the greater opportunities that Indiana offered them. In later years some recalled that they were doing well in England or Wales but had been lured by reports that they could do even better in Indiana.[25] Nevertheless, particularly in the first half of the nineteenth century, many of these people were wary of Great Britain's future and had left because of the threat of poverty, if not poverty itself. This was true of most of the immigrants who joined the Hornbrook colony north of Evansville and of many farmers who came in later years. For some, "distress" had less to do with economics than with the caprices and prejudices of landlords and aristocrats. The case of John Ewbank and the refusal of his landlord to renew his lease because of Ewbank's conversion to Methodism has already been noted. But the unusual and romantic story of Ralph Shaw also illustrates the wide variety of circumstances that compelled some English people to immigrate to Indiana. Shaw was a "scholarly young man" with little money who fell in love with the daughter of an English nobleman. Denied permission to marry, the couple ran off together, sailed for New York in 1835 where they got married, and then proceeded to Delaware County, Indiana, where they purchased eighty acres of land and taught school. True to the storybook nature of their lives, they inherited a portion of her father's estate in the 1850s and apparently lived affluently ever after.[26] How many young couples ran off in this manner is impossible to say, but clearly immigration afforded new possibilities to young lovers who were kept apart by parents in England.

Some skilled industrial and craft workers left England for Indiana out of sheer economic desperation. In the remarkable experience of James Holcroft it is seen that Indiana served as a safety valve not just for workers experiencing trouble in England, but for those who had immigrated to eastern states only to find hardship there as well. Holcroft was a young Lancashire calico maker and cotton worker of outstanding skill and wide experience who had also learned the plasterer's trade. Nevertheless, he lost his work and tramped through England, "foot-sore, penniless and alone," and ended up borrowing £7 from his father for passage to America in 1848. Although he easily found work in a Rhode Island cotton mill, amazing his fellow workers with his advanced skills by operating six looms simultaneously, Holcroft aroused the jealousy of his foreman, quarreled with him, had his wages docked, and so "threw his looms out of gear" and in disgust prepared to return to England. Fortunately he then heard that he could find plastering work in Richmond, Indiana, where he became a contractor, and eventually made a fortune in real estate in Blackford County. Such a dramatic reversal of fortune was not typical, but neither was it uncommon.

For skilled and ambitious immigrants like Holcroft, Indiana became a place of deliverance from poverty and frustration and a place of almost boundless opportunity.[27]

The distressed circumstances of some of the early English and Welsh immigrants are exemplified by those who arrived impoverished or in debt. It is striking that some arrived virtually penniless, a condition that seems more characteristic of the destitute Irish who arrived en masse in the wake of the potato famine. When Robert and Mary Smith landed in New York from Cambridgeshire in 1833 they had five dollars to their name and had to walk the entire distance from New York to Evansville, while Mary carried their infant in her arms. Robert "worked while on the way in order to meet the necessities of life," and they arrived in Indiana one dollar ahead. He then carried mortar for bricklayers until he could afford to rent farmland; eventually he purchased 125 acres.[28] Such a scenario was not uncommon among the English heading for Indiana. Richard Chapman, though an apprenticed blacksmith, was even more destitute than Smith when he emigrated alone from Woodford near Salisbury in 1851 and arrived in New York on a freezing February day in 1852 "with only a nickel in his pocket." Yet Chapman had the advantage of having skills that were still in demand, and he easily found blacksmithing work for a couple of years in New York, during which time he was able to send for his wife and child. Then he moved his family to Jefferson County, Indiana, where he set up his own shop and became successful enough to purchase 240 acres of land.[29] It was by such means and determination that poor English and Welsh people became successful, even wealthy, citizens of Indiana.

### The Surge of Nineteenth-Century Immigration

Whatever their social and economic situation, the great majority of English and Welsh immigrants came to Indiana not to join an English settlement but to make it on their own, as individuals or families, as Americans. This was particularly true after the 1830s when the frontier was passing and the state was reaching a new stage of growth. Indiana was developing a market economy, losing its subsistence agriculture and developing some industries. And because Indiana's diversifying economy offered a greater variety of opportunities and its farmland remained a bargain, emigration from England and Wales to Indiana surged in the 1840s and 1850s.

From the census figures the magnitude and direction of English and Welsh immigration to Indiana can be seen. Between 1850 and 1860 the numbers living in the state nearly doubled to more than nine thousand. Most of these people were a small part of a significant surge of British immigration to the United States that occurred between 1845 and 1857 and that numbered more than a half million individuals (including Scots).[30] The size of the English and Welsh population living in Indiana increased slightly through the rest of the century and exceeded eleven thousand in 1890 before falling in subsequent decades. At the county level one can see that the English and Welsh were scattered throughout the state, with predictable concentrations in urban counties and in areas of early settlement, where the British had been the dominant immigrant group. The figures showing their percentage among the foreign born demonstrate this rather well. As late as 1850 the English comprised significant percentages of the foreign born in a number of counties, reaching 42 percent in Grant, 61 percent in Lagrange, and 43 percent in Benton (where an English colony had opened up the prairie lands to cultivation). But these proportions fell off dramatically as other ethnic groups entered the state, although Floyd, Fountain, Vanderburgh, and Clay counties actually had increasing proportions of English and Welsh people living in them.

It is impossible to know exactly which areas in England and Wales all of these immigrants came from, but a sample of 253 case studies taken from letters, journals, and mostly county histories does allow some reasonably safe generalizations.[31] Throughout the late eighteenth and early nineteenth centuries Yorkshire was the most common county of origin. This can be explained by its large population employed in both textiles and agriculture. Lancashire, a high-wage industrial county, was second to Yorkshire only through the mid-1850s, when most of the industrial traumas and occurrences of technological displacement were over. By that time more people were leaving Lincolnshire, and after the Civil War Durham joined Yorkshire as an important source of Indiana's immigrants. The London area, of course, was also a prominent source of immigrants throughout the century, many of them having gone there from various parts of Great Britain. As for the Welsh, it appears that the vast majority left industrial South Wales, although some of these originally had come from the north.[32] These case studies also show a clear occupational trend: the proportion of farmers fell steadily after midcentury, from roughly 60 percent of those heading to Indiana to under 30 percent in the years after the Civil War. The balance was being made up increasingly by craftsmen, miners, and laborers.[33]

More can be learned about these people by examining the research that historians have done with the United States ship passenger lists, which provide each immigrant's name, age, family status, occupation, and some related information.[34] Unfortunately, the lists rarely specify passengers' exact destinations, and the handful of Indiana-bound English and Welsh that have been identified are too few to be of much help to the historian.[35] Yet it is very likely that what was true of the entire population of British immigrants to the United States at large was also true of those who came specifically to Indiana, at least as far as a few basic patterns are concerned. In the early decades of the nineteenth century British immigration was to an astonishing degree a family movement: in 1831 more than three-fourths of the English and Welsh traveled with other family members—more than any other nationality arriving in the country. At the same time craftsmen and some industrial workers were showing more interest in the United States than were agriculturalists, though Indiana attracted more farmers, as the sample of case studies clearly shows. Most of these people were not desperately poor or victims of unemployment, though some feared what the future might bring them in an increasingly industrialized Great Britain. By 1841, however, there were more immigrants who appear victims of a depressed British economy. There were fewer agriculturalists and more industrial workers affected by cyclical unemployment. Many of the immigrant farmers of the midcentury period felt threatened by the end of Great Britain's protective Corn Laws in 1846. These were largely poorer tenant farmers laboring on heavy soils without the means to invest in more productive "scientific" farming and thereby compensate for falling grain prices. Unskilled laborers were also there on the cramped sailing vessels, as were miners and building trades workers. The movement also began to include more individuals, though it was still principally a family or "folk" immigration in character. But by the mid-1880s a very different kind of immigration occurred. The ideal of becoming an independent American farmer was giving way to more basic economic considerations as reasons for immigration. Increasing numbers were "birds of passage" or seasonal immigrants making repeated trips to America aboard the safer and faster steamships and lacking firm commitments to settle permanently in America. It was more of a "labor migration" composed of individuals from urban areas with experience in either the building trades, mining, or some form of unskilled labor. There was also a smattering of farmers, especially to agricultural states like Indiana.[36]

### Agricultural Immigrants

Indiana's seemingly boundless land attracted English and Welsh immigrants from diverse backgrounds to a life of agriculture, including those who apparently had little or no prior farm experience, as was the case with various coal miners, carpet weavers, textiles workers, engineers, and

with Saunders Hornbrook himself.[37] Some of these people were no doubt taken in by the "agrarian myth" of American farm life being one of carefree self-sufficiency, only to confront the harder realities and leave farming and perhaps America altogether.[38] Yet the transition was often made with great success. When George Wright emigrated from Derbyshire in 1852 he landed with eighty dollars and "knew how to do but little else besides milking a cow." But Wright gained farming skills as a laborer in Indiana, then bought his own farm and became a "highly skilled agriculturalist" with one of the "model farms" in Shelby County.[39] The few immigrant farm laborers from England at least had farm experience that could be applied in Indiana. Usually they worked on farms in eastern states or in Indiana and acquired knowledge about American farming conditions before renting and then buying their own land.[40]

Those who had farmed in England or Wales typically were not destitute or even poor. Most sold assets to help finance their land purchases in America. Yet many had been losing money as English farmers and feared a dismal future in which they and their sons would not have farms of their own and would fall to the status of farm laborer or even an industrial worker in England. This was true of the previously mentioned Mr. Peck, a member of the English settlement north of Evansville. He felt that he was "likely to lose all" if he remained in England because of the depression in English agriculture after the Napoleonic Wars, and so he felt compelled to leave while he still could with his life savings of £500. Peck's new English neighbor, Mr. Maidlow, left Hampshire because he was losing money on the farm that he rented there at sixteen shillings per acre (roughly four dollars, more than the *purchase* price of most land in Indiana), and he dreaded the loss of all of his capital. These and other rather desperate English immigrants at the settlement were now facing severe hardships in what was still a wild part of Indiana; but they were now landowners and few expressed regrets. One who did was an immigrant farmer from Devon. He had felt compelled to immigrate for the same reasons as the others, but when asked if he repented leaving England, he answered, " 'I do . . . a good deal, and so does my poor wife,' and then he burst into tears."[41]

But the majority of English farmers who came to Indiana were not just successful, they were also carriers of some of the most advanced and efficient methods of cultivation and raising livestock—what in fact were known as the "English methods" of agriculture.[42] No other immigrant group was as widely praised for its agricultural efficiency and productivity. The English were known as "progressive farmers" and regarded as "the most practical and scientific farmers in the state," who raised the standards of Indiana's agriculture, in spite of the fact that many eventually had to abandon some of their labor-intensive methods to make profits in America, where labor was scarce and land was abundant.[43] Some introduced new breeds of livestock into the state. Yorkshireman Richard Sedgwick, who was in Wayne County by 1808, imported the first Shorthorn bull into the region, and thirty years later Robert Smith from Chatteris worked with another man to bring the first Jersey bull into Indiana. After George Davis emigrated from England to Lake County in 1869, he crossed various breeds of hogs to produce the new "Victoria" breed, which won Davis numerous prizes in the Chicago Fat-Stock shows in the late 1870s and early 1880s.[44]

One particularly important contribution that English farmers made to Indiana's agriculture was that they helped to dispel the common misassumption that the prairie lands in the region were not suitable for cultivation.[45] This happened in Benton County in 1850 when a small colony of Englishmen led by Francis Greenwood settled near White Oak Grove and opened up the area to successful farming. What these English settlers did not anticipate was that "the bleak prairie and the winter winds were too much for them," and all "had a good cry and wished themselves back in the old home," as "the low land . . . and cheerless surroundings were in sharp contrast to the well kept hedge rows and gardens of old England." But eventually, with the support of fellow Englishmen who joined them, they adjusted to their new environment, became successful farmers, and attracted more farmers to the area.[46]

### Industrial Immigrants

The English and Welsh in Indiana were remarkably diverse in their skills and backgrounds. This diversity can be explained by the uniqueness of Great Britain's economy, especially its comparatively high degree of industrialization and urbanization. Because Great Britain led the world in textile production throughout the nineteenth century and had more textile workers than any other nation, it was inevitable that some of these workers would join the stream of immigrants flowing toward America. Their numbers were greatest during the early decades of the century, when new technologies displaced some weavers and spinners in Great Britain and when America still hungered for certain textile technology and skills.[47] Most headed for New England and other eastern states where textile work was most readily available. However, Indiana proved attractive, too, because work in textiles was becoming more available, and for many, temporary work in textiles was a good way to reach the long-term goal of farming one's own land.

Of 253 case studies of nineteenth-century English and Welsh immigrants in Indiana, at least 24 (nearly 10 percent) had worked in textiles before their immigration.[48] All but one had immigrated before the mid-1850s, and they came to Indiana with various work experiences and goals. Some weavers and cloth dressers first settled in eastern states, worked at their trade, and then proceeded to Indiana with their savings to buy farmland. This pattern of mobility among textile workers in their long-term pursuit of land was strikingly familiar for a number of immigrants, among them William Thomas, a cloth dresser from Wales who immigrated in 1816 and went to Pittsburgh and then to Ohio, where he continued his trade and erected a small mill. Finally, sixteen years later Thomas entered Dearborn County to carry on cloth dressing and wool carding, and then he bought his farm.[49]

By the 1840s a wide variety of English textile workers could resume their work in Indiana. Textile operatives were leaving Yorkshire and heading directly to Indiana to work in mills that were already established there, and reed makers for cotton and silk manufacturers as well as cotton machinists were able to follow their craft in the state. Most were weavers, including those who had worked on England's industrialized power looms and those who still worked on preindustrialized hand looms. Whether they were prompted mainly by dislocation and unemployment or by a desire to seek a better life, the English textile workers were using the budding mills of Indiana as stepping-stones to something better. Mark Sharp, for example, worked in a woolen mill near Leeds and was also working with his own hand loom until he left England in 1847. A few months later he arrived in Lafayette, Tippecanoe County, where he found work in Hoagland's woolen factory. Soon he was able to open his own butcher shop and carry on a successful business.[50] James Nichols is another example. He left Yorkshire for Indiana in 1865 to work for his uncle, George Ellis, who had emigrated from Leeds thirty-five years earlier and established the Wabash Woolen Mills in Terre Haute in 1853. While Nichols could have remained in the woolen business with his uncle, he chose to open his own grocery business, which brought him the independence he was seeking.[51] Some English cotton machinists, like John Isherwood, worked in eastern states at their trade but found related, more remunerative work in Indiana—in Isherwood's case, work on locomotives and in gas works.[52]

But it appears that most of the textile workers from England and Wales who immigrated to Indiana intended to become farmers. Typical was William Brummitt, a Yorkshire weaver like his father. "In 1856, growing tired of his trade, he determined to come to America, procure land

and become a farmer," and so he immigrated directly to Porter County and two years later purchased three acres of uncleared land, which by 1880 had become the nucleus of an impressive 325-acre farm.[53] Other weavers and lace makers had made the same type of move in the 1820s and 1830s, though they had found it necessary first to work in mills in eastern states as skilled workers or overseers to acquire the capital necessary for farming.[54] Farming one's own land was a long-term goal that many were able to realize in Indiana.

It is hard to overestimate the importance of mechanics, machinists, and engineers in America's economic development. Some economic historians see them as the key players who made American industry competitive with Great Britain's.[55] Of course, many of these skilled persons had come from Great Britain in the first place, and this was true for those in Indiana too.[56] Some immigrant guidebooks emphasized the state's need for mechanics,[57] and considerable numbers from England and Wales responded to this need. Not every immigrant mechanic or machinist found in Indiana what he expected. When William Faux traveled through Evansville in 1819 he met "a few English mechanics" who regretted their immigration and thought "they could do better" in England.[58] But generally, skilled workers like these could reasonably expect to double or even triple their wages in Indiana. The mobility, both geographical and occupational, of many of these immigrants is impressive. James Lees, a machinist from Duckinfield, near Manchester, had spent a few years in Canada with his parents and then returned to England, until he immigrated again in 1849. He lived for a year in the eastern states and then in 1850 moved to Cannelton, on the north bank of the Ohio River in Perry County. He was given charge of the repair shop in a cotton mill, after which he became an engineer, and then established his own foundry and machine shop. Becoming "one of the leading citizens of Cannelton," Lees achieved a degree of upward mobility that was seldom heard of in England, and his was not an isolated case.[59]

As with immigrants from the textile industries, those who were mechanics, engineers, or machinists probably were drawn to Indiana most often by the lure of farm ownership. From available case studies it can be learned that these people usually entered farm life in Indiana after working at their trade a number of years in America, for they were not able to purchase their farms outright. Most apparently bought up the cheaper uncleared lands and endured the rigors of bringing them under cultivation. James Ewen was a machinist who left England in 1849 and used his skills in railroad shops in Chicago and other places for five years until he came to Lake County in 1854. Ewen was one of the first settlers in North Township and bought forty acres of wild land on which he built a crude log shanty and farmed and hunted until he could buy a larger farm.[60] Cornishman James Parnell was a mechanic who truly thought in the long term. In 1845, at age nineteen, he "carried out a desire of long standing" by immigrating to the United States. For twenty-three years he worked for high wages in Ohio making patterns and working in railroad shops, and then he achieved his ultimate goal and became a highly successful livestock farmer in Hancock County, Indiana.[61] Even in later decades, despite diminished agricultural opportunities, such long-range goals were reachable. Thomas Alderson began working in the coal mines of Durham at the age of nine. Before immigrating to America in 1879, he worked as a blacksmith, a fireman, and an engineer on a railway train. Going directly to Clay County, he worked there as a stationary engineer in the coal mines for twenty-two years. He then went to Greene County, where he bought a small farm in 1903 and gradually built up his holdings to become a prominent farmer and stock raiser.[62] The valuable and adaptable skills that mechanics, engineers, and machinists possessed were gateways to profitable employment and successful farming in Indiana. Men with such skills had choices before them and, with the help of letters from friends and family already in America, were able to plan their immigration carefully and acquire sufficient capital before setting out as farmers.

Some machinists and engineers of comfortable social and economic positions in Great Britain also immigrated to Indiana in the midnineteenth century. These were hardly desperate men. Edward Sinker, for example, was a widely experienced Welsh machinist who superintended major ironworks at various places in Great Britain. He was in charge of repairing the naval vessels in Portuguese ports and was an engineer on the project to bridge the Menai Strait. Yet with boundless ambition he headed to Indianapolis in 1849 where he set up his own boiler repair business. The venture quickly grew into the highly successful Western Machine Works, and Sinker became one of the city's "most esteemed" and well-known citizens.[63] Or consider the case of Timothy Harrison. He was born to "one of the old and eminently respectable families of Yorkshire," enjoyed a literary education at the prestigious preparatory school at Rugby, and had "scholarly tastes and habits." He immigrated to Indiana in 1856 to exploit the training in mechanical engineering that he had received at the Leeds Locomotive Works. Harrison purchased a woolen mill in Henry County and gradually expanded his interests into various manufactures to become a leader in the commercial and industrial development of Wayne County.[64]

*Edward Sinker, founder of the Western Machine Works, Indianapolis.*

Along with textile workers and mechanics came numbers of other skilled persons, especially building trades workers, miners, and various craftsmen. Carpenters like William Woodward, who emigrated from London in 1844, and Benjamin Turnock, who emigrated from Staffordshire in 1840, came to Indiana specifically to become farmers. Meanwhile, fellow Englishmen in the building trades found ample opportunity to utilize their craft in Indiana and enjoy other types of occupational mobility. Stonemasons like John Matthews, who had worked on London's Parliament buildings, prospered by opening and operating quarries, while Charles White left stonemasonry altogether to become a merchant in Shelby County.[65]

As with textiles, American coal mining was based largely on the experience of Great Britain, the world's leading coal producer throughout most of the nineteenth century. About forty thousand British miners entered the United States during the 1840s and 1850s alone, and it was their skills, methods, and technology that opened up most mines and established craft mining in the United States. It was also their ideas and leadership that led to the industry's first unions.[66] The impact that these immigrants had on early America was truly profound.

Among those Britons who opened up and developed the coalfields of southwestern Indiana were Richard Freeman, who became known as "the father of the coal industry in Knox County," and his brother Job, who was credited with making Linton, Greene County, known as "the Pittsburg of the West." The sons of a Staffordshire miner, the Freemans immigrated in 1850. They started out as miners themselves and opened up coal mines in Indiana. Eventually the Freemans became coal mine owners and operators and by the turn of the century were among the state's leading coal magnates.[67] A nearly identical story involved Daniel H. Davis, who emigrated from South Wales in 1857 with the intention of "accumulating a great fortune." He came to Clay County ten years later to establish the Davis Coal Company, which became the foundation for Davis's extensive ownership of banks, trusts, and real estate.[68] Though such success was extraordinary, many other English and Welsh miners came to Indiana and through similar mobility realized their ultimate goal: to get out of mining altogether. Usually they mined first in Pennsylvania, and then in Indiana, until they had sufficient capital to take up farming. But a number of others chose to become saloon and hotel keepers, grocers, merchants, or even lawyers.[69] The relatively high wages that miners earned and the diverse openings that existed in the Indiana economy made such a deliverance from the bowels of a coal mine common among the English and Welsh immigrants.

The story of Frank Straughan is especially touching. Blinded at age thirteen, he was compelled to enter the Durham mines as a laborer until he and his parents immigrated directly to Indiana in 1882. Straughan was sixteen at the time and resumed laboring in the mines in Rosedale, Parke County, to earn enough money to pay for the surgery that might restore his sight. In spite of the expensive and painful surgery, Straughan remained blind. He returned to the mines and worked there until he was twenty-four, when he was able to open a candy store with his earnings. He never regained his sight, but he did enjoy a profitable business and the admiration of all who knew him.[70]

The social and occupational mobility exhibited by the miners was also enjoyed by millers, tailors, shoemakers, potters, and other "pre-industrial craftsmen."[71] These persons had transferable skills, though sometimes they had to undergo considerable adjustment to fit American situations, as did Samuel F. Smith, a Yorkshire shoemaker who immigrated in 1835. Smith had to relearn his craft because on the Indiana frontier he initially had to use wooden pegs instead of shoe nails.[72] The famed potters of Staffordshire are especially worthy of mention. Clays from the "Mississippi chalk banks" were lying ready in Perry County for exploitation by people like Englishman James Clews, who had the necessary skills. For two decades he was a maker of fine blue cobalt pottery in Staffordshire. Then he ran into money problems, was forced to sell his assets to settle his debts, and immigrated in the mid-1830s to Troy, where he attempted to reestablish what he had lost in Staffordshire. In spite of importing at least forty highly skilled potters from Staffordshire, his effort failed. By 1860 another Staffordshire potter, Samuel Wilson, was in Troy making "Rockingham and yellow ware" in his own Indiana Pottery Company. This is one of many examples of how English and Welsh immigrants brought unique skills to Indiana.[73]

## The Transfer of Skills and Technology

The flow of skilled laborers and technology from Great Britain to America, what historian David Jeremy has called "the Transatlantic Industrial Revolution," was important for the economic development of many states, including Indiana.[74] Understandably, the British government was alarmed by this outflow of talent, and until 1824 it sought to maintain British leadership in manufacturing by prohibiting the emigration of skilled artisans and persons with valuable technological knowledge. Thus some of the early English and Welsh immigrants who left for Indiana actually risked imprisonment in Great Britain when they violated these laws. John Sutcliffe, a Methodist clergyman who was also skilled at making reeds for silk looms, had heard of the better opportunities that awaited craftsmen in America.

*Humphrey Griffith of Dolgelly, Wales.*

Fortunately he had a friend who was a captain of a sailing vessel and who was willing to help him evade government inspection. With the help of the ship's stevedores, Sutcliffe was hidden in the ship's hold, and his valuable reed-making tools were hidden in a firkin of butter. In such a risky fashion he virtually escaped to America in 1812. Going first to Kentucky and then to Fayette County, Indiana, in 1828, Sutcliffe combined his two callings and realized the opportunities that had attracted him in the first place.[75] In a similar way Humphrey Griffith of Dolgelly (Merionethshire), Wales, had served a seven-year apprenticeship as a watch and clock maker in Shrewsbury and then worked at his craft in London until 1817, when he decided to break the law and emigrate. Griffith managed to slip away to Dublin, and from there he was able to make the voyage to America, working for a short while in Pennsylvania and Ohio and then coming to the vicinity of Indianapolis in 1822. He was the first clock and watchmaker in the city and made the clock for the original Statehouse, which was said never to need maintenance or regulating. Perhaps because of his trade, Griffith was known for his "punctuality in all things," and with shrewd investments in business and real estate he was twice able to visit his native homestead in Dolgelly.[76]

Throughout much of Indiana's economic history English and Welsh immigrants were conspicuous in inventing and improving various machines and devices and using mechanical and engineering skills that had originated across the Atlantic. Some of these people were able to combine their mechanical pursuits with farming and thus realize what were probably long-term agricultural goals. This was true of men like Richard Sedgwick, who emigrated from Yorkshire to Indiana in its territorial days. A successful farmer and also a mechanic, he reportedly built the first fanning mill, which was apparently a forerunner of the threshing machine. Others made the first wooden pumps, fanning mills, and similar devices, all of which served Indiana's early economic development.[77]

As Indiana's economy became more diversified after the Civil War, its new industries attracted British workers to the state. Some of these new industries were largely dependent on the skills and technology brought to the state by English and Welsh immigrants, some of whom were actually recruited by American businessmen. Henry Legg was a highly skilled plate glass maker and for twenty years was the foreman of the casting department of the Thames Plate Glass Works in his native London. In 1872 he was invited to come to New Albany, Indiana, to become chief foreman of the casting department of the new DePauw American Plate Glass Works. But this was just the beginning of an important immigration of skill: Legg was able to return to London in 1874 to bring over his family of seven members, together with "several skilled plate glass workers and their families," as well as a device called the "box and coal furnace" and "Dinas brick" from Wales. These items were used in glass furnaces in Great Britain and were then used in American glass furnaces.[78]

A similar story involves the United States Encaustic Tile-Works of Indianapolis, said to have been the largest establishment of its kind in the world. With easy access to highly suitable clays for decorative flooring tiles, the company, organized in 1877, "procured a number of skilled workmen from England," and after eighteen months of experimentation got under way. By the mid-1880s the firm employed three hundred persons, including many English operatives, and its superintendent visited England and brought back "a number of additional families" who had the appropriate, specialized skills.[79] The factory's product was soon in great demand in every state, as well as in a number of foreign countries. Such contributions, along with an Anglo-Saxon bias, led later writers to say that "no class of foreign-born citizens have done for America what the English have."[80]

Welshmen also became catalysts in Indiana's early industrialization, since industrial South Wales was a source of advanced skills. William Bowen, the son of the Welshman who built Belgium's second blast furnace, immigrated to Pottsville, Pennsylvania, in 1859 at age nineteen. Apparently he had been well taught by his father, for with a brother in 1874 he established the Bowen Brothers Foundry in Hobart, Lake County, Indiana.[81] Twenty years later another Welsh immigrant, William Richards, was undertaking a similar enterprise in tinplate manufacturing. Having learned his skills from his father, who was a highly successful tinplate maker in Glamorganshire, Richards left Wales in 1890, probably frustrated by the crippling impact of new American tariffs on Welsh tinplate exports. After a year's employment in a Pittsburgh steel plant, the twenty-seven-year-old Richards went to Madison County, Indiana, and with his brother rolled the very first sheet of tinplate in Elwood. Later he took part in the building of the Morewood Tin Plate Company in nearby Grant County and then headed it for nine years, after which he became the director and paymaster of the Indiana Rubber and Insulated Wire Company in Jonesboro. He became known as one of the foremost businessmen of Indiana.[82]

Of course, English and Welsh immigrants could also acquire their skills in America and put them to good use in Indiana. George Ellis emigrated from Leeds in 1829, and he gained most of his knowledge about how to manufacture woolen fabrics in Philadelphia. In 1853 he moved to Terre Haute where he established the Wabash Woolen Mills, which by 1880 included more than eleven hundred spindles and produced one thousand yards of cloth daily. Not every English iron roller had learned his skills in the old country. John Knight, for example, led an interesting life as a sailor before he immigrated in 1856. After twenty years of service in the United States Navy he entered his first rolling mill in Dearborn County and became an ironworker.[83] A particularly interesting case of technology flowing eastward across the Atlantic is that of William Hoadley, Jr., whose family emigrated from Yorkshire in 1842 only to return to England four years later with an American-made planing mill and machine for making buckets. Hoadley hoped to introduce this American technology to England and make his fortune. But "owing to the hostility felt there against American improvements," his enterprise failed and he returned to America. He settled in New Albany and bought a sawmill and flour mill—only to learn later that others made fortunes out of this same bucket scheme in England.[84] In these and other cases Indiana both received from and offered skills to English and Welsh immigrants.[85]

## Forces in Assimilation: The Civil War and Anglo-American Culture

The English and Welsh in Indiana shared a characteristic that helped make them Americans: a deep hatred toward slavery and an eagerness to participate in the Civil War. A few had previously owned slaves themselves in the South before freeing them and leaving for Indiana, and though one English preacher in Fort Wayne supported slavery on a biblical basis, the great majority of English and Welsh immigrants loathed the very idea of slavery.[86] Matthew Foster, an immigrant from Durham, passed through Indiana in 1817 on his way to St. Louis, but was so repulsed by the agitation to make Missouri a slave state that he returned to Pike County, Indiana, to settle on an idyllic site that he had noticed on his way to the West.[87] Herefordshire native James Powell was highly active in the Underground Railway while living in Ohio and continued abolitionist activities after he came to Indiana in 1854.[88]

British immigrants were among the first to respond to Lincoln's call to arms. Not only did Indiana's English and Welsh participate enthusiastically in the Civil War, but they also did so within such a short time of their immigration. It is not known why Dawson Smith left his wife and children in Yorkshire in 1864, sailed for America, and "at once allied himself with the causes of the American Union . . . and immediately went to the front." Afterwards he went to White County, Indiana, and "took charge of the woolen mills" in Monticello.[89] William Stockdale was another who immigrated during the war and fought bravely in it. Jeremiah Winter emigrated from Norfolk in 1858, enlisted four years later, fought his first battle at Gettysburg, and then farmed in White County.[90] The list goes on. Some were killed, and others suffered, perhaps, a worse fate in the infamous Andersonville Prison. Henry Nobes, a native of London who enlisted in the Seventy-second Indiana Infantry, emerged from that terrible place a skeletal eighty-three pounds, and he carried the physical and emotional scars with him for the rest of his life.[91]

The Civil War not only killed and maimed these immigrants, but it also tore apart their families in several ways. William Matthews was refused permission to enlist from his father, an immigrant stonemason from London, so he ran off to Indianapolis and joined the army anyway.[92] Even more poignant is the story of Jonas Rhodes, whose four sons all went off to face the carnage. One son joined the Confederate Army after having married the daughter of a slaveholder. One son died in battle, his body never found, and two others died shortly after their return from the war.[93]

The Civil War provided an opportunity for the English and Welsh in Indiana to prove their patriotism, their commitment to the Union, and their manhood; for some it satisfied a yearning for adventure. But the war was also an occasion for sacrifice, and for some to fight for black freedom. William Stockdale is an example of this. Having immigrated during the war, he immediately enlisted, lost an eye and a leg in battle, and received these reassuring words from his father still in Manchester: "You fought in a good cause—and you where [were] one I may say that where [were] the means of giving the blacks freedom."[94]

Near the turn of the century the character of English and Welsh immigration to Indiana was changing. Because American industries were outperforming Great Britain's there was no longer much need for British technology or the skilled persons who provided it. Historian Dean R. Esslinger has shown that after the Civil War South Bend's English immigrants were increasingly composed of manual and semiskilled workers, although the English and Germans continued to achieve a higher status than all other ethnic groups.[95] This pattern was very likely experienced in Indiana's other cities as well. Some English and Welsh industrial workers continued to immigrate to the state, along with laborers, craftsmen, miners, and farmers, but they were no longer as prominent or as highly valued as they once were. Indeed, the English worker in particular was now earning the reputation for being too demanding, prone to strike, and even too tradition minded to learn new techniques himself in America.[96] The fact that the English were active in the formation of American labor unions was not something that every Hoosier would applaud.[97]

In addition, there was lingering distrust between some English immigrants and native-born Americans. The latter harbored traditional resentment for the English that stemmed from the Revolution and the War of 1812. Tension between the two countries flared up again during the time of the Mexican War, the Civil War, and in the 1890s over policy in South America. Also, heavy English investment in American railways, land, mining, and cattle companies fueled fears on the part of some Americans that the British were out to exploit and dominate America once again. English immigrants in Indiana must have felt these tensions at times, especially when they celebrated Victoria Day and displayed vestiges of their ethnicity. For their part the English found some Americans' uncouth behavior and shrill and strident nationalism abrasive and threatening. Some English immigrants in America who spoke fondly of their place of birth were met with hostile accusations of disloyalty, and it was not unknown for English farmers in the Midwest to paint enormous American flags on their barns so as to leave no doubt about their patriotism.[98] Many more had to prove it during the Civil War.

But whatever cultural friction there was between English immigrants and their Hoosier hosts it was outweighed by general good will and mutual appreciation. Generally,

IHS C5238

*George J. Eacock, attorney, was born in Suffolk County, England, in 1853 and immigrated to Lafayette, Tippecanoe County, in 1873.*

the English and Welsh were welcomed for their abilities, and most Indianans saw them as cousins rather than true foreigners.[99] As rising numbers of peoples from southern and eastern Europe entered Indiana, the English immigrants and native-born Americans saw more clearly their common set of cultural traits, beliefs, prejudices, and their related political heritage. The bulk of Indiana's population, after all, was derived from the British Isles, and so the British in Indiana were not total strangers. Indeed, though their assimilation was not always easy, the English had a higher intermarriage rate with the native-born Americans than did any other ethnic group, and their voting behavior and largely Republican political ideology also closely paralleled that of the native born.[100] Assimilation was most rapid and thorough among the children of English immigrants, for more so than any other ethnic group they were hardly distinguishable from most of the native-born population. Their sense of ethnic identity and what few immigrant institutions they had seldom lasted to a third generation.[101]

The assimilation of the English in Indiana was seen perhaps most clearly in the state legislature. Unlike other immigrant politicians, the English born did not rise through leadership in ethnic organizations, and they avoided the appearance of being ethnic leaders. Among those who rose to political prominence in Indiana was William Baxter, a woolen factory manager from Yorkshire who had also read law. He immigrated in 1848 at age twenty-four, traded wool in Philadelphia and Indiana before entering politics, and was elected to the state House and Senate as a Republican in the 1870s. Baxter was recognized for his leadership in the reform of prisons and capital punishment and for his involvement in the temperance movement.[102] Another Yorkshireman in the state legislature was William Carr, a stonecutter who immigrated in 1854, worked at his trade in various American cities, and was elected as a Democrat in 1880. He, too, was "identified with the leaders of progression and improvement."[103] Another English immigrant, Elijah Halford, became Benjamin Harrison's private secretary after a career as a journalist and managing editor of the *Indianapolis Journal*.[104]

In the world of art two English immigrants in Indiana were widely praised for their particularly valuable contributions. George Winter, trained partly in New York, headed west in 1836 and in 1837 settled in Logansport, where he won fame painting portraits of the Miami and Potawatomi Indians. And John Herron, who came to Indiana in 1847, made a fortune in real estate. He bequeathed money to the Art Association of Indianapolis, which used the money to build the John Herron Art Institute (now the Indianapolis Museum of Art), as well as the influential John Herron Art School (now the art school for Indiana University-Purdue University at Indianapolis).[105]

## The Twentieth Century

In the twentieth century English and Welsh immigration to Indiana, and to the United States generally, declined dramatically. More precisely, the immigrants were rejecting America for the British Commonwealth countries as their choice of destination. From 1905 on Canada took in more Britons than the United States did, while other members of the Commonwealth and Empire also increased their share. And by World War I only 18 percent of all English and Welsh immigrants came directly to the United States, as opposed to roughly 75 percent in 1841.[106]

Several factors explain this shift in direction. First of all the United States was not as attractive to Britons as it had been in the past. American industries had little need for imported skills and were getting plenty of cheap unskilled labor from southern and eastern Europe, while cheap and profitable farmland was much harder to come by. At the same time the Dominions were having greater appeal, due to some extent to a growing imperial consciousness and loyalty on the part of the immigrants, but more to the inducements that these destinations offered them: assisted passages, prearranged employment and housing, and free or very cheap land. To reinforce this trend the Empire Resettlement Act of 1922 was passed to facilitate the movement of surplus labor from Great Britain's industrial cities and poor farming districts to those parts of the Dominions that suffered labor shortages—all at a time when the United States was shutting its doors to large-scale immigration.[107]

The English and Welsh never filled the generous immigration quotas that were granted to them by the discriminatory Immigration Act of 1924 (commonly known as the Johnson Bill). The years of large-scale immigration from Great Britain to the United States were over. In fact, during the Great Depression more English and Welsh returned to Great Britain than arrived in America. This decline is clearly seen in the census figures for Indiana: after 1920, when there were more than eight thousand English born and eighteen hundred Welsh born in the state, these numbers fell to a little more than five thousand and two hundred respectively. In each decade from 1950 to 1980 only about one thousand English and a couple dozen Welsh immigrated to Indiana.[108]

Those who did come to Indiana from England or Wales between 1900 and 1950 included many whose essential motives and characteristics were not altogether different from those who had arrived earlier. But because laborers and farmers were much fewer in number, certain skilled persons and especially professional people became relatively more prominent. This trend grew in later years to become what was commonly referred to as a "brain drain" from Great Britain to America. Most simply possessed skills or could perform tasks that were more highly rewarded in Indiana than in Great Britain, though the era of significant technological transfer was over. The enormous steel works of Gary were built with American know-how (which of course was based on British know-how). Yet Welshmen like Thomas Howells from Cardiff were involved with their construction, though few Britons performed manual tasks in these later ironworks.[109] Others included D. T. Jones, a tin mill foreman from South Wales who arrived in Gary in 1916 to become the night superintendent in Gary's Sheet and Tin Mill. Some left the tin mills of South Wales directly for those in Gary, along with electricians and people who worked as foremen. For a sense of community, these immigrants organized in 1916 the Welsh Daffodils Society (the daffodil is the national flower of Wales), which in the 1930s merged with the larger Cambrian Welsh Society, organized in 1926. Each year the society commemorated St. David's Day with a banquet and song festival featuring traditional Welsh songs and hymns. By the mid-1950s there were approximately 150 Welsh families in Gary, and though most were naturalized citizens they celebrated their Welshness through cultural events like the national *Gymanfa Ganu* (singing festival), held each year in various parts of the country.[110]

Coal miners also continued to come from Great Britain to Indiana well into the twentieth century, and something of the nature of this movement can be seen in the stories of the four Davies brothers and the James and Moses families, who left the Aberdare area in South Wales to mine in Jasonville, Greene County. These people were part of a tradition of Welsh mining in Greene County that dated back a couple of generations, and they were maximizing their earning power by following long-established networks between Glamorganshire and the United States. Like many of their predecessors, these more recent Welsh immigrants first mined in Pennsylvania or West Virginia before coming to Indiana, quite willing to follow the best economic opportunities. The four Davies brothers had started out for Pennsylvania but then heard of better work in Jasonville and settled there instead. John Davies was killed in a mining accident in Jasonville in 1920. Some sense of the importance of networks and faster steamships is captured by the experience of the Moses family. John Moses followed relatives from Wales to Indiana in 1908, and he was followed by family members two years later.

And though acquiring American citizenship in 1915, they returned to Wales in 1919, only to immigrate once again to Indiana a year later.[111] Immigrants could carefully compare the two countries and choose between them, knowing that their decisions were not irreversible.

The "special relationship" between Great Britain and America that one often hears mentioned was born out of the common cultural and political roots of British colonization, reinforced over time by the steady immigration of millions of British people and forged by twentieth-century alliances, especially their common struggle in World War II. While more professional people participated in the slowing emigration from England and Wales, the Second World War also affected the emigration in interesting ways. Besides the thousands of British war brides who came to the United States with their American husbands soon after the war, there were some Britons who had been evacuated to the Dominions or the United States for safety, and though most eventually returned to Great Britain some did stay or came back to the United States in later years. One English war evacuee who left an enduring legacy to the state of Indiana was Joyce Isabella Mann, who was born in Norfolk in 1886 and became a governess to Europe's nobility after her own family had gone bankrupt. Having escaped to America from the Nazi threat in 1940, from 1943 to 1953 she was in service in Houston, Texas, to Kenneth Dale Owen, descendant of Robert Owen, and from 1954 in New Harmony, where she remained for the rest of her life. Mann was active in the preservation of the historical records of the Owen community and gave a large portion of her own wealth to the New Harmony Workingmen's Institute Library.[112]

The modern postwar era saw smaller numbers of English and Welsh immigrants arrive in Indiana, but the proportions of those with professional qualifications were far higher than ever before. From the late 1950s through the mid-1960s the United States took in more surgeons and physicians from England than from any other nation, and during the 1970s and 1980s about half of the British immigrants to the United States were professional, technical, or managerial workers—mainly doctors, academics, nurses, engineers, and secretaries. The "brain drain" from Great Britain to America was on, to the benefit of states like Indiana, and to the grave concern of many British observers.[113]

Although these modern-day immigrants arrived mainly by jet aircraft, some characteristics of the people who had sailed over a century before can be seen in them: they, too, were ambitious, adventurous, and talented people who saw a brighter future in America. Interviews with recent immigrants to Indiana and other states reveal that economic considerations were the most important, but by no means the only reasons for their decision to immigrate. Attractive offers to work in laboratories, companies, or universities had much more than simply economic appeal. In addition, like an echo of the war brides of a half century ago, Americans living in Great Britain as students, businessmen, or military personnel have brought back English or Welsh spouses, while many British students living in America met spouses and stayed. Some also expressed their exasperation with the comparatively rigid heirarchical tradition in British society and institutions, while others were angry with the higher taxes of Labour governments and what they saw as progressive dependency in society. And, like English and Welsh immigrants of long ago, some were just bored with life and wanted to start over in a new country.[114]

As Americans and Britons view each other today, usually through the lenses of television and the movies, there is for many a mutual attraction or at least a fascination that is probably unique in the world. This is true because each sees in the other more similarities than the many interesting differences that exist. They see the legacy of British immigrants. The role that these immigrants played in the history of Indiana's birth, growth, and development cannot be ignored.

## Notes

1. Cornelius Pering to S. Edwards, 27 Aug. 1833, Pering Family Papers, 1821–1920, S 1052, Indiana Division, Indiana State Library, Indianapolis.

2. Mrs. Susannah Hine Pering to Mrs. L. Edwards, Chard, Somerset, 27 Aug. 1833, ibid. It is not possible to determine the number of English or Welsh immigrants in Indiana at this time. The first U.S. census to enumerate immigrants by country of origin was that of 1850, at which time there were 5,550 English and 169 Welsh.

3. Charlotte Erickson, "British Immigrants in the Old Northwest, 1815–1860," in David M. Ellis, ed., *The Frontier in American Development* (Ithaca, N.Y.: Cornell University Press, 1969), 323–56.

4. For interesting details on the English experience during these events, see James Madison, *The Indiana Way: A State History* (Bloomington and Indianapolis: Indiana University Press and Indiana Historical Society, 1986), 18–27; John D. Barnhart and Dorothy L. Riker, *Indiana to 1816: The Colonial Period* (Indianapolis: Indiana Historical Bureau and Indiana Historical Society, 1971), 94–178; Howard H. Peckham, *Indiana: A Bicentennial History*, The States and the Nation Series (New York: Norton, 1978), 21–30; J. P. Dunn, Jr., *Indiana, A Redemption from Slavery*, American Commonwealths (Boston: Houghton Mifflin and Co., 1888), chapters 2 and 5. The English who came to America in the 1770s had a very low ratio of women to men, and they were generally people of means, some of them taking with them a servant or two. See Charlotte Erickson, "English," in Stephan Thernstrom, ed., *Harvard Encyclopedia of American Ethnic Groups* (Cambridge, Mass.: Belknap Press of Harvard University Press, 1980), 323.

5. *National Cyclopedia of American Biography*, 63 vols. (New York: James T. White, 1898–1984), 16:268; William Wesley Woollen, *Biographical and Historical Sketches of Early Indiana* (Indianapolis: Hammond and Co., 1883), 376–77.

6. *History of Dearborn, Ohio and Switzerland Counties, Indiana* (Chicago: Weakley, Harraman and Co., 1885), 786–87.

7. For just some of the numerous cases see Charles Blanchard, ed., *Counties of Morgan, Monroe and Brown, Indiana* (Chicago: F. A. Battey and Co., 1884), 196–97; *Biographical Memoirs of Hancock County, Indiana* (Logansport, Ind.: B. F. Bowen, 1902), 240; *Portrait and Biographical Record of Madison and Hamilton Counties, Indiana* (1893; reprint, Evansville, Ind.: Unigraphic, 1973), 528–29 (here see the case of the Havens brothers), 586; *History of De Kalb County, Indiana* (Indianapolis: B. F. Bowen and Co., Inc., 1914), 586.

8. Sedgwick was also the second white man married in Wayne County. *Biographical and Genealogical History of Wayne, Fayette, Union and Franklin Counties, Indiana*, 2 vols. (Chicago: Lewis Publishing Co., 1899), 1:488.

9. August J. Reifel, *History of Franklin County, Indiana* (1915; reprint, Evansville, Ind.: Unigraphic, 1971), 114.

10. *Portrait and Biographical Record of Madison and Hamilton Counties*, 387.

11. Ibid., 586; Captain Lewis C. Baird, *Baird's History of Clark County, Indiana* (1909; reprint, Evansville, Ind.: Unigraphic, 1972), 896. See also the case of James Jones, mentioned above. Not all of the English immigrants were willing to fight in the conflict. Thomas Patterson paid someone to take his place in the Virginia militia in 1813, before he entered Indiana. See the Thomas Hodgson Book, 1775, SC 764, Indiana Historical Society Library, Indianapolis. On the American policy toward the English see Harry C. Allen, *Conflict and Concord: The Anglo-American Relationship since 1783* (New York: St. Martin's Press, 1959).

12. Charlotte Erickson, *Invisible Immigrants: The Adaptation of English and Scottish Immigrants in Nineteenth-Century America* (Leicester: Leicester University Press, 1972). On the native born not seeing the English as foreigners see R. T. Berthoff, *British Immigrants in Industrial America, 1790–1950* (1953; reprint, New York: Russell and Russell, 1968), 132. In his study of immigrants in South Bend, Dean R. Esslinger found that the English were unique for not forming ethnic neighborhoods in the city. Esslinger, *Immigrants and the City: Ethnicity and Mobility in a Nineteenth-Century Midwestern Community* (Port Washington, N.Y.: Kennikat Press, 1975), 52. Those Welsh who were less fluent in English tended to be more clannish. See Berthoff, *British Immigrants*, 111.

13. The story of this "English colony" is reconstructed from *History of Dearborn, Ohio and Switzerland Counties*, 461–62, 560, 986, and Archibald Shaw, ed., *History of Dearborn County, Indiana* (Indianapolis: B. F. Bowen and Co., Inc., 1915), 212–15, 226, 227. Together these sources cite at least twenty-two Yorkshire families.

14. Reifel, *History of Franklin County*, 129–30; Ernie Hernandez, *Ethnics in Northwest Indiana* (Gary, Ind.: Post-Tribune, 1984), 170; T. H. Ball, ed. in chief, *Encyclopedia of Genealogy and Biography of Lake County, Indiana* (1904; reprint, Evansville, Ind.: Unigraphic, 1974), 113–14; Jesse Setlington Birch, *History of Benton County and Historic Oxford* (Oxford, Ind.: Craw and Craw, Inc., 1942), 24–25.

15. On providing English marriage partners see the case of John Henney's father in *Biographical Record of Bartholomew County, Indiana* (Indianapolis: B. F. Bowen, 1904), 213.

16. William Faux, *Memorable Days in America* (London: W. Simpkin and R. Marshall, 1823), 242, 243. For another favorable account by an English settler in the area see the letter of T. Cawson, 1 Jan. 1820, SC 546, Indiana Historical Society Library, in which

Cawson boasts that "my dog and cat eat more venison in one month than any nobleman in England can eat in a year." Yet Cawson admitted that "I often sighed to be again in my native land; but I am now satisfied." He also noted that "we have emigrants arriving from England every week." On the colonies of Morris Birkbeck and George Flower and the one established by Saunders Hornbrook see Morris Birkbeck, *Notes on a Journey in America, from the Coast of Virginia to the Territory of Illinois* (Philadelphia: Caleb Richardson, 1817) and John E. Iglehart, "The Coming of the English to Indiana in 1817 and Their Hoosier Neighbors," *Indiana Magazine of History* 15 (June 1919): 89–178. By 1840 most of the English colonists in Vanderburgh County had drifted into Evansville, and their village of Saundersville had vanished.

17. Robert Owen's well-known work in New Lanark cannot be discussed here, and for that matter the New Harmony colony had little to do with British immigrants, save Owen himself and perhaps a few others. These communities' history is adequately discussed in Frank Podmore, *Robert Owen, A Biography* (New York: Haskell House Publishers, 1971); G. D. H. Cole, *The Life of Robert Owen*, 3d ed. (London: Frank Cass, 1965); Donald E. Pitzer, ed., *Robert Owen's American Legacy: Proceedings of the Robert Owen Bicentennial Conference* (Indianapolis: Indiana Historical Society, 1972); and Richard E. Banta, "New Harmony's Golden Years," *Indiana Magazine of History* 44 (Mar. 1948): 25–36.

18. R. Carlyle Buley, *The Old Northwest: Pioneer Period, 1815–1840*, 2 vols. (Bloomington: Indiana University Press in association with the Indiana Historical Society, 1950), 2:608–9. See also the references in the preceding note. The man who did the selling for George Rapp was Richard Flower, son of George Flower.

19. Faux, *Memorable Days in America*, 241–43.

20. James B. Lane, *"City of the Century": A History of Gary, Indiana* (Bloomington: Indiana University Press, 1978), 15.

21. *History of De Kalb County*, 586.

22. Faux, *Memorable Days in America*, 247.

23. *History of Dearborn, Ohio and Switzerland Counties*, 742–44.

24. Ibid., 925, 938; *Biographical and Genealogical History of Wayne, Fayette, Union and Franklin Counties*, 1:458–59; Jesse W. Weik, *Weik's History of Putnam County, Indiana* (Indianapolis: B. F. Bowen and Co., 1910), 381–82. Other immigrants of elite backgrounds of course came to the more settled parts of the state. See the case of Cambridge-educated surgeon Elam Perkins in *Biographical Record and Portrait Album of Tippecanoe County, Indiana* (1888; reprint, Evansville, Ind.: Unigraphic, 1972), 392–93, and the case of Dr. Henry Plowman, son of a nobleman who was fluent in five languages, in John H. B. Nowland, *Sketches of Prominent Citizens of 1876* (Indianapolis: Tilford and Carlon, Printers, 1877), 421.

25. James Tate, for example, was farming and butchering in his native Yorkshire but was "favorably impressed with the reports given of the country across the sea" and immigrated to see if the stories were true. Samuel E. Alvord, *Alvord's History of Noble County, Indiana* (Logansport, Ind.: B. F. Bowen, 1902), 264–65. Others were doing well but were actually recruited to Indiana, as was wagonmaker William Lewry in 1855. Weston A. Goodspeed and Charles Blanchard, eds., *Counties of Porter and Lake, Indiana* (1882; reprint, Evansville, Ind.: Unigraphic, 1970), 396.

26. John S. Ellis, *Our County [Delaware], Its History and Early Settlement* ([1898]; reprint, Evansville, Ind.: Whipporwill Publications, 1987), 61.

27. Benjamin G. Shinn, ed., *Biographical Memoirs of Blackford County, Ind.* (Chicago: Bowen Publishing Co., 1900), 363–65.

28. Frank M. Gilbert, *History of the City of Evansville and Vanderburg[h] County, Indiana*, 2 vols. (Chicago: Pioneer Publishing Co., 1910), 2:63–64.

29. *Biographical and Historical Souvenir for the Counties of Clark, Crawford, Harrison, Floyd, Jefferson, Jennings, Scott and Washington, Indiana* (Chicago: John M. Gresham and Co., 1889), 215. See also the case of James Grawcock, who took on ditch digging to secure his foothold in Indiana in 1853. Weston A. Goodspeed and Charles Blanchard, eds., *Counties of Whitley and Noble, Indiana* (1882; reprint, Evansville, Ind.: Unigraphic, 1970), 482–83.

30. *Historical Statistics of the United States: Colonial Times to 1957* (Washington, D.C.: Bureau of the Census, 1961), 56–57.

31. This "unscientific" sample of case studies was taken from immigrant letters and journals and mostly from the wide variety of publications that fall under the rubric "county histories," some of which are referred to in this work. The county histories were taken from fifty-three of Indiana's ninety-two counties, evenly spread to cover the entire state, and both rural and urban areas. These cases are also fairly spread over the period from the late eighteenth century through 1880—with a few from the late nineteenth and early twentieth centuries. There is obviously a bias here, in that these cases are mostly from those who "made it," some of them subscribing to the book in order to have their story told in it. However, the information used in this study—the immigrants' origins, occupations, and early experiences—is not much affected by the bias.

32. Alan Conway, "Welsh Emigration to the United States," in *Dislocation and Emigration: The Social Background of American Immigration*, vol. 7 of *Perspectives in American History* (Cambridge, Mass.: Charles Warren Center for Studies in American History, Harvard University, 1973), 177–271. William E. Van Vugt, "Welsh Immigration to the U.S.A. during the Mid-Nineteenth Century," *Welsh History Review* 15 (1991): 545–61.

33. This trend is supported by the studies cited in n. 34.

34. The pioneer in this new scholarship on the British is Charlotte Erickson, whose studies include "Who Were the English and Scots Immigrants to the United States in the Late-Nineteenth Century?," in D. V. Glass and R. Revelle, eds., *Population and Social Change* (New York: Crane, Russak, 1972), 347–81; "Emigration from the British Isles to the U.S.A. in 1831," *Population Studies* 35 (July 1981): 175–97; "Emigration from the British Isles to the U.S.A. in 1841: Part I. Emigration from the British Isles," *Population Studies* 43 (1989): 347–67, and "Part II. Who Were the English Emigrants?," *Population Studies* 44 (1990): 21–40. See also William E. Van Vugt, "Running from Ruin? The Emigration of British Farmers to the U.S.A. in the Wake of the Repeal of the Corn Laws," *Economic History Review*, 2d ser., 41 (Aug. 1988): 411–28, and "Prosperity and Industrial Emigration from Britain during the Early 1850s," *Journal of Social History* 22 (Winter 1988): 339–54.

35. See the compilations of ship lists with Indiana-bound immigrants from Great Britain provided by Michael Cassady in *The Hoosier Genealogist* 23 (Sept. 1983): 55–61; 25 (June 1985): 26; 25 (Dec. 1985): 84, 92; and 27 (Sept. 1987): 66–68. These lists are from 1850, 1853, 1855, and 1867 and provide information on fewer than fifty English or Welsh immigrants, who were mostly craftsmen, laborers, and farmers.

36. This very general picture is based on the studies cited in n. 34.

37. For examples of immigrants with nonagricultural backgrounds taking up farming in Indiana see Goodspeed and Blanchard, eds., *Counties of Porter and Lake*, 706; *Biographical Memoirs of Greene County, Ind.*, 2 vols. (Indianapolis: B. F. Bowen and Co., 1908), 2:775; Blanchard, ed., *Counties of Morgan, Monroe and Brown*, 612–13.

38. Charlotte Erickson, "Agrarian Myths of English Immigrants,"

in O. Fritiof Ander, *In the Trek of the Immigrants* (Rock Island, Ill.: Augustana College Library, 1964), 59–80; Wilbur Shepperson, *Emigration and Disenchantment: Portraits of Englishmen Repatriated from the United States* (Norman: University of Oklahoma Press, 1965).

39. Edward H. Chadwick, *Chadwick's History of Shelby County, Indiana* (1909; reprint, Evansville, Ind.: Unigraphic, 1977), 777–78.

40. For examples of English farm laborers immigrating to Indiana see *History of Warrick, Spencer and Perry Counties, Indiana* (1885; reprint, Evansville, Ind.: Unigraphic, 1965), 795; Goodspeed and Blanchard, eds., *Counties of Whitley and Noble,* 433; *Portrait and Biographical Record of Montgomery, Parke and Fountain Counties, Indiana* (Chicago: Chapman Bros., 1893), 596; Goodspeed and Blanchard, eds., *Counties of Porter and Lake,* 762.

41. Faux, *Memorable Days in America,* 246, 258.

42. These "advanced methods," pioneered by the English and Dutch, were based on land-intensive uses of the soil and an efficient blend of livestock farming and mixed crops. This diversified agriculture was crucial for the growth of the northern United States economy. See William L. Barney, *The Passage of the Republic: An Interdisciplinary History of Nineteenth-Century America* (Lexington, Mass.: D. C. Heath, 1987), 46.

43. Such accolades can be found in many accounts, among them Joseph Claybaugh, *History of Clinton County, Indiana* (Indianapolis: A. W. Bowen and Co., 1913), 483–84; Benjamin G. Shinn, ed., *Blackford and Grant Counties, Indiana,* 2 vols. (Chicago: Lewis Publishing Co., 1914), 1:386; Gilbert, *History of the City of Evansville and Vanderburg[h] County,* 2:63; Chadwick, *History of Shelby County,* 777–78.

44. These three accounts are found in, respectively, *Biographical and Genealogical History of Wayne, Fayette, Union and Franklin Counties,* 1:488; Gilbert, *History of the City of Evansville and Vanderburg[h] County,* 2:63; Goodspeed and Blanchard, eds., *Counties of Porter and Lake,* 727–28.

45. Paul W. Gates, *The Illinois Central Railroad and Its Colonization Work* (Cambridge, Mass.: Harvard University Press, 1934), 12–13.

46. Birch, *History of Benton County,* 24–25.

47. See David Jeremy, *Transatlantic Industrial Revolution: The Diffusion of Textile Technologies between Britain and America, 1790–1830s* (Oxford: Basil Blackwell, 1981); Erickson, "Emigration from the British Isles to the U.S.A. in 1831."

48. See n. 31.

49. *History of Dearborn, Ohio and Switzerland Counties,* 944. John Howard, a poor weaver from Oldham, whose son James would establish the famous Howard Ship Yards of Jeffersonville, Indiana, had heard of the "glowing possibilities of the New World" and sailed in 1819, eventually proceeding to Cincinnati where he erected a small mill and engaged in wool carding and cloth dressing. James, also born in Oldham, worked for his father until he was apprenticed to a steamboat builder in Cincinnati and then set up his own highly successful business in Jeffersonville in 1834. See Baird, *History of Clark County,* 330–31, 431–32. See the similar case of the parents of Thomas Boardman in H. W. Beckwith, *History of Vigo and Parke Counties* (1880; reprint, Evansville, Ind.: Unigraphic, 1974), 146–49.

50. *Biographical Record and Portrait Album of Tippecanoe County,* 576.

51. Beckwith, *History of Vigo and Parke Counties,* 300–1, 241–42.

52. *History of Dearborn, Ohio and Switzerland Counties,* 776–77.

53. It seems likely that Brummitt sent favorable letters back to family members in Yorkshire, for a year later his elder brother also emigrated, though he first spent four years lumbering in Michigan before buying his own land in Indiana. Goodspeed and Blanchard, eds., *Counties of Porter and Lake,* 393.

54. Charles Blanchard, ed., *Counties of Clay and Owen, Indiana* (Chicago: F. A. Battey and Co., 1884), 441; Charles Blanchard, ed., *Counties of Howard and Tipton, Indiana* (Chicago: F. A. Battey and Co., 1883), 449; Goodspeed and Blanchard, eds., *Counties of Porter and Lake,* 706.

55. For example, see W. Elliot Brownlee, *Dynamics of Ascent: A History of the American Economy,* 2d ed. (Chicago: Dorsey Press, 1988), 153–55.

56. In 1890 a tenth of all machinists in the United States were British immigrants. Berthoff, *British Immigrants,* 73–74.

57. John M. Peck, *A New Guide for Emigrants to the West: Containing Sketches of Michigan, Ohio, Indiana, Illinois, Missouri, Arkansas, with the Territory of Wisconsin, and the Adjacent Parts* (Boston: Gould, Kendall, and Lincoln, 1843), 255.

58. Faux's observation is recorded in Iglehart, "The Coming of the English to Indiana," 160.

59. *History of Warrick, Spencer and Perry Counties,* 761.

60. Goodspeed and Blanchard, eds., *Counties of Porter and Lake,* 693.

61. *Biographical Memoirs of Hancock County,* 474–75.

62. *Biographical Memoirs of Greene County,* 2:774–75.

63. This description comes from the *Indianapolis Sentinel,* which reported Sinker's death in a long article in the 6 Apr. 1871 issue. The *Indianapolis Evening News* put the story of Sinker's death, from typhoid, on the front page in the 5 Apr. issue and described the great sadness that his workers felt over his death. For a description of Sinker's life see Berry R. Sulgrove, *History of Indianapolis and Marion County* (1884; reprint, Evansville, Ind.: Unigraphic, 1974), 102, 464–65.

64. *Biographical and Genealogical History of Wayne, Fayette, Union and Franklin Counties,* 1:176–77.

65. This paragraph is based on the cases found in *Portrait and Biographical Record of Madison and Hamilton Counties,* 818; *Pictorial and Biographical Memoirs of Elkhart and St. Joseph Counties, Indiana* (1893; reprint, [South Bend, Ind.: Whipporwill], 1982), 393; Blanchard, ed., *Counties of Morgan, Monroe and Brown,* 633; Chadwick, *History of Shelby County,* 438–39.

66. Priscilla Long, *Where the Sun Never Shines: A History of America's Bloody Coal Industry* (New York: Paragon House, 1989). On the British role in unions see n. 97.

67. George E. Greene, *History of Old Vincennes and Knox County, Indiana,* 2 vols. (1911; reprint, Evansville, Ind.: Whipporwill, 1988), 2:225–26, 217; *Biographical Memoirs of Greene County,* 1:336–39.

68. *National Cyclopedia of American Biography,* 18:402–3.

69. For such cases of English and Welsh miners in Indiana see *Biographical Memoirs of Greene County,* 2:774–75; Greene, *Old Vincennes and Knox County,* 2:306; Blanchard, ed., *Counties of Clay and Owen,* 361, 465, 468, 472.

70. *Portrait and Biographical Record of Montgomery, Parke and Fountain Counties,* 184–85.

71. *History of Posey County, Indiana* (1886; reprint, Evansville, Ind.: Unigraphic, 1967), 627; Shinn, ed., *Blackford and Grant Counties,* 1:302–4; Goodspeed and Blanchard, eds., *Counties of Porter and Lake,* 737.

72. "Autobiography of Samuel F. Smith," SC 1372, Indiana Historical Society Library. Smith saw only a bleak future for shoemakers in Yorkshire because of their overabundance.

73. *Tri-State Trader* 8 (26 June 1977): 45–46; Logan Esarey, *A History of Indiana, from its Exploration to 1922* (Dayton: National Historical Association, 1928), 905; *History of Warrick, Spencer and Perry*

*Counties,* 775–76. Berthoff makes the unbelievable claim that six hundred skilled potters were imported to Troy from Staffordshire. *British Immigrants,* 75.

74. Jeremy, *Transatlantic Industrial Revolution.* See also Berthoff, *British Immigrants,* and H. J. Habakkuk, *American and British Technology in the Nineteenth Century: The Search for Labour-Saving Inventions* (New York: Cambridge University Press, 1962).

75. Frederic Irving Barrows, ed., *History of Fayette County, Indiana* (Indianapolis: B. F. Bowen & Co., 1917), 1014–15.

76. Sulgrove, *History of Indianapolis and Marion County,* 161–62.

77. See cases in *Biographical and Genealogical History of Wayne, Fayette, Union and Franklin Counties,* 488–89; Logan Esarey, *History of Indiana from Its Exploration to 1922;* also *An Account of St. Joseph County . . . ,* ed. John B. Stoll, 3 vols. (Dayton: Dayton Historical Publishing Co., 1923), 3:498–99.

78. *Biographical and Historical Souvenir for the Counties of Clark, Crawford, Harrison, Floyd, Jefferson, Jennings, Scott and Washington,* 96–97.

79. Sulgrove, *History of Indianapolis and Marion County,* 476.

80. Chadwick, *History of Shelby County,* 777.

81. Goodspeed and Blanchard, eds., *Counties of Porter and Lake,* 670.

82. Shinn, ed., *Blackford and Grant Counties,* 2:727.

83. Beckwith, *History of Vigo and Parke Counties,* 241–42; *History of Dearborn, Ohio and Switzerland Counties,* 797–98.

84. Blanchard, ed., *Counties of Morgan, Monroe and Brown,* 616–17.

85. For an example of how English millers could learn from their American counterparts, see the story of Thomas Blackwell, who immigrated in 1866 and studied American milling techniques for a year and a half before returning to England. Blackwell immigrated a second time and became a prosperous miller in Porter County. Goodspeed and Blanchard, eds., *Counties of Porter and Lake,* 291.

86. Chadwick, *History of Shelby County,* 395–96, 633–34. See also the William W. Steevens letters published in *Old Fort News* (spring 1971): 16 n. 3.

87. "The Pike County, Indiana, Ancestors of John Foster Dulles," SC 587, Indiana Historical Society Library.

88. Blanchard, ed., *Counties of Howard and Tipton,* 449.

89. *Biographical History of Tippecanoe, White, Jasper, Newton, Benton, Warren and Pulaski Counties, Indiana,* 2 vols. (Chicago: Lewis Publishing Co., 1899), 1:451–52.

90. William Stockdale Letters, 1865–83, SC 1412, Indiana Historical Society Library; *Biographical History of Tippecanoe, White, Jasper, Newton, Benton, Warren and Pulaski Counties,* 2:868–69.

91. *Biographical Record and Portrait Album of Tippecanoe County,* 487–88. For other cases of English and Welsh immigrants suffering from imprisonment at Andersonville and similar traumas, see Blanchard, ed., *Counties of Clay and Owen,* 472; Shaw, ed., *History of Dearborn County,* 744; *Portrait and Biographical Record of Montgomery, Parke and Fountain Counties,* 615–16; and Barrows, ed., *History of Fayette County,* 738–39.

92. Blanchard, ed., *Counties of Morgan, Monroe and Brown*

*Counties,* 633–34. William was also an immigrant. His two brothers also saw action in the Civil War.

93. Lane, *"City of the Century,"* 16.

94. Stockdale Letters, 28 Apr. 1867.

95. Esslinger, *Immigrants and the City,* 86–87.

96. Berthoff, *British Immigrants,* 66.

97. Ibid., 89; Clifton Yearley, *Britons in American Labor* (Baltimore: Johns Hopkins Press, 1957); Amy Zahl Gottlieb, "The Influence of British Trade Unionists on the Regulation of the Mining Industry in Illinois, 1872," *Labor History* 19 (summer 1978): 397–415.

98. See the case of Samuel Clark in *History of McHenry County, Illinois* (Chicago: Inter-State Publishing Co., 1885): 646–47.

99. Berthoff, *British Immigrants,* 132.

100. Ibid., 134; Erickson, "English," 319–36; Philip R. VanderMeer, *The Hoosier Politician: Officeholding and Political Culture in Indiana, 1896–1920* (Urbana and Chicago: University of Illinois Press, 1985): 127–29.

101. Erickson, "English," 320, 331–33.

102. *Biographical and Genealogical History of Wayne, Fayette, Union and Franklin Counties,* 107–8.

103. Goodspeed and Blanchard, eds., *Counties of Whitley and Noble,* 242–43.

104. *Pictorial and Biographical Memoirs of Elkhart and St. Joseph Counties,* 341.

105. Peckham, *Indiana,* 168–71; Buley, *Old Northwest,* 2:579–80.

106. Erickson, "English," 335 and "Emigration from the British Isles to the U.S.A. in 1841: Part I," 351.

107. Kenneth Lines, *British and Canadian Immigration to the United States since 1920* (San Francisco: R & E Research Associates, 1978). Ronald A. Wells explores the role of "the heightening imperial consciousness" in the redirection of the movement, as evident in the popular press, in "The Voice of Empire: *The Daily Mail* and British Emigration to North America," *The Historian* 43 (Feb. 1981): 240–57.

108. Lines, *British and Canadian Immigration;* Erickson, "English," 335.

109. Berthoff, *British Immigrants,* 67.

110. *Gary Post-Tribune,* 10 June 1956.

111. Written interviews with Thomas R. Davies and Margaret Orr, 28 Mar. 1992. The author would like to thank Pamela Wasmer for her assistance.

112. Mary Louise Robson, *Wings of the Morning: Isabella Mann* (New Harmony, Ind., 1967).

113. Francesco Cordasco, ed., *Dictionary of American Immigration History* (Metuchen, N.J. and London: The Scarecrow Press, Inc., 1990), 202; Erickson, "English," 336. The brain drain was real: Great Britain was for a time losing nearly 50 percent of its graduating scientists and engineers. See "Young Men Go West," *The Economist* (14 Oct. 1967): 193–94.

114. Written interviews with immigrants Gillian Winifred Stockton, 9 June 1992; with David Peerless, 8 June 1992; and Valerie Hall, 17 June 1992. See also the interviews in Lines, *British and Canadian Immigration,* 33, 38, 43.

# FRENCH

AURELE J. VIOLETTE

*Even if immigrants from France had been prone to resist assimilation, their numbers relative to the larger population would have made the retention of French ways and customs difficult. All indicators point to the fact, however, that French immigrants came to the United States with the intention of becoming Americanized as quickly as possible. A high percentage of French immigrants purchased property within a short time of their arrival, and few immigrants to Indiana ever returned to France permanently.*

There is a tendency in studies that deal with the French in connection with the history of Indiana to limit the discussion to the early explorers, missionaries, voyageurs, and settlers, who, in the late seventeenth and eighteenth centuries, created for France a vast empire in North America that stretched from Canada to the Gulf of Mexico. In this view, the French impact on Indiana ended when France lost its political and military control over the region in the mideighteenth century.

During the first decades of the nineteenth century, however, another phase in the history of the French in Indiana began as new French immigrants settled in Indiana, and, although they never attained the numerical significance of the Germans and the Irish,

they left a lasting impact on the history of Indiana. Unlike their predecessors, the new French immigrants had no ties to French Canada, and their decisions to emigrate were often directly related to the turbulent political and economic history of France in the period after 1789.

The first immigrants were few in number and were drawn to Indiana by a wide range of individual impulses. The same missionary zeal that had inspired the missionaries from Canada in the seventeenth century attracted French clergy, many of whom were also religious refugees from the French Revolution, to the Indiana missions. Stephen Theodore Badin, who arrived in the United States from revolutionary France in March 1792, became the first priest ordained in the United States and, until his death in 1853, ministered to the needs of Catholics scattered throughout Kentucky and Indiana.[1] Simon William Gabriel Bruté de Rémur, a member of a distinguished French royalist family, was trained as a medical doctor before joining the Society of St. Sulpice. Fellow Sulpician Benedict J. Flaget, who had been appointed bishop of the newly created Diocese of Bardstown in Kentucky, recruited Bruté for the American missions. In 1834 Bruté became the first bishop of the Diocese of Vincennes in Indiana.[2]

Political refugees and utopians could also be found among the early-nineteenth-century French immigrants to Indiana. Jacques Garnier de Saintes, as a member of the National Convention in 1792, voted for the execution of Louis XVI. Later, during Napoleon Bonaparte's regime he was appointed president of the criminal court at Saintes and was made a chevalier of the Legion of Honor. He was exiled from France in 1815 when the Bourbons returned to power and later settled in New Albany on the Ohio River, serving as an agent for the French Agricultural and Manufacturing Society, also known as the Vine and Olive Company, which was attempting to attract French settlers to a colony on the Tombigbee River in Alabama.[3]

Several years after Garnier de Saintes was forcibly exiled from France, a group of self-imposed exiles left France to create a new life in America. In 1823 a number of French utopians, who included Madame Marie Fretageot, her son Achille, her nephew Victor Colin Duclos, the artist and naturalist Charles Lesueur, and several others, left Le Havre to establish their residence at William Maclure's School of Industry in Philadelphia. Shortly after the group's arrival Maclure purchased an interest in Robert Owen's community at New Harmony in Posey County, Indiana. In the fall of 1825 Madame Fretageot and the others who had accompanied her to America sailed from Pittsburgh down the Ohio River on Maclure's "Boatload of Knowledge" bound for New Harmony, where they participated in the founding of Owen's community.[4]

Beginning in the 1830s the first communities established by settlers from France began to appear along the Ohio River as Indiana became the destination for increasing numbers of immigrants from France.[5] The movement of immigrants from France to Indiana reflected the general pattern of French immigration to the United States in the nineteenth century, with a gradual increase in numbers through the 1850s, after which a steady decline began.[6] The 1850 census, the first that specified place of birth, reported 2,337 French-born residents of the state of Indiana. The number grew to 6,251 in the 1860 census and reached a peak of 6,363 in the 1870 census, the largest number of French born enumerated at any decennial census.

The great majority of immigrants from France to Indiana in the nineteenth century had roots in the regions of eastern France that bordered Luxembourg, Switzerland, and the German states. These were the regions that corresponded to the historic provinces of Alsace, Lorraine, and Franche-Comté, although by the nineteenth century these provinces no longer existed as administrative units. In 1790 the new revolutionary government reformed France's administrative system, and the département system replaced the former system of administration. Four departments were created from Lorraine: Meuse, Meurthe, Moselle, and Vosges. Alsace was divided into Bas-Rhin and Haut-Rhin, and the departments of Doubs, Haute-Saône, and Jura were formed from the Franche-Comté.[7] (See Figure 1.)

The location of this region on the frontier between France and Germany helps to explain its linguistic and religious diversity. Dialects akin to those spoken in the neighboring German states were spoken throughout Alsace (except for the area around Belfort) and the eastern districts of Lorraine. French predominated throughout the remainder of the region. Similarly, several religious influences competed with one another. As a rule, French-speaking regions adhered to Catholicism; the only major exception at the beginning of the nineteenth century was the Lutheran enclave around Montbéliard. A majority in Alsace was also Catholic, although Lutherans were heavily represented in Bas-Rhin, and Mulhouse in Haut-Rhin was a Calvinist center. Anabaptists and Jews also were scattered throughout this region of eastern France.

Historians have traditionally explained the emigration from eastern France in the first few decades of the nineteenth century in terms of a variety of political, demographic, and economic factors. Unlike other groups who were driven to emigrate by cataclysmic episodes, emigrants from France seem to have responded less to specific events in making their decisions to emigrate, although certainly the military occupation of eastern France in 1815, the famines of 1816–17 and 1827–30, as well as the revolutions of 1830 and 1848 contributed to many decisions to emigrate.[8]

There is little doubt that overall economic conditions in France in the first half of the nineteenth century—a period when France was beginning to make the transition to an industrial society—accounted, in large part, for the emigration. In rural areas, periodic famines, the progressive fragmentation of the land, the increasing encroachment of cultivation on commons, and the strict enforcement of laws against poaching and stealing wood compelled many peasants to emigrate. Urban workers similarly did not experience any improvement in their lot. Wages in the factories of eastern France remained very low, and unemployment frequently brought stark misery to the urban poor.[9]

The fact that most emigrants from eastern France could be classified as peasants and lower middle class—village shopkeepers and artisans, for example—whose economic condition was probably deteriorating suggests the importance of economic factors.[10] However, economic

factors offer only part of the explanation. The emigration from eastern France probably should be viewed as part of a broader process of migration that encompassed Switzerland, the states of southwestern Germany, and the departments of eastern France. The first five decades of the nineteenth century witnessed a steady movement of peoples throughout the Rhine region. Many Swiss and Germans passed through eastern France on their way to Le Havre and other ports of embarkation. In the same period shipping companies began to recruit emigrants throughout the region in order that their ships, which had brought raw materials from America, would not have to make the return trip empty. Agents for various colonization schemes recruited extensively in eastern France.[11] Land speculation companies in the United States distributed brochures that painted an idyllic picture of America, where fortunes could be easily made. All these influences contributed to an emigration fever that swept throughout the region and which probably reached its climax during the California gold rush years. The "mirage des Eldorados" on the horizon—the promise of fortunes to be made in America—served as a powerful magnet.[12] That emigration from France probably had less to do with economic conditions in France than with prosperity in the United States is suggested by the fact that years of economic depression in the United States coincided with the years of lowest immigration from France.[13]

The question then becomes why some emigrants from eastern France decided to settle in Indiana. The sources are unanimous in indicating the significance of letters written to family, friends, and former neighbors by those who had

already preceded them to the United States as the single most important factor affecting the choice of a destination. An official in Sélestat in Bas-Rhin reported in 1841 that, "l'émigration aux États-Unis ne vient pas des agents d'émigration, mais des lettres d'Alsaciens déjà établis là-bas." ("Emigration to the United States is not caused by emigration agents but by the letters of Alsatians already settled there.")[14]

For many of the earliest French immigrants, however, Indiana was not their original destination. It was only after they had settled elsewhere initially that they were attracted to Indiana by the promise of land, work on the Wabash and Erie Canal, or other employment. There were several points in neighboring states that channeled immigrants to Indiana. Immigrants from German-speaking regions of eastern France tended to follow the established paths of German migration and in the early decades of the nineteenth century gravitated to the Ohio River city of Cincinnati, from which they gradually settled the southern Indiana counties along the Ohio River. French-speaking immigrants came from a number of widely scattered points. Around 1818 over five hundred families from Lorraine settled in several towns along Lake Ontario in upstate New York. The establishment of these towns—collectively known as the LeRay settlements—were part of an ambitious colonization scheme undertaken by James LeRay de Chaumont. The villages of Cape Vincent, Rosiere, Chaumont, Theresa, and Le Raysville

## Figure 1. Departments of Eastern France in the Midnineteenth Century

attracted the most French immigrants, some of whom later moved on to various points in the Midwest, including northern Indiana.[15]

A number of French towns in Stark County, Ohio, also provided many French settlers to northern Indiana. The Stark County settlements originated when a group of French immigrants from the Belfort region, headed by Theobold Frantz, settled in the area around Canton.[16] The enthusiastic letters of these original settlers to their countrymen brought others—both Catholic and Protestant—to eastern Ohio. The names of several of the towns in the Canton area reveal the French origins of many of their founders: Paris, Strasbourg, Massillon, Louisville, and Belfort.[17]

In southern Indiana, a few French immigrants came from the French colony established at Sainte Marie, Illinois. This colony was the accomplishment of Joseph and Jacques Picquet of Strasbourg, who in 1837 organized the Colonie des Frères to purchase land in Jasper County, Illinois. Their intention was to create a utopian colony based on Catholic principles; the site for the colony was selected primarily because of connections the founders had with Bishop Bruté, whose diocese at that time included eastern Illinois.[18] However, the major center of French influences in the regions surrounding southern Indiana was Louisville, Kentucky, which was founded in the late 1770s and named in honor of King Louis XVI. Louisville, as well as the neighboring towns of Portland and Shippingport, had a very strong French identity in the early decades of the nineteenth century. French Catholic clergy were among the first inhabitants of Louisville. Most of the early settlers of these towns were French, and the French were heavily involved in shipping as well as mercantile and financial affairs. The major houses were built in a French style; French was spoken in the streets and in the churches; and to Louisville's inhabitants the Ohio, which separated Kentucky from Indiana, was known as *La Belle Rivière*. Probably the most important event in the life of the city in the first half of the nineteenth century was the visit in 1825 of the Marquis de Lafayette.[19]

By 1830 the population of Louisville was beginning to increase rapidly; the Louisville and Portland Canal that bypassed the Falls of the Ohio had opened, and community leaders looked optimistically toward continued growth and prosperity in the future when Louisville would become a major entrepôt and the gateway for immigrants to the West.[20] In 1835 a group of prominent Louisville merchants made an attempt to attract more settlers from France to Kentucky and Indiana by arranging the publication and distribution in the French-speaking areas of Franche-Comté and western Lorraine of a guide to provide potential immigrants with information on the United States in general and the Ohio River area of Indiana and Kentucky in particular. The guide was typical of many similar guides published in France in the early nineteenth century. It provided information on the geography, history, population, political system, and economy of the United States and offered reasons for emigrating. The United States was bustling with commercial activity. The climate was temperate. The soil was fertile, and there was plenty of good land available. The educational system was well developed. Freedom of religion prevailed, and, for women, the United States was a veritable "paradise." French immigrants to the United States could also expect a warm welcome from Americans who remembered fondly the assistance provided by France to the United States during the Revolutionary War. More than anything else, however, the guide emphasized the ample resources and prosperity of the place, and for potential French emigrants, the existence in Kentucky and Indiana of people who spoke their language. Settlers were advised, though, that if they were not used to working very hard, to purchase land in Kentucky, but if they had developed habits of hard work, then Indiana should be their destination![21]

Equally important in influencing immigrants to settle in Indiana was the Catholic Church, which engaged in numerous activities that directed French immigrants to Indiana. The Catholic Church in Indiana maintained close contacts with France throughout the nineteenth century because France served as the primary source of clergy. In addition, strong financial ties existed between the Church in Indiana and an organization founded in 1822 to provide financial assistance to the American missions—at first, primarily those in Louisiana and Kentucky. This organization was known as the Society for the Propagation of the Faith and was based in Lyons in eastern France where it also collected funds for the American missions among the inhabitants of the region.[22]

Because of these ties to France, American clerics frequently traveled to France in search of clergy and subsidies for their endeavors. Bishop Benedict Flaget, whose Bardstown diocese at the time included Indiana, began the practice of sending his emissaries to France when he sent Fathers Guy Chabrat and Stephen Badin to France on such a mission in 1820. Flaget, then in his seventies, embarked upon a four-year trip between 1835 and 1839 during which he visited Rome and spent eighteen months preaching under the sponsorship of the Society for the Propagation of the Faith to large audiences over a wide area of eastern and central France.[23]

More significant for Indiana, however, was the two-year sojourn of Bishop Bruté to France, which began

*Simon William Gabriel Bruté, the first bishop of Vincennes.*

*Julian Benoit.*

shortly after his appointment as head of the Diocese of Vincennes in the spring of 1834. Bruté's purpose was to recruit clergy for the new diocese, and he visited seminaries throughout France. Among the approximately twenty priests and seminarians who accompanied Bruté when he sailed from Le Havre on his return voyage in June 1836 were Célestine de la Hailandière and Maurice de St. Palais, who would follow Bruté to the see of Vincennes, and Julian Benoit, a young seminarian from Septmoncel in the Jura with whom Bruté had lived while visiting Lyons. Another clergyman recruited on this trip to France, who would play a significant role in the establishment of the Catholic Church in Indiana, was August Bessonies; he remained in France to complete his seminary studies and did not depart for the Indiana missions until 1839.[24]

Bruté's successors as bishop continued the practice of personally visiting and sending their agents to France.[25] These trips to France not only resulted in the collection of funds, equipment, and personnel for the Indiana missions, but also directly and indirectly promoted the settlement of French immigrants in Indiana. Frequently, servants, teachers, gardeners, carpenters, ironworkers, and other craftsmen accompanied these travelers on their return. De la Hailandière on an 1839 trip engaged the services of Jean-Marie Marsile, an architect from St. Servan, Prosper Eluère, an accomplished ironworker, and Jacques Roquet,

a woodworker, to participate in the design and construction of church structures in the Vincennes diocese, including the Cathedral of St. Francis Xavier in Vincennes. Bishop St. Palais persuaded Camille de Buisseret, a member of a French noble family and an attorney with a law degree from the Sorbonne, to settle in Vincennes.[26]

Also contributing to the growing number of clergy and settlers in Indiana by the 1840s were the religious communities recruited in France. The first institution established in Indiana by a community of French nuns—the Sisters of Providence from Ruillé-sur-Loir—was St. Mary's Female Academy near Terre Haute, which opened its doors in 1841. This institution later became the College of Saint Mary-of-the-Woods, and the Sisters of Providence played a major role in the establishment of orphanages and parochial schools throughout Indiana.[27] In the following year Bishop de la Hailandière gave Father Edward Sorin and a contingent of Holy Cross brothers from Le Mans the property that had been purchased in the 1830s by Father Badin at Ste. Marie des Lacs near South Bend. By 1843 the first buildings had been constructed, and in 1844 Father Sorin had acquired a charter from the Indiana legislature for an institution of higher learning that would become the University of Notre Dame.[28] In 1855 Holy Cross sisters, who had arrived in Indiana in 1843, established Saint Mary's Academy near Notre Dame. Like the Sisters of Providence, the Sisters of the Holy Cross contributed significantly to the expansion of Catholic institutions throughout Indiana.[29]

The Catholic Church in Indiana, however, was not only serving those who, for whatever reason, had already found their way to Indiana, but also in the 1830s and 1840s was actively promoting Catholic immigration to Indiana. This was a period when anti-Catholicism was beginning to express itself—sometimes quite violently—in many areas of the United States. Even Indiana did not escape its manifestations.[30] Many Catholic clergy thought of creating a safe haven for their coreligionists on the Indiana frontier where Catholics could establish their own colonies, practice their religion freely, and be protected from the nativism that was spreading throughout other areas of the country. The Vincennes Emigrant Society emphasized the Catholic character of the region in a communication to the *Freeman's Journal* in 1842.[31] And in 1846 Rev. Joseph Kundek, a Croatian-born priest who had arrived in southern Indiana in 1838, wrote a letter to the Leopoldine Society in Vienna expressing this vision clearly:

> I believe that [Catholic] settlements are the most apt means to safeguard and to spread our holy religion in America, because in this manner the members of the same faith unite as it were into one family, live together, mutually share their religious sentiments and impressions, as one body attend the divine service, receive from their pastor all the comforts of religion as they desire, have the opportunity of having the necessary instructions imparted to their children in school, mutually support one another in commerce and occupations, and thus form a society that meets all their interests. Such colonies and settlements are according to my conviction the best means to protect the Catholic immigrants against the loss of their faith, to safeguard them against the inducements and seductions of our adversaries, and to enable them to preserve incorrupt the sacred treasures of religion and to transmit it to their children.[32]

Kundek spent his entire career in southern Indiana working to realize his dream of a Catholic colony in Dubois County. Several towns in that area, including Jasper, Celestine, and Fulda, owe their establishment and German-Catholic character to Kundek. The town of Ferdinand was probably Kundek's major accomplishment. He purchased the land for the town, arranged to have it platted, and advertised extensively in the German-language press of Cincinnati for immigrants to populate it.[33]

In most cases the endeavors of the Catholic clergy to attract their coreligionists to Indiana were much less formal than Kundek's organized schemes. Another clergyman who played a major role in the establishment of the church in Indiana was Rev. Julian Benoit, who had returned from France with Bishop Bruté in 1836. One of his first assignments was the parish of St. Mary's at Derby in Perry County. While organizing a number of other parishes in Perry County, Benoit began writing to friends in Belgium and France, recommending that they direct emigrants to Perry County where land could be purchased for $1.25 an acre and where there were coreligionists and a church with a resident priest who spoke their language.[34] Benoit's message added only one new element to the message of the Louisville merchants who a few years earlier had published the *Guide des émigrans français*. Immigrants to Indiana could expect to find cheap land and people who could speak their language, and they could also practice their Catholic faith in a nonhostile environment.[35]

## Settlement Patterns, 1850–1880

French-born immigrants to Indiana at the time of the 1850 census were concentrated in two regions. In southern Indiana several counties in close proximity to Cincinnati and others along the Ohio River had begun to attract settlers from France, and in the northern half of the state Allen County—with 532 French-born residents—had already achieved the distinction it would retain throughout the nineteenth century as the Indiana county with the largest concentration of French-born settlers. Dearborn, Floyd, Harrison, and Ripley counties joined Allen County in recording more than one hundred French-born residents. In the three census enumerations that followed the 1850 census, Allen County and the Ohio River counties continued to attract the most French immigrants, although, as Indiana's economy and system of transportation expanded, new concentrations developed in Marion, St. Joseph, and Knox counties. Indiana counties that could have been added to the list of those which, at various times between 1850 and 1880, counted more than one hundred French-born residents were Adams, Clark, Dubois, Franklin, Jefferson, Jennings, Knox, Marion, Marshall, Perry, Posey, St. Joseph, Spencer, and Vanderburgh.

A statistical breakdown of those immigrants who came from German-speaking or from French-speaking departments of France is not possible. Censuses in the nineteenth century did not compile that information, and surnames are not an accurate indication, as many French-speaking immigrants had Germanic or Anglicized surnames. Both groups were represented early in the settlement of Indiana, and German-speaking

Alsatians and Lorrainers played a large role in the establishment of such towns as St. Leon and New Alsace in Dearborn County, North Vernon in Jennings County, and Napoleon in Ripley County.[36] The fact that settlement patterns of immigrants from the German states across the Rhine coincided closely with the pattern of immigrants from France suggests the origins of most immigrants from France in the German-speaking departments.[37] The German-speaking French seem to have blended and identified more with fellow German-speaking immigrants than with the Francophone immigrants to Indiana.

County and local histories are the best sources for identifying those areas of Indiana where the Francophone element was concentrated. They reveal that only Allen and Floyd counties and a few settlements in neighboring counties ever had a strong French element. Allen County, the largest county in Indiana, was a major point on the Wabash and Erie Canal and was developing into the center of a highly productive agricultural region. New Albany in Floyd County was located directly across the Ohio River from Louisville and was in 1850 the most populous city in Indiana. Other French settlements could be found at St. Croix and Leopold in Perry County and St. Louis and Frenchtown in Harrison County.

These settlements, while containing a French majority, also attracted settlers of other nationalities and, more commonly, French-speaking settlers from Belgium or the French cantons of Switzerland, with which many Indiana French had family connections. The first immigrants to respond to Father Benoit's appeal, for example, came from Belgium and France. By the time they began arriving in Perry County in 1841 and 1842, Father Benoit had been replaced by Rev. August Bessonies, who purchased forty acres north of what was then called simply "The Chapel" for the establishment of a town. In recording the deeds to the property Bessonies noted that it was his intention "to promote both the temporal and spiritual welfare of the French people coming from Europe."[38] The town Bessonies laid out was named Leopold in honor of both the king of Belgium and the Leopoldine Society that had provided funds for the construction of a church and the purchase of land. In 1843, following the expansion of the church to accommodate the new immigrants, "The Chapel" became St. Augustine parish. Some German and English settlers also took up residence in this forested area of Perry County, but Leopold retained a French identity for several decades. While the widespread use of the French language began to fade after 1879, when the last French pastor of St. Augustine was replaced, special missions were still being preached in French in the church as late as 1897.[39]

Another Perry County locale that also attracted French settlers was St. Croix, located on Big Oil Creek about six miles from Leopold. Beginning around 1849 several French families from Louisville, led by John Dupaquier, began settling near St. Croix, attracted to the area by cheap land and a French priest in nearby Leopold who could attend to their spiritual needs.[40]

In Harrison County the largest French settlement was in Spencer Township near St. Bernard Church, a log structure built in 1849. Five families led by Theodore Henriott, who left France in 1840 with the object of establishing a Catholic colony in America and growing grapes for wine, settled this area. The group believed that the land they selected in Spencer Township would be ideal for that purpose. Over the next few years about fifty French families settled in the area, and when a post office was established the settlement was officially designated Frenchtown. The first resident pastor was appointed to St. Bernard Church in 1858, and until 1888 services were conducted in French. Another French settlement in Harrison County was St. Louis, a few miles south of Frenchtown. A French family named Béry from Louisville settled St. Louis around 1847; this settlement, however, never developed into a town and was eclipsed by Frenchtown.[41]

The largest and oldest French settlement in southern Indiana developed in one of the most picturesque regions of the state—along a collection of hills known as Knobs that rise about six hundred feet above the Ohio River and extend into the interior of Indiana. Many of these hills are located in Floyd County. Although the exact date of their settlement is unknown, many French immigrants settled in Floyd County, and by 1850 the county ranked second in the state behind Allen County in the number of French-born residents. Most of those who settled in Floyd County had their origins in the Franche-Comté and the French-speaking districts of Lorraine.

The largest concentration of French immigrants was found in New Albany Township, which included the city of New Albany. In New Albany these immigrants worked in the shipyards, foundries, shops, and other establishments that were making New Albany a center of manufacturing for the state.[42] A smaller community could be found southwest of the city in a settlement that was known by various names over the years. Originally probably called Porrentruy after the canton in Switzerland from which some settlers emigrated, it was also known as Frenchtown, the French Settlement, and the French Creek Settlement. It was located on Budd Road at the foot of a heavily wooded hill called *Le Ballon* (balloon). The settlers were primarily of Swiss, Belgian, and French extraction,

This log cabin ("Petite Maison") was built by a French settler in the French Creek Settlement in New Albany Township. This photograph was taken around 1896.

and some of them were veterans of Napoleon's armies. The first immigrants arrived around 1830 and were supposedly drawn to the area by the beauty of the hills that reminded them of their homeland.[43]

The settlement developed initially along the creek that flowed through the area and whose bed became a thoroughfare in dry periods—the *grande rue* to some. Some inhabitants of the French Creek Settlement worked in New Albany. Others engaged in small-scale agriculture, growing grapes and maintaining gardens and orchards whose products were then sold in the markets of New Albany. For a while a local sabotier made wooden sabots (shoes), and Floyd County sabots could be purchased as far south as New Orleans for fifty cents a pair.[44]

The French Creek Settlement never became very large or prosperous. It was probably at its peak between 1840 and 1860 when about forty families were living in the vicinity. Thereafter a period of decline set in as the children of the original settlers began to move away, and by the 1880s the area had acquired a reputation for lawlessness.[45]

Another Knobs community whose history was different from that at French Creek was developed about six miles to the north in the vicinity of Floyds Knobs in Lafayette Township.[46] The essential difference between the two communities was the presence of a church in Lafayette Township that served as the focal point of the community's religious and social life. Catholic immigrants from Ireland originally settled this area before Floyd County was carved out of Clark and Harrison counties in 1819. By 1823 a small log church had been built that served as the nucleus of the parish known as St. Mary's-of-the-Knobs, which at first was visited occasionally by French priests from Louisville and Bardstown. In the late 1830s the church began to be served regularly by priests residing in New Albany and

Jeffersonville. Among the first of the priests was Rev. Louis Neyron, another of Bishop Bruté's 1836 recruits, who served St. Mary's from Holy Trinity Church in New Albany, a parish that he had founded and which also contained a sizable French element.[47]

The French inhabitants of the Floyds Knobs settlement were primarily farmers, although many also engaged in barrel making and worked in the quarries that provided stone for the construction of New Albany and Louisville. The first generation of French immigrants retained the language, songs, dress, and customs of their native land, but by the 1870s the use of the language was beginning to decrease, and after 1873 the sermons at St. Mary's were delivered only in English rather than in English, German, and French as had been the custom for many years.[48]

While some French immigrants were establishing themselves in southern Indiana, others were beginning to settle in Allen County in the northern part of the state. In 1840 only a few French-born immigrants had made their way to Allen County. Among them was Rev. Julian Benoit, who had been sent by Bishop de la Hailandière in 1840 to become pastor of St. Augustine Church in Fort Wayne, a congregation that included a few French but was primarily made up of French-Canadians, Irish, and Germans. Other early French settlers included Jean Baptiste Bequette, a silversmith who manufactured

St. Mary's-of-the-Knobs, Lafayette Township, Floyd County.

"ear-bobs for Miami belles" and Lucien P. Ferry, who became the first city attorney when Fort Wayne received its city charter in 1840. Bernard Poirson had also reached Allen County by 1840; he became the first tavern keeper in Washington Township when he opened "French Mary's Tavern" in the township.

By the time of the 1850 census over five hundred French immigrants had settled in Allen County and had already established a pattern that would characterize their settlement for the next several decades. They tended to settle in only a few Allen County townships: Wayne Township, which included the city of Fort Wayne, and the rural Perry, Washington, St. Joseph, and Jefferson townships. Cedar Creek, Lake, and Adams townships also recorded at least fifty French-born residents between 1850 and 1880. The remaining twelve Allen County townships never attracted French settlers in any significant numbers. (See Figure 2.)

Since most of the French immigrants settled in rural townships, they probably were drawn to Allen County by the availability of land and employment opportunities that would allow them to save money to purchase land. The settlement pattern also suggests that proximity to a Catholic church was a consideration. The rural parishes whose congregations were composed of a high percentage of French immigrants were St. Vincent de Paul in northern Washington Township, St. Louis de Besançon in Jefferson

Township, St. Leo in Cedar Creek Township, St. Michael in St. Joseph Township, and St. Patrick in Lake Township. The official dates of establishment of these parishes do not always indicate their foundation, as in most cases religious services were held in private homes by itinerant clergy long before parishes were founded and the first church structures built.[49] St. Vincent de Paul was established in 1846 when the first church was constructed. In eastern Allen County, St. Louis de Besançon was established in 1851 by Rev. August Bessonies. St. Leo (1856) in the town of Leo and St. Michael (1874), in what was called Pierr Settlement on St. Joe Center Road near its intersection with Hazelett Road, were usually served by priests from other parishes in the area.[50] St. Patrick in Arcola (1866) was the only Allen County parish with a sizable French element to which a French-speaking priest was never assigned.

St. Augustine Church in the center of Fort Wayne was the oldest Allen County parish, having been founded by Father Badin in the 1830s; when Father Benoit undertook the construction of the present Cathedral of the Immaculate Conception in 1859, St. Augustine Church was moved to another area of Cathedral Square. It was subsequently destroyed by fire. Most French who resided in Fort Wayne were members of the Cathedral parish and, although they engaged in a wide variety of occupations and lived throughout the city, a number of

## Figure 2. Allen County Townships with French-Born Residents, 1850–1880

Source: U.S. Census

| EEL RIVER | | PERRY | | CEDAR CREEK | | SPRINGFIELD | | SCIPIO | |
|---|---|---|---|---|---|---|---|---|---|
| 1850 | 4 | 1850 | 63 | 1850 | 7 | 1850 | 0 | 1850 | 0 |
| 1860 | 7 | 1860 | 109 | 1860 | 100 | 1860 | 17 | 1860 | 0 |
| 1870 | 6 | 1870 | 83 | 1870 | 83 ● St. Leo | | 1870 | 38 | 1870 | 0 |
| 1880 | 9 | 1880 | 58 | 1880 | 75 | 1880 | 23 | 1880 | 0 |

| LAKE | | WASHINGTON | | ST. JOSEPH | | MILAN | | MAUMEE | |
|---|---|---|---|---|---|---|---|---|---|
| 1850 | 19 | 1850 | 83 St. ● | | 1850 | 125 | 1850 | 17 | 1850 | 0 |
| 1860 | 61 | 1860 | 100 Vincent | | 1860 | 113 | 1860 | 19 | 1860 | 0 |
| 1870 | 51 | 1870 | 69 | 1870 | 21 | 1870 | 21 | 1870 | 1 |
| 1880 | 43 | 1880 | 52 | 1880 | 76 | 1880 | 20 | 1880 | 0 |

● St. Patrick

St. ● Michael

| ABOITE | | WAYNE | | ADAMS | | JEFFERSON | | JACKSON | |
|---|---|---|---|---|---|---|---|---|---|
| 1850 | 19 | 1850 | 87 | 1850 | 21 | 1850 | 82 | 1850 | 0 |
| 1860 | 14 | 1860 | 223 | 1860 | 66 | 1860 | 218 | 1860 | 22 |
| 1870 | 14 | 1870 | 188 | 1870 | 75 | 1870 | 178 ● | | 1870 | 27 |
| 1880 | 14 | 1880 | 200 | 1880 | 58 | 1880 | 141 St. Louis | | 1880 | 29 |

| LAFAYETTE | | PLEASANT | | MARION | | MADISON | | MONROE | |
|---|---|---|---|---|---|---|---|---|---|
| 1850 | 0 | 1850 | 5 | 1850 | 0 | 1850 | 0 | 1850 | 0 |
| 1860 | 4 | 1860 | 36 | 1860 | 4 | 1860 | 15 | 1860 | 4 |
| 1870 | 0 | 1870 | 33 | 1870 | 1 | 1870 | 23 | 1870 | 16 |
| 1880 | 0 | 1880 | 16 | 1880 | 5 | 1880 | 16 | 1880 | 12 |

concentrations of French settlers developed. The earliest settlement probably grew up in the area of the James F. Sallot residence on South Lafayette Street. Sallot was born in Courchaton, Haute-Saône, in 1810 and with his wife Josephine Claude Julliard left France in 1846 on a sailing vessel for a three-month voyage to New Orleans. They came immediately by boat up the Mississippi and Ohio rivers and eventually made their way to Allen County. They settled in the Arcola area but after six years moved to Fort Wayne, where they purchased land south of Fort Wayne in what is now the south central area of the city. Their homestead eventually became a social center for other French families, many of whom purchased property in the area that became known as Frenchtown—an area bounded by the Pennsylvania Railroad tracks on the north, Hanna Street on the east, Lafayette Street on the west, and Pontiac Street on the south.[51] Later, another concentration of French settlers developed north of the city in the Spy Run Avenue area near the French brewery established in the 1860s by Charles Centlivre.

Outside of Fort Wayne two predominantly French parishes served as the focal point of French settlement in the rural areas of the county. St. Vincent de Paul parish was located north of the city in a settlement that at various times was called Pichon Settlement, Nouveau Gaul, New France, and Academie. Most of the original settlers of the area were French, who began settling in Washington, St. Joseph, and Perry townships in the early 1840s. Many of them originated in Haute-Saône and Doubs and the area of Switzerland that bordered on Doubs.[52] Father Benoit began attending the settlement in 1843 and at first said Mass in private homes. The first church—a log structure built on the east side of Auburn Road—was erected on land donated in 1846 by Isadore Pichon, an original settler and former soldier in Napoleon's army who had participated in the invasion of Russia.

The first resident pastor at St. Vincent was appointed in 1856, and in 1861 Rev. August Adam, who had recently arrived from France with Father Edward Sorin of Notre Dame, began a long pastorate during which considerable expansion took place. A frame church was built about 1863 on the northwest corner of the Old Auburn Road, with members of the congregation, numbering about eighty families, providing most of the materials and labor for its construction. A parish school was built, and in 1866 Father Adam established the Academy of Our Lady of the Sacred Heart as a boarding school for girls. Both the parish school and the academy were placed under the direction of the Sisters of the Holy Cross from Notre Dame; advertisements for

the academy emphasized the fact that the girls would be taught by French-speaking teachers. Following Adam's reassignment in 1870, the parish was entrusted to the care of Holy Cross priests from Notre Dame, who remained in the parish until 1897. During that period St. Vincent was always served by a French-speaking priest, as were the mission churches for which St. Vincent was responsible.[53]

Another concentration of French settlers was found in Jefferson Township. Many of the settlers there were related to those at St. Vincent and came from the same French-speaking areas of eastern France. Their origins were reflected in the name eventually selected for the village where a church was constructed—Besançon, named after a city and diocese in France from which many of the settlers emigrated. Before the church was built, religious services were held in the log cabin home of Joseph Dodane, one of the original settlers. Dodane, with Claude Francis Lomont, financed the construction of the first frame church named in honor of St. Louis, a medieval king of France.[54]

After 1864 St. Louis usually had a French-speaking resident pastor. When Rev. August Adam became pastor in 1870 the congregation numbered about six hundred, and Adam, as he had done previously at St. Vincent, began the construction of a larger church to accommodate the growing membership. To finance the new building Adam asked each parish family to raise a calf until it was three years old. The public sale of the cows yielded three thousand dollars for the church, which can still be seen on old US Route 30 about three miles east of the city of New Haven.[55]

### The Immigrant Experience

The French immigrants who were creating communities like Besançon already had endured many hardships. Many, after making the very difficult decision to emigrate, had to make what must have been painful farewells to friends and family whom they probably would never see again. They had endured a long sea voyage and an equally arduous trek overland to Indiana. If they were farmers they had cleared the land and had built their first log homes.[56]

Most French immigrants to Indiana in the mid-nineteenth century were probably under the age of thirty at the time of their entry into the United States.[57] They emigrated as individuals and as family groups. Once the decision had been made to emigrate, they would gather their belongings—everything from household items, spinning wheels, tools, farming implements, seeds, vine cuttings, and wagons to food for the trip—and travel by foot, river barge, or wagon to one of the ports where it was possible to secure passage to the United States. Most immigrants left from Le Havre, although Bordeaux, Nantes, and Marseilles also served as points of departure. The passage across the Atlantic could last, depending on the route, from one to three months and ended, for most immigrants, at either New York or New Orleans.[58]

From these points the immigrants took many routes into the interior. Immigrants whose port of entry was New Orleans would usually travel up the Mississippi and Ohio to Louisville or Cincinnati. If they entered through New York, a variety of routes became possible. The earliest immigrants usually walked or rode in wagons across Pennsylvania to Pittsburgh or Wheeling, where they would embark on a riverboat for the trip down the Ohio. As transportation facilities improved, other means of conveyance—stagecoach, canal, or railroad—became available. Many immigrants to northern Indiana followed the route formed by the Erie Canal across New York State to Buffalo, across Lake Erie to Toledo, and, after it had opened, the Wabash and Erie Canal across northwestern Ohio and Indiana.[59] Travelers taking this route usually spent about a month making the trip from New York to Indiana.

The conditions the immigrants found in Indiana were quite primitive. Indiana still retained a distinct frontier character when the first French settlers began arriving. Dense forests covered much of the state, and wild animals roamed throughout Indiana. In some places where French settlers established themselves—like some low-lying areas around New Albany and Jefferson and Jackson townships in eastern Allen County—swamps added to the hardships the settlers faced. Some immigrants purchased land immediately after arriving in Indiana. Others secured employment in manufacturing or on the canals and railroads to earn money to purchase a farm, which was the primary goal of most French immigrants.[60] In the state as a whole, as well as in those areas where French immigrants were concentrated, agriculture was the occupation pursued by most. Of 535 French-born residents of Allen County, for example, whose occupation was indicated in the 1870 census, 371 listed farming, and many others had occupations that were directly related to farming.

French immigrants who settled in urban areas engaged in a wide variety of pursuits. They were ordinary laborers, craftsmen, manufacturers, shopkeepers, merchants, and trained professionals.[61] As a group the French seem to have been especially enterprising and ambitious. John B. Beugnot was born in France in 1833. Beugnot came with his parents to Stark County, Ohio, where the family resided for five years before purchasing a farm in Jefferson Township, Allen County, where John learned the cooper's trade. Beugnot later became the owner of several cooper shops and stave factories in New Haven and Fort Wayne. Frank Belviy, who came to New Albany in the early 1850s, maintained a grocery business for many years at Sycamore and Sixth streets. Francis Bercot was a saloonkeeper and proprietor of a boardinghouse on Columbia Street in Fort Wayne. François Houppert emigrated from Lorraine and lived, at various times, in Madison, North Vernon, and Indianapolis, where he engaged in the making and importing of wines. John Joquel from Nancy was a dealer in oil and lamps before opening a successful book and stationery establishment in Fort Wayne in 1876. Dr. Adrian E. Fauvre, who was born in Bourges, practiced medicine in both Indianapolis and Fort Wayne for many years. August Lanternier, who arrived in Allen County with his parents in 1854, became one of the leading florists in Allen County.

Some businesses founded by French immigrants were quite long-lived. Two well-known Fort Wayne establishments, for example, lasted over one hundred years—until the 1970s. One of these was a dry goods business established by Peter Pierre, a French immigrant who was given one hundred francs by his father in 1851 to join a brother who had already settled in Fort Wayne. For a while after his arrival Pierre was an itinerant peddler in southern Allen and northern Wells counties, selling pins, needles, thread, and other trinkets out of a trunk strapped to his back. In 1857 he entered into a partnership with his brother in a dry goods business on Calhoun Street. The partnership lasted for sixteen years, after which Peter began his own business as "P. Pierre, Broadway Dry Goods." Prosperity followed, and the business was passed down in the Pierre family until the store was closed in May 1973; at the time of its closing it was the oldest dry goods business in Indiana under the continuous management of the same family.[62]

Another prominent Fort Wayne French-owned business was the Centlivre Brewery. Two brothers from Belfort—Charles Louis and Frank Centlivre—established the "French Brewery" in 1862. The brewery, which was located north of Fort Wayne along the west bank of the St. Joseph River, not only quickly became one of the largest breweries in the Midwest, but a nearby park, stables for horse racing, and boat rides provided by Centlivre also made the area around the brewery a popular place of recreation for Fort Wayne residents who could reach the brewery easily on a special streetcar line.[63] These few typical examples suggest that French immigrants adjusted very quickly to the

*This statue of Charles L. Centlivre, the founder of the Centlivre Brewery in Fort Wayne, was erected by the employees of the brewery in 1911. The statue was removed to the roof of Hall's Old Gas House restaurant on Superior Street in 1974 after the brewery closed.*

economic environment found in Indiana and were able, in many cases, to achieve prosperity within a few years of their arrival. The French probably assimilated much more easily into the general fabric of American life than most other immigrant groups. The relative insignificance of their numbers was probably the main reason. Immigrants to Indiana from France were always a distinct minority within the state—both as a percentage of the total population and as a percentage of the foreign-born population. The highest percentages in both categories were attained at the time of the 1860 census when the French born accounted for 0.5 percent of the total population of the state and 5.2 percent of the foreign-born population. Thereafter the percentages declined steadily until by 1980 the French born constituted a miniscule 0.02 percent of the total population and 1.0 percent of the total foreign-born population. (See Table 1.)

Even if immigrants from France had been prone to resist assimilation, their numbers relative to the larger population would have made the retention of French ways and customs difficult. All indicators point to the fact, however, that French immigrants came to the United States with the intention of becoming Americanized as quickly as possible. A high percentage of French

### Table 1: French Born in Indiana as a Percentage of the Total Population and as a Percentage of Foreign Born

| Year | Total Indiana Population | Total Foreign Born | Total French Born | % Total Population | % Foreign Born |
|------|------|------|------|------|------|
| 1850 | 988,416 | 55,537 | 2,337 | 0.2 | 4.2 |
| 1860 | 1,350,428 | 118,284 | 6,251 | 0.5 | 5.2 |
| 1870 | 1,680,637 | 141,474 | 6,363 | 0.4 | 4.5 |
| 1880 | 1,978,301 | 144,178 | 5,010 | 0.3 | 3.5 |
| 1920 | 2,930,390 | 150,868 | 3,254 | 0.1 | 2.2 |
| 1930 | 3,238,503 | 135,134 | 2,160 | 0.1 | 1.6 |
| 1940 | 3,427,796 | 110,992 | 1,459 | 0.04 | 1.3 |
| 1950 | 3,934,224 | 100,630 | 1,400 | 0.03 | 1.4 |
| 1980 | 5,490,260 | 101,802 | 1,065 | 0.02 | 1.0 |

Source: James H. Madison, *The Indiana Way: A State History* (Bloomington and Indianapolis: Indiana University Press and Indiana Historical Society, 1986), Appendix A.

immigrants purchased property within a short time of their arrival, and few immigrants to Indiana ever returned to France permanently. French immigrants also tended to

*Residence, beer garden, and brewery of Charles L. Centlivre. The original brewery was destroyed by fire in July 1889 and was replaced by a much larger structure.*

apply for naturalization soon after entry into the United States.[64] Some in the first generation intermarried with members of other nationalities and faiths. Some were attracted to politics and ran for elective office within a few years of their arrival. French immigrants served as township assessors, trustees, constables, county commissioners, and city council members. Francis Gladieux, a native of Alsace who settled in Jefferson Township of Allen County in 1853, became a prosperous farmer, served as a county commissioner for nine years, and was one of the first French immigrants to be elected to the lower house of the Indiana legislature.

The process of assimilation was probably somewhat slower in rural areas where isolation and the proximity of other French settlers made it easier to retain old ways, at least through the first generation. The cultural characteristic that defined the French—language—was probably the best indicator of the degree of assimilation. Most immigrants who settled in urban areas learned English quickly. Preaching in French, for example, was abandoned early in 1856 in the cathedral at Vincennes.[65] In rural areas, if there was a church served by a French priest, the use of French persisted longer, but even in most rural parishes French had been replaced by English by the 1880s. One of the last parishes still served by a French priest—St. Louis in Besançon—received its first non-French pastor in 1902 when Rev. John F. Noll was assigned to the parish. A parish historian reported later that at the time of Noll's arrival "the people were thoroughly Americanized and worked in perfect harmony with him."[66]

The process of assimilation is also revealed by the history of the mutual aid societies founded by French immigrants and their descendants. Like other immigrant groups, the French formed mutual aid societies to provide certain financial benefits in times of need. The first such society in Indiana was the Lafayette Benevolent Society of

Fort Wayne (Société de Bienfaisance Lafayette), which was incorporated in 1861. A requirement for membership was French birth or an ability to understand and speak French: "Qu'il soit Française de naissance ou d'origine ou qu'il comprenne & qu'il parle la langue Française." (That he be French by birth or origin or that he understand and speak the French language.)[67] The successor of the Lafayette Benevolent Society was the French-American Society of Allen County formed in 1902. Like its predecessor, this society paid death benefits to its members' survivors, but it differed in that only French ancestry was a prerequisite of membership.[68]

The French-American Society of Allen County was the last such French organization in the state of Indiana. Members of the society met regularly at Langard Hall (also known as the French-American Hall) on the corner of Barr and Columbia streets in Fort Wayne. Membership in the society grew steadily in the years before the First World War, and several annual events sponsored by the organization were very popular. The most well known was the society's annual picnic held at Centlivre Park,

beginning in 1903. While the picnic provided Allen County French with the opportunity to hear French music and converse in French, the picnic quickly became a community-wide event, with thousands of people who were not French in attendance.[69]

**The Last Hundred Years**

French immigration to Indiana was largely a nineteenth-century phenomenon. French immigrants began settling in Indiana in the 1840s, and over the course of the next two decades their numbers continued to increase. At the time of the 1880 census, however, a decline in absolute numbers of French-born residents was noticeable, marking the beginning of a trend that was never reversed. Indiana remained the destination of many French immigrants, but they no longer arrived in sufficient numbers to replace those who had died.

Not only did the immigration slow considerably in the last decades of the nineteenth century but the reasons why immigrants selected Indiana also changed. The search for land became less important. Some late-nineteenth-century immigrants were miners who came to work in the mines of western Indiana. Others were former French soldiers or inhabitants of those areas ceded to Germany after the Franco-Prussian War.[70] Glassworkers were also attracted to Indiana after 1887 when the discovery of natural gas led to the establishment of many glass factories in Indiana. By the time of the 1900 census a number of new concentrations of French-born residents had developed in some gas boom counties. Blackford, Grant, Delaware, and Madison counties during the height of the boom experienced increases in French-born residents. Some were drawn to these counties from other areas of Indiana by the promise of employment, but new immigrants from eastern France were also recruited.[71]

Despite these new immigrants, however, the downward trend continued throughout the twentieth century until the number of French-born residents in the state became statistically insignificant. Allen County, which had always had the largest concentration of French settlers, at the time of the 1910 census reported, for the first time since 1850, less than five hundred French-born residents. The same pattern was also evident in other Indiana counties that had attracted French settlement in the past. Some Indiana counties, such as Knox, Vigo, and Vanderburgh, seemed to have resisted the general trend when the 1920 census revealed an increase in French-born residents. However, this situation was not the product of any new wave of immigration but resulted from the inclusion in the 1920 census figures of the residents of these counties who were

*Four generations of Pierres, circa 1890. Peter Pierre (seated) and his mother Catherine Heckbour were both born in France. Peter established a successful dry goods business in Fort Wayne, which was carried on by his son Joseph (standing).*

*Golden wedding anniversary celebration of Francis Gladieux and Mary Lomont in Zulu, Indiana, 6 August 1910. Francis and Mary were born in France and immigrated as young children with their families to Allen County. Their anniversary celebration was one of the last gatherings in Jefferson Township involving significant numbers of the original French settlers.*

born in regions retroceded by Germany to France after World War I.

Another twentieth-century demographic trend was the increasing urbanization of the French in Indiana. Whereas in the nineteenth century most of the French born could probably be classified as rural, by 1930 the majority of French born were urban dwellers. The 1940 census broke down the French-born population at the time of the 1930 and 1940 censuses into three categories: urban, rural-nonfarm, and rural-farm. Of 2,160 French-born residents recorded in 1930, 70 percent were classified as urban, 16 percent as rural-nonfarm, and 14 percent as rural-farm. By the time of the 1940 census the total number had shrunk to 1,459, but the percentages remained essentially unchanged: 72 percent, 15 percent, and 13 percent, respectively.[72] By 1980 the French-born residents of Indiana numbered only 1,065 and were found primarily in the most urbanized counties of the state, with the exception of Monroe County where Indiana University is located.[73] This situation reflected the general trend of European immigration to the United States over the course of the nineteenth and twentieth

centuries. By the end of the twentieth century the overwhelming majority of immigrants were skilled professionals who were attracted to large urban areas or, in the case of Monroe County, to a major university.

The author wishes to thank the following individuals for their assistance: Rev. Charles Banet, St. Joseph College, Rensselaer, Indiana; Elmer D. Denman, Indiana University-Purdue University Fort Wayne; Gladys Lomont, Besancon, Indiana; and Bobbi Shadle, Indiana University-Purdue University Fort Wayne.

## Notes

1. See J. Herman Schauinger, *Stephen T. Badin: Priest in the Wilderness* (Milwaukee, Wis.: Bruce Publishing Co., 1956), and George R. Mather, *Frontier Faith: The Story of the Pioneer Congregations of Fort Wayne, Indiana, 1820–1860* (Fort Wayne: Allen County-Fort Wayne Historical Society, 1992), 70–75. Badin was trained for the priesthood at the Sulpician seminary in Baltimore, which later became known as St. Mary's Seminary. Because Badin was the first priest ordained in the United States, nineteenth-century sources frequently refer to him as the "proto-priest" of the United States. Many early Indiana missionaries and bishops were themselves members of or had close connections with the Society of St. Sulpice. See Christopher J.

Kauffman, *Tradition and Transformation in Catholic Culture: The Priests of St. Sulpice in the United States from 1791 to the Present* (New York: Macmillan, 1988).

2. On his career see Charles Lemarie, *Monseigneur Bruté de Rémur, premier évêque de Vincennes aux États-Unis (1834–1839)* [Paris: C. Klincksieck, 1974?], and James Roosevelt Bayley, *Frontier Bishop: The Life of Bishop Simon Bruté,* ed. Albert J. Nevins (Huntington, Ind.: Our Sunday Visitor, Inc., 1971). France continued to provide clergy for the Catholic Church in Indiana throughout the nineteenth century. The three bishops who followed Bruté to the see of Vincennes were French born: Célestine de la Hailandière, 1839–47; John Stephen Bazin, 1847–48; and James Marie Maurice d'Aussac de St. Palais, 1849–77. Many of the early Catholic clergy in Indiana had ties to the former French province of Brittany. As the century progressed the German-speaking provinces of eastern France began to provide most of the clergy recruited in France. On the Breton influence on the early church in Indiana see Charles Lemarie, *Les missionnaires bretons de l'Indiana au XIXe siècle* (Angers: Lemarie, 1973).

3. Edward D. Seeber, "A Napoleonic Exile in New Albany," *Indiana Magazine of History* 44 (June 1948): 175–77.

4. "Diary and Recollections of Victor Colin Duclos, 1825–1833," in *Indiana as Seen by Early Travelers: A Collection of Reprints from Books of Travel, Letters and Diaries prior to 1830,* ed. Harlow Lindley (Indianapolis: Indiana Historical Commission, 1916), 536–48; Donald F. Carmony and Josephine M. Elliott, "New Harmony, Indiana: Robert Owen's Seedbed for Utopia," *Indiana Magazine of History* 76 (Sept. 1980): 161–261. The artist Lesueur lived at New Harmony until 1837 and left many drawings of the people, structures, and conditions at New Harmony in the 1820s and 1830s. See Jacqueline Bonnemains, "Charles-Alexandre LeSueur en Amérique du Nord (1816–1837)," *Annales du Muséum du Havre* no. 42 (June 1993): 1–65.

5. The middle decades of the nineteenth century witnessed the greatest immigration from France to the United States, with the 1840s recording the largest number of French immigrants to the United States. Between 1821 and 1830 United States immigration authorities counted only 8,470 immigrants entering the country from France. The number jumped to 45,520 in the following decade, and between 1841 and 1850, 77,220 immigrants from France entered the United States. In the 1850s the number declined slightly to 76,050, after which a steady—if somewhat irregular—pattern of decline became apparent. United States immigration statistics for the nineteenth century, however, can only suggest broad trends because the methods for counting immigrants from France changed over the course of the century. Between 1820 and 1869, for example, United States immigration figures included all arrivals from France— permanent immigrants as well as occasional travelers. Between 1869 and 1906 the figures included those whose last domicile was France and who announced their intention to make the United States their permanent domicile. Between 1907 and the outbreak of the First World War the "French" figures included Walloons, Swiss Romands, and French Canadians. On this subject see Henri Bunle, "L'immigration française aux États-Unis," *Bulletin de la Statistique Générale de la France et du Service d'Observation des Prix* 14 (Jan. 1925): 199–222; Louis Chevalier, "L'immigration française au XIXe siècle," *Études d'histoire moderne et contemporaine* 2 (1947): 127–71; Ronald Creagh, *Nos cousins d'Amérique: Histoire des Français aux États-Unis* (Paris: Payot, 1988), 435; Patrice Louis René Higonnet, "French," in *Harvard Encyclopedia of American Ethnic Groups,* ed. Stephan Thernstrom (Cambridge, Mass.: Belknap Press of Harvard

University Press, 1980), 380.

6. For purposes of this study, information on 4,738 immigrants to Indiana from France in the nineteenth century was collected. Of these the date of entry into the United States was obtained for 965 immigrants. Of the 965, 56 entered the United States before 1831, 143 between 1831 and 1840, 294 between 1841 and 1850, and 305 between 1851 and 1860; the remaining 158 entered the United States after 1861.

7. See Jean Houpert, *Les Lorrains en Amérique du Nord* (Sherbrooke, Quebec: Éditions Naaman, 1985), 135, 198–200; A. Gain, "La Lorraine allemande: Foyer d'emigration au début du XIXe siècle," *Le Pays Lorrain* (May–June 1926): 193–205, 259–66; René Remond, *Les États-Unis devant l'opinion française, 1815–1852,* 2 vols. (Paris: Librairie Armand Colin, 1962), 1:67–69; Norman Laybourn, *L'émigration des Alsaciens et des Lorrains du XVIIe au Xxe siècle,* 2 vols. (Strasbourg: Association des Publications près les Universités de Strasbourg, 1986), 2:3–357. The place of birth was obtained for 395 immigrants to Indiana from France. Alsace-Lorraine was indicated as the place of birth of 34, Alsace 128, Lorraine 54, and Franche-Comté 71. On the specific towns of origin of several Francophone families in Indiana see Charles H. Banet, *Courchaton, Département de la Haute-Saône, Registres paroissiaux, 1670–1792, Actes de la Commune, 1793–1852* (Rensselaer, Ind.: C. Banet, 1980); Charles H. Banet, *Records of Coulevon, Département de la Haute-Saône: Registres paroissiaux, 1556–1792, extracted from the Baptismal (Birth), Marriage and Death Registers for the Catholic Parish of Saint George at Vesoul* (Rensselaer, Ind.: By the author, 1985); Charles H. Banet, *French Immigrants in Allen County, Indiana, 1850–1870* (Fort Wayne, Ind.: Public Library of Fort Wayne and Allen County, 1981); Alfred Rondot, comp., *Place or Town of Origin of Allen County, Indiana French Surnames, 1800–1900 Found in the Courchaton, Haute-Saône, France Register, 1670–1852* (n.p., 1980).

8. On this period in French history see André Jardin and Andre-Jean Tudesq, *Restoration and Reaction, 1815–1848,* trans. Elborg Forster (New York: Cambridge University Press, 1983); Nicole Fouché, *Émigration Alsacienne aux États-Unis, 1815–1870* (Paris: Publications de la Sorbonne, 1992), 111–38.

9. André Jean Marc Prévos, "Frenchmen between Two Rivers: A History of the French in Iowa" (Ph.D. diss., University of Iowa, 1981), 140–41; Paul Leuilliot, "L'émigration alsacienne sous l'Empire et au début de la Restauration," *Revue Historique* 165 (1930): 254–79; Carl A. Brasseaux, *The 'Foreign French': Nineteenth-Century French Immigration into Louisiana,* vol. 1, *1820–1839* (Lafayette: University of Southwestern Louisiana, 1990), xiii–xxv.

10. Creagh, *Nos cousins,* 271; Remond, *États-Unis,* 1:68–74; Jardin and Tudesq, *Restoration,* 305; Mack Walker, *Germany and the Emigration, 1816–1885* (Cambridge, Mass.: Harvard University Press, 1964), 47.

11. Most of the colonists recruited by Henry Castro between 1842 and 1845 to several French settlements near San Antonio, Texas, came from Bas-Rhin, Haut-Rhin, Meurthe, Moselle, Doubs, and Jura. Lorenzo Castro, *Immigration from Alsace and Lorraine: A Brief Sketch of the History of Castro's Colony in Western Texas* (New York: Geo. W. Wheat & Co., 1871), 5–7; Joseph Strebler, *Alsaciens au Texas* (Strasbourg: Culture Alsacienne, 1975), 83–85.

12. Chevalier, "L'immigration," 157–62.

13. Remond, *États-Unis,* 1:67.

14. Chevalier, "L'immigration," 161–62; Creagh, *Nos cousins,* 270; Fouché, *Émigration Alsacienne,* 98ff., and especially Remond, *États-Unis,* 1:69ff.

15. See Creagh, *Nos cousins,* 258–59; Mary Gilbert Kelly, *Catholic*

*Immigrant Colonization Projects in the United States, 1815–1860* (New York: The United States Catholic Historical Society, 1939), 23–25.

16. French settlement of the area began in 1826 with the arrival of the first French families. In March of that year five French families left Le Havre for New York. One family remained behind in New York to earn money in order to continue its travels west. The remainder left immediately by way of the Hudson River, the Erie Canal, and lake schooner to Cleveland. They lived in a barn for about a month while their leader Theobold Frantz searched for a place to settle. He decided on Canton when he approached it from the north and saw the cross of St. John's Catholic Church, supposedly exclaiming: "Je n'irai pas plus loin; c'est ici que j'ai trouvé la première croix depuis que nous avons quittes New York, et c'est ici, près de cette croix, que je m'établirai." William H. Perrin, ed., *History of Stark County, with an Outline Sketch of Ohio* (Chicago: Baskin and Battey, 1881), 465.

17. Many of the French surnames found in the Allen County, Indiana, area—Belot, Bobay, Gerardot, Gladieux, Jacquay, Julliard, Monnier, and Vernier, for example—are also found among the original French settlers of Stark County, Ohio. See Houpert, *Les Lorrains*, 162–63; Edward T. Heald, *The Stark County Story*, 4 vols. (Canton, Ohio: Stark County Historical Society, 1949–59), 1:164–66, 274–76, 378–79. While Stark County probably had the largest concentration of French immigrants, there were also French settlements in Clark, Darke, Defiance, Fulton, Holmes, Miami, Paulding, Shelby, and Wayne counties in Ohio. On French communities near the Indiana border in Darke County, Ohio, for example, see William M. Miller, "A French Community in Ohio," *The French Review* 20 (Oct. 1946): 8–13.

18. Mary Borromeo Brown, *The History of the Sisters of Providence of Saint Mary-of-the-Woods*, vol. 1, *1806–1856* (New York: Benziger Brothers, Inc., 1949), 787–89.

19. See Robert A. Burnett, "Louisville's French Past," *The Filson Club History Quarterly* 50 (Apr. 1976): 5–27 and Huntley Dupre, "The French in Early Kentucky," ibid., 15 (Apr. 1941): 78–104. For a detailed list of French inhabitants of Louisville see Benedict J. Webb, *The Centenary of Catholicity in Kentucky* (Louisville: Charles A. Rogers, 1884), 518. On Lafayette's visit to Louisville and Jeffersonville in Indiana see Edgar Ewing Brandon, comp. & ed., *A Pilgrimage of Liberty: A Contemporary Account of the Triumphal Tour of General Lafayette through the Southern and Western States in 1825, as Reported by the Local Newspapers* (Athens, Ohio: The Lawhead Press, 1944), 256–70. For the broader context of Lafayette's visit see Sylvia Neely, "The Politics of Liberty in the Old World and the New: Lafayette's Return to America in 1824," *Journal of the Early Republic* 6 (summer 1986): 151–71.

20. See Carl E. Kramer, "City with a Vision: Images of Louisville in the 1830s," *The Filson Club History Quarterly* 60 (Oct. 1986): 427–52.

21. *Guide des émigrans français dans les états de Kentucky et d'Indiana ou renseignemens fidèles sur les États-Unis de l'Amérique en général, et sur les états de Kentucky et d'Indiana en particulier, indiquant les mesures et précautions à prendre avant de s'embarquer ainsi que les moyens d'y émigrer agréablement, d'y doubler sa fortune, de la mettre à l'abri de tous risques, et de s'y établir dans une situation à se créer une fortune de quatre-vingt à cent mille francs, après douze ans d'absence, avec de faibles capitaux et un travail modéré* (Paris: Artiius Bertrand, 1835). Books, pamphlets, and articles in periodicals—particularly in the Catholic press—dealing with Indiana were not uncommon in France in the early nineteenth century. Some were records of travel in the region, but most focused on the activities of the early Catholic clergy and were frequently published in order to raise funds and recruit clergy for the church in Indiana. Among the early travel accounts would be that of a French traveler who visited Louisville and New Albany in July 1817: Edouard DeMontulé, *Voyage en Amérique, en Italie, en Sicile et en Egypte, pendant les années 1816, 1817, 1818 et 1819*, 2 vols. (Paris: Dalaunay, 1821). Another nineteenth-century traveler recounted his trip from New Orleans up the Mississippi to Louisville and New Albany. He visited the French settlement at the Knobs and from there went to Lanesville, where relatives resided: M. J. Dulieu, *Mississipi et Indiana: Souvenirs d'Amérique* (Paris: Jules Lecuir, [1862]). Bishop Benedict Flaget's account of the early church in Kentucky was probably the earliest publication describing the accomplishments of the nascent church on the Kentucky and Indiana frontiers, and like others of its genre it contained an appeal for financial assistance: *Appel de B. J. Flaget, évêque de Bardstown (Kentucky) à ses compatriotes de France* (Paris: De l'imprimerie d'Ad. LeClerc, 1820). See also [Rev. Stephen T. Badin], *Origine et progrès de la mission du Kentucky: Par un témoin oculaire . . .* (Paris: LeClerc, 1821); *Oeuvres des Soeurs de la Providence, établie à Sainte-Marie-des-Bois, au diocèse de Vincennes (États-Unis)* (Paris, 1843); [Amédée Desgeorge], *Monseigneur Flaget, évêque de Bardstown et Louisville* (Paris: J. Lecoffre, 1851); *Mission de Notre-Dame du Lac, sur les bords du Lac Michigan, dans le nord de l'état d'Indiana* (Le Mans, 1852); J. M. et Félicité de Lamennais, *Lettres inédites adressées à Mgr Bruté, de Rennes, ancien évêque de Vincennes, recueilliés par M. H. de Courcy et précédées d'une introduction par M. Eugène de la Gournerie* (Nantes: Forest et E. Grimaud, 1862).

22. Annabelle M. Melville and Patrick Foley, *Louis William DuBourg: Bishop of Louisiana and the Floridas, Bishop of Montauban, and Archbishop of Besançon, 1766–1833*, 2 vols. (Chicago: Loyola University Press, 1986), 2:583; Edward John Hickey, "The Society for the Propagation of the Faith: Its Foundation, Organization, and Success (1822–1922)" (Ph.D. diss., Catholic University of America, 1922). Another organization known as the Leopoldine Society was formed in Vienna in 1828 to perform the same function. See Bernard Thompson, "The Leopoldine Society," *St. Meinrad Historical Essays* 1 (Nov. 1929): 203–12.

23. Remond, *États-Unis*, 1:137–43; Webb, *Centenary of Catholicity in Kentucky*, 382–84.

24. Remond, *États-Unis*, 1:125–28; John Kraka, "Célestine de la Hailandière: Second Bishop of Vincennes, 1839–1847," *St. Meinrad Historical Essays* 3 (May 1934): 134–40.

25. Célestine de la Hailandière, for example, returned to Europe in 1839 and 1845, and Maurice de St. Palais visited France in 1845 and three times during his episcopacy—in 1851, 1859, and 1869. Father Julian Benoit returned to France in 1841, 1865, and 1874. Benoit also made extended trips to New Orleans in 1853 and 1860 to raise funds for the Indiana church among French coreligionists in Louisiana. See *Biographical Sketch of Rt. Rev. Julian Benoit: Domestic Prelate to His Holiness Leo XIII, and Vicar General of the Diocese of Fort Wayne, By a Clergyman of the Episcopal Household* ([Ft. Wayne, Ind.?], 1885), 11.

26. On the activities of the early Catholic Church in Indiana see H. J. Alerding, *A History of the Catholic Church in the Diocese of Vincennes* (Indianapolis: Carlon and Hollenbeck, 1883); Thomas T. McAvoy, *The Catholic Church in Indiana, 1789–1834* (New York: Columbia University Press, 1940); William McNamara, *The Catholic Church on the Northern Indiana Frontier, 1789–1844* (Washington, D.C.: Catholic University of America, 1931); Mary C. Schroeder, *The Catholic Church in the Diocese of Vincennes, 1847–1877* (Washington, D.C.: Catholic University of America Press, 1946).

27. See Brown, *History of the Sisters of Providence* and Mary Theodosia Mug, *Life and Life-Work of Mother Theodore Guerin*,

*Foundress of the Sisters of Providence at St. Mary-of-the-Woods, Vigo County, Indiana* (New York: Benziger Brothers, Inc., 1904). On 11 July 1992 Pope John Paul II signed the "Decree on the Heroic Virtues of Mother Theodore Guerin," conferring the title of "Venerable" on this French-born nun who founded the Sisters of Providence. This designation indicates that Mother Theodore's cause for beatification has been formally accepted by the Catholic Church; Mother Theodore is the first person from Indiana to be recognized in this manner by the Catholic Church.

28. Etienne and Tony Catta, *Basil Anthony Mary Moreau*, trans. Edward L. Heston, 2 vols. (Milwaukee, Wis.: Bruce Publishing Co., 1955), 1:490–518; Arthur Hope, *Notre Dame: One Hundred Years*, rev. ed. (South Bend, Ind.: Icarus Press, 1978), 1–49; John T. Wack, "The University of Notre Dame du Lac: Foundation, 1841–1857" (Ph.D. diss., University of Notre Dame, 1967); Edward Sorin, *Chronicles of Notre Dame du Lac*, John M. Toohey, trans., James T. Connelly, ed. (Notre Dame, Ind.: University of Notre Dame Press, 1992). The early French influence in northern Indiana and the establishment of Sacred Heart Parish at Notre Dame is also chronicled in Joseph M. White, *Sacred Heart Parish at Notre Dame: A Heritage and History* (Notre Dame, Ind.: Sacred Heart Parish, 1992). The letters of twenty brother-founders of the Congregation of the Holy Cross to Edward Sorin, the superior at Notre Dame, and to Father Basil Moreau, the founder-director of the Congregation at Le Mans in France, not only provide information about one group of French immigrants and the establishment of Notre Dame but also provide vivid details of the challenges of coping with the primitive conditions on the Indiana frontier in the 1840s. *Adapted to the Lake: Letters by Brother Founders of Notre Dame, 1841–1849*, ed. & trans. George Klawitter (New York: Peter Lang, 1993).

29. See M. Eleanore Brosnahan, *On the King's Highway: A History of the Sisters of the Holy Cross of St. Mary of the Immaculate Conception, Notre Dame, Indiana* (New York: D. Appleton and Co., 1931). The early history of the Sisters of the Holy Cross has also been chronicled most recently in Sister M. Georgia Costin, C.S.C., *Priceless Spirit: A History of the Sisters of the Holy Cross, 1841–1893* (Notre Dame, Ind.: University of Notre Dame Press, 1994). Two other Indiana colleges were established by French congregations, but they survived only a few years: French Eudists established St. Gabriel's College in Vincennes in 1837, and in 1857 three brothers of Christian Doctrine from Verilize established St. Maurice Institute in Decatur County. Other religious congregations originating in France were the Sisters of Our Lady of Charity of the Good Shepherd from Angers, who began charitable work in Indianapolis in 1873, and the Little Sisters of the Poor from St. Servan in Brittany, who began working among the aged in Indianapolis in the same year. Schroeder, *Catholic Church*, 192–93; Alerding, *History of the Catholic Church*, 615–16, 622–24.

30. See Brown, *History of the Sisters of Providence*, 216–19, 363–69; Lemarie, *Les missionnaires bretons*, 169; Kelly, *Catholic Immigrant Colonization Projects*, 79.

31. Kelly, *Catholic Immigrant Colonization Projects*, 6.

32. Rev. Joseph Kundek to Leopoldine Society, 12 Oct. 1846, quoted in Albert Kleber, *Ferdinand, Indiana, 1840–1940* (St. Meinrad, Ind., 1940), 15–16.

33. Ibid., 11–36; Kelly, *Catholic Immigrant Colonization Projects*, 66–76. See also Francis S. Holweck, "Two Pioneer Indiana Priests," *Mid-America* 12 (July 1929): 63–81.

34. Kelly, *Catholic Immigrant Colonization Projects*, 77–78; James Mosby, comp., *The Living History of Perry County* (Evansville, Ind.: Unigraphic, 1977), 103, 104. In 1840 the Reverend Benoit was

reassigned to Fort Wayne in Allen County. When in 1857 Fort Wayne was selected to become the seat of a new diocese, Benoit was nominated to become its first bishop but was passed over in favor of John Henry Luers who had been born near Munster in Westphalia. A consideration prompting church authorities to select Luers was the fact that the Western church had been dominated too long by the French clergy and that a German bishop should be appointed over a Catholic population that already by the 1850s included more Germans than French. Schroeder, *Catholic Church*, 139.

35. The overwhelming majority of immigrants from France—both French and German speaking—were Roman Catholics who retained their ties to the church after settling in Indiana. However, eastern France also provided immigrants of other faiths. Some of the earliest Amish families in the Leo area came to Allen County in 1852 and 1853 from Alsace by way of Stark County, Ohio. John Christian Wenger, *The Mennonites in Indiana and Michigan*, no. 10 of *Studies in Anabaptist and Mennonite History* (Scottsdale, Pa.: Herald Press, 1961), 10; William C. Ringenberg, "Development and Division in the Mennonite Community in Allen County, Indiana," *Mennonite Quarterly Review* 50 (Apr. 1976): 114–31. Protestants from Alsace settled in the Hubbles Corner area in Dearborn County and established the oldest Lutheran Church in the region in 1833. Ripley County History Book Committee, *Ripley County History, 1818–1988* (Dallas, Tex.: Taylor Publishing Co., 1989), 110. There was also a small French Reformed element in Allen County in the 1840s and 1850s. George Ross Mather, *Frontier Faith: The Story of the Pioneer Congregations of Fort Wayne, Indiana, 1820–1860* (Fort Wayne: The Allen County-Fort Wayne Historical Society, 1992), 201–2. A few Jewish merchants from Alsace and Lorraine established businesses in several Indiana cities. Isaac Lauferty and his son Alexander in the 1870s established a private banking house in Fort Wayne. Moses Kahn from Frauenburg near Metz attended Indiana University and later became a well-known clothing merchant in Bloomington. Several Jewish merchants were prominent in Muncie's business community, including Lipman and Henry Marks from Forbach in Lorraine, who established L & H Marks & Co. Alexander L. Shonfield, "Preface to the History of the Jewish People and a Sketch of the Jewish Congregation in the City of Muncie, Indiana," publication [no. 9] of the Indiana Jewish Historical Society (Fort Wayne, Ind.: Indiana Jewish Historical Society, 1977), 27–38.

36. *Ripley County History*, 110; Houpert, *Les Lorrains*, 140–41.

37. See Erika E. Griffith, "The Growth and Decline of the German Element in Indiana, 1772–1972: A Description and Interpretation of German Influence upon the Development of Indiana" (M.A. thesis, Butler University, 1972), 60.

38. Deed Book C, Perry County Recorder's Office, quoted in Thomas James de la Hunt, *Perry County: A History* (Indianapolis: The W. K. Stewart Co., 1916), 105.

39. Mosby, comp., *Living History of Perry County*, 104. For the names of some of the original French and Belgian settlers in Perry County see de la Hunt, *Perry County*, 110.

40. Alerding, *History of the Catholic Church*, 321; Lemarie, *Les missionnaires bretons*, 311 n.

41. David G. Lidikay, "Frenchtown: Some Thoughts and Comments about Its History and Development," *Southern Indiana Genealogical Society Quarterly* 1 (Oct. 1980): 69–70; F. A. Bulleit, comp., *Illustrated Atlas and History, Harrison County, Indiana* (Corydon, Ind.: F. A. Bulleit, 1906), 55.

42. For information on the original French settlers of Floyd County see "French Settlement on Buffalo Trail," undated manuscript, Stuart Barth Wrege Indiana History Room, New Albany-Floyd County Public Library; "Family Names Occurring at Floyd Knobs

between 1836–1850 (Records at Holy Trinity Church, New Albany),” ibid.; Alice L. Green, “French Settlements in Floyd County,” *Indiana Magazine of History* 11 (Mar. 1915): 64–69.

43. *The New Albany Valley News*, 3 Dec. 1959; George Yater, “Old French Colony once Tended Vineyards on Floyd County Knobs,” undated newspaper article, Stuart Barth Wrege Indiana History Room, New Albany-Floyd County Public Library.

44. Green, “French Settlements,” 68; “Porrentruy, an Old French Settlement,” undated manuscript, Stuart Barth Wrege Indiana History Room, New Albany-Floyd County Public Library; “Down in Porrentruy: A Quaint Old French Settlement among the Indiana Hills,” undated newspaper article, ibid.

45. *New Albany Ledger*, 24 Oct. 1890; *New Albany Tribune*, 16 Jan. 1935.

46. The 1850 census recorded 115 French-born residents of Lafayette Township. Another 130 resided in the city of New Albany, and 45 were residents of New Albany Township, which would include the French Creek Settlement. “1850 Indiana Foreign-Born by Township” (Unpublished manuscript, Indiana Historical Society, Education Division, 1991), 17.

47. Louis Neyron served as a physician in Napoleon’s army during its invasion of Russia and was taken prisoner by the Prussians at the Battle of Waterloo. He later decided upon a religious career and was recruited by Bishop Simon Bruté for the Indiana missions. “100th Anniversary of the First Catholic Church in Floyd County,” newspaper clippings and photographs, Stuart Barth Wrege Indiana History Room, New Albany-Floyd County Public Library.

48. Henry Verst, *Floyd Knobs, Indiana: History of St. Mary Parish and a Story of Floyd Knobs, 1800–1938* (New Albany, Ind.: Floyd County Printing Co., n.d.), 28; “St. Mary’s of the Knobs,” undated manuscript, Stuart Barth Wrege Indiana History Room, New Albany-Floyd County Public Library.

49. Detailed information on the establishment of these parishes, as well as the clergy who served them, the religious communities that operated their schools, and parish organizations is available in H. J. Alerding, *The Diocese of Fort Wayne, 1857–September 22-1907: A Book of Historical Reference, 1669–1907* (Fort Wayne, Ind.: The Archer Printing Co., 1907).

50. On St. Michael’s see also William T. Kaiser, “Saint Michael’s Church—Pierr Settlement—Saint Joseph Township,” *Allen County Lines* 4 (Dec. 1979): 23–24.

51. *Fort Wayne Weekly Sentinel*, 20 Apr. 1898; *Fort Wayne Journal-Gazette*, 5 July 1914. The area was also known as Lasselleville and the Lasselle Addition. Some French families in this area attended St. Peter’s Church (established 1871). On the long career of the Reverend Julian Benoit in Fort Wayne see Mather, *Frontier Faith*, 79ff.

52. Edward T. Erpelding, “Saint Vincent de Paul Parish, 1853–1966” (M.A. thesis, Saint Francis College, Fort Wayne, Ind., 1967), 4.

53. In addition to St. Leo and St. Michael, St. Vincent’s priests were responsible, for a number of years, for the mission at Girardot Settlement (known as Ege after 1885) in Noble County. This settlement was founded by a French immigrant Gabriel Girardot, in whose home the first Mass was celebrated in 1856 by Rev. Francis Deschamps, the first resident pastor at St. Vincent. Girardot had arrived in the United States without his family in 1853. As he cleared the land and prepared a home for his family, he vowed to build a “church in the wilderness” to thank God for the safe relocation of his family to Indiana. The church was dedicated in 1863 by Bishop Luers and Father Benoit and was built entirely by Girardot who also constructed the pews, altar, and other furnishings. Only a few French families settled in the area and by the 1870s non-French settlers were beginning to outnumber the French. *Immaculate Conception Church, Ege, Indiana. Mass of Consecration. Most Rev. John M. D’Arcy, D.D. November 14, 1989*, program, 5–6.

54. B. J. Griswold, *The Pictorial History of Fort Wayne*, 2 vols. (Evansville, Ind.: Unigraphics, 1971), 1:644.

55. Joseph A. Hession, *Historical Sketch of St. Louis Parish, Besancon, to Commemorate the Seventy-Fifth Anniversary (1871–1946) of the Present Church and the One-Hundredth Anniversary (1846–1946) of Saint Louis Parish* (n.p., n.d.). The new church was built around the old church, which was left standing within the enclosure of the new and used for services until the construction of the new church was sufficiently advanced to shelter the congregation. *Monroeville News*, 24 Jan. 1973. In 1910 the golden wedding anniversaries of three couples who had been among the earliest French settlers of Jefferson Township served as the occasion for celebrations attended by hundreds; these were among the last such gatherings in Jefferson Township involving significant numbers of original French settlers. See *Fort Wayne Daily News*, 25 July, 6, 27 Aug. 1910.

56. Many of the original log homes constructed by the French settlers were still being used as residences as late as 1919. See *Fort Wayne Journal-Gazette*, 9 Feb. 1919.

57. Of 830 French immigrants to Indiana whose approximate age at the time of their entry into the United States could be determined, 128 were under ten years of age, 202 were between eleven and twenty, 235 were between twenty-one and thirty, 144 were between thirty-one and forty, and 141 were over forty-one.

58. Brasseaux, ‘Foreign French,’ xxvi. See also Phyllis Michaux, ed., “Instructions from the Ohio Valley to French Emigrants,” *Indiana Magazine of History* 84 (June 1988): 161–75; “The High Cost of Emigration,” *French Ancestors: Heritage of the French Settlers in Western Ohio* 1 (July–Aug. 1988): 55.

59. Brasseaux, ‘Foreign French,’ xxv–xxvi; Brown, *History of the Sisters of Providence*, 545.

60. Some French immigrants were not immune to California fever and headed west to accumulate the money needed to purchase land. Jacques Joseph Banet, who immigrated in 1848 to Floyds Knobs, went to California between 1852 and 1859, working in the goldfields around Sacramento while his wife did laundry and cooking for the miners. The Banets later returned to Allen County where his wife’s father, Francis Xavier Lacroix, had established residence in 1852. Another Allen County resident, John Peter Maire, returned from California with enough gold to purchase an eighty-acre farm and with the nickname that he would bear the remainder of his life— “California John.”

61. Among the occupations of French immigrants to Indiana in the nineteenth century were architect, attorney, baker, barber, basket maker, blacksmith, boatman, brewer, brick maker, bricklayer, broom maker, butcher, cabinetmaker, candy maker, carpenter, chair manufacturer, chambermaid, clerk, clothing merchant, cooper, cutter, dining room girl, distiller, domestic, dressmaker, dry goods merchant, dyer, engineer, farmer, ferryman, florist, gardener, general contractor, glassblower, grinder, grocer, hardware merchant, hoop maker, horticulturist, hotel worker, housekeeper, housemaid, ironworker, laborer, machinist, mason, medical doctor, merchant, miller, miner, molder, music teacher, musician, notary public, operator of boardinghouse, owner of brickyard, owner of brewery, painter, policeman, proprietor of bookstore, proprietor of bakery, printer, railroad worker, saloonkeeper, saw dresser, servant, shoe clerk, shoemaker, tailor, tanner, teacher, tinner, upholsterer, vintner, wagon

maker, waitress, watchmaker, weaver, and wooden-shoe maker. See Bunle, "L'immigration," 206–7.

62. *Old Fort Bulletin* (May–June 1973): 16.

63. See Randolph L. Harter, *Charles L. Centlivre and the Centlivre Brewery* (Fort Wayne, Ind.: R. Harter, 1984).

64. Of 547 immigrants to Indiana whose date of entry into the United States and declaration of intent or naturalization are known, 274 either applied for citizenship or were naturalized within five years of entry, 102 between six and ten years, 57 between eleven and fifteen years, and 114 after sixteen years.

65. Schroeder, *Catholic Church,* 87.

66. Hession, *Historical Sketch,* 6. This information is confirmed by Gladys Lomont, a lifelong resident of Jefferson Township. She was born in 1903 and recalls that by the time of the First World War French was spoken only occasionally by older residents of the township. Gladys Lomont, interview with author, 6 May 1992.

67. "Acte d'Incorporation & Constitution de la Société de Bienfaisance Lafayette de Fort Wayne, Indiana," Miscellaneous Records (1866), Allen County Recorder's Office. The charter members of the Lafayette Benevolent Society were Augustine H. Carier, Claude F. Eme, Xavier Valroff, François Bercot, Louis T. Bourret, François S. Aveline, François D. Lasselle, Jean Baptiste Chauvey, and Jules Albert. The society initially met in F. D. Lasselle's hall on Calhoun Street. Between 1864 and 1876 its meetings were held in Anton Fisher's hall on East Main Street. After 1876 a meeting place was established in the Foster's Block on Court Street, where the society maintained a library of French works. T. B. Helm, *History of Allen County, Indiana, with Illustrations and Biographical Sketches of Some of Its Prominent Men and Pioneers. To Which Is Appended Maps of Its Several Townships and Villages* (Chicago: Kingman Brothers, 1880), 95. The French in New Albany in 1866 organized a mutual aid society known as the French Mutual Aid Society of New Albany. See *Constitution et statuts organiques de la Société Française de Secours Mutuels de New Albany (Indiana), fondé le 15 Septembre 1866 et incorporé le 21 du même mois* (New York: Imprimerie de J. A. Flauraud, 1880).

68. "Articles of Association of the French-American Society of Allen County," Miscellaneous Records (1915), Allen County Recorder's Office.

69. See, for example, *Fort Wayne Journal-Gazette,* 6 Sept. 1910 and 28 July 1913. In 1923 the designation of the society was changed to the Lafayette Legion. By that time the society had ceased to be active as a social organization, although death benefits continued to be paid to its members until the Legion's official dissolution in 1947.

70. Ibid., 15 June 1914.

71. The only new concentration of French settlers of any significance to result from the gas and glass booms developed on the south side of Hartford City in an area that was known by some as Frenchtown, where many glassworkers from France and Belgium took up residence.

72. U.S. Department of Commerce, Bureau of the Census, *Sixteenth Census of the United States: 1940,* vol. 1, *Population. Second Series. Characteristics of the Population* (Washington, D.C.: Government Printing Office, 1941–43).

73. U.S. Department of Commerce, Bureau of the Census, *Characteristics of the Population. General Social and Economic Characteristics. Indiana* (Washington, D.C.: Government Printing Office, 1983).

# GERMANS

GILES R. HOYT

> The ultimate effect of the virulent anti-Germanism of the period 1917–22 is not well researched. The German family names of those who died in battle during World War I and are listed in the Indiana War Memorial in Indianapolis indicate that many young men fought more or less willingly. German Americans of any generation were and always had been Americans first. This included the commander of the American Expeditionary Force in World War I, Gen. John J. Pershing (originally Pfoerschin). Ironically, Bismarck Street in Indianapolis was renamed Pershing during the war.

## I. Introduction

Although Indiana had a smaller percentage of immigrants than other states and a greater influx of Old Stock Americans, particularly from the South and Appalachian area, several immigrant groups were large enough to have an impact on the development of the Hoosier state.[1] Immigrants from German-speaking areas of Europe constitute the largest among these groups. For this reason it cannot be the nature of an essay of this type to present a complete study of the German—or rather, German-American—presence in Indiana in all of its details. This essay, however, will show the complexity of the German presence in Indiana, give examples of German-American influence, and discuss the most significant institutions and personages with German origins. The need for a truly comprehensive study remains, and it is hoped that this essay can make a contribution in that direction.

What constitutes this group of German Americans for the purposes of this essay? Because of the geographic and political diversity of their European origins, German Americans will be understood as Americans whose roots reach back to the regions and countries that form the supranational German-speaking parts of Europe.[2] The definition is thus not legalistically based on the notion of citizenship, but on common bonds of ethnicity, language, culture, and history. In this sense then, Germans migrated to Indiana from a variety of areas, including other states of the United States where they first settled, e.g., Pennsylvania. In Europe these areas include all of the German-speaking regions of the Austro-Hungarian Empire; ethnic German enclaves in Russia, Bohemia, and Romania; the largest part of Switzerland, Liechtenstein, and south Tyrol in Italy; and the west Rhine areas of Alsace, Lorraine, and Luxembourg. Prior to 1871—the founding year of the Second Reich—people defined themselves as citizens of a given sovereign kingdom, duchy, or autonomous city-state (Bavaria, Baden, Mecklenburg, Bremen, etc.).[3] Political-geographic divisions were exacerbated by linguistic differences. A Saxon speaking his Low German dialect, or Plattdeutsch, could not easily, if at all, understand a person from Württemberg speaking in a broad Swabian dialect. This seems to contradict the notion of language as one of the common bonds. But just as England had the Queen's English, German speakers (and readers) have High German in literature, the press, and schools.

Perhaps more significant a factor in fragmenting the German-speaking groups was religious differences in the land that spawned the Reformation. Unlike the Irish,

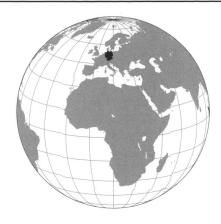

who were predominantly Roman Catholic, the Germans were divided almost equally into Catholics and Protestants. The latter group was further divided among Lutherans and Evangelical-Reformed (Calvinists). In addition, there were several groups of Anabaptists who had fundamental differences with the Protestant state churches as well as among themselves. To these groups can be added the smaller number of German-Jewish immigrants to indicate the complexity underlying any simple appellation "German." In fact, as late as 1898 at the grand opening of Das Deutsche Haus (The German House, after 1918 Athenaeum) in Indianapolis, the festival play stressed as its major theme the unity of all the German-speaking groups through their joint contributions to building America.[4] Thus, in a sense, many German-speaking people in America came to be called "Germans" only in the context of their being German Americans. Especially for the intellectuals arriving before 1871, Germany existed as a "Kulturnation," a cultural ideal rather than as a political construct.

In the 1990s there is a great deal of discussion about the nature of ethnicity and its positive or negative impact on cultural pluralism in the United States. It is significant that German-speaking immigrants were the first non-English-speaking immigrant group in America. They defined to a great extent what ethnicity meant in America and opened American society to others.[5] Orlando Patterson, in *Ethnicity: Theory and Experience,* makes a useful distinction between an ethnic group that chooses to emphasize common cultural traits "as their most meaningful basis of their primary, extra-familial identity" and a culture group that shares consciously or unconsciously an "identifiable complex of meanings, symbols, values, and norms."[6] In terms of ethnicity and culture, German Americans in Indiana constitute an identifiable group. In the 1990 census, based on a statistical sample, 2,085,487 Hoosiers claimed German ancestry, the largest of any group, the next largest being Irish Americans with 965,602 out of

a total of 6,479,714. (See Table 1.) Indiana ranks ninth among the fifty states in terms of the number of people claiming German ancestry.[7]

The 1980 census also showed immigrants from Germany constituting the largest group from any one country in Indiana with 11,818 people. The next largest group were those born in Mexico with 9,460.[8] Politically speaking, however, there is no "German" vote as such, and German Americans, along with Irish Americans, Americans of East European descent, and Old Stock Americans of New England origin, belong to the group known as "white" on most government and other lists. German Americans have ceased being a group easily identifiable in the American mainstream.

While there was some repatriation of German immigrants, the vast majority came to the United States and to Indiana with the idea of staying.[9] Even during and immediately after World War I, when German Americans suffered the most because of their heritage, over 90 percent had their United States citizenship or had applied for citizenship. There had never been any thought among Hoosier German Americans of establishing an independent German state in America, such as was considered by radical idealists in Hermann, Missouri, or by some emigration societies in faraway Germany. But neither did Hoosier Germans cast aside their cultural heritage. Rather they sought to retain for themselves and their offspring essential aspects of customs, traditions, language, music, and values governing public and private behavior. Here and elsewhere German-speaking immigrants and their children greatly influenced the development of American mainstream culture—from kindergarten and the Christmas tree to graduate education and symphony orchestras. The political ideals of German immigrants were almost always much more in line with indigenous American political principles than those they left behind. They understood the advantages of a democratic government based on rational, Enlightenment principles of individual and natural rights, equality before the law (i.e., no class of citizens privileged by birth alone), separation of church and state, and free enterprise, but with a strong sense of social responsibility and justice. It can be demonstrated that the reinforcement of these values is one of the greatest contributions of German immigrants to Indiana and to the United States as a whole.[10]

Antebellum Indiana mirrors the general trends of German immigration for the Midwest. The European areas most prominently represented are the western part of German-speaking areas: the Palatinate, Baden, Alsace, Switzerland, Westphalia, Hesse, Hannover, Württemberg, and Bavaria. Travel from those areas generally followed major waterways, particularly the Rhine.

Germany, the later immigration through 1880 brought considerable numbers of people from the eastern German provinces, including Pomerania, Mecklenburg, and Silesia.

Emigration was not always made easy by the various provincial governments, and considerable debate focused on the issue of large-scale emigration and its effect on a given area. Frequently proof that young males had served their time in the military, or a substantial fee, if such was not the case, had to be provided before permission to depart was granted. Many communities, provinces, landholders, and officials required the payment of a "leave tax." This, combined simply with the logistics of travel and migration, often made for a daunting adventure.[11]

## II.  The Early Period—Colonial Period to 1816

Unlike England, Spain, and France, Germany, exhausted from the Thirty Years' War (1618–48) and with no centralized power, did not have a colonial presence in the New World. Germans came, however, with the earliest colonizing groups. It is impossible to say exactly when the first German-speaking persons arrived in Indiana. During the early French period of the area comprising the present state of Indiana, German names appear among the inhabitants of Fort Vincennes (Sackville), established in 1727. Gen. George Rogers Clark captured the fort twice during the American Revolution, and his force contained many German Americans. Capt. Leonard Helm was commander of Fort Vincennes and agent for the Indians of the Wabash valley.[12] Two German-American officers, Capt. Frederick Geiger and Col. Luke Decker, were among Gen. William Henry Harrison's troops that moved against the Prophet in 1811 at the Battle of Tippecanoe.

Religious groups generally referred to as Anabaptists, particularly the Moravians, began their long presence

Table 2, derived from the 1880 United States census, gives an indication of the origin of German immigrants and the Indiana counties in which they settled. It is apparent that immigrants from specific German-speaking areas clustered in certain places. The number of German born from Oldenburg in Franklin County shows that an area settled primarily by Germans from Oldenburg in Germany in the 1840s continued to attract people from that area. Also quite remarkable is the large number of immigrants from Mecklenburg and Prussia who settled mainly in La Porte County, reflecting a chain migration. Whereas German immigration in the period up to 1860 was dominated heavily by people from west and southwest

## Table 1. Indiana Ancestry—1990 Census

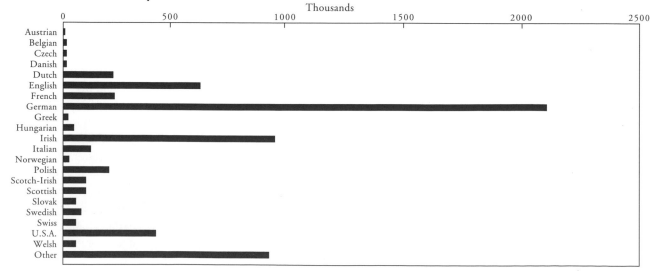

in Indiana in the 1790s.[13] Arriving in 1792, John Heckewelder was the most important early Moravian preacher in Indiana. A scholar of languages, he mastered the Indian dialects of the area and later was sent by President George Washington to act as counselor and interpreter of Indian languages to Gen. Rufus Putnam, who was negotiating a peace treaty with the Indians at Vincennes.[14] A Moravian mission among the Delaware Indians on White River near present-day Anderson was established in 1801 by John Peter Kluge and Abraham Luckenbach. They were sent from the center of Moravian religious activity in Bethlehem, Pennsylvania. One of the earliest Quaker families in the Richmond area was the Hoover family, descended from Andrew Hoover (Huber), a Hannoverian who arrived in Germantown, Pennsylvania, in the early 1700s.[15] David Hoover surveyed the area around Richmond and was delighted with its potential. The family moved to the Middle Fork area in 1806.

In 1796 a number of Swiss immigrants from the Canton Waadt organized a company to buy land on the Ohio River in the area of present Switzerland County where they founded the town of Vevay and introduced viticulture to Indiana.[16]

One of the most unusual and interesting communities in early Indiana—even before statehood—was New Harmony in Posey County, established by the Anabaptist sectarian Johann Georg Rapp and his followers. They came from the Iptingen area near Stuttgart, Germany.[17] Early in life Rapp had become fascinated with the customs and ceremonies of the early Christians, and he developed a theology of simple, communistic Christianity and began a charismatic preaching and colonizing career. Rapp and his group felt increasingly isolated from the society around them because of their basic Anabaptist doctrine that opposed infant baptism, confirmation, oaths of allegiance, and military service. Believing that they were fulfilling the prophecy of the Sunwoman of Revelations 12:6 who "fled into the wilderness, where she hath a place prepared of God," Rapp, his son Johannes, and two elders sought a place in the western wilderness of America for the thousands of separatists whom they believed would follow them.[18] They bought five thousand acres twenty-five miles west of Pittsburgh at three dollars an acre and established the town of Harmony. Rapp met 300 of his people in Baltimore where they arrived on the ship *Aurora* on 4 July 1804. Another party of 260, led by Frederick Rapp, the brilliant business manager of the Harmonists and adopted son of George Rapp, arrived the next month in Philadelphia.

In 1814 the society sold Harmony to a German American for one hundred thousand dollars and bought three thousand acres in southwest Indiana on the Wabash River. The Rappites established a brewery, a distillery, mills, and factories and manufactured cotton and woolen goods. By 1819 the Harmonists were providing for nearly all of their needs and selling more than twelve thousand dollars' worth of agricultural produce annually. In the following year their manufactured goods were valued at fifty thousand dollars.[19] Branch stores were established in Vincennes; Shawneetown, Illinois; Louisville, Kentucky; Pittsburgh, Pennsylvania; and other places. Rappite products and manufactured articles found ready markets throughout the Ohio and Mississippi valleys, from Pittsburgh to New Orleans. A report from the English colony at Albion, Edwards County, Illinois, states that the manufactures of the Rappites were given preference over all others, and that in the years 1818–24 the English settlers had purchased one hundred fifty thousand dollars' worth of goods from the Rappites.[20] Based on German principles of hard work and thrift, the community prospered and had the highest per capita income in the state by 1818. Life was also filled with song, since music was both a diversion and a staple of religious life, and flower gardens abounded. An English visitor, George Flower, stated: "With surprise all who went to Harmony observed with what facility the necessaries and the comforts of life were acquired and enjoyed by every member of Rapp's community. When compared with the privations and discomforts to which individual settlers were exposed in their backwoods experiences, the contrast was very striking."[21]

The Rapp community's considerable capital was expanded through commerce. The Farmers Bank of Harmony was one of the first such institutions in the state and one of the soundest.[22] The Harmonist story in Indiana ended in 1824 when the Rappites sold the town to Robert Owen of Scotland for one hundred fifty thousand dollars and moved back to Pennsylvania. A few Rappites remained in the state "and these were the agitators for a large German immigration in the southern part of Indiana."[23]

Jacob Schnee (1784–1838), a Lutheran pastor and real estate dealer, came in the wake of the Rappites.[24] Schnee was a Pennsylvania German who dreamed of a Lutheran community based on Christian principles, though not a communal society with shared property. He agreed to purchase the Harmony, Pennsylvania, property from Mennonite Abraham Ziegler, who had originally purchased it from Rapp. This endeavor failed as a result of the economic crises during the post–Napoleonic period that also affected the young United States. Money was simply very scarce. After the breakup of Robert Owen's secular commune at New Harmony in 1827, Schnee and a group of twelve to fifteen families of Pennsylvania

## Table 2. Germans in Indiana by County in 1880

| County | Germany | Other Germany | Baden | Bavaria | Berlin | Bremen | Hamburg | Hanover | Hesse | Hesse Cassell | Hesse Darmstadt | Hesse Hessburg |
|---|---|---|---|---|---|---|---|---|---|---|---|---|
| Adams | 127 | 21 | 49 | 51 | 1 | 1 | 4 | 72 | 1 | 0 | 6 | 0 |
| Allen | 926 | 132 | 230 | 247 | 1 | 6 | 4 | 312 | 2 | 19 | 185 | 0 |
| Bartholomew | 375 | 12 | 18 | 32 | 0 | 2 | 2 | 76 | 13 | 1 | 34 | 0 |
| Benton | 32 | 4 | 16 | 19 | 0 | 0 | 0 | 9 | 2 | 1 | 6 | 0 |
| Blackford | 25 | 0 | 6 | 6 | 0 | 0 | 0 | 0 | 0 | 0 | 17 | 0 |
| Boone | 37 | 1 | 12 | 5 | 0 | 0 | 0 | 1 | 4 | 2 | 2 | 0 |
| Brown | 18 | 2 | 14 | 0 | 0 | 0 | 1 | 1 | 2 | 0 | 0 | 0 |
| Carroll | 49 | 0 | 15 | 16 | 0 | 0 | 0 | 1 | 6 | 0 | 3 | 0 |
| Cass | 149 | 8 | 78 | 151 | 0 | 4 | 7 | 66 | 32 | 9 | 31 | 0 |
| Clark | 363 | 14 | 224 | 93 | 2 | 0 | 0 | 31 | 20 | 14 | 39 | 0 |
| Clay | 64 | 4 | 45 | 82 | 0 | 0 | 3 | 15 | 9 | 6 | 7 | 0 |
| Clinton | 30 | 2 | 12 | 8 | 0 | 1 | 0 | 3 | 1 | 1 | 7 | 0 |
| Crawford | 35 | 1 | 10 | 10 | 0 | 0 | 0 | 1 | 0 | 0 | 0 | 0 |
| Daviess | 86 | 9 | 33 | 30 | 0 | 0 | 0 | 6 | 15 | 1 | 7 | 0 |
| Dearborn | 1097 | 7 | 194 | 639 | 0 | 0 | 1 | 411 | 22 | 4 | 34 | 0 |
| Decatur | 218 | 7 | 21 | 55 | 4 | 2 | 3 | 157 | 6 | 1 | 5 | 0 |
| De Kalb | 165 | 52 | 39 | 0 | 2 | 3 | 1 | 8 | 6 | 19 | 11 | 0 |
| Delaware | 45 | 5 | 6 | 5 | 0 | 0 | 0 | 1 | 1 | 1 | 8 | 0 |
| Dubois | 66 | 10 | 271 | 477 | 1 | 0 | 0 | 346 | 47 | 28 | 43 | 0 |
| Elkhart | 454 | 7 | 47 | 58 | 0 | 2 | 1 | 11 | 13 | 1 | 27 | 0 |
| Fayette | 199 | 4 | 37 | 26 | 0 | 0 | 0 | 12 | 3 | 0 | 4 | 0 |
| Floyd | 942 | 24 | 143 | 143 | 0 | 0 | 0 | 51 | 28 | 3 | 51 | 0 |
| Fountain | 180 | 0 | 14 | 15 | 0 | 0 | 0 | 3 | 2 | 0 | 4 | 0 |
| Franklin | 196 | 17 | 116 | 538 | 0 | 1 | 9 | 383 | 86 | 5 | 63 | 10 |
| Fulton | 44 | 3 | 17 | 36 | 0 | 0 | 5 | 14 | 8 | 3 | 19 | 0 |
| Gibson | 245 | 5 | 38 | 118 | 0 | 1 | 0 | 65 | 13 | 0 | 15 | 0 |
| Grant | 24 | 2 | 3 | 5 | 0 | 1 | 1 | 4 | 3 | 0 | 0 | 0 |
| Greene | 67 | 0 | 3 | 5 | 0 | 0 | 0 | 0 | 0 | 0 | 0 | 0 |
| Hamilton | 23 | 2 | 13 | 44 | 0 | 0 | 0 | 2 | 3 | 6 | 23 | 0 |
| Hancock | 48 | 8 | 10 | 17 | 0 | 0 | 0 | 12 | 4 | 1 | 40 | 0 |
| Harrison | 178 | 4 | 98 | 140 | 1 | 0 | 0 | 18 | 6 | 3 | 67 | 0 |
| Hendricks | 39 | 0 | 13 | 5 | 0 | 2 | 1 | 1 | 1 | 0 | 2 | 0 |
| Henry | 17 | 4 | 12 | 8 | 0 | 0 | 0 | 2 | 3 | 1 | 7 | 0 |
| Howard | 32 | 0 | 6 | 40 | 0 | 0 | 0 | 11 | 5 | 0 | 3 | 0 |
| Huntington | 287 | 5 | 65 | 64 | 0 | 1 | 1 | 17 | 10 | 1 | 32 | 0 |
| Jackson | 363 | 5 | 54 | 74 | 1 | 1 | 0 | 328 | 4 | 1 | 8 | 0 |
| Jasper | 93 | 2 | 39 | 25 | 0 | 1 | 0 | 19 | 8 | 0 | 0 | 0 |
| Jay | 48 | 8 | 49 | 26 | 0 | 0 | 0 | 7 | 2 | 1 | 1 | 0 |
| Jefferson | 419 | 17 | 176 | 145 | 1 | 2 | 3 | 34 | 33 | 5 | 28 | 0 |
| Jennings | 271 | 3 | 57 | 81 | 0 | 0 | 0 | 26 | 10 | 0 | 9 | 0 |
| Johnson | 65 | 0 | 9 | 3 | 0 | 0 | 4 | 3 | 1 | 0 | 3 | 0 |
| Knox | 320 | 14 | 34 | 55 | 0 | 1 | 1 | 54 | 1 | 0 | 3 | 0 |
| Kosciusko | 160 | 3 | 13 | 37 | 0 | 1 | 0 | 2 | 7 | 2 | 9 | 0 |
| Lagrange | 57 | 3 | 13 | 14 | 1 | 0 | 1 | 3 | 2 | 4 | 9 | 0 |
| Lake | 514 | 104 | 56 | 113 | 2 | 2 | 4 | 117 | 38 | 29 | 45 | 0 |
| La Porte | 904 | 67 | 73 | 101 | 0 | 0 | 14 | 89 | 7 | 5 | 13 | 0 |
| Lawrence | 13 | 1 | 9 | 15 | 1 | 0 | 0 | 0 | 0 | 0 | 6 | 0 |
| Madison | 40 | 5 | 16 | 32 | 0 | 0 | 0 | 3 | 3 | 0 | 7 | 0 |
| Marion | 1548 | 152 | 594 | 527 | 14 | 13 | 17 | 344 | 182 | 20 | 291 | 0 |
| Marshall | 168 | 1 | 118 | 122 | 0 | 0 | 1 | 4 | 6 | 3 | 21 | 2 |
| Martin | 24 | 1 | 6 | 16 | 0 | 0 | 0 | 1 | 0 | 0 | 1 | 0 |
| Miami | 129 | 6 | 63 | 95 | 0 | 2 | 2 | 31 | 5 | 5 | 59 | 0 |
| Monroe | 36 | 0 | 10 | 4 | 0 | 0 | 0 | 2 | 0 | 0 | 0 | 0 |
| Montgomery | 42 | 1 | 4 | 8 | 0 | 0 | 0 | 2 | 6 | 0 | 2 | 0 |
| Morgan | 18 | 0 | 24 | 9 | 0 | 0 | 0 | 5 | 1 | 0 | 2 | 0 |
| Newton | 28 | 18 | 11 | 9 | 0 | 1 | 0 | 2 | 2 | 0 | 2 | 0 |
| Noble | 171 | 5 | 139 | 46 | 0 | 0 | 1 | 27 | 4 | 3 | 22 | 0 |
| Ohio | 13 | 0 | 6 | 5 | 0 | 1 | 0 | 144 | 0 | 0 | 1 | 0 |
| Orange | 4 | 0 | 1 | 0 | 0 | 0 | 0 | 1 | 0 | 0 | 0 | 0 |
| Owen | 82 | 0 | 7 | 13 | 0 | 0 | 1 | 6 | 0 | 2 | 1 | 1 |
| Parke | 15 | 1 | 1 | 2 | 0 | 0 | 0 | 0 | 0 | 0 | 3 | 0 |
| Perry | 74 | 26 | 101 | 224 | 0 | 3 | 7 | 77 | 38 | 5 | 87 | 7 |
| Pike | 21 | 1 | 6 | 17 | 0 | 0 | 0 | 64 | 0 | 5 | 8 | 0 |
| Porter | 157 | 12 | 20 | 62 | 0 | 1 | 1 | 22 | 19 | 9 | 2 | 0 |
| Posey | 116 | 20 | 157 | 238 | 1 | 1 | 0 | 41 | 20 | 72 | 252 | 0 |
| Pulaski | 26 | 11 | 86 | 23 | 1 | 0 | 0 | 4 | 4 | 0 | 6 | 0 |
| Putnam | 77 | 0 | 8 | 7 | 0 | 0 | 0 | 2 | 0 | 1 | 0 | 0 |
| Randolph | 107 | 7 | 14 | 18 | 1 | 0 | 0 | 7 | 7 | 0 | 15 | 0 |
| Ripley | 198 | 11 | 252 | 394 | 0 | 3 | 1 | 825 | 35 | 3 | 22 | 0 |
| Rush | 37 | 8 | 9 | 35 | 0 | 1 | 0 | 1 | 3 | 7 | 3 | 0 |
| St. Joseph | 125 | 7 | 159 | 580 | 0 | 1 | 0 | 7 | 11 | 39 | 11 | 66 |
| Scott | 10 | 2 | 3 | 5 | 0 | 0 | 0 | 0 | 5 | 2 | 0 | 1 |
| Shelby | 137 | 5 | 60 | 88 | 0 | 0 | 2 | 1 | 17 | 13 | 6 | 22 |
| Spencer | 241 | 15 | 205 | 402 | 0 | 2 | 3 | 2 | 121 | 47 | 0 | 17 |
| Starke | 27 | 3 | 17 | 32 | 0 | 0 | 0 | 0 | 1 | 4 | 0 | 0 |
| Steuben | 40 | 2 | 16 | 15 | 0 | 0 | 0 | 1 | 0 | 1 | 0 | 7 |
| Sullivan | 31 | 0 | 6 | 5 | 0 | 0 | 0 | 0 | 0 | 2 | 1 | 2 |
| Switzerland | 163 | 3 | 7 | 3 | 0 | 0 | 0 | 0 | 25 | 2 | 0 | 0 |
| Tippecanoe | 587 | 20 | 181 | 143 | 0 | 11 | 0 | 2 | 106 | 37 | 12 | 44 |
| Tipton | 50 | 0 | 7 | 15 | 0 | 0 | 0 | 0 | 2 | 7 | 1 | 14 |
| Union | 5 | 0 | 12 | 3 | 0 | 0 | 1 | 0 | 6 | 1 | 0 | 0 |
| Vanderburgh | 0 | 0 | 0 | 0 | 0 | 0 | 0 | 0 | 0 | 0 | 0 | 0 |
| Vermillion | 22 | 2 | 1 | 0 | 0 | 0 | 0 | 0 | 1 | 3 | 0 | 3 |
| Vigo | 569 | 33 | 197 | 166 | 6 | 3 | 2 | 8 | 225 | 52 | 10 | 50 |
| Wabash | 148 | 1 | 41 | 128 | 0 | 8 | 0 | 0 | 4 | 12 | 1 | 11 |
| Warren | 76 | 1 | 7 | 5 | 0 | 0 | 0 | 0 | 3 | 1 | 1 | 3 |
| Warrick | 178 | 45 | 81 | 115 | 0 | 0 | 33 | 0 | 43 | 14 | 29 | 39 |
| Washington | 46 | 1 | 2 | 5 | 0 | 0 | 0 | 0 | 0 | 1 | 1 | 1 |
| Wayne | 149 | 24 | 138 | 92 | 1 | 23 | 2 | 9 | 548 | 16 | 2 | 12 |
| Wells | 84 | 0 | 20 | 18 | 0 | 0 | 2 | 1 | 7 | 0 | 0 | 6 |
| White | 114 | 0 | 8 | 31 | 0 | 0 | 0 | 0 | 16 | 1 | 0 | 4 |
| Whitley | 159 | 8 | 25 | 40 | 0 | 1 | 1 | 1 | 31 | 5 | 1 | 19 |
| Totals | 16201 | 1061 | 5356 | 7674 | 42 | 110 | 149 | 4452 | 1997 | 573 | 1819 | 341 |

| County | Holstein | Lippe Detwold | Mecklenburg | Nassau | Oldenburg | Pomerania | Prussia | Saxony | Westphalia | Wittenberg | Württemberg | Total |
|---|---|---|---|---|---|---|---|---|---|---|---|---|
| Adams | 0 | 0 | 3 | 0 | 5 | 0 | 325 | 22 | 3 | 0 | 32 | 723 |
| Allen | 4 | 0 | 9 | 4 | 2 | 0 | 1464 | 58 | 3 | 33 | 141 | 3782 |
| Bartholomew | 6 | 0 | 8 | 0 | 3 | 0 | 304 | 9 | 0 | 5 | 19 | 919 |
| Benton | 0 | 0 | 0 | 2 | 0 | 0 | 78 | 1 | 0 | 2 | 19 | 191 |
| Blackford | 0 | 4 | 0 | 0 | 0 | 0 | 5 | 0 | 1 | 0 | 10 | 74 |
| Boone | 0 | 0 | 0 | 0 | 3 | 0 | 35 | 3 | 0 | 0 | 20 | 125 |
| Brown | 0 | 0 | 0 | 0 | 1 | 0 | 13 | 0 | 0 | 0 | 1 | 53 |
| Carroll | 0 | 0 | 0 | 0 | 0 | 0 | 120 | 0 | 0 | 0 | 16 | 226 |
| Cass | 15 | 0 | 16 | 1 | 3 | 0 | 339 | 8 | 3 | 4 | 92 | 1016 |
| Clark | 0 | 0 | 1 | 98 | 11 | 0 | 246 | 19 | 0 | 22 | 95 | 1292 |
| Clay | 0 | 0 | 1 | 7 | 0 | 0 | 216 | 8 | 0 | 2 | 58 | 527 |
| Clinton | 0 | 0 | 0 | 0 | 1 | 0 | 11 | 0 | 0 | 0 | 8 | 85 |
| Crawford | 0 | 0 | 0 | 0 | 1 | 0 | 0 | 15 | 0 | 0 | 9 | 82 |
| Daviess | 0 | 0 | 0 | 7 | 0 | 0 | 82 | 0 | 0 | 0 | 4 | 280 |
| Dearborn | 3 | 0 | 1 | 2 | 15 | 0 | 442 | 40 | 3 | 5 | 60 | 2980 |
| Decatur | 1 | 0 | 0 | 0 | 44 | 0 | 73 | 4 | 3 | 4 | 8 | 616 |
| De Kalb | 11 | 0 | 69 | 0 | 0 | 8 | 208 | 8 | 1 | 14 | 62 | 687 |
| Delaware | 0 | 0 | 0 | 1 | 0 | 0 | 15 | 5 | 0 | 5 | 9 | 107 |
| Dubois | 0 | 2 | 0 | 5 | 46 | 0 | 540 | 17 | 4 | 3 | 26 | 1932 |
| Elkhart | 0 | 0 | 10 | 3 | 0 | 0 | 155 | 17 | 1 | 7 | 60 | 874 |
| Fayette | 0 | 0 | 0 | 0 | 0 | 0 | 16 | 3 | 0 | 1 | 11 | 316 |
| Floyd | 5 | 0 | 0 | 43 | 5 | 0 | 142 | 19 | 4 | 4 | 42 | 1649 |
| Fountain | 2 | 0 | 0 | 0 | 0 | 0 | 30 | 3 | 0 | 2 | 18 | 273 |
| Franklin | 1 | 1 | 0 | 0 | 193 | 0 | 263 | 11 | 0 | 14 | 54 | 1961 |
| Fulton | 0 | 0 | 7 | 0 | 0 | 0 | 69 | 7 | 0 | 4 | 25 | 261 |
| Gibson | 0 | 3 | 2 | 8 | 8 | 0 | 145 | 1 | 0 | 0 | 19 | 686 |
| Grant | 0 | 4 | 0 | 1 | 0 | 0 | 16 | 0 | 0 | 0 | 4 | 68 |
| Greene | 0 | 0 | 0 | 0 | 0 | 0 | 53 | 6 | 0 | 0 | 0 | 134 |
| Hamilton | 0 | 0 | 0 | 0 | 1 | 0 | 26 | 1 | 0 | 0 | 30 | 174 |
| Hancock | 0 | 0 | 2 | 0 | 0 | 2 | 128 | 4 | 3 | 3 | 4 | 286 |
| Harrison | 0 | 0 | 0 | 74 | 4 | 0 | 122 | 17 | 0 | 1 | 23 | 756 |
| Hendricks | 0 | 0 | 0 | 1 | 0 | 0 | 10 | 0 | 0 | 0 | 7 | 82 |
| Henry | 0 | 0 | 1 | 0 | 3 | 0 | 20 | 1 | 0 | 1 | 12 | 92 |
| Howard | 2 | 0 | 0 | 2 | 0 | 0 | 29 | 2 | 0 | 0 | 8 | 140 |
| Huntington | 0 | 0 | 25 | 0 | 2 | 0 | 135 | 3 | 0 | 1 | 50 | 699 |
| Jackson | 1 | 2 | 0 | 34 | 12 | 0 | 263 | 6 | 0 | 1 | 12 | 1170 |
| Jasper | 0 | 0 | 17 | 0 | 12 | 0 | 141 | 9 | 0 | 1 | 7 | 374 |
| Jay | 0 | 0 | 1 | 0 | 3 | 0 | 71 | 3 | 0 | 0 | 79 | 299 |
| Jefferson | 0 | 0 | 1 | 0 | 7 | 0 | 351 | 15 | 2 | 6 | 98 | 1343 |
| Jennings | 20 | 0 | 0 | 0 | 3 | 0 | 96 | 8 | 0 | 2 | 14 | 580 |
| Johnson | 0 | 0 | 1 | 0 | 0 | 0 | 16 | 1 | 0 | 0 | 12 | 118 |
| Knox | 4 | 27 | 3 | 0 | 4 | 4 | 775 | 7 | 4 | 2 | 18 | 1331 |
| Kosciusko | 0 | 0 | 1 | 0 | 0 | 0 | 50 | 1 | 0 | 1 | 25 | 312 |
| Lagrange | 0 | 0 | 18 | 0 | 1 | 0 | 36 | 13 | 0 | 10 | 39 | 224 |
| Lake | 35 | 20 | 125 | 8 | 5 | 159 | 1251 | 28 | 16 | 2 | 91 | 2764 |
| La Porte | 34 | 0 | 1013 | 0 | 1 | 5 | 2068 | 43 | 4 | 17 | 142 | 4600 |
| Lawrence | 0 | 0 | 0 | 0 | 0 | 0 | 80 | 0 | 0 | 3 | 4 | 132 |
| Madison | 0 | 0 | 3 | 2 | 0 | 0 | 19 | 2 | 0 | 0 | 16 | 148 |
| Marion | 21 | 4 | 60 | 65 | 13 | 16 | 2712 | 171 | 13 | 71 | 554 | 7402 |
| Marshall | 0 | 0 | 0 | 0 | 0 | 0 | 153 | 24 | 0 | 0 | 82 | 705 |
| Martin | 0 | 0 | 0 | 1 | 0 | 0 | 3 | 0 | 0 | 0 | 2 | 55 |
| Miami | 0 | 0 | 7 | 2 | 3 | 0 | 120 | 16 | 1 | 9 | 73 | 628 |
| Monroe | 1 | 0 | 0 | 0 | 0 | 0 | 16 | 0 | 0 | 0 | 4 | 73 |
| Montgomery | 0 | 0 | 0 | 3 | 0 | 0 | 11 | 2 | 0 | 1 | 18 | 100 |
| Morgan | 0 | 0 | 0 | 1 | 0 | 0 | 77 | 11 | 0 | 5 | 12 | 165 |
| Newton | 5 | 0 | 0 | 0 | 1 | 1 | 79 | 2 | 0 | 0 | 2 | 163 |
| Noble | 0 | 0 | 131 | 1 | 1 | 0 | 248 | 5 | 0 | 1 | 115 | 920 |
| Ohio | 0 | 0 | 0 | 0 | 0 | 0 | 91 | 5 | 4 | 0 | 1 | 271 |
| Orange | 0 | 0 | 1 | 0 | 1 | 0 | 5 | 0 | 0 | 0 | 1 | 14 |
| Owen | 0 | 0 | 1 | 0 | 0 | 0 | 34 | 0 | 0 | 0 | 33 | 181 |
| Parke | 0 | 0 | 0 | 0 | 0 | 0 | 5 | 0 | 0 | 0 | 2 | 29 |
| Perry | 0 | 0 | 2 | 22 | 14 | 0 | 390 | 25 | 4 | 0 | 92 | 1198 |
| Pike | 0 | 0 | 0 | 0 | 1 | 0 | 132 | 1 | 0 | 0 | 2 | 258 |
| Porter | 265 | 0 | 201 | 4 | 0 | 11 | 469 | 24 | 1 | 6 | 22 | 1308 |
| Posey | 5 | 32 | 3 | 3 | 2 | 0 | 410 | 15 | 1 | 0 | 107 | 1464 |
| Pulaski | 0 | 0 | 288 | 1 | 1 | 8 | 316 | | 0 | 4 | 13 | 792 |
| Putnam | 0 | 0 | 1 | 0 | 0 | 0 | 17 | 1 | 0 | 0 | 3 | 117 |
| Randolph | 0 | 0 | 0 | 0 | 12 | 1 | 27 | 1 | 0 | 1 | 44 | 263 |
| Ripley | 0 | 1 | 1 | 3 | 48 | 0 | 429 | 86 | 5 | 11 | 52 | 2380 |
| Rush | 1 | 0 | 0 | 0 | 0 | 2 | 29 | 3 | 0 | 1 | 7 | 147 |
| St. Joseph | 4 | 0 | 39 | 3 | 0 | 0 | 1932 | 85 | 2 | 11 | 300 | 3382 |
| Scott | 0 | 0 | 0 | 7 | 0 | 0 | 8 | 0 | 0 | 0 | 8 | 51 |
| Shelby | 1 | 0 | 0 | 1 | 3 | 0 | 81 | 6 | 0 | 2 | 13 | 458 |
| Spencer | 2 | 1 | 0 | 6 | 13 | 0 | 238 | 7 | 1 | 8 | 98 | 1429 |
| Starke | 5 | 1 | 9 | 0 | 10 | 2 | 210 | 2 | 0 | 0 | 16 | 339 |
| Steuben | 1 | 0 | 3 | 0 | 0 | 0 | 22 | 3 | 0 | 0 | 14 | 125 |
| Sullivan | 0 | 3 | 0 | 0 | 0 | 0 | 34 | 2 | 0 | 0 | 5 | 91 |
| Switzerland | 0 | 0 | 0 | 0 | 1 | 0 | 34 | 0 | 0 | 0 | 1 | 239 |
| Tippecanoe | 1 | 0 | 12 | 0 | 10 | 1 | 479 | 80 | 7 | 26 | 201 | 1960 |
| Tipton | 0 | 0 | 0 | 0 | 0 | 0 | 27 | 4 | 0 | 2 | 16 | 145 |
| Union | 0 | 0 | 0 | 1 | 0 | 0 | 5 | 0 | 0 | 0 | 3 | 37 |
| Vanderburgh | 7 | 16 | 19 | 33 | 48 | 0 | 1464 | 90 | 33 | 0 | 283 | 6379 |
| Vermillion | 0 | 0 | 0 | 0 | 0 | 0 | 31 | 1 | 0 | 1 | 1 | 66 |
| Vigo | 2 | 2 | 9 | 1 | 4 | 0 | 621 | 66 | 3 | 60 | 190 | 2279 |
| Wabash | 0 | 1 | 0 | 2 | 0 | 0 | 101 | 1 | 3 | 3 | 71 | 536 |
| Warren | 0 | 0 | 0 | 0 | 0 | 0 | 15 | 5 | 0 | 0 | 19 | 136 |
| Warrick | 1 | 3 | 0 | 1 | 107 | 0 | 222 | 3 | 5 | 0 | 29 | 948 |
| Washington | 0 | 0 | 0 | 4 | 0 | 0 | 13 | 7 | 0 | 0 | 0 | 81 |
| Wayne | 2 | 1 | 0 | 1 | 15 | 0 | 491 | 29 | 0 | 23 | 59 | 1637 |
| Wells | 1 | 0 | 0 | 0 | 0 | 0 | 9 | 11 | 0 | 0 | 48 | 207 |
| White | 0 | 0 | 38 | 0 | 0 | 1 | 160 | 5 | 0 | 19 | 32 | 429 |
| Whitley | 10 | 1 | 1 | 2 | 0 | 0 | 58 | 5 | 0 | 17 | 28 | 413 |
| Totals | 449 | 107 | 2164 | 472 | 706 | 221 | 23135 | 1237 | 138 | 464 | 4289 | 77557 |

Germans arrived to found the Harmony Institute. It was not successful for a variety of reasons, and Schnee's followers moved to Indianapolis after only one planting season. Schnee returned to the area the next year and leased 806 acres for twenty-one years, calling it Schneeville. He established a mill, one of the earliest in Harmony Township, took a prominent part in the political life of Posey County, and ran for the General Assembly on the Whig ticket. He was defeated in that race by Robert Dale Owen who ran on the Democratic ticket. Schnee did serve, however, at least one five-year term as judge of the circuit court of Posey County. In 1835 he served as one of the road commissioners appointed to survey and build a state road from New Harmony to Evansville and was appointed president of one of the six county agricultural societies formed by the General Assembly to improve agriculture in the state.[25] In 1836 he inaugurated the first county fair in the backwoods of southwestern Indiana.

### III.   The First Wave of German Immigration—1816–48

From the period following the American Revolution to the end of the Napoleonic wars in Europe, concluding with Napoleon's defeat at Waterloo in 1815, emigration from Central Europe was very limited. With the ending of hostilities, however, emigration intensified for various reasons. The extremely conservative policies of Prince Fürst von Metternich, the Austrian chancellor who dominated postwar politics in Europe, led to the restoration of old-line monarchies in most of Europe, ending the dream of Republicans for a new political order that would guarantee more individual freedoms and prosperity in peace. On the economic side, overpopulation, poor harvests, and the devastating effect of England's industrial revolution on Germany's home industries led to widespread poverty and unemployment. At times some communities found it more feasible to finance their impoverished citizens' departure for America rather than to keep them on welfare.

Another reason frequently given for emigration was the onerous military conscription policies followed by German and Austrian provincial governments, particularly Prussia. Standing armies were maintained at considerable expense both to the governments involved and the citizenry. The latter paid high taxes and gave up their sons for extended service, often as long as five years, for low pay and poor living conditions. Conscription was not a factor in the United States until the Civil War, and there was no draft for a standing army until the twentieth century.[26] This was a major emigration factor for the pacifist Anabaptist groups for whom military service was a sin.

Emigration was seen then by many as the only way out of misery; consequently it continued almost unabated through the 1830s and 1840s.[27] There were certain organizational patterns to this emigration. In fact, service to immigrants on both sides of the Atlantic existed as a business during all phases of emigration. This entrepreneurial activity might also be viewed as spurring emigration as much as other innovations that after 1815 greatly altered the structure of German emigration, including changes in migration financing, mobility and transportation systems, range of origins and destinations, and the composition of emigrants "with respect to their ideas about America."[28] Also, letters and reports from established immigrants to friends and relatives provided the "pull" that combined with the "push" factors in Europe to create a chain migration as people followed each other to the newly opened areas such as Indiana.

Settlement of Indiana extended from the south to the north, and German immigration to Indiana followed that pattern as well. Topography also played a role in that much of the northern part of the state consisted of wetlands that were more difficult to farm. Development of areas adjacent to the Ohio River extended from both the south and the east. Migration, particularly from Ohio, was vitally important in bringing German immigrants into southern and eventually central Indiana. To some extent settlement of southern and southeastern Indiana is a by-product of the growth of Cincinnati, which was certainly the major starting point for the majority of early German pioneers into Indiana.[29]

Immigration into parts of northern Indiana did, of course, take place, although somewhat later than into southern and central parts of the then new state. Johann Schreyer, for example, came from his native Bavaria in 1843 and settled eight miles northeast of Plymouth, Indiana.[30] His farm consisted of forty acres near a public highway leading to Plymouth, the county seat. By 1846 he had eight acres under cultivation and was about to build a larger house, "all of wood, as is the custom in this country."

In addition to the skills and labor potential German immigrants brought, they brought capital so badly needed by their new country. Contrary to what is often thought, immigrants, particularly German immigrants, were not necessarily poor. The official estimated worth of each emigrant from Bavaria between 1835 and 1855 was 95 dollars, and even for the relatively poor area of Baden it was still about 40 dollars per person or 3.5 million dollars.[31] Of the immigrants to Dubois County, a high percentage were single and at a productive age, i.e., between fifteen and sixty-five.[32] German statistical tables indicate that the amount of gold carried by emigrants during the early part of the nineteenth century varied from $76 to $318 per person. In addition to money, they also brought wearing apparel, tools, watches, books, and jewelry. If one estimates the personal property of the emigrant at $150, and since approximately 4,297,980 immigrants arrived at the port of New York from 5 May 1847 to 1 January 1870, the national wealth of the United States for this period was increased by five billion dollars. Some German immigrants from districts near the Rhine were considered to be rather wealthy since in 1832 they brought with them between three and four thousand pounds sterling. In 1843 one hundred thousand Germans had made arrangements to immigrate to the United States and together possessed approximately five million dollars. However, to follow the Dubois County example, many who settled there were poor and had scarcely enough money to buy land, although it did not take long for the Germans to catch up and surpass the native born. The real estate evaluation in Dubois County in 1850 was $402,176, $225,816 to native born, $172,610 to Germans, and $3,750 to other foreign born. Germans at that time constituted 25 percent of the population. By 1860 it was $2,131,904, $1,140,725 to Germans, $917,688 to native born, and $73,491 to other foreign born.[33] Again German Americans were approximately 25 percent of the population, indicating their much higher per capita net worth.

Religion constituted the central point in the life of the majority of early German (and other) immigrants. It provided a spiritual and psychological framework for understanding life and its difficulties. The church was the physical manifestation of their belief system; it connected them with the cultural life of the world they left behind and, at the same time, gave support in their new surroundings. It provided counseling, helped educate children, maintained culture and language, rendered help in times of need, and served as a center for social activities. The use of German in church functioned to preserve "the right faith" and to protect the young especially from outside influences, much as it still does for the Amish. Religion could also be a source of bitter rivalry among denominations and divisiveness among German Americans.

For German Americans in Indiana church life developed organizational patterns different from what they had been used to in Germany. This was particularly true for the Protestant denominations, but as more Catholics came to Indiana from all over Europe the process of change strongly affected them as well. Changes within the churches occurred from the need to adapt to the American environment. On the Indiana frontier local control within congregations became imperative because of distances and the lack of a strong synodic hierarchy. The

American tradition of separation of church and state provided no financial support for the competing denominations but offered and guaranteed religious freedom. The effect ultimately was the same for German Americans as for other groups—the proliferation of denominations and subdivisions within them.

Initially, however, German immigrants of various Protestant denominations often joined together to build churches because of economic necessity. For example, in Indianapolis the stately old Zion Evangelical United Church of Christ (UCC), as it is now known, was formed in 1841 as the German United Evangelical Protestant Lutheran and Reformed Zion Church. With the arrival of more Germans it became possible for churches to be formed by individual denominations, and a "settling out" occurred that gave form to religious life through the early part of the twentieth century.

German immigrants arriving in either cities or in farming towns devoted their attention to establishing a church and a church school after securing a place to live. Hundreds of churches were founded in Indiana by German immigrants and their descendants. In Indianapolis alone, by 1870, there were at least nine churches of German origin with as many as twenty by 1910. Among Indianapolis's churches with a German-American background are: First Lutheran, Zion Evangelical UCC (which still has services in German), Friedens UCC, St. John's Lutheran, St. Peter's Lutheran, Emmaus Lutheran, St. Paul's Lutheran, St. Mary's Catholic, Sacred Heart Catholic, First German Evangelical (now Lockerbie Square United Methodist), First German Methodist, Nippert Memorial (German Methodist), and five German Reformed churches. Several churches (Ebenezer Lutheran-1836, Mt. Pisgah Lutheran-1837) date from the city's earliest immigration. Relative latecomers who may be considered to have German origins are the Mennonites and the Wisconsin Lutheran Evangelical Synod, which established churches in Indianapolis in 1951 (Mennonite Church) and 1971 (Divine Savior Lutheran Church) respectively.[34] In Richmond there were several churches serving a large German-speaking population: St. John's Lutheran (1844), St. Andrew Catholic (1846), St. Paul's Lutheran (1853), and German Methodist Episcopal (1860).[35] In the Oldenburg-Batesville area of southeast Indiana the Huntersville Evangelical Protestant Church and the Oldenburg Holy Family Catholic Church were founded in 1847.[36] The early German churches in Evansville were Trinity Lutheran (1841), First German Methodist Episcopal, German Baptist, and Emanuel Lutheran. There were also several Evangelical congregations, Zion, St. John, Bethel, and St. Paul, as well as the Catholic parishes Holy Trinity (1849), St.

*Confirmation class of Evangelifchen Immanuels Gemeinde, Hammond, 1903.*

Mary, St. Boniface, and St. Anthony.[37] The larger cities also had synagogues such as the Jewish Temple in Indianapolis. In most areas of Indiana where Germans settled the groundwork was laid for the religious life of German Americans during the 1840s and 1850s. The very early significance of German-American places of worship both for the German immigrants and their children as well as for the religious life in the state as a whole cannot be doubted.

To understand both the religious life and the settlement patterns of the German immigrants—since they tended to cluster around their churches—it is useful to examine the various religious groups. They tend to fall into the following broad categories: Anabaptists, Catholics, traditional Protestant denominations (Evangelical, Lutheran, Reformed), American Evangelical Protestant denominations (especially Methodist and Baptist), Jewish, and, finally, the anticleric Freethinkers. Any attempt at completeness in treating these groups would require several volumes. Several more fully researched examples will be used to indicate basic patterns.[38]

The earliest Mennonite movement into the area was mentioned above. The Moravians, Pennsylvania Germans like the Mennonites, also came after the 1818 St. Mary's Treaty with the Indians opened the central Indiana area.[39] The Moravians established the community of Hope,

Indiana, in Bartholomew County which they originally named Goshen. That name, however, had just been claimed with the United States Post Office by Goshen in Elkhart County, a Mennonite town. The congregation in Hope was founded by Martin Hauser and other settlers from Salem, North Carolina, with the help of a two hundred-dollar grant from the Provincial Church Board in Bethlehem, Pennsylvania. The first services were held in a rough log church on 17 June 1830, but the formal organization was completed with the visit of Ludwig David von Schweinitz, the official representative from the Church in Bethlehem.[40] Hauser became the first pastor.

The Lutherans also established an early foothold in Indiana. The first Lutheran survey missionary, i.e., circuit-riding minister, to pass through Indiana was George Foster in 1805;[41] the most important of the early pastors was Friedrich Konrad Dietrich Wyneken.

As early as 1829 a Pennsylvania Lutheran named Henry Rudisill and his wife arrived in Fort Wayne, a village of about one hundred fifty, mostly French and Indians. The Rudisills were the first Germans as well as the first Lutherans. Through Rudisill's communications with the Immigration and Mission Committee of the Lutheran Synods in the East, he was responsible for an influx of Germans to Fort Wayne. By 1836 the village had about five hundred people. Pastor Jesse Hoover, a Pennsylvania

Lutheran who traveled the breadth of northern Indiana ministering to the scattered Protestant families, established a congregation in that area. It may have been Hoover's reports to the Mission Committee of Pennsylvania that caused them to send young Wyneken to Fort Wayne.[42] Before finally settling there, he toured the northwestern corner of Ohio, entered Michigan, came back through Michigan City, and followed the Wabash to Fort Wayne. After this trip Wyneken composed a pamphlet that had far-reaching effects in attracting German pastors to America and establishing a strong Lutheran presence—*The Distress of the German Lutherans in North America.*[43]

In 1841, at the request of the Mission Committee, Wyneken traveled to Germany where he established mission societies in several cities, including Dresden and Leipzig, and recruited a number of young pastors for work in America. An untiring voice of Lutheran theology, upon his return to Indiana in 1843 he worked harder to promote the pure Augsburg Confession. He left Indiana in 1845 to accept a call to St. Paul's Church in Baltimore. He left there in 1849 to become pastor of the mother church of the Missouri Synod, Trinity Lutheran in St. Louis, and in the fall of 1850 he was elected president of the synod to succeed the venerable Prof. C. F. W. Walther. Wyneken returned to Indiana to Adams County in 1859. In 1864 he took charge of Trinity Lutheran Church in Cleveland, Ohio, where he died in 1876. Fort Wayne had in the meantime become a force in the Lutheran Church-Missouri Synod with the founding of Concordia Seminary.

In southern and southeastern Indiana parishes and whole communities were founded by several of Indiana's great Catholic German missionaries and colonizers in the 1830s and 1840s: Father Joseph Ferneding was the first German Catholic missionary to Indiana, Father Joseph Kundek established five settlements in Dubois County, and Father Franz Josef Rudolf worked in the Oldenburg area. Also of considerable importance is Father Xavier Weniger who worked throughout the Midwest to establish parishes.

Rev. Joseph Kundek, born in Croatia in 1810 and ordained in 1835, read the reports of the Leopoldine Society on the missions in North America.[44] He asked to be sent to the American mission field and was put in charge of the area centered at Jasper where he arrived in September 1838.[45] He became the first pastor of St. Joseph Church, presumably named after the Austrian Emperor Franz Josef from whose family Kundek had obtained a grant.[46] By 1840, 110 German families had arrived in Jasper.

Shortly after his arrival in Dubois County Kundek set out to explore the countryside, hatchet and compass in hand. He observed that the fertile land between the port of Troy on the Ohio River and Jasper would accommodate a large number of settlers. With the help of a grant from the Leopoldine Society, Kundek purchased several large tracts of land where Ferdinand would be founded. He established the site, named for the Austrian emperor, and advertised in the Catholic-German publication *Der Wahrheitsfreund* printed in Cincinnati. The first brave souls ventured north from the Ohio on the Troy-Jasper road, which at best was barely passable. Looking for a settlement in Ferdinand, they found nothing more than a clearing where a clapboard with "Ferdinand" on it had been nailed to a big oak tree. Several decided to stay and brave the woods. Some of the earliest settlers included John and Anna Beckmann, Andrew and Catherine Kempf, and Joseph and Margareth Schneider, to all of whom children were born in Ferdinand as early as 1842. By the year 1844 there were 242 families in the Jasper parish.

Kundek's intent was to establish a large region to be settled exclusively by German Catholics so that faith, language, and tradition would continue to interact and be preserved in the new environment.[47] Kundek's vision of a cultural landscape in Dubois and Spencer counties is visible to the present.[48] In all, Kundek built four parishes: Ferdinand, Fulda, Celestine, and Rockport. He also sought to solidify the Catholic presence in the area by establishing a monastery. After several attempts and a visit to Europe in 1851, he was successful in bringing Benedictines to southern Indiana. The order's monastery at Einsiedeln, Switzerland, complied with Kundek's request, and St. Meinrad Abbey was founded in 1853. Kundek's unrelenting labors for his flock and thousands of miles in the saddle took a toll on his health. Although a man of strong constitution, he died in 1857 at the age of forty-seven.

Kundek's legacy was further strengthened by the founding of the Convent of the Immaculate Conception in Ferdinand. In August 1867 four Benedictines arrived, Sister Mary Benedicta Berns, who was the first mother superior, Sister Mary Xaveria Schroeder, Sister Mary Rose Chappelle, and Sister Mary Clara Vollmer.[49] St. Meinrad and Immaculate Conception remain centers of learning and caring to this day.

The town of Oldenburg was established on land bought by two Germans from the area of Oldenburg, Germany, John Plaspohl and John Ronnebaum. Together with Father Joseph Ferneding, they had considerable success attracting German settlers to the area. Father Ferneding was the first pastor of St. Paul's at New Alsace, and he established many other churches in southeast Indiana.[50] In 1834 Father Ferneding took up residence in New Alsace and began ministering to all the incipient Catholic

*Oldenburg, Indiana, scene 1887.*

communities in southeastern Indiana. He too hailed from the Province of Oldenburg. A noninheriting son of landed peasants, he studied theology in Münster and followed a call from Bishop Fenwick of Cincinnati to serve German immigrants in the Midwest. Indeed, he served numerous Catholics and helped found many parishes in the region.[51]

Father Franz Josef Rudolf was the priest at Oldenburg from 1844 to 1866 when Oldenburg became the center for Catholicism in southeast Indiana. A convent was established in 1851 after the arrival of the Sisters of the Third Order of St. Francis in late 1850 headed by Mother Theresa Hackelmeier from Vienna. A Franciscan friary was established in 1866.

German immigrants also interacted with the American evangelical movements that had origins in English and Scottish Methodism. Unlike the Congregationalists, Presbyterians, and Lutherans, the Methodists, even more so than the Baptists, were not confined to a particular society, nationality, or region. As early as 1801 circuit riders from Kentucky had crossed the Ohio River and preached to the early settlers in Clark County, Indiana. Methodism had thus established itself in the area.[52] Its less rigid doctrine, recognizing all forms of baptism as valid, proved attractive to a broad spectrum of people. It also had a strong central organization behind a preacher who was sent to one area to minister. Methodists saw in the German immigrants to the Midwest a source of converts and as early as 1835 Bishop Emery, who was responsible for the area, sent out a plea for preachers who could speak in German.[53] William Nast, a highly educated German with

a degree from the University of Tübingen, converted to the Methodist Episcopal Church in 1835. He was licensed to preach and was sent to the Ohio Conference where he founded the first German Methodist Episcopal Church in Cincinnati in 1838.[54] Under Nast's influence, John Kiesling was among the first "saddlebag preachers" to carry Methodism to the early German settlements in Indiana. By 1860 there were congregations established in the southern portion of the state, notably in Lawrenceburg, Aurora, Batesville, New Albany, Huntingburg, and Santa Claus, as well as the north and middle sections of the state, including Fort Wayne, Indianapolis, Columbus, Terre Haute, South Bend, and Michigan City.[55] The work among the Germans in the state was organized into separate districts under presiding German elders. One of the unique aspects of Methodism that attracted the Germans was the camp meeting. German Methodists established a campground at Santa Claus, where summer camp was held in German even after World War I. It might be noted here that Jesse Stork, the son of German Methodists from Holland, Indiana, Dr. and Mrs. H. W. Stork, was reputed to have been the first American casualty of the Spanish-American War.[56]

German Methodists as well as other denominations frequently occupied the same general area. For example, in Dubois County, Lutherans settled in the northern part, Catholics in the central and southern parts, and German Methodists in the southwestern part. No one church dominated a whole county. There were eighteen churches in Dubois County in 1860 with a total membership of

4,950. For a time the Methodists, including a considerable number of German Methodists, ranked first, with Catholics and Lutherans ranking second and third respectively.[57] In Richmond the German Methodist Episcopal Church was founded in 1860 and coexisted with the Lutheran and Reformed churches already present.[58] It is clear that from the beginning the Germans were highly diversified in their religious persuasions in spite of some clustering in certain areas.

Clustering along lines of European regional origin also took place as outlined above regarding the large number of immigrants from the Oldenburg region who settled in southeastern Indiana. Other such clustering included rural settlement patterns in southwestern Franklin County. In other areas of German settlement, people from specific areas coalesced around provinces of origin: for example, Dubois County, and in other states such as Wisconsin, as well as along the Missouri River.[59] In southwestern Franklin County this was not the case except for some clustering of Protestants from Hannover. Settlement patterns were in fact very fluid until 1875. In Franklin County a relationship existed between the immigrants from Hannover and Oldenburg because men and women from these two German provinces preferably intermarried within these groups.[60]

Both German- and French-speaking Swiss immigrants, like their German and Austrian fellow immigrants, were spread evenly throughout the new state.[61] Clustering did occur in the area of Switzerland County where Swiss settlement began in 1796 with the arrival of winegrower Jean Jaques Dufour. The town of Vevay was laid out in 1813, and by 1816 the population of Switzerland County numbered 1,832. The Swiss Colonization Society, begun in Cincinnati in 1856, founded a second settlement farther down the Ohio River in 1857. This almost purely German-speaking town was called Tell City and had a population of 1,230 by July 1858. While growth was strong early on, the projected population of 100,000 did not occur. By 1990 the population had reached about 9,000. Tell City's Swiss Days festival shows that the town remains quite conscious of its Swiss origins.

German Swiss were also present in Indianapolis among the Catholic religious orders and among the Mennonite and Amish groups. In these groups, however, their unique Swiss origins were subordinated to the overarching identity of the larger group to which they belonged. An exception was Berne in Adams County where a considerable number of Swiss Mennonites settled and where a Swiss-German dialect is still understood by a few elderly people. According to William A. Fritsch, Fulda in Dearborn County was home to a prosperous Swiss-German settlement, although there seems to be little evidence of this.[62]

Frequently names of Indiana towns indicate where their founders came from. Although this in itself does not necessarily mean that a larger number of immigrants from the same area settled there, it may indicate a mass or chain migration from a given area. For example, New Elsass in Dearborn County was founded in 1839 by Frank Anton Walliser, an Alsatian.[63] By 1880 there were 55 immigrants from Alsace in the county along with 203 immigrants from France, many of whom may have emigrated from Alsace before 1871 when it became part of Germany. In addition, there were 1,097 immigrants listed in the 1880 census as coming from "Germany," with no province given. A number of those could have come from Alsace as well.

It was much more likely that German-speaking immigrants, regardless of province of origin, would tend to live close together whenever possible. This principle of association or grouping with people of like culture led to seventeen distinct German communities in southwestern Indiana.[64] For example, in Evansville the German element settled in Lamasco on the north side of the city and in Independence on the west. Religion and church membership tended to focus German speakers in a given area or neighborhood for settlement. In the rural community of White Creek in Bartholomew County, German-speaking Lutherans settled as did Catholics in Ferdinand. On Indianapolis's south side, German-speaking Catholics moved into the area around Sacred Heart Church. It is useful to remember in observing these early settlement patterns that "there was no thought of maintaining an alien culture because America was young and there were diverse cultures here on every hand."[65]

J. Heinrich Kessens Zur Oeveste, a farmer from the Oldenburg area, left Bremerhaven for America in March 1834. The letters he and his family wrote home over the next fifty years describe life in the White Creek farming community in Bartholomew County. After arriving in Cincinnati Zur Oeveste worked on the canal and in an inn near "Dehten" (Dayton) to save enough money to buy land. On 10 October 1841 he announced the birth of a son and that the family would be moving to Indiana. He planted corn, potatoes, and some fruit. He commented that one could imagine how much work it was to begin in the green bush. Trees were cut off one to two feet above ground, the wood was burned, and the big trees were left but ringed so they died.

In a letter from "Batalimer Counti an der Weit Krick," dated 6 December 1842, Zur Oeveste announces they can live on their own and more peacefully than in Germany because "one pays only $1.50 in taxes for a year." Five years from the time the land was bought, taxes are increased slightly. Zur Oeveste writes again on 25 September 1844 stating that now he has nineteen acres under plow, three strong horses, ten cows, twenty to thirty pigs, sheep, and geese. He further comments that prices are good, horses sell for thirty to forty dollars, and milk-producing cows for eight to ten dollars. He has also been successful in establishing fruit trees and berry bushes and notes that there is much more fruit than in Germany.

Aspects of everyday life, farming, folkways, and religion fused in the more isolated rural regions of the state where German Americans clustered. The religious calendar and the farm calendar overlapped, with specific days for blessing seeds in the spring. There was the blessing of St. Agatha's bread on her feast day—bread was placed in the attic of the barn or farmhouse as a protection against fire.[66] Corpus Christi—considered the beginning of the planting season—was observed with parades. German-American Catholicism of the early period seems to have been a mixture of folk, German, and more orthodox Catholic elements. For rural life the centrality of religion cannot be disputed. Particularly among German-American Catholics one can speak of a fusion of religious and local political life. In Dubois County Father Kundek established the Church's control right from the beginning. To this day Dubois County remains heavily Democratic in its party affiliation, although there was some conflict between the Protestant minority, who tended to be Republican, and the Catholics. But both parties expressed their pride in being Americans by staging the biggest Fourth of July celebrations with music, dance, and of course, beer. However, a negative element, which was a political factor in the pre–Civil War period, was the strong nativist movement along the Ohio River and elsewhere in the state.[67]

As the western frontier developed and there was more and more need for the skills they possessed, Germans moved to Indiana's cities where they took on an increasingly important role in the fast-growing state. German Americans became wheelwrights, bakers, blacksmiths, gunsmiths, butchers, and brewers. The key to moving beyond subsistence living was specialization of activity, particularly in community groups.[68] The Germans were specialists of the first order.

They constituted the first large non-Anglo-American ethnic group to settle in American cities. From the very beginning German cultural life became a part of the fabric of midwestern cities.[69] Germans were the first to explore the possibilities of a multiethnic, pluralistic urban society, and they paved the way for other ethnic groups.[70]

German immigrants were present in considerable numbers in early Indianapolis. Between 1840 and 1850 the city's population increased from 2,692 to 8,095, of which 802 adults and 243 children or 12.9 percent of the population were born in German states. Considering that some of the migrants into Indiana were from German Pennsylvania, the number of German Americans no doubt was higher. By 1849 the area bounded by New York, Market, East, and Noble (now College) streets was described as "Germantown" because of the concentration of Germans living there.[71]

At the early date of 1837 Rev. Abraham Reck organized Mt. Pisgah Lutheran Church. Rev. Theodore Kunz organized the German United Evangelical Protestant Lutheran and Reformed Zion Church in 1841. Its members were, as the church's name suggests, of various denominational varieties, including Confessional Lutheran and German State Evangelical. Reverend Kunz, being of the latter persuasion, soon left to form St. Paul's Lutheran Church. These churches maintained parochial schools as well.

The professions of Indianapolis Germans in 1850 reflect the highly skilled nature of the majority, although a fair number (115) were laborers, but of these 42 were property owners. Thirty-two were carpenters, 26 shoe-makers, 13 tailors, 12 coopers, 11 blacksmiths, 10 grocers, and 9 merchants, with a wide variety remaining. The German merchants held property worth an average of $4,367.[72]

The first Indianapolis German band was organized in 1841 by Abraham Protzmann and was the first organized musical activity of that nature in the city. The first German newspaper was the *Indiana Volksblatt,* a conservative Democratic weekly edited by Julius Boetticher beginning in 1848.[73]

Evansville experienced similar migration by Germans in the early period. Lamasco, a town northwest of Evansville, became a center for the large German immigration that had begun there in the early 1830s and then picked up rapidly about 1843. Growth of the new town continued through the 1840s and in the 1850s. Most of the German settlers were skilled craftsmen who could supply many of the needs of the Evansville people with fine handiwork. In fact, the Germans developed a style of domestic architecture distinctly different from that in Evansville that is known as the Lamasco type architecture.[74]

Most of the early German churches were established in Lamasco. The history of the Catholic Church in Evansville began in 1836 when Bishop Simon Bruté of Vincennes sent Father A. Deydier to Evansville.[75] The Reformed Jewish congregation B'nai Israel was organized in 1857 with the temple completed in 1865. Among the other German churches are: Trinity Lutheran (Missouri Synod), established in 1841 and the oldest German church; Zion Evangelical, organized in 1849 with the present church built in 1855; St. John's Evangelical Protestant, a more liberal, independent church; and Emanuel Lutheran, established in 1855 at First and Franklin streets. Both Zion and St. John's maintained parochial schools until it was felt that the public school's German instruction was satisfactory.

Although German-American historians early on noted the lack of a central point of immigration for Indiana and thus a slow development in terms of German immigration, Fort Wayne, along with Indianapolis, is cited as attracting many Germans around 1840.[76] This is certainly evidenced by the founding in Fort Wayne of Concordia College, an important Lutheran seminary.[77]

The first bishop of the newly established bishopric of Fort Wayne was Johann Heinrich Luers, who was born in 1819 in Lütten near Oldenburg. He had immigrated at the age of thirteen with his parents. After studying in Cincinnati he became pastor of St. Joseph Catholic Church. He was recognized as an expert in church history and had a large library. He died in 1871.

Germans figured prominently in the development of many smaller cities and towns during Indiana's early history. Richmond's early German immigrants tended to blend well with the Quaker migrants who had started settling the area in the 1820s. One of the earliest was John Petersen from Astrup.[78] He left Germany in 1827 through the then new seaport of Bremerhaven on a tobacco-passenger ship to Baltimore. He traveled from Pittsburgh and Wheeling down the Ohio River to Cincinnati. There Petersen heard about Indiana and came to Richmond as a stonemason to work for $1.50 a day on the National Road. As part of a chain migration, Fred Schultz, Petersen's brother-in-law, came also. Petersen was followed by his widowed mother, sister, and other relatives. Like Petersen, 90 percent of all German immigrants to the area came from the kingdom of Hannover.

The Germans got along well with Quakers since their attitudes toward the work ethic, plain clothing, and pacifistic and abolitionist thinking were similar. Also, the Germans did not approve of hard spirits, and Quakers at that time had nothing against beer. One of the Quaker leaders, Andrew Hoover, was German born. Intermarriage, though first resisted, was possible. Petersen married Eliza Hunt, daughter of a prominent Quaker family. Accumulation of wealth and property was seen as a legitimate Christian goal by both groups.[79] The first German church was St. John's Lutheran. The congregation met in Petersen's home until Rev. John Schultze, formerly of East Germantown, Pennsylvania, and a graduate of a mission school in Berlin, was called to the pastorate in 1844. In 1846 the congregation purchased land, built a simple church, and established a parochial school

offering instruction in the first six grades. The school existed until 1934. The first German school, however, was founded by John Stammeyer in 1843 or 1844.[80]

The Germans tended to settle in the southern part of the city where they developed a close-knit community known later as "South-end Dutch." As primarily northern Germans they spoke Plattdeutsch or Low German. St. Andrew's Catholic Church was established in 1846. By 1835 Richmond, in the northern reaches of the Vincennes diocese, was accessible to missionary priests only in the spring and fall of the year. Father Joseph Ferneding served as missionary for the new diocese.[81] John Henry Moorman and Bernard Brokamp were instrumental in helping Father Ferneding establish a parish. The first pastor, Father Vincent Bacquelin, spoke no German. He was replaced by bilingual Father William Doyle after the diocese received complaints from the Germans that they did not have a German-speaking priest.

In the 1850s Richmond became a commercial center and a rail and road hub for eastern Indiana. By 1857 as many as seven hundred wagons a week were passing through Richmond. As early as 1847 Wayne County orchards were producing twenty thousand bushels of apples, twenty-five thousand hogs, and thirty-five thousand barrels of surplus flour for shipment to Cincinnati.[82] Germans engaged in virtually every line of business, owning the three largest dry goods stores and two wholesale notions houses. One of the well-known companies established by early German immigrants was Gaar, Scott & Co., the second-largest producer of threshing machines in the United States. Abram Gaar, a Bavarian Lutheran from Dinkelsbühl, moved to the Palatinate, but when this region was also Catholicized by militant princes he moved to America. Clamour Bartel and his second wife left Astrup in 1854 with their six children, including four-year-old Adam.[83] Clamour and his older sons worked on the National Road. Adam lived with an aunt and eventually went to work for Knollenberg's retail notions store and later for Emswiler and Crocker. Adam bought out Emswiler and Crocker and established the Adam H. Bartel Co., which still exists. Adam and his wife Mathilda Knollenberg built a large home at 16th and South streets. He was a keen student of history, studied his roots in Hannover, had a collection of paintings, and helped found the First English Lutheran Congregation "after realizing the need to adapt to the English-speaking society which dominated Richmond, then as now."[84]

Germans arrived in the Lake County area almost as early as did native-born Americans. Chicago was at an early date one of the largest German centers in the Midwest, and for many Germans it became a gateway into the Calumet

Region when they heard of the opportunities and land available there. Among them were Henry Reese, Heinrich D. Eggers, John F. K. Vater, and Henry Schrage who founded the Whiting area. Ernst Hohman, Joseph Hess, and Jacob Rimbach settled the Hammond area. Whiting, Tolleston, Miller, Hessville, and Schererville were founded by Germans; the greatest concentration, however, was in Hammond. Germans also started to settle in Hammond's St. John's Township in 1837 and by 1850 comprised more than half the population.[85] The first Germans in the area were Catholic, such as John Hack who settled near the present site of St. John.[86] In 1838 German Lutherans began the settlement of Hanover Township, which included the villages of Brunswick, Klaasville, and Hanover Center. In 1850 Germans constituted 14 percent of Lake County's population.[87]

## IV. The Forty-Eighters Arrive—1848–61

Each generation brought a different type of German immigrant. Certainly the best educated, most politically and socially motivated, and most vocal of any generation of German immigrants were those who came following the Revolution of 1848. German intellectuals, who mainly came from the educated middle class, had long chaffed under the yoke of the German class system that had been reinforced during the post–Napoleonic period. Some of the Forty-eighters, as they came to be called, like the political refugees of National Socialism in the 1930s, considered themselves exiles who would one day return to Germany. For the most part the Forty-eighters were totally disaffected by German politics and saw in the young, undeveloped American society an opportunity to work for a better society here. They grasped the issues of American politics quickly and became activists for various causes, particularly equal rights, the abolition of slavery, and women's rights. Some became very well known nationally, such as Carl Schurz, Civil War general and cabinet member, but a larger number figured prominently in local political and social life, such as John Holtkamp of Richmond, Theodore Hielscher of Indianapolis, and Martin Klauss of Evansville.

The Forty-eighters found much they appreciated and much to criticize in the frontier state of Indiana. They criticized both the Germans who came before them and the Yankees with their seemingly single-minded interest in making money without any consideration for higher ideals and social considerations. Earlier German immigrants were craftsmen or farmers and adherents to a religious faith. The Forty-eighters, with their liberal and socialist orientation, had turned away from the Church that had not supported the democratic aspirations of the people but sided with the princes. The Forty-eighters were imbued with rationalist thought that held the tenets of organized religion to be spurious at best. They were impatient with the earlier immigrants' conservatism and materialism, regardless of the fact that the earlier settlers had paved the way for them in the raw frontier.[88]

In general the Forty-eighters found the American political virtue of tolerance in a classless society commensurate with their ideals. The lack of "higher" intellectual idealism and the less than refined attitude toward the arts and domestic life gave them a desire to maintain German values in that regard and, beyond mere retention, infuse these values as much as possible into the nascent American society.[89]

The vehicle for this retention and development of German values in America was the *Verein,* meaning club or association of like-minded individuals dedicated to a cause or ideal. For the secular-inclined person the Verein assumed the function of a quasi-church, providing direction and purpose. In fact, it was possible to divide the Germans into *Vereinsdeutsche* and *Kirchendeutsche* (society- and church-oriented Germans). The former were primarily an urban phenomenon, since the city was the natural gathering point for intellectual German immigrants who wished to work for the inclusion of German idealism into American society and the general maintenance of that idealism. According to Theodore Stempfel, *Vereinsleben* (club life) began in Indianapolis in earnest with the founding of the Indianapolis *Turngemeinde* or Turner Society in 1851. For Stempfel, a member of the generation of immigrants who followed the founders, the German presence in Indianapolis, and the United States in general, began with the arrival of the founders of the Turner societies.[90]

Turners based their social and educational ideas on the teachings of Friedrich Ludwig Jahn (1778–1852), the father of modern gymnastics. Jahn's theories of physical and mental health incorporated the ideals of German patriotism, middle-class virtues, and progress through education. He became the patriarchal figurehead of the Revolution of 1848. The German liberal intellectuals who fled the repression of post–1848 Germany revered Jahn and endeavored to instill his values, as they perceived them, in their fellow Germans and especially their young. The Turnverein (gymnastic society) became the center of German political and educational activity in the United States and in Indiana cities. The Turner movement contributed much to the development of American education, particularly physical education.[91]

A variety of secular German organizations other than Turnvereins were founded during this time, primarily in cities and larger towns. Vereins can be classified according to the following typology with examples from Indianapolis:

Educational—Freidenker (1870), Turner (1851, reorganized 1870), Deutsch-Englischer Schulverein (1859)

Sport and physical education—Turner, Soccer Club (1954)

Music and arts—Männerchor (1854), Sängerchor (1885)

Mutual benefit—open Preussen Unterstützungsverein

Fraternal—Free Masons

Veterans' organizations—German army (Fort Wayne, Civil War veterans)

Commercial interests—Indianapolis Vegetable Growers Association established in the early 1920s "with the objective of promoting their vegetables on the local market."

Lobbying and influencing local, state, and national politics—Freimänner Verein (abolitionist)[92]

By 1900 Indianapolis had over fifty German Vereins—which does not include all the church-related Vereins. Other cities showed a proliferation of Vereins as well. The pattern persists to this day. The oldest continuously existing singing society in Indiana is the Indianapolis Männerchor, founded in 1854.

The arrival of the Forty-eighters in Indiana coincided with a virtual explosion in the number of German-language newspapers and periodicals published in Indiana. Indiana had, over the course of time, over two hundred German-language periodicals. Many had a short life span, others lasted for more than fifty years. The growth of German-language journalism in Indiana was part of a national trend. In 1840 there were forty German newspapers in the United States, in 1848 twice that, in 1852, 133, in 1860, about 266. In fact, the pre–Civil War period, 1848 to 1861, was the golden age of German-American newspapers.[93]

Publication tended to be located in the cities where intellectuals usually settled.[94] During this period Indianapolis saw the founding of *Die Freie Presse von Indiana* (The Free Press of Indiana), a four-page weekly established by Theodore Hielscher for a group of Germans opposed to slavery and the Democratic party. It supported free soil and abolition principles. Fort Wayne had *Der Fort Wayne Demokrat,* 1856–58, an irregularly issued weekly edited by E. Engler. It continued as the *Indiana Staats-Zeitung* under Gustavus J. Neubert. These papers were more conservative than similar papers in Chicago or on the East Coast and tended to reflect issues discussed in the English-language press as well, particularly abolition and states' rights. Concerned primarily with events in America

rather than in Germany, the German-language press in Indiana became an important part of the mainstream of Hoosier journalism.

## V. Indiana Germans in the Civil War

One of the major topics of the German-language press was the preservation of the Union. German intellectuals brought with them the ideal of political union under a republican government. This ideal, lost in the failed republican movement in Germany after 1848, was similarly challenged in America by the secession of the slave-holding states of the South. German Americans wrote and spoke forcefully for the cause of preserving the Union and for the abolition of slavery, and when war came, they served in numbers far beyond their proportionate share of the population.

There were, of course, many reasons why German immigrants became involved in a bloody struggle in their new homeland. Many of the immigrants were young men of military age and with military backgrounds. Signing up meant certain citizenship without fuss and a bounty for doing so. The North particularly needed their skills with artillery, cartography, and engineering. There were numerous full German regiments and such were encouraged by politicians in the North.[95]

The Turner Hall in Indianapolis was one of the principal locations of abolitionist activities in the city. Fort Sumter was bombarded beginning 12 April 1861, and by 18 April all of the unmarried Turners marched, accompanied by their own band, to Camp Morton to enlist in the Union army.[96] Enlistment was on a three-month basis, and when the Turners returned after three months, a number of them met with prominent German-American citizens to press for the establishment of an all-German regiment. The *Freie Presse* announced on 8 August 1861 that Governor Morton had granted permission. By 24 August 1861 the 32nd (First German) Regiment was organized, and August Willich, who had served as an officer in the German Revolution of 1848 and had a hand in the organizing of the 9th Regiment in Ohio, was given command with the rank of colonel.[97] The 32nd under Willich distinguished itself under fire numerous times. On 17 December 1861 three companies of the 32nd defeated over three thousand Texas Rangers at Rowlett's Station. This engagement backed the Confederate invaders out of central Kentucky and provided the Union with another victory, rare in the first year of the war.

Willich was recognized for his ability to control his troops under fire. On the second day of the battle of Shiloh, Willich decided his troops were firing too wildly. He rode to their front and put them through the manual of arms while they were directly under fire. In September 1863 Willich took his troops up the rocky face of Missionary Ridge and assaulted the Confederate fortifications. The 32nd was one of the first regiments to plant the colors at Missionary Ridge. The 32nd joined Sherman's army on the march to Atlanta. After the capture of Atlanta the three-year veterans of the 32nd were mustered out in Indianapolis on 7 September 1864.[98]

Other Hoosier Germans who served as officers include: Capt. Jacob Bieler of the Morton Battery; Lt. Col. Frank Erdelmeyer, who served as commander of the 32nd Indiana Regiment after Willich's successor Col. Henry von Tebra; and Capt. Adolph Metzner, who was captain of Company A and topographer for the 32nd. Captain Metzner's 104 sketches and paintings of the war give a vivid pictorial history of the 32nd. Later he and Erdelmeyer ran a drug business at 915 New Jersey Street in Indianapolis.

German Americans supported the Union's war effort in many ways. Herman W. Sturm, who had a successful machine shop in Indianapolis, built up the arsenal established by Gov. Oliver P. Morton since each state was required to support its regiments. Sturm moved in rank from captain to colonel as he successfully produced over eight hundred thousand dollars' worth of war materials. Later, he and Gen. Lew Wallace served as secret United States agents to assist Mexico against French intervention in that country.[99] Albert Lange, born in 1801 in Charlottenburg, lived in Terre Haute. The liberal movement attracted Lange to this country in 1829, where he edited a paper in Cincinnati, moved to Hancock County, Indiana, married, farmed, moved to Terre Haute, practiced law, drifted into politics, joined the Whig party under Zachary Taylor and Millard Fillmore, and was United States counsel at Rotterdam. Back in Terre Haute, he served as mayor. In 1860 he was made state auditor and "proved of great assistance to Governor Oliver P. Morton during the Civil War."[100]

## VI. The Great Migration—1870–90

At the conclusion of the Civil War the United States, despite the agony of the Reconstruction period, was moving slowly toward unprecedented growth. It also was the beginning of the second major wave of German-speaking people entering the country. Even during the 1860s more than 700,000 Germans arrived in the United States. (See Table 3.) The second major migration year was 1882 with more than 250,000

### Table 3. German Immigration since 1820

| Decade | Total Immigration | German | % of Total |
|--------|-------------------|--------|------------|
| 1820–29 | 128,502 | 5,753 | 4.5 |
| 1830–39 | 538,381 | 124,726 | 23.2 |
| 1840–49 | 1,427,337 | 385,434 | 27.0 |
| 1850–59 | 2,814,554 | 976,072 | 34.7 |
| 1860–69 | 2,081,261 | 723,734 | 34.8 |
| 1870–79 | 2,742,137 | 751,769 | 27.4 |
| 1880–89 | 5,248,568 | 1,445,181 | 27.5 |
| 1890–99 | 3,694,294 | 579,072 | 15.7 |
| 1900–09 | 8,202,388 | 328,722 | 4.0 |
| 1910–19 | 6,347,380 | 174,227 | 2.7 |
| 1920–29 | 4,295,510 | 386,634 | 9.0 |
| 1930–39 | 699,375 | 119,107 | 17.0 |
| 1940–49 | 856,608 | 117,506 | 14.0 |
| 1950–59 | 2,499,268 | 576,905 | 23.1 |
| 1960–69 | 3,213,749 | 209,616 | 6.5 |
| 1970–79 | 4,493,000 | 66,000 | 1.5 |
| 1980–88 | 4,711,000 | 55,800 | 1.2 |
| Total | 53,993,312 | 7,026,258 | 13.0 |

Source: U.S. Bureau of the Census, *Historical Statistics of the United States: Colonial Times to 1970* (Washington, D.C., 1975), 15; U.S. Bureau of the Census, *Statistical Abstract of the United States* (Washington, D.C., 1990), 10.

registered arrivals from Germany—more than the over 220,000 who had come during 1854, the peak year of the pre–Civil War period.

Many of the German-speaking immigrants arriving after the Civil War came from the eastern provinces of Germany and tended to be from a different socioeconomic background. They faced an American environment different from that which greeted their countrymen earlier in the century.[101] Whereas the vast majority of German-speaking immigrants up to the time of the Civil War had come from southwestern, western, and northwestern Germany, the post–Civil War period saw the majority coming from the eastern areas, including Silesia, Pomerania, and Saxony. The majority of the former (western Germany) were farmers or craftsmen, the majority of the latter (eastern Germany) were hired hands or laborers. This group tended to have less capital to work with than earlier immigrants. As is still the case, the eastern areas tended to be poorer than the western.

What the newer immigrants faced was no longer an ever-moving frontier with vast amounts of open land, but rather a fairly developed economy, one that to a great extent, in the Midwest at least, had been developed largely by earlier German immigrants and their American-born children. Therefore the newer immigrants were frequently dependent on the older ones for work and capital, creating a tiered society within the German community that is still evident today.[102]

Early German immigrants, particularly those who were successful, generally argued for liberal immigration laws.

Frequently state governments actively advertised in Europe seeking German immigrants to help develop their states. Indiana did much less of this than did other states. During the Civil War, however, Governor Morton appealed to would-be German immigrants with a well-written pamphlet depicting Indiana as an attractive settlement choice. Morton, hoping to attract Germans to build up Indiana's postwar economy, stressed attractions that Europeans would be looking for: *Bürgerrecht*—the right to citizenship that places one on an even legal basis with the native born; guarantee of job opportunities and high pay; inexpensive land for cultivation, "through which it is easily possible in a few years by diligence and desire to work for an immigrant to obtain property and establish a home"; low taxes; all kinds of opportunities to change one's place of residence at will; inexpensive foodstuffs in comparison to wages; numerous and inexpensive schools. Even the Civil War was cited as being responsible for more advantages for the immigrant because of the shortage of labor and war-induced economic opportunities.[103]

Germans came and changed the social and physical landscape of Indiana. In the cities the number of Vereins, clubs, and fraternal organizations continually increased in number throughout the period following the Civil War, including German-American Civil War veterans' organizations. The Turners revived their societies, most of which had become dormant while the members were supporting the war effort. On 1 January 1865 John F. Mayer, Charles Koehne, Matthias Moesch, and George F. Meyer organized the Indianapolis Turnverein, superseding the former Turngemeinde. By May 1867 a two-story building had been erected on East Maryland Street, and classes under teacher William Muecke were under way.[104] An indication of the varieties of German-American societies that existed during this period is evident in the parade held in Indianapolis in 1866 under the auspices of the German School Association.

Musical societies also held their pageants and festivals during the early post–Civil War period. A special hall was built in Indianapolis for the great songfest of the North American Singers' Union held in 1867. Forty-one musical societies were represented with 798 delegates from many cities, including Madison, Evansville, Richmond, Terre Haute, and Jeffersonville, Indiana; Cleveland, Cincinnati, Columbus, Akron, and Dayton, Ohio; and Chicago, Illinois, Wheeling, West Virginia, Allegheny City, Pennsylvania, and others. The success of this event put Indiana and Indianapolis on the German-American musical map. These musical and artistic endeavors typically constituted the primary source of such activity in virtually all communities where Germans had settled in significant numbers.

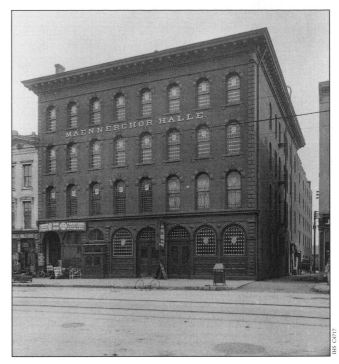

*Maennerchor Halle, Indianapolis, ca. 1900.*

IHS C4717

In 1874 the Indianapolis Männerchor moved to the large Union Hall because its performances were so well attended. In 1867 three operas were given in Indianapolis on successive nights, *Die Zauberflöte, Faust,* and *Der Freischütz.*[105] In 1871 Bernard Vogt brought an orchestra together, although previously in 1862 Max Leckner had founded a philharmonic society. In 1872 the Indianapolis Liederkranz was founded from the song sections of the Druiden and Rothmänner lodges. Among similar music-based interest groups in other Indiana cities the Evansville Germania Männerchor is one important example. In South Bend, of the twenty-eight active social organizations between 1850 and 1880, six were distinctly German. The Turnverein was clearly the most important and probably the largest, but there were also active German-American chapters of the Masons and Odd Fellows, and the Männerchor met weekly in its hall on Sycamore Street.[106]

Social groups functioned beyond merely providing entertainment and diversion. They were also support groups that prepared members for leadership both within the German-American and the broader urban community. The role of the Turnvereins in the Civil War and the political activity that preceded it gives an indication of the potential of German-American organizations. Dean Esslinger's study of German Americans in South Bend indicates that of the twelve German community leaders between 1850 and 1880, no fewer than eleven were officers in German societies.[107]

Churches and church-related organizations also prospered during the period after the Civil War when German immigration was at its zenith. For example, in Indianapolis the German Reformed Synod formed two new congregations in the 1880s. Sacred Heart Catholic Church was established on the south side in 1875, and St. Mary's Catholic Church erected two schools in 1876. Two orphanages were established, one by the Lutheran Orphanage Association in 1883 and one prior to that by the Zion Evangelical Church. The latter structure, designed by Vonnegut and Bohn Architects, still serves youth as the Pleasant Run Children's Home.

A philanthropic activity originating from the German-American community of Indianapolis that served the entire community was the Protestant Deaconess Society under the leadership of Rev. Christopher Peters of Zion Evangelical Church. D. A. Bohlen designed a building on Senate Avenue that housed a teaching hospital that was supported by the society.[108] In Richmond successful businessman Adam Bartel helped establish an English-language Lutheran church and an orphanage. As German Americans prospered and immigration continued, growth of German-American organizations and institutions also continued unabated.

Nowhere is the activity of German Americans more apparent than in the German-language press that flourished during the 1870s, 1880s, 1890s, and on through the early part of the twentieth century up to World War I. The life of Indiana's German Americans is chronicled in the numerous periodicals, books, and newspapers published during this time. There were over two hundred German-language newspapers and periodicals published in Indiana.[109] Insofar as they are preserved, they constitute one of the primary sources of information about the life of Indiana's German Americans.

Evansville had several German newspapers. The first, *Der Volksbote,* originally edited by J. Rohner in 1851, continued to flourish. Frederick Keller, who had studied theology at Heidelberg, served as editor for several German newspapers, including *Der Volksbote.* Keller died in Evansville in 1876 while editing *Die Union.* The *Union* and the *Demokrat* were Evansville's German evening and morning papers respectively. The *Union* sold out to the *Demokrat.* At the beginning of World War I the *Demokrat* was the only German paper in Evansville, having existed for over fifty years and edited at the time by Frederick Lauenstein.

Most of the smaller local German papers in southern Indiana, for example those in Tell City and Rockport, were pushed out by the larger Louisville and Evansville papers. Henry Lange, who also wrote several volumes of poetry,

published a paper in New Albany. Jeffersonville's longtime German newspaper editor was E. G. Engelhardt, who published the *Beobachter aus Indiana.* He also published a number of books and pamphlets. Huntingburg had its *Huntingburg Signal.* Richmond and Berne also were home to German-language papers and religious periodicals.

In Indianapolis the German-American press flourished. There was the *Indiana Volksblatt und Telegraph,* a continuation of the *Volksblatt* established by Julius Boetticher in 1848. Other papers included the *Indiana Freie Presse,* the *Tribüne,* and the *Telegraph* as dailies. The *Spottvogel* appeared as a popular weekly as did the Catholic *Die Glocke.* Some of the very articulate and influential editorial writers included Julius Boetticher, Adolf Seidensticker, Frederick Keller, Carl Beischlag, T. B. Jeup, and Philip Rappaport.

Terre Haute had several German papers, among them the *Terre Haute Journal.* In Lafayette Francis Johnson edited the *Deutsch Amerikaner* and published several books in English. Although Logansport still maintained a German weekly, the many Chicago German-language papers supplied the needs of Crown Point, South Bend, and Hammond. In Fort Wayne the daily *Freie Presse und Staatszeitung,* ably edited by Herman Mackwitz, was the only major German-language paper still being published after World War I.

The German-language press helped in the retention of the German language. The language base was also refreshed by the constant influx of new immigrants although, except for some rural groups, English tended to dominate for second- and third-generation German Americans. The use of the German language in Indiana is a complex phenomenon related to immigration patterns and socioeconomic structures. Also, the linguistic map of the state with regard to the varieties of German spoken is quite complex. Along with standard or High German, there are a number of dialects spoken in Indiana. The Amish of Indiana speak Pennsylvania German, a recognized world dialect. In addition, in Dubois and contiguous counties there are those who still speak Franconian and Badisch, southern and southwestern German dialects respectively, and Oldenburger Platt, a northern or Low German dialect.[110]

There was little homogeneity about the way even standard German was spoken, and regional peculiarities developed. In Vanderburgh County, for example, the St. Wendel area had a peculiar way of mixing High German and English words unique to that community.[111] In rural and small town settings a unique blend of regional German developed, as in the Jasper-Ferdinand area.[112]

The Church represented the strongest factor in the preservation of the German language over a number of generations. This was particularly true for the Missouri Synod Lutherans who, at a meeting of their general conference in Fort Wayne, decided to suppress English in synodical educational institutions even if it meant special tutoring of students in German.[113] Religious expression and language were closely linked in the minds of many. "If you weren't confirmed in German, you weren't confirmed."[114]

Schools provided language and culture maintenance as well as an introduction into general American life. Indiana's public schools still left a great deal to be desired, lagging behind other midwestern states—ninth out of ten in literacy and seventh in terms of money spent per pupil at the end of the nineteenth century.[115] Many German Americans felt the need for maintaining their own parochial schools where the German language was used. In the cities German was taught along with English. In many of the parochial schools German was the main medium of instruction.

Eventually German influence was felt in the public school system as more German Americans became involved on school boards.[116] Nowhere is that more apparent than in Indianapolis where the German-English School had already introduced the two elements for which German Americans are most responsible in American education—physical education and manual technical training. The former was the province of the Turners whose *Turnlehrerseminar* became the Normal College for Physical Education and ultimately in 1941 the Indiana University School of Physical Education, now at Indiana University-Purdue University at Indianapolis (IUPUI). It is the oldest such school in the United States.

One of the most successful German-American private schools in Indiana was the German-English Independent School in Indianapolis, established in 1859, which had a manual training aspect in its curriculum based on the German *Gewerbeschule*.[117] The school served as an incubator for educational models that its past members and students would apply to the public school system. In 1888 the Indianapolis School Board, whose members included such prominent German-American citizens as John P. Frenzel, Clemens Vonnegut, and Jacob W. Loeper, provided for a Manual Training Department at Shortridge High School. The department was continued until 1894 when Manual Training High School was opened with German immigrant Charles E. Emmerich as principal. The school was later named for him. The school was a source of well-educated and skilled workers for Indianapolis's automotive and machine tool industries. Indianapolis became known for its excellent educational programs with Shortridge and Manual in the forefront; it also became a center for German-language pedagogy with

Robert Nix, head of language education at Shortridge, city supervisor for foreign languages, and author of numerous textbooks, in charge.

In the fields of art and architecture Indiana's German Americans also made considerable contributions. In the very heart of Indianapolis is the Soldiers and Sailors Monument created by two German artists: Bruno Schmitz from Koblenz and Rudolf Schwarz who came with Schmitz and stayed in Indiana. The monument, commissioned after an international competition in 1887 and the tallest war memorial in the country at the time, was the only work done by Schmitz in the United States. Schwarz did the group sculptures on the monument as well as the Oliver P. Morton statue at the state capitol and numerous monuments throughout Indiana and the Midwest. These include the soldiers monuments in Franklin, Terre Haute, Crawfordsville, and Vincennes, Indiana.

The "Hoosier Group" of artists who were born in Indiana and not all of German background were supported by the efforts of Herman Lieber, a successful Indianapolis businessman. The artists in the group studying at the Royal Academy in Munich included ultimately J. Ottis Adams, William Forsyth, Otto Stark, Theodore C. Steele, August Metzner, and Samuel Richards. It was somewhat of a foregone conclusion that the first group of Hoosier artists ever to go abroad to study art went to Germany, mainly because of German influence on Indiana's cultural life.[118]

One of the German-born artists fascinated by the American West was Berliner Wilhelm J. Reiss who came to Indianapolis in 1884. He also served as an editor of the German-language daily *Telegraph* in Indianapolis from 1901 to 1906. Hoosier-born German artists include William Miller and John Henry Niemeyer. Born in Indiana of German parents were such artists as Otto Stark, who was art director at Arsenal Technical High School from 1889 to 1919, and Louis F. Mueller, who also studied at the Royal Academy in Munich and received a rare cash award there for his work. Recognized Indiana-born German-American artists include Anna Hasselman, Simon P. Baus, Charles Reiffel, and Lillian Weyl.[119]

In 1888 Bernard Vonnegut and Arthur Bohn established an architectural firm. Vonnegut and Bohn were responsible for such significant buildings as the John Herron Art Institute, the Jewish Temple, Shortridge High School (now Middle School), and The German House (known since 1918 as the Athenaeum), the Federal Building in Vincennes, and the Student Union at Indiana University, Bloomington. Indiana's oldest architectural firm in continuous existence, Bohlen, Meyer, Gibson &

Associates, was founded by Diedrich A. Bohlen who immigrated to Indianapolis from the kingdom of Hannover in 1851. His firm's legacy includes in Indianapolis the City Market, Roberts Park Methodist Church, and the former Tomlinson Hall. Bohlen also designed the Oldenburg Immaculate Conception Convent and Academy, Assumption Cathedral in Evansville, and the Chapel at St. Mary-of-the-Woods College in Terre Haute. Bohlen's son Oscar joined the firm in 1884 after which such landmarks as the Murat Temple and the Majestic Building in Indianapolis and the French Lick Springs Hotel were designed.

Notable also is Swiss-German architect Adolf Scherrer who completed the design of the present state capitol building. George E. Kessler, born in Frankenhausen, Germany, was the leading architect for the boulevard and park systems in Indianapolis, Fort Wayne, South Bend, Terre Haute, and elsewhere in the country.

Much of the energy and genius of Hoosier German Americans continued to be applied to business. German Americans in general were less inclined toward speculation and also did not become the ultrawealthy robber barons of nineteenth-century American business. In many cases, however, they did prosper and contribute heavily to the development of industry in Indiana. In general, capital and labor continued to flow into the United States from Germany after the Civil War. For example, the Northern Pacific Railroad was refinanced through the Deutsche Bank.[120]

Throughout the state German Americans were engaged in the accumulation and application of capital. Money brought by German immigrants was generally carefully and conservatively invested, frequently in "rock-solid" enterprises. German-American names in industry include the South Bend carriage and later-to-be automotive factory of the Studebaker brothers, Americans "proud of their Pennsylvania-German origin."[121] Founded in 1852, the Studebaker Corporation was producing twenty thousand wagons a year by 1879 and had a capital investment of three million dollars, the largest in the state.[122] In Evansville the cigar factory of Herrmann Fendrich, born in 1813 in Baden-Baden, employed over two thousand people with a daily output of four hundred thousand cigars offering brand names such as "Diamond Joe" and "Charles Denby." Herman Hulman, Sr., of Terre Haute had a profitable wholesale business that he expanded to Illinois and Evansville. He was the head of a family that, allied through marriage with the Fendrich family, presently controls large diversified holdings, including the Indianapolis Motor Speedway.

Evansville also had a number of famous German-American entrepreneurs. John A. Reitz from Dorlar,

Westphalia, came to Evansville in 1836, started a sawmill in 1845, and became a "lumber king." His eldest son, Francis Joseph Reitz, expanded into the furniture business and became president of the City National Bank of Evansville. The Reitz, home is a landmark in Evansville with its exquisite Renaissance decor. Henry Reis, born in 1847 near Mainz, worked for some time in a drugstore before he worked his way up from clerk to president of the Old State National Bank in Evansville. Henry V. Bennighof from Rhein-Hessen came to Evansville in 1852 and became involved in the Evansville Savings Bank where he was elected trustee and then president. "Many German business men and artisans have helped to build up these banks and they have done their part faithfully, as no bank has ever failed in Evansville," that is until the Great Depression.[123] This holds true also for Indianapolis where Otto N. Frenzel became president of Merchants National Bank, and his brother John P. Frenzel became president of the Indiana Trust Company. Theodore Stempfel, writer and chronicler of German-American life in Indianapolis, also was an executive in the latter bank.

In Indianapolis German Americans were involved in virtually every business conceivable. Clemens Vonnegut, Jr., son of the founder of Vonnegut Hardware Company, joined together with Carl von Hake, a large real estate holder, in taking over the Indianapolis Coffin Company. Theodore Kruse and H. C. Dewenter had the only firm in Indiana making heating and cooling equipment. Begun in 1884, it became one of the largest firms of its kind in the country. The Lewis Meier Company was one of the country's largest manufacturers of work clothes. Its president, Henry Severin, Jr., together with Speedway's Carl G. Fisher, built the Hotel Severin, one of the capital city's most prestigious hostelries. Paul H. Krauss had the oldest and largest custom shirt factory in Indiana and introduced steam cleaning in Indianapolis. William Wiegel started a factory in 1871 that built showcases; it became the state's largest.

Everywhere in the state Hoosier Germans had breweries. In 1889 the Indianapolis breweries founded by C. F. Schmidt, Peter Lieber, and Caspar Maus formed the Indianapolis Brewing Company with Albert Lieber as president. August Hook, father of druggist John A. Hook, founded the Home Brewing Company in 1891. The American Brewing Company began in 1897.[124] The famous Chicago restaurant, the Berghoff, hails from the Berghoff family in Fort Wayne and its brewery. The Simon Hack brewery in Vincennes was southwestern Indiana's showpiece.

While a number of German Americans seemed to have the elusive knack for generating capital and successfully

*Guedelhoefer Wagon Company, ca. 1910s, Indianapolis.*

running businesses, the majority of the German Americans provided the second element to the economic equation—capital plus labor. Particularly during the later immigration periods, when industry began to replace agriculture as the primary employer of labor, newer immigrants made a livelihood working for others as tradespeople, craftsmen, or factory workers. This was a life calling for six long workdays per week.

The life of one working-class German-American woman, Catharina Schulte Feil, is chronicled in a series of letters dated from 1861 to 1893 to her mother, brothers, and sisters in Germany. Her life may typify in some ways the lot of working-class German immigrants. After immigrating alone to the United States, Feil settled in Indianapolis where she worked in a bakery on South Illinois Street. She was married twice—first to a man named Feil and then to a man named Gutknecht. Her first year was, according to a letter dated 11 August 1861, pretty bad. On 1 January 1862 Feil wrote that her husband of one year had died; she spoke, however, with resolution about her struggle to make a go of it.[125] Though her life was one of working from early morning until evening, she

was convinced that life was still better in America.[126] She was, in fact, relatively successful, and her letter of 10 November 1889 describes with some pride the installation of natural gas in her home.

German-American workers in Indiana were strong supporters and exerted leadership in the labor movement that began in earnest in the 1880s. The newly industrialized German Reich had an early trade union tradition, a relatively new idea in the United States. In Germany local workers' associations began at the same time as the revolutionary upheaval of 1848. Out of the thirty-eight unions listed by the Indianapolis Central Labor Union in 1896 Germans were officers in sixteen of them and were active members in most of the others.

This leadership phenomenon was, of course, part of the social stratification among German Americans that ran parallel to that of society as a whole. However, there was an unusually large number of German Americans in the trades and among skilled workers. They tended to be upwardly mobile and were more heavily represented in leadership positions than their numbers warranted.[127] This is partly because of the skills and capital they often

*Wedding photograph of Clara Hoenke and Herman Jaeger,*
*Tolleston, Lake County, ca. 1890.*

brought with them and because, as the first non-Anglo immigrant group, they found social and economic acceptance more readily than other groups.

German Americans by and large did not seek political office beyond the state level. Until about 1850 English-speaking immigrants dominated the political scene. Thereafter politicians came to recognize the Teutonic influence in middle America. Even Abraham Lincoln struggled with German grammar and at one time owned a German newspaper.[128] The "German" vote was a factor to some extent, although normally voting by German Americans followed a line similar to that of the rest of American society, certainly more so than the more unified Irish-American group.

German Americans were represented in Indiana politics.[129] Indiana has had five treasurers of German descent. The first was August Lemcke who came originally from Hamburg. After living in Posey County, Lemcke moved to Evansville, held several positions in the city administration, and was elected sheriff of Vanderburgh County for two consecutive terms. He was elected state treasurer and after his term in office settled in Indianapolis.

German-American judges include George Ludwig Reinhard from Lower Franconia. He came to the United States in 1857 in time to fight with the 15th Indiana Regiment at Shiloh and Stones River. After the war he studied law and was elected prosecuting attorney for Spencer and Warren counties. He was appointed judge there in 1882. Gov. Alvin P. Hovey appointed him to the appellate court in 1891. Later Reinhard became dean of the law school at Indiana University in Bloomington. He also authored several law books. Peter Maier immigrated to Ohio, then to Evansville where he was elected judge of the circuit court in Vanderburgh County. Johannes Kopelke of Crown Point was born in 1854 in Buchwald near Neustettin. He studied law at Ann Arbor, Michigan, served in the state senate, and was appointed judge of the Lake County superior court in 1911.

John Kleiner, a German schoolmaster, served as mayor of Evansville and then was elected to Congress from Indiana's first district. William Heilman, a successful businessman who manufactured portable sawmills and other machinery, was elected to the state senate, then to the federal House of Representatives also from the first district. John W. Boehne, born in Vanderburgh County, amassed a fortune in the foundry business in Evansville, served twice as mayor of the city, and also was elected to Congress. Charles Lieb of Rockport, born in Flehingen, Germany, in 1852, became a leading banker. Lieb served three terms in the state legislature, then was elected to Congress.

Hoosier Germans were somewhat interested in what was going on in Germany after the unification of the country under Bismarck. Although they took pride in German accomplishments, they were much more interested in American politics and society because they were now Americans in a growing country with unique political ideals of liberty and equality—this in spite of a sometimes massive nativist resentment and Puritan outrage at German conviviality.

## VII. Settling in, Cultural Maintenance—1890–1917

"The Gay '90s" period was a time of economic growth, political calm, and rich social life. It was also a time of more or less hidden social tensions and a distinct change in the patterns of immigration that fed German-American cultural life. Fewer and fewer German immigrants arrived after the peak years of the 1880s. Between 1880 and 1889 more than 1.4 million Germans immigrated to the United States. This was 27.5 percent of the total number of all immigrants, but between 1900 and 1909 slightly more than 320,000 came, or only 4.0 percent of the total immigration.[130] Socioeconomic changes in Germany were working against emigration. Although the change from workers tied to the land to labor as a free market variable was a slow development in German political and economic thought, it became increasingly refined as Germany became a net labor importer rather than an exporter of population.[131] By 1893 Germany had ceased to be an emigration country and turned into a net labor-importing country.

Germany also maintained a foreign policy that would lead it into conflict with other major European powers, particularly England and France. The former tried to control German expansion on the seas, and the latter had a long tradition of keeping suppressed Germany's national and territorial aspirations. Germany had not forgotten the devastating invasions of Louis XIV and Napoleon. Throughout the fin de siècle period Europe's fuse was burning ever shorter. This would ultimately affect the lives of German Americans in Indiana in very significant ways.

The United States also was developing a foreign policy that brought it close to European attitudes toward territorial hegemony. The Spanish-American War in 1898 established American dominance in the Western Hemisphere as originally expressed in the Monroe Doctrine and established American presence in the Pacific when the United States, after its defeat of the Spanish, took over the Philippines. Many liberals, including many German Americans, felt this attitude was the European kind of imperialism they had objected to in their homeland. They felt, possibly quite rightly, that it would lead to ongoing conflicts and an abrogation of American ideals of nonoppression. While Indiana's German-American intellectuals were less vehement about the war, concerns were expressed. This may have helped set the stage for the anti-German hysteria and distrust of German Americans that was to explode in this country during World War I.

The political concerns of Hoosier German Americans perhaps are nowhere better expressed than in the minutes of the meetings of the State Federation of German Societies. For example, during its fourth convention held in Indianapolis on 3 August 1907 President Joseph Keller's speech remarked on the accomplishments of the organization in past years: incorporation of the organization by the United States Congress and the president, holding an Immigration-Congress in Baltimore, successfully resisting nativistic attacks, defeat of the Hepburn-Dolliver Bill and the tabling of the Littlefield Bill that would have restricted immigration, and the establishing of a national alliance with the Irish.[132] Keller

mentioned the following political and social causes the federation supported and for which it received support from candidates for the legislature: raising teachers' salaries, establishing a pension for teachers, and resistance to the tightening of temperance laws. The state board had a bill developed for old age benefits for teachers and a law was passed; the Federation of German Societies of Indianapolis introduced a bill for the increase of teachers' salaries which passed in the state legislature. The restrictive Dillingham-Gardener Immigration Bill was fought with all means available. President Keller said he was well aware of the need for the societies to band together on a citywide basis and he urged Evansville and Terre Haute to move in that direction.

There was also a report from the Committee for Personal Freedom. This antitemperance, antinativism group requested that Indiana's German Americans should join with members of other ethnic groups in order to defeat attempts on personal freedoms. The speaker remarked on how German Americans were widely dispersed throughout Indiana ("*das zerstreute Deutschthum*"), and that it was difficult for them to organize. The board was directed to publish the report in all German newspapers in the state and to translate it into English.

There was also a report on the Committee for German Language and Physical Education ("*Turnen*"). The committee recommended that all societies give prizes for pupil essays in German and that the federation support increased requirements for entrance and graduation of physical education teachers. The Normal College of the North American Gymnastics Union was moved to Indianapolis in 1907. The federation praised the college's goal of preparing teachers to teach gymnastics, and also preparing them for maintaining the "German Character" in America.

In the reports from the various areas of the state, Logansport German societies were trying to get the German Catholic Society to join their federation. Obviously, the Germans now felt more closely linked by ethnicity as concerns for ethnic survival became stronger. All German Americans were affected by the temperance movement and nativist tendencies. A letter from Philip Rappaport to the board of the State Federation of German Societies, postmarked Washington, D.C., comments on the fewer numbers of German immigrants and on the need to stand up against exaggerated puritanical moralism. In the German republican tradition of the Forty-eighters he states: "Respect of the law can never be regarded more highly than respect of the person, and just as one can have little respect for a bad person, one cannot expect that a bad law will be respected."[133]

*Float, 1905 Turnfest, Indianapolis.*

Taking a very progressive position, a committee was established to study the development of "Municipal Employment Bureaux" to advance the working and middle class such as was being done in Germany. Germany had pioneered social benefit programs and was far ahead of the rest of Europe in this regard. Intellectuals such as Philip Rappaport followed events in Germany carefully and found certain aspects of its social policies to be of potential benefit to the United States.

The German societies supported German-American political causes and a broad range of cultural interests. German societies played a strong role in the development of music, the arts, and a vigorous social life in Indiana's cities, organizing parades, concerts, balls, picnics, dances, and feasts. Through such events German traditions and styles gradually were incorporated into America's way of life. Many Hoosiers of non-German background participated in the activities of Hoosier-German societies. Vice President Charles W. Fairbanks was a frequent speaker at German-American events and a member of the Indianapolis Männerchor. The German Club *(Der Deutsche Klub)* at The German House (Athenaeum) in Indianapolis is described as "a social organization, in which there are almost as many American members as there are Germans. Summer night concerts have been a feature of the Klub for the season, and bowling parties are held nearly every evening. It is a great place for meeting of friends and is accessible."[134]

There was indeed intermingling and integration of the German element into the population of Indiana as a whole. Except for rural enclaves, Germans settled next door to Anglo Americans or those of Scotch-Irish background, leading to close contact and intermarriage.[135] This was certainly the case in Indiana.[136] The result was an intermingling of customs, traditions, and techniques,

often with unique American variations. There remained, however, a sufficient number of distinct German cultural groups and proponents of the "German Way of Life" so that tension continued. This becomes apparent in reading the minutes of the State Federation discussed above. Large numbers of German Americans believed that the German language, culture, and religious life should be strongly present in America. Second- and third-generation German Americans, while aware of their German heritage, involved themselves deeply in the development of American culture. This was very much the case in literature and music. Theodore Dreiser, one of the giants of American literature, was born in 1871 in Terre Haute, the son of a Moravian mother from Ohio and a German immigrant father. "The father's stern religiosity, the mother's flowing tenderness, the family's unceasing poverty—this trio of forces worked at shaping the young Dreiser."[137] Dreiser's first language was German. His friend H.L. Mencken, a fellow German-American literary giant, commented that this was probably the reason for the unique rhythms of his prose.[138] Dreiser's novel *Jennie Gerhardt* (1911) chronicles the life of a German-American family similar in many ways to Dreiser's own. The novel focuses on the daughter Jennie and her entrance into the

*Theodore Dreiser (right) with Sullivan, Indiana, native Will Hays, president of Motion Picture Producers and Distributors of America, Inc., Hollywood, 1931.*

American mainstream of life. *Jennie Gerhardt* defines in Dreiser's stark, realistic style American life in the Midwest for the working middle class.

In music Paul Dresser, brother of Theodore Dreiser (Paul modified the family name), became one of America's leading songwriters and gave Indiana its state song, *On the Banks of the Wabash Far Away.* Ragtime music was enriched by the contributions of sisters Julia Niebergall and May Aufderheide, both of Indianapolis.

The Hoosier German contribution to the musical life of Indiana continued overtly until World War I. In Indianapolis German singing societies held four or five concerts a year, and "until the World War the conducting and singing were in German, with well-paid, professional directors."[139] While the singers were mostly German or of German descent, the associate membership included hundreds of non-Germans. Liederkranz director Frederic Krull, born in Indianapolis, received his training in Berlin, where his uncle Carl Voigt was music director under three emperors. Krull's contribution to Indiana's repertoire is considerable: he set thirty poems of James Whitcomb Riley to music. Herman Lieber and Leo Rappaport secured financial backing for organizing and incorporating the fifty-piece Indianapolis Orchestra with Alexander Ernestinoff as director. The orchestra performed until 1917 and remained financially secure. The Indianapolis Männerchor, with its own recognized musical talents, presented concerts, as it still does, and brought many classical music events to the city.[140] Similar musical patterns developed in other cities and villages in Indiana, often with the Männerchor in the lead, as in Evansville and Fort Wayne. In Columbus T. J. Koch created a superb chamber orchestra. Richmond had its Liederkrantz Singing Society and the Knollenberg Orchestra.[141]

## VIII. The Hammer Effect—World War I, Prohibition, and the Great Depression

When in 1898 Hoosier Germans in Indianapolis celebrated the opening of the completed Das Deutsche Haus and declared it a symbol of their achievements, no one would have thought that only twenty years later the German community would feel compelled to change the building's name to the Athenaeum or that in 1919 there would be a law banning the teaching of German, the language of the "Hun," from all public schools in Indiana.

The United States allied itself with England in the European war for various reasons: sincere solidarity with England, especially on the part of East Coast Americans; profiteering from the sale of war materials to the British; and bad German and very clever British foreign relations

with the United States. The war was to be the war to save democracy and, ironically, the war to end all wars. The fact that England had been the traditional enemy of American democracy and had a rigid class system that was certainly less than democratic seemed to make no difference. Indeed, the United States had waged war twice to obtain and maintain its freedom from England. But American involvement in World War I was less about European politics than American international aspirations and nationalist assertiveness—externally and internally. For better or worse, it was a time of "norming," of having all citizens commit to a certain American way of life, including language, political identity, and, as much as possible, customs.

The German-American National Alliance had missed the point in its plea to Washington to remain neutral in an essentially European war being waged by the aristocracies of Europe, which were cruelly sacrificing their youth in a vicious stalemate.[142] The object of America's involvement seemed to be to establish the United States as a nation among nations with its own cohesive identity. This was enforced with remarkable vigor and the abrogation of the civil rights of all "foreigners," particularly German Americans. The American Protective League was formed with two hundred thousand untrained spies to keep an eye out for subversion. Hysteria gripped the land: in St. Louis on the morning of 5 April 1918 German-born Robert P. Prager was seized by a mob of two hundred and hanged as a lesson in patriotism; Boy Scouts burned German newspapers on the streets of Columbus, Ohio; the National Guard burned German-language books in Wisconsin; and musical organizations purged German composers, including Schubert and Schumann, from their repertoire. The Council of National Defense, created by Congress in 1916, established councils in each state.[143] The German language was forbidden in schools, in churches, and over the telephone by state councils of defense. In some places, any language except English was forbidden for public use. In Indiana the Indiana State Teachers' Association even advocated the elimination of all foreign languages from the elementary schools, and after the passage of the McCray Bill in 1919, it was illegal to teach German in any school, public or private. The ban was not lifted until 1923.[144]

The ultimate effect of the virulent anti-Germanism of the period 1917–22 is not well researched. The German family names of those who died in battle during World War I and are listed in the Indiana War Memorial in Indianapolis indicate that many young men fought more or less willingly. German Americans of any generation were and always had been Americans first. This included the commander of the American Expeditionary Force in World War I, Gen. John J. Pershing (originally Pfoerschin). Ironically, Bismarck Street in Indianapolis was renamed Pershing during the war.

In Fort Wayne, as in most Indiana cities, the war brought often subtle but long-standing tensions to the surface. This was the time "for the Anglos to gain the upper hand in the long-term cultural clashes with the German ethnics."[145] German cultural traits and activities were driven from any preeminence in the public arena.

The effects on individuals, families, and communities were considerable. Richmond's excellent German language program in its schools was dropped.[146] The Richmond Kriegsverein of 1871, a veterans' group, disbanded for its own personal safety when threats made it advisable. After the 1917 law declaring Germans enemy aliens was passed, many German Americans throughout the state discovered that their parents had failed to complete papers on them. Prominent Richmond citizen John Feltman was declared an enemy alien after arriving in this country with his parents at age two. He had to apply for naturalization at age seventy-five. Families changed names, burned records, and pretended to be other than German in origin. Donald M. Royer notes in Richmond that "as late as 1988 one detects a sense of timidity among some German-Americans about their ethnic identity. They would rather not 'come out' as it were. . . . Anti-German prejudices were much more subdued in Richmond during World War II, but the legacy of World War I still seems to linger in the self-feelings of some residents of German ancestry."[147] World War I did the most toward loss of community identity, loss of language, and loss of neighborhood.

So it was also in that most German of Hoosier counties, Dubois County. The nativist English-language press outside Dubois County's German areas mounted attacks against the German Americans with the demand they speak English and disband their German clubs.[148] This led to conflict—a majority felt times were changing and that alignments with Germany should be dropped. "Of the few who would talk about this period in Dubois County history, the memories are of bitterness at losing their language and their connection with their past."[149] After the war life went on as before, but without the German language in public places and in the schools, without the old German names for organizations, and with a sense of isolation bordering on alienation and internal discontent.

On a personal level, Hoosier German-American author Kurt Vonnegut, Jr., perhaps describes best the effect of anti-Germanism in Indiana:

> As I have said in other books, the anti-Germanism in this country during the First World War so shamed and dismayed my parents that they resolved to raise me without acquainting me with the language or the literature or the music or the oral family histories which my ancestors had loved. They volunteered to make me ignorant and rootless as proof of their patriotism. This was done with surprising meekness by many, many German-American families in Indianapolis, it seems to me. Uncle John [Rauch— prominent Indianapolis lawyer] almost seems to boast of this dismantling and quiet burial of a culture, a culture which surely would have been of use to me today.[150]

In addition to the anti-German and generally antiforeign nativism of World War I came a devastating blow to the remnants of German-American social life— prohibition. It also affected other ethnic groups—like the Irish with their whiskey and the Italians with their wine. Prohibition involved more than forbidding the production, sale, and imbibing of alcoholic beverages— it was an attack on the personal freedoms of a large number of people. Beer was and is a symbol of *Gemütlichkeit*, of conviviality for German Americans. First, American mainstream society forced them to stop using their language, to change the names of their societies, and break contact with the land of their origin, and then another core element of their way of life was also outlawed. They were made to feel more and more like second-class citizens.

The third blow to German Americans hit all groups equally: the Great Depression beginning in 1929. Frugality and industriousness, acclaimed German-American virtues, were not enough to save them from the economic ravages of deflation and unemployment. The depression called into question the economic structures that had been the basis of American prosperity. Further, it had a leveling effect on all groups and forced them to accommodate each other's needs for mutual survival.

## IX. The World in Turmoil—From Isolationism to World War II

After World War I America seemed to withdraw into itself in great self-absorption leaving Europe to its own devices. Many Americans of all backgrounds felt that the United States's participation in the war had been a mistake.[151] American politicians were very frustrated that the Europeans had not seemed to learn very much from the Great War and from the excellent example that the Americans felt themselves to be.[152]

German Americans, who in spite of everything were still voters, joined the isolationist trend in droves.[153] President

Woodrow Wilson was unable to get the Senate to ratify the Versailles Peace Treaty and the Covenant that would establish the League of Nations. In the 1920 presidential election Warren G. Harding and the Republicans won in a landslide on an isolationist ticket. Many German Americans, lifelong, even generations-long, members of the Democratic party, deserted it, some never to return. Harding lost no time in concluding a separate peace with Germany and making it plain the United States would never join the League.

The rising trend in Europe toward fascism was generally regarded with great suspicion by virtually all Americans. Fascism did not represent a useful model for the United States to follow in order to escape its economic troubles. As was shown during World War I, Pan-Germanism was not on the minds of German Americans. German intellectuals had never appreciated the militaristic class system in Europe, including the Junker of Prussia and the new militarists of Weimar and then Nazi Germany. It was the very thing German intellectuals had tried to eliminate in 1848 and during the failed Weimar Republic from 1919 to 1933. They did not succeed. In America there was no such system and no need for it. During the Third Reich the German ambassador in America, Dr. Hans Heinrich Dieckhoff, reported to the German Foreign Office that the German element in the United States was much weaker than assumed, that of Chicago's 700,000 German Americans 40,000 belonged to German-theme clubs but only 450 to the Nazi-supported Bund. He concluded that there was no possibility at all that the Germans in America would use their political power for the benefit of the Reich. After a failed rally in Madison Square Garden in February 1939, German-American organizations and their press worked hard to expunge the Bund.[154]

While German Americans had lost their position in American society and their children had been forcefully cut off from the German language, there was a resurrection of German culture. Some churches and clubs used German again, and the Indianapolis Männerchor, which had renamed itself the Academy of Music during the war, reclaimed its original name.

During the 1920s and 1930s there was an ethnic mobilization in some areas to improve the economic situation. This was seen in Indianapolis with gardeners on the south side and in Dubois County, especially among the county's Catholic population. There were self-help networks, e.g., girls serving as domestics. The domestic networks were implemented with the help of the Catholic Church. Also, young men helped in agricultural networks for low wages. There was a flourishing moonshine industry, also known as "Dubois Dew." This was a significant source of survival income for Dubois Countians during the 1920s and early 1930s. The industry was highly organized with market connections throughout Indiana and Illinois.[155] Similar, though more legal, networks existed for produce and for labor among Indianapolis's German-American gardeners.

President Franklin D. Roosevelt's New Deal in many ways worked against such networks, causing the federalization of many aspects of life. Americans would see an increasing involvement of government in the economic and the social life of the nation. The Extension Agency became the representative of Roosevelt's programs. The townsfolk and Protestants in Dubois County liked the federal programs, and gradually rural Catholic resistance was undermined.[156] There was also resistance, however, to the Rural Electrification Act (REA). Many farmers thought it was bad luck to have poles put up on their land. Local pastors wanted electrification and were instrumental in achieving it, but it was not accomplished until the 1940s. Unity through kith and kin had been undermined by New Deal dependence on outside powers and the need to bring the local economy into the national economy.[157]

The process of joining the American mainstream had always proceeded apace even before World War I and the New Deal. German Americans as a group had been in the United States in large numbers since colonial times so they were part of the mainstream anyway. However, in such places as Dubois County, "religious tradition was undoubtedly the most powerful factor in restraining assimilation."[158] Also, there was a rural versus urban lag in development—the REA did not reach outlying nonurban areas until after World War II. Neither did the automobile and road system break up rural America until after World War II.

Immigration from Germany continued to decline through the 1920s and 1930s, except for the exiles from fascism.[159] Many of these people preferred the larger cities and clustered on the East and West coasts. Some, like writer Thomas Mann, remained Europeans and considered their stay in America to be temporary.

In 1941 Japan attacked Pearl Harbor, and the United States was at war with the Axis Powers of Japan, Germany, and Italy. During World War II about one-third of the eleven million Americans in the armed forces were of German stock, among them Gen. Dwight D. Eisenhower, Gen. Carl Spaatz, both of Pennsylvania-German background, and Chester Nimitz, commander of the Pacific Fleet. Gen. Walter Krueger, field commander in the Pacific Theater, was born in Germany. The amphibious tanks used to cross the Rhine were perfected by Donald Roebling, grandson of John Augustus Roebling who built the Brooklyn Bridge. The Indiana War Memorial list of casualties again includes a large number of Hoosier Germans.

## X. Rebuilding Bridges—1948 to the Present

For the second time in less than twenty-five years Germany and the United States were at war. Again there was suspicion and concern about German Americans, and internment camps existed for them as well as for Japanese Americans. There were still in this country almost six and a half million Americans of German birth or whose parents had been born in Germany. The American focus in Europe, however, was less on ridding the world of the "Hun" than on eliminating a horrendous ideological threat, fascism, the main proponent of which was Germany but which had started in Italy and included Spain. Also, most of Eastern Europe was ruled by dictators. Indeed, not a few European intellectuals, including some British, were intrigued with the strong man/strong society concept inherent in fascism.

In the aftermath of World War II with the extreme devastation everywhere in Europe and with the growing threat of the communist ideology seemingly even more pernicious than fascism, outreach to Germany from the United States was quick in coming. In 1948 when the Soviets blockaded Berlin, an airlift was established to bring provisions from the West to the beleaguered city. During the years of the Cold War the Federal Republic of Germany, founded in 1949, became a vital ally with the United States with whom strong political, economic, and military cooperation was established. For the first time Germany (West) and the United States faced, and ultimately withstood, a common threat.

Thousands of American troops, many of German descent, reestablished some contact with Germany, and many entered into family relationships through marriage. The experiences of American military men and the women they married derived largely from the Rhine-Main and southern German areas. This has strongly influenced the kind of cultural life German Americans and their clubs developed, giving Bavarian folk costumes and Oktoberfest-style entertainment prominence in German-American celebratory events.

The physical and economic devastation in Europe and the political repression in Eastern Europe caused increased immigration. Many of the more than ten million ethnic German expellees and refugees from eastern Europe found their way to Canada, the United States, and to Indiana. The increase in immigration to Indiana from German-speaking areas of Europe between 1940 and 1960 was considerable according to census figures: in 1940 there were 18,784 German born and 4,405 Austrian born; in 1960 the former had increased to 85,393, the latter to 10,823. Once the German "economic miracle" of reconstruction was in full swing, emigration dropped drastically and many an immigrant of the early 1950s returned to Germany.

Ongoing changes in the world economy has brought Indiana and Germany closer together. Presently there are at least thirty-six companies with investments by German-owned companies in Indiana, including Boehringer-Mannheim, Miles Laboratories, and Knauf Fiberglass, to name a few. A considerable number of Indiana firms have Germany as a direct or indirect trading partner. By and large, German-based firms in America do not contribute a great deal to German-American activities, preferring to underplay their connection to Germany for psychological and economic reasons. Indeed, the corporate culture of many large firms tends to be transnational and culturally neutral.

The increasing number of school exchanges, sister-city relationships, and citizen-based partnerships has led to the reestablishment of long term positive connections between Germany and Indiana's German Americans as well as with all Hoosier citizens. A prime example is the sister-city relationship between Jasper, Indiana, and Pfaffenweiler, Baden-Württemberg, Germany. Jasper was the recipient of many immigrants from Pfaffenweiler during the 1800s. Mutual visits and student exchanges are reinforcing the link between these communities and descendants' families. Indianapolis has a strong partnership with Cologne, the magnificent old city on the Rhine. Exchanges between the two partners have included museum collections, orchestras, and young people.

*Logo for the sister cities of Jasper, Indiana, and Pfaffenweiler, Germany.*

On both sides of the Atlantic the familial and cultural relationships between two communities is a prime example of the "roots" movement, reflecting the desire to reaffirm personal and family identity—and possibly self-esteem—as well as a sense of continuity in an ever-shifting social environment. America's bicentennial in 1976 acted as a catalyst for historic awareness. Alex Haley's *Roots* with its African-American focus provided the magic word for the rapidly growing genealogical movement spanning all ethnic groups. For the German Americans the year 1983, marking the tricentennial of German immigration, became an added and eventually even more significant catalyst for the rediscovery, documentation, and celebration of their specific heritage that had been shattered by two wars. For German Americans in Indiana and nationally the ethnic revival has no political connotation as such. There has been no "German vote" since the 1950s that would cause politicians to be concerned with German Americans as a voting block.[160]

Also there is no group in Indiana, other than the Amish, that is maintaining German as a first language. German is studied as the language of choice in schools, where it is fairly close behind French, but both languages are far behind Spanish. Indiana would have a long way to go to catch up to the bilingualism that existed before World War I.

That is not to say that there are not Hoosier German authors and poets writing about German-American experiences in both German and English. A poet who has received considerable critical acclaim is Norbert Krapf, who incorporates many themes from his background in Jasper, Indiana.[161] Kurt Vonnegut is a novelist of international fame. Christiane Seiler writes poems in German and English. Seiler's works have been included in a number of anthologies as have those of her fellow academician Ingeborg Hinterschiedt.[162] The question of "Germanness" remains germane to a number of writers.

During the past few decades new German-American organizations have been established. These include the Deutscher-Verein of Jasper and the German-American Klub of Indianapolis, both vibrant organizations with strong memberships. Their purpose is basically celebratory and social. The Indiana German Heritage Society was founded by former members of the governor's commission for the celebration of the 1983 tricentennial of the founding of Germantown, Pennsylvania, the site of the first major German immigration to North America. The society, headquartered in Indianapolis in the Athenaeum, supports research in Hoosier German history and heritage. It supports a publication series along with the Max-Kade German-American Program at IUPUI.[163]

*Banner of the Fort Wayne, Indiana, German Veterans Association. Michael C. Hawfield (right) and Eberhard Reichmann.*

A number of new festivals have been started based on Indiana's German heritage. These include the Freudenfest in Oldenburg, the Strassenfest in Jasper, and the German Fest in Fort Wayne. Indianapolis's German organizations have a number of fests held at the clubhouses of the Saengerchor, the Liederkranz, the Athenaeum, or at German Park. Out of old traditions new traditions develop that maintain ethnic themes and which appeal to the general public.

Much has been done to collect and preserve the material and spoken culture of Hoosier Germans.[164] The German-American collections of the Indiana Historical Society Library and the Indiana State Library have been indexed and made available in annotated listings.[165] A much greater awareness of the import of German contributions to life in Indiana exists as a result of such work.

The renewed interest in ethnic background in this country is an interesting phenomenon given the pervasiveness of mass culture. This interest has the same origin as the desire in Germany to cling to regional traditions and dialects—all expressions of the search for identity and meaning. Critical voices can be heard regarding "hyphenated" Americans who believe in their group's superiority and are intolerant of others. Since German Americans participate fully in all other aspects of American life and do not exclude others from their celebrations, this concern does not seem warranted. A somewhat more valid criticism has been aimed at the economic motivation and lack of authenticity in some German-American clubs and celebrations.[166]

In that regard, German-American culture takes its origins from its adaptation of German customs and traditions to the American environment. This culture is rooted in its own past of over three hundred years and hence is distinct from Central European cultural

*The United States's first Summer Graduate Institute for Teachers on German Heritage, Indiana University-Purdue University, Indianapolis, 1986.*

manifestations; it is the result of continuous interaction with an Anglo-American and multiethnic environment and thus is inseparable from American culture. This is why German visitors to the United States find German-American celebrations and festivals different from those in Germany. In fact, German visitors' reactions often range from finding the celebrations quaint to strange. "German" in German American means the values and cultural markers understood to be present in this really very American cultural heritage.

## Notes

1. Indiana differs from its neighbors in the Old Northwest in having a small foreign population. In 1850 an estimated 55,000 foreign-born inhabitants comprised less than 6 percent of the total population compared to an average of 12.2 percent in the Old Northwest as a whole. Ohio had 11 percent, Wisconsin 36.2 percent, the highest. Gregory S. Rose, "The Distribution of Indiana's Ethnic and Racial Minorities in 1850," *Indiana Magazine of History* (hereafter cited as *IMH*) 87 (Sept. 1991): 226.

2. For a discussion of this problem and an overview of Germans in America see Kathleen Neils Conzen, "Germans," in *Harvard Encyclopedia of American Ethnic Groups*, ed. Stephan Thernstrom (Cambridge, Mass.:

Belknap Press of Harvard University Press, 1980), 405–20.

3. For information on the early German immigrations see: Lucy F. Bittinger, *The Germans in Colonial Times* (Philadelphia and London: J.B. Lippincott Co., 1901; reprint, New York: Russell and Russell, 1968); Albert B. Faust, *The German Element in the United States, with Special Reference to Its Political, Moral, Social, and Educational Influence,* 2 vols. (Boston: Houghton Mifflin Co., 1909); Daniel Haberle, *Auswanderung und Koloniergründung der Pfälzer im 18. Jahrhundert* (Kaiserslautern: H. Kayser, 1909); Friedrich Kapp, *Aus und über Amerika,* 2 vols. (Berlin: J. Springer, 1876); Gustav Körner, *Das Deutsche Element in den Vereinigten Staaten von Nordamerika, 1818–1848* (1880; reprint, New York and Frankfurt: Peter Lang, 1986); Peter Marschalck, *DeutscheÜberseewanderung im 19. Jahrhundert* (Stuttgart: E. Klett, 1973); Günter Moltmann, *Germans to America: 300 Years of Immigration, 1683–1983* (Stuttgart: Published by Institute for Foreign Cultural Relations in Cooperation with the Inter Nationes, Bonn-Bad Godesberg, 1982); LaVern J. Rippley, *The German-Americans* (Lanham, Md.: University of America Press, 1984); Frank Trommler and Joseph McVeigh, eds., *America and the Germans: An Assessment of a Three-Hundred-Year History,* 2 vols. (Philadelphia: University of Pennsylvania Press, 1985); Victor W. Von Hagen, *The Germanic People in America* (Norman: University of Oklahoma Press, 1976), 3.

4. Festival play at the opening of Das Deutsche Haus. Germania and Columbia, personifications of the two respective cultures, are shown together admonishing all strident provincialists to work together for the good of all in America.

5. "The ultimate irony, however, may be that the melting pot theorists were only too accurate: a major reason why Germans in the long run were unable to retain succeeding generations within the definitions of

the ethnicity they 'invented' was because America proved ready to accept so much of what that ethnicity was designed to keep alive." Kathleen Neils Conzen, "German-Americans and the Invention of Ethnicity," in Trommler and McVeigh, eds., *America and the Germans,* 2:145.

6. Orlando Patterson, "Context and Choice in Ethnic Allegiance: A Theoretical Framework and Caribbean Case Study," in *Ethnicity: Theory and Experience,* eds. Nathan Glazer and Daniel P. Moynihan (Cambridge, Mass.: Harvard University Press, 1975), 308–9. Discussed in John G. Rice, "The Swedes," in *They Chose Minnesota: A Survey of the State's Ethnic Groups,* ed. J. D. Holmquist (St. Paul: Minnesota Historical Society Press, 1981), 272.

7. Bureau of the Census, *1980 Census of Population, Ancestry of the Population by State: 1980, Supplementary Report* (Washington, D.C.: Department of Commerce, 1983).

8. Bureau of the Census, *1980 Census of Population General Social and Economic Characteristics: Indiana* (Washington, D.C.: Department of Commerce, 1984).

9. For a discussion of repatriation see Günter Moltmann, "American-German Return Migration in the Nineteenth and Early Twentieth Centuries," *Central European History* 8 (Dec. 1980): 378–92.

10. Letters from friends and family in Germany show their understanding and appreciation of a democratic government and their commitment to it. Although most immigrants did not run for office themselves, they were an electoral force in the United States and were actively involved in politics, as were subsequent generations.

11. Ralph Langbein and Wiebke Henning, "Staat und Auswanderung im 19. Jahrhundert," *Zeitschrift für Kulturaustausch* 39 (1989): 292–301.

12. William A. Fritsch in *German Settlers and German Settlements in Indiana* (Evansville: [s.n.], 1915), describes the following incident regarding Helm. When an English force under Col. Henry Hamilton came south to recapture Vincennes, it found Helm in command of the fort with but one soldier, the French inhabitants having fled. Fritsch cites Mann Butler in *A History of the Commonwealth of Kentucky* (Louisville: Published for author by Wilcox, Dickerman and Co., 1834), who "tells us how Captain Helm, at the approach of the English, bravely placed a loaded cannon before the entrance of the fort and upon their coming within hailing distance, commanded them to halt, emphasizing his demand by brandishing a firebrand and shouting that he would shoot if they came nearer. Hereupon the English proposed a parley in which they agreed that Captain Helm and his men should have free passage from the fort with their arms. Imagine their surprise when Captain Helm, with his command of one man, stepped forward!" Clark then returned, recaptured the fort, and reinstated Helm. Fritsch, *German Settlers and German Settlements in Indiana,* 6–7.

13. The tenets of faith, on which most Anabaptist groups agree, include opposition to infant baptism, confirmation, oaths of allegiance, and military service. Anabaptists include the Quakers, Hutterites (also known as Moravian Brothers), Mennonites, Amish, and Dunkards, all of whom appear in Indiana. The Anabaptist movement in central Europe derived from an individualistic, pietistic response to the formality of established Protestant religions established by John Calvin, Huldrych Zwingli, and Martin Luther.

14. Fritsch, *German Settlers and German Settlements in Indiana,* 7.

15. Donald M. Royer, *The German-American Contribution to Richmond's Development, 1833–1933* (Indianapolis and Richmond: Indiana German Heritage Society and Richmond German Heritage Society, 1989), 8.

16. Fritsch, *German Settlers and German Settlements in Indiana,* 9.

17. Among the more important works on the Rappite community, especially regarding the Indiana years, are the following:

John C. Andressohn, "Three Additional Rappite Letters," *IMH* 45 (June 1949): 184–88, and "Twenty Additional Rappite Manuscripts," ibid., 44 (Mar. 1948): 83–108; Karl J. R. Arndt, *Documentary History of the Indiana Decade of the Harmony Society, 1814–1824,* 2 vols. (Indianapolis: Indiana Historical Society, 1975–78), and "The First Wabash Song," *IMH* 38 (Mar. 1942): 80–82, and *George Rapp's Harmony Society, 1785–1847* (Rutherford, N.J.: Fairleigh Dickinson University Press, 1972); Fritsch, *German Settlers and German Settlements in Indiana,* 10–16; Elfrieda Lang, "The Inhabitants of New Harmony According to the Federal Census of 1850," *IMH* 42 (Dec. 1946): 355–94; Hugo Karl Polt, "The Rappites and New Harmony, Indiana," *American-German Review* 10 (Oct. 1943): 17–20; Richard D. Wetzel, *Frontier Musicians on the Connoquenessing, Wabash and Ohio: A History of the Music and Musicians of George Rapp's Harmony Society (1805–1906)* (Athens: Ohio University Press, 1976); Otis E. Young, "Personnel of the Rappite Community of Harmony, Indiana, in the Year 1824," *IMH* 47 (Sept. 1951): 313–19.

18. For a discussion of the Sunwoman and the significance for Rapp see Karl J. R. Arndt, "The Indiana Decade of George Rapp's Harmony Society, 1814–1824," in *Proceedings of the American Antiquarian Society* (1970; reprint, Worcester, Mass., 1971), 2–4.

19. Donald E. Pitzer and Josephine M. Elliott, "New Harmony's First Utopians, 1814–1824," *IMH* 75 (Sept. 1979): 233.

20. Fritsch, *German Settlers and German Settlements in Indiana,* 13.

21. Quoted in ibid., 14.

22. John D. Barnhart and Donald F. Carmony, *Indiana: From Frontier to Industrial Commonwealth,* 4 vols. (New York: Lewis Historical Publishing Co., Inc., 1954), 1:300–13. The Rappites loaned the state $5,000 to shore up its economy in 1823, but they refused a loan request from Indiana's first governor, Jonathan Jennings, for personal use.

23. Fritsch, *German Settlers and German Settlements in Indiana,* 15.

24. Mary Lou Robson Fleming, "Jacob Schnee: Preacher, Publisher, Printer and Utopian Community Pioneer," *Pennsylvania Folklife* 32 (Spring 1983): 128–38. See also Arndt, *Documentary History of the Indiana Decade of the Harmony Society.*

25. Gayle Thornbrough and Dorothy Riker, comps., *Readings in Indiana History, Indiana Historical Collections,* vol. 36 (Indianapolis: Indiana Historical Bureau, 1956), 384.

26. See interviews in Darrel E. Bigham, *Reflections on a Heritage: The German Americans in Southwestern Indiana* (Evansville: Indiana State University Press, 1980), 5, passim.

27. For a discussion of emigration from Germany see Mack Walker, *Germany and the Emigration,* Harvard Historical Monographs, vol. 56 (Cambridge, Mass.: Harvard University Press, 1964). See also Peter Assion's discussion of Germans' perceptions of their political and economic situation in Europe as a factor in emigration: "Die Ursachen der Massenauswanderung in die Vereinigten Staaten—Objektive Zwänge und ihre subjektive Wahrnehmung," *Zeitschrift für Kulturaustausch* 39 (1989): 258–65. A very useful commentary on perceptions of life in the United States, specifically Indiana, compared to Europe is provided by Johann Wolfgang Schreyer in an 1846 letter from Plymouth, Indiana, to his family in Bavaria. He notes the taxes are minimal, no conscription, public land is free from taxation for five years; and he comments that one owes it to one's children to immigrate to the United States, even if one is older, for "the result of this emigration will surely be so valuable that the younger descendants will thank the ancestor who has afforded them the blessings of this land." See Donald Carmony, ed., "Letter Written by Johann Wolfgang Schreyer," *IMH* 40 (Sept. 1944): 292–94.

28. Günter Moltmann, "The Pattern of German Emigration to the United States in the Nineteenth Century," in Trommler and McVeigh, eds., *America and the Germans,* 1:16.

29. Gary W. Stanton, "Brought, Borrowed or Bought: Sources and Utilization Patterns of the Material Culture of German Immigrants in Southeastern Indiana, 1833–1860" (Ph.D. diss., Indiana University, 1985), 63.

30. Schreyer's experiences are given in his 1846 letter cited above.

31. Stanton, "Brought, Borrowed or Bought," 53.

32. Information concerning immigration to Dubois County is taken from Elfrieda Lang, "Some Characteristics of German Immigrants in Dubois County, Indiana," *IMH* 42 (Mar. 1946): 29–46.

33. Ibid., 35, 38–39.

34. George T. Probst, *The Germans in Indianapolis, 1840–1918,* rev. and ed. Eberhard Reichmann (Indianapolis: German-American Center and Indiana German Heritage Society, 1989), 9, 73, 110, 127–28.

35. Royer, *German-American Contribution to Richmond's Development,* 1.

36. David S. Dreyer, *A History of Immigration to the Batesville Vicinity* (Indianapolis: Bredensteiner Printing Co., 1987), 1.

37. Bigham, *Reflections on a Heritage,* 4.

38. There is no monographic study giving an overview of the history of the German religious movements in Indiana. There are some individual church histories and references in broader studies on religion in the Midwest, including Indiana.

39. Mennonites is the name given a broad spectrum of Anabaptists, i.e., people who believe that baptism and congregational allegiance should come only when a person is old enough to freely choose. The name derives from Menno Simons (1496?–1561), a Dutch reformer whose field of activity was mainly northern Germany. Included are the Mennonite Church, the General Conference Mennonite Church, Old Order Amish Mennonite Church, Hutterian Brothers, and Mennonite Brethren Church, among others. See John C. Wenger, *Glimpses of Mennonite History and Doctrine* (Scottsdale, Pa.: Herald Press, 1949), and *The Mennonites in Indiana and Michigan* (Scottsdale, Pa.: Herald Press, 1961). The Moravians trace their origin to Jan Hus (1372–1415), the early Bohemian reformer who was executed for his beliefs. Like the Mennonites, Quakers, and other groups, the Moravians were persecuted in Europe and sought religious freedom in America. Count Nikolaus Ludwig von Zinzendorf, banished from Europe in 1736, preached among the Indians and with his followers was responsible for settlements in Georgia and North Carolina. Bethlehem, Pennsylvania, however, became the center of the Moravian Church in North America, established in 1741. It is from here that settlers moved into Indiana. See John Taylor Hamilton, *A History of the Church Known as the Moravian Church, or the Unitas Fratrum, or the Unity of the Brethren, during the Eighteenth and Nineteenth Centuries* (New York: AMS Press, 1971).

40. He described his visit in a journal. See note 44.

41. Rudolph F. Rehmer, "Indiana Lutherans at the Nineteenth Century Crossroads," in *American Lutheranism: Crisis in Historical Consciousness? 1988 Essays and Reports of the Lutheran Historical Conference,* vol. 13 (1990), 72. For a discussion of the early German Lutheran pioneers in Indiana see Robert E. Smith, "'Help in the Name of Jesus!' The Spirituality of German Lutherans in Indiana, 1816–1847," in *Studies in Indiana German-Americana,* vol. 2 (Indianapolis: Indiana German Heritage Society, 1995).

42. Ibid., 13.

43. The German title is *Die Noth der deutschen Lutheraner in Nordamerika. Ihren Glaubensgenossen in der Heimath an's Herz gelegt von Fr. Wyneken, Pastor in Fort Wayne, in Indiana.* The first American edition appeared in Pittsburgh in 1844.

44. A biographical overview of Kundek and his effect on the cultural life of Dubois County is provided by Dunstan McAndrews, *Father Joseph Kundek, 1810–1857: A Missionary Priest of the Diocese of Vincennes* (St. Meinrad, Ind.: St. Meinrad Archabbey, 1954). See also Angela Sasse, "Pioneer Roman Catholic Missionary in Southern Indiana," in *Studies in Indiana German-Americana,* vol. 2.

45. Kundek's work is described in Albert Kleber, *Ferdinand, Indiana, 1840–1940: A Bit of Cultural History* (St. Meinrad, Ind.: Abbey Press, 1940). Kundek's correspondence from Indiana will be included in a revised edition of Norbert Krapf, ed., *Finding the Grain* (1996). See note 161.

46. "St. Joseph Church, Jasper, Ind.: 1880–1980," 100th Anniversary Booklet (n.p., 1980), 1.

47. Kundek wrote in a 1846 letter to the Leopoldine Society: "I believe that settlements are the most apt means to safeguard and to spread our holy religion in America, because in this manner the members of the same faith unite as it were into one family, live together, mutually share their religious sentiments and impressions, as one body attend the divine service, receive from their pastor all the comforts of religion as they desire, have the opportunity of having the necessary instructions imparted to their children in school, mutually support one another in commerce and occupations, and thus form a society that meets all their interests. Such colonies and settlements are according to my conviction the best means to protect the Catholic immigrants against the loss of their faith, to safeguard them against the inducements and the seductions of our adversaries, and to enable them to preserve incorrupt the sacred treasure of religion and to transmit it to their children." Quoted in Kleber, *Ferdinand, Indiana,* 15–16.

48. For an overview of the religious landscape of Dubois County see Elfrieda Lang, "German Influence in the Churches and Schools of Dubois County, Indiana," *IMH* 42 (June 1946): 151–72.

49. Kleber, *Ferdinand, Indiana,* 125. A detailed history of the convent and its various missions in education and other service is provided by M. Frederica Dudine, *The Castle on the Hill: Centennial History of the Convent of the Immaculate Conception, Ferdinand, Indiana, 1867–1967* (Milwaukee: Bruce Publishing Co., 1967). The Benedictines replaced a number of Sisters of Providence who had taught in Ferdinand schools from 1862 to 1867.

50. Dreyer, *History of Immigration to the Batesville Vicinity,* 9.

51. Stanton, "Brought, Borrowed or Bought," 86. See also Philip Gleason, *Conservative Reformers: German-American Catholics and the Social Order* (Notre Dame, Ind.: University of Notre Dame Press, 1968).

52. William W. Sweet, *Religion on the American Frontier, 1783–1840,* vol. 4, *The Methodists* (New York: Cooper Square Publishers, 1964), 64 ff. See also Elisabeth K. Nottingham, *Methodism and the Frontier: Indiana Proving Ground* (New York: Columbia University Press, 1941); F. C. Holliday, *Indiana Methodism* (Cincinnati: Hitchcock and Walden, 1873).

53. Gustavus E. Hiller, "The German Methodist of Indiana," *The Indianapolis Area of the Methodist Episcopal Church: First Quadrennium, 1920–1924* ([Indianapolis?: n.p., c. 1924?]), 107–9.

54. For information regarding Nast's early missionary experiences see Donald E. Byrne, *No Foot of Land: Folklore of American Methodist Itinerants* (Metuchen, N.J.: Scarecrow Press, 1975), 190–92.

55. For information on the development of German Methodist churches see Herbert L. Heller, *The Indiana Conference of the Methodist Church, 1832–1956* ([n.p.]: Under the auspices of the Historical Society of the Indiana Conference, 1957), 197–205.

56. Hiller, "German Methodist of Indiana," 109.

57. Lang, "German Influence in the Churches and Schools of Dubois County," 153–54.

58. Royer, *German-American Contribution to Richmond's Development*, 1.

59. Stanton, "Brought, Borrowed or Bought," 66.

60. Ibid., 79.

61. For a more complete overview of Swiss-German immigration see Leo Schelbert's essay in this volume.

62. Fritsch, *German Settlers and German Settlements in Indiana*, 22.

63. "The names of such villages as Elberfeld, Haubstadt and Darmstadt indicate their early settlers, whose descendants still love their mother tongue and German customs." Ibid.

64. Manfred E. Haas, "Early German Settlements," in James E. Morlock, ed., *Was It Yesterday?: A Companion Volume to The Evansville Story* (Evansville: University of Evansville Press, 1980), 56.

65. Ibid., 57.

66. Juliet Anne Niehaus, "Ethnic Formation and Transformation: The German-Catholics of Dubois County, Indiana, 1838–1979" (Ph.D. diss., New School for Social Research, 1981), 120. The prevalence of this fusion exists in the legends and folktales of present-day Hoosier Germans. See Eberhard Reichmann, *Hoosier German Tales, Small and Tall* (Indianapolis: German-American Center and Indiana German Heritage Society, Inc., 1991), especially 107–23.

67. Kleber, *Ferdinand, Indiana*, 77. "The Nativist Movement was an important factor in the formation of the German-Catholics of Dubois County into an ethnic community." Niehaus, "Ethnic Formation and Transformation," 123.

68. Royer, *German-American Contribution to Richmond's Development*, 1. Royer notes regarding Germans in Richmond: "It is an established fact that a significant number of German settlers brought with them craft skills in woodworking, cabinetmaking, stone and brick masonry and construction which they used in the building of the National Road, railroad lines, and bridges across the Whitewater River, especially the Old National Road Bridge. They were also instrumental for the construction of scores of flour, woolen and sawmills along the Whitewater River." Royer comments that the various histories hardly mention the German contribution.

69. James M. Bregquist, "Germans and the City," in *Germans in America: Retrospect and Prospect*, ed. Randall M. Miller (Philadephia: The German Society of Pennsylvania, 1984), 41.

70. Ibid., 53.

71. Probst, *Germans in Indianapolis*, 3.

72. Ibid., 16.

73. Körner mentions that an earlier paper, the *Hochwächter*, was published in Indianapolis by Georg Walker in 1845. These were the first German newspapers published in Indiana. Körner, *Das Deutsche Element in den Vereinigten Staaten von Nordamerika*, 237.

74. Henry A. Meyer, "Early Evansville," in Morlock, ed., *Was It Yesterday?*, 27.

75. Ibid., 31.

76. Körner, *Das Deutsche Element in den Vereinigten Staaten von Nordamerika*, 237.

77. Ibid., 243.

78. Royer, *German-American Contribution to Richmond's Development*, 37.

79. Ibid., 41. "John Wesley . . . put one aspect of the 'work ethic' this way: 'Earn all you can, save all you can, and give all you can to the Lord.'" "To this the English Quakers and German settlers gave their hearty approval." Ibid., 43.

80. Fred Bartel, *The Institutional Influence of the German Element of the Population in Richmond, Indiana, Papers of the Wayne County Historical Society* 1, no. 2 (Richmond: Nicholson Print.,1904), 21.

81. Royer, *German-American Contribution to Richmond's Development*, 47.

82. Ibid., 54.

83. Ibid., 59–63.

84. Ibid., 63.

85. Powell A. Moore, *The Calumet Region: Indiana's Last Frontier* (Indianapolis: Indiana Historical Bureau, 1959), 348.

86. Ibid., 78. There is very little research on the Germans in the Lake County area.

87. Elfrieda Lang, "The Inhabitants of Center Township, Lake County, Indiana, According to the Federal Census of 1850," *IMH* 44 (Sept. 1948): 283, and "An Analysis of Northern Indiana's Population in 1850," ibid. 49 (Mar. 1953): 17–60.

88. Theodore Stempfel in *Fünfzig Jahre Unermüdlichen Deutschen Strebens in Indianapolis* (Indianapolis: German-American Center and Indiana German Heritage Society, Inc., 1991), 2–3, considered the year 1848 the real beginning of the history of the Germans in Indianapolis: "During the first quarter of this century the bulk of German emigrants was recruited mainly from the lower middle class in Southern Germany. . . . Politically immature, their aspirations and endeavors were completely geared toward improving their material condition. The days of severe hardship in the old fatherland had made them accustomed to all kinds of privations; therefore, most of them succeeded through perseverance and frugality to work their way up to a comfortable life in a relatively short period of time. The struggle for existence, the responsibility of family, house and farm required all of their time and energy."

89. This is precisely the argument of Stempfel: "Without arrogance one can surely maintain that the German refugees at the end of the 1840s and the beginning of the 1850s represent the best element within the entire immigration ever to reach American soil. Among the '48ers were men like Karl Heinzen, Friedrich Hassaureck, Gustav Struve, August Becker, Friedrich Hecker, Karl Schurz, Heinrich Tiedemann, August Willich, Franz Sigcl, Ludwig Blenker, Max Weber, Jakob Müller, Eduard Dorsch, Lorenz Brentano, Nikolaus Muller, and many others who achieved national reputation in their adopted new fatherland in the fields of letters and politics as well as in public life. A burning desire for freedom inspired them, and after only a few years they became the driving force in the agitation against the institution of slavery.

The idealists of 1848 have contributed immensely to the cultural development of America. American history provides proof that they have always been among the most loyal adherents and the most solid supporters of the republic in times of peace and war. They were the leaven in American culture but, unlike the immigrants of former decades who promptly stripped off their nationality, they preserved their native customs and manners, yet became quickly Americanized in the political sense." Stempfel, *Fünfzig Jahre Unermüdlichen Deutschen Strebens in Indianapolis*, 3–4.

90. "Thus, at the beginning of the 1850s, societies for the cultivation of German language and song, sociability and customs, and especially Turnvereins ['gymnastic societies'] were created in all larger American cities with a German population. It stands to reason that the '48ers showed their primary interest in the Turnvereins, since many of them were already members of Turnvereins in Germany where they played an important role in political and social life under the leadership of Jahn. The intrepid, at times aggressive, demeanor of their members brought them into discredit with their [German] government so that they were persecuted and punished for being allegedly dangerous to the

state. For this very reason, the Turners gained the sympathy and interest of all those who were politically oppressed in this country. The essence of the idealistic aspirations of the '48ers finds expression in the slogan: 'True liberty, education, and prosperity for all,' and this is also the motto which underlies all Turnvereins in America." Ibid., 4.

91. For an overview of the Turner movement in the United States see Horst Ueberhorst, *Turner unterm Sternenbanner* (Munich: Heinz Moos Verlag, 1978).

92. Giles R. Hoyt, "German Vereine in Indianapolis," in *Das Ohiotal—The Ohio Valley. The German Dimension,* ed. Don Heinrich Tolzmann (New York: Peter Lang, 1993), 102–3.

93. Rippley, *German-Americans,* 163. Fully half of the Forty-eighters were active in journalism. Carl Schurz defined the purposes of the German press as: 1. Explain America to immigrants; 2. Promote cooperation among the Germans in America; 3. Inform German Americans about Germany; 4. Teach the German immigrant about the 'open-handed' generosity of the United States.

94. Bibliographies of the German-language press in Indiana include: Karl J. R. Arndt and May E. Olson, *German-American Newspapers and Periodicals, 1732–1955: History and Bibliography* (Heidelberg: Quelle and Meyer, 1961), 110–31, and *German Language Press of the Americas,* 3d ed., 2 vols. (Munich: Verlag Dokumentation, 1973– ), 1:111–30; Oscar L. Bockstahler, "The German Press in Indiana," *IMH* 48 (June 1952): 161–68; John W. Miller, *Indiana Newspaper Bibliography* (Indianapolis: Indiana Historical Society, 1982). The most complete annotated listing of the German-language press published in Indiana is James Ziegler, *The Indiana German-Language Press: A Bibliography* (Indianapolis: Max Kade German-American Center at IUPUI and Indiana German Heritage Society, 1994).

95. Rippley, *German-Americans,* 59.

96. Probst, *Germans in Indianapolis,* 49.

97. Mark A. Lause, "General August Willich: A Cincinnati Republikaner and the Paradox of the Modern State," in Tolzmann, ed., *Das Ohiotal—The Ohio Valley,* 57–63.

98. Probst, *Germans in Indianapolis,* 50–52.

99. Ibid., 52; Fritsch, *German Settlers and German Settlements in Indiana,* 39.

100. Fritsch, *German Settlers and German Settlements in Indiana,* 24.

101. A good, brief overview of the emigrant-immigrant experience is given by Jörg Nagler, "Von Auswanderer zum Einwanderer: Zur Situation deutscher Immigranten in den Vereinigten Staaten während der zweiten Hälfte des 19. Jahrhunderts," *Zeitschrift für Kulturaustausch* 39 (1989): 303–11.

102. For a discussion of this phenomenon see Klaus Bade, "German Emigration to the United States and Continental Immigration to Germany in the Late Nineteenth and Early Twentieth Centuries," in *Labor Migration in the Atlantic Economies: The European and North American Working Classes during the Period of Industrialization,* ed. Dirk Hoerder (Westport, Conn.: Greenwood Press, 1985); John Bodnar, *The Transplanted: A History of Immigrants in Urban America* (Bloomington: Indiana University Press, 1985); Charlotte Erickson, *American Industry and the European Immigrant, 1860–1885* (Cambridge, Mass.: Harvard University Press, 1957); Hartmut Keil and John Jentz, eds., *Deutsche Arbeiterkultur in Chicago von 1859 bis zum Ersten Weltkrieg* (Ostfildern: Scripta Mercaturae Verlag, 1984).

103. Oliver P. Morton, *Die Auswanderung nach den Vereinigten Staaten von Nord-Amerika. Indiana eine passende Heimstatte für Emigranten,* trans. C. J. Beleke (Indianapolis: Joseph J. Bingham, 1864). This was an excellent and highly detailed advertisement for Indiana. Comparative statistics on health, income, taxes, and other information were provided. In terms of advertising the Hoosier state's positive attributes for a foreign audience, the piece remains unsurpassed. It was written with great understanding and sensitivity about what Germans would care to know.

104. Probst, *Germans in Indianapolis,* 56.

105. Ibid., 68.

106. Dean R. Esslinger, *Immigrants and the City: Ethnicity and Mobility in a Nineteenth-Century Midwestern Community* (Port Washington, N.Y.: Kennikat Press, 1975), 109–10.

107. Ibid., 110.

108. Probst, *Germans in Indianapolis,* 112.

109. See above, note 94, for a listing of works on Indiana's German-language press.

110. For an overview of German dialects spoken in Indiana see Joseph C. Salmons, "But Hoosiers *Do* Speak German," *Yearbook of German-American Studies* 21 (1986): 155–66. For a more detailed look at dialects in Dubois County see Peter Freeouf, "Dialect Leveling and Preservation in the German of Dubois County, Indiana," *Studies in Indiana German-Americana,* vol. 1 (Indianapolis: Indiana German Heritage Society, 1988), 14–24.

111. Bigham, *Reflections on a Heritage,* 14.

112. "The common Catholic dialect of the Jasper-Ferdinand area represents a koiné development which has eliminated whatever primary dialect characteristics were present in the speech of the earliest German settlers." Freeouf, "Dialect Leveling and Preservation in the German of Dubois County," 22.

113. Probst, *Germans in Indianapolis,* 131.

114. Bigham, *Reflections on a Heritage,* 7. Similarly, Elfrieda Lang remembers her grandmother expressing great concern that the young girl would not go to heaven when the language of her confirmation in Posey County was switched to English in 1917–18.

115. James H. Madison, *The Indiana Way: A State History* (Bloomington and Indianapolis: Indiana University Press and Indiana Historical Society, 1986), 180.

116. Probst, *Germans in Indianapolis,* 100.

117. An overview of this important educational institution is provided in Theodore Stein, *Historical Sketch of the German-English Independent School of Indianapolis: "Our Old School"* (Indianapolis: Cheltenham-Aetna Press, 1913).

118. "The German community was especially influential in cultural affairs. One man in particular, Herman Lieber, a native of Düsseldorf who had transformed his book bindery into the only art gallery in Indianapolis, was the major force in the nascent artistic life of the city." Martin Krause, *The Passage: Return of Indiana Painters from Germany, 1880–1905* (Indianapolis: Indianapolis Museum of Art and the Wallraf-Richartz-Museum Cologne, 1990). This splendid book gives a scholarly but highly accessible overview of the work of the Hoosier Group.

119. Probst, *Germans in Indianapolis,* 106 ff.

120. Rippley, *German-Americans,* 88.

121. Fritsch, *German Settlers and German Settlements in Indiana,* 48.

122. Esslinger, *Immigrants and the City,* 11.

123. Fritsch, *German Settlers and German Settlements in Indiana,* 51–52.

124. Probst, *Germans in Indianapolis,* 85 ff.

125. "Der liebe Gott hat ja alles diese Opfer von mir verlangt. Ich habe es auch alle mit Ergebung in Gottes Willen angenommen. Meine Lieben, ich darf freudig an meine Jugendjahre zurückdenken, das[s] ich gegen jederman meine Pflicht erfüllt habe gegen Gott und jeder [*sic*] Mensch." (God has required all these sacrifices from me. I have accepted them all in submission to God's will. Dear Ones, with joy I can think back on my youth and that I fulfilled my duty to everyone and to God.)

126. "Ich sehe ein, ich mache besser mein Leben hi[e]r wie in Deutschland." (I realize I can have a better life here than in Germany.) She also noted that single immigrant girls had a good life here; they could earn two dollars a week cooking, scrubbing, and washing.

127. Esslinger, *Immigrants and the City,* 107.

128. Rippley, *German-Americans,* 73.

129. Fritsch, *German Settlers and German Settlements in Indiana,* 41 ff.

130. Willi Paul Adams, *The German-Americans: An Ethnic Experience,* trans. and ed. by LaVern J. Rippley and Eberhard Reichmann (Indianapolis: Max Kade German-American Center, IUPUI, 1993), 6.

131. Klaus J. Bade, "German Emigration to the United States and Continental Immigration to Germany in the Late Nineteenth and Early Twentieth Centuries," *Central European History* 8 (Dec. 1980): 374.

132. *Protokoll der Vierten Staats-Konvention.* Staats-Verband Deutscher Vereine von Indiana. Abgehalten am 3. August 1907 Nachmittags 2 Uhr, in der Halle des Unabhängigen Turnvereins, Indianapolis, Indiana (Indianapolis: Gutenberg Co., 1907).

133. "Die Achtung vor dem Gesetze kann nie höher stehen als die Achtung vor dem Menschen, und so wenig man Achtung vor einem schlechten Menschen haben kann, kann man erwarten, dass ein schlechtes Gesetz geachtet wird." Ibid., 18.

134. Quoted in Probst, *Germans in Indianapolis,* 179.

135. Germans tended to intermarry with Anglo-Saxons more readily on the frontier than in old established areas. See Rippley, *German-Americans,* 29.

136. Royer, *German-American Contribution to Richmond's Development,* 39; Dreyer, *History of Immigration to the Batesville Vicinity,* 10; Bigham, *Reflections on a Heritage,* 19.

137. Philip L. Gerber, *Theodore Dreiser* (New York: Twayne, 1964), 27.

138. H. L. Mencken's relationship to Indiana is discussed in Val Holley, "H. L. Mencken and the Indiana Genii," *Traces of Indiana and Midwestern History* 3 (winter 1991): 4–15.

139. For an overview of musical life in Indianapolis with emphasis on the German contribution see Martha F. Bellinger, "Music in Indianapolis, 1821–1900," *IMH* 41 (Dec. 1945): 345–62, and "Music in Indianapolis, 1900–1944," ibid. 42 (Mar. 1946): 47–65.

140. Josef Keller, *Festschrift zur Feier des Goldenen Jubiläums des Indianapolis Männerchor am 23. 24. und 25. Juni 1904* (Indianapolis: Gutenberg Co., 1904).

141. Royer, *German-American Contribution to Richmond's Development,* 78.

142. Charles Nagel, a prominent German-American citizen, pleaded with his fellow German Americans to observe current events. He described the new American type: that he was an American politician, but celebrated his German heritage. Nagel could not understand why Americans turned away from neutrality since Germany's strength was on land, England's on the sea. Germany was not a threat to the United States. In fact, England was harming United States trade more than Germany. The United States would not permit its enemy to carry munitions on passenger ships, something it was doing. England had also received a loan from the United States, helping them to drag the war on longer. "No Cause for War" (an address delivered before The Germanistic Society at The German House, Indianapolis, 24 Mar. 1916).

143. Rippley, *German-Americans,* 185 ff.

144. Probst, *Germans in Indianapolis,* 153. Ironically, during subsequent years foreign language instruction was eliminated in most elementary schools on the grounds that it was too expensive and negatively affected the children's ability to learn English.

145. Clifford Scott, "Hoosier Kulturkampf: Anglo-German Cultural Conflicts in Fort Wayne, 1840–1920," *Journal of German-American Studies* 15 (1980): 15.

146. Royer, *German-American Contribution to Richmond's Development,* 89 ff.

147. Ibid., 92.

148. Niehaus, "Ethnic Formation and Transformation," 147.

149. Ibid., 148.

150. Kurt Vonnegut, Jr., *Palm Sunday: An Autobiographical Collage* (New York: Delacorte Press, 1981), 21.

151. Gerhard L. Weinberg, "From Confrontation to Cooperation: Germany and the United States, 1933–1949," in Trommler and McVeigh, eds., *America and the Germans,* 2:45–58. In fact, during the 1920s German-American relations improved steadily. Americans invested in the German economy and worked to reduce pressure of reparations to the detriment of France.

152. Frank Trommler, "The Rise and Fall of Americanism in Germany," in ibid., 2:332–42, quotations 332. Trommler quotes Georges Clemenceau, "America? That is the development from barbarity to decadence without the detour through culture," and Heinrich Heine, "Worldly utility is their true religion and money is their God, their one all-powerful God." European ambivalence toward America is found in the terms "Americanization" and "Americanism," popular from ca. 1900 through the 1920s.

153. Rippley, *German-Americans,* 196.

154. Ibid., 205.

155. Niehaus, "Ethnic Formation and Transformation," 161.

156. Ibid., 185.

157. Ibid., 187.

158. LaVern J. Rippley, "Ameliorated Americanization: The Effect of World War I on German-Americans in the 1920s," in Trommler and McVeigh, eds., *America and the Germans,* 2:217.

159. A review of the problems surrounding research in exile life is given in John M. Spalek, "Research on the Intellectual Migration to the United States after 1933: Still in Need of an Assessment," in ibid., 2:287 99.

160. Rippley, *German-Americans,* 217.

161. Norbert Krapf, ed., *Finding the Grain: Pioneer Journals, Franconian Folktales, Ancestral Poems* (Jasper, Ind.: Dubois County Historical Society, 1977) and *Somewhere in Southern Indiana: Poems of Midwestern Origins* (St. Louis: Time Being Books, 1993).

162. Lisa Kahn, ed., *Deutschschreibende Autoren in Nordamerika* (Freeman, S.Dak.: Pine Hill Press, 1990), 36–41.

163. The archives at IUPUI hold one of the best collections of German Americana in the Midwest.

164. E.g., the collection of German-American folktales, legends, and anecdotes in Reichmann, ed., *Hoosier German Tales.*

165. The Indiana Historical Society Library's collection is described in Paul Brockman, "Guide to the German Ethnic History Collection at the Indiana Historical Society," in *Studies in Indiana German-Americana,* 1:72–83.

166. Niehaus sees in the Strassenfest and DeutscherVerein of Jasper an inauthentic representation of the area's German heritage. It is a "movement that is clearly reactionary in that it fosters a sense of common identity when in fact the community is cross-cut by heavily divergent economic interests." Niehaus, "Ethnic Formation and Transformation," 216–17. She implies that it is exclusionary in that newcomers, primarily non-German stock people with different values, are not part of the group. However, she does allow that whereas formerly Catholics and Protestants in Dubois County did not socialize together, they now work and celebrate together in the DeutscherVerein and at the Strassenfest.

# GREEKS

CARL CAFOUROS

*It was natural for immigrants to desire their children to imitate them. Generally the immigrant generation was ethnocentric. They viewed Greek culture as superior, thus it was necessary to preserve it as long as possible wherever they settled. Their actions were also motivated out of fear. Immigrants did not understand American ways. They depended on their children for advice; if the children broke away the immigrants' security would disappear. The real danger in preserving Hellenism in Indiana, as elsewhere, came as the children matured into young adults.*

To understand why Greeks immigrated to the United States and to Indiana one must understand the circumstances that influenced them to leave their old countries. Greece and the other Balkan states developed differently than the countries of western and central Europe. The cultural and philosophical estrangement of eastern and western Europe began with the division of Christianity between the Orthodox and Roman Catholic communions in the eleventh century, and Islamic conquest completed the process. While the West was evolving out of the bondage of feudalism, the Balkan peninsula passed under Ottoman rule in the fifteenth century. The Turkish conquest isolated the Orthodox from western European scientific and economic developments. Due to Islamic conservatism and antagonism toward western Europe, the conquered Greek provinces regressed into underdeveloped agricultural backwaters, and only the Orthodox Church preserved Greek identity and culture during the period of domination. Due to Ottoman misrule, the Greeks did not develop industries and a middle class capable of economic and political administration similar to that of the developing western European nations.

Greek merchant princes of the diaspora instigated the Greek war of independence, although upon achieving independence the revolutionary leaders' attempts to form a stable government were fruitless. Great Britain, France, and Russia intervened, establishing the boundaries of the new state without regard to Greek ethnic considerations and financially sapping Greece with large loans. The philhellenic European powers suppressed the Byzantine aristocracy and placed the seventeen-year-old Bavarian Prince Otho on the throne. The new Greek kingdom was saddled with an inexperienced ruler and large loans that kept the country perpetually bankrupt.[1]

There was a continuity in governmental style despite the revolution. After independence the government did not redistribute the land to the peasants equitably, and Turkish landlords were replaced by wealthy Greek supporters of the king. The Greek peasants remained tenant farmers. Growing opposition to Otho resulted in his ouster in 1862. He was replaced by George I, a prince of Denmark. A liberal constitution was granted in 1864.

In the late nineteenth century the primary sources of discontent in Greece were the tax and political systems. Revenue collection was an archaic system. The tax burden on farmers averaged 10 percent of their annual crop. Contractors bid for the right to collect the taxes, and the highest bidders received the government contracts for tax collection. The tax system was regressive and abusive, encouraging ruthless collection practices in order to insure an adequate profit to the contract holders. The tax monies

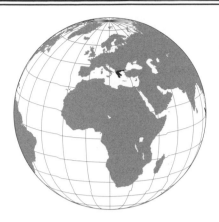

collected from the rural provinces were spent on internal improvements in the cities, while those scheduled for the agricultural areas were canceled.[2] Parliamentary deputies from rural provinces lacked knowledge of the peasants' problems because agricultural laborers as an occupational group held low status in Greek society.[3]

Greece in the late nineteenth century was a land of contrasts. It was a scenic land populated by approximately two and a half million people. The country's terrain was primarily mountainous, lacking mineral wealth in commercial quantities. The population was educated in and extremely proud of its Hellenic history and traditions. Despite its internal problems and economic weaknesses, the nation genuinely desired to resurrect itself into an economic and political power in the world. Independence revived Greek nationalism. The emerging intelligentsia desired to lead the nation on a crusade to re-create the Byzantine Empire. The chief foreign policy initiative of the Greek state was union of the "unredeemed" Greeks of Crete, the Aegean Islands, Macedonia, and other Greek-speaking provinces of the Ottoman Empire with the kingdom. Also important was industrialization of the country, which was aided by foreign capital. Essential to economic growth was completion of the transportation system; the largest projects undertaken were the Corinth canal and the railroad network. By western European standards the achievements were paltry, but in an underdeveloped country any improvement was significant.[4] The most significant transformation was the urbanization of the rural population in response to increased economic opportunities offered in the kingdom's cities. Also the desire for economic opportunity stimulated immigration to the United States.

The Greek economy remained agriculturally based, despite attempts at industrialization. In such a country agricultural tragedy stimulates immigration to foreign countries. Disaster struck the Greek farmers around 1890. The immediate cause of Greek immigration to the United States was the decline in the demand for currants. In 1863 French vineyards were ravaged by a disease that

killed the grapevines. The French wine industry placed large orders for Greek currants to continue their wine production. Given the increased demand, many Greek farmers speculated in the future of currants, chopping down their olive groves to create vineyards. By 1890 French vineyards recovered, and the demand for Greek grapes dropped dramatically. Economic depression beset the Greek agricultural community with the fall in the price of currants.[5] Faced with financial ruin, farmers sought economic opportunities elsewhere. Traditionally, Greeks migrated to other areas of the Balkans when faced with economic problems. Nationalism, mutual suspicions, and persecution between Greece, Bulgaria, and Romania stifled the usual destination of Greek immigrants. Consequently, Greeks began to immigrate to the United States and other countries.

Greeks were among the last Europeans to immigrate to the United States. Their immigration to America occurred on a small scale in the eighteenth and early nineteenth centuries. They settled New Smyrna, Florida, in the 1760s. Greek orphans were brought to this country by Congregationalist missionaries in the 1820s. The first Greek Orthodox church in the United States was founded in New Orleans in 1864 by Greek cotton merchants. Large-scale Greek immigration to the United States began in the 1890s and ended in the early 1920s. The peak years were between 1907 and the post–World War I years. Statistics concerning Greeks arriving in the United States are questionable. There are two primary reasons for the problem. Initially, the Greek government did not keep accurate figures on departures, especially during the early years, because the Greek government assumed the immigrants would return quickly to Greece. The other reason concerns interpretation of the concept of nationality. Ethnicity to Greeks is eternal; it cannot be changed or obliterated. If a person's father is Greek, then he or she is also Greek, despite place of birth or current residence. The American criterion of nationality was diametrically opposed to the Greek interpretation. The United States policy accepted the country of a man's birth as his nationality. While American authorities considered Greek ethnics emigrating from Turkey, Bulgaria, or Serbia as Turks, Bulgars, and Serbs, the Greek government claimed them as Greek citizens. According to American statistics, 186,204 Greeks immigrated to the United States between 1820 and 1910.[6] The Greeks claim twice that number as immigrants to this country. Despite these differing figures, approximately 95 percent of the Greeks entering the United States during the period 1899–1910 were males,[7] the vast majority being rural adolescents from the Peloponnesus region of Greece.

**Greece**
o National Capital
· City
— International Boundary

Miles   100

## The Pioneer Years

Once in this country Greek immigrants headed for every region of the United States, searching for employment and locations to establish businesses. Upon arrival, a Greek immigrant would go to the home of an established friend or relative from the same village back in the Old Country. The new immigrant brought messages from home and asked about available jobs. The host Greek would arrange either a position locally or suggest a better locale to find employment. The story of Frank B. Papatheofanis's immigration to this country and state is illustrative of many Greek immigrants' experience.

He was known affectionately as "Uncle Frank" by those who knew him personally. He was born in 1888 in Tripolis, which is in the Peloponnesus. Uncle Frank came to the United States in 1903 when he was fourteen years old, with the financial assistance of relatives in Wheeling, West Virginia. Once in Wheeling he went to work shining shoes for his sponsors. Many Greek immigrants began their new lives in this country as bootblacks. Young Greeks without funds who wanted to come to America would contact established Greeks from their home villages for sponsorship. The patron would advance money to pay transportation costs in exchange for the immigrant's labor. Uncle Frank worked for his sponsors until he repaid his debt. The patron provided food, shelter, and minimal monthly pay. The workers shared a common sleeping and eating room above their workplace. Uncle Frank received five dollars per month, half of which he sent to his mother in Greece to help his family. A bootblack's hours were long; Uncle Frank's workday began at 6:30 A.M. and continued until 11:00 P.M., seven days a week. The cost of a shoe shine was five cents. Uncle Frank worked nearly three years to repay his debt of seventeen dollars. He

shined shoes for the first two years and operated a shooting gallery during his third year. Eight months after Uncle Frank left Greece his brother Angellos immigrated. Angellos financed himself and traveled to Cleveland where he went to work as a bootblack for a Greek named Mavros. After settling his account in 1906 Uncle Frank left Wheeling to join his brother in Cleveland. The two brothers pooled their resources and began to explore opportunities elsewhere. In 1907 Angellos came to Indianapolis to survey the city. He liked the city and sent for Uncle Frank to join him. The brothers established two shoe shining parlors in downtown Indianapolis. They prospered and over the years diversified the shoe shining parlors by adding dry cleaning and other business interests. Uncle Frank ran his business, The Star Service Shop, for sixty-five years, retiring in 1972.[8]

The development of Greek communities around the country was a function of economics. The primary reason for emigration from Greece was a desire for economic advancement by impoverished rural Greeks from southern Greece. The average Greek immigrant to this country and state in those years was an adolescent male of peasant stock with little formal education. However, his ambition and persistence to be successful more than compensated for his apparent lack of skills. The United States was viewed by many Europeans as the land of opportunity where the streets were "paved with gold." Letters home and advertisements by ship lines helped maintain that stereotype and the flow of immigrants. The intent of most Greek immigrants was to come to the United States to become wealthy and return to Greece. Once in this country the immigrants generally preferred to live in cities due to the increased economic opportunities present there. Agricultural labor was disdained as most had experienced that lifestyle in the Old Country and few had the resources to enter into farming properly. The Greek communities of Indiana developed in this manner.

## The Greek Communities of Indiana

The Greek immigrants who resided in Indiana initially had no intention of remaining in the state or the country. The vast majority of the pioneer Greeks in Indiana were single males without family ties to the state, and their acculturation to American society took years to complete. Some actually returned to Greece upon achieving their financial goals.[9] Yet it was that group of seemingly uprooted individuals that transplanted the seed of Hellenism to Indiana. Wherever Greeks settled they attempted to restore their old lifestyles. Each Greek parish became a unique community, independent of each other, analogous to the city-states of ancient Greece.

In general the Greeks lived in close proximity to each other and their places of employment or business. They desired to live near friends and relatives for companionship and economic concerns. Immigrants could save money that otherwise would be spent for transportation by living close to their places of employment. When a sufficient number of Greeks settled in an area they established a *kinotitos,* a community council, to establish an Orthodox church. The *kinotitos* became the governing body of the Greeks in each city. The primary goal of such a council, after establishing a church, was the hiring of a priest and management of the communal properties.

Orthodoxy was a common link that bonded Greek immigrants to a community wherever they resided in the state. In the Old Country it was the religion of 99 percent of the population. The Holy Synod of Greece did not believe that immigrants to the United States would remain there permanently and did not provide an administrative structure for the parishes established in this country. Each community was autonomous.

The reason the Greeks retained Orthodoxy in America is simple to understand: in the United States Greek Orthodoxy was the badge of Hellenism. The Church served as the link that kept Greek immigrants attached to the motherland, nurtured their patriotic hopes, and preserved their faith and language in America. Since most of the Greek immigrants were adolescents or young adult men, absence from home and family made them more fervent in the retention of their faith and culture. Churches became the center of the Greek communities in this state and country. Social life of the immigrants revolved around the liturgical calendar of the Orthodox Church and Greek traditions; therefore church communities coalesced to meet the needs of their members. A community provided immigrants with a forum for comradeship, mutual aid, and shared cultural values.

In the 1920s the more established Greek businessmen in each community organized chapters of the American Hellenic Educational Progressive Association (AHEPA), a nationwide fraternity. The fraternity not only helped the Greeks learn about the United States and to forge business contacts, but also provided a forum for social activities beyond communal religious contacts.

With increased immigration Greeks established themselves in various Indiana cities. By 1912 Greeks resided in Anderson, Connersville, Elkhart, Evansville, Franklin, Gary, Hammond, Indiana Harbor, Kokomo, La Porte, South Bend, and Whiting.[10] The Indianapolis community hosted the largest group of Greeks in the state numbering 180 in 1908[11] and 249 by 1910.[12] Continued immigration led to further expansion. By 1923, in addition to the above cities, Greeks lived in

Alexandria, Auburn, Bloomington, Bluffton, Bushville, Columbus, Doubesville, East Chicago, Elwood, Fort Wayne, Frankfort, Huntington, Kendallville, Lafayette, Logansport, Muncie, New Castle, Peru, Richmond, Terre Haute, and Wabash.[13] Thus the general pattern of Greek settlement was concentrated in northern and central Indiana. While they settled in the various cities listed above, the majority of Greeks resided in Allen, Marion, Lake, and St. Joseph counties. In those counties the Greeks numbered enough to establish Hellenic Orthodox churches, which were and remain the center of Hellenism in Indiana.

## Indianapolis

According to the census reports in 1900, of the eighty-two Greeks residing in Indiana, twenty-nine lived in Indianapolis.[14] The city was a major rail center of the New York and Pennsylvania railroads, and most of the Greeks worked at the rail yards, although some were peddlers. The only Greek known to be self-employed was Peter Floros, who was a confectioner with a store at 45 West Washington Street.

Greeks did not dominate an area of Indianapolis by themselves. The various Orthodox Christian communions formed a Balkan neighborhood composed of Serbians, Romanians, Bulgarians, Macedonians, and Greeks on the near west side of Indianapolis around Military Park on West Street. The neighborhood was bounded roughly by Illinois Street on the east, White River on the west, Maryland Street on the south, and New York Street on the north. In the 1920s there were two other concentrations of Greeks in the city. A considerable number resided on the east side from the 1920s through the 1940s. That neighborhood was bounded by Fulton Street on the west, Randolph Street on the east, Michigan Street on the north, and Washington Street on the south. The focal point of the east side neighborhood was Highland Park. The main attraction was the park's hill, which the Greeks named Greek Hill. Affluent Greeks in the 1920s lived on the exclusive north side between 35th and 40th streets on North Illinois Street. John Zazas, the wealthiest Greek in town, built his mansion at 4356 North Meridian Street in the 1920s.

The Greek community of Indianapolis was composed of young men who had been raised in the various *epiarchies* (provinces) of the Peloponnesus, which were the regions most affected by the economic crisis in the 1890s. They were of poor peasant stock who came to the United States to better themselves and their families in Greece. While their educational levels varied, few of the immigrants had a complete course of schooling in Greece. Once in America and Indianapolis the Greeks suffered

IHS C100

*Pantelis L. Cafouros, ca. 1893.*

from their inability to communicate effectively. For that reason, many young Greeks were forced into low-paying jobs to earn their livelihoods since the proper use and knowledge of English were unnecessary.

In the fall of 1906 Pantelis Cafouros started a night school for Greeks to expand their knowledge of English. Cafouros, who was literate in Greek, German, French, Italian, Bulgarian, Turkish, and English, came to the United States in 1893. Being proficient in so many languages, he served as an interpreter at the local municipal courts for other immigrants. Cafouros found his idea of a school well received by the local Greeks. He rented a room on the fifth floor of the Magnolia Building, which was located on South Capitol Avenue. To aid the school the students constructed the classroom furniture. The first night of the class was held on 22 October 1906 with thirty students in attendance. Wishing to make the opening night an auspicious occasion, Cafouros asked Gov. J. Frank Hanly to make the inaugural address. As headwaiter of the Claypool Hotel, Cafouros had served Governor Hanly many times, and due to that relationship the governor agreed to come and address the members of the Greek night school. After a five-minute speech by

the governor, the class applauded and attempted to sing *America* for their esteemed guest. After that song they sang the Greek national anthem, the governor departed, and the lesson commenced.[15]

Peter Floros, one of the first Greeks to enter the United States, arrived at New York City in 1882. Floros learned the confectioner's trade in Chicago. He moved to Indianapolis and established a confectionery at 45 West Washington Street by 1900. Floros was also the first Greek to establish his own family in Indianapolis. The first two Greek children born and baptized in Indianapolis were his daughters. The baptism of his second daughter Anna was written up in the *Indianapolis News* on 2 February 1907. The article describes the Greek Orthodox sacrament of baptism in full detail. Greeks believe in infant baptism and full body immersion. The baptism was performed in Floros's home; the baptismal font was a regular tub.[16]

In early twentieth-century Greece the birth of a man's first son resulted in a celebration, with the jubilant father firing a twenty-one-gun salute to mark the arrival of another soldier against "those who oppressed Greece." James Cafouros, born on 25 August 1911, was the first Greek boy born in Indianapolis. Pantelis Cafouros wanted the whole city to take notice of the event, so he purchased one hundred dollars worth of fireworks and then received permission from police and city officials to fire the salute. At 8:30 P.M. that evening the show began from the roof of his restaurant, the Devil's Cafe. The fireworks display was reportedly the largest seen in the city up to that time, attracting the attention of thousands. At the conclusion of the last explosion Cafouros, surrounded by other Greeks, opened up his cafe and distributed cigars.[17] Cafouros also was the father of the second Greek boy born in the city. The birth of this son, George, was celebrated differently.

The Soldiers and Sailors Monument stands in the center of downtown Indianapolis. The city's landmark, its beauty was hidden at night by darkness. Comments by tourists and friends sparked Cafouros's next act. George was born on 28 April 1913. Thinking of the city's honor and to celebrate the birth of his son, Pantelis offered to donate five hundred dollars toward a fund to illuminate the monument. While expressing gratitude to him for his generous offer, the project was taken over by the state and city governments. The reason given was that private citizens should not sacrifice themselves financially for projects that governments should sponsor.[18]

Despite its small size, in 1900 the Greeks of Indianapolis formed a community council for the formation of an Orthodox church. An itinerant Greek priest and Pantelis Cafouros and William Laspazis spearheaded the effort to establish a Greek Orthodox church in Indianapolis.

*Pantelis L. Cafouros (left) owned the Paradise and Devil's Cafe, Indianapolis, ca. 1910.*

They rented a room on the third floor of a downtown bank, and the priest supported himself by working alongside other Greeks at the rail yards. Discouraged by the situation, the priest departed for the Old Country in 1903.[19] The first attempt to found a church was a failure.

The community council began its second church in 1905. Council members elected officers and hired Father Nicholas Velonis as pastor. The church occupied a rented room in another office building located at 27 South Meridian Street. Community dues were six dollars a year, and Father Velonis received a salary of fifty dollars per month.[20] The new parish was named Holy Trinity; the church was formally incorporated 29 January 1910. The management of the community's property and funds were placed under the control of eleven directors.[21]

As the community continued to grow the church facilities on Meridian Street proved inadequate. The search for a new location went on for several years, and in 1912 a plan to construct a church within the Greek neighborhood caused a factional split that resulted in nonconstruction. In 1914 the community purchased a two-story wooden house adjacent to the aborted construction site. The first floor of the house was converted into the sanctuary, and the priest lived on the upper floor. This second church was retained until 1919

when the Zenite Metal Company purchased the community's properties.[22] The proceeds of the sale were used to construct a brick church at 231 North West Street and to purchase a parsonage near the new church. This site served the community's need for the next forty years.

From the early 1900s through the 1960s Greek-owned businesses—dry cleaners, restaurants, florists, confectioners, bakeries, taverns, and billiard halls—thrived in downtown Indianapolis. One Greek owned a theater. Michael Harakas started his own hotel on West New York Street.

In 1960 the community constructed a new church at 4011 North Pennsylvania Street. In 1981 construction of the Cultural Center was completed. Since 1974 the community has sponsored its annual Greek Food Festival. The community is composed of six hundred families. The community of Holy Trinity includes the Greek Orthodox faithful of Indianapolis, Anderson, Muncie, Columbus, Bloomington, Terre Haute, Crawfordsville, Kokomo, and Lafayette.

## Old World Loyalties and the Schism

Greek immigrants remained patriotic to Greece as evidenced by their massive remigration to fight in the

Balkan Wars. Their progeny remain interested, generally speaking, about the welfare of Greece, as evidenced by their various relief efforts for Greece. Their interest and political influence was instrumental in establishing the American trade embargo against Turkey in the mid-1970s in the wake of the Turkish invasion of Cyprus. Indiana Congressman John Brademas, utilizing his unique talents, was a crucial leader in that process.

The Balkan peninsula has been referred to as the "tinder box" of Europe, and the Balkan Wars can be viewed as two of the more senseless conflicts in man's inhumanity to man. To the Greeks of Greece and the diaspora the wars were of tremendous significance as part of the "Great Idea," which was the campaign to recapture the glories of the Byzantine Empire. Greek ethnocentricism and patriotism were at fever pitch during the first quarter of the twentieth century, and the Balkan Wars were strategic moves intended to enhance Greek influence in the world. Inspired by Italian success against Turkey, Greece formed the Balkan League that declared war on and defeated the Ottoman Empire in 1912. By the Treaty of London, 30 May 1913, Turkey ceded its European provinces to the allies, except for Constantinople and parts of Thrace.

Within a year after the second Balkan War, World War I erupted in Europe. The Greeks divided into two factions: the Royalists, who promoted neutrality, and the Venizelists, who contended that Greece could best achieve its territorial aspirations by joining the Allies. The Venizelists, headed by Eleutherios Venizelos, led Greece into World War I on the side of the Allies. But despite Allied promises Greece did not obtain fulfillment of its territorial ambitions. After the war Greek Americans unsuccessfully attempted to influence American foreign policy in favor of Greek claims.

With the war over, the Royalists renewed their struggles against Venizelos. The elections of 1920 brought the Royalists to power and the return of King Constantine to the throne. Constantine failed to receive diplomatic recognition from the United States due largely to his opposition to the Allies in World War I. The king launched a war against Turkey that Greece lost, leading to his abdication in 1923. The Turks deported 1.5 million Greeks from Asia Minor to Greece.

Turkey's defeat of Greece had two effects on Greeks in the United States. Greek immigrants began to reassess their Old World loyalties. They withdrew from the arena of Greek politics, and their interest in Greek cultural affairs began to subside. Life and interest in American developments filled the void for the second generation. Given Greece's problems, America became accepted as their permanent new home throughout the decade of the 1920s. Also in the 1920s, the naturalization rate

among the Greeks of Indianapolis and elsewhere increased dramatically. By becoming United States citizens, Greek Americans eventually learned they would be able to help Greece more by staying in this country than by returning to the motherland.

The breakdown of concern for purely Greek affairs also resulted from the civil war in the Greek-Orthodox parishes in the United States. The scattered parishes in the United States were officially under the control of the Ecumenical Patriarchate of Constantinople until 1908 when authority shifted to the Holy Synod of Greece. The local church community in the United States remained a self-governing community, often, as in Indiana, incorporated by the state. Holy Trinity in Indianapolis, for example, annually elected eleven directors entrusted with overseeing the community's funds and properties. The most important piece of property belonging to any community was the church building itself. Every dues-paying member was a co-owner of the communal properties, and each member had a vested interest in the efficient operation of the church. Under such decentralized conditions the directors of Holy Trinity and the other parishes hired and discharged priests as they could any employee. Noting the lack of organization of the American parishes, the hierarchy of the Church of Greece set out to rectify the situation. It formed an archdiocese in the United States in 1918 under Alexander, Bishop of Rodostolou, a Venizelist. Upon the return to power in Greece of the Royalists in 1920, Bishop Alexander was refused funds, among other things. He responded by forming the Association of Canonical Hellenic Clergymen and refused to work with the Holy Synod of Greece. Alexander was then declared a schismatic. Bishop Germanos, a Royalist, came to the United States in 1922 to establish synodical control. The rivalry between Germanos and Alexander for control of this nation's Greek parishes heated up and provoked secession movements and court battles for control of church properties.

The Indianapolis Greek community kept abreast of homeland politics through locally distributed newspapers, the *Atlantis* and the *National Herald,* the former favoring the Royalists while the latter sided with the Venizelists. Old Country politics, in Indianapolis as elsewhere, was the immigrant's passion, and the Greeks of the capital city mirrored the struggle for religious control. The battle in Indianapolis would be long and bitter, pitting Venizelist rank and file against the largely Royalist board of directors. Being in the minority, and having no effective voice in governing the parish, the Venizelists withdrew from Holy Trinity in 1923 and formed Saint James Greek Orthodox Church at 45 South West Street, with Father Simon Mataxakis as pastor. The bitter separation sundered the community, and friends, who found themselves differing on the ideological aspects of the debate, would not speak to each other or socialize outside their factional circles. The Venizelists, however, always intended Saint James to be a temporary abode. The leaders intended to reenter Holy Trinity, and they filed a suit against their Royalist counterparts in Marion County Superior Court in the spring of 1923. The Venizelists, arguing that they were the true Holy Trinity representatives who had been deprived of trustee rights, won a stunning victory and were granted possession of the records, monies, and all properties belonging to Holy Trinity. Royalist court appeals fell short, and they vacated Holy Trinity in 1927, having lost a final case in the Indiana Supreme Court in 1929. The former Holy Trinity tenants shared a facility with Syrians at the Saint George Syrian Orthodox Church on North Sherman Drive, and from 1930 to 1933 worshiped at the Romanian Orthodox Church on West Market Street.

The schism split the Greek community and thus divided its limited financial resources between two churches. By 1928 Holy Trinity had $175 in its bank account and owed $3,000 on its mortgage. Despite financial help from Harry Alexander and Gregory Dale the collapse of the church was imminent, and in 1931 Railroadmen's Savings & Loan Association became the new property owner via an auction of Holy Trinity's properties.

The financial collapse of Holy Trinity was the lowest point in the history of the Greek community of Indianapolis. The Venizelists continued to hold church services at 231 North West Street, but the atmosphere was different. Instead of having full control over the properties, the Venizelists paid rent to an impersonal company in order to hold services in their own church. Though immediately calamitous, in the long run the foreclosure of the mortgage and the loss of proprietary rights proved beneficial. Historically the Greeks have worked together when adversity threatened them, and in this case it led to putting aside factional disputes for the common goal of restoring Holy Trinity to its rightful owners. To accomplish that end a new Holy Trinity corporation was formed on 31 March 1934 to buy back the church and its associated properties from Railroadmen's Savings & Loan Association.

With the formation of this new corporation, the Royalist-Venizelist controversy in Indianapolis came to an outwardly peaceful end. The Royalists resumed attendance for services at 231 North West Street with the Venizelists. The problem of funding the church gravitated into the hands of John Zazas. Though considered autocratic by some, Zazas nonetheless provided an efficient administration when the situation warranted it and, in effect, saved Holy Trinity and restored it to the whole Greek community. The final wounds of divisiveness healed during the 1940s.

On a national level the open schism came to an end when the prelates of the Holy Synod of Greece and the Ecumenical Patriarchate chose Athenagoras, Metropolitan of Corfu, to serve as Archbishop of North and South America. John Zazas was a member of the archdiocesan council. Administratively, financial matters and management remained the responsibility of the local communities, but the appointment and discharge of priests came under the jurisdiction of the new archbishop.

## Gary

The city of Gary was founded in 1906 as an industrial city. Greeks began to migrate there to seek their fortunes. As in Indianapolis, the early Greek immigrants in Gary formed a community council to meet their collective needs. The event that coalesced the Greek community to action to found their parish was the death in 1911 of the first Greek of the Gary community. The religious bond between the community dictated that his friends invoke the last rites in a Greek Orthodox church. The body was taken to Chicago for services, and it was then that serious discussion began for a Greek Orthodox church in Gary. The community was quite small, consisting of ten Greek families who held their first organizational meeting in the spring of 1912. The first worship services of the new church were held in 1913 in a rented store building at 1259 Madison Street. Priests from Chicago came to celebrate the Divine Liturgy. In 1915 the Gary congregation petitioned the Holy Synod to assign it a priest, and Father Nicholas Mandilas of Corfu, Greece, was assigned as the first permanent pastor.

The major concern of the new parish was expansion to meet the needs of a growing community since the rented store proved to be inadequate to house the church. Leaders of the community traveled to Indianapolis, South Bend, and Marion, Indiana, and to Cleveland and Toledo, Ohio, to ask financial help of other Greek communities in building a new church. Late in 1913 the Gary congregation laid plans to acquire a new church site.

In 1916 the community purchased a parcel of land at the intersection of 14th and Madison streets to build a church. At the same time some members of the congregation decided that a more appropriate place would be near other immigrant churches at 13th and Jackson streets. Leaders of the community loaned the parish $10,000, and the 13th Street property was purchased for $3,500. The loan was repaid in 1919, and the 14th Street property was sold the same year for $3,000. Groundbreaking for the new church occurred in 1917.

Disruptions in the local economy due to World War I delayed completion, forcing church services to be conducted in a tent on the property during the winter of 1918. The first service in the new church was held on Easter Sunday 1919, and the dedication service of Saint Constantine Church was held on 27 September 1919. According to existing records the dedication was the most pretentious celebration among foreign-born citizens ever held in Gary. The Hierarchical Divine Liturgy lasted over four hours. An estimated crowd of over four thousand persons attended the dedication, including the Greek consul of Chicago. Donations collected that day amounted to $3,000.

The Greek community of Gary numbered some three hundred persons in 1919. The new church cost $50,000 to build and an additional $25,000 to furnish. After 1924 the parish name was changed to Saints Constantine and Helen. The mortgage debt was repaid by 1942.

The growth of the Greek community in the Gary area was tremendous. In 1920 the community numbered 1,392. By 1930 the immigrant population of the parish was 3,344; the second generation numbered 730. By 1976 the size of the community equaled 7,000 persons.

In 1950 the church expanded by constructing a Hellenic Community Center at a cost of $150,000. In the late 1950s church leaders decided the time had come to move the church, and in 1961 a committee was authorized to search for a site to build another new church. In 1967 the community purchased thirty-seven and a half acres at 8000 Madison Street in Merrillville, Indiana, for $200,000.

The old church and the Hellenic Community Center were sold in 1971. Groundbreaking for the new Saints Constantine and Helen Greek Orthodox complex in Merrillville was on 20 September 1970. The Cultural Center and Great Hall were opened for church services in 1971. Construction on the new church began 18 August 1974. The new church was officially opened 21 December 1975 and designated a cathedral on 20 May 1976. The church serves about eleven hundred families. The size of the community was estimated at seven thousand in 1988.[23]

### East Chicago

The first known Greek to settle in East Chicago was Nicholas Mavronicholas, who arrived in 1904. His brother arrived the following year. The Rozzos brothers, Tony and George, arrived by 1907, the Dollas brothers arrived in 1908, and other immigrants followed in a small steady stream. Since their numbers were not large enough to establish a Greek Orthodox church, the religious needs of the community were met by attending services at neighboring Greek churches in Chicago or Gary, or by

*Consecration of Saints Constantine and Helen Greek Orthodox Church, 1971, Merrillville.*

seeking assistance of other Eastern Orthodox churches in the geographical area. In 1916 the community founded the Saint George Greek Society, whose purpose was to establish a Greek Orthodox church in East Chicago. The inconvenience of traveling to other Orthodox churches for religious services was undoubtedly burdensome to the Greeks of East Chicago. In response, the society rented a room at the Katherine House, a Baptist settlement house that opened in 1919, to hold their church services. Priests from Chicago conducted the Divine Liturgy on Sundays. Organizational difficulties plagued the society, and in 1921 it disbanded. Society funds were kept in escrow at the Union National Bank to assist future attempts to establish a parish. The second attempt to found a church began in 1927 when members of the Calumet Chapter No. 157 of the Order of AHEPA agreed to form the Plato School Organization. The goal of that organization was the establishment and maintenance of a Greek evening school. Greek parents wished to transmit their language to their children so that instruction in the Greek language would preserve Greek traditions, history, and the Greek Orthodox faith. The Saint George Society transferred its treasury to the new organization to stabilize it financially. In 1929 the

Greek population of East Chicago was large enough to support its own church, and in the fall of 1929 a consortium of East Chicago Greeks decided to incorporate as the St. George Greek Orthodox Community. Their application for a charter was granted 22 October 1929. John Contolukas was elected the first president of the community. The treasury was formed from donations by the board of trustees. A rented building at 3801 Euclid Avenue was the original site of the new church. The Bishop of Chicago appointed Father Thales Demetriades as the parish priest. In 1931 the Plato School Organization and the church corporation merged to form a new corporation known as the St. George Greek Orthodox Church and Plato School. The school funds were used to purchase land for the construction of a church. From 1929 through 1937 church services were held at the Euclid Avenue address.

On 25 April 1937 the community decided to build a new church. Construction began 5 October 1937, and the building was completed 17 December 1937. The first Divine Liturgy was held in the new church 17 April 1938. The mortgage was paid off 9 November 1942.

The Sunday School was founded in 1948. The aim of the program was to instruct the youth of the community in the teachings of the Greek Orthodox faith. Members of the congregation served as teachers and assistants throughout the years.

The Greek community experienced a dramatic increase in size in the 1950s, which caused the community to expand its facilities again. In 1954 land on Grand Boulevard was purchased with the idea of constructing a Hellenic community center. Construction of the six-hundred-seat hall was completed on 27 October 1957. The community's next project was the building of a parish home for the priest and his family. Construction began in 1965 and was completed two years later.

By the 1970s the Greeks of East Chicago began to move to the suburbs. That exodus planted the idea of relocating the church and community. In February 1977 the community decided to sell its properties in East Chicago and to relocate farther south in Lake County. Ultimately, the community purchased twelve acres of land in Schererville. The size of the community in 1979 was nearly one thousand persons.[24]

## Hammond

The first known Greek immigrant to settle in Hammond was James Bereolos. He arrived in Chicago in 1892 seeking a better economic life, and in 1896 he moved to Hammond. During the Spanish-American War he embarked upon his first business venture, a restaurant named the "Maine." He was joined by his brother Gust, and together they entered upon a series of business ventures.

In 1906 James Bereolos returned to his home village, married, and came back to Hammond with his wife Elpis. The following year their son Peter was the first of the second generation of Greeks born in Hammond. The Bereolos brothers were joined in Hammond by their cousins the four Brahos brothers, Peter, George, William, and Nicholas, by 1906. In 1908 George Brahos went to Greece and returned with his bride Mary. In 1909 their daughter Helen Brahos Senes was the first girl of Greek parentage born in Hammond.

The Greek community of Hammond grew dramatically during the years 1910–35. Many of the immigrants became entrepreneurs, entering service-type businesses. Sam Shufakis was exceptional among the early Greeks in Hammond. He became fluent in English and was active in the political and civic life of his adopted city. He was the first Greek to be elected to the Hammond City Council, serving from 1918 to 1921.[25] The spiritual needs of the community were met by traveling to the various established Greek churches in Chicago, Gary, and other neighboring communities. While the need for a local church was recognized, the development of it was hampered for years, primarily for economic reasons.

The establishment of Hammond Chapter #123 of the Order of AHEPA in 1926 catalyzed the local Greek community into organizing itself. The AHEPA chapter spearheaded the community effort to raise funds for the establishment and maintenance of a Greek Orthodox church in Hammond. On 24 October 1936 members of the AHEPA arranged a general assembly meeting of the Greek community to establish a local church. The general assembly decided to incorporate a not-for-profit organization to be known as the Greek Orthodox Center, Inc. Its purpose was to provide for the religious, social, and educational needs of its members. The organization's charter was issued on 19 November 1936, and it was amended in 1937 by changing the name of the corporation to Hellenic Orthodox Church, St. Demetrios, Inc.

On 8 November 1936, 110 men and women attended the organization's general assembly meeting. The AHEPA chapter donated 50 percent of its treasury for the establishment of a church. A parish council of eleven persons was elected. The council selected the following officers: Peter Brahos, president; John T. Pappas, vice president; Charles Tsatios, secretary; P. C. Primer, treasurer. Dues were set at one dollar per month.

On 19 November 1936 the organization's charter was issued, and the council approved a one-year lease of the Odd Fellows Hall, 617 State Street. Work proceeded to transform the rented space into a sanctuary. The council applied for recognition by the Greek archdiocese and for assignment of a priest. The first pastor was Rev. Nicholas Spelliotis. The first church service was held on 20 December 1936.

In January 1937 negotiations were begun for purchase of the State Street property, and by April the purchase was completed. The community assumed a mortgage of ten thousand dollars, which was paid off 27 July 1942.

After World War II the second generation began to assume the leadership duties of the community. On 27 July 1948 a lot at 7021–33 Hohman Avenue was purchased for $6,800. Plans for a new church and rectory were drafted, and construction of the facilities began in May 1951. The new church was consecrated in June 1958, and the mortgage was paid off in October 1958.

On 4 January 1959 the general assembly of the community approved plans for an "educational unit" addition to the church at an estimated cost of $140,000. Construction of the facility began 31 January 1960. It opened in October 1960, and the construction debt was retired. Additional properties adjacent to the church properties were purchased to provide additional space for expansion between the years 1965 and 1972.

On 24 October 1976 the parish celebrated its fortieth anniversary. More than five hundred parishioners of St. Demetrios gathered at Wicker Park to celebrate forty years of community progress.[26]

## South Bend

The first-generation Greek immigrants in South Bend and the Michiana area came from the village of Theologion, near Sparta, Greece. The first known Greek in the area was Thomas Sarantos who arrived in 1890. Six months later the Chaporis family arrived. The first Greek child, Stathoula Chaporis, was born on 21 May 1895. In 1901 Eustice Poledor moved to South Bend from Philadelphia where he had lived since 1896.

The Greek community continued to expand due to new immigration, intercommunity migration, and natural population growth. The early Greeks in South Bend, Elkhart, Goshen, and Mishawaka entered the local economic life generally as self-employed entrepreneurs. Their goal was financial independence. During the period 1926–50 approximately 125 businesses were owned and managed by Greeks. Generally, they engaged in service-oriented businesses such as restaurants, confectioneries, fruit stores, shoe shine parlors, dry cleaners, repair shops, billiard parlors, and liquor stores.

By the mid-1920s the Greek community in the Michiana area numbered some five hundred persons, so the size of the community was sufficient to maintain a Greek Orthodox church.

The South Bend Chapter #100 of the Order of AHEPA was established in April 1926. The chapter's creation was apparently the result of the Fort Wayne Greeks' establishment of an AHEPA chapter the previous year. The establishment of the AHEPA chapter and a vesper service by Bishop Philaretos Johanides of Chicago in 1926 catalyzed the local Greeks into establishing St. Andrew parish. Prior to forming the parish local Greeks attended services at St. Michael's Russian Orthodox Church or SS. Peter and Paul Serbian Orthodox Church.[27] The bishop appointed a building committee, and Eustice Poledor and family donated the site for construction. By March 1926 Bishop Johanides granted the community its petition to establish a church. Articles of incorporation were filed with the state of Indiana on 9 July 1926. Instead of building, the community decided to purchase St. Paul's German Evangelical Lutheran Church. Renovations were completed, and the first church services were held on 12 September 1926.[28] The church was consecrated in 1930.[29] The first pastor was Father Philotheos Mazokopakis, who served until 1936 when he was elected bishop and returned to Greece.[30] Under his pastorate the parish began an aggressive building program, including the construction of a Greek school, community hall, and chapel. This complex of buildings was to serve the community's educational, religious, cultural, and social activities for the next thirty years. The second priest, Father Arcadios Arcadion, served for the next fifteen years, and his main concern was the unity and welfare of the entire Michiana Greek community. During his pastorate St. Andrew parish included the Greeks living in La Porte, Michigan City, Mishawaka, Elkhart, Goshen, Warsaw, Fort Wayne, Peru, Logansport, and Rochester.[31]

During 1951–54 community activities centered on parish property expansion. Numerous building plans were discussed, and it was decided to relocate the church to new facilities. In April 1954 the parish made a purchase offer for Grace Methodist Church.[32] The offer was accepted, renovations were completed, and relocation to the new church was accomplished by the end of 1956.[33]

In 1976 the parish celebrated its golden anniversary. That same year it instituted its Grecian Festival. The festival and the Grecian Ball became fund-raisers for the parish. In 1978 plans for a new church were laid, fund-raising efforts were increased, and in 1982 plans were completed. Groundbreaking took place 3 April 1983; the church was officially opened 4 December 1983.[34]

St. Andrew Church has a pan-Orthodox congregation. Besides Greeks, the congregation is composed of converts and Orthodox Christians of Russian, Serbian, Egyptian, Syrian, and Armenian backgrounds.[35]

## Valparaiso

The youngest Greek Orthodox parish in the state is St. Iakovos in Valparaiso. In 1980 a group of Greek Americans in Porter County formed a social group called the Hellenic Friendship Circle. Dena Adams was the founder. During one of the circle's meetings the idea of establishing a local Greek Orthodox church was conceived. In August 1980 the first organizational meeting was held at Time Low Foods offices where plans were discussed to start a satellite church derived from Saints Constantine and Helen in Merrillville. A community council was formed by the Greeks residing in Porter County, and on 17 November Bishop Iakovos of Chicago met with the council in Valparaiso and presented the archdiocesan rules and regulations for establishing a church in the archdiocese. The bishop appointed an interim council, and dreams of a new church became reality.

The first Divine Liturgy of the new parish was held 4 January 1981 with 115 persons in attendance. In March 1981 the parish was incorporated under Indiana law adopting the name Greek Orthodox Church of Porter County. On 15 September 1981 Bishop Iakovos granted the new parish its charter. In December 1981 the parish council was sworn in by the bishop. He named the church St. Iakovos in October 1982. The parish consisted of 76 members.

On 26 June 1983 Father Chris Constantinides arrived as the first pastor. He increased parish membership to 125 pledging members. Besides the obvious spiritual needs of the community, the main objectives of the parish have been the renovation of the church and payment of its debt. In 1987 the interior decoration of the church was completed, as well as the installation of new carpeting and the refinishing of the pews. The parish conducted luncheons, festivals, rummage sales, and all sorts of fund-raisers since its inception to pay off its mortgage. All its efforts were successful; on 13 October 1987 the parishioners "burned the mortgage."

## Social Life

Many comments have been made about the clannishness of Greeks. Greek immigrants became urbanized because employment and business opportunities were in the cities. They chose to live in close proximity to one another for the comradeship of fellow countrymen

*Greek Independence Day celebration, Indianapolis, 1939.*

and for economics. Immigrants found their first homes in compact inner-city areas in quarters native Americans no longer inhabited. Middle-class and wealthy Americans were not willing to live in close proximity to factories and office buildings because of the blighting of older neighborhoods caused by industrial expansion in downtown areas. The simplest, most profitable use for a house so located was to subdivide it into apartments. The closeness of such housing to downtown areas meant that immigrants could save on transportation costs. Although the settlement patterns in each city were unique, various urban ghettos in the state's municipal areas developed in this manner.

During the early years Greek immigrant social life was small-scale and community based. Businessmen and workers had little time or capital to expend on entertainment. The social activities of pioneer Greeks set the pattern for various communities around the state. As the size of a community grew the magnitude of activities increased proportionately, for celebrations as such were communal in nature. Of the semisecular holidays, Greek Independence Day, 25 March, was the most important. In the larger communities of New York and Chicago parades commemorated the annual event. In the smaller communities it was celebrated by church services and private merrymaking.

The main celebrations during the pioneer years revolved about the feasts of the Church and other Orthodox religious observances. The main periods of fasting were the Christmas Fast, the Great (Lenten) Fast, and the first two weeks of August in preparation of the dormition of the Theotokos (Assumption of the Blessed Virgin Mary). The Great Fast covers forty-eight days of Lent, and the rules of fasting are severe. During fasting periods Orthodox Christians abstain from eating meats, eggs, and dairy products. In addition to the major fasting periods, observant Orthodox fast every Wednesday and Friday throughout the year. Of the various religious holidays, Holy Week and Pascha celebrations remain solemn and joyous. The Resurrection service of the Orthodox Church is quite impressive.

The most widespread celebrations were Name Day parties, Saint Basil Day (New Year's Day), and weddings. When an Orthodox child was born his or her name was chosen from lists of the saints of the Church or Old Testament luminaries. Instead of celebrating a person's actual date of birth, the Greeks commemorated that event on the feast day of the individual's patron saint. A typical celebration would be an open party at the celebrant's home. Guests would make the rounds of the persons celebrating a particular day; Saint Basil's Day was celebrated on the eve of the day. Individuals would have

parties at their homes or businesses, and the parties consisted of games of chance and cutting the Vasilopita, a round loaf of sweet bread containing a gold coin. The person who received the piece of bread containing the coin was supposed to be extremely lucky for the coming year. Another indicator of good fortune for the coming year was gauged by success at the card table. If a person won substantially at cards the winner would usually expand his business, as *Tyche* (i.e., luck) smiled on him. The losers would be more conservative in the new year. Such gambling began on Saint Basil's Eve and continued throughout the evening.

Since foreigners were viewed with disdain and Greeks preferred to associate with other Greeks, social contact between Greeks and native Hoosiers was infrequent during those years. To most Americans Greeks possessed an incomprehensible language and strange religious practices, which seemed out of place in the United States. Greeks felt more comfortable within their individual communities due to the language barrier. Thus immigrant Greeks attempted to translate Greek society to their new environment. Greek culture and language was transmitted to the second generation through intentional isolation.

The second generation lived in two worlds: the Greek world of their parents and friends and the world of their American friends. Greeks were determined to preserve their culture in Indiana and in the United States. The immigrant generation in Indiana and elsewhere was under pressure by the church hierarchy and their own consciences to preserve Hellenism in the state and the country. The primary worry was that if their children were illiterate in the Greek language, then Greek culture and faith would not survive. The language question was vital to the immigrants in a practical sense. Immigrant parents depended upon their children as translators as necessity dictated. The main problem for members of the second generation came when they started school. Generally the second generation Greek-American children were unable to speak English when they reached school age. In the nativist, conformist era following World War I teachers and fellow students put indirect pressure on Greek and other foreign students fluent in foreign languages to discard their native tongues as useless baggage in the melting pot of America. The effect of public ridicule was to repress the open use of the native tongue, and Greeks acculturated themselves to the situation. They spoke Greek among themselves, but in public they conversed in English.

To accomplish the goal of educating its children, each Greek community in the state established its "Greek school." Such schools were at various levels of professionalism. Classes were held for several hours per meeting after regular school concluded. Teachers were recruited from among the congregation of the church, while wealthier Greeks hired tutors to instruct their children. Curricula included Greek grammar, poetry, philosophy, and history. On Greek Independence Day students presented a program for their community demonstrating their mastery of their lessons by reciting in Greek.

Greek children in Indiana and the country were exposed to the realities of life at an early age. Their free time was minimal. Parents wanted their children close to them to help around the house or family store. Greek family life was close-knit, loving, and patriarchal. Sons were expected to help their fathers because it was their duty. If the parents owned a business, it was assumed the son would eventually take it over from the parents. At the same time Greek parents urged their children "to be someone" better than their parents through higher education. The professions of law and medicine were highly esteemed by the immigrant generation and were impressed upon their children as goals to pursue. Academic excellence was prized along with athletic accomplishment. The second generation was exposed to Americans on a different level than their parents. In attempting to achieve their goals, second-generation Greeks moved beyond the self-imposed isolation of their parents' Greek-only social world.

Such development was the central paradox of the Greek-American experience throughout the United States. The immigrant generation wanted their children to be educated and upwardly mobile in society yet still retain their Greek heritage. Changes were inevitable. The second generation was exposed to a world unknown to their parents, and they generally wanted to be accepted by their American peers.

It was natural for immigrants to desire their children to imitate them. Generally the immigrant generation was ethnocentric. They viewed Greek culture as superior, thus it was necessary to preserve it as long as possible wherever they settled. Their actions were also motivated out of fear. Immigrants did not understand American ways. They depended on their children for advice; if the children broke away the immigrants' security would disappear. The real danger in preserving Hellenism in Indiana, as elsewhere, came as the children matured into young adults.

The principal generational conflict involved the desire of second-generation youth for a social life and dating. Such activities were discouraged by immigrant parents unless they had a hand in arranging matches for their children. The idea of dating was problematic. Traditionalists put emphasis on arranged marriages with other Greeks, which caused a great deal of conflict among the young of every community. The pressure on daughters was greater than on sons. Parents of girls thought they were helping their daughters because arranged affairs were the only socially acceptable way for daughters to find a husband. Parents made the arrangements and then informed their daughter of their decision. Conventional Greek wisdom held that marriage came first, and love would develop later in the relationship. Not wanting to be dominated or in defiance of parental interference, a young Greek woman might choose a non-Greek as a boyfriend. The young women wanted to marry men they loved. Ethnicity was unimportant in such matters. The immigrant generation did not agree with such ideas, fearing that intermarriage would destroy Greek culture in the state and nation.

A serious relationship with a non-Greek was socially unacceptable. The problem was complex and caused anxiety for many young Greek-American women. A Greek girl was not free to date a Greek boy without her parents' approval, and if she had a relationship with a non-Greek she faced possible ostracism by the community. Gradually the stigma attached to intermarriage faded into insignificance. The majority of the second generation remained loyal to the Orthodox Church, proving their parents' fears of intermarriage to be groundless.

Another problem confronted by the second generation was that of the Greek liturgical language. The second generation had been taught to speak, read, and write demotic Greek at home and at school. The Divine Liturgy was composed and chanted in Byzantine (i.e., medieval) Greek. Those who were fluent in Greek could follow the services completely, while those who were not proficient in Greek were at a distinct disadvantage. Sermons also were preached in Greek. Sexes were segregated during the services; the men occupied the right side of the church while the women stood on the left. After World War II such segregation was discarded. The liturgy is celebrated bilingually today.

The Greeks immigrated to the United States during a period of economic depression, overseas expansionism, and national self-doubt. The wave of immigrants arriving in the United States after the Civil War is referred to as the New Immigration. Its distinguishing characteristic was the origin of the immigrants. The "new" immigrants emigrated from eastern and southern Europe. This change in immigration patterns would stimulate eugenicist treatises, urging immigration restriction and culminating in the National Origins Acts. American nativism and xenophobia culminated in the drive for 100 percent Americanism and a resurgence of the Ku Klux Klan, which was particularly strong in Indiana. While some ethnic groups were targeted by nativist groups in Indiana, available evidence indicates that the Greeks were not harassed. The reasons for such tolerance was multifaceted.

*Modeling of a nineteenth-century Greek court dress, 1961
International Fashion Revue, Gary.*

The number of Greeks was miniscule compared to the total population of the state. Greeks acculturated themselves to the American way of life: they were conservative, industrious, and entrepreneurial. Certain Greeks anglicized their names to remove the possibility of prejudice. In Marion County the Greeks had a considerable business presence in the city. A lieutenant of Klan leader D. C. Stephenson was impressed by the business acumen and ambition of the local Greeks, which undoubtedly shielded them from outward forms of violence.[36] Lake and St. Joseph counties were not controlled by the Klan. The main prejudices against the Greeks manifested themselves in linguistic humor when Greek was spoken in public and in Greeks' exclusion from social clubs.

Given the general nonacceptance of immigrant Greeks in social clubs along with their own prejudices, Greeks formed their own social clubs. Where the concentration of Greeks from a particular province in the Old Country was numerous a club organized on that premise would be established. In Indianapolis there was no evidence that such a club developed. However, in Lake County such provincial clubs were established. The two national Greek

immigrant fraternities that arose in the 1920s were the American Hellenic Educational Progressive Association and the Greek American Progressive Association. Both fraternities were attempts by Greeks in Indiana and the country as a whole to adapt to life in this country. The key to understanding the philosophy of each is contained in the first word of its official name. The American Hellenic Educational Progressive Association, referred to as AHEPA, placed its emphasis in acculturating Greeks to American society and stressed loyalty, the use of English, and naturalization. The AHEPA was founded in 1922 in Atlanta, Georgia, in response to antiforeign activities of the Klan. The organization spread rapidly among Greek communities. In Indiana, AHEPA chapters were established in Hammond, East Chicago, Gary, South Bend, Fort Wayne, Anderson, Muncie, and Kokomo. The Indianapolis chapter began in 1929. The organization is still vital with its emphasis today on philanthropic issues, and it has been referred to as the "right arm of the Church." The Greek American Progressive Association, better known as GAPA, was formed in reaction to the conformist platform sponsored by AHEPA. There was a GAPA chapter in Indianapolis, but it ceased operations fifty years ago. There is an active chapter of GAPA in Lake County. Besides the political agendas of such clubs, they sponsored community entertainment that supplemented the activities of the parishes. They also were an avenue for Greeks from around the state to socialize with each other at the annual state lodge conventions. The AHEPA developed auxiliary clubs for the spouses and minor children of members and was instrumental in aiding Greece during World War II and the Cold War years.[37]

## Epilogue

Today, for subsequent generations of Greek Americans in Indiana and the United States, social life is not as restricted as was experienced by the immigrant generation. There are several reasons for this development. First, the second generation acculturated to American society, given its greater exposure to it. Secondly, American public opinion toward the Greeks changed dramatically in 1940. In October of that year Greece refused to capitulate to the Axis. The Greeks repulsed the Italian invasion of their country and went on the offensive in Albania. Their victories were heartening to the Allies, as there had been few Allied victories in the war to that time. In the end Greece was defeated by the German army. As a result of the war Greeks were viewed sympathetically by Americans, and Greek Americans took pride in being Greek. Also, American society became more liberal and appreciative of its diverse population base. The civil rights movement of the 1960s stimulated a revitalized ethnicity in the United States. The xenophobic concept of America as a melting pot was replaced by tolerance and genuine interest, resulting in what the author terms the "beef stew" concept of American ethnicity. By the mid-1970s the process of philosophical change was completed. Greek communities around the state began to sponsor annual festivals, which help introduce Greek language, art, traditions, and the Orthodox faith to society as a whole.

It has been one century since the Greeks immigrated in large numbers to the United States, and in that time, despite the fear of the immigrant generation, Hellenism is alive in Indiana.

## Notes

1. Lewis Sergeant, *Greece in the Nineteenth Century: A Record of Hellenic Emancipation and Progress, 1821–1897* (London: T. F. Unwin, 1897), 212–13. Otho is characterized as "absolutely ignorant of kingcraft, utterly incompetent to govern, incapable of nothing but the indefinite increase of the national debt and escorted by an army of hungry Bavarians."

2. Percy F. Martin, *Greece of the Twentieth Century* (London: T. F. Unwin, 1913), 127–29.

3. Theodore Saloutos, *The Greeks in the United States* (1964; reprint, Cambridge, Mass.: Harvard University Press, 1975), 7.

4. Ibid., 1–3.

5. V. Gabrieldes, "The Overproduction of Greek Currants," *Economic Journal* 5 (June 1895): 285–88.

6. Senate Document No. 756, 61st Cong., 3d sess., in Reports of the Immigration Commission, *Statistical Review of Immigration, 1820–1910* (Washington, D.C.: Government Printing Office, 1911), 13.

7. Ibid., 47.

8. Interview with Frank B. Pappas, Indianapolis, Ind., 4 Sept. 1978.

9. See Theodore Saloutos, *They Remember America: The Story of the Repatriated Greek-Americans* (Berkeley: University of California Press, 1956). The book is rare as it has been out of print since the 1950s.

10. George N. Helmis, *Greek-American Guide for 1912* (New York: The Helmis Press, 1912), 342.

11. Spyro A. Kotakis, *E Ellenes en Ameriki* (Chicago: Spyro A. Kotakis Publishing Co., 1908), 190.

12. Carl Cafouros, "The Community of Indianapolis: A Microcosm of the Greek Immigrant Experience" (Master's thesis, University of Illinois at Urbana-Champaign, 1980), 19.

13. Nick Nickolson, *Greek Directory of 1923* (Chicago: Greek Directory Publishing Co., 1923), 311–53.

14. United States Department of the Interior, United States Census Office, *Twelfth Census of the United States, 1900* (Washington, D.C., 1901), 1:733, 748, 797.

15. *Indianapolis News,* 23 Oct. 1906.

16. Ibid., 2 Feb. 1907.

17. *Indianapolis Star,* 26 Aug. 1911.

18. Ibid., 30 Apr. 1913.

19. Cafouros, "The Community of Indianapolis," 11.

20. Ibid., 12.

21. Ibid., 18.

22. Ibid., 19.

23. Millie Melton, *75 Years 1913–1988 Album* (Gary, Ind.: SS. Constantine & Helen Greek Orthodox Cathedral, 1988), 20–22.

24. Anthony Kanavos, "History of St. George 'Hellenic' Greek Orthodox Church, 1929–1979" (Unpublished private report, 1979).

25. Spiro J. Senes, "A Fifty Year History of the Hammond Greek-American Community" (Unpublished private report, 1986), 5.

26. Ibid., 6–15.

27. Milton Kouroubetis, *The Greeks of Michiana: A Microcosm of the Greek Experience in America* (South Bend, Ind.: Northern Indiana Historical Society, 1987).

28. Ibid., 137–39.

29. Ibid., 156–60.

30. Ibid., 161–69.

31. Ibid., 162, 171–73.

32. Ibid., 185.

33. Ibid., 189–93.

34. Ibid., 219–20.

35. Ibid., 218.

36. Pappas interview.

37. For more information on the history of the AHEPA see Saloutos, *Greeks in the United States.*

# HISPANICS

SAMUEL SHAPIRO

In many ways the experiences of the Mexican workers in East Chicago, Gary, and Hammond, the industrial cities of the Calumet, were not unlike those of the southern and eastern European immigrants who had preceded them. They got the dirtiest, most difficult, and most dangerous jobs in the mills and the oil refineries.

## Beginnings

### ....The Saga of Our Parents
Valentin Martinez

> We fled from our country, Mexico
> From civil disorder and anarchy
> From lack of work and opportunity,
> To save our children from calamity.

(First stanza of a *corrido* [ballad] printed in *Mexican American Harbor Lights*, 1992, p. 11. Later stanzas are printed at the head of each section of this essay.)

*S*in Indios, no hay Indias (Without Indian laborers, there are no Indies). This proverb sums up a basic fact about the Spanish Empire in the Americas—its dependence on dense Indian populations that could be put to work for the benefit of the conquistadores. And it helps explain why there was no large-scale Hispanic migration to Indiana until the second decade of the twentieth century, long after the collapse of the Spanish

Empire in America. Central Mexico, the site of the Aztec Empire, and Peru and Bolivia, the realm of the Inca, became the first and most important viceroyalties of the Spanish Empire. What is now Indiana, like most of the rest of the present-day United States, was of little interest to Spain. The Ottawa, Potawatomi, Shawnee, and Miami of this far northern area, few in number and living on a simple hunter-gatherer level, could not have provided the rich tribute that Cortés, Pizarro, and their followers found in Mexico City and Cuzco. In the sixteenth century only about four thousand Native Americans lived in the Calumet swamps along the southern shore of Lake Michigan that was to become the center of Hispanic migration to Indiana in the twentieth century.[1]

Spanish explorers of the sixteenth century did in fact probe *el norte* to see if they could find another rich Tenochtitlán (Mexico City) there. Francisco Vásquez de Coronado and his chosen thirty got as far as Lindsborg, Kansas, in 1542 and spent a month examining the area. But there were no Seven Cities of Cíbola, no gold, and no Indian civilization worth plundering. The Spaniards admired the landscape and saw its potential agricultural wealth, but it was not what they were looking for. They turned southwest and went back in disgust.[2] Thus they left immensely valuable wheat lands to be fought over ("Bloody Kansas") more than three centuries later. As late as 1700 what is now the American Southwest was still *tierra despoblada* (empty acres).[3]

As is well known, the first European explorers of the Hoosier state were French. Père Jacques Marquette and Louis Jolliet passed through the state, and René Robert Cavalier de La Salle made a treaty with the Native Americans of the South Bend area in 1679 under the Council Oak.[4] Explorers, missionaries, coureurs de bois, and soldiers threw a thin veil of settlements over vast parts of North America and tried to establish an empire for the Bourbon kings of France along the St. Lawrence, the

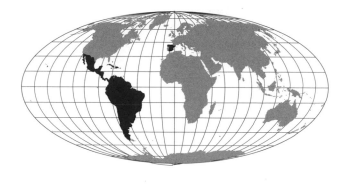

Great Lakes, and the Mississippi. But their valiant efforts, in a second Hundred Years' War, were in vain. The French left many names on the land—Vincennes, Detroit, La Porte, Terre Haute, Terre Coupee, and much fascinating history—but English language, government, and culture were to be dominant in the Hoosier state.

Even during the nineteenth century, as agriculture and industry boomed and tens of thousands of immigrants from more than fifty foreign nations came to Indiana, only a handful of the Spanish speaking arrived. Under the dictatorship of Porfirio Díaz, the longest in the history of the Western Hemisphere (1877–80, 1884–1911), many Mexican peasants were not free to leave, being tied to the land by a system of debt peonage. In Indianapolis, the state capital and largest city, no Hispanic name was recorded by the census until 1870, although Hispanics may have lived there between censuses.[5] A handful of exiles and a number of men seeking work crossed into the United States in the 1890s, but almost all of them remained in the border states of California, Arizona, New Mexico, and Texas. The census of 1910, taken at the very end of the *Porfiriato* and the beginning of mass migration to the North, showed only 162,000 Mexican-born residents in the United States.[6]

Even East Chicago, which was to become and remain the most Hispanic city in the Hoosier state, had only a handful of Mexican Americans before the First World War. Magdaleno Castillo, a resident-to-be, served in the Spanish-American War. The memorial volume *Mexican American Harbor Lights* lists only two Mexican Americans arriving in East Chicago in 1910, one in 1911, three in 1912, none in 1913, and two in 1914.[7] A relative deluge came later, seventeen in 1918, twenty-five in 1919, and thirty-two in 1920. Manuel Lara, the first known Mexican to settle in Gary, arrived in 1911, "worked in the tin mill, got married, served in World War I, and became a respected member of the community."[8] Later arrivals, because they were imported as strikebreakers and came in such large numbers, were not so easily assimilated.

## World War I

Filled with sorrow and distress,
We said goodbye and ventured forth
On the long and arduous journey,
To the Colossus of the North.

During the last quarter of the nineteenth century, Lake County, where nearly one of every two Hoosier Hispanics (44,526 of 98,788—45 percent) still lives, became one of the most industrialized areas in the world. The once useless marshlands along the southwest shore of Lake Michigan, shunned for so long by Native Americans and Europeans alike, suddenly revealed their potential to the entrepreneurs of the Gilded Age. Since before the Civil War a dense network of railroads easily and cheaply delivered to the Calumet coal from a dozen midwestern fields, ore boats brought the remarkably rich iron ore from the Mesabi Range on the shores of Lake Superior to deep water ports on the Indiana shoreline, and both carried away finished steel products. Nearby steel-consuming cities such as Chicago, South Bend, Detroit, Cleveland, Toledo, Milwaukee, and Indianapolis clamored for steel rails, bridges, structural steel for buildings, sewing machines, bicycles, and, soon, automobiles. And immigrants from all over Europe, fleeing from economic distress or political and religious persecution, found cheap passage across the Atlantic on ships that had brought bulky American exports—steel, wheat, lumber, cotton—to Europe. In its first census in 1910 Gary, founded by the United States Steel Corporation in 1906, had 4,480 native whites (27 percent), 8,242 foreign-born whites (49 percent), and 3,681 native whites of foreign or mixed parentage (22 percent), but too few Mexicans to enumerate separately.[9]

One of the smaller side effects of that gigantic upheaval, the First World War, was that it brought substantial numbers of Mexicans to the Hoosier state. Steel production, already booming and vastly profitable before the war, reached new heights of production and profitability. (In 1916–17, US Steel had total profits of $888 million.)[10] But the tens of thousands of Czechs, Slovaks, Hungarians, Serbs, Croats, Greeks, Poles, Romanians, etc., who made up the labor force in steel, the railroads, meat packing, and other industries, could no longer be augmented by additional immigration.

One solution was to bring in native whites from depressed areas of the Appalachians and the Ozarks. Another was to recruit southern blacks, who were anxious for the better economic opportunities and

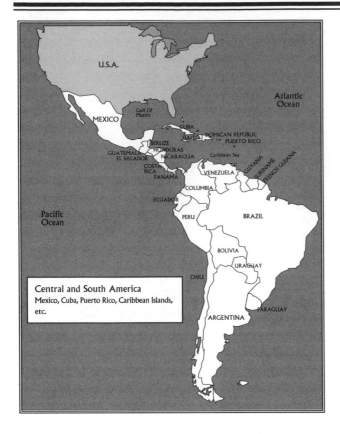

Central and South America
Mexico, Cuba, Puerto Rico, Caribbean Islands, etc.

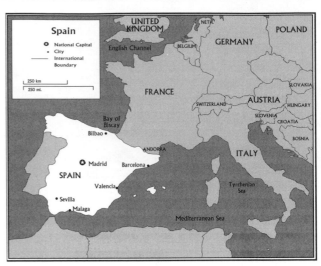

the relative freedom of the North. In 1910 Gary had only 383 black residents; ten years later there were 5,299.[11]

## The Steel Strike of 1919

For we had a glorious dream
A dream, a dream of tomorrow,
That our children would have,
A better, nobler life than ours.

Last to arrive were the Mexicans and Mexican Americans. During the war the federal government had enforced an uneasy truce in the essential steel mills; steelworkers were portrayed as patriotic industrial heroes even as inflation eroded their tragically low wages.[12] With the war over, steel industry leaders were determined to retain the twelve-hour day, the seven-day, eighty-four-hour workweek, and wages that the Interchurch World Movement found to be "below healthful existence." US Steel chairman Judge Elbert H. Gary, with 228,000 men on his payroll in 1914, insisted that "the workmen prefer the longer hours. . . . The workmen themselves are unwilling to have the hours of labor decreased." In 1917 Big Steel (U.S. Steel) had net profits of $253 million while steel wages were less than five dollars a day.[13]

After a preliminary organizing drive, John Fitzpatrick, president of the Chicago Federation of Labor, and William

Z. Foster, a former member of the International Workers of the World, called a strike to begin on 22 September 1919. At the end of a week, 365,000 steelworkers were on strike, 90,000 of them from the Chicago district that included northern Indiana. In East Chicago 7,000 men joined the strike, leaving only 200 workers in four of the nineteen mills.[14]

The steel company leaders, who had shown their determination and ruthlessness in crushing the Homestead Strike in 1892 (five months) and other steel strikes in 1901 and 1909 (fourteen months), used every weapon in their arsenal to reassert control of the rebellious labor force.[15] Pickets and union organizers were beaten up and blacklisted, and newspapers denounced the conservative union as "a hot bed of anarchy" and a red anarchist element. Strikers were arrested and released only if they promised to return to work. Even priests and ministers urged the men to return to the mills.

Hundreds of businessmen belonging to the Loyal American League were deputized, armed, and sent out to patrol the streets, and the state militia was sent to Gary and East Chicago. As the strike went into its second week, fifteen hundred federal troops under Gen. Leonard Wood were sent into northwestern Indiana from Chicago's Camp Sheridan. The troops, quartered on steel company property (as if to show whose side they were on), set up a stockade and arrested hundreds of pickets and demonstrators.[16]

Still the strike went on. The steel companies noted that their black laborers, 10 percent of the work force at Big Steel, economically more desperate and separated from white workers by racism, did not join the strike; therefore, more blacks were recruited by the steel companies. The companies noted also that the strike ballot had been printed in English, Hungarian, Italian, Czech, and Slovak but not in Spanish since there were only a few Mexican steelworkers. The industry's own GO BACK TO WORK leaflets were also printed in seven languages but not in Spanish.

Recruiters in the appropriate places were notified and substantial numbers of Mexicans were brought in as strikebreakers. The widow of Ignacio Maravilla recalls how her husband and his brother Candido were recruited (*renganchado*) by the Inland Steel Company and brought into the plant by boat from Chicago because the pickets were blocking the entrance to the mill. All but one of the Mexicans listed as arriving in Indiana Harbor that year came from deep inside Mexico: one each from Zacatecas and Nuevo León, four from Michoacán, five from Guanajuato, six from Jalisco, seven from Mexico City, and one from Texas.[17] One out of three married men left their wives behind since they were not certain whether they would return to Mexico themselves or bring their families to Indiana later on. Six of ten were under thirty years of age, nine of ten were under forty. They were a splendid reserve army of labor, in the most productive years of their lives, unencumbered with dependents, which made housing them easier and schools unnecessary, and uninformed about the strike they were being used to break.[18] Inland Steel brought in forty to fifty Mexican strikebreakers every day, most of whom eventually went back to Mexico or did not survive.[19]

Within a few weeks the strike was seen to have failed; it was officially called off after three months on 8 January 1920.[20] The steel barons had skillfully used the tactics of divide and rule, setting blacks and Mexicans against European immigrants just as Hernán Cortés had used Tlaxcalan allies to defeat the Aztecs of Tenochtitlán in 1521. The steel companies left the Calumet a legacy of ethnic hatred, and they held back decent wages and working conditions in the industry for a generation.[21]

Although most of the Mexican workers had limited skills, were illiterate, and could speak only rudimentary English, Inland Steel found them to be excellent laborers. The steel mills no longer required the highly skilled workers of earlier years; a small group of trained men could run a blast furnace, a Bessemer converter, or a blooming, plate, rail, or bar mill. Common laborers could do most of the work, and at the standard pay of forty-two cents an hour. The craftsmen of the Amalgamated Association of Iron, Steel, and Tin Makers reached their high point of twenty-four thousand members in 1891, but that figure was only 5 percent of the half million steelworkers of 1919.[22] Mexicans did not organize or complain about low wages because in rural Mexico pay on a hacienda was sixteen cents a day; in Jalisco, from which place so many came to the Hoosier state, the pay was only thirteen cents and a few tortillas. Nor did they complain about poor housing, although many of them lived in Indiana in flimsy tenements "so overcrowded, so filthy, and so filled with vermin that they are worse than hog wallows."[23] Back home most of them lived in barns, shacks, abandoned warehouses, or huts made out of straw.

Few Mexicans in the 1920s made the troublesome, expensive, and even dangerous decision to become American citizens—less than 6 percent of the foreign born according to the 1930 census.[24] Unable to vote or to organize a union, they would be no menace to businesses' control of the Calumet cities. In boom times more Mexicans could be brought up to fight the union and keep down wage demands. And in the economic crises that were characteristic of capitalism in general and of the steel business in particular they could be sent back where they came from. During the short, sharp recession of 1921, when Inland's output dropped 400,000 tons, half the company's Mexicans were laid off; in that year 9,000 Mexicans entered the United States and 106,000 returned to Mexico.[25] Here was a businessman's dream of a reserve labor force that could be turned on and off like a faucet.

## The 1920s

> We crossed the border,
> Apprehensive, but with hope
> Forebodingly, to a distant land,
> And to an unknown tongue.

"I see countless toilers in factory, mill, and shop—bare-bodied men who move like specters amid the heat and glow of furnace and forge, of molten streams of metal and red-hot, yielding, lapping sheets of steel—and heaving wharfmen loading cargoes on far-extending piers." (Gov. J. Frank Hanly, in his speech at the first banquet of the Gary Commercial Club, at the Gary Hotel, 25 November 1907.)[26]

In many ways the experiences of the Mexican workers in East Chicago, Gary, and Hammond, the industrial cities of the Calumet, were not unlike those of the southern and eastern European immigrants who had preceded them. They got the dirtiest, most difficult, and most dangerous jobs in the mills and the oil refineries. After plutonium and dioxin, gasoline and molten steel are among the most dangerous materials in the world. In 1917, for example, in an all too common kind of accident, thirteen laborers cleaning out a pit were incinerated by a river of liquid steel.[27] Abraham Olivo's grandfather lost a leg when a steel beam fell on it.[28] In a typical mill, almost one of four immigrants—3,273 over five years—was injured or killed.[29] Every steelmaker was either injured himself or knew workers who lost fingers, hands, legs, or their lives. In those days there was no workmen's compensation program, no pension, and no social security system. Wounded veterans of the industrial "wars" dragged out their lives in poverty. Indeed, until 1927 there was no hospital in East Chicago; injured or sick people were taken to Gary.[30]

Working conditions in the mills were so bad that steelworkers were in "a frame of mind of more or less chronic rebellion, largely physical reaction from exhaustion and deprivation."[31] In 1923, yielding to a "wrathful storm" of public opinion, Judge Gary capitulated and agreed to inaugurate the eight-hour day.[32] In 1924, to meet the demand for steel during the boom, Inland introduced the three-shift program; wages remained at three dollars a day for common labor. Grievances and work stoppages were endemic throughout the 1920s, but with the steel companies, the municipal, state, and national authorities, and the newspapers equating labor unions with bolshevism, nothing was done to alleviate the situation.

> We toiled in so many places,
> Wandering from state to state.
> Searching for the proper soil,
> To stop and plant our roots.

Housing conditions were as bad as the conditions inside the factories. An overwhelming majority of the Mexicans lived on Block and Pennsylvania avenues, on the wrong side of the tracks, just across the street from the Inland Steel mills where so many of them worked. Here speculative builders put up eighteen-by-eighteen-foot wooden barracks with nine-by-nine-foot rooms a few feet apart from one another, with an outside communal faucet and an outhouse. A social worker noted that "the health of Mexicans seems to be worse up here. They have more money but less air and fresh vegetables, and they are more crowded."[33]

Since so many workers were solos (bachelors or married men who had left their families back in Mexico), many Mexican women ran boardinghouses to add to the family income. The daughter of a survivor of those hard, hard days recalls that her parents housed fifty-two boarders, cooking and washing with only one black hired helper.

> I remember a group of very clannish men from
> Monterrey who were brought to work in the steel
> mills. When my mother told them that she did not
> have enough room to house all of them, they said that

*Spanish Castle Meeting Hall, built in 1931 as the headquarters of the Union Espanola, a benefit society for the sick organized in Gary in 1913 for Spanish-descent residents.*

some of them would sleep in the beds while others worked. The beds were never cold.[34]

The Calumet was a man's world, with all the dislocations attendant upon that circumstance. One pioneer remembered that women were so rare in the early days that the sight of one "made men lay down their tools and smile in sheepish pleasure." A *corrido* (Mexican folk song) laments the flightiness of wives who took advantage of the skewed sex ratio to violate patriarchal customs (*machismo*), and of children who looked down upon their old-fashioned parents:

> Even my old woman has changed on me—
> She wears a bob-tailed dress of silk,
> Goes about painted like a *pinata*
> And goes at night to the dancing hall.

> My kids speak perfect English
> And have no use for our Spanish
> They call me "fader" and don't work
> And are crazy about the Charleston.

> I am tired of all this nonsense
> I'm going back to Michoacan;
> As a parting memory I leave the old woman
> To see if someone else wants to burden himself.[35]

Inland's Mexican-American steelworkers did not have much leisure. After twelve hours of exhausting work in the mill many of them had strength enough only to eat and sleep. Some of them never saw nearby Lake Michigan. They got one day off every two weeks. For recreation there were many pool halls, more than a hundred saloons (in spite of Prohibition), and a number of bordellos.[36] In the 1920s northwest Indiana was a frontier community, and in some ways it resembled the legendary cow towns Laredo, Abilene, and Dodge City of a half century before. Even in the mid-1960s Julian Samora, a sympathetic Chicano sociologist, noted that the population of East Chicago "is still demographically abnormal, and consequently prostitution, divorce, gambling, alcoholism, narcotics addiction, and other dysfunctions are still a problem."[37]

Piled on top of loneliness, low pay, exhausting work, miserable housing, and diseases such as rickets, pneumonia, typhoid, tuberculosis, and syphilis was the pervasive racism of the area in the "tribal twenties." The "normal" American aversion to dark-skinned people was exacerbated in the Calumet by memories of the steel strike and by Mexican-American refusal in many cases to dissolve in the melting pot, speak English, and become citizens. Some wives even returned to Mexico to have their children born there and retain their Mexican citizenship.

Raymond A. Mohl records numerous examples of prejudice and hostility at all levels of society:

—"Nearly every negro carries a gun, . . . while the Mexicans carry long knives."

—"Next to the bad negroes, the bad Mexicans were declared the worst offenders."

—In 1924, after a shooting, when four hundred suspects were arrested: "Unmistakable signs of indigestion have already been caused by the latest dose of Mexican chile superimposed on already weird Hungarian goulash."

—"On the north side they will not rent to Mexicans."

—The Gary Hotel "refused to admit Mexicans" and Mexicans were "unwelcome and unwanted" at movie theaters, restaurants, barber shops.

—Father John DeVille: "You can americanize the man from southeastern and southern Europe, . . . but you can't americanize a Mexican."

—Our "large alien population is the basic cause of unemployment."

—The Mexican "is bountifully fed and housed, whether he works or not."

Only rarely was there a voice of sympathy and compassion:

—"The agony and suffering that all of these people endure is beyond comprehension by any who have not experienced it."[38]

But not all Mexicans wallowed in vice and crime. Like other immigrant groups Indiana's Mexican Americans built churches and organized fraternal groups. Coming from a country with no tradition of popular financial support for the church, and with a powerful tradition of anticlericalism (the government was executing priests in the 1920s) devout Mexicans in East Chicago at first attended Mass in Polish, Italian, or Croat parishes in Gary or southside Chicago. But, like other immigrants, they longed to hear their own language, Spanish, in church on Sunday mornings— especially as many of them spoke no other language. As no native priest was available Father Octavius Zavatta, a Spanish-speaking Italian of the Community of the Precious Blood, was sent to say Mass in St. Anthony's Church on Todd Street. For two dollars a week the community arranged to have a bus on the corner of Washington and Pennsylvania at 9:30 to take all comers to ten o'clock Mass.[39]

In 1927, eight years after the arrival of Mexican strikebreakers in the Calumet, the community achieved what was common for ethnic groups in America but uncommon and not even possible in Mexico at that time, a Mexican priest, a refugee from religious persecution, Father Apolinar Santa Cruz, and a church they had paid for themselves, Our Lady of Guadalupe, at 3855 Pennsylvania Avenue in the heart of the barrio. From their meager earnings in the mills and boardinghouses the Mexican community had raised $1,677.65 in 1925, raffled off an automobile the following year, and got donations of material from Inland, Youngstown, and Atlas Cement.[40] When the first East Chicago Spanish church burned to the ground in 1939 a new one was promptly built the next year.[41] It was not until forty years later, in 1967, that the much smaller Hispanic community in Indianapolis had regular Sunday Masses in Spanish.[42]

By the end of the decade there were dozens of Catholic and Protestant religious organizations, orchestras, *mariachi* bands, folklore dance groups, baseball teams, theater groups, language associations, and parades on Mexican national holidays. In 1925 Rosa de Lima Buitron became the first Mexican American to graduate from high school, and in 1927 Ramon Gonzalez Arriaga was the first Mexican American to become a home owner. By contrast, the first Mexican Social Club in Indianapolis was not organized until 1958.[43]

*Zactecas baseball team, early 1930s.*

Between 1927 and 1929 the Senoras of Yesteryear recorded that 118 Mexicans arrived in Indiana Harbor. By then, among the solos who were still the most common newcomers, women came and also whole families: for example, Arnulfo Vasquez, his wife, their two sons and two daughters.[44] Mexicans in Gary owned twenty-seven businesses: a grocery, two tailor shops, four barbershops, nine restaurants, and eleven pool halls.[45] The frontier age was over, and a more stable society was emerging. Then came the Crash of 1929 and the Great Depression— a tragedy for all Americans but a special disaster for the Mexicans of the Calumet.

## The Repatriations, 1930–32

> We picked the fruit and lived in tents,
> We set the tracks and lived in boxcars,
> We sought to earn our daily bread,
> On the heaviest, dirtiest task.

Alongside the pleasant aspects of American society which William Dean Howells insisted were most characteristic, there has always been an ugly side to life in the United States and in Indiana. The first settlers had hardly achieved statehood in 1816 before they began to plan the elimination of the Native Americans. In 1838, by the infamous "Trail of Death," the Native Americans of northwest Indiana were sent on a death march to the West.

Slavery was excluded from the Northwest Territory by the Ordinance of 1787, but Indiana went beyond that and made several efforts to exclude blacks themselves. When blacks arrived in the Calumet in the 1920s as part of the Great Migration they were rigidly segregated. At Froebel High School in Gary, for example, they were barred from most extracurricular activities and were not permitted to use the school swimming pool until 1943. Even then parental pressure forced the school board to allow blacks to swim only on Fridays, the day before the pool was cleaned.[46]

Brown-skinned Mexicans were considered almost as undesirable as blacks. One employer explained that, "We use no Mexicans. We have more refined work and have not had to resort to the greasers. They use them (at the mill) for rough work, and around blast furnaces."

Although Mexicans were 9 percent of US Steel's work-force in 1928, only 2 percent of them held skilled jobs. One foreman dismissed a job applicant with the comment, "If you have not worked as a machinist in this country, you are not a machinist." Without a union to defend their rights the Mexicans were helpless. Often they had to pay a bribe to get a job. One employment manager admitted that, "When I hire Mexicans at the gate, I pick out the lightest among them. No, it isn't that the lighter colored ones are any better workers, but the darker ones are like the niggers."[47]

The Ku Klux Klan, which attacked blacks, Catholics, Jews, and foreigners, was more powerful in Indiana than in any other state, since it virtually took control of the Republican party by 1924.[48] The Mexicans of the Calumet Region and elsewhere were a target for the wrath of the Klan: Mexicans generally had brown skin; they kept to themselves in ramshackle, miserable housing in slum neighborhoods; they spoke English badly, or not at all; they frequented pool halls, speakeasies, and brothels; they liked to play cards and arrange cockfights; some of them smoked marijuana or sniffed cocaine; most of them were not citizens and few seemed interested in changing their allegiance; they took white men's jobs; most were Catholics, despised by the Klan as faithful slaves of the pope in Rome. If the Klan found few recruits in East Chicago it was only because there were so few native-born Protestants there who were eligible for membership.[49]

As long as the mills kept pouring out metal the steel masters of the Calumet saw to it that their labor force was not overly interfered with. But when the Great Depression devastated the steel industry and tonnage at Inland fell to 15 percent of capacity, thousands of Mexicans, along with ethnics from every other country, were laid off. The frail system of private charity rapidly broke down; even doubling municipal taxes in 1931 did not provide enough funds to care for the unemployed. By then five hundred Mexicans had voluntarily returned south of the Rio Grande by car, truck, or bus.[50]

Faced with municipal bankruptcy, political and industrial leaders decided to apply the remedy they had used in 1921. Paul E. Kelley, transportation agent for Inland Steel and an officer of the American Legion, wrote to officials in Washington and bluntly explained: "Here is our problem, to rid the community of Mexicans."[51] The Hoover administration was sympathetic but had no funds; American citizens of Mexican origin, moreover, were not subject to deportation. Kelley, along with Judge M. E. Crites and Russel F. Robinson, decided to handle the problem on a local level.

After employing thousands of Mexicans for as long as fifteen years Kelley now discovered that they "cannot stand our severe winter season." Furthermore, they were lazy; "These Mexican people will be content to sit idly by, and let us feed them." Many of them had tuberculosis or syphilis. Horace S. Norton of Gary, faced with the same problem of superfluous laborers, came to the same conclusion: "The kindest thing which could be done [for] these people would be to send them back to Mexico. They do not assimilate and are unhappy here."[52] In order to persuade the federal authorities and public opinion (and perhaps himself) that it would be proper and even humanitarian to return these forlorn children of the tropics to their ancestral home, Kelley invented an imaginary labor shortage in the *bajio* (plateau) region of central Mexico. Indiana's Mexicans were needed, he wrote, "to replace Chinese and Japanese, who have left some of the most fertile land in the world destitute of workers." East Chicago could no longer bear the burden of supporting them.

Having conjured up this totally imaginary scenario of Mexicans eager to return to an expectant "mother country," Kelley took steps to make it come true. A stag party at the Knights of Columbus raised some money for "community uplift[!]"[53] Inland and US Steel loaned the American Legion additional funds, and the railroads agreed to a special fifteen-dollar excursion fare from the Calumet to Laredo, Texas.

The deportees were promised that special trains would meet them at the border to take them where land and jobs awaited. Those who refused to go voluntarily would be dropped from the Indiana relief rolls. Kelley himself would accompany the *repatriados* to see that all went well and that the passengers did not abandon the train somewhere inside the United States. Four trains, with nine cars and three hundred passengers apiece, left East Chicago on 2 June, 25 July, 23 August, and 27 September, arriving in Laredo two days later. A total of nearly a half million Mexicans, a third of those living in the United States and many of them citizens born or naturalized here, were on similar trains from Cleveland, Chicago, Detroit, Los Angeles, and elsewhere. There was no comparable effort to send unemployed Belgians, Italians, Croats, Serbs, or Bulgarians back home.

Abraham Olivo, a sixteen-year-old head of a family of four (his father had been murdered in New Mexico ten years earlier), was a passenger on one of the trains from East Chicago. His recollections, videotaped and on deposit at the East Chicago Public Library and the Indiana Historical Society Library, give the lie to Paul Kelley's self-serving racism. Olivo was born in Kansas City in 1916 and hence was a citizen of the United States as were his younger sister and brother, yet all of the Mexicans were treated like deportable aliens. Those without citizenship papers were denied work at the mills or welfare; one teenage repatriate recalled that Mexicans were "forced . . . or sort of fooled" into boarding the trains.[54] When Abraham Gonzalez was laid off at Youngstown Sheet and Tube he was told to sign papers that he thought would qualify him for welfare aid. Instead, they were documents in which he "agreed" to repatriation. "It was a tremendous shock to all the Gonzalez family, but there was nothing they could do."[55]

These deportations in 1932 were no more "voluntary" than those of black slaves from Sierra Leone in 1800, of the Miami and Potawatomi from South Bend in 1838, of the Japanese Americans from San Francisco in 1942, of the Jews from Warsaw in 1943, or the Bosnian Muslims, Croats, and Serbs from areas in what had been Yugoslavia in the 1990s.

The American Legion did not furnish food for the two-day journey; Olivo remembers that he distributed box lunches from the East Chicago parish of Nuestra Senora de Guadalupe. Nor were there any trains or welcoming committees to meet the arrivals. They were taken across the Rio Grande to Nuevo Laredo and "dumped," while Paul Kelley got on a northbound train and went home. Kelley reported that the trip had been a splendid success and that "there was no difficulty or trouble of any sort." Doubtless Kelley was right, for himself and the ruling class he represented; a fifteen-dollar train fare would save hundreds of dollars in welfare expenses. A young woman forced to board one of these deportation trains in Gary saw things in a different light:

> This is my country, but after the way we have been treated, I hope never to see it again. . . . As long as my father was working and spending his money in Gary stores, paying taxes and supporting us, it was all right, but now we have found we can't get justice here.[56]

Meanwhile, the forlorn Olivo family slept on the cement in the railroad station in Nuevo Laredo. That night a thief stole the family's few belongings and their small store of money. Henry Lopez, an eleven-year-old on one of the deportation trains, also remembered that in Nuevo Laredo "everything was in a turmoil and completely disorganized." His family also was robbed of all their belongings.[57] The next day, remembering their parish church back home in Indiana, the Olivos sought out the local church of Nuestra Senora de Guadalupe where they were given a few tortillas to eat. Young Abraham, although he spoke hardly any Spanish, managed to learn that there was work on the Martin Gomez Dam in a town called Camaron. The Olivos were able to hitch a ride there on an ox-drawn cart. Sixteen-year-old Abraham got a job as a laborer; the family's first housing was a mud hut, their bedding *petates* (straw mats). There, holding a variety of jobs, the Olivos remained for the next eleven years.

### Migrant Workers

Climate and crops played a dominant role in the history of antebellum America. In subtropical regions where crops like tobacco, rice, and cotton required year-round labor, slave labor was established. North of the Ohio River slavery did not pay because corn belt fields were idle in the winter.

But there are crops and operations that require a considerable amount of seasonal labor. Detasseling corn; weeding, harvesting, and canning tomatoes and cucumbers; harvesting and processing sugar beets; and picking apples, peaches, and cherries created a demand for cheap, unorganized, and seasonal labor. Mexican migrant workers from the Southwest began to be brought in to fill that demand early in the twentieth century.

When in her sixties, Pilar Gamez remembered with simple but moving eloquence what it was like to work in the Iowa sugar beet fields in 1932. She was eleven years old.

> We'd start out early in the morning. Papa was so impatient that sometimes we got to the fields before the sun had time to dry the dew. We'd get our shoes soaking wet, and that made matters much worse, for me at least, for my shoes were too little, and they'd shrink when they dried. But, I had to wear them, for that was a matter of pride, too. No matter how poor we were, then and at other times, we were kept in shoes. When, later, we knew white American children, we couldn't understand why they went barefoot, for they were not any poorer than we were. But, oh, if only Papa had let us go barefoot that summer!

> The ground was baked white and hard. A terrible drought that year. I worked with Papa—that was another thing about him. I was his daughter, and there was to be no foolishness with strange boys around. So there we worked, Papa breaking the ground with the hoe as close to the plant as he dared; me, down on my hands and knees, pulling the weeds out of the broken earth, and especially around the plant. My two brothers worked near us always, so Papa could keep an eye on them, too. They took turns, hoeing and weeding, and as I said, the young one brought us water.

> There we worked, up one row, down the other, ten rows to the acre. That's a detail I'll never forget. It was awful, except that always there was Papa there, encouraging us. He called me his little bone—I was so skinny. *Mi huesita!* My little bone! My brothers were bones, too.

> "Let's see if we can get to the end of the row," Papa would say, or something like that. And on we went, under that blazing sun, stopping only to eat the only thing we had—a cold fried potato sandwich.[58]

In 1967–68, an average year, 214,000 agricultural migrants were brought into the Midwest and Great Lakes states, comprising nearly a quarter of the hired farm working force.[59] American citizens avoid the hard work and low wages paid for farm labor, and the growers prefer foreigners if they can get them. Despite the passage of the Immigration Reform and Control Act of 1986, which granted amnesty to three million undocumented workers and tried to cut down illegal immigration and raise wages, there was still a surplus of migrant farm workers. Forged documents (a social security card and a resident alien card) cost $900, and overtaxed federal and state officials are swamped trying to enforce the regulations. In 1992 the average migrant family made $7,200 a year, half the poverty level of $14,000.[60]

Conditions in the migrant camps are only marginally better today, sixty years later, than when Pilar Gamez was a child. In August 1990 a family of ten arrived from the Rio Grande valley and were at work detasseling corn in a field on the outskirts of Fort Wayne. Later they harvested tomatoes and cucumbers. They were getting the minimum wage of four dollars an hour and since everybody worked the total pay was substantial. The father was back home in McAllen, Texas, where he had recently bought an expensive 1989 Trans-Am automobile; his children were working to make the payments. Housing for the family consisted of ramshackle barracks, much the worse for wear. An older man, an uncle of some of the children, told me that in previous days things had been much worse; they lived in tents or former chicken shacks. Food was a mush of beans and potatoes. The children had some schooling back in Texas and irregularly during the school year in Indiana. But their frequent moves, and their isolation from any community other than their own, made it impossible for them to become acculturated or literate. All they knew how to do generation after generation was poorly paid, unskilled seasonal labor. Many of the children were bright and lively but they seemed to have no future except in the fields.[61] Even in the 1990s, despite the passage of protective legislation on the state and national levels, ten- and eleven-year-old children were working in the fields in Tipton County.[62]

### Return to the Calumet

> Our dream sustained us and stilled,
> Our uncertainties and anxieties,
> Still we reached the land Indiana,
> City of East Chicago, by the lake.

Quite a few of the Mexican-American deportees of 1932 had to come to the United States twice to establish a permanent residence. Henry T. Lopez, for example, born in Miller, Indiana, in 1921, was deported at the age of eleven. He returned to East Chicago in 1936 and was hired by Inland Steel as soon as he graduated from high school. He returned to Inland after service in the Air Corps (1942–45), rose to the position of yard superintendent, and worked for the company for thirty-nine years.

Abraham Olivo was another returning deportee. In 1938 he married Esther in Mexico. She, like Olivo, had been expelled from the United States (Long Beach, California) six years earlier. Abraham's younger sister Carlotta had married

a resident from Gary and was living in that city. In 1943, in the midst of the wartime boom, Carlotta persuaded Abraham to return to Indiana. Despite the skills he had acquired in Mexico as a truck driver, pipe fitter, construction worker, and machine repairman, he had to take a dirty, dangerous, low-paying job as a common laborer cleaning out coke pits. A white foreman told him he did not like the idea of having to supervise "Greasers, Niggers, or Chinese."

Olivo quit; but Doc Howard, Inland Steel labor relations chief, rehired him and sent him to another factory, the plant where seventy-six-inch hot steel was rolled. It was common to assign Latin Americans to these unpleasant jobs. "They made 'tropicals,' that is, people from Mexico, Puerto Rico, or Cuba, work in the open hearth because they felt that they could take the heat."[63] Of course, as previously indicated, when Paul Kelley wanted to get rid of superfluous Mexican workers he claimed that they could not take the cold in the Calumet.

Olivo joined the Steel Workers' Union and got a promotion within a week. With two years out for service in the Pacific, Olivo worked thirty-six years for Inland, retiring as a head hooker at $8,000 a year.[64]

By 1937 steel production had recovered from its abysmally low depression levels, and the industry enjoyed thirty years of prosperity. Although top-level jobs were still out of reach for Mexican Americans, steel employees benefited from the kind of company loyalty that one associates with Japanese firms. *Mexican American Harbor Lights* (p. 31) records their longevity records with pride:

20–29 years—one
30–39 years—seventeen
40–47 years—eighteen

With the mills prospering, there was plenty of money in the community to support small businesses. The following is a list of Mexican-American enterprises:

> Four *panaderias* (bakeries), two beauty salons, one coal company, an herb shop, three ice cream parlors, one laundry, one meat market, one poultry shop, one "*Productos Mexicanos*," thirty restaurants, one sewing machine store, two theaters, five barbershops, three pool halls, twenty-four grocery stores, five hotels, three jewelry stores, three bookstores, six newspapers, four printing shops, three record shops, one rooming house, six shoe making and shoe repair shops, eight *Tortillerias*.[65]

All these varied enterprises gave a much needed variety to the opportunities available to members of *la raza* in the Calumet. But these were overwhelmingly small mom-and-pop businesses. On a national level, as late as 1987, the average receipts for Hispanic businesses was only

*Garza food store, East Chicago, established in 1927 or 1928. The store began processing and manufacturing chocolate, later expanding to include processed cheese and sausage.*

$59,000 a year, and eight out of ten had no paid employee.[66] But at least the immigrants and their children could enjoy Mexican food, music, herbal medicines, Spanish books, plays, films, and salespeople who spoke their language. Throughout the state, even in small towns and places with a very small Mexican-American population, there is likely to be a Mexican restaurant or grocery within driving distance. Acculturation works both ways—Hispanic Americans learn to speak English, and other Americans learn to like tacos, chile con carne, and bean burritos. And on an intellectual level, translated versions of novels by Alejo Carpentier of Cuba, Carlos Fuentes of Mexico, and Gabriel García Márquez of Colombia—a Nobel Prize winner—have won a wide audience in this country.

### The War Years (1942–45)

> Here we labored in the steel mills
> On the railroads and cement plants
> In the lowest paying jobs
> On the heaviest, dirtiest tasks.

The cyclical steel industry is like an oversensitive thermometer that exaggerates the rise and fall of the American economy. During the Great Depression, when the gross national product fell by more than 50 percent, Inland Steel's output fell by more than 80 percent. But when the Japanese attacked Pearl Harbor on 7 December 1941, and Hitler petulantly declared war on the United States a few days later, demand for and output of steel rose to unprecedented levels. Jeeps and trucks, landing craft and artillery shells, rifles and bullets, railroad cars and oil pipelines, and submarines, aircraft carriers, and battleships

were ordered in previously unheard-of quantities, and the Calumet, America's premier steel center, was uniquely qualified to provide the essential raw material.

Once again, as in 1910, 1919, and the later 1920s, an unskilled, illiterate immigrant, even if he could not speak English, could walk up to the factory gate and begin work the next day—no questions asked. A disgruntled worker could walk off the job, go to another mill, and be hired the same day. This time, as in 1917–18, the labor shortage was exacerbated by the demands of the armed forces which took millions of young workers away from farms and factories for the duration. Once again, as in earlier boom times, Mexican Americans in northwest Indiana and elsewhere wrote to their relatives and friends in Kansas City and Laredo, Jalisco and Guanajuato, Durango and Aguascalientes, telling them about steady jobs at excellent pay. Inland and other steelmakers, along with defense plants, beet sugar and tomato growers and processors, once again sent *enganchadores* ("hookers," recruiters) to the South and Southwest to supply the labor force that could no longer be brought from Europe or the Orient. The mills also offered free passage to Puerto Ricans, American citizens who had the rights of passage to the mainland. Of the sixty-five brief biographies published in James B. Lane's *Latinos in the Calumet Region* (1987), fourteen subjects were from the Commonwealth of Puerto Rico, one from Colombia, one from Cuba, and one from Honduras. Thus a new Caribbean flavor was added to northwest Indiana's previous Mexican chile con carne. On a much smaller scale, Eli Lilly and Company brought educated professionals and semiprofessionals to Indianapolis from its pharmaceutical branches in various Latin American countries.[67]

This time at least there was no suspicion of the loyalty of the Spanish speaking and their children. In 1898 some officials had worried—needlessly—about whether

*Key shop owned by Vincent Alvarez, East Chicago, 1930s.*

Mexican Americans would fight against *la madre patria,* Catholic Spain. And in 1917 the United States had gone to war against Imperial Germany partly because of the Zimmermann Telegram, in which communication Germany's foreign minister had suggested that Mexicans and Mexican Americans could be persuaded to attack the United States and recover the lands of the Mexican Cession of 1848.[68]

But during the Second World War Mexican Americans were as patriotic—or even more patriotic—as any other ethnic group. In the days after Pearl Harbor a few Chicanos—remembering racial and religious prejudice, the Klan, the infamous expatriations—expressed fear that they would be rounded up as security risks: "They don't have to deport me! I'm going on my own. . . . I belong to Mexico. *Soy puro mexicano!* (I'm 100 percent Mexican)."[69] But unlike black Americans, who served in segregated Jim Crow units throughout the war, or the Japanese Americans, who were evacuated from the West Coast and sent to internment camps for the duration, Hispanic Americans were accepted into the armed services on *almost* equal levels.

Almost—but not quite. Aliens, like citizens, were subject to the draft. And because the overwhelming majority of Hispanics were considered unskilled—in the Calumet in 1928, 79 percent were classified as laborers, 19 percent semiskilled, and less than 2 percent skilled[70] and the situation had not drastically changed by 1941—few of them could qualify for an exemption as an essential civilian worker. And none of the members of the East Chicago draft board, "the few key people in the community who informally and frequently met to adjust the community's course," were of Hispanic origin.[71] Whereas an American of older stock might be exempt from service on various grounds, few Hispanics "were ever exempted, reclassified, or found to be too essential to be drafted."[72] The author of *Among the Valiant: Mexican-Americans in World War II and Korea,* Raúl Morín was drafted in spite of his age (thirty-two), his wife, and his three children. So was Abraham Olivo, a steelworker with four children. Olivo was denied an exemption while some younger unmarried men were classified as "essential war workers."[73]

Hispanics made excellent soldiers; because of the hard work so many of them were doing on farms and in factories they were in excellent condition. Basic training was not as difficult as working in a steel mill, harvesting beets, or picking tomatoes. They were brave and accustomed to following orders. General Douglas MacArthur was quoted as saying: "Send us more of these Mexican boys: they make good jungle fighters."[74] It is worth noting that of the seventeen Mexican Americans who won the Congressional Medal of Honor

(five posthumously) during World War II and Korea, all were combat infantrymen and not one was a commissioned officer.[75]

Nevertheless, for the Hispanics of Indiana as for most Americans World War II was "the Good War." Every month for four years the steel mills in Gary, East Chicago, and Indiana Harbor, and the oil refineries in Hammond set new production records. Needed industrial capacity was added at an astonishing rate.

> On March 3, 1942, American Steel Foundries broke ground for its Cast Armor Defense Plant, and began production six months later. In a short time, Cast Armor hired almost six thousand employees, many of them women.[76]

The personal narratives printed in *Mexican American Harbor Lights* (1992) are full of examples of "Rosita the Riveter," Mexican-American women who overcame the racial prejudice of corporation executives, the social preferences of their husbands, and their own hesitation and fears and went to work outside the home: Florence Vasquez was "a defense worker at Inland Steel." Juanita Vasquez was hired in 1942 at Youngstown Sheet and Tube, "the first Mexican American to be employed in the Accounting Department. I retired in 1981."

Margarita Ruiz Maravilla "worked as a factory laborer with pick, shovel, and wheelbarrow at the Buffington plant of the Universal Atlas Cement Company in Gary." Luz Diaz "started to work at the Inland Steel Company in 1943. . . . I finally retired in 1948."[77] Note that these women, and many others, remained at work after the war ended.

Some Mexican *padres de familia* insisted on retaining old customs in the midst of wartime upheaval. Regalado Munoz, a bigamist with a family back in Mexico, threatened to leave his East Chicago wife if she tried to work outside the house.

> Regalado started earning double what he earned before. My mom was also offered work at Inland during the War but had to turn it down. Regalado told my mom he would leave her and go to Mexico if she accepted this offer.

The unfortunate Señora Munoz, who had been forced into marriage at sixteen in order to escape brutal whippings by her father, also had to quit high school in the ninth grade; her grandfather "believed in the Mexican style for all girls to get married, and for men to work." When her husband died in 1956, she was a widow left with seven children, no savings, no pension from Inland, and $280 a month from social security. At thirty-three she made a last effort to obtain an education, but it was too late.

My mom also started going back to school. Mostly there were Latinos that attended class with her. None of them knew how to read and write. She only went a half year and that was all.[78]

Señora Munoz married again, had two more children (for a total of nine), was divorced, and finally obtained a job at the East Chicago police station. She successfully raised her large family as a single parent. "My mom knows many people and is very popular. She is now 62 years old and moves around without no trouble at all." Surely this Chicano woman was as brave as any of those Congressional Medal of Honor winners.

Wartime and postwar prosperity greatly eased racial and religious tensions in the Calumet. With more jobs available than people to fill them, the angry confrontation of striker and scab was a relic of the past. Northwest Indiana's Hispanics had a share in postwar prosperity and a common pride in having helped defeat the racist dictatorships of Adolf Hitler and Hideki Tōjō.

### Postwar Readjustments

But worked and lived we did,
In a secure environment for the children,
In the Democratic republic, the United States
Grateful are we in our adopted land.

As in 1919, the end of a world war brought renewed labor conflict to the steel mills of the Calumet. During the first fifteen years after Germany and Japan surrendered there were five major strikes: 1946 (30 days); 1949 (42 days); 1951–52 (55 days); 1956 (34 days); 1959 (116 days); and hundreds of local walkouts.[79] Big Steel and Little Steel grudgingly accepted the existence of the steelworkers' union. However, there were prolonged and bitter battles over wages, pensions, sick leave, incentive pay, vacations, "equal pay for equal work," maintenance of membership clauses, "management's right to manage," and health insurance plans.[80]

This time, at least, no militia or regular army troops were sent into the steel cities to crush the unions. Nobody was shot, and there were no Mexican-American or black strikebreakers. Public opinion and the National Labor Relations Board would have barred any such tactics. The labor movement was at its height, and after the 1956 merger of the American Federation of Labor and Congress of Industrial Organizations (AFL-CIO) fifteen million union members supported the United Steelworkers of America (USWA). Only a few members of *la raza* had become foremen or white-collar workers, but Hispanic workers in the mills were solidly and understandably

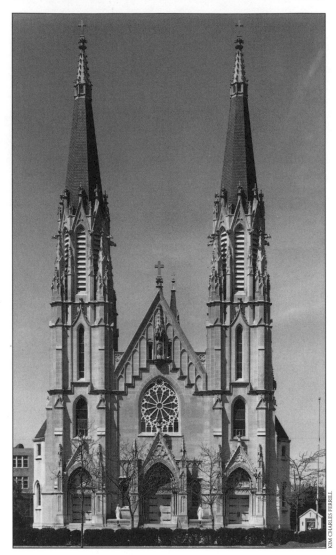

KIM CHARLES FERRILL

*St. Mary's Church, Indianapolis, responded to an expanding Spanish-speaking community by offering Sunday Mass in Spanish beginning in 1967.*

loyal to the union that had done so much for them. In 1970 Jesse Arredondo was elected president of East Chicago Local 1010, the largest in the USWA, representing 18,700 steelworkers.[81]

Eventually, both management and the unions realized that their century-old strife was too costly for both sides; the four-month-long strike in 1959 cost both labor and management over $1 billion each. In long-drawn-out negotiations that often threatened to break down over a fraction of a penny, the two sides hammered out agreements on all the issues that divided them. United States Steel's chief negotiator declared himself enthusiastic about the labor-management Cooperative Wage Study (CWS), and steelworker president David McDonald called it a "wonderful achievement."[82]

Nobody benefited more from the achievement of labor peace, pay increases, and the elimination of wage inequities in the mills than the Mexican Americans. This first postwar agreement gave sizable increases to the "labor" jobs at the bottom of the pay scale still held by so many Mexicans.[83] And by now the second and third generations, in a pattern similar to that of other ethnic groups, had jobs that would have been closed to their fathers and mothers thirty years before. In *Mexican American Harbor Lights* the authors proudly list dozens of "firsts" in prestigious occupations: police officer, accountant, chemist, welder, airline supervisor, pharmacist, water department foreman, real estate broker, marketing agent, civil servant, chief cost clerk, schoolteacher, jail turnkey, superintendent, priest, state trooper, insurance agent.[84]

Indianapolis also, despite its much smaller Hispanic population (8,450—about 1 percent according to the 1990 census), could show Spanish-speaking men and women in white-collar work, businesses, and the professions: publisher of a Spanish newspaper, accountant, surgeon, attorney, stockbroker, detective, auto mechanic, director of Hispanic Center, pastor of Methodist church, architect, retired captain in U.S. Army, civil service, CEO of construction company, professor at IUPUI, director of bilingual education, social worker.[85] These job categories may not seem very impressive, but it is important to remember that a great many of these people were the children of illiterate migrants who came to central Indiana to pick tomatoes in Tipton County. For them to get an education and move out of the migrant stream into the professions and the middle class was a remarkable achievement.

Also, the Mexicans began showing the effects of the melting pot. While attending school at Bloomington under the GI Bill of Rights Sam Maravilla met and married a fellow student, Beverly Dornberg. He went on to become the first Mexican from Indiana Harbor to become a professional chemist. Thirty-one years earlier his father Jose had been brought to Inland Steel as a scab, and his mother, Esperanza, went to work as a laborer during the Second World War.[86]

One area in which the Calumet's Mexicans did not keep up with other ethnic groups was politics. Living in the barrios on Block and Pennsylvania in Indiana Harbor, or south of the Wabash tracks in Gary, planning some day to return to Mexico or fearful of being forcibly repatriated as in the 1930s, many Mexicans spoke English very poorly or not at all. Ignacio Maravilla, also a strikebreaker for Inland Steel in 1919, did not enroll in a basic English class with his wife Margarita until they had been in Indiana more than thirty years.[87] A 1974 South Bend study found that nearly seven out of ten residents of Spanish origin over forty were "functionally illiterate" (four years of schooling or less).[88] The Mexican community tended to be poor, young,

school dropouts, and people with those characteristics tend not to be interested in politics or the vote.

The postwar boom in the steel industry made large fortunes for a few sticky-fingered politicians, for the businessmen who ran the mills, and for substantial shareholders of US Steel, Bethlehem, Youngstown Sheet and Tube, and Inland Steel, along with modest but rising wages for steelworkers, possible. The armed forces, in which three hundred thousand Chicanos (a disproportionate number) served, using steel bombs and shells (many of them produced in northwest Indiana), had destroyed the steel-making facilities of Germany and Japan. America's allies England and France were also devastated. With no effective competition, the untouched plants of the Calumet were fabulously profitable. In the fifteen years after the war, steel production went up 25 percent while the work force declined by almost half.[89] It was easy to raise wages and, with government approval, to raise steel prices as well. The Korean War (1950–53) led to another boom in the cyclical industry. Inland built four new blast furnaces in 1952 and added 2,300 workers to its current force of 18,000. East Chicago as a whole needed 10,000 more men as workers.

Thus the sons and daughters of the second and third generation of Mexican Americans in the Calumet enjoyed the blessings of steady work (except for five postwar strikes in fourteen years), union membership, rising pay scales, and the chance to get better jobs both inside and outside the mills. A 1959 study showed that the first generation to arrive in the Midwest had been occupationally downgraded as compared with their fathers who had remained in Mexico. Only 54 percent of those who remained in Mexico were menial laborers, as against 83 percent of the immigrant generation. But the second generation in the United States was moving up; only 32 percent were doing unskilled labor in factory or field.[90]

Top management jobs were still barred to most ethnics. Tony Barreda, for example, a second-generation Mexican American, was the first Chicano promoted to quality control foreman at Inland. But Barreda could rise no higher, so he resigned to become a community organizer and the head of the Union Benefica Mexicana (UBM), a social and mutual help association.[91] Gabriel Fraire, born in Mexico, came to East Chicago with his family at age thirteen and worked for three decades at Inland Steel, ending up as a foreman. "An intelligent and hard worker," he could rise no higher.

> With age comes wisdom and a saddening. For the last thirty-one years I have worked in East Chicago, Indiana for the same corporation. In the last twenty-five of those thirty-one years I have realized no

*Union Benefica Mexicana poster, East Chicago, 1988, announcing the celebration of Mexican independence.*

change in my status or position in their hierarchy of management. From the beginning I knew why but tried to ignore the obvious. . . .This is frustrating and demoralizing, the worst part being that I have watched young men who worked for and trained under me rise to positions as supervisors. That was heartbreaking.[92]

The social structure in the steel city resembled that on the haciendas which so many of the older Mexicans had abandoned a half century before. Instead of the land-holding *caciques* (bosses), there were steel barons Elbert H. Gary, William Palmer Gleason, and Ben Fairless of United States Steel, and Joseph Block and his sons Philip D., Leopold, and E. J. "Jimmie" Block, who founded Inland Steel in 1897 and passed the presidency on to Joseph's grandson and namesake in the 1950s. Instead of the *capataz* (foreman) of the hacienda, there were plant superintendents and union committeemen who handled labor matters. Under the leadership of USWA president David J. McDonald it was hard to tell management from the union. The two had comparable salaries, dressed alike, held meetings and took vacations in the same exotic places, and had a common devotion to "putting out fires" in wage disputes.[93] And, as the sturdy base of the social pyramid, the *peones* (workers) of the system were the men in the mills. Many of the newest peons were housed

in Pullman sleeping cars sitting on the tracks on company property.[94] At least the despots had turned benevolent since the violence of earlier times, and there was some sense of noblesse oblige in corporation boardrooms. You paid your men reasonable wages, did not shoot them when there were strikes, and did not ship them back to Mexico when they had to be laid off.

The industrialists and politicians who ran East Chicago also spent a lot of money on urban renewal in the boom years of the fifties and sixties. During the depression, World War II, postwar readjustment, and Korea, the city's always inadequate infrastructure had been allowed to decay. Now, using tax money and federal funds, there was a carnival of construction: schools, bridges, a new fire station, a new central police station, a new sewage plant, a new library, widening Chicago Avenue, and building a section of the Chicago-Detroit Expressway. The Inland Steel Foundation contributed a million and a half dollars to remodel St. Catherine's Hospital and add a new wing dedicated to two of the Block brothers—where the city did not have a hospital thirty years before. East Chicago won the National Clean-Up, Paint-Up, Fix-Up competition for cities of its size four times in six years.[95] The Chicanos, like other inhabitants of the Calumet, certainly benefited from these municipal improvements, but there was still the psychological pain of discrimination.

> While waiting at a bus station to see a friend off to Florida [in the 1950s], two Garyites were approached by the police and asked where the person had been living. When told "Pullman City," the temporary home of the contract workers, the officer said "good riddance." He also informed these individuals that as soon as their friend departed they were to "get the hell out of here."[96]

*First place float, Gary Golden Jubilee Parade, 1956.*

*GLAD (Gary Latin American Democrat Club) float in East Chicago parade, 1966.*

The conductor on the South Shore to Chicago line has been heard to call out "Mexico!" as the train approaches the East Chicago station.

Everything still depended on the steel business. In 1966, the year Youngstown opened a new hot strip mill and began construction of a new blast furnace, the Indiana Security Division reported only 3 percent unemployment in northwestern Indiana. And here, after thirty good years, many young Chicano men and women continued to make the mistake of neglecting their education. A high school diploma had never been a requirement for a job in the mills. It was quite usual for young men to drop out of school, get a job at Inland, and pursue their further vocational education in the plant while earning a salary. Formal education was never a high priority for Chicanos in earlier generations, especially since the teachers often tended to be hostile, even violent, to the Spanish speaking. It seemed natural to quit school at fifteen or sixteen, follow your father through the factory gate at Inland or Youngstown, contribute a salary to the family budget, buy a car, and get married. Carmelo Cruz, born

in San Guzman, Puerto Rico, a third-grade dropout, started working for US Steel in 1948 as a laborer at $1.25 an hour. After twenty-five years in 1978 he was earning $30,000 a year. Why bother with school?[97] A 1991–92 study showed that only 69 percent of United States teenagers completed high school in four years, a serious enough problem. But only 42 percent of Hispanic youth graduated on schedule.[98]

Even as the mills continued to expand the shadows of trouble appeared. Outsiders driving through Gary on the Indiana Toll Road to or from Chicago might be troubled by the stench and smoke from the mills. "Calumick," the Indian word from which the region takes its name (from the French word Calumet), actually means "the act of smoking together." Steelworkers never complained about the dirty air; it was, one of them said, "the smell of money." Even a century before lithographs of factory towns liked to show dense black clouds billowing from factory chimneys and railroad smokestacks. Like the fashionable corpulence of Diamond Jim Brady and Lillian Russell, the black clouds were a sign of prosperity.

Now personal thinness and clean air were in fashion, and the latter was enforced by clean air acts and the Environmental Protection Agency. Steel making is a dirty business, and cleaning it up is expensive. In 1982 Inland reported that the corporation had spent $200 million for pollution control during the previous ten years, with an annual operating cost of nearly $25 million. Thus one-fifth of a billion dollars had to be taken out of profits, wages, and expanded facilities while steel plants overseas kept producing in the old, dirty, and low cost way. "Meanwhile steel imports reached a monthly record of 2,200,000 tons in February."[99] The Steel Belt was about to turn into the Rust Belt.

## Hard Times

Once again, when the American economy caught a cold, the Calumet contracted pneumonia. The destruction of industry in Japan and Germany turned out to be a blessing in disguise. The new plants that rose in Yawata (Kitakyūshū) and Yokohama, in Dortmund, Essen, and Wolfsburg, were built from scratch, brand-new, incorporating state-of-the-art industrial techniques and skillful management. Volkswagen Beetles, Toyotas, Nissans, Hondas, Japanese television sets, motorcycles, and sewing machines began flooding into this country.

Foreign cars did not use any steel from Inland or Youngstown Sheet and Tube. Even in prosperous years the Calumet's mills kept downsizing and laying off men; recessions in 1969–70, 1973–75, and 1981–82 made a bad situation worse. Lake County was still ranked fourteenth in the state in manufacturing output in 1975 ($5.7 billion). But wages of as much as $35,000 or $38,000 a year (for skilled work with overtime) were becoming scarce. A lot of Hispanics got bad news:

> Less than two years after he was married, Jesus [Osario, 22, born in Talanga, Honduras, 7th grade school dropout] was laid off his job. . . . "My manager walked up to me with my check in his hand and said, 'Sorry, Jesus, we just don't need you here any more.'"

For the next five years Jesus mowed lawns, pulled weeds, washed cars, sold his blood, and subsisted on food stamps. "We eat a lot of traditional Honduran-style foods, like beans and chicken, but that's mostly because it is so cheap. Maria really likes steak, when we can afford to get it."

> A couple of months before the wedding, [James Vargas, high school graduate] was again laid off [at Inland]. . . . Jim was called back to work on and off again over the next two years. A few days after

they found that Gail was pregnant, he was placed on permanent furlough . . . . "There used to be opportunity for people—for everyone. But now that the mills are slow, so is Northwest Indiana."[100]

Between 1982 and 1987, during the height of the Reagan administration, the number of employees in the Calumet fell 34 percent. In 1985 the unemployment rate in Lake County was over 13 percent. Twenty-eight thousand men were out of work. In 1990, fifty-three thousand persons in Lake County were receiving food stamps, one out of every nine residents, the second-highest percentage in the state. Thirty-three thousand persons, two-thirds of them children, were receiving welfare, sixth among the Hoosier state's ninety-two counties.[101] Since Hispanics made up as much as half the population in Lake County cities like East Chicago, and were largely at the lower end of the socioeconomic ladder, they had more than their share of hardship and suffering.

Thousands of Chicanos, along with the Calumet's other ethnic groups, were getting pink slips. Per capita income in the Calumet, once near the top of Indiana's ninety-two counties, began an inexorable slide that continued throughout the Reagan years of the 1980s. The Calumet's per capita income, which was 107 percent of the state average at the beginning of the decade, was only 97 percent of it seven years later. Moreover, one-fifth of that income, one of the highest ratios in the state, was in the form of dividends, interest, and rent ($1 billion out of $5 billion). Very little of that went to Hispanics, and none to Chicanos like Jesus Osario and James Vargas.[102] A lot of it doubtless went to the yacht owners for whom Mayor Robert A. Pastrick of East Chicago built a 220-slip marina in 1988. Perhaps the unemployed steelworkers could go down to the waterfront and watch the yachts.

> The golf links lie so near the mill
> That nearly every day
> The laboring children can look out
> And see the men at play.

When the coke ovens, blast furnaces, and rolling mills were roaring Lake County's population shot up. Since the beginning of the century men had traveled thousands of miles to take dirty, exhausting, and dangerous, but well-paying jobs in the steel factories. As the nation recovered from the Great Depression and the demand for steel rose, Lake County's population increased by as much as 25 or 40 percent a decade. It was second only to Marion County-Indianapolis.

Lake County Population (in thousands)

|          | 1940 | 1950 | 1960 | 1970 |
|----------|------|------|------|------|
| Number   | 260  | 293  | 368  | 513  |
| Change   | NA   | 33   | 75   | 145  |
| Percent Change | NA | 12 | 26 | 39 |

Then, in the 1970s, the growth curve faltered and slowed. And in the following two decades the Calumet's population plummeted.

|                | 1980 | 1985    | 1990 (in thousands) |
|----------------|------|---------|---------------------|
| Number         | 546  | 523     | 476                 |
| Change         | 33   | minus 23| minus 47            |
| Percent Change | 6    | minus 4 | minus 9[103]        |

The 1992 interpretation of the 1990 Clean Air Act required that coke ovens reduce toxic emissions by 90 percent. Ten coke mills in northwest Indiana were among those to be held to this standard, and the cost to the industry as a whole was estimated to be as much as $510 million. Bethlehem Steel lost $71.5 million in the third quarter of 1992.[104] Inland Steel's cash flow fell to zero in 1982 and again in 1991–92.[105]

Of course, the industry has recovered before from long spells of drowning in red ink. But the industry's competitors south of the border do not have to contend with clean air acts and minimum wage laws. In Monterrey, Mexico's steel city, the steel plants are spewing out toxic gases. Wages in Mexico are also less than a quarter of those in the Calumet. One of the first acts of the Clinton administration was to impose tariffs on foreign steel. Passage of the North American Free Trade Agreement (NAFTA) may cause the virtual dismantlement of the steel industry in Lake County. It will be deeply ironic if the industry that brought so many workers to Indiana from Mexico will abandon them and move to the place from which the workers originally came.

## Mexican American—or Chicano?

Strong family feelings are considered to be part of the Hispanic heritage, but the family biographies in *Mexican American Harbor Lights* and *Latinos* are full of references to sons and daughters who have moved to Chicago, Los Angeles, Hawaii, the Philippines, Germany, and elsewhere. The first generation of arrivals in East Chicago tended to remain on Block and Pennsylvania avenues near the mills and their fellow Mexican Americans. Their children and grandchildren fanned out all over the city, and even outside it and the state. Eight of the brothers and sisters of Pilar Gamez, the little girl who worked in the Iowa beet fields, remained in East Chicago. But three others moved away to Tennessee, Texas, and the Philippines. And all of her four children also moved out of town:

> Ronald, who with his wife Alicia and their three children, live in Lynwood, Il; and Don and Charlotte and their five children in Winona, IN; Sylvia and her husband Lupe Alvarez, and three children in Highland, IN; and Judith and her husband, Larry Waldrop and their two children in Blountville, Alabama.[106]

Note the size of the Gamez family and that one of her daughters, Señora Waldrop, has apparently married a non-Mexican.

Between 1980 and 1990 the white population of Lake County fell 11 percent, and the black population 7 percent. Only the early age of marriage and the unusually large number of children among Hispanics have kept their population from an absolute decline. In the decade of the 1980s Lake County's Hispanic population increased only 1.7 percent—732 persons in ten years, an average of about 70 each year. In 1919 during the steel strike Big Steel (US Steel) and Inland brought in more Mexicans than that in a single day.

Structural changes in the United States economy and in the economy of the Mexican-American community fostered a renewed and heated debate about the conditions and the goals of Chicanismo. Should Mexican Americans try to assimilate, forget Spanish, join the Republican or Democratic parties, and aim at equality? Or should they insist on preserving their differences, proudly call themselves Chicanos, organize a *La Raza Unida* party, and aim at a bilingual society like those in Canada, Belgium, and Switzerland? *El Plan de Aztlan,* drawn up at the Chicano National Liberation Youth Conference in Denver, is the manifesto of Mexican-American nationalism, and Rodolfo "Corky" Gonzales is its poet laureate:

> I am Joaquin,
> Lost in a world of confusion,
> Caught up in the whirl of an
>     Anglo society
> Confused by the rules,
> Scorned by attitudes
> Suppressed by manipulations,
> And destroyed by modern society.
>     My fathers
> Have lost the economic battle
> And won
>     The struggle of cultural survival.[107]

Ask ten people of Hispanic background what they think about this controversy and you will get ten different answers. One steelworker, watching the 16 September parade in East Chicago in 1990, complained that his son had refused to speak Spanish, even at home. "People laugh at that old stuff, Pop. They make fun of you at school if you have a Spanish accent. It's embarrassing, man." When the younger man was laid off at Inland (because he had less seniority than his father), he became a truck driver and moved to Los Angeles. Then came an opportunity for a good job for someone who was bilingual—and, of course, the son could not qualify. "He asked me, 'Pop, how come you didn't teach me Spanish?' And I told him, 'How come you didn't want to learn it?'"

At the same parade the author was introduced to a Puerto Rican steelworker. The author tried to interview him in Spanish but he insisted that he did not understand that language, although he was born and raised in Ponce, Puerto Rico, "*la perla del sur*" (the Pearl of the South). I tried to buy him a taco from one of the street vendors but he insisted that he wanted a hot dog: "I don't eat that Mexican junk. And don't call me Francisco—my name is *Frank*." Finally, he got so angry that he walked away. I wonder if he will want his grandson to recover his *Borinquen* (Puerto Rican) heritage. It is often the case that the third generation wants to remember what the first generation tried to forget.

Chicanismo, ethnic nationalism, state and federal laws providing for Spanish-language ballots, and court interpreters, have spawned a backlash—the English-only movement. There have been heated disputes about bilingual education in Gary, East Chicago, and Indianapolis: one alderman proposed that anyone seeking a grocer's retail license should have to pass an English-language proficiency test. "If you don't know English, you can't understand the laws. You have to know more than Mexican." Across the barricade Raul Yzaguirre, president of the National Council of La Raza, protested bitterly that "U.S. English is to Hispanics as the Ku Klux Klan is to blacks."[108]

The debate over the Spanish language and Hispanic ethnic nationalism is most heated in those states and cities where there are sizable minorities or local majorities. These are the same places that have elected Spanish-surnamed mayors, governors, congressmen, and senators: Herman Badillo, borough president of the Bronx, Mayor Henry Cisneros of San Antonio (now secretary of education in the Clinton administration), Governors Raul Castro of Arizona and Robert Martinez of Florida, Representatives Ed Roybal of East Los Angeles, Henry B. Gonzalez and Eligio "Kiki" de la Garza of Texas, Cuban-born Elena Ros-Leitenan of Florida, and Senator Joseph Montoya of New Mexico. All these officials can and do make rousing speeches in Spanish to their special constituencies, but since they have to court English language voters as well, they avoid nationalist extremes.

Indiana's statewide Hispanic population is so small—99,000 out of 5.5 million, only 1.7 percent—that it has never attained the critical stage that leads to nationalist movements. Few of the Chicanos interviewed in East Chicago had ever heard of fiery nationalists like Gonzalez, Reies Tijerina, or *El Plan de Aztlan*. A recent and excellent study of St. Joseph County's Hispanic population (2.1 percent, a little higher than the statewide average) suggests that Spanish in the Hoosier state will fade away like all the other immigrant languages that were formerly spoken here:

Language Spoken

| Language | Total Pop. (%) | Under 18 | Over 18 |
|---|---|---|---|
| Spanish only | 11 | 4.5 | 18 |
| English only | 24 | 42 | 7 |
| Both languages | 65 | 54 | 75 |

The handwriting on the wall seems clear—and it is in English. Three out of every four Hispanics still speak their ancestral language, and one out of ten speaks no other. But the increase in English monolingualism from 7 percent among older people to 42 percent among the young shows where the future lies. And, when given the choice by bilingual investigators, more than three out of four of the respondents (79 percent) felt more comfortable in English and preferred to reply to the interview in that language.[109] Monica Medina, a third-generation Mexican American who has a degree from Indiana University and speaks English without a trace of any accent, left East Chicago because she did not like its Hispanic flavor and insists that she has "no allegiance to Spanish culture." Still she found her bilingualism an essential tool in her job as director of the Hispanic Center in Indianapolis. [110]

## Chicanos and Blacks

Black Indianans, four and one-third times more numerous than Hispanics, are found scattered over the Hoosier state. Ten counties (Allen, Delaware, Elkhart, Grant, Lake, Madison, Marion, St. Joseph, Vanderburgh, and Vigo) have five thousand black residents or more, sometimes a lot more (Lake 116,000, Marion 169,000). Only four counties (St. Joseph 5,200, Allen 5,800, Marion 8,500, and Lake 44,520) have over five thousand Hispanics.

How will these two minorities relate to each other? A social scientist might predict that their common lower-class

CHARLES GUTHRIE

*El Centro Hispano (Hispanic Center), 617 E. North St., Indianapolis, located in the old St. Joseph's Hall, 1990.*

status and their shared suffering at the hands of the white majority might cause them to become allies. Or, they might become enemies fighting over their inadequate share of America's bounty, the scraps from the table of the wealthiest country in the history of the world. And, in fact, both results have occurred in the Calumet, where blacks from the Old South and brown-skinned people from the tropics met each other in the schools, the mills, and the barrios.

Sometimes the encounter was violent. David Menchaca, a Chicano, attended Gary West Side High School from 1972 until his graduation in 1976. Residential segregation led to a student population of 70 percent black, 29 percent Latino, and 1 percent white. "Actually," David recalled, "there were so few whites that you could count them on your fingers and toes." The two groups took out their frustrations on each other:

> Race fighting was commonplace then, and the odds were "usually six or more to one" in favor of the Blacks. David recalls a big fight one day at the first lunch period: "I had come downstairs, and all my friends were gone. It was then that I realized I was

being watched by some very threatening eyes. I hit the front door at a dead run, but unfortunately didn't run fast enough. I got caught a block away and received a beating I'll never forget.[111]

Older and wiser heads tried to cooperate and work together on such matters of joint concern as housing, school segregation, fair employment, crime, and corruption. At a crucial meeting of the Gary City Council, 18 May 1965, Mexican-American councilman John Armenta cast a critical vote to give subpoena powers to a proposed Human Rights Commission drafted by black city councilman Richard Gordon Hatcher. The bill passed five to three, one of its opponents having been ejected from the council chamber. Armenta's vote had made the difference.[112]

Chicanos also supported Hatcher when he ran for mayor of Gary. The racket-tainted Democratic party was making such an obvious effort to defeat a reform candidate that Hatcher had to raise most of his campaign funds outside the city. Once again the Hispanic voters of Gary, led by Armenta and Dr. Manuel J. Vargas, supported Hatcher, and their backing was crucial. Hatcher won the Democratic primary by 3,000 votes and the general election by an even narrower margin, 1,865 votes. What Jesse Jackson was later to call the "Rainbow Coalition" had again made the difference.[113]

Within a year and a half the Chicano-black coalition broke up. Armenta and Hatcher squabbled over patronage, and Vargas denounced what he called the "preprogrammed thinking of Hatcher's yes-men." Hatcher made speeches extolling black nationalism, and Armenta ran against him for mayor in 1971. As a result of white flight from a city with a black mayor, Gary was now more than 55 percent black. Hatcher won again, this time by a wide margin of 34,000 to 21,000, with Armenta receiving less than 3,000 votes. Hatcher would doubtless have won anyway, but such a failure to show any political muscle at all on the part of *la raza* was embarrassing.[114]

## After Seventy-Five Years

> We progressed slowly, it is true
> Overcoming by faith and hard work
> Illuminated by the light of our dream,
> Our dream that starred the night.

It is nearly seventy-five years since the arrival of the first substantial number of Spanish-speaking people in Indiana, brought to Lake County to help break the steel strike of 1919. Although Hispanics were less than 2 percent of the Hoosier state's population in 1990, they are growing three times as fast, in percentage terms, as black Hoosiers and seventy times as fast as whites. In fact, as a consequence of differential rates of birth, emigration, and immigration, the 2 percent of Indiana's people who are Hispanic had a slightly larger absolute growth than the 90 percent who are classified as white.

Population Change, 1980–90

|  | Increase | Percent Increase |
|---|---|---|
| White | 11,883 | .2 |
| Black | 17,603 | 4.2 |
| Hispanic | 12,270 | 14.2[115] |

And these official statistics, impressive as they are, doubtless understate the growth of Indiana's second largest minority. The 1980 census returns, for example, gave Indianapolis 6,818 Hispanics. But Monica Medina, on the basis of her work with the community as director of the Hispanic Center, believes that there were 13,000. And Professor Daniel Briere of the University of Indianapolis, who has collaborated on a study of the Hispanic people of Indianapolis, believes that the true number might be as many as 15,000. Undocumented workers afraid of being deported, Spanish-speaking residents who did not receive a Spanish-language census form, and members of what Oscar Lewis has called "the culture of poverty" who have little or nothing to do with the government, went uncounted. And thus the Hispanic community has not benefited from some of the programs that are distributed on the basis of population.

The growing Hispanic minority, still very small in the Hoosier state, is part of the second-largest, fastest-growing minority in the nation: over twenty million Mexican Americans, Puerto Ricans, Cubans, Central Americans, South Americans, and Spaniards.[116] On a national level, Mexicans have risen from the tenth largest ethnic group (seven million people) in 1980 to seventh place (eleven million people) in 1990. If this trend continues, Hispanics will be nearly one-fifth of the United States population by 2050.[117]

For reasons discussed previously, Hispanic people remain considerably below average in per capita income, the most convenient measure of social status. In 1972 average income by ethnic groups was as follows:[118]

Jews—172 percent of average
Japanese—132
Polish—115
*Mexican—76*
*Puerto Rican—63*
Black—62
Native American—60

However, despite the continuing problems of racial prejudice, lower-than-average levels of education and income, and the decline of the manufacturing sector of the American economy in the 1990s, many Hispanic people are making it the way earlier immigrant groups did. *Latinos in the Calumet Region,* a 1987 collection of biographies, like the later *Mexican American Harbor Lights,* is full of individual success stories. The sixty-six earlier narratives tell of people who arrived from tiny villages in Mexico, rural Puerto Rico, Castro's Cuba, often penniless, unskilled, illiterate, speaking no English, who made a place for themselves and for their children in America. These are some of the positions held by members of these families: secretary, paralegal, manufacturer, surgeon, high school teacher, welder at Inland Steel, policeman, member of air force and army, chief of staff at Lake County Medical Clinic, electrician at Inland, labor relations mediator at Inland, crane operator at Inland, mail carrier, US Steel employee ($30,000), housing manager, millwright at Inland, medical records clerk, marine corps member, foreman, pilot, bilingual teacher, professor, mechanic in navy, engineer, undercover agent, and community organizer.

Chicano nationalism may be eroded by the same thing that Werner Sombart blamed for the failure of socialism in America: "Apple Pie," that is, the elevated living standard of the average American. *Harbor Lights* is full of stories of discrimination, poverty, and suffering, but the overall tone is one of gratitude, pride, and patriotism:

> The dream we had for our children
> Took flesh and became reality.

## South Bend as a Laboratory

With 5,201 Hispanics (2.1 percent of the population) St. Joseph County is very close to the state average of residents from Spanish-speaking countries. As noted above, it is one of only four counties with more than five thousand Hispanics. The presence of the University of Notre Dame, with its extensive ties to the Catholic community and the Chicano studies program established there by Professor Julian Samora (the first Mexican American to get a degree in sociology), makes it an excellent laboratory for studying the state of the Hispanic community at the beginning of the last decade of the century. Here are some of the conclusions of a 1992 study directed by Professor Martin F. Murphy (himself married to a Hispanic from the Dominican Republic).

— The Hispanic population of St. Joseph County is growing seventeen times faster than the general population (slightly higher than statewide growth, noted above).

— The population is very diverse on all demographic variables: place of birth, Hispanic tradition and language, educational levels, income, and place of residence in the county. Most originated in Mexico.

— Hispanics are still having a lot of children; their population is twice as young as that of the general county population (median age seventeen vs. thirty-three). The average household has twice as many persons as the county average (4.7 vs. 2.5)(children and extended family).

— Younger Hispanics are moving up the social ladder, as noted above. But one out of four in the age group 16 to 24 has dropped out of school.

— Employment: there is a trend toward multiple income families, stable jobs, little lost work time for illness, injury, or layoff, and continued high blue-collar employment in manufacturing (about 50 percent). Four out of five Hispanic women have worked outside the home.

— The average Hispanic is bilingual (65 percent, with another 11 percent who speak only Spanish).

— Hispanics feel they are discriminated against, especially by the local newspapers and television.

— Hispanic income is still much lower than the average. With twice as many persons as the average household, median household income is $23,000 as against the Indiana average of $28,000. Twenty-nine percent of the population lives below the poverty level, almost twice the national average of 16 percent.

— A higher-than-average percent of the county's Hispanics has some form of health insurance (83 percent vs. only 68 percent for Hispanics on a national level). But one out of five never sees a physician.

— Eighty-one percent are Catholic, 16 percent belong to some other Christian denomination.

— Sixty-three percent of eligible voters are registered. Forty-three percent feel that local politicians represent Hispanic interests badly or very badly. Fifty-five percent feel that local media coverage of Hispanic topics is bad or very bad. Fifty-six percent feel that non-Hispanics in the county do not understand or treat them well.[119]

Hispanics in Indiana have progressed a long way from the brutal racism of the expatriation proceedings during the Great Depression; but they still have a long way to go in the areas of education, high-status jobs, and acceptance by the community.

### Assimilation and Intermarriage

Sociologists have delineated more than a half dozen kinds of assimilation: cultural, structural, behavioral, identification, attitude, civic, etc. When a Mexican American, a Puerto Rican, or a Cuban speaks English, takes an Anglo first name, becomes a fan of football (instead of soccer) or basketball (in place of bullfighting), celebrates Christmas instead of *Posadas* and *el Día de Los Reyes,* and eats hamburgers, hot dogs, and pizza instead of tacos, *asopao* (Puerto Rican chicken), or *judíos y christianos* (Cuban black beans and rice), he is assimilating. Finally, like John Hernandez, who grew up in an otherwise completely Anglo community in Hebron, Indiana, never learned Spanish, or ate much Mexican food, he may say that "he does not even consider himself a Mexican."[120]

Marriage with a member of a different ethnic group can be another measure of assimilation. Sociologists view it "as the surest means of assimilation and the most infallible index of its occurrence."[121] I have mentioned above Sam Maravilla, first generation to be born in the United States, who attended Indiana University, met Beverly Dornberg there and married her. Sam's nephew Rodrigo, of the next generation, also went to Bloomington, and met and married Virginia Ann Johnson there. Gregory, Rodrigo's son, went to Harvard and is likely to marry anybody with whom he falls in love.[122] The first generation of migrants had much less opportunity to meet non-Hispanics and generally looked with disfavor on those who married outside of *la raza.* Parents arranged a suitable marriage; "in 1917, the olden days, young Mexicans weren't allowed to date. It was a mystery how my parents ever married."[123] One young woman of twenty-three, not allowed to date by her old-fashioned parents, secretly dated a young man twice and then married him.[124] When Carmen, the daughter of Juanita Torres (born in Caguas, Puerto Rico) married a non-*Borinquen* (Puerto Rican) but a Catholic graduate of Bishop John Noll High School, her mother was unhappy because "she married out of her own race." Prejudiced white students at Froebel High School in Gary were so unhappy when Miguel Rosario dated a young black woman (Patricia Morgan) that they beat her up and smeared black paint on her white and pink dress. Later the couple married; he became a doctor. Their son Renaldo was beaten up as his mother had been; he suffered a concussion from being hit over the head with a baseball bat.[125]

A 1983 Notre Dame dissertation investigating Chicano intermarriage confirms commonsense expectations about the subject. Mexican Americans who "marry out" are more likely:

—to be better educated and to have better-educated parents
—to have non-Mexican friends and schoolmates
—to have an Anglo first name
—to speak English at home
—to be of the second or third generation in the United States
—to feel that it is all right for a wife to earn more than her husband
—to have a mother who works outside the home
—to reject separatist Chicano ideology
—to have a higher socioeconomic status
—to belong to non-Mexican organizations
—to have served in the military or live near military bases
—to have fewer children.[126]

About one of five Chicanos marries outside *la raza* and the rate is increasing. In the long run, Indiana's Hispanic population will doubtless assimilate and become simply "Americans." A pertinent example is the way the Celts, Basques, Greeks, Romans, Franks, Muslims, Visigoths, and English intermarried and assimilated in France so that (except for the most recent arrivals) everybody there is French, drinks wine, is likely to follow the Tour de France, be passionate about gastronomy, etc. America's twenty million Hispanics already have abandoned the bullfight for baseball and football. When Hispanics vote they vote Democratic or Republican (Nixon got 30 percent of the Hispanic vote) and not for *La Raza Unida* party. They move around the country, intermarry, and lose all trace of a Spanish accent. Tacos and fajitas seem as "American" as pizza, frankfurters, doughnuts, and Budweiser. But some residual feelings of ethnicity remain.

## A *Puchero* (Argentine Stew), not a Melting Pot

Yes, much we suffered and endured
But the struggle was won,
For the dream we had for our children,
Took flesh and became reality.

Still, even if the most notable feature of Hispanic ancestry is a last name like Cardenas, Sepulveda, Rosales, Hernandez, or Muñoz, something of an ethnic heritage survives. Anthony Quinn, son of a Mexican mother and an Irish father, does not even have a Chicano given name or surname. But he *feels* himself to be Chicano, and that's what counts. The Hispanic Americans who came to Indiana to work in the fields or factories were "tried in the crucible" of these painful experiences and emerged as strong as the steel they made for so many decades. In their reminiscences a Spanish verb keeps popping up— *aguantar,* to suffer or survive. So perhaps the best way to end this account of their seventy-five-year story is to repeat the words William Faulkner used to end his account of the similar triumphant suffering of the black people in his fictional Yoknapatawpha County:

They endured.

## Notes

1. James B. Lane, *"City of the Century": A History of Gary, Indiana* (Bloomington: Indiana University Press, 1978), 4.

2. Herbert E. Bolton, *Coronado: Knight of Pueblos and Plains* (New York: Whittlesey House, 1949), 291–305.

3. L. H. Gann and Peter J. Duignan, *The Hispanics in the United States* (Stanford, Calif.: Hoover Institution on War, Revolution, and Peace/Boulder, Colo.: Westview Press, 1986), 10.

4. John D. Barnhart and Donald F. Carmony, *Indiana, from Frontier to Industrial Commonwealth,* 4 vols. (New York: Lewis Publishing Co., 1954), 1:33–34. The Council Oak was destroyed in early 1992.

5. Charles Guthrie, Dan Briere, and Mary Moore, *The Indianapolis Hispanic Community* (Indianapolis: University of Indianapolis Press, 1995).

6. Gann and Duignan, *Hispanics in the United States,* 36.

7. Senoras of Yesteryear, *Mexican American Harbor Lights* (East Chicago, Ind.: By the authors, 1992), 4 (hereafter cited as *MAHL*).

8. Lane, *"City of the Century,"* 71. See also *Gary Post-Tribune,* 10 June 1956.

9. *1910 Census,* vol. 2, *Population* (Washington, D.C.: Government Printing Office, 1913), 568.

10. William Z. Foster, *The Great Steel Strike and Its Lessons* (New York: B. W. Huebsch, Inc., 1920), 150.

11. *1910 Census,* 2:568; *1920 Census,* vol. 3, *Population* (Washington, D.C.: Government Printing Office, 1922), 297.

12. Raymond A. Mohl and Neil Betten, *Steel City: Urban and Ethnic Patterns in Gary, Indiana, 1906–1950* (New York: Holmes and Meier, 1986), 27.

13. Ibid., 30; Lane, *"City of the Century,"* 38.

14. Foster, *Great Steel Strike,* 100–1; *Lake County Times,* 22 Sept. 1919.

15. Foster, *Great Steel Strike,* 12–13.

16. Mohl and Betten, *Steel City,* 28–29; Foster, *Great Steel Strike,* 170–91.

17. *MAHL,* 4.

18. Lane, *"City of the Century,"* 71.

19. *MAHL;* Ciro Sepulveda, "La Colonia del Harbor: A History of Mexicanos in East Chicago, Indiana, 1919–1932" (Ph.D. diss., University of Notre Dame, 1976), 54.

20. Foster, *Great Steel Strike,* 1.

21. The standard history of this paranoid period in American history is Robert K. Murray, *Red Scare: A Study in National*

*Hysteria, 1919–1920* (Minneapolis: University of Minnesota Press, 1955).

22. Foster, *Great Steel Strike*, v, 151.

23. Lane, *"City of the Century,"* 74.

24. Gann and Duignan, *Hispanics in the United States,* 37, 40, 44.

25. Paul S. Taylor, *Mexican Labor in the United States: Chicago and the Calumet Region* (Berkeley: University of California Press, 1932), 36; Sepulveda, "La Colonia del Harbor," 62.

26. Lane, *"City of the Century,"* 27.

27. Sepulveda, "La Colonia del Harbor," 43.

28. Abraham Olivo, interview with the author, 1990.

29. David Brody, *Steelworkers in America: The Nonunion Era* (Cambridge, Mass.: Harvard University Press, 1960), 101.

30. Sepulveda, "La Colonia del Harbor," 38–39.

31. Commission of Inquiry, quoted in ibid., 42.

32. Brody, *Steelworkers in America,* 273–74.

33. Lane, *"City of the Century,"* 72.

34. *MAHL,* 12–13.

35. Lane, *"City of the Century,"* 61, 73.

36. James B. Lane and Edward Escobar, eds., *Forging a Community: The Latino Experience in Northwest Indiana, 1919–1975* (Chicago: Cattails Press, 1987), 138.

37. Ibid., 218.

38. Mohl and Betten, *Steel City,* 93, 94, 95, 96, 97, 99.

39. Sepulveda, "La Colonia del Harbor," 78.

40. Ibid., 83–84, 81; *MAHL,* 36.

41. Lane and Escobar, eds., *Forging a Community,* 188–91.

42. Guthrie, Briere, and Moore, *The Indianapolis Hispanic Community.*

43. Ibid.

44. *MAHL,* 6.

45. Lane, *"City of the Century,"* 72.

46. Ibid., 232.

47. Ibid., 73.

48. Larry R. Gerlach, *Blazing Crosses in Zion* (Logan: Utah State University Press, 1982), 56; Richard K. Tucker, *The Dragon and the Cross* (Hamden, Conn.: The Shoe String Press, 1991), 101.

49. Archibald McKinlay, *Twin City: A Pictorial History of East Chicago, Indiana* (Norfolk, Va.: Donning Co., 1988), 105.

50. *Lake County Times,* 15 Apr. 1931.

51. Paul E. Kelley to the Department of Labor, 4 Mar. 1932, copy in East Chicago Public Library.

52. Sepulveda, "La Colonia del Harbor," 140; Olivo interview; Lane, *"City of the Century,"* 74.

53. Lane and Escobar, eds., *Forging a Community,* 175.

54. Ibid., 178.

55. *MAHL,* 60.

56. Lane, *"City of the Century,"* 75.

57. *MAHL,* 60.

58. James B. Lane, *Latinos in the Calumet Region* (Gary: Indiana University Northwest, 1987), 2.

59. *Aztlan:* Thematic Issue, Chicanos in the Midwest, vol. 7, no. 2 (summer 1976): 153.

60. *New York Times,* 4 Nov. 1992.

61. Interviews with the author, Aug. 1990.

62. Monica Medina, interview with the author, 9 Feb. 1993.

63. Lane, *Latinos,* 13.

64. Olivo interview.

65. *MAHL,* 55–56.

66. Earl Shorris, *Latinos: A Biography of the People* (New York: W. W. North and Co., 1992), 321.

67. Guthrie, Briere, and Moore, *The Indianapolis Hispanic Community.*

68. Barbara Tuchman, *The Zimmermann Telegram* (New York: Macmillan, 1966).

69. Raúl Morín, *Among the Valiant: Mexican-Americans in World War II and Korea* (Alhambra, Calif.: Borden Pub. Co., 1966), 15.

70. Gann and Duignan, *Hispanics in the United States,* 42.

71. McKinlay, *Twin City,* 156.

72. Morín, *Among the Valiant,* 27.

73. Olivo interview.

74. Morín, *Among the Valiant,* 203.

75. Ibid., passim.

76. McKinlay, *Twin City,* 150.

77. *MAHL,* 14, 15, 20.

78. Lane, *Latinos,* 9, 10.

79. Lane, *"City of the Century,"* 239, 259, 242–43, 244–46, 262.

80. Ibid., 244; *MAHL,* 99; Jack Stieber, *The Steel Industry Wage Structure: A Study of the Joint Union-Management Job Evaluation Program in the Basic Steel Industry* (Cambridge, Mass.: Harvard University Press, 1959).

81. *MAHL,* 99.

82. Stieber, *Steel Industry Wage Structure,* 170.

83. Ibid., 56.

84. *MAHL,* 12–17.

85. *La Estrella Hispanica* (Indianapolis), various dates 1985–86.

86. *MAHL,* 22–23.

87. Ibid., 15.

88. *Aztlan,* 311.

89. Ibid., 245.

90. June Drenning Holmquist, *They Chose Minnesota* (St. Paul: Minnesota Historical Society Press, 1981), 101.

91. Interview, 16 Sept. 1990.

92. Lane, *Latinos,* 15.

93. Stieber, *Steel Industry Wage Structure,* 170.

94. Lane and Escobar, eds., *Forging a Community,* 207.

95. McKinlay, *Twin City,* 168.

96. Lane and Escobar, eds., *Forging a Community,* 208.

97. Lane, *Latinos.*

98. *South Bend Tribune,* 29 Mar. 1993.

99. McKinlay, *Twin City,* 172.

100. Lane, *Latinos,* 20, 39.

101. *The Indiana Fact Book* (Bloomington and Indianapolis: Indiana University Press), 113, 114, 260.

102. Ibid., 103.

103. Ibid., 260.

104. *South Bend Tribune,* 29 Oct. 1992.

105. *Value Line,* Aug. 1992.

106. Lane, *Latinos,* 5.

107. Rodolfo Gonzales, *I Am Joaquin* (Santa Barbara, Calif.: La Casa Publications, 1967).

108. James Crawford, *Hold Your Tongue: Bilingualism and the Politics of English Only* (Reading, Mass.: Addison-Wesley, 1992), 5, 148.

109. Michael Murphy, "The Hispanic Population of St. Joseph County," computer print-out, 1992.

110. Medina interview.

111. Lane, *Latinos,* 45.

112. Lane, *"City of the Century,"* 281.

113. Ibid., 287–89, 290; Richard Gordon Hatcher speech, South Bend, Ind.,11 Aug. 1967, *South Bend Tribune,* 12 Aug. 1967.

114. Lane, *Latinos,* 12, and *"City of the Century,"* 296, 300.

115. *Indiana Fact Book,* 63.

116. Frank L. Schick and Renee Schick, comps. and eds., *Statistical Handbook on U.S. Hispanics* (Phoenix, Ariz.: Oryx Press, 1991), xv.

117. *Time,* 1 Mar. 1993, p. 72.

118. Thomas Sowell, *Ethnic America: A History* (New York: Basic Books, 1973), 5.

119. Murphy, "The Hispanic Population of St. Joseph County."

120. Lane, *Latinos,* 34.

121. Armando I. Abney-Guardado, "Chicano Intermarriage in the United States: A Sociocultural Analysis" (Ph.D. diss., University of Notre Dame, 1983).

122. *MAHL,* 23.

123. Ibid., 11.

124. Lane and Escobar, eds., *Forging a Community,* 218.

125. Lane, *Latinos,* 7, 13.

126. Abney-Guardado, "Chicano Intermarriage," passim.

# HUNGARIANS

LINDA DÉGH

*In 1882, when steamship agents offered to book passage for a group of thirty-two villagers of Hegykő, Sopron County, to bring them to South Bend as laborers for Studebaker's wagon factory and Oliver's plow plant, the Hungarians did not hesitate. These farmhands displayed extraordinary entrepreneurial skills, mobility, and a readiness to sacrifice for a better future. They were already accustomed to migrating to labor sites. Temporarily it did not bother them to do the most strenuous labor under utter deprivation in the hope of fast money-making. Their motivation was to save every penny, return home as soon as possible, pay off debts, and become prosperous farmers.*

Today's America is only the embryo of a gigantic new world: its struggles only its birthing pains. Time carries a new humanity in its womb whose language may be as little English, as little Roman, as is today's French or Spanish, and whose social system may not resemble anything we now know. The phenomena we encounter on this continent alert us to these concerns of world history. This America is a great school: where the perspective of the philosopher, the historian, the statesman broadens; where there is little to imitate, but everything is interesting and educational (1877).[1]

The Hungarian-American subculture is a small but diverse part of the patchwork of Indiana ethnics. It does not stand out as a solidly knit community or even as a string of communities united by common threads of identity. Although the image of Hungarians or Magyars[2] has been romanticized into stereotypical roles by movies and other forms of popular culture, in reality Hungarians are often divided among themselves, stubbornly clinging to separate regional identities brought from the Old World. From 1870 to 1956 disparate groups of Hungarian immigrants have settled in Indiana for different reasons, a fact which helps explain their lack of solidarity.

The first Hungarians to move to the United States were exiles of the unsuccessful 1848–49 revolution against the Hapsburg Empire. Hungarians, led by Lajos Kossuth, revolted against Austrian rule and attempted to establish an independent kingdom of Hungary, but because of the overwhelming military strength of Austria and her allies the revolution failed. Rebels fled to America and attempted to start a new life in the midwestern and southern United States. The fallen champion Kossuth, meanwhile, toured Britain, France, and the United States to plead for support for the restoration of the Kingdom of Hungary; he was hospitably welcomed in America, where at least fifteen communities with Hungarian names had been established, including a county and five settlements bearing the name of Kossuth. These communities soon faded into obscurity, including one in Washington County, Indiana, which by 1990 contained only scattered houses, a general store, and a church. The name remains, but the residents do not recall who Kossuth was, nor does the cemetery preserve any evidence of Hungarian presence.

This first group of revolutionary exiles to America, numbering eight hundred to nine hundred people, soon

Mass immigration from Hungary to America (including Hungarians and national minorities) began in the 1870s and affected mostly the agricultural population. Between 1870 and World War I, more than two million people crossed the ocean. As in other European agricultural countries with economies based on large land ownership, industrialization and farm mechanization forced Hungarian farmworkers to seek their livelihood elsewhere in industrial towns, where they resorted to road building, construction work, or mining—at home or abroad. Bankrupt farmers, landless farmworkers, sharecroppers, and servants took seasonal work in major European mining places and construction sites to provide the means to return home to old-fashioned farming.

In 1882, when steamship agents offered to book passage for a group of thirty-two villagers of Hegykő, Sopron County, to bring them to South Bend as laborers for

dispersed to urban centers—New York, Boston, Chicago, New Orleans—where they linked up with other elite émigrés, patriotic and politically conscious old nobility, intellectuals, and successful business entrepreneurs, and launched the symbols that would later form the core of a constructed Hungarian-American identity. On 15 March 1928, the eightieth anniversary of the revolution, the unveiling of a statue of Kossuth on Riverside Drive in New York City and a joint political statement by Hungarian Americans and Hungarian government representatives reinforced Kossuth's figure as the symbol of Hungarian freedom. The 15 March anniversary date is celebrated uniformly by all Hungarian settlements around the world, including those in Indiana. The so-called Kossuth pilgrimage of 1928, which politicians from Hungary launched as a reminder of the territorial mutilation of Hungary by the winning powers in 1919, was sponsored by 272 Hungarian-American organizations, 87 churches, and 41 newspapers. The patriotic elite supported other demonstrations and appeals for "Justice for Hungary"[3] throughout the interwar years, and, as a result, a federation of Hungarians abroad was founded. This liaison was manipulated according to changing political ambitions, but it continued to sport the name of Kossuth and Hungarian freedom on its banner.

The official programming of the patriotic holiday popularized Kossuth's folk image, which spread through the Hungarian-American masses and surfaced in oral tradition and popular chapbooks. Hungarian immigrants in Indiana still carry scraps of the story in their hearts. John Béres of Gary, telling the story in 1967, said that when Kossuth toured America he visited the South incognito and helped Abraham Lincoln liberate slaves; he helped the poor and was worshiped by everyone. Mary Scobie of Crown Point remembered that her grandmother kept a piece of tricolored armband that she wore as a schoolgirl at a celebration on Kossuth's behalf in Indianapolis. "He was the best-looking man she ever saw," Mary said. "Looked like Daniel Boone and tamed wolves."

*Sitting in this mid-1890s photograph is András Rónai (Andrew Rooney), who settled in East Chicago in 1884. He was the father of Andrew Rooney (the child in the photo?), who in 1934 was elected as the first so-called ethnic mayor of East Chicago.*

Hungary
○ National Capital
• City
— International Boundary

125 Mi.

Studebaker's wagon factory and Oliver's plow plant, the Hungarians did not hesitate. These farmhands displayed extraordinary entrepreneurial skills, mobility, and a readiness to sacrifice for a better future. They were already accustomed to migrating to labor sites. Temporarily it did not bother them to do the most strenuous labor under utter deprivation in the hope of fast money-making.[4] Their motivation was to save every penny, return home as soon as possible, pay off debts, and become prosperous farmers.

Contemporary American observers were stunned by what they saw of these "alien population" groups, who banded together in shabby tenements on the outskirts of industrial towns, close to working places, in complete isolation from mainstream society. In 1907 John Holliday of Indianapolis used harsh words to describe the living conditions of a group composed "almost entirely of illiterate peasants from Austria-Hungary who differ greatly in enterprise and intelligence from the average American citizen." He could not conceal his dismay at "these people who have no social advantages whatever, their only place of recreation being the saloon and coffee house," who "crowd together in the most densely populated districts of the cities," who settle in Indianapolis "in communities by themselves, where they continue to speak their native languages, and are slow to assimilate American ideas," and who "possess little pride in their personal appearance and live in dirt and squalor." Mentioning Hungarian boarders specifically, he speaks of thirty men, two women, and a sickly, pale, barefoot child living in four rooms on the second floor of a dirty, dilapidated house. Their diet was tasteless—lots of soup made from a five-cent soupbone

with cabbage and noodles. Except for family photos, the boarders did not decorate their living quarters. Holliday expressed indignation at the "constant influx of the foreign population" as labor for developing industry because the immigrants did not attempt to integrate. He found these new arrivals inferior to early pioneers who undertook a dangerous journey and struggled to build their new existence. "The immigrant of today is allured by fairy tales of a country unrivalled in its wealth and opportunity to get riches."[5]

Holliday's mistake was to compare immigrant farm workers, who temporarily accepted the hardest body-breaking industrial labor in a foreign environment for a better peasant existence in their native land, with pioneer farm entrepreneurs who built their new peasant wealth on new land carved out of the wilderness. These Hungarian workers had no need to integrate and learn English since their goal was to return to their homeland as soon as possible. All they wanted was to work and earn the money they needed to take home. The immigrant laborer was a temporary hired hand who took advantage of the opportunity to earn better wages in America's booming industries. The immigrant was a peasant, a proud bearer of a rich cultural tradition, and he was not ready to relinquish his roots for marginal company-town living. Committed to his goal, he took up unskilled labor temporarily, as so many guest workers from underdeveloped agricultural countries have done ever since, anywhere in the industrialized western world. Repeatedly, in some six to eight migrations between 1903 and 1920, Hungarian guest workers made the crossing and invested their earnings to build their farms at home in Hungary. What their life was like until the decision had to be made to return or to stay for good is well documented in the Hungarian-American press and in accounts of surviving descendants.

Holliday accurately described the austere communal living conditions of single transitory male workers in the institution known as *burdos ház* (boardinghouse), a place that accommodated the workers' need for minimum living expenditures so that the maximum amount of earnings could be saved. Similar was the description of Géza D. Berkó: this "peculiar commonwealth was presided over by the landlady, whose subjects enjoyed the same rights with her as did her husband."[6] The *burdosasszony* (the missus), wife of a fellow worker, took care of cooking, washing, and cleaning in the house where residents took turns sleeping according to their work shifts. Except for Sunday church services and occasional visits to the saloon, the men had no social life. Berkó saw the *burdoscsalád* (boarder family), "this new form of community," as the hotbed of debauchery, criminality, and destroyer of Hungarian morality.[7] In retrospect, D. Sütő of Griffith (in

*Mr. and Mrs. Martin Hévizi's wedding in 1909. The bride, angry at her parents for arranging her marriage at age fifteen to a man of thirty-seven, cut out the couple's heads in the Szilágyi family photograph (right). The family, newly arrived from Hungary to Harrisburg, Pennsylvania, eventually settled in the Calumet Region.*

1972) remembered his years as a boarder when he worked for US Steel. He kept returning to the same landlady, herself from a village neighboring his own, six times between 1911 and 1922. Her husband found him a better job and introduced him to a greenhorn (*grinór*) girl who became his wife.

The exploitation of the workers was painted by the Hungarian-American press in dark colors: the Magyars were a farming folk used to open prairies, but they always had the toughest jobs—in dark mines, factories, foundries, and steel mills, near roaring machines and sparkling fires, where the sun never shone. Describing the inhuman conditions, reporters underscored in their romantic depictions the difference between industrial labor as opposed to farm life on the Magyar prairies. The mental state of laborers spending years in ethnic and cultural isolation is well demonstrated by the rich body of folk songs, often in letter form, in which the immigrant calls

out in pain, addressing his beloved in the Old Country, complaining about hard labor, extreme fear of the American working place, solitude, and homesickness.[8] The poem of György Kemény about the grinders of South Bend, for example, laments the sufferings of the Magyar toiling in Oliver's dark, airless, sunless, infernal shop. His blood is the sacrifice making farmers happy and prosperous. In essence, the plow iron becomes the soul of the foundry worker, crying as it breaks the soil.[9] A folk song noted in 1913 has an apparent reference to the South Bend grinding shop:

> Are you surprised that I'm so pale?
> It's the ninth year I've spent in the Oliver shop
> I grind iron for farmers.

With time passing and conditions changing, temporary workers had to decide whether to stay or return. Staying meant breaking out from isolation, learning the language and basic skills, settling with family, and changing their loyalty from the homeland to their new land of choice. When economic and political conditions in Hungary and the United States forced people to stay at the place where they happened to be, shortly before or after the First World War, several pockets of Magyar peasants became more visible in the United States. The peasant immigrants, including ethnic minorities originating from all parts of historic Hungary and speaking regional dialects, became the bearers of a specific Hungarian-American culture. After World War I and the breakup of the Hapsburg Empire, a new group, peasant refugees from Romania (Transylvania), Yugoslavia, and Czechoslovakia, escaping minority status in newly formed nations, joined the Hungarian immigrants already in the United States, reinvigorating fading traditions. Young men in particular fled from military service, afraid of the brutal drilling by the hostile powers.

In spite of the great diversity of Hungarians, with their uneven representation of cultural dialects, religions, and loyalties, these four generations of peasant immigrants—the foreign born, and their first- , second- , and third-generation American-born offspring—comprised the largest, most conspicuous group that established the image and identity of the Hungarian American as it is celebrated today. The group as a whole was nicknamed *öreg Amerikások* (Old Americans). However, this group, totaling about four hundred fifty thousand Magyars in the United States, never settled anywhere en masse or created a solid, closed ethnic residency, but instead spread out in the suburban regions of industrial towns, making their living from heavy industry. Only 1 percent ever returned to farming. The majority of Hungarians landed in New York and found their way to mines and factories in New Jersey, Pennsylvania, Ohio, Virginia, Michigan, Illinois, and Indiana. At the turn of the century 50 percent lived in "rural, non-farm areas," compared to 35 percent in 1910, a peak year when Indiana counted thirty thousand Hungarians. But not even Cleveland, reputed as the American Debrecen,[10] had a stable Hungarian population amounting to more than 10 percent of the total population.[11] In reality, the settlement pattern was determined by job opportunities. Thus, the original chain migration built on family, neighborhood, and village connections did not help create American outposts for Hungarians as was the case of several Indiana German settlements. Young people moved easily from one company town to the next, irrespective of family ties; and settlements increasingly showed the presence and intermarriage of Hungarians from diverse regions. Indiana settlers of the first two generations show a strong relationship to specific working places in the above-listed states where they once worked or had acquaintances.

Hungarian Hoosiers can be located primarily in two regions: in St. Joseph County and the residential areas of the city of South Bend; and in the industrial area known as the Calumet Region—Gary, East Chicago, Indiana Harbor (these latter two commonly known as the "Twin Cities"), Hammond, Whiting, and suburban residential towns such as Highland, Griffith, Munster, Schererville, Merrillville, and others. South Bend and some mining places in the Terre Haute strip-mining area attracted earlier job seekers directly from Hungary at the turn of the century. Some Hungarians were brought early on to jobs in railroad construction, packing companies, slaughterhouses, and the Malleable Castings Company in the Haughville section of Indianapolis. As peasant immigrants of central and eastern Europe did everywhere else, these Hungarians isolated themselves from the native population. The Calumet Region became a secondary settlement for Hungarians after the building of US Steel (in Gary) and other companies during the early years of the 1900s. Already experienced in industrial labor in America, Hungarian immigrants came as pioneers to build their own place. Families in the 1970s still liked to remember those heroic times. Mrs. Frank Jakab drew a vivid picture of her arrival—she was a farmwife whose husband wanted to make enough money to add more acreage to their farm in Hungary. Her husband wrote, telling her to sell everything and join him in Gary. When she met him at a shack where the railroad tracks ended, it must have seemed like the end of the world. Looking around she saw nothing but sand dunes; sticks marked the stretch where Broadway was to be built. "You have destroyed us," she charged. "Why did you bring me to this miserable place where there is not even a bed to sleep in?" Soon ethnic neighborhoods were constructed by the same settlers who built the industrial plants that provided for their employment; their villagelike homes accommodated their traditional sense of decent living.

Many professionally trained persons, intellectuals of diverse categories, began to emigrate from Hungary after the First World War. They did not join the settling trend of peasant immigrants in the United States and did not seek companionship with them. Peasantry constituted a solid subculture in Hungary and was isolated from the elite—not only as servants, the poor, and the powerless are isolated from masters, the rich, and the powerful, but also as they are separated by different standards of education, worldview, language, and the arts. Thus, as Joshua Fishman observes: "New arrivals . . . either passively entered into already existing Hungarian-American institutions, or ultimately assimilated into general American society and lost their Hungarian identity."[12] With no common ground for these professionally trained immigrants to associate with those they saw as lower-status Hungarians, their own ethnic survival was doomed by dissociation among themselves. The urban-elite émigrés belonged largely in two categories: the educated immigrants—businessmen, public servants, lawyers, doctors, engineers, many Jewish intellectuals among them—who left in the period between the two wars because they saw no future or job security in their truncated country; and those who left after the end of the Second World War and were admitted as Displaced Persons (DPs) following the dissolution of refugee camps in Austria—exiles with intent to return, old nobility, military men, politicians, determined immigrants who sought security and a better life, Jews fearful of Hungarian anti-Semitism after surviving concentration camps, and others fearful of Communism. These prototypes, however, constitute only a small minority in Indiana towns. The immigrants of Indianapolis, for example, today represent only a symbolic community that meets at political, social, and ritual commemorative programs, or that hosts cultural events related to distinguished Hungarian or Hungarian-American visitors. Their children and grandchildren no longer claim Hungarian identity.

The latter category of Displaced Persons also includes the so-called freedom fighters, those who took their opportunity to leave Hungary when the 1956 revolutionaries lifted the barbed wires at the Austrian border. Although an estimated two hundred thousand people (one-third women, two-thirds men) left Hungary in 1956–57, many of them returned. At that time, thirty-two thousand were admitted to the United States after screening at Camp Kilmer; eventually, sixty thousand were processed through the camp and released to sponsors who helped them to settle down, find jobs, and blend in. The majority of freedom fighters, however, were not politically motivated. Rather, they had suffered in Hungary from forced ideological and physical isolation from the prosperous and democratic world they dreamed about; they wished to leave behind their limitations. These newcomers were mostly young people, half of them under twenty-five years of age, some of them children who left without the knowledge of their parents. Many were students eager for higher education; among the professionals were physicians, technicians, engineers, electricians, and skilled workers. Only a fraction were farmers. Calumet Region Hungarian churchmen informed their congregations about the new arrivals, and families opened their purses and hearts to assist the homeless. The Ladies Aid Association and the Martha Circle, from one of the two Hungarian Protestant churches, in cooperation with St. Emery's Catholic Church in Indiana Harbor, held bake sales, made sausages and csiga-noodles, and collected clothing and household goods for the invited refugees. A few families and several young men were sponsored and given jobs at local factories upon recommendation by venerable old Hungarian steelworkers. But the sponsors' enthusiasm soon soured. The freedom fighters did not want to become factory workers; they were not lured by the comfortable homes that their sponsors showed could be earned with hard and honest labor nor by the gold watch that they could expect upon retirement. These new people did not want to work in industry; they wanted to leave the factory as soon as possible to continue their education and build a career in a skilled profession. A world's difference separated peasant thrift and the goals of these immigrants, who soon vanished into the mainstream. A child asked to identify his or her ethnic background might say something like: "My mother is English and Dutch; my dad is Hungarian. We traveled to Hungary last summer, but I could not speak to any of my relatives because I was not taught the language." Julianna Puskás's observation on the diverse nature of the post–1945 settlers seems correct: she claims each arrival constitutes a new closed community that cannot find even the most flexible ethnic ties compelling; the differences are bigger than the identity of being Magyar. As she explains, ethnic consciousness did not hold these dissimilar Hungarian groups together even with the thin thread that bonded other new immigrants like Croats, Slovaks, and Finns. Puskás attributes this lack of cohesion to the specifics of the social and political history of Hungary.[13]

## Who Are the Magyars in Indiana?

Opening the telephone directory of any sizable city or industrial region, the ethnographer will find Hungarian presence in the large number of common Hungarian names. One can find plenty of listings of Szabó (tailor), Kovács (smith), Varga (cobbler), Ács (carpenter), Kocsis (coachman), Juhász (shepherd), Molnár (miller), Biró (judge), Borbély (barber), Kerekes (wheelwright), and other surnames that indicate an occupation. Others feature physical character, mood, or temper, such as Kiss (small), Nagy (big), Balogh (awkward), Vastagh (thick), Vigh (pleasant), Joó (good), Mérges (angry), or Szép (pretty). People often bear the name of the geographical location where they originated, such as Szegedi (from Szeged), Veszprémi (from Veszprém), and Szilágyi (from Szilágy). The multiethnic character of Hungarians is indicated by such common names as Magyar, Tóth (Slovak), Török

(Turkish), Németh (German), Oláh (Romanian), Horváth (Croatian), Rácz (Serbian), and Lengyel (Polish), and often people keep their foreign-sounding names (spelled in Hungarian), such as Lakcsik, Roncsák, Vukovics, Klusovszky, Hoffer, or Trimmel. Others may not be so easy to identify. In the desire to preserve their original names, some Anglicize the spelling and write Yuhas (Yuháss), Chizmar (Csismár), Kish (Kiss), Rooney (Rónay), and Sillaghe (Szilágyi), while those favoring assimilation simply translate their names into English, like Good (Joó), Shepherd (Juhász), King (Király), and Cook (Szakács).

Dialing any number of these listings may lead to a great diversity of life stories and interpretations of what Hungarianness means, how it is related to Americanization, and how far it is being claimed and maintained. The variety is infinite, ranging from the newcomer who tries to cope and make a living, to the veteran custodian of Hungarian values who still survives the succumbing generation, to the conscious and unconscious preserver of a selected set of traditions, to the young seeker of "roots" who makes a pilgrimage to Hungary and relearns the forgotten mother tongue, and even to the individual whose Hungarian family name—handed down by a single unknown and long-dead immigrant grandparent—is the only connection to a Hungarian ethnic past.

Regardless of the individual's place in the timetable of the immigration process, Hungarians have never represented a large number in America, nor has their presence greatly fluctuated. In the peak years between 1907 and 1910, as previously noted, two million Hungarian job seekers came to the United States, and thirty thousand came to Indiana. Hungarians are shown sporadically and in low and slowly declining numbers in the censuses between 1910 and 1980 in almost all the larger Indiana cities, townships, and industrial counties. Often fewer than a hundred Hungarians appear, except for the already mentioned St. Joseph, Lake, and Marion counties, where more accumulation and continuity were established as opposed to other places where transiency seemed the rule. In 1980 there were 794 foreign-born Hungarians in St. Joseph County, 705 in the Calumet cities, and 1,830 in Marion County. Nowhere else was the total number of foreign-stock Hungarians beyond four figures. The 1980 count of the population of Hungarian ancestry in Indiana was 44,312, of which 18,382 were of single ancestry. This is indeed a modest number compared to the 1,776,902 Americans in the United States who claim to be of Hungarian ancestry.

Prior to 1918 Hungarians were included with the minorities of the Austrian Empire; and after the war Magyars of the post–World War I states were listed as Romanians, Slovaks, and Yugoslavs. Unfamiliarity with the "foreigner's" nationality and culture often caused local officials to identify Magyars erroneously by a meaningless nickname "Hunyáks"; the more general nickname, "hunkey," in the sense of "greenhorn," was good-naturedly accepted by Calumet Hungarians. The Magyars were lumped into the same category with their Balkan neighbors, who were settled in miserable tenements close to the working places, divorced from the residential areas where Americans had their nice homes. One can get a taste of the territorial segregation of ethnics crammed together, away from the "Sunny Side" where the bosses lived in the boom years of industry, from the comments of an Irish railroadman reminiscing with a Magyar woman, Mrs. Green, née Elizabeth Préda, about the troubles they saw in the Calumet Region. They recalled a note posted on the entrance of the steel factory: "Don't apply if you are Irish." In the vicinity of Inland Steel, the Irish were neighbors of the Hungarians, and they supported each other if they were out of work. Mrs. Green, who kept boarders before she married a British immigrant, took the needy in for free.

This 1967 photograph shows Mrs. Arthur Green, née Elizabeth Préda, standing across from the Inland Steel Company entrance. A prominent Hungarian businesswoman, for years she ran the old Baltimore Hotel, which housed immigrant workers and endless charitable cases, evidence of her renowned good will.

Roman Catholic Hungarians (representing the majority religion of the Old Country) also suffered from religious prejudice: Mrs. Mary McGuam of East Chicago remembers that when her father, a Linton coal miner, enrolled her in the local grade school in 1908, the principal told a teacher to "take this foreign child to the Catholic school." Ironically, her denomination later helped elevate her status through her marriage to the respected Irish funeral director of that community.

## The Magyar Self-Image and How Others See It

According to a widespread saying first noted in the fifteenth century by Italian humanist Coelius Rhodiginus, "Extra Hungariam non est vita, et si est, non est ita" (There is no life outside of Hungary, and if there is, it's not the same). This proud identification of Hungarians with their homeland was often cited and fitted to the national ideology at a time when, ironically, Hungarian masses were forced by historic events to leave their country. For the immigrants and their descendants in America, this saying became more meaningful, even crucial to their ethnic survival. It contributed to the formation of a complex Old Country image that is reinforced by nostalgic expatriates in their everyday talks and folkloric images.

Another key feature of the Hungarian national stereotype also influenced the culture formation of Hungarian Americans: the historically developed self-image of Magyars is that of the self-contained isolate, caught between East and West in the heart of Europe, with neither kin nor friends. The territorial position of the country between East and West had previously prompted scholars to portray the complexity of Magyar culture as due to lasting interethnic contacts with Germanic and Slavonic neighbors. However, a pride in distinctiveness, and the nostalgic "we are alone" mood, prompted nationalists to search for traces of a venerable "Asian" ancestry. In support of this national ideal, propagated by poets, patriots, and philosophers, ethnographers followed Jacob Grimm's mythology construct (1835) and plowed through folklore to find the Asian roots of modern Hungarian folk culture. Despite the fact that central European cultural features layered prominently over the distant "Asian" residues, some nationalists continued to stress the romantic image of the Asian Magyars, an image which seemed to follow in the path of their mythical, valiant Hun brethren in fulfillment of a historic destiny.

According to the popular myth, Attila the Hun was the "scourge of God" whose mission was fulfilled by the Magyars. Conqueror Árpád and his dynasty, the first holy King Stephen (1001–1038) and his virgin son St. Emery, elected Magyars to defend European Christianity against pagan Mongolian and Turkish invaders. Popular authors often argued that the noble Asian roots of Hungarians helped them to resist invasion, annexations, and subjugation by foreign powers. The miracle that the small nation survived and could absorb other nations, while great powers disappeared from the stage of history, was often attributed to the people's origin and distinctiveness.

Related or unrelated to these features, the self-portrayal of the Hungarian national character was forged in the nationalist movement of the nineteenth century, combining positive and negative elements. Magyars came to be characterized as melancholic, meditative, and sparing of words, like their ancestors on the Asian Steppe and the Great Hungarian Plain. Yet they are also known for their straw-flame temperament, making them impulsive and emotional. They take their pleasure mournfully, cry while they drink, and listen to the tunes of the gypsy fiddler. Hungarians are daring soldiers and generous hosts, yet they bear the burden of the "Turanian curse"[14]—they cannot get along with each other.

Throughout history, outsiders have also contributed to the Hungarian folk image, and certain of these traits have become part of the ethnic self-image. Officials and pleasure travelers viewed "the people of the Puszta"[15] as exotic riders of wild horses. The Magyar tenderized his meat under the saddle,[16] danced the passionate csárdás,[17] ate hot paprika and goulash (a characterization echoed by the American press in the late 1980s when Hungary's defiance of Moscow's dictum was attributed to a specific "Goulash Communism"). The betyár (outlaw), who took refuge in the csárda (inn)[18] and who was featured in sympathetic nineteenth-century European literature and in hostile Hapsburgian reports, was portrayed as a rebel against an unjust law and as the embodiment of freedom against foreign rule. On the other hand, Magyars were often confused with Gypsies because Gypsy musicians arranged and popularized their national and folk music.

In addition, sensation mongers took advantage of the remoteness of Hungary from the urbanized western world. The twentieth-century literary resuscitation of the trial protocols of Countess Elizabeth Báthory (1560–1614)[19] as the vampire lady contributed as much to the belief that Hungary is the hotbed of witchcraft and vampirism as did Bram Stoker's novel Dracula, composed of elements of Romanian history and folklore, and of legendary Székely ethnogenesis (descent from Attila the Hun).[20] Stoker's Dracula figure was further developed by the American film industry, and the Hungarianness of the vampire count was confirmed in the public eye by the performance of Béla Lugosi, a Hungarian-American actor. Lugosi's portrayal and folkloric props became the models for further film, television, and cartoon versions, as well as the source of a new, fast-spreading vampire belief known to every American child. The belief that Dracula was Hungarian has not been rejected altogether.

## The Hungarian-American Ethnic Model: Local vs. National in the Indiana Subcultural Chapter

In Hungary peasant culture developed more regionally than nationally. Whereas individuals were well versed in the subjects of local folk education and were loyal to local traditions, they were ignorant of the overall national culture established by school education. The situation, however, changed on the American scene. Peasant immigrants at the outset continued their loyalty to native local heritage and maintained regional identities even when under pressure to disperse and intermingle. In Indiana both the St. Joseph County and the Calumet settlements are characteristic of the blending of regional Hungarians, yet individuals still adhered to separate Old Country traditions and maintained identification with home rules of life while on the road to Americanization.

Consciousness of Hungarian national identity and its symbols, however, began to infiltrate local identity features in the American settlements quite early. The romantic nationalist image of the late nineteenth century was recast to fit the nostalgic mood of elite expatriates. This image was stronger and far more attractive for the masses of homesick immigrants than their more divisive, less prestigious peasant ancestral traditions, and the new image helped them to unify through the development of a set of standardized, homogenized identity symbols. In other words, substituting the culture symbols of the immigrant elite for the weakening local tradition meant admission to the "noble Hungarian nation" in exile. Hungarian ethnicity is not so much loyalty to a distant "foreign-born" ancestor as a determination by individuals to maintain chosen Hungarian values. The construction of a homogenized Hungarian-American culture was conveyed by social, beneficent, and religious organizations whose regional and local chapters followed the guidance of their national or global headquarters. Enthusiastic clergymen assumed leadership in the promotion of a patriotic national culture; thus it is no surprise that the "official" characterization of Hungarians was accepted, or that the burden of inherited local and regional customs, demeaned as marks of backwardness, soon disappeared. Calendar and life cycle rituals were supplemented by Hungarian and American patriotic national commemorative celebrations that were supervised by elite community leaders and filled the ethnic recreational needs of the settlers who were eager to learn and improve themselves in the new situation.

The first step in this upward move was a closer identification with the immigrant elite. As Mr. Joe Zsigrai of Hammond and Mr. Miklós Pálla of Whiting explained it: "In America I am a Mister, just like the President, or anybody else; nobody can order me around: 'Do this, do that'; my name is not 'Hey Johnny, you lazy dog.'" The sensation of a newly acquired dignity by former farmhands made it easier for them to blend into the mainstream. While the imported repertoire of regional folk costumes,

*This couple from the 1930s wears a "created" national costume, made up of elements of Hungarian symbols.*

dances, music, and foods was suppressed and moved from the public to the private area of consciousness (and later almost completely forgotten), a modest but unanimously accepted stock of new Hungarian-American forms emerged and, over the decades, became important symbols of Hungarianness. Among these are the *magyar ruha* (Hungarian dress, a fabricated festive fantasy costume); the csárdás pair dance; Gypsy music; a few popular folk and imitation-folk melodies; and a menu of festive dishes limited to stuffed cabbage, gulyás, chicken paprikás, kolbász (smoked sausage), csiga and other homemade noodles, kalács (milk bread), kifli (horns with walnut filling), rétes (strudel), and palacsinta (crepes). None of these ethnic menu items can be missing from weddings, funerals, associational banquets, church commemorations, dedications, 15 March and Fourth of July picnics, and the most enduring of Hungarian feasts: the Wine Harvest Dance and the pig-slaughter dinner. The minutes of organizing associations, as well as photo-illustrated yearbook reports and locally compiled cookbooks, give us excellent information on the conspicuous similarity of the ritual ethnic feast in South Bend[21] and the Calumet Region.[22] Consistent use for almost a century has converted these ingredients of dubious origin into fresh folklore forms that express a newly shaped Hungarian self-identity.

If one can say that prior to 1914 the immigrant elite acted destructively upon original peasant traditions, one might also note that since 1956 the freedom fighter immigrants have temporarily assumed leadership in the revival and reassertion of Hungarian ethnic arts. The ambition to teach dances, songs, and crafts, to organize festivals, and to teach the grandchildren of immigrants the forgotten language was greatly motivated by the teachers' own needs. Nevertheless, the political ethnic revival movement, claiming the recognition of a multiethnic America, activated latent awareness of folk traditions resulting in the revitalization of fading forms of folklore. In the spirit of the bicentennial anniversary of the country, as Manning Nash pointed out:

> American culture in the domain of ethnicity has moved from melting pot to tolerance and on to "consensual pluralism," where cultural difference in ethnic modes is positively valued. Ethnicity is seen as the legitimate expression of identity, with political claims. But the pluralism is under the overarching notion of citizen-American which encompasses a wide variety of ethnic modes. Ethnic categories, groups, organizations are encouraged to make public displays . . . not seen as the exclusive province of the ethnic category or group—all can participate.[23]

This situation energized the new immigrant intelligentsia and reached out to the young generation of American-born enthusiasts. Offering workshops in Indianapolis, Hammond, and Gary, together they tried, in a typical "straw-flame" mode, to create Hungarian ethnic performing groups without much success.

## The Ethnic Process: (1) Formation of Hoosier Subcultures

From the time that the earliest immigrant laborers dared to travel to the new world, Hungarian villagers had been informed about America. Contemporary reports described how the villages were affected by the successful departure and easy moneymaking of daring entrepreneurs who sent home pictures of themselves in elegant attire, sporting gold watches on gold chains,[24] and how the villagers enthusiastically anticipated prosperity on their return. As already noted, in the preliminary stages the newcomers lived in boardinghouses, isolated between two worlds. They arrived from their village to another villagelike settlement, inhabited by other peasants, some their kind and some similar but speaking other languages. The boardinghouse was one of the favorite themes of the Hungarian-American entertainment business. Scenes of an idyllic country-style life in the boardinghouse were featured by acting troupes in the artificial, folksy Magyar style in which sultry dialogues, drinking, and carousing were accompanied by a Gypsy band. Musical sketches on Columbia Records were popular repertory pieces on the Sunday Hungarian Family Hour program that aired from Hammond from 1920 to 1948. The show was hosted by Cornelius Szakatics, who had originally settled in South Bend. The Hungarian-American press also used the boardinghouse and its residents—the burdos, the missus, and the mister—as anecdotal characters to caricature life's realities. Newsmen touring Hungarian settlements for good stories might write about an incident overheard in gossip, such as a sexual rivalry with burlesquelike consequences. Many informants in the Calumet Region narrated juicy boardinghouse stories, and even more people spoke of their real life as boarders in their youth.

In 1969 Mr. Dénes Székely, age seventy-five, gave a detailed description of boardinghouse life in Indiana Harbor as it was when the ethnic community had already taken shape:

> Let's see, you rent a house and five-six people move here, you understand? Here's a bed, there's another, a third . . . there's room for a fourth. Two men in each, how much is this? Then, three-four beds can go into the dining room also. The boarding woman had ten, twelve boarders. She had to cook, wash, make food, make lunch buckets for the men. You know how much they paid? Eight dollars per month. The sister of my wife had twelve. Yeah. Six upstairs in the attic, it was hard to pass between the beds, next to them were the bags. Every man had his suitcase, therein he had his booze . . . they sold the brandy by the gallon. It was cheap. Whiskey, white spirit was cheap, they fixed it with water, as they liked it. Yeah, you went to the saloon, you gave five cents to the saloonkeeper for the whiskey, for the beer . . . oh yeah, the saloonkeeper was Magyar, yeah, all were. I didn't know other than Magyar.

Continuing the conversation, Székely related how he married his boarding lady when her husband died suddenly:

> I told my buddy with whom we shared a bed, "Poor woman, she has no money to bury her husband, let's do something. It can't be that the city takes him and throws him somewhere. . . . Let's figure out some-

thing. All right, let's go.—Where?—Let's go in the saloons, all we know, everywhere, Romanians, Polacks, Italians, all, let's go."

They went from saloon to saloon, and the men were so sorry for the poor woman they collected one dollar from everyone.

> Honest to God, I collected the dough in my cap. The Hungarian saloonkeeper gave us free drinks. We made so much money that we could buy a headstone. I didn't know then that she's going to be my wife, no, no, I didn't. We buried him. Didn't let him rot. I went to the undertaker, McGuam, the old man, was a good man. I told him, this woman has no money. Nothing. He said, okay. We had made pictures of the dead to send to the old country.[25] Still, there was money left.

Székely never learned English but became a respected member of the Indiana Harbor Hungarian-American community. He was elected church warden of the First Hungarian-Reformed Church of Indiana Harbor, which is still holding services on Ivy Street. Like his contemporaries, he made the transition from seasonal worker to skilled foundry laborer and then took up businesses of different sorts. Such men became bartenders, saloon keepers, contractors, butchers, grocers, auto mechanics, and electricians. Many of the stories follow a common progression: journey from Hungary to America with humble beginnings, departure, adventure, attempt to return, disillusionment and detachment, and finally success. In each life story there is a stylistic dissociation, as if the past were being told by another person: the young peasant of the past as opposed to the dignified American entrepreneur of the present. This attitude change can best be seen in the golden jubilee books, historical volumes put together by community members, containing individual family genealogies and life stories in abstract. Eighty percent of these, sometimes with photos, were written in Hungarian until 1910, and 90 percent in English after 1960. While vital statistics are given accurately in these texts, the immigrant, after detailing turbulent years, presents himself as a dignified and loyal American. Typically he is a war veteran and a member of civic clubs, his wife is active in bowling and charity benefits, and their children go camping, excel in sports, and make good grades in school. All are devout members of their church.

*The candy store of Mr. and Mrs. Szücs on Melrose Avenue in East Chicago in 1910. The overhead gaslight is reported to have been the first in the city.*

Nevertheless, these foreign born could never make the decision to completely detach themselves from their place of birth, much less give up their cultural loyalty to ancestral heritage. One person who told how she felt about her loyalties was Mrs. Róza Saley (Szalai), née Virág, mother of four children, active businesswoman, churchwoman, and holder of numerous offices (she was particularly active during World War II in the Independent Hungarian Political Club as a member of the Committee of War Mothers of Hungarian Origin). She was fifteen when she was brought to Lorain, Ohio. "I am a guest of sixty years in America," she said. "We arrived at Ellis Island on June 1, 1914. Miss Liberty met us. They took us to Ellis Island; I saw there many kinds of immigrant people. I became deaf and mute because I did not understand what they said . . . this is where my American life began."[26] With her husband, she moved to Indiana Harbor in 1921, postponing indefinitely, like many others, her hopes of returning. In time, the immigrant entered a new phase of adjustment that led to the foundation of the ethnic enclave.

Without any radical or conscious effort to give up old values, assimilation began by learning basic skills, learning new concepts and essential English words, changing everyday habits in eating and clothing, changing the daily schedule, operating appliances, writing checks, and so forth. When the small neighborhoods in this sample emerged from 1912 to 1925, they seemed perfect cells to accommodate cultural heritage on a broad base.

Like other ethnic nuclei around the industrial areas, small Hungarian neighborhoods sprang up and expanded into self-sufficient settlements. Bankers, lawyers, doctors, food merchants, restaurateurs, mail carriers, and pawnshop owners catered to the immediate needs of their patrons in South Bend,[27] Gary, and East Chicago. At the same time, the local chapters of the most important Hungarian-American institutions—benevolent fraternities, political clubs, and churches—also began to take shape, providing for the physical and spiritual welfare of the community. Local chapters of national insurance and death benefit associations were founded, but of these only the Verhovay Aid Society (now renamed the William Penn Association) survives. The celebration of its seventy-fifth anniversary in South Bend in 1984 seemed a ritual display of the upward mobility of Hungarian Americans[28] and reflected the erosion of traditional Hungarian values. Its program—sandwiched between the American and Hungarian national anthems and the invocation and benediction of the Roman Catholic and Calvinist pastors—followed the routine of ethnic celebrations of all kinds, practiced and polished by generations. Official speeches were made, and a woman in national costume sang so-called folk

These Hungarians probably made up one of the numerous mutual benefit societies that blossomed in most ethnic communities. Here they gathered for music and refreshments, and we can only guess as to the meaning of the currency in the hand of the figure standing far left and the pistol in the hand of the gentleman standing behind the table.

songs (magyar nóták), accompanied by a Gypsy band. The banquet's menu was to be "homemade" Hungarian, but as Mihály Hoppál notes, "The 'Hungarian breaded chicken' differed only in name from the Kentucky fried chicken."[29] The social event ended, of course, with dancing, but no Hungarian tunes were played because the orchestra did not know any. This event was, noted the author, a display of symbols that the group wanted to use to distinguish itself as Hungarian from other ethnics. Otherwise, "neither the dances, nor the Gypsy music, nor the costumes, nor the language were Hungarian."

The role of the parish churches in both South Bend and the Calumet Region had an overall stronger influence on ethnic preservation than the above-mentioned fraternities and clubs. As elsewhere in Hungarian America, the church fulfilled not only spiritual but also—and maybe more important—cultural and social needs and provided for the welfare of its members. The parishes were founded as little Hungarian islands in the strange world and ended up as true representatives of Hungarian-American loyalty. The parishes, mainly Roman Catholic in South Bend[30] and in almost equal division Calvinist and Catholic in the Calumet Region, still persist in spite of the current decline of the population because of the memory of their former significance. Without the churches, no ethnic survival would have been possible.

If the village church was both physically and symbolically the center of spiritual life in Hungary, the ethnic parish not only retained this position but also increased its relevance, becoming the center of all social, political, and cultural activities. To assume the role of religious and national leadership, the churches had to undergo fundamental changes. The Old Country village church represented the establishment in the face of the humble, subservient village folk, whereas the new was entirely the creation of the parishioners, who not only built their church but also hired and paid their clergymen. Early on, missionary churchmen from Hungary resented their changed position and complained about the demands of their congregations. One of them, in Whiting, complained in a petition to his superiors:

> Bingo, picnics, drinks, raffles are not God's concerns . . . nothing had upset me more than these excesses in our Hungarian community life. After many years of learning, do I need a theology diploma to become a "good butcher" and a "good picnic organizer?"[31]

Actually, the changed relationship drew pastor and congregation closer to each other in a more pleasant, domestic, ethnic union. Turning the house of worship into a symbolic national center raised the awareness of the national identity of immigrant peasants. "The forming of communities and associations during this period became the schools of Hungarian consciousness. In the strange environment, they began to celebrate March 15 and October 6[32] with great enthusiasm . . . they put on shows, marched with banners and brass band," writes Puskás.[33]

As time passed, however, new problems emerged. Conflicts arose between the Hungarian-Reformed Church, the American-trained Hungarian diaspora theologians, and the American Presbyterian Church. Switching from purely Hungarian language services to English preaching—for the benefit of the new American-born generations—caused disagreement between the membership. While the American Presbyterian Church was accused of "soul thievery" and "pagan blasphemy,"[34] the preservation of language and culture was the real issue, not the hegemony of the Hungarian or American synod. Yet language shift did not destroy ethnic tradition; fifty-five years later the same church maintains its ethnic pride and style despite the dying out of the foreign-born generation and the resultant diminishing attendance at its Hungarian language services.

The ethnic enclave, the irrational, nostalgic imitation of the hometown, was founded by the immigrant generation seeking temporary shelter in the alien world. For a while essential values could be maintained. It was sufficient to adjust to the industrial environment, the multilingual neighborhood, and the mainstream minimally, while nurturing the illusion of a little Hungarian-American island as reality.

*A Hungarian family at the casket of little Alex Galambos, East Chicago, 1921.*

No matter how short-lived or how much reserved to the immigrant generation it was, the ethnic neighborhood was essential for sustaining tradition and feeling comfortable with peers. Seven regional Hungarian dialects in the Calumet Region, an indication of the dissolution of an original settling of home village neighborhoods, have been noted. Intermarriage between peasants from diverse regions became more common—if they hailed from the same religion. Subgroup formation could be identified according to who came directly from Hungary, who moved there from other previous locations, the time that they moved there, what generation they belonged to, and above all, what their denomination was. This last category involved cultural differences which, in the Old Country, divided Protestants from Catholics.[35] This division increased under the influence of the Hungarian-American Church in that the parishes provided for year-round social, ritual, and political activities for their members.[36] In Gary, for example, the membership of Holy Trinity Catholic Church and the Carolina-Avenue Reformed Church never met; and, if the members did not happen to share the same employer, they were not likely to know each other. Nevertheless, these differences did not affect basic Hungarian ethnicity in terms of an identical set of conventions that regulated and normalized worldview, ethics, rules of behavior, and taste. As long as the ethnic enclave existed, the most important community events, the life-cycle rituals, were maintained according to the guidance of traditional texts to be recited by the masters of ceremonies.[37] Likewise, there was an essential agreement on housing and habitat patterns, interior decoration, use of space, and application of religious and family-oriented symbols, such as the traditional flower garden in front of the house, and the bench in front of the fence to chat with neighbors—all corresponding to Old Country forms. Thus, the original idyllic peasant village appeared as a faint reflection, blurred by the haze of industrial pollution. The two deer on Steve and Ida Csalas' front lawn in Indiana Harbor, the pink flamingos on the side of the fountain of the Leslie Huszárs' Valparaiso yard, and the revolving silver Christmas tree in the Steve Vargos' living room in Carlisle—all are indications of taste adjustment. They symbolize a longing for lost nature in the midst of industrial filth.

Did those who dreamed about returning to the Old Country really hope for fulfillment? The majority of the immigrant generation had to postpone the return to peasant life until after retirement from industrial work. Retirees from East Chicago, Crown Point, Gary, Hammond, and Munster, who moved to Florida, Louisiana, and California, built their farmhouses and planted wine grapes, fruits, and vegetables for their own pleasure. For twenty-five years Balázs Csikós was an iron caster in Gary and a stubborn dreamer of farming. He bought land from his savings and peddled produce to the Chicago market until trucking companies ruined his business. Later he hired pickers and sold his tomato crops to the canning plant. In retirement he built a house in Plant City, Florida. At age eighty-six, he and his wife had driven from Florida to reunite with his old cronies at the 4 July Hungarian picnic in Black Oaks, the popular recreational site in the Calumet Region: they drank wine and sang mournfully, accompanied by the Gypsy fiddler. This American patriotic outdoors feast has become a homecoming, reuniting the generations. American-born Frank Tóth, son-in-law of the Csala couple of Indiana Harbor, explained that for him the eating of the roast pork (*pecsenye*) means so much ethnic and family tradition that he comes every year and instructs his children to follow suit.

As long as the Indiana-Hungarian neighborhoods had a majority of their immigrant generation, they were culture-forming and culture-maintaining entities. But as the initial Old Country values shifted slowly to a new Hungarian-American consciousness, there emerged a new folklore rooted in the old heritage but based on contemporary issues of everyday life. As the memory of the old faded, the emergent new became central in the cultural spectrum of the group. Old stories about magic healing, bewitching of cows, and the wisdom of supernaturally endowed coachmen—as well as stories of folk heroes of Hungarian history—were replaced by American-style ghost stories and by local character anecdotes focusing on the acculturation process. For example, the greenhorn housewife did not know how to ask for sauerkraut, and when she lost her temper and cursed the salesperson (*szarok rád!* [Shit you!]), he finally understood what she wanted; or the man applying for the "citizen paper" kept repeating "It's hard, it's hard," and the judge (whom he addressed as "George") thought he knew the name of President Warren G. Harding and granted him citizenship. Funny yarns were as popular as horror stories about work in the steel mills, danger, crime, and violence—involving not only Hungarians, but other ethnics as well. Many of the popular stories are native Hungarian; others are variants that spread through Hungarian colonies either by word of mouth or the Hungarian-language press.

## The Ethnic Process: (2) Toward Integration

The ethnic community eventually outlived its usefulness. What had brought it to life also led to its demise. The children and grandchildren of the immigrants were born in America and, even if they were confined to the colony, their education departed sharply from that of their elders. They found the environment suffocatingly exotic, limited, out-of-date, and hindering progress. The generation in conflict had to choose between family adherence or self-reliance, and between language loyalty or moving upward on the social scale. Most parents wished a better life for their children than what they had and did not force language maintenance. In fact, immigrant women learned English from their children. Changes in naming children also occurred. While older children received Hungarian first names, those born in later years were given fashionable English names (particularly after the Great Depression when mutual dependency was eased, or during World War II when military involvement of immigrant boys elevated the pride of being American).[38]

At the same time, parents could not comprehend the world toward which their offspring gravitated. One can sense the irreconcilable gulf between parents in the colony and their status-oriented children when listening to their bilingual conversations in which Hungarian questions are answered in English. The American-born children's broken Hungarian mixes regional dialect with English; John Csomor, Jr., of Hammond saw a loud blue jay and noted: *Esment nojzol a bluebird,* combining a dialect word for "again" (*esment*) with the English noun "noise," Hungarianized into a verb with the suffix "-ol," and adding the English bird name. He had meant to talk to the author in Hungarian. The natural language of the ethnic compound known as "Hunglish" is a creole mirroring the acculturation process of Hungarians, the adaptation of English through practical life and oral communication.[39]

Thus, with the passing of the immigrant generation, ethnic neighborhoods were vacated and turned over to other nationality groups reaching the ethnic stage. The American-born first and second generations moved to

*A fund-raiser for the World War II effort by Hungarians in Gary at Füzy Hall.*

suburbia, away from the smoky chimneys of the Twin Cities (East Chicago and Indiana Harbor); old church and library buildings were sold to newcomers. Survivors of the original settlers—widows and widowers, isolated by old age and loss of community, live on in the alienated old neighborhoods like custodians of a ghost town, communicating over the telephone with their friends or children in the suburbs.[40] The folklore they brought with them from the Old Country, and created in the new, lives on in memory and bears fresh fruits as they revive the past, putting together bits and pieces of new information gathered from rare visitors, television, newspapers, dreams, and fantasies.

For the first American-born generation, the meaning of ethnicity is different. In the first place, it is an option to choose, to retain and to develop creatively images and emblems of ethnicity or to reject them completely. In the cultural spectrum of American borns, ethnic heritage occupies only a small compartment that is reserved for special occasions or for self-gratification. They are select elements displayed more for the general public than for insiders. What is chosen for these occasions is usually spectacular or attractive and classy, taken more from the national (elite) than from the regional heritage as a more usable item in status-promoting social activities. While everyday life—home decoration, eating habits—no longer contains traces of homeland ethnicity, a few display items appear prominently at festive occasions, particularly in the performance of dances and music, in the parading of costumes, and in the preparation of special dishes. When the International Institute in Indianapolis invited local ethnics to introduce their specialties to the public in 1986, the Hungarian women were dressed in Matyó[41] blouses with black skirts and boots and sporting an embroidered kerchief (all mass-produced and exported by the Folk Arts and Crafts Cooperative of Hungary); they served *paprikás krumpli* (potato stew in paprika) and green salad and sang sentimental pseudo-folk songs. This hybrid, new ethnic revival appears as a response to the national appeal of ethnic Americans; it is a conscious self-stereotyping, a message to others, but also a nostalgic gesture toward the in-group and an attempt to preserve elements of a distant past that the new generations do not understand.

The desire to renew ties with the Old Country is a new phenomenon, the awakening of a new consciousness for the second American-born generation. For well-adjusted Americans, it is a romantic trip to join chartered flights to Hungary and experience the country shrouded by controversial family accounts. The image of Hungary as the source of superior morality and excellence, the scene of suffering and humiliation, and the epitome of agricultural backwardness and servility had shifted slowly toward an irrationally idyllic, earthly paradise as spatial and temporal distance grew.

For the most recent visitors, little was left to connect past and present. Modern Hungary was not the country left behind by ancestors or depicted by Hungarian-American visionaries. Travelers often expressed disappointment at not finding the romantic mud-walled, straw-roofed ancestral cottage that they had been told about in their childhood. In many cases, visitors, influenced by public opinion concerning conditions in this former Communist country, related encounters and situations involving scare and dare. To counteract the image of "Red Commies," there was always a hero or a suffering victim—Magyars could not be featured as all bad.

The Hungarian-by-choice may be a member of a totally integrated family, as is Elizabeth Kovács. Born in Indianapolis of post–World War II upper-middle-class parents, she was educated in California. She picked up a pamphlet about Hungarian folk dance and was so impressed with the music and the dance that she went to Hungary to learn the language and the customs of her ancestry. Upon her return, she joined a Hungarian folk dance ensemble. Married to a non-Hungarian, she keeps active in the ensemble, teaches classes, and helps raise Hungarian consciousness among the young, all without support from her family—her fully assimilated brother does not condone her involvement.

The American-born children of the 1956 "freedom fighters" seem most susceptible to the festival movement propagated by both American and Hungarian agencies. Lacking roots and continuity, however, the movement is superficial, following the performance guidelines given by festival agencies to other central and east European amateur performing groups throughout the United States. The similarity of costumes and foodstuffs of Magyars, Germans, Serbs, Polacks, Slovaks, and Croats shows artificiality, pretense, or an ersatz myth of ethnic distinctiveness. Yet, for the active and passive participants in ethnic festivities, for those who volunteer to fix the food and make the costumes, as well as for those who come to watch the event and consume the food, the show certainly carries a message. As the fabrication is repeated and polished, and if political, economic, and cultural conditions are favorable, the fake can turn out as the genuine voice of ethnic Magyars, unique and important, a contribution to multicultural America.

Symbols of ethnicity can be maintained by later generations in various ways. Some pray, some curse, others count in Hungarian. One makes Hungarian nut rolls every Christmas—the legacy of his only Hungarian ancestor, his grandmother. This pastry is his only tie to his Hungarian heritage. Ethnicity may be active or latent; depending on circumstances it may be recalled or completely forgotten.

## Isolation and Ethnic Distinctiveness

Following World War I the flow of Hungarian peasants to America was interrupted. For a long time there was no way to return to Hungary, no chance to visit. All contacts were one-sided, gifts were sent from America to families in Hungary. The relative affluence of Hungarians in heavy industry was beneficial to the poor peasant villagers between the two wars and briefly during the economic collapse following World War II. The wars were big turning points in the Americanization of Hungarian immigrants. As the editor of the *Amerikai Magyar Népszava jubileumi diszalbuma* (American Hungarian Voice of the Folk) wrote:

> Is there any Hungarian anywhere in America who would not defend the American flag with the same enthusiasm as the Hungarian? Is there anyone who is not enthused by the sound of the American hymn? No, there isn't! America would not be America if one could live here without the American air, the surrounding atmosphere; the impact of the spirit emanating from the innumerable typically American institutions cannot help but spontaneously impress a genuinely American character on people's heart, soul and even appearance.[42]

Nevertheless, people felt an obligation to help the village of their birth and their poor kin. Contractor Paul Csontos of Hammond had a cross erected in his hometown as a tribute to his parents' memory. Many families not only made donations toward charities, repair of churches, construction of school buildings, and electrification in their native land, but they also sent tools, chemicals, and agricultural equipment, thus contributing to village modernization. Their families received packages, foodstuffs, and clothing, strengthening slackening ties between expatriates and their hometown. While the one-way, donor-recipient relationship was developed into an almost businesslike deal, in terms of sending money for land, cattle purchases, and other needs, a gulf between cultural values widened due to the lack of the intimate personal contact necessary to maintain warm familial feelings. Lack of a systematic chain migration and remigration between home and diaspora settlements (which was an institutionalized integrative force among Italians, Greeks, Irish, and other nationalities) contributed to the cultural isolation of ethnic Hungarian Americans. The awareness of the "we are alone" feeling surfaced again between the two wars and awakened a new nostalgia for the fading image of the Old Country. But World War II hostilities, with Hungary being on the other side, followed by the Communist takeover after the war, further increased the feeling of isolation. This feeling continued until the 1960s, when the "new ethnicity" movement coincided with Hungary's growing interest in reaching out to children of immigrants with programs to encourage Hungarian language maintenance in America.[43] A changed relationship was initiated in the form of a reversal of gift giving. Packages of books, records, musical instruments, embroidery patterns, folk art objects, and spices for traditional cookery arrived in America in great quantity. Learning of the language, history, literature, and folklore was initiated by Hungarian-American professionals of the Displaced Persons generation, who offered college-level courses to the children of immigrants and encouraged them to continue their education in Hungary in vacation camps and free universities. The opening of this new chapter in Old Country/New Country collaboration, however, did not depend on a tradition that had existed before the cultural rift created by the prolonged separation during the most critical stage of the ethnic process. The ethnicity package that was offered therefore often contained sterile, mass-produced, romanticized, and long-defunct archaic folk art products that became the paraphernalia of the festival-producing generation.

Maintenance of personal contacts with peers could have reaffirmed the homeland pattern of Hungarian culture on the diaspora, but isolation forced Hungarian Americans to create their own folk culture out of memories and new experiences in day-to-day living in their interethnic environments. Linguistic specialty also contributed to the discoloration of Hungarian ethnicity. Whereas Slavs, Germans, and Latins can communicate because of linguistic similarities, the original Hungarian language relationship with the Finnic-Ugric language group does not link Hungarian Americans with the culturally and geographically far-removed Uralic peoples.

The sharing of a common history with Slovaks, Serbs, Croatians, and Romanians in the Hapsburg Empire would have served as an obvious cultural affinity for Hungarians had the memory of national intolerance in the old empire still not lingered and kept mutual mistrust alive. Hungary's policy toward its minorities seems to survive today in that ethnic Hungarians in the United States still call themselves American Hungarians, meaning Hungarians who live in America, as opposed to German Americans, African Americans, or Italian Americans, meaning Americans who originate from Germany, Africa, or Italy. The unsigned article "Politika" in the tenth anniversary volume of the *Amerikai Magyar Népszava* illustrates the desire not to be classed with minorities in the native country:

We Hungarian immigrants are regarded as nationalities here in America as much as the German, the Irish, the Italian, the Russian and the other immigrant folk, and like the Slovak, the Romanian and the Swabian in Hungary. No matter how we loved our country of birth, it is an unchangeable fact that we had left it, and that no one has invited us here . . . we have chosen America as our new country. Therefore, despite the veneration and love we feel toward our native land, we have to become true children of the country we chose. In no way can we assume the role of our Old Country minorities.[44]

When one considers the interethnic relationship between Hungarian peasant colonies in Indiana and former minorities in Austria-Hungary, certain ambiguities arise. Old hostilities could have been forgotten by simple workingmen had they not been reminded of past ills by the provincial nationalism of the immigrant elite. Even during the 1960s and 1970s, brawls erupted in the pubs in Gary and the canteens of Inland Steel and the Youngstown Sheet and Tube Company because of injured national pride in the distant past, supported by almost mythical evidence. Many stories circulated, like the one about a Serbian who reproached a Magyar for the Bosnian Occupation in 1866, who, in turn, tried to hit the Serb for the murder of Franz Ferdinand, the crown prince of Austria, whose assassination led to the outbreak of World War I.

On the other hand, neighbors can establish friendships on the basis of cultural proximity. Mrs. Margie Hévizi's good friends in Gary were a Romanian couple, who taught her herbal medicine; Mrs. Ida Csala of Indiana Harbor was inseparable from Mrs. Mary Bodnár and Mrs. Elsie Csmerka, both Slovaks. The immigrants knew as much Hungarian as the Hungarians knew former minority languages. As Mrs. Bodnár expressed it: "We were the same, poor but sharing; it didn't matter what language we spoke." In some settlements, ethnic and racial animosities—if they ever existed—have been reconciled or forgotten. For a while, peasant immigrants stereotyped blacks as they did their joke characters, the archetypal Gypsies; however, tolerance and a mutual effort toward understanding now seem more common. Social classes and professions are more often the subject of jokes than are nationalities; stock characters are hillbillies (ignorant country bumpkins unfamiliar with factory work), peddlers, tax collectors, plant foremen, ministers, businessmen, and saloonkeepers. In this advanced phase of integration, the children and grandchildren of the foreign-born generation seldom marry within their own ethnic group. Yet awareness of ethnic ancestry is present in everyone's consciousness, and young people often attend ethnic celebrations on both sides of their family. Indeed, to be American with an ethnic background is fashionable; and for some, having a Hungarian background is a source of pride.

The accidents of history, the long-lasting isolation of Hungarian Americans from the Old Country, the peculiarity of the language, the hereditary national prejudice against culturally similar neighboring ethnics, and the ideological, social, and cultural segmentation of the immigrant generations singly and together have contributed to the specific formulation of a Hungarian-American identity.

## Notes

1. From the travelogue of Aurél Kecskeméthy, *Éjszak-Amerika 1876-ban* (North America in 1876) (Budapest: Ráth, 1877), 418. All translations from Hungarian to English in this essay are the author's responsibility.

2. The self-designation of Hungarians as Magyars and their country as Magyarország originates from the Ugric period descriptive of their tribal position.

3. This was the name of the plane piloted by György Endresz and Sándor Magyar across the ocean in 1931, symbolically linking Hungary with the United States.

4. Julianna Puskás, *Kivándorló magyarok az Egyesült Államokban 1880–1940* (Emigrant Hungarians in the United States 1880–1940) (Budapest: Akadémiai Kiadó, 1982), 198–202.

5. John H. Holliday, "The Life of Our Foreign Population" (Typescript, Indiana Historical Society Library, Indianapolis), 1, 3, 13, 14.

6. Géza D. Berkó, ed., *Amerikai Magyar Népszava jubileumi diszalbuma* (n.p., 1910), 41–42.

7. After conducting ethnographic research in the Calumet Region, Andrew Vázsonyi presented a detailed evaluative report on the boardinghouse as an institution, with particular emphasis on sex life and morality. Andrew Vázsonyi, "The *Cicisbeo* and the Magnificent Cuckold: Boardinghouse Life and Lore in Immigrant Communities," *Journal of American Folklore* 91 (Apr.–June 1978): 641–56.

8. Dezsö Nagy's two-volume anthology *Az Amerikás magyarok folklórja* in *Folklór Archivum* 8 (1978), 11 (1979) (Budapest: MTA Kutatócsoport) is fairly representative of what could be gleaned from the Hungarian-language American press. The three kinds of newspapers—elite, working class, and denominational—give a very heterogeneous picture. It would be impossible to show the close interaction between newsmen and the readership in the creation of a specific ethnic diaspora folklore, but it is notable that editors reached out to the working people, inviting compositions from correspondents and folk poets from the industrial towns. While these editors utilized materials contributed by the working class and wrote about them with sentimental compassion, they published traditional folklore with the air of elite superiority. The phonetic transcript of English words in the context of Hungarian verse and prose emphasized the inability of the uneducated rustic to learn proper English, to use concepts correctly, or to relinquish the heavily accented dialect of their village. The linguistic adaptation could just as well have been taken as a sign of the ability to make cultural adjustments. Materials comprising lyric and ritual (life cycle and calendar-related) poetry and prose narratives form a stable body of the folklore of the immigrant generation of peasant ancestry. The Hungarian-language press certainly helped its broad dissemination.

9. Berkó, ed., *Amerikai Magyar,* 247.

10. Debrecen, a large agricultural town in northeast Hungary, also known as "the Calvinist Rome" for its stronghold of Calvinists, acquired this name in America because its relatively large Hungarian population is Calvinist.

11. Puskás, *Kivándorló magyarok,* 199–200.

12. Joshua Fishman, *Hungarian Language Maintenance in the United States,* vol. 62 of Uralic and Altaic Series (Bloomington: Indiana University, 1966), 8.

13. Puskás, *Kivándorló magyarok,* 109.

14. Hungarian Americans often remember this curse. Remembering the Great Depression when the Calvinists built their church in Indiana Harbor, many mentioned that those were the good times when they were all brothers and shared the lean potato soup; "now they are enemies, all rich people who would not give to the other." During a conversation with Mrs. John Kovács and Mrs. Imre Szabó (in Whiting, Ind., 1975), the meaning of the curse to them came clear:

Mrs. Kovács: They did not care that the community progresses; they cared only for what went into their pockets. They had to sell the Hungarian House. Now it belongs to the Slovaks. 'Cause they stick together; the Hungarians are each other's enemies. They are envious of each other.

Mrs. Szabó: Yeah, if he had the opportunity, he would take the life of the other, only that he should have more. Like the old proverb says, "átok verte meg a Magyart, hogy az soha össze nem tart" (the Magyars were cursed that they never hold together).

15. Puszta: desert or prairie—here it means the Great Hungarian Plain.

16. This nomadic practice has not been continued anywhere in modern times; yet on a talk show, Zsa-Zsa Gabor claimed that she had done it herself back in Hungary at her family's farm.

17. Csárdás: a lively Hungarian national couple dance named so in the nineteenth century but composed of a great variety of folk dance motifs.

18. Csárda: the name of the wayside inn where the lady innkeeper harbored and entertained the betyárs (outlaws) and cattlemen, fugitives from the unjust law, as depicted in nineteenth-century folklore, folk art, and literature.

19. The "World Champion Lady Vampire of All Times" may have been the innocent victim of a family feud between the powerful Báthorys over her estate.

20. Bram Stoker's Dracula introduced himself as a Székely of "Attila's Blood," true to the legend of this Hungarian subculture, which for centuries provided military defense for the kingdom of Hungary on the southeast borders of Transylvania. Dracula professes the priority of the Hun-Székelys in Hungary and also claims the "historic mission" of the Magyars, "when Árpád (chieftain of Magyar tribes) and his legion swept through the Hungarian fatherland, he fought us here when he reached the frontier . . . the Honfoglalás (Conquest) was completed there. . . . And when the Hungarian flood swept eastward, the Székelys were claimed as kindred of the victorious Magyars, and to us for centuries was trusted the guarding of the frontier of Turkeyland."

21. Mihály Hoppál, "Ethnic Symbolism: Tradition and Ethnicity in a Hungarian and an American-Hungarian Community," *Folklór Archivum* 18 (1989), 155–84; also Mihály Hoppál, "Amerikai Magyar Családi Fényképek," in *Néprajzi Látóhatár* 1 (1992).

22. Péter Niedermüller, "The After Life of Peasant Culture: Objects and Rituals," in *Folklór Archivum* 18 (1989): 190–243.

23. Manning Nash, *The Cauldron of Ethnicity in the Modern World* (Chicago: University of Chicago Press, 1989), 121.

24. Puskás, *Kivándorló magyarok,* 185.

25. It is remarkable that the American funeral home industry has helped maintain an important part of the final lifecycle ritual in Hungarian tradition: the wake and the feast of the dead. The McGuam family, the community undertakers, catered to this practice for fifty years. To be given a decent burial is a must. At the funeral of Mrs. Steve Bolla of Indiana Harbor in 1965, the author felt as if she were at an Old Country village wake, as she was surrounded by praying, singing, and lamenting members of her parish. She asked the minister if he could tell the difference between a Hungarian and an American wake. He said yes, an American service takes fifteen minutes, but for a Hungarian it is a full day and an afternoon. The minister is also more in demand at a Hungarian wake; he has to deliver four sermons in both languages.

26. At the request of her children, Róza Saley (Szalai) had typed her life history as she remembered it on her eightieth birthday. See Miklós Kontra, "Virág Róza Jött Amerikába" (Róza Virág came to America), *Magyar Nyelv* 3 (1984): 344–49.

27. Hoppál, "Ethnic Symbolism."

28. Ibid.

29. Ibid, 167.

30. Nineteen parishes. For the Catholic parishes and their functions from 1900, see Hoppál, "Ethnic Symbolism," 155–56.

31. Manuscript from the Ligonier Archive of the Hungarian-Reformed Church.

32. Six October is the commemoration of the execution of thirteen generals of the 1848 revolution, as deserters from the Austrian Army, on that day in 1849.

33. Puskás, *Kivándorló magyarok,* 242–43.

34. Tenth Anniversary Yearbook: First Hungarian Reformed Church of Indiana Harbor Celebrates 1925 to 1935, comp., Rev. Sándor Mircse.

35. Until 1949 village elementary education in Hungary was parochial, Roman Catholic or Greek Catholic, Reformed (Calvinist), Lutheran, or Jewish.

36. "The Hungarians are divided religiously, but united nationally. At their gatherings and banquets they always use their national costumes, sing their folk songs, dance their folk dances, and play their folk music," reports the East Chicago Community Council in its newsletter in 1959, concerning ethnic minorities in the East Chicago community. Niedermüller listed calendar community events of the Hungarian-Reformed parish of Indiana Harbor in 1926, 1933, 1934, 1936, and 1938–42, offering an excellent overview of the mix of Hungarian and American celebrations serving religious, social, charitable, and business purposes. Yet these monthly occasions are just a part of the numerous communal activities besides church attendance that create a strong bond between parish members.

37. The Calumet community had several eminent tradition-bearers who safeguarded the maintenance of celebratory life. Imre Lábas of East Chicago, Imre Baráth of Gary, and József Almásy and József Kállay of Indiana Harbor were among the experienced poets, best men, masters of ceremonies, singers, and dancers who continued skills learned in the Old Country. Several handwritten songsters containing ritual poetry, occasional greeting formulas, and folk and popular song texts are in the author's possession, giving an account of an active transplanted tradition.

38. "Hungarians of South Bend point with pride to the fact that the first American soldier—a member of the American Expeditionary Force of 1917—to fire a cannon on a European battlefield was 'one of their boys' named Stephen Ács Jr." Puskás, *Kivándorló magyarok,* 307.

39. *Beyond Castle Garden: An American-Hungarian Dictionary of the Calumet Region,* collected and compiled by Andrew Vázsonyi and edited by Miklós Kontra, with an ethnography by Linda Dégh (Budapest, 1995) contains about 2,500 words, idioms, expressions, sayings, sentence constructs, stories, and conversational formulas.

40. Linda Dégh, "Dial a Story, Dial an Audience: Two Rural Women Narrators in an Urban Setting," in *Women's Folklore, Women's Culture,* eds. Rosan A. Jordan and Susan J. Kalčik (Philadelphia: University of Pennsylvania Press, 1985), 3–25.

41. Matyó is the name of the people in a small ethnic region in Borsod-Abauj County, famous for its characteristic folk art, mass-produced and marketed by tourist arts and crafts shops in Hungary.

42. Berkó, ed., *Amerikai Magyar,* 209.

43. In 1970 the Hungarian government initiated a so-called Mother-Tongue Movement to reintroduce diaspora Hungarians in the Western world to the Hungarian. Activating the strongly politicized World Federation of Hungarians, this effort was partially successful, although many American Hungarians were suspicious of the government's real intentions and stayed away. The program brought together diaspora community leaders, clergymen, and teachers with Hungarian intellectuals at biannual conferences held in Hungary, and it activated language and history education, and arts and crafts and dance workshops, mostly under the aegis of churches, led by members of the post–World War II emigrant generations.

44. Berkó, ed., *Amerikai Magyar,* 208.

# IRISH

William W. Giffin

*The Irish in Indiana did not experience the intense social ills typical of eastern slum life. However, they did not escape entirely social problems associated with poverty. For example, the Irish immigrants in Indiana had a high illiteracy rate, even in rural areas. In the counties of northern Indiana there were more illiterates among the natives of Ireland than in any other group in 1850.*

Descendants of the Emerald Isle entered Indiana in the eighteenth century. The Irish were represented among the relatively few fur traders and pioneers who were active in Indiana before it became a state in 1816. Irish immigrants came to Indiana in great numbers after statehood during the years 1816 to 1860. The influx of Irish natives peaked in Indiana during the period 1860–1920, when the Irish were most identifiable as an ethnic group. The history of the Irish in Indiana from 1920 to 1992 is largely the story of descendants of immigrants from Ireland who came to the United States in the nineteenth century.

The Irish appeared on the Indiana record in the early eighteenth century when the occupants of the territory north of the Ohio River were the Miami, other Native Americans, and French colonial inhabitants. Immigrants from Ireland formed the largest non-English foreign-born contingent arriving in the English colonies in the eighteenth century. These Irish newcomers were largely people of Scottish ancestry whose families had settled in Northern Ireland (Ulster). Until the 1760s English colonists (including the Irish) made no attempt to settle west of Pennsylvania in territory occupied by native people and claimed by France. English colonial businessmen had little success breaking into the fur trade with the western Indians who dealt almost exclusively with the French. Catering to Indians by placing trading posts near their towns, France established Fort Ouiatenon, Fort Miamis, and Post Vincennes on the Wabash-Maumee water route. This virtual French monopoly of the western fur trade was broken by English colonists during the 1740s.[1]

A native of Ireland played a major role in this turn of events. George Croghan arrived in Pennsylvania after emigrating from Dublin in 1741. He shortly established an extensive fur trading enterprise in the Great Lakes region. His trade connections extended westward to the Wabash River. During the 1740s Croghan and his Pennsylvania associates obtained an increasing share of the western fur trade at the expense of the French. By the end of the decade some of the Miami and other tribes of the Wabash country were traveling to Pickawillany (in present western Ohio) to deal with the Irishman. According to a frontier historian Croghan was successful in winning Native American customers because he was fair and tactful in his dealings with them, unlike fur traders of English descent who often showed their contempt for Indians. Also, the man from Dublin was successful because he was unusually enterprising and offered quality trade goods at low prices.[2] A Croghan biographer, describing him as a fascinating character with an unusually generous and charitable nature, wrote:

> Croghan took snuff, drank heavily, loved to dress richly, and to live on a grand scale. When he addressed himself to his contemporaries, his native background stood out like a beacon—orally, in his strong, Irish brogue, and, on paper, in a handwriting and spelling so unschooled as to approach illiteracy. A master of conviviality, his easy good nature made him an idol on the frontier.[3]

Becoming aware of his amicable contacts with Native Americans, officials of colonial Pennsylvania and the British government engaged Croghan's services in Indian diplomacy. Croghan became the leading negotiator with the western Indian nations before the American Revolution. The aim of the diplomacy was to loosen the ties between France and the Miami and other western nations. Croghan was successful in promoting this goal before 1754. For example, while at Pickawillany in 1751 he received a group of Wea and Piankashaw from the Wabash country and accepted their petition to be taken under English protection. The rivalry between the fur traders of England and France caused friction between the two nations, which brought them into armed conflict. Croghan failed to persuade most of the Native Americans not to side with France in the ensuing French and Indian War. But the Irishman apparently did not lose his favorable reputation among the natives of the western country. He accomplished another assignment in Indian diplomacy after the war with France. Croghan was called upon to negotiate an end to Pontiac's War, which involved many Indian nations across the Great Lakes region. Native American forces captured most of the British forts in that area in 1763. Croghan's diplomatic expedition took him to Vincennes and to Fort Ouiatenon on the Wabash River (near present Lafayette) in 1765. Finally Croghan met with Pontiac, who was the Ottawa leader of the Indian campaign. Pontiac agreed to make peace on Croghan's promise that the British would not permit settlements in the western country. In large measure Pontiac's War had been a response to Native American concern about the consequences of an influx of colonial settlers into lands just beyond the Allegheny Mountains, which had begun for the first time at the opening of the decade.[4]

During the rest of the eighteenth century relatively few people migrated from the East to settle in Indiana or in the Great Lakes region, but some of those who did so were of Irish descent. Croghan's promise to Pontiac related to the Royal Proclamation of 1763, which prohibited unauthorized settlement west of the Allegheny Mountains. In the face of this proclamation, population movement beyond the Alleghenies was minimal and there was no English colonial settlement in Indiana before the War for Independence. Settlers from the states began arriving in Indiana during the American Revolution. Settlement was confined to three areas of southern Indiana until the end of the century. The earliest and westernmost of the new settlements was along the Wabash River at Vincennes. A few migrants arrived in 1779 when it was in the hands of an American army under the command of George Rogers Clark, but more of them located there after the end of the war. By 1786 the Vincennes area contained a few hundred English-speaking newcomers whose cultural heritages conflicted with those of the old French inhabitants of the town. The resulting ethnic friction led Col. J. M. P. Le Gras, a local magistrate, to view many of the English-speaking newcomers as aggressive and undesirable. Le Gras found Daniel Sullivan to be especially troublesome. Undoubtedly Sullivan was of Irish origins. The early eastern settlements were on Clark's Grant near the Falls of the Ohio River (present-day Clark and Harrison counties) and in the Gore (near the present Ohio boundary and including modern Dearborn County). The settlers of these areas were mainly old stock Americans, a great proportion of whom were of Irish ancestry. The Irish-stock settlers of this period were largely, but not exclusively, related to persons who had emigrated from northern Ireland and who had settled earlier in the backcountry of the Carolinas and in Kentucky.[5]

With the turn of the century came important changes for people living in Indiana. In 1800 the United States Congress created the Indiana Territory with Vincennes as its capital. The population of the territory increased from about twenty-five hundred in 1800 to about sixty-four thousand in 1815. Newcomers located in the old eighteenth-century settlement areas in Indiana as well as in new ones such as the Ohio River towns in the southeast (Lawrenceburg, Vevay, Madison, and Jeffersonville). The ethnic characteristics of the territorial population did not change much after 1800. Yet nationality diversity was somewhat greater, and the presence of the foreign born was more evident during the Indiana territorial period. Some of the natives of Ireland living in Indiana were well known to the territory's citizenry. William Prince was born in Ireland in 1772. After immigrating to the United States, Prince moved to Knox County, settling there by 1800. Prince married a woman of French descent, Therese Tremble, and took an active role in the public life of Vincennes. At various times during the territorial years he was Knox County sheriff, Vincennes postmaster, and county justice of the peace. Prince was known throughout

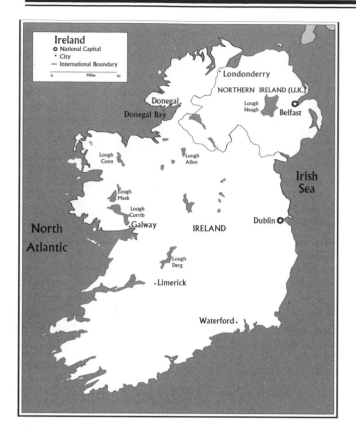

Indiana as a member of the territorial council chosen in 1809 and as territorial auditor (1810–13).[6] James Dill was another highly visible native of Ireland. He located in Dearborn County after living in Kentucky. Dill was an avid supporter of territorial governor William Henry Harrison, who often appointed him to office. Dill made a vivid impression when serving in court as prosecuting attorney. One of his contemporaries wrote:

> When Gen. Dill appeared in court, it was in the full costume of the gentleman of the last century—his knee breeches and silver buckles and venerable cue neatly plaited and flowing over his shoulders, seemed a mild protest against the leveling tendencies of the age; but nothing could impair the hold which the . . . courtly and witty Irishman had on the friendship of the people of this county.[7]

Natives of Ireland were the first settlers of some areas of the Indiana Territory. James McGuire was born in 1785 at the seaport town of Dundalk in Ireland's Leistner province. McGuire joined the English army when an adolescent. He traveled with his regiment to Canada and subsequently made his way to Ohio. In 1808 McGuire moved to Lawrenceburg, Dearborn County, where he entered the Indiana territorial militia and rose through its ranks. McGuire removed from Lawrenceburg to the Dearborn County countryside and thereby became the first settler of

Laughery Township. One of his neighbors wrote: "When I moved to Laughery, in 1814, Major James McGuire lived one mile below me in the block house kept up in time of war."[8] Likewise, John Kelso emigrated from Ireland to New York, moving from there to the Indiana Territory in 1813. The Irishman was the first settler in an area that became Kelso Township, Dearborn County.[9]

In 1813, when John Kelso arrived in Dearborn County, the territorial capital was removed from Vincennes to Corydon, where steps were taken to advance the Indiana Territory toward statehood. The United States Congress authorized a state constitutional convention after the census of 1815 determined that the territory exceeded the congressionally mandated population requirement for statehood. The Irish participated in the state-making process in Indiana. The constitutional convention held at Corydon in 1816 was composed of forty-three elected delegates, who apparently represented an approximate cross section of the territory's population with respect to nativity. Eleven of the delegates were natives of northern states and twenty-six were natives of southern states. Six of the delegates were born in European countries, four in Ireland, one in Germany, and one in Switzerland. Convention delegates Patrick Beard, James Dill, William Graham, and David Robb were natives of Ireland. When it became the nineteenth state in the Union in 1816, Indiana's Irish population was still composed largely of descendants of immigrants from northern Ireland. As most other pioneers, the Irish lived in the southern third of Indiana where most of them were involved in homestead farming.[10]

The 1815 population census of the Indiana Territory was taken in a seminal year in history. The Atlantic world entered an era of peace following the end of the War of 1812 in America and the conclusion of the Napoleonic Wars in Europe. These armed conflicts had almost completely stopped immigration to the United States during the previous two decades. The peace permitted the resumption of emigration from Europe. During the next one hundred years immigration to the United States occurred on a massive scale. The initial period of this new mass immigration was 1815–60. The total number of immigrants arriving in America increased dramatically each passing decade with the result that a grand total of about five million immigrants entered the United States during the period. The newcomers came mainly from the countries of northern and western Europe. Especially large numbers of immigrants came from the British Isles and from the German provinces. Ireland led all countries by sending about two million people to the United States. The Irish immigrants came from all the provinces of Ireland, but compared to the past relatively few of them originated in Ulster. Many factors combined to bring about this mass immigration. Some rural people had been displaced by the forces of industrialization and modern scientific farming that were on the rise in northern and western Europe in the first half of the nineteenth century. The catastrophic potato famine in Ireland during the 1840s was a factor contributing to the extraordinary scale of emigration from Erin. In addition immigrants had countless individual motives for pulling up roots. As most European immigrants of the period, the bulk of the Irish newcomers located in the northeastern quadrant of the United States between 1815 and 1860. Indiana was not among the states in this region that received the greatest numbers of Irish immigrants during this period. Indeed, fewer foreign-born persons located in Indiana than in many northeastern states.[11]

Yet there was an unprecedented increase in the number of Irish immigrants in Indiana during the years from 1816 through 1860. Meanwhile, Indiana passed through its pioneer phase when homestead farms were isolated by the absence of transportation improvements. In the three decades before the Civil War the construction of roads, canals, and railroads reduced the isolation of country folk, and commercial farming expanded. Further, the pace of industrialization and urbanization increased.

There was a small increase in the Irish immigration to Indiana during the years 1816–32. Also, Irish Catholic newcomers became somewhat more visible in the population during this period. Although no systematic statistical record of the foreign born was made, the presence of Irish natives was recorded in comments made by contemporaries. Some of the commentators were early travelers whose observations were later published. Isaac Reed, a Presbyterian missionary, noted that when he resided in New Albany in 1818 some of the inhabitants of the town were from Ireland.[12] Karl Postel, who was a foreign traveler touring Indiana during the 1820s, also referred to the Irish. He wrote:

> For adventurers of all descriptions, Indiana holds
> out allurements of every kind. Numbers of Germans,
> French, and Irish, are scattered in the towns, and
> over the country, carrying on the business of bakers,
> grocers, store, grog shops, and tavern keepers.[13]

The history of the Catholic Church in Indiana provides the best source of information about the Irish during 1816–32. The clergy and parishioners of the Catholic Church in this state were still predominantly French. French Jesuit priests had introduced the Wabash country to Catholicism, and Vincennes had become a center for the Church's activities there in the French colonial era. Missionary priests had been attending to the spiritual needs of Catholics outside of Vincennes since the early eighteenth century. By 1830 there were Catholic families in Vincennes, Princeton, Washington, Evansville, New Albany, St. Mary-of-the-Knobs, Vevay, Dover, Montgomery, Mount Pleasant, Columbus, Shelbyville, Indianapolis, Fort Wayne, and South Bend. The Church estimated that there were 20,000 Indiana Catholics in a total state population of about 345,000 in 1830. The Catholic population was composed chiefly of persons of French and English stock. The latter were related to English Catholic families that had immigrated to Maryland and then migrated to Kentucky before coming to Indiana. Yet the Catholic record of the time contains evidence that Irish people were among the communicants of the Church in Indiana. For example, Irish immigrants settled in Dearborn County during the early years of statehood. In 1820 Catholic parishioners, who were mainly Irish and English, erected a log church building at Dover in Kelso Township. The parish was served by priests from Bardstown, Kentucky, who traveled a Bardstown, Cincinnati, and Vincennes circuit. Bishop Benedict Joseph Flaget of the Bardstown diocese was responsible for Catholics in Indiana during this period.[14]

Similarly, the presence of the Irish was recorded in the history of the Catholic Church in Floyd County. Irish immigrants were among the earliest settlers in the vicinity of Little Indian Creek in Lafayette Township. Nineteenth-century Floyd County historians referred to this area as the Catholic or Foreign Settlement. The Irish immigrants who located there included Thomas Pierce, who departed Ireland in 1818 and lived for a time in Pennsylvania. In 1820 Pierce settled on Little Indian Creek, where he was a farmer and surveyor. He was apparently accompanied on his journey from Ireland by the Byrns family (county Loud), which was composed of a mother, five sons, and three daughters. Shortly after the arrival of Pierce and the Byrns family, a Catholic church was organized on Little Indian Creek by Father Abraham, a Catholic priest from Bardstown, Kentucky. Thomas Pierce donated land for the church building. The Irish Catholic settlers erected a log church by the creek at the foot of the knobs. Other Irish newcomers joined the congregation after 1820. Nicholas Duffey and his large family located in the Catholic Settlement in 1821. John Coleman, also from Ireland, joined this Catholic community in 1825. He was one of the initial schoolteachers and justices of the peace in that part of Floyd County. As the years passed, still other Irish immigrants came to the vicinity making it an even more identifiable Catholic settlement.[15]

In summary, the history of the Irish in Indiana between 1816 and 1832 resembled the Irish story earlier in the century. The number of Irish increased moderately, and they were generally found in the southern half of the state, especially in Ohio River counties. General settlement in northern Indiana was minimal in 1830. According to a distinguished state demographic historian, only twelve Irish people settled in northern Indiana between 1820 and 1830.[16] Pioneer farming continued to be the chief pursuit of the Irish. Irish Catholics in the population were somewhat more evident than in the past.

The Irish population increase in Indiana during the period 1832–46 was substantially greater than it ever had been in the past. Significant numbers of Irish immigrants came to Indiana to work in canal construction during the 1830s. The Wabash and Erie Canal was Indiana's first major artificial waterway. The Wabash and Erie Canal scheme was grandiose. It projected the linking of Lake Erie at Toledo with the Ohio River at Evansville. The canal was expected to connect Fort Wayne, Logansport, and Lafayette in the north to Terre Haute, Washington, and Evansville in the south. Canal construction was confined to the northernmost section during the first half of the decade. The influx of Irish construction workers began in 1832, marking the start of canal excavation at Fort Wayne. The canal project created a demand for construction workers that was too great to be met by the laborers who were available in northern Indiana. Labor procurers advertised in newspapers throughout the state. In August 1832 the *Indianapolis Indiana Journal* published an advertisement that stated:

**Cash for Canal Hands**

We wish to employ laborers on the Wabash and Erie Canal, 12 miles west of Fort Wayne. The situation is healthy and dry. We will pay $10 per month for sober and industrious men.[17]

When such efforts to secure men in Indiana proved to be insufficient to meet canal needs, labor contractors acting in the interests of the canal traveled through Ohio, Pennsylvania, and New York, attempting to recruit immigrants, most of whom were Irish and German. The canal agents offered a contract under which the immigrant would receive an advance on the cost of transportation to Indiana in exchange for a deduction from his wage. Most of the immigrants who acceded to the blandishments of the Wabash and Erie Canal labor agents were Irish.[18]

There was little about Indiana canal construction work to recommend it to Irish immigrants in the East. Employment in canal excavation was hard and dirty, while in midsummer it was also hot and thirsty work. Canal diggers lived in primitive and unsanitary shelters, worked in unhealthy environments, and moved in social circumstances that were conducive to rowdiness and heavy drinking. Furthermore, workers were usually out of contact with the church of their faith. In addition to facing these repellant features of work and life on the canal, married Irish immigrants had to choose between two undesirable alternatives when deciding to take canal construction work in Indiana. A married man could choose to move west alone, thereby exposing himself and his family to problems of separation, or he could go to Indiana in the company of his family, thereby subjecting it to the crudities inherent in life on a canal under construction.[19] Another problem confronted the Irish immigrant considering an offer of canal work in Indiana. Many self-described canal agents were confidence men who bilked or exploited immigrants. An example was reported in the *Fort Wayne Sentinel* (27 August 1842) that stated:

A number of stone-cutters, chiefly Irish, and many with their families, have arrived here the past week, from New York on their way to Lafayette to work on the canal. . . . They were engaged by G. M. Nash . . . who advertised in the New York papers and by bills posted . . . that he was authorized by Messrs. Moorehead & Co. of Lafayette to engage them to work on the canal. Nash got $6.50 from each and gave them passage to Toledo. From Toledo, Moorehead & Co. would give them passage to Lafayette, where their fares would be returned. The Company denies all knowledge of Nash and needs no stone-cutters since the locks are made of wood. These families are to be pitied. Induced by high wages, now [they have] . . . no money and no jobs.[20]

Eventually the Irish-American press attempted to dissuade Irish immigrants from taking jobs in canal construction. Its aim was to shield natives of Ireland from fraud and exploitation. Nevertheless, many Irishmen continued to ignore this advice and went west as construction workers.

Irish newcomers worked in canal construction because it offered them comparatively high wages. The canal worker's wage was ten dollars a month in 1832. The monthly wage rose to thirteen dollars in 1837 as the demand for construction labor increased. These wages were high in comparison to the remuneration commonly available to Irish immigrants in eastern cities, where most Irishmen were required to work as unskilled laborers receiving the lowest wages. A large majority of the Irish came out of rural and agricultural backgrounds and consequently lacked manufacturing skills. Also, countless eastern employers refused to hire Irish Catholics except as unskilled laborers. Many Irish immigrants found canal employment alluring because it appeared to offer a means of escape from urban poverty in the East.[21]

The incursion of Irish canal workers into Indiana during the 1830s was undoubtedly substantial. It may be assumed that thousands of immigrants were hired for canal construction during the course of the decade. Their total number is not known because the state did not keep careful records concerning canal building, and it did not systematically count the immigrants working on the Wabash and Erie Canal in the 1830s. Yet sometimes the number of canal workers was officially reported. The *Journal of the House of Representatives of the State of Indiana* stated that 205 immigrants were hired for canal work from March to June 1833. Private observers noted that there were approximately one thousand construction workers on the canal near Fort Wayne in the summer of 1833. There were from one to two thousand immigrants working on the canal between Fort Wayne and Huntington in 1834 and in 1835. Indiana residents who witnessed the influx of immigrants were impressed by the scene. A Presbyterian minister in Fort Wayne, making a missionary report in 1834, wrote that great numbers of German and Irish immigrants were arriving there. The number of immigrants appeared to be great in comparison to the small size of villages in northern Indiana. The Fort Wayne population was less than nine hundred in 1830.[22]

Labor was arduous for the Irishmen excavating the Wabash and Erie Canal. The work required walking miles through the unpopulated countryside, wading through marshes, and removing trees in wooded areas. Their chief activity was digging and shoveling dirt in the ditch, often under a blazing sun. The canal diggers worked under the supervision of canal contractors who organized them into labor gangs. In describing the work method, canal historian Paul Fatout wrote:

> They built canal banks by using one-horse carts, usually four carts to a squad. Four men filled a cart, which then pulled away to dump the load on the fill perhaps a hundred yards distant. Shovelers, spacing the process so that they had a cart filled by the time an empty one returned, were on a sort of production belt that meant steady digging and heaving.[23]

An 1860 memoir recalling Fort Wayne in the early canal days described a view of the men working there. The memoir stated, "the 'Old Fort,' or rather one building of it, [was] tenanted by some Irish family. . . . The canal was then being dug at that point, and eastward, and when the season for labor began, hundreds of Irishmen, and horses and carts, could be seen at one view."[24]

Life in a Wabash and Erie Canal labor camp was harsh. Irish immigrants were sheltered in crudely erected log shanties. A shantytown stretched over a great distance by the side of the excavation in each of the areas where the canal was under construction.

The canal labor camp was a predominantly male society. Most of the Irish workers were single men or married men who were separated from their families. Father Stephen Badin, a Catholic priest, visited the canal west of Fort Wayne in 1834. In reference to the Irish in labor camps there, he wrote that there were "very few of the devout sex, and few children among them."[25] Thus, some of the canal workers were accompanied by their families. Father Simon Lalumiere, a Catholic priest serving in Terre Haute, recorded that he attended many families and single men when he visited Catholics on the Wabash and Erie Canal between Lafayette and Coal Creek in 1842.[26]

Some of the conditions of work and life on the Wabash and Erie Canal were detrimental to the health of the men, women, and children in the labor camps. Mosquitoes were prevalent all along the canal route and there were mosquito infestations in marshes and lowlands on the canal line. Consequently, those working or living at the canal excavation commonly came down with the ague and other malarial fevers spread by disease-bearing insects. Illness was also the consequence of conditions in the construction camps. The workers' shanties were inevitably unsanitary. The crude shelters were small, overcrowded, located in primitive settings, and occupied by men doing dirty labor. Further, apparently inadequate attention was given to the removal of waste from the camps. Illness naturally occurred in these circumstances. The Irish in the shantytowns suffered from dysentery and sometimes contracted cholera. Dysentery and the ague were physical trials but were rarely fatal. Other malarial fevers were more likely to cause death. Victims of cholera usually died. The high mortality rate for the Irish on the canal became legendary. The name of Richard Doyle, an Irish canal worker, was the first entry in the burial record started by Father Badin when he was a missionary priest at Fort Wayne. The link between mortality and canal building was symbolized by burial markers along the canal route near Fort Wayne.[27]

Irish newcomers who were constructing canals in Indiana experienced other indignities. In some respects they were treated as a class apart from others. They carried the stigma of being poor people in an affluent land. Father Badin characterized the Irish canal workers as "the lower class of the Irish."[28] Canal contractors regarded Irishmen as unqualified to be employed as skilled laborers. Thus men of other national backgrounds were engaged as skilled artisans and were paid higher wages to erect canal structures such as aqueducts. Meanwhile, Irishmen were hired to work with picks and shovels.[29] They were also set apart by their faith. The Irish Catholics were working in a heavily Protestant state, containing denominations and sects that were suspicious and fearful of the Catholic Church.[30]

The hard life in the Wabash and Erie Canal camps led many Irishmen to behave in ways inconsistent with accepted behavior in polite society in the 1830s. Excessive drinking and rowdiness were by-products of the canal construction experience.[31] Initially the canal commissioners attempted to preclude liquor problems. In 1832 the canal contracts stated that, "the party of the first part [William Rockhill, contractor] shall not permit any workmen in his employ while they are engaged in constructing this Section [at Fort Wayne] to drink distilled spirits of any kind under the liability of forfeiting this contract at the option of the party of the Second part [Samuel Lewis, Canal Commissioner]."[32] The liquor provisions of the canal contracts were only enforced for a short time. Drinking distilled spirits was common in Indiana pioneer society during the 1830s, and prohibition was not the prevailing viewpoint on liquor usage then. Subsequently, whiskey drinking was virtually sanctioned by canal contractors. In reference to the prevalence of drinking on the canal, one source stated, "and every gang of workmen boasted a 'jigger boss' whose duty it was to carry a large tin pail of whiskey along the line and issue a small drink or jigger whenever it seemed needed. His judgment was the only limit or guide."[33] Also shanties from which jiggers of whiskey were dispensed were set up along the canal works by local liquor merchants who took much of the workmen's wages. In 1834 Father Badin observed that the Irish canal laborers in Indiana were "too fond of drinking."[34] In the next decade Father Lalumiere reported, "I have much trouble with my Irish boys on the [Wabash and Erie] canal, they will drink."[35] The Irishmen drank because the liquor was available, because it was their custom, and because whiskey was seen as a medicinal for malaria. Undoubtedly the Irishmen who drank to excess saw whiskey as a means of diversion from loneliness and boredom and viewed the hard spirits as a way of temporary release from the grim work camp experience.[36]

Irish life on the Wabash and Erie Canal in the 1830s was further complicated by ethnic friction among the emigrants from Ireland. There were two feuding groups of Irish canal workers. They were commonly known as the Fardowns and the Corkonians, whose animosities were rooted in the history of Ireland. The Fardowns were Protestants of Scottish ancestry who had emigrated from Ulster in Northern Ireland. The Corkonians were Catholic emigrants from Ireland. Corkonians and Fardowns were members of organized groups headed by leaders who advocated forms of ethnic nationalism. Some Irishmen entered these associations upon their arrival in the United States, for example in New York City. Others joined later in canal construction areas. Undoubtedly, few of the Irish canal workers were active in these associations. However, at times most of the Irish on a canal were caught up in the feuds of the organized ethnic nationalists. The two groups shared a history of violent conflict in America as well as in Ireland. Men in the Corkonian and Fardown associations fought on canal construction projects in New York, Pennsylvania, and Maryland. Riots involving hundreds of men occurred on the Chesapeake and Ohio Canal, where the militia was called out after deaths and many injuries. This was the background of the troubles among Irish immigrants on the Wabash and Erie Canal.[37]

The troubles in Indiana began after September 1834 when Corkonian and Fardown members and leaders appeared on the Wabash and Erie Canal. These activists included men who had been involved in canal riots in the East. According to a contemporary source, during the following nine months Corkonians and Fardowns "manifested their ill will to each other by merciless beatings on such of each party as chanced to fall in the power of the other."[38] The Corkonians and the Fardowns occupied ethnically segregated construction camps. The Corkonians were on the upper part of the canal line, and the Fardowns were on the lower section of the line. Corkonians and Fardowns deliberately hired themselves to canal contractors on different parts of the line because they feared for their safety in ethnically mixed camps. The beatings were confined almost exclusively to the Irish laborers on the canal. Since local people were not involved, the civil authorities made little effort to suppress the violence. In any case, law enforcement would have been difficult because there was no justice of the peace along great lengths of the canal in newly organized counties. Hostilities escalated in the summer of 1835. Members of each party took great precautions for their safety before traveling from one part of the canal line to another. Tensions reached a critical level during the week before the 12 July anniversary of the Battle of the Boyne. The battle near Belfast in 1690 was a historic clash between Catholics and Protestants. The forces of King William of Orange, a Protestant, had defeated an Irish-French army supporting James II, a Catholic. Alarming stories circulated among the Irish in the canal camps as the anniversary approached. Corkonians and Fardowns heard rumors that were essentially the same. It was said that their enemies shortly would attack their camp at night in an attempt to burn their shanties and murder them in their beds. Corkonian and Fardown camps were evacuated at night. Men, women, and children concealed themselves in the dark woods and avoided the use of light or fire so that their hiding places would not be revealed. In the daytime armed men worked on the canal. The work continued "until some idle report would get in circulation, that the other party was *marching* to fight them, at which times they would leave their work and hasten with great rapidity to the supposed point of danger."[39] Such alarms and responses were frequent from 4 to 10 July. Meanwhile, the two sides agreed to hold a showdown on the Boyne anniversary and chose a field of battle. On 10 July one of the canal engineers reported "that all the workmen on the lower end of the line were armed and marching to the reputed battle field."[40] Indeed, both groups stopped working on 10 July and began to "march towards the centre of the line for a general battle."[41] According to the *Fort Wayne Sentinel,* eight hundred Corkonians, most of whom were armed, assembled at Lagro on 10 July while "at the same time about 250 armed Fardowns advanced to Wabash, seven miles from Lagro, on their way to attack their adversaries."[42] David Burr, a canal commissioner, reported that there were seven or eight hundred armed men with three or four hundred on a side. Burr met Fardown leaders as they moved up the canal line to a point near his residence and then he talked to Corkonian spokesmen. Each side told Burr virtually the same story. The terror of possible violence at night could be borne no longer. Civil authority would not or could not protect them. They wished to work in peace, but they chose to fight in daytime to preclude nighttime depredations. A battle would end the problem by driving one of the parties away from the canal.[43]

Burr and some other local residents persuaded the two parties to suspend hostile activities while Burr attempted to negotiate a settlement. Father Lalumiere met with the Irish Catholics. According to a church historian, "His presence . . . made the laborers instantly disperse. He exhorted them to behave as true Irishmen, and true Catholics, worthy of the country of their adoption."[44] Meanwhile, militia units and civil authorities from communities along the canal were called into action and made a show of force. Eight ringleaders were arrested and taken under a strong guard to Indianapolis because there was no secure jail in the area. Further, the authorities regarded the ringleaders as "the cause of contention" and therefore wished to separate them from their countrymen.[45] The jailed men were freed shortly by a writ of habeas corpus issued because of irregularities in the legal proceedings.[46] This event was summarized in Gov. Noah Noble's annual message to the legislature, in which he wrote, "During the past summer the foreign laborers upon the line of the canal, resuscitated some of their old party animosities, which so often were the cause of collision in their native country, Ireland, and while under great excitement, from five to seven hundred on a side

assembled for several days, armed for battle, to the great terror of the citizens of that vicinity."[47] The anticipated battle among Irishmen was averted by the combination of diplomacy and force. Subsequently the canal board required each contractor to dismiss and blacklist any laborer who engaged in a brawl. Thereafter times were more peaceful. Yet the troubles among Irishmen did not end. The *Indiana Documentary Journal* reported fighting between Corkonians and Fardowns on the Central Canal in 1837. Meanwhile Bishop Simon Bruté of the Diocese of Vincennes urged the Catholic Church to devise means of deterring Irish immigrants from joining militant associations when they arrived in New York, to discover the leaders of such associations, and to find ways of appealing to the consciences of the men involved in them. Later these associations were condemned in a Catholic Church pastoral issued in New York.[48]

The Wabash and Erie Canal was not the only internal improvement project that attracted Irish construction workers to Indiana during the 1830s. An unknown number of Irishmen participated in early road building. National Road construction began at Richmond at the opening of the decade, continued to Indianapolis by the middle of the decade, and reached Terre Haute by 1839. National Road laborers receiving eight to twelve dollars a month were among the first Irish who settled in Indianapolis. Irish and German laborers working on the National Road augmented the Catholic population of Terre Haute. A construction boom in Indiana during the second half of the decade began in 1836 when the state legislature enacted the Mammoth Internal Improvements Act, which authorized eight construction projects involving road, canal, and railroad building. The authorization provided for the construction of the Wabash and Erie Canal from Lafayette to the Ohio River, the Whitewater Canal in the state's southeast, and the Central Canal through Indianapolis to northern and southern termini on the Wabash and Erie Canal. The implementation of this grand scheme brought an even greater demand for construction workers and higher wages paid to canal laborers. Thus, more Irish immigrants came to Indiana to work on the canals. For example, Irishmen were laboring on the Central Canal near Indianapolis by 1837. However, all of the state-sponsored improvements projects were stopped in 1839 since the financing of the transportation scheme broke down in the midst of the national economic depression that followed the panic of 1837. The construction projects languished through the first half of the next decade as the depression continued and the state was unsuccessful in reorganizing its finances. The demand for canal diggers was minimal, and Irish immigrants had little incentive to come to Indiana seeking canal and road construction work during that time.[49]

Irish Catholics who came to Indiana during 1832–46 were devoted to their faith. Immigrants who were separated from their families and friends in Ireland needed their church for support as they became accustomed to living in America, as well as for its spiritual guidance. Thus, the record of the Catholic Church reveals a notable part of Irish history in Indiana. The Catholic Church in Indiana was initially hard pressed in caring for the increasing number of Irish and German Catholic immigrants entering the state. Only four Catholic priests were serving in Indiana in 1834. Bishop Simon Bruté of the Diocese of Vincennes, formed in 1834, was responsible for the spiritual needs of Catholics in the whole state. In 1835 Bishop Bruté estimated that there were six to seven hundred Catholics in Fort Wayne and fifteen hundred to two thousand more on the canal route. In addition, there were Catholics living elsewhere in the state. Father Badin and Father Lalumiere made trips to visit Catholics in the towns and in the construction camps on the Wabash and Erie Canal. Father Lalumiere enrolled Irish and German canal workers in a temperance society that he founded.[50]

The growth of the Catholic Church in Indiana was evidently related to the transportation improvements that were made in the 1832–46 period. The Catholic population increased particularly in towns located on recently constructed canals and roads as well as in towns on the Ohio River. During the 1830s Irish Catholics in Indiana towns and settlements were usually cared for by priests of French birth. Later the national origins of the priests became more diverse as the number of Catholic parishioners and priests increased. By the early 1840s the list of priests serving in Indiana included Irish and German names. When a church building was not available in a town, a visiting priest said Mass in a local Catholic home as had been the custom in earlier times. As a consequence of Catholic population growth in the early 1830s, Catholic parishes were organized and Catholic churches were built in many Indiana towns in the years after 1835. The Catholic congregations were ethnic mixtures, composed largely of Irish and German parishioners.

The Catholic Church became more vital in Fort Wayne, Logansport, Lafayette, and other Wabash and Erie Canal towns after 1832. Most Catholics in Fort Wayne were of French ancestry before 1832. Yet Fort Wayne Catholics were predominantly Irish and German shortly after the arrival of canal construction workers in 1832. In the early 1830s Catholics were organized by Father Badin, who spoke fluent English. Father Badin collected money for a church building in 1834, when many of the Irish and Germans began arriving in Fort Wayne. Father Lalumiere visited Fort Wayne while touring the eastern part of the diocese in late winter 1835 where he noted that one hundred fifty Catholic families were worshiping in a newly erected chapel, apparently a small and plain structure. Father M. Ruff (born in Metz, France) attended Fort Wayne Catholics in 1835. He spoke French, English, and German. The Catholic population increased sufficiently to permit the assignment of the first resident pastor to Fort Wayne in 1840. He was Father Louis Mueller, who was of German birth. In consequence of personality differences, Father Mueller was eventually opposed by his parishioners, mainly the Irish and French. Father Mueller was required to confine himself to work among Catholics outside the city, chiefly Germans. The next resident priest was Father Julian Benoit, who arrived in 1840 and completed the building of St. Augustine Church, begun by his predecessor. During the 1840s Father Benoit apparently cared for the Irish and French communicants, while the German-speaking parishioners were attended by a priest of German birth who assisted Father Benoit.[51]

The arrival of Irish immigrants contributed to the growth of the Catholic Church in canal towns west of Fort Wayne. In the mid-1830s several Irish families settled at Lagro, later a wheat shipping port on the canal. Catholics erected a frame church in Lagro in 1838. The arrival of Irish workers made Peru a permanent Catholic mission station by 1834. A Catholic church was founded in Peru in 1838. There was an influx of Catholics into Logansport during the mid-1830s when the canal was being constructed in Cass County. In 1838 Father John Claude Francois organized a Catholic congregation in Logansport; it was composed mainly of Irish laborers employed on the canal. A small frame chapel erected near the canal bank was used until a stone church was built in Logansport in 1839.[52]

The Catholic presence in Lafayette apparently was minimal during the 1830s before the Wabash and Erie Canal entered Tippecanoe County. Catholic activity in Lafayette increased with the arrival of Irish canal workers. In 1840 there were about fifteen Catholic families in Lafayette, and in response to their petition for regular visits by a missionary priest, Father Augustus Martin, Father John Claude Francois, and Father Simon Lalumiere successively made trips to Lafayette. Mass was read in the homes of Frank Daily and James H. McKernan. Describing Catholic worship in the absence of a church structure in Lafayette, a local church historian, writing later in the century, reported: "Mass in those days was offered in the houses of different members of the congregation, and when they all assembled it was quite a gala day. Whilst the priest heard confessions in one room the women were preparing dinner in another. All who were present were expected to dine at the house where mass was said. The men assembled out of doors, discussing fluctuations of the currency. . . . Every one kept open house in turn."[53] There were twenty-five Catholic families in Lafayette in 1843 when Lafayette's first resident priest, Father Michael Clark, held services in a rented room in a building occupied by a religious bookstore. In response to a growing Catholic population, St. Mary and Martha's Church was built in Lafayette in 1844.[54]

The appearance of Irish immigrants stimulated Catholic Church activity in towns on the National Road, including Richmond, Indianapolis, and Terre Haute during the 1832–46 period. In the 1830s traveling priests visited Richmond Catholics, some of whom were Irish (such as the O'Hara family), and said Mass in private homes. Father Michael O'Rourke occasionally made trips to Richmond during the early 1840s. Father O'Rourke was the resident priest at Dover in Dearborn County. Father John Ryan was Richmond's first resident priest. He organized a Richmond parish composed of Irish and German families and built St. Andrew's Church in 1846. Mass was celebrated by missionary priests in the residences of Catholic families in Indianapolis (including those of Michael Shea and John O'Connor) prior to the opening of the first Catholic Church in Indianapolis (Holy Cross) in 1840.[55]

While there were a number of Catholics living in Vigo County, there was only one Catholic resident of Terre Haute during the early 1830s when traveling priests occasionally visited the area. A few Terre Haute Catholics erected a church in 1838, when the National Road construction was nearing their town. The 1838–41 records of Terre Haute's St. Joseph's Church show an increasing number of Irish family names, including Murphy, Byrne, Dugan, Cahill, and Kelly, as well as some English and German names. Father Lalumiere became resident priest at Terre Haute in 1842. The largest group in his congregation was composed of the Irish with some Kentuckians (English stock) and Germans.[56] Describing the Terre Haute parish in 1845, one of Father Lalumiere's parishioners wrote, "We have but a small congregation [about sixty communicants] and they with few exceptions are very poor, living by daily labor of the hardest, and who can scarce spare time to practice their religious duties."[57]

There was comparable Catholic activity involving the Irish in towns and settlements near the Ohio River from 1832 through 1846. In Floyd County the old Irish Catholic settlement on Little Indian Creek (Lafayette Township) was enlarged by Irish and German newcomers during the 1830s. Father Louis Neyron (a Frenchman) brought about the replacement of the Catholic settlement's old log chapel. In 1837 a new brick building called St. Mary's Church was erected on a hill overlooking the creek valley. Patrick Byrns and Patrick Duffey made the bricks for the building. These natives of Ireland were among the first settlers of the area. Also in Floyd County during the early 1830s, the New Albany Catholics attended St. Mary's Church in Lafayette Township. New Albany Catholics also heard Mass said in private homes when a traveling priest visited their city. The augmentation of the local Catholic population led to the organization of Holy Trinity parish in New Albany and to the erection of a church building there (circa 1836). The members of the Holy Trinity congregation had Irish, German, French, and English family names. The Irish names included McKenna, Dougherty, Mullin, Flannagan, McGuire, O'Brien, and Riley. In Dearborn County the old Catholic parish at Dover (Kelso Township) was still composed of Irish and English families. The Dover parish had grown enough by 1840 to justify the assignment of Father Conrad Schneiderjans as its first resident priest. Also, that growth prompted the replacement of the old log church with a new frame one. During 1842–46 Father Michael O'Rourke was assigned to St. John the Baptist parish at Dover.[58]

The years 1846–60 formed another distinct period of Irish history in the state of Indiana. Indiana was no longer in its pioneer phase; roads, canals, and railroads connected previously isolated communities and prompted further urban and industrial growth. The Irish immigration to Indiana was much larger than in the past. While many natives of Ireland resided in rural areas of the state, the Irish foreign-born population became more urban in the decade before 1860.

Several factors gave impetus to Irish immigration to Indiana after 1846. A terrible potato famine caused an exodus from Ireland during those years. In 1847, as the national economy was improving, the Indiana legislature refinanced the state debt in ways that permitted private companies to complete the construction of some canals begun earlier. Wabash and Erie Canal construction was resumed in earnest, the work being completed in 1853. This demand for labor again provided a motive for Irish construction workers to come to Indiana. The 1830s pattern of Irish life on the Wabash and Erie Canal was repeated in southern Indiana after 1846 when canal construction was in progress between Terre Haute, Washington, and Evansville. In the early 1850s the canal was under construction in Pike, Gibson, and Vanderburgh counties. Sixty-odd years later Gibson County witnesses to the canal work related their memories to the author of a county history. One observer stated: "On these heavy works there was a large number of men, carts, and teams at work for nearly three years. . . . They had a very large plow on these works which the writer has seen drawn by eight yoke of heavy oxen. Shanties for the people and rough stables for the horses and oxen were scattered so thickly that it looked like a string town for many miles along the canal. . . . There were a hundred boarding shanties [on the canal line in] Gibson County. Some of these shanties were eighty feet long and would have bunks for as many as fifty boarders. . . . Nearly all of the people who lived near the works were Irish. They had no trouble getting all the whiskey they required."[59] As in the past, canal work endangered the health of Irish laborers and caused the deaths of many of them. Unsanitary conditions in canal shantytowns fostered cholera epidemics. Hundreds of people died in a cholera outbreak on the canal south of Covington in 1849.[60] Recalling an extraordinarily high number of deaths in a cholera epidemic on the canal in Gibson County, a witness stated: "The stricken would die within three or four hours. On the old Potter farm . . . so many people were sick and dead that the canal people hired a cooper . . . to make boxes for coffins. . . . There was a general stampede from the works. Cold weather came, and work was resumed. There were three dead Irishmen found in a blacksmith shop . . . two miles north of Oakland City."[61]

The Irish came to Indiana to be employed on railroad lines constructed before 1860. The first significant railroad in Indiana was completed in 1847; it linked Madison and Indianapolis. Railroad construction was so extensive during the 1850s that all the state's larger cities had rail connections by 1860. Many Irish immigrants came to Madison to work on the railroad there. Similarly Irish newcomers located in Indianapolis as a consequence of railroad work. A group of Irish immigrants took residence in South Bend in 1851, after working on the

construction of a railroad connecting Buffalo, South Bend, and Chicago. Another group of Irish families settled in South Bend later in the decade after finishing work on a railroad joining Philadelphia, South Bend, and Chicago. Irish Catholic laborers were found in large construction camps along new rail lines in Indiana, where they received the support and guidance of traveling Catholic priests. For example, in 1853 or 1854 Father John Baptist Corbe gave the last rites to a sick Irish workman in a railroad construction camp in Vigo County where about two hundred Catholic families were living. Also, Father Patrick McDermott attended Catholic mission stations along the Evansville and Crawfordsville Railroad when it was under construction in the early 1850s.[62]

Irish workers contributed much to the building of roads, canals, and railroads in Indiana. These transportation improvements aided the state's population growth at midcentury by facilitating migration and immigration to Indiana. During the 1850s the number of Irish immigrants in Indiana almost doubled, and the number of foreign born in the state grew twofold. The number of natives of Ireland in Indiana increased from 12,787 in 1850 to 24,495 in 1860. Meanwhile, the Indiana foreign-born population grew from 55,537 to 118,184. Thus, Irish immigrants comprised 23 percent of the foreign born in Indiana in 1850 and 21 percent of the state's foreign born in 1860. It should be noted that the foreign born were but a small proportion of the total population of Indiana, which was 988,416 in 1850 and 1,350,428 in 1860. Only 8.8 percent of the state's total population was foreign born in 1860.[63]

*Samuel D. McIntosh, a native of Ireland, came to Delphi, Indiana, in 1845 and made and sold saddlery. About 1855 he erected this frame house, which fire destroyed in 1929.*

Table A. Indiana Census of Population*

| Year | Born in Ireland | Foreign Born | Total |
|---|---|---|---|
| 1850 | 12,787 | 55,537 | 988,416 |
| 1860 | 24,495 | 118,184 | 1,350,428 |
| 1870 | 28,698 | 141,474 | 1,680,637 |
| 1880 | 25,741 | 144,178 | 1,978,301 |
| 1890 | 20,819 | 146,205 | 2,192,404 |
| 1900 | 16,306 | 142,121 | 2,516,462 |
| 1910 | 11,266 | 159,663 | 2,700,876 |
| 1920 | 7,271 | 150,868 | 2,930,390 |
| 1930 | 3,931 | 142,999 | 3,238,503 |
| 1940 | 2,657 | 110,631 | 3,427,796 |
| 1950 | 2,352 | 100,630 | 3,934,224 |
| 1960 | 1,673 | 93,202 | 4,662,498 |
| 1970 | 1,152 | 83,198 | 5,193,669 |
| 1980 | 825 | 101,802 | 5,490,224 |

*Based on United States Department of Commerce, Bureau of the Census, *Census of Population* for the years 1850–1980.

Examinations of federal census records reveal that Irish immigrants became less concentrated in southern Indiana during the 1850s. While natives of Ireland were living in every Indiana county, the numbers of Irish immigrants were greatest in the southern reaches of the state in 1850. Many Irish canal and railroad laborers were working on construction projects in southern Indiana at midcentury. Further, the foreign born generally were more heavily concentrated in southern Indiana because the state had been settled from south to north and because many early immigrants had come to Indiana via the Ohio River. A disproportionate percentage of the Irish lived in a few Indiana counties. The ten counties with the greatest numbers of persons born in Ireland contained 53 percent of the Irish immigrants in all of the state's counties in 1850. Seven of these counties with high Irish populations in 1850 were in southern Indiana (Daviess, Dearborn, Floyd, Jefferson, Jennings, Pike, and Vanderburgh), two of them were in central Indiana (Marion and Tippecanoe), and one was in northern Indiana (Allen). In consequence of general demographic and economic trends, the distribution of Irish immigrants in Indiana began to shift northward during the 1850s. The 1860 census revealed that five of the ten Indiana counties with the greatest populations of persons born in Ireland were in the southern section (Dearborn, Floyd, Jefferson, Vanderburgh, and Vigo), that three of them were in the central section

(Marion, Tippecanoe, and Wayne), and that two were in the northern section (Allen and La Porte). Irish population gains were greater in the state's central and northern counties during the 1850s than in its southern counties. During the same decade Irish immigrant populations actually declined in a few of the southern counties, including Daviess, Pike, and Jefferson.[64]

Irish immigrants tended to locate in counties on new transportation routes in all sections of Indiana during the 1850s. The Wabash and Erie Canal, the Indianapolis and Madison Railroad, and the National Road passed through nine of the ten Indiana counties containing the greatest numbers of Irish immigrants in 1850 and in 1860. Many Irish construction laborers eventually settled along transportation routes where they had worked. Some Irish newcomers probably purchased canal land at the bargain prices that the Wabash and Erie Canal trustees had advertised in their attempt to recruit immigrant workers. Other Irish construction workers did not settle near the canals, roads, or railroads that they had built. Many of them had been transients. In 1834 Father Badin had advised against the erection of chapels at canal construction locations because Catholic workers were at such places only temporarily. There was an Irish exodus following the completion of canal building in Pike County, where the number of persons born in Ireland fell from 683 in 1850 to 35 in 1860. Nevertheless, the number of Irish laborers

Table B. Number of Persons Born in Ireland for the Ten Indiana Counties with the Greatest Irish Foreign-Born Populations*

| County | 1850 | 1860 | 1870 | 1880 | 1890 | 1900 | 1910 | 1920 |
|---|---|---|---|---|---|---|---|---|
| Allen | 406 | 697 | 982 | 1,030 | 843 | 598 | 449 | 292 |
| Cass | | | 963 | 732 | 616 | 479 | 298 | 164 |
| La Porte | | 877 | 666 | | | | | 105 |
| Lake | | | | | 505 | 573 | 729 | 908 |
| St. Joseph | | | | 618 | 636 | 551 | 466 | 345 |
| Grant | | | | | | 371 | 200 | |
| Madison | | | | | | 478 | 259 | 160 |
| Marion | 492 | 1,748 | 3,760 | 4,064 | 4,127 | 4,009 | 3,383 | 2,488 |
| Montgomery | | | 626 | | | | | |
| Tippecanoe | 917 | 1,645 | 1,926 | 1,238 | 959 | 636 | 395 | 189 |
| Wayne | | 884 | 956 | 852 | 593 | 427 | 247 | 131 |
| Clark | | | 873 | 664 | 447 | | | |
| Daviess | 838 | | | | | | | |
| Dearborn | 813 | 866 | | | | | | |
| Floyd | 451 | 835 | | | | | | |
| Jefferson | 1,313 | 970 | 972 | 568 | | | | |
| Jennings | 367 | | | | | | | |
| Pike | 683 | | | | | | | |
| Vanderburgh | 498 | 730 | | 534 | 424 | | | |
| Vigo | | 949 | 1,391 | 1,396 | 1,097 | 809 | 624 | 366 |

*Based on United States Department of Commerce, Bureau of the Census, *Census of Population* for the years 1870–1920. Also, "1850 Census Foreign-Born for Indiana," unpublished manuscript, 1991, Indiana Historical Society, Education Division; "1860 Census Foreign-Born for Indiana," unpublished manuscript, 1991, Indiana Historical Society, Education Division.

who had worked on canals, roads, and railroads undoubtedly was not large enough to account entirely for the Irish population increase during the 1850s. Apparently additional Irish immigrants were attracted to Indiana by the promise of economic opportunity, especially in the cities on new transportation lines. The transportation improvements fostered economic growth, creating employment for immigrants in the cities and providing the foreign born with the means of access to them. Irish population increases were especially great in counties with economically booming cities. For example, the Irish foreign-born populations of Marion County (Indianapolis) and Vigo County (Terre Haute) more than tripled between 1850 and 1860, when there was less than a doubling of the number of Irish immigrants in the state. Conversely, the Irish immigrant population of Jefferson County decreased by about one quarter during the 1850s as that county's principal city (Madison) entered a period of economic decline.[65]

During the period 1816–60 most Irish immigrants in Indiana were located in rural areas, where they lived in villages or on farms. A demographic study revealed that in 1850 farming was the occupation of 53 percent of the Irish immigrants in northern Indiana, which was the most rural section of the state. Ninety-one percent of the state's total population was rural in 1860, when few Indiana counties had cities with populations of twenty-five hundred or more. Thus, most of the Indiana counties with Irish immigrant populations were entirely rural in 1860.[66]

In 1860 Indiana's Irish population was much more urban than the state's general population. Only 8.6 percent of the total state population was urban, i.e., located in cities with minimum populations of 2,500. But at least one-third of the Irish foreign born lived in urban places (8,685 of 24,495). Naturally, the proportion of the Irish living in cities was highest in Indiana counties with urban centers. For example, 93.5 percent of the natives of Ireland in Floyd County (New Albany) were urban dwellers (781 of 835). Irish immigrants were a comparatively urban people in all of the regions of the United States, especially in the Northeast where most Irish newcomers were concentrated.[67]

In some respects Irish urban experiences in Indiana reflected Irish life in major eastern cities before 1860. In New York City and in Boston the great mass of Irish workers were in the lowest paying occupations, i.e., unskilled labor for Irish men and domestic service for Irish women. Similarly, in South Bend during this period between one-half and two-thirds of the Irish workingmen were employed as laborers. In Terre Haute in 1860, 69 percent of the foreign-born Irish workingmen and women were laborers (45 percent) and domestic servants (24 percent). Irish immigrants accumulated relatively

little property in Indiana cities and elsewhere because so many of them received low wages for unskilled work. In 1860 the median values of personal and real property owned by the Irish immigrants in South Bend were lower than the comparable figures for immigrants of other European nationalities in that city. Also, the average values of real and personal property owned by Irish natives in Terre Haute were found to be low in 1860. Indiana's urban and rural Irish immigrants had different statistical profiles regarding occupations and property ownership. Relatively few of the rural Irish in the state were employed in unskilled labor by midcentury. In 1850 only about 26 percent of the Irish men were laborers in the largely rural counties of northern Indiana. The remainder of the Irish in those twenty-one counties were employed in agriculture, businesses, professions, and skilled crafts. Irish immigrants in the latter occupations in all parts of Indiana included persons who possessed surplus capital or craft skills. Immigrants in this category either possessed financial assets or skills upon arrival in the United States or acquired them after entry into the country. Many of the Irish who came to Indiana during 1816–60 had lived in other states (chiefly in the Northeast) or in Canada. Irish newcomers lacking capital or skills tended to locate in Indiana cities that seemed to offer the best opportunities for their advancement.[68]

In other respects there were great contrasts between the experiences of the urban Irish in Indiana and elsewhere. In Boston and New York City impoverished Irish immigrants were ill housed in densely populated slum areas, where they were exposed to social problems involving crime, ill health, and illiteracy. Undoubtedly, population densities were comparatively low in immigrant residential areas of Indiana cities. The Irish in Indiana did not experience the intense social ills typical of eastern slum life. However, they did not escape entirely social problems associated with poverty. For example, the Irish immigrants in Indiana had a high illiteracy rate, even in rural areas. In the counties of northern Indiana there were more illiterates among the natives of Ireland than in any other group in 1850.[69]

Also, the social life of the urban Irish in Indiana contrasted with that of the Irish in the East during the 1850s. There were differences in residential patterns and in organizational activities. The Irish in Indiana did not form great immigrant ghettos like those found in Boston. In Indiana the urban Irish were generally dispersed. Yet there were varying degrees of residential concentrations of foreign-born Irish in the state's cities. In 1850 Irish immigrants resided in all five Lafayette wards, but 51 percent of Lafayette's Irish-born population lived in the city's first ward and another 22 percent resided in its fifth ward. Natives of Ireland living in Terre Haute in 1860 were almost evenly distributed in that city's five wards, each of which contained less than one quarter of the total Irish immigrant population. In 1860 foreign-born Irish men were evenly distributed in Madison's nine wards, but the concentrations of the Irish men were somewhat greater in wards 8–9 (south) and in wards 1–3 (north). Ethnic residential segregation was also weak in South Bend. But Irish residents of South Bend were especially found in the fourth ward (east side) and in the third ward (west side) in 1860. Urban Irish immigrants were dispersed because they chose residences in close proximity to their workplaces. For instance, many Irish women lived in Terre Haute's second ward because it contained affluent neighborhoods where they were employed as domestic servants. Thus more female natives of Ireland resided in the second ward than in any other Terre Haute ward in 1860. In South Bend Irish employees of Notre Dame lived on the east side in the fourth ward, while Irish employees working for westside factories and railroads resided in

the third ward. The Irish laborers who were engaged in the construction of the railroad incline plane west of Madison took residence in the western part of Madison. Prior to 1860 the Irish newcomers in Indiana evidently were not active in establishing the kind of benevolent and fraternal organizations that formed much of the social life of Irish immigrants in eastern cities.[70]

Newcomers from Ireland in the urban East formed cultural institutions including churches, schools, and newspapers in efforts to maintain their Irish heritage. The Irish in Indiana had a somewhat similar cultural history before 1860. As previously indicated, the urban and rural Irish in the state were much involved in the organization of Catholic parishes and in the erection of Catholic Church edifices between 1830 and 1860. Catholic congregations were initially composed of ethnic mixtures, including Irish and German parishioners. After 1846 Catholic parishes in Indiana became more segregated along nationality lines. During the 1840s the German population increase was great enough to permit the formation of German-language

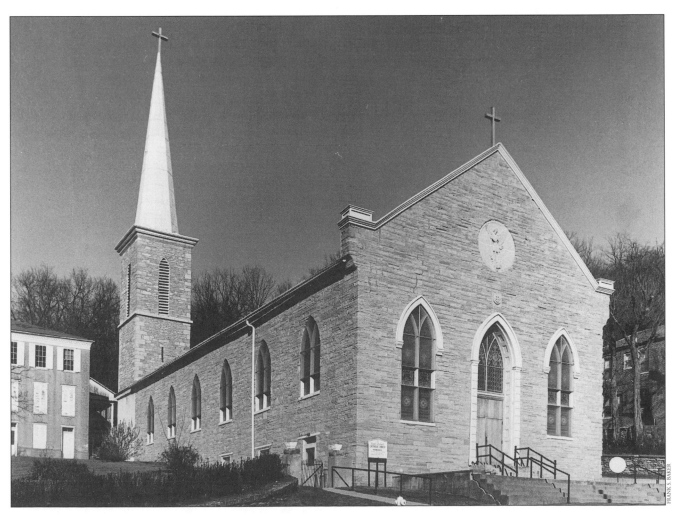

*St. Michael's Catholic Church, Madison, Indiana, ca. 1987.*

churches. A predominantly Irish congregation remained in the initial Catholic church of a city when the German communicants withdrew to form a separate parish. This occurred in a number of Indiana cities. The phenomenon began in 1848 in Fort Wayne and in Evansville, which had the largest German populations in the state. The parishioners of St. Michael's Church of Madison became largely Irish after the founding of a German church in 1851. Likewise, chiefly Irish Catholic parishes were created in Lafayette in 1853 and in New Albany in 1854 when new German parishes were formed. In Indianapolis, the Irish proportion of St. John's congregation increased after St. Mary's Church (German) was opened in 1858.[71]

Some Catholic parishes were principally Irish when they were organized in the 1850s. The Irish composed most of the congregation of North Madison's St. Patrick's Church which was built near the Irish neighborhoods there. The Irish outnumbered the Germans in the congregation of South Bend's first Catholic church, which was opened on the city's east side in 1853. Initially known as St. Alexis, it was called St. Joseph after 1860. In 1859 the Irish on South Bend's west side founded St. Patrick's Church. In 1860 a predominantly Irish parish appeared in Richmond when Irish communicants withdrew from the first Catholic church there and formed St. Mary's Church.[72]

Indiana's Irish were involved in other cultural institutions. At least one parochial school was maintained in virtually every largely Irish Catholic parish in Indiana cities by 1860. Irish ethnic newspapers evidently were not published in Indiana before the Civil War. The *New York Irish-American* and other Irish newspapers appeared elsewhere. Yet Irish immigrants were associated with Indiana newspapers. For example, John Dowling (born in Ballinrush, Ireland) was editor of the *Terre Haute Wabash Courier* during the 1830s.[73]

The Irish were active in Indiana politics and government during 1816–60. The Irish immigrants soon became a factor in nineteenth-century party politics. Irish voters supported the Democratic party, which adopted positions that were sympathetic to immigrants in contrast to the Whig party which took nativist stands. The Democrats used their control of the 1850–51 state constitutional convention to ease voting requirements for immigrants. Three of the six foreign-born delegates to the constitutional convention were natives of Ireland. The 1851 state constitution provided that aliens could vote providing that they declared their intentions to become citizens and met a minimal residence requirement. During the 1850s many Irish aliens sought the franchise under these terms. A study of county naturalization records shows that three-fourths of the Irish aliens in Terre Haute who declared their intentions regarding citizenship during the decade did so in the general election years of 1854, 1856, and 1860. Also, in each instance most of these Irish men declared their citizenship intentions during the week preceding election day.[74]

Nativism and the Know-Nothing movement formed part of the background of Irish involvement in Indiana politics during the 1850s. Anti-Catholic attitudes were common in early nineteenth-century Indiana, and such attitudes intensified as the state's Catholic population increased and as attacks were made on the Catholic Church. Stories alleging immorality in Catholic convents were circulated. In 1853 large crowds in Indianapolis heard Father Alessandro Gavazzi, a defrocked priest, accuse the Church in Rome of possessing inordinate power, criticize Catholic education, and recall the Inquisition. Similarly, in 1853 anti-Catholic columns appeared in the *Terre Haute Wabash Courier.* The demise of the Whig party in the first third of the decade left a vacuum that was partially filled in 1854 with the emergence of the anti-Catholic Know-Nothing political movement. The Know-Nothings supported severe naturalization laws and the restriction that only natives of the United States be eligible for office.[75] Nativists saw the Democrats as the Catholic immigrant party. A writer in the *Terre Haute Daily Wabash Express,* who generally regarded Democrats as "riff raff," stated:

> Perhaps there never was a political gathering in this county [Vigo] which partook so much of Irish elements as the so-called Democratic meeting which met at City Hall on Sat. Eve. There were about 300 persons present and . . . there were not 40 native born citizens there.[76]

At the height of the Know-Nothing movement Catholics were harassed in some cities. Nativist political issues sometimes led to violence. For example, in Gibson County there were fights between native and Irish men. There were some election day riots involving nativists and Irish in 1854. The Republican party, which was formed at mid-decade, did not reject Know-Nothingism and soon began to absorb the nativist vote. Meanwhile the Democratic party roundly condemned nativism. Know-Nothings and Republicans believed that Democrats purchased the votes of Irish immigrants and that the Irish men voted repeatedly at elections. Indeed, each party charged the other with vote fraud in the 1856 election. After the Democratic successes in the latter election the Know-Nothing faction died and the Republican party repudiated nativism. But in 1858 the Republican platform did not advocate religious liberty, and the Republican ticket did not include a Catholic, but did carry an Irish Protestant.[77]

Irish immigrants had been elected to Democratic party positions and to public offices in Indiana before 1860. Democrat Patrick M. Brett (born county Tipperary) was Daviess County auditor (1841–44). William Stewart was Marion County clerk (1850–56) and secretary of the Democratic national convention in 1852. Cornelius O'Brien (born county Kilkenny) was Dearborn County clerk (1851–56) and a delegate to the Democratic national convention in 1856. At least twenty-five natives of Ireland were among the 1,513 legislators who served in the Indiana General Assembly from 1816 to 1850. Most of the foreign-born Irish legislators were Ulstermen. There were only nine Catholics among all the legislators during that period.[78]

Irish immigrants were interested in public affairs abroad as well as at home in the years before the Civil War. Many of Indiana's Irish newcomers were concerned about events in Ireland and were solicitous about the welfare of its people. The Irish in Indiana took steps to aid Ireland during the time of its terrible potato famine. The Committee for Irish Relief was formed in Terre Haute in 1846. It collected $1,441.65, which was sent to Ireland in 1847. Also in 1847, $1,200 for famine relief was raised in Fort Wayne through the efforts of Irish immigrants who organized a public meeting at the courthouse, held a dinner at a public house, and made appeals in local churches. Corn was shipped from Madison to Ireland during the famine. Undoubtedly the Irish in Indiana had warm feelings for the land of their birth, and some expressed these sentiments. John Ford and Martin Flanagan (county Galway natives) were the first residents of a farming community in Bartholomew County (near Columbus). Sweet Ireland was the name that they gave to the settlement.[79]

The years 1860–1920 formed another distinct period in the history of the Irish in Indiana. By 1920 Indiana's population was predominantly urban and its economy was diversified with modern industry and agriculture. The number of Irish immigrants in Indiana was greater during this time than ever before or after. Irish newcomers were among the builders of modern Indiana. Irish workers were employed in railroad construction, which created a railroad network connecting the state's markets. Irish immigrants enlarged an expanding labor pool, which was fundamental to the acceleration of industrialization in the state. The disproportionate number of Irish immigrants who located in cities swelled Indiana's urban population. Also, the Irish community in Indiana was most evident as an ethnic group during the period 1860–1920. As their numbers increased, the Irish were further identified with ethnic cultural institutions. The social identity of the Irish community was defined by its ethnic residential patterns and by its new ethnic organizations.

Natives of Ireland remained prominent in Irish life in Indiana from 1860 to 1920. The Irish immigrant population of Indiana grew during the 1860s and rose to its highest number (28,698) in 1870. The size of foreign-born Irish population in Indiana declined during the 1870s, and this trend of the 1870s continued through the remainder of the period as the number of Indiana residents who had been born in Ireland fell to 25,741 in 1880, to 20,819 in 1890, to 16,306 in 1900, to 11,266 in 1910, and to 7,271 in 1920. The smaller numbers of Irish immigrants in Indiana after 1870 reflected a late nineteenth-century change in the country's immigration pattern in which the national origins of most immigrants shifted from the countries of northern and western Europe to those of southern and eastern Europe. By 1910 there were more foreign-born Hungarians and Polish peoples in Indiana than Irish and English. Although the state's Irish foreign-born population declined after 1870, the Irish immigration to Indiana was comparatively large through the end of the century, and Irish newcomers were influential. There were more than twenty thousand Irish immigrants in Indiana from 1870 through 1890. The Irish immigrant population in Indiana remained greater than it was in 1850 until after 1900.[80]

The Irish remained widely distributed in Indiana. As late as 1920 at least a few Irish immigrants lived in every county of the state, except Warrick. While in the earlier period Irish immigrants mostly had been concentrated in the southern section of Indiana, Irish newcomers arriving after 1860 were more often found in the state's central and northern sections. After 1860 fewer of the ten Indiana counties with the greatest numbers of persons born in Ireland were located in the southern third of Indiana. In 1870 three of the counties with high Irish populations were in northern Indiana (Allen, Cass, and La Porte), four of the counties were in central Indiana (Marion, Montgomery, Tippecanoe, and Wayne), and three were in southern Indiana (Clark, Jefferson, and Vigo). In 1900 four of the ten Indiana counties with the greatest populations of persons born in Ireland were in the northern section (Allen, Cass, Lake, and St. Joseph), five of them were in the central section (Grant, Madison, Marion, Tippecanoe, and Wayne), and one was in the southern section (Vigo). The northward movement of the foreign-born Irish population was part of a larger late-nineteenth- and early-twentieth-century phenomenon involving the growth of industries and urban populations in the central and northern counties of Indiana.[81]

Irrespective of state section, the foreign-born Irish population of the 1860–1920 period was still concentrated in the Indiana counties containing cities with good transportation connections, expanding populations, and industries. For example, in 1900 six of the ten counties with the highest numbers of Irish immigrants were on the old Wabash and Erie Canal line and on the National Road (Allen, Cass, Marion, Tippecanoe, Vigo, and Wayne). More significantly, these six counties contained expanding urban and industrial centers on railroad lines built in the latter half of the nineteenth century. Four of the ten counties with the greatest numbers of Irish newcomers also contained growing industrial cities on railroads constructed during the same era (Grant, Madison, Lake, and St. Joseph). Irish immigrants were attracted by the economic opportunities found in Indiana towns and cities that prospered following railroad building.[82]

While many of the Irish lived in rural areas of the state, Irish immigrants in Indiana became increasingly urban during 1860–1920. The rural Irish were sometimes found in Catholic farming areas such as the old Catholic Settlement on Little Indian Creek in Lafayette Township, Floyd County. There were small Irish concentrations in many towns, including Cannelton (Perry County), whose cotton mills employed Irish workers in the late nineteenth century. Yet a disproportionate number of the Irish lived in cities. The Irish immigrants were more urban than Indiana's general population throughout the period. Thus in 1920, 71.8 percent of the Irish foreign born were urban, while that figure was only 50.6 percent for the total state population.[83]

The Irish were heavily employed in factory and construction work in Indiana cities after 1860. In some respects the employment experiences of the Irish who came to Indiana in the late nineteenth century were different than those of the Irish who entered the state before the Civil War. Earlier the urban Irish were restricted largely to low paying unskilled jobs. But a study of the census of 1880 in South Bend found that only 23 percent of the Irish were common laborers. Sixty-eight percent of the Irish employed in South Bend were factory employees or skilled workers in 1880, while 8 percent of them were in businesses and professions. The Irish worked in factories elsewhere; for example, in Madison a native of Ireland owned a starch factory that gave employment to Irish immigrants. The Starch Works located on the near south side of Indianapolis employed Irish women. As in the past, Irish men were hired as construction workers. Irish workmen were employed in the erection of the Union Station in Indianapolis and in the construction of the University of Notre Dame campus. The occupations and income of urban Irish put them near the bottom of the economic ladder, and their upward economic mobility was difficult. Although they had made gains in property ownership, the Irish in South Bend still owned less personal and real property than other European immigrant groups there in 1870.[84]

Indiana's Irish community experienced its greatest visibility during 1860–1920. In the late nineteenth century Irish society in Indiana was more sharply defined than it had been before 1860. Irish residential areas in cities were more identifiable than before. At least in some instances, the urban Irish became more residentially segregated in Indiana than in the past. Even so, they did not form exclusively Irish neighborhoods. The residential segregation of the Irish increased in the third ward and in the fourth ward of South Bend from 1870 to 1880. The Irish district in the fourth ward was on the east side near Water Street between Hill Street and St. Joseph's Church. The Irish neighborhood in the third ward was on the west side near the railroad tracks in the vicinity of St. Patrick's Church. Irish immigrants who had arrived before 1870 remained in these South Bend neighborhoods, where newcomers from Ireland joined them in the 1870s. By 1880 notable concentrations of the Irish had developed in these South Bend wards through the accretion of immigrants from Ireland during a period covering more than two decades. Predominantly Irish urban neighborhoods were sometimes identified by nicknames with ethnic connotations. The fourth ward Irish neighborhood in South Bend was nicknamed "Dublin." Irish neighborhoods that formed in other cities during the late nineteenth century had identities sharp enough to be remembered during the 1930s by people interviewed in a study of the Irish in Indiana made by the Federal Writers' Project. "Irish Town" in the southwest section of Fort Wayne was remembered by Patrick Murphy in the 1930s as he recalled his arrival in Fort Wayne in 1880. The Federal Writers' Project records noted "Irish Hollow" in Madison. Also, "Bog Hollow" of New Albany was recalled as an Irish settlement in an area resembling the bogs of Ireland; it was located between the Southern Railroad and the Ohio River. "Irish Hill" in Indianapolis was located south of Washington Street and west of Shelby Street. Ninety percent of the Irish in Marion County once lived in "Irish Hill," according to the Federal Writers' Project.[85]

Public awareness of Irish society in Indiana was raised as a variety of Irish organizations appeared in the state for the first time after 1860. Two Irish regiments were formed in Indiana during the Civil War. They were among several Indiana military units that were recruited chiefly along nationality lines in the 1860s. The Thirty-fifth Regiment was the first Irish regiment. It was commanded by Col. John C. Walker. His troops wore green hats signifying their Irish identity. After mustering in on 11 December 1861 the Thirty-fifth was sent to Kentucky and then to Tennessee. The Sixty-first Regiment was the second Irish regiment, and it was consolidated with the Thirty-fifth in Nashville. This enlarged Irish regiment participated in military action in Tennessee in the battle of Perryville (8 October 1862) and in a skirmish at Dobbins' Ford (9 December 1862), where it lost five killed and thirty-five wounded. Later under Gen. William Rosecrans, the Thirty-fifth participated in the battle of Stones River where it lost twenty-nine killed and seventy-two wounded. It also suffered heavy losses in the battle of Chickamauga (19–20 September 1863). After reenlistment and furlough in the winter of 1863–64, the Thirty-fifth returned to active duty as part of the Second Brigade of the First Division of Fourth Corps and was tested again. At Kennesaw Mountain regimental losses were eleven killed and fifty-four wounded. The Thirty-fifth entered Atlanta on 9 September 1864. Later the Irish regiment marched with the Fourth Corps in pursuit of retreating Confederates. Still later it was assigned to Franklin, Tennessee, engaging in action there and in the battle of Nashville. In June 1865 the Thirty-fifth was sent to Texas where it was mustered out in September. A public reception for the Irish regiment was held on the Statehouse grounds in Indianapolis on 21 October 1865.[86]

The Irish formed benevolent, fraternal, temperance, military, and musical organizations in Indiana during the latter decades of the nineteenth century. While they often had multiple purposes, all of these associations met the Irish immigrants' need for companionship with others who shared their immigrant experiences and cultural heritage. Most of these organizations were founded in the 1870s and 1880s. The benevolent associations were established on the principle of mutual aid and typically provided benefits when members suffered illness or death. The United Irish Benevolent Association was organized in Indianapolis in 1870. According to its constitution, the aims of the association were to provide benevolence and "to promote the social welfare of Irish citizens; to create a fraternity of sympathy, an identity of interest, and a union of power among them."[87] Its membership was limited to persons of Irish birth or ancestry who were between the ages of eighteen and fifty and were free of any physical infirmities likely to shorten life. The association had one hundred fifty members in its first year of existence. The United Irish Society existed in Indianapolis in the 1870s and in the 1880s. The St. Patrick's Temperance Benevolent Society appeared in Indianapolis in the 1870s, while the St. Patrick's Benevolent Society did so in the 1880s. The Hibernian Benevolent Society was active in Terre Haute between 1857 and 1917. The Young Men's Hibernian Society in Lafayette was a branch of the Irish Catholic Benevolent Union; it had 15 members when it was established in 1871 and 107 members in 1888. The Irish Catholic Benevolent Association was meeting in Fort Wayne in 1874. The Catholic Hibernian Benevolent

Society of Evansville had 60 members in 1874 when it was established; it was still active in 1892. The Father Matthew Total Abstinence and Benevolent Society was founded in Logansport in 1870; it was still meeting in 1886.[88]

The Ancient Order of Hibernians (AOH) was one of the larger and more enduring of the Irish organizations formed in Indiana after 1860. It claimed antecedents in a fourteenth-century Irish society with ties to St. Patrick. Established in the United States in 1836, the AOH was reorganized as a nationwide association in 1871. Membership was restricted to natives of Ireland until 1884 when persons of Irish ancestry were also admitted to the order. The membership policy change was influenced by a decline in emigration from Ireland. In the order's early years the Hibernians were essentially a fraternal association interested in the celebration of St. Patrick's Day. Subsequently the order broadened its program to include the provision of insurance benefits, advocacy of Irish independence, and criticism of the stage Irishman. The first AOH division in Indiana was founded in Knightsville (Clay County) in 1871. It was organized by Thomas McGovern, who became the first state delegate. Units of the Ancient Order of Hibernians were founded in Indianapolis in 1873, in Terre Haute in 1879, in Lafayette and Logansport in 1883, in South Bend in 1885, and in other cities. The AOH was active in Indiana cities through the end of the century. Also, the Hibernians were organized at county and state levels in Indiana. AOH offices included county delegate and state president. For example, John W. McGreevy of Logansport was elected state president in 1884 and reelected in 1886.[89]

Listings in city directories reveal varying levels of Hibernian activity in Indianapolis from 1873 to 1900. An increasing interest in the Ancient Order of Hibernians in Indianapolis during the 1870s was indicated by the growing number of its lodges there. In 1874 the local AOH was composed of Lodge Nos. 1 and 2, each holding weekly meetings. The AOH was designated as a benevolent organization for the first time in 1878. Meanwhile it continued to expand, and by 1879 there were six AOH lodges that met either weekly or bimonthly. During the 1870s each lodge listed a president and a secretary. AOH county officers were named for the first time in 1879. The countywide organization of the AOH in Marion County was broadened in the early 1880s as the office of AOH county treasurer was added to the offices of county delegate and county secretary. Yet, AOH activity declined in Indianapolis during the 1880s when there were as few as two AOH lodges during that decade. The lodges met bimonthly, which was less frequent than in the past. Undoubtedly, the decline of the AOH in the 1880s involved membership losses to other Irish organizations that were founded in Indianapolis during the decade. The other associations did not survive the 1880s, and Hibernian activity increased again from 1890 to 1900. The number of AOH lodges in Indianapolis grew from three in 1889 to six by the end of the century. In 1898 the Indianapolis AOH listed a county headquarters in St. John's Hall and a county organization composed of the offices of president, secretary, and treasurer.[90]

Irish women's organizations were founded in Indiana after 1860. Such groups included the Maids of Erin, which appeared in Indianapolis in 1876. The Sodality Society of the Church of the Assumption in Evansville was established in 1878. Alice Doyle, N. Haney, and Mary Shea were the officers of this society for young ladies in 1885. Also, local female units of the Ancient Order of Hibernians were organized in Indiana cities including Fort Wayne and Terre Haute. AOH Ladies' Auxiliaries Nos. 1 and 2 met in Terre Haute in 1904 and remained active through 1920. These Terre Haute auxiliaries held twice-monthly meetings in St. Joseph's and St. Ann's churches respectively. Each of these associations was headed by a president, a secretary, and a treasurer. The female Hibernians in Terre Haute also had a county organization with offices of president, secretary, and treasurer.[91]

The various other Irish organizations in Indiana included fraternal orders such as the Friendly Sons of St. Patrick, found in Indianapolis in 1881, and the Knights of Erin, located in Terre Haute in 1882. The Emmet Guards, a military association of Irish men, was active in Indianapolis at various times from 1870 through 1890. The Emmet Guard Band marched in Indianapolis in the early 1890s. Also, the Hibernian Rifles appeared in Indianapolis in 1898. Irish temperance groups in the state included the St. Patrick's Total Abstinence Society of Indianapolis, which was active in 1878 and remained so through 1890. The St. Joseph Total Abstinence Society of Terre Haute met from 1879 through the end of the century.[92]

A great deal of the social life of the Irish in Indiana was related to the Catholic Church. As previously indicated, many of the Irish ethnic organizations had ties with churches in Catholic parishes that were chiefly Irish. In addition, the Irish joined Catholic associations found in Indiana in the late nineteenth century. These groups included the Knights of Father Matthew, the Catholic Knights of America, and the Knights of Columbus. The significant social role of the Catholic Church was exemplified by St. John's Church in Indianapolis. It was a center of Irish social life in Indianapolis during 1870–1900. St. John's Church sponsored activities including lectures, cultural entertainments, lawn festivals, card parties, and weekend retreats.[93]

KIM CHARLES FERRILL

*St. John's Catholic Church, Indianapolis, Indiana, 1995.*

In the late nineteenth century, the Irish in Indiana observed St. Patrick's Day as an occasion for religious observance and as a day of great celebration. The Ancient Order of Hibernians often took the lead in St. Patrick's Day celebrations in Indiana after 1871. Nevertheless, the Irish Delegate Assembly, which met regularly in Indianapolis, invited representatives of Irish associations from across the state to attend an Indianapolis meeting on St. Patrick's Day, 1879. The events included a parade and an address by the Most Reverend Francis Silas Chatard, bishop of Indianapolis, on "The Social Mission of the Irish Race." "There was always a big celebration on St. Patrick's day and a dance at night," according to Irish immigrant Patrick Murphy who lived in Fort Wayne during the 1880s.[94]

Also, Patrick Murphy recalled that the Irish in Fort Wayne regularly held dances on Saturday and Sunday nights. Old Irish dances including reels, jigs, hornpipes, and breakdowns were sometimes performed. According to Murphy, at times doors were taken off hinges and placed on carpeted floors so that the dancers would have a hard surface for dancing the hornpipe. Such dances and parties were sometimes held in the homes of the Irish. In early twentieth-century Indianapolis, "Greenhorn" parties to welcome immigrants were held in Irish homes, where rugs were rolled up for dancing.[95]

The Irish in Indiana were identified with cultural institutions as well as with social organizations during the period 1860–1920. Additional predominantly Irish Catholic congregations were created. Catholic parishes had begun to divide along ethnic lines before 1860, and this trend continued afterward. In Jeffersonville the English-speaking Catholics, who were largely Irish, separated from the German parishioners of St. Anthony's Church and formed the congregation of St. Augustine's Church, which was opened in time to be blessed on St. Patrick's Day, 1868. St. Joseph's Church congregation in Terre Haute became mainly Irish in 1865 when German communicants formed St. Benedict's parish. In 1869 there was an increase in the Irish proportion of the congregation of St. Vincent de Paul Church in Logansport when German communicants formed a parish. In South Bend St. Patrick's congregation remained predominantly Irish after 1870, although it was composed of persons of different nationalities. Polish peoples living in South Bend attended St. Patrick's until 1877 when they formed their own parish. Similarly, some of the Belgians residing in South Bend attended St. Patrick's for two decades before they founded their own parish in 1898. Chiefly Irish congregations were formed in new Catholic churches constructed in urban neighborhoods where Irish newcomers settled in greater numbers after 1860. For example, in 1865 St. Patrick's (initially St. Peter's) Church of Indianapolis was erected at the terminus of Virginia Avenue, which was near the eastern edge of the city's southside Irish community. Parochial schools that were started in predominantly Irish parishes before 1860 still offered Catholic education, and new ones were opened during this period. For instance, a school was erected in the Church of the Assumption parish of Evansville in 1881. The list of the leading promoters of the Assumption school contained many Irish names including Patrick Raleigh, Michael Gorman, Joseph Dillon, C. J. Murphy, Eugene McGrath, John J. Nolan, Charles McCarthy, and John McDonough.[96]

As in the era before 1860, the press was not a cultural institution developed by the Irish in Indiana before 1920. Undoubtedly the Irish read the daily newspapers and publications of the Catholic press. Nevertheless, Irish individuals were involved in newspaper publications in the state. The *Indianapolis Western Citizen,* 1876–84, was published by Thomas McSheey who was a native of county Kerry, Ireland. John F. Joyce (Irish ancestry) held positions as copyboy, reporter, and editor of the *Terre Haute Gazette,* 1876–1906. Gabriel Summers (Irish ancestry) published the *South Bend News* and the *South Bend Times* and, after a merger, the *South Bend News-Times,* 1908–20. Also, Joseph Patrick O'Mahony published the *Indiana Catholic* in the World War I period.[97]

Changes in Irish demographic history in Indiana became increasingly evident after the turn of the century. Some Irish neighborhoods began to show signs of change by 1920; however, in many places urban Irish residential patterns were still typical of the late nineteenth century. The old-style residential pattern was found in the relatively new city of Gary where 57 percent of the Irish immigrants were located in two of that city's ten wards (the first and the seventh) in 1920. The greatest concentrations of Irish immigrants in South Bend were still in the third and fourth wards; however, their numbers were much smaller than in the past. The nineteenth century-style residential segregation of the Irish began to decline. There were indications of increasing geographical mobility among the Irish by 1920. A movement of the Irish out of their old eastside and westside South Bend neighborhoods began in 1915. Undoubtedly many of the Irish leaving those South Bend areas were not of the immigrant generation. Also, the population of St. John's parish in Indianapolis was declining by 1915. Families moved away as the city encroached upon the old Irish residential areas. No Indianapolis ward held more than 15 percent of the city's Irish-born population in 1920.[98]

The number of foreign-born Irish in Indiana was decreasing while the number of Irish born in the United States was increasing. The Irish immigrant population of Indiana fell from 16,306 in 1900 to 7,271 in 1920. During those decades the number of persons born in Ireland declined in every Indiana county but one. Natives of Ireland increased in Lake County as immigrants were attracted by Gary's industrial expansion during the opening decades of the century. Meanwhile, persons of Irish stock (i.e., parentage) were forming a larger proportion of Indiana's Irish population. There were more than twice as many persons of Irish stock as there were natives of Ireland in 1910. Specifically, 24,556 people in Indiana reported that both their parents were born in Ireland, while only 11,266 indicated that they were natives of Ireland. The Irish made up 10 percent of the persons of foreign stock in Indiana in 1920.[99]

Irish ethnic associations in Indiana began to fade during 1900–20 as the state's Irish immigrant population fell. The ethnic organizations were fewer in number and variety. The Irish benevolent societies tended to disband earlier than the Irish fraternal associations. The Hibernians were still organized in Fort Wayne in 1907 and in Logansport in 1913. The Hibernian units in Terre Haute and in Indianapolis survived through 1920.[100]

Most of the Irish living in Indiana and elsewhere in the nation moved slowly upward on the path of economic advancement in the late nineteenth century. The Irish in Indiana moved farther in that direction after 1900 as the

*Samuel Kingan brought his meatpacking plant from Northern Ireland to Indianapolis in 1862, where it continued in business until 1966. The Irish made up a large portion of Kingan's workforce.*

state's Irish stock population grew. Yet at the beginning of the century a large number of the Irish were still tied to relatively low-paying jobs in Indiana. Many of the Irish across the nation experienced poverty and its attendant social problems at this time. For instance, according to a federal report in 1901 the Irish had the greatest proportion of inmates in all charitable and penal institutions in the United States. These conditions were reflected in Indiana, although they were not as severe as elsewhere. Thus, the Irish were disproportionately represented in the Indiana state prison population. In 1902 there were ninety-three foreign-born state prison inmates including forty-eight Irish, twenty-seven Germans, and seven English. Nevertheless, by World War I the Irish in Indiana were typically hardworking employees in blue-collar occupations in the state's factories and skilled crafts.[101]

A number of the Irish were employed in the state's businesses and professions before World War I. For example, many Irish men started construction companies. In 1895 Daniel Foley founded the American Construction Company, which built streets and bridges. Foley was a native of county Kerry, Ireland, and a resident of Indianapolis. Also, the Irish were involved in grocery, drugstore, furniture, saloon, hotel, manufacturing, and other businesses in Indiana. Irish entrepreneurs in Indianapolis included Michael O'Connor, who was the owner of a wholesale grocery firm, and William J. Mooney, who was the co-owner of a wholesale drug company. Irish-owned furniture stores in Indianapolis included G. P. McGoughall and Son, Madden Furniture, and Michael Clune's firm. Mary Kennedy (the daughter of an Irish immigrant) purchased a drugstore in Lawrenceburg after her graduation from pharmacy college in 1905. Stephen J. Hannagan (whose parents were born in Ireland) bought a saloon in Lafayette after he had worked a number of years in local factories. Patrick H. McCormick, who was born in county Limerick, Ireland, owned the St. Denis Hotel in Columbus. Gabriel Summers (Irish ancestry) was the president of the South Bend Iron Bed Company, a manufacturing firm. The professions entered into by the Irish in Indiana included law, teaching, medicine, and the clergy. For example, Dr. E. J. Brennan (born in Kilkenny, Ireland) was a staff member of Indianapolis City Hospital. Brennan was also on the faculty of the Central College of Physicians and Surgeons and a member of the Indianapolis Board of Health in the late nineteenth century.[102]

The church and politics served as avenues of social advancement for the Irish in America before 1920. The hierarchy of the Catholic Church in America was dominated by the Irish. In Indiana, however, the Catholic prelates were of French and German origins. Nevertheless, an Indiana native of Irish ancestry, the Reverend Denis O'Donoghue, was appointed auxiliary bishop of the Indianapolis diocese in 1900 and then named bishop of Louisville in 1910. Other Irish men and women in Indiana devoted their lives to the Catholic Church. Many Irish priests were assigned to Catholic parishes in Indiana during 1860–1920. Some of them were natives of Ireland, for example, Father Hugh O'Neill (county Waterford) and Father Patrick McDermott (county Roscommon). They served St. Patrick's parish in Indianapolis between 1868 and 1885. Many of the Irish women teaching in Indiana were on Catholic parochial school faculties. Politics enhanced the careers of Irish lawyers in Indiana. A large proportion of the Indiana legislators of Irish ancestry were attorneys. Also, the Irish who were successful in business in Indiana were often involved in politics. Most of those listed herein as examples of the Irish in businesses were also active in politics. Some Irish men with political connections became policemen and firemen in Indiana cities and some of them became chiefs. John Kennedy and James J. Daugherty were Terre Haute fire chiefs in 1894 and 1900, respectively.[103]

The Irish were a significant force in American urban politics from 1860 to 1920. The Irish in Indiana were not numerous enough to constitute the kind of strong voting blocs that strengthened the hands of Irish politicos elsewhere. However, many of Indiana's Irish politicians possessed the skills requisite to political success. The state's Irish voters were identified with the Democratic party, and Irish candidates for office were usually on the Democratic ticket in Indiana. Irish politicians played important roles in Democratic party leadership. Thomas Taggart of Indianapolis was a powerful figure in state and national Democratic party affairs. Taggart was Democratic state chairman (1892–94) and Democratic national committee chairman (1904–8). In addition, he was a member of the party's national committee (1900–16) and a delegate to all of its national conventions from 1900 to 1924. Taggart worked in association with William Hunter O'Brien, who was born in Lawrenceburg. O'Brien was chairman of the Democratic state central committee, treasurer of the Democratic national committee (1908), and delegate to Democratic national conventions in 1900, 1904, 1916, and 1920. Also, O'Brien was mayor of Lawrenceburg (1885–94, 1898–1902), state senator (1903, 1905), and auditor of the state (1911–15).[104] Taggart and O'Brien were Protestants. Taggart was a native of county Monaghan in Northern Ireland. O'Brien (whose father was born in county Kilkenny) followed his mother (Jane Hunter O'Brien) into the Methodist Church. Also, five Protestants of Irish ancestry were elected mayor in

Indianapolis during 1860–1900. Republicans Daniel McCauley and John Caven were mayors of Indianapolis in the 1860s and 1870s. Thomas Mitchell, a Democrat, was elected mayor of Indianapolis in 1873. Democrats Thomas L. Sullivan and Taggart were Indianapolis mayors in the 1880s, 1890s, and early 1900s.[105]

There was a marked increase in the involvement of Irish Catholics in Indiana politics and government during 1860–1920. Irish Catholics, usually running as Democrats, were elected to a great variety of offices during that period. Irish Catholic Democrats held various offices in municipal government. David J. Hefron was mayor of Washington (1871–75). Patrick H. McCormick (born in Ireland) was mayor of Columbus before 1900, and Thomas W. O'Connor was mayor of Monticello (1909–13). Irish Catholic Democrats on town and city councils included Timothy E. Howard, who was on the South Bend council (1878–84). Michael H. Farrell was on the Indianapolis board of aldermen (1889–91), and Stephen J. Hannagan was on the Lafayette council (1896–1910). John C. Lawler served three terms on the Salem council before 1900. John B. Kennedy (born in county Kilkenny) was on the Lawrenceburg council before 1912. Irish Catholic Democrats in other municipal offices included Charles McKenna (born in Ireland), who was elected street commissioner of New Albany in 1869. James Deery was elected Indianapolis city clerk in 1883. Michael Sweeney was Jasper city marshal for four terms before 1900. John Francis McHugh was Lafayette city attorney (1889–95). Michael Maloney was appointed postmaster of Aurora in 1913.[106]

Irish Catholic Democrats held many Indiana county positions during the 1860–1920 years. For example, John W. McGreevy was elected Cass County attorney in 1885. Also, Thomas Hanlon of county Clare, Ireland, was Floyd County auditor (1875–83, 1899–1908). John Sweeney of county Cork, Ireland, was Perry County sheriff (1878–80), and John F. Joyce was Vigo County clerk (1909–17).[107]

Meanwhile, Irish Catholic Democrats were elected to state offices in Indiana. For instance, Matthew L. Brett of Washington was state treasurer (1863–65). James H. Rice of New Albany was state auditor (1883–87). Timothy E. Howard of South Bend was state supreme court judge (1893–99). Joseph H. Shea of Seymour was judge of the fortieth circuit (1907–12) and judge of the state appellate court (1913–16).[108]

Justin Walsh, in *The Centennial History of the Indiana General Assembly, 1816–1978*, found that many Irish candidates were elected to the Indiana General Assembly after 1860. There were twenty-two natives of Ireland among the 1,966 members of the General Assembly during 1850–90. The 1,712 members of the General Assembly during the 1890–1930 era included at least

125 legislators of Irish ancestry (five of whom were natives of Ireland). The Irish comprised many of the Catholic members of the legislature whose numbers rose from thirty-three during 1851–89 to ninety-three during 1891–1929. In a study of Indiana legislators of the 1896–1920 era, Philip R. VanderMeer found that the proportion of foreign-born Irish lawmakers in the legislature was about the same as the percentage of the foreign-born Irish in the total population. Also, VanderMeer noted that 85 percent of the lawmakers of Irish parentage were Democratic. Moreover, he reported that all of the Catholic legislators of Irish parentage were Democrats.[109]

The Irish in Indiana were interested in political issues concerning Ireland as well as in American politics during 1860–1920. Consequently, some of them became Fenians. American Fenianism was founded in 1859 as a militant Irish republican movement promoting the independence of Ireland from Great Britain. In 1859 the Indianapolis Circle of the Fenian Brotherhood was organized by Father Edward O'Flaherty, who recruited Fenian members throughout Indiana. The Fenians in Indianapolis were quiet during the Civil War until 1865 when a leadership dispute split the local brotherhood into two factions, one of which became defunct after a year. In 1866 the Fenians staged one of the largest meetings ever held in Indianapolis and subscribed a large amount of money on the occasion of a visit to Indianapolis by the Fenian president, who was engaged in a national publicity and fund-raising campaign for the brotherhood. American Fenians were most noted for organizing an army that conducted an unsuccessful invasion of Canada in the interest of Irish independence. In 1866, under the command of Capt. James Haggerty, one hundred thirty armed Fenians went from Indianapolis to Buffalo, New York, where they joined a Fenian army. The invasion's failure left Indianapolis Fenians in disarray. But they reorganized and hosted a Fenian state convention in Indianapolis in 1868 when Indiana was divided into northern and southern Fenian districts. The renewal of internal dissension caused the Fenian organization to disband near the end of the decade. Subsequently, ex-Fenians in Indianapolis joined other Irish organizations. These included a military club called the Emmet Guards in honor of Robert Emmet (1778–1803), who was executed for his role in the Irish insurrection of 1803.[110]

Some of the Irish in Indiana participated in Irish nationalist movements in the 1880s. The Irish National Land League was founded in Ireland through the efforts of Michael Davitt (1846–1906), who was convinced that Irish nationalism required a pressing attack on the British landholding system in Ireland. Charles Stewart Parnell (1846–1891), who was leader of the Irish party in Parliament, was president of the Land League. The Irish National Land League was organized in the United States in 1880 in order to secure the moral and the financial support of Irish Americans. Davitt informed the American press that the league, while seeking the abolition of landlordism, gave legal assistance and shelter to Irish tenants facing evictions. Subsequently, Irish Americans formed league branches in cities across the nation and donated hundreds of thousands of dollars to the league. The Indianapolis branch of the Irish National Land League was organized in 1881; it was active through 1886. The Irish National Land League Association of Indiana was also founded in 1881. The state association was headed by officers from Michigan City, Rushville, and Indianapolis in 1883. A further expression of Irish nationalism in the 1880s was the naming of Parnell Hall, which was a meeting place of Irish groups in Indianapolis.[111]

Also, Irish nationalism appeared in Indiana during World War I. Irish nationalists who had opposed British rule in Ireland were not eager to see the United States join Great Britain in the war in Europe. Thus, protests about American favoritism toward the Allies were made at joint German-Irish rallies staged in several Indiana cities in 1915. Similarly, Joseph Patrick O'Mahony's *Indiana Catholic* was the most important of the newspapers in the state taking the anti-British/pro-German editorial position. Nevertheless, many Irish Hoosiers fought and died in World War I.[112]

The twentieth-century Irish experience in Indiana was different after the First World War. During the period 1920 to the present the Irish in Indiana largely have been comprised of the descendants of immigrants who had come from Ireland after 1815. The number of natives of Ireland in Indiana fell steadily from 7,271 in 1920 to 2,352 in 1950. During those years over half of the Irish newcomers lived in Lake and Marion counties.[113]

Irish Catholics were concerned about the rise of the Ku Klux Klan in Indiana during the 1920s. Indiana had the highest ratio (92 percent) of native-born white population in the United States in 1920, and the Klan benefited from widespread nativism in the state. The Klan decried immigration as Indiana's total foreign-born population shrank from 159,663 in 1910 to 142,999 in 1930. The number of the state's foreign-born Irish declined sharply during the 1920s. In the main, Klan antiforeignism was directed at Indiana's immigrants from southern and eastern Europe, but its anti-Catholic venom spilled over on the Irish. William J. Mooney, who was the son of an Irish immigrant and a Catholic Democrat, related stories of Ku Klux Klan crosses burned on his porch in Indianapolis in the 1920s, according to his grandson William J. Mooney III. Dennis John O'Neill was among the Irish who criticized the Indiana Klan. In 1926, after graduating from Notre Dame, O'Neill was employed by the *Indianapolis Times,* covering state politics as a news reporter. O'Neill and editor Boyd Gurley started an investigation of Klan involvement in state politics. Their work led to a series of articles that exposed the Klan's corrupt political dealings and contributed to its decline in Indiana. In 1928 the *Times* was awarded a Pulitzer Prize for its Klan exposé.[114]

The Irish became less and less visible as an ethnic group in Indiana after 1920. Previously identifiable Irish neighborhoods disappeared as their residents dispersed. Meanwhile, the Irish left urban Catholic parishes where they had predominated. Also, fraternal and benevolent organizations with Irish names died out. Exoduses from old Irish areas in South Bend and Indianapolis were in progress during World War I, and Irish residential dispersals in these cities continued during the 1920s. In the 1930s former Irish neighborhoods in Fort Wayne, Madison, and New Albany remained only as memories, for example, of people interviewed by Federal Writers' Project researchers investigating the state's Irish history. As their residential patterns changed the Irish often removed from one Catholic parish to another. Thus, the Irish were found in several Catholic parishes in some Indiana cities. By 1920 Irish Catholics in Terre Haute were attending St. Patrick's, St. Ann's, and St. Margaret's churches as well as St. Joseph's Church, which most of the Terre Haute Irish had attended at an earlier time. Mutual aid groups such as the Hibernian benevolent societies faded away before 1930 as did most of the Irish fraternal associations. The Ancient Order of Hibernians survived in some Indiana cities after 1920, but its membership dwindled. For example, the AOH was active in Terre Haute until near the end of the 1920s. Only AOH Division Nos. 1 and 2 existed in Indianapolis in 1936, while in earlier times there had been six Hibernian units in that city.[115]

In consequence of these trends, studies covering Indiana history since World War I note little activity of the Irish as an ethnic group. In their famous analysis of Middle America, Robert and Helen Lynd hardly refer to the small Irish minority in Muncie. In the 1930s some Federal Writers' Project researchers concluded that the Irish in Indiana had been assimilated completely and had lost their distinctive ethnic identity. Irish immigrants had settled in rural Madison Township of Dubois County in the nineteenth century. A Federal Writers' Project scholar who studied the history of Dubois County reported that the Irish of Madison Township had become amalgamated in the larger population and that the Irish group there had lost its national characteristics.[116] A Federal Writers' Project report on Indianapolis and Marion County stated, "The Irish

made no effort to perpetuate their customs . . . and much of the transplanted culture of Erin has died out."[117]

Yet, paraphrasing Mark Twain, the report of the death of Irish ethnicity in Indiana was exaggerated. In some instances the Irish continued to act as an ethnic group, although they were less identifiable than in the past and less visible than groups of other national origins. An Irish residential concentration remained from the 1920s to the 1940s in the neighborhood of St. Luke's Church on Gary's east side. This reflected the fact that the numbers of Irish immigrants settling in Lake County increased through 1920. Indeed, Lake County received a large proportion of the state's Irish immigrants after 1920. There were church congregations with sizable numbers of communicants of Irish ancestry in Catholic parishes across Indiana in the 1930s and in the decades thereafter. For example, during the 1930s Catholic families of Irish origins were still attending St. Mary's Church near Floyd Knobs. This was the old Floyd County (Lafayette Township) church located in what nineteenth-century commentators called the Catholic Settlement on Little Indian Creek. Likewise, some Irish ethnic associations were found in Indiana during the depression decade and afterward. In 1936 the Ancient Order of Hibernians had 527 members in Indianapolis. The AOH members there met bimonthly for entirely social and educational purposes. A St. Patrick's Day celebration on the Sunday preceding 17 March and a picnic on or near 4 July were annual events of the Indianapolis Hibernians. The Irish in Indiana remained connected with their ethnic heritage in a variety of individual and personal ways. Some remembered the immigration histories of their parents or grandparents. Undoubtedly, many Hoosiers with roots in Ireland identified with the Fighting Irish of Notre Dame, which became increasingly successful on football fields after World War I. In the 1930s shamrock was growing on Patrick Flanigan's farm in the Bartholomew County "Sweet Ireland" settlement, which had been started by his immigrant father. Flanigan had visited Ireland and had returned with some of the shamrock. In the middle of the century, Martin Joseph Cleary owned the Fort Wayne Lincoln Life baseball team, which he publicized as the Shamrocks. Cleary's ancestors were Irish.[118]

The pace of socioeconomic progress among the Irish hastened in the twentieth century. After World War II the Irish advanced rapidly into the middle and upper-middle classes. Many of the children and grandchildren of Irish immigrants obtained the benefits of an academic education. In addition, others secured advanced training in professional schools and in graduate schools. Consequently, there were more professional and business people of Irish background during the latter twentieth

**Table C. Number of Persons Born in Ireland for the Ten Indiana Counties with the Greatest Irish Foreign-Born Populations***

| County | 1930 | 1940 | 1950 | 1980 |
|---|---|---|---|---|
| Allen | 160 | 97 | 103 | 44 |
| Cass | 78 | 44 | | |
| La Porte | 75 | 49 | 74 | 41 |
| Lake | 720 | 474 | 517 | 144 |
| Porter | | | 25 | 25 |
| St. Joseph | 286 | 198 | 183 | 55 |
| Howard | 54 | | | |
| Madison | 75 | 55 | 31 | 22 |
| Marion | 1,442 | 1,086 | 883 | 227 |
| Tippecanoe | 87 | 44 | | 48 |
| Wayne | | | 27 | |
| Vanderburgh | | 29 | 25 | 17 |
| Vigo | 153 | 95 | 64 | 25 |

*Based on United States Department of Commerce, Bureau of the Census, *Census of Population* for the years 1930, 1940, 1950, 1980.

century than in earlier times. They included lawyers and physicians, workers in insurance companies and banks, and professors and technicians. For example, William P. Flynn was an Indiana National Bank board chairman, and Andrew Sweeny was a State Life Insurance Company founder. In 1980 the occupational distribution of the Irish Catholics was similar to that of the urban Anglo-Saxon Protestants.[119]

The Irish in Indiana remained active in politics and government after 1920 and maintained their ties to the Democratic party. In 1928 William J. Mooney was state campaign director for Democratic presidential candidate Al Smith. Frank E. McKinney, an American Fletcher National Bank board chairman and a director of the Indiana Bell Telephone Company, was the Democratic party national chairman during part of the Truman administration. As in the past, Irish politicians were elected to a variety of offices. Reginald H. Sullivan served as mayor of Indianapolis (1930–35, 1939–43). He was an Irish Protestant Democrat, as were a number of the mayors elected before him in that city. Al Feeney was the first Irish Catholic Democrat elected mayor of Indianapolis; he died in office in 1950. Later, John J. Barton was Indianapolis mayor. Another Irish Catholic Democrat, James H. Maguire, was mayor of Kokomo (1948–51).[120]

Many candidates of Irish ancestry were elected to the Indiana General Assembly in the twentieth century. At least 83 of the 1,258 assembly members were of Irish origins during 1930–70. In that period the Irish comprised 10 percent of the lawmakers (777) whose ancestry was known. Almost all of the Irish Catholic lawmakers of the period were Democrats. While only 5.2 percent of the assembly members were Catholic during 1891 to 1929, 14.1 percent of them were Catholic during 1931–69.

Several Irish women won seats in the General Assembly during the 1960s. Anna Maloney, a retired teacher, represented Lake County in the House of Representatives (1961–72). During her career Maloney served as president of the Indiana Federation of Teachers and held membership in several professional women's associations. In 1965 Kathrine Margaret O'Connell Fruits and Cecilia M. Logan were elected to Marion County seats in the House. Fruits was a homemaker. Logan was an accountant. Both had been Democratic precinct committeewomen and leaders in county and state Democratic women's clubs. Sheila Ann Johnston Klinker represented Tippecanoe County in the House (1983–84). Klinker, who was a teacher and an athletic coach, had been a Democratic state convention delegate and a worker in Democratic gubernatorial and congressional campaigns. All of the female Irish legislators were Democratic and Catholic. Fruits, Logan, and Klinker were representative of a growing number of Indiana families that were Irish on one side. Other state lawmakers with some Irish ancestry included Republican William Doyle Ruckelshaus, who became known nationally as deputy attorney general in the Nixon administration. Ruckelshaus was a Catholic of German and Irish origins. Similarly, Democratic state senator and lieutenant governor Frank Lewis O'Bannon of Corydon was a Methodist whose family lines were Irish, English, Dutch, German, and French.[121]

In the second half of the twentieth century most of the Irish in Indiana were generations removed from their immigrant forebears. In 1980 there were only 825 Irish immigrants in Indiana. Yet in 1990 almost a million Hoosiers claimed Irish ancestry. Irish Hoosiers increasingly married across nationality lines and sometimes outside the family's traditional faith. In consequence family memories of Ireland grew dimmer. The Irish ethnic group became less visible and less conscious of itself than it had been in the 1930s. Yet the relatively few Irish immigrants of the recent period remembered well the Emerald Isle. Noreen Hall of county Cork immigrated in 1949 and located in Highland (Lake County). In 1984 she still remembered that her Christmases in Ireland "were beautiful, and holy." Mary Jones of county Mayo also settled in Highland after departing Ireland in 1955. She fondly recalled Irish folk dancing, which she taught in Indiana for sixteen years.[122] The great bulk of Irish Hoosiers who were born outside the immigrant generation remained tied to their Irish family histories in various ways. A 1978 account of the Irish in Indianapolis stated: "Capt. [David T.] Shea wears the 1889 fireman's badge issued his grandfather, Jeremiah, who came from County Kerry. His brothers, Joseph and James, also are fire captains, and

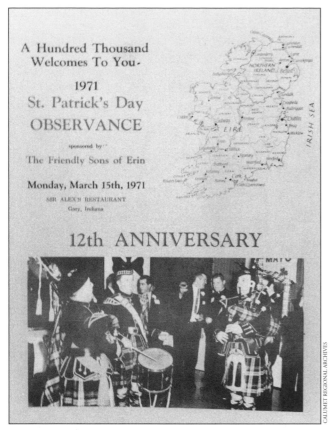

A Hundred Thousand
Welcomes To You-

1971
St. Patrick's Day
OBSERVANCE

sponsored by

The Friendly Sons of Erin

Monday, March 15th, 1971

SIR ALEX'S RESTAURANT
Gary, Indiana

12th ANNIVERSARY

*Friendly Sons of Erin celebration in Gary, 1971.*

three other brothers . . . are firemen."[123] Similarly, the historic devotion of the Irish family to the Catholic Church was seen in the life of Edward T. O'Meara, whose parents were immigrants from county Tipperary. The Most Reverend O'Meara was archbishop of the Archdiocese of Indianapolis (1980–92).[124]

There were many Irish societies in Indiana in 1892 when immigrants still made up a large part of the state's Irish community. One hundred years later it was unusual for Irish Hoosiers to organize along ethnic lines, but in some places there were associations rooted in Irish organizational history. Established in 1959 in Lake County, the Friendly Sons of Erin was still active in the 1980s when it gave Shamrock awards and John F. Kennedy awards for public service. The venerable Ancient Order of Hibernians is still alive and well in Indianapolis. The Irish American Heritage Society and the Irish Step Dancers also are active in Indianapolis. At least once a year on St. Patrick's Day, the Irish in Indiana comprise a community that is conscious of itself and visible to others. For example, the Irish of Terre Haute gather at St. Patrick's Church for a parade starting at the intersection of 19th and Poplar streets, which is painted with a green shamrock on a field of white. On 17 March the descendants of Erin in Indiana, as those elsewhere, are happy to be Irish and everyone else is welcome to be Irish.[125]

## Notes

1. Maldwyn A. Jones, *American Immigration* (Chicago: University of Chicago Press, 1974), 22; John D. Barnhart and Dorothy L. Riker, *Indiana to 1816: The Colonial Period* (Indianapolis: Indiana Historical Bureau and Indiana Historical Society, 1971), 71–93.

2. Albert T. Volwiler, *George Croghan and the Westward Movement, 1741–1782* (Cleveland: The Arthur Clark Company, 1926), 21–23, 36; Nicholas B. Wainwright, *George Croghan: Wilderness Diplomat* (Chapel Hill: The University of North Carolina Press, 1959), 3, 14–15; Barnhart and Riker, *Indiana to 1816,* pp. 98, 105; Eugene H. Roseboom and Francis P. Weisenburger, *A History of Ohio* (Columbus: The Ohio State Archaeological and Historical Society, 1961), 20.

3. Wainwright, *George Croghan,* 4.

4. Ibid., 16–21, 38; Barnhart and Riker, *Indiana to 1816,* pp. 123, 124, 125–26, 152–55; John D. Barnhart and Donald F. Carmony, *Indiana: From Frontier to Industrial Commonwealth,* 4 vols. (New York: Lewis Publishing Company, Inc., 1954), 1:49; Roseboom and Weisenburger, *History of Ohio,* 27–28.

5. Barnhart and Carmony, *Indiana,* 1:77–79, 98–99; Leonard C. Helderman, "Northwest Expedition of George Rogers Clark, 1786–1787," *Mississippi Valley Historical Review* 25 (Dec. 1938): 317–24; Jones, *American Immigration,* 22, 108.

6. Rebecca A. Shepherd, Charles W. Calhoun, Elizabeth Shanahan-Shoemaker, Alan January, eds., *A Biographical Directory of the Indiana General Assembly,* vol. 1, *1816–1899* (Indianapolis: Indiana Historical Bureau, 1980), 319.

7. Barnhart and Carmony, *Indiana,* 1:152.

8. Archibald Shaw, ed., *History of Dearborn County, Indiana: Her People, Industries and Institutions* (Indianapolis: B. F. Bowen and Co., Inc., 1915), 148–49.

9. *Atlas of Dearborn County, Indiana* (Philadelphia: Lake, Griffing and Stevenson, 1875), 18.

10. Barnhart and Carmony, *Indiana,* 1:151.

11. Jones, *American Immigration,* 92–97, 108–10, 117–18.

12. Harlow Lindley, ed., *Indiana as Seen by Early Travelers,* vol. 3 of *Indiana Historical Collections* (Indianapolis: Indiana Historical Commission, 1916), 463, 473.

13. Ibid., 524.

14. Thomas T. McAvoy, *The Catholic Church in Indiana, 1789–1834* (New York: Columbia University Press, 1940), 16–20, 169; Herman J. Alerding, *A History of the Catholic Church in the Diocese of Vincennes* (Indianapolis: Carlon and Hollenbeck, 1883), 29, 81, 379–80; Charles Blanchard, ed., *History of the Catholic Church in Indiana,* 2 vols. (Logansport, Ind.: A. W. Bowen and Co., 1898), 1:251–52; J. Lawrence Richardt, "A Narrative History of Saint Joseph Church, Terre Haute, Indiana, 1838–1872" (M.A. thesis, Indiana State University, 1969), 6–7, 9; Shaw, ed., *History of Dearborn County,* 404.

15. *History of the Ohio Falls Cities and Their Counties,* 2 vols. (Cleveland: L. A. Williams and Co., 1882), 2:302, 309–10, 314; Alerding, *History of the Catholic Church in the Diocese of Vincennes,* 341–42.

16. Elfrieda Lang, "Irishmen in Northern Indiana before 1850," *Mid-America: An Historical Review* 36 (1954): 190–91.

17. Quoted in Charles R. Poinsatte, *Fort Wayne during the Canal Era, 1828–1855: A Study of a Western Community in the Middle Period of American History,* vol. 46 of *Indiana Historical Collections* (Indianapolis: Indiana Historical Bureau, 1969), 59.

18. Richardt, "Narrative History of Saint Joseph Church," 31; Poinsatte, *Fort Wayne during the Canal Era,* 60–61.

19. Jones, *American Immigration,* 130–31.

20. Quoted in Poinsatte, *Fort Wayne during the Canal Era,* 60.

21. Jones, *American Immigration,* 131; Poinsatte, *Fort Wayne during the Canal Era,* 60–61.

22. Richardt, "Narrative History of Saint Joseph Church," 31; Alvin Fay Harlow, *Old Towpaths: The Story of the American Canal Era* (New York: D. Appleton and Co., 1926), 267; Poinsatte, *Fort Wayne during the Canal Era,* 63, 144; Barnhart and Carmony, *Indiana,* 1:418.

23. Paul Fatout, *Indiana Canals* (West Lafayette, Ind: Purdue University Studies, 1972), 85.

24. *History of Allen County, Indiana* (Chicago: Kingman Brothers, 1880), 93.

25. Quoted in William McNamara, *The Catholic Church on the Northern Indiana Frontier, 1789–1844* (Washington, D.C.: The Catholic University of America, 1931), 61.

26. Richardt, "Narrative History of Saint Joseph Church," 31.

27. Fatout, *Indiana Canals,* 58; Poinsatte, *Fort Wayne during the Canal Era,* 62.

28. McNamara, *Catholic Church on the Northern Indiana Frontier,* 61.

29. Fatout, *Indiana Canals,* 85.

30. Emma Lou Thornbrough, *Indiana in the Civil War Era, 1850–1880* (Indianapolis: Indiana Historical Bureau and Indiana Historical Society, 1965), 634.

31. John H. O'Donnell, "The Catholic Church in Northern Indiana: 1830–1857," *The Catholic Historical Review* 25 (July 1939): 140.

32. Quoted in Poinsatte, *Fort Wayne during the Canal Era,* 61.

33. Ibid., 61–62.

34. McNamara, *Catholic Church on the Northern Indiana Frontier,* 61.

35. Richardt, "Narrative History of Saint Joseph Church," 42.

36. Fatout, *Indiana Canals,* 59.

37. Mary Salesia Godecker, *Simon Bruté de Rémur: First Bishop of Vincennes* (St. Meinrad, Ind.: St. Meinrad Historical Essays, 1931), 361–62; Harlow, *Old Towpaths,* 236–37, 267; Barnhart and Carmony, *Indiana,* 2:447; Lang, "Irishmen in Northern Indiana," 191–92; Fatout, *Indiana Canals,* 58, 69; Poinsatte, *Fort Wayne during the Canal Era,* 62–63; Willis Richardson, "History of the Wabash and Erie Canal" (Master's thesis, Indiana University, 1925), 77–78; *Indianapolis Indiana Journal,* 31 July 1835; David Burr to Gov. Noah Noble, 30 Dec. 1835, *Indiana Documentary Journal, 1835,* House Report no. 18, pp. 1–4.

38. *Indiana Documentary Journal, 1835,* p. 2.

39. Ibid.

40. Ibid.

41. Ibid.

42. Quoted in *Indianapolis Indiana Journal,* 31 July 1835.

43. *Indiana Documentary Journal, 1835,* pp. 2–3.

44. Godecker, *Simon Bruté,* 345.

45. *Indiana Documentary Journal, 1835,* p. 3.

46. Ibid.

47. *Indiana House Journal, 1835–1836,* p. 26.

48. *Indiana Documentary Journal, 1835,* p. 3; Barnhart and Carmony, *Indiana,* 2:447; Godecker, *Simon Bruté,* 361–62.

49. Richardt, "Narrative History of Saint Joseph Church," 7; Edward A. Leary, *Indianapolis: The Story of a City* (Indianapolis: The Bobbs-Merrill Co., Inc., 1971), 35; Barnhart and Carmony, *Indiana,* 2:447.

50. Alerding, *History of the Catholic Church in the Diocese of Vincennes,* 29; Blanchard, ed., *History of the Catholic Church in Indiana,* 1:51; O'Donnell, "Catholic Church in Northern Indiana," 141; McNamara, *Catholic Church on the Northern Indiana Frontier,* 61–62; Richardt, "Narrative History of Saint Joseph Church," 42.

51. Poinsatte, *Fort Wayne during the Canal Era,* 141–48; Herman J. Alerding, *The Diocese of Fort Wayne, 1857–Sept. 22, 1907: A Book of Historical Reference 1669–1907* (Fort Wayne, Ind.: Archer Printing Co., 1907), 203.

52. McNamara, *Catholic Church on the Northern Indiana Frontier,* 62; Thomas B. Helm, ed., *History of Cass County, Indiana* (Chicago: Brant and Fuller, 1886), 435–36; Jehu Z. Powell, ed., *History of Cass County, Indiana,* 2 vols. (Chicago: The Lewis Publishing Co., 1913), 1:435–36; Alerding, *Diocese of Fort Wayne,* 208–10, 211–12, 213–14.

53. *Biographical Record and Portrait Album of Tippecanoe County, Indiana* (Chicago: The Lewis Publishing Co., 1888), 284–85.

54. Ibid., 285; Alerding, *Diocese of Fort Wayne,* 217–18.

55. Alerding, *History of the Catholic Church in the Diocese of Vincennes,* 421–25, 469–70; Andrew W. Young, *History of Wayne County, Indiana: From Its First Settlement to the Present Time* (Cincinnati: Robert Clarke and Co., 1872), 407; *History of Wayne County, Indiana,* 2 vols. (Chicago: Inter-State Publishing Co., 1884), 2:150–51; William R. Holloway, *Indianapolis: A Historical and Statistical Sketch of the Railroad City* (Indianapolis: Indianapolis Journal Print., 1870), 239; Berry R. Sulgrove, *History of Indianapolis and Marion County, Indiana* (Philadelphia: L. H. Everts and Co., 1884), 406.

56. Alerding, *History of the Catholic Church in the Diocese of Vincennes,* 452–57; Richardt, "Narrative History of Saint Joseph Church," 18–30.

57. Quoted in Richardt, "Narrative History of Saint Joseph Church," 41.

58. *History of the Ohio Falls Cities,* 2:209–10, 310, 314–15; Shaw, ed., *History of Dearborn County,* 404–5; Alerding, *History of the Catholic Church in the Diocese of Vincennes,* 333–34, 341–42, 379–80.

59. Gil R. Stormont, *History of Gibson County, Indiana* (Indianapolis: B. F. Bowen and Co., Inc., 1914), 98.

60. Fatout, *Indiana Canals,* 141.

61. Stormont, *History of Gibson County,* 99.

62. O'Donnell, "Catholic Church in Northern Indiana," 137–38, 143; Donald T. Zimmer, "Madison, Indiana, 1811–1860: A Study in the Process of City Building" (Ph.D. diss., Indiana University, 1974), 61; "Jefferson Co.-261.4-Irish" (roll 11, frame 1157), "Marion Co.-260.5-Ethnology" (roll 16, frame 0798), Federal Writers' Project, Indiana/Writers' Program, Indiana, Original Manuscripts (microfilm), Indiana State University Library, Terre Haute, Ind. (hereafter cited as FWP); John Aylward, "Immigrant Settlement Patterns in South Bend, 1865–1917" (typescript, Northern Indiana Historical Society), 4–5; Barnhart and Carmony, *Indiana,* 2:38; Richardt, "Narrative History of Saint Joseph Church," 43; Charles E. Robert, *Evansville: Her Commerce and Manufactures* (Evansville, Ind.: Courier Company, 1874), 532.

63. Percentages computed by author. See Table A.

64. See Table B; Gregory S. Rose, "The Distribution of Indiana's Ethnic and Racial Minorities in 1850" (typescript, Indiana Historical Society, Ethnic History Project, 1989), 16–17.

65. Poinsatte, *Fort Wayne during the Canal Era,* 60; Elbert J. Benton, "The Wabash Trade Route in the Development of the Old Northwest," *Johns Hopkins University Studies in Historical and Political Science* 21 (Jan.–Feb. 1903): 97–98; McNamara, *Catholic Church on the Northern Indiana Frontier,* 62; "1850 Census Foreign-Born for Indiana" (Unpublished manuscript, Indiana Historical Society, Education Division, 1991), 6; "1860 Census Foreign-Born for Indiana" (Unpublished manuscript, Indiana Historical Society, Education Division, 1991), 7; Table B.

66. Lang, "Irishmen in Northern Indiana," 193; Barnhart and Carmony, *Indiana,* 2:14.

67. Computations by author. Figures obtained from the nationality by township section of "1860 Census Foreign-Born for Indiana," 14–63.

68. Jones, *American Immigration,* 130; Dean R. Esslinger, *Immigrants and the City: Ethnicity and Mobility in a Nineteenth-Century Midwestern Community* (Port Washington, N.Y.: Kennikat Press, 1975), 87–88, 94; Sharon Bryant Hinkle, "Irish Immigrants in Terre Haute, Indiana in 1860: A Comparative Study" (M.A. thesis, Indiana State University, 1987), 10, 20, 22; Lang, "Irishmen in Northern Indiana," 192–93, 195–96; Thornbrough, *Indiana in the Civil War Era,* 552; Poinsatte, *Fort Wayne during the Canal Era,* 65.

69. Jones, *American Immigration,* 132–34; Lang, "Irishmen in Northern Indiana," 197; Thornbrough, *Indiana in the Civil War Era,* 552.

70. "1850 Census Foreign-Born for Indiana," 37; Hinkle, "Irish Immigrants in Terre Haute," 41, 59, 61; Zimmer, "Madison, Indiana," 59, 62, 72; Esslinger, *Immigrants and the City,* 52–54; Aylward, "Immigrant Settlement Patterns in South Bend," 4–5.

71. Poinsatte, *Fort Wayne during the Canal Era,* 148; Robert, *Evansville,* 534; *Biographical Record and Portrait Album of Tippecanoe County,* 289; *History of the Ohio Falls Cities,* 2:210; Alerding, *History of the Catholic Church in the Diocese of Vincennes,* 334, 373–74, 428; Sulgrove, *History of Indianapolis,* 407; Alerding, *Diocese of Fort Wayne,* 227–28, 255–56.

72. Alerding, *History of the Catholic Church in the Diocese of Vincennes,* 351–52, 472–73; Alerding, *Diocese of Fort Wayne,* 277–78; Timothy E. Howard, *A History of St. Joseph County, Indiana,* 2 vols. (Chicago: The Lewis Publishing Co., 1907), 1:417–20; Aylward, "Immigrant Settlement Patterns in South Bend," 5–6; Young, *History of Wayne County,* 408; *History of Wayne County,* 2:152–53.

73. Shepherd, et al., eds., *Biographical Directory, 1816–1899,* pp. 104 5.

74. Thornbrough, *Indiana in the Civil War Era,* 60; Barnhart and Carmony, *Indiana,* 1:398–99, 2:97; Poinsatte, *Fort Wayne during the Canal Era,* 228–29; Hinkle, "Irish Immigrants in Terre Haute," 86.

75. Thornbrough, *Indiana in the Civil War Era,* 60–61, 634, 639; Barnhart and Carmony, *Indiana,* 2:141; Richardt, "Narrative History of Saint Joseph Church," 39; Carl Fremont Brand, "The History of the Know Nothing Party in Indiana," *Indiana Magazine of History* 18 (Mar. 1922): 53, 72–73; ibid. (June 1922): 177.

76. Richardt, "Narrative History of Saint Joseph Church," 39–40.

77. Brand, "Know Nothing Party in Indiana," 68, 76, 202, 284, 297; Stormont, *History of Gibson County,* 97; Thornbrough, *Indiana in the Civil War Era,* 76–77, 640.

78. Shepherd, et al., eds., *Biographical Directory, 1816–1899,* pp. 37, 296, 373; Justin E. Walsh, *The Centennial History of the Indiana General Assembly, 1816–1978* (Indianapolis: Indiana Historical Bureau, 1987), 115, 721.

79. Richardt, "Narrative History of Saint Joseph Church," 32; Poinsatte, *Fort Wayne during the Canal Era,* 228; "Jefferson Co.-261.4-Irish" (roll 11, frame 1165), "Bartholomew Co.-261.4-Irish" (roll 1, frame 1865), FWP.

80. See Table A; Clifton J. Phillips, *Indiana in Transition: The Emergence of an Industrial Commonwealth, 1880–1920* (Indianapolis: Indiana Historical Bureau and Indiana Historical Society, 1968), 369.

81. See Table B; United States Department of Commerce, Bureau of the Census, *Fourteenth Census of the United States Taken in the Year 1920,* vol. 3, *Population 1920: Composition and Characteristics of the Population by States* (Washington, D.C.: Government Printing Office, 1922), 303–4.

82. See Table B.

83. *History of the Ohio Falls Cities,* 2:310; Thornbrough, *Indiana in the Civil War Era,* 552; Urban Irish computations by author based on figures in *Population 1920,* p. 304 and *A Report of the Seventeenth Decennial Census of the United States, Census of Population: 1950,* vol. 1, *Number of Inhabitants* (Washington, D.C.: Government Printing Office, 1952), 19.

84. Esslinger, *Immigrants and the City,* 88–89, 94–95; "Jefferson Co.-261.4-Irish" (roll 11, frame 1159), FWP; Kathleen Van Nuys, *Indy International* (Indianapolis: The Indianapolis News, 1978), 55; Aylward, "Immigrant Settlement Patterns in South Bend," 6.

85. Esslinger, *Immigrants and the City,* 52–54; Aylward, "Immigrant Settlement Patterns in South Bend," 5; "The Irish in Fort Wayne in 1880," "Allen Co.-261.4-lrish" (roll 1, frame 0775), "Jefferson Co.-261.4-Irish" (roll 11, frame 1160), "Floyd Co.-261.4-Irish" (roll 7, frame 0558), "Marion Co.-260.5-Ethnology" (roll 16, frame 0798), FWP; Frederick D. Kershner, Jr., "From Country Town to Industrial City: The Urban Pattern in Indianapolis," *Indiana Magazine of History* 45 (Dec. 1949): 329.

86. Thornbrough, *Indiana in the Civil War Era,* 126; William H. H. Terrell, *Indiana in the War of the Rebellion: Report of the Adjutant General* [reprint of volume 1 of the report published in 1869] (Indianapolis: Indiana Historical Bureau, 1960), 561, 571; William H. H. Terrell, *Report of the Adjutant General of the State of Indiana,* 8 vols. (Indianapolis: A. H. Conner, State Printer, 1865–69), 2:352; Sulgrove, *History of Indianapolis,* 346; *History of Allen County,* 72; Carl Wittke, *The Irish in America* (Baton Rouge: Louisiana State University Press, 1956), 142.

87. Holloway, *Indianapolis,* 279.

88. Thornbrough, *Indiana in the Civil War Era,* 552–53; Phillips, *Indiana in Transition,* 465; Holloway, *Indianapolis,* 279–80, 257; *Indianapolis City Directory for 1878,* p. 68; *Indianapolis City Directory for 1883,* p. 39; Sulgrove, *History of Indianapolis,* 407; *Terre Haute City Directory and Business Mirror for 1858,* p. 28; *Terre Haute City Directory, 1915–1916,* p. 76; *Biographical Record and Portrait Album of Tippecanoe County,* 301; *Fort Wayne City Directory, 1874–75,* p. 290; Robert, *Evansville,* 514; *Evansville City Directory for 1892,* p. 54; Helm, ed., *History of Cass County,* 451.

89. Wittke, *Irish in America,* 196–97; Kerby A. Miller, *Emigrants and Exiles: Ireland and the Irish Exodus to North America* (New York: Oxford University Press, 1985), 533–34; Philip Flanagan, "The Ancient Order of Hibernians," "Marion Co.-261.4-Irish" (roll 16, frame 0818), FWP; *Terre Haute City Directory, 1879–80,* p. 267; *Biographical Record and Portrait Album of Tippecanoe County,* 301; Helm, ed., *History of Cass County,* 452, 537; Howard, *History of St. Joseph County,* 1:462.

90. *Indianapolis City Directory, 1874,* p. 503; *Indianapolis City Directory for 1878,* p. 74; *Indianapolis City Directory for 1879,* pp. 55, 63; *Indianapolis City Directory for 1882,* p. 52; *Indianapolis City Directory for 1886,* p. 69; *Indianapolis City Directory for 1889,* p. 93; *Indianapolis City Directory for 1900,* p. 134; *Indianapolis City Directory for 1898,* p. 134.

91. *Indianapolis City Directory, 1876,* p. 619; *Evansville City Directory for 1885,* p. 31; *Terre Haute City Directory, 1904,* p. 62; *Terre Haute City Directory, 1920,* p. 44; Alerding, *Diocese of Fort Wayne,* 204.

92. *Indianapolis City Directory for 1881,* p. 60; *Terre Haute City Directory, 1882,* p. 64; Holloway, *Indianapolis,* 292, 294; *Indianapolis City Directory for 1890,* pp. 79, 81; *Indianapolis City Directory for 1898,* p. 122; *Indianapolis City Directory for 1878,* p. 68;

*Terre Haute City Directory for 1879–80*, p. 268; *Terre Haute City Directory for 1900*, p. 37.

93. Thornbrough, *Indiana in the Civil War Era*, 552–53; Phillips, *Indiana in Transition*, 465; *Indianapolis City Directory for 1879*, p. 56; *Terre Haute City Directory for 1879–80*, p. 268; Powell, ed., *History of Cass County*, 1: 224–25; Van Nuys, *Indy International*, 57.

94. Thornbrough, *Indiana in the Civil War Era*, 553; "Allen Co.-261.4-Irish" (roll 1, frame 0775), FWP.

95. "Allen Co.-261.4-Irish" (roll 1, frame 0775), FWP; Van Nuys, *Indy International*, 55.

96. Alerding, *History of the Catholic Church in the Diocese of Vincennes*, 335–37, 431, 458; Alerding, *Diocese of Fort Wayne*, 320–21, 277–78, 351–52, 395–96; *History of the Ohio Falls Cities*, 2:446–47; Richardt, "Narrative History of Saint Joseph Church," 60; Helm, ed., *History of Cass County*, 437; Powell, ed., *History of Cass County*, 1:436; Howard, *History of St. Joseph County*, 1:421–22; Esslinger, *Immigrants and the City*, 28, 112–13; Aylward, "Immigrant Settlement Patterns in South Bend," 7; Holloway, *Indianapolis*, 182, 240–41; Sulgrove, *History of Indianapolis*, 407; Shaw, ed., *History of Dearborn County*, 404; Robert, *Evansville*, 534; Joseph P. Elliott, *A History of Evansville and Vanderburgh County, Indiana* (Evansville, Ind.: Keller Printing Co., 1897), 279.

97. Shepherd, et al., eds., *Biographical Directory, 1816–1899*, p. 256; Justin E. Walsh, ed., *A Biographical Directory of the Indiana General Assembly*, vol. 2, *1900–1984* (Indianapolis: Indiana Historical Bureau, 1984), 2, 407; Phillips, *Indiana in Transition*, 588.

98. Urban Irish computations by author based on figures in *Population 1920*, pp. 307, 308; Aylward, "Immigrant Settlement Patterns in South Bend," 7; Van Nuys, *Indy International*, 57.

99. Table A; United States Department of Commerce, Bureau of the Census, *Thirteenth Census of the United States Taken in the Year 1910*, vol. 2, *Population 1910: Reports by States, with Statistics for Counties, Cities and Other Civil Divisions, Alabama–Montana* (Washington, D.C.: Government Printing Office, 1913), 548; Philip R. VanderMeer, *The Hoosier Politician: Officeholding and Political Culture in Indiana, 1896–1920* (Urbana: University of Illinois Press, 1985), 124.

100. Alerding, *Diocese of Fort Wayne*, 204; Powell, ed., *History of Cass County*, 1:398; *Terre Haute City Directory, 1920*, p. 44.

101. Hasia R. Diner, *Erin's Daughters in America: Irish Immigrant Women in the Nineteenth Century* (Baltimore: The Johns Hopkins University Press, 1983), 107–8; John J. D. Trenor, "Proposals Affecting Immigration," *The Annals of the American Academy of Political and Social Science* 24 (July–Dec. 1904): 229.

102. Shepherd, et. al., eds., *Biographical Directory, 1816–1899*, pp. 130, 248; Van Nuys, *Indy International*, 56–57; Shaw, ed., *History of Dearborn County*, 911; *Past and Present of Tippecanoe County, Indiana*, 2 vols. (Indianapolis: B. F. Bowen and Company, Publishers, 1909), 2:862; Walsh, ed., *Biographical Directory, 1900–1984*, p. 407; *Pictorial and Biographical Memoirs of Indianapolis and Marion County, Indiana* (Chicago: Goodspeed Brothers, Publishers, 1893), 150.

103. Phillips, *Indiana in Transition*, 464; Blanchard, ed., *History of the Catholic Church in Indiana*, 1:94, 105; Sulgrove, *History of Indianapolis*, 407; Alerding, *History of the Catholic Church in the Diocese of Vincennes*, 432, 434; *Terre Haute City Directory, 1894*, p. 30; *Terre Haute City Directory, 1900*, p. 19.

104. VanderMeer, *Hoosier Politician*, 48; Wittke, *Irish in America*, 113; *Pictorial and Biographical Memoirs of Indianapolis and Marion County*, 128–29; Shaw, ed., *History of Dearborn County*, 1007–9; Walsh, ed., *Biographical Directory, 1900–1984*, p. 321.

105. Leary, *Indianapolis*, 122–23, 146–47.

106. Shepherd, et al., eds., *Biographical Directory, 1816–1899*, pp. 97, 123, 176, 192–93, 231, 248, 253, 297, 381; *Past and Present of Tippecanoe County*, 2:862; Shaw, ed., *History of Dearborn County*, 556–57, 910–11; *Biographical and Historical Souvenir for the Counties of Clark, Crawford, Harrison, Floyd, Jefferson, Jennings, Scott and Washington, Indiana*, 2 pts. (Chicago: John M. Gresham and Co., 1889), pt. 2, pp.100–1.

107. Helm, ed., *History of Cass County*, 536–37; Shepherd, et al., eds., *Biographical Directory, 1816–1899*, pp. 163, 380–81; Walsh, ed., *Biographical Directory, 1900–1984*, p. 222.

108. Shepherd, et al., eds., *Biographical Directory, 1816–1899*, pp. 37, 192–93, 328, 351.

109. Walsh, *Centennial History of the Indiana General Assembly*, 258, 399, 703, 721; VanderMeer, *Hoosier Politician*, 126–33, 140–42.

110. Wittke, *Irish in America*, 153–57, 197–98; Thornbrough, *Indiana in the Civil War Era*, 553; Holloway, *Indianapolis*, 280.

111. Wittke, *Irish in America*, 164–66; Miller, *Emigrants and Exiles*, 539–40; *New York Times*, 19, 20 May 1880; *Indianapolis City Directory for 1881*, p. 60; *Indianapolis City Directory for 1883*, p. 39; *Indianapolis City Directory for 1885*, p. 41; *Indianapolis City Directory for 1886*, p. 60.

112. Phillips, *Indiana in Transition*, 588–89; Barnhart and Carmony, *Indiana*, 2:375–76.

113. Table A; Table B.

114. Phillips, *Indiana in Transition*, 368–69; Table A; Van Nuys, *Indy International*, 57; Dennis Clark, *Hibernia America: The Irish and Regional Cultures* (New York: Greenwood Press, 1986), 131.

115. Alerding, *History of the Catholic Church in the Diocese of Vincennes*, 453, 459; "Floyd Co.-261.4-Irish (roll 7, frame 0558), "Allen Co.-261.4-Irish" (roll 1, frame 0775), "Jefferson Co.-261.4-Irish" (roll 11, frame 1160), FWP; *Terre Haute City Directory, 1904*, p. 62; *Terre Haute City Directory, 1927*, p. 26; "Marion Co.-261.4-Irish" (roll 16, frame 0818), FWP.

116. Robert S. Lynd and Helen Merrell Lynd, *Middletown: A Study in Contemporary American Culture* (New York: Harcourt, Brace and Co., 1929), 293, 332; Clark, *Hibernia America*, 124; "Dubois Co.-260.5-Ethnology" (roll 5, frame 1882), FWP.

117. "Marion Co.-260.5-Ethnology" (roll 16, frame 0798), FWP.

118. Ernie Hernandez, *Ethnics in Northwest Indiana* (Gary, Ind.: Post-Tribune, 1984), 154; Table B; Table C; "Floyd Co.-260.5-Ethnology" (roll 7, frame 0561), "Marion Co.-261.4-Irish" (roll 16, frames 0818-0819), "Bartholomew Co.-261.4-Irish" (roll 1, frame 1865), FWP; Walsh, ed., *Biographical Directory, 1900–1984*, p. 76.

119. Leonard Dinnerstein and David M. Reimers, *Ethnic Americans: A History of Immigration and Assimilation*, 2d ed. (New York: Harper and Row, Publishers, 1982), 110; Van Nuys, *Indy International*, 56.

120. Kershner, "Country Town to Industrial City," 329; Van Nuys, *Indy International*, 55, 56, 57; John H. Fenton, *Midwest Politics* (New York: Holt, Rinehart and Winston, 1966), 175; Walsh, ed., *Biographical Directory, 1900–1984*, p. 277.

121. Walsh, *Centennial History of the Indiana General Assembly*, 566, 703, 721; Walsh, ed., *Biographical Directory, 1900–1984*, pp. 145, 238, 257, 279–80, 320, 364.

122. Table A; The exact number of persons reporting Irish ancestry was 965,602, United States Department of Commerce, Bureau of the Census, "Selected Social Characteristics: 1990, Indiana" [1990 CPH-L-80. Table 1], Ethnic History Project, Indiana Historical Society; Hernandez, *Ethnics in Northwest Indiana*, 153.

123. Van Nuys, *Indy International*, 56.

124. *The Criterion,* 17 Jan. 1992; *Indianapolis Star,* 11, 16, 17 Jan. 1992.

125. Hernandez, *Ethnics in Northwest Indiana,* 154; Michael F. Funchion, ed., *Irish American Voluntary Organizations* (Westport, Conn.: Greenwood Press, 1983), 61; Nationalities Council of Indiana, Inc., club list (Indiana Historical Society, Ethnic History Project, 1992); Jack McGinley, telephone interview with the author, Indianapolis, 22 Oct. 1992; Juanita Taylor, telephone interview with the author, Indianapolis, 21 Oct. 1992; Pat Spellacy, telephone interview with the author, Indianapolis, 21 Oct. 1992; *Terre Haute Tribune-Star,* 16 Mar. 1992; Patrick H. Cahill, telephone interview with the author, Terre Haute, Ind., 22 Oct. 1992.

# ITALIANS

JAMES J. DIVITA

*While Gregori painted and Mother Mary Magdalen prayed, Italian workers and peasants arrived in the state to market their labor in mines, mills, shops, quarries, and stores. They immediately settled together on the same streets, probably within the shadow of their employer or the means of transportation to their employer. This was the Italian village in the Hoosier city.*

## Italians in Indiana before Statehood, 1679–1816

The first Italian to set foot in present Indiana was Enrico Tonti, who camped along the St. Joseph River near the site of South Bend in early December 1679. Born at Gaeta in the kingdom of Naples ca. 1650, he was the son of that city's governor. As supporters of the anti-Spanish Masaniello revolt, he and his family were forced to flee to France. There he joined the navy, held the rank of captain, and distinguished himself in battle against the Spanish at Messina. The explosion of a grenade, however, cost him his right hand. An iron or brass substitute encased in a glove was fitted over the stump.

Tonti desired to accompany the great French explorer Robert Cavelier, Sieur de La Salle, on an expedition into the North American interior. La Salle was initially hesitant to employ a one-handed man (how could he paddle a canoe?), but he soon recognized Tonti's physical strength and his positive attributes. The La Salle party traversed the Great Lakes and sailed southward on Lake Michigan until they came upon the mouth of the St. Joseph River. They ascended the St. Joseph searching for a route that would lead them westward to the "Father River." After locating the headwaters of the Kankakee River, Tonti and the others floated past lifeless oaks and through the marshes of present Lake and Newton counties, Indiana, until they entered the open prairies of the Illinois country.

Tonti remained an active explorer and fur trader in the Midwest until his death in 1704. He built forts along the Illinois River and explored much of the Mississippi River valley. The Neapolitan was highly respected among the Indians who called him "Thunder Arm": his well-aimed iron hand was a good weapon against foes.[1]

The first Indiana residents of Italian origin lived at Vincennes, the first permanent European settlement in the state, established by the French in 1732. Often descendants of soldiers in the Carignan Regiment settled along the frontier. This regiment, raised by Tommaso Francesco di Savoia, Prince of Carignano, was originally composed of Piedmontese recruits who entered French service. Numbering over four hundred officers and men, it was the only regiment transferred to Canada (1665). A French visitor to Vincennes in 1796 commented that the population spoke "pretty good French," but that it was "intermixed with many military terms and phrases" that betrayed its Carignan origin.[2]

Several Italians lived at Vincennes before 1816, the year Indiana became a state. Michelangelo Babini, born at Livorno in Tuscany, had been a lieutenant of Spanish carabineers in Louisiana and was now a prominent fur merchant. Lorenzo Badazone was a well-known, successful businessman. Joseph André, called "The Italian" by his neighbors, was from Pavia near Milan. He married at Detroit in 1774 and was killed by Indians at about age fifty in 1801.[3]

The most famous Italian at Vincennes, however, was Francesco Vigo. Born at Mondovì, Cuneo Province, in 1747, he enlisted in the Spanish army and was stationed in Louisiana. Seeing business opportunities around him, he resigned from the army to become a merchant and fur

trader at Vincennes. As a supporter of George Rogers Clark and the American cause during the Revolution, he accepted $12,000 in Virginia currency and promissory notes of questionable value to provision Clark's forces.

After Indiana became American in 1783, Vigo became the largest landholder in the vicinity. He was appointed a colonel in the local militia; advised President George Washington on Indian affairs (1789); participated, with William Henry Harrison, in a convention that discussed whether slavery should be permitted in the Indiana Territory (1802); served as a trustee of Vincennes University (1806); helped establish the first free library west of the Alleghenies; and had a county named after him (1818). The United States secretary of war described him as "a man of the most scrupulous regard for truth, disinterestedness, and honor."[4]

Wars in Europe during the French Revolution and Napoleonic period resulted in various naval blockades, restricted markets, and a slower flow of goods. Reduced fur prices and rising prices for merchandise ruined Vigo financially and forced him to mortgage most of his land. The old Italian died in 1836, leaving an estate of $77.62.[5]

After his death Vigo's heirs continued to press the United States government, which had assumed Virginia's territorial claims in the West, to reimburse them for the credit extended Clark. Finally in 1876, forty years after Vigo's death and almost a century after Clark captured Vincennes, the government paid $49,898.60, thereby recognizing the claim with interest.

Today a major attraction in Vincennes is the George Rogers Clark Memorial along the banks of the Wabash River. Nearby is the statue of Francesco Vigo, with eyes directed toward the memorial and right arm leaning on several money bags—Vigo, the Italian who helped make Indiana American.

### Italians in Pioneer Indiana, 1816–65

Federal census takers in 1850 counted eight Italian born in Indiana,[6] but ten years later they enumerated a hundred Italian born in a state population of 1,350,428.

*Francesco Vigo, drawn from life by Charles Alexandre Lesueur. Without his financial and moral support, George Rogers Clark could not have captured Vincennes from the British. The county in which Terre Haute is located is named in his honor.*

Twenty reported their native state, all but one (a Neapolitan) born north of Rome (seven Genoese, five Sardinians, four Tuscans, and three Lombards). They lived in twenty-five of the state's counties, nineteen each in Vanderburgh and Marion counties, eleven in Ripley County, and ten in Tippecanoe County. Of fifty-two who reported occupations, fifteen engaged in farm work; eleven were skilled (toy or fringe manufacturers, shoemaker, seamstress, tanner, etc.); nine were laborers; nine were involved in the sale of food or drink (confectioners, peddlers, clerks, etc.); and eight were sculptors, artists, or musicians. Generally speaking, all pre–World War I immigrant occupations were already represented. The richest Italians were an Evansville toy maker ($2,000 in real property), a confectioner in Laurel, Franklin County ($1,700 in real property), and a stevedore in Vevay, Switzerland County ($1,200 in personal property)! Of the one hundred, sixty-three were male, thirty-seven female.[7]

Despite their paucity among Indiana's permanent pioneer residents, several Italian born had a notable impact despite their brief sojourn in the state. They were clerics

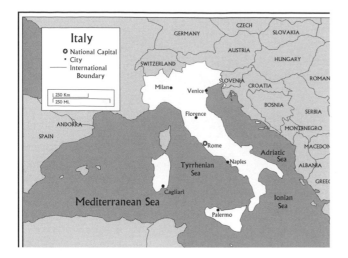

who reflected the romanticism and nationalism of their native land and transported their zeal to Indiana. Three Italians accepted a mission call to the Midwest in 1816 and served at Vincennes through 1820. They were Vincentians, members of a Catholic religious order that cared for the sick and conducted religious revivals. The best known of the trio was Joseph R. Rosati (1789–1843), born at Sora in the kingdom of Naples and ordained at Rome in 1811. He would become the first bishop of St. Louis (1826).[8] The other two Vincentians were John Baptist Acquaroni and Andrew Ferrari from Porto Maurizio near Genoa. Ferrari was stationed at Vincennes with the intention of establishing a novitiate there. Indeed, they fanned the flames of faith until a resident priest replaced them.

In 1853 Pope Pius IX ordered Archbishop Gaetano Bedini to tour the United States and report on the growing Catholic Church there on the way to his diplomatic post in Brazil. Anti-Catholic riots broke out in Louisville, Cincinnati, and wherever else Bedini visited. The papal emissary was shadowed by anti-Catholic speakers, the best of whom was Alessandro Gavazzi. Son of a law professor at the University of Bologna and a cleric at age sixteen, Gavazzi liked to dwell on the need for Italian unification and the excesses of Italy's rulers. Although Bedini did not visit Indiana, Gavazzi was invited to address a receptive audience at the Masonic Hall in Indianapolis on 28–30 October 1853. He spoke English imperfectly and gesticulated wildly. He accused Bedini of complicity in the execution of revolutionaries, criticized the establishment of a Catholic school system, and insisted that papal pretensions contradicted American democracy.[9] That Gavazzi was invited to Indiana and was received so warmly reveals the political and intellectual atmosphere in the state at that time. In February 1854, less than four months after auditors enthusiastically cheered him, nativists organized the state's first chapter of the Know-Nothing movement. Its program denounced alleged papal influence in politics and education, called for severe restrictions on immigration and the repeal of naturalization laws, and demanded that only native-born Americans be eligible to hold political office. In 1855, just before they were absorbed into the newly organized Republican party, Indiana Know-Nothings numbered between thirty and fifty thousand.[10]

The atmosphere that brought Gavazzi to the forefront also had an international aspect. Robert Dale Owen (1801–1877), son of the founder of the communal experiment at New Harmony and a former Hoosier congressman, was United States minister to the kingdom of Naples and Sicily from 1853 to 1858. Although a fighter for liberal issues like women's rights and prison reform, like the Know-Nothings he was unsure that immigration and democracy were compatible. He thought it better to end immigration into the United States than to permit newcomers to settle and then refuse them citizenship. He also thought that naturalized citizens who returned permanently to their birthplaces should be stripped of their American citizenship.[11] Owen did not press the Franklin Pierce administration to adopt such a policy because it was inopportune; the number of immigrants from southern Italy was negligible in his day.

## Italians and Indiana's Economy, 1865–1930

Italians abandoned their homeland by the thousands just as the dream of political unification became real. The fundamental problem facing the new government was economic, but the government did not know how to formulate a coherent policy of national economic development. Since the various parts of the country were former independent states and at different economic levels, the leaders with their northern backgrounds had limited, narrow experience at handling a national problem complicated by an increasing population.

Formulation of a coherent national policy was hindered by cabinet instability (fifty-seven governments in the sixty-one years between 1861 and 1922). Lack of a strong program and little action were the keys to staying in power. Unused to popular participation in government, ordinary people were not surprised when politicians used their positions for personal gain, and cynical political coalitions brought former opponents together. Furthermore, the country's meager financial resources were not used for internal improvements but for colonial expansion. The government, however, could not be accused of misusing its popular mandate; until 1912 only 10 percent of the population was eligible to vote.

Whenever the government tried economic reform, the impact was disastrous. When taxes were raised to fund public programs, investment capital disappeared, industrialization languished, and emigration from Venetia, Piedmont, Liguria, and Tuscany commenced. When promises of land reform were left unfulfilled, a sizable portion of the army was stationed in the South to control malcontents. When the government sought to implement free trade and abolish tariffs, unemployment increased because southern industry needed protection from foreign competition to survive. In 1887 the government engaged in a trade war with France and other countries, resulting in high tariffs on Italian agricultural products. Consequently, mass emigration affected the Abruzzi, Campania, Basilicata, Calabria, and Sicily. A Mishawaka Italian born in Calabria reported that in his hometown the travel agent represented several steamship companies and never needed to seek clients to earn a living. In 1907, 285,731 Italians entered American ports, the largest number in any single year.[12]

Emigrants after 1900 were primarily owners of small plots unable to provide sufficient income for a family, younger sons, recently married men, and adventurers. A Richmond housewife born in Bisaccia, Avellino Province, described her hometown:

> Five or six families were rich, owned everything, and you worked for them. If you were poor you stayed that way unless you left. Nothing ever happened in our town and nothing ever changed much.

Men arrived without their families, sought to accumulate a fortune rapidly, and then return home to buy land, invest in some way, or send the fare for their families to join them. Italians contributed to the over $5 million that was remitted abroad through the Gary post office in 1910.[13]

To some, *La Merica* was a country of strangers to which economic necessity had driven them. About one-third of the immigrants returned home, and many entered and departed the United States several times. By 1913 one out of every twenty Italians had lived in America.[14] Even today English-speaking retirees who receive Social Security checks can be found in Italian villages.

To Indiana businessmen, whether immigrants were permanent residents or migratory, tall or short, made little difference as long as the low wages they accepted helped maximize company profits. Judge Elbert H. Gary, board chairman of United States Steel Corporation, understood the situation well when, in the early 1920s, he declared that the greatest threat to the continued existence of American free enterprise was the immigration quota system that limited the inflow of cheap labor.[15]

Federal census takers indicated how well the Indiana economy attracted Italian immigrants.[16]

| Year | Italian born |
|------|-------------|
| 1870 | 95 |
| 1880 | 198 |
| 1890 | 468 |
| 1900 | 1,327 |
| 1910 | 6,911 |
| 1920 | 6,712 |
| 1930 | 6,873 |

In 1910, the peak year, Italians lived in sixty-nine of the state's counties, with the largest concentrations in Lake (1,279), Vermillion (811), Marion (663), Cass (479), and La Porte (471). This pattern reflected Italian employment in the metallurgical, fuel, food, and railroad industries. Every city with more than ten thousand people also had Italian residents. The largest concentrations were located in Indianapolis (658), Gary (639), Elkhart (267), Logansport (237), and La Porte (223).[17]

Generally speaking, Italians settled in Indiana because out-of-state companies located their facilities along rail lines here and because of the national need to exploit Indiana's natural resources. Standard Oil Company and United States Steel Corporation, eastern-based firms, employed Italians in northern Lake County. Italians in the stone quarries of Logansport worked for the Casparis Stone Company of Columbus, Ohio, or the France Stone Company of Toledo, Ohio. Bedford Quarries Company of Chicago operated one of the limestone quarries employing Italians at Oolitic. Italian coal miners in Parke County populated Diamond, a town originally platted by the Brazil Block Coal Company, whose president lived in Chicago. The Ohio Oil Company prospected in east central Indiana. The United Mine Workers Union, with national headquarters in Indianapolis, recruited miners for western Indiana jobs. Italians settled in Richmond, Logansport, Fort Wayne, and Elkhart because the Pennsylvania and New York Central railroads situated repair shops and yards there. Even Indianapolis Sicilians, self-employed in produce, settled in the Hoosier capital because it was a rail hub giving them easy access to the sources of the fruits and vegetables they sold. Several had lived in Columbus, Cincinnati, Chicago, or even New Orleans before settling in Indiana.

The Hoosier state exploited its natural gas, oil, coal, and limestone deposits at the beginning of the twentieth century. The discovery of natural gas in 1886 and oil in 1889 created a boom atmosphere in nineteen counties of east central Indiana. Italian workers took jobs in Adams, Madison, and Delaware counties. Cheap, available energy encouraged the growth of glass manufacturing in this area. Standard Oil also decided to develop refining facilities at Hammond and Whiting because pipelines could easily connect the refineries to the new oil fields. Alas, overexploitation led to decline after 1910. Italians, as their jobs disappeared, relocated. In 1900 the southern portion of rural Adams County was part of the natural gas/oil field. More Italians worked there than in Lake, St. Joseph, Allen, or Vigo counties. By 1920 census takers found no Italians in Adams County but growing populations in the other counties.[18]

Already by 1890 Italians worked in the coal mines of Clay, Vermillion, and Vigo counties in west central Indiana. Within the next ten years Diamond in Parke County became a lively coal miners' town. Many of the miners came from Venetia, Trentino, Piedmont, and Emilia and had experience working with stone and wood. Platted in 1893 and incorporated in 1903, Diamond had a population of 1,070 in 1910. Raccoon Township, which included Diamond, had 2,821 residents.[19] In October 1910, however, a thirty thousand dollar fire originating in the Italian Social Club destroyed twenty-three businesses and several houses. The volunteer bucket brigade worked through the night, but to no avail.[20] Since the property loss was only partially covered by insurance and the coal veins were becoming too thin to work profitably, the town began to decline. Italians moved away, the population of the town fell to 352, and the population of the township decreased to 1,674 in 1920.[21] Today Diamond is a platted town site reverting to nature.

A story with a happier ending can be told about Clinton in Vermillion County, where coal was profitably mined after 1884. From 17 Italian born in 1890, the number of Vermillion County Italian born peaked at 1,387 (second only to Lake County) in 1920. Since the Crown Hill mines and Bunsen Coal Company were beginning to operate west and southwest of Clinton in 1910–11, just as the mines around Diamond began to close, Italians transferred to the new location. Even their houses in Diamond were dismantled and reassembled there. They developed a whole new neighborhood and business district in the northwest corner of Clinton. "Four to five trains a day carried miners to work" at Centenary, Blanford, or Universal, a retired Piedmontese miner and butcher pointed out. "Each mine had a whistle and at 5 p.m. you could identify which mines were working by the sound of the whistle. There were some Sicilians out there, but usually they were Piedmontese and Venetians who had strong backs and were good workers." In 1910 Vermillion ranked fourth among Indiana counties in coal production. The smallest biweekly payroll was $150,000 in cash. Clinton reached a population of eleven thousand in 1920 and then began to decline. The area's mines could not compete with southern operators who paid nonunion workers lower wages.[22] Some Italians tried to weather the crisis, accepted a shorter work week, or remained until the mines laid them off. Then they moved away or tried to find work in Terre Haute or Danville, Illinois. The town, therefore, did not disappear. Today Clinton is a town of five thousand and home of the Little Italy Festival.

The "iron horse" and its upkeep provided a livelihood for immigrants in Richmond, Logansport, and Elkhart. By 1910 Italians generally had replaced the Irish in maintaining roadbeds and in the menial tasks within the repair shop. Both trackmen and repairmen worked seven days a week, twelve hours per day (choice of two shifts, either 6 A.M. to 6 P.M. or 6 P.M. to 6 A.M.). "Working for the Pennsy was steady and secure," recalled a Logansport railroader whose father had come from the Abruzzi, "especially good if you were willing to work hard and didn't have much education." A trackman could earn ninety cents a day in 1914 and a roundhouse worker could earn as much as $3.20 a day. In the 1920s trackmen worked a six-day week for eighteen dollars. "With extras you could bring home $1,500 a year. The hard part was getting paid only twice a month." Before World War II, Italians were unable to obtain riding jobs—engineer, conductor, brakeman. However, they were always offered a spot on a gang that maintained a section of track. "My first job when I was 16 was wiping off steam locomotives in the roundhouse," the Logansport railroader laughed, "but I rose to track foreman. At first I was part of a five-man section gang. Four of us were Italian—Pasquale, Donato, Di Genova, and Gallo." Railroaders traveled to where they were needed. One Logansport interviewee had moved his family to Kentland, Crown Point, and North Judson, wherever the company sent him. He was the better kind of section hand, a family man who lived along the right-of-way, assigned a length of track, whose lifetime occupation was maintenance. The other kind of section hand was an unmarried man, a temporary or summer employee, who was supervised by a foreman-padrone.[23] A padrone was an English-speaking Italian who obtained a job for a newcomer in return for a fee or percentage of the worker's pay. (See also p. 290.) These workers were the veterans of the camp car. "It wasn't much more than a boxcar with beds," remembered a Richmond Italian who had lived in one in 1914. Some cars were filthy, and, because they were windowless, they were foul smelling. With no permanent home, this kind of worker was dependent on the foreman not only for the job but also for life itself. Breakfast was a cup of coffee, maybe with sausage and bread; lunchtime was usually only bread. The foreman kept strict account of what was eaten and deducted its cost from the worker's pay. Once when section gang members complained that the bread was moldy, the *padrone* threw it at them and exclaimed, "Take that you pigs; you never had better bread than that at home."[24]

Whoever experienced the 1922 strike against the Pennsylvania Railroad never forgot the experience. "I moved up to the roundhouse and repaired air brakes," remembered an eighty-year-old Richmond railroader. "Then they decided to pay us on a piece work basis and require a clock-in and clock-out. When the other guys went on strike for better pay, the boss told me that if I joined them, it would be the end of my job. I went out with them because otherwise they'd beat me up." The company obtained a restraining order, specifically naming Italian and other strikers, from a federal court in Indianapolis,[25] and successfully hired replacements for those who still did not return to work. Some strikers moved from Logansport to find factory jobs in Mishawaka. Others abandoned the state to take steel mill jobs in Warren, Ohio. Still others accepted small jobs but eventually returned to the railroad. "My father was very proud and refused to return even after the foreman came to our house to try and persuade him," a Logansport real estate saleslady recalled. "They listed him by name in that court order. He walked five miles to work in the quarry west of town. He came home covered with dust and looked like a ghost. Exhausted too, but he never worked for the railroad again."

Logansport Italians quarried crushed stone, and Bedford Italians quarried quality limestone. Exploitation of this natural resource began after the Civil War when Bedford and Lawrence County were first served by a railroad. Among buildings constructed with Bedford limestone were the Indiana Statehouse, the Vanderbilt mansions in New York and North Carolina, and the Chicago Public Library.

About twenty Italians were employed as cutters by David Reed as early as 1882. He brought them into his quarry, a few miles north of Bedford, because local labor was scarce. By 1910 Lawrence County's Italian-born population peaked at 242, mostly from the Abruzzi and Calabria. Although Germans and Austrians were also employed in the quarries and mills, most foreign workers were Italian. Reed's Station, where most Italians lived, had a post office and an Italian-owned grocery store. "The bar there was run by my brothers," said a Bedford lady whose father was born in Calabria. The company furnished housing for the workers who paid cheap rent, five to six dollars per month. Houses were all painted an unattractive green. A nearby mill was operated almost exclusively by Italians, one of whom was the efficient foreman. Owners viewed Italians as more reliable workers than the local population, but they considered Italians less

capable of accomplishing more complicated tasks.[26] Yet Italians continued to work at tasks local labor shunned.

The native population, however, viewed the Italians as unwelcome interlopers—foreigners who took away their jobs. Suffering the impact of the 1907 recession, some local men moved against the Italians. Following the destruction of Italian-owned property by arson, handbills were posted and shoved under the doors of houses occupied by Italians. "All Italians must vacate and not be found here after February 20. Those that stay will suffer the penalty. By order of COMMITTEE."[27] Anonymous letters were also sent to quarry managers, warning them not to employ Italians. The managers, however, responded by offering a two hundred dollar reward to anyone who brought about the arrest and conviction of those who intimidated and frightened away foreign labor "necessary for the performance of certain parts of our work."[28]

The paper threat was not the story's end. Posters appeared denouncing the United States government for permitting the immigration of foreign labor, an attitude which in turn was denounced as Know-Nothingism.[29] Meanwhile, a "dago army," composed of recruits from Lawrence and Monroe counties, engaged in target practice to prepare for any eventuality.[30] After rock throwing and stabbing incidents at Sanders in Monroe County, sixty local men armed with shotguns confronted Italians armed with revolvers and shotguns. Gov. J. Frank Hanly then consulted the county sheriff to ascertain whether the National Guard needed to be deployed.[31] Tension, aggravated by the use of liquor on both sides, remained through the summer of 1908. A war of words accompanied the incidents when the editor of the *Bedford Daily Democrat*, dismayed at so much publicity for foreign laborers in the rival *Bedford Daily Mail*, branded the *Mail's* editor, a Mayflower descendant, the "Italian editor" and renamed his paper "The Bladder."[32]

Protests against the Italian presence continued through 1910, after which immigrants began to leave the area.[33] Hearing about a shortage of workers, the Donato brothers—Crescenzo D. (Chris) and Ismael D. (Harry)—decided to take their chances and find employment at Bedford.[34] Members of a family of woodcarvers from Rivisondoli in the Abruzzi, they immigrated to America and studied at the Cooper-Union Art Institute in New York. By the 1920s Chris became Bedford's only Italian quarry owner and contractor. "He always paid his workers five cents an hour more than anyone else," his grandnephew, an Indianapolis developer, commented, "but he always carried a checkbook. If he saw an employee loafing, he fired him and immediately paid him off by

*Solimano Grocery in Logansport, 1890. Laurence and Mary Brizzolara Solimano with son Charles (left) at the corner of Pearl and Broadway. Solimano, a Genoese, operated a confectionery and fruit store in Indianapolis during the 1870s.*

check." His quarries supplied limestone for several federal buildings in Washington, D.C. His business was so profitable that he was able to retire at age forty-six.

Harry was a subcontractor, carver, and sculptor. He produced statuary for the courthouse grounds at Bloomington and Bedford and sculpted the entranceway for the Chicago Tribune Tower, the Maiden pillars for Chicago's Museum of Science and Industry (modeled after those on the Acropolis), the decorations on the Indiana State Library, and the columns and facade of SS. Peter and Paul Cathedral in Indianapolis.[35]

Not only did Italian labor strengthen the economies of the coal mining, railroading, and quarrying centers of Indiana, but it also contributed to the state's industrialization. Between 1900 and 1930 Standard Oil of Whiting, Inland Steel of East Chicago, United States Steel of Gary, Ball-Band, Bendix, and Studebaker in South Bend-Mishawaka, and General Electric in Fort Wayne provided them jobs. In 1930 Lake County had 2,037 Italian residents; St. Joseph County 782; and Allen County 241.[36]

Gary, the Miracle City of the Twentieth Century as it was once styled, was founded in 1906 on the sandy, barren shore of Lake Michigan. Immigrants lived in "The Patch," a several square-block area separated from the better part of town by both the Wabash and Pennsylvania railroad tracks. Italians were usually young male southerners, mostly illiterate, who continued to work for the railroad or sought a construction or steel mill job. Like other foreigners, they accepted jobs which the native born thought were too dirty or hot. Mill management viewed them as stupid, but their slowness to react to orders usually arose from not understanding English. Only with great determination could they study the new language after working eighty-four hours a week.[37] Conditions in the mill were exemplified in a booklet that steel management published in Italian and other languages in 1917. It took seventy-six pages to spell out the plant's safety rules and regulations. On the last page the company forbade the workers playing jokes or not being serious on the job, for these activities were safety hazards. The booklet then concluded by forbidding workers giving money or gifts to foremen.[38]

Italians were willing to live in the shacks turned boardinghouses that the real estate promoters had erected in this unregulated part of the city. After a twelve-hour workday, they rented a bed and were assigned a sleep shift. Boardinghouse owners could obtain a 50 percent return on their real investment each year. Yet some workers saved enough of their seventeen-cent hourly average wage to return home, pay passage for the family, or even start a small business.[39]

The attempt of steelworkers to improve working conditions resulted in the infamous 1919–20 strike, during which Gov. James P. Goodrich protected company property and strikebreakers by using military force to assist local police. The foreign born deeply resented this antistriker stance and the unsympathetic attitude of many native born. Disgusted by their defeat, immigrants returned home or refused to work under the old conditions.

The labor troubles of this era seemed to speed up the process of tightfistedness that resulted in self-employment and movement to a better neighborhood. While newspapers reported the antics of Italian bootleggers during Prohibition, newspaper advertisements and city directory listings indicate that a respectable number of Italians ran fruit stores, saloons, shoe repair shops, bakeries, restaurants, and even an auto dealership. Some began to move away from their enclave at 17th Avenue and Broadway to a new area south of 35th Avenue called Glen Park.

Woeful tales should be balanced by at least one success story. Marcello Gerometta (1883–1948), born in Udine, learned the bricklaying trade in Italy and Germany. He arrived in Gary (1907) and was employed as a foreman by a local builder for two years before deciding to become a contractor. He built 285 houses for United States Steel, an apartment house, several business and office structures, and St. Mark's Catholic Church. He constructed and owned the city's largest hotel, the two million dollar, four hundred-room Hotel Gary at 6th Avenue and Broadway. Completed in 1928, the hotel helped accommodate 12,000 conventioneers in Gary that year. Undaunted when the depression reduced hotel occupancy and he lost his fortune, Gerometta purchased a hundred frame dwellings built by the steel company and rehabilitated them with basements and modern plumbing. After World War II he supervised the construction of the east wing of Methodist Hospital and the new Holy Angels Church. His success is illustrated by the fact that he resided north of the Wabash Railroad tracks and the tribute which a pioneer Gary architect paid him: "Gerometta probably was Gary's best contractor. He was more interested in quality than profits. He always took great pride in his work."[40]

Compared to their compatriots in Gary, Logansport, or Clinton, the Italians of Indianapolis were in their own genre: self-employed. They divided rather neatly by origin, occupation, and neighborhood. Many immigrants in the Hoosier capital were Sicilian from Termini Imerese and Trabia, Palermo Province, engaged in the sale of fresh

On Saturdays during the 1920s Indianapolis Sicilians peddled fruits and vegetables in towns like Greenfield, shown in this photo. Others moved permanently to Richmond, Rushville, Bloomington, Crawfordsville, and Terre Haute to serve customers better.

fruits and vegetables, and lived on the southeast side. A group of Calabrians lived northeast of the Sicilians. They worked for the gas and rubber companies and would leave two restaurants as monuments to their presence. Scattered on the north side were immigrants from Basilicata, Campania, Calabria, Lombardy, and the Friuli. They were grocers, painters, musicians, tailors, barbers, shoemakers, printers, and terrazzo/marble workers.

Italians already resided in Indianapolis before the Civil War. Of the nineteen reported in the 1860 manuscript census, one family of seven was in the grocery business and three others earned a living as "plaster of paris image makers."[41] Later fruit peddlers set up stands at important downtown intersections. Several natives of Genoa succeeded each other in operating a confectionery/ice-cream store at 11 South Illinois Street from 1877 to 1900. The federal census of 1870 reported 18 Italian born in Indianapolis, indicating no increase during the previous decade. By 1900, however, 282 lived there, with the number growing to 658 in 1910, 754 in 1920, and 794 in 1930.[42] A sizable portion of this increase was due to the arrival of Frank Mascari, a twenty-five-year-old fisherman from Termini. An elderly widow on Merrill Street reported:

> He was my uncle and godfather. He came to America
> to try his luck after his father got a Black Hand threat
> and a boat full of fishermen who were his friends
> never returned.

After investigating the business possibilities in New Orleans and Louisville, Mascari visited Indianapolis in 1882 and was attracted to the conservative, predominantly middle-class city with a growing population. He opened his fruit store on Virginia Avenue south of East Washington Street. Before long, his three brothers and his brother-in-law arrived. In the 1890s wives, children, sisters, and friends appeared, and by 1910 those not related by blood would probably be related through marriage.[43] Mascari's prognosis was accurate: Indianapolis was an economic opportunity for Sicilians and other Italians. By the outbreak of World War I, Italians dominated the city's produce business. Of the fifty-four fruit and vegetable dealers operating in 1910, thirty-three were Italian.[44] They occupied many of the stands in City Market and sold produce from pushcarts and wagons drawn along the curb around the Marion County Courthouse. One of their best-selling commodities was the banana, which they had shipped up from New Orleans on the Illinois Central rail line. The Italians reputedly introduced this exotic fruit to the Indianapolis market, and several of them were nicknamed the "banana kings."

The appearance of the automobile gave the ambitious Italian greater mobility. Merchandise could be trucked to customers at curbside in outlying areas like Broad Ripple, Franklin, and Greenfield. If a steady business was possible, the Italian relocated his family to other Indiana communities like Noblesville, Bloomington, Greensburg, Lafayette, Terre Haute, Greencastle, Wabash, Marion, or Anderson, thus establishing a produce network throughout central Indiana.

Northsiders also contributed to Indianapolis life. Grocer Ferdinando Montani from Calvello, Potenza Province, had five sons who were musicians. They helped organize the musicians union local and performed at many public events and private social gatherings. Fresco painter Giovanni Gioscio decorated churches and public buildings in Indiana, the Midwest, and elsewhere. His paintings still exist in old St. Joseph's in Indianapolis and in Catholic churches in Connersville and Avilla. Calabrian tailors fitted the carriage trade at Kahn's Tailoring. Friulani, some of whom had worked at Clinton before the decline of coal mining, installed marble altars, church mosaics, and terrazzo floors everywhere around central Indiana.

We should note that not all Indiana Italians settled in cities or towns. Nationally, 12 percent of the Italian immigrants were attracted to agriculture. As early as 1860 some Italians were farmers in Ripley County. In later decades, the point of attraction appears to be the farmland around North Judson in Wayne Township, Starke County. The number of ditches that traverse the township, lying southeast of the Kankakee River, indicates the former existence of the marshland that Tonti observed during his 1679 expedition. Access to North Judson was easy. Four rail lines crossed there, providing connections to Chicago, South Bend, and Logansport. In 1900, 10 Italian born lived in the county; by 1910, 26; and in 1920, 112.

*William Boilini family farm at North Judson, ca. 1930. Left to right: William Boilini, Jr., Joseph Mordini, Malfesa Picchietti Mordini, John Boilini, Theresa Picchietti Boilini, William Boilini, and Frank Boilini.*

Several families from Modena and Lucca settled east and south of North Judson: Picchietti, Boilini, Bertucci, Amidei, Seghetti, and Simoni.[45] They grew onions and potatoes for an urban market and shipped cheese daily by rail to Chicago retailers. The Italians were attracted by fresh air and the chance to be one's own boss. Many, however, supplemented their income from truck farming by working for a railroad or opening a store in town.

Italian immigrant success in Indiana might be measured by the responses of Italians entering or departing the United States: "To what state are you going?" Or "What state are you leaving?" From 1908 to 1914 inclusive, 1,560 continentals (from Piedmont to Venetia) headed for Indiana while 720 left the state for Italy; in the same period, 3,318 peninsulars (from Liguria to Sicily) looked to Hoosierland, while 1,556 returned to the Old Country.[46] With a repatriation rate at around 46 percent, Indiana retained its Italian immigrants better than the nation, whose rate was over 60 percent. The difference may be attributed to a favorable business climate that encouraged the ambitious immigrant to seek opportunities for self-employment outside the factory. Interestingly, no interviewee in Indianapolis could remember anyone who departed for Italy permanently.

### Italians and the New Environment, 1890–1950

Considering the total number of Italian immigrants that the new environment of the Hoosier state attracted, it is noteworthy that two celebrities, Luigi Gregori (1819–1896) and Mother Mary Magdalen Bentivoglio (1834–1905), were part of that migration.

Gregori was a Vatican art cataloger and papal portraitist. The Royal Academy in his native city of Bologna awarded him a gold medal for a historical oil painting. Then in 1874 Father Edward Sorin, founder of the University of

Notre Dame, on the recommendation of two cardinals, employed Gregori to decorate the new Sacred Heart Church. Gregori immediately became popular with visitors who enjoyed watching him paint the Stations of the Cross and a series of biblical scenes in the church. Sorin also gave Gregori the task of decorating the inside of the Golden Dome and the corridor walls of the present administration building. He painted on mixing bowls in the campus kitchen until he mastered the technique of producing an undistorted figure on a curved surface. For the corridors he undertook a series of twelve murals depicting scenes from the life of Christopher Columbus, using administrators and faculty members as models. The largest mural, measuring nineteen feet in width by eleven and a half feet in height, showed the Discoverer's return and reception at the Spanish court. The United States Post Office chose it as one of the subjects in its first commemorative stamp series, the Columbian Exposition issue of 1893. Visitors to Notre Dame's administration building and campus church are confronted by Gregori's artistic skills reflected in his paintings, which remain minutely perfect and vivid despite the years. Here an Italian master worked to enrich the Hoosier artistic heritage.[47]

Countess Annetta Bentivoglio was a member of the well-known Bologna noble family. In 1864 she was admitted to the Poor Clares religious community and took the name Mary Magdalen. When the Italian army occupied Rome (1870), Mother Mary Magdalen immigrated to the United States to establish an overseas branch that could become a refuge in case the Italian government suppressed her order. In 1897 she and seven sisters established a Poor Clare monastery in Evansville with the full support of Bishop Francis Silas Chatard of Vincennes-Indianapolis, one of Mother Mary Magdalen's Rome acquaintances. Eight years later she died in the Ohio River city, where her body remains incorrupt.[48]

While Gregori painted and Mother Mary Magdalen prayed, Italian workers and peasants arrived in the state to market their labor in mines, mills, shops, quarries, and stores. They immediately settled together on the same streets, probably within the shadow of their employer or the means of transportation to their employer. This was the Italian village in the Hoosier city.

The Italian language supposedly brought immigrants together. The fact was that only the educated few spoke the Tuscan dialect, the Italian literary language. "There were two kinds of Italians in our neighborhood," reported an Indianapolis lady whose father was born in Termini. "There were the *paesani,* the ones who came from our town, and the *strani,* the ones who came from somewhere else. My mother didn't like *strani.*" An East Chicago laboratory technician, whose father came from the Marches, said that the Italian kids he played with always spoke English. "We couldn't understand their dialect, so we had to use English." "I don't know if they came from the same town as my folks, but they must have come from some place nearby, because we could understand them," recalled a longtime Logansport

*On 31 October 1920 Italian and other immigrants gathered on the lawn of the Indiana Statehouse to dedicate a monument to the first Italian to see the New World.*

resident whose parents came from Civitella Alfedena in the Abruzzi. "My mother always amazed me," said a Clinton college graduate whose parents were Piedmontese. "She could do business with all the Italians, even the Sicilians." "John Bova Conti was an educated man," his grandson, an Indianapolis butcher, boasted. "He knew three languages, English, Italian, and Sicilian."

Italian immigrants, because of the use of regional dialects, were always reminded of these differences. Interestingly, these differences were transmitted to their American-born descendants. "There weren't many Sicilians around Clinton," a Terre Haute resident recalled. "We always viewed them as the lowest of the low." Italians in Mishawaka formed two neighborhoods: Calabrians settled north of the St. Joseph River while Romagnols, Piacentini, Venetians, and other northerners lived south of the river. They generally worked for Mishawaka Woolen Manufacturing Company (later renamed Uniroyal, makers of Ball-Band footware), conveniently located on the riverbank. The northerners were welders or bosses. "They always thought they were better than us," a Calabrian complained, "it's true, though, that they had more education." "You want me to serve those Sicilians?" exclaimed a priest from the Marches when the bishop asked him to establish a parish on the southeast side of Indianapolis. "Never trust a *Napoletan*," a Logansport real estate saleslady quoted her Abruzzese mother, "they bargain even with God." "We were about the only *Romani* in all of East Chicago," boasted a lady born near the Italian capital. An East Chicago steelworker believed: "It was always easier to get promoted or a better job if you were a *paesano* of the boss." "I heard that Sicilians carry guns in their boots. Is that true?" wondered an Indianapolis Italian whose father was born near Naples. A church volunteer, a member of one of three Roman families who settled in Elkhart, grimaced and said: "I'm tired hearing about those *Foggian'*. Italians from other places came here too!" "We were going to have guests and my dad wanted to serve wine during Prohibition," an Indianapolis non-Sicilian northsider remembered. "We went down to see the Sicilians, because we knew they made their own. But none would sell us any."

The family, hometown, church, social club, natural leaders, and the experience of the workplace provided unity and stability for the minority village within the Hoosier city.

For centuries the family served Italians as the center of social life, a social welfare agency, and a bulwark against social injustice and government tyranny. So it was transported across the ocean: brother enticed brother, a son persuaded an elderly parent to immigrate, a cousin knew that a familiar face and friendly handshake would welcome

him to the new land. The major social events were the parties after baptisms, weddings, and funerals, when relatives and friends gathered to share in the joy or grief of the occasion over pasta, wine, and pastries. Given the number of births, marriages, and deaths, these parties were frequent. The purchase of the first car indicated new prosperity and permitted one to show off by visiting relatives who had settled outside the village. All was sealed by attending the family picnic replete with food, breeze, ball, and snooze. Even today faded photographs of these events are fondly preserved.

Criticism of family members was common within the family circle, but criticism was never to be repeated to outsiders. Public criticism of a family member was resented. Naturally, sibling rivalry existed, and parents might have a favorite offspring. "Whenever I had a dispute with my brother," a Logansport church secretary reported, "my mother and dad always supported my brother." "Italian families always were that way," continued her female cousin. Furthermore, the oldest son was second in authority only to the father and took his role whenever the father was absent. Sometimes family loyalty could be abused. Frank Mascari's niece recalled that her father was once hurriedly summoned to a brother's house. "He found him lying on the floor with a gun to his head, saying that he would use it unless someone gave his son $1,500 to pay a gambling debt. My father was soft; he gave him the money, which they never paid back."

Women also contributed to family solidarity. At least in public, they supported male decision making and impressed the hierarchy of authority and obedience on the children. Privately, however, the situation might be different. "And who do you think wears the pants in that house?" was a common inquiry about family dynamics before women wore slacks and shorts.

"What my dad said was the law, although my mother would have her say first," an East Chicago bricklayer remembered about his Italian Protestant mother. "When he wanted to cut her off, he would say 'Missus, *cuoc' le fagiol'* (cook the beans!). That would do it, and she'd go in the kitchen." A couple born in Sinagra, Messina Province, living on a farm outside Crown Point, was asked, "Who's the boss in this family?" "I am," announced the ninety-two-year-old husband proudly. "Bullasheet" responded his smiling, eighty-nine-year-old mate.

Part of the woman's authority arose from her childbearing and economic contribution. No husband could prove virility without his wife giving birth to sons. The amount of income that the wife produced by providing room, board, and clean clothes for single workers in Clinton, Gary, and Fort Wayne could match her husband's income. If he was self-employed, she frequently worked with him in the shop, store, or stand.

Marriages were generally arranged by the fathers of the couple, sometimes by maiden aunts, godmothers, or family friends. A Mishawaka Calabrian lamented:

> I took my mother to visit her lady-friend who had a daughter. When we left, I said to the daughter, "I hope you can come to the dance coming up." My mother told my father that I liked the daughter and he spoke to her father about me.

He has been married, but not happily, for a half century.

A seventeen-year-old Indianapolis girl was sitting on her front porch when a boy, just returned from the army during World War I, spied her and asked his father: "Who's that girl?" His father made arrangements, but she balked for a long time until her father threatened her. "After we were married, he'd go to Cincinnati to pick up produce. He had another girl there," she recalled. "When he mistreated me and was away so often, I went to the priest. Those Irish priests at the Chancery just said, 'Why didn't you just say no to your father?' They didn't understand that he would have killed me."

Adults could use the direct approach to marriage. An elderly Indianapolis lady reminisced:

> My father was left with three kids after my mother was killed in an explosion. Friends told him about a widow. So one Saturday afternoon, on the way home from the Market, he stopped at her house, knocked on the door, and said, "My children need a mother. I want to marry you. Will you have me?" She looked him over and invited him to come back for supper. My father and stepmother were happily married for many years.

Marriages were sometimes arranged to keep family wealth in a limited circle. One Terminese father married all of his sons and daughters to the sons and daughters of a *paesano* in Columbus, Ohio. Sometimes marriages were arranged with relatives, and church records show dispensations for consanguinity. Marriages occurred between children of business partners and fellow factory workers. A marriage arranged with a richer family was very desirable. By the late 1920s, however, children were rebelling against the system. So fathers were forced to accept dating—preferably in groups or with a chaperone—to see if the couple liked each other. By 1940 the traditional practice had pretty much broken down.

Offspring for whom marriages were not arranged generally married non-Italians. One lady's father had been a loner among Indianapolis produce merchants.

"My brothers didn't marry Italians," she pointed out. She herself had chosen to marry a man of Italian ancestry, but he was from out of state. "My husband was Scotch-Irish," a Bedford informant said. "He could never understand why my family always kept coming over, and we had so much company. It got to the point that we had words over it." A woman of Sicilian origin married a Kentuckian by choice. "He had nothing," she said. A friend cattily laughed: "He thought Italians in the produce business had money, but he found it tough working in the Market."

Many arranged marriages were successful, and romance blossomed after the ceremony. Divorces occurred infrequently, and only among descendants of immigrants does one find divorce with its legal entanglements and emotional complications. Although divorce was unusual, womanizing was not, especially with non-Italian women. The penalty for ogling another Italian's wife or daughter was severe, but non-Italians did not react that way. An Elkhart railroader, recalling the section gangs, concluded: "Like the Americans, our men had problems with blondes and booze." A priest, however, who heard the confessions of Italians pointed out: "The girls around here are all pretty clean."

Except for a few Waldensians in Clinton, Italians were usually baptized Catholics. Many of them, however, were nonpracticing because of anticlericalism and identification of the church with exploiting landowners. Some northerners in Mishawaka and Fort Wayne were anarchists or socialists ideologically opposed to Catholicism, but most were simply uninvolved in church life except at times of "hatch, match, and dispatch"—birth, marriage, and death.

The Catholic Church responded slowly to the presence of Italians in Indiana. Ultimately, four parishes were

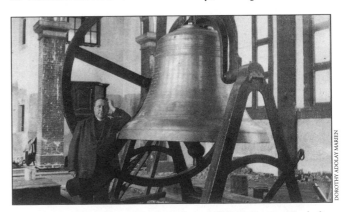

*Father Marino Priori, founding pastor of Holy Rosary Catholic Parish in Indianapolis, inspects the 7,000-pound San Salvador bell before its installation in the west campanile (1924). Readers of his* Eternal Light *magazine donated the bell to the church.*

DOROTHY ADOLAY MARIEN

established to serve them: Holy Rosary in Indianapolis, St. Joseph in Fort Wayne, St. Anthony in Gary, and Immaculate Conception in East Chicago. All were organized to counter Protestant missionary zeal or because of Catholic lay agitation.

Catholic authorities in Indianapolis reacted soon after the Methodists began providing Bible lessons for Italian children and arranged for the Sicilian-born minister Nicolò Accomando to open a mission there. In 1909 Father Marino Priori, born in Montefalcone Appennino, Ascoli Piceno Province, founded Holy Rosary parish. Two years later Methodist mission membership peaked at seventy-two, and Priori hurriedly began construction of a brick church and opened a parish school. Interdenominational rivalry over the city's Italians ended in 1920 when the mission closed because its members moved to other cities and national subsidies ceased.[49]

St. Joseph's Mission for Italians was founded by Father Anthony Petrilli in a two-story house on Bass Street near Fairfield Avenue on Fort Wayne's south side in 1913. The inspiration behind the mission came from Loreto J. Starace, Neapolitan lawyer and journalist, who, on his own initiative, assembled Italians to sing hymns and pray together since they had no church. Only when Starace pleaded with the bishop to save the faith of the city's Italian shopkeepers, railroaders, and factory workers was the bishop sufficiently moved to found St. Joseph's.[50] Because Starace returned to Italy for military duty upon the outbreak of World War I, Petrilli lost a strong ally to continue the mission. The local pastor did not want an Italian church erected close to his church, so he persuaded the bishop to move Petrilli's mission west of St. Mary's River. In this location the church attracted fewer Italians because it was removed from their neighborhood. Discouraged by this situation and his lack of acceptance by diocesan clergy, Petrilli returned to his native

*Father Anthony Petrilli (right with straw hat) and St. Joseph parishioners inspect their church during its construction (1916).*

Montefalcone Valfortore, Benevento Province, in 1919. Two years later Petrilli's successor convinced the bishop to suppress the parish.[51]

Several false starts and no financial support from the Catholic bishop convinced Gary Italians to petition the Episcopal bishop of Northern Indiana to organize an Italian parish. In response, Accomando, now an Episcopal priest, founded St. Antonio Mission at 19th Avenue and Adams Street in 1917. The Catholic bishop, who had branded Italian immigrants "not the better class" and ungrateful for the efforts in their behalf,[52] now concluded that Gary was "a hot-bed of proselytism."[53] He granted permission to Father John Baptist DeVille, native of Moena in Trentino-Alto Adige, to open St. Anthony chapel to serve Italians and Hispanics at the new Gary-Alerding Settlement House, 15th Avenue and Van Buren. DeVille mounted a successful effort to reclaim the Latin Episcopalians, but by the time Accomando closed St. Antonio's in 1927, Italians were already abandoning the central district for better, outlying neighborhoods.

Carmelite sisters arrived in East Chicago to open a children's home and evangelize spiritually lukewarm immigrants in 1913. Fearful of Methodist efforts in the city, the sisters successfully persuaded forty-five Italians to petition the bishop for their own church. Italian Precious Blood fathers, recently expelled from the Mexican missions, opened the storefront Sacred Heart Mission near 148th Street and Tod Avenue. Here they remained until 1927, when they closed the mission unexpectedly and returned to Italy.

The pride of East Chicago Italians was hurt because they had no church. After all, other national groups from Poles and Lithuanians to Hungarians and Romanians had their own churches. Local leaders traveled to Fort Wayne to petition the bishop for a priest. He sent Father Michael A. Campagna, born at Castro dei Volsci in Lazio, to organize Immaculate Conception parish in 1933.[54] Campagna's personal magnetism resulted in popular enthusiasm among unemployed masons and parishioners, who salvaged bricks from repaved city streets and an abandoned brickyard to build a church and hall at 149th Street and Olcott Avenue within two years.

The irony of church as village symbol is that Italians did not provide sufficient financial support for its maintenance. Since the property of the church in Italy was maintained by the state or a wealthy local patron, Italians did not have a tradition of voluntary contributions. No Italian parish in Indiana depended solely on its own parishioners for economic survival, and, even then, both Priori and Campagna left their pastorates under a financial cloud. The power of symbol is revealed in the Protestants' most successful effort among Hoosier Italians, the Hill Crest

Community Center at 8th and Oak streets in Clinton. Hill Crest was a Presbyterian mission founded in 1911 and merged with the downtown congregation in 1962.

Italians found attending Mass at Sacred Heart Catholic Church inconvenient since the church was built outside their neighborhood in the older part of town. The Irish-born pastor always insisted on Mass attendance and church membership before conducting a funeral, an important transitional event in a community where mining fatalities were not uncommon. Popular disaffection increased, and on the night of 16 November 1909 five men planted ninety-two sticks of stolen dynamite in the facade of the five-month-old church. Because only three sticks exploded the building was spared total destruction.[55] Two months after the explosion, on 21 January 1910, businessman and elder John W. Robb proposed that property be purchased for an Italian Presbyterian mission in the North End, the Italian neighborhood. Soon Calogero Benedetto Papa, Italian-born lawyer, arrived to serve as minister. The Catholics sent Priori of Indianapolis to canvass the neighborhood, but to no avail. Hill Crest Mission, designed by Philadelphia architect Isaac Pursell, was dedicated on 29 October 1911.[56] Financially, Hill Crest was in the same situation as all other Italian religious institutions in Indiana. Most of its support would come from friends and outside organizations.

Very dedicated lay workers succeeded Papa, who departed for economic reasons in 1913. They gave Hill Crest its future. "My parents were not devout Catholics. The Reverend [L. O.] Brown and Miss [Elizabeth] Pfander contacted us and showed interest in our needs and so we went there," explained a longtime member. A Terre Haute resident recalled that "Miss Pfander once brought us Christmas gifts where we wouldn't have had any. My mother was very impressed because they were not used but new toys." Then in 1922 ground was broken east of Hill Crest for a gymnasium addition, the only church gymnasium in town. "It was the center of social activity in our neighborhood," informants declared. "Our friends went there and so did we." "They stressed settlement house activities, including sewing classes, basketball playing, and Americanization classes," reported a retired school principal whose parents came from Asiago, Vicenza Province. "It was a real social center where you could go with your friends."[57] Unlike the situation in Gary where Catholics worked to reclaim Italian Episcopalians, later pastors of Sacred Heart parish took the soft approach by generally ignoring Hill Crest. This attitude may have been the legacy of the 1909 dynamiting incident that resulted from the use of the hard approach.

Through World War II Hill Crest leadership effectively used its social and recreational programs to introduce

*Clinton's Hill Crest Presbyterian Mission conducted English and citizenship classes for Italian and other immigrants in the early 1920s. Judge G. E. Bingham and teachers Mollie Gohn (left) and Dorothy Kruzan sit before the citizenship group at the Vermillion County Courthouse in Newport.*

the North End's young people to its religious program.[58] Not one contact mentioned any theological conflict with Sacred Heart, and, when specifically questioned on that point, returned to basketball, caring staff, and picnics as reasons for their interest in Hill Crest. In 1953, 275 enrolled in Sunday School classes; in 1956 church membership peaked at 173.

A desire for spiritual direction could bind a people, but so could the need for insurance coverage and social activity. In some cases the mutual aid society or social club supplemented the church as a symbol of community unity, in other cases the society or club was itself that symbol. Italians organized a society, club, or lodge in every one of their settlements no matter what its size. The mutual aid society normally provided income during a member's illness and benefits for his family after his death. An Italian government survey reported that almost 30 percent of the 1,400 Italian mutual aid societies in foreign countries existed in the United States, and in 1908 one-fourth of them (102) were located in states that surrounded Chicago.[59] Unlike those organized in other states, however, Indiana's societies or clubs were seldom religious. Probably the state's first club was Indianapolis's Società italiana di Mutuo Soccorso Umberto Primo (Humbert I Italian Mutual Aid Society), already organized by 1891. The earliest act of incorporation found in the State Archives is that of the Association of the Italian Cristoforo Colombo Benevolenza Society No. 2 of Clinton, Indiana, notarized 23 April 1896. Four clubs still exist as symbols of *Italianità*. Two of them organized in Mishawaka where no one ever proposed the erection of an Italian church. A third was formed after it became clear an Italian church would not be organized (Elkhart). The fourth, in East Chicago, helped found the church and viewed it as a second anchor for the Italian community.

Loggia Cesare Battisti Musicale (Cesare Battisti Musical Lodge) was organized in East Chicago (1919) by Augusto Vespaziani, Louis Ferrini, and Leo Bonaventura as a social club sponsoring a band. Members soon affiliated with the Unione Siciliana (founded 1895, renamed Italo-American National Union in 1925), a Chicago-based fraternal order that provided life insurance. Formerly when a friend died, lodge members passed the hat around in order to pay for the funeral and provide something for survivors. Shortly thereafter, sick benefits were added to the members' coverage. Now social activity was combined with a patriotic name and insurance protection. In 1933 the leadership of the Cesare Battisti Lodge advocated the establishment of a permanent Italian parish. In 1941 the lodge purchased its own club rooms at 148th Street and Olcott Avenue, only one block north of Father Campagna's church. The lodge dedicated its own hall on the club room site in 1956. When asked which institution—the lodge or church—played a greater role in the life of the Italian community, a retired bricklayer, who was a member of both Immaculate Conception and Battisti, replied unhesitatingly: "The lodge." Indeed, the church did close for financial reasons in 1994 while the lodge contemplated moving to larger facilities in a better location. Six lodge members have been honored by the Italian Republic. Battisti events continue to attract crowds, and it is one of the most active Italian clubs in the state.

The Italian American Relief Association was founded on Harrison Street in Elkhart probably in 1916 (incorporated in 1926). Originally funds were collected to start an Italian church. When that did not prove feasible the funds were used to start the club. The membership decided that if the club ever folded, its property would pass to St. Vincent's parish. "Although many members came from my hometown," a retired railroader born in Volturara Appula, Foggia Province, recalled, "the club was open to all Italians. We paid sick benefits and attended funerals. We paid for a member's funeral not by collecting dues, but by visiting the home of the deceased after the funeral and each member donating $10." Members also took turns attending a sick member overnight to give his family relief and time to sleep. Otherwise, drinking, smoking, and card playing were the ordinary pastimes. In early May a banquet or some ceremony marks the feast day of Maria SS. della Sanità (Our Lady of Good Health). "She's the patron saint of Volturara, but other Italians join in," pointed out a club member of Calabrian background.

The Edmondo DeAmicis Mutual Aid Society was founded in 1917 at the home of the Gianesi family, 306 West 10th Street, Mishawaka. It provided sick and death benefits to its sixty-three charter members. Guglielmo Ricci was its first president. In 1930 the DeAmicis Club constructed its meeting hall at 11th and Spring streets. Besides insurance coverage, the club offered members social activities such as dances every Saturday night and a chance to exhibit their physical abilities in the athletic rivalries with neighborhood Belgian organizations. Originally the club was drawn from among the northern Italians who lived south of the St. Joseph River, but later some northside Calabrians also joined.

The other major southside organization was the Italian Liberty Club, organized by John Nicolini, with 45 members in 1921. It was noted for its brass band and its members' interest in current affairs. "They were more political than anyone else," a northsider commented, "and some of their members were on the radical side." Club rooms were located at 401 West 9th Street. In 1953, to unite all southside men in one organization, the Liberty Club with its reportedly 235 members merged with the DeAmicis Club.[60] Edward Baldoni was the first president after consolidation.

The Società italiana di Mutuo Soccorso Maria SS. DiLoreto (Our Lady of Loreto Italian Mutual Aid Society), Mishawaka, was organized in 1933 by natives of Platì in Calabria. A *paesano* had died penniless and had to be buried at public expense. Platesi felt ashamed that this had happened to one of their own. So Frank Portolese and Anthony Catanzarite went door-to-door to recruit members for a mutual aid club north of the St. Joseph River. At first they met in members' homes, then in a rented room on Battell Avenue. Then eleven members remortgaged their homes as collateral for a twelve thousand dollar loan to build a clubhouse at 914 Division in 1941.

Simultaneous with all these organizational moves to achieve strength by utilizing the financial and social resources of their community, Italian immigrants also sought to improve their position vis-à-vis the broader community through political action and affiliation with national organizations. Sometimes the mutual aid society became a springboard for a political candidate, and sometimes the society decided to affiliate with the Sons of Italy or the Italo-American National Union.

Italians ran for political office. The first successful candidate appears to be Pietro Savio, Clinton councilman. Leo Bonaventura, born in Sinagra, Sicily, and first president of the Battisti Lodge, served as East Chicago constable from 1912 to 1924. In 1921 Louis Salzarulo, born in Bisaccia near Avellino and Sons of Italy lodge member, was elected to represent the Italian neighborhood in the Richmond City Council despite Ku Klux Klan activity. Banker Louis Ferrini, born at Tivoli near Rome, was an East Chicago councilman from 1926 to 1930.

In Gary, after the 1919–20 steel strike and the end of precitizenship voting privileges in Indiana, several steps were taken to politicize Italians. At first they voted the way the *padrone* or the foreman wished. The candidate whom their friends preferred was elected, but Italians received nothing in return, complained Nicolò Accomando in his news magazine. To counteract Klan impact and to safeguard Italian interests, Accomando supported the candidacy of two lawyers, James F. Pace for state representative and Donald (Donato) A. Lepore for justice of the peace, in the 1926 primary election. Although both candidates were defeated, Accomando saw a silver lining. They had received sufficient votes to indicate eloquently that, with good organization and intelligent leadership, Italians could do much locally and statewide.[61]

Besides organizing a Sons of Italy lodge in 1923, Gary Italians also organized the Roosevelt League. Its purpose was to obtain recognition among non-Italians of the contribution that Italians made to Indiana's political life. Its first officers were Dr. Antonio Giorgi, Pace, lawyer Paul Giorgi, and Accomando.[62] Like most Italian immigrant voters at the time, the Roosevelt League was Republican. Allegiance to the GOP became difficult to defend when it became obvious that the anti-immigrant Klan worked closely with corrupt Republicans like Gov. Edward L. Jackson. Nationally, Republicans were identified with President Herbert C. Hoover and the Great Depression. In November 1934, twenty-three-year-old Democrat Daniel Perrotta was elected to one of the nine seats on the Gary City Council. He became a reformer, wishing to clean up the city's vice. Although Perrotta had gangster connections, he publicly demanded an investigation into organized crime. In late September 1935 he charged that high city and county officials supported organized gambling. A few weeks later Perrotta was beaten, shot, and dumped along a country road. Perrotta, the son of an immigrant contractor, received one of the largest funerals in Gary history, but his murder was never solved.[63] This is not exactly what proponents of the Roosevelt League had desired.

The political awakening of Hoosier Italians resulted in efforts to form a Sons of Italy grand lodge for Indiana. In July 1925 representatives of five lodges assembled in Indianapolis. Representing Richmond were Luigi Salzarulo, Francesco DeLaura, and Francesco Marino. From the Indianapolis lodge came Francesco DeGiulio, Angelo Mannella, and Nunzio Mazza. Indiana Harbor sent Alberto Guerrera, Pietro Cozza, and Leo Bonaventura. Hammond's representatives were John Filecia, Elia Barrelli, and D'Onofrio Maggi. The new Gary lodge was represented by Ferdinando Marando, Angelo Largura, and Martino Mazzari. These politicians, businessmen, and professionals were the elite of the Italian communities around the state. DeGiulio of Indianapolis was chosen president promoter and Salzarulo of Richmond secretary promoter.[64]

The movement to form a grand lodge was slowed by the simultaneous effort to federate all mutual aid societies in the state under the name Sons of Italy. A second set of talks, however, was conducted in East Chicago in October 1925. For the next several years, the major actions keeping the idea of a grand lodge alive were the East Chicago lodge's polling the other lodges on the topic in 1928 and Silvester Yaney of Fort Wayne proposing the formation of a grand lodge in 1940. Efforts succeeded only after a meeting in Gary twelve years later. The first grand convention was held at Fort Wayne in June 1953. Dominic J. Colone of Fort Wayne was elected grand venerable.

Membership in societies, clubs, and lodges ran from ten to several hundred. Success usually depended on the willingness of members to serve as officers and officers to arrange activities. Personality conflicts, the traditional fear of "somebody's trying to act big," Italian regional differences, and Indiana parochialism handicapped the effectiveness of these organizations. Hard feelings and schisms occurred in the women's groups as well. The introduction of Social Security under President Franklin D. Roosevelt and the younger generation's residing outside the old neighborhoods resulted in reduced interest and the dissolution of many of these groups.

Nearly every Italian community in the state had *padroni* or *prominenti;* some had both. A *padrone* (plural *padroni;* the boss) was someone who knew English and had strong connections with the political or economic establishment. These connections were used to assist immigrants to find and retain jobs as well as take care of legal obligations (e.g., court appearances and citizenship applications). In some cases the *padrone* actively recruited workers in his native town and paid the transatlantic fares for these recruits. In other cases the immigrant approached the *padrone* when he wanted a better job.

Generally the *padrone's* services were not free. He expected a percentage of his client's salary for a stated or unstated period of time; or he required that the fare advanced should be repaid with interest; or he received the salaries of his recruits and paid them what he deemed proper; or he accepted a fee for using his knowledge and relations with government agencies for the client's benefit. This kind of *padrone* existed in Indianapolis, Logansport, Fort Wayne, and Mishawaka.

The *prominente* (plural *prominenti;* the conspicuous one) existed in every Italian community. Generally professional in occupation, but maybe a priest or saloon keeper, a person with some education or observable leadership qualities or wisdom, the *prominente* was frequently respected, feared, and envied simultaneously. The stereotypical *prominente* had a pasta belly and wore a suit and tie. At lodge meetings members deferred to him, and at lodge activities he was identified by the ribbon or sash he wore across his chest. Ask any knowledgeable immigrant or descendant and he can easily identify *prominenti.*

The minority village had its internal unity, but the dominant society defined its parameters and set the rate or degree of acceptance of immigrants in Hoosierdom. Fortunately, Italians were neither so numerous, unique, nor threatening that a dominant society with a tendency toward Know-Nothingism could reject their presence. Suspicions, however, did exist toward newcomers of foreign birth, foreign language, dark skin, peculiar customs, and the Catholic religion.

Italians were particularly proud of their participation on the Allied side during World War I. When the Rome government called for the return of military-age men, immigrants in Lake and Vermillion counties responded.[65] When the names of Americans killed and wounded were published, some of those names were of Italian origin. A Gary soldier named Saladina lost his life; several veterans were memorialized by a plaque in the Battisti Lodge meeting hall in East Chicago. An Italian general's portrait, Italian flags, and Italian names among those who served are found in the World War Memorial at Indianapolis. Italian immigrants financed the bust of Christopher Columbus on the grounds of the Indiana Statehouse in 1920. Italians were on the road toward integration into American society.

The euphoria evaporated rapidly. While Italians did not experience violent confrontations with the Ku Klux Klan or face-offs of the magnitude of those in Bedford in 1908, they experienced petty harassment and limited job opportunities. Parades of hooded men intimidated them. "Since many of us were self-employed, the Klan didn't make much difference. But if you wanted a job teaching or in government, there were never any openings," reported an Indianapolis northsider. "Everybody made their own wine, some made beer and whiskey," remembered a Clinton lady whose father was born near Turin. "Once they broke into our house, made all of us sit while they broke the wine barrel open and let the wine spill out. And then they even broke the bottles. My father had an idea who it was and always called them 'horse thieves.'"

"The only time I remember a clash with the Klan was during a parade on horseback in Clinton," a former school principal said. "A Klanner dismounted to cane an Italian drunk sitting on the curb with his head down. He didn't remove his hat when the American flag passed. At that point, one of the policemen, a big Italian, stepped forward to protect the drunk and said, 'If you touch this man, I will let these people,' nodding toward us Italians standing around, 'mob you.' The Klanner withdrew."

A Logansport woman reported the difficulties her father, an auto mechanic, faced in the 1920s. "He lost a number of jobs in garages because he was an Italian Catholic. The boss would say, 'Your work's okay, but the Klan doesn't like people like you working here.'" Her cousin, a Kokomo investment broker, continued: "My father told me that Klanners paraded in their robes on horseback. One of his friends who ran a store noticed the fancy boots one of the Klanners was wearing. Several days later, a customer came in his store wearing the same fancy boots he saw in the parade. He chased him out of the place with a meat cleaver." "Sure, they paraded here," said an East Chicago school administrator, "but that's about all." "If you wanted a better job, it was good if you were a Mason," concluded a retired steelworker.

During the anti-immigrant Klan era, Italians not only sought political power through organization, as already recounted, but also gloried in the achievements of the Benito Mussolini regime in Italy. How much of this was nationalistic pride and how much of it was compensation for insecurity in the new environment is difficult to ascertain. Of course, socialists in Clinton and atheists in Mishawaka were not supporters of *Il Duce,* but they were a minority. When an Italian leftist in St. Joseph County ripped the Italian flag because it bore the royal coat of arms, a South Bend restaurateur became a hero in immigrant circles for beating him so badly that the leftist's arm and leg were broken.

In these years immigrants saw no conflict between democracy in America and Fascism in Italy. In 1924 the Richmond Sons of Italy lodge voted $2.50 to buy an American flag and place it alongside the Italian flag *come rispetto di questa nazione* (as a sign of respect for this country).[66] The following year members voted to donate $10 to the Italian government to help it pay its war debt to the United States.[67] Masses for the repose of deceased members of the Italian royal family were celebrated at Holy Rosary Church in Indianapolis several times between 1926 and 1933. "I remember taking the train to Vincennes with my father for the dedication of the Vigo statue in 1935," an Indianapolis grocer's son recalled. "They played the 'Star-Spangled Banner' and then 'La Giovanezza.'" During the Italian song several men actually raised their right arms in the Fascist salute."

The Fascist government encouraged nostalgia for Italy and Italo-American solidarity. At the Discovery Day dinner (1932), in the presence of Mayor Reginald H. Sullivan, five Indianapolis Italians were awarded the Italian medal of merit: tailor Frank DeJulio, lawyer Harry E. Raitano, tailor Angelo Mannella, produce merchant Nunzio Mazza, and restaurateur Fred Iozzo.[68] The person responsible for all this Italian government activity was the distinguished surgeon, Dr. Vincent A. Lapenta, royal Italian consular agent at Indianapolis and a knight officer of the crown of Italy.

Immigrants applauded the acquisition of Ethiopia to benefit poor Italy (1936), but the growing rapprochement with Nazi Germany led Hoosier Italians to question the Duce's farsightedness. The divorce of American freedom from Fascist dictatorship occurred dramatically on 11 December 1941, when Germany and Italy declared war on the United States. On that same day, far from general staff

headquarters and diplomatic missions, Sons of Italy lodge members met at their clubhouse in Richmond, Indiana, to discuss whether they should change the name of their organization.[69] On 22 January 1942 the minutes of the lodge meeting were recorded in Italian for the last time.[70]

The war had an immediate effect on Hoosier Italians in other ways. Those who were not American citizens and were identified with Italy were taken into custody by the FBI. Nationally, four thousand were arrested; in Indianapolis the best known was Lapenta.[71] For years he had been invited to public forums to discuss Italy's role in international affairs. He immigrated to America in 1907 and settled in Indianapolis four years later. In South Bend the FBI arrested Francesco Rizzo, an Italian naval captain married to a Mishawaka girl. He was the owner of the El Tropico nightclub. He had recently addressed the Congressional Club, but had wrongly predicted that the European war would soon end and that the United States would keep out of war. The press also emphasized that his wife's family was from Forlì Province, the Duce's birthplace.[72] Guilt by association.

Government agents descended on Italian neighborhoods to interrogate enemy aliens, usually apolitical men and women who had resided in the United States for several decades but had not bothered to apply for citizenship. Embarrassed and fearful, they had to answer questions about the guns, cameras, and shortwave radio sets in their possession. "They saw my brother's aerial and paid us a visit. He was a ham radio operator," said a lady born in Indianapolis. "I had to go to the police station with someone who could identify me because my mother went to visit her family in Sicily while she was pregnant and I was born there," said another interviewee. In Mishawaka Pat Jermano was quizzed about the name of his club, Maria SS. DiLoreto. The agent wanted to know the meaning of "SS." "He thought it referred to Adolf Hitler's elite body guard," recalled a club member. Jermano was hard pressed to explain that "SS" stood for *Santissima* (most holy) as in "Mary Most Holy of Loreto."[73]

War, however, is serious business. In June 1942 Army Air Corps Maj. Raymond Salzarulo was lost in the Battle of Midway. His brother Robert was a second lieutenant in the Army Air Corps. He flew three missions from England over Germany, was shot down in 1944, and was held prisoner until the end of the war. A third brother, Frank, was a captain of infantry; a fourth brother, Bill, was a lieutenant commander in the navy; and a fifth brother, Albert, was a lieutenant in the signal corps. All were sons of Louis and Maria Scotece Salzarulo, natives of Bisaccia, Avellino Province, residing at Richmond.[74]

On 19 February 1944, S. Sgt. John Aloysius "Johnny" Bushemi of Gary, professional photographer and son of a

Sicilian immigrant, was recording the action on the island of Eniwetok in the Pacific when an enemy mortar shell shattered his legs and wounded him in the neck. His last words were: "Be sure to get those pictures back to the office right away."[75] The American Legion post near his home was named in his memory.

Italy joined the Allied side in September 1943. William and Clarence Marocco and Angelo and Henry Ricci of Logansport visited the three thousand Italian prisoners of war held at Camp Atterbury south of Indianapolis, encouraged them to form a band, and arranged for Logansport's USO Council to sponsor the band in a holiday grand concert on 28 December 1943.[76]

Indiana Italians also became interested in providing relief for Italian war victims. Under the chairmanship of Holy Cross priest Salvatore Fanelli, assistant at St. Joseph's parish in South Bend, Notre Dame and Italian clubs in St. Joseph County collected more than three tons of clothing, over two tons of nonperishable foodstuffs, and almost sixty-five hundred pounds of powdered milk for Italian relief.[77] Other cities conducted similar drives.

Before World War II the Sons of Italy lodge in Richmond was always very careful to counterweigh an Italian act with an American one, donating to an American charity when donating to an Italian one. In June 1925 members approved the spending of ten dollars to send a telegram congratulating King Victor Emmanuel III of Italy on his silver anniversary of ascending the throne. Two weeks later they voted to contribute ten dollars to the Fourth of July Committee and telegraph greetings to President Calvin Coolidge in Washington.[78] From 1940 to 1943 the lodge contributed only to the American Red Cross. Beginning in 1944 members donated funds primarily for Italian relief and Italian orphans. This interest in Italy climaxed in 1948 when the lodge authorized the sending of a cablegram to the leading Rome newspaper "to urge the people to vote against cominists [sic]. All members in favor of this act."[79]

World War II forced immigrants and their descendants to clarify their identity. They became Americans ready to stand by and sacrifice for their new country. They remained Americans even when, proud of their roots, they sought to improve conditions in the Old Country.

### Decline and Revival since 1945

The establishment of an immigration quota system (1924) contributed to the reduction of Italian born in Indiana from 6,873 in 1930 to 3,868 in 1970. The latter census also indicated that a subculture may survive through offspring: an estimated 14,067 Indiana residents were children of an Italian-born mother and/or father.[80]

General prosperity after World War II, the decline of industries that traditionally employed Italians, and increased opportunity for their descendants to obtain an education leading to professional and skilled jobs encouraged moving to suburbia. Ethnic solidarity retreated before social mobility. Young married couples with children did not want to occupy the narrow housing of their fathers and mothers if they could afford a two-bedroom, ranch-style house surrounded by grass and trees. The automobile could bring them in to visit the old folks and attend the few Italian events that interested them. Golfing, boating, gardening, the right schools, the big game, business associates, and bridge partners distracted them from the cohesion of family, traditional social customs, and the insurance benefits of the old organizations. "Our kids' activities and other friends at school or work don't bring us together as Italians very much," explained a Richmond-born lady whose father had emigrated from Roseto Valfortore in Apulia.

Integration into American life was essential. Several immigrants and their descendants sought elective and appointive office. Alfred A. (Fred) Ferrini of East Chicago ran unsuccessfully for Indiana secretary of state on the Republican ticket in 1948—a year when strong Democratic candidates were elected president and governor. Italian Americans have sat on city councils in Fort Wayne (Sam Talarico), Indianapolis (David Page and Frank Short), and Richmond (Louis Salzarulo, Frank and Philip Marino). They have served as party chairmen in Cass (Frederick Sabatini), St. Joseph (Ideal Baldoni), and Marion (Anthony Maio and Providence Benedict) counties, and in Richmond (Andrew Cecere) and Mishawaka (Sam Mercantini). They have experience as commissioners in Cass County (Peter J. D'Andrea and Anthony Sabatini) and St. Joseph County (Henry Ferrettie and Joseph Zappia), as Vermillion County sheriff (Dom Costello), as police chiefs in Richmond (Dan A. Mitrione) and Fort Wayne (Albert J. Bragalone), as mayors of Michigan City (Joseph LaRocco), East Chicago (Dr. John B. Nicosia), and Elkhart (Peter Sarandos), and as Marion County assessor (William S. Mercuri and Frank Corsaro). They have been elected judges (John M. Ruberto of Gary and Frank J. Treckelo of Elkhart).

Italian born and Italian Americans have served as state legislators. Paul "Jerry" Roland of Indianapolis was elected in 1964. Sam and John Bushemi and Victoria Caesar represented Lake County. One legislator in the 1975–76 session had been born in Villarosa, Enna Province, Sicily (Representative Marion Bushemi), and two were of Italian ancestry (Senator Ralph J. Potesta, whose family came from Pontecagnano-Faiano, Salerno Province, to East Chicago in 1920; and Representative Anthony Pizzo, M.D., of Bloomington, whose parents came from Cinisi, occasion by presenting a Columbus statue to the city of Mishawaka.

The great manifestations of *Italianità* in Indiana are the Little Italy Festival in Clinton, the Holy Rosary *festa* in Indianapolis, and the ethnic days observed in the north. Stand in the park adjacent to the bridge over the Wabash River at Clinton on Labor Day weekend. Look south to observe a green, white, and red banner—the Italian flag—suspended from the bridge. The colors match the stripes on the street sign posts all over town. Gondola rides on the river are also available. The mellow-colored Four Seasons fountain stands guard at the riverbank. Find the intersection of 9th and Pike streets. Observe there the statue of the male immigrant carrying his valise and waving to friends upon arrival at his new home. Drive down to the Holy Rosary-Danish Church Historic District in Indianapolis on a June weekend. You will discover thousands of central Indiana residents drooling over cannelloni, fettucine, sausage and green peppers, antipasto, and spumoni. Try the wine, take a chance on a fruit basket, test your luck at cards. Listen to the bells. Pin a donation to the veil of Mary. Visit Merrillville, South Bend, or Fort Wayne on a summer weekend. Make noise, join the crowds, sample the food, and have fun as the nationalities celebrate themselves.

In 1990, of the 5.5 million residents in the state, an estimated 125,297 have an Italian ancestor. They are sufficiently numerous to provide a little blush to the blandness of Indiana, the least cosmopolitan state in the Old Northwest, and to interpret its down-home heartland atmosphere. One of them, Angelo Pizzo of Bloomington, delighted local moviegoers by writing the screenplay for that popular, "gym-dandy" film *Hoosiers*.

*In 1970 Philip Marino (seated under city seal) was elected president of the Richmond Common Council. His father Frank (right), born in Cosenza and a council member since 1942, was elected vice president. Together with Louis Salzarulo, who served with the elder Marino on the council for a dozen years, they exemplify an Italo-American presence in the political life of Indiana cities.*

Palermo Province, to Logansport in 1920). Robert N. Sabatini was elected from Logansport in 1988.

As death removed Italian-born grandparents, and as a sense of "do your own thing" arose during the 1960s and 1970s, a search for roots became popular. Italian descendants were pleased that the dominant group loved Italian cuisine. They used "the kitchen" and their cultural inheritance as a foundation for their ethnic pride.

After 1970 we find Sons of Italy lodges and Italian clubs active in East Chicago, Merrillville, Logansport, Mishawaka, Elkhart, and Fort Wayne. The American Italian Benevolent Society and the Italian American Women's Club operate in Lake County. The Columbus '92 Commission organized in 1989 to plan an appropriate observance of the Columbus Quincentenary in Marion County. It sponsored a gala dance, Columbus Mass, and rededication of the Columbus bust on the grounds of the Indiana Statehouse. Italians also marked the

**Indiana townships with at least fifty Italian-born residents (1980)**

| County | Township | Number | Town |
|---|---|---|---|
| Lake | North | 253 | Hammond, East Chicago |
| Lake | Calumet | 231 | Gary |
| St. Joseph | Portage | 200 | South Bend |
| Lake | Ross | 139 | Merrillville |
| St. Joseph | Penn | 131 | Mishawaka |
| Wayne | Wayne | 73 | Richmond |
| Marion | Washington | 68 | Indianapolis |
| Vermillion | Clinton | 67 | Clinton |
| Porter | Portage | 66 | Portage |
| Elkhart | Concord | 65 | Elkhart |
| Marion | Center | 62 | Indianapolis |
| Lake | St. John | 59 | Schererville |
| Allen | Wayne | 50 | Fort Wayne |

**Indiana counties with more than one thousand residents with Italian ancestors (1990)**

| | | | |
|---|---|---|---|
| Lake | 18,829 | Delaware | 2,233 |
| Marion | 18,589 | Wayne | 2,119 |
| St. Joseph | 10,034 | Johnson | 1,982 |
| Allen | 7,808 | Madison | 1,724 |
| Porter | 5,889 | Clark | 1,549 |
| Elkhart | 4,139 | Vermillion | 1,502 |
| Tippecanoe | 3,570 | Howard | 1,499 |
| Hamilton | 3,401 | Hendricks | 1,370 |
| Vigo | 2,962 | Cass | 1,265 |
| Monroe | 2,879 | Kosciusko | 1,046 |
| La Porte | 2,454 | Grant | 1,009 |
| Vanderburgh | 2,408 | | |

## Conclusion

Italians have played many roles in the Hoosier state. Explorer, priest, revolutionary, banker, painter, saint, bootlegger, gangster, steelworker, restaurateur, banana king, doctor, railroader, politician, builder, miner, quarry worker, war casualty, policeman, lawyer, and even farmer.

The Italian subcultural experience falls into four periods. From 1890 to 1920 the immigrant's main concern was his quest for economic advancement. His job and family security were essential. This was the era of menial tasks, *padroni,* and mutual aid societies. From 1920 to 1939 the immigrant continued to search for economic opportunity. Because of the quota system, few Italians were new arrivals and those residing in the state had opted to be American. Economic improvement was held in tandem with the desire to improve relations with the institutions of the broader society. This was the era of political clubs, political candidates, *prominenti,* and church activity. Ambivalence yet remained between Italian tradition and American assimilation, some wanting to forget the old language, others wanting to create at least parity between the two loyalties. Then came the era of the Second World War, 1939 to 1945. Italians were tested and found to be Americans with Italian roots. The fourth period, since World War II, shows immigrants and their descendants secure in their American commitment. Some have assimilated to such a degree that only an Italian family name remains. Others accept the notion that Americans are *e pluribus unum,* one people emerging from many nationalities. They are proud to be Italian American while living and working in an environment that is not definably Italian.

Three interviewees met this author over dinner in Logansport (1983). They exhibited different attitudes toward their Italian roots. The oldest was an eighty-year-old housewife born in Pescocostanzo in the Abruzzi. "You should be like a tree. To survive, you should sway with the breeze." Her daughter was in her sixties. She was a high school graduate and had lived in Indianapolis and had worked for the state. "During World War II, other workers would deliberately make some remark about Italy in my presence. I'd say, 'Hey, my family came from Italy, but I'm an American.'" Her cousin, an investment broker in his midfifties, had attended Notre Dame and had earned a business degree. "I'm an Italian American. If you don't like the Italian part, tough."

## Notes

1. For Tonti's memoirs of his Indiana passage see vol. 1 of *Illinois Historical Collections* (Springfield, Ill.: H. W. Rokker, 1903), 128–31, and Arville L. Funk, "La Salle in Indiana," *Outdoor Indiana* (Feb. 1965): 2–5. See also Francis Parkman, *The Discovery of the Great West: La Salle* (New York: Rinehart and Co., 1956), 94, 121–24; Erik Amfitheatrof, *The Children of Columbus: An Informal History of the Italians in the New World* (Boston: Little, Brown and Co., 1973), 39–41, 47; Michael A. Musmanno, *The Story of the Italians in America* (Garden City, N.Y.: Doubleday and Co., 1965), 5.

2. Constantin François Chasseboeuf de Volney, *Tableau du Climat et du Sol des États-Unis d'Amérique,* 2 vols. (Paris: Courcier, 1803), 2:401. For the Canadian exploits of the Carignan Regiment see George M. Wrong, *The Rise and Fall of New France,* 2 vols. (New York: The Macmillan Co., 1928), 1:374–80.

3. Frederick Burget, trans., "Register of Baptisms, Marriages, and Burials of Post Vincennes, 1749–1830," III, pp.16, 50; IV, p. 23, Genealogy Division, Indiana State Library; Joseph Henry Vanderburgh Somes, *Old Vincennes: The History of a Famous Old Town and Its Glorious Past* (New York: Graphic Books, 1962), 94, 100.

4. Bruno Roselli, *Vigo: A Forgotten Builder of the American Republic* (Boston: Stratford Company Publishers, 1933), 263.

5. Dorothy Riker, "Francis Vigo," *Indiana Magazine of History* 26 (Mar. 1930): 23. See also Eric Pumroy, "Francesco Vigo: Italian on the American Frontier" (Paper presented before the American Italian Historical Association, Washington, D.C., 11 Nov. 1984).

6. The 1850 statistics in "1850 Census Foreign-Born for Indiana" (Unpublished manuscript, Indiana Historical Society, Education Division, 1991). It reported four Italian born in Marion County, one each in Brown, Franklin, Jefferson, and Vigo counties.

7. Joseph C. G. Kennedy, *Eighth Census of the United States, 1860,* vol. 1, *Population of the United States in 1860 Compiled from the Original Returns of the Eighth Census* (Washington, D.C.: Government Printing Office, 1864), 130, reported 92 natives of Italy and 329 natives of Sardinia in the state's population. The number of Sardinians is suspect, however, since the previous figure, for Sweden, is also 329. Subsequent data comparisons always used 421, the printed statistic (92 plus 329), as the number of Italian born in 1860. See Department of Commerce, Bureau of the Census, *Sixteenth Census of the United States: 1940 Population,* vol. 2, *Characteristics of the Population* (Washington, D.C.: Government Printing Office, 1943), part 2, p. 693. The state's 1860 manuscript census, computerized by the Indiana Historical Society, yielded the names of 95 Italian born and 5 Sardinian born. This data, better fitting the general trend, was the basis of the analysis given here.

8. For Rosati's description of how the local population received him during his ministry at Vincennes see Frederick J. Easterly, *The Life of Rt. Rev. Joseph Rosati, C.M.* (Washington, D.C.: Catholic University of America Press, 1942), 43–44.

9. For his autobiography see Father [Alessandro] Gavazzi, *Lectures in New York*, 3d ed. (New York: DeWitt and Davenport, Publishers, 1853), 17–117; *Indianapolis Morning Journal*, 1 Nov. 1853.

10. Carl F. Brand, "The History of the Know Nothing Party in Indiana," *Indiana Magazine of History* 18 (Mar. 1922): 53; Robert F. McNamara, *The American College in Rome, 1855–1955* (Rochester, N.Y.: The Christopher Press, 1956), 4; Emma Lou Thornbrough, *Indiana in the Civil War Era, 1850–1880* (Indianapolis: Indiana Historical Bureau and Indiana Historical Society, 1965), 61; Logan Esarey, *A History of Indiana from 1850 to 1920*, 2 vols. (Fort Wayne: The Hoosier Press, 1924), 2:620.

11. Robert Dale Owen to Secretary of State William L. Marcy, 12 Apr. 1855, quoted in Richard William Leopold, *Robert Dale Owen: A Biography*, vol. 45 of Harvard Historical Studies (Cambridge, Mass.: Harvard University Press, 1940), 319; Louis M. Sears, "Robert Dale Owen's Mission to Naples," *Indiana History Bulletin* 6, Extra No. 2 (May 1929): 51; Sexson E. Humphreys, "New Considerations on the Mission of Robert Dale Owen to the Kingdom of the Two Sicilies, 1853–1858," *Indiana Magazine of History* 46 (Mar. 1950).

12. Salvatore Saladino, *Italy from Unification to 1919: Growth and Decay of a Liberal Regime* (New York: Thomas Y. Crowell Co., 1970), 59, 114. For other worthwhile studies see Betty Boyd Caroli, *Italian Repatriation from the United States, 1900–1914* (New York: Center for Migration Studies, 1973) and Gino C. Speranza, "The Effect of Emigration on Italy" (1904), reprinted in Francesco Cordasco and Eugene Bucchioni, *The Italians: Social Backgrounds of an American Group* (Clifton, N.J.: Augustus M. Kelley, Publishers, 1974).

13. Powell A. Moore, *The Calumet Region: Indiana's Last Frontier*, vol. 39 of *Indiana Historical Collections* ([Indianapolis]: Indiana Historical Bureau, 1959), 371.

14. Caroli, *Italian Repatriation from the United States*, 41.

15. Yet Judge Gary particularly disliked strikers who were of foreign origin, Catholic, and socialist. John M. Blum, "Nativism, Anti-Radicalism, and the Foreign Scare, 1917–20," *The Midwest Journal* 3, no. 1 (Winter 1950–51): 51.

16. Summary statistics in *Characteristics of the Population* [1940], part 2, p. 693.

17. Department of Commerce and Labor, Bureau of the Census, *Thirteenth Census of the United States, Abstract of the Census*, vol. 2, *Population* (Washington, D.C.: Government Printing Office, 1913), 596, 618–19, 623–25.

18. Department of the Interior, Census Office, *Census Reports, Twelfth Census of the United States, Taken in the Year 1900*, vol. 1, *Population* (Washington, D.C.: United States Census Office, 1902), part 1, p. 748; Department of Commerce, Bureau of the Census, *Fourteenth Census of the United States, State Compendium—Indiana* (Washington, D.C.: Government Printing Office, 1924), 49.

19. *Thirteenth Census of the United States, Abstract* [1910], 583.

20. *Indianapolis News*, 20 Oct. 1910; *Indianapolis Star*, 21 Oct. 1910.

21. *Fourteenth Census of the United States, State Compendium* [1920], 17, 21.

22. Eugene Clayton, "An Economic Analysis of Labor Conditions in the Indiana Coal Industry in 1932" (M.A. thesis, Indiana University, 1941), 50–51.

23. Edwin Fenton, *Immigrants and Unions, A Case Study: Italians and American Labor, 1870–1920* (New York: Arno Press, 1975), 243.

24. Dominic T. Ciolli, "The 'Wop' in the Track Gang," *The Immigrants in America Review* 2 (July 1916): 64. For mention of Italians who built the Illinois Central Railroad trestle over Richland Creek, Greene County, in 1905–6 see *Indianapolis Star*, 16 Dec. 1979. At 2,295 feet, it was the third longest trestle in the world. For the construction of the Bender Road and Boonville-New Harmony overpasses in Vanderburgh County by the New York Central Railroad (1910) and Italian fatalities see *Indianapolis News*, 16 Feb. 1984.

25. District Court of the United States for the District of Indiana, No. 557, *In Equity, The Pittsburgh, Cincinnati, Chicago, and St. Louis Railroad Company* v. *The International Association of Machinists*, 24 July 1922.

26. Oliver C. Lockhart, "The Oolitic Limestone Industry in Indiana," *Indiana University Studies* 8 (Sept. 1910): 97.

27. Text in *Bedford Daily Mail*, 28 Jan. 1908.

28. Ibid., 31 Jan. 1908.

29. Ibid., 4, 14 Feb. 1908.

30. Ibid., 21, 22 Feb. 1908.

31. Ibid., 11 May 1908.

32. *Bedford Democrat*, 5 Mar. 1908; *Bedford Daily Democrat*, 25, 29 (see cartoon) Aug. 1908.

33. Joseph A. Batchelor, *An Economic History of the Indiana Oolitic Limestone Industry*, Indiana Business Studies, no. 27 (Bloomington: The School of Business, Indiana University, 1944), 139, 143.

34. The family name was Di Donato, but the brothers simplified it by dropping "Di" and using "D." as a middle initial.

35. For printed biographies see *Indianapolis News*, 18 June 1947; *Indianapolis Star*, 31 Jan. 1949; and *Indianapolis News*, 28 Nov. 1974.

36. Department of Commerce, Bureau of the Census, *Fifteenth Census of the United States: 1930; Population* (Washington, D.C.: Government Printing Office, 1933), vol. 3, part 1, pp. 720–23.

37. Isaac James Quillen, "The Industrial City: A History of Gary, Indiana to 1929" (Ph.D. diss., Yale University, 1942), 345.

38. Illinois Steel Company's rules and regulations for safety in the plant, published in January 1917, Indiana Room, Gary Public Library.

39. Richard J. Meister, "A History of Gary, Indiana: 1930–1940" (Ph.D. diss., University of Notre Dame, 1966), 14. For specific examples see *Gary Post-Tribune*, 19 June 1983.

40. *Gary Post-Tribune*, 7 Feb. 1948. For further information on Gerometta see Quillen, "Industrial City," 397; Meister, "History of Gary," 41; Moore, *Calumet Region*, 290; and Thomas H. Cannon, ed., *History of the Lake and Calumet Region of Indiana*, 2 vols. (Indianapolis: Historians' Association, 1927), 2:77–78.

41. "1860 Census Foreign-Born for Indiana" (Unpublished manuscript, Indiana Historical Society, Education Division, 1991).

42. U.S. Secretary of the Interior, *The Statistics of the Population of the United States, Ninth Census*, vol. 1, *Population* (Washington, D.C.: Government Printing Office, 1872), 390; summary of 1900 to 1930 statistics in *Fifteenth Census of the United States: 1930*, 2:321.

43. Marriage records of St. Mary's parish, Indianapolis, lists over twenty Italian weddings between 1892 and 1909.

44. Fruit sellers' list in *Indianapolis City Directory for 1910*, p. 1623.

45. "Starke County," *Plat Books of Indiana Counties* (Rockford, Ill.: W. W. Hixson and Co., [1920]).

46. U.S. Bureau of Immigration, *Annual Report of the Commissioner-General of Immigration* (Washington, D.C.: Government Printing Office), appropriate years.

47. For specific information on Gregori see *Notre Dame Scholastic*, 30 Nov. 1878, p. 205; 14 Oct. 1882, p. 83; 17 Nov. 1883, pp. 170–71; and 20 Mar. 1886, p. 436.

48. For further information on Mother Mary Magdalen see Gabriel Francis Powers, *A Woman of the Bentivoglios* (Notre Dame, Ind.: Ave Maria, n.d.); and *Commemorating the Diamond Jubilee of the Poor Clares in Evansville, Indiana* (Pamphlet published by the Poor Clares, 1972).

49. For details about the Methodist mission see James J. Divita, *The Italians of Indianapolis: The Story of Holy Rosary Catholic Parish, 1909–1984* (Indianapolis: Holy Rosary Parish, 1984), 15–26, and "The Indiana Churches and the Italian Immigrant, 1890–1935," *U.S. Catholic Historian* 6 (Fall 1987): 333.

50. Bishop Herman J. Alerding to Loreto Starace, 24 Aug. 1913, Fort Wayne Diocesan Archives.

51. Divita, "Indiana Churches and the Italian Immigrant," 339.

52. Alerding to Mother Maria Teresa, 2 Jan. 1915, Fort Wayne Diocesan Archives.

53. Alerding to Rev. J. E. Burke, 14 Mar. 1920, ibid.

54. Michael A. Campagna, *A Little Love* (n.p., 1972), 35.

55. *Clintonian,* 19 Nov. 1909.

56. Ibid., 31 Oct. 1911.

57. Also see Tommie Gatherum, "Basketball at Hill Crest Community Center in Clinton, Indiana," in Chester L. Larkins, ed., *Memories of Growing Up in the Midwest* (Leawood, Kans.: Inter-Collegiate Press, 1982). Another short article in this collection is written by Paul Kelly, who coached at both Clinton and Sullivan, Indiana.

58. For other details see James J. Divita, "Hill Crest Mission," Synod of Lincoln Trails *Trailmarker,* Feb. 1985, p. 3. This article appeared on the seventy-fifth anniversary of Robb's proposal to found the mission.

59. Italy Commissariato dell' emigrazione, "La Società italiane all'estero nel 1908," *Bolletino dell' emigrazione* no. 24 (1908): 96–105. For the development of societies in Italy see Fenton, *Immigrants and Unions,* 15–17.

60. David Eisen, ed., *A Mishawaka Mosaic* (Elkhart, Ind.: Bethel Publishing, 1983), 118–19; *South Bend Tribune,* 15 Jan. 1953; *Mishawaka Enterprise-Record,* 21 June 1984.

61. *Americans All,* Mar. 1926, p. 8; Apr. 1926, p. 34; May 1926, p. 8.

62. Ibid., Feb. 1926, p. 16.

63. Meister, "History of Gary," 291–92; James B. Lane, *"City of the Century": A History of Gary, Indiana* (Bloomington: Indiana University Press, 1978), 191.

64. *Americans All,* July–Aug. 1925, p. 13.

65. *Clinton Saturday Argus,* 4, 18 June 1915.

66. Loggia Colonia Italiana Wayne County No. 933, Richmond, Ind., *Processi Verbali,* 10 Nov. 1924, p. 63; 21 Dec. 1924, p. 64.

67. Ibid., 20 Dec. 1925, p. 80.

68. *Indianapolis News,* 11 Oct. 1932.

69. Loggia Colonia Italiana of Wayne County No. 933, *Official Record,* 11 Dec. 1941, p. 118.

70. Ibid., 22 Jan. 1942, p. 120.

71. *Indianapolis Star,* 16 Dec. 1941.

72. *South Bend Tribune,* 12 Dec. 1941; *Indianapolis News,* 26 Feb. 1940. After a brief internment, Rizzo was drafted into the U.S. Army, received U.S. citizenship, served in the intelligence division, and was discharged after two years with a citation from President Franklin D. Roosevelt. *Indianapolis Star,* 18 Dec. 1988.

73. For another version of this incident see *South Bend Tribune,* 9 Oct. 1983.

74. Raymond's death was heavily publicized in the Italian-American press: *Il Progresso Italo Americano* (New York), 30 June, 12 July 1942; *Il Giornale d'Italia* (San Francisco), 30 June 1942; and *L'Unità del Popolo* (New York), 4 July 1942. His loss exemplified the sacrifice Italian immigrants and their families were willing to make for America at war. Louis received much publicity when he had the cathedral bell in Bisaccia recast in Raymond's memory. *Time,* 29 June 1953, p. 26. Raymond's posthumous son, Raymond, Jr., a graduate of the Air Force Academy, was shot down over Vietnam in 1966. *Indianapolis News,* 2 Mar. 1973.

75. Lane, *"City of the Century,"* 219.

76. Souvenir ticket in the possession of Anita Ricci of Logansport. For further information on Italian POWs at Atterbury see Dorothy Riker, comp., *The Hoosier Training Ground* (Bloomington: Indiana War History Commission, 1952), 36–41.

77. *South Bend Tribune,* 26 July 1944; 6 May, 10 June 1945.

78. *Processi Verbali,* 7 June 1925, p. 71; 21 June 1925, p. 72.

79. *Official Record,* 14 Apr. 1948, p. 232.

80. U.S. Department of Commerce, Bureau of the Census, *1970 Census of Population* (Washington, D.C.: Government Printing Office, 1973), 1:16–604.

## Interviewees/Oral Sources

Joe Airola, Clinton; Jerry Barbar, East Chicago; Thomas Benedict, Indianapolis; Fred J. Bertucci, North Judson; Edward Boilini, Indianapolis; Caroline Formento Bonacorsi, Clinton; Mary Book, Indianapolis; Rev. Michael T. Bradley, Indianapolis; Msgr. Joseph D. Brokhage, Indianapolis; Olympia Buffo, Clinton; Alex Butch, Logansport; Clara Mercurio Caito, Indianapolis; Rose Gatto Caito, Indianapolis; Peter and Mary Bianchi Calacci, East Chicago; Vito Carapezza, Clinton; Rev. Fred Cardinali, Fort Wayne; Rev. David Carkenord, Elkhart; Mary C. Caruso, Fort Wayne; Thomas E. Castaldi, Sr., Fort Wayne; Armand Catapano, Elkhart; Andrew C. Cecere, Richmond; Mary Jo O'Neill Coll, Indianapolis; Maggelina Caito Corsaro, Indianapolis; Josephine Palumbo Corso, Logansport; Dr. Thomas A. Cortese, Sr., Indianapolis; Dorothy Markello Cox, Terre Haute; Joe D'Andrea, Logansport; Ann (Ninfa) Gatto DeHilt, Indianapolis; James Della Rocco, East Chicago; Charles DeMeo, Richmond; Rocco and Rose Marie Mozzone Di Brita, Fort Wayne; Dominick J. Di Michele, East Chicago; Albert J. Dinelli, Calumet City, Illinois; Sarah Nicoletta Dine (Dionisio), Richmond; Albert M. Donato, Jr., Zionsville; Msgr. John J. Doyle, Indianapolis; Furi Farinelli, East Chicago; Margaret Pesavento Fenoglio, Clinton; Henry Ferrettie, Mishawaka; John W. Gioscio, Indianapolis; Marie Meno Glover, Bedford; Margaret C. Griffiths, Clinton; Carmel Ricci Grusenmeyer, Logansport; Carole Hensel, Fort Wayne; Jay Doria Huber, East Chicago; Bruno Iacoli, Rosedale; Anthony A. and Elizabeth Nadolny Ianigro, Elkhart; Louis and Louise Ianigro, Elkhart; Dominic F. and Betty Iozzo, Cicero; Margaret Iozzo, Cicero; Margaret Murello LaGrotto, Indianapolis; Mrs. Dominic (Nellie) Landolfi, Fort Wayne; Catherine Lapenta, Indianapolis; Katherine Bertucci Laudato, North Judson; Peter and Beverly J. Lenzo, Indianapolis; Jennie Devanis Lepri, Clinton; Patra Lese, Elkhart; Nick and Jennie Lombardo Leto, Fort Wayne; Frank A. and Vicki Lobraico, Indianapolis; Rev. Wayne McLaughlin, Clinton; Helen Cassino Maddalone, Fort Wayne; A. Chick Maggioli, Mishawaka; Josephine "Fanny" Mancini, Connersville; Becky Manley, East Chicago; Elmer and Dorothy Adolay Marien, Indianapolis; Philip Marino, Richmond; Michael J. Mascari, Beech Grove; Salvatore and Mary Sansone Mascari, Indianapolis; Mr. and Mrs. Tony Matury, Lowell; Mike Mazza, Indianapolis; Salvatore Mazza, Indianapolis; Al and Ida Caito Meyer, Greenwood; Tudie P. Miceli, Greenwood; Margaret Filicicchia Minardo, Indianapolis; John and Raffaela Montani, Indianapolis; Helen Finley Murello, Indianapolis; Frances Caito Navarra, Carmel;

John Negovetti (Negovetich), East Chicago; Edward (Al) Papa, Elkhart; Joseph and Carmela Gervasio Pappano, Richmond; Nicholas and Kate Bessignano Pasquale, Logansport; Thomas and Mary D'Andrea Pasquale, Logansport; Frances Palumbo Perrone, Logansport; Irma Pesavento, Clinton; Joseph T. Pinella, Indianapolis; Ross (Rosario) Portolese, Mishawaka; Rev. Joseph Pusateri, East Chicago; Sylvia Doria Razzini, East Chicago; Msgr. Francis J. Reine, Indianapolis; Anita Ricci, Logansport; Lawrence Ricci, Kokomo; Mary LeDonne Ricci, Logansport; Joe Rodino, Elkhart; Virginia Abel Ronzone, Elkhart; Dorothy Baird Kruzan Rottet, Clinton; Fausto "Fred" Sabatini, Logansport; Florence Salaroglio, Clinton; Albert C. Salzarulo, Richmond; Frank Salzarulo, Indianapolis; Rev. Augustine J. Sansone, Indianapolis; Natale Schmizzi, Osceola; Rev. Fred Schroeder, Logansport; Bruno and Dolores Seghetti, North Judson; Nello and Laura Seghetti, North Judson; Madeleine Meo Sgro, Indianapolis; Rev. James J. Shanahan, Clinton; Santina Picchietti Shoemaker, North Judson; Joe Siciliano, Elkhart; Josephine Mascari Sigreto, Indianapolis; Josephine Venezia Spallina, Indianapolis; Mary Spinnato, Indianapolis; Josephine Sansone Stinnett, Indianapolis; Charles E. Stoeckley, Avilla; Msgr. Curt Suelzer, Fort Wayne; Quin Tarquinio, Richmond; Rev. Hal Thomas, Fort Wayne; Michael Timpe, Indianapolis; George Torhan, East Chicago; Frank A. Trimboli, Mishawaka; Florence Auer Turner, Clinton; Rita Boilini Vanek, North Judson; Rose Pappano Vecera, Richmond; Edith Castagna Vignocchi, Clinton; Frank Violi, Mishawaka; Domenick "Pete" and Connie Viterisi, Fort Wayne; Mike Yaney, Elkhart.

# JAPANESE

JUSTIN H. LIBBY

*Unlike the trend in many United States cities, immigrants to Indianapolis no longer cluster in insular ethnic neighborhoods as they did in the early 1900s, and this is true for the Japanese Americans who have become permanent residents. Because they do not live in close proximity, Indianapolis does not have a Japanese district similar to other cities such as Los Angeles. This settlement pattern has contributed to their assimilation into Indiana's society.*

Immigrants to the United States of Japanese ancestry have had a history of both resilience and adaptation. After suffering from discriminatory laws and racial hostility in the first half of the twentieth century, Japanese immigrants have assimilated into American society by striking a balance between their own ethnicity and an accommodation to the predominant values and behavior of American life. Japanese immigrants have made an important contribution to the communities where they have settled.

Immigration of people of Japanese ancestry to Indiana has been predominantly a post–World War II phenomenon, although they have been present in the state since the late nineteenth century. Five Japanese people were recorded in an 1880 Indiana count of foreign-born population, while by 1890 the number in the state had risen to 25. In 1880 the number of Japanese in the United

States had risen to 401 and increased to 2,039 according to the census of 1890. Like most newcomers to the American shores, Japanese immigrants met some racial prejudices, but in general anti-Asian sentiment was more prevalent along the Pacific slope than in the Midwest. In spite of initial resentments to their presence in Indiana, the new residents proved in time to be productive and resourceful citizens.[1]

Most of the first-generation immigrants to America, known as Issei, were young males from rural Japan. The purpose of this study, therefore, is to focus on Issei immigrants and their descendants. The majority of the first generation arrived in the United States between the years 1890 and 1924, and each successive generation has been comparatively homogeneous in age and cultural experience. Japanese Americans may be identified, as well as their place in society, by the generation to which they belong. The differential age groupings that arose were primarily a result of the discriminatory immigration laws.

Japanese immigration to the United States resulted from a breakdown of the barriers in their isolated homeland. In 1854 Commodore Matthew Perry and his American ships forced an agreement of residency and trade with the United States. Under the Tokugawa Shogunate travel was banned, but during the 1868 Meiji Restoration in Japan greater contact with the West was encouraged by the new leaders. Most of the earliest immigrants, therefore, were those who took advantage of this new freedom to travel outside the country.

Immigration of any real substance began in 1885 when Japan allowed young male laborers to go to Hawaii to work under contracts on sugar plantations. Their numbers grew rapidly.[2] In 1890 there were only 2,039 people of Japanese ancestry on the islands, but that number jumped to 24,326 within ten years.[3] The years 1900 to 1908 are of great importance in the history of Japanese immigration to the United States mainland. While many immigrants came directly from their homeland, even more came from Hawaii. In 1906 the Pacific states demanded exclusion legislation for the Japanese similar to existing laws that prohibited Chinese immigration.

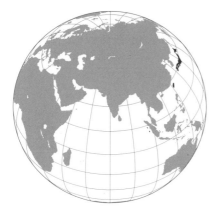

Subsequently, in 1907 the governments of the United States and Japan reached a Gentlemen's Agreement, which provided that Japan would prevent immigration of workers to the West Coast of the United States while the Theodore Roosevelt administration would ease discriminatory legislation along the Pacific slope. After reaching a peak of 30,824 immigrants to the mainland in 1907, emigrations from Hawaii were stopped by the Gentlemen's Agreement.[4] These immigrants instead turned to Brazil after Canada and Mexico also limited their quotas.

Locally, the movement of Japanese immigrants to Indiana was limited to small numbers during this time. According to the Dillingham report on United States immigration, 66,590 immigrants from all over the world reported their final destination as Indiana during the twelve fiscal years 1899 to 1910, and only 18 were reported as Japanese.[5]

In an article in the *Indianapolis Sentinel* dated 23 July 1905 the reporter asked why the Japanese had come to America, specifically Indianapolis, and were they here permanently or did they intend to return to Japan. Three Japanese men in the city were interviewed and were said to represent three distinct types of Japanese in America.

Ikko Matsumoto, a jeweler on South Meridian Street, was the best known and one of the most influential Japanese in the state. He had resided in Indianapolis nearly twenty years making it his permanent home, and for this reason he was said to represent the rarest class of Japanese found in America.

A bamboo dealer on East Washington Street, S. Kawai, had motives that were exactly opposite of Matsumoto's. He was here to learn as much as possible about American methods in business and education and then he intended to return to Japan.

The third type of Japanese in Indiana was said to be represented by I. Takito, an art dealer on Massachusetts Avenue. He had been a wanderer in Indianapolis for a short time. After graduating from an agriculture college in Japan, he came to the United States to pursue his studies at the University of Michigan. Takito decided to sell art goods supplied by his father, a wealthy Japanese farmer.[6]

Although these three men were said to be fair representatives of their fellow countrymen throughout the United States, the author asked if there was a hidden motive behind their reasons for coming here. The "little brown men with their sharp eyes and keen intellects" were said to be scattered through the country "always watching, watching, watching." The author wrote that the supreme object in coming to this country was to learn all they could and return to Japan to use that knowledge for the betterment of their native country.

In the same article it was explained that young men came to America because they were said to be the quickest to learn and the best at adapting to strange environments. These Japanese were assumed to be "well versed in mathematics and science" and attracted little attention.

Also mentioned were three Japanese college students, Kikijirio Nagai, Shun Suzuki, and Maysama Hondu, who were working their way through Wabash College and compiling excellent records. The author's final answer to the question "why are there Japanese in Indianapolis?" was that they are "here to learn, learn, learn."[7] In another newspaper article appearing in the *Indianapolis Star* on 28 August 1906 two Japanese students were identified as living in Kokomo. Twenty-one-year-old Atsumi Motokichi and twenty-three-year-old Inomata Tadasu commented that they believed the English language would become the universal tongue, and they had come to this country to master the language and learn American social customs. Motokichi was a cousin of the Japanese ambassador to the United States, Takahira Kogoro, and thus of royal blood, while his companion was the son of Capt. Inomata Arima of the Japanese Imperial Army, who had just distinguished himself in the Russo-Japanese War.

During their vacations from Defiance College in Defiance, Ohio, the young men were working as common laborers in Kokomo and Marion for the Western Interurban Company. They were learning electrical engineering so they could return to Japan as instructors. Arima was said to be proficient in mathematics, while Motokichi was an expert in languages and expected to enter the diplomatic service in the future.[8]

Although present in the state, Japanese in Indiana were limited in numbers at the beginning of the twentieth century. Those who were here made news because their presence was unusual. During the fiscal year ending 30 June 1908, 5,865 immigrants entered Indiana and 4,155 left, but only two of these were Japanese.[9] It should be noted that a significant rise in people of Japanese ancestry living in Indiana would not occur until after a forced relocation inland from the West during the Second World War.

During and right after the First World War a series of national discriminatory laws placing explicit restraints regarding immigration to the United States were passed. These new statutes were enacted partly in response to a fear of immigration to the United States during the Great War, as well as a response to the public's view that uncontrolled immigration would eventually produce a threat to social and economic stability. A literacy requirement was imposed in 1917; four years later Congress passed an exclusionary law fixing quotas for all immigrants based on their national origins. Terminating the Gentlemen's Agreement of 1907, the Immigration Act of 1924 tightened these quotas, effectively preventing Japanese from entering the United States for the next twenty-eight years.

These immigration restrictions greatly affected the Japanese population in the United States, as did the economic and racial prejudice that inhibited opportunities. During the 1920s Japanese immigration back to their homeland rose to 80 percent, thereby causing an inversion of the earlier immigration patterns.[10] Ironically, during these years of immigration restraints the Japanese population within Indiana grew slowly from five in 1880 to eighty-one in 1920 yet decreased to a low of twenty-nine by 1940 as many former immigrants decided for various reasons to return to Japan. Following the Second World War, however, there has been a steady increase of Japanese living in Indiana.

From 1920 to 1950 the majority of the Japanese population in Indiana lived in central and northern Indiana with the exception of southwestern Vanderburgh County where many came to reside. Other counties with a constant Japanese-American community from 1910 to 1950 were Marion, Lake, Vigo, and St. Joseph. From 1910 to 1940 more Japanese lived in urban Indiana communities than rural communities, more were foreign born than were natives until 1940, and men outnumbered women nearly two to one.[11]

The proportionately small number of Japanese in Indiana may be explained by the large number who lived in the Pacific Coast states and Hawaii before and after World War II. From 1890 to 1950 Hawaii had a larger Japanese population than the entire mainland.[12] Remote from the West Coast ports of entry and offering few work opportunities not found in the West, Indiana attracted very limited numbers of Japanese.

In the United States, the primary occupations of more than 90 percent of Issei men were farming, business, and blue-collar work, and all the professional and clerical workers added up to less than 10 percent of this first generation.[13] Issei, with agricultural backgrounds, came primarily from southern Japan, specifically from the prefectures of Hiroshima, Fukuoka, Kumamoto, Wakayama, and Yamaguchi. Many of those who remained in the United States established permanent homes by sending "calls" to Japan for women to marry. Couples were often brought together through an exchange of photos; hence, the term "picture brides."[14] As Issei married and had children a second generation, called Nisei, came to have a larger stake in American life.

Nisei were generally born between 1910 and 1940, while the majority of the third generation, known as Sansei, were born after World War II. Nisei possessed one advantage that had been denied to their parents. They were United States citizens by birth, not "aliens ineligible for citizenship." Most of the Issei spoke Japanese and little English, while most of the Nisei spoke English and very little Japanese. This caused a gap between the first and second generations of Japanese Americans who were permanent residents. In the 1930s three-quarters of Issei were Buddhists, while half the Nisei were Christians.[15] Nisei suffered from many of the same racial prejudices as had their parents, although they were not subject to all the legal discriminations endured without citizenship.

Japanese Americans, citizen and alien alike, faced hostile civic groups between 1920 and 1941, including special Asian-exclusion leagues, labor organizations, the Native Sons and Daughters of the Golden West, and the American Legion.[16] Ulysses Sigel Webb, attorney for the

Native Sons and Daughters of the Golden West, brought suit to void Japanese citizenship asking for a reversal of the United States Supreme Court decision "in the Wong Kim Ark case of 1898, which upheld the right of citizenship of a Chinese born in this country."[17] Concerned with the large numbers of Japanese settling in California, Webb successfully upheld the validity of the Alien Land Law of California and drafted the amendment to the Federal Immigration Law adopted in 1926.[18] Japanese immigrants and their American-born children were depicted as threats to national security and the American way of life. In previous years the American Legion, with headquarters in Indianapolis, tried to play an influential role in setting the policy for the Japanese in the United States. The organization set up special committees to lobby for the exclusion of all Japanese immigrants and the barring of Japanese Americans and their descendants from citizenship. The Legion appeared successful when such a law was enacted in 1924.[19]

The Japanese attack on Pearl Harbor on 7 December 1941 led to extremists' attacks on and fears of the Japanese Americans. Many Americans believed that those of Japanese ancestry had remained loyal to the Tokyo government and were potential subversives.[20] Congressmen, the press, farmers' associations, and patriotic organizations called for the evacuation of all Japanese from the West Coast, while government spokesmen not only did little to allay the anxieties of the public but actually encouraged this removal policy.

On 19 February 1942 President Franklin D. Roosevelt signed Executive Order 9066, which gave military commanders the power to remove "dangerous persons" from designated areas and to construct relocation camps to house them.[21] Japanese Americans were not mentioned specifically, but shortly after the order American citizens with at least one-sixteenth Japanese blood were barred from living, working, or traveling on the West Coast. Although no charges of disloyalty were brought against any person, more than 110,000 citizens and aliens—men, women, and children—were transferred to relocation camps, where they were kept behind barbed wire and guarded by armed soldiers. Sixty-four percent of the Japanese interned were American citizens. The American Civil Liberties Union called the removal of Japanese-American citizens, along with Japanese aliens from the Pacific Coast, an "invasion of the liberties of American citizens on the basis of racial origin."[22] Nonetheless, permanent camps were established in the deserted and barren regions of Tule Lake and Manzanar in California, Poston and Gila River in Arizona, Minidoka in Idaho, Heart Mountain in Wyoming, Granada in Colorado, Topaz in Utah, and Rowler and Jerome in Arkansas.[23]

Eventually the mass evacuation order was reversed in 1944 by the Supreme Court decision *Endo* v. *United States,* effective 2 January 1945. Mitsuye Endo of Sacramento, California, petitioned for a writ of habeas corpus, contending that her detention in camp was unlawful, and all nine justices agreed that the War Relocation Act had no right to detain loyal American citizens in camps. As a result the West Coast mass exclusion orders were revoked, but these families had already lost most of their homes, businesses, and possessions as their property had been stolen, sold, or confiscated.[24]

At the American Legion's national conventions from 1942 to 1944 a series of resolutions were passed that supported the military internment of Japanese-American citizens. All were later rescinded after World War II. Resolution Number 281, from the convention of 1942, expressed its views concerning both alien and native-born Japanese.

The resolution noted that there had been no complaints from the Japanese as to their loss of privileges or their confinement in the camps. Furthermore, the Legion opposed the campaign to allow two thousand Japanese students to leave camp to continue their education at various schools and colleges because the sons of Legion members had been drafted into military service, thereby cutting short their educational programs. In addition, it was proposed that those Japanese who "escaped" to states east of the Rockies were to be taken into custody and confined again. This document was rescinded in November 1946, but it was representative of the views of a large segment of the American population at the time.[25]

As the Japanese were released from the camps and allowed to move eastward, many settled in cities that they would not have visited without the forced relocation camps. This directly affected the Japanese population in Indiana. During World War II Indiana had a small Japanese-American population, and before the war there was no strong anti-Asian prejudice in the state. Indiana's 1940 population of 3,427,796 included only 29 Japanese Americans, and of that number 20 were Nisei or American born, while only 9 were Issei or Japanese born.[26] In contrast to Indiana in 1940, California, Oregon, and Washington had a Japanese-American population of 112,985, about 1.1 percent of the total population of the country.[27] Out of the approximately 285,000 Japanese in the United States in 1940, 93,717 or 33 percent were in California and 157,905 or 55 percent were in Hawaii, while the remaining 12 percent resided throughout the country.[28]

In 1940 nearly half the counties in Indiana had no persons other than whites or blacks living there, while the major concentration of the Japanese Americans was in the larger cities of Gary, Indianapolis, and South Bend.[29] Unlike residents of the West Coast states, most Indiana residents had no contact with, or direct knowledge of Japanese Americans, and during World War II there was little possibility of a Japanese attack on Indiana.

During this time there were no groups in Indiana such as the Joint Immigration Committee or the Native Sons and Daughters of the Golden West advocating exclusion of the Japanese Americans. There were no state leaders in Indiana similar to Attorney General Earl Warren and Gov. Culbert Olsen of California, Sen. Rufus Holman (R. Oregon), and Rep. Leland Ford (R. California) who endorsed the exclusion policy. On the federal level there were no prominent Indiana leaders, including Paul McNutt, head of the War Manpower Commission, or 1940 Republican presidential nominee Wendell Willkie, who publicly supported the exclusion policy.[30]

When Congress debated and passed Public Law 503 on 19 March 1942, no representative or senator from Indiana spoke. This law implemented Executive Order 9066 by providing a "penalty for violation of restrictions or orders with respect to persons entering, remaining in, leaving, or committing an act in military areas or zones." The entire congressional debate on the bill lasted barely ten minutes in each house, was discussed by five members of the House and three members of the Senate, and was approved by a voice vote in each house.[31]

During the war some members of the Indiana congressional delegation discussed various subjects involving Japanese Americans, including the Japanese prisoners of war, comparison of Japanese Americans and Chinese Americans, and the identification and registration of enemy aliens. Representative Charles Halleck of Rensselaer, who later would become Republican minority leader of the House, supported a bill in February 1944 to allow all citizens to renounce their citizenship, become enemy aliens, and be treated accordingly.[32] On 11 January 1943 Republican congressman Raymond Springer of Connersville introduced a bill to require certain persons to be fingerprinted and carry identification cards, which was to apply to, among others, Japanese Americans.[33] Springer addressed the question of relocation by opposing the War Relocation Authority appropriation in 1943 since part of it would be used to send Japanese aliens into other sections of the country to farm and work in the labor force. Specifically, he was concerned about the intrusion upon voters in his section of Indiana.

An analysis of twenty Indiana newspapers in sixteen cities around the state suggests considerable interest in the issues of "fifth-column" activities of the Japanese living along the West Coast. The newspaper coverage led many Hoosiers to be "anxious, angry, and afraid" of Japanese Americans.[34] On 18 February 1942 the *Muncie Evening Press* included a guest editorial, written by a woman traveler, which suggested that every Japanese American, whether born in the United States or not, "Must be put into concentration camps at once." The editorial stated that the president or Congress should act to "put them all behind barbed wire and keep the sexes separate."[35]

On 19 December 1944 the *Indianapolis News* published one of the few editorials with a positive view of the Japanese Americans that appeared in any Indiana newspaper during the entire war. The editorial entitled "Our Japanese-American Patriots" commended an American Legion post in New York for inviting into its membership sixteen Japanese Americans who had been removed from an Oregon post. Of the new inductees fourteen had served overseas, two had been killed in action against the Nazis, ten had been awarded the Purple Heart, and two would be killed in action in the Pacific, one on Leyte and the other while on a volunteer mission.[36] The article demonstrates that not all posts followed the national Legion resolutions. The Japanese veterans admitted to the New York post were among the thirteen thousand Japanese Americans serving in the United States Army who had "outstanding records and have been cited for gallantry repeatedly."[37] Indiana residents reacted to the issue of Japanese Americans much like in other areas of the country by voicing their opinions through editorials in newspapers.

The sentiments toward Japanese Americans during the war were to encourage or discourage the increased migration to Indiana. Under the War Relocation Act cited earlier, the evacuation was important to Indiana because Japanese Americans who passed governmental clearance were permitted to leave the camps and to settle in areas outside the restricted zones. About thirty-five thousand, many of them older Nisei, took advantage of the opportunity to move eastward and obtain employment or to enter college in the Midwest or in the East. After initial resistance from schools in the East, because it was against their policy to accept the students or because of the institution's involvement in classified research for the government, midwestern cities such as Chicago, Cleveland, and Minneapolis appeared more hospitable to the Japanese people.

The National Student Relocation Council (NSRC) was formed on 29 March 1942 to coordinate the efforts of church leaders, educators, government personnel, the Japanese American Citizens League, the YMCA, and the YWCA who were trying to secure placements for Japanese-American students. Although only 111 institutions were given government approval by 11 September 1942, more than 300 colleges and universities had agreed to accept

Nisei. The majority of the schools were private and religious institutions rather than public universities.

There was a school in Indiana open to Japanese Americans. Earlham College in Richmond accepted these students due, in large part, to the persistence of the school's president, William C. Dennis. Earlham had a direct connection with Japan for more than fifty years through its graduates and religious affiliations. Beginning in 1942 Dennis pursued both government approval to admit Japanese-American students at Earlham as well as to gain their acceptance by the Richmond community.[38]

For each student the Federal Bureau of Investigation needed to approve the school chosen, conduct a loyalty check of the student, and be assured adequate financial resources were available. One final prerequisite needed before a student left the internment camp was a letter of acceptance by community leaders where the school was located.

The mayor of Richmond, Indiana, wrote such a letter in support of two students who were American citizens of Japanese descent and who sought to complete their education at Earlham College. During a later mayoral campaign in 1942 the incumbent mayor publicly denied his earlier letter of support of the college's plan to enroll the Japanese-American students, fearing it might cost him the election. A controversy had developed in the Richmond community, and President Dennis dealt firmly with the latent hostility and racism generated by the election. He wrote to a waiting student in a camp that the great majority of the people of Richmond were "thinking right about the matter," and he proceeded with the admittance of Japanese-American students.[39]

After being forcibly relocated the Nisei wanted to leave the camps and return to school. They discovered Earlham by various means including the NSRC, recommendations by professors at their preevacuation schools, an article in a magazine, and through friends of their families. The Midwest was foreign territory to the Nisei; however, Earlham College gave them an opportunity to continue their educations.

During World War II about twenty Nisei studied at Earlham College. Many of their parents had come from Japan to work on the railroads of the West Coast and later settled permanently. While still in the West these Issei moved into a variety of other occupations, becoming respected members of their communities. Following Executive Order 9066, these Japanese-American families were evacuated, relocated, and interned before the Nisei students were released to attend Earlham.

After reaching the school the students were interviewed by reporters of the student newspaper, the *Earlham Post*. One Nisei commented that he did not think American

*Earlham College students Rose Takano and Henry Tanaka at the front entrance of Earlham Hall, 1943–44.*

citizens would be interned while another Nisei said that a small group of Kibei, who had pro-Japanese sympathies, deserved to be relocated but not at the expense of the innocent majority. Another Nisei expressed anger about the economics involved in the evacuation, which allowed Caucasians to pay the Issei $750 for furniture worth $3000 and $300 for a brand-new Pontiac.[40]

Recently, researchers at Earlham studied a core group of five former Japanese-American students from the World War II period. Each student was influenced by his or her experience at the college, but all made important contributions to the campus and the Richmond community and thereby altered the lives of many Hoosiers with their presence.

One student, Grant Noda, was the son of agricultural workers in California before they were relocated. He became familiar with Earlham after reading a magazine article on Quaker colleges. Ernest Wildman, a Quaker and professor at the college, housed Noda and another Japanese-American student who did house and farmwork, such as milking the cows and feeding the farm animals. Noda shared a room with one of the professor's sons, Bill Wildman, and the two became lifelong friends.[41]

A female Japanese-American student, Rose Takano, was in high school when she was interned but was able to leave the camp with the help of a Quaker faculty member at Stanford University. After graduating from high school in 1943, the Stanford family friend introduced her to Earlham and to the Steintorf family. While at Earlham she stayed with the Steintorfs and became an officer in the Little Y, a branch of the YWCA.[42]

The third student was Henry (Hank) Tanaka, the son of an Oregon family of restaurant operators. He lived with the Wildman family at Earlham along with Grant Noda. Tanaka experienced the racism that did exist in Richmond when he and several other students went to Millers Cafeteria, a nearby restaurant. A black student with Tanaka was refused service, and Tanaka climbed onto a table to speak about racial attitudes to the other diners. Tanaka became a conscientious objector at Earlham and was drafted as a C.O. in the Medical Corps. After becoming a psychiatric social worker and a pioneer in new methods of treatment for mental illness, Tanaka retired as director of Hill House at Case Western Reserve University in Cleveland, Ohio, in 1990. A year later he was honored by Earlham as a distinguished alumni.[43]

Another Japanese-American student at Earlham, Edward (Eddie) Uyesugi, made his presence known in the community. He arrived at the school with his older brother in August 1942 and became a star running back on the football team. An issue centering on interracial dating that involved Uyesugi created a serious problem. He began dating Ruth Ann Farlow, and anticipating that there would be a problem, the couple tried to keep it a secret. They were discovered, and teachers and administrators attempted to stop the relationship from becoming serious. To appease President Dennis, Farlow made it appear that she was dating other men by dancing with them at student dances.[44] Uyesugi and Farlow later married and settled in Indiana where he was a practicing ophthalmologist. Patients from all over the world sought him out after he pioneered new ways of treating ailments of the eyes.

Uyesugi's older brother changed his name to Newton Wesley while he was at Earlham to avoid discrimination as a Japanese American. Shortly after his arrival Wesley went for an interview with the editor of the local newspaper, the *Palladium-Item,* in response to a series of anti-Japanese articles. This meeting helped diffuse the discrimination situation in the community.[45]

Before being sent to a relocation camp, Wesley applied directly to Earlham College and was told to avoid getting into any trouble, since the behavior of the first students to leave the camps would directly influence whether or not other students would be allowed to depart for college. The Nisei interviewed said they experienced a drive to be one of the "model minority," and similar parental expectations were reinforced by societal pressure.[46]

Several of the students and faculty members at Earlham admitted they had preconceived notions of the Nisei, including the lack of a sense of humor. The Japanese-American students did not fit these stereotypes because each was an individual person. In comparison to the large numbers of people on the West Coast, many Hoosiers did not seem to be adamantly opposed to loyal Japanese-American students attending college. Reasons for this more receptive attitude by some in the Midwest may have been a less vulnerable geographic location during the war, less contact with Japanese over the years thus producing less racial hatreds, and a lack of economic competition with Japan. The Nisei found themselves in new situations, different from being Japanese on the West Coast, and Americans from the Midwest generally found them to be intelligent, ambitious, and highly motivated.

On 29 January 1943 an article in the *Indianapolis News* entitled, "City Has Choice on Jap Migrants," commented that Indianapolis could accept or reject "relocated" workers. Interned Japanese, who were American citizens, were being permitted to enter employment elsewhere in the country under regulations that required investigation of the individual and ascertainment of the willingness of a community to receive them. These internees were said to be available to help meet the manpower shortage and had backgrounds in agriculture, service occupations, and business.[47]

One Japanese-American family, the Takayoshis, became Indianapolis residents in 1943 after living in internment camps in the West. In 1942 they were told to go to the Puyallup Assembly Center near Seattle, Washington, later to be taken to the Minidoka internment camp near Twin Falls, Idaho, and to bring only what they could carry. Despite the fact that Yoshi and Kim Takayoshi and their children were American citizens the family was interned. Not fearing they would be harmed, the family decided it was best to go to the camp to prove their innocence and their loyalty to their homeland, the United States.[48] When the opportunity came to volunteer to fight in the war, Yoshi and two of his brothers enlisted. His brothers were accepted but Yoshi was rejected because of an old shoulder injury. Hearing about a job opportunity in Wisconsin, Yoshi left the camp to investigate the employment possibilities. He stopped in Indianapolis en route and decided to settle in the community after finding a job and housing. Yoshi operated a filling station in the city for many years and expressed his gratitude for a supportive employer. He and his wife became members of a Baptist church, raised their children in the city, and have lived in

Indianapolis for nearly fifty years. They said they have been satisfied residing in Indiana, and received only a few minor negative comments when they initially moved to the state.[49]

In northwest Indiana in the middle 1980s there were two dozen Japanese-American families, and two Nisei from this group experienced internment during World War II. They were Purdue University Calumet mathematics professor Theodore S. Chihara of Highland and Catherine Yamamoto of Crown Point, a children's librarian at the Lake County Public Library in Merrillville. Although neither became embittered by his/her confinement, both recall the anguish of their parents. Yamamoto was eleven when her family was taken from its farm home near Auburn, Washington, and interned initially in California and subsequently in Colorado. She rationalized that she and her sisters would have stayed on the farm for life if they had not been forcefully relocated.[50]

Other Japanese Americans from northwest Indiana suffered from the World War II experience in a different way since they were still living in Japan at the time. Dr. Takamitsu Nakamura of Munster, an ear, nose, and throat specialist in Hammond; Theresa Tatko Takahashi Ozug of Merrillville; and Yukiko Dawson of Valparaiso endured B-29 bombings that flattened their home cities of Osaka, Tokyo, and Yokohama. Nakamura was seven when his family fled to the mountains in order to escape almost daily air raids on Osaka. Ozug was fourteen when nightly raids began in June 1944 over her home in Yokohama.

Another Japanese American from northwest Indiana was visiting his mother's homeland with his family when the war broke out. Sam Schultz, owner of the House of Kobe restaurant in Schererville, was born in Seattle, Washington, although his mother was a native of Kamakura, Japan. Although only visiting Japan, his family was imprisoned by the military, and Schultz's mother and sister died when the camp was hit by Allied bombs. He survived the ordeal and returned to America.[51]

Schultz, whose maternal family line is Inouye, married a native of Saga, which is twenty miles north of Nagasaki. The family served as a liaison for the Japanese community in northwest Indiana and found that many of the third- and fourth-generation Japanese are descendants of immigrants from the Hiroshima area. Japanese did not move to the Midwest in large numbers until 1946, when nearly thirty-six thousand former internees migrated to the Chicago area.[52]

The loyalty of people of Japanese ancestry was questioned both in the United States and abroad during the World War II period. Two longtime Indianapolis Japanese-American residents were interviewed after the attack on Pearl Harbor. The article was printed in the *Indianapolis Star* on 8 December 1941 titled "Native-Born Japs Here to Back U.S." The two Japanese expressed their wholehearted support of the United States government in its hostilities with Japan and declared their determination to fight if needed. Professor Toyozo W. Nakarai had been a teacher at Butler University for fifteen years, and Harry Sasaki operated a coffee and tea stand in the city market for nearly thirty years.[53]

Thirty-three thousand Japanese Americans did fight in World War II, while many of their relatives were held behind barbed wire.[54] Some Japanese refused to enlist, but others stressed that they could prove their loyalty to the United States by enlisting and distinguishing themselves in the war. On 22 January 1943 the War Department directed that a Japanese-American Combat Team be activated on 1 February and be composed of the 442d Infantry Regiment, the 522d Field Artillery Battalion, and the 232d Engineer Combat Company. An all-Nisei army group, the 442d Regimental Combat team was engaged in some of the bloodiest fighting of the European war in the vicinity of Serravezza, Carrara, and Fosdinovo, Italy. This unit absorbed Hawaii's 100th Battalion, which was made up of Japanese Americans who had been inducted into the army before Pearl Harbor was attacked, and emerged as the most decorated combat unit in American military history.[55] The unit suffered more than 9,000 casualties including 600 dead, and, among other awards, earned more than 3,600 Purple Hearts, 810 Bronze Stars, 342 Silver Stars, 47 Distinguished Service Crosses, a Medal of Honor, and 7 distinguished unit citations.[56] Sen. Daniel Inouye (D. Hawaii) was a member of this unit and still carries a war infirmity suffered while fighting in Italy.

In the Pacific theater several thousand Japanese Americans served a valuable military role as interpreters. Assuming that Americans could not understand Japanese, Japan's military forces often failed to code their messages. In 1942 *Life* magazine stated that when the war started less than one hundred persons in America had a real mastery of Japanese, and army intelligence officers agreed.[57] There were Nisei on every battlefront reading captured Japanese documents and passing information on to allied commanders.[58] Gen. Douglas MacArthur's chief of intelligence, Charles Willoughby, credited Nisei Americans with saving over one million Allied lives.[59]

Japanese Americans proved their commitment to a country that had distrusted their loyalty. The incarceration of an entire ethnic group without any hearing or any formal charge brought against a single member has been described as the worst assault on civil rights in United States history. In 1975 President Gerald Ford revoked Roosevelt's Executive Order 9066, saying "we now know what we should have known then—not only was the evacuation wrong but Japanese-Americans were and are loyal Americans."[60] The presidential Commission on the Wartime Relocation and Internment of Civilians concluded in 1983 that the wartime mistreatment of Japanese Americans was based on broad historical causes that shaped those decisions, including race prejudice, war hysteria, and a failure of political leadership.[61]

After a compromise agreement five years later, President Ronald Reagan signed bill HR442-PL 100-383 on 10 August 1988, which approved $1.25 billion in reparations to Japanese Americans interned during World War II.[62] A federal commission concluded that the internment was not based on military necessity, and more than twenty-five thousand claimants have received the $20,000 redress checks Congress authorized, a small amount considering what they lost. More than seventy-two thousand former internees were still alive in 1991, and several living in Indiana received this compensation.[63]

Other laws that affected the Japanese were passed at the end of World War II. The concept of family unity was carried into the War Brides Act of 28 December 1945 (Public Law 271) and the Fiancees Act of 29 June 1946 (Public Law 471) allowing these people to enter the United States as nonquota immigrants. The first ships arrived bringing wives and children of soldiers to the United States in April 1946 and by 30 June 1949, 113,135 war brides, 327 war grooms, and 4,537 children of armed forces personnel were admitted to the country. Of the 757 Japanese admitted under these laws, 752 were wives and five were children of American citizens.[64]

In 1952 the California State Supreme Court declared unconstitutional the 1913 Alien Land Act that made those aliens who were "ineligible for citizenship" also ineligible for ownership of agricultural property. Earl Warren, a chief justice of the Supreme Court known for his pursuit of social justice later in his life, had been the California state attorney general who ruled that American-born Japanese could not acquire voting residence; as governor of California from 1943 to 1953 he oversaw the relocation of the Japanese during World War II.

Another progressive step was made when the Issei were allowed to become naturalized citizens and, hence, given the right to vote under the McCarren-Walter Act of 1952. Over President Harry S Truman's veto, Congress passed this new law with the support of the American Legion and the Japanese American Citizens League, two usually incongruent groups.

Locally, the time period from 1940 to 1950 revealed demographic changes as the Japanese-American population in Indiana grew by almost eleven times, from 29 to 318. In the 1950 Indiana census of counties and cities of 10,000

inhabitants or more, Japanese were distinguished by sex, and males outnumbered females by 18 percent in the counties and by 24 percent in the cities, narrowing the earlier gender gap. In this poll there were a total of 150 men and 104 women in the counties and a total of 98 men and 60 women in the cities. Marion, Lake, and Allen counties had the highest number of Japanese, while Indianapolis, Fort Wayne, and Gary had the largest urban populations in the state. Of the 318 people of Japanese ancestry counted in 1950, more than half, or 160, were not living in the eleven major cities of the state at that time but were living in smaller towns or rural communities.[65] Like many other sections of the country Indiana would experience a continued growth in the population of Japanese Americans born outside and within the state after World War II. Sansei, or third generation, were born either in the wartime internment camps or shortly after the conflict.

The 1960 census showed Japanese in Indiana numbered 1,903. During the second half of the twentieth century census figures of citizens of Japanese ancestry became more difficult to distinguish because of intermarriage. As increased numbers of Japanese aliens moved to the United States and to Indiana for business reasons, census figures are assumed to include a percentage of residents who do not intend to become citizens.

In an article in the *Indianapolis News* dated 9 May 1963 the United States Immigration and Naturalization Service reported that of the 27,892 aliens registered as residents for that year in Indiana 310 were originally from Japan. Of the total registrations, 24,429 aliens indicated they now considered Indiana their permanent home.[66]

United States immigration policy was reformed in the Hart-Celler Act of 1965, whose provisions took effect in 1968 by abolishing the national origins quota system and the designation of the Asia-Pacific Triangle. Japanese immigration would be less restricted with higher ceilings allowed; however, persons naturalized in the United States from Japan steadily decreased from 2,673 in 1966 to 1,548 in 1975.[67]

In the 1970 census for Indiana the population with Japanese ancestry was documented by sex as well as urban and rural residence, and the females outnumbered the males 62 percent to 38 percent, reversing the previous trend. The total in this count was 2,100, differing 179 from the official census count for the state of 2,279. The urban areas had the highest population of 1,626 with 41 percent male and 59 percent female. The rural nonfarm residences included 392 people with 28 percent male and 72 percent female, and the smallest group was rural farm with 37 percent male and 63 percent female. The urban areas had 1,626 people, the rural nonfarm area had 392 people, and the rural farm area had 82 people, which corresponded with the urban jobs of the Japanese immigrants admitted for the year 1975.[68] The predominant occupations were professional, technical, and kindred workers, managers, administrators, sales and clerical workers, with the smallest number employed as farmers or farm managers.[69] This report showed the rise of Japanese immigrants, especially Nisei and Sansei, from jobs in the agricultural sector to the professional and service-oriented fields.

Many of the Americans in Indiana of Japanese ancestry have contributed to their communities as doctors, dentists, businessmen, businesswomen, and professors. One example is Hidetaro Suzuki, who was born in Tokyo in 1937. Suzuki's parents loved music and were thrilled that he, as a toddler, sang in tune. At the age of four they bought a violin for him, and he began lessons. During World War II Japanese children were rounded up and sent to the mountains for safekeeping. Each child was told to select one possession to take, and Suzuki chose his violin. To the dismay of his violin teacher, Suzuki pursued an interest in baseball as the catcher on his school team.[70]

At the age of fourteen Suzuki won first prize in the Japanese National Violin Competition. As a result he played one hundred concerts a year for a period of five years. After graduating from the Toho School of Music in 1956 his exceptional music talent led to his acceptance at two prestigious American music schools, Curtis Institute of Music in Philadelphia and Julliard School in New York. He accepted an all-expenses paid Curtis scholarship to study with Efrem Zimbalist in Philadelphia. The Fulbright Commission paid his boat trip expenses between Yokohama and Seattle and train trip expenses between Seattle and Philadelphia. Although the Fulbright grant stipulated he return to Japan at the end of his studies, Suzuki chose to move to Canada with his wife and son.[71]

Suzuki had met and married Cuban-born Zeyda Ruga, a gifted pianist, at Curtis while both were students. They had a son, Kenneth, while still in Philadelphia and then they moved to Quebec, where Suzuki became the symphony's concertmaster for sixteen years. They increased their family again with the birth of twins, Elina and Nantel, while living in Quebec. With performances all over the world the family traveled on a Japanese passport, a Cuban passport, an American passport, and two Canadian passports. They were asked to explain this combination everywhere.[72]

Rising emotions over French nationalism made it uncomfortable for foreigners to live in Quebec, so when Suzuki heard of the opening for concertmaster of the Indianapolis Symphony Orchestra he auditioned and won the position.[73] He had difficulty getting a work permit to settle in the United States; the problem was related to his travel money from Fulbright and the expectation he was to have returned to Japan. The legal snarl in the United States delayed the family's move for a year. The Indianapolis Symphony Orchestra president and its manager traveled to Washington, D.C., to solve the immigration problem. Zeyda said she knew she was going to love Indianapolis because a lot of places would have dropped them because of all the trouble and delay.[74]

In addition to being the Indianapolis Symphony Orchestra concertmaster, Suzuki has served as a faculty member of Jordan College of Music at Butler University. Furthermore, he also founded the chamber series, Suzuki and Friends, which he has directed since 1980 and in which he frequently performs with his wife.[75] The Suzuki family has made an important addition to Indiana, as attested by Suzuki receiving the TRACI award given by the Metropolitan Arts Council for his contribution to the "advancement of culture in Indianapolis."[76]

A 1977 *Indianapolis News* article featured another longtime member of the community, Rev. James Sugioka, who had lived here for thirty-five years and was a retired Disciples of Christ minister and an active participant in civil rights. Sugioka was a graduate electrical engineer but returned to the classroom at the Christian Theological Seminary, calling Butler University his alma mater.[77] A Japanese-American faculty member at Butler, Dr. T. Z. Nakari, was a professor of the Old Testament and Hebrew and was considered one of America's outstanding teachers. He later retired to Tennessee.

Other Japanese Americans in Indiana have brought their talent to the state. In honor of the United States Bicentennial in 1976, a group of Japanese-born women formed a group known as the Minyo Dancers, who perform ancient folk routines that originated among laborers to lighten their workdays. The Indianapolis women were schooled in their interpretive motions and steps by Tsutomu Matsuda of Tokyo, president of the Federation of Minyo Dancers in Japan, and have added younger native Japanese women to the group to ensure its continuance in Indianapolis.[78]

Tsuru (Betty) Bunnell, the current Minyo Club president and an original member, says the dancers introduce Japanese culture to American society. All eighteen dancers are of Japanese ancestry; sixteen are from Japan and two are from Hawaii, and all came to Indiana by marriage. Bunnell came to the United States in 1957, first to Pennsylvania and then to Indianapolis because of her husband's job. The Bunnells have lived in New Palestine for the last twenty years, and she works at the Japanese Sakura Mart grocery store in Indianapolis. Her first impression of Hoosiers was that they were not very friendly, but now says she is very happy and

*The Minyo Club, Indianapolis.*

comfortable after making many friends, including the Minyo dancers.[79] These women have combined Japanese tradition with their American lives.

Another local group known as the Japanese American Citizens League was founded in 1976 and is part of the national organization established by a Nisei in 1922 to promote Japanese civil rights. One of its original objectives was to prove that American-born Japanese were entitled to citizenship, so they adopted the lobbying techniques of other American pressure groups. The techniques used by the organization to obtain its goals revealed the differences between the Issei, who were more passive in their relationship with the American government and society, and the Nisei, who sought change with more vigor and activism. Today the league still lobbies for the rights of all Japanese Americans. Many residents in Indiana have joined the group and are active in the community, subscribing to its weekly paper the *Pacific Citizen*.[80]

Members of the local Japanese American Citizens League included nurseryman Jim Maeda, a University of California at Davis graduate; Seattle-born and raised George Umemura, who earned an Indiana University doctorate in business administration and handled marketing for Eli Lilly and Company; and Prof. Terry Ishihara from Terre Haute, an Idaho native educated at the University of Arizona and a Rose-Hulman Institute faculty member with a doctorate in mechanical engineering.[81]

Officers of the Japanese American Citizens League in 1977 included Hawaii native Walter Nakatosukasa, a microbiologist in pharmaceutical research, and Charles Matsumoto, who has a pharmacology doctorate. Both Southport residents were University of Washington at Seattle graduates. Membership chairman during the same time was Ken Matsumoto, an Arizona native with a University of California, Berkeley, chemistry doctorate. George Hanasono, the representative to the International Center in Indianapolis, is Reverend Sugioka's nephew. Hanasono came to Indiana in 1974 as a pharmaceutical researcher with degrees from the University of California, Los Angeles, and the University of Southern California, a University of Iowa doctorate, and advanced study at the University of Montreal. These Japanese Americans achieved success through their accomplishments in higher education and became involved citizens in Indiana.[82]

By 1980 Indiana's population with Japanese lineage had grown to 2,503. It is difficult, however, to distinguish Japanese aliens from residents who planned to make Indiana their permanent home. Since many Japanese companies have located in Indiana, managers and their families have temporarily moved to the state with no intention of becoming citizens of the United States. Nonetheless, these foreign nationals are counted in the census records, which prevents accurate Japanese-American statistics of the permanent residents.

In the 1980 Indiana census figures 1,291 persons were recorded as Japanese foreign born and 1,212 were classified as natives to the state of Japanese ancestry. Some Japanese Americans in Indiana married individuals of different ethnic backgrounds from themselves; therefore, their children could report belonging to more than one ancestry group. In a 1980 ancestry of population study by the census bureau of Japanese in Indiana, 3,806 persons reported at least one genealogy, 2,746 persons reported a single descent, and 1,060 persons reported a multiple lineage. Consequently, an exact figure of Japanese Americans is very difficult to derive from the census data that allows reporting of more than one ancestry group.[83]

In a census count of Indiana foreign born for 1980 by township, a pattern is evident that the largest Japanese populations and companies are based in Wabash Township in Tippecanoe County with 172 people, Bloomington Township in Monroe County with 89 people, and eight townships in Marion County with a total of 299 people. Most of the Japanese population, however, was dispersed all over the state covering 151 different townships in 57 counties.[84]

Unlike the trend in many United States cities, immigrants to Indianapolis no longer cluster in insular ethnic neighborhoods as they did in the early 1900s, and this is true for the Japanese Americans who have become permanent residents. Because they do not live in close proximity, Indianapolis does not have a Japanese district similar to other cities such as Los Angeles.[85] This settlement pattern has contributed to their assimilation into Indiana's society.

Many Japanese Americans have retained traditions brought with them or learned by their parents, such as dance, food, and educational advancement. Some of the immigrants have contributed their experience and knowledge to promote Indiana to outside interests. One Japanese native turned Hoosier is Mari Yamamoto Regnier, who is a key player in Indiana's efforts to attract future Japanese industries. She conducts seminars on doing business with the Japanese, works with lawyers at Barnes & Thornburg of Indianapolis to help them establish smooth communication with Japanese clients, is on the board of the Japan-America Society of Indiana, and has published articles in Indiana and Japan about the experiences of Japanese businesses in the Hoosier state.[86]

The Japanese population in Indiana increased by 47 percent during the decade between 1980 and 1990, jumping from 2,503 to 4,715.[87] Statisticians have attributed

Officials of Subaru-Isuzu Automotive, Inc., celebrate in March 1995 after receiving the prestigious ISO-9002 award for meeting an international standard of quality in automobile manufacturing. The company was the first car producer in North America to earn the certificate.

this increase to the number of Japanese businesses expanding their operations to Indiana, one example being the Subaru-Isuzu automotive plant in Lafayette. The 1980 census reported 195 Japanese in Tippecanoe County, and the 1990 census reported 813. While most of these Japanese are in Indiana only temporarily, they are still considered a part of Indiana's statistics.

Recently, Japanese foreign nationals have experienced harassment and discrimination due to war memories from fifty years ago and economic competition worsened by the United States recession. On 14 August 1989 a bomb threat was received by a Japanese company on the anniversary of the 1945 Japanese surrender that ended World War II, although no bomb was found.[88] The anniversary of the Japanese bombing of Pearl Harbor also raised racial animosity for some Hoosiers, especially World War II veterans. In a 7 December 1991 editorial by a Japanese American who is a copy editor for the *Indianapolis Star*, the racial insults and questions of loyalty were discussed to make readers aware of the injury and ill feeling such attitudes caused citizens with Japanese ethnic backgrounds.[89]

Members of the Japan-America Society of Indiana are working to change "heartless hostility into Hoosier hospitality," according to an *Indianapolis Star* article on 19 February 1992. The not-for-profit Indiana society, founded in June 1988, is one of about thirty similar organizations in the National Association of Japan-America Societies, the oldest of which are in Boston, Los Angeles, and San Francisco. Initially, the Indiana society's purposes "were to help Americans and Japanese deal with culture shock, to prevent misunderstandings and to help both sides correct inaccurate preconceptions." It now serves as a network among American and Japanese companies, providing a good mechanism for discussion.[90]

Recently the society eased tensions in an Indiana community. The message, "Don't Forget Pearl Harbor," was painted on the garage owned by a Johnson County resident. The message was strategically placed so that Japanese executives would see it every day as they drove to work at their business in Franklin. The Japan-America Society of Indiana arranged a seminar that included speeches by both Japanese and American executives. About fifteen hundred people attended a Cherry Blossom Festival organized by the wives of the Japanese executives later the same day. The next day the Pearl Harbor message on the garage was covered with a coat of paint.[91]

The 350-member organization, about 60 percent American and 40 percent Japanese, helps organize outings to golf courses, Conner Prairie, University of Notre Dame football games, Indianapolis Symphony Orchestra performances, and Indianapolis Indians baseball games. The society also helps promote events that involve primarily Japanese culture, such as the sold-out performance by Kodo, a group of Japanese percussionists.[92] Consequently, Hoosiers have been exposed to an increasing number of people of Japanese ancestry and their culture.

Since World War II the numbers of Americans of Japanese heritage in Indiana have continued to grow, and in 1990 they lived in eighty-nine out of the ninety-two counties, indicating that the state has a widespread population. It is apparent from the 1990 statistics that Japanese Americans have not settled in one major area of the state since forty counties have numbers of ten residents or below. The counties with the largest populations are Marion with 824, Tippecanoe with 813, Bartholomew with 258, St. Joseph with 247, and Hamilton with 229. There is a correspondence of larger Japanese populations in counties with Japanese businesses and American colleges and universities, suggesting that many of the Japanese counted may be foreign nationals who are in the state for a short time.[93]

As a result of the presence of Japanese industries in Indiana interest has risen in the Japanese language, and it is being taught in some form at more than fifty school districts in the state. A different kind of school, the Indiana Japanese Language School, was established in 1981 and met at Orchard Country Day School in Indianapolis. The school meets on Saturdays for four hours to help Japanese students in kindergarten through grade twelve maintain their native language, improve their mathematics skills, and understand the culture of Japan. When the school first opened there were 15 students; in 1989 the number had risen to about 250. This growth reflects the acceleration of Japanese business interests in the state. The majority of students at the language school are children of Japanese employees whose companies have transferred them to Indiana for from one to five years.[94]

With this larger population the number of Japanese restaurants and grocery stores has also increased in the state so that those of Japanese ancestry enjoy their traditional food along with many Hoosiers from different ethnic backgrounds. Shoji (George) Sato is a sushi chef at Sakura, one of two Japanese restaurants in Indianapolis that has more authentic food. He is from Ibaraki prefecture near Tokyo and learned his trade from a chef in Japan. Seven years ago a Japanese friend who was working in Detroit, Michigan, called Sato about a job as a sushi chef. Sato took the job but found that crime committed near the restaurant and toward customers made him uncomfortable.

Sato married a Japanese girl before he came to the United States, where he planned to work and then send for her if the situation were acceptable. When the owner of the restaurant in Detroit decided to open another one in Indianapolis, Sato was willing to move. He has lived in the Indianapolis area for six years now and considers the people nice, the city clean, and life more comfortable. Sato sent for his wife, and they have two young children. Their son and daughter have green cards and at the age of eighteen will have the option to choose American or Japanese citizenship. At this point Sato and his family are planning to stay in Indianapolis, but he wants his children to learn the Japanese language.[95]

Sakura, the restaurant where Sato works, was opened because of the many Japanese companies in Indiana, and on the weekends many Japanese drive from cities such as Columbus and Bloomington to eat there. The majority of the customers, however, are non-Japanese, partly because the people of Japanese ancestry are spread all over the state.

Another employee at Sakura is a waitress named Shizue Addison, who has worked there for about six months but has lived in Indiana for a total of twenty-two years. She was born in the southern part of Japan in Miyazaki on Kyushu Island and met her ex-husband in Japan. Addison has a son and a daughter and has had positive experiences living in the Indianapolis area. She is glad there are Japanese restaurants and grocery stores in Indiana so she no longer has to call someone in Japan to have items sent to her. When Addison goes to Japan to visit she said she misses her home in Indiana after a week or two and wishes to return.[96]

Since 1880 the Japanese immigrants who have made Indiana their permanent home have assimilated into communities where they have settled while balancing their own ethnicity. Those who decided to build a life for themselves here were attracted to the state for different reasons, yet all have endured economic hardship and deprivation, ethnic hostility, wartime hysteria, and racial discrimination. Achieving success by overcoming all those vexatious conditions and becoming model citizens has earned the Japanese the respect of all Americans, and in particular the residents of the state who call Indiana home.

## Notes

1. U.S. Department of Treasury, *Arrivals of Alien Passengers and Immigrants in the United States 1820–1892* (Washington, D.C.: Government Printing Office, 1893), 99 (Government Printing Office is hereafter cited as GPO); Department of the Interior, Census Office, *The Abstract of the Eleventh Census: 1890* (Washington, D.C.: GPO, 1894), 33. The first source lists twenty-five Japanese living in Indiana in 1890; the second source lists eighteen.

2. Thomas Sowell, *Ethnic America: A History* (New York: Basic Books, 1981), 160.

3. Yamato Ichihashi, *Japanese in the United States: A Critical Study of the Problems of the Japanese Immigrants and Their Children* (Stanford, Calif.: Stanford University Press, 1932), 393.

4. Ibid.

5. William Dillingham, *Abstracts of Reports of the Immigration Commission* (1910–11), Sen. Doc. No. 747, 61st Cong., 3d sess., 105.

6. *Indianapolis Sentinel,* 23 July 1905.

7. Ibid.

8. *Indianapolis Star,* 28 Aug. 1906.

9. Ibid., 17 Jan. 1909.

10. June Drenning Holmquist, ed., *They Chose Minnesota: A Survey of the State's Ethnic Groups* (St. Paul: Minnesota Historical Society Press, 1981), 558.

11. U.S. Department of Commerce, *Characteristics of the Population: Indiana* (Washington, D.C.: GPO, 1941), 12.

12. Harry H. L. Kitano, "Japanese," in *Harvard Encyclopedia of American Ethnic Groups,* ed. Stephan Thernstrom (Cambridge, Mass.: Belknap Press of Harvard University Press, 1980), 561–62.

13. Sowell, *Ethnic America,* 168.

14. Harry H. L. Kitano, *Race Relations* (Englewood Cliffs, N.J.: Prentice-Hall, 1974), 214.

15. Sowell, *Ethnic America,* 170.

16. Kitano, "Japanese," 565.

17. R. L. Lapica, ed., *Facts on File Yearbook: Person's Index of World Events,* 62 vols. (New York: Facts on File, Inc., 1942–93), 2:204. The yearbooks are indexed for convenience.

18. *The National Cyclopaedia of American Biography,* 86 vols. (New York: James T. White and Co., 1898–1994), 37:466.

19. William Pencak, *For God & Country: The American Legion, 1919–1941* (Boston: Northeastern University Press, 1989), 258.

20. Kitano, "Japanese," 565.

21. Ibid., 566.

22. *Facts on File Yearbook,* 2:204.

23. Kitano, *Race Relations,* 57.

24. Harry H. L. Kitano, *Japanese Americans: The Evolution of a Subculture* (Englewood Cliffs, N.J.: Prentice-Hall, 1969), 40.

25. "Military Control Over Japanese Internment Camps Urged," American Legion National Convention, Kansas City, 1942 "Resolutions," as quoted in *American Legion MSS,* Indianapolis, Ind., 66.

26. U.S. Department of Commerce, Bureau of the Census, *Sixteenth Census of the United States, 1940. Population,* vol. 2, *Characteristics of the Population Part 2: Florida–Iowa* (Washington, D.C.: GPO, 1943), 676 (hereafter cited as Bureau of the Census for the appropriate year).

27. Jacobus tenBroek, Edward N. Barnhart, and Floyd W. Matson, *Prejudice, War, and the Constitution* (Berkeley: University of California Press, 1968), 352.

28. U.S. Census Department, *Japanese, Chinese and Filipinos in the United States, 1940–1970* (Washington, D.C.: GPO, 1973), Appendix Λ, 119.

29. Bureau of the Census, 1940, p. 842.

30. U.S. Commission on Wartime Relocation and Internment of Civilians, *Personal Justice Denied* (Washington, D.C.: GPO, 1982), 72–86.

31. *Congressional Record,* 77th Cong., 2d sess., 19 Mar. 1949, pp. 2722–27, 2729–30.

32. Ibid., 78th Cong., 2d sess., 16 Feb. 1944, p. 1779.

33. Ibid., 78th Cong., 1st sess., 11 Jan. 1943, p. 117.

34. tenBroek, Barnhart, and Matson, *Prejudice, War, and the Constitution,* 208.

35. *Muncie Evening Press,* 18 Feb. 1942.

36. Kitano, *Japanese Americans,* 41.

37. *Indianapolis News,* 19 Dec. 1944.

38. Jackson Bailey et al., "Japanese-American Students at Earlham College: A Case Study of Wartime Experience and Racism" (Unpublished manuscript, Earlham College), 25.

39. Ibid., 30.

40. Ibid., 32.

41. Ibid., 39.

42. Ibid., 35.

43. Ibid.

44. Ibid., 43.

45. Ibid., 37.

46. Ibid., 41.

47. Roger Daniels, *Concentration Camps USA: Japanese Americans and World War II* (New York: Holt, Rinehart, and Winston, Inc., 1972), 99.

48. Yoshitaka and Kimiko Takayoshi, interview with author, 7 Jan. 1992, Indianapolis.

49. Ibid.

50. Ernie Hernandez, *Ethnics in Northwest Indiana* (Gary, Ind.: Gary Post-Tribune, 1984), 141.

51. Ibid., 142.

52. Ibid., 143.

53. *Indianapolis Star,* 8 Dec. 1941.

54. Kitano, "Japanese," 567.

55. Sowell, *Ethnic America,* 174.

56. Kitano, *Race Relations,* 60.

57. Joseph D. Harrington, *Yankee Samurai: The Secret Role of Nisei in America's Pacific Victory* (Detroit: Pettigrew Enterprises, 1979), 5.

58. Sowell, *Ethnic America,* 174.

59. Harrington, *Yankee Samurai,* 260.

60. Hernandez, *Ethnics in Northwest Indiana,* 143.

61. Roger Daniels, *Coming to America: A History of Immigration and Ethnicity in American Life* (New York: HarperCollins, 1990), 303.

62. "Internees Gain Reparations," *Congressional Quarterly Almanac,* 100th Cong., 2d sess. (Washington, D.C.: Congressional

Quarterly, Inc., 1988), 44:80–81.

63. *Indianapolis Star,* 26 Jan. 1992.

64. William Dillingham, "Dillingham Report," *Immigration Monthly Review,* 2, no. 7 (Jan. 1950): 93.

65. Bureau of the Census, *Population: 1950,* Table 47, pp. 14–129.

66. *Indianapolis News,* 9 May 1963.

67. Thernstrom, ed., *Harvard Encyclopedia of American Ethnic Groups,* 1074.

68. Ibid., 1069.

69. Ibid., 1075.

70. *Indianapolis Star,* 25 Mar. 1984.

71. Hidetaro Suzuki, fax interview, 27 Jan. 1993, Indianapolis.

72. Laura Gaus, "Suzuki: Worth the Wait," *Indianapolis Magazine* 19 (Sept. 1982): 16.

73. Ruth Fark Banta, "Music the Suzuki Way," *Indianapolis Monthly* 6 (Feb. 1983): 60.

74. Gaus, "Suzuki," 16.

75. *Indianapolis Star,* 13 Jan. 1991.

76. Indianapolis Symphony Orchestra, *Symphony on the Prairie Program,* 10th Anniversary Season, Conner Prairie (Indianapolis: Indiana State Symphony Society, 1991), 22.

77. *Indianapolis News,* 2 Dec. 1977.

78. *Indianapolis Star,* 13 Jan. 1980.

79. Tsuru (Betty) Bunnell, interview with author, 20 Jan. 1993.

80. *Indianapolis News,* 2 Dec. 1977.

81. Ibid.

82. Ibid.

83. U.S. Department of Commerce, Bureau of the Census, *Ancestry of the Population by the State: 1980,* Supplementary Report PC-80-S1-10 (Washington, D.C.: GPO, 1983), 23, 41, 59.

84. Bureau of the Census, *Indiana's Foreign-Born for 1980,* Summary of Computer Tape 3A, Indiana (Washington, D.C.: GPO, n.d.).

85. Susan McKee, "The Immigrants," *Indianapolis Monthly* 7 (Oct. 1983): 65.

86. *Indianapolis News,* 2 May 1989.

87. U. S. Department of Commerce, Bureau of the Census, *Census of Population and Housing: 1990,* Summary Tape File 1A, East North Central Division, vol. 1, *Indiana–Ohio* (Washington, D.C.: GPO, 1991).

88. *Indianapolis News,* 20 Jan. 1990.

89. *Indianapolis Star,* 7 Dec. 1991.

90. Ibid., 19 Feb. 1992.

91. Ibid.

92. Ibid.

93. Ibid.; Bureau of the Census, *Census of the Population and Housing: 1990,* Summary Tape File 1A.

94. *Indianapolis News,* 16 Oct. 1989.

95. Shoji (George) Sato, interview with author, 27 Jan. 1993.

96. Shizue Addison, interview with author, 27 Jan. 1993.

# JEWS

CAROLYN S. BLACKWELL

*Before the existence of the general store the Jewish peddler was well known to Indiana settlers. He played a dual role: one as a trader who brought goods that could not be found in the wilderness, another as a carrier of news from other settlements, which served to lessen the isolation of the settlers. The Jewish peddler lived a life of loneliness, discomfort, and hard work, but in return he gained a foothold on the frontier. When the railroad ended the need for peddlers, their understanding of the American economic system enabled them to make the transition to store owner.*

"And the Lord shall scatter you among the peoples, and ye shall be left few in number among the nations." (Deuteronomy 4:27)

There is no simple definition of a Jew. One definition characterizes Jews as a cultural group, primarily religious, but not exclusively, bound together by a common language of prayer, customs, literature, and a sense of a "common destiny." Jews are not united throughout the world by national ties, but are part of the community in which they live.[1] But Jews do share the tradition of Judaism and in a historical context a sense of community. Jewish populations are scattered throughout

the world, thus Jews are multicultural and bring with them not only Jewish history and traditions but also varying religious practices and cultural attributes of their country of origin.

The Jewish experience in Indiana began with a slow trickle of immigrants, mainly as traders. From 1760 to 1780 David and Moses Franks, Barnard and Michael Gratz, Joseph Simon, and Levy Andrew Levy, all Philadelphia businessmen, were associated with frontier land ventures and commercial enterprises around the Ohio, Illinois, and Wabash rivers. These men pioneered trade routes over which goods from the East flowed into Indiana and Illinois.[2]

During the American Revolution Jews contributed to the colonist cause in several ways. In July 1778 George Rogers Clark asked Moses Henry, interpreter and envoy to the Indians, to accompany Father Pierre Gibault from Cahokia to Fort Sackville (Vincennes). The purpose of this trip was to persuade the residents to support the American cause.[3] Another assistant to Clark's expedition was Isaac Levy (Levi), a Hungarian-born Jew who was a medical doctor and trader. Levy had wandered south from New York and was in Lexington, Virginia, when the Revolution began. He enlisted in a local company under Capt. Benjamin Harrison. Levy was one of the recruits assigned to George Rogers Clark, who had been directed to break the British hold on the Northwest. Levy's responsibilities were to provide supplies and medical treatment for the men. According to his military pension application, Levy was stationed at Vincennes. Later he joined the French firm of Gratiot & La Croix and settled in Cahokia.[4]

Along the river highways of the Ohio and the Wabash, individual Jewish settlers found their way to frontier settlements. The early Jewish immigrants were scattered and were often the only Jews in the community. Religious practices were difficult to observe, if at all, and many married Christians. Among the first immigrants was Phineas Israel, who came to Connersville from England in 1816. For some reason his neighbors called him Johnson, so he called himself Phineas Israel Johnson. Two years later his brother David, with a wife and child, came from

Vincennes Judah practiced law and began his political career. He was an outspoken Jacksonian supporter and served as a delegate to the Democratic convention in 1824. Judah was elected six times to the Indiana House of Representatives during the period 1827 to 1840 and served as speaker of the House during the twenty-fifth General Assembly. He married a gentile, Harriet Brandon, and raised his children as Christians.[6]

John Jacob Hays was the first Jewish resident of Fort Wayne. He served as Indian agent from 1820 until 1823. His duties included apportioning money to the Indians for land ceded by them and trying to gain and maintain the trust of the Indians in the hope that more land could be gained by peaceful means. Prior to his appointment as Indian agent, Hays lived in Cahokia and served as collector of internal revenue for the Illinois Territory. One of Hays's most prized possessions was the license certifying his marriage to Marie Louise Brouillet of Vincennes in 1801, which was presented to him by his old friend William Henry Harrison.[7]

England and settled in Brookville. The Johnsons traded with the local Indians for furs in exchange for "ornaments." In 1820 David Johnson moved to Cincinnati, and Phineas moved westward, eventually settling in St. Louis.[5]

Samuel Judah was an early Jewish settler who contributed to the political life in Indiana. Judah graduated from Queens College, Rutgers University, in 1816 and studied law for two years in the office of George Wood, a noted New Brunswick, New Jersey, attorney. After passing the bar in the fall of 1818, Judah went to Merom, Indiana, where he lived only a year before settling in Vincennes. In

After 1825 Jewish history in Indiana is based upon waves of immigration. The first wave began during the 1820s and consisted primarily of German-speaking Jews

Table 1. Indiana Jewish Population

American Jewish Yearbook *(New York: The American Jewish Committee and Philadelphia: Jewish Publication Society of America),* for 1900-50, 1970-90; Jacob Marcus, To Count a People: American Jewish Population Data, 1585–1984 *(Lanham, Md.: University Press of America, 1990), for 1859, 1878, 1960.*

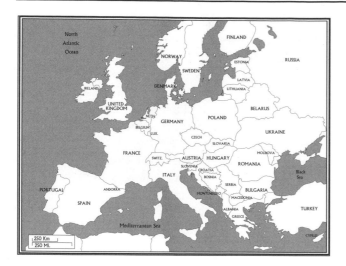

from central Europe and was part of the larger German immigration. The Jewish immigrants left Germany for economic reasons and because of civil inequalities. A large number of the German-Jewish immigrants came from Bavaria, where the legal position of Jews was fragile. The following observation was made by a German-Jewish newspaper: "The Jewish emigration appears to be less due to greed for gain than to consciousness of being unable in any other way to achieve independence or to found a family."[8]

The second wave of immigrants began in the 1880s and was composed almost entirely of Yiddish-speaking (blend of Hebrew and German) Jews from eastern Europe (Poland) and Czarist Russia. The causes of the mass immigration were the pogroms and poverty. This wave lasted until Congress passed the immigration law of 1924.[9] However, it was the German and East European waves that established Jewish communal life in Indiana. This was achieved by "chain migration." In the Jewish experience chain migration usually meant a single young male came first and was followed by brothers and/or cousins. Later they married women from nearby Jewish communities. As these families prospered more relatives were brought from Europe.

During the early years of the twentieth century a much smaller wave occurred. This was a group of Sephardim, primarily from Monastir in Macedonia and Salonika. Ladino (blend of Spanish and Hebrew) was the primary language of the Sephardim, which differed from the Yiddish spoken by the Ashkenazim, thus setting them apart not only from other Jews, but also from non-Jews.[10]

The fourth wave began in the 1930s and continued until the 1950s. This wave came in two stages: those who sought to flee Nazi persecution prior to World War II and those who survived the Holocaust. These refugees were from all over Europe and changed the Jewish communal life in Indiana. The most recent wave of

immigration is that of Soviet Jews that began in the 1970s and still continues. The assistance given to these immigrants is under the direction and supervision of the Jewish Welfare Federation.

An overview of Jewish demography in Indiana shows Jewish population to be about 20,000 to 23,000 or .4 percent of the total population. The Jewish population has remained fairly stable during the twentieth century. In 1859 there were 3,000 Jews in Indiana. By 1900 the population had increased to 25,000, and in 1990 the number was 18,300. The number of Jews has decreased as they have migrated to larger urban centers.[11]

Indiana and Ohio were the first states west of the Alleghenies to establish permanent Jewish communities. While individuals had settled in Indiana during the territorial period, organized Jewish communities did not appear until over two decades after statehood.[12] The pattern of community development was from north to south. In 1848 Indiana's first Jewish congregation (Achduth Vesholom) was founded in Fort Wayne. Congregation Israel was organized at Lafayette in 1849. Evansville congregation B'nai Israel (1853) and Indianapolis Hebrew Congregation (1856) followed.[13] As Jews became more urban the population shifted from small towns and cities to larger urban areas. Today 80 percent of the Jewish population live in Indianapolis, Gary, South Bend, Fort Wayne, and Evansville, in that order.[14]

## German Jews

German Jews (Ashkenazim) did not blend (or unite) with American Jews any more than did German Catholics with American-born Catholics. Old American Jews were descendants of many nationalities, but they stressed their Sephardic (Spanish) origins. After 1820 Americans perceived Jews as a nationality group, not a religious

*Temple Israel, Lafayette, ca. 1940. The congregation was founded in 1849.*

group, and identified them according to language. Thus, German Jews were considered German. Immigrant German Jews came to consider themselves to be German Americans of the Jewish faith. However, Jews moving to Indiana faced a major difficulty in maintaining their religious identity because the Jewish population was scattered and unorganized. Therefore, Jewish life was slow to develop. Many of the earlier German-Jewish immigrants were assimilated when they married Christians, no longer practiced Judaism, and raised their children as Christians. German language and culture were preserved only within the family.

Assimilation of German Jews decreased as Jewish marriages became more feasible and the practice of Judaism resumed. By the 1840s German Jews dominated Jewish life in Indiana. Their allegiance to religious liberalism provided the basis for the success of the Reform Judaism movement in the United States. (In 1824 the Reform movement had started independently in South Carolina.) The Reform movement allowed Judaism to adjust to American cultural patterns and modified its service to reflect the standards of the Protestant middle class.[15]

The first formal Jewish congregation was established officially in Fort Wayne on 26 October 1848. Whenever a Jewish community is established, the selection of a burial ground precedes the building of a house of worship. The proper care and burial of the deceased is considered a primary and sacred obligation of the community. Thus, the Society for Visiting the Sick and Burying the Dead was formed and purchased a burial ground on 13 October 1848 for two hundred dollars. The primary purpose of the society was to give personal assistance and financial aid to the sick and to bury the dead.

Until 1859, when the first formal house of worship was purchased, the congregation of thirty members met in the home of Frederick Nerdlinger. At its founding the congregation was German Orthodox, and, in keeping with orthodoxy, men and women worshiped in separate rooms. Also, the services and minutes of meetings were in German.

On 6 October 1861 the name of the congregation became Achduth Vesholom (Peace and Unity). The Einhorn prayer book, which contained both German and Hebrew, was introduced. The following year saw the gradual introduction of Reform Judaism into the ritual. By January 1866 men, women, and children were allowed to sit together during services.[16]

During the nineteenth century the relationship between German Jews and American non-Jews, including Germans, was one of cooperation and acceptance. The relationship between the German Jew and the non-Jewish population is seen in the Ligonier experience. In 1854 Frederick William Straus and Solomon Mier, both twenty-one years of age, arrived in Ligonier, Indiana, from Germany. At that time Ligonier was a northeastern Indiana village of three hundred people. Construction of the Lake Shore and Michigan Southern Railroad through Ligonier is probably what attracted the two young men to the village.

Straus opened a small general store, and by 1860 he was able to bring his two brothers, Mathias and Jacob, from Germany. In 1868 the store was sold and the brothers founded the Citizens Bank. In 1928 the bank merged with the banking house of Solomon Mier and became the American State Bank. The bank remained solvent through the depression years.

The Straus brothers became successful land brokers and bankers. They established banks in Ohio, Michigan, Illinois, Minnesota, North Dakota, and southern Ontario, Canada. Mier "became one of the largest farm land dealers in the Midwest."

German Jews worked in the Ligonier community and helped to introduce many improvements. In 1876 Straus and John B. Stahl, a Presbyterian, were the driving force behind the project to erect a public elementary and high school. Mier was the "prime mover" behind the installation of the first sewer and disposal systems. He insisted that the waterworks be publicly owned.

In 1908 a library became a reality for the town. This was accomplished through Carnegie funds and many donations in the form of money and books by the Straus, Mier, Jacobs, and Goldsmith families, and many other members of the Jewish community. In July 1974 the library's board of directors volunteered to set aside a room dedicated to the more than one hundred years of Jewish contributions to the town of Ligonier: "The city of Ligonier is proud to pay this tribute to the Jewish residents who were such an integral, vital, and forward-looking segment of this small midwestern community."[17]

Today no Jewish families remain in Ligonier. The decline began in the 1920s as young Jews went to college, married, or moved to larger cities. The last Jewish resident, Durbin Mier, died in 1981.

During the 1850s and 1860s German Jews settled throughout northern and central Indiana at Lafayette, Plymouth, Wabash, Huntington, North Manchester, and Indianapolis. There was little interethnic conflict, and German Jews felt secure, particularly in Indianapolis where there was a large and active German community. Indianapolis German Jews supported and participated in the German associations of the city, such as the Maennerchor and the Deutsche Haus Athenaeum.[18]

Mayer Messing, a rabbi from Prussia, became the first Jewish religious leader in Indianapolis to participate in civic life. He was a founder and first president of the

*Ligonier confirmation class of 1919. From left to right: Henrietta Schloss, Rose Selig, Rabbi Robert Minda, Alfred Ackerman, and Catherine Baum.*

Indianapolis Humane Society and served on the boards of the Industrial Home for the Blind, the Fresh Air Mission, and the Indiana Red Cross.[19]

After 1871 German-Jewish emigration from Germany slowed down to a trickle as the long-desired German unification became a reality. The early- and midnineteenth century immigrants had achieved remarkable success by the 1880s: from pack peddlers to well-to-do business people and civic leaders. The early German-Jewish peddler helped further the economic growth of the area when he settled and started his various endeavors. Consequently, he became well known in his community, and as his participation in civic matters increased so did his respectability. In the nineteenth century and over a relatively short period of time, German Jews in Indiana found a level of security, acceptance, and respect never before accorded them. Yet their American acculturation and integration did not diminish their love of German culture and language.[20]

During the German immigration (1830–80) a large number of Indiana cities and towns were built. Also, it was during this period when Indiana Jewish congregations were established. As German immigration became a pioneering force in Indiana history, so did German-Jewish immigration become a pioneering force in Indiana Jewish history.

### Eastern European Jews

During the period 1880–1924 a large number of Polish, Russian, Lithuanian, Slovak, and Romanian Jews immigrated to the United States. These immigrants were young and poor and possessed some industrial skills, usually in the garment trades.[21] The eastern European Jews were primarily orthodox, and Yiddish was their medium of communication.[22] German-Jewish immigrants spread throughout the country, but eastern European Jews settled in large numbers in New York City and other large cities in the Northeast and Midwest. Gradually they began to move to Indiana from the East Coast and large midwestern cities such as Chicago.[23] Though German Jews established congregations and contributed to the economic and civic areas of their communities, it was the East European Jews who began a communal life and provided the foundation for a lasting Jewish community.

The settlement pattern was usually in the working-class neighborhoods and in areas with other eastern European Jews. An example is the south side of Indianapolis, where a small group of Polish Jews established a neighborhood as early as 1870. This group started one of the first *shuls*[24] on the south side. The group's early years were characterized by meetings in rented rooms and frequent changes of rabbis who held other jobs. For example, Isaac Silverman also ran a butcher shop. In 1876 the congregation became known as Chevro Bene Jacob. Finances were extremely tight, and one of the members, Samuel Steinberg, quit work every Friday at noon to collect money from members to pay the rent for the meeting room and to hire a rabbi for the High Holidays. The congregation survived and grew, and in 1882 a building was purchased at 352 South Meridian Street and the congregation's name changed from Chevro Bene Jacob to Sharah Tefilla.[25]

Eastern European Jews differed from German Jews in both religious and secular culture. The eastern European immigrants were poor and possessed a "communal tradition" that had been fostered in the *shtetls* (self-contained rural communities). Religious observances were followed with a zeal foreign to American Jews. Also, they professed socialist and/or Zionist sentiments that differed from the attitudes of American Jews who were basically middle class and anti-Zionist. Much has been written about the division and conflict between the newly arrived eastern European Jews and the established German Jews, who were embarrassed by their coreligionists' language (Yiddish), dire economic condition, and their passionate religious and political feelings.[26]

The major portion of Gary's Jews originally came from eastern and southeastern Europe. Their cultural tradition appeared to be related to their "unique Jewishness." Thus, a Jew living in Russian-dominated Lithuania was neither Russian nor Lithuanian, but one whose family happened to live in Lithuania—maybe for several generations. These Jews did not wish to acculturate into a hostile culture, but attempted to maintain Jewish culture within Jewish religious tradition.

In Gary two congregations were established, Temple Beth-El (Orthodox) in 1907 and Temple Israel (Reform) in 1910. As in other congregations, the temple became a community center that offered a variety of social services and activities. Temple Beth-El printed a monthly *Bulletin* that had articles on Zionism and local Jewish news and achievements. The *Bulletin* was a source of information, fostered "ethnic pride," and warned against taking on

The second house of Temple Beth-El, Gary, built in 1912.

the ways of American Protestants. One issue stated: "Don't drop Jewishness."[27]

In the early 1900s Jews from Russia, Poland, Hungary, and Romania began to settle in Vincennes. The Jews rented a room for *Shabbat* services and High Holidays, which were conducted by men of the community who had attended the *cheder*[28] of their respective communities. The *shochet* also served as the Hebrew teacher for the young boys. Albert Rosenberg, in "Memories of Hovas Hochim Congregation in Vincennes," speaks of the fascination of observing the men in their prayer shawls reciting the Torah and after services listening to their tales of the *shtetl*.

Hovas Hochim Congregation was formed in 1935 and followed Orthodoxy. The membership consisted of thirty families from Vincennes, Washington, Princeton, and Jasper, Indiana, and Lawrenceville and Olney, Illinois. During the years following 1935 the congregation was able to afford a rabbi—usually a rabbinical student from Cincinnati—for the holidays by selling tickets to these services.

The building that had been purchased in 1935 to serve as a place of worship was enlarged in order to provide a meeting room and space for community events. The congregation was active and had community suppers, seders, and Purim plays.

The congregation began losing members either to death or migration to other parts of the country, and there were no new members arriving in the community. In 1965 the congregation was dissolved.[29]

### Sephardic Jews

In 1907 a much smaller wave began to settle in Indianapolis—Sephardim from the Ottoman Empire (Macedonia and Salonika). The motivation for the immigration was the prospect for job opportunities and was political in the sense that conditions were deteriorating in the Ottoman Empire.

Some of these immigrants had worked in large cities such as Detroit, Chicago, Cincinnati, or New York before settling in Indianapolis. Kahn Tailoring Company, a German-Jewish firm, employed many of the immigrants.[30] Sephardim also were fruit peddlers (wholesale and/or retail), bakers, and shoemakers. Others owned their own stores that usually were groceries, candy stores, and clothing stores.

During the depression the need for men's clothing decreased drastically, and Kahn's laid off many workers; nearly 50 percent were from the Sephardic community. With the loss of paychecks, families set up small stands outside the city market where the rent for a stand was low. The stands sold pens, socks, shoelaces, fruits, and vegetables. Some of the women's clubs wanted the market to ban the outside stands. The Jewish Welfare Federation fought this action, fearing that if the stands were banned the stand holders would be placed on relief rolls.

The federation appointed an unemployment committee to make personal visits to Jewish employers and to request that they hire unemployed Jews. In 1931 Edith Steinberg, wife of Rabbi Milton Steinberg of Beth-El-Zedeck Congregation, took over the supervision of the committee. Through her efforts and personal contacts one-third of the job applicants were placed.[31]

One indication of cultural identity is language. The Sephardim primary language was Ladino, while the Ashkenazim, whose country of origin might be Russia, Poland, Hungary, or Romania, spoke one or another mutually understood Yiddish dialects. Communication was difficult, if not impossible, except through a third common language, usually English. This cultural difference represented different histories, experiences, values, and other customs such as the Sephardic practice of naming a child after a living relative, which was not done by the Ashkenazim. Before World War II intermarriage between Ashkenazim and Sephardim took place rarely, if at all.[32]

### Indiana Jews during World War II

After 1933 the attention of Indiana's Jews turned to Germany. National and Jewish organization leaders debated throughout the 1930s and 1940s about refugee policies, rescue possibilities, and monetary assistance.[33] Indiana's Jewish communities were small in comparison to those in Chicago or New York and were not sharply divided as to how to respond. The Jewish Welfare Fund raised money to aid refugee causes and to support Palestine.

*Family of Jewish displaced persons arrive in Indianapolis from Germany, 1949.*

Once war was declared by the United States, Jewish men throughout Indiana served in the armed forces. On the home front the Jewish Welfare Board sponsored a USO at the Kirshbaum Center in Indianapolis. The Council of Jewish Women maintained a day lounge at Camp Atterbury. Jews opened their homes to Jewish soldiers for *Shabbat* dinners and the Passover seder for those stationed at Fort Benjamin Harrison and Camp Atterbury. The Jewish community of Vincennes offered support services for the soldiers stationed at George Field in Lawrenceville, Illinois.[34]

### Soviet Jews

During the 1960s various Soviet writers began to draw attention to the persistence of anti-Semitism in Russia and of the desire of some 80 percent of the Jewish population to immigrate if the opportunity were presented. A paradox in Russia existed: Jews were oppressed and openly humiliated in the press, yet were not permitted to leave the country.[35] A small trickle of immigration to Israel had been permitted, usually elderly Jews seeking to be reunited with family members. After the June 1967 war the Soviet Union placed a ban on immigration to Israel.

In May 1968 a young Jewish man in Moscow wrote a letter to the Supreme Soviet renouncing his citizenship and speaking out against forced Jewish assimilation. He received an exit visa for Israel in 1969. The *Washington Post* published his letter in December 1968. Other letters found their way to the West, resulting in tremendous publicity. In 1973 the character of immigration changed when a ruling was made by United States Attorney General Elliot Richardson. Emigrés found that when they arrived in Vienna they could request referral to Jewish agencies that were willing to assist them in gaining entry to the United

States or to countries other than Israel. Supported by American Jewish communities and the Jewish Welfare Federation, more and more Jews chose the United States.

Once an individual decided to come to the United States the Hebrew Immigration Aid Society (HIAS) of Rome took over. In Rome the immigrant was provided with vocational counseling, and courses in English and American history and culture. The national office of the Jewish Welfare Federation processed the applications and placed the immigrants in Jewish communities throughout the United States.[36]

In Indiana the Indianapolis Jewish Welfare Federation and the Interreligious Resettlement Effort of Fort Wayne particularly are active in assisting this group. Under the direction of the Jewish Welfare Federation the various congregations sponsor the immigrants. Classes in English and acculturation are under the direction of the Board of Jewish Education. The individuals and/or families are provided with housing and given assistance in finding employment.

It is difficult to present a profile of Soviet immigrants. Overall, their language is Russian, and a few speak some English. Their level of education varies from university to technical, artisan to construction worker, and tailor to hairdresser. Many have non-Jewish spouses and are nonpracticing in religious observances. They identify themselves as Jews by birth, not by religion.[37]

With the dissolution of the Soviet Union, the character of Soviet immigration again has changed. Earlier, Jews came because of oppression, lack of freedom, and anti-Semitism. However, not all Jews faced these conditions; some had good jobs, owned their own houses, and maintained religious traditions within the family. One such individual stated she and her husband were university educated and had held excellent positions in one of the southern republics. Her husband's immediate superior was Russian, and they worked well together at the management level. The change brought about by *glasnost* and *perestroika* allowed ethnic sentiments to surface. When the collapse of the Soviet Union occurred the Jews, being the minority, were forced out of their positions of authority. Street demonstrations against minority groups became common and "one learned what areas of the town to avoid." Faced with the threat of aggressive anti-Semitism and economic insecurity, she and her family came to Indianapolis. Supported by the Jewish community, they are taking English and computer classes, have become members of one of the synagogues, and have enrolled the children in the Hebrew Academy.

Through the teaching of grandparents, the family maintained the religious traditions in their home. She spoke of a grandfather who had a Talmud that had come from Israel and how he tried to read to them. It is of great importance that the children be offered the opportunity to live as Jews. Her view of life in Indianapolis: "the freedom, no one pays any attention to you, you can go where you please."[38]

## Economic and Civic Life

The economic and civic contributions of Jews to the cities and towns of Indiana cannot be neglected. Jews have been involved in many professional and occupational areas. However, their most outstanding endeavor has been in the area of retailing and manufacturing. These Jews supported civic and social projects not only financially but also through service. Jewish men were elected to the office of mayor in Gary, Madison, Marion, New Harmony, and Ligonier (three were elected). The majority of these men were local businessmen.[39]

Before the existence of the general store the Jewish peddler was well known to Indiana settlers. He played a dual role: one as a trader who brought goods that could not be found in the wilderness, another as a carrier of news from other settlements, which served to lessen the isolation of the settlers. The Jewish peddler lived a life of loneliness, discomfort, and hard work, but in return he gained a foothold on the frontier. When the railroad ended the need for peddlers, their understanding of the American economic system enabled them to make the transition to store owner.[40]

Jews abandoned their packs and began to settle in the developing towns and cities. One of the earliest to open a store was Adam Gimbel, a German Jew from Biedesheim, Bavaria. According to Knox County records, Gimbel purchased a "Pedlar's License" to "retail Dry Goods" on 24 May and 4 July 1842, 12 October 1843, and 12 April 1844. According to information in tax records, he and his brother owned a business by 1848. By 1855 Adam Gimbel's seven brothers had joined him in the business. The early Jewish community of Vincennes developed around this family.

In 1857 a three-story brick building was built on the corner of Main and Second streets, the progress of which was followed carefully in articles published in the *Western Sun*. After a family tragedy Gimbel moved to Philadelphia in 1866, but in 1868 his son Jacob reopened the store. The Gimbels expanded over the years and opened stores in Philadelphia, New York, and Pittsburgh, and in 1928 Saks Fifth Avenue became a subsidiary.[41]

Adam Gimbel served on the Vincennes City Council for twenty-four years. Jacob "Jake" Gimbel was active in the county Democratic party organization. On 14 March

Table 2. Jews in Five Major Indiana Cities

|  | 1878 | 1905 | 1937 | 1948 | 1968 | 1980 | 1990 |
|---|---|---|---|---|---|---|---|
| Evansville | 378 | 800 | 1,765 | 1,350 | 1,100 | 1,200 | 520 |
| Fort Wayne | 275 | 500 | 1,960 | 1,200 | 1,225 | 1,350 | 1,100 |
| Gary (Calumet) | 1,200 (1918) | 2,200 (1927) | 2,450 | 2,500 | 6,800 | 5,000 | 2,300 |
| Indianapolis | 500 | 2,300 | 10,850 | 7,200 | 8,800 | 11,000 | 10,000 |
| South Bend (Elkhart) | 125 | 1,200 (1912) | 2,972 | 2,660 | 3,245 | 1,900 | 1,800 |

American Jewish Yearbook *for 1980 and 1990; Marcus,* To Count a People, *for remaining years.*

1890 the *Vincennes Commercial* (Republican paper) printed a political cartoon that depicted Gimbel as "Boss Gimbel" and accused him of attempting to run the Democratic party.[42]

Jewish businessmen gradually earned respect for their business methods and skills and for their contributions to the community. This acceptance and integration into the community is illustrated by Jewish families in the northern Indiana communities of Plymouth, Wabash, Huntington, and North Manchester. In these communities a formal Jewish congregation did not exist. Only Wabash founded a congregation (1868) and had its own Jewish cemetery.[43] Jews in other communities prayed either in private homes or rented rooms. For special occasions such as weddings and burials a rabbi from a larger city conducted the service. Otherwise, the Jews attended services in Fort Wayne or South Bend.

The early merchants of these towns were German Jews with the exception of David Marx of Huntington. Marx was born 6 August 1845 in Strasbourg, Alsace. Alsace was then French, but Marx was of German ancestry.

While working as a traveling salesman, Marx met Amelia Levi of Huntington. They married in 1874, and that same year he formed a partnership with his brother-in-law Jacob Levi. A year later, 1875, Marx was the sole operator of their business, a clothing store. This was the beginning of D. Marx & Sons. Today the store is in the fourth generation of family management.

David Marx was a member of the Huntington Board of Trade. The first president of the board was Leopold Levy. Levy was elected on the Republican ticket to the office of state treasurer for two terms (February 1899–February 1903). Frank Summer Bash (*History of Huntington County*) wrote: "Mr. Levy was a successful businessman, a public spirited citizen, and a competent state official. While a resident of Huntington, he was always ready to aid any and every movement for the promotion of the general welfare."[44]

The Lauer brothers, Meyer and Levi, were born in Volkerhausen, Saxony. Meyer was the first to come to America where he worked as an apprentice in a Cincinnati cabinet factory. When his brother Levi joined him, they left Cincinnati and became pack peddlers. In 1858 they came to the Plymouth area and continued as peddlers until they saved enough money to open a clothing and general store in 1861. Marc Lauer, a grandson of Meyer Lauer, stated the relationship between Jews and non-Jews was good then. This rapport is supported by the membership of Jews in clubs and organizations of the community and by their "joining in" with their neighbors for social gatherings and in support of local civic causes.[45]

An account of the history of the store of Beitman and Wolf is also a history of the Wabash Jewish community. They were German Jews who started as peddlers and opened businesses in Wabash. In the 1840s Charles Herf and B. Moses owned grocery stores, and Michael and Leonard Hyman owned a dry goods and clothing store. In 1863 Benjamin Wolf opened a butcher shop, and in 1865 he purchased the M. and L. Hyman Store. He formed a partnership in 1868 with David Beitman under the name Wolf and Beitman (later changed to Beitman and Wolf). The store sold groceries, household goods, and clothing until 1934 when it became a clothing store for men and women.

Benjamin Wolf also owned several farms and bought and sold horses. He was one of the organizers of the Wabash National Bank. In 1902 he sold his share in the bank and was one of the incorporators of the Farmers and Merchants Bank of Wabash. The Wolf and Beitman families took part in the civic life of Wabash. The families belonged to the Rotary and Kiwanis clubs and were among the founders of Rodef Sholem Congregation and Rodef Sholem Cemetery in 1868.[46]

Prior to World War I, 147 Jews lived in Wabash.[47] Many of them worked in the Pioneer Hat Factory; one of the owners was Nathan Meyers. With the closing of the factory Jews began to leave Wabash, and by 1979 only four families remained.[48]

Jacob Oppenheim opened Oppenheim's New York Cheap Store in 1875 in North Manchester. The name of the store was intended to reflect the merchandise carried. "New York" implied the highest quality, and "cheap" was synonymous with value.[49] The store did a cash and credit business as most of the merchants did at that time. Oppenheim's first ledger shows that sales, as well as records of credit owed by customers, were recorded in Yiddish until they were written in English for billing purposes. Ben Oppenheim took over the store after his father's death. He was a founder of the North Manchester Telephone Company, and in 1943 the Kiwanis Club gave him the "Star Service Award" for community service.[50]

Economic endeavors and civic contributions were repeated throughout the Jewish communities of Indiana. In Lafayette Solomon Loeb, his brother Louis, and brother-in-law Samuel Hene opened Loeb's first dry goods store in 1869. The family supported education and community development as illustrated by service on the Lafayette School Board and support of Purdue University and Columbian Park.[51]

In 1838 the first Jews to settle in Evansville were the Gumbert family. Simon Gumbert was licensed to practice medicine in 1855. Other German Jews began to come down the Ohio River, and by 1850 there were enough male Jews for a minyan.[52] Most were merchants, but some such as Gumbert and Moses Weil, who was admitted to the bar in 1869, entered the professions. Jacob Eichel led the way for community improvements when he proposed building the first electric plant and laying brick streets. William A. Gumbert was a patron of the arts and helped found the Old Broadway Theater League and the Evansville Children's Theater.[53]

The pattern was repeated in Indianapolis as newly arrived Jews exchanged their packs for horse and wagon, then a small store. If successful, the small store would become larger. One such individual was Leopold Strauss, a German Jew from Frankfurt. He came to Indianapolis in 1865 and worked as a clerk in Morris and Lewis Greisheimer's Eagle Clothing Store. By 1871 Strauss was a partner, and in 1879 he bought the store from the Greisheimers. The Eagle Clothing Store grew, and Strauss became one of the retail leaders of the city.

*L. Strauss and Co., Indianapolis, 1906.*

He was the first local retailer to fix prices instead of bargaining, as was the custom. In 1899 he formed a partnership with Abram L. Block of Brooklyn, New York. The name of the store was changed later to L. Strauss and Company. Strauss was a founder of the Indianapolis Merchants' Association.[54]

Many Jews contributed to the growth of Indianapolis: Louis Wolf, Gustave A. Efroymson, William H. Block, Henry Kahn, Samuel E. Rauh, Louis Newberger, and Nathan Morris to name a few. These early citizens helped to secure the Jewish community, and when new immigrants arrived they quickly formed organizations to assist their acculturation.[55]

Very few Jews were farmers; some owned land but leased it to others to farm. However, Louis Ruderman of Columbia City bought thirty-one acres near LaOtto in Noble County and began farming in 1922–23 by planting onions. Louis was joined by his nephew Abe who farmed the land and his brother Morris who served as bookkeeper. Together the three men formed A & M Ruderman Farms. The Rudermans were commercial growers of iceberg lettuce, potatoes (sold to potato chip companies), and spearmint and peppermint that were distilled into oils.[56]

One venture that sought to deal with the great influx of eastern European Jews was the pioneering farm "Utopias." Om Alam was one such group that tried this experiment in New Odessa, Oregon, in late 1881. The group's motto spoke of labor in the fields as a way of achieving physical and spiritual renewal for Jews. The goal of proving to the world that Jews were qualified for physical labor also was stressed. To gain experience the individuals wanting to join the group in New Odessa first worked on farms in Long Island, New York, Connecticut, and Indiana. One such individual was reported to have refused a job in the city (New York) to work for lower wages on a farm in Vincennes.[57] However, the majority of Jews remained urbanites and were employed in various businesses and professions.

Indiana Jews have served in the armed forces since the Civil War. During that war Jews from Evansville were part of Companies A, B, and C; others from the Wabash area also were part of Indiana regiments. One outstanding soldier was Frederick Knefler, son of one of the founders of the Indianapolis Hebrew Congregation. He enlisted in the 11th Indiana Regiment and made his way through the ranks as lieutenant and captain, and Gov. Oliver P. Morton appointed him colonel of the 79th Regiment. By the end of the war he had attained the rank of brevet major general and was the highest ranking Jew in the Union army.[58]

During the First World War Col. Abram Ullman Loeb, a member of Gen. John J. Pershing's staff, participated in the first American invasion in France. Sidney Kraus, a Naval Academy graduate, served as head of a branch of the United States Aeronautical Service in 1941.[59] These are just a few examples of the many Indiana Jews who have served their country.

## Communal Life

Local Jewish community life developed in an irregular way, and Jewish organizations reflected this formation. Organizations evolved in response to the needs of the community at its various stages of growth. When several families came to live in an area, the first cooperative effort was the formation of a burial society and the purchase of land for a cemetery. This necessitated a levy of dues and the employment of individuals to maintain the cemetery and keep records. As more Jews arrived, leaders formalized the community by writing a constitution and bylaws that provided a name for the congregation and/or society, officers, qualifications for membership, and monetary assessments. Standing committees were formed to deal with the problems of the congregation, such as the need for a temple for religious observances and a place for business meetings.[60]

Jewish social and organized life in Indiana was slow and took different paths with each wave of immigration. German Jews organized their social and religious life in a more complex fashion. They organized a seminary for rabbis (Hebrew Union College, Cincinnati, 1875), organizations to assist new immigrants, homes for the elderly and orphans, and fraternal organizations.

Eastern European Jews, feeling alienated in a new country, organized *landsmanshaften* (organizations of immigrants from the same area). In the *landsmanschaft* fraternal organization, the new immigrant found friends and/or acquaintances from his area, which gave him and his family a sense of security and belonging.

Sephardic Jews also organized their lives around synagogue and social and educational activities. As Jews became "Americanized," German Jews, who had distanced themselves from eastern European and Sephardic Jews, began to associate with them. Jews now work together in community organizations, and each city with a sizable Jewish population has its own committees that oversee Jewish communal life.[61]

Prior to the Civil War era, Jews established community organizations as a way of dealing with the problem of loss of identity as Jews. Because Jews were widely scattered throughout Indiana, it was difficult to maintain their Jewish traditions and identity. In Fort Wayne and Indianapolis the early congregations drew members from the surrounding small towns such as Huntington and Kokomo. As more Jews arrived in Indiana leaders

*Louis Vollrath Grocery and Meat Market, 125 W. Morris Street, Indianapolis, 1905.*

began to formalize the congregations and achieve the funding necessary to construct synagogues. The dedication of a synagogue demonstrated a favorable growth pattern, membership support, able leadership within the Jewish community, and acceptance by the non-Jewish community.[62]

Jewish life in Indiana became centered around the synagogue. Each congregation was independent. If congregations chose to be part of a nationwide synagogue movement, the ties were weak.

During the early phase of Jewish life in Indiana, most Jews belonged to some type of congregation/community, but since the Jewish population was small, they saw themselves as members of a congregation rather than a community. Protestant religious life was congregation-centered and this fit in well with Jewish religious life. Jews saw belonging to a congregation as a way of establishing their identity. When Jews with different religious practices began to arrive, they formed their own congregations. The Reform and Conservative movements reinforced the differences between congregations, and finally the traditional synagogues gave in to the trend to distinguish

between the various religious practices and formed Orthodox bodies.[63]

The early congregations in Indiana practiced traditional Judaism. They were concerned with meeting the needs of their members and did not appear to have ideological differences. These congregations followed Jewish law when organizing.

The Reform movement precipitated ideological or denominational splits.[64] The German Jews stimulated the change that occurred during the mid-1800s. The first German Reform congregations were Har Sinai, Baltimore (1842) and Temple Emanu-El, New York (1845). The leading force of the Reform movement in America was Rabbi Isaac Mayer Wise, a German-speaking immigrant from Bohemia, who came to the United States in 1846 and settled in Cincinnati, which became the center of the Reform movement. In 1875 he founded Hebrew Union College, the oldest rabbinical college in the nation.

In 1856 Rabbi Wise visited Jewish communities in Terre Haute and Vincennes. His memories reflect two different situations. He observed that Jews in Terre Haute "live in peace and concord among themselves and with their neighbor[s] reaching each other the cordial and supporting hands of brothers." However, a different situation awaited him in Vincennes. Rabbi Wise wrote, "brethren in this place are very poor, poor indeed with exception of S. Judah, Mr. Joseph and some young men, as our friend Hersher—rest are very poor, cannot afford to support any thing or person except families—(Gimbels were among poor [then]) could not offer help."[65]

Rabbi Wise dedicated the new synagogue of the Indianapolis Hebrew Congregation on 24 October 1858. In his speech he compared the United States to ancient Greece: "We see a conflux of different and dissimilar people, all contributing their peculiarities and characteristics to the common stock, rendering the American mind a composite of the excellencies of all nations and climes." He congratulated those in attendance with the statement that "they were enabled to contribute some valuable elements to this social fabric."[66]

Indiana Jews contributed to the development of Reform Judaism. In 1870 Henry Adler of Lawrenceburg was willing to give ten thousand dollars in trust to Rabbi Wise and his congregation for the "establishment and support of a rabbinical college." Temple Israel of Lafayette was a charter member of the Union of American Hebrew Congregations (central organization of Reform Judaism). One of its rabbis, Julian Morganstern, served as president of Hebrew Union College from 1921 to 1947.[67]

The Midwest and the South became strong centers of the Reform movement. In Indiana during the 1860s and 1870s Reform Judaism spread as German Jews became more acculturated. Congregations were established as Reform, or traditional congregations changed to Reform. The Congregation Ahavath Shalom (Lovers of Peace) of Ligonier was established in 1865 as a traditional congregation. About 1876 the Einhorn prayer book was replaced by the Reform prayer book. Over the next ten years changes occurred: the Hebrew school became the Sabbath school; English replaced German as the language for the sermon; and Bar Mitzvah for boys only was replaced by confirmation for both boys and girls.[68]

In some congregations the change was not without conflict. In 1866 Achduth Vesholom of Fort Wayne introduced Reform Judaism. Some members left and formed their own congregation that lasted several years before the members returned to Achduth Vesholm. In May 1874 the congregation joined the Union of American Hebrew Congregations, which had been established in 1873.

Congregation B'nai Israel (1857) of Evansville was established by German Jews and supported Reform. However, as the Jewish population of Evansville grew and became more diverse new synagogues were established.

In 1873 eastern Europeans established Congregation B'nai Moshe and practiced traditional Judaism. In 1883 a Conservative congregation, Adath Israel, was founded.[69]

The Conservative movement was a product of conflict felt by Jews who considered themselves part of Western culture and felt comfortable in the United States, but wanted to practice a more traditional Judaism.[70] One such individual was Bernhard Felsenthal of Madison. Individuals from varied geographical areas (Alsace, Bohemia, England, German states, and Poland) composed the Madison congregation and had different attitudes toward Judaism from liberal to orthodox. These differences caused a delay in the organization of the congregation. Led by Gottlieb Wehle, compromises were made: the synagogue school was to use only Hebrew, and the service followed the orthodox ritual but was in German. Felsenthal, aware of attitudes against orthodox practices, began to develop ideas based on the changes in the synagogue. In 1859 he published one of the first guidelines for adapting traditional Judaism to American life, which brought him recognition and involvement in the Conservative movement.[71]

The compromises sought to preserve traditional Judaism but adapt it to American life. Each congregation was able to determine its extent of change. Some wanted only "mixed seating" and more formal and quiet behavior, while others wanted an organ and more use of English.[72]

As Jewish life became more congregation-centered, the role of women began to extend to the synagogue. Jewish women are the core of family life and act as "the glue that holds the family together." In this role women are the transmitters of Jewish culture and tradition. An all-male board and/or trustees administered the early congregations. However, women formed organizations within the congregation and supported the religious and social life of the congregation.

In 1887 the Hebrew Ladies Benevolent Society in Evansville was founded with fifty-nine charter members. Its constitution and bylaws were written in German and English. Membership qualifications were: "Any Hebrew lady of blameless reputation can become a member of the society by fulfilling the conditions of the Constitution and being in good health; no married lady may be admitted whose husband is not a member of Congregation B'nai Israel." The organization's purpose was "benevolence, which shall preeminently consist of mutual assistance of members in case of sickness and in doing the funeral honors in case of death."[73]

Jewish women were concerned not only with the congregation but also with the needs of the community at large. In 1900 a Jewish Shelter House was established to give assistance and, if needed, temporary housing for individuals and families in need. The Jewish women in

Indianapolis ran the shelter. Emma Eckhouse was a founder of the Nathan Morris House, which offered vocational training and assistance to new immigrants adjusting to American life.[74]

The women of the Richmond Sisterhood played a major role in the development of a Jewish community in their city. The first meeting of the sisterhood was held on 18 December 1919. Minnie Unger and Hannah Fred were appointed to write a constitution modeled after a sisterhood in Paducah, Kentucky. The women decided to join the National Federation of Temple Sisterhoods, which was a branch of the Union of American Hebrew Congregations. The need to establish a connection with a national Jewish organization influenced the decision to affiliate with a Reform organization, and the group felt comfortable with the Reform. However, the religious services held by the men in rooms behind their various businesses reflected traditional Judaism.

The women touched all phases of Jewish life in Richmond. They hosted social events, ran a religious school, organized religious events such as a Passover seder, and carried out philanthropic and defense responsibilities. The sisterhood was more advanced than the congregation, which did not have a constitution or a national affiliation.

An example of defense action is seen in an incident that occurred in February 1921. Conflict arose when it was reported that Dr. Woodburn had addressed the Women's Club of Richmond, stating "that most of the Bolshevists were Jews." The sisterhood decided to ask Dr. Englander of Hebrew Union College how to handle the matter. The steps taken by the sisterhood forced Woodburn to make "a qualified retraction." Woodburn claimed that he was misquoted and responded that he had stated "some of the Bolshevists were Jews."[75]

In 1925 the annual report of the sisterhood showed that the membership included "nine from Connersville, one from Carthage, one from Eaton, Ohio and two from Oxford, Ohio had signified their intention of joining." In a limited way Richmond was a regional center for Jewish communal life.[76]

Hannah Greenbaum Solomon of Chicago wanted to further the interests of Jewish women. She was a member of the Women's Committee for the World's Parliament of Religions. In 1890, while attending one of the meetings, she sought and received approval to arrange for a Jewish Women's Congress. Solomon founded the National Council of Jewish Women in 1893 and served as its first president. The council was dedicated to serve "Faith and Humanity through religious education and philanthropy." The vice president (1893–96) for Indiana was Mrs. Etta L. Nussbaum of Marion. Local councils were established in Indianapolis (1896) and Terre Haute (1898).[77]

The report of the first national convention of Jewish women in 1896 listed the number of members and activities of local councils. Indiana councils were as follows: Marion (twenty-one), running a Sunday school for the congregation; Wabash (twenty-three), literary group; Peru, just started and attended a Jewish Chautauqua; Fort Wayne, Bible study and lectures; Lafayette, being formed; Indianapolis, winter school for poor girls, forty attended, taught darning, patching, and how to make over clothes.[78] Indiana Jewish women have contributed much in the past not only to the Jewish community but also to the community at large. Today they are still active participants in their congregations and Jewish and civic organizations.

Jewish communal life flourished outside the congregation. The first American Jewish fraternal organization was B'nai B'rith (Sons of Covenant), which was founded in 1843 in New York.[79] The Thisbe Lodge 24 is the oldest fraternal organization in Evansville. It was founded 7 February 1859 and stressed "Benevolence, Brotherly Love, Harmony."[80] B'nai B'rith sponsored the Anti-Defamation League (ADL), which is nonsectarian and speaks out against anti-Semitism, bigotry, and attacks on the fundamental rights of human beings. The ADL has carried out this goal vigorously, especially in its recent response against hate crimes in the United States and "ethnic cleansing" in Bosnia and Herzegovina. Congressman Lee Hamilton of Indiana, chairman of the House Subcommittee on Europe and the Middle East, wrote to the ADL in 1992 commending its early response to the atrocities.[81]

The present Jewish Welfare Federation was established in 1905 as the Jewish Federation of Indianapolis. The federation movement started in Boston in 1895 as an organization of Jewish charities. In Indianapolis, as in other cities, German Jews controlled the federation, although mainly eastern European immigrants were the recipients of the services. The goals of the federation were: centralize fund-raising; support local and national Jewish organizations; and provide educational opportunities. During its early years the federation's efforts were directed primarily toward financial assistance, employment, health care, and legal aid for new immigrants. As immigration decreased the federation turned to community projects such as a Jewish community center, adult education classes, and social gatherings.

The Jewish Welfare Fund was established in 1927 as an autonomous agency of the federation. Its purpose was to support projects not assisted by local and national Jewish organizations. By intent, the board was more representative than the federation board and included members from Zionist, Sephardic, and Orthodox communities. In 1948 the Jewish Federation and the

Jewish Welfare Fund merged and reorganized as the Jewish Welfare Federation. The organization continues fund-raising activities for national and local projects such as the Bureau of Jewish Education, Jewish Community Center Association, Jewish Family and Children's Services, Jewish Social Services, Park Regency (retirement housing), and Hooverwood (home for the elderly). The federation has addressed contemporary issues by establishing, for example, the New Americans Committee to assist Russian resettlement.[82]

The Jewish Federation of Indianapolis worked with synagogues in Gary, Hammond, Valparaiso, Whiting, and East Chicago. In 1930 the charitable organizations of these communities were placed under the umbrella of the Gary Jewish Welfare Federation, and in 1958 it became the Northwest Federation.

The federation is an expression of *Tzedakah* (a way of life, contingent on the idea it is God's will to aid the poor and the traveler). There are different levels of *Tzedakah,* the highest being the giver who anonymously assists an unidentified recipient.[83]

In 1939 the Jewish Federation of Indianapolis organized a Public Relations Committee in an effort to inform the non-Jewish community about Judaism and the situation in Nazi Germany. In 1947 this committee became the Jewish Community Relations Council (JCRC). Its goals were: "promote interfaith activities; maintain good relations between Jews and non-Jews; promote high ethical standards among Jews; protect Jewish rights; support civic and community welfare programs; and publicize the Jewish contribution to American life." Since its inception, the goals have been expanded to include the defense and support of Israel, support for Soviet Jews, and educational programs on the Holocaust. The JCRC cooperates with groups in the non-Jewish community on domestic issues that appear to undermine civil liberties and social and economic justice. The council works to develop and maintain interreligious coalition ties on various community projects.

The JCRC is headed by an executive director and governed by an elected board that represents all parts of the community—synagogues, women's groups, men's groups, federation agencies, etc. Though the group is diverse and expressive of differing views, it is united in preserving Jewish identity and resisting anti-Semitism.[84]

In 1892 a Hebrew Free Loan Society was organized in New York City and was based on the principle in Deuteronomy 23:19, "Thou shalt not lend upon usury to thy brother." Thus, money could be loaned without interest to fellow Jewish brothers in need. In December 1907 twenty-four men founded the Lafayette Orthodox Hebrew Free Loan Association. The origin of the

*Jewish Community Center ballroom dance class, Indianapolis, 1953.*

$28.60 capital investment is unclear, but it probably was from membership dues and initiation fees of the founders.[85]

The Free Loan Association's constitution clearly outlined guidelines for membership, dues, criteria and responsibilities of the board of directors, and loan requests. The bylaws specified the maximum loan (six hundred dollars) to any one member; a married couple was considered one member. The constitution also established a minimum payment schedule and specified the procedure for loan application.

The depression years of 1929 to 1938 were difficult for the Free Loan Association. It was forced to borrow money in July and October 1929 (one thousand dollars), 1930 (fifteen hundred dollars), and 1938 (five hundred dollars) from a commercial bank in order to meet its loan requests.[86] Several methods were used to solve the lack of resources. In January 1931 the membership voted (on recommendation of the board) to issue eighty shares in the Free Loan Association at twenty-five dollars per share with a member's purchase limited to eight shares. The money obtained from selling shares was placed in a reserve fund and kept separate from the capital funds. A member could borrow from the reserve fund for a fee.[87] During the years 1934–38 some members were embarrassed by their need to borrow money, so a number system was used instead of names to designate borrowers.[88] The success and caring spirit of the Free Loan Association was due in a large measure to the efforts and years of service of Jacob Singer. He served continuously as president from 1907 to 1960.

Communal organizations met not only religious and physical needs but also offered opportunities for the immigrant to socialize with his *landsman* (countryman). Most Indiana cities and towns lacked the large number of

Jews necessary to form a network of *landsmanshaften* (organization of people from same region/country) as in New York City so organizations such as the Workmen's Circle filled this void.[89]

The Workmen's Circle (Arbeiter Ring) was a fraternal order of Jewish workingmen sympathetic to the Socialist party. The Workmen's Circle was founded in 1892 by a small group of eastern European immigrants in New York City. By 1908 Indianapolis had organized a branch of the Workmen's Circle. Its goals were along the lines of the national organization: support socialism, stress the study of Yiddish culture and language, and assist the members in the event of illness and death.[90] By 1913 Indianapolis had two branches meeting at the Communal Building at 17 West Morris Street. Later, Branch 175 was able to purchase a building at 1218 South Meridian Street.

The Workmen's Circle manifested its support of socialism by holding May Day banquets, conducting debates on the American socialist movement, and raising funds for the Socialist party and the defense of incarcerated socialists. The maintenance of Jewish identity and transmission of Yiddish culture was a major part of the circle as reflected in the support of a Yiddish library, Yiddish afternoon school, and Hebrew Immigrant Aid Society.

In late 1918 a decrease in eastern European immigration and the rise of Jewish workingmen to shopkeepers and small merchants forced the circle to admit non-Jews with socialist sympathies. During the 1920s and 1930s a conflict between the left and right wings of the Socialist party weakened the circle. By the 1950s membership had decreased drastically, and the Workmen's Circle closed.[91]

Jewish education is centered primarily around the synagogue. During the early phase of communal development Jews were concerned with achieving integration into the general society, and public education was one way to effect this. Also, very few Jewish communities could provide the financial and institutional support necessary for a community school. Therefore, the responsibility for Jewish education fell on the synagogues.[92]

Education was treated in a unique manner in Terre Haute. The Jewish community had established two congregations: Terre Haute Zion Gemeinde in 1858 (it became Reform Temple Israel in 1882) and the Orthodox Temple B'nai Abraham in 1889. In 1935 the two congregations merged in order to "promote and preserve the Jewish community of west central Indiana." The congregation is affiliated with the Union of American Hebrew Congregations, maintains two synagogues, and offers members the choice of Reform or Orthodox services. A Reform rabbi, assisted by an Orthodox rabbi, oversees the services and educational programs in both temples.

There is a Sunday religious school and an afternoon Hebrew school. Also, there is an active youth group that promotes Jewish life.[93]

The most important educational force in the Gary Jewish community was the Hebrew Educational Alliance founded during the 1920s. In conjunction with the Sunday school, almost all Jewish children received some type of formal Jewish education. Classes were held at Temple Beth-El until a Jewish Community Center was constructed and classrooms were available. The students attended classes five days a week, after the regular public school day. The courses taught were Hebrew, Jewish history, the Bible, "Ceremonials," and the foundations of Judaism. The alliance provided a library of Hebrew and Yiddish books and sponsored social activities for the students. A publication of Temple Beth-El described the alliance's role as teaching "the youth of Gary the rich cultural heritage of Judaism" and making children "conscious as Jews in a religious and Jewish-Nationalistic sense."[94] The alliance served as a bridge between life in eastern Europe and life in American society while helping to preserve Jewish identity.

The day school movement is relatively new in Jewish education. The push for day schools began in the 1960s as the need to preserve both Jewish identity and tradition was reawakened in the aftermath of the Holocaust and the Six-Day War. Indianapolis was one of the last of the larger American Jewish communities to found a day school. The barriers encountered by supporters ranged from financial to ideological.[95]

The Indianapolis Hebrew Academy founded in 1970 is an independent day school serving the entire Jewish community in the Orthodox tradition. The goals of the school are to promote the ideals of Judaism and love of God and the Torah and to educate children to become intelligent creative persons. The school offers a curriculum that includes Jewish and secular studies for preschool, elementary, and high school levels. It also offers a Midrashic program (study of rabbinical commentary on the moral teachings of the Bible) for junior high and high school students.[96]

Jewish education beyond the high school level is found in three areas: the colleges of Jewish studies, seminaries and yeshivas, and Jewish studies programs in colleges and universities. In Indiana Jewish studies programs are located at Indiana University, Bloomington, and Purdue University, West Lafayette. The programs—whatever name and format—have acquired an importance in the structure of Jewish education. The status of the programs is enhanced because those who participate are independent of the formal Jewish community and are recognized as scholars in the general university community.[97] Organizations such as the Association for Jewish Studies and the Midwest

*Golden Age Club, Jewish Community Center, Indianapolis, 1954.*

Jewish Studies Association serve to link Jewish educators and provide a forum for the exchange of ideas and scholarship.

Additional and informal education is offered through institutions such as Jewish community centers, B'nai B'rith, and the Hillel Foundation (Indiana University, Bloomington). Adult education is usually under the guidance of community centers or synagogues. On the occasion of the 125th anniversary of the Indianapolis Hebrew Congregation, Rabbi Jonathan Stein said, "Historically, the family is the link from generation to generation. Parents teach their children and the children teach their children. Judaism is not a religion of the synagogue alone." He also spoke of the lack of education in Judaism among adults. The Indianapolis Hebrew Congregation began various adult education classes such as B'nai Mitzvah (group study equivalent to Bar and Bat Mitzvah classes) and Torah study.[98]

Though Zionism was powerful organizationally in Europe, it never was held as an ideology in the United States. The main objective of Zionism, as outlined by Theodor Herzl, was "to establish for the Jewish people a

publicly and legally assured home in Palestine."[99] However, in the United States this ideal was transformed from establishing a national homeland into a program of "support [to] the Jews in Israel (or Palestine)."[100]

From 1897 to 1922 there was opposition by the Jewish religious groups to Zionism. Zionism secularized the traditional Jewish hopes for a return to Zion (Palestine) by emphasizing the national rather than the religious character of Judaism.

Reform Jews viewed Judaism as a religion with a universal message. Also, Reform Jews feared that Zionism and its nationalistic sentiment would weaken their position as loyal Americans.[101] The antinationalist position of the Reform Jews was reflected in a series of resolutions from 1890 to 1918. One such resolution was adopted at Indianapolis in 1906. It stated: "We herewith reaffirm that religion is the tie which unites the Jews, the synagogue is the basic institution of Judaism and the congregation its unit of representation."[102]

Zionist meetings were held in Fort Wayne as early as 1912 on a regular basis and open to both men and women. In 1919 Minnette Baum of Fort Wayne, with the assistance of Mrs. Greemsfelder of Greenwich, South Carolina, organized a local chapter of the World Zionist Organization (WZO) of America. The organization raised money to send a nurse to work in Palestine. The organization was dissolved after a year due to anti-Zionist pressure. However, in 1922 Baum asked the Daughters of Israel, the women's auxiliary of the Orthodox congregation of B'nai Israel, to join the WZO of America. Because of conflicts with male members, the women broke away and affiliated with Hadassah. The purpose of Hadassah was "the education and development of an awareness of the need of a Jewish homeland."[103]

Many of the immigrants to Palestine were East Europeans who had come from the same regions and/or were relatives of American Jewish immigrants. During the Nazi era the Jews in Palestine were prepared to offer sanctuary to endangered European Jews. Attitudes began to change toward Zionism during the 1930s when the Jews in Palestine began to stand up to Arab rioters and British restrictions on Jewish immigration.

With the memory of the Holocaust and the formation of the state of Israel in 1948, American Jews began to support Zionism. Fund-raising for Israel became a major concern of Jewish community organizations.[104] Today, Indiana Jewish communities support Israel and Zionism as a cultural concept that sees Jews as a distinct group based on national ideas in the Jewish tradition and representing Jewish identity. Also, Indiana Jews are committed to maintaining Jewish life and preserving Jewish identity in the diaspora.

American society is characterized by immigrants from many countries. The ideology of America supports integration of immigrants, religious toleration, and political rights.[105] Anti-Semitism in the United States was never as virulent as in European countries and was directed toward religious and social discrimination.

In 1861 Dr. Arnold Fishel requested to serve as chaplain of the Cameron Dragoons, a New York regiment of mainly Jewish recruits. Secretary of War Simon Cameron refused based on a congressional act signed by President Abraham Lincoln that stated, "chaplains must be regular ordained ministers of some Christian denomination." On 5 January 1862 the Board of the Indianapolis Hebrew Congregation passed a resolution that instructed David Dessar, secretary, to write a letter to Congressman Albert G. Porter requesting to "have the obnoxious Chaplain clause . . . stricken from the statutes." Rabbi Isidor Kalisch of the Indianapolis Hebrew Congregation circulated a petition signed by seven thousand people, many of whom were Christians, supporting the Jewish request to amend the act to include "Jewish religion."[106]

At the Republican State Convention in 1916 there were three candidates from Lake County: Julius Friedman for lieutenant governor, Mayor Roswell O. Johnson of Gary for governor, and Frank Heighway for superintendent of public instruction. Johnson was forced to withdraw based on an accusation of support by "special interest" groups that would benefit from his election.

Friedman was asked to withdraw his name because the party did not want to nominate three men from Lake County. He refused and was asked again to pull his name after Johnson withdrew. Again Friedman refused. Johnson and his allies called for Friedman's withdrawal because of "the fact that he [Friedman] is a Jew and engaged in wholesale liquor business," and claimed, "Lake County Republicans didn't want to be represented by that kind of a man."[107]

At times prejudice is due to someone being perceived as different. Sol Strauss came to Paoli after World War I. He was a German Jew who had graduated from Heidelberg University and served in the German air force during the war. Strauss opened a general clothing store, and some residents would not shop "the Jew's store" because he "had bombed 'our boys.'" He often walked along Main Street and was accused of wanting "to spy on our window displays." A quote by a resident expresses a lack of insight and sensitivity: "People were very prejudiced, insensitive to him, and he learned to live with it." After Strauss's death a local attorney who shared his confidence said, "this man loved Paoli." In his will Strauss left a trust for civic projects, one of which was a library for children.[108]

In the 1920s the Ku Klux Klan became active in Indiana. It was a movement that espoused the superiority of native-born white Protestants, and its targets were blacks, Catholics, and Jews. Jews were considered to be "insoluble and indigestible in a Protestant America."[109] The Klan used the economic weapon of threatening to boycott Jewish-owned businesses and in its organ, *The Fiery Cross,* urged people to support only "100 percent American businesses."[110] The Klan also kept a watch on schools and the teachers. Sam Goldman of Rushville graduated from Earlham College and was certified as a teacher. He was hired to teach at nearby Straughn, but pressure by the Klan kept him from teaching.[111]

There was disagreement over how to respond to the Klan's propaganda. Rabbi Jacob Bienenfeld, editor of the *Indiana Jewish Chronicle* (1922–23), defended the Klan's constitutional right of freedom of expression and thought it best to maintain silence. However, B'nai B'rith did develop a response to the Klan. It asked members to help organize anti-Klan sentiment among businessmen and professionals, monitor violations of the law by the Klan, and report violations to the Jewish community.[112]

In Indiana as recent as the 1980s, acts of vandalism have defaced Jewish memorials, synagogues, and cemeteries. One of the earliest incidents occurred in Fort Wayne in May 1864. Several gravestones of children were destroyed.[113] The Anti-Defamation League monitors anti-Semitic actions and attitudes throughout the United States. A recent poll by the ADL found that one in five adults hold strongly anti-Semitic views. However, the percentage rate of anti-Semitism has declined from 29 percent in 1964 to 20 percent in 1992.[114]

Within the contemporary Jewish community various groups have "culturally converged" and are held together by common aspects of Jewish-American life such as support of Israel, the promotion of family life, and preservation of the memory of the Holocaust. Currently there is a strong movement within all segments of the Jewish community to maintain religious tradition and preserve Jewish identity.

Within a culturally diverse society Jews have made contributions to the cultural, intellectual, and economic life of Indiana. Jews have achieved integration into the community-at-large, but at the same time have maintained their identity.

## Notes

1. Morris N. Kertzer, *What Is a Jew?* (New York: Collier Books, 1978), 3–4.

2. Jacob Marcus, *The Colonial American Jew, 1492–1776,* 3 vols. (Detroit: Wayne State University Press, 1970), 2:739–45. Marcus writes of the acquisition and confirmation of land grants pursued by the Franks, et al., through the Indiana, Illinois, and Wabash land companies. Particular attention is given to the many legal difficulties encountered due to the changing of control over the territories involved (2:752–63).

3. Hubbard Madison Smith, *Historical Sketches of Old Vincennes* (Vincennes: [s.n.], 1902), 158.

4. Samuel Rezneck, *Unrecognized Patriots: The Jews in the American Revolution* (Westport, Conn.: Greenwood Press, 1975), 200. In 1832 Levy was granted an annual pension of ninety-six dollars. "Pension Applications," W773, National Archives, Washington, D.C.

5. Lance Jonathan Sussman, *A Chronology of Jewish History in Richmond, Indiana, 1816–1980* (Fort Wayne: Indiana Jewish Historical Society, 1981), 3.

6. Ruth Marcus Patt, "Samuel Judah, Class of 1816: Rutgers's First Jewish Graduate," *Journal of the Rutgers University Libraries* 47 (Dec. 1985): 77–90.

7. Joseph Levine, *John Jacob Hays: The First Known Jewish Resident of Fort Wayne,* Publication no. [1] of the Indiana Jewish Historical Society (Fort Wayne: Indiana Jewish Historical Society, 1973), 1–12.

8. Joseph Blau and Salo Baron, eds., *The Jews of the United States, 1790–1840: A Documentary History,* 3 vols. (New York: Columbia University Press, 1963), 3:803–4. Quote taken from *Allgemeine Zeitung des Judentums,* 28 Sept. 1839.

9. Arthur Hertzberg, *The Jews in America: Four Centuries of an Uneasy Encounter* (New York: Simon and Schuster, 1989), 153.

10. Jack Glazier, "Stigma, Identity, and Sephardic-Ashkenazic Relations in Indianapolis," in *Persistence and Flexibility: Anthropological Perspectives on the American Jewish Experience,* ed. Walter P. Zenner (Albany: State University of New York Press, 1988), 49.

11. Jacob Marcus, *To Count a People: American Jewish Population Data, 1585–1984* (Lanham, Md.: University Press of America, 1990), 64; *American Jewish Yearbook* (New York: The American Jewish Committee and Philadelphia: Jewish Publication Society of America, 1991), 207.

12. Daniel J. Elazar, *Community and Polity: The Organizational Dynamics of American Jewry* (Philadelphia: Jewish Publication Society of America, 1980), 51.

13. Isaac Landman, ed., *The Universal Jewish Encyclopedia,* 10 vols. (New York: The Universal Jewish Encyclopedia, Inc., 1939–43), 5:557. The first Jewish settlement is said to have been established in Rising Sun in 1825. However, no records remain in this community.

14. Lance J. Sussman, "Reflections: The Writing of Indiana Jewish History," *Memoirs and Reflections,* Publication no. 17 of the Indiana Jewish Historical Society (Fort Wayne: Indiana Jewish Historical Society, 1983), 31–33.

15. Carolyn S. Blackwell, "German Jewish Identity and German Jewish Emigration to the Midwest in the Nineteenth Century," in *German American Emigration and Settlement Patterns,* ed. E. Reichmann (forthcoming).

16. Ruth G. Zweig, *The First Hundred and Twenty-Five Years,* Publication no. 2 of the Indiana Jewish Historical Society (Fort Wayne: Indiana Jewish Historical Society, 1973), 2–8.

17. Lois Fields Schwartz, *The Jews of Ligonier: An American Experience,* Publication no. [10] of the Indiana Jewish Historical Society (Fort Wayne: Indiana Jewish Historical Society, 1978), 4–31.

18. George T. Probst, "The Germans in Indianapolis, 1850–1914" (M.A. thesis, Indiana University, 1951), 64, 65, 69.

19. Judith E. Endelman, *The Jewish Community of Indianapolis: 1849 to the Present* (Bloomington: Indiana University Press, 1984), 29.

20. Blackwell, "German Jewish Identity."

21. Roger Daniels, *Coming to America: A History of Immigration and Ethnicity in American Life* (New York: HarperCollins, 1990), 227.

22. Sussman, *Chronology of Jewish History in Richmond,* 9.

23. Daniels, *Coming to America,* 223–26.

24. Yiddish meaning synagogue.

25. Endelman, *Jewish Community of Indianapolis,* 61–62.

26. Daniels, *Coming to America,* 227.

27. Raymond A. Mohl and Neil Betten, *Steel City: Urban and Ethnic Patterns in Gary, Indiana, 1906–1950* (New York: Holmes and Meir, 1986), 172–73.

28. Every *shtetl* had a *cheder,* a school where young males learned to read and write and studied the Torah.

29. Albert Rosenberg, "Memories of Hovas Hochim Congregation in Vincennes," taken from text of speech given to the Bureau of Jewish Education, 21 Sept. 1986 (Indianapolis Jewish Historical Society). One of the Torah scrolls was given to the Jewish Community Center in Bloomington, Indiana, and another to the Bureau of Jewish Education in Indianapolis.

30. Glazier, "Stigma, Identity, and Sephardic-Ashkenazic Relations," 49.

31. Endelman, *Jewish Community of Indianapolis,* 37, 163–64. Kahn Tailoring Company was founded in 1866 by Henry Kahn, a German Jew, and evolved from custom tailoring to mass production, becoming one of the country's largest makers of men's suits and military uniforms.

32. Glazier, "Stigma, Identity, and Sephardic-Ashkenazic Relations," 50–51, 59.

33. For more about the refugee crisis see David S. Wyman, *Paper Walls: America and the Refugee Crisis, 1938–1941* (Amherst: University of Massachusetts Press, 1968).

34. Endelman, *Jewish Community of Indianapolis,* 186–87; Rosenberg, "Memories of Hovas Hochim Congregation," 3.

35. Ronald Sanders, *Shores of Refuge: A Hundred Years of Jewish Emigration* (New York: Schocken, 1988), 602–3. The writers who spoke to this situation were the non-Jewish poet Yevgeni Yevtushenko in 1961 and Andrey Sakharov in 1971. Twenty-six Jewish intellectuals in Vilnius (Vilna), Lithuania, sent a letter to the first secretary of the Central Committee of the Lithuanian Communist party, outlining the position of Soviet Jews.

36. Sanders, *Shores of Refuge,* 606–8.

37. Jewish Welfare Federation File, M463, box 122A, folder 4, Indiana Historical Society Library, Indianapolis.

38. Interview with new immigrant (name withheld by request).

39. Joseph Levine, *From Peddlers to Merchants* (Fort Wayne: Indiana Jewish Historical Society, 1979), 1.

40. Rudolf Glanz, *Studies in Judaica Americana* (New York: Ktav Pub. House, 1970), 120–21.

41. Richard Day, "A Report on the 'Gimbel Buildings,'" in *Memoirs and Reflections,* Publication no. 17 of the Indiana Jewish Historical Society (Fort Wayne: Indiana Jewish Historical Society, 1983), 44–50, 55–56.

42. Landman, ed., *Universal Jewish Encyclopedia,* 5:557; Day, "A Report on the 'Gimbel Buildings,'" 55.

43. The congregation was reorganized in 1873 under the name Rodef Sholem. In 1888 it purchased the First Christian Church building and converted it to a temple. The congregation dissolved in 1946, and the building is now a Lutheran church. For further information see the Wabash File, Indiana Jewish Historical Society, Fort Wayne.

44. *Huntington Herald-Press,* 24 Jan. 1974.

45. Levine, *From Peddlers to Merchants,* 1, 4.

46. An acre of ground for Jewish burials was purchased in 1854 by C. Herf, M. Hyman, and L. Hyman. When the Rodef Sholem Congregation was organized, the land was donated to the temple. Additional land was acquired in 1913 (one and one-quarter acres) and although a Jewish community is no longer in Wabash, a trust fund maintains the cemetery. There are about three hundred Jews, including four Jewish Civil War soldiers, from Wabash and surrounding areas buried there.

47. Marcus, *To Count a People,* 68.

48. Levine, *From Peddlers to Merchants,* 6–14.

49. Ibid., 23.

50. Ibid., 25.

51. Lafayette File, Indiana Jewish Historical Society, Fort Wayne.

52. Minyan: Ten Jewish males thirteen years of age or over are needed to hold a regular prayer service.

53. Evansville File, Indiana Jewish Historical Society, Fort Wayne.

54. Endelman, *Jewish Community of Indianapolis,* 34–35.

55. For a more complete account of the economic and civic contributions see ibid., chapter 2.

56. Abe Ruderman, "Memoirs of a Jewish Farmer in Indiana," Publication no. 19 of the Indiana Jewish Historical Society, Fort Wayne (Fort Wayne: Indiana Jewish Historical Society, 1985), 17–19.

57. Uri D. Herscher, *Jewish Agricultural Utopias in America, 1880–1910* (Detroit: Wayne State University Press, 1981), 24, 38.

58. Evansville File, Indiana Jewish Historical Society, Fort Wayne; Ethel and David Rosenberg, *To 120 Years! A Social History of the Indianapolis Hebrew Congregation (1856–1976)* (Indianapolis: Indianapolis Hebrew Congregation, 1979), 25.

59. Landman, ed., *Universal Jewish Encyclopedia,* 5:558; *100th Anniversary-Washington Avenue Temple, 1857–1957, Congregation B'nai Israel, Evansville, Indiana* (Fort Wayne: Indiana Jewish Historical Society).

60. W. William Wimberly II, *The Jewish Experience in Indiana before the Civil War: An Introduction,* Publication no. 6 of the Indiana Jewish Historical Society (Fort Wayne: Indiana Jewish Historical Society, 1976), 3.

61. Sidney L. Markowitz, *What You Should Know About Jewish Religion, History, Ethnics and Culture* (New York: Citadel Press, 1955), 93–94.

62. Wimberly, *Jewish Experience in Indiana before the Civil War,* 3–4.

63. Elazar, *Community and Polity,* 100.

64. The first attempt of reform was in 1824 by Beth Elohim (Sephardic-traditional congregation) in Charleston, South Carolina. It was the "German wave" of immigrants that pioneered the Jewish Reform movement in the United States. The main force behind the Reform movement was Rabbi Abraham Geiger of Frankfurt, Germany, who in 1836 founded a journal, *The Scientific Journal of Jewish Theology.* For further reading on the history of the Reform movement see Howard Morley Sachar, *The Course of Modern Jewish History* (New York: Dell, 1977), 153–59 and Sefton D. Temkin, "A Century of Reform Judaism in America," in vol. 74 of *American Jewish Yearbook* (New York: The American Jewish Committee and Philadelphia: Jewish Publication Society of America, 1973), 3–75.

65. Jacob Marcus, *Memories of American Jews, 1775–1865,* 3 vols. (Philadelphia: Jewish Publication Society of America, 1955), 3:7–8.

66. Rosenberg and Rosenberg, *To 120 Years!,* 19-20.

67. Sussman, "Reflections," 33–34.

68. Schwartz, *Jews of Ligonier,* 16–17, 21.

69. For additonal information see: *100th Anniversary-Washington Avenue Temple, 1857–1957*; Joseph P. A. Elliott, *A History of Evansville and Vanderburgh County, Indiana* (Evansville: Keller Print Co., 1897); and Evansville File, Indiana Jewish Historical Society, Fort Wayne.

70. For a history of the Conservative movement see Moshe Davis, *The Emergence of Conservative Judaism* (Philadelphia: Jewish Publication Society of America, 1963). A major force behind the movement was Isaac Leeser of Philadelphia. He formed the first Jewish theological seminary in 1855, which failed. Philadelphia Jewish leaders started the Jewish Theological Seminary in New York in 1886 and were successful. Glazier, "Stigma, Identity, and Sephardic-Ashkenazic Relations," 104–7.

71. Elizabeth Weinberg, "August 3, 1855—The Dedication (Synagogue in Madison, Indiana)," Publication no. 21 of the Indiana Jewish Historical Society (Fort Wayne: Indiana Jewish Historical Society, 1986), 17–21.

72. Evansville File, Indiana Jewish Historical Society, Fort Wayne.

73. Ibid.

74. Rosenberg and Rosenberg, *To 120 Years!,* 165–66.

75. Sussman, *Chronology of Jewish History in Richmond,* 23–26.

76. Ibid., 27–28.

77. *The First Fifty Years: A History of the National Council of Jewish Women, 1893–1943* (n.p., 1943), 9–22.

78. *Proceedings—First Convention of the National Council of Jewish Women—November 15–19, 1896* (Philadelphia, 1897), 77–78.

79. Sachar, *Course of Modern Jewish History,* 173. The organization borrowed its secret ritual from the Masons. Its earliest founders—Henry Jones, William Renau, Isaac Rosenberg—were Masons of high degree. The early meetings were characterized by secret passwords from Hebrew and German sources, initiations, and other rituals. By the midnineteenth century membership in a lodge was a "coveted social distinction."

80. *Evansville Courier Press,* 14 Apr. 1976.

81. *ADL on the Frontline,* Sept. 1992, p. 8.

82. Jewish Welfare Federation File, M463, collection guide, "Historical Note," Indiana Historical Society Library, Indianapolis.

83. Ernie Hernandez, *Ethnics in Northwest Indiana* (Gary, Ind.: Post-Tribune, 1984), 79.

84. Endelman, *Jewish Community of Indianapolis,* 178–79, 248–50; Dr. Marcia Goldstone, conversation with the author, 1992.

85. Chester E. Eisinger, *A Brief History of the Lafayette Orthodox Hebrew Free Loan Society, 1907–1960,* Publication no. [9] of the Indiana Jewish Historical Society (Fort Wayne: Indiana Jewish Historical Society), 1–2. Eisinger includes a list of founders.

86. See constitution and bylaws in ibid., 20–26.

87. Ibid., 3, 7.

88. Ibid., 4–6.

89. Endelman, *Jewish Community of Indianapolis,* 71. Endelman notes that Hungarian Jews did organize the Indianapolis Juedische Bruder Verein in the early 1890s, but apparently this was an exception.

90. Maximilian Hurwitz, *The Workmen's Circle: Its History, Ideas, Organization and Institutions* (New York: The Workmen's Circle, 1936), 11–15.

91. Endelman, *Jewish Community of Indianapolis,* 71–73; "Workmen's Circle Minute Book (in Yiddish), 1918–1926," Indiana Historical Society Library.

92. Elazar, *Community and Polity,* 260–61.

93. Oded Rosen, ed., *The Encyclopedia of Jewish Institutions: United States and Canada* (Tel Aviv, Israel: Mosadat Publications, Inc., 1983), 120.

94. Mohl and Betten, *Steel City,* 173.

95. For further comment on barriers to day school education see Endelman, *Jewish Community of Indianapolis,* 225–27, and Elazar, *Community and Polity,* 208–11.

96. Rosen, ed., *Encyclopedia of Jewish Institutions,* 120.

97. Elazar, *Community and Polity,* 212.

98. Lloyd B. Walton, "125 Years of Judaism," *Indianapolis Star Magazine,* 19 Oct. 1980.

99. Werner Keller, *Diaspora: The Post Biblical History of the Jews* (New York: Harcourt, Brace & World Inc., 1969), 425. For a general discussion of the rise of Zionism see Walter Laqueur, *A History of Zionism* (New York: Schocken Books, 1976), 40–83, 270–331.

100. Elazar, *Community and Polity,* 100.

101. Naomi Wiener Cohen, "The Reaction of Reform Judaism in America to Political Zionism (1897–1922)," in *The Jewish Experience in America,* ed. Abraham J. Karp (Waltham, Mass.: American Jewish Historical Society, 1969), 149–50.

102. Ibid., 153.

103. Esther Kretzmann Schwartz, "History of Zionist Organization and Hadassah in Fort Wayne, Indiana," in *Articles by or about Jews,* Publication no. [16] of the Indiana Jewish Historical Society (Fort Wayne: Indiana Jewish Historical Society, 1982), 9, 11, 16.

104. Keller, *Diaspora,* 483.

105. Calvin Goldscheider and Alan S. Zuckerman, *The Transformation of the Jews* (Chicago: University of Chicago Press, 1984), 157.

106. Rosenberg and Rosenberg, *To 120 Years!,* 25–26.

107. Account given to the Indiana Jewish Historical Society, Fort Wayne, by Bernard Friedman; *Gary Republican,* 15 Apr. 1916.

108. Ruth Uyesugi, "The Jew Who No One Really Knew," in *Articles by or about Indiana Jews,* Publication no. [16] of the Indiana Jewish Historical Society (Fort Wayne: Indiana Jewish Historical Society, 1982), 1, 2, 4.

109. Wyn Craig Wade, *The Fiery Cross: The Ku Klux Klan in America* (New York: Simon and Schuster, 1987), 178–79.

110. James H. Madison, *Indiana through Tradition and Change: A History of the Hoosier State and Its People, 1920–1945* (Indianapolis: Indiana Historical Society, 1982), 48–49.

111. Sussman, *Chronology of Jewish History in Richmond,* 20.

112. Endelman, *Jewish Community of Indianapolis,* 121.

113. Zweig, *First Hundred and Twenty-Five Years,* 8.

114. ADL Special Report: Survey on Anti-Semitism and Prejudice in America, 1992.

# KOREANS

ELISABETH E. ORR

*The first-generation immigrant children grew up with Korean values at home but were exposed to American culture and values through school, friends, and the media. Thus they often had little interest in marrying someone from Korea or even less in having their marriages arranged by their parents. Many married Americans, while others married Korean Americans who had had similar experiences while growing up in the United States. Those who opted to marry spouses they met in Korea often had problems when they found that their expectations for marriage differed from those of their Korean spouses.*

The history of Koreans in Indiana and the United States stretches back nearly a century. Though the first Koreans arrived in the United States in the 1890s, they did not come to Indiana until the 1910s. During the 1920s and 1930s there were twelve Koreans in Indiana.[1] Little is known about these early immigrants. They may have been farmworkers or students, as were most Koreans on the West Coast at that time. However research shows that they did not lead easy lives. For example, Mary Paik (pronounced pack) Lee came to the United States in 1905 when she was five years old, arriving with her parents who fled Korea as political

refugees. Lee's stories of her early life in this country are full of hardship, discrimination, and disappointment. In the early twentieth century many Americans had hostile feelings toward any group of people who were not native-born Americans. Life was especially difficult for nonwhite immigrants. Further, the small numbers of other Koreans and Asians in the United States at that time increased their sense of isolation. Early Korean immigrants found themselves the victims of racism and economic hardship, but through years of hard work and determination they were able to build new lives in America, far away from their Korean homeland. Their lives were very different from those of Koreans who came to the United States in the 1970s, 1980s, and 1990s. In telling her life's story during the 1980s in California, Mary Paik Lee reflected on the change in lifestyle for Koreans living in the United States:

> Years of backbreaking work without enough food and relaxation took its toll on my parents, but they just hung on through sheer will power. Their wretched physical condition was painful to see. The fourth generation of young Koreans growing up [currently] in comfortable homes with every advantage open to them will find it difficult to realize the sacrifices made by the first generation.[2]

Recent immigrants have arrived to find a sizable Korean community already in place in Indiana. They have worked very hard to be successful, and their high levels of education and skill have helped them enter the job market looking for professional positions, well above anything dreamed of by those who immigrated during the 1900s. When Byong Chul Kim, an engineer, arrived in Indianapolis from Seoul, Korea, in October 1978, he joined a community of nearly four thousand Korean immigrants in the state of Indiana. To Kim the United States represented economic opportunities and personal freedoms unavailable in Korea at that time. Kim was typical of many Koreans coming to the United States since the early 1970s. He did not have to face the blatant

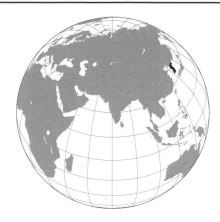

racism of earlier generations, nor was he confronted with a lifetime of backbreaking manual labor. Kim's experiences in the United States involved increasing his economic opportunities rather than escaping political oppression:

> [My dad] wrote to me and said, "Why don't you come and try the United States. . . ." He said that there were a lot of opportunities over here. So, I decided I would come over and give it a try. . . . After coming to the states, I went to IUPUI and did my graduate work while I was working, so I've been working as an engineer for eleven years.[3]

Over the last three decades Indiana has become home to thousands of Korean immigrants and their American-born children. Before the passage of the 1965 Immigrant Act opened the doors to people of all national origins, the population of Koreans remained small in Indiana as it did in the rest of the United States. After the 1965 act the Korean population began to grow rapidly until Koreans became one of the largest groups entering the United States during the 1970s and the early 1980s. In 1980 there were over 350,000 Koreans in the United States.[4] That number has continued to grow during the 1980s and early 1990s, though at a slower rate.

Unlike Chicago, Los Angeles, and New York, Indiana has not been an initial port of entry for Korean immigrants. After arriving in the United States, Koreans have been drawn to Indiana because of career and educational opportunities, as well as to join relatives already settled in the state. The majority of Korean Hoosiers now live in the Indianapolis area, where they have tended to settle on the east side of town. Though they are scattered throughout the state, Indianapolis is the heart of the Korean community in Indiana.

The recent Korean immigrants have become well known for their success in educational endeavors and entrepreneurship and play an important role in the economic life of American cities. Koreans in Indiana strive to fulfill the American dream of educating their children, owning their own homes, and having successful careers. They are hardworking and well educated. Through Korean-owned businesses, organizations, and churches, these immigrants have become a permanent feature in Indiana.

Korean immigration to the United States can be categorized into three phases. The first phase began in 1903 with the importation of Korean laborers to sugar plantations in Hawaii and ended in 1924 with the enactment of the Oriental Exclusion Act, which cut off the inflow of all Asian immigrants due to a rise in American xenophobia toward foreign, especially non-European, influences. The second phase took place during and after the Korean War. Due to close relations between South Korea and the United States, Korean students began coming to the United States to study. Although these students came only intending to obtain an education, many eventually stayed. During the same period Korean wives of American servicemen immigrated to the United States, and Korean children were brought over to the United States for adoption by American couples. The third phase began with the 1965 Immigration Act, which abolished discriminatory quotas based on national origins. From 1965 to the present, Koreans have been one of the largest immigrant groups entering the United States.

In 1903 the first shipload of Koreans arrived in Honolulu to work on Hawaiian sugarcane plantations. This was the first sizable group to arrive in the United States or its territories at one time. Large-scale immigration to Hawaii followed due to negotiations between sugar planters and the offices of the American minister at Seoul, Horace D. Allen, and some American missionaries in Korea at that time. Allen and a friend, David W. Deshler, then junior partner at American Trading Company operations at Inchon, Korea, schemed to recruit Korean labor for Hawaiian plantations. Deshler arranged transportation for the laborers from Korea to Japan and profited by booking passage through his transportation company. (Deshler held shares in the company.) Historians disagree on Allen's motivation for convincing Korean Emperor Kojong to allow Korean workers to go to Hawaii. Allen seems to have believed that Hawaii would provide economic opportunities for the poor laborers.[5]

In 1902 there was a cholera epidemic in Korea. The country had also entered a second year of drought, followed by rains and flooding and then a plague of locusts. These disasters caused widespread famine in Korea. Allen believed that conditions in Hawaii had to be better.[6]

Opportunities for Koreans in Hawaii were advertised in Korean newspapers. Mild weather, high wages, free room and board, and education in the English language were

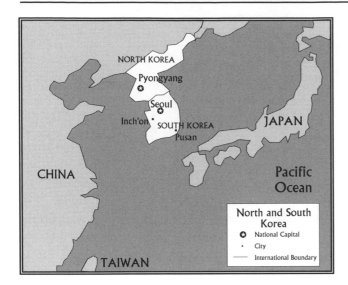

North and South Korea
⊗ National Capital
• City
— International Boundary

among the advantages touted by the ads. All of this seemed too good to be true, and it was. Hot, humid weather, grueling work, and poor food and medical care awaited them. Their wages no longer seemed high when the immigrants were confronted with the cost of living in Hawaii.

The only way most Korean laborers could afford to pay for passage from Korea to Hawaii was to borrow heavily from Deshler's company, which had been created specifically for this purpose by the Hawaii Sugar Planters Association. Even so, with all the advertisements and easy credit for ship fare, few Koreans signed on. Korean identity was so strongly tied to familial loyalty and responsibility that even when disaster struck, as in 1902 and 1903, few Koreans were willing to leave their homeland. The first shipload of 101 laborers signed up only after being persuaded to do so by American missionaries. Between 1901 and 1902, only 16 Koreans came to Hawaii and the United States, but between 1903 and 1905 over 7,000 arrived.[7] Most were young, unmarried males. The men hoped to return to Korea after making a small fortune in Hawaii. Conditions were harsh in Hawaii for these early Korean immigrants, and many left Hawaii in search of better economic opportunities on the West Coast, especially in California.[8]

In 1905 there was a sudden halt to Korean immigration to Hawaii. Korean reticence toward leaving family and homeland, rising opposition to Korean politicians and American missionaries, the recall of Horace Allen, and, most important, the establishment of Japanese hegemony over Korea were reasons for the end of Korean immigration. The Japanese saw Korean immigration as a threat to their newly established protectorate. Immigration was suspended on 17 November 1905 with the signing of a secretly negotiated treaty formalizing Japanese control over Korea. With

this move the Japanese government intended to protect Japanese immigrants in the Hawaiian Islands from Korean competition.[9] At times Koreans had acted as strikebreakers against Japanese workers, who often organized strikes and demanded wage increases. Such practices did little to endear Korean laborers to the Japanese government.[10]

Of the 7,226 Koreans who came to Hawaii between 1903 and 1905, 6,048 were men, 637 were women, and 541 were children.[11] The majority of the men had been manual laborers in Korean towns and cities but were also soldiers, policemen, and servants. Few farmers came, probably because land ownership produced an optimism for future investment that manual laborers and urban workers lacked. What the Koreans found in Hawaii was anything but what the advertisements had depicted. Plantation work was a never-ending cycle of sugarcane cultivation.

When Korean immigration ceased in 1905, most Korean men in Hawaii did not have wives, and there were few single Korean women on the islands. Although other Korean immigration had been terminated, the importation of brides began in 1907 and continued until 1924. Because Korean hostility to Japanese hegemony was intense, the Japanese looked for ways to appease overseas Koreans who were especially adept at stirring up foreign sympathy for Korea's plight. By granting exit visas to young Korean women who agreed to marry Korean men overseas, the Japanese hoped to "calm political passions."[12] These marriages were called "picture bride" marriages and were arranged as follows: the couple exchanged pictures through an intermediary, then if both parties agreed to the match, the woman came to Hawaii and married the man.

The men described life in Hawaii in glowing terms to their prospective brides in hopes of persuading them to come. A common practice was for the man to send a picture of himself as a young man in Korea. The young woman had no way of knowing that she was not really marrying the handsome, young stranger in the photograph. Many picture brides arrived in Hawaii with high expectations, only to be met at Honolulu Harbor by a weathered old man, tanned dark by the sun. The brides confronted an additional shock in the drudgery of plantation life. It is likely that many picture brides came from desperate situations in Korea since they willingly came to marry men about whom neither they nor their families knew much. Between 1910 and 1924 approximately 1,000 picture brides came to the islands and 115 went to the West Coast.[13]

Like the European immigrants, the Koreans came to the United States for new opportunities, to escape oppression, and to start new lives. Realizing that sugarcane plantations did not offer economic mobility, many Koreans returned home, although a sizable number settled along the West Coast, particularly in California.[14] The Hawaiian Islands served as a stepping-stone for Korean laborers who hoped to enter the United States mainland.[15] By 1922 a majority of Korean workers had left Hawaii.[16]

Unlike European immigrants who simply changed their names to fit in, Korean immigrants were seen as physically different and were frequently the victims of discrimination.[17] Nevertheless, early Korean immigrants found ways to survive. Many opened stores because they were not allowed to hold other jobs due to discrimination and white hostility. Koreans became successful shopkeepers and owners of ethnic enterprises such as restaurants and grocery stores.[18] Korean immigrants linked economic success to ethnic solidarity. Koreans worked together to survive by trading labor with each other on their farms or by contributing money into a *kae,* a community fund that allowed members to borrow money.[19] The *kae* was especially useful to Koreans attempting to lease or buy land to farm. Without strategies like the *kae,* few Korean immigrants would have been able to do more than work as field hands or manual laborers.

During this same early period of immigration, Korean students came to the United States to obtain their degrees from American colleges and universities. Between 1910 and 1919, approximately 541 students were admitted to American schools and universities.[20] Japanese hostility toward student visa applications was strong because many of the students became leaders of the Korean independence movement in America. This movement was an attempt by Korean students and immigrants to gain Korean independence from Japan. One of the most famous of these student leaders, Syngman Rhee, later became the first president of the Republic of Korea (South Korea) from 1948 to 1960.

Another manifestation of Korean nationalism in the United States was the organization of Korean churches. A high percentage of Korean immigrants had ties to churches at home, especially to the Methodist and Presbyterian denominations that had sent large numbers of missionaries to Korea. In America, Korean churches provided not only worship services in Korean but also acted as meeting places for social gatherings and Korean language schools. The Korean church in America also became the center of the Korean independence movement. Such activities strengthened solidarity among the immigrants. Through politicized community organizations and a deep involvement in the Korean independence movement abroad, Korean immigrants were able to preserve their identity.

In 1924 Congress passed an immigration act that limited entry of immigrants based on country of origin. The act favored northern and western European immigrants while virtually eliminating immigrants of non-European origin.[21] The Immigration Act of 1924 was devastating for prospective Korean immigrants. Restrictive policies in both Japan and the United States resulted in a low number of Koreans being admitted to the United States and Hawaii between 1920 and 1940. In 1920 there were 1,677 Koreans on the mainland, in 1930 there were 1,860, and in 1940 there were 1,711. In Hawaii, too, the population was static: 1920–4,950; 1930–6,461 (picture brides and resultant new births); 1940–6,851.[22] Although some Korean students were allowed to come to the United States during this period, they were the rare exception. For example, between 1921 and 1940, 289 students were allowed to come to the United States, but they were forced to leave after finishing school.[23]

The United States declaration of war against Japan was hailed by Korean immigrants in the United States as the beginning of the end in their fight for independence from Japan. They threw themselves into the American war effort wholeheartedly, volunteering in the armed services whenever possible, investing heavily in war bonds, and volunteering in the National Guard. They also proudly wore badges identifying themselves as Koreans so that white Americans would know that they were on their side.[24]

Unfortunately Koreans were often treated very badly by white Americans during World War II, especially on the West Coast, because they were thought to be Japanese. The United States government officially identified Koreans as "enemy aliens" in its 1940 Alien Registration Act. Such treatment was horrible for Korean immigrants, who themselves despised the Japanese. Koreans could do little to prove themselves, however, since Korea was under Japanese control and was officially considered by the United States government to be loyal to Japan.[25] Nevertheless, the defeat of Japan, which resulted in Korean independence, was cause for great celebration among the Korean immigrant community.

After World War II the relationship between the United States and Korea grew closer as the United States established a military government in South Korea while the Soviet Union occupied North Korea. One result of closer relations between South Korea and the United States was a more liberal United States policy on student visa applications. Although the actual number of Korean immigrants did not increase, many of Korea's top students came to American universities to obtain specialized training for their careers in Korea. In 1958 alone, 1,387 Koreans were admitted as nonquota entries for study but not permanent residence.[26] The entrance of even small numbers of Koreans was a significant departure from earlier United States policy of nonentry for Koreans and other Asians.

During the late 1950s and early 1960s most Koreans in Indiana were engaged in educational pursuits. Many students of various ages and with a variety of goals made use of the opportunity to study here. For example, in 1955 Yangja Cho came from Kwangju, Korea, to study at John Herron Art School in Indianapolis. She planned to stay for three years if she could stand being away from her family for so long.[27] In November 1955 Dr. Chang Mo Moon, superintendent of Severance Medical College and Hospital in Seoul, Korea, arrived in Indianapolis for a one-year stay as administrative resident at Methodist Hospital. He intended to learn American principles of hospital administration so that he could apply those methods in Korea. One of Moon's children was in the United States at the same time, studying at Ohio State University.[28] Kyoung Sook Kim came to attend high school in Indianapolis in 1962. She lived with an American family and was a student at North Central High School. She found the lives of American teenagers a striking contrast to her life in Korea, where she had attended an all-girls school. She found it difficult speaking English constantly but hoped "to stay here and attend college in order to learn more about everything in this country."[29]

Among the earliest known Korean residents in Indianapolis were Han Won Paik and Chinok Chang Paik and their three children. The Paiks moved to Indianapolis in 1962 after they completed graduate degrees at Northwestern University in Illinois. He majored in physics, and she studied mathematics. Mr. Paik went on to finish his graduate work at Indiana University in Bloomington and then became a professor at IUPUI. Mrs. Paik taught math and statistics at IUPUI in addition to raising three children. She later became an actuary for an insurance company in Indianapolis. The Paiks came to the United States to get an education and ended up staying because of better academic and career opportunities. Also Mr. Paik had relatives in the United States when he arrived in 1958, which was added incentive for settling here. Reflecting on the difficulty of their early years, Mrs. Paik commented:

> [We had] hardships with everything. Language, [it was] hard to study, I was expecting, and all kinds of things were coming together. My husband said, "You can't work like this." You know, if I did not study, if I left school, then the immigration law would have forced me to separate from him, to go back home to Korea. It was desperate. I just had to go to school. On finals' day I took my exams and then in the evening I went to the hospital and I had my daughter.[30]

Like many others, the Paiks managed to surmount personal difficulties in order to stay in this country.

There were only three or four Korean families in Indianapolis when the Paik family arrived in 1962. In the 1990s when Koreans came to Indiana, they had many others to help them to adjust, but early immigrants like the Paiks simply had to rely on themselves. When the Paiks arrived, Americans were not as accustomed to seeing Asians and were not always welcoming.[31]

Koreans who arrived in the 1950s and early 1960s reported finding strong racial discrimination in the United States. Sometimes other students made them feel like outsiders by calling them names or by staring at them wherever they went. Store clerks often treated them with disrespect. Charles Chae, who settled in Indianapolis in the 1960s, said, "Sometimes kids followed me when I went out because I looked so different. There were not many Asians in Indy then."[32] Such treatment was uncomfortable at best, but it was generally borne in silence with quiet perseverance. In the end optimism prevailed. Mr. Paik summed up the feelings of many: "Though I and other Koreans sometimes have felt discrimination, never in human history has a country valued so much or given so much for basic human life, especially for a foreigner; only in this country we call America."[33] Gratitude to America and the freedom and opportunity it provided helped the Koreans of the 1950s and 1960s to endure much of the discrimination they experienced.

Discrimination was not the only problem immigrants had. Some came to the United States already in difficult situations. One such group was Korean women married to American servicemen. Many entered the United States during and after the Korean War and thus were part of the second wave of Korean immigration. From 1952 to 1982 over forty thousand Korean women came to the United States as spouses of American citizens.[34] Many, though not all, were uneducated and from poor families. While some

*Han Won Paik and Chinok Chang Paik on his sixtieth birthday, Indianapolis, 1988.*

HAN WON AND CHINOK PAIK

undoubtedly married for love, others married servicemen in hopes of entering the United States and increasing their social status. Due to cultural differences and language barriers, however, most of the marriages did not last long, leaving the women in desperate straits. Without family or friends in the United States and lacking acceptance by the Korean immigrant community, many of the ex-wives of servicemen found themselves without allies. Some were able to return to Korea, but many others remained in the United States, eking out an existence with few job skills and little education.

Also in this second wave of Korean immigration were Korean children adopted by American parents. Many of these children had lost their families during the war, and United States adoption represented one of their only real options since Koreans rarely accept children unrelated to them into their families. Coming to the United States opened up a world of opportunities for Korean orphans who might otherwise have faced grim lives. Since the Korean War, over forty thousand Korean children have been adopted by Americans.[35]

Several Indiana organizations acted as adoption agencies for Korean children. One was the People's Temple Apostolic Church, which in 1959 created a program through which American couples could adopt biracial Korean children fathered by American servicemen. These children were in particular need since they were not adoptable by Korean standards. The church established a fund to pay for the costs of transporting the children to the United States and for legal fees arising from the adoption procedures. A number of families in the Indianapolis area were involved in this project. The church's minister and his wife adopted three Korean children, a boy and two girls.[36] Thus the second wave of Korean immigrants was made up of students, wives of servicemen, and adopted children.

There were other Koreans who wanted to immigrate at this time but could not. Their reasons for wanting to leave Korea were varied but were centered around a lack of opportunities and an increasingly dictatorial Korean government. After the Korean War, South Korea's population exploded with an influx of war refugees from the North. The rapid population growth was accompanied by industrialization and rapid urbanization.[37] In order to keep prices low on exported Korean manufactured goods, wages had to be kept low. The Korean government helped industry maintain low wages by prohibiting strikes and using to their advantage the surplus of workers willing to work for low wages or to cross picket lines during a strike.[38] In addition, a scarcity of educational opportunities at the university level in Korea caused fierce competition, and many Koreans looked elsewhere to find economic and educational success. The United States was also attractive to Koreans because American popular culture and consumer goods had flooded Korea during and after the Korean War. Koreans saw the United States as a land of opportunity and freedom. Until 1965, however, few were allowed to immigrate.

After the passage of the 1965 Immigration Act, eliminating national origin quotas, Koreans began immigrating to the United States in large numbers. This was the third wave of Korean immigration, and it has continued through the early 1990s. By 1980 it was estimated that there were over 350,000 Koreans in the United States, with the great majority having come during the third wave. By 1980 there were 3,295 Koreans in Indiana.[39] Since then, the population has grown slowly as the number of immigrating Koreans has decreased considerably. Comparing his early years in Indianapolis to the present, Charles Chae said, "When I first came here in the late 60s there were only a few Koreans in Indy. It was very difficult. I had an American friend in town which helped but there were less than fifteen Korean couples in town then. Now there are more than five hundred [couples]."[40]

During the late 1960s and throughout the 1970s and 1980s, many Koreans continued to take advantage of educational opportunities as well as to fill the need for doctors, engineers, and scientists in the United States. The family preference provision in the 1965 Immigration Act allowed individuals who had already immigrated to bring over as many of their immediate family members as they wished. Entire families immigrated in order to give their children an American education. Though this placed a heavy burden on the parents of these children, they believed that Korea held a limited economic future and that the United States held a better future in the long run. It was not uncommon for parents to send their children to live with relatives so that they could attend school in the United States. Esther Lee, a young medical student at IU Medical School, whose parents sent her to the United States when she was fifteen years old, said:

> My parents thought that in order for us to get educated it would be best to send us to the United States. It really is true that the United States is the country where if you study hard and try, you can be successful whereas in a lot of other countries that may not always be true. . . . I may not have had the opportunity to pursue my career if I had been back home.[41]

Children from less affluent families did not have the opportunity to pursue professional careers because education in Korea was very expensive. Also, until recently young women did not generally pursue graduate school studies since they might have been considered unmarriageable in Korea. According to Haekyung Lee, a professor with a Ph.D. at Indiana University in Bloomington, "When I was in school [in Korea], my parents' friends always warned them that it would be hard to find a husband for me because I was too smart. The attitude was that a woman shouldn't be more than a man."[42] Such women often found more educational freedom in the United States. Indiana drew many Koreans, men and women, to its universities and colleges. A large student population arose in Bloomington (several hundred Korean students including foreign students and Korean Americans), while smaller numbers attended schools in Lafayette, Muncie, Terre Haute, and South Bend. In contrast to second-wave immigrants, many of the foreign students receiving their degrees from Indiana schools in the 1980s and 1990s returned to Korea to look for jobs. The pre-1980 Korean students often tried to stay because job opportunities were better in this country. Another difference was that most students of the 1950s, 1960s, and 1970s attended school on scholarships awarded for outstanding academic achievement, while those of the 1980s and 1990s benefited from Korea's economic boom and their parents paid their tuition. Though this meant that the quality of students decreased, it also meant that more Korean students had access to an American education.

Numerous other third-wave immigrants came to Indiana on the family exemption which allowed immigrants to bring over family members to join them. Following Korean tradition, many adults sent for their elderly parents in order to take care of them during their old age. Also many young Koreans returned to their homeland to find spouses and brought them back to the United States. Others sent for their families after first establishing themselves in jobs.

Families formed the basic unit of support within the Korean community. Traditionally Korean families have been large because of the value placed on children, especially sons. A woman's role was to produce sons and to raise the children to respect their elders and place family loyalty above all else. Though some of these values have been modified in the United States, Korean immigrants still teach their children to respect adults and to value family relationships. Children are taught to respect their parents and, unlike many American families, do not develop a friendship type of relationship with their parents even in adulthood. This has created problems for some families when children try to behave like the perceived American ideal they have seen on television and in some of their American friends' families.

The Paik grandchildren, the one on the far left celebrating his first birthday, Indianapolis, 1994.

Because many Koreans have immigrated in order to give their children an American education, and thus have sacrificed their own professional success, they are very careful to emphasize high academic achievement. Good grades are generally expected, and most Korean children in the United States are closely supervised by their parents to make sure that they are doing well in school. Above all, educational success is nourished by constant encouragement and prodding. Many Korean parents also direct their children toward specific kinds of careers beginning at an early age. In Korea, a bachelor's degree is considered a basic requirement for many jobs, and so immigrants often urge their children to attain the highest levels of education possible. This is the reason that Korean students earn a disproportionately high percentage of graduate degrees. Though such pressure produces a high rate of success, it may also take its toll. One young Korean mother spoke with frustration about her husband's expectations for their four-year-old son and year-old daughter. "Even though my husband was raised here [in the United States], he wants my son to be a medical doctor and my daughter, she can do anything she wants because she's a woman."[43] She had other plans. "I know that my son is very gifted in music. Once he listens to music he knows it and he can sing along. So, I don't mind him being a musician but my husband will go against it. He says, '[My son will be a musician] over my dead body.'"[44]

Children sometimes resent their parents' high expectations, especially in comparison to their other classmates. Kiju Hansen, a fourth grader in Fort Wayne, complained, "My mother tells me that I always have to do better, even if I'm doing the best out of everyone in my class."[45] His mother Sook-Ja Hansen explained, "In Korea we don't accept mediocrity as good enough. It's not enough to be at the top of your class if no one else is working very hard. We expect our children to do the best they can regardless of how everyone else is doing."[46]

In the short run, it is easier for children to adjust to life in the United States than it is for adults. They learn English more quickly and easily than their parents and are exposed to American culture every day in school. The children generally feel fairly comfortable with English and American culture within a year's time, in contrast to their parents, who often feel like outsiders in some way for the rest of their lives. Problems do arise, however. Very young children, and those born in the United States, tend to identify themselves as Americans but run into problems when others see them as Asians. Byong Chul Kim related the story of his children's confusion over their identity. "The biggest problem they have is when you see advertisements with Asians in them and they laugh at them and say, 'See the Chinese over there.' They do not know that they're different."[47]

To overcome identity problems, parents try to raise their children with a feeling of pride in being Korean and with a knowledge of Korean language and culture. This is not an easy task. Though most parents speak Korean at home, children often cannot speak it fluently but rather are more likely to be able to understand certain words and phrases. Up until the time that they go to school children usually speak Korean exclusively, since that is what they are exposed to at home. Once they enter grade school, however, they are surrounded by English-speaking children and teachers and begin to feel more comfortable speaking English than Korean. Many Korean parents reported speaking to their children in Korean and receiving responses in English. Another related problem has been a growing generation gap between parents and their American born or raised children. In a sense these children have had to choose between Korean and American customs of behavior in order to feel accepted at school and in American society. American informality, individuality, and freedom of expression have often been seen by Korean parents as a lack of respect. Such problems have not gone unnoticed by the Korean community in Indiana. Since its founding in 1971 the Korean Language School in Indianapolis has taught children about Korean language and culture. Each weekend parents have brought their children to the campus of IUPUI for classes. Many of the teachers have been Korean foreign students who are uniquely qualified to teach immigrant children, since they have come from Korea so recently themselves.

Another group of Korean children with special needs were those adopted by American parents. Adoptive parents have tried to teach their children about their Korean heritage and to instill a sense of identity and pride in them. One way this was done is through the Korean Language School in Indianapolis where adopted children and their parents can study Korean language, culture, and customs alongside the children of Korean immigrants.[48] Such interaction provides adopted children with good Korean role models, as well as making them aware of their ancestry. Another group that provides support for adoptive families with Korean children is Ours of Central Indiana. This organization is a support group that celebrates Korean holidays and culture. Adoptive families have the opportunity to meet other interracial families and share experiences.[49] Other more informal activities such as eating Korean food, wearing traditional Korean clothing for special events, and taking tae kwon do lessons all contribute to adopted children's pride in being of Korean ancestry.

Adopted children have come to the United States through special channels. From 1983 to 1989 Korean adoptions in Indianapolis were handled largely through Bethany Christian Services in Indianapolis. During these seven years American couples adopted over two hundred Korean children through Bethany. After 1989 the adoption of Korean children came to a halt except for the placement of special needs children. The cessation of adoptions grew out of Koreans' feeling that Korea, as an industrialized nation, should support its own orphans. After the 1988 Seoul Olympics, there was an increase in negative publicity by the Korean media, which viewed foreign adoptions as the exportation of human beings, as opposed to the American view that the children should go to loving homes, American or otherwise.

Just as in Korea, marriage and family are extremely important among Koreans in Indiana. Koreans emphasized the stability and strength of Korean marriages and frequently noted that the divorce rate among Koreans, at home and abroad, has been extremely low. In comparison to American couples, Koreans rarely got divorced. Married couples who moved to Indiana together frequently commented on the fact that immigration pushed them even closer together than they might have been in Korea. In Indiana they found their strongest allies in each other, whereas in Korea they would have been surrounded by family and friends. Although marriages were strained by the upheaval of immigrating, in the long run they were strengthened.

Couples who immigrated together and were both Korean faced a variety of challenges. Korean women grew more assertive as they worked full time and began to feel more independent and autonomous. Also, their jobs left little time for housekeeping and supervising children, according to traditional Korean standards. One woman who had recently married remarked:

> My husband wants to think he is more dominant [and better] than me in everything we do. But my beliefs and values are different. Even though he was raised here, his parents had the typical Korean marriage where his mother was nothing.[50]

In Korea women rarely had jobs outside the home, and their identities were tied to their roles as housewife and mother. It was considered shameful for a woman to hold a job. It shamed her husband because people assumed that he was not making enough for them to live on. "Why else would a woman work?" was the traditional assumption. In this view women did not hold jobs unless they had to. In the United States this view has changed since the 1960s and the emergence of the women's movement. So upon immigrating, nearly all Korean women have held full-time jobs. It has not been seen as shameful in the United States by Koreans, and it has helped families make ends meet. Nevertheless, Korean men still expected their working wives to keep up their traditional duties: keeping the house spotless, cooking elaborate, time-consuming meals, and disciplining the children and supervising their homework.

In the face of change, many Korean husbands reacted by becoming more traditional and conservative just at the time when their wives were moving in the opposite direction. Men reacted against the fear that they were losing out on what generations of Korean men expected from their wives. Women found that they liked the new self-confidence and sense of identity gained through working. Though this caused conflict within Korean marriages, few couples were ready to give up. A businessman in Indianapolis, whose wife enjoyed working full time as a nurse, related a story about his marriage:

> My wife has changed a lot since coming here in the sense that she speaks out now. She was very reserved when she first came here. This causes conflict now but we are working on it. In Korea we say it is like a bow and arrow. When you draw the arrow back in the bow, you are initially going in the opposite direction from your goal but it is necessary to do this in order to go forward. So too with conflict in marriage. Sometimes it is necessary to step backwards or go through conflict in order to resolve problems.[51]

Though many immigrants faced cultural conflict within their marriages, they rarely chose divorce as the answer. The solution was often found in compromise. Many couples reported that their marriages were a combination of Korean and American values. Though the wife may still be responsible for home and children, she and her husband

*Korean high school students perform a native dance at Eagle Creek reservoir in Indianapolis in 1975.*

may now discuss financial decisions together. If she has her own business, she probably manages it in her own way. When asked how his marriage differed from an American marriage, Jae Hong Choi of Indianapolis replied, "We don't kiss all the time or talk about our emotions like American couples, otherwise we are very much like American couples."[52]

In their spare time Korean couples continue to follow traditional styles of socializing. When couples get together they form separate groups of men and women. Most men and women have friends of the same sex, especially once they are married. Even their hobbies differ. Among Korean men in Indiana sports are the most popular kind of hobby, with golf being the hands-down favorite. In Indianapolis there are many informal groups of Korean golfers. Women are more likely to have solitary hobbies that fit into their busy schedules such as reading, gardening, or shopping. Both men and women belong to a variety of clubs organized in Indianapolis by the Korean community like the tennis, chess, photography, and volleyball clubs.

In contrast to traditional Korean marriages were mixed marriages between American men and Korean women. As discussed earlier, many of these marriages were between American servicemen and Korean women with little education. If the woman was uneducated, her English skills were probably nonexistent, and her job skills were minimal. Because her husband probably spoke little Korean, the couple had little ability to communicate. The marriage would deteriorate as the husband's frustration grew and the wife's fear and alienation increased, and the marriage often ended in divorce. Chinok Chang Paik often worked as a translator at Fort

Benjamin Harrison in the Indianapolis area for Korean women involved in problems with their American husbands. She believed that 90 percent of all such marriages ended in divorce, and that they usually did not last more than two or three years.

Servicemen and their Korean wives were by no means the only examples of Korean/American mixed couples, however. Numerous Korean men and women met their American spouses in Korea or the United States. Those who were educated or came from economically advantaged families in Korea have had an easier time adjusting to American life. Mixed marriages have been much more common between Korean women and American men than the reverse. The most frequently cited reason for this discrepancy is that American men are more likely to view women as equals. American marriages, especially among the younger generation, are more of a partnership than the hierarchical relationship of Korean marriages. Several women in mixed marriages commented that because they were not traditional Korean women, they were more comfortable with an American-style marriage. One such woman was Sheena Kotarski of Indianapolis. She married an American serviceman and had a happy marriage. She felt that her independent, freethinking ways made her more suited to marriage with an American than with a Korean.

Another woman, Sook-Ja Hansen, was attending a Korean university when she met her American husband, who was in the Peace Corps at the time. When she eventually informed her family of her decision to marry an American, they were very upset. Though they had not planned to arrange her marriage, a tradition still practiced in Korea today, her parents had hoped that she would choose a promising young Korean man, possibly someone from her university. Though she had disgraced her family, they eventually came to accept her husband. The fact that he was educated helped her family to accept her marriage. Nevertheless, she and her husband found their early life in Korea difficult and soon decided to move to the United States:

> It's much easier living here with my husband than in Korea. In Korea we used to stand apart at bus stops and get onto the bus at different entrances because people would say terrible things to us. Many Korean people are very prejudiced against mixed marriages.[53]

Living in Fort Wayne, the Hansens had a typical American marriage. Both worked full time and shared household jobs. They both actively participated in raising their son.

Many mixed couples in Indianapolis did not take part in Korean community activities because they feared the prejudice of other Koreans. Mixed couples frequently socialized with other mixed couples or American couples because they felt more comfortable and accepted. In the Fort Wayne area, approximately 50 percent of all Koreans were in mixed marriages. Korean immigrants in this area were more accepting of mixed marriages than in Indianapolis. Mixed couples were more active in the Korean church and community activities in Fort Wayne because they felt more comfortable in such a setting. Though she had not felt excluded, Sook-Ja Hansen said that there was some discrimination stemming from the mistaken belief that only lower-class Korean women would marry American men. "Once they get to know you and find out what kind of a person you are, they are not so reluctant to be friendly."[54]

Most Korean parents expressed the hope that their children would marry other Koreans or Korean Americans when they grew up. Marrying Americans was discouraged because of the difference in values between the two cultures. Parents worried that their children's marriages would end in divorce if they married Americans. Equally important was the concern that their children would grow farther away from them, thus increasing the generation gap and the alienation the parents felt in the United States. The first-generation immigrant children grew up with Korean values at home but were exposed to American culture and values through school, friends, and the media. Thus they often had little interest in marrying someone from Korea or even less in having their marriages arranged by their parents. Many married Americans, while others married Korean Americans who had had similar experiences while growing up in the United States. Those who opted to marry spouses they met in Korea often had problems when they found that their expectations for marriage differed from those of their Korean spouses. This was especially a problem for Korean-American women who married Korean men and then discovered that their husbands were even more traditional than they had imagined.

Regardless of what kind of marriage Korean immigrants entered into, all agreed that Indiana was a good place to settle and raise a family. Indiana offered traditional values that resembled Korean culture more than some of the large metropolitan areas in the United States, where Korean youth gangs have become a problem. Also, in many very large cities husbands and wives have found the high cost of living to be an added stress. In contrast, Korean gangs are nonexistent in Indiana, and the cost of living is less than in many other areas of the country.

Perhaps the most frequently cited reason by third-wave immigrants for settling in Indiana was job opportunity. Koreans have been very successful in the United States in part because of their strict work ethic. Doctors, college professors, engineers, businesspeople, and assembly workers were among the primary occupations of Koreans in Indiana. Unlike Chicago, Los Angeles, and New York, which were initial ports of entry, Koreans often came to Indiana after having lived elsewhere in the United States. Many were transferred to Indianapolis by their employers. For those who arrived directly from Korea, friends, Korean businesses, or Asian Help Ministries, a nonprofit organization, helped them find employment. Others found work here after graduating from an Indiana college or university. Many immigrants commented that they came to Indiana for undergraduate work but then found themselves staying longer and longer to finish graduate degrees. As the years passed the students realized that family and friends in Korea had gone on with their own lives and that living in the United States had begun to feel more comfortable in many ways than life in Korea. Jae Hong Choi, a polymer scientist with AT&T in Indianapolis, was one such person. "I decided the American way of doing things was more to my liking. Confucian society is very conservative. For example, you can't express yourself freely to your elders. It is really quite strict. Also career opportunities were greater here at the time [when I decided to stay]."[55]

Doctors and college professors, many of whom came in the 1960s and early 1970s, were among the earliest third-wave Korean immigrants in Indiana. In Indianapolis alone there were over a dozen Korean doctors. Dr. Heun Yune was one of the early medical doctors in Indianapolis. He found Indianapolis an excellent place to practice medicine. Having finished his medical training at Vanderbilt University in Tennessee during the early 1960s, he received a number of invitations from an American colleague to return to Vanderbilt medical school as a full-time faculty member. He eventually did so in 1966 and then accompanied his American mentor to the IU Medical School in 1971, where he has practiced ever since. Dr. Yune was fairly typical of Koreans arriving at this time. He had an excellent command of English since he had worked with Americans during the Korean War and attended medical school in the United States. Because he spoke English fluently and his job placed him in the midst of American society, he quickly became immersed in American culture and felt comfortable with it. He also did not have the luxury of a large Korean community to depend on. When asked his opinion on those coming to Indiana during the 1980s and 1990s he replied that, "It is all too easy for them to remain insulated from American society by relying on others."[56] Dr. Yune and his family had a variety of friends, American and Korean, and he believed that this was healthier in the long run

than having only Korean friends. This type of attitude personifies early third-wave immigrants who were firmly established in the United States by the 1970s and 1980s.

Korean professors at Indiana universities and colleges also were well integrated into American society because they too spoke fluent English and dealt with Americans on a daily basis. Koreans taught in fields such as mathematics, physics, chemistry, economics, business, and home economics, where what they learned in Korea was transferable to the United States. Areas such as literature, history, and the social sciences required greater familiarity and training in western culture than was generally available in Korea. Also language proficiency was not as much of a barrier in mathematics and the sciences as in other fields. Teaching in Indiana was not always easy for immigrants, who sometimes mentioned that they had been harassed by students. Chinok Chang Paik taught mathematics at IUPUI and explained that some students blamed her for their bad grades, saying that they could not understand her and thus could not be expected to do well on exams. Paik felt such complaints were discriminatory since most of the students understood her and did well on exams if they studied. Another professor at Indiana University in Bloomington spoke of similar experiences. Haekyung Lee remembered one student who had tried to blame her poor performance on Lee's English ability. Fortunately, such experiences were not the norm and resulted more from students looking for excuses than from a lack of ability on the part of Korean professors.

Until the 1980s Korea provided few economic opportunities. Stagnating business opportunities forced Koreans to look elsewhere for economic growth. The United States had a much stronger economy and more jobs. Many of the highly trained Koreans who immigrated, however, faced language barriers and cultural conflicts. Sometimes they were unable to find work in their chosen fields and turned to entrepreneurial endeavors. This is one reason that Americans think of Koreans in connection with small businesses, such as greengroceries, restaurants, and wig shops across the country.[57]

In Indiana small business opportunities were widely pursued by Korean immigrants. By the early 1990s Indianapolis alone boasted several Korean grocery stores and a half dozen Korean restaurants. Bloomington had one grocery store catering to all Asians and a tae kwon do studio. Other Korean communities throughout the state also had businesses that catered to them. Most businesses established by Koreans were not ethnically based however, and the majority engaged in business unrelated to Korean food or tae kwon do. Convenience stores, non-Korean food restaurants, insurance agencies, wig shops, import/export companies (with Korea as well as other countries), and consulting firms were among the many enterprises run by Koreans in Indiana. Upon arrival in the United States, many Korean businessmen were able to establish themselves quickly because they brought a fair amount of money with them from Korea. During the 1980s Korean entrepreneurs were the largest group of Korean immigrants coming to the United States since American immigration policy no longer gave priority to medical doctors but shifted its stance to favor those who wanted to establish businesses with savings brought from Korea. Thus businesspeople have outnumbered others in the last decade.

Assembly line workers composed one of the largest groups among Koreans in Indiana. They were generally well-educated people who lacked the proficiency in English necessary to obtain white-collar jobs comparable to the ones they held in Korea. Though factory jobs paid fairly well, Korean immigrants tended to feel they had lost status when they took such jobs. Factory work in Korea was considered the domain of the uneducated and lower classes, so when finding themselves faced with the prospect of assembly work, many felt they had lost face among their peers. The apparent loss of status was very difficult for many Koreans to deal with and added to the stress of adjusting to life in the United States.

Women who worked outside the home found job opportunities much more plentiful in the United States than in Korea. In Korea most employers did not hire women because they believed, in accordance with Confucian values, that jobs with a lot of responsibility or those that paid well should go to men. Many Korean women found it liberating to pursue their careers without being judged negatively by society. Though it was difficult to balance family and career, Korean women enjoyed developing their careers. Dierdra Moon, a graphic design artist in Indianapolis, balanced taking care of her two young children and her husband as well as cooking and cleaning house. Still, she looked forward to going back to work soon. "As a woman, being here is great."[58] This is not to imply that Korean women were typical American working women. They were not. Over and over again the women and their husbands emphasized that though they worked, most of them were still very traditional. They had careers, but they were the ones responsible for children and the home, not their husbands. Sometimes their husbands helped out a little with household chores, but this was the exception. Many Korean women accepted this way of life because they were raised to believe that their roles as adult women would be very traditional. Thus they tried to combine tradition and modernity to form a compromise they and their families could live with.

Drawn by education, family ties, and job opportunities, the Korean population in Indianapolis reached approximately eight hundred by the mid-1970s.[59] By this time the Koreans had established a small, informal community with an interdenominational Korean church as the nucleus. The church was established in January 1971, and the congregation met in the United Methodist Church at 38th and Meridian streets. Approximately thirty people attended the first service. The minister who served the Korean congregation, Ki Chong Lee, was Methodist and arranged for the use of the American church's facilities. The founding of this congregation arose out of the need for Korean language services. In 1969 a number of Korean immigrants had decided that there was a need for a church and that the population was large enough to support it. This interdenominational church became a place where people could worship as well as socialize.

Nearly ten years later the original church split into several different denominations. The size of the congregation had grown over the years with increased immigration and births, and a number of these members broke off to establish Korean churches within their own denominations. The reasons for this were numerous. Many members had strong loyalties to specific denominations and wanted to establish churches in their own denominations. Other conflicts developed over personal affiliations, and loyalties brought over from Korea, and still others involved strained relations among church members due to the frustrations of immigration and the problems of adjusting to a new culture. The Korean Catholic Church held its first Mass in February 1977, and the Korean Presbyterian Church was established in the early 1980s. The original interdenominational church soon became the Korean Methodist Church. The Baptists eventually established their own church, too. Between 120 and 150 people attended the Presbyterian church during the 1980s and 1990s. Other churches were smaller, with congregations ranging from a few dozen to around a hundred. By the early 1990s there were a half dozen Korean churches serving nearly two thousand people in the greater Indianapolis area. Though less than half that number actually attended services on a regular basis, the churches did play an important role for many in the Korean immigrant community.

Churches were also important because they were a place where all Koreans, Christian and often non-Christian, met and felt at home with other people who understood their language and culture. In addition, Korean churches in Indiana became a substitute for territorial ethnic communities. The church became the focus for strengthening the immigrants' psychological defenses against an alien American culture. In their nonreligious roles churches acted as cultural brokers between immigrants and American society.[60] The church

*A grouping of Korean churches in Indianapolis, 1995: Korean Baptist Church (upper left); Korean Presbyterian Church (upper right); Korean Bethel Christian Church (lower left); and The First Korean United Methodist Church (lower right). All photos by Robert M. Taylor, Jr.*

community also served as a surrogate extended family in situations where kinship ties were severed or weakened by immigration. Because the role of the extended family in Korea was so important, the church became a vital element in the lives of many immigrants.

Although Koreans emphasized that the primary purpose for attending church was religious, members attended church for social reasons too. "The church really is an important part of the Korean people, even back home and especially in the United States. It is their only link back home."[61] Due to extensive missionary work by the Presbyterians and Methodists, many immigrants were Christians in Korea, and it was natural for them to look to the church for leadership once they arrived in the United States.[62] Non-Christians too were at least familiar with the church in Korea because of its high profile in building hospitals, schools, and universities. Churches often acted as a family, especially for new arrivals. "Church plays a big role in a social service way for a lot of immigrants. I think a lot of Korean churches do that function because there's no one else to do it."[63] Church members picked up newcomers from the airport, helped them to find jobs and housing, translated legal documents, and acted as court translators. The church also provided a place where Koreans could mingle with other Koreans at least once a week.

Although the church provided an inviting community, it was sometimes a barrier to learning English and assimilation. New immigrants often found refuge within the church and only ventured into American society to work. Those workers in Korean-owned businesses could avoid all contact with American society. Immigrants who came in the 1960s and early 1970s believed the church could be a hindrance to acculturation for more recent arrivals. They emphasized that the best way to get used to living in the United States was to experience it. These veteran immigrants had been forced to immerse themselves in American culture in order to survive and felt that many newcomers, in the 1980s particularly, insulated themselves from American society. Veterans opined that by relying on other church members for friendship and advice instead of overcoming embarrassment over poor English skills and fear of the unknown, it took the newcomers longer to feel comfortable in American society.

Many of these early immigrants were attending American churches by the late 1980s because they were more comfortable there and were tired of the conflict they experienced in some of the Korean churches. The Korean clergy did not usually speak or read English, which tended to alienate those who came in the late 1960s and early 1970s. Parents feared that their children would not be able to relate to a minister who could not communicate with them while American churches could

easily serve that purpose. Churches outside the Indianapolis area often avoided these problems because their congregations were made up of a different kind of membership. Fewer new immigrants settled in Fort Wayne, for example, because of fewer job opportunities, which meant a smaller core of Koreans to persuade relatives to settle there. Most of the Fort Wayne Korean population had lived there since the 1970s and were completely immersed in American society. Thus the Korean language congregation at First Presbyterian Church in Fort Wayne was a comfortable mix of all ages, with nearly 50 percent of the couples being mixed. Founded in 1978, the Fort Wayne church began with a part-time minister and in 1984 hired a full-time minister, the Reverend Dr. Joseph B. Doh. Though it had a small congregation throughout the 1980s and early 1990s, the church actively encouraged self-sufficiency among its members by providing English lessons. In addition, Dr. Doh spoke both English and Korean fluently so that he was able to communicate with all his congregation. The Korean United Methodist Church in Bloomington met different needs than either the Indianapolis churches or the Fort Wayne church. Founded in 1981 by a group of Korean students, the Bloomington congregation included students at Indiana University as well as other Korean Bloomington residents. Because the Korean community was smaller in Bloomington than in Indianapolis and socialized informally around Indiana University, the church focused more exclusively on religion than other churches. Foreign students were very active in services, Bible studies, children's education, and the Korean school. However, the church's large student population meant that its membership was transient.

Besides churches, the Korean community established a number of other organizations, some based on mutual

*Koreans preparing to play soccer on Independence Day, 15 August, early 1990s. The Korean Society and Korean churches come together annually to celebrate this event.*

interests, others for the purpose of meeting people and working to strengthen the bond between Koreans in Indiana. Among nonreligious organizations in Indiana the Korean Society of Indiana was one of the most active. According to Dr. Han Won Paik, the Korean Society was initially founded as a social group by Korean community leaders including Dr. Paik and Dr. Kilchul Kim, a respected member of the group of early immigrants in the Indianapolis area. Founded in 1971, the organization grew out of an informal arrangement among friends "who got together and started taking turns going to Chicago to pick up Korean groceries for their friends here in Indianapolis."[64] Though there were three Korean grocery stores in Indianapolis by the early 1990s, there were none in the early 1970s. The closest stores were in Chicago. Thus out of this group grew the idea for a social club that any Koreans in the area could join for the mutual benefit of all. It was significant that the Korean Society was not affiliated with any church, since to do so would have excluded nearly half of all Koreans in the Indianapolis area. The early leadership was taken on by medical doctors and technicians who were well respected in the Korean community. At this time members began recruiting heavily from other occupations, such as businessmen, assembly workers, and students. Jay Park, president of the Korean Society in 1989 and 1990, reminisced about his role in the 1970s:

> I became involved in the mid-1970s while I was a student at Butler. I encouraged Korean people to register and join the Korean Society. . . . By 1977 I had become more nationalistic [than before] and I decided to work for the Korean community. Koreans in the U.S. needed to help each other and be a cohesive group for mutual benefit. I still believe it is important that Koreans put the Korean Society above other affiliations because we must all work together before reaching out to others.[65]

Nonetheless, by 1979 the Korean Society became inactive and remained so until 1987. The reasons for this lull may be attributed to conflict between certain factions within the organization. The factions were built around professions or friendships and were not unusual in other Korean organizations, where personal loyalty was often placed above group loyalty. After seven years of inactivity, the Korean Society was resurrected in 1987 with the intention of pulling in as many kinds of Koreans as possible. At the first meeting, held at Warren Central High School in the Indianapolis area, sixty people attended. They elected Jay Park as president and appointed a committee of five representatives, one from each of the

five churches, to run the society. Since that time the society has been quite active. Promoting friendship among Koreans in the metropolitan Indianapolis area was one of the primary goals, and toward this end members held social gatherings such as their annual Christmas party in December. Members also helped new immigrants find jobs, aided in translation and legal problems, and provided many kinds of informal education about American society and basic "how to" information. The society has tried to be involved in a variety of ways in its members' lives. In 1991 the society sponsored an area soccer team of Korean children who wanted to attend a soccer tournament in Chicago for Koreans from all over the Midwest. The team needed money for meals and to stay in Chicago overnight. Without outside help, the team had little hope of attending but because of the donations by a number of Korean Society members, the team was able to attend the tournament.

Over the years the membership of the society changed in accordance with the changing face of the Korean community. During the 1970s it was made up of early immigrants to the Indianapolis area, especially doctors and medical technicians, as well as professors and students. After beginning again in the 1980s, businessmen were among its most active members. Assembly line workers were also very supportive.

Other Korean-sponsored groups were organized around specific interests or for meeting certain goals. A particularly active group during the 1980s was the Society of Friends of Korean Studies (SOFOKS), which has been involved in reinstating Korean studies as part of the East Asian Studies program at Indiana University in Bloomington. This organization was different from other Korean groups in that it was open to anyone, including non-Koreans, interested in furthering the Korean studies program. Another part of the group's effort was directed toward bringing Korean students to Indiana University in an exchange program. Dr. Heun Yune was the founder of SOFOKS and one of its most active supporters. He feels that because he lives in the United States it is important for him and other Korean immigrants to contribute to American society instead of only looking back to Korea.

Professional organizations were also part of the Korean community. The Korean Scientists and Engineers, a national organization, had a very active chapter in Indiana. Korean medical doctors were members of American medical associations, but their wives organized the Indiana Korean Medical Auxiliary and raised money to help support rural health care in Korea. While talking about his work as a scientist at AT&T, Jae Hong Choi commented that people often were surprised at how active the Korean Scientists and Engineers association was. "Koreans are a

*Korean Society members write names in the Korean alphabet for visitors during a multicultural activity at the Indiana State Museum, Indianapolis, 1994.*

cohesive group and have tended to be very active in community organizations."[66]

The importance of involvement in Korean community activities and church groups was a theme echoed by many immigrants. In Indianapolis and other areas where large numbers of Koreans lived it was relatively easy to be active in a variety of things. Moreover, it fulfilled the need of all Korean immigrants to maintain some kind of tie to their homeland. Nearly all Korean immigrants thought about returning to Korea on a permanent basis. All of them visited Korea when they could afford it. Many had investigated the possibility of returning to Korea in the late 1980s when Korea's economic and political situation seemed to have stabilized; however, the longer Koreans lived in the United States the more likely they were to stay. "In the early days there was always the dream for me that I might go back, in that when I got out of school I might go back to the friends I had known and the society that I had grown up in."[67] But for Byong Chul Kim this proved to be only a dream, especially after he was settled in a job, got married, and had children. At that point the United States had become a second home. Others repeated the same sentiments but, like Kim, stayed

in the United States. Although many people mentioned missing their families and friends, several also said they did not miss the conflict, expectations, and disappointments that came with such relations. Some mentioned the fact that their children had been born in the United States and it would have been very difficult to move them. Others thought that they had changed so much that, though they longed to return, they would no longer feel comfortable in Korean society. Though she wanted to return to Korea because "it is home," Haekyung Lee thought that she "would like to stay here because I fear that I can't fit in to Korean society again. My personality probably fits better in American culture than Korean culture now. I've become too aggressive [for a Korean woman]."[68] Lee also wanted the opportunity to continue her research and career opportunities in the United States. In the end Lee was ambivalent about what she would do. Mentioning her daughter as a factor she said, "There are better opportunities for my daughter here but I know that if she is a very bright student she will meet discrimination. It's hard for minority students."[69] Ties to Korea were very important to Koreans, and many sent their children to Korea every summer or every few years to learn what it meant to be Korean. Celebrating holidays in the Korean tradition was another means of keeping close ties to Korea. At Christmas and on New Year's Eve many Korean children dressed in traditional Korean clothing. A few people celebrated the Chinese New Year though even in Korea not many people observe this holiday anymore. For the most part Koreans in Indiana celebrated the same holidays that other Americans celebrated. They generally served special Korean dishes but otherwise their celebrations were very similar to American celebrations.

By the 1990s the Korean population in Indiana was just under 5,500, and it was expected to grow slowly over the next decade. In the Indianapolis area there were 1,144 Korean immigrants and people of Korean ancestry, which was by far the largest concentrated group in the state. Lafayette ranked second with 647, followed by Bloomington (514), Hammond/East Chicago (441), and South Bend (310).[70] The presence of Korean immigrants over the last three decades has added to the increasingly heterogeneous makeup of Indiana. Struggling to negotiate the cultural conflicts between American and Korean societies, Korean immigrants tried to build new lives in a foreign land. Life has not always been easy. For many first-generation immigrants loss of status, their lack of proficiency in English, and fear of an unknown culture have held them back from truly becoming active members of American society. Persistence and hard work have paid off for many Koreans though. Over the years, as they toiled to build a promising future for themselves and their children, they grew to love their new country and to call it home, albeit a second home. Koreans and their descendants have a long, well-established history in the United States and with each passing year continue to add their hard work, values, and traditions to the multiplicity of ethnic groups that inhabit the state of Indiana. No longer identifying themselves as only Korean, the second and third generations pursued their goals and aspirations as Americans, just as generations of immigrants and their children had before them.

## Notes

1. U.S. Census, 1920 and 1930.

2. Mary Paik Lee, ed., *Quiet Odyssey: A Pioneer Korean Woman in America* (Seattle: University of Washington Press, 1990).

3. Byong Chul Kim, interview with author, 1 Apr. 1990.

4. See Koreans in the United States in the general U.S. Census Reports for 1980, pp. 354, 593.

5. Lee Houchins and Chang-Su Houchins, "The Korean Experience in America, 1903–1924," *Pacific Historical Review* 43 (Nov. 1974): 549–50.

6. Ibid., 550–51.

7. Ibid., 553; H. Brett Melendy, *Asians in America: Filipinos, Koreans, and East Indians* (Boston: Twayne Publishers, 1977), 125.

8. Houchins and Houchins, "Korean Experience in America," 555.

9. Ibid., 553–54; Melendy, *Asians in America*, 125; Illsoo Kim, *The New Urban Immigrants: The Korean Community in New York* (Princeton, N.J.: Princeton University Press, 1981), 220.

10. Kim, *New Urban Immigrants*, 20.

11. Houchins and Houchins, "Korean Experience in America," 554.

12. Ibid., 559.

13. Ibid., 559–60; Kim, *New Urban Immigrants*, 24; Melendy, *Asians in America*, 125.

14. Kim, *New Urban Immigrants*, 21.

15. Ibid.

16. Houchins and Houchins, "Korean Experience in America," 562.

17. For an excellent autobiographical account of early Korean immigrant experience in the United States see Lee, *Quiet Odyssey*. Lee and her family were among the first Koreans to go to Hawaii. They soon moved to California, where she still lives.

18. Ronald Takaki, *Strangers from a Different Shore: A History of Asian Americans* (Boston: Little, Brown and Co., 1989), 13.

19. Ibid., 274–75.

20. Houchins and Houchins, "Korean Experience in America," 558.

21. Takaki, *Strangers from a Different Shore*, 7, 418.

22. Melendy, *Asians in America*, 129.

23. Ibid.

24. Takaki, *Strangers from a Different Shore*, 364.

25. Ibid., 365.

26. Melendy, *Asians in America*, 130.

27. *Indianapolis Star*, 24 Sept. 1955.

28. *Indianapolis News*, 2 Nov. 1955.

29. *Indianapolis Times*, 3 Mar. 1963.

30. Han Won Paik and Chinok Chang Paik, interview with the author, 23 Nov. 1990.

31. Ibid.

32. Charles Chae, interview with the author, 25 Oct. 1990.

33. Paiks interview.

34. Pyong Gap Min, "The Korean American Family," in *Ethnic Families in America: Patterns and Variables*, eds. Charles H. Mindel, Robert W. Habenstein, and Roosevelt Wright, Jr. (New York: Elsevier, 1988), 218.

35. Ernie Hernandez, *Ethnics in Northwest Indiana* (Gary, Ind.: Post-Tribune, 1984), 145.

36. *Indianapolis News*, 25 Feb. 1960.

37. Luciano Mangiafico, *Contemporary American Immigrants: Patterns of Filipino, Korean, and Chinese Settlement in the United States* (New York: Praeger Publishers, 1988), 80.

38. Takaki, *Strangers from a Different Shore*, 437.

39. U.S. Census, 1980. The actual figure for Indiana was 3,940. Charting the growth of the Korean community in Indiana is problematic because population figures for Koreans in Indiana are nonexistent between 1940 and 1970.

40. Chae interview.

41. Esther Lee, interview with the author, 15 Apr. 1990.

42. Haekyung Lee, interview with the author, 13 Nov. 1990.

43. Anonymous.

44. Ibid.

45. Sook-Ja and Kiju Hansen and Yol Min, interview with the author, 12 July 1992.

46. Ibid.

47. Kim interview.

48. Jae Hong Choi, interview with the author, 11 Nov. 1990.

49. Melitta Payne of Bethany Christian Services, interview with the author, 30 Sept. 1991.

50. Anonymous.

51. Ibid.

52. Choi interview.

53. Sook-Ja Hansen, interview with the author, 14 July 1992.

54. Ibid.

55. Choi interview.

56. Dr. Heun Yune, interview with the author, 15 July 1992.

57. Bong Youn Choy, *Koreans in America* (Chicago: Nelson-Hall, 1979), 226.

58. Dierdra Moon, interview with the author, 29 Apr. 1990.

59. Choy, *Koreans in America,* 348. Choy cites *Tongn-A Ilbo,* a Korean language publication, 1 Jan. 1976, as the source of this information.

60. Kim, *New Urban Immigrants,* 187.

61. Esther Lee interview.

62. Christianity claims the highest number of adherents in Korea. According to the 1984 *Mission Year for Prayer and Study,* published by the Presbyterian Church (USA), of the 40 million inhabitants of the Republic of Korea in 1984, 31 percent were Christian, 26 percent were Shamanist, 26 percent were Buddhist, 14 percent were New Religionist, and 13 percent were Confucian. These figures are misleading, however, to the extent that many people combine religions without conflict. For example, Confucianism is generally practiced with Buddhism because the former is a code of ethics while the latter is an organized religion and is spiritual in nature.

63. Paiks interview.

64. Sung Jay Park, interview with the author, 10 July 1992.

65. Ibid.

66. Choi interview.

67. Kim interview.

68. Haekyung Lee interview.

69. Ibid.

70. U.S. Census, 1990.

# THE LOW COUNTRIES

ROBERT P. SWIERENGA

> *Indiana offered opportunities aplenty for the poor farm tenants and laborers of the grain region of the northern Netherlands. Beukma wrote lengthy and enthusiastic letters to his homeland offering to assist friends and relatives "provided they were solid people" and not afraid to work. "Here I have found what I was looking for—bread and freedom; now I have no worry about the future of my children," Beukma wrote on 4 July 1836.*

The Low Countries[1]—Belgium, the Netherlands, and Luxembourg—lie astride the Rhine River delta outlets to the North Sea. For centuries these lands have been western Europe's gateway to the Atlantic world. Thousands of European immigrants and vast quantities of cargo passed yearly through the ports of Antwerp, Rotterdam, and Amsterdam, en route to the New World. Historically, the Low Countries formed part of much larger empires, those of Charlemagne in the eighth and ninth centuries, the Burgundian and Hapsburg rulers in the fifteenth and sixteenth centuries, and Napoleon in the early nineteenth century.[2] The Hapsburg King Charles V (1500–1558) is credited with creating the modern Netherlandic state. In the seventeenth century the Spanish King Philip's brutal rule sparked a successful revolt that led to the creation of the Dutch Republic. After Napoleon's defeat, the Netherlands, Belgium, and Luxembourg were politically united in the Kingdom of the Netherlands, but the union lasted for only fifteen years, from 1815 to 1830.

Attempts to unify the Low Countries were always undermined by the abiding cultural and religious differences spawned by the Protestant Reformation and the ensuing Eighty Years' War (1566–1648). These religious wars left the region north of the Rhine River staunchly Reformed or Calvinist and the region to the south Catholic. Linguistically, the Low Countries comprise four language groups: Dutch, French, Frisian, and German, and the language borders overlap the religious and political borders. Netherlanders in the northern province of Friesland speak the Frisian language. The Dutch language is spoken in the remainder of the Netherlands and also in the heavily populated Flemish region of northern Belgium. The dialect of French called Walloon is spoken in the southern region, while German or the local Germanic dialect of *Letzeburgesch*[3] is spoken in the southeastern Belgian province of Luxembourg and the adjacent nation of Luxembourg. The Belgian Luxembourg province had been carved out of the Grand Duchy of Luxembourg in 1839.[4]

Culturally, the three primary religions are the Dutch Reformed in the north, the Flemish Catholics in the center (both Hollanders and Belgians), and the Walloon and Luxembourg Catholics in the south. The sociocultural distinctiveness and exclusiveness of these very diverse regions was carried to North America by the immigrants. The Protestant Dutch immigrated in the greatest numbers, followed closely by the Flemish Catholics. The more sparsely populated Walloon and Luxembourg areas in the south never experienced overseas immigration.

The Dutch and Belgian presence in America is historic, dating back more than 350 years to the founding of New Netherlands in the years 1614–24.[5] Belgians, both Flemish and Walloon, were numerous among the pioneer settlers of this "Dutch" outpost. Immigration has been continuous since then, but the pace fluctuated depending on push and pull factors. There are three distinct phases: the commercial expansion of the seventeenth century, the free immigration

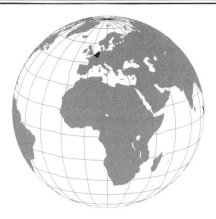

Table 1. Decadal Immigration into the United States from Belgium and the Netherlands, 1820–1989

| Period | Belgium | Netherlands |
|---|---|---|
| 1820–1840 | 50 | 2,539 |
| 1841–1850 | 5,074 | 8,251 |
| 1851–1860 | 4,738 | 10,789 |
| 1861–1870 | 6,734 | 9,102 |
| 1871–1880 | 7,221 | 16,541 |
| 1881–1890 | 20,177 | 53,701 |
| 1891–1900 | 18,167 | 26,758 |
| 1901–1910 | 41,635 | 48,262 |
| 1911–1920 | 33,746 | 43,718 |
| 1921–1930 | 15,846 | 26,948 |
| 1931–1940 | 4,817 | 7,150 |
| 1941–1950 | 12,189 | 14,860 |
| 1951–1960 | 18,575 | 52,277 |
| 1961–1970 | 9,129 | 30,606 |
| 1971–1980 | 5,329 | 10,492 |
| 1981–1989 | 6,335 | 10,663 |
| Total | 209,824 | 372,657 |

Source: *1989 Statistical Yearbook of the Immigration and Naturalization Service* (Washington, D.C., 1989).

of the nineteenth century, and the planned immigration following the Second World War.

Colonization of New Netherlands began as an adjunct to the fur trading ventures of the Dutch West India Company, and it culminated in 1664 with the English conquest, although Dutch culture remained firmly rooted for many generations. After a hiatus of 180 years, the great immigration began in the 1840s and continued until the First World War and the quota law of 1921. The peak decade for the Dutch came in the 1880s (53,700), followed by the 1910s (43,700). The Belgian immigration crested after 1900 and remained high until the war (1900s–41,600; 1910s–33,700).[6] (See Table 1.) After the devastating Second World War, the Dutch immigration exceeded the Belgian because the Dutch government actively sponsored the overseas resettlement of its dispirited people, even to the extent of providing passage money for the poor. Between 1951 and 1960, 52,000 Netherlanders and 18,500 Belgians immigrated to the United States. About half as many arrived in the 1960s and even fewer since 1970. Besides many working-class folk, both nations also suffered a "brain drain" of professionals in the postwar exodus.

The major causal factors in the nineteenth-century immigration were economic hardships, accentuated by religious dissent. Belgium and the Netherlands were the most densely populated European nations, and the overwhelmingly rural population suffered from a lack of available land. Nor could the sluggish industrial sector absorb the surplus, except in Wallonia which was the first region of Europe to experience the industrial revolution. Periodic economic crises such as the potato blight and inflation in the 1840s, and the collapse of grain prices in the 1880s due to the new competition from North America, the Ukraine, and elsewhere, prompted many farm laborers to immigrate to the American frontier. Also, thousands of Protestant Dutch departed to gain religious freedom from the oppressive policies of the Dutch King Willem I (1815–40) and his ministers, who defended the monopoly of the national

Hervormde (Reformed) Church. The orthodox Calvinists seceded in 1834 and suffered police harassment for nearly a decade until the government granted their rights.

The Dutch Calvinists spearheaded the trek to North America in the 1840s and established the major colonies in the Midwest. The initial surge set off a chain migration of family and friends in the ensuing decades, prompted by tens of thousands of "America letters" sent to the homeland urging them to come. The Lowlands, however, never witnessed a mass exodus of desperate people, such as the famine Irish. Immigrating Lowlanders were primarily people of middling status who envisioned a diminished future for themselves and their children. The Netherlands ranked twelfth and Belgium thirteenth among the fifteen major European nations in the proportion of their population that immigrated overseas in the years from 1850 to 1920.[7]

The primary settlement region of the Lowlanders was the Great Lakes and upper Midwest. But Indiana, because of its strong southern heritage and frontier expansion from southeast to northwest, attracted the smallest immigrant population of any state in the Old Northwest. Indiana's proportion of foreign born peaked in 1860 at 9 percent and declined gradually thereafter. Hence, Indiana attracted only a few thousand Dutch and Belgians, while Luxembourgers numbered in the mere hundreds.

## Belgians

Belgian immigrants planted four major settlements in Indiana in the nineteenth century: two Walloon and two Flemish.[8] Like the settlement of the state generally, the

Belgium, Netherlands
and Luxembourg

⊙ National Capital
• City
— International Boundary
  Province Boundary

0      Miles      40

Belgians first settled in the south and only later in the middle and north. The older of the Walloon colonies, dating from the 1830s, is the town of Leopold in far southern Perry County; the newer colony was founded after the Civil War in the glass manufacturing center of Hartford City, immediately north of Muncie. The major Flemish settlements developed after 1880, and both were in northern St. Joseph County at Mishawaka and South Bend. Eventually Mishawaka became the most concentrated and long-lasting Belgian community in Indiana with one quarter of Indiana's total Belgian population.

The Walloon immigration ended before the turn of the century, whereas the Flemings began arriving in the 1880s and continued until the 1950s. The Walloons, from the hilly Ardennes region, were attracted to similar terrain along the Ohio River. By contrast, the Flemish farmers from the northern Belgian lowlands chose the level plains of northern Indiana to carry on farming until the region developed an industrial base.

The Perry County settlement near Evansville dates from 1815 when John A. Courcier, a Walloon immigrant and veteran of the War of 1812, received a government land grant there. John and his wife Mary are thought to be the first permanent Belgian residents of Indiana.[9] In the late 1830s the Courciers were joined in this Catholic region by other Walloons from the Belgian province of Luxembourg, who were attracted by construction jobs on the Wabash and Erie Canal and the "America letters" of the first diocesan priest in Perry County, French Father Julian Benoit (1808–1885). Benoit effectively served St. Augustine Parish in Leopold intermittently from 1836 to 1840 before being reassigned to Fort Wayne. By that time at least a dozen Belgian families had become pioneer farmers in the county,[10] all raising large families and sinking their roots deep in the soil. The Belgians gradually improved their farms and replaced their primitive log cabins and homemade furnishings with homes constructed of sawed lumber and store-bought furniture and curtains.

Leopold Township was created in 1847, some years after the village of Leopold had been platted. The name of this primitive frontier settlement honored the first Belgian king, Leopold I. Upon learning of the town in the United States named for him, the appreciative king donated several gold candelabra for St. Augustine Church.[11] In 1850 Belgians comprised 10 percent of the total population in Leopold Township, and on the eve of the Civil War this growing community included 73 percent of all Belgians in Indiana. Over the years they intermarried so frequently that a descendant of one family probably has ancestors in one or more other families.[12]

St. Augustine Church soon outgrew its original tiny log sanctuary. In 1866 Belgian masons led by Peter George and his son began building a new stone church from local sandstone.[13] After many financial struggles the congregation finally dedicated its sanctuary in 1873, but another thirty years passed before the tower, spire, chimes, and bells were installed. Belgian-born Father Hyppolite Pierard ably served the parish in these years.

The most prominent object in St. Augustine Church was the statue of Our Lady of Consolation, which was commissioned in 1866 in thanksgiving for the safe return of Leopold's sons from the Union army. The statue was crafted in Belgium as a replica of the original in the home church in Luxembourg province that the immigrants cherished dearly. One of the Leopold veterans, Lambert Rogier, who had survived the ordeal as a prisoner at the infamous Andersonville Confederate Prison, actually went to Belgium to accompany the statue to Leopold and thereby fulfill his vow.[14]

Leopold Township reached maturity as the premier Belgian center in southern Indiana in the 1870s when its population surpassed 650, one-third of whom were first-generation immigrants. Two-thirds of the Belgians in Perry County lived in the township and another one-fifth lived in the adjacent township of Oil. Together, nine out of ten Belgians in Perry County resided in these two core townships. All of the Belgians farmed except for a half dozen merchants, craftsmen, and teachers. Joseph Meunier and Joseph Genet operated dry goods stores in the village of Leopold. The Georges and Joseph Pierard worked as stonemasons, and Henry Goffinet and Frank John George taught school. Joseph Labelle ran a hostelry in the river town of Cannelton.

In the twenty years after 1880 the Belgian population grew by 65 percent to 1,100. Since the pace of Belgian immigration to Perry County slowed after the Civil War, most of the increase came from internal growth. Families with six or more children were common among the Belgian Catholics. By 1900 first-generation Belgians comprised only 15 percent of the population, compared to 30 percent in 1880. Clearly, the children and grandchildren of the pioneers were now in the majority.

Despite the generational shift, the census marshal in 1900 found little occupational change from 1880. All but nine family heads were farming, and as could be expected in a native agricultural community, more than 90 percent owned their own farms. "Big barns and small houses" was the hallmark of Belgian farmers.[15] They invested every spare dollar in developing their land and buying more whenever possible, in order to put their adult sons on the land. Leopold Township by 1880 was overcrowded and had become a beehive ready to swarm. In the next years the Belgians began expanding outward like a giant oil slick into the surrounding townships of Clark, Union, and Anderson, each of which had one hundred or more inhabitants of Belgian birth or ancestry by 1900.

Leopold itself in 1900 remained a church village with a few stores, such as Meunier's general store, implement dealer Joseph Genet, Joseph Thiery's grocery, and the butcher shop of John P. James. A stonemason, carpenter, blacksmith, and miller rounded out the craftsmen. Four young men were teachers: William D. Devillez, brothers Alfred and Peter F. James, and Frank George, who had moved to the future county seat, Tell City. Since the illiteracy rate (age 12+) was below 10 percent and all but twenty-two adults could speak English in 1900, the schools were clearly fulfilling their role.

During the agricultural depression of the 1920s and 1930s, young people began to leave the community for work elsewhere and to pursue higher education, causing Leopold like thousands of villages across rural America slowly to decline. Massive soil erosion in the hilly region also made continued farming unprofitable, and landowners during the Great Depression abandoned their homesteads or lost them at tax sales. The United States government came to the rescue and took a hand in hastening Leopold's demise. Congress in 1935 designated the upland ridge

area of southern Indiana to become part of the Hoosier National Forest and began buying up land from the willing sellers, most of whose land was yet held by the founding families who are permitted to live out their lives there. By 1990 the Forest Service owned more than 125,000 acres and the purchases continue.[16] Thus, after one hundred and fifty years the Belgian colony of Leopold, by a twist of fate, is slowly reverting to its native forest flora and fauna, and the town will eventually cease to exist. It is ironic that this historic community maintained its ethnocultural homogeneity for five and six generations and more, only to be dislocated by the government for the greater public good.

A second Walloonian colony in southern Indiana developed in New Albany (Floyd County) on the left bank of the Ohio River, where several dozen families from the Belgian province of Luxembourg settled in the 1840s. Most farmed around the city, but several were tradesmen in town. Farmers' sons found summer work on Ohio River steamboats and winter work in the pork-packing plants of New Albany and in Louisville and Portland on the Kentucky side of the river. Later, in the 1880s and 1890s, some thirty to forty families worked in the thriving glass factories of New Albany. By 1910, however, all had departed the county for the Muncie area, following the rapid decline of the glassworks.[17]

Two businessmen in New Albany of Belgian ancestry contributed in special ways to Indiana in 1883. Washington Charles DePauw (1822–1887) endowed the university at Greencastle that bears his name, and John F. Baker (1850–?) operated the largest cigar factory in the city. DePauw was born in Salem, Indiana. His grandfather Charles was a Huguenot Protestant from Ghent who joined French soldier and statesman Lafayette (1757–1834) in America in 1777 to fight on the patriot side in the Revolution. His father John Baptiste was a surveyor (who platted the town of Salem in 1814, which later became the seat of Washington County), a lawyer, judge, member of the Indiana Constitutional Convention of 1816, and nine times elected to the state legislature.

Washington DePauw was an outstanding businessman in New Albany who began with a saw and gristmill, expanded into farming and banking, and then during the Civil War became the largest grain dealer in Indiana by supplying the Union army. After the war he built rolling mills and iron foundries, but the apex of his career came in the 1880s when he invested half a million dollars in a successful plate glass works in New Albany that broke the monopoly of European glassmakers. In 1883 DePauw gave $600,000 to the financially strapped Indiana Asbury College, which was renamed DePauw University in 1884. The Greencastle school received $1.5 million from

DePauw's estate in 1887. He also endowed DePauw Female College of New Albany and contributed to church building projects and benevolent institutions throughout Indiana and the neighboring states.[18]

John F. Baker's Belgian-born father, John B., immigrated to Kentucky in 1832 and moved to New Albany in 1848. After farming for five years he began building steamboats for the Ohio River trade. John F. was a journeyman cigar maker until 1876, when he opened the largest cigar factory in New Albany and employed "a greater number of workmen" than any other cigar works. Subsequently, Baker sold the factory and invested in an insurance company and opened the Centennial Saloon. He belonged to the Odd Fellows and other lodges, served as president of the Brewer and Liquor Dealers Association, and was president of the Democratic Union Club of New Albany.[19] Neither DePauw nor Baker evidenced any Belgian self-identity, and New Albany and Floyd County never had as viable a Belgian community as Leopold to the west. DePauw was a Protestant, and Baker's wife was of German ancestry.

While the Walloons in Leopold farmed, those in Hartford City and the nearby six-county area (Blackford, Delaware, Grant, Hamilton, Jay, and Madison counties) worked in glass manufacturing. This east-central region around Muncie was rich in silica sand, and the discovery of natural gas in 1886 fostered a booming glass industry that brought newfound prosperity. At its height Hartford City had eleven glass factories, and the nearby city of Matthews (in adjacent Grant County) had sixteen plants.[20]

The American glass industry had long relied upon the Walloon Belgians of the Liège district for skilled workers. News of the new factories in the Muncie area reached Belgium quickly, and a large group of workers decided to immigrate in order to seize the opportunity in the American Midwest. They found good-paying jobs for skilled craftsmen and wrote back home urging family and friends to join in the bonanza. By 1900 nearly 1,500 persons of Belgian birth, plus another 750 of Belgian parentage, lived in the six-county region around Hartford City. The heart of the community was on the south side of Hartford City in "Belgian Town" around St. John the Evangelist Church. Alexandria in Madison County was a secondary center.

Almost every Belgian adult male in the area worked in the window glass factories as blowers, cutters, flatteners, "snappers," gatherers, and packers. Most were blowers and flatteners. Over 40 percent of the workers at the Hartford Glass Company were Belgians. They comprised 80 percent of the blowers, 60 percent of the snappers, 75 percent of the flatteners, 50 percent of the cutters, and 100 percent of the gatherers. Blowers in 1898 earned $130 per month, cutters $125, and gatherers $90, which was three

to five times the rate in Belgium. Living costs in America were no higher than in the homeland.[21] Since 35 percent of the Belgians in Blackford County in 1900 could not speak English, their foremen and supervisors came from the ranks of immigrants from the Liège region who had been in America for a decade or two. Approximately 20 percent of the Belgians in Hartford City in 1900 had first worked in glass factories in Ohio and Pennsylvania. The rest were new immigrants who came mainly in the years 1887 through 1893. This was a prosperous community. More than two-thirds owned their own homes by 1900, and fewer than 10 percent (mostly wives) were illiterate.

The United States economic depression of the 1890s that began in 1893 ended the boom times. The census marshal in Blackford County in 1900 counted only thirty Belgian immigrants who had arrived in town during the hard years 1894–99. The glass industry, along with all manufacturing industries, experienced a "shaking out" in these tough times. Poorly managed companies closed or were absorbed by the few larger companies that concentrated their operations in Hartford City.

The members of the American Window Glass Workers Association became very fearful of the imported Belgian blowers. When in 1906 rumors circulated in Muncie of the possible influx of thousands of Belgian glass workers who were thrown out of work in Europe, labor officials actually went to East Coast ports to meet incoming groups of Belgians and count the glass workers. They were relieved to find only two in one group of five hundred.[22] But even consolidation and more efficient operations could not stave off decline. Soon only the American Window Glass Company remained, and it, too, closed its doors in 1928, bringing to an end the glass era in the Muncie region.

During the demise of the glass industry, the Belgian craftsmen either found other work or migrated elsewhere. Most departed. Between 1900 and 1910 the number of Belgian born in the six-county region dropped from 1,500 to below 500. By 1930 the federal census marshals counted only 170 first-generation Belgians in the entire glass region (Table 2). Nevertheless, Belgians remained the third largest foreign-born group in Blackford County behind Irish and Germans.[23]

With the glass boom, Hartford City needed a Catholic church to serve the many Belgians as well as Irish and French families. The bishop of Fort Wayne in 1894 upgraded the parish and sent a resident pastor, Father Charles Dhe, to St. John the Evangelist parish, and in three years the congregation dedicated a new $10,000 church building with adequate space for a school. St. John is proud of its Belgian sons who served the Catholic church: Bishop Leo Pursley, Father Leo A. Piquet, Father Emil

| COUNTY | 1850 | 1860 | 1870 | 1880 | 1890 | 1900 | 1910 | 1920 | 1930 FB | 1930 NB | 1940 |
|---|---|---|---|---|---|---|---|---|---|---|---|
| ADAMS | | | 1 | 1 | 1 | | | 1 | 7 | 2 | 8 |
| ALLEN | | | 14 | 3 | 9 | 6 | 12 | 35 | 38 | 68 | 56 |
| BARTHOLOMEW | 1 | | 4 | | | | 3 | 3 | 3 | 14 | 3 |
| BENTON | | | | 1 | | 4 | 2 | 1 | | 1 | |
| BLACKFORD | | | | | | 479 | 146 | 95 | 73 | 106 | 49 |
| BOONE | | | | | | | | | | 1 | 1 |
| BROWN | | | | | | | | | | | 2 |
| CARROLL | | | | | 1 | | | | | | |
| CASS | | | 4 | 1 | 2 | 5 | 4 | 7 | 6 | 7 | 8 |
| CLARK | 1 | 1 | 1 | | | | 2 | 1 | 1 | 1 | |
| CLAY | | 1 | 18 | 5 | 39 | 67 | 55 | 26 | 23 | 62 | 16 |
| CLINTON | | 3 | 2 | 1 | 1 | | | | | | 1 |
| CRAWFORD | | | 1 | 1 | 1 | | | | | 1 | |
| DAVIESS | | | | | | 1 | | 1 | | | |
| DEARBORN | | 2 | 2 | | | | | 6 | | | 1 |
| DECATUR | | | | 1 | | | | | | | |
| DE KALB | | | 1 | 1 | | 6 | 3 | | 3 | 10 | 3 |
| DELAWARE | | | | 1 | 7 | 187 | 25 | 28 | 25 | 41 | 18 |
| DUBOIS | | 1 | 3 | 2 | 1 | | | | | 2 | |
| ELKHART | | 1 | 6 | 4 | 23 | 2 | | 6 | 9 | 22 | 17 |
| FAYETTE | | | | | | 1 | 3 | | | 1 | 3 |
| FLOYD | 27 | 21 | 36 | 23 | 39 | 16 | | 7 | 3 | 16 | 2 |
| FOUNTAIN | | | 3 | | 1 | 4 | 3 | 5 | 4 | 14 | 3 |
| FRANKLIN | | | 3 | | | 1 | 5 | | 1 | 6 | |
| FULTON | | | 7 | | | | | | | 1 | |
| GIBSON | | | | | 1 | | | 1 | 1 | 1 | 4 |
| GRANT | | | | | 17 | 339 | 34 | 58 | 40 | 42 | 28 |
| GREENE | | | 1 | | | 10 | 41 | 55 | 30 | 21 | 18 |
| HAMILTON | | | | | | 93 | 3 | | 1 | 1 | 3 |
| HANCOCK | 1 | | | | | 10 | 12 | 2 | 1 | 2 | 1 |
| HARRISON | | 23 | 3 | 12 | 5 | 3 | 4 | 1 | | 5 | |
| HENDRICKS | | | | 1 | | 1 | | | | 3 | |
| HENRY | | | 1 | | | | 3 | 6 | 3 | 5 | 3 |
| HOWARD | | | | | 33 | 21 | 12 | 27 | 24 | 35 | 11 |
| HUNTINGTON | 6 | | 4 | 1 | | 1 | 6 | 20 | 7 | 7 | 7 |
| JACKSON | | | | | | | | | | | |
| JASPER | | | | 2 | 1 | 3 | 3 | | 1 | 2 | |
| JAY | | | | 4 | 18 | 77 | 9 | 10 | 7 | 19 | 3 |
| JEFFERSON | 3 | 1 | | | 1 | 2 | | 1 | 1 | | 1 |
| JENNINGS | | | | | 1 | 1 | 1 | | | | 1 |
| JOHNSON | | | | | | | | | | | |
| KNOX | | 1 | 11 | 12 | 6 | 4 | 166 | 127 | 114 | 100 | 86 |
| KOSCIUSKO | | | | 1 | 1 | 2 | 2 | 2 | 4 | 4 | 1 |
| LAGRANGE | | | | | | | | 2 | 1 | 2 | |
| LAKE | | 4 | | 1 | 1 | 5 | 35 | 45 | 54 | 101 | 39 |
| LA PORTE | | 9 | 3 | 2 | 3 | 1 | 4 | 51 | 35 | 46 | 33 |
| LAWRENCE | | | 5 | 5 | 1 | 2 | | 5 | 2 | 7 | 1 |
| MADISON | | | | | 1 | 301 | 38 | 24 | 24 | 44 | 24 |
| MARION | | | 6 | 4 | 11 | 7 | 25 | 24 | 22 | 70 | 19 |
| MARSHALL | | | | 1 | 1 | | 2 | 4 | 10 | 8 | 9 |
| MARTIN | | | | | | 5 | 1 | 3 | 1 | 4 | 1 |
| MIAMI | | | | | 47 | 1 | 2 | 4 | 5 | 5 | 5 |
| MONROE | | | | | | 2 | 2 | 1 | 2 | 7 | 1 |
| MONTGOMERY | | | | | | | | | | 3 | |
| MORGAN | | | | 2 | | | 4 | | | 3 | |
| NEWTON | | | | 1 | 4 | 4 | 1 | 1 | 3 | 2 | 1 |
| NOBLE | | | | | | 1 | | 1 | | 4 | 2 |
| OHIO | | | | | | | | | | | |
| ORANGE | | | | | | | | | | | |
| OWEN | | | | | 2 | | | 1 | 1 | 2 | 1 |
| PARKE | | | | 5 | 13 | 15 | 8 | 3 | 1 | 4 | |
| PERRY | 58 | 243 | 213 | 194 | 203 | 143 | 97 | 57 | 25 | 267 | 7 |
| PIKE | | | | | | | | 1 | | | |
| PORTER | | | 1 | | 3 | 5 | 2 | 4 | 4 | 5 | 4 |
| POSEY | | | | | | | 21 | | 1 | 21 | |
| PULASKI | | | 1 | | | | | 4 | | | |
| PUTNAM | | | | | 1 | | 1 | | 4 | 1 | 1 |
| RANDOLPH | | | | | | | 12 | | 2 | 4 | 1 |
| RIPLEY | | | | | | | | 2 | | | |
| RUSH | 1 | | | | | | | | 1 | 4 | |
| ST. JOSEPH | 4 | 20 | 83 | 155 | 261 | 672 | 1386 | 1606 | 2513 | 2320 | 2000 |
| SCOTT | | | 1 | | | | 4 | | | | 1 |
| SHELBY | | | 1 | | | | | | | | |
| SPENCER | | | | | | | 1 | | | 2 | |
| STARKE | | | | | | 1 | 1 | 2 | 2 | 5 | 3 |
| STEUBEN | | | | | | | | 1 | 2 | 1 | 2 |
| SULLIVAN | | | | | | 2 | 55 | 13 | 13 | 11 | 10 |
| SWITZERLAND | | | 1 | | | | | | | | |
| TIPPECANOE | | | 2 | 3 | 3 | 6 | 6 | 13 | 7 | 19 | 7 |
| TIPTON | | | | | | | | | 6 | 5 | 2 |
| UNION | | | | | | | | | | | |
| VANDERBURGH | | | | 1 | 1 | 1 | 2 | 8 | 5 | 11 | 6 |
| VERMILLION | | | | | 1 | 2 | 5 | 47 | 18 | 9 | 16 |
| VIGO | | 1 | 5 | 19 | 12 | 2 | 9 | 49 | 41 | 81 | 34 |
| WABASH | | | | | | | 7 | 6 | 3 | 5 | 4 |
| WARREN | | | 1 | 1 | 1 | | 5 | 2 | 1 | 4 | 1 |
| WARRICK | | 4 | | 1 | | | | | | 1 | |
| WASHINGTON | | 1 | 1 | | | | 1 | 1 | 2 | 4 | 2 |
| WAYNE | | | | 2 | | 1 | 1 | 5 | 2 | 4 | 2 |
| WELLS | | | | | | | | | 5 | 6 | 2 |
| WHITE | | | | 1 | | | 2 | | | 1 | 1 |
| WHITLEY | 1 | 1 | 13 | 7 | | 1 | 1 | 1 | 6 | 2 | |
| TOTALS | 103 | 334 | 462 | 486 | 733 | 2576 | 2298 | 2526 | 3254 | 3728 | 2600 |

FB = Foreign Born　　　NB = Native Born　　　Source: Federal Population Census

Joseph Goossens, Monsignor Victor Leopold Goossens, Brother John Patoux, and the brothers Fathers Ralph G. and Leo A. Hoffman. The latter pastored the Belgian St. Monica's Church on Mishawaka's north side.[24]

As in Leopold Township, Hartford City was not nourished by a continuing flow of fresh Walloon immigrants after 1900. The old patois (provincial) French died out with the first generation, and the children became largely assimilated. But some families continued Old Country customs and food ways by brewing homemade beer, making wine, baking Christmas cookies and fruit tarts, and frying waffles according to grandmothers' recipes. Waffle irons that had been stowed in shipping trunks were treasured possessions. The Christmas tarts and cookies went to the milkman, mailman, teachers, and all helpful friends as tokens of appreciation. On New Year's Day families brought tarts and cakes to their neighbors with a kiss on both cheeks and wishes of *"Bonne Anné et une bonne santeé,"* meaning a good New Year and good health. In return they received a glass (or two) of the "house wine."[25]

Traditional delicacies included potatoes fried in special beef fat and dishes garnished with leeks and shallots consisting of pig tails, feet, liver, hearts, and calf heads. To get just the right flavor of coffee, Belgians purchased one hundred-pound bags of beans through the Sears, Roebuck & Company mail order stores and roasted the beans themselves according to original recipes. Belgians enjoyed dancing and music, and bands even led funeral processions from the home of the deceased to the parish cemetery and back for refreshments after the graveside committal.[26] But the last of the Belgian pioneers passed away by the 1980s, and the memory of the motherland and its culture today is dim indeed.

The premier "Belgian Town" in Indiana for one hundred years was located in the northern city of Mishawaka in St. Joseph County. The community took shape in the decades after the Civil War and reached maturity in the 1920s. The first Belgian in the St. Joseph River valley was Father Louis de Sceille (1795–1837), the founder of the Notre Dame settlement. He came to America in 1832 and carried on missionary work among the Potawatomi Indians at Pokagon until his untimely death in 1837.[27] In 1833 Father de Sceille recruited three of his former altar boys from Hansbeke, all skilled craftsmen, to immigrate to St. Joseph County. But they had difficulty finding work and after a year returned to Belgium. However, eleven years later in 1845, two brothers of one of the remigrants, Bernard and Edward Reyniers, both blacksmiths, decided to come. Bernard brought his wife and two children to Mishawaka. In that same year their son Désiré (1845–1926) became the first child born to Belgian parents in the city. The Bernard Reyniers family were the only Belgians in all of St. Joseph County in the 1850 census. They were joined by five families during the 1850s, forming the nucleus of the later community.[28]

Désiré Reyniers served with the 138th Indiana Volunteers in the Civil War. After mustering out he worked briefly as a shoemaker and then for the rest of his life was a blacksmith at the Mishawaka Iron Company and later at the Niles Plow Company. Désiré and his wife raised ten children and did their part in boosting the Belgian presence in the area.[29]

From the outset more than three-fourths of the St. Joseph County Belgians lived in Mishawaka, mainly in the bustling Flemish community of "Belgian Town" on the city's southwest side. This region was originally swampy muck land that drained several streams flowing into the St. Joseph River. The Flemish settlers were skilled in land drainage and soon created prosperous truck farms on the peat soils. Later, as the city encroached, they turned the farms into substantial middle-class properties with well-kept lawns and gardens.[30]

Between 1870 and 1900 the number of Belgians grew from 88 to 347 in the city and from 91 to 672 in the county. (Between 1895 and 1905 the population really exploded with the arrival of more than 500 Flemish immigrants.) By 1912 Mishawaka counted 1,355 Belgians, in 1919 there were 1,702, and by 1926 about 2,000. Mishawaka's population had a higher percentage with Belgian ancestry than any other city in the United States at 12 percent.[31]

The number of Belgian retail merchants and professionals increased apace. Beginning in 1870 Belgian businessmen opened groceries; tailoring and dry cleaning shops; dairies and bottling works; dry goods, furniture and jewelry stores; offices for real estate, insurance, doctors and dentists; barbers and beauty shops. The West End State Bank and De Vos Funeral Home stood near the anchor of the community, St. Bavo's Roman Catholic Church, on West 7th Street. There were also a number of building contractors and tradesmen, shoemakers, electricians, a coal dealer, and later auto gasoline stations and repair shops. Contractor A. C. Colpaert employed many Belgian craftsmen and was a leading developer in South Bend.[32]

The number of Belgian groceries grew from one in 1901 (that of Bruno De Vreese) to nineteen in 1932. But the rise of major supermarket chains such as Atlantic and Pacific created strong competition that underpriced the small corner groceries. This revolution in food merchandising coincided with the decline of parochialism among third- and fourth-generation Belgians that weakened their loyalty to the neighborhood grocers. The small shops gradually had to close or merge into the national chains. By 1942 only

*St. Bavo's Roman Catholic Church, Mishawaka, ca. 1950s.*

fifteen Belgian grocers were operating, and ten years later only two survived. The ethnic dry goods and variety stores suffered the same fate. By 1972 the last Belgian grocery had closed and only one dry goods store was in business. This was Henry Van Volsem's store, which has been in business since 1907 at the same location and is today run by a descendant of the founding family.[33]

Apart from the shopkeepers and clerks, almost all the men worked in factories, in metals, rubber, shoes, wood, and textiles. Most found employment at the Mishawaka Woolen Mills or "Ball-Band" wool boot factory founded in 1877 (later owned by Uniroyal) and in the foundries and machine shops of Dodge Manufacturing Company and Darch & Company iron smelting. Ball-Band, an immense factory with 1.5 acres of floor space, employed so many "fresh" immigrants that it was fondly known as the "Belgian Shoe College." In 1909 the majority of Ball-Band's sixteen hundred workers were Belgians. Many Belgian farmers also worked in the factory during the winter season.[34]

Belgian ambition and determination in business and industry is equaled only by their enthusiasm for religious, social, and recreational activities. Social life revolved around St. Bavo's Church (founded in 1903) and its ethnic clubs, the Broederenkring (Brothers' Circle) mutual benefit society, Ernest Derho's Athletic Club for the active

men, and the Mishawaka Homing Pigeon Club, which continued the Old Country pastime of training and racing homing pigeons.

Founded as a Flemish church, St. Bavo's was blessed with pastors who served effectively for many years; only four priests led the congregation in seventy-seven years (1903–1980). The church, which was dedicated in 1905, underwent a $70,000 refurbishing in the 1980s, and the congregation continues to thrive. The Belgian School at St. Bavo's, which was administered by Father Achille Schockaert for many years and taught by nuns, complemented the church, but its classes were taught in English to prepare the children to take a place in their adopted country.[35]

The Broederenkring (later called simply the BK Club) was organized in 1925, and its club building served for decades as the social center of the community. Besides various civic activities, the BK Club promoted the unique Belgian sports of archery, bowling, and darts. The BK Athletic Association organized American-style football, baseball, and basketball leagues. The most popular contests in the 1930s pitted the Belgian champions against the rival Italian Catholics of the southside De Amicis Club.[36] After the Second World War the BK Club of Mishawaka alternated its monthly meetings with its sister organization in South Bend, the Volkskring (People's Circle). In 1961 an umbrella organization, the St. Joseph County Belgian-American Civic and Democratic Club, was formed to link the two societies. The BK Club continues today as the largest civic society in Mishawaka, although since 1962 persons not of Belgian ancestry were admitted and now comprise half of its members.[37]

The Homing Pigeon Club is the oldest club in Mishawaka, dating from the early 1890s. It staged elaborate races according to Old Country rules and regulations, and many a Belgian backyard boasted a "pigeon house." In 1912 over one hundred men participated but eventually, as the pioneer generation died off, the Mishawaka club combined with its South Bend counterpart. By 1985 the club had dwindled to only twenty-eight aged members, most in their eighties and nineties, who still raced pigeons in the Belgian tradition.[38]

Other Mishawaka Belgian clubs that thrived during the heyday of ethnic social life in the 1920s were the Belgian-American Club, the Belgian Bicycle Club, Archery Club, and KTK Fraternity. The Belgian-American Club was formed in 1915 to raise relief funds for the mother country by sponsoring dances and picnics. After the war it evolved in 1923 into the Aalter Kermis Club. Aalter was a village near Hansbeke, from which a large part of the Mishawaka Belgians had originated. The club's main activity was to stage an annual street fair on the day of the original Kermis (festival) in Aalter, which was about the time of the

American Labor Day. The Archery Club perpetuated the old Flemish heritage of shooting wooden birds with specially designed "long bows."

Raymond Vander Heyden, who was for years known around town as "Mr. Belgium," introduced bicycle racing in 1913 when, after a visit to the homeland, he returned with a Belgian-made racing cycle. He built the city Velodrome, and soon the Belgian Bicycle Club was scheduling a full slate of races every weekend. Periodically, European stars came to test the mettle of the local talent. Interest in this immensely popular sport peaked in the 1920s, and in the 1940s the sporting club quietly disbanded.[39]

The KTK Fraternity grew out of the St. Bavo's basketball team, and in the late 1930s it evolved into the Belgian bowling league, which in 1985 still had four men on the KTK team. The alleys are in the basement of the BK Club building. In 1954 forty-five men who wished to promote fishing and hunting formed the Belgian-American Conservation Club. Thus there were clubs for every taste that helped to preserve the ethnic community.[40]

Not to be outdone, the numerous Belgian merchants in Mishawaka founded the Belgian-American Businessmen's Association in 1939, and it remained active for a quarter century. Non-Belgian men married to Belgian women were also accepted as members. Besides promoting networking and mutual support, during the Second World War the club provided special Christmas packages for Belgian-American men in the armed forces. After the war it turned its civic interests to providing academic scholarships for Belgian-American youths to attend colleges and universities. Prior to the war, these young people seldom attended high school beyond the mandatory age of fourteen and later sixteen. After the war, however, the GI Bill and the Businessmen's Association scholarships encouraged more young people to complete high school and go to college. This significant behavioral shift prompted Henry Verslype to assert that the GI Bill "completed the Americanization that had started at Ellis Island so many years before." Verslype also notes, however, that about half of the graduates of parochial grade schools in Mishawaka attended parochial high schools, where ethnocultural values were inculcated.[41]

Because "Belgian Town" was a homogeneous neighborhood nourished with new immigrants for more than one hundred years, until at least the 1960s, people spoke Flemish at home, in the streets, and at church. This considerably slowed the pace of Americanization, and it was not until the years after World War II that Mishawaka's Belgians visibly lost their ethnic identity.[42]

The Belgians in nearby South Bend had a very different experience. They did not settle in one neighborhood but intermingled throughout the city and in the farm country

*Belgian war bride (right), Terre Haute, 1946.*

IHS MARTIN COLLECTION 56849

to the west. South Bend's Belgians, unlike those in Mishawaka, had to learn English quickly in order to communicate with neighbors and fellow workers. Throughout its history, South Bend had only one-third the density of foreign-born Belgians as Mishawaka. The original Belgians in South Bend moved the short distance from Mishawaka in search of work in factories such as the Oliver Chilled Plow Works and Studebaker Corporation. Economic opportunities in the larger city were more compelling to them than the possible loss of ethnic solidarity. South Bend's population also included Germans, Irish, New England Yankees, Poles, Swedes, Hungarians, Italians, and other nationalities.[43]

For religious services the Belgians at first attended the Irish and Polish parishes. Finally, in 1896 the first Flemish-speaking priest, Father Henry Paanakker, C.S.C. (Congregation of the Holy Cross), arrived to preach and hear confession in the native tongue. Within two years Father Paanakker succeeded in building a Flemish church, Sacred Heart of Jesus, to serve the 104 Belgian families that the priest had located and visited throughout the parish. The next year a parochial school opened with 110 pupils meeting in the basement of the new church. Some more active and progressive members formed a chapter of the St. Vincent De Paul Society to meet financial needs of Belgians in times of unemployment, sickness, and death. For leisure time, the parish formed a dramatic club "Voor Moedertaal en Broedermin" (For Mother Tongue and Brother Love).[44]

Founders of Sacred Heart Church were Edward De Wispelaere, one of the earliest immigrants in South Bend in 1885, Joannes Baptiste Nieuwland, whose funeral in 1898 was the first in the new church, and trustees P. Debaets, E. Haerent, and A. Sargent. When Father Paanakker became ill in 1906, a son of the parish, Father Julius Nieuwland,[45] who was a professor at the University of Notre Dame, served as interim pastor for a few years, as did Father Charles L. Stuer of St. Bavo's Church in Mishawaka. Finally, Stuer successfully recruited a Flemish-speaking priest, Father Charles Fisher, who served longer than any predecessor. In 1907 the congregation had 625 souls, including 4 Holland families. Because of the increasing secularization of South Bend Belgians, the Sacred Heart congregation did not continue to flourish. Finally, in 1972 so few attended Mass that the church was closed and the doors padlocked.[46]

As in Mishawaka, South Bend's Belgian pigeon fanciers formed a Homing Pigeon Club (1912), and ethnic leaders also organized a Belgian benevolent society, the Volkskring Club, to provide emergency relief, find jobs, and do everything possible "to make good American citizens of them." The society began in 1925 with fifty members and continued to attract the upwardly mobile, such as South Bend Mayor Edward F. Voorde (1910–1960), who in 1959 was reelected to his sixteenth term as president of the Volkskring. The South Bend Mutual Sickness Relief Society (or Ziekevereeniging) was also active in the 1920s as an insurance society.[47]

As elsewhere, the Belgians in South Bend willingly became naturalized American citizens and were loyal Democrats. Some held leadership positions, such as Mayor Voorde. He was a tavern owner who became chair of the county Democratic organization in 1952 and served two terms as mayor in 1955–60. He died in office, the victim of an auto accident that occurred while returning from a mayoral function, and his funeral at Sacred Heart Church was one of the largest in South Bend history. Voorde's son John was an at-large councilman in the 1960s in South Bend, as was fellow countryman Joe De Kever in the 1970s in Mishawaka.[48]

In Mishawaka, Belgians controlled the Third Ward on the west end and represented the ward in the city council for much of its history. In 1900 Peter Tollens (1860–1909) became the first Belgian councilman. He was an importer of the famous Belgian draft horses and a pigeon fancier. August De Groote, a machine shop foreman and second-generation Belgian, followed Tollens. Predan Ghyselinck served in the 1930s. Other Belgian Americans held county and city offices in Mishawaka and South Bend as assessor, treasurer, clerk, fire captains and chief, health officers, and park board members.[49]

Belgians in Indiana also fought in every American war beginning with the War of 1812, but none proved to be more frustrating to them than World War I. When the Germans overran their homeland in 1914–16, Belgians volunteered to return and serve in the army only to find that transatlantic shipping companies refused to transport them to Antwerp for fear of attracting German U-boat attacks. Eventually, unknown hundreds of Belgians managed to reach the European war theater and defend their mother country, including at least twenty-five from St. Joseph County, whose names were printed in the Belgian (Moline, Illinois) newspaper *Gazette Van Moline*.[50]

In 1917, when the United States entered the war against Germany, thousands of Belgian men volunteered or were drafted to fight with the American Expeditionary Forces in Europe. At the signing of the Armistice in November 1918, Mishawaka citizens celebrated the defeat of the hated German Kaiser Wilhelm with a big party that included burning an effigy of the Kaiser and speeches honoring Belgian veterans, all accompanied by the Belgian band playing patriotic and national airs. If World War I had hundreds of Belgian-American soldiers, World War II had thousands.[51]

Comparing the St. Joseph, Blackford, and Perry County settlements, it is obvious that Mishawaka remained the quintessential Belgian town, because Flemish immigrants continued to settle there throughout the first half of the twentieth century. The Walloon immigration greatly declined after 1900, while the Fleming immigration continued. From 1902 to 1910 less than one in five Belgian immigrants to the United States were Walloons. In the 1920 census 72 percent of the Belgian foreign stock reported Flemish as their mother tongue, 21 percent spoke French, and 4 percent spoke either German or Dutch before immigration.[52]

What accounts for the differential in Walloon-Flemish immigration? The answer lies in demographic and economic conditions in Belgium. The Walloon provinces had lower birthrates, and the region was heavily industrial, containing mines, glass and arms factories, and iron and steel works. With relatively fewer mouths to feed and industrial jobs available close at hand, Walloons were not compelled to immigrate overseas. But the entirely rural and traditional Flemish provinces had a tripling of population in the nineteenth century, and the land could not sustain the number of new farm families. Immigration to the United States with its open spaces seemed to be the answer for Flemish farm folk. Hence, the immigration of Walloons dropped sharply in the 1890s, while the Flemish continued to immigrate after 1900. The Fleming immigration did shift, however, from a folk to a labor immigration in the decade before World War I. Many single men and married men without their wives immigrated in order to establish themselves in the labor market. The men worked to earn passage money for their fiancées, parents, wives, and children. Some single men also returned to their home village to find a bride to bring back to the United States.[53]

Belgian immigrants in the decades before the First World War (the peak immigration years) were poor, minimally educated laborers and farmers, and a few craftsmen. Many were illiterate. After the literacy test went into effect in 1917 at Ellis Island, the educational level rose to the sixth-grade level. Despite the handicap in formal schooling, the Belgians were willing to work, and they could get by on little. They were survivors.[54]

The Catholic church and family networks were the institutions that sustained them. As in the Old Country, the immigrants looked to the parish priest for guidance and advice. Henry Verslype of Mishawaka recalls hearing his pastor in the early 1920s admonish his congregation, "Tuesday is Election Day. Don't forget to vote the straight Democratic ticket." The people took such advice as "a matter of course" and without resentment, Verslype noted, because the pastor was the respected leader of the community and God's agent for their good.

As the second generation reached maturity in the interwar years, the forces of Americanization became more apparent. More young people completed public high school and entered white-collar jobs in firms outside the ethnic community. The word of the parish pastor carried less authority outside the realm of religion than it had for the first generation. The increasing social contacts with non-Belgians led to intermarriages with other nationalities. A careful study of 911 Belgian marriages in Mishawaka from 1903 to 1946 shows a rapid increase in intermarriages in the 1930s and 1940s. The following figures show the in-group marriage rate in Mishawaka for five time periods: 1903–6, 81 percent; 1907–16, 88 percent; 1917–26, 85 percent; 1927–36, 60 percent; and 1937–46, 42 percent. The melting pot of the public high school, where most marriage partners were found, seems to be the key institutional factor causing assimilation.[55]

The third generation who came of age after the Second World War are entirely English-speaking, upwardly mobile in their jobs, and able to blend into the dominant society. Many dropped the prefixes of their family names, "De," "Van," "Van Der," and "Van De," or Anglicized the names altogether, so as not to call attention to their foreign ancestry.[56] The long-standing Flemish-Walloon distinction, which continues to be salient in the homeland, is also being subsumed under the national label "Belgian." In the 1980 census 94 percent of persons of Belgian ancestry referred to themselves by the name of the country.[57] For some this may be merely a matter of adjusting to a self-identity that Americans can understand, but for many the regional cultural differences in the homeland have become meaningless. The same phenomena have occurred among the Dutch immigrants. The "Roots" phenomenon of the 1970s and the revival of ethnic interest and pride among the third and fourth generation led to a strengthened sense of Belgian identity in centers such as Mishawaka, but it is likely only a final flash in the inevitable process of assimilation.

## Netherlanders

Descendants of the Old Dutch of New York, New Jersey, and Pennsylvania were the first Hollanders to settle in Indiana. As early as 1809 Col. John Paul (1758–1830) of Germantown, Pennsylvania, whose father was a native of Holland, came to the Indiana Territory from Danville, Kentucky, and settled with his family of three plus a niece at the present site of Madison on the Ohio River in Jefferson County. Colonel Paul first went west in 1778 with the military expedition of Gen. George Rogers Clark in the campaign against the Indians of the Ohio country.[58]

Paul was a good judge of land and acquired many choice tracts throughout southern Indiana. Besides dealing in real estate and farming, Paul helped lay the foundation of government. He was the first representative of southeastern Ohio in the Northwest Territory Assembly and in 1816 was elected senator from Switzerland and Jefferson counties to the first state legislature where he served as the first presiding officer of the state. At the local level he was the first clerk and recorder of Jefferson County, which he named along with Madison, and he platted the town of Xenia, Ohio. This energetic Dutchman cut a wide swath through frontier Indiana and left his mark.

At the conclusion of the War of 1812, in 1816 and 1817 several dozen Dutch Reformed families migrated from Kentucky to Switzerland County, Indiana. A strong restlessness and wanderlust had previously driven them from their New Jersey base to the large Conewago colony near Gettysburg, Pennsylvania, in the 1760s. Then in 1780, even before the end of the War of Independence, they continued west into the Kentucky wilderness around Harrodsburg. Between 1789 and 1802 these veritable Daniel Boones had pushed into the Ohio country in covered wagons, driving their cattle before them, and purchased large tracts of land near the Salt River in a region that became known as the "Low Dutch Tract."[59]

After the second war with England ended in 1815, and with the promise of Indian peace on the frontier, these Dutch Americans sought land north of the Ohio

River near Colonel Paul's town of Madison and founded a colony in Pleasant Township of Switzerland County in 1817 called "Dutch Settlement." Their aim, according to a petition in 1783 to the Continental Congress, was "to settle together in a body for the conveniency of civil society and propagating the Gospel *in their own language* [italics added]. Prominent among the newcomers were four families of the Frisian Banta clan, plus the Van Arsdales, Voorheeses, Van Nuyses, Demarests, Schomps, and others. The Voorhees family produced the prominent Hoosier politician, Daniel W. Voorhees, "the tall sycamore of the Wabash," who served in Congress in the Civil War era. Some of these Kentucky Dutch later settled south of Indianapolis in Johnson County around Hopewell.[60]

Other Conewago Dutch settled in Dearborn County. In 1819 Abraham Brouwer (Brower) and his son Jeremiah H. (1798–1866) of New York City, both medical doctors, practiced in Lawrenceburg and Elizabethtown, Ohio, respectively (Elizabethtown was one mile inside the Ohio border). Both were towns on the main road from Cincinnati to Vincennes (present National Route No. 50). Jeremiah Brouwer was a president of the Indiana State Medical Society. In 1822 William S. Ward (ca. 1795–1857), another Dutch Yorker, arrived in nearby York Township with his family of thirteen and took up shoemaking and farming. His son Isaac B. was a carpenter and later opened a florist business, and his youngest daughter, Rhoda A. Larimer, became associate editor of the *Lawrenceburg Press*. There were doubtless numerous other Dutch Americans of the old stock throughout early Indiana, but their sense of Dutchness had largely disappeared before migrating, and they carried little ethnic identity to Indiana.[61]

The dispersion of the "Old Dutch" immigrants throughout the Midwest led to chance meetings with the new immigrants of the nineteenth century. One of the first "Young Dutch" in Indiana was the enterprising farmer Klaas Janszoon Beukma of Leens, province of Groningen. In 1835 Beukma, a widower with three sons and a daughter, departed the Netherlands under a cloud because of his "treasonous" support of Belgian independence. After arriving in New York, he traveled westward through the Hudson and Mohawk valleys to Schenectady. Along the way he met people "who could still speak a slightly antiquated Dutch [but] often I found them less than charming and with very little knowledge or interest in the land of their ancestors."[62]

After traversing the Ohio Canal from Cleveland to Portsmouth and thence by the Ohio River through Cincinnati, Beukma was pleasantly surprised to meet an elderly farm woman of Dutch ancestry who "could still make herself understood in her beloved Dutch. . . . She wanted me to read to her from her Nederduitsche [Dutch]

Bible." But her children did not understand a word, she lamented, and thought their mother mentally deranged when she spoke Dutch.[63]

Beukma found the Dearborn County land unappealing, and upon learning of the Wabash Canal project and the rich soils of northwestern Indiana, he traveled by covered wagon in the fall of 1835 to Lafayette in Tippecanoe County. Since the canal would link Lake Erie with the Ohio and Mississippi River systems, he correctly reasoned that Lafayette would become a regional trading center. He purchased a 282-acre farm in Washington Township with a log dwelling and two outbuildings plus livestock for $995. It was situated near Americus on the now state highway from Logansport to Lafayette. The rich river-bottom portion of the farm yielded corn, oats, potatoes, and garden vegetables for the growing urban market.[64]

Indiana offered opportunities aplenty for the poor farm tenants and laborers of the grain region of the northern Netherlands. Beukma wrote lengthy and enthusiastic letters to his homeland offering to assist friends and relatives "provided they were solid people" and not afraid to work. "Here I have found what I was looking for—bread and freedom; now I have no worry about the future of my children," Beukma wrote on 4 July 1836. Three years later he bought another farm for $500 only two miles from Lafayette and moved there, placing one of his sons on the old place.[65]

The Lafayette market for fresh vegetables was unlimited, and the Beukmas prospered greatly by applying their traditional knowledge of farming muck soils. Ironically, however, after thirteen years of success two of Beukma's sons caught the California gold fever in 1849 and died there in 1850 and 1851. His son Willem was spared because he had returned to Groningen from October 1847 to May 1849 to seek a wife and recruit relatives and friends for a new colony that he and his father planned in Plainfield, New Jersey. Beukma's daughter married a son of T. J. Aapkens, who had come with his family from Defiance, Ohio, and had opened a brick factory. But the young couple also moved away by 1860.[66] Thus, despite conditions favorable to immigration both in Groningen and Indiana in the 1840s, Beukma's numerous appeals fell on deaf ears until 1847, when the mass immigration spearheaded by the Dutch Calvinist Seceders brought six Frisian families and singles (eighteen persons) to the Lafayette area.[67] This became the nucleus of the oldest Dutch Reformed settlement in Indiana. The newcomers, in turn, enticed others to follow. One wrote: "Because of the language barrier we would be pleased to have a Holland preacher and medical doctor here."[68] This need was fulfilled, but not immediately since the colony grew slowly, reaching a total of 148 Dutch born by 1850.

The dark loam prairie soils interspersed with woodlands, all located near a major market center, enticed the Luite Boelkens family in 1860 to relocate from Wisconsin to the Lafayette area, where his married brother and other fellow Groningers were prospering as tenant farmers. Boelkens found work for $2.50 per day, his twelve-year-old son earned $10 a month, his fourteen-year-old daughter worked for $2 a week, and his three younger children found summer jobs planting and hoeing corn for 65 cents a week, plus board. All worked for Americans and had learned enough English to get by.[69] "There is work here and money to be earned," Boelkens wrote his family in Groningen, but big landlords had driven land prices up to $160 per acre. Nevertheless, "all the Hollanders are making a good living." Boelkens continued:

> The harvests have been exceptionally good here. Wheat is $1.00 a bushel, rye 50 cents, corn 36 cents, butter 20 cents a pound, eggs 12 cents a dozen, pork 5 cents and 6 cents a pound, beef 3–5 cents a pound. There is a slaughterhouse here. Every day 300 to 400 cows and oxen are slaughtered. I was there 8 days ago. At that time there were 138 tongues on a long table which were slaughtered in the forenoon. And there is another slaughterhouse where 800 to 1000 hogs are butchered every day. Most of the meat is sent to London in casks. There is a railroad here which runs directly to New York, and from Lafayette to Kansas. Hundreds of trains pass every day. We see at least 50 come and go every day. The best potatoes cost 25 cents a bushel, apples 20–25 cents a bushel.[70]

Three years later Boelkens noted that his oldest son, now age fifteen, hired out with an American for $88 for four months. "He does not waste a dollar," the proud father added. His younger son earned $1.25 a day working for the same farmer. A daughter did housework for a farm widow for 75 cents a week, plus room and board. After slaughtering six of his hogs, Boelkens reported to his envious family in Holland: "We will eat pork three times a day for a whole year," and added, "this is the best country we have found in America. There can be no more beautiful or better land than what we have here. . . . I dare say that we have never been better off on this earth." With an overflowing heart, the pietistic Boelkens gave thanks to God. "He will take care of us, if we will but come to Him in sincerity."[71]

By 1866 the family reported earning $100 per month in the summer when all the children were working. "On Sunday we go to church. We have a good life and plenty of money." But twenty-year-old Anje Boelkens confessed to her uncle and aunt in Groningen that she could no longer write a letter "very well" in Dutch and "I do not know much about Holland."[72] Prosperity in America exacted its price.

The prewar immigrants were a mixed group religiously, including Reformed, Seceders, and Roman Catholics, as well as agnostics and modernists who "did not have conscientious scruples with regard to the Sabbath day." This was the behavior criteria by which the more orthodox judged the rest. Those who worshiped attended either St. Boniface Catholic Church, the German Reformed Church, or the Baptist Church.[73]

The lack of a Reformed church turned the more devout away from Lafayette for several decades. Finally, in 1861 the Groningers Jan Balkema and his son Edward, together with Luite Boelkens, organized Dutch-language services in Balkema's home.[74] Three years later the Reverend John R. Schepers, also a Groninger, who had affiliated with the United Presbyterian (Scottish) Church in Michigan, agreed to come to Lafayette to organize a Dutch congregation, Second Presbyterian. The church began with twenty-two charter members, but quickly doubled and tripled in size as Schepers gathered the Hollanders in the community and the new arrivals from Holland. The congregation worshiped until 1889 in a small frame structure built in 1866 to seat one hundred and fifty, located on Hartford Street at Fourteenth in the northwestern section of the city. In 1896 the once-enlarged building was moved one block to Fifteenth Street and Hartford, and another large wing was added to accommodate the growing flock.[75]

In 1869 the congregation left the English-speaking denomination for the ethnically homogeneous True Holland Reformed Church (later renamed Christian Reformed Church). Some members farmed in Fairfield Township immediately north of Lafayette but gradually, as the city changed to an industrial and service economy centered around Purdue University, the Dutch congregation became an urban one. By 1880 it counted 146 "souls" and reached 530 in 1910, 600 in 1924, 700 in 1957, and 575 in 1991. The founding of a Christian school in 1950 helped hold the community together. The main growth spurts came in the years immediately after the First and Second World Wars. The congregation nearly succumbed in the 1880s. In 1880 twelve influential farm families moved to Fowler, twenty-five miles to the northwest, and more seriously, in 1888 twenty-seven families—more than one-half of the congregation—seceded to join the more Americanized sister denomination, the Reformed Church in America. First Reformed Church, located on East Fifteenth Street, in turn mothered congregations in Seafield and Goodland in the 1890s, but neither survived. The Fowler CRC congregation also disbanded in 1890 because all the families moved back to Lafayette. Seven Dexter (Americanized from Dijkstra) families from Friesland were the major clan in Goodland, settling in a "chain migration" that began in 1861 and continued until 1893. They were supporters of the Goodland Reformed Church.[76]

The high point of the Dutch in Tippecanoe County was in 1920, with fifteen hundred persons of Dutch birth or ancestry. The Christian Reformed Church then totaled five hundred and the Reformed Church in America three hundred. These two Reformed congregations thus included more than half of the Hollanders in the county. Apart from the customary church societies for men, women, and youth, the Lafayette Reformed folk did not create social clubs and benevolent societies like the Mishawaka Belgians. In 1900 half of the Dutch in the county farmed in the rural townships, primarily in Fairfield some twelve miles north, and the rest lived and worked in Lafayette. Of 265 Dutch in the city labor force in 1900, 45 percent were unskilled laborers including female domestics, 25 percent were skilled craftsmen led by carpenters, and 13 percent were semiskilled workers. No more than a dozen men can be identified as factory workers. Businessmen comprised only 12 percent, and 4 percent were professionals (clerics, teachers, a professor, etc.). All but eight men could speak English, most were naturalized citizens, and 37 percent of the families owned their own houses.[77] The Lafayette Dutch began at the bottom rung of the socioeconomic scale and gradually worked up into the middle class. Lafayette also served as an immigrant beacon that led to Dutch Reformed settlements in counties immediately to the north—Benton and White in the 1870s, Newton in the 1880s, and Jasper in the 1890s.

While the Groningers in the Lafayette region immigrated in hopes of economic improvement, a colony of more than fifty Frisian Mennonites, who settled in the Goshen area in 1853–54, left the Netherlands because of their religious convictions. As pacifists they sought to escape compulsory military service and the high taxes to support the same. Two pastors of these "plain people," Ruurd J. Smid (changed to Smith) and Ruurd J. Symensma, both farmers, came with the group that comprised more than half of the congregation in the village of Balk, municipality of Gasterland, Friesland.[78]

After landing in Philadelphia, they followed the trail of the German Mennonites westward to Zoar and Waynesburg, Ohio, and then on to Goshen. In Goshen, with the help of German fellow believers, they purchased a block of 320 acres for $3,200, of which 50 acres were cleared and in crops. The property was ten miles south of Goshen, along what became known as "Holland Settlement Road" near the village of New Paris.[79]

Over time the small farm colony attracted other family and friends from the Gasterland congregation, such as four DeVries (changed to Defrees) brothers,[80] and the families Zondervan, Smink, Dal, Postma, Visser (Fisher), Duiker (Duker), Swart, Rystra, and Huitema (Hygema), all of whom arrived before 1860. Immediately after the Civil War, another nine families and a few singles came from Gasterland. Most lived in Jackson Township, although Bauke Ferwerda (Ferverda) bought a farm near Nappanee that remains in the family, while son Hiram settled on a farm near New Paris.[81] The post–Civil War immigrants raised the number of Dutch in Elkhart County in 1870 to nearly one hundred and fifty (including forty-five children born in Indiana). By 1900 about ten families had spilled over into Jefferson Township of Kosciusko County to the south.[82]

Because the "Amish" Frisian colony in New Paris was too small to support a full-fledged church, it met monthly and later biweekly in private homes, and Pastor Ruurd Smith conducted worship in the Frisian language. On alternating Sundays the Hollanders worshiped with the local German-speaking Mennonite congregation. Pastor Smith preached at the Holland services for more than thirty-five years until his retirement in 1889. Smith's retirement brought an abrupt end to Frisian services, and the Balkers joined with the Germans to form the Salem Mennonite Church of New Paris.[83] Thus, the Dutch Mennonites in one generation lost their national identity and went over to the Amish. Most remained with the very conservative Old Mennonites, while a few families, the Hygemas in particular, joined the more liberal Mennonite Brethren faction. All prospered greatly as farmers. One son of the Balkers, Piebe Swart, made a significant literary contribution by translating from Dutch into English *The Complete Works of Menno Simons,* which was first published in Elkhart in 1871.[84] That some shred of ethnic identity remained with the second generation is evident from the 1878 family history of Hiram Benjamin Ferverda of North Webster, who closed with the exclamation: "We are proud of our Dutch heritage." But neither Hiram's father nor any of his siblings married Hollanders, and the descendants scattered throughout north-central Indiana where no Hollanders lived.[85] The Frisians were simply absorbed by the other Mennonites of the region.

In the 1880s a second group of Hollanders settled in Goshen. These were a dozen orthodox Calvinist families from the province of Zeeland who developed celery farms on the muck land east of town.[86] Whether they learned of Goshen from the Frisian Mennonites is not known, but the groups considered each other to be theologically misguided and certainly kept their distance.

In 1904, 9 families, led by the Hoogenbooms, formed the East Goshen Christian Reformed Church with 50 souls. The Calvinist groups grew slowly, reaching 21 families with 117 souls in 1915. In 1935 they only had 25 families and 132 souls. One reason for the lack of growth was that in the years immediately after World War I a number of families moved to Grand Rapids, Michigan, a Dutch Calvinist center, to take advantage of higher-paying jobs in the booming furniture industry and other factories.[87]

Other Dutch religious minorities in Indiana were a few Amsterdam Jewish families in Indianapolis and Roman Catholics in several major cities—Evansville, Fort Wayne, Vincennes, Indianapolis, and, after 1900, South Bend and Mishawaka. The seven Jewish families, plus a few singles, in Indianapolis in 1870 were typical itinerant clothing and cigar merchants, who had previously lived in England, Pennsylvania, New York, and Michigan. Most resided in Ward 5 with a few in Ward 7.[88]

Dutch Catholics, along with a few Protestants, began filtering into Evansville on the Ohio River in the late 1840s and 1850s, settling among German Catholics from Prussia, Oldenburg, and Hannover. Most of the Dutch hailed from the Achterhoek region of the province of Gelderland on the German border. The Dutch in Vanderburgh County increased from 150 to 200 between 1860 and 1880 but then declined by 1890 to only 100. In 1930 there were 131 persons of Dutch birth or parentage in the county, all but 9 in Evansville. Clearly, Evansville never became a Dutch center, and the Dutch there intermarried with Germans and quickly lost their identity.

In the 1850s a few Catholic families from the provinces of Gelderland and Overijssel settled in Vincennes and among the Belgians in Leopold. Following the Civil War more families from Overijssel immigrated to Fort Wayne where they found factory work, while others went to Indianapolis and Terre Haute.

The major Dutch Catholic center in Indiana developed among the Flemish Belgians in St. Joseph County. Gradually, Dutch families moved to Mishawaka and South Bend in the 1880s and 1890s, but the main wave arrived after 1900, especially between 1920 and 1930, when the number of Dutch Catholics doubled from 300 to 550, including more than 300 Dutch born. Since most worked in the Ball-Band factory, it is clear that the attraction of St. Joseph County was its booming economy and employers who favored Flemish workers.

Orthodox Dutch Calvinists built the largest settlement in the Calumet district of Lake County, centered around Munster and Highland on the Sauk Trail. This area, like most of northwest Indiana at the time, was classified as "swampland" or "low prairie" by the federal government,

and the heavy clay soil required drainage ditching systems before it could be farmed. By 1930, more than 1,650 persons of Dutch birth or ancestry lived in northern Lake County (Table 3), and today the number surpasses 5,000. The four Reformed churches in 1990 alone counted 2,500 souls.[89] The first families, led by Peter Jabaay, moved into Munster between 1854 and 1857 as a spillover from the earlier colonies in Roseland, South Holland, and Lansing, Illinois. They opened farms on a fertile strip of lowland running from four to five miles along the north side of Ridge Road (US Highway No. 6), stretching to the Little Calumet River. When the Cady Marsh was reclaimed in 1871, the Hollanders also expanded south of the ridge. Drawing upon their traditional skills of draining and tilling swampland, they prospered and in the words of a visiting physician from Hammond developed a proverbial "Happy Valley."[90]

The founding families originated in the Old Country village of Strijen near Rotterdam in the province of Zuid-Holland. They crossed the ocean together in 1855 and headed for the cheap but fertile lands along the Calumet River. Jacob Monster (who fortunately changed his name before giving it to the village of Munster) ran a general store and post office and served on the town council, school board, and as road supervisor. With oxen and sled he also deepened the Hart Ditch cut through the sand ridge, which hastened the drainage of Cady Marsh. By 1860 the colony included 54 residents, 37 of whom were Dutch. The next years brought a sharp increase to 23 Dutch families totaling 125 persons in 1870.[91] Munster became the church village for the 60 to 70 farm families along the ridge. Hammond, the larger city to the north, was the market center, although for everyday needs the Hollanders patronized Munster's and Klootwyk's general store in the Dutch village. Surprisingly, two saloons run by Americans survived in this "puritan" village, but no orthodox Hollander would cross their thresholds.[92]

*The Jacob Munster family, ca. 1900.*

| COUNTY | 1850 | 1860 | 1870 | 1880 | 1890 | 1900 | 1910 | 1920 | 1930 FB | 1930 NB | 1940 |
|---|---|---|---|---|---|---|---|---|---|---|---|
| ADAMS | | | | 11 | 1 | 1 | 2 | 6 | 2 | 15 | |
| ALLEN | | 4 | 17 | 146 | 17 | 33 | 40 | 49 | 42 | 171 | 35 |
| BARTHOLOMEW | | 1 | | 4 | | 3 | 3 | 2 | | 6 | |
| BENTON | | 2 | 1 | 36 | 21 | 9 | 9 | 13 | 7 | 24 | 4 |
| BLACKFORD | | | | 1 | 1 | | | | | 1 | |
| BOONE | | | | 1 | | | | 13 | | 9 | 1 |
| BROWN | | | | 0 | | 1 | | | 2 | 5 | 1 |
| CARROLL | | | 6 | 4 | 4 | 1 | 5 | 5 | 6 | 14 | 3 |
| CASS | | 2 | | 4 | 1 | 12 | 2 | 9 | 6 | 35 | 8 |
| CLARK | | 2 | 1 | 2 | 1 | | | 1 | 2 | 9 | |
| CLAY | | 1 | 10 | 5 | 6 | 5 | 2 | 3 | 1 | 10 | |
| CLINTON | | 2 | 9 | 3 | 2 | 2 | 2 | | 2 | 11 | 5 |
| CRAWFORD | | 1 | 1 | 1 | | 1 | | | | | |
| DAVIESS | 2 | 2 | | 10 | | | | | 1 | 2 | |
| DEARBORN | 5 | 17 | 4 | 17 | 4 | 1 | 2 | 2 | 2 | 10 | 1 |
| DECATUR | 2 | 3 | 4 | 9 | 1 | 3 | 2 | 1 | | 10 | |
| DE KALB | | | 3 | 1 | | 2 | 3 | 3 | 2 | 10 | |
| DELAWARE | | | | 3 | 2 | 47 | 35 | 27 | 22 | 37 | 19 |
| DUBOIS | | 6 | 1 | 12 | 10 | 6 | 4 | 3 | 2 | 7 | 1 |
| ELKHART | | 36 | 99 | 103 | 121 | 102 | 104 | 90 | 117 | 283 | 90 |
| FAYETTE | 1 | 2 | 1 | 1 | 1 | | 6 | 2 | | 10 | 3 |
| FLOYD | | 3 | 7 | 2 | 1 | 3 | 6 | | 1 | 9 | 2 |
| FOUNTAIN | | 3 | | 1 | 9 | 43 | 74 | 58 | 55 | 127 | 36 |
| FRANKLIN | 2 | 4 | 11 | 8 | | 1 | | 5 | 1 | 9 | 1 |
| FULTON | | 4 | | 1 | | 2 | | | | 4 | |
| GIBSON | | 1 | 3 | 5 | 4 | 2 | | 6 | 3 | 7 | 2 |
| GRANT | | | | 8 | | 6 | 6 | 10 | 6 | 15 | 12 |
| GREENE | | 1 | | 0 | | | | | | 4 | |
| HAMILTON | | | | 1 | | 2 | | | | 4 | 1 |
| HANCOCK | | | 2 | 0 | | 1 | | 1 | 4 | 10 | |
| HARRISON | | | 1 | 0 | | 1 | 1 | | | 5 | |
| HENDRICKS | | | | 2 | 1 | | 4 | 3 | 16 | 28 | 19 |
| HENRY | | | | 2 | | | 14 | | | 10 | 1 |
| HOWARD | | | | 1 | 1 | 1 | 3 | 10 | 4 | 14 | 1 |
| HUNTINGTON | | | 6 | 3 | 3 | 5 | 5 | 4 | 6 | 17 | 2 |
| JACKSON | 0 | 14 | 8 | 11 | 3 | 3 | 6 | 5 | | 9 | |
| JASPER | | | | 69 | 52 | 141 | 156 | 195 | 181 | 414 | 174 |
| JAY | | | 1 | 1 | | | 2 | | | 6 | |
| JEFFERSON | 1 | 2 | 1 | 6 | 3 | 3 | 5 | 3 | 1 | 9 | 2 |
| JENNINGS | | | 9 | 3 | 1 | 1 | | 1 | | 4 | |
| JOHNSON | 2 | 1 | 2 | 3 | 4 | 7 | 8 | 4 | 15 | 18 | 13 |
| KNOX | | 9 | 8 | 22 | 6 | 3 | 2 | 2 | 1 | 26 | |
| KOSCIUSKO | | | 7 | 12 | 12 | 27 | 22 | 18 | 13 | 47 | 5 |
| LAGRANGE | | 1 | | 3 | 1 | 7 | 1 | | 2 | 8 | 1 |
| LAKE | | 28 | 76 | 122 | 151 | 230 | 477 | 415 | 437 | 1221 | 344 |
| LA PORTE | | 38 | 18 | 16 | 9 | 17 | 17 | 47 | 43 | 82 | 37 |
| LAWRENCE | | | | 0 | | | 1 | | 2 | 10 | 1 |
| MADISON | | 1 | 21 | 0 | | 19 | 12 | 5 | 7 | 38 | 6 |
| MARION | 1 | 13 | 32 | 65 | 88 | 120 | 220 | 268 | 262 | 520 | 188 |
| MARSHALL | | 7 | 11 | 11 | 4 | 5 | 7 | 8 | 11 | 33 | 10 |
| MARTIN | | | | 0 | | | | | | 1 | |
| MIAMI | 1 | | 2 | 1 | 3 | 3 | 3 | 4 | | 9 | 5 |
| MONROE | | | | 1 | 2 | 2 | 4 | 6 | 3 | 7 | 2 |
| MONTGOMERY | | | 3 | 8 | 4 | 4 | 2 | | 1 | 11 | 2 |
| MORGAN | | | | 0 | | | | | | 5 | 1 |
| NEWTON | | | 5 | 3 | 66 | 95 | 94 | 55 | 39 | 82 | 44 |
| NOBLE | | 1 | 3 | 2 | 1 | 4 | 6 | 4 | 5 | 9 | 8 |
| OHIO | 2 | | | 0 | | 1 | | | | 2 | |
| ORANGE | | 1 | | 0 | | | | | | 1 | |
| OWEN | | | 1 | 1 | 3 | | | 1 | | 2 | |
| PARKE | | | | 0 | 1 | 1 | 1 | 1 | | 2 | |
| PERRY | 6 | 11 | 15 | 17 | 12 | 6 | 4 | | 1 | 19 | |
| PIKE | | 1 | | 1 | | | | | 1 | 2 | 1 |
| PORTER | | | 2 | 5 | 10 | 25 | 14 | 7 | 9 | 33 | 23 |
| POSEY | 5 | | 21 | 15 | 5 | 4 | 3 | 1 | | 7 | |
| PULASKI | | 1 | 2 | 1 | | | | 4 | 1 | 8 | 1 |
| PUTNAM | | 1 | | 0 | | | | | | 4 | 2 |
| RANDOLPH | | | 1 | 1 | | | | | | 2 | |
| RIPLEY | | 2 | 21 | 13 | 3 | 4 | 2 | 1 | | 11 | |
| RUSH | | 1 | | 3 | 2 | 4 | 3 | 4 | 2 | 12 | |
| ST. JOSEPH | 2 | 8 | | 16 | 17 | 27 | 112 | 137 | 234 | 316 | 190 |
| SCOTT | | 4 | | | 1 | | | | | 1 | |
| SHELBY | | 2 | 7 | 1 | 2 | 5 | 1 | 1 | | 4 | 3 |
| SPENCER | | | 5 | 2 | 1 | | 1 | | | 7 | |
| STARKE | | | 5 | 6 | 3 | 8 | 24 | 10 | 4 | 15 | 9 |
| STEUBEN | | 2 | 5 | 2 | | | | 1 | | 6 | |
| SULLIVAN | | 1 | | 2 | | | 1 | 1 | 1 | | 1 |
| SWITZERLAND | | | | 0 | | | 1 | | | | |
| TIPPECANOE | 25 | 148 | 248 | 279 | 369 | 443 | 437 | 368 | 325 | 940 | 228 |
| TIPTON | | 1 | | 3 | | | | | | 4 | |
| UNION | | | 19 | 0 | | | | | | 2 | 1 |
| VANDERBURGH | 1 | 81 | 73 | 89 | 28 | 27 | 19 | 17 | 17 | 114 | 8 |
| VERMILLION | | | | 1 | | | 2 | | 2 | 4 | 1 |
| VIGO | 2 | 24 | 28 | 65 | 36 | 53 | 57 | 51 | 33 | 139 | 29 |
| WABASH | | | | 0 | | 1 | 4 | 4 | 1 | 4 | 4 |
| WARREN | | 3 | 1 | 4 | 7 | 18 | 20 | 8 | 4 | 9 | 3 |
| WARRICK | | | | 30 | 1 | 2 | 1 | | | 5 | 4 |
| WASHINGTON | | 1 | | 0 | | | | | | | |
| WAYNE | 5 | 4 | | 9 | | | 1 | 2 | 4 | 25 | 4 |
| WELLS | | 1 | 3 | 0 | 1 | | | 1 | 1 | 5 | 1 |
| WHITE | | 3 | 22 | 48 | 31 | 63 | 40 | 26 | 14 | 63 | 13 |
| WHITLEY | | | 1 | 8 | 2 | 2 | 1 | | 1 | 7 | 0 |
| TOTALS | 60 | 513 | 873 | 1395 | 1157 | 1678 | 2126 | 2018 | 1992 | 5286 | 1617 |

FB = Foreign Born          NB = Native Born

The founding of the Dutch Reformed Church in Lansing in 1861 enhanced the settlement in Munster by greatly shortening the travel to church each Sunday. Then in 1870 the entire Munster contingent of the Lansing church seceded (except Jacob Munster and his wife) and organized its own congregation affiliated with the more isolationist-minded Christian Reformed Church. At the turn of the century the Munster Christian Reformed Church grew rapidly with immigrants fresh from the Netherlands and others moving out from Chicago. It reached its apogee in 1915 with 650 souls, after mothering in 1908 a daughter church in Highland ten miles east that already numbered 466 souls in 1915. Dutch settlers had first moved into Highland in the 1890s, led by Jacob Schoon.

The Dutch farmers at first raised the typical American field crops of hay, corn, and wheat, but by the 1870s they had turned to their forte, the intensive truck farming of vegetables and fruits for the South Chicago markets—cabbages, cauliflower, pickles, tomatoes, sweet corn, potatoes, melons, and after 1900 primarily onions, onion sets, and sugar beets.[93] The Chicago food processing firm of Libby, McNeill & Libby opened a plant in Highland about 1904 to take the tomatoes, cabbages, and pickles of the Dutch and other farmers. At harvest time the plant processed sixty tons of cabbage daily into sauerkraut.[94] The kraut plant of Herman Meeter, a Highland Hollander, and Schrum's dill pickle plant also bought Dutch produce. Beets went to the Holland Sugar Beet Company and later to railroad receiving stations for processing elsewhere.

Of 150 Dutch in the workforce in North and Calumet townships in 1900, 89 percent were farmers or farm laborers. The others were day laborers, a few carpenters and clerics, a huckster, and a salesman. The Dutch generally eschewed factory work, finding the shop floor confining, hostile, and un-Christian. They longed to own their own land and to keep things "Dutch." For the same reasons the twenty-five single young women who worked as domestics all served in Dutch households, and one widow supported herself at home as a dressmaker. These were poor folk struggling to achieve financial security on the land and in their own communities. By 1900, 40 percent owned their own farms, two-thirds free of mortgages. But 60 percent were yet tenant farmers trying to climb the agricultural ladder.

The huge Chicago market provided the Dutch truck farmers the opportunity for prosperity. First by ox cart, then horse and wagon, and after World War I increasingly by motor truck, they brought their vegetable crops in season daily (except Sunday) to the Chicago commission houses at the South Water and later Randolph Street

KEN SCHOON

*C. P. Schoon standing in an onion field, Munster, ca. 1920.*

markets and to the 71st Street Market in Englewood. Alternatively, they raised their crops under contract to commercial food processors, set up farm stands, or peddled their produce from house to house in the steel mill towns of Hammond, Whiting, East Chicago, and Gary. Edna Ferber's novel *So Big* (1924) forever immortalized the Dutch truck farmers at the apogee of this business in the 1920s.[95]

The most typical Dutch crop in the ridge communities was onion sets. For thirty years, 1920–50, the farmers from South Holland to Highland devoted more than three thousand acres (one-third of all cropland) to this crop, of which they gained a virtual national monopoly with over 75 percent of the market. The labor-intensive, onerous handwork seemed to suit the Dutch temperament, and it brought economic prosperity to many, although only the most successful survived the Great Depression.[96]

The penetration of Chicago industry and residential suburbs into the Calumet Region of Hammond and Gary brought Munster and Highland into the metropolitan orbit. In 1905 the National (later American) Brick Company opened a factory near the towns to exploit the "blue" clay soil. Some Hollanders worked seasonally as day laborers at the kilns that provided most of the "Chicago common" bricks for the booming metropolis. Such off-farm earnings enabled many families to survive the early "lean years." World War I hastened the Americanization process, and in the 1920s and 1930s the Dutch language gave way to English in the churches and on the streets. In historian Lance Trusty's apt words, "the old tongue inevitably faded away in Munster, victim of time and the times."[97]

Because of the large concentration of Hollanders, Munster and Highland boasted of its Dutch social and civic organizations—a community band and chorus, a commercial club and agricultural societies, and sporting activities. But most social activities were church-centered, such as the Young Men's and Young Women's societies and their adult counterparts. Dutch Calvinists were a staid lot compared to their Catholic compatriots in Mishawaka and South Bend with their dance halls, carnivals, bicycle racing, and pigeon fanciers. The Munster and Highland Calvinists separated themselves "from the world," i.e., the alien culture, by each establishing Christian day schools to educate their youth in biblical perspectives.[98] As a supporter noted many years later, these "hardy pioneers" had "no means, no money, no experience, no background, nothing but sincere convictions that this was a way of life they wanted for their children and children's children."[99] This practice opened them to "reproach and ignoring" from Americans and even from the more Americanized fellow Dutch. But as a defender stated later, "it was forced on us to a great extent by our immigrant ways, but also by the militant mind of the church." The county superintendent of schools required all eighth-grade students of the nonaccredited "Dutch Schools" to take state exams in the public school, which the students successfully passed each year. During their first decade, instruction in English gradually became the norm. Until the 1930s the Dutch private schools in Lake County had larger enrollments than the tax-supported public schools, which served the non-Dutch and the Reformed Church in America families who rejected the separatist principle.[100]

After 1900 Munster's twin city of Highland grew rapidly around three Dutch families: the Schoons, with more than six hundred progeny by 1956, the Zandstras, and the Van Tils. Bartel H. Zandstra had sixteen children, many of whom assumed leadership positions in the church, schools, civil life, and business such as the Zandstra Farms, the oldest operating business in Highland. The ninth child, Bartel (1903–1983), became a leading Democratic politician in Lake County and the state and in the 1950s was a candidate for lieutenant governor.[101]

Henry Van Til and John Groot opened the Farmers and Merchants Bank in 1914. Sam Van Til operated a neighborhood grocery on Jewett Street in Highland in the 1930s, and in the next decade his son Nick opened a similar store on Jackson Street in Hammond. Nick E. Leep's Pleasant View Dairy, founded in the 1920s, was Highland's largest business for many decades, after surviving the violent "milk war" of 1932 when large Chicago dairies tried by intimidation to drive out the Dutch competition. In the 1950s Nick Van Til branched out into Van Til's Supermarkets with stores in Hammond, Highland, Schererville, and Merrillville. Van Til's Farm Market on Ridge Road, owned by a relative of Nick, has also been a Highland landmark for

many generations. Until 1950 Highland remained a stable Dutch village of truck farmers, downwind of the Calumet Region petroleum refineries and steel mills. But by 1990 it had evolved into a Chicago bedroom community of twenty-five thousand. The Dutch influence, while muted, remains evident among leading business and civic leaders and in the two Christian Reformed churches and the Christian school. Due to church evangelism programs, however, these institutions are increasingly multiethnic.[102]

As urban life encroached on the market gardeners of the Calumet Region and land values shot upward, some Dutch in Lake County, most of whom belonged to the Reformed Church, moved south thirty-five miles to DeMotte in Jasper County, a town on the Illinois Central Railroad line, where a Dutch farm colony was founded in the 1870s. In 1874 land on Chicago's south side, fifteen miles from the city center in Roseland and South Holland, was worth $1,000 an acre, compared to only $150 to $200 an acre in Munster and Highland, and even less in DeMotte.

The Otis brothers of Chicago, Charles and Lucius, foresaw the remarkable opportunities in the prairie counties of northern Indiana where absentee landlords had retarded settlement.[103] They purchased thousands of acres southwest of DeMotte near Thayer and recruited dozens of Dutch immigrants as sharecroppers by furnishing milk cows and farm equipment on favorable terms. Pioneers on the Otis Estates were the Groningen and Frisian families Walstra, Peterson, Sipkema, Sytsma, Roorda, Bozeman, Nanninga, Kammenga, and Hoffman.[104] By 1880 sixty-nine Dutch born lived in Keener Township, Jasper County (Table 3). The number doubled by 1900 because in the early 1890s a second wave of Dutch arrived from Roseland, Lansing, and Highland. They were spurred by the Roseland real estate dealers and promoters, John Cornelius Ton and his brother Richard, who purchased a large parcel of recently drained swamplands north of DeMotte and advertised it heavily in Roseland and surroundings as an ideal Dutch truck gardening colony. Within a year they began "buying out the American farmers of that vicinity" in order to create a "large and enterprising" Dutch settlement. "The outlook is cheering," reported a visiting Dutch Reformed Church organizer, although several crop failures later tried the faith of the farmers and caused some to leave. Besides raising cabbages and pickles, the Dutch specialized in asparagus and later in dairying and chicken and turkey hatcheries.[105]

The founding of a Dutch Reformed church in 1893 ensured DeMotte's growth by providing "solid" preaching and psalm singing. The church building site was selected two miles west of town at "Dutch Corner" to draw in the families from Roselawn and Thayer. First Reformed Church had 450 souls in 1920, and the Christian Reformed Church had 200 in 1935. It had begun in 1932 when thirty-two families seceded from First Reformed for the more "Dutchy" denomination. Previously in 1920 twenty-six families (100 persons) had withdrawn to form the English-speaking American Reformed Church after First Reformed refused "so radical a change" as to allow English in the second service. Half of DeMotte's population of 200 became members of the new church located in town on the main highway, Route 53.[106]

By 1930, 700 Dutch born lived in northern Jasper and Newton counties. DeMotte grew rapidly in the years of "white flight" from Chicago in the 1950s when thousands of Dutch in the southside districts of Englewood and Roseland left within a decade. In 1990 DeMotte's four Calvinist churches (two Reformed Church in America and two Christian Reformed Church) surpassed 2,750 souls, making the town the second largest Dutch Protestant settlement in Indiana today.[107] DeMotte, like Munster and Highland, had a Christian day school and the usual panoply of church societies, music clubs, and activities to absorb the rare leisure time of its Dutch folk. The community band provided music for the Fourth of July picnic and the ice cream socials. The town's relative geographic isolation has preserved a stronger sense of Dutchness than in the Lake County towns. Walter Roorda (1931–1993) of Bethel Christian Reformed Church, who owned a furniture store in town, represented the district for twenty-five years in the Indiana House of Representatives.[108]

Because of new colonies like Munster, Highland, and DeMotte, Hollanders with modest or poor finances prospered in the region, provided they could tolerate the unrelenting toil and maintain strong family units in which their wives and children played a vital part. They readily moved out of the Chicago area to cheaper lands yet remained in ethnic enclaves within reach of the city. The largest influx occurred in the 1950s when the Dutch in the southside Chicago districts, notably Roseland and Englewood, fled before the encroaching black migration.

Several hundred Dutch Protestants also settled in and around Indianapolis and Muncie in the years after 1890. The smaller group in Muncie, eight families (forty persons in 1900), migrated from western Michigan to find work in the iron mills making nuts and bolts. The much larger group in Indianapolis was composed primarily of dairy farmers from Friesland—the Bottemas, Bosmas, Bloemhofs, Bultstras, DeGroots, Koldykes, Meyers, Nautas, Nydams, Postmas, Schoenemans, and Tacomas. Cash (Kerst) Bottema, a milkhand who immigrated on a cattle boat in 1891, founded Bottema Farms, Mutual Milk Dairy, and Brown Brothers Packing Company. He served as president of the Holstein-Friesian Breeders Association of Indiana and was an original stockholder of the Marion County Farm Bureau.[109]

By 1911 seventeen families organized a Dutch Reformed church to carry on the faith. Christian Park Reformed Church, now located on Wentworth Boulevard, serves several hundred second- and third-generation families. Pastor Allen B. Cook served as the general contractor, and the men of the congregation assisted him in building a new church in 1948. In 1978 the congregation was led by a Dutch immigrant pastor, the Reverend Harmen Heeg, whose family had settled in Canada after the Second World War. Meanwhile, in 1961 the Christian Reformed Church also established a congregation in the capital city, which presently has about 150 members. The Reverend Jack Zandstra, a son of Bartel H. of Highland, organized the congregation. In 1930 Marion County counted 262 Dutch born and 520 of Dutch ancestry out of a population of 425,000. There were 203 Dutch born in 1980, living mainly in the western and northern suburbs.[110] In the 1950s a second immigrant wave arrived, including several dozen families expelled from the former Netherlands East Indies (now Indonesia) by the revolutionary leader President Sukarno. These mainly secular Dutch comprised the majority of the 62 charter members of the Netherlands Club, founded in 1974, to keep alive the Dutch language and culture.[111]

The Dutch settled throughout Indiana in an essentially American environment. While the Catholics chose the cities of Evansville, Fort Wayne, Indianapolis, and other rising urban centers where they were quickly absorbed, the Protestants' religious solidarity and distaste for factory work led them to found farm colonies in largely unsettled regions—Lafayette, Goshen, Munster, Highland, and DeMotte. Remnants of these enclaves survive to the present day.

## Luxembourgers

The Grand Duchy of Luxembourg is smaller than Rhode Island—its territory covers only one thousand square miles, and its population was less than three hundred thousand in the 1940s. The total immigration to the United States was only forty-eight thousand in the great century of immigration, 1815–1915. Most carved out farms in the heavily forested lands of Minnesota, Wisconsin, Illinois, and Iowa among fellow Roman Catholic Germans and Belgian Luxembourgers. Cincinnati was an early destination and jumping-off point to the West, but Chicago quickly superseded it. Some five hundred Luxembourg families had settled in Ohio by 1890, in contrast to only fifty to sixty families in all of Indiana. It is estimated that between seventy-five thousand and one hundred thousand Luxembourgers presently live in the United States, mostly in the Chicago area and points west.[112]

The Luxembourg overseas immigration began in earnest during the potato crisis of the 1840s when more than four thousand people came to America. These desperate rural folk were strongly influenced by the extensive immigration of nearby Belgians from the province of Luxembourg.[113] In the 1850s six thousand Luxembourgers immigrated to America, followed by four thousand to five thousand in the years immediately after the American Civil War, seven thousand to eight thousand in the 1870s, and six thousand in the 1880s. Most came from the thin-soiled Ardennes region (the Luxembourg District), where rural poverty and land hunger gave "America letters" a strong appeal, and immigrant agents found ready customers.[114] Adult males outnumbered females by more than two to one, and there were more single immigrants than families. They reached the European ports of Le Havre and Antwerp by train and then set sail for New York, where they again boarded trains for Chicago and points west.[115]

After 1870 Luxembourgers increasingly settled around American cities: Chicago, St. Paul-Minneapolis, New York, Dubuque, and Milwaukee, where they engaged in truck farming. In Indiana, Michigan City and La Porte on Lake Michigan attracted several dozen families from the Moselle area and the Alzette valley near Mersch. Ten families settled among several hundred Belgian Luxembourger families in Perry County along the Ohio River. Paul Gilles and family arrived in the 1850s. By 1880 he and his unmarried son Theodore were farming in Troy Township, while his oldest son, Paul, Jr., was married and working in a fur factory in nearby Tell City.[116] In addition to the La Porte and Perry County settlements, half a dozen Luxembourg families in 1890 lived in Jay County on the Ohio border in the compact village of Trinity. This was the only pure Luxembourg settlement in Indiana. Individual families and individuals were scattered in many other counties. Only three Luxembourgers lived in the capital city of Indianapolis in 1880. It is noteworthy that the Congregation of Holy Cross at Notre Dame in St. Joseph County included Luxembourg priests, brothers, and nuns. Luxembourg farmers rarely subdivided their land among their sons, so the younger generation went into the professions or followed the frontier westward to homestead new lands.[117]

Luxembourgers were traditionally conservative in religion and culture, and they devoted themselves to their families and daily work. Their motto, "True to God, to friends, and to fatherland," captures the essence. Wherever they settled they joined German Catholic churches and enrolled their children in parish day schools. Catholic education was deemed an absolute necessity to protect their youth from the liberal Protestantism and secularism in the public schools. No sacrifice was too great for church and school. "To travel four, six, eight or more miles on a Sunday to attend Mass was regarded as of no consequence." The church and its sacraments were the focal point of their lives from baptism through confirmation, marriage, death, and burial in holy ground. They seldom found Luxembourgers for their mates because the marriage pool was too small, but German Catholics were quite acceptable. "Mixed" marriages (with non-Catholics) were strongly condemned. Wakes were elaborate, imposing events, and families visited graves weekly to pray and carefully tend the flowers and substantial headstones of family and friends. Most venerated in statuary and festivals was "Our Lady of Luxembourg, Comforter of the Afflicted," who, since the seventeenth century, was their most prominent national symbol.[118]

Table 4.   Luxembourgers in Indiana by County, 1860–1940

| County | 1860 | 1890 | 1940 |
|---|---|---|---|
| ADAMS | | | 1 |
| ALLEN | | 4 | 1 |
| BENTON | | 4 | |
| CASS | | 1 | |
| ELKHART | 1 | | 1 |
| FLOYD | 1 | | |
| FRANKLIN | 7 | | |
| GREENE | 1 | | |
| HOWARD | | | 1 |
| JASPER | | | 2 |
| JAY | | 8 | |
| JEFFERSON | 1 | | |
| JOHNSON | 1 | | |
| LAGRANGE | | | 5 |
| LAKE | | | 15 |
| LA PORTE | 6 | | 4 |
| MADISON | | | 1 |
| MARION | 8 | 1 | 4 |
| MARSHALL | | 3 | 2 |
| NEWTON | | | 2 |
| PARKE | 1 | | 1 |
| PERRY | 13 | | |
| RIPLEY | 2 | | |
| RUSH | 1 | | |
| ST. JOSEPH | 2 | 4 | 10 |
| STARKE | | | 6 |
| VIGO | 3 | | 4 |
| WARRICK | 1 | | |
| WASHINGTON | 1 | | |
| WAYNE | 2 | | |
| TOTALS | 52 | 25 | 60 |

After becoming naturalized citizens, Luxembourgers voted the Democratic ticket at the polls. The Democratic party was the choice of all Catholic immigrants because it rigorously fought against Whig-Republican blue laws, protected immigrant freedoms and legal rights, and favored decentralized government power. During the Civil War young Luxembourg men fought to preserve the Union. Luxembourg immigrants usually had to learn some English to get by in their work, but if they settled in a German community they preferred to use German, which they learned in school. Their native tongue, Luxembourgesch, died out quickly. The use of German ended abruptly during the First World War and the nativist era that followed.[119]

## Summary

Lowlanders historically comprised less than 5 percent of Indiana's population (based on 1980 ancestry figures), and they were relatively inconspicuous. Nevertheless, their clustering in rural colonies and urban neighborhoods gave them an enduring presence and greater cultural impact than their numbers would otherwise warrant. Whether Catholic, Calvinist, or Mennonite, they were colonists par excellence.

Over the generations the Dutch Calvinists succeeded in maintaining a stronger sense of ethnicity than Catholic Dutch, Belgians, or German Luxembourgers. Although Belgian born surpassed Dutch born by nearly two to one (Tables 2 and 3), the 1980 census question on ancestry revealed eight times as many single-ancestry Dutch as Belgians, and twenty-two times as many multiple-ancestry Dutch. Only 12,500 Belgians were cognizant of their ancestry, compared to 210,000 Dutch.[120] The Dutch clearly had far less outmarriage than Belgians, who have all but lost their ethnic heritage.

Reasons for the difference lie in modes of settlement, church institutional structures, and religious beliefs. Dutch Protestants planted farm colonies in scarcely populated regions—Lafayette, Goshen, Munster, Highland, and DeMotte. Catholic Dutch and Belgians, on the other hand, settled primarily in rising cities—New Albany, Hartford City, Mishawaka, South Bend, Evansville, Fort Wayne, and Indianapolis. Leopold was the only long-term rural Belgian colony. Since city life broke down ethnic communities more rapidly than rural life, the Catholics paid the price.

Church structures and religious beliefs are even more important than environmental factors. Nearly all Dutch Reformed churches were ethnically homogeneous and used the Dutch language in worship until at least the 1920s. The urban Catholic parishes were generally of mixed nationality, and even rural parishes became mixed over time. None was exclusively Dutch, and a few had a Dutch-speaking priest for the confessional booth. The Belgians belonged to an international church with a standard Latin Mass; they readily shared the "common bonds of faith" with French and German coreligionists. Since every major city had a Catholic church, Catholic immigrants could readily disperse.

Calvinists, on the other hand, established their own churches, led by Dutch-speaking pastors, who taught their flock to remain separate from the world. "In isolation is our strength" was the motto of the Christian Reformed Church for its first hundred years, until the 1950s. Religion was the determining factor in the rate of Americanization, but ultimately the Lowlanders, like most Europeans, became largely assimilated.

The author wishes to thank the following individuals: Herbert Brinks and the staff of Heritage Hall at Calvin College; Larry Wagenaar and the staff of the Joint Archives of Holland at Hope College; Mary Anthrop; Phyllis Gaillard; Judy Hoffman; Carl Pansaerts; Angeline Reagan; Ronald Redder; Evelyn Roorda; Kenneth Scheeringa; Gregory S. Rose; Kristine A. J. Smets; Lance Trusty; and David Zandstra.

## Notes

1. Much of the Netherlands and Belgium lie near or below sea level; hence the application "low" or "nether" lands. Luxembourg, however, is inland, east of the Ardennes Mountains, and its terrain is hilly and above sea level.

2. J. A. Kossmann-Putto and E. H. Kossmann, *The Low Countries: History of the Northern and Southern Netherlands* (Rekkem, Belgium: Flemish-Netherlands Foundation, "Stichting Ons Erfdeel vzw," 1987), 5–6, 19–20.

3. Louis M. deGryse, "The Low Countries: Belgians, Netherlanders, and Luxembourgers," in *They Chose Minnesota: A Survey of the State's Ethnic Groups*, ed. June Drenning Holmquist (St. Paul: Minnesota Historical Society Press, 1981), 199.

4. Nicholas Gonner, *Luxembourgers in the New World* (orig. in German, [Dubuque, Iowa, 1889]), English trans. and eds., Jean Ensch, Jean-Claude Muller, and Robert E. Owens (Esch-sur-Alzette, Grand Duchy of Luxembourg: Editions-Reliures Schortgen, 1987), 48; Paul Robert Magocsi, "Luxembourgers," in Stephan Thernstrom, ed., *Harvard Encyclopedia of American Ethnic Groups* (Cambridge, Mass.: The Belknap Press of Harvard University Press, 1980), 686–89.

5. Henry A. Verslype, *The Belgians of Indiana: With a Brief History of the Land from Which They Came* (Nappanee, Ind.: Evangel Press, 1987), 23; Robert P. Swierenga, "Dutch," in *Harvard Encyclopedia of American Ethnic Groups*, 284–95; and Pierre-Henri Laurent, "Belgians," ibid., 179-81.

6. G. Kurgan-Van Hentenryk, "Belgian Emigration to the United States and Other Overseas Countries at the Beginning of the Twentieth Century," in *Two Studies on Emigration through Antwerp to the New World*, eds. G. Kurgan and E. Spelkens (Brussels: Center for American Studies, 1976), 9–49.

7. Compiled from data in Brian R. Mitchell, *European Historical Statistics, Seventeen Hundred Fifty to Nineteen Hundred Seventy* (New York: Columbia University Press, 1979), 29–34, 145.

8. This account relies heavily on the excellent book by Verslype, *Belgians of Indiana*. The author is an amateur historian who spent a lifetime among his countrymen in Mishawaka. For general overviews

of Belgian immigration, including brief references to Indiana, see Laurent, "Belgians," 179-81; Frank VandePitte, "Belgische immigranten in de Verenigde Staten, 1850–1920" (Unpublished licentiate thesis, Rijksuniversiteit Gent, 1988); and Gerrit Verrijken, "Aspecten van de emigratie naar Amerika, Inzonderheid de Verenigde Staten, vanuit Antwerpen (1856–1914)" (Unpublished licentiate thesis, 1984). Between 1850 and 1856 the Belgians shipped almost six hundred beggars and prisoners to the United States until American government protests stopped the practice. Most apparently went to Missouri; there is no evidence that any settled in Indiana. See R. Boumans, "Een onbekend aspect van de Belgische uitwijking naar Amerika: De gesubsidieerde emigratie van bedelaars en oud-gevangenen (1850–1856)," *Bulletin des Seances de l'Academie Royale des Sciences d'Outre-Mer* 11 (1956): 378–83.

9. Verslype, *Belgians of Indiana,* 35. County historians designate Andrew Peter as the first native Belgian to establish a home in a wilderness clearing that later became the town of Leopold, but they did not give his date of arrival. See Doris B. Leistner, "Perry County Ancestors," *Tell City News,* 22 Apr. 1991.

10. Verslype, *Belgians of Indiana,* 35–36; Charles Blanchard, ed., *History of the Catholic Church in Indiana,* 2 vols. (Logansport, Ind.: A. W. Bowen and Co., 1898), 1:190–203, esp. 193; Verrijken, "Aspecten van de emigratie," 163.

11. Verslype, *Belgians of Indiana,* 37–39.

12. Ibid., 49; Leistner, "Perry County Ancestors."

13. The George family hailed from Hachy, Belgium. The youngest son, Frank John George, after working as a stonemason for a time gained a minimal education and became a schoolteacher and eventually the Perry County school superintendent. Verslype, *Belgians of Indiana,* 38–39.

14. Ibid., 39.

15. Carl S. Pansaerts, "Big Barns and Small Houses: A Study of the Flemish-Belgians in a Rural County, Lyon County, Minnesota, 1880s–1940s" (M.A. thesis, University of Minnesota, 1989).

16. Verslype, *Belgians of Indiana,* 40; Ellen Sieber and Cheryl Ann Munson, *Looking at History: Indiana's Hoosier National Forest Region, 1600 to 1950* (Washington, D.C.: U.S. Forest Service, 1992), 8, 86.

17. VandePitte, "Belgische immigranten," 69, 100–1, 120–21; Verrijken, "Aspecten van de emigratie," 162–63.

18. Verslype, *Belgians of Indiana,* 33–35; Philemon D. Sabbe and Leon Buysse, *Belgians in America* (Tielt, Belgium: Lanno, 1960), 54–55.

19. *Biographical and Historical Souvenir for the Counties of Clark, Crawford, Harrison, Floyd, Jefferson, Jennings, Scott, and Washington, Indiana* (Chicago: John M. Gresham and Co., 1889), 67–68.

20. Verslype, *Belgians of Indiana,* 40.

21. VandePitte, "Belgische immigranten," 28, 45–46, 100–1, 134–38, 145–47. This work is full of detailed data on employment, wages, and living costs of Belgians in the United States.

22. *Indianapolis News,* 15 Nov. 1906.

23. Federal population census, Blackford County, 1930; VandePitte, "Belgische immigranten," 45–46.

24. Verslype, *Belgians of Indiana,* 41–42; Blanchard, ed., *History of the Catholic Church,* 1:294.

25. Verslype, *Belgians of Indiana,* 42–43.

26. Ibid., 43, citing a paper of Mary C. Sablon presented at the 1976 bicentennial celebration in Hartford City.

27. Father de Sceille was born in Sleydinge, the scion of one of the oldest and wealthiest families in the Belgian Diocese of Ghent. After serving as a pastor at Aalst and Hansbeke, he immigrated with two Dominicans, Theodore Van den Broek (a Hollander) and Adrain Van de Weyer. After serving as an itinerant priest in Indiana and

southern Michigan for three years, in 1835 he became the priest at Pokagon. Verslype, *Belgians of Indiana,* 45.

28. The Mishawaka families in 1860 were Deserdaue, Buysse, De Gryse, and Reyniers, and in South Bend the Smith and Vanderza families plus four singles, De Rue, Luskey, Sinkel, and Vanessche. Verslype, *Belgians of Indiana,* 47–48.

29. Ibid., 47.

30. *South Bend Tribune,* 20–21 July 1975; Janet Manspeaker and Reg Wagle, "Mishawaka as Melting Pot," in *A Mishawaka Mosaic: Mishawaka, Indiana, 1833–1983,* ed. David Eisen (Elkhart, Ind.: Bethel Publishing Co., 1983), 112–17.

31. Verslype, *Belgians of Indiana,* 48–54; VandePitte, "Belgische immigranten," 39. For 1870 the author accepts Verslype's careful tally of Belgians in St. Joseph County as more accurate than the census totals published in Table 2.

32. Verslype, *Belgians of Indiana,* 48–51; *South Bend Tribune,* 20–21 July 1975.

33. Verslype, *Belgians of Indiana,* 51–69, based on the author's careful analysis of Mishawaka city directories; *South Bend Tribune,* 20–21 July 1975.

34. Manspeaker and Wagle, "Mishawaka," 115; VandePitte, "Belgische immigranten," 101–2; Royal L. La Touche, *Chicago and Its Resources Twenty Years After, 1871–1891: A Commercial History Showing the Progress and Growth of Two Decades from the Great Fire to the Present Time* (Chicago: Chicago Times Company, 1892), 146–47.

35. Verslype, *Belgians of Indiana,* 140, 167, 168–84; Manspeaker and Wagle, "Mishawaka," 113.

36. Manspeaker and Wagle, "Mishawaka," 116–17; *South Bend Tribune,* 20–21 July 1975.

37. Verslype, *Belgians of Indiana,* 140, 150–55.

38. Ibid., 158–67, provides a longtime member's insights into the intricate practices of the Pigeon Club; Manspeaker and Wagle, "Mishawaka," 117.

39. Manspeaker and Wagle, "Mishawaka," 117; *South Bend Tribune,* 20–21 July 1975.

40. Verslype, *Belgians of Indiana,* 157, 140; Manspeaker and Wagle, "Mishawaka," 116–17; *South Bend Tribune,* 20–21 July 1975.

41. Verslype, *Belgians of Indiana,* 157–58, 112–13.

42. Ibid., 60, 187.

43. Ibid., 76; *South Bend Tribune,* 20–21 July 1975.

44. Verslype, *Belgians of Indiana,* 76–78.

45. The Reverend Julius Arthur Nieuwland (1878–1936) was born in Hansbeke, Belgium, and came to South Bend in 1880 with his parents. He graduated from Notre Dame in 1899 and was ordained a priest in the Congregation of Holy Cross. In 1904 he earned a Ph.D. degree from Catholic University of America and thereafter was professor of botany at Notre Dame (1904–18), and dean of the school of science and professor of organic chemistry (1918–36). He helped develop "Neoprene," an oil-resistant rubber. While a professor, he continued to be a "humble priest of God," hearing confessions in Flemish at St. Bavo's Church in Mishawaka and Sacred Heart of Jesus in South Bend. Verslype, *Belgians of Indiana,* 73–78, 119.

46. Ibid., 77–79; *Christian Intelligencer,* 21 Aug. 1907.

47. Verslype, *Belgians of Indiana,* 74–75, 150.

48. Ibid., 75, 124–26.

49. Ibid., 124–26.

50. Ibid., 127–31.

51. Ibid., 135–39.

52. James Paul Allen and Eugene James Turner, eds., *We the People: An Atlas of America's Ethnic Diversity* (New York: Macmillan, 1988), 58.

53. Verslype, *Belgians of Indiana*, 50–51, 82, 96.

54. Ibid., 292.

55. Compiled from data gathered by Verslype, ibid., 185–87. Belgian women married non-Belgian men twice as often as Belgian men married non-Belgian wives.

56. Ibid., 294.

57. Allen and Turner, eds., *We the People*, 58.

58. *Biographical and Historical Souvenir for the Counties of Clark, Crawford, Harrison, Floyd, Jefferson, Jennings, Scott, and Washington*, 203–6.

59. Jacob Van Hinte, *Netherlanders in America: A Study of Emigration and Settlement in the Nineteenth and Twentieth Centuries in the United States of America*, ed. Robert P. Swierenga, trans. Adriaan de Wit (Grand Rapids, Mich.: Baker Book House, 1985), 54–55. The Conewago colony numbered 170 families at its height, but then was utterly abandoned. Mary Lynn Spykerman Parker, "New Jersey to Pennsylvania to Kentucky to Indiana to Kansas," *Dutch Family Heritage Society Quarterly* 6, no. 1 (1992): 13–15; ibid., no. 2 (1992): 48–53.

60. Van Hinte, *Netherlanders in America*, 55; *History of Dearborn, Ohio, and Switzerland Counties, Indiana* (Chicago: Weakley, Harraman and Co., 1885), 1153.

61. *History of Dearborn, Ohio, and Switzerland Counties*, 168–69, 965–66. See Charles Minnick, sheriff of Porter County, in *Counties of Porter and Lake, Indiana* (Chicago: F. A. Battey and Co., 1882), 106; Parker, "New Jersey to Pennsylvania," lists all the known Conewago families and all the primary and secondary sources.

62. Van Hinte, *Netherlanders in America*, 56–57.

63. Ibid.

64. Henry S. Lucas, *Netherlanders in America: Dutch Immigration to the United States and Canada, 1789–1950* (Grand Rapids, Mich.: W. B. Eerdmans, 1989), 35–36.

65. Ibid., 36–37; Willem Beukma's Travel Diary, 1847–1863 (translated typescript, Heritage Hall Archives, Calvin College, Grand Rapids, Mich.).

66. Lucas, *Netherlanders in America*, 37, 235, 243–44; Beukma, Travel Diary; federal population census, Tippecanoe County, 1860.

67. These were the families of J. Bolman, Jelle DeBildt, J. DeJong, J. W. DeJong, Hein G. Holwerda, and Willem J. Jong. Lucas, *Netherlanders in America*, 37–38. Holwerda settled in Prairie Township, White County, north of Lafayette.

68. Van Hinte, *Netherlanders in America*, 119.

69. L. T. Boelkens and Martje J. Nieuwenhuis to Relatives, 16 Nov. 1860, Boelkens Letter Collection, Heritage Hall Archives, Calvin College.

70. Ibid.

71. Boelkens letter, 16 Aug. 1863, ibid.

72. Martje J. Nieuwenhuis to Melo Nieuwenhuis, [1866], ibid.; Anje L. Boelkens to Uncle and Aunt, [1866], ibid.

73. Christian Reformed Church, *100 Years of God's Grace, Lafayette, Indiana, 1865–1965* (Lafayette, Ind., 1965), 9. The descendants of John Anthrop (Entrop) of Rotterdam, who arrived in 1853, comprised one of the largest clans of Dutch Catholics. See "History of the Anthrop Family" (1929), typescript in possession of Mary G. Anthrop, Lafayette, Indiana.

74. Christian Reformed Church, *100 Years of God's Grace*. Jan Geerts Balkema, a carpenter, immigrated in 1850 with his family of six from Kloosterburen, Groningen. Boelkens, a blacksmith, immigrated from Uithuizermeeden, Groningen, in 1853 with a family of ten and first settled for several years in Wisconsin. See Robert P. Swierenga, *Dutch Emigrants to the United States, South Africa, South America, and Southeast Asia, 1835–1880: An Alphabetical Listing by Household Heads and Independent Persons* (Wilmington, Del.: Scholarly Resources, 1983), 9, 20. Balkema's home was at Seventeenth and Tippecanoe Avenue.

75. *100 Years*, 9–11; *History of Tippecanoe County and the Wabash Valley* (Dayton, Ohio: National Historical Association, Inc., 1928), 283. The area was in Ward 4 in 1860 and Ward 7 in 1900.

76. *100 Years*, 11–18; First Reformed Church, *100 Years, 1888–1988* (Lafayette, Ind., 1988), 3–9; *Christian Intelligencer*, 11 June 1890; "The Dexter Families," clipping from an unidentified newspaper from Boswell, Indiana. The Goodland congregation began with fifteen families (thirty-seven souls) in 1890, but it remained a "feeble church" without a regular pastor. Moreover, many of the twenty-five Dutch farm families in the area showed "little interest" in religious matters, and eventually in 1912 the Goodland RCA disbanded. The disappointing story can be pieced together from the Minutes, Classis of Wisconsin, Reformed Church in America, 1890–1912.

77. The data were compiled from the 1900 federal population census manuscripts. Twenty-three women were unable to speak English; ten had been in the United States less than ten years. In 1900, 425 were Dutch born and 811 were American born.

78. Marie Yoder, "The Balk Dutch Settlement Near Goshen, Indiana, 1853–1889," *Mennonite Historical Quarterly* 30 (Jan. 1956): 33–34; Lucas, *Netherlanders in America*, 247–48; Van Hinte, *Netherlanders in America*, 167–73.

79. Yoder, "Balk Dutch," 36; Van Hinte, *Netherlanders in America*, 170–71; Lucas, *Netherlanders in America*, 248.

80. See "Jared Defrees" biographical sketch in *Pictorial and Biographical Memoirs, Elkhart and St. Joseph Counties, Indiana* (Chicago: Goodspeed Bros., 1893), 362. The entry has some errors. For information on the various DeVrieses see Swierenga, *Dutch Emigrants to the United States*, 67–68.

81. See Hiram and Eva Ferverda family memoirs, "Early Beginnings," published in 1978, Heritage Hall Archives, Calvin College.

82. The 1865–69 arrivals were Bauke Ferwerda (Ferverda), the Wemyer family, John Belt, Jacob and Henry DeVries, Aye VanderVeer, Richard Pelsma, Klaas Duisterhout (changed to Darkwood), and Frederick Krull. 1880 federal population census, Elkhart County.

83. Yoder, "Balk Dutch," 38–42; Van Hinte, *Netherlanders in America*, 172–73.

84. Lucas, *Netherlanders in America*, 521.

85. Ferverda and Ferverda, "Early Beginnings," 3–4.

86. The Goshen Calvinists included the Klaaysens, Hoogenbooms, Blackports, Vanderriders, VanderMaases, Geenes, and Zylmans. The latter were likely Frisian. See 1900 federal population manuscript census, Elkhart County. The families all resided in Ward 4 of Goshen City.

87. Christian Reformed Church Yearbooks, 1905–35; Van Hinte, *Netherlanders in America*, 769, citing *De Grondwet*, 9 Dec. 1919.

88. The Jewish families were Louis Siegers, Martin Meyer, Henry Levy, brothers Isaac, J., and Sam Speelman, Isaac Solomon; and the singles were Samuel Boss and Jacob Speelman. Levy was born in England and Meyer in Hannover, and both had Dutch wives. Isaac Speelman and Solomon had English-born wives, which was common among Dutch-Jewish immigrants in the nineteenth century.

89. Superb local histories are Lance Trusty, *Town on the Ridge: A History of Munster, Indiana* (Hammond, Ind.: Regional Studies Institute, Purdue University Calumet, 1982); David Zandstra, "The Calumet Region," *Origins* 4, no. 1 (1986): 16–21; no. 2 (1986): 48–54. See also federal population censuses; Reformed Church in America Yearbooks, 1900, 1920, 1990; Christian Reformed Church Yearbooks, 1935, 1990; Munster Christian Reformed Church, *Diamond Jubilee*

*Anniversary Book, 1870–1945* (Munster, Ind., 1975), 1; Munster Christian Reformed Church, *Centennial of the First Christian Reformed Church, Munster, Indiana, 1870–1970* (Munster, Ind.,1970), 1; Trinity Reformed Church, *Dedication December 1, 1957* (Munster, Ind., 1957), 1. For Highland see Diamond Jubilee Committee, *Highland Indiana Diamond Jubilee, 1910–1985* (Highland, Ind., 1985); Henry Bakker, *Highland First Christian Reformed Church, Seventy-Five Years of History, 1908–1983* (Highland, Ind., 1983). The author also benefited from David Zandstra's detailed information about historic Munster in a letter of 14 June 1992.

90. *Diamond Jubilee,* 1.

91. Trusty, *Town on the Ridge,* 6–8. The seven founding family groups, who were living in North Township in 1860, were Jabaay, Munster, Kooy, Klootwyk, Slykhuis, Van Bodegraven, Bouwman, and an unmarried carpenter Jacob Kats.

92. Ibid., 14.

93. Ibid., 8, 16.

94. *Highland Indiana Diamond Jubilee,* 8; Bakker, *Highland,* 5–6.

95. Zandstra, "Calumet Region," 16–20.

96. Ibid., 51–53, provides a detailed description of onion set cultivation. See also David Zandstra, "The Dutch of Highland, Indiana," paper presented to the 1993 conference of the Association for the Advancement of Dutch-American Studies, Calvin College.

97. Trusty, *Town on the Ridge,* 16–17.

98. The Munster Christian School was established in 1906 and the Highland Christian School in 1909. See "A History of Highland Christian School," *Highland Christian School 75th Anniversary, 1909–1984* (Highland, Ind., 1984). Highland's charter stated that the instruction would be "according to the Calvinistic Principals [*sic*] of the tenets of the Christian Reformed Church, both in the Holland and the American Language." The entire charter is published in "Happy 75th Birthday Highland Christian School," Highland Historical Society *Newsletter* 7 (Feb. 1984), 4.

99. *Illinois Observer,* Apr. 1957.

100. First Christian Reformed Church Highland, *Fiftieth Anniversary, 1908–1958* (Highland, Ind., 1958), 9; Trusty, *Town on the Ridge,* 19–21.

101. Ernie Hernandez, *Ethnics in Northwest Indiana* (Gary, Ind.: Post-Tribune, 1984), 166–68; *Highland Indiana Diamond Jubilee,* 10–13; Nick and Joan Huizenga, "Surrounded by Witnesses: History of Nicholas and Joan Huizenga, Their Forebears, Their Children" (Typescript booklet, n.p., n.d.); "Highland Remembers Bartel Zandstra," Highland Historical Society *Newsletter* 6 (May 1983), 3. Other issues of this newsletter in the years 1983–87 contain articles, photographs, and stories of the Dutch in Highland.

102. "Strack & Van Til Celebrate 50 Years," Highland Historical Society *Newsletter* 9 (Oct. 1986), 5; full-page ad in *Highland Indiana Diamond Jubilee;* Zandstra, "Dutch of Highland," 10–11.

103. Paul W. Gates, *Landlords and Tenants on the Prairie Frontier: Studies in American Land Policy* (Ithaca, N.Y.: Cornell University Press, 1973), chapters 4 and 6.

104. *Centennial History of DeMotte, 1876–1976* (DeMotte, Ind., 1976), 13–14; *50th Anniversary of First Christian Reformed Church, DeMotte, Indiana, 1932–1982* (DeMotte, Ind., 1982).

105. Lucas, *Netherlanders in America,* 327–28; Van Hinte, *Netherlanders in America,* 553; *Christian Intelligencer,* 21 Feb. 1894; First Reformed Church [of DeMotte], *Centennial Booklet, 1893–1993* (DeMotte, Ind., 1993), 5–7.

106. *Christian Intelligencer,* 18 Apr. 1900; Minutes, Classis of Wisconsin, Reformed Church in America, 1895; Chicago Classis (RCA) Minutes, 1919–22, 1932–33, Joint Archives, Hope College, Holland, Michigan; "DeMotte Church Still Growing," *DeMotte Citizen,* undated clipping (ca. 1970); *The First Reformed Church, DeMotte, Indiana, 1893–1953; Seventy-Fifth Anniversary, 1893–1968, First Reformed Church DeMotte, Indiana; Fiftieth Anniversary, 1920–1970, The American Reformed Church, DeMotte, Indiana;* RCA Yearbooks, 1900, 1920; CRC Yearbook, 1935.

107. RCA Yearbook, 1990; CRC Yearbook, 1990, Heritage Hall, Calvin College, Grand Rapids, Michigan. The new Christian Reformed Church edifice built in 1955 seated 600 and served 134 families. *Illinois Observer,* Aug. 1955, Jan. 1956, Sept. 1958.

108. *The Banner,* 9 Aug. 1993.

109. Kathleen Van Nuys, "Dutch Influence Lives On," *Indianapolis News,* 7 Oct. 1977, reprinted in Kathleen Van Nuys, *Indy International* (Indianapolis: Indianapolis News, 1978), 9–11.

110. Christian Park Reformed Church, Indianapolis, Indiana, *Dedication Services, September 11–12, 1949;* Van Nuys, "Dutch Influence Lives On," 9; CRC Yearbook, 1991; federal population censuses, Marion County, 1930, 1980.

111. Van Nuys, "Dutch Influence Lives On," 10–11.

112. Gonner, *Luxembourgers,* 108–9, 114–15, 197–98; Magocsi, "Luxembourgers," 686–87.

113. Gonner, *Luxembourgers,* 54.

114. Ibid., 25–35.

115. Ibid., 60–73, 82–84.

116. Federal population census manuscripts, Perry and La Porte counties, 1860, 1880.

117. Gonner, *Luxembourgers,* 115–16, 196.

118. Ibid., 253–55.

119. Ibid., 275–77.

120. Bureau of the Census, *1980 Census of Population, Ancestry of the Population by State: 1980 Supplementary Report* (Washington, D.C.: Government Printing Office, 1983). The 1990 census question on ancestry, based on a sample, revealed thirteen times as many Dutch as Belgians claimed their heritage (198,589 and 14,942, respectively). See 1990 CPH-L-90, Table 1 "Selected Social Characteristics: 1990, Indiana," U.S. Department of Commerce, Bureau of the Census, Ethnic and Hispanic Branch, 1990 Census Special Tabulations.

# MIDDLE EASTERNERS

FRANK W. BLANNING

*Why so few arrivals? In part because the Middle Eastern area has a history that permeates the thinking, conversation, and general spirit of its people, and a continual consciousness of their historical roots discourages leaving.*

## Introduction

Since 1955, with the founding of the National Association of Arab-Americans, United States residents with ethnic ties to the region generally called the Middle East have been popularly identified as Arab Americans. Both designations might be confusing. The area is referred to by the British as the Near East, by the French as the Near Orient, and by the United Nations as Eastern Asia. Logically thinking of an Arab as a person from the region called Arabia, we know that immigrants from Egypt, Palestine, Lebanon, and Syria do not have ethnic ties to the land of Arabia, although those countries do use the Arabic language. For some clarity then, using language to define the immigrants, Americans today call those originally from the above countries Arab Americans. Those few who came to America from Middle Eastern Afghanistan, Turkey, and Iran, where languages other than Arabic are used, are today identified as Afghan Americans, Turkish Americans, Iranian Americans, Armenian Americans, and Kurdish Americans.

According to United States census documents prior to World War II, Middle Easterners were a small percentage of the immigrants who came to the United States and to Indiana; Europeans made up the bulk of new Americans. The 1880 census for Indiana reported only one Palestinian living in Marion County, one Egyptian residing in Vanderburgh County, and three Turks and four Persians in other counties. The 1890 census reported the Indiana population as being 2.5 million persons, with 216 individuals having Middle East ancestry. No foreign born were identified as being from a country in the Middle East.[1] In 1898 the *Indianapolis News* reported the country of origin of steerage passengers arriving in New York. Of 905 bound for Indiana, 34 arrived from "Turkey in Asia," the name given to the Middle East region at that time.[2] The *Indianapolis Sun* in 1910 informed its readers that Indiana's foreign born spoke twenty-five different languages, but it did not identify the Middle East languages of Arabic, Afghan, Pashtu, Persian, Farsi, or Turkish in its listing.[3]

Why so few arrivals? In part because the Middle Eastern area has a history that permeates the thinking, conversation, and general spirit of its people, and a continual consciousness of their historical roots discourages leaving. It holds them, and the regional culture gives them a level of comfort. "If history can be defined as mankind's recorded past, then the Middle East has had more history than any other part of the world. . . . The main breakthroughs to civilization occurred in the Middle East."[4] A piece of land provides food, but more than basic sustenance, land gives Middle Easterners a feeling of belonging to a secure and stable place. Those who came first to the United States were primarily from a landless Christian minority. These immigrants found employment, friendship, and support from similarly landless Christian immigrants who recently, and quickly, had become prosperous Americans. Economic and upward social mobility came rapidly. The first who came made quick adjustments, joining the American working class. Estimating from census figures, city and county historical sources, and ethnic-oriented stories printed in city and county newspapers, it appears that the number of Indiana residents with Middle East ancestry in 1920 was around 3,600.[5]

Arriving in New York the immigrants stayed in the East where late-nineteenth-century United States industrial and business expansion provided quick employment, and where established fellow Middle East immigrants provided

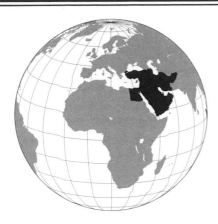

friendly settling-in assistance. The American westward expansion caught the attention of a few, and Chicago and Detroit were their first stopping points. Those who later moved on into Indiana migrated into an area with a triangular pattern, with Chicago, Detroit, and central Indiana the triangle points. Some came westward via the Ohio River. Arriving at Switzerland County by way of Cincinnati, and to Clark and Jefferson counties via Louisville, Syrians from the Levant moved north and west to Rush, Henry, Wayne, Monroe, and Johnson counties. Slow northern and westward movement continued, and from 1890 to 1915 the counties of the middle part of Indiana, the towns of Fort Wayne and Terre Haute, and then Indianapolis, had small concentrations of Middle Easterners. Bloomington and Monroe County attracted a few, and one or two others settled in other southern Indiana counties bordering the Ohio River.

Middle East immigration virtually ceased when restrictive United States admission quotas were imposed in 1924. Later, following the World War II period, restrictions were eased. Admitted were persons from southern Europe, Asia, Africa, and the Middle East who had American relatives or who possessed skills that American officials believed would be valuable and needed. The Immigration and Nationality Act of 1965 gave preference to professionals, and a number of medical doctors immigrated. Information available from the 1960 census "Ancestry of Population in Indiana" report put the Middle East figure at 5,619; by 1990 the figure was 8,911.[6]

The 1960 to 1990 increase in Middle Eastern population also has been attributed to factors other than the easing of quotas. Following the end of World War II American economic expansion could supply work opportunities. Indiana colleges and universities attracted foreign graduate students, some from the Middle East, who sought professional and technical education and training. International exchange scholarship and fellowship programs, funded in part by both the United States and foreign government academic and economic development grants, were made available to both scholars and trainees. Still, among the many immigrants coming to the United States after 1948, comparatively few were Middle Easterners. Indiana, Illinois, and Michigan received only 25,000, although 331,000 immigrated to other states between 1948 and 1985. More than half were Christian, another third were Muslim.[7]

Unlike the nineteenth- and early-twentieth-century immigrants, the midcentury arrivals were primarily an educated elite. However, as with the earlier, more humbly circumstanced immigrants, there was some hesitation about leaving their homeland. A Syrian, who came to Rushville in 1945, told friends that his father had been against his leaving. The father said his sons would be needed to help the family at home and to provide for the parents' old age security. Others heard rumors of social and political problems in America and read news reports of the hardships some new Middle Eastern ethnic Americans encountered.

Having few coreligionists in the United States and knowing America's Judeo-Christian foundation and its sectarian religious structure, most Muslims saw no sense in leaving their generally safe place of familiar Islamic laws and customs. Islam is the predominant religion of the Middle East, and it is the official state religion in almost all of the region. The United States, with its separation of church and state, is nominally Judeo-Christian. Despite a small influx of Middle East Muslims to middle America after 1950 and evidence of an increasing Muslim presence, they remained an American minority. Each year the Syrian Orthodox Church in Indianapolis has a food festival that attracts several thousand people, 85 percent of whom are ethnic Christian Middle Easterners from all over Indiana.

*The Arab display at the International Festival, Gary, ca. 1956–57.*

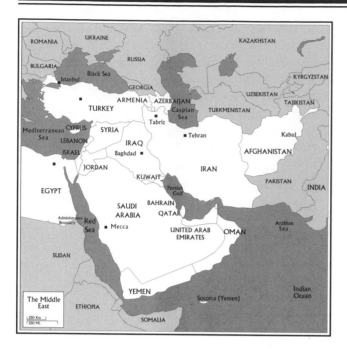

The Middle East

Today a supermarket in Bloomington, as well as grocery stores in other Indiana cities, have sections devoted to Middle East food. They are popular with Muslims, Christians, and Jews. There are restaurants serving Mediterranean specialties in several urban areas. Indiana Muslims, Middle Eastern Jews, and Christians share an identification with a common geographical origin as well as their religious heritage. The lists of medical professionals in Indiana hospitals contain many Middle Eastern names, and scholars from the region are found in research and teaching positions in Indiana colleges and universities.

Some tourists and students came to Indiana from the nations of Saudi Arabia, Kuwait, Iraq, Yemen, and the Arab Emirates. A few tourists applied for and received residence, as did a small number of students.

The nation of Israel has a population made up primarily of first- and second-generation immigrants. Those who leave for the United States are listed as coming from their original homelands and are included in another chapter of this history.

## The People

The Middle East is perceived by many as a puzzling place of mystery and intrigue: a region enveloped in romance, the excesses of rich rulers, and the corruptions of dictatorial political leaders. It is a region of extremes, where great wealth and grinding poverty, tribal rivalry and regional loyalty, and small productive fields and endless desert exist side by side. It bears a long history of friction and suffering: "A place wracked with chronic and irreconcilable tensions."[8] Indiana residents had some

knowledge of the Turkish Muslim people through Gen. Lew Wallace. A Crawfordsville, Indiana, native, the author of *Ben-Hur* was minister plenipotentiary and envoy extraordinary of the United States to Turkey in the 1880s, from which he sent long letters to friends and publications in Indiana.[9] His reports included historical documentation and anecdotes covering the more than four centuries of Ottoman rule in the central Middle East. Wallace traveled through much of the Ottoman territory, the traditional "Middle Ground" between East and West, on the Great Silk Route.

The Middle East is known also for important contributions to art, architecture, literature, entertainment, athletics, government, communication, business, and industry. The traveling exhibits of the treasures of Tutankhamen and the art of the Mamelukes show long-practiced art and craft skills, as do the jewel collections of Tocpaki. The Great Pyramids, the rock-cut structures of Petra, and the mountaintop buildings of the Afghans and the Iranians are beacons for architectural students. Ancient writings show sophisticated civil service and industrial organization. Today Middle Easterners fill key world positions; one, Dr. Butros Butros Ghali, an Egyptian, is secretary general of the United Nations. In the United States, former Senators James Abourezk and James Abdnor and the 1993 Senate Majority Leader George Mitchell claim Middle Eastern ancestry. Diplomat Philip Habib, poet Khalil Gilbran, and former New Hampshire governor and onetime presidential chief of staff John Sununu are among Americans of Middle East background.

Hoosier educational institutions, particularly in higher education, have Arab-American scholars of international reputation, many of whom immigrated since 1950. There are skilled ethnic Middle Eastern medical doctors in Indiana hospitals and medical schools: Dr. William Nasser is a distinguished Indiana cardiologist, and Dr. Homayoon Shidnia, a physician born in Iran, is an assistant director of the radiation-oncology department at the Indiana University Medical Center in Indianapolis. Afghan immigrant Dr. Sami Ahmadsai is a noted northern Indiana physician, Dr. Karim Mushref is a family physician in Fort Wayne, and Dr. Assef Rahmany practices in Highland. An ethnic Egyptian, Dr. Hassan El Shami, is on the Indiana University folklore faculty, and Dr. Ilya Harik, originally from Lebanon, is a distinguished political scientist there. Indiana architect Mazen Ayoubi is Kurdish. Dr. George Irani, from Lebanon, is a social scientist at Franklin College. Dr. M. Nazif Shahrani, an ethnic Afghan, teaches anthropology at Indiana University and directs its Middle East Studies program. There are two American Afghans, Dr. Zarjon Baha and Professor Sayyed M. Kazem, on the Purdue University engineering faculty. Ethnic Turks, too, can be found in various Indiana educational institutions. From 1985 to 1991 Professor Salih Altoma served as chairman of Indiana University's Department of Near Eastern Languages and Cultures. Indiana's list of prominent ethnic Middle Easterners is long.

## Syrians and Lebanese

"The January 2, 1920, issue of the [Terre Haute] Tribune carried advertisements for four Syrian grocery stores, all friendly competitors. . . . Geo. Nasser & Son had sugar-cured bacon for 32 cents a pound. . . . Over at Azar's Grocery a customer could purchase beef steak for 12 cents a pound. . . . Enterprise Market was offering three boxes of Red Cross macaroni for 25 cents. . . . Republic Meat Market had . . . fresh sausage for 15 cents a pound. . . . Most of the eleven Syrian grocery stores still established in Terre Haute [in 1975] are owned and operated by first generation Americans who learned the grocery store business by working in their families' stores."[10]

In the late nineteenth and early twentieth centuries, Christian Syrians from the Mount Lebanon area constituted the largest group of immigrants from the Middle East to the United States. They still constitute a majority. In a 1990 study of the half million Middle East immigrants, it was found that "over 125,000 were Lebanese Maronites (affiliated with the Roman Catholic Church); there were also 100,000 Greek Orthodox; 50,000 Melkites (a combination of Roman Catholic and Greek Orthodox), 25,000 Moslems, 10,000 Protestants, and 140,000 unaffiliated."[11]

Why did they leave the Middle East? In a minority there, Syrian Christians lived comfortably with the Muslim majority. Still, there were religious, political, and social tensions. "As followers of . . . honored, if lesser, prophets,

*William and Latefee Kassis with sons George, Charles, and Mose in their Kassis grocery store, 220 Wabash Avenue, Terre Haute.*

Christians and Jews enjoyed a wide measure of toleration under the jurisdiction of their own religious hierarchies, although their communities were more heavily taxed as the price they paid for protection by the Muslim army."[12] By 1890 there were other ethnics, coming primarily from uncertainty about safety under the continuing protection of a weakening Muslim Ottoman Empire.

Travelers in the Middle East told stories of wealth and work opportunities in America. American Christian foreign missionary societies were working in Syrian schools and medical centers, encouraging good scholars to study in the United States. Some of the students had learned to use the English language in Christian missionary schools; others had gained a familiarity with "foreign ways" working for Europeans. "In Aleppo [Syria], where European merchants lived [during the Ottoman period], Christians acted as their [the Europeans] intermediaries, helping them buy goods for export and distribute those brought in from Europe; Syrian Christians were important in the trade between Damietta and the Syrian coast."[13]

Single men usually immigrated first, sending for wives and families as soon as they could. The earliest Indiana arrivals found that peddling, requiring little investment, was a fast way to make money. The first Syrian peddler was a man named Francis Riszk, and he peddled as far south as Indianapolis. Thirty-one peddlers went to Alexandria. Syrians found work in the glass factories of the Fort Wayne region and settled there. They were from the Saydnaya district of Syria and encouraged others in the Old Country to join them. One went from Fort Wayne to Winchester to start a dry goods store. In 1892 David and Saada Kafoure of Indianapolis opened a dry goods business, and Najeeb and David Kafoure were dry goods peddlers.[14] Other Syrians settled in northern Indiana, opening stores, restaurants, and small manufacturing shops, some of which are still operating as family businesses. Most of the first Syrian specialty stores in Indianapolis, such as Nick Shaheen's Oriental Rug Emporium on the Circle and Dayan's Linen Store, operated by a Jewish Syrian, are no longer in business. Kafoure's store on Willard Street, near the present Eli Lilly offices, opened in 1892 and closed fifty years later.

Newly arriving Syrians generally did not move westward from eastern coastal cities; the few who did move west settled in the larger urban areas of Pennsylvania, Michigan, Illinois, and Minnesota. "From 1910 through 1930 . . . over 88 percent of the Syrians lived in or near urban centers, almost half of them on the East Coast. Of the remainder, about 2 percent farmed and the rest were businessmen in small towns or rural areas."[15] Those who came to Indiana first joined earlier immigrants.

In 1891 Iskander Freije, a Syrian, brought the first Arabian horses to America to exhibit at the Chicago World's Fair. He remained in the Chicago area after the exhibition, and between 1893 and 1915 many of his former Syrian neighbors and their families joined him. A short comment in the *Indianapolis Star* noted that "David Frieje, a naturalized Syrian citizen of Indianapolis, is anxiously awaiting the arrival of his wife Martha, whom he left in Palestine eight years ago, and his 7-year-old daughter, Salomey, whom he has never seen."[16] Other Freijes (Friejes) prospered in the villages and cities of Indiana.

In the later years the pattern of receiving families, neighbors, and friends continued. A number of new arrivals chose to settle in Indianapolis because it was the railroad and warehousing center of the United States. Others moved to regions of mid-Indiana where there were often small manufacturing businesses.

Syrian names were sometimes Anglicized: Hanna became John, Youssef became Joseph, and Fadallah became Fred. Kafoure was and continues to be a family name prominent in Indianapolis as are Osman, Neiman, George, and Malouf. In a family history the late Michael Kafoure wrote, "It is here we adopted Americanized spelling of the name Kfouri to Kfourey, Kafourey and finally Kafoure." In a later chapter, edited for the family by Michael's brother William, he tells of the reasons they left the simple life of their Syrian town of Talia. "Word of a new 'Garden of Eden' across the ocean reached Talia and to some it was their door to a new life.... They could not see through the ... thousands of miles over the ocean that separated them, the unknown culture and the people and their language. And to top it all, it took 30 days to cross the Atlantic Ocean. But they came."[17]

Peddling continued as a major source of Syrian employment in Indiana up to the 1920s. Peddlers in the South Bend area who had saved some money emulated Chicago Syrians and established peddler material supply stores for others. Terre Haute was particularly attractive to new immigrants, in part because it welcomed and helped them. In 1907 George and David Kafoure opened a grocery store there, staked to grocery supplies and fifty dollars in cash by Anton Hulman, Sr., proprietor of Hulman's Wholesale Grocery. The Kafoures called their store "The D and G Grocery," located at 4th and Sycamore. Within twenty years there were sixty Syrian groceries in Terre Haute. "No big chain grocery could compete, their customers were too loyal," says Syrian food expert Helen Corey in an interview. Corey's articles and books about Middle Eastern foods keeps contemporary cooks aware of Syrian delicacies.[18]

Syrian women participated in the peddling trade, successfully distributing sewing and other handiwork supplies to farm women. "My Grandmother peddled dresses, kitchen stuff, and spices," relates one Syrian. "Extended family enterprises were common, and the pooling of funds, thrifty living practices, and long working hours built family bank accounts. This allowed for the sending of money for passage to relatives in Syria."

Syrian immigrants stressed acculturation and the use of English, but in Terre Haute the use and preservation of the Arabic language in the home and at social or church events was encouraged. Peddling, considered a temporary occupation, ended when enough money was accumulated to set up a business. A home in a community with accessible schools was one of the first investments a family made. Children, following secondary schooling, worked at factory employment or enrolled in higher educational professional programs, preferably medicine and engineering. The first Syrian doctor, a general practitioner named Dr. Waheeb Zarick, started a Marion County practice in 1920. Today the practice of medicine continues to be a sought after profession by Syrians as well as other ethnic Middle Eastern Americans.

"We are like the thousands of other Americans of Lebanese and Syrian heritage," writes Anthony R. Abraham of Michigan City in a public letter distributed to his compatriots. "[We] quietly pursue daily activity ... accomplishing deeds of community and religious good without the blare of personal trumpets, or the razzle-dazzle of publicity releases."[19] The new immigrants and their progeny were known by their Indiana neighbors as activists for neighborhood causes and regular attendees at school events. There were forty-six Middle Eastern names on the roles of the Indiana militia that went off to World War I, and descendants proudly boast that criminal court records in Indiana did not show a single Syrian name in that first fifty-year period. The legacy of good participative citizenship continues to this day. In 1940 George Riszk, a building contractor, donated land and equipment for a park on East 30th Street in Indianapolis; the building on the site was named the Northeast Community Center.

Although rapidly absorbed into the life of Indiana communities, Syrians maintained their Middle Eastern religious practices. In the 1990s religion remains a major source of personal and collective ethnic expression. Most Syrians and Lebanese in Indiana are either Christian Maronites or communicants in the Syrian Eastern Orthodox Christian Church, and in central Indiana today there are six Eastern Orthodox churches organized and operating. Syrian and Lebanese Christians find the Roman Catholic Church and Roman Catholicism also appropriate for worship in the absence of an Orthodox church, and thus are never without a "church home."

*St. George Syrian Orthodox Church, 28th and Sherman, Indianapolis, founded in 1926. This photograph, ca. 1932, shows the visiting Metropolitan Germanos Shahadi and to his right Father John Corey, pastor of the church.*

Christian family life, family customs, and family values, which were developed long before the time of their arrival in America, are preserved and strengthened in their religious lives.

Family life and kinship, a source of ethnic strength for Indiana Syrians, also blunts their total assimilation and loss of identity. Alice Mesalam of Indianapolis remembers this very well. Loyalty to their adopted land, to new and old friends, and to each other is one of the family treasures she relates in a memoir. She writes, "Dad and his brothers settled in the Elwood area, because that part of the state had a natural gas boom . . . and peddling was good. They peddled until they had enough money to open a grocery store. Dad and Uncle George opened one together, on the corner of South L Street. Uncle George's family lived next to the store, we lived a block away." She tells of the second floor of her home. "Dad fixed his own altar. He hung his Icons, had a red silk cloth draped over them, and a red votive light. Each night he would read his bible there, before his beloved Icons. . . . I don't remember of Dad ever giving us a beating, but his look, when displeased, was more than enough. We were not abused, but each of us were expected to go to the store after school and help out. . . . Easter was always a special time for Dad, the best of times for all of us. We would boil and dye eggs a deep red with onion skins, and then test them to make sure there were plenty of strong ones. On Easter Sunday, when company would come, we would beat our eggs against those of our guests to see who had the strongest. Which eggs would crack first? . . . This was a time for Mom to make Baklava. She would have the sheets of dough all over the kitchen tables."[20]

The 1924 Johnson-Reed Immigration Act allowed one hundred Syrians a year to enter the United States. However, with a substantial base of Syrians already installed in Indiana, Syrians were not totally thwarted in adding to their numbers. Syrian Americans traveled to Syria, married, and brought their brides home on a "brides quota" visa. Others came in through Canada as tourists, secured extensions, and finally were able to qualify for residence in Indiana.

*Interior of St. George Christian Orthodox Church, Indianapolis.*

Family togetherness, practiced in Syria, was a way of keeping expenses down. "My father and my uncle, the Ajamie brothers, lived together on Willard Street in Indianapolis," said Marie Ajamie in an interview. "They married brides chosen by their families, and with my brothers, sisters, and cousins we all lived together under one roof." She noted that the rent was three dollars a week, and when their landlord tried to raise it to five dollars the family went into mourning. The landlord relented. Brides for single men were sometimes chosen by their families in Syria. Indiana-born Bill Kafoure's father wrote home to Lebanon that he wanted a wife, and a reply said that a man in Beirut had four lovely daughters. "He answered, 'Fine, send one to me.' My mother arrived in New York, they were married in the Orthodox Cathedral there, and then they returned to Terre Haute. They stayed with friends in separate places, and consummated the marriage three days after arrival and after a wedding party."[21]

## The Afghans

Indiana has always counted ethnic Afghans among its population, according to Hussain M. Farzad, an administrator at Indiana University and chairperson of

the Afghan Cultural Association of Indiana. "At a celebration [in 1991] of Eid-ul-Fitr,[22] a holiday marking the end of the fasting month of Ramadan, there was a large gathering of Muslims at Lafayette," he recalls. "There was a good representation of American Afghans in the assemblage, one working in the Capitol building in Indianapolis and several others who said they came from families which had migrated to northern Indiana from Chicago after World War II."[23]

In discussing his native land, Farzad noted that over 99 percent of the population are Sunni or Shia Muslim, though several thousand are Hindus and Sikhs, Jews, and Christian Armenians living mostly in urban centers. He said Afghanistan is a mountainous country of about 650,000 square kilometers (the size of Texas or France) sitting at the crossroads of the great civilizations and empires of the Middle East, Central Asia, and the Indian subcontinent. The ethnic variety of the country's population (about 1.5 million people) reflects its geographic location. "The largest group are the Pashtuns, or 'Afghans,' who make up roughly half . . . speaking a language called Pashto, related to Persian but quite distinct. . . .The second largest linguistic group is the Persian speakers . . . northeast of Kabul [the capital] and known as the Tajiks. In the far north are about three million Turkic speakers, Turkomans and Uzbeks. . . . The remote massif of central Afghanistan is home to the Hazaras, who speak a variety of Persian called Hazaragi."[24] The Hindu Kush, with peaks as high as 25,000 feet, go through the center of the country, shutting off people in their valleys during long winters of deep snows.

The Afghan people's origin is unknown. "They first appear in history . . . around the year 1000."[25] In the fifteenth century they were ruled by the Mogul Dynasty, in the eighteenth by the Iranians and the Turks, and in the nineteenth the British attempted to move in but failed to fully implement a conquest. The war that made international headlines in the 1980s was a result of internal conflict, with the Soviet Union supporting an unpopular regime. Afghans have a history of independent living in mountain and valley enclaves; early Afghan immigrants, mostly artisans, continued their independent living practice in Indiana.

In 1966 a long association with Indiana University began. President Herman B Wells had a personal friendship with Afghan educator Dr. Toror Etemadi, president of Kabul University. Also, Wells had developed a collegial relationship with economic scholar Dr. Baqi Zai when he was doing research at the university in 1950. Zai married an Indiana woman and returned to Afghanistan, where he became a leading government figure. On a visit to Afghanistan, Wells arranged for an exchange program aimed at developing university administrators, and the Indiana University School of Education began an extensive program of cooperative training. First, Dr. William Porter, then Professor Christian Jung and Dean Thomas Schreck, all of Bloomington, lived in Kabul as resident directors. Economist Dr. Taulman Miller followed. Afghan educational leaders, primarily well-educated members of the Afghan elite, conducted research in Indiana and did study for advanced degrees, and Afghan students were a part of the international educational exchange programs of the 1960s and 1970s.[26]

In 1978 a Marxist regime came to power in Afghanistan, which precipitated an exodus of several thousand people. Most settled in Los Angeles, Washington, D.C., and New York City, where there were concentrations of Afghan Americans. However, Indiana's reputation as a welcoming and warmly accepting state, made during the Indiana University-Afghan exchange years, was not forgotten. Several engineers came to Indiana at that time and found employment in technical fields. Others entered the arts or education. For example, Parwin M. Farzad became a costumer for the opera program at the Indiana University School of Music; Dr. Jumaqul Bandawal, of Muncie, a consultant for Indiana primary and secondary schools; Dr. Mohamed Hussein Razi, an international student adviser at Vincennes University; and Dr. Youssef Ayoubi, a leading accountant in Indianapolis.

*Nabil Jadallah and his sister Jamila Jadallah wear their native Jordanian clothing at the 1961 International Fashion Revue in Gary.*

## The Palestinians

"Living in Beirut as a stateless person for most of my growing up years, . . . I did not feel I was an Arab, a Lebanese, . . . or 'a southern Syrian.' I was a Palestinian."[27] "Palestinians are everywhere in the world."[28] They have been in Indiana for generations, although they were not always identified by their fellow Hoosiers as Palestinians. In Palestine they suffered under many of the same masters as did their central city of Jerusalem, which "since the inception of Christianity. . . has been subject to more than ten foreign dominations."[29] With a never-ending love for their land, Palestinians often ask the question, "Whose country is this, anyway?"[30] In the year 860 B.C., according to one Old Testament scholar, "its boundaries extended from the base of the Golan Heights of present-day Syria westward to the Mediterranean Sea, then southward to Gaza, . . . north to beyond the eastern edge of the Dead Sea, and finally northwest to touch Lake Tiberias at the foot of the Golan."[31] A contemporary commentator writes, "Palestine, though small in size, has the diversity of a continent."[32]

Palestinians also cherish a unique culture that has absorbed invaders but has not lost its heritage. Phoenician trader patterns, Persian artistry, Judeo-Christian insights, and Muslim devotion are woven into the Palestinian experience.

In Indiana there are Palestinian Christians, Palestinian Muslims, and Palestinian Jews. Counted as Syrian or Lebanese by the census after 1960, the 1990 Census Special Tabulations lists 471 Hoosiers as Palestinians.[33] Indiana Palestinians say their own tabulation sources count many more.[34] They are found in Indiana medical practice, public service positions, business establishments, and educational institutions. Among them is Fred E. Musleh, who heads a consulting engineering firm; Mina Khoury, an international trade entrepreneur; and the Banura family, which operates one of the most popular and successful restaurant businesses in Indianapolis.

The first Palestinians to come were Christian; the later arrivals (post–1949) are about 60 percent Muslim. "[Palestinian] immigrants continue to arrive today and constitute the largest group of post–World War II immigrants [from the Middle East]."[35]

## The Turks

Turkey, then the center of the Muslim Ottoman Empire, sent few immigrants to the United States in the nineteenth or early twentieth centuries. The Ottomans of those years, experiencing the end of what had been a vital Middle Eastern political, military, and cultural entity, were impoverished. To have any reasonable means of support for their families, Turkish men sought year by year work outside Turkey, moving to Islamic countries or to southern Europe.

Why did so few Turks join the 1880–1920 flood of immigrants to America? Those who did cross the Atlantic Ocean were accustomed to a cultural pattern unique to the geographical and cultural setting of their home region of Anatolia, a peninsula located between the Mediterranean, Black, and Aegean seas. They quickly felt homesick and lonely in the United States, and as soon as they could many went home to the way of life and language they understood. Before 1935 there were a few itinerant Turkish laborers in the South Bend–Michigan City area. Although little is known about them from recorded Indiana population data, it is known that they lived in barrack-type housing and had little contact with their neighbors.

The Ottoman Empire (1299–1922) enveloped the Balkans, most of southwest Asia, the North African coast, and Turkish Anatolia. The United States census of 1860 counted Turkish immigrants in the three categories of Turkish language speakers, Muslims, and citizens of the Ottoman Empire. Only fifteen people in the United States were recorded as "Turkish Language Speakers" in 1860. "Of about 360,000 immigrants from Ottoman Turkey in the period 1820–1950, probably less than 10 percent were Turks. Moreover, the rate of return migration was exceptionally high among Turks: of some 22,000 Turks who came between 1899 and 1924, an estimated 86 percent went back to Turkey."[36]

English language usage proved a barrier Turks could not easily cross. They were also bewildered by the unfamiliar American working habits and the unfriendliness they encountered. One historian, Oscar Handlin, writes in a commentary on Turkish ethnic adjustment, that they "formed lonely little cliques wherever a few gathered." They were predominantly young men staying together in large or small groupings, eating Turkish food on feast days, and praying in corners of rooms in their homes or in available mosques. "Observers of Turkish-American communities in the 1940s and 1950s reported that most had retained their Turkish way of life without acquiring the lifestyle of their new country beyond the requirements of their jobs. Prior to the 1930s the vast majority of Turkish immigrants were motivated by economic incentives and moved from the lower strata of Turkish society to the lower strata of American society; very few, if any, achieved prosperity. Until the 1950s no Turks attained distinction in any field in the United States, except for several wrestlers."[37]

The establishment of the Republic of Turkey in 1923 caused a considerable increase in the return migration of Turkish Americans. World War I and frequent regional and internal conflicts in Turkey had decimated the male population, and the new government encouraged citizens to return home. In addition, the Immigration Act of 1924 set a yearly admission quota of one hundred for Turks entering the United States. Those few allowed immigration cards were primarily skilled workers or special professionals who had some English language facility.

In 1950 modified United States immigration regulations permitted entry visas to graduate students and skilled technicians. The government of Turkey became an important postwar partner of the Allies, and a brigade of Turkish soldiers fought with American soldiers as a part of the United Nations force in the Korean War in the 1950s. Robert College, an American missionary endeavor located near Istanbul, had for several generations provided an English-language liberal arts education for gifted young people of the region; an American technical college was established in Ankara; and American-Turkish military agreements gave additional exposure to American institutions. The Turkish-American community in Indiana encouraged and supported scholars arriving in the United States, and associations of Turkish-American engineers, agronomists, and medical doctors arranged with Indiana's universities, business firms, and hospitals for exchanges with colleagues in Turkey. Erdogan Kumco, a distinguished professor at Ball State University in Muncie, is a Turkish American well known in international academic circles. Ilhan Bosgoz is a professor at Indiana University. Although those who have come and stayed since 1950 have added a great deal to Hoosier life, Turkish Americans are still not found in great numbers in Indiana.

## Iranians

With a population of about thirty-six million, there are eight identifiable cultural groups in Iran, at least seven religions, and four recognized languages, plus several local colloquial dialects of Farsi, the official language. The Shia branch of Islam is the dominant religious faith. "In the broadest sense, then, Iranian is a national designation, not an ethnic one. A more restricted meaning of the term would be 'a person whose mother tongue is Persian,' which would include Zoroastrians, Jews, and most Bahais, as well as Muslims, and exclude such Muslim peoples as

Turks, Kurds, Baluchi, and Arabs."[38] Iran, the Persia of history, is neither an Arab nor an Arabic-speaking nation. Iranian scholars have long worked freely in European centers of learning and have exchanged ideas with academics there for centuries. Geographic location gives Iran a trading base which in turn continually brings in foreigners and foreign influence.

Iranians came to the United States in very small numbers before 1900. Census documents show that barely 130 entered in the years 1842 to 1903, and there were too few for listing in the years 1904 to 1924. This changed in the three decades following World War II. In 1976 there were an estimated 34,000 Iranians who immigrated. According to the *Harvard Encyclopedia of American Ethnic Groups,* "Immigrants from Iran have been predominantly individuals or individual families." Indiana colleges and universities were the destination of students. Medical centers, industrial areas, and research centers in South Bend, Terre Haute, Fort Wayne, and Indianapolis attracted others. Permanent resident status was requested by a significant number of those who came temporarily, several of whom were skilled professional persons. Dr. Hormoz Bromand, one of the first Iranian scientists to come to Indiana, was a food chemist and meat standards expert at the Stark and Wetzel meat plant in Indianapolis. In addition, he started two consulting companies for research in food and nutrition. Dr. Cyrus Behrozzi is associate dean of the School of Social Work at Indiana University, with offices in Indianapolis.

Iranians are historically an individualistic people who have long associated with foreign cultures. In Indiana they have not joined ethnic groups or Iranian associations. Iranian Muslims have followed Islamic traditions in their homes and worshiped in mosques, but rather than forming "Iranian Medical" or "Iranian Engineer" groups they have been active in American professional groups, labor unions, and local school boards. Iranian Americans have been generous in giving both time and money to the Red Cross and a wide range of charities. There is a Society for the Promotion of Persian Culture in Indianapolis, and events such as the celebration of the traditional festival that marks the beginning of the Persian New Year (called "Now Ruz" in the Persian language) are attended by Iranians and their neighbors and friends.

There are incomplete records of immigration to the United States by some of the Iranian border minorities, including Armenians, Jews, and Assyrians. In the nineteenth and early part of the twentieth centuries, groups of these immigrants traveled together; what arrival information exists indicates that Armenians made up the largest percentage of early Iranian ethnic groups. Affiliation of Armenian, Assyrian, and Jewish Hoosiers with church or social groups already active in Indiana made moot their identification as ethnic Iranians.

The decades of the 1950s and 1960s witnessed increased contacts between Iran and the United States. The strategic location of Iran, Iranian resources, and Iran's history of international commercial intercourse brought Americans and American businesspeople to Iran. In turn, professional and economic opportunities in the mid-1950s drew Iranians to Indiana. Some came for temporary employment but decided to stay once they had become somewhat established. Applications for permanent residence multiplied. Two Iranian engineers started a consulting firm in Lafayette, invited colleagues to join them, and, as their success grew, so did the ranks of Iranian immigrants. Professional counterparts in Iran, fiancées, and relatives of the new Hoosier American Iranians soon joined them. Of 30,262 Iranians who entered the United States between 1945 and 1976, 2,373 were physicians.[39] Marriage to United States citizens and the start-up of families helped sway the decisions of a few to stay in Indiana.

The first student groups to arrive after 1950 did not stay after completion of their degree work. This situation changed quickly in 1978. The turmoil that followed the overthrow of the royal regime, the rise of a fundamentalist Islamic government, and the "drawing in" of Iranian culture led to a large increase in immigration to the United States, primarily by Iran's middle and upper classes. The United States embassy in Tehran was put under siege when the deposed Shah was given medical treatment in New York, and diplomatic relations between the two nations were severed. Embassy personnel were held hostage.

There were several thousand Iranian students studying in the United States at the time, more than two hundred in Indiana, who wished to finish their work before returning home. Although this group had come on temporary residence visas, the situation in their homeland led a number of them to extend their visas. Extensions became permanent for some; American immigration policy recognized the contributions these professionals would make if allowed to stay. Although California, New York, and Illinois received the greatest number of immigrants, Indiana, as of 1990, was the home of 931 Iranian-born residents.

### Egyptians

Early converts to the Christianity of St. Mark, Egyptians established an indigenous church called Coptic ("Egyptian" in Arabic). Today Egypt is 86 percent Sunni Muslim and 14 percent Copt.[40] A few Copts joined their fellow Christians from Syria in immigrating to Indiana in the last part of the nineteenth century. As in the Levant, the nineteenth-century Christian missionary movement was active in Egypt. Beginning in the early post–Civil War period, the Presbyterian Church in Indiana supported an exchange with the Coptic Church in Egypt. The Presbyterians established schools and medical centers. Like their Syrian brethren, the Egyptians began their lives in Indiana first as peddlers and then as proprietors of small stores and other business establishments. In 1930 there were two Egyptian doctors in general practice in South Bend, a surgeon in Fort Wayne, and several Egyptian doctors who had come to practice in Indianapolis under church auspices.

Because they were so few, Egyptian immigrants in the 1875 to 1915 period were included in the "Turkey in Asia" groupings. It was somewhat different in the 1970s and 1980s. With an Egyptian "open door" economic policy and a change in Egypt's relationships with the Soviet Union, Israel, and the United States, Eygpt–United States associations developed. Beginning in 1978 Egyptian undergraduates could study for a year in the United States under a special "Sadat-Carter Peace Fellowships" initiative. Other scholars took advantage of expanded Fulbright exchange programs. The Indiana State Police Training Academy trained Cairo and Alexandria police officers. The University of Notre Dame established relationships with Egyptian archaeologists, and the Indianapolis Museum of Art hosted curators of Pharaonic, Islamic, and Mameluke art exhibits brought from the Egyptian Museum in Cairo. Eli Lilly and Company in Indianapolis, once one of Egypt's major suppliers of insecticides, continues to market pharmaceuticals there. The United States consul general in Egypt reported that his records showed very few Egyptians leaving for permanent stays in America.[41] However, many American-trained Egyptians are working in Egypt today. The group also includes the minister of education, the head surgeon of a major hospital, the president of the largest Egyptian bank, and the dean of Cairo University. In 1990 the federal census counted only 388 foreign-born Egyptians living in Indiana. There is no count available of the many who came to Indiana and returned to their homeland.

Several other Middle East immigrants, primarily Armenians, Assyrians, and Kurds, came to Indiana as individuals or in small groups. They were minorities who knew of a glorious past and lived in a dreadful present. A majority of them came to America as refugees.

## Assyrians

The 1990 Census Special Tabulations records 398 persons of Assyrian ancestry living in Indiana. None are

*International Festival in Gary, sponsored by the Gary International Institute, ca. 1956–57.*

listed in the "Foreign-Born Population by Place of Birth" category because Assyrians came from what are now parts of Iran, Turkey, Iraq, Syria, and Lebanon. Assyrians chose Chicago as their first destination. In 1935 a northern Indiana ethnic population study, a project of several libraries initiated by the East Chicago Public Library, indicated four families living in the East Chicago region.[42] Although some families of Assyrians moved to neighboring states, the Chicago group remains the core of religious and social activity. Christian missionaries had been operational in their home regions and encouraged some young Assyrians to go to the United States for their education. Few returned home, and those who stayed do not usually identify themselves as Assyrians.

## Kurds

The Kurds have long been a "forgotten" people, mainly found today in regions of Iran, Iraq, and Turkey. Primarily Muslim, the few who came to the United States were sponsored by Christian church groups or Muslim friends. Those who stayed soon assimilated into the general population and do not have an ethnic identity in census data. The 1985–91 conflicts in the Iran and Iraq regions and the Kurds' long-standing enmity with the Turks caused tragic displacements of thousands of Kurdish people. The 1991 Gulf War saw even more suffering and great loss of life among the Kurds of northern Iraq.

## Armenians

The Armenians claim to be the first of the early Christian converts. Their faith added to their uniqueness as a small, highly civilized people of artistic and literary accomplishments living in Muslim territory just north of present-day Turkey and Iran. "The Armenian Apostolic Church derives its name from the apostles Thaddeus and Bartholomew, who according to tradition began the conversion of the Armenians to Christianity between A.D. 43 and A.D. 68."[43] Armenia was in the path of many of the barbaric invasions between the tenth and sixteenth centuries. In the sixteenth century the land was conquered by the Ottoman Turks.

The long years of Muslim Ottoman hegemony saw the Christian Armenians as a partially protected minority. Primarily farmers or craftsmen, a few developed skills in finance and in governmental affairs. To the Muslims, however, they were always an outside minority—religious infidels. During the final thirty years of the Ottoman Empire, Armenian nationalist zeal erupted in bloody conflicts. Just before World War I Ottoman massacres killed more than a million Armenians.

American missionary groups had been deeply involved with Armenians since the middle of the nineteenth century, establishing a Protestant Armenian Evangelical Church. As had some Syrians, early Armenian immigrants learned about the United States in mission schools. At first single men immigrated to the United States. Speaking the Armenian language, fifteen hundred of them are listed in the "mother tongue" statistics of the 1890 census.

"After 1890 the emigration of Armenians from Turkey escalated in direct correlation with the deteriorating state of Armeno-Turkish relations. . . . Refugees fortunate enough to escape from Turkey to the United States rapidly increased the Armenian immigration rate, until it reached 2,500 annually in the middle and late 1890s."[44] After 1890 immigration to the United States increased with over fifty thousand Armenians arriving by 1914. Following World War I more than ten thousand Armenians, primarily women and children survivors of massacres and deportations, came to America. A restrictive national quota system stopped the Armenian immigration after 1924, but the Displaced Persons Act of 1948 and the Immigration and Nationality Act of 1965 allowed many thousands to leave what was perceived as the cultural and economic harassment of Syria, Egypt, Iran, Bulgaria, Lebanon, and Soviet Armenia. A literate people, carrying with them a mastery of jewelry and rug making, Armenians tended to live in large urban population centers where such expertise was marketable. Cities on the two coasts, primarily in the Northeast and Mid-Atlantic states and those in the Napa Valley of California, became Armenian centers, but groups also came to the Chicago and Detroit areas. A 1960 library survey found fifteen Armenian families in East Chicago, Indiana, who worshiped with Eastern Orthodox Armenian Christians in

Chicago.[45] The 1990 census shows 1,056 people of Armenian ancestry in Indiana, the fourth largest (after Syrian, Lebanese, and Iranian) of the ethnic North Africa and Southwest Asia area Americans.

### Kuwait, Saudi Arabia, Iraq, the Gulf Emirates

"In 1910, (the Standard Oil Company of New Jersey) head Geologist had concluded that there was oil potential in the Middle East region known today as Iraq; but until after the (World War I) war, New Jersey Standard did nothing about it."[46] In the middle of this century new and extensive oil reserves were found.

Saudi Arabia, Kuwait, Iran, Iraq, and the Gulf Emirates, newly rich, mounted massive education and training projects with special study in the United States. Indiana colleges and universities were heavily involved. Immigration patterns changed as the situations of individual students changed. Telephone contact and affordable air travel for vacation trips home changed previous perceptions. Middle East television stations broadcast many programs, films, or news documentaries that portrayed the United States as a somewhat romantic, rich, and attractive place. Middle Easterners with available travel funds came as tourists, some as students, and still others came as employees of American firms doing business in the Middle East. Marriage with Americans and acculturation led to applications for immigration. For Muslims, reluctance to leave the culture and the traditions of their Middle East environment for the perceived unfamiliar Christian culture of America gradually began to disappear. Although there are criticisms of "brain drain," United States immigration laws continue to look with favor on applications for changes from student to permanent resident status, particularly when the new residents are well-educated contributors to American society. Arab Americans in the larger cities celebrate the Eastern Orthodox and Muslim holidays along with traditional national, Jewish, and Christian holidays. Middle Eastern food, in restaurants started originally by Christian Middle East immigrants, is popular with Muslims and Jews as well as Christians, and joint celebrations of religious feasts are not uncommon. Organizations for Muslim students have developed on campuses where only those of Christians and Jews had existed. Middle East studies programs have become a part of college and university curricula; Middle East history and Islamic studies were added to world history offerings.

The discovery of oil in the Middle East made other significant, if sometimes subtle, changes in the patterns of Middle Eastern society. Nations such as Jordan and nearby regions without oil were partial beneficiaries of oil wealth

*Dancers at the first Middle Eastern festival, Indianapolis, 10 June 1995.*

as they provided workers, teachers, technicians, and business skills to the oil-wealthy regions. Migration within the Middle East, the movement of people from the less affluent countries to the newly rich, affected patterns of immigration to America and Europe. With newly earned money for travel, education, and resettlement abroad, there was a wave of movement by people with abilities and skills. "I left Iran and came to the United States in 1950 because I wanted to see the country I had come to admire," said Dr. Sidnia, a radiologist at an Indianapolis hospital. "I left the West Bank of the Jordan River for medical training in Egypt, then on to a clinic in Saudi Arabia, and then to New York where I took some training so I could pass United States medical licensing examinations," said a doctor practicing in Kokomo. "In 1969, I had an engineering specialty, was offered a position in Indiana, and my wife, two sons, a daughter and I have lived here happily," said an Afghan in Lafayette. He added that his brother, also an engineer, had joined him later and now worked in South Bend. Fieldwork opportunities, library facilities, and supportive colleagues prompted serious scholars to request a change from student to resident visas. American academic institutions, libraries, and research centers have gained needed high-quality personnel. Saad Eddin Ibrahim, the distinguished Arab scholar, came to the United States from Egypt, received a doctorate, and then taught at DePauw University in Greencastle. He and his American wife returned to Egypt where he continues teaching and research and where she holds a senior position with the Ford Foundation office in Cairo.

The 1990 United States census showed that there were 1,541 individuals in Marion County with ethnic ties to the Middle East, 1,450 of whom lived in Indianapolis. These modest numbers, throughout the state as well as in central Indiana, might be deceptive. The contributions of

Indiana's ethnic Middle Eastern residents are seen in almost every segment of educational, cultural, business, and professional activity. While their identity may be hidden by their reluctance to form Arab, or Middle East, enclaves or clubs, their useful Indiana citizenship is expressed wherever they live.

*Editor's Note:* Dr. Frank W. Blanning, the author of this informative contribution on Middle Easterners, passed away on 28 November 1994. At the time of his death he was in the process of revising the essay, in particular adding material to several sections. Time did not allow the editors to locate someone to complete the revisions, and not wanting to deprive the reader of this overview it has been published as is, but with the understanding that more information would have been forthcoming.

## Notes

1. 1880 to 1890 United States Census.

2. *Indianapolis News,* 26 Nov. 1898.

3. *Indianapolis Sun,* 21 Sept. 1910.

4. Arthur Goldschmidt, Jr., *A Concise History of the Middle East,* 3d ed. (Boulder, Colo.: Westview Press, 1988), 15.

5. Early census information did not list persons from the Middle East in precise national identification terms. However, in interviews, the author heard personal accounts of ethnic Middle Easterners' business or social activities. He was told that many of these were reported in the social function columns of small town and county weekly newspapers. Previously noted Indianapolis newspaper articles refer to some religious or special holiday activities of the few Middle Easterners living in or near the capital city.

6. U.S. Department of Commerce, Bureau of the Census, 1960 and 1980 Census Special Tabulations. The 1990 census reports only 2,533 "foreign born" Middle Easterners in Indiana. While "foreign born" counts would not include ethnic Middle East children or adults born in the United States, Dr. George Irani, a native of Lebanon and currently a professor at Franklin College, told the author that his cursory research indicated that the total ethnic Middle East population and the "foreign born" population were far too low. One reason for this, according to Irani, was the lack of ethnic awareness on the part of many American assimilated young people. The young people, and often their parents, hesitated to designate ethnic origins on census forms. Irani also noted that there were a substantial number of Palestinians in Indiana who were not counted in the Middle East categories because of their statelessness.

7. U.S. Immigration and Naturalization Service.

8. Patrick D. Gaffney, "The Mother of Challenges," *Notre Dame Magazine* (spring 1991): 15.

9. Lew Wallace Collection, Indiana Historical Society, Indianapolis, Ind.

10. *Terre Haute Spectator,* 11 Oct. 1975.

11. Leonard Dinnerstein, Roger L. Nichols, and David M. Reimers, *Natives and Strangers: Blacks, Indians, and Immigrants in America* (New York: Oxford University Press, 1990), 143.

12. Alixa Naff, "Arabs," in Stephan Thernstrom, ed., *Harvard Encyclopedia of American Ethnic Groups* (Cambridge, Mass.: Belknap Press of Harvard University Press, 1980), 128.

13. Albert Hourani, *A History of the Arab People* (New York: Oxford University Press, 1991), 397.

14. Michael Kafoure, "Early Syrian-Lebanese Arabic Immigrants Settling in Indianapolis, 1890–" (1980).

15. Naff, "Arabs," 131.

16. *Indianapolis Star,* 17 Nov. 1905.

17. Michael Kafoure, *History of the Kafoure Family in America* (Edited and published by William G. Kafoure, 1984), 3.

18. Helen Corey, *Helen Corey's Food from Biblical Lands: A Culinary Trip to the Land of Bible History* (Terre Haute, Ind.: Helen Corey, 1989).

19. Anthony R. Abraham, a leader in the Syrian community of Indiana, wrote an open letter. Titled "Who Are We," it was directed to his fellow Lebanese and Syrian Americans. It was given to the author by Alice Mesalam of the St. George Syrian Orthodox Church in Indianapolis in 1991.

20. Christmas letter from Alice Mesalam to her family and friends, Dec. 1990, copy in the possession of the author.

21. In February 1991 fourteen ethnic Lebanese and Syrian Americans met with the author at the Mesalam home in Indianapolis. The two anecdotes recorded here were given orally by Marie Ajamie and Michael Kafoure.

22. The Arabic Eid-ul-Fitr (Ramazan Bayram in Turkish) is an Islamic holiday, marking the end of the fasting month of Ramadan. Ramadan is observed as one of the twelve lunar months of the Islamic calendar and is the third of the Five Pillars of Islam (the other four are Witness, Worship, Tithing, and Pilgrimage). During Ramadan, from daybreak until sunset, devout Muslims refrain from eating, drinking, smoking, and sexual intercourse. Commemorating the first revelations of the Holy Koran to the Prophet Muhammad, the Ramadan month is followed by a feast, or an Eid.

23. Hussain M. Farzad, interview with author, Indiana University, Bloomington, Ind., May 1992.

24. Jeri Laber and Barnett R. Rubin, *"A Nation Is Dying": Afghanistan under the Soviets, 1979–87* (Evanston, Ill.: Northwestern University Press, 1988), 2.

25. Arthur Bonner, *Among the Afghans* (Durham, N.C.: Duke University Press, 1987), 26.

26. Farzad interview. Farzad, an Indiana University administrative officer, was a participant in the first Indiana University–Afghanistan exchanges.

27. Fawaz Turki, *The Disinherited: Journal of a Palestinian Exile* (New York: Monthly Review Press, 1972), 8.

28. Interviews with Indiana Palestinians, spring 1992.

29. George E. Irani, *The Papacy and the Middle East: The Role of the Holy See in the Arab-Israeli Conflict, 1963–1984* (Notre Dame, Ind.: University of Notre Dame Press, 1986), 62.

30. Thomas L. Friedman, *From Beirut to Jerusalem* (New York: Farrar Straus Giroux, 1989), 284.

31. Charles D. Smith, *Palestine and the Arab-Israeli Conflict* (New York: St. Martin's Press, 1988), 1.

32. Hazem Zaki Nuseibeh, *Palestine and the United Nations* (New York and London: Quartet Books, 1981), 15.

33. 1990 United States Census, Ancestry of Population of Indiana section.

34. Mina Khoury, interview with author, Feb. 1991.

35. Alixa Naff, *The Arab Americans* (New York: Chelsea House Publishers, 1988), 85.

36. Talat Sait Halman, "Turks," in Thernstrom, ed., *Harvard Encyclopedia of American Ethnic Groups,* 993.

37. Ibid.

38. John H. Lorentz and John T. Wertime, "Iranians," in ibid., 522.

39. Ibid., 522, 523.

40. The author lived in Egypt as a professor for twenty years. Although some of the information about the land and the people came from the author's observations, the primary sources were his Egyptian colleagues, several of whom are historians.

41. Author's interview with the U.S. Consul, U.S. Embassy, Cairo, Egypt, Jan. 1967.

42. East Chicago Public Library, *Ethnic Residents of the East Chicago Region* (1935).

43. Robert Mirak, "Armenians," in Thernstrom, ed., *Harvard Encyclopedia of American Ethnic Groups,* 138.

44. Ibid.

45. In 1960 the East Chicago Public Library, in cooperation with other libraries in the northern Indiana area, did a survey of ethnic groups and their organizations and institutions.

46. David Fromkin, *A Peace to End All Peace: Creating the Modern Middle East, 1914–1922* (New York: Henry Holt and Co., 1989), 534.

# NATIVE AMERICANS

ELIZABETH GLENN AND STEWART RAFERT

*The treaties made between 1803 and 1809 took from Indian control primarily the southern portions of present-day Indiana. The rapidity of land loss, the insidious divide-and-conquer approach to treaty making, and the relatively few Indian leaders involved in the treaties combined to bring about political and religious responses from Native Americans.*

In 1679 René-Robert Cavelier, Sieur de La Salle, led the first recorded expedition of Euro-Americans into what was to become Indiana. When the expedition had descended the St. Joseph River to its portage with the Kankakee River, one member, Father Louis Hennepin, reported, "This place is situated on the edge of a great plain, at the extremity of which on the western side is a village of Miamis, Mascontens and Oiatinon gathered together."[1] This simple statement is the first mention of ethnic groups different than any others in this volume—the Native Americans or American Indians, who were here before all others.

From 1668 to 1673 the French received indirect information about peoples along the Ohio River in the southern extremity of the state. La Salle learned in 1668 from the Iroquois in the Northeast that

> this river [Ohio] took its rise three days' journey from Seneca, that after a month's travel one came upon the Honniasontkeronons and the Chiouanons, and that, after passing the latter, and a great cataract or waterfall, one found the Outagame and the Iskousogos.[2]

Jacques Marquette and Louis Jolliet, traveling down the Mississippi, reported passing the mouth of the Ohio [Waboukigon] River and elaborated on its population:

> This river flows from the lands of the East, where dwell the people called Chaouanons in so great numbers that in one district there are as many as 23 villages, and 15 in another, quite near one another. They are not at all warlike, and are the nations whom the Iroquois go so far to seek, and war against without any reason.[3]

These brief early accounts about Native Americans in Indiana belie the complexity of earlier and later history. They do suggest what peoples resided in Indiana at the time of the first recorded European contact, namely the Miami, Wea, and Mascouten in the extreme north and, most likely, the Shawnee (Chiouanons) in the extreme south. The French already knew the Miami, Wea, and Mascouten through contact earlier in the 1600s in present Wisconsin; and, until displaced into Illinois, the Shawnee were, to the French, "heard about" peoples with earlier contacts east of the Ohio River location.

It would be almost fifty years after La Salle's exploration before the French would establish permanent posts in present Indiana and provide a fuller historical record of the indigenous peoples in the region. To conjecture about Native American peoples in Indiana prior to La Salle's expedition, the archaeological record of the region's prehistory is necessary. Although too little space prevents other than a cursory description of prehistory, the following brief four-part review will give at least an impression of the complexity of Native American occupation and some notion of major cultural developments.[4]

Paleo-Indian (ca. 9,500–8,000 B.C.). Both evidence and logic indicate that the first opportunity for human occupation within the present state limits occurred as the ice packs of the Wisconsin glaciation receded. At that time small, nomadic, hunting-intensive groups utilized the area's resources. The primary evidence for this early

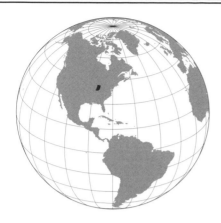

paleo-Indian occupation in the state today is a wide distribution of fluted spear points.[5]

Archaic (ca. 8,000–1,000 B.C.). During the transition to modern climatic conditions varied cultural adaptations occurred. These cultural responses have been grouped into two major patterns: northern boreal archaic (Glacial Kame, Red Ochre, Old Copper) and southern shell midden sites. Both show more generalized hunting and gathering than the previous period and are demonstrated in the south by large shell midden sites of long occupancy with an obvious dependence on eating mussels, and in the

north by smaller, perhaps more nomadic populations known primarily by their burial sites. As climatic conditions became more recent during the late Archaic, more complex features associated with burial practices and plant domestication began to develop and continued into the next period.

Early (Adena) and Middle Woodland (ca. 1,000 B.C.–900 A.D.). The hallmarks of this prehistoric phase are earthworks, burial mounds, pottery, and established horticulture. By far the most noted sites from this era are conical burial mounds, with and without internal tombs, and widespread earthwork complexes. It has long been the opinion that this lengthy and diverse period was characterized by intense cultural activity and widespread exchange networks and that burial ritual was a dominant theme of that activity. Recent work in archaeoastronomy, illustrated by earthwork/mound orientation, has added a new interpretation to that cultural intensity.[6] The Mounds State Park in Anderson, Indiana, exemplifies this period.

Middle Mississippian/Late Woodland/Upper Mississippian (ca. 900 A.D. to contact). This is a complex period characterized by a variety of archaeological

*Excavation of Mound F at Angel Mounds.*

phenomena. Part of the variety is caused by the number of influences from surrounding states and beyond that overlap Indiana. In southwestern Indiana one finds Middle Mississippian with affinities to the southwest; in east central Indiana Upper Mississippian Fort Ancient is found with associations to the east; in central Indiana the Oliver Focus is found with associations to both the northeast and northwest; Upper Mississippian Oneota materials are found in the northwest; and northern Late Woodland expressions are found in the north. With the exception of the extreme north, the few cultural generalizations that can be made about this complex period are that the sometimes palisaded settlements are larger than in preceding periods, horticulture is intensive, and the bow and arrow becomes the projectile tool of preference. A palisaded, temple mound-dominated Middle Mississippian site, Angel Mounds near Evansville, is an interesting example from this period.[7]

From the archaeological period preceding contact, one would hope to find evidence of continuity from prehistory to known historic tribes so that specific peoples could be traced both backward and forward in time. The effects of the protohistoric period were, unfortunately, too great to make such assignments with certainty. Diseases introduced in even such far-off localities as the Southeast and Atlantic coasts could travel the trade routes to the interior causing epidemics and unrecorded changes in demography. Trade goods gradually replaced local technologies, and the competition for trade goods caused unrecorded relocations of peoples. Trade and demographic factors also "reconfigured" peoples; that is, groups became extinct, fragmented, recombined, and renamed. These factors, combined with too few well-known transitional sites, make assignments difficult. Even the oft given associations between some of late Fort Ancient with the Shawnee and the eastern expression of Oneota with the Miami and/or Illinois recently have been called into question.[8] Despite this equivocation, the Miami, or their predecessors, were the most likely occupants of northern Indiana as one enters the Historic Period, and most late-prehistoric materials in the state were probably associated with Central Algonquian-speaking peoples.

**Furs, Souls, Routes, and Allies**

Although Native American culture was never static, from the time of contact with the European world the native cultures of the region saw the direction and rate of change accelerated by the needs and offerings first of the French, then the English and Spanish, and lastly, the Americans. The successive French desires for furs, souls, a transcontinental route to the Orient, and allies in its "contest for continent" with Great Britain were all to influence the natives directly and indirectly. As the contest for continent was resolved in Great Britain's favor, the same objectives, except for missionary efforts, were pursued so major cultural adjustments for the tribes in the region were not necessary. However, the United States's desire for land began a dramatically different second cycle of adjustment for Native Americans in the region.[9]

In 1679 La Salle explored the territory the French hoped to control and exploit. Traveling through present northwest Indiana, he crossed a portage near today's South Bend that connected the watershed of the Great Lakes with that of the Mississippi. When crossing the portage the French explorers discovered a Miami, Wea, and Mascouten village. The French then paddled on to the Kankakee River, the beginning of a route that would eventually take them through Illinois to the Mississippi. By the end of the seventeenth century the French were surely aware of other routes in the state that would connect the Great Lakes country with the Mississippi—the Maumee River/Wabash River portage at Fort Wayne; the Maumee River/Eel River portage near Fort Wayne; the Elkhart River/St. Joseph of the Maumee portage in Noble County; and the St. Joseph of Lake Michigan/Tippecanoe River portage.

By the end of the 1600s the French were concerned with the potential for British influence in the region since the Ohio River and its northern tributaries afforded the British similar access from the East to the furs and Indians of the Upper Great Lakes. The fur trade involved a reciprocal relationship between the incoming Europeans and the indigenous peoples. Simply stated, the fur trade depended on the Native American to trap and exchange furs for European manufactured goods (goods primarily of metal, cloth, and glass).[10] This process began by the 1500s with the demand of each side so great for what the other provided that its effects preceded actual contact. One effect was competition for positions of direct access between the tribes north and south of the St. Lawrence River leading to the Iroquois Beaver Wars that dominated the 1600s. The history of those wars is not a concern here, but they did have an effect on the native population of this area. To avoid Iroquois incursions, northern and, eventually, southern Indiana were vacated by the peoples who had traditionally lived there. By the time La Salle ventured across the St. Joseph portage and found a village of Miami, Wea, and Mascouten, these were peoples already known to the French as refugees from west of Lake Michigan. As La Salle made his exploratory trip in 1679, tribes like the Miami were returning to what may have been their traditional territories.

As the fur trade moved west with the French in the latter half of the 1600s, its direct influence was even more profound. The Indian economy was nearly self-sufficient with group membership rights and available resources shared by all. Therefore a strong sense of territory prevailed, and located within that territory were villages surrounded by horticultural resources and environments favorable for hunting, fishing, gathering, and finding resources necessary for tools, utensils, weapons, clothing, and housing. Production also emphasized the use of available resources (stone, hides, bone, furs, shell, soil, and plants) to make the necessary tools, weapons, utensils, vehicles, residences, and clothing in a household-by-household jack-of-all-trades replication of the known technology. This cultural self-sufficiency was ameliorated somewhat by far-reaching trade networks along which prized luxury goods, such as copper, fine chert or obsidian, mica, and saltwater mollusk shells, and some necessities were traded.

The introduction of European manufactured metal-edged tools and utensils, metal containers (kettles), cloth, muskets, glass beads, and the other standard stock of the early trade, presented a highly desirable choice for the Native Americans. However, it eventually disrupted the traditional technological production with the replacement of metal for stone, wood, antler, and bone tools and weapons; metal kettles for clay, wood, bark, or leather containers; and, most certainly, cloth for leather and fur clothing, since furs and skins were the primary trade commodities. Decorative or luxury items were no less affected. Glass beads, ribbons, and metal ornaments replaced shell, porcupine quill, and stone decorative elements for personal or clothing adornment. Preference for the new materials that could neither be made nor repaired by the traditional economy and a loss of traditional technology created a dependency on the trade. A new economic adaptation rapidly developed away from self-sufficiency toward the acquisition of goods made and controlled by another cultural tradition and the fluctuations of a distant market system. As dependency on the trade became established, indebtedness ensued and more furs could be demanded to eradicate the debt, thus worsening the dependency. Moreover, as male economic activities turned toward fur trading, female economic and management functions became more important.

Native dependency on the fur trade had a far-reaching impact on political systems and population. The most common tie was intermarriage between the trader in the field and a daughter of an often prominent member of a tribe. Intermarriage created strong primary relationships for trading purposes. In subsequent generations a large population of Métis (mixed-bloods) developed in the Great Lakes region. This population specialized in the trade and, as the trade diminished, provided many individuals who would play important roles as members of Great Lakes tribes.

Indian villages or bands became tied to locations of trading posts or other outlets for goods, and relocation gave access to better or cheaper goods. Some tribes adopted new political and strategic objectives such as a middleman role in the trade network, control of important portages/routes, or military alliance with one or another European power.

Although trade dominated the French contact period economically, the missionary effort was also of great importance to French goals. Converting from traditional beliefs to Catholicism did not have the same appeal to the Native Americans as converting from stone to metal tools. Native religion was characterized by a belief in a supernatural that was immanent in nature. The supernatural sphere often expressed itself to the individual through visionary experiences, and the efficacy of one's supernatural power became manifest through success in activities such as hunting, fishing, and healing. The intermediary with the supernatural was the shaman, and, for many groups indigenous to the Upper Great Lakes region, the Midiwewin was an intertribal association of religious specialists whose high-ranking members maintained the most sacred knowledge and enacted the most elaborate rituals. The differences between Native and European religious systems often meant that early baptisms were heavily biased toward infants and the sick and dying. Other conversions were motivated by the observation that proselytized Indians seemed to facilitate easier access to trade goods. Strong cultural effects of the vigorous missionary effort did not appear until much later in the contact period.

The competition for control of the territory between European nations also became a concern of the region's Indians. Native Americans were used as auxiliaries by colonial armies and, as each contest became more intense, the regional tribes, separately or in combination, used their choice of alliance for political and trade leverage. In this multifaceted political interaction with various Euro-American interests, the duality of Indian leadership (separate civil and war leaders) was probably an advantage and thus persisted through much of the early contact period.

The major usually inadvertent influence on Native Americans introduced by the European traders, explorers, missionaries, soldiers, and politicians was disease. Measles, mumps, chicken pox, smallpox, and tuberculosis, to name a few, were diseases previously unknown in the New World and, because of this, no resistance to them had developed in its indigenous populations. Several epidemics swept across the Upper Great Lakes/Ohio River region with devastating results. Smallpox epidemics afflicted tribes in Indiana in 1733, 1752, 1757, 1762–64, 1781–82, 1787–88, and 1801. The Wea had a measles epidemic in 1715, and scarlet fever affected the Miami and Potawatomi in 1793–94.[11] Particularly vulnerable were the very old (the tradition carriers) and the very young (the strength of the next generation) with obviously destructive effects on the ability to sustain both a culture and a population. Often, so many people were sick at a given time that the ability to sustain the normal pattern of life was impossible. During the measles epidemic in 1715 the Wea were unable to fulfill their military obligations to the French,[12] and the smallpox epidemic of 1733 caused the Miami to abandon their towns and disperse into northern Indiana.[13]

Alcoholic beverages were purposefully introduced, even after their deleterious effects on Native Americans were well known. Used by traders to undersell their competition and by politicians to gain a concession, alcohol became an uncontrollable commodity.

## French, English, and Indians: The Trading Period

By the 1650s in the region of present-day Wisconsin the French initiated contact and established a trading relationship with many of the tribes that were later associated with Indiana. In 1679 La Salle encountered representatives of those previously contacted tribes, the Miami, Wea, and Mascouten, in northern Indiana. The Miami and Wea, in combination with the Piankashaw, a group located in Illinois and western Indiana, were culturally and linguistically affiliated with the Illinois tribes just to the west. These three groups, all to be associated with Indiana through the 1700s on, were so culturally similar that there is a common assumption that they had, in the not too distant past, been one "tribe." Despite their cultural closeness, the Miami, Wea, and Piankashaw were politically autonomous throughout the historic period. The Mascouten, the third group encountered in the village by La Salle, was at this point allied with but not linguistically related to this Miami/Illinois group. From what little is known about the Mascouten language it is thought to be another dialect of the Fox/Sauk/Kickapoo language group.[14]

By 1700 the Wea had settled on the Wabash (probably at their longtime location near present Lafayette) and, shortly after the turn of the century, at least some of the Miami proper occupied land at the head of the Maumee (at present Fort Wayne). Early in the 1700s the Mascouten and the closely affiliated Kickapoo established themselves near the Wea along the middle Wabash. Another Central Algonquian group, the Potawatomi, very soon followed the Miami into the St. Joseph River valley of northern Indiana. The Shawnee also had come to the Ohio River valley in southern Indiana by 1700.

The French established posts at present Fort Wayne (Fort Saint Philippe, later named Fort Miamis) near the Miami town of Kekionga and at Ouiatenon (near Lafayette) among the Wea, and later, the Kickapoo and Mascouten. All of these groups were long accustomed to European trade. The posts monitored the route to the new French province of Louisiana and secured the trade in the region from the English after attempts to persuade the Miami and Wea to locate farther north failed. Somewhat later (ca. 1732), the French established Post Vincennes and attracted the Piankashaw to that vicinity.

Even as the French established a presence to keep the British at bay, British interests began penetrating the region. The lower prices and often better goods available through the British traders motivated the Ohio and Wabash tribes to make agreements with the British through the efforts of Indians allied to the British such as the Iroquois. The economic competition between France and Britain itself became an instrument of change for the area's tribes. Alliances shifted as elements of groups such as the Miami, Wea, Piankashaw, and Shawnee dealt with the British, while the Potawatomi remained relatively constant with the French. These opposing interests also created divisions within tribes. During the second quarter of the 1700s the Miami were split politically over the issue of alliance. The basically pro-French contingents remained at Kekionga and Tippecanoe. The pro-British contingent, under La Demoiselle (Old Briton), formed an active trading community, Pickawillany, near present Piqua, Ohio. This split persisted until 1752 when a French/Indian force destroyed Pickawillany and killed La Demoiselle. Despite this fragmentation, by the mid-1700s the Miamis' position in the area was enhanced by their role as effective middlemen in the trade cycle.

As the area's trade competition escalated into the military conflict that was the French and Indian War, the majority of the tribes of the region realigned themselves with their old friends the French. When Britain achieved dominance over Canada in 1760, former Indian allies of the French discovered the disadvantage of both a noncompetitive trading situation and an alliance with the losing side. The French practice of giving presents and goods to maintain Indian loyalty and goodwill was discontinued by the British who considered it an unnecessary expense. The end of hostilities also encouraged the illegal movement of British colonists west, exposing Indian lands to a new threat. The Indians responded in 1763 with Pontiac's War. The inability to sustain this uprising emphasized to the Upper Great Lakes tribes the reality of their economic dependency, engendered by a century of involvement in the European-controlled fur trade/alliance system. However, the widespread military

# Treaty Cessions
# 1795–1809

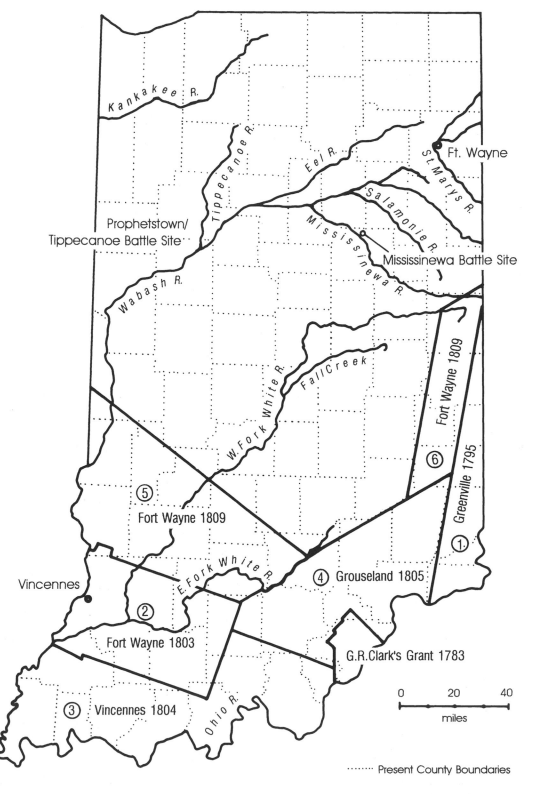

Kankakee R.

Eel R.

St. Marys R.

Ft. Wayne

Tippecanoe R.

Salamonie R.

Prophetstown/
Tippecanoe Battle Site

Mississinewa R.

Mississinewa Battle Site

Wabash R.

Fort Wayne 1809

Fall Creek

W. Fork White R.

⑥

Greenville 1795

⑤
Fort Wayne 1809

①

Vincennes

E. Fork White R.

④ Grouseland 1805

②
Fort Wayne 1803

G.R.Clark's Grant 1783

Ohio R.

③ Vincennes 1804

0        20        40
miles

········· Present County Boundaries

P.K.Goffinet

successes of the Indians during Pontiac's War also demonstrated to the British their own vulnerability as a small minority in Indian lands. British authorities attempted to regulate trade and, through the Proclamation of 1763, to establish a boundary between colonists and Indian country.

The changes for the Native Americans were not extensive during the brief British domination of the West. The fur trade continued, still run by the French and the Métis intermediaries with whom they usually did business. France ceded Louisiana to Spain, and the Spanish, now just across the Mississippi, offered a trade option and a political alternative.

Enormous change came in the aftermath of the American Revolution. The transition from French/British to American territory would eventually call upon a whole new adaptive strategy. Until the American Revolution, the relationship of the Native Americans to Europeans was based on the trade/mission/military auxiliary complex. This complex involved the Indians themselves as an integral part of the fur trade, the object of the mission effort, and as necessary allies in the contest for continent. The ultimate American goal was quite different—to acquire the land for colonization and development by its own citizens   without Indians.

Much has been written about the United States's shifts on Indian policy from demand by right of conquest, to confrontation, to negotiation, all used ultimately for territorial expansion. Also much has been written about the framework of territorial development beginning with the Northwest Ordinance of 1787 through the peopling of Indiana with Anglo Americans and the completion of statehood under that document.[15] In response to the territorial demands of the United States, Native Americans were forced more and more to react to events and policies not of their making and, often, in direct opposition to their interests. To the Indians of Indiana this was less apparent before the War of 1812 but unquestioned after—a factor that affected deeply their strategies and responses to circumstances in two stages during the preremoval period of American control.

## American Period

The American Revolution in what is now Indiana included George Rogers Clark's incursion into the Illinois country; the acquiescence of Vincennes to American occupation; the capture of Vincennes for the British by Lt. Gov. Henry Hamilton after an expedition down the Wabash from Detroit; Clark's daring march to retake Vincennes; and the pro-American expedition by LaBalme from Vincennes to Fort Miamis with its disastrous defeat

*Little Turtle, Miami leader.*

by the Miami. Although Native Americans negotiated with Clark and accompanied and then left Hamilton, the Vincennes aspect of the conflict was not their affair. The 1780 LaBalme expedition against the trading post and Indian towns at Fort Miamis was their affair and resulted in the expedition's total defeat by a Miami confederation led by Little Turtle.[16] The American Revolution in the West ended for the Miami and their confederates on that note. Little wonder that the results of the 1783 transatlantic peace negotiations in which the British relinquished their territory to the United States and subsequent American attitudes about its rights of conquest were mystifying to the region's Indian population, particularly since, with the exception of the established French/Métis trading communities along the Wabash and the new Clark's Grant at the Falls of the Ohio, Indiana was still the "land of the Indians."

In 1783 the distribution of the American Indian population in the region had not changed dramatically since early in the century. Long-established trading communities drew and held concentrations of Native American populations: the Miami, Delaware, and Shawnee in the area of Kekionga, the Wea and Kickapoo at the now dwindling post of Ouiatenon, and the Piankashaw at Vincennes. The Potawatomi were in the north near the St. Joseph and Kankakee river trading posts. "Jack-knife" posts,[17] primarily at the mouths of Wabash tributaries, drew concentrations such as the Potawatomi and Wea to Kethtippecanunk and the Miami to Kenapacomaqua near the mouths of the Tippecanoe and Eel rivers, respectively. Other villages, less reported, existed between the older centers.

Despite the appearance of population stability, three changes in the composition of Native American inhabitants should be noted. Tribes from the former British colonies in the East, having lost their land, traversed this far west. Notable among these exiles were bands of Delaware and a small group of Nanticoke, both originally from the mid-Atlantic area. Another change was the expansion of Potawatomi settlement into much of the northern third of Indiana. Lastly, groups known to have been in and around the Indiana region for all or a part of the preceding century faced extinction or, more often, absorption into other tribes such as the assimilation of remnants of the Mascouten by the Kickapoo by the early 1800s.

Throughout the early American period this heterogeneous population faced a complex set of circumstances. Within an international context the region's Indians had been players in the continental competition between first France and Britain and then Britain and the United States. The French influence was still present in the trade system and local population. The British climate still existed in trade and politics. In fact the British, who continued to occupy Detroit after relinquishing the site, were geographically and politically closer to the region's Indians than if confined to their Canadian territory. The principal demand of the United States was for land. American intentions were not lost on the Native Americans of the area and, if they were, the British were nearby to remind them.

The United States directed its diplomacy to establishing a boundary between Euro-American and tribal lands, opening more land for frontier settlement. Newly elected President George Washington, urged on by Gen. Josiah Harmar and Gov. Arthur St. Clair, initiated a military response to meet Indian resistance to further loss of land. American armies and militia under the command of first Harmar and then St. Clair invaded the Indian territory in 1790 and 1791. Meanwhile, American militia harassed settlements along the Wabash. The objective of the military action was the demoralization of the concentration of Indian villages in the Wabash/Maumee region. A confederation of Indian tribes led by Miami war leader Little Turtle defeated both armies, giving St. Clair's the most one-sided defeat ever suffered by an American army.[18]

Little Turtle is credited as the strategist for the varied approaches used against Harmar and St. Clair. The Shawnee war leader, Blue Jacket, assisted in carrying out the plan against St. Clair. The victors held councils afterwards to consider what should be done: should these

military successes be followed by driving settlers out of the disputed territory north of the Ohio, or should the military advantage be used to negotiate an advantageous peace? Despite numerous councils, neither option was pursued. A more subtle factor operating to cause indecision may have been that the traditional Indian political duality between peace and war leaders interfered with the ability of the components of the confederation to come to a necessary consensus.

The native inertia allowed Gen. Anthony Wayne to prepare a larger, better trained and equipped army, the Legion of the United States, for the third major invasion of Indian territory. As Wayne marched north from the Cincinnati area in 1793 and 1794 he constructed a line of forts, including Fort Recovery on the site of St. Clair's defeat. Attrition in his ranks occurred, and at times his army or line of supply was quite vulnerable. The Indians, however, could not take complete advantage of these weaknesses, in part because American forces frequently destroyed their food supply causing economic hardships. As Little Turtle watched Wayne's preparations, he advised against confrontations with this larger, very different army. He became a participant, however, when the more militant Shawnee Blue Jacket assumed command for the conflict that took place at Fallen Timbers in northeastern Ohio on 20 August 1794. This brief encounter, lasting only an hour and ten minutes with nearly equal losses on each side (thirty-three United States and forty Indians killed), began with an Indian advantage, but when the legion's lines held and advanced, the Indian force retreated and was then put to rout. The Indians fell back to Fort Miamies, a British fort constructed in the region during the preceding year, and found the gates closed and locked against them. The Indian coalition broke up completely. Negotiations from a position of strength was no longer an option.[19] By August 1794, after repeated destruction of crops and villages and an epidemic in 1793–94, the Native Americans of the region were hungry, impoverished, and without provision for the coming winter. The British, upon whom they depended for supplies, did not have sufficient resources to alleviate the problem. The failure of the British to give the military support promised particularly demoralized the Indians. These factors more than the single battle at Fallen Timbers led to the Treaty of Greenville in 1795, which began the process of alienating Indian lands of the Old Northwest Territory to the United States government and ended, with the exception of the War of 1812, formal Indian/white warfare in what was to become Indiana.

In the immediate post-Greenville years a portion of the region's Indians relocated. Fort Wayne and its immediate area now belonged to the United States, and the diversified

Indian population there began to disperse. The Shawnee moved east into Ohio, the Delaware built a number of villages along the White River, and the Miami moved from Kekionga to the upper Wabash and its tributaries.

When the Indiana Territory was formed in 1801 and William Henry Harrison was appointed territorial governor, alienation of Indian lands and rapid settlement of the territory with pioneers were his primary objectives. He inaugurated a series of treaties with the Miami, the Piankashaw, the Wea, the now independent Eel River Miami, the Kickapoo (and the absorbed Mascouten), the Potawatomi, and the Shawnee, as well as more recent "immigrants" from the East such as the Delaware (including the Munsee and the Nanticoke), the Ottawa, and the Wyandot. The treaties made between 1803 and 1809 took from Indian control primarily the southern portions of present-day Indiana.

The rapidity of land loss, the insidious divide-and-conquer approach to treaty making, and the relatively few Indian leaders involved in the treaties combined to bring about political and religious responses from Native Americans. The political response emphasized Native American interests separate from entanglements with Euro-American objectives—namely the preservation of their own land and way of life. Tecumseh focused nativist attitudes in the early 1800s.[20] He expressed his views, delivered to Native Americans over a wide area of the eastern United States, to Joseph Barron, Harrison's interpreter, in 1810:

> The great spirit said he gave this great island to his red children. He placed the whites on the other side of the big water, they were not contented with their own, but came to take ours from us. They have driven us from the sea to the lakes, we can go no farther. They have taken upon themselves to say this tract belongs to the Miamis, this to the Delawares & so on. but the Great Spirit intended it as the common property of all the Tribes, nor can it be sold without the consent of all.[21]

Espousing this philosophy, Tecumseh began the process of developing a united front—a confederacy—among Native Americans north and south to confront the rapid loss of their resources. Treaty making halted in 1809 despite determined efforts from Harrison to acquire more cessions.

Tecumseh's brother Tenskwatawa (The Prophet) was a visionary who led a nativistic revitalization movement.[22] As the result of a series of illusory experiences, he preached that a return to some of the old ways, the incorporation of his new ways, and a rejection of white ways (including material goods and alcohol) would lead to the deliverance of the Indian. He provided religious ceremonies and beliefs to

*Tecumseh, from a pencil sketch drawn by Pierre Le Dru.*

Indian people at a time when personal and cultural disintegration was prevalent. In Indiana his influence was particularly strong among the Shawnee, Delaware, Potawatomi, and Kickapoo, and he attracted to his Indiana base, Prophetstown, near present Lafayette, groups of Indians from as far away as Wisconsin. As a dynamic and charismatic religious leader his message provided much of the impetus for his brother's political movement.

These religious and political adaptations helped bring on the War of 1812. The prelude to the war, the Battle of Tippecanoe, was the result of a Harrison-led expedition against Prophetstown. When war was officially declared, initial expeditions focused on areas of resistance to Harrison's treaty progress, such as the Miami villages along the lower Mississinewa. During the course of the war at least twenty-five Indian villages and towns in Indiana were struck and destroyed. These included villages (and crops) of Miami, Potawatomi, Kickapoo, Winnebago, Delaware, Nanticoke, and Wyandot. Of the nineteen total campaigns or engagements in Indiana, fifteen were initiated by United States troops or militia. Those initiated by the Indians were the sieges of forts Fort Wayne and Harrison, an attack on the Vallonia blockhouse, and the highly publicized Shawnee attack on the settlement at Pigeon Roost.[23]

# Location of Indian Towns in Indiana
## between 1795 and 1809

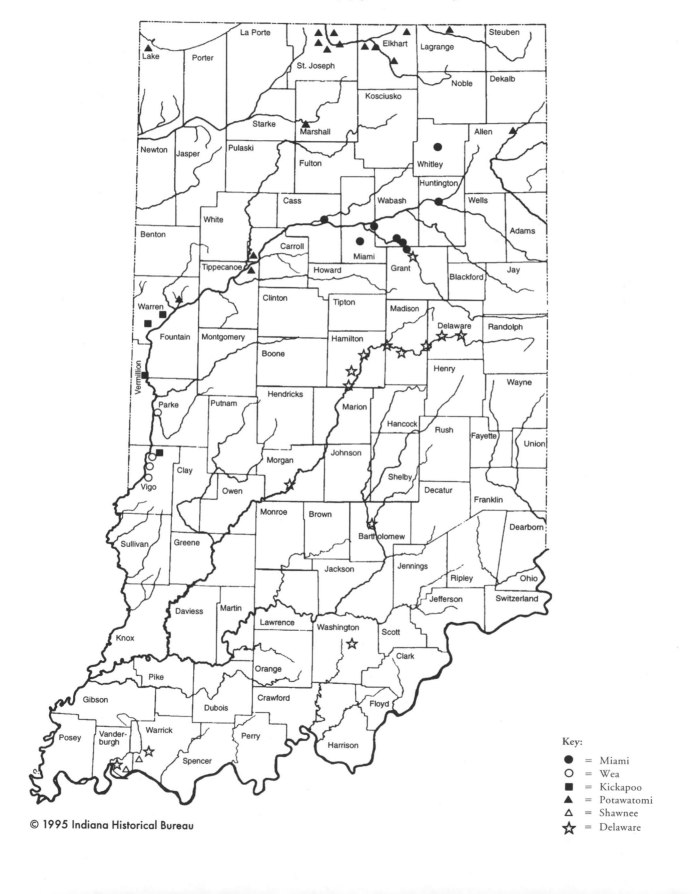

Key:
- ● = Miami
- ○ = Wea
- ■ = Kickapoo
- ▲ = Potawatomi
- △ = Shawnee
- ☆ = Delaware

© 1995 Indiana Historical Bureau

The end of the war brought about drastic changes for the tribes. Warfare ended as a solution to the intrusion of ever-increasing numbers of Euro-Americans. Strong, experienced leaders such as Little Turtle (Miami), Pacanne (Miami), Blue Jacket (Shawnee), Five Medals (Potawatomi), and Tecumseh (Shawnee) died shortly before or during the War of 1812, making political changes necessary. The defeat of the British lessened the desire to resist. Although the Miami (including the Eel River band), the Delaware, and the Potawatomi returned to their prewar locations in Indiana, the Piankashaw and the majority of the Wea and the Kickapoo settled farther west in Illinois and Missouri.

During the early period of Indiana statehood Native Americans made profound adjustments to new circumstances. Federal officials launched a new wave of Indian policies as they resumed land acquisition treaties in 1818. In a series of treaties the United States acquired large land cessions from the Miami, Delaware, and Potawatomi to be followed shortly by similar cessions by the Piankashaw, Wea, and Kickapoo. These were not cessions of distant hunting and trapping grounds; they came from the heart of Miami and Delaware occupation areas in central Indiana. With the new treaties came the first mention of an official removal policy. In 1818 the

*Chief Menominee statue near Plymouth. In the summer of 1838 more than 150 Indian lives were lost to disease, fatigue, and the side effects of winter on the "Trail of Death." Among the dead was Chief Menominee.*

INDIANA STATE LIBRARY

Delaware, part of whom had already moved from Indiana west of the Mississippi, acquiesced to a removal clause and prepared for removal in 1820. Attached to these treaties were individual allotments given primarily to Indian leaders (treaty signatories) and Métis tribal members. Ideally this plan was designed to reinforce the European rather than the Indian concept of land use, but in fact it was a form of bribery. "Civilization" was promoted by granting the Miami implements of agriculture, a gristmill, and a sawmill.

From 1818 through 1840 the Indiana treaty negotiations followed each other in rapid succession. The effective land base of the Miami, Wea, Kickapoo, Delaware, and Wabash Potawatomi was ceded at the treaties at St. Mary's (New Purchase) in 1818, which, with the exception of the Big Miami Reserve and some small reserves, relinquished all lands south of the Wabash. In 1821 at Chicago, in 1826 at Mississinewa Paradise Springs (now Wabash), in 1828 at Carey Mission, and in 1832 at Tippecanoe the Potawatomi and Miami ceded their effective land base north and west of the Wabash and Miami rivers. The largest remaining single Indian landholding, the Big Miami Reserve, was reduced in 1834, and in the next two years the Potawatomi ceded their smaller reserves and agreed (not unanimously) to remove.[24] The forced removal of the Potawatomi, effected by the military and fittingly called the "Trail of Death," took place in 1838.[25] In 1838 and 1840 the Miami ceded the last of the Big Reserve and all but one small reserve and a number of individual allotments. The Miami, with the exception of five families who were allowed to remain in Indiana, also agreed to remove to Kansas Territory. By 1840 the United States held all land previously used and occupied by Native Americans with the exception of a single communally held reserve (Meshingomesia's) and a scattering of individual allotments, all held by Miami, the last Indian group in "the Land of Indians" to be removed.

Indian land loss during the twenty-two-year period from 1818 to 1840 was quite rapid. Out of the resistance of the Miami and Potawatomi to removal from their homeland a strong political adaptation developed. Both the Miami and Potawatomi had a large population of Métis, many of whom were traders. During this critical time the Métis acted as cultural intermediaries during the constant negotiations. The astute leadership of, for example, John B. Richardville, Francis Godfroy, and Metocinyah, a traditional leader, for the Miami delayed and frustrated the treaty and removal process. Leaders bought time and gained concessions that in the end permitted a number of Miami to avoid removal and remain in Indiana with some assets for survival. Despite the delays the process was unrelenting and, in return for

# Treaty Cessions
# 1817–1840

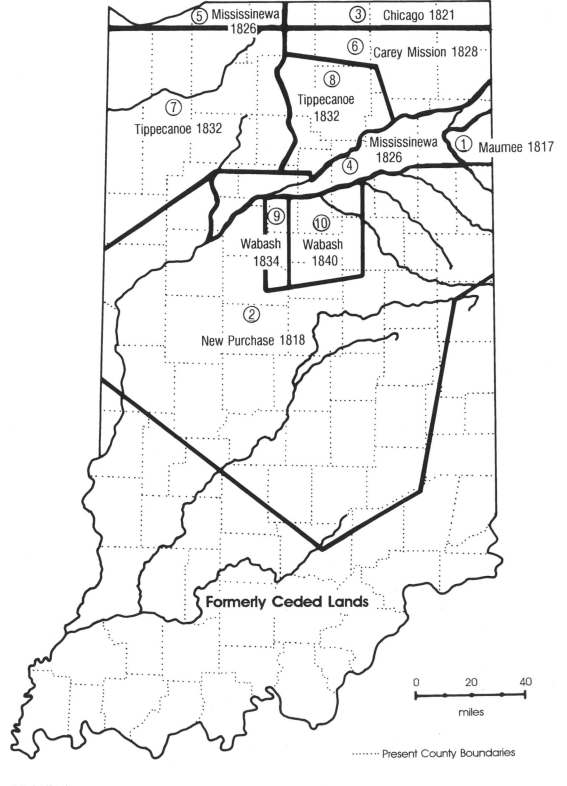

⑤ Mississinewa 1826

③ Chicago 1821

⑥ Carey Mission 1828

⑧ Tippecanoe 1832

⑦ Tippecanoe 1832

Mississinewa 1826

① Maumee 1817

④

⑨ Wabash 1834

⑩ Wabash 1840

② New Purchase 1818

**Formerly Ceded Lands**

```
0        20        40
|--•--•--•--•--|
      miles
```

······ Present County Boundaries

P.K.Goffinet

their land, the various tribes received cash annuities, land allotments, gifts, salt, the elimination of debts claimed by traders, and desultory attempts to acculturate them to a new way of life.

The most numerous targets of the misapplied and often unscrupulous treaty process and ultimate removal between 1818 and 1840 were primarily the Delaware, Potawatomi, and Miami (including the Eel River), who probably numbered, at the beginning of the period, fewer than four thousand individuals. In 1824 after the removal of the Delaware and other remnant groups, such as the remainder of the Wea and Kickapoo, the longtime agent of Indiana's Indian agency, John Tipton, gave the number of Potawatomi, Miami, and Eel River under his supervision as 1,368, 848, and 225, respectively—a total of 2,441 individuals.[26]

· After two hundred years of contact with Euro-Americans, the Native American population experienced rapid and disruptive cultural changes. Many of the earlier changes were voluntary to accommodate participation in the fur trade. Changes that occurred during the post–War of 1812 period, however, were forced by rapidly deteriorating conditions and the manipulation of white officials and speculators. It was during this period that the best cultural descriptions of the region's Native Americans were recorded. The most notable examples are Charles C. Trowbridge's descriptions of the Miami and Shawnee and George Winter's paintings of the Miami and Potawatomi.[27] The descriptions that remain from this period are records of the way of life of peoples who were believed to be disappearing. It was perceived that extinction, assimilation, or removal were to be the fate of all Indiana's Indians. The Mascouten were extinct, and assimilation programs were well under way for all eastern Native Americans. Forced or self-removal had already effected the westerly movement of the majority of the Piankashaw and Wea, the Delaware and Nanticoke, and the Kickapoo, Shawnee, and Potawatomi, leaving only the Miami as an intact tribe wholly within Indiana by 1840.

## Post-Removal

The history of the Indiana or Eastern Miami tribe began on 6 October 1846 with the removal from Peru of 323 Miami to the Osage Subagency in Kansas Territory. Provisions of the Miami treaties of 1838 and 1840 allowed 126 Miami to remain in Indiana. Forty-three of this group belonged to the family of John Baptiste Richardville, the wealthy half-Miami, half-French chief who died at Fort Wayne in 1841. Twenty-eight more belonged to the family of Francis Godfroy, another wealthy mixed-blood chief who died near Peru in 1840. The remaining 55

*Frances Slocum monument, Peru.*

belonged to the family of Metocina, a Miami chief who died along the Mississinewa in today's Grant County in 1832. Metocina's descendants were led by his son Meshingomesia. In 1845 Congress passed a resolution permitting the descendants of Frances Slocum, the elderly white captive, and her Miami husband Shepaconah (Deaf Man) to stay in Indiana, adding another 22 to the tribe. This small group, totaling 148, was the nucleus of today's Miami tribe of Indiana.[28]

Within a few years of removal the Indiana tribe was augmented by another group of Miami. In this case Mazequah, one of the chiefs taken west, got into a serious dispute with the Western Miami and returned to Indiana with his two wives, nephew, and brother-in-law, along with Peshewah ("Wildcat" or Francis Bruell), Osandiah, Joseph White, "Benjamin," and Black Raccoon. In all, eleven families or 101 individuals returned to their homeland. They petitioned the Indiana legislature and the commissioner of the Bureau of Indian Affairs to remain, and their attorney wrote that he was "not aware of any objections that are or can be urged against paying them their annuities in Indiana."[29] On 1 May 1850 Congress passed a joint resolution allowing the Indians to remain.[30]

Although Joseph White and Osandiah returned to Kansas within a few years, most of this group settled on the Godfroy reserve near Peru, increasing the influence of the Godfroy family in tribal affairs.

By 1850 the Miami Indians had largely defeated federal removal policy if one judges by the number of Indians removed. By that year half the tribe had legally obtained exemption from removal, and some 250 Miami resided in familiar haunts in Indiana. The Western Miami population was also about 250. These figures fluctuated somewhat as families moved for months or sometimes years between Indiana and Kansas.

Most of the 250 or so Miami in Indiana in 1850 lived on some eight thousand acres of land remaining from treaty reserves in Miami, Wabash, and Grant counties. Outside that area the Peter Langlois family lived on a reserve near Lafayette, while the descendants of Chief Francis Lafontaine lived on a reserve west of Huntington and Joseph Richardville and James R. Godfroy (married to Archangel Richardville) lived with their families on reserves on the St. Mary's River near Fort Wayne.[31] The reserves chosen for Miami residence were all located on rivers where Miami people could continue their annual subsistence cycle of hunting, fishing, horticulture, and gathering edible and medicinal plants. While game animals had grown scarce, the rivers still abounded in fish, and river bottomlands contained a variety of soil types supporting many kinds of edible plants and fruit-bearing shrubs and trees. The Miami lands between Peru and Marion were connected by a series of trails and paths, making for easy communication by horse or on foot.

Consolidation of the tribal population on a small land base ended much of the mobility that the Miami had enjoyed before removal. The influx of settlers prevented the use of large hunting territories and forced the Miami to make more intensive use of their remaining land. The last hunting bands, consisting of ten to twenty-five people, went on winter hunts east of Kokomo in the late 1840s. One such group of five men and six women left in the fall of 1847 and returned in the early spring of 1848. The men hunted and trapped game animals for meat and fur, while the women stayed in camp and prepared the meat and hides.[32] Coincidentally, the last bear was hunted and killed in Indiana in 1847.

The generation after removal was a period of relative stability in which Miami leaders and tribespeople could adapt at their own pace to the changes brought on by the rapid settlement of northern Indiana. While Miami people continued to adopt many elements of the surrounding Euro-American culture, they retained much of their own culture. The scarcity of game animals encouraged increasing reliance on the rivers for food. Miami men speared, trapped, netted, and shot fish with bow and arrow, the specific method depending on the species of fish and the season. Miami people continued to grow the soft white corn they had used as a trade item in the eighteenth century. For home use it was made into hominy. A number of edible plants such as the milkweed, young pokeweed, dandelion, Jerusalem artichoke, and wild mustard were gathered, some of them introduced from Europe or Asia after contact. As whites cleared or drained more land, such plants spread readily, particularly along the edges of clearings.[33] Wild blackberries, raspberries, and gooseberries were popular food items, as were wild plums, grapes, cherries, and the fruits and nuts of various trees.

Nearly all marriages in the generation after removal were by "Indian custom." Often a leader would choose a marriage partner for a young man. A gift such as a pony would be given to the young woman's parents. Later clan affiliation would depend on whether the couple went to live with the husband's or the wife's family. Plural marriages among the tribal elite were still common. Francis Godfroy was best known for his two wives, but at least eight other Miami men had plural marriages as late as the 1860s. Such marriages created kin relationships with a much larger group of people and were a sign of status as well. The death of marriage partners was common, as was divorce, so that most people were married several times. Ozahshinquah, a daughter of Frances Slocum, was married five times and had children by each of her husbands. William Godfroy had a plural marriage for a time and five other wives during his long life (1822–1911). The Miami also had a rigid taboo against marrying within a clan, even though the relationship might be quite distant by non-Indian standards. With such a large number of marriages between the six acceptable clans of a small group, kinship relationships quickly became extremely complex.

When death came to the less acculturated Miami living along the Wabash and the Mississinewa, they were buried in village or family cemeteries, usually in unmarked graves. In testimony given in 1872, Pecongeoh (Charles Peconga), a son of Meshingomesia, described Miami burial customs:

> When a person dies, they go and bury him, but still they say his spirit is there at the house yet. They say that when they don't make an adoption, the spirit still stays there and all the rest of the family keep dying off. . . . The one that is adopted does not take the place of the one that died—it is in order to get the spirit of the one that is dead to Heaven, the same thing that you would call a funeral.[34]

Usually favorite objects were placed in or on the grave. Years later Mrs. Sarah Wadsworth recalled seeing the

# Major Miami Sites
## circa 1847–1872

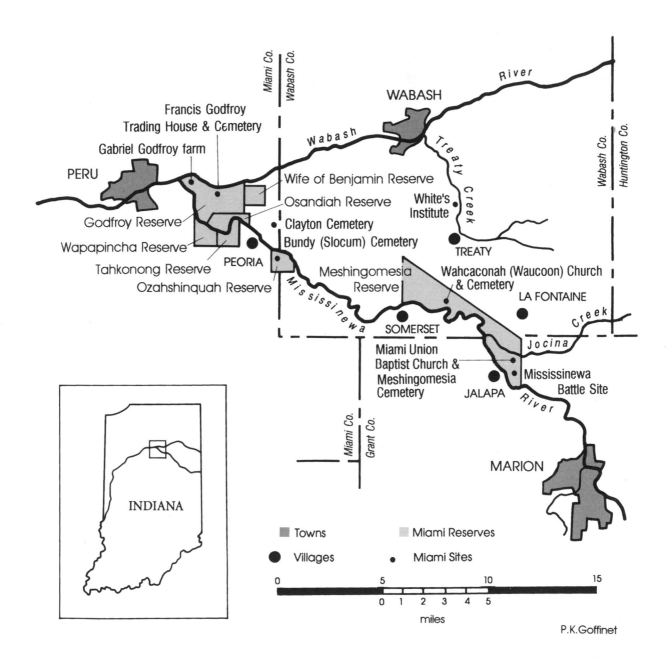

P.K.Goffinet

burial of Peshewa in 1855 when she was a girl living in Miami County. She stated that the assembled group ate and then placed food near the head of the deceased. A favorite horse of Peshewa was killed for the journey to the spirit land.[35] At the time many Miami still believed that the spirit of the dead remained for four or five days where the person had lived. Often a pole with a white flag attached was raised over a grave so that the Great Spirit would know where the deceased lay.[36]

The more acculturated Catholic Miami who lived away from the main body of the tribe had Christian burial services and were buried in marked graves, often in a portion of a larger non-Indian graveyard. The Lafontaine family west of Huntington had a large burial plot in Mount Calvary Cemetery. The first burial in the family plot was that of Topeah, or Francis Lafontaine, the chief of the Miami tribe who died near Terre Haute in 1847 on his way back from Kansas.

After the death of Lafontaine, Meshingomesia was chosen to lead the Indiana Miami. Meshingomesia was long noted for his prudent leadership of the largest group within the tribe. He favored the adoption of white culture, but in the protected environment of a reservation where change could take place slowly. He managed many of the everyday affairs of his group of some sixty people, choosing wives for young men and marrying them, ordering miscreants off the reservation, and selecting places where houses could be built. He had a firm idea of Miami treaty rights and resisted the demands of government officials if they were contrary to tribal needs.

In 1854 Commissioner of Indian Affairs George Manypenny summoned Eastern and Western Miami leaders to Washington, D.C., to negotiate a new treaty. The main purpose of the treaty was to "capitalize" the permanent annuities of the 1826 Miami treaty to end after a set term. Accordingly, $231,004 was set aside for the Indiana tribe at 5 percent interest, or $11,550 per year, which would be paid to tribal members until 1881, at which time the principal would be divided among all the tribespeople.[37] Meshingomesia led the Miami delegation which included his son Pecongeoh, Peter Bondy, Pimyotamah, and Keahcotwah (Buffalo). Gabriel Godfroy accompanied the group but was too young to serve as a delegate.

Meshingomesia accepted the capitalization and eventual ending of annuities, but otherwise used the treaty negotiations to consolidate Indiana Miami rights. Several times he was asked to sell the reservation bearing his name, but he refused. To counter the efforts of mixed-blood Miami from outside the Miami community to join tribal rolls, the Miami delegation inserted language in the treaty that no one should receive annuities unless he or she was added to the tribal roll "by the consent of the said

Miami Indians of Indiana, obtained in council, according to the custom of [the] Miami tribe of Indians."[38] A few years earlier the Office of Indian Affairs had added sixty-eight people to Miami rolls from the village of Papakeechi (Flat Belly), who had moved to Michigan to avoid removal, and from the family of Josetta Beaubien, the half-sister of John Baptiste Richardville. Neither group was accepted by the tribal council.

To ascertain who should receive annuity payments under the 1854 treaty a tribal roll or census was prepared. The new roll included the original families permitted to remain in Indiana as well as the group that returned from Kansas and their descendants. Although 302 names are listed, when duplications and the names of deceased tribespeople are eliminated, the roll indicates a population of 278.[39] Women at that time outnumbered men by 50 percent, or three to two, indicating evidence of the violence of the period before removal.

Most of the names on the 1854 roll are Miami, implying that most people still spoke the language. The non-Miami names were from the more acculturated Miami of mixed French-Miami marriages. The descendants of Pierre Langlois who lived near Lafayette fell into this category, as did some of the Richardville, Aveline, Godfroy, Goodboo, Bondy, and Lavonture families. Some of the Métis Miami still spoke French, while other Miami spoke little French or English. Among the early settlers around the Miami reserves were some Scotch Irish who migrated to northern Indiana from Virginia. These people were of old American stock, long acquainted with hunting, trapping, fishing, and making use of edible and medicinal plants. They had little or no formal education and lived not much differently than the Indians themselves. Soon they were working for Miami people and began marrying among them. Their children were always regarded as Miami Indians.

Important changes came to the Miami communities along the Wabash and the Mississinewa in the 1850s and 1860s. Land was slowly cleared, usually under contract with a white sharecropper. Contractors often built log houses for the Miami, and the older practice of living in tents or bark-covered shelters died out completely. Meshingomesia, Peter Bondy, Thomas Richardville, and other Miami leaders converted to the Baptist faith and encouraged tribespeople to do likewise. In the mid-1860s Meshingomesia allowed a Baptist church and a one-room school to be built on the south end of the reservation to encourage the adoption of Euro-American ways. While the Miami continued much of their annual subsistence cycle, they also purchased many everyday manufactured items in local country stores. In earlier times the Miami had purchased such items from traders. They were long accustomed to using food items such as rice, coffee, mustard,

*Plains Indian children at White's Institute, Treaty, Indiana, Wabash County.*

pepper, nutmeg, cinnamon, allspice, vinegar, baking powder, and molasses, as well as tools such as commercially made hoes, shovels, scythes, and whetstones, and personal items such as combs, tobacco pipes, and mirrors. Miami homes were furnished with chairs and tables, plates, cups and saucers, mugs, coffee pots, knives, forks, spoons, and blankets.[40] Miami personal attire by the 1860s was "citizen clothing" except for ceremonial occasions. Some Miami women continued to apply elaborate silk applique and beadwork to leggings, blankets, shawls, and moccasins.

Some examples of Miami usages of common items will illustrate the persistence of an Indian viewpoint. The Miami used hatchets or hand axes much as everyone else for cutting, clearing, and shaping wood. At the same time they believed that one could "split a storm" or tornado by sinking a hatchet into a nearby tree in the direction from which the storm was coming. Another example shows in the Miami use of ponies or horses. When the Miami rode in groups, even into town, they tended to ride single file. They were very reluctant to use their horses for farmwork and accumulated them in large numbers as a sign of wealth and status.

Changes in the world at large began to have a more profound and disturbing impact on the Miami tribe after the Civil War. Very few Miami served in the war, a sign of tension between the tribe and the federal government, as well as a sign of the scarcity of men. Less than one-fifth of the Meshingomesia reserve was cleared, and timber theft became an acute problem, often in the guise of bogus leases to whites. In November 1867 the aging Meshingomesia

wrote the commissioner of Indian Affairs asking that the last communal reservation in Indiana be allotted or divided among his family. In his letter he stated:

> Some of my band have been attending the schools of the whites and are disposed to engage in agricultural pursuits . . . they are reluctant to build houses and barns and make other permanent improvements unless they have the title to the land upon which they make such improvements and are guaranteed that they can hold and enjoy the same.[41]

It is difficult to assess how much influence white advisors such as Samuel McClure of Marion had in this controversial decision. In general, judging by what happened to these Miami lands, it could be said that the pressure for allotment was considerable. Congress passed enabling legislation in 1872, and in 1873 the reservation was split into sixty-three "farms" for those entitled to a share in the land. The allotments ranged from 77 to 125 acres. The land could not be taxed or sold until 1 January 1881, at which time the allottees were to be made United States citizens.[42]

Many of the allotments from the Meshingomesia reservation were made to children, who were required by law to have non-Indian guardians. A few of these guardians were honest, but most improved their wards' land through personal loans. Later, when the ward defaulted on the loan, the guardian recovered an improved farm with fences, house, barn, and other outbuildings.[43] When citizenship came in 1881 most of the Meshingomesia reserve allotments were heavily mortgaged. By 1890 whites owned two-thirds of the former reservation, and many of the Meshingomesia Miami had moved to Marion, hardly the outcome Meshingomesia had expected.

Another threat to Miami landownership came through attempts at taxation by local officials. As early as 1870 Grant County officials attempted to tax the Meshingomesia reserve. Initially the Grant County Circuit Court ruled in favor of local assessors, but the decision was overturned on appeal to the state supreme court.[44] Miami, Wabash, Huntington, and Allen counties placed many Miami treaty reserves on tax rolls during the 1870s. The Miami challenged property taxes on the basis that they were not United States citizens and the land was exempt through treaty provisions. In 1880 the commissioner of Indian Affairs issued a lengthy report on the tribe concluding that Indians who lived on treaty grants could not be taxed. The commissioner's opinion had no effect on local officials who continued to tax Miami lands.[45]

About 1870 the Miami began to experience high death rates. The Miami community may have become less healthy as the population concentrated in a few nearby clusters. In New England the denser settlement patterns that resulted when Indians quit seasonal hunts and took up fixed locations had encouraged the spread of infectious diseases.[46] At any rate the Indiana Miami died in such numbers that the tribal population actually declined from 330 in 1870 to 319 in 1881. In contrast, the tribal population had risen 18.7 percent from 1855 to 1869.[47]

The high mortality of the 1870s brought charges and countercharges of witchcraft between the Godfroy and the Meshingomesia Miami. As a Godfroy descendant told the story years later, "between the years 1872 and 1878 the Godfroy Band of Indians died like flies. They held a council and decided that Chief Me-shing-o-me-sia and his Indians were using witchcraft upon their people."[48] A modern scholar correlates witchcraft with the rapid decline in communal life that accompanies Indians' transition to private citizenship and the termination of state management of their lands. This was certainly happening to the Indiana Miami. As communities rebuild stability, charges of witchcraft tend to die out.[49]

The 1880s found the locus of the rural Miami population shifting to the Godfroy reserves of Miami County as the Meshingomesia land rapidly disappeared from Indian ownership. While the Meshingomesia Miami lost some two-thirds of their land during the 1880s, the Godfroy Miami and the nearby Bondy family lost only 20 percent of their land and retained 1,759 acres in 1890. (Bondy family landholdings on the Miami-Wabash County line declined from 805 acres to 542 acres during the 1880s.)[50] While the per capita payment of $695 made in 1881 from the Miami

capital fund undoubtedly helped for a time, the ending of annuities was a blow to the Miami cash economy. The decline in agricultural prices that set in during the decade of the 1880s was a further blow to those Miami families that had some farm income. To add to the economic woes of the Miami, local officials continued to tax Miami lands. (See map of Miami sites ca. 1847–1872.)

In 1886 the Miami won a major victory in the struggle against taxation of their lands. In a case involving eighty-two acres belonging to a Richardville descendant, the federal district court at South Bend ruled that while the state could enforce criminal and civil law on Indian lands, taxation of such lands was forbidden because it "might work a forfeiture or affect substantially the Indian right of exclusive and free enjoyment."[51] Following this decision the Indiana Supreme Court affirmed nontaxation of Miami treaty lands in 1891. The same year the state legislature passed a statute making the taxation of Miami lands unlawful and encouraging Miami owners to sue where lands were taxed to clear the title from any cloud created by tax assessment.[52]

Miami leaders were keenly aware of the need to maintain a tribal land base and moved swiftly to remove the burden of taxation from their lands. Gabriel Godfroy sued Miami County in 1891 and by 1897 had won a permanent injunction against further attempts at taxation.[53] Camillus Bundy, leader of the Miami who lived on the Ozahshinquah reserve, went further than Godfroy and sought the help of the Interior Department in instituting a suit in federal court to recover the taxes that were wrongfully collected. Calling himself "attorney in fact" for the Indiana Miami, Bundy circulated a petition among the Miami, many of whom signed with an "X," supporting his position. While allowing that the Meshingomesia Miami had been made citizens in 1881 and that their land could be taxed after that date, he asserted that the remainder of the Miami had never been made citizens, and their treaty lands remained exempt.

Commissioner of Indian Affairs Daniel Browning agreed with Bundy's logic and issued a report in 1897 that echoed the commissioner's report of 1880. Browning then requested a decision from the assistant attorney general for the Interior Department as to whether the federal government should press the cases or leave litigation to the Miami. On 23 November 1897 Assistant Attorney General Willis Van Devanter issued an opinion *against* Miami tax exemption, a staggering reversal of five federal court decisions supporting the Miami. Van Devanter based his decision on the legislation of 1881, which divided the capital fund from the 1854 treaty, saying that since that time the federal government had not recognized the Indiana Miami as a tribe.[54]

Van Devanter's opinion on Miami taxation had a devastating long-range effect on the tribe. The denial of the Indiana Miami tribal government meant that Miami treaties were voided, and the consequences were immediate and dire. Miami children were sent home from federal Indian schools in Lawrence, Kansas, and Carlisle, Pennsylvania, taxes were again levied on Miami treaty grants, and the Miami were told they could not sue for tribal rights in federal courts. By coincidence, Willis Van Devanter's father, Isaac Van Devanter, had been the attorney for the Meshingomesia Miami. Later Willis Van Devanter was appointed to the United States Supreme Court where he wrote several key decisions concerning Indian law. His 1897 decision stripping the Indiana Miami of federal status was inconsistent with later cases and is difficult to explain.

After the decline of the 1870s Miami population began to grow rapidly in the 1880s. At that time more Miami were marrying non-Indians, which increased the number of families. In addition, family size was increasing and mortality appears to have lessened. Tribal population increased from 318 in 1881 to 440 in 1895, when a new tribal roll was made. While the population increased only 14.7 percent in the twenty-seven years from 1854 to 1881, the increase from 1881 to 1895 was 38 percent.[55] At the very time tribal population began this rapid increase land losses accelerated, forcing many families off the land and into nearby towns. The Meshingomesia Miami bore the brunt of this forced migration.

The rapid growth of the Indiana Miami population that began in the early 1880s was not reflected in federal census returns. One can generally assert that census returns on Indians have reflected the legal and social status of Indians rather than the actual count of Indians in the state. Federal rolls of Indiana Miami made from 1854 to 1968 and more recent tribal rolls prepared for the federal government give a much more accurate picture of the tribal population. The increases in Miami population are similar to those of other tribes for which there are accurate enumerations. The 1890 and 1900 federal censuses are reasonably accurate for Miami Indians, but beginning in 1910 enumeration of the Miami dropped rapidly, reaching a low point in 1920. The latter year was also the low point for enumeration of Indians in Indiana. There is no evidence that the actual number of Indians declined. Rather, at a time when the national mood swung heavily toward "100% Americanism," many Indians chose not to identify themselves as such for the census enumerators. This underenumeration of Miami Indians did not begin to change until the 1960s.

Near the end of the nineteenth century outsiders again predicted the end of the Miami tribe, much as they had in the 1820s and 1830s. The perspective from within the tribe was different, one of anger over loss of land and federal recognition but not resignation. In the year 1902 representatives of the Godfroy, Meshingomesia, and Bundy groups created a formal tribal organization. Leaders peppered the Bureau of Indian Affairs with letters asking for assistance with treaty rights, recovery of land, and in pressing lawsuits in federal courts. The Miami leadership also engaged attorneys from Chicago to help with the complexities of federal Indian law.[56] The bureau repeatedly informed the Miami that the tribe had no legal status. Negative responses from Washington did not deter the efforts of Miami leaders to press for tribal rights. In 1903 Camillus Bundy initiated the Miami reunion, a tribal institution that continues to the present. Because fewer Miami lived in the countryside near each other the reunion took on importance as a social institution. It was also an occasion to discuss tribal business and often was preceded by a council meeting.

By 1920 the land issue was critical for the Miami as holdings dropped to 449 acres in Butler Township, Miami County, and on the west edge of Waltz Township in neighboring Wabash County. The Miami population on the land dwindled to only eleven families with a population of sixty-four.[57] Each year it seemed some important feature of Miami folklife was lost. In 1917 Polly Wildcat (or Mongosa) died, the last Miami who spoke no English. In 1921 the last fish were smoked for preservation at the Godfroy home. In 1922 the new owners of the Godfroy house tore down the log portion on the east side, which had been built in 1822 as Francis Godfroy's Mount Pleasant trading post. The loss of Miami foodways, folkways, language, crafts, and general knowledge of subsistence was steady.[58]

A low point for the Miami seemed to occur in 1923. In that year Camillus Bundy, a respected leader in the tribe and the last living child of Ozahshinquah, lost his 114-acre

*The Godfroy House, ca. 1900. Francis Godfroy (war chief of the Miami) built the right part of the house in 1822.*

farm to mortgage foreclosure. Bundy had argued for years that this portion of a treaty grant to his mother should never have been taxed. Reacting to the foreclosure, Bundy called a meeting at his house in September 1923 concerning full federal rights for the Miami tribe. This meeting became the foundation for the Miami Nation, the present tribal organization.[59]

In addition to renewing their struggle for treaty rights the Miami began the Ma-con-a-quah or Muk-kons-kwa (the Miami name of Frances Slocum) pageant to portray Miami customs for the Miami and whites. When enacted for Miami audiences the performance was called a powwow, and there was no charge. For non-Indians the performance was called a pageant, and the admission charge was fifteen to thirty cents. The Miami advertised: "Come, see and hear the Indians tell their history in their own way." The group of fifteen to thirty Miami, including children, performed over northern and central Indiana and in southern Michigan and western Ohio. Performances were an important source of money for tribal legal expenses and delegations to Washington, D.C. The group also enhanced the pride of the Miami people in themselves and asserted pride in Indian identity at a time when it was unpopular to do so. Many of the children who participated in the pageant later became tribal leaders.[60]

About the same time that the Miami renewed their struggle for treaty rights after World War I, the Potawatomi of southwestern Michigan began going to the University of Notre Dame at South Bend to exchange market baskets for food. The Pokagon Potawatomi produced large quantities of various kinds and sizes of utilitarian baskets that were sold or traded from households or at nearby rural market centers. Annually, from about 1921 up to the mid-1930s, numbers of Catholic Potawatomi would go to Notre Dame with wagonloads and Model-T loads of basketwork at Easter, Thanksgiving, and Christmas. The university would feed the visitors at its central kitchens and provide each family with a basket of staples. Many of the Potawatomi arrived festively dressed in tribal garb. These traditional gift exchanges supplied the university with all the containers it needed until the elders with the skills and disposition for the craft died and as more Potawatomi went into the wage economy, some of them in the South Bend area.[61]

The revitalization of the Miami leadership and culture during the 1920s did not affect the loss of land and hardship on the Miami people. Camillus Bundy summarized the Miami situation in a letter to President Calvin Coolidge in 1927:

> Once having been recognized by the Congress and government of this union no one has the right to dissolve us and destroy us as a race. But they have been doing so, and are doing so, and through it all we have been reduced to a plight which is a reproach upon this nation.[62]

At the time Bundy was urgently seeking aid for the Miami, Indian affairs had reached a crisis point throughout the United States. Specialists in law, education, and health visited Indian communities throughout the country and found appalling conditions. Removing the federal government from Indian affairs had not solved the "Indian problem" as many nineteenth-century reformers had hoped.[63]

The Meriam Report, as the survey of Indian affairs came to be called, showed that much of the previous reform was misguided and damaging in the context of tribal societies. Most Indians were not going to become small farmers, and destroying tribal governments did not help Indians adjust to modern society. With the coming of the New Deal many suggestions of the Meriam Report were incorporated in the landmark Wheeler-Howard or Indian Reorganization Act of 1934. Among other items,

## THE
# Ma-Con-a-Quah
## Company of Miami Indians

#### Who Are Real Indians Will Come to

## Beachwood   Park

#### Located on Huffman's Lake near

## Etna Green and Atwood

## On   T H U R S D A Y
# J U L Y   4th

**These Indians will be arrayed in their Gay Indian Costumes.**

The Company will give an Historical Indian Pageant portraying the life, costumes, and characteristics of the real American Red Man.   Come and hear the Indian Songs, see the Indian Dances, the  Adoption,  Hunting Trip, etc., on July 4th in the Afternoon at 2:30 and Evening at 7:30.

## Children from 8 to 12 years . . 15c
## Persons over 12 years . . . . . .30c

Refreshments and Lunch Served on  the  Grounds. Many Other Attractions.

## EVERYBODY   INVITED!

STEWART RAFERT

*Broadside of the 1920s announcing a Ma-con-a-quah pageant.*

the legislation encouraged the formation of tribal charters and tribal governments. The Miami of the Meshingomesia and Bundy clans had reorganized in 1923 and were ready to seek federal recognition for the Miami tribe under the new law. As part of the process they obtained a state charter as "The Miami Nation of Indians of the State of Indiana" on 30 September 1937.

In February 1938 the Miami Nation sponsored legislation that would bring a variety of tribal claims before the United States Court of Claims. When this legislation received noncommittal support from the Interior Department it was rewritten and resubmitted in 1939 to focus on the settlement for Miami lands in the 1826 Miami treaty. This legislation, which died in committee, anticipated the post–World War II Miami claims under the 1826 treaty. Later, in 1939, the Interior Department supervised the selection of an attorney to prosecute Indiana Miami claims. Because of pending Indiana Miami claims, the Bureau of Indian Affairs encouraged the Western Miami tribe to obtain a charter under the Oklahoma Indian Welfare Act, which supplemented the Wheeler-Howard Act. The Western Miami charter was approved on 10 October 1939, enabling the sister tribe to participate in claims under nineteenth-century treaties.[64]

The Great Depression of the 1930s worsened conditions in the already economically depressed Miami community. Local officials regarded Miami needs as a federal responsibility, while the federal government insisted the Miami needs were a local responsibility. Only a few Miami were high school graduates, and even the Miami with some education had great difficulty competing for jobs with non-Indians. Hunting, fishing, trapping, and gathering edible and medicinal plants became urgent activities again. Unfortunately for the Miami, state game law enforcement was tightened at the very time that many Miami returned to the rivers and countryside for subsistence activities. From 1930 to 1940 the tribe asserted hunting and fishing rights according to treaties in state and federal courts. The cases were uniformly rejected on the basis that the tribe had no federal status.[65]

The 1930s were the twilight of Miami subsistence activities, the final period when living off the land and rivers made an important difference to tribespeople. A few families continued to raise the traditional Miami corn, drying it on platforms and braiding the shucks of the seed corn ears to hang long strings of corn for drying as they had for centuries. Fur prices remained high enough that Miami men could trap and skin muskrat, fox, raccoon, skunk, and mink for sale to fur buyers in Wabash and Peru. In the early spring people gathered tonic greens such as wild onion and young pokeweed. Later in the season skunk cabbage, young milkweed, dandelion, shepherd's purse, plantain, ground cherry, cattail root and shoot, and Jerusalem artichoke were gathered. Many of the Miami who had been displaced from the countryside returned to favorite haunts to gather plants. Some of the fur-bearing animals such as muskrat and raccoon were eaten, as well as rabbit and squirrel. Men continued to spear and net fish, as well as hunt them with bow and arrow. Young rabbits and squirrels were popular, as were ducks. In the summer raspberries, blackberries, wild plums, and other fruits were gathered. In the fall people would gather apples from abandoned farmsteads as well as hickory nuts and walnuts.[66] Most families, even those living in town, supplemented their diets with some of the above items. Sharing of food, firewood, and coal was common and important. Nearly all Miami babies were born at home with the help of a midwife or one of the two or three local doctors willing to charge a few dollars for a birth.[67]

The arrival of electricity and home refrigeration in the countryside near the end of the 1930s lessened the need for old methods of food preservation. World War II brought jobs and a degree of prosperity unknown before. The war also took most young men away from home and introduced them to new skills and ideas. For the Miami, as for most tribes, World War II was a great dividing line between generations. The war also disrupted the Miami claims process and Indian claims in general. After the war began the tribal council passed a resolution of support for the American war effort, stating that "every family is represented by our boys at the front" and promising to forget for the duration of the war the obligations of the United States toward the tribe.[68] These good intentions were sorely tested in 1944 when Grant County officials sold the acre of land on which the Miami Baptist Church and Indian school were located for unpaid taxes. The land had always belonged to the tribe and was tax exempt as church land. The commissioner of Indian Affairs replied to the complaint of the tribal government that the tribe had lost federal protection in 1897, and there was nothing that could be done.[69]

When World War II ended Indian affairs took a new turn with passage of the Indian Claims Commission Act in 1946. The legislation created a three-person board to review all grievances against the federal government arising before 1946. Congress allowed the commission ten years to examine claims and limited attorneys' fees to 10 percent of final awards. The intent of the legislation was to achieve a final settlement of all obligations of the federal government to tribes, leading to a "final solution" of the age-old "Indian problem." Once the commission began hearings the Justice Department militantly defended government interests, taking an adversarial role toward tribes. By 1960 the Claims Commission had dismissed 88 of 105 claims and often sought delays while it played one tribe against another. When an award was finally made it was based on values at the time of original treaties with no adjustment made for interest or loss in value of the dollar.[70]

The Indiana Miami tribe had been pressing various claims against the federal government since 1859. The loss of federal recognition by administrative fiat in 1897 had intensified tribal claims because the tribal government was eliminated from the judicial process. Tribal leaders had little formal education and few financial resources. Federal denial of Miami claims and, worse yet, the denial of the right to make a claim was intensely frustrating. Further, Congress had legislated differently for the Meshingomesia and other Miami clans, heightening clan rivalry. Few outsiders, including claims attorneys, could appreciate the depth of Miami alienation from Anglo-American jurisprudence.

In October 1949 the Indiana Miami initiated the claims process by signing a contract with attorneys that was approved by the Bureau of Indian Affairs. Ira Sylvester Godfroy, William Godfroy, and John A. Owens, descendants of chiefs Francis Godfroy, John B. Richardville, and Francis Lafontaine, were plaintiffs for the tribe.[71] Representatives of the Miami Nation held back because they had pursued a much broader range of claims and federal recognition of the tribe in the 1930s. There was some sentiment among leaders of the Miami Nation that a settlement on land claims could prejudice tribal sovereignty. This concern was not unfounded, as one intent of the Claims Commission was to prepare the way for termination of tribal governments once claims were settled.[72]

As soon as the Miami filed claims of thirteen million dollars on land they had lost in Indiana, the Delaware, Potawatomi, Kickapoo, and the Six Nations of the Iroquois filed counterclaims to the Miami territory.[73] Teams of anthropologists and ethnohistorians formed the Great Lakes–Ohio Valley Project and spent a number of years sorting through the competing claims to assess tribal use and occupancy of the state. In 1956 the commission awarded the Indiana Miami 75 cents an acre for land the government had paid 6.4 cents for in 1818. Tribal officials appealed, and in 1960 the commissioners awarded $1.15 an acre, or $8,091,400 to the Indiana and Oklahoma Miami tribes. When the tribal roll was completed in 1968 about 3,066 Indiana Miami were found eligible to share in the award, which came to a little over $1,200 each after legal expenses and treaty payments were deducted.[74] Much of the money went for consumer goods and did little to alleviate the long-term poverty of a large portion of the tribe. In 1979 Congress

appropriated $1,373,000 on the final Indiana Miami award from the Claims Commission. The Muskogee, Oklahoma, office of the Bureau of Indian Affairs was so slow in amending the tribal roll that eleven years elapsed before the money was paid in 1990.[75]

World War II and postwar nationwide movements of Native Americans also affected Indiana. In a movement that primarily sought economic opportunity, Native Americans migrated from all areas of the country into Indiana's industrial areas. The resulting population distribution contrasts with that found earlier. The indigenous Miami were and are found primarily in the upper Wabash and, secondarily, with the indigenous Potawatomi in the South Bend area. More recent migrants tend to be dispersed throughout the state or concentrated in cities. Of the more recent migrants the Cherokee are the most concentrated (in east central Indiana), the most numerous nonindigenous group, and the most active in their own subtribal activities.

Other issues of great emotional significance affected the Indiana Miami after World War II. In the mid-1960s federal watershed control efforts led to construction of the Mississinewa dam that flooded fourteen thousand acres of the Mississinewa valley dear to the memory of generations of Miami people. Much of the former Ozahshinquah and Meshingomesia reserves were flooded, and the new reservoir made the relocation of several Miami cemeteries necessary. The largest and best known was the Bundy (or Frances Slocum) cemetery, located on land Camillus Bundy had tried to protect from mortgage foreclosure in the 1920s. Many Miami of several clans had family buried there. Closest of kin were required by Army Corps of Engineers rules to be present during disinterment. Remains and burial objects were put in surplus army footlockers and reburied in a new cemetery located on high ground a mile and a half away.[76] Many families were concerned that not all remains were removed from the many unmarked graves, some dating to the 1830s. Moving the cemeteries and flooding the lower Mississinewa valley again caused the Miami to feel powerless in the face of bureaucratic authority.

Protection of Miami cemeteries and other prehistoric and historic Indian burial sites throughout Indiana became a high priority of the Miami tribe during the 1980s. Tribal chairman Ray White, Jr., testified before the Kentucky and Indiana legislatures and spoke before professional archaeological societies to strengthen protection of native burial complexes and sites. The destruction of a large archaic burial site near Uniontown, Kentucky, in 1988 spurred protests and action from Native American leaders around the country and stimulated Kentucky and Indiana to pass legislation making such destruction a felony. The amateur excavation and destruction of Windsor Mound, a few miles east of Muncie in Randolph County, the same year emphasized the need for such legislation. The hasty and careless removal of artifacts from one of the best-preserved Adena mounds in Indiana was a loss to the citizens of the state and a great concern to professional archaeologists.

In the mid-1970s Oliver Godfroy of Peru returned to federal court with the nearly century-old Miami claim for tax exemption on treaty reserves. The land involved was seventy-nine acres of a treaty grant set aside for Francis Godfroy in 1838. Gabriel Godfroy, the plaintiff's grandfather, had first sued for tax exemption on the land in 1878. The case, *Swimming Turtle* v. *Board of Commissioners of Miami County*, involved a review of all the earlier applicable cases, as well as the meaning of Article III of the Northwest Ordinance in a modern context. That article stated in part that "The utmost good faith shall always be observed toward the Indians; their lands and property shall never be taken from them without their consent." On 25 August 1977 Judge Allen Sharp ruled that Godfroy:

> who had made every reasonable effort consistent with realities of modern society to maintain his status as an Indian was an "Indian" as defined in Article III of the Northwest Ordinance which exempts Miami Indian land from taxation by state or its political subdivision.[77]

While Godfroy's parcel was virtually the only treaty grant land left in Miami hands, the court victory was an important symbol to the Miami tribe as it supported "Indianness."

The Indiana Miami activities concerning land claims and tax exemption in the 1960s and 1970s repeated those of the 1920s and 1930s with the exception that the tribe was at last achieving some success. A new opportunity opened in 1978 when the Bureau of Indian Affairs established guidelines for tribes that sought federal recognition. In a minor irony of history, the regulations for achieving federal recognition were published just as the Indian Claims Commission—established to terminate federal rights—issued its final report. Recovering federal legal rights was one of the oldest goals of the Indiana Miami tribe, going back to 1897 when recognition was administratively removed.

Within five months of the publication of the federal guidelines, the Indiana Miami tribe notified the Bureau of Indian Affairs that it would petition for federal acknowledgment. In January 1980 the Indiana House and Senate overwhelmingly passed a joint resolution supporting federal recognition of the tribe.[78] In the ensuing two years a number of tribal meetings were held to discuss federal recognition. Lora Siders, the tribal

*A Miami general meeting, 1984, Wabash, Indiana.*

secretary, began updating tribal rolls, and in 1982 the tribe hired one of the authors of this essay, Stewart Rafert, to assist with the many technical issues of a petition. Tribal funding was supplemented by a series of grants from the Administration for Native Americans, Department of Health and Human Services.

The Miami petition was submitted in July 1984, reviewed by the Branch of Acknowledgment and Research, the office that would make a decision, and additional evidence was submitted in 1985. Unfortunately for the tribe the Branch of Acknowledgment slowed its work and nearly came to a halt under pressure from federally recognized tribes that did not want competition from new tribes for scarce federal funds, from budget cutters who did not want more Indians added to federal rolls, and from those opposed to Indian gaming. In the ensuing years over thirty completed petitions of other tribal groups have been filed, while the Branch of Acknowledgment has taken an increasingly painstaking approach to each case.[79] The Pokagon Potawatomi of Dowagiac, Michigan, several of whose tribal members had migrated to the South Bend, Indiana, area as early as the 1920s, submitted their petition in 1985 and were caught in the same slowdown as the Miami. In May 1989 Phil Alexis and Ray White testified before the Senate Select Committee on Indian Affairs concerning the difficulties and great expense of the recognition process for the Potawatomi and Miami. The Pokagon group turned to Congress and gained federal recognition in September 1994.

The 1980s saw a resurgence of Miami tribal life in Indiana despite the frustrations of nonrecognition. Early in the decade the tribe established its first modern offices and began actively intervening on behalf of Miami Indians as well as other Indians within Indiana and the nation. Office needs expanded until the tribe purchased the old Peru High School complex in 1990.[80] With funding from bingo and other business enterprises, the tribe renovated the building and opened the Little Turtle Day Care Center in 1991 and began serving meals for the elderly. The Junior Council of the tribe sponsored a number of fund-raising activities as well as prizewinning floats in the Circus City Parade and the Three Rivers Festival in Fort Wayne.[81]

Native American awareness and activities in Indiana intensified throughout the 1980s and into the 1990s, shifting from the anger of the 1970s to a multifaceted approach to Indian issues and awareness. The Miami, Potawatomi, and other Indian organizations sponsored many powwows, raising public awareness that an active Indian population existed in the state. Indian groups also sponsored floats in parades, returned to beadwork, basketry, and other traditional crafts, and joined together to combat stereotypes and to raise public awareness of Indian issues. Of perhaps greater importance, the state's Native Americans spoke with an Indian perspective on issues key to all citizens, such as preservation of heritage, respect for ancestors, and protection of the state's wildlife and natural resources.

In Indianapolis Jan Hammel of the American Indian Movement (AIM) often raised important issues that were then shaped by various Indian constituencies. AIM-inspired charges motivated the formation of the Inter-tribal Council of Indians in the early 1980s, which dealt primarily with burial issues. LeRoy Malaterre and other Indians in the greater Indianapolis area initiated the American Indian Council in 1976.[82] The council has sponsored a traditional powwow annually since that date and has kept its statewide membership informed of midwestern powwows, other Indian events, and critical issues. Oowanah Chasing Bear, a Kiowa Apache, founded the Red Hawk Native American Support Group in the late 1980s to insure that key events in American Indian history are remembered. The Red Hawk Group also sends food and supplies several times a year to needy people on reservations.[83]

Non-Indian groups and organizations have broadened their perspectives to include and assist Indiana's Indians in important ways. Various historical organizations in Fort Wayne, South Bend, Lafayette, and other cities now include Indian input into their displays and living history exhibits. The Minnetrista Cultural Center in Muncie, opened in 1989, invited Miami Indians to create an exhibit of their culture and has since assisted all the tribes

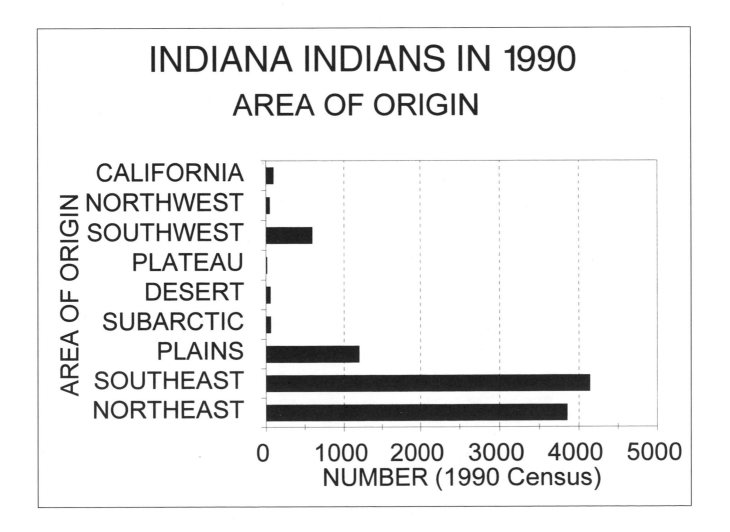

INDIANA INDIANS IN 1990
AREA OF ORIGIN

that have been associated with Indiana to meet on regular occasions to plan conferences and workshops on all aspects of Indian culture.[84] In 1992 Gov. Evan Bayh recognized the need to facilitate communication among the state's Indians and citizens by creating a state Indian Commission. The commission will serve as a clearinghouse for the state's Native Americans to express their needs and ideas and will raise the awareness of the general citizenry of the Indian population in many ways.

The 1990s began on a difficult note for the Indiana Miami when the Bureau of Indian Affairs made a negative preliminary ruling on the Miami petition in July 1990. While the federal government conceded that recognition had been illegally removed from the tribe in 1897, Branch of Acknowledgment staff were unwilling to restore legal status. Instead they maintained that the tribe met all the acknowledgment criteria until World War II, but after World War II did not show sufficient evidence of a tribal community or political influence over tribal members.[85] After the negative finding the tribe employed attorney Arlinda Locklear and anthropologist Jack Campisi of the Native American Rights Fund and the authors of this

essay to prepare a rebuttal to the finding. The rebuttal was filed in June 1991. Preparation of additional technical evidence cost in excess of one hundred thousand dollars. On 9 June 1992 the Branch of Acknowledgment again made a negative ruling on the Miami petition.[86] In September 1992 tribal officials filed suit over the decision. Among tribal officials and elders there was again the feeling that justice delayed was justice denied.[87]

For a century and a half outsiders have expected the Indians of Indiana to disappear. Instead, the Miami tribe has done everything within its power to maintain its treaty status and the rights conferred for signing over much of the land of Indiana. While the Miami people closely resemble other citizens of Indiana in their lifestyles, goals, and desires, the claims of a Miami heritage, earned through a long and not yet completed struggle, are powerful. The other Indians of Indiana, who now far outnumber the Miami, have similar claims to a rich Native American heritage. The pressures to assimilate will remain strong, but the Indians of Indiana by and large have chosen to honor their ancestors and their children by maintaining a precious identity for the future.

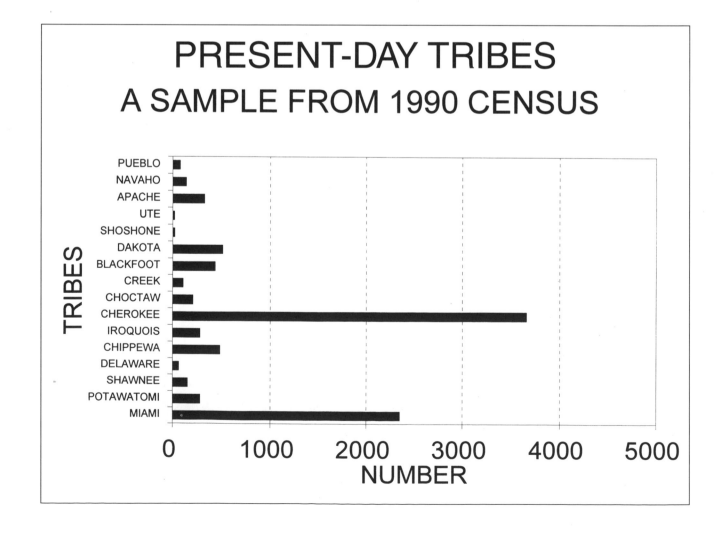

## Notes

1. Father Louis Hennepin, *A Description of Louisiana,* trans. John Gilmary Shea, March of America facsimile series, no. 30 (Ann Arbor, Mich.: University Microfilms, 1966), 140.

2. From Pierre Margry, vol. 1, p. 116, translated and interpreted by William A. Hunter, "History of the Ohio Valley," in *Northeast,* vol. 15 of *Handbook of North American Indians,* ed. Bruce G. Trigger (Washington, D.C.: Smithsonian Institution Press, 1978), 588–89.

3. Reuben Gold Thwaites, ed., *The Jesuit Relations and Allied Documents,* 73 vols. (Cleveland: Burrows Bros. Co., 1896–1901), 59:145.

4. There are few recent syntheses of Indiana's prehistory. The most recent with that intention is James H. Kellar, *An Introduction to the Prehistory of Indiana* (Indianapolis: Indiana Historical Society, 1983). A collection of articles providing more recent interpretations of some periods of central Indiana prehistory is in Ronald Hicks, ed., *Native American Cultures in Indiana: Proceedings of the First Minnetrista Council for Great Lakes North American Studies* (Muncie, Ind.: Minnetrista Cultural Center and Ball State University, 1992).

5. John T. Dorwin, *Fluted Points and Late-Pleistocene Geochronology in Indiana,* vol. 4, no. 3 of *Prehistory Research Series* (Indianapolis: Indiana Historical Society, 1966).

6. Donald R. Cochran, "Adena and Hopewell Cosmology," in *Native American Cultures in Indiana,* 26–40.

7. A full description of this site is found in Glenn A. Black, *Angel Site: An Archaeological, Historical, and Ethnological Study,* 2 vols. (Indianapolis: Indiana Historical Society, 1967).

8. A recent examination of this issue, past and present, has been made by James A. Brown, "Ethnohistoric Connections," in *At the Edge of Prehistory: Huber Phase Archaeology in the Chicago Area,* eds. James A. Brown and Patricia J. O'Brien (Kampsville: Published for the Illinois Department of Transportation by the Center for American Archeology, 1990), 155–60.

9. An excellent treatment of the history of Indiana during the prestatehood period is John D. Barnhart and Dorothy L. Riker, *Indiana to 1816: The Colonial Period* (Indianapolis: Indiana Historical Bureau and Indiana Historical Society, 1971). A collection of articles pertaining to the contest for continent from the perspective of the Indiana region is found in John B. Elliott, ed., *Contest for Empire, 1500–1775: Proceedings of an Indiana American Revolution Bicentennial Symposium* (Indianapolis: Indiana Historical Society, 1975).

10. For a detailed description of the fur trade in Indiana see Bert Anson, "The Fur Traders in Northern Indiana" (Ph.D. diss., Indiana University, 1953). For a developmental discussion see Elizabeth J. Glenn, "Miami and Delaware Trade Routes and Relationships in Northern Indiana," in *Native American Cultures in Indiana,* 58–70.

11. Helen Hornbeck Tanner, ed., *Atlas of Great Lakes Indian History* (Norman: Published for the Newberry Library by the University of Oklahoma Press, 1987), 169–71.

12. *Collections of the State Historical Society of Wisconsin,* vol. 16 (Madison: Published by the Society, 1902), 322–26.

13. Ibid., vol. 17, pp. 181, 185.

14. Ives Goddard, in Trigger, ed., *Northeast,* 583–87.

15. A standard holistic work is R. Carlyle Buley, *The Old Northwest: Pioneer Period, 1815–1840,* 2 vols. (Indianapolis: Indiana Historical Society, 1950). Specific topics relating to this region are covered in *Pathways to the Old Northwest: An Observance of the Bicentennial of the Northwest Ordinance* (Indianapolis: Indiana Historical Society, 1988).

16. The most recent biography of Little Turtle is Harvey Lewis Carter, *The Life and Times of Little Turtle: First Sagamore of the Wabash* (Urbana: University of Illinois Press, 1987).

17. A useful concept discussed by Jacqueline Peterson in "Many Roads to Red River: Métis Genesis in the Great Lakes Region, 1680–1815," in *The New Peoples,* eds. Jacqueline Peterson and Jennifer S. H. Brown (Lincoln: University of Nebraska Press, 1985), 60. She defined "jack-knife" posts as: "subsidiary trading outlets run by a single trader and his employees or by one or more trading families related by blood or marriage." Settlements at South Bend and Peru started as jack-knife posts.

18. Wiley Sword, *President Washington's Indian War: The Struggle for the Old Northwest, 1790–1795* (Norman: University of Oklahoma Press, 1985) is a recent intensive analysis of this period.

19. Ibid., 258–311.

20. There are a number of biographies of Tecumseh, the most recent of which is by R. David Edmunds, *Tecumseh and the Quest for Indian Leadership* (Boston: Little, Brown, 1984).

21. Logan Esarey, ed., *Messages and Letters of William Henry Harrison,* 2 vols. (reprint, 1975; vols. 7 and 9 of *Indiana Historical Collections,* 1922), 1:457.

22. R. David Edmunds has written a recent biography on Tecumseh's brother, *The Shawnee Prophet* (Lincoln: University of Nebraska Press, 1983).

23. Tanner, ed., *Atlas,* 106–11, provides a convenient listing and location map of the War of 1812 battles in the West. The Mississinewa confrontations are discussed in Elizabeth J. Glenn, "The Ethnohistoric Report on the Battle of Mississinewa," *Archaeological Reports* 14 (1977).

24. The texts of all American Indian treaties are found in chronological order in Charles J. Kappler, comp. and ed., *Indian Treaties, 1778–1883* (New York: Interland Publishing Co., 1972).

25. Published primary accounts of the Potawatomi removal provide excellent examples of how this policy was effected, e.g., Irving McKee, ed., *The Trail of Death: Letters of Benjamin Marie Petit* (Indianapolis: Indiana Historical Society, 1941); "The Attempted Potawatomi Emigration of 1839," *Indiana Magazine of History* 45 (Mar. 1949): 51–80; "A Continuation of the Journal of an Emigrating Party of Potawatomi Indians, 1838, and Ten William Polke Manuscripts," ibid., 44 (Dec. 1948): 392–408; and "Jacob Hull's Detachment of the Potawatomi Emigration of 1838," ibid., 45 (Sept. 1949): 285–88, all edited by Dwight Smith.

26. Nellie Armstrong Robertson and Dorothy Riker, eds., *The John Tipton Papers,* 3 vols. (Indianapolis: Indiana Historical Bureau, 1942), 1:facing p. 408; Sarah Jane Tucker, *Indian Villages of Illinois Country,* Illinois State Museum *Scientific Papers* 2, no. 1 (1942): Plate XLIX.

27. Charles C. Trowbridge, *Meearmeear Traditions,* vol. 7 of *Occasional Contributions* (Ann Arbor: University of Michigan Press, 1938); *Shawnee Traditions,* vol. 9 of ibid. (1939); *The Journals and Indian Paintings of George Winter, 1837–1839* (Indianapolis: Indiana Historical Society, 1948).

28. Bert Anson, *The Miami Indians* (Norman: University of Oklahoma Press, 1970), 206, 211–12, 225–26; Stewart Rafert, *The Miami Indians of Indiana: A Persistent People, 1654–1994* (Indianapolis: Indiana Historical Society, 1996).

29. A. A. Cole to Commissioner of Indian Affairs, 12 Feb. 1850, Office of Indian Affairs, Letters Received, RG 75, M234, National Archives, Washington, D.C.

30. *Resolution 6, May 1, 1850,* 31st Cong., 1st sess.

31. Miami Indians of Indiana, Census Roll of 1854, RG 75, National Archives. The 1854 Miami roll gives the locations of all the Miami groups.

32. Testimony Pursuant to Congressional Legislation of June 1 1872, RG 75, ISP Shelf 8, Entry 310, p. 287, National Archives. Copies of this document are in the Indiana Historical Society Library, Indianapolis, and the Minnetrista Cultural Center, Muncie.

33. William Cronon, *Changes in the Land* (New York: Hill and Wang, 1983), 51.

34. Testimony, 410–11.

35. Sarah Wadsworth interview, 10 Oct. 1909, Jacob P. Dunn Papers, Notebook 1, Indiana State Library, Indianapolis.

36. *Journals and Indian Paintings of George Winter,* 194 n.

37. Charles J. Kappler, ed., *Indian Affairs: Laws and Treaties,* 2 vols. (Washington, D.C.: Government Printing Office, 1904), 2:643–44.

38. Ibid., 2:644.

39. Stewart J. Rafert, "The Hidden Community: The Miami Indians of Indiana, 1846–1940" (Ph.D. diss., University of Delaware, 1982), 170.

40. Ibid., 115–16.

41. Meshingomesia to Commissioner of Indian Affairs, 21 Nov. 1867, Office of Indian Affairs.

42. *U.S. Statutes at Large,* 17:213.

43. Rafert, "Hidden Community," 33–39.

44. *Me-shing-go-me-sia and Another* v. *The State and Another,* 36 Indiana 310 (1871).

45. Rafert, "Hidden Community," 33–39; Land Division, Letter Book 37, RG 75, pp. 51–70, National Archives.

46. Cronon, *Changes in the Land,* 101.

47. Rafert, "Hidden Community," 176, 179.

48. Clarence Godfroy, *Miami Indian Stories* (Winona Lake, Ind.: Light and Life Press, 1961), 81.

49. William Simmons, *Spirit of the New England Tribes: Indian History and Folklore* (Hanover, N.H.: University Press of New England, 1986), 116–17.

50. Landholdings were calculated from deed books in the Miami and Wabash County Recorder's Office, 1880–1890.

51. *Wau-pe-man-qua* v. *Aldrich,* 28 F. 489, 497 (1886).

52. *Acts of Indiana,* 57th General Assembly, regular session, 1891, pp. 115–16.

53. Miami County, Indiana, Circuit Court, Order Book No. 44, p. 171.

54. *Decisions Relating to the Public Lands* (Washington, D.C.: Government Printing Office, 1898), 25:426–32.

55. Rafert, "Hidden Community," 186–88.

56. Ibid., 206–7; Edward B. Stark and Charles A. Denison to Commissioner of Indian Affairs William A. Jones, 4 Mar. 1902, Office of Indian Affairs, Letters Received, RG 75, National Archives.

57. Thirteenth Census, 1920, Butler Township, Miami County, Ind.

58. Interviews by author with LaMoine Marks, 24–25 Aug. 1989.

59. Memorandum, Carmen Mary Ryan, 29 Oct. 1964, Miami Nation of Indians of Indiana, archives, Peru, Indiana.

60. Interview by author with Lora Siders, 9 July 1985.

61. James A. Clifton, *The Pokagons, 1683–1983* (Lanham, Md.: University Press of America, 1984), 116–17.

62. Office of Indian Affairs, Letters Received, 8 June 1927, RG 75, 28876, National Archives.

63. William T. Hagan, *American Indians* (Chicago: University of Chicago Press, 1979), 152–53.

64. Anson, *Miami Indians,* 260.

65. Rafert, "Hidden Community," 160–63.

66. Interviews with LaMoine Marks, 24–25 Aug. 1989.

67. Interview with Lora Siders, 9 July 1985.

68. Resolution, 11 Oct. 1942, Miami Nation of Indians of Indiana, archives.

69. Land Division, Letters Sent, 2 Dec. 1944, RG 75, 43361, National Archives.

70. James S. Olson and Raymond Wilson, *Native Americans in the Twentieth Century* (Urbana: University of Illinois Press, 1984), 137, 140, 143.

71. Agreement of 31 Oct. 1949, Miami Nation of Indians of Indiana, archives.

72. Olson and Wilson, *Native Americans in the Twentieth Century,* 137.

73. Ibid., 139.

74. Anson, *Miami Indians,* 284–88.

75. Payment was announced at the fall meeting of the Miami Nation of Indians, 21 Oct. 1990.

76. Interviews by author with Herman and Wyneeta Bundy, 24 Nov. 1980 and Phyllis Miley, 13 Oct. 1993.

77. *Swimming Turtle* v. *Board of Commissioners of Miami County,* 441 F. Supp. 374 (1975).

78. [Indiana] Senate Concurrent Resolution No. 9, 21 Jan. 1980.

79. "Summary Status of Acknowledgment Cases," Branch of Acknowledgment and Research, Bureau of Indian Affairs, 22 Oct. 1993.

80. *Kokomo Tribune,* 14 Nov. 1990.

81. Indiana Miami Tribal Newsletter, 29 Mar. 1992.

82. Newsletter, American Indian Council [Lebanon, Ind.], Mar. 1993.

83. Ibid., Jan. 1991.

84. *Peru Daily Tribune,* 31 May 1991.

85. *Kokomo Tribune,* 18 July 1990.

86. *Fort Wayne News-Sentinel,* 10 June 1992.

87. *Peru Daily Tribune,* 12 Sept. 1992.

# PEOPLES OF THE PACIFIC:

## Australians and New Zealanders, Pacific Islanders, Filipinos

JAMES A. BALDWIN

*Most Filipinos in Indiana today are part of the fourth wave of Filipino immigration to the United States, the immigration of English-speaking, highly trained professional people and their families, most of whom arrived after United States immigration laws were liberalized in 1965. These immigrants have made their mark on Indiana most notably in the field of medicine.*

The Pacific Ocean, together with its associated seas and islands plus the continent of Australia, covers almost half of the earth's total surface area. This enormous geographic region extends from Southeast Asia's Malay Peninsula eastward to the west coast of South America and from the Gulf of Alaska southward to the fringes of Antarctica. That portion of this region from the Philippines south to Australia lies as far from Indiana as it is possible to be and still be on the surface of the earth. In fact, the antipode of Indianapolis—the point where a line connecting Indianapolis and the center of the earth would emerge on the other side of the globe—is located off the southwest tip of Australia. When it is noon in Indianapolis it is midnight in most of Indonesia.

The three hundred million people who today live throughout this vast region are descended from perhaps the most migratory assemblage of peoples that the world has ever known. As early as forty thousand years ago seafaring peoples had reached Australia from Asia. By 3000 B.C. Polynesians had set out on perilous canoe voyages that took them across thousands of miles of open and uncharted ocean. By A.D. 1000 Polynesian navigators had discovered and settled the distant archipelagoes of New Zealand and Hawaii. Finally, beginning in 1788 (after enduring a six-month voyage more than halfway around the world) Europeans began arriving in large numbers in Australia and, starting with a missionary settlement in 1814, in New Zealand as well.[1] This migratory tradition of the far-flung peoples of the Pacific has brought many of them—particularly Australians, New Zealanders, Pacific Islanders, and Filipinos—to North America and to Indiana. Today there are approximately seven thousand people living in Indiana whose roots lie in the Pacific region (Table 1).

### Australians and New Zealanders

Over the last two centuries tens of thousands of mostly British and Irish immigrants have moved, willingly or unwillingly, to Australia and New Zealand, largely displacing the indigenous populations of both lands. The British government originally developed Australia as a penal colony, and British courts continued to ship convicts there as late as the 1860s. New Zealand, in contrast, was the goal of organized groups of farmers and other settlers sponsored by the Church of England or Presbyterian congregations in Scotland.

News of the discovery of gold in California in 1849 reached Australia before it reached the East Coast of

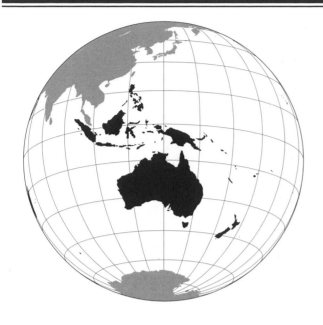

reported 61. By 1890 Australians were living in twenty-five of Indiana's counties, with the greatest number in Marion (11), Allen (8), and Elkhart, Lake, and Madison counties (4 each). By 1930 there were 98 Australians residing in Indiana, a figure that had increased only to 104 by the time of the 1940 census. The 1940 census reported that Indiana's Australian-born population was concentrated in Lake (41) and Marion (18) counties. Within Lake County the city of East Chicago reported 18 Australian-born residents, more than any other city in the state. Of the Australian-born population in 1930, 62 (or 63 percent) were male; in 1940, 61 (or 59 percent) were male.[5]

The 1960 census, however, reported 277 Australian-born individuals in Indiana, of whom only 67 (or 24 percent) were male. This dramatic shift in the sex ratio of the Australian-born population of Indiana, from 59 percent male in 1940 to 76 percent female in 1960, reflects the post–World War II influx of war brides. The 1960 census also recorded 372 individuals for whom at least one parent had been born in Australia, resulting in a total of 649 people of Australian "stock" living in Indiana. By 1980 the census recorded 317 Indiana residents who were born in Australia. The same census also recorded 585 individuals who claimed to have one or more Australian ancestors. The 1990 census recorded 434 Australia-born residents of Indiana, while 826 individuals claimed Australian ancestry. These figures are up 37 and 41 percent, respectively, from the comparable 1980 figures.[6]

Temporary Australian visitors to Indiana over the years have included noted Melbourne journalist Richard Hughes. Hughes toured the United States in the months just before the Japanese attack on Pearl Harbor, reporting to his readers back home on American attitudes toward a war in which Australia—but not America—was already a participant. Desiring to gauge the sentiments of a "typical" American small town, Hughes spent a few days in Columbia City, Indiana. "You won't find this place on any map," he wrote of the county seat of Whitley County. "It's only a pinpoint on the State map of Indiana—Wendell Willkie's State. But it is magnificently typical of dozens of little Mid-West farm towns I have seen." Hughes lodged in a Columbia City hotel where he noted approvingly that "there are not so many flies as in an Australian country pub. And Berghoff's beer isn't as good as Victoria beer, but it is better than Sydney beer." After interviewing a number of local citizens, including State Highway Commissioner James Adams, Hughes concluded that "Columbia City [already] feels it is in the war, and it doesn't like the feeling."[7]

Even though Australians have always outnumbered New Zealanders in Indiana, New Zealand seems to have sent the first immigrant from the Pacific region to take up

the United States, and by the end of 1850 some eight thousand Australians (many of them British ex-convicts or escaped convicts) had arrived in California. The original name of San Francisco's notorious Barbary Coast district was "Sydney-Town," the neighborhood where many of these Australians settled.[2] Australian immigration to the United States has never equaled the high-water mark of 1850. During the 1880s, for example, less than a thousand Australian immigrants came to North America each year, while during the depression years of the 1930s approximately two thousand per year arrived. The peak twentieth-century year for Australian immigration was 1946 when over six thousand Australians arrived, most of them war brides accompanying American servicemen back to the States.[3] In recent decades, though, more Americans have settled in Australia than Australians have settled in the United States. During the 1970s, for example, an average of two thousand Australians came to the United States annually, while about five thousand Americans set out each year for a new life in Australia. Australians settling in the United States have continued to favor California: in 1970, 30 percent of United States residents of Australian (or New Zealand) descent lived in California.[4]

The earliest evidence of Australians settling in Indiana comes from the 1860 federal census, which revealed that 7 individuals born in Australia were living in the state, scattered from Vanderburgh County in the south (1) to Lake County in the north (3). It is likely that at least some of these Australians arrived in California during the gold rush a decade earlier but had come east along with many of those Hoosiers who had failed to find riches in the goldfields. The 1880 census recorded a total of 22 Australian-born people in Indiana, while the 1890 census

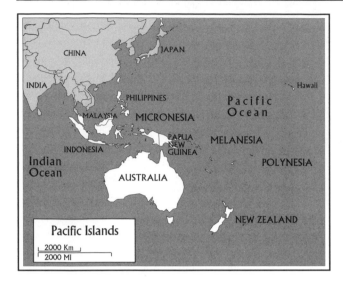

*Geoffrey J. Bannister, former New Zealander and president of Butler University in Indianapolis since 1989.*

residence in the Hoosier state. While the first Australians living in Indiana were not recorded until 1860, the 1850 census reported a single Indiana resident claiming New Zealand birth, an individual living in the Gibson County community of Princeton. The 1880 census counted 7 Indiana residents who had been born in New Zealand, 1 in Fort Wayne, and 6 in Crawfordsville. The 6 individuals in Crawfordsville were probably members of a single family. Eighty years later, as recorded in the 1960 census, Indiana was home to 44 individuals who had been born in New Zealand. Of these, 32 were females, an imbalance again reflecting the influx of the World War II war brides. The 1960 census also recorded 73 people who had been born in the United States with at least 1 New Zealand parent, resulting in a total of 117 people of New Zealand stock living in Indiana. The 1990 census recorded 134 individuals living in Indiana who had been born in New Zealand, an increase of 28 percent from the 105 New Zealand-born individuals living in Indiana in 1980.[8]

Australians and New Zealanders living in Indiana, because of their small numbers and because they have come from two countries very similar to the United States in culture, social structure, and language, have tended to assimilate quickly and with little difficulty.[9] Among recent arrivals in Indiana from Down Under is former New Zealander Geoffrey J. Bannister, president of Butler University in Indianapolis since 1989.

## Pacific Islanders

Geographers classify the many islands and island chains that sprinkle the map of the Pacific Ocean into four great regions: Indonesia, Melanesia, Micronesia, and Polynesia. Indonesia (the "Indian islands," known in earlier centuries as the East Indies) is in large part the archipelago now occupied by the Republic of Indonesia.[10] Melanesia (the "black islands") extends eastward from Indonesia to embrace all of the large islands of the Southwest Pacific from New Guinea to the Fiji Islands. Micronesia (the "small islands") lies in the western Pacific to the north of New Guinea and includes the Mariana Islands (the largest of which is Guam), the Caroline Islands, and the Marshall Islands. Polynesia (the "many islands") includes all of the islands within a large triangle in the mid-Pacific extending from Hawaii to Easter Island to New Zealand and embracing such island groups as Samoa and Tonga.[11] Individuals originating in each of these island regions have settled in Indiana.

The 1980 census recorded that there were 210 Indiana residents who had been born in Indonesia. That census also recorded that there were a total of 241 people of Indonesian descent living in Indiana. The 1990 census counted 542 Indonesia-born residents of Indiana, an increase of 158 percent since 1980.[12] Many of these Indonesian residents originally came as students to Indiana's colleges and universities. A few, however, were probably members of a community of mixed European (mostly Dutch) and Indonesian descent that left Indonesia after its independence from the Netherlands in 1949. Many of these, in turn, immigrated to the United States from the Netherlands, most of them from 1958 to 1962 under a special quota established for refugees displaced by World War II. Indiana was one of fifteen states (plus the District of Columbia) where members of this refugee community of "Indos" settled. By the 1970s, however, most of the members of this community from Indiana and elsewhere in the northern United States had relocated to southern California where the climate was more to their liking.[13]

Melanesians were first recorded in Indiana by the 1980 census, which discovered that there were six "other Melanesians" (that is, not ethnic Fijians, who were separately recorded) living in Indiana, and that four individuals living in Indiana claimed to have been born in Fiji.[14] The 1990 census recorded three individuals of Melanesian (not otherwise specified) ethnic origin in Indiana, living—one each— in Delaware, Monroe, and Vigo counties.[15] It is probable that each of these individuals was associated in some way with the three universities located within those counties (Ball State, Indiana, or Indiana State).

Micronesia, unlike Indonesia or Melanesia, is a region in which the United States has been active militarily and politically for almost a century. As a consequence of the transpacific ties that have developed between the United States and the region, emigration from Micronesia, most particularly from Guam and the islands of the former Trust Territory of the Pacific Islands, has been of much greater magnitude than immigration to the United States from Indonesia or Melanesia. Spain ceded Guam to the United States in 1898 after the Spanish-American War. The Northern Mariana Islands (to the north of Guam), the Caroline Islands, and the Marshall Islands were taken from Japan following World War II and administered under the supervision of the United Nations as the Trust Territory of the Pacific Islands.

The Guam Organic Act of 1950 provided for an elected territorial government for Guam, and, as American citizens, its inhabitants obtained the right to move without immigration restrictions to the United States. The Trust Territory of the Pacific Islands has since 1986 been divided into four political units: the Commonwealth of the Northern Mariana Islands (which enjoys a relationship to the United States similar to that of Puerto Rico), the Federated States of Micronesia (an independent state consisting of the central and eastern Caroline Islands), the Republic of the Marshall Islands (also an independent state), and the Republic of Palau (the westernmost island group of the Carolines). Like the people of Guam, the

people of the Northern Marianas are United States citizens. And, under the "compacts of free association" that have been agreed to by the United States and the other Micronesian political entities, Micronesians are permitted free access to the United States even though they are not American citizens.[16]

Guam, according to the 1990 census, had a population of 133,152, of whom just under 63,000 were ethnic Guamanians. These Chamorros are the descendants, with a mixture of Spanish and Filipino elements, of the Micronesian population that inhabited the island when it was discovered by Magellan in 1521. The 1990 census also revealed that a total of 49,345 ethnic Guamanians lived on the United States mainland or in Hawaii.[17] Thus, of the total Guamanian population, only 56 percent now live in Guam, while 44 percent live in the United States. Although the first Guamanians seem to have come to the United States mainland in the early 1920s, many more came in the 1950s to take jobs with the United States military and, after 1962, to escape the devastation caused by Typhoon Karen. Over half of the ethnic Guamanians now living in the United States reside in California, most near military bases or shipyards.[18]

## Table 1. Peoples of the Pacific in Indiana, 1850–1990

| | Year | 1930 | 1960 | 1980 | 1990 | Change '80–'90 |
|---|---|---|---|---|---|---|
| Australians | 1860 | 98 | 277 | 317 | 434 | 37% |
| New Zealanders | 1850 | | 44 | 105 | 134 | 28% |
| Indonesians | 1950s | | | 210 | 542 | 158% |
| Fijians | 1980 | | | 4 | N.A. | N.A. |
| Other Melanesians | 1980 | | | 6 | 3 | -50% |
| Guamanians | 1980 | | | 161 | 217 | 35% |
| Other Micronesians | 1960 | | 20 | 19 | 15 | -21% |
| Hawaiians | 1980 | 1 | | 672 | 528 | -25% |
| Samoans | 1980 | | | 60 | 151 | 152% |
| Tongans | 1980 | | | 4 | 15 | 275% |
| Other Polynesians | 1980 | | | 16 | 15 | -6% |
| Pacific Islanders (not specified) | 1960 | | 8 | | 13 | N.A. |
| Filipinos | 1904 | 77 | 540 | 4,174 | 4,754 | 14% |
| Totals | | 180 | 889 | 5,748 | 6,821 | 19% |

Notes: "Year" indicates the year when the particular group is first documented in Indiana. Statistics for Australians, New Zealanders, Indonesians, and Fijians refer to individuals born in the countries indicated and living in Indiana. Statistics for all other groups refer to persons who claimed that particular ethnic heritage, regardless of where they were born.

Source: U. S. Bureau of the Census, various reports [see notes for references].

The 1980 census reported that there were 161 people of Guamanian ancestry in Indiana. The 1990 census reported that this figure had grown to 217. The latter census also reported that Guamanians could be found in forty of Indiana's ninety-two counties, with the largest number in Marion (58), Starke (19), and Allen (14) counties. Many of these Guamanians have come to Indiana as a result of marriage to an Indiana military person or because they serve in or work for a branch of the United States military. By far the largest concentration of Guamanians in Indiana is in Marion County's Lawrence Township, until recently the site of Fort Benjamin Harrison. Thirty-five Guamanians lived in Lawrence Township in 1990.[19] One important Guamanian with ties to Indiana was Frank G. Lujan, who earned a J.D. degree from Indiana University, Bloomington, in 1967. Lujan returned to Guam where, after a career as a lawyer, he was elected senator in the territorial legislature and also served as attorney general of Guam.[20]

The 1960 census reported that twenty people in Indiana had been born in the Trust Territory of the Pacific Islands or had one or both parents born there. The 1980 and 1990 censuses provide data for an ethnic category called "other Micronesian," that is, for individuals whose ethnic heritage lies anywhere in Micronesia but Guam. The 1980 census reported nineteen such individuals, while the 1990 census reported fifteen such "other Micronesians" in Indiana, with the largest number (four) in Vanderburgh County.[21] It is safe to assume that most of these individuals were from the island groups of the former Trust Territory of the Pacific Islands. Many Micronesians from the Trust Territory came originally to the United States to attend school or college. Beginning in the late 1970s there have been as many as two thousand Micronesian students per year enrolled in American colleges and universities. The total number of "other Micronesians" in the United States in 1990 was 6,808, with by far the largest portion living in Hawaii (1,848), California (1,566), and Oregon (631).[22] Most Micronesian students likewise attend colleges and universities in Hawaii or on the United States West Coast (or on Guam).[23] For reasons of distance and climate, very few Micronesian students have chosen to attend colleges in Indiana.

In 1898, the year that the United States took Guam from Spain, the United States also annexed the previously independent Hawaiian Islands. This act was quickly followed the next year by the division, with Germany, of the Samoan archipelago, America assuming sovereignty over the smaller and easternmost islands of the chain. These two island groups, now the state of Hawaii and the territory of American Samoa, maintain to this day a significant United States presence in Polynesia. It is not by

accident, then, that native Hawaiians and Samoans today comprise over 95 percent of the Polynesian population that has settled in Indiana. The 1990 census reported that 709 individuals of Polynesian ethnic origin lived in Indiana: 528 Hawaiians, 151 Samoans, 15 Tongans, and 15 "other Polynesians."[24]

Following two centuries of introduced disease, poverty, and the large-scale in-migration of Chinese, Japanese, Filipinos, and other ethnic groups, native Hawaiians (including full- and part-Hawaiians) now comprise only about 12 percent of the population of the state of Hawaii. Native Hawaiians have been immigrating to the American mainland since the early nineteenth century, when many came to the West Coast of North America to participate in the California gold rush or the fur, fishing, and timber trades of the Pacific Northwest. The Owyhee River of Oregon, where many native Hawaiians trapped and fished, is in fact named after an archaic spelling of Hawaii.[25] The 1990 census reported that of the 211,014 ethnic Hawaiians in the United States, 138,742 lived in Hawaii and 72,272 lived on the mainland. Of the mainland Hawaiian population, well over half (42,285) lived in California, Oregon, or Washington.[26]

The 1980 census reported 672 individuals of Hawaiian ancestry in Indiana, while the 1990 census counted 528 ethnic Hawaiians. The latter census also reported that ethnic Hawaiians lived in sixty-seven of Indiana's ninety-two counties, with the largest numbers being found in Marion County (91) and Lake and St. Joseph counties (33 each).[27] Many of Indiana's native Hawaiians are spouses of Hoosiers who served in the military in Hawaii, or students or faculty from Hawaii at one of Indiana's colleges or universities.

American Samoa is currently an unincorporated territory of the United States, its people having the status of United States "nationals," not American citizens. Western Samoa, in contrast, has been a sovereign state since achieving independence in 1962 from New Zealand, by whom it had been administered as a United Nations Trust Territory. The inhabitants of both Samoas, however, have been able to immigrate to the United States, particularly if they had some association with the United States military. Samoans have indeed immigrated to the United States and also to New Zealand in relatively large numbers. According to the 1990 census, 151 ethnic Samoans were living in Indiana.[28]

Individual Samoan sailors, who were employed on European and American sailing ships as early as the 1840s, probably reached various United States ports where those who settled were quickly absorbed into the general population. Samoans began immigrating to Hawaii in small numbers in the 1920s, many of them sponsored by the Mormon Church, which was then active in mission work in both Samoas.[29] The 1920 census recorded only six Samoans in the United States, all of them in California. The immigration of Samoans to the United States, however, began in earnest when the United States Navy closed its base at Pago Pago in American Samoa in 1951. Samoan civilians working for the navy were permitted to transfer to other navy installations, and from 1950 to 1970 perhaps twenty thousand American and Western Samoans (most of them navy workers or enlistees with their families) came to the United States, mainly to California or Hawaii.[30]

The 1990 census counted 62,964 ethnic Samoans living in the United States. Samoans continue to be highly concentrated in California and Hawaii (31,917 in California, 15,034 in Hawaii). In 1990 the population of American Samoa was only 46,773, while the population of Western Samoa was approximately 190,000. There were also about 44,000 Samoans (mostly Western Samoans) living in New Zealand.[31] Thus the number of Samoans living overseas is today equal to just less than half the combined population of the two Samoan homelands. The number of Samoans living in the United States, though, is now greater than the population of American Samoa.[32]

The 1980 census showed that 60 ethnic Samoans lived in Indiana, of whom 19 were recorded as being born in Western Samoa. The 151 Samoans in Indiana, according to the 1990 census, are dispersed across the state, being found in forty of the state's counties. The largest numbers are found in Marion (19), St. Joseph (16), and Clark (15) counties. Within Marion County, the largest number (9) live in Lawrence Township near the former Fort Harrison.[33] Indiana's Samoan population, like the state's population of other Pacific Islanders, consists mostly of spouses of present or former United States military personnel as well as enlistees or employees of the military.

In addition to native Hawaiians and Samoans, Tongans have been enumerated separately by the census since 1980. The 1980 census indicated that there were 4 residents in Indiana of Tongan ancestry, while the 1990 census recorded 15 people of Tongan ethnic origin in the state. These 15 individuals were located in St. Joseph County (10), Kosciusko County (3), and Marion and Morgan counties (1 each).[34] Nationwide there are a total of 17,606 Tongans in the United States, 63 percent of whom are located in California and Hawaii. An additional 3,904 Tongans (22 percent of the total) live in Utah, reflecting the long-standing missionary connection between Polynesia and the Mormon Church.[35]

The 1990 census recorded two additional categories of Pacific Islanders residing in Indiana: 15 individuals classified as "other Polynesian" and 13 individuals classified

as "Pacific Islander, not specified." The "other Polynesian" category includes Tahitians, Cook Islanders, and Maori (the indigenous people of New Zealand). The 1990 census thus indicated that there was a total of 957 Pacific Islanders living in Indiana (excluding Indonesians), of whom 528 (55 percent) were Hawaiians, 217 (23 percent) were Guamanians, and 151 (16 percent) were Samoans. The largest single concentration of Pacific Islanders in Indiana is within Marion County's Lawrence Township (61 individuals), once the home of Fort Harrison.[36] This is a geographical reflection of the close historical and economic ties that have existed between Pacific Islanders, particularly Guamanians, Hawaiians, and Samoans, and the United States military.

## Filipinos

From 1898 to 1946 the Philippine Islands were the site of America's most ambitious experiment in colonialism. Having received the Philippines as a spoil of the Spanish-American War, the United States established a territorial form of government for the islands in 1902, after suppressing a short-lived but bloody insurrection led by Emilio Aguinaldo. The Philippines became an internally self-governing commonwealth in 1935 and, following occupation by the Japanese from 1942 to 1945, achieved full independence as the Republic of the Philippines in 1946.

Since independence the United States has continued to maintain an especially close relationship with the Philippines. An agreement dating from the time of independence allowed the American military to maintain bases in the Philippines until the closing—sparked by the volcanic eruption of Mount Pinatubo—of Subic Bay Naval Base in 1992. Also, until 1992 Philippine citizens were permitted to enlist in the United States military. The fact that the goal of United States colonization of the Philippines was the eventual independence of the islands fostered much goodwill there toward the United States.[37] Carlos P. Romulo, Philippine author, statesman, and foreign minister during the early 1950s, always referred in a respectful way in his speeches and writings to "Mother America."[38] Finally, in more recent years, America has been the chosen place of residence for Philippine politicians in exile (first Benigno and Corazon Aquino, and then Ferdinand and Imelda Marcos).

Since the very beginning of American interest in the Philippines three prominent Hoosiers have played important roles in strengthening the links between the United States and that island nation, and these links have aided in the establishment and growth of a Filipino community within Indiana that is today the third largest

Asian- or Pacific-American ethnic community in the state. These three Hoosiers were Albert J. Beveridge, Elmer Burritt Bryan, and Paul V. McNutt. Beveridge, Republican United States senator from Indiana from 1899 to 1911, was one of the leading turn-of-the-century advocates of American imperialism. In 1898, in a campaign speech entitled "The Taste of Empire," he argued that, "If England can govern foreign lands, so can America. If Germany can govern foreign lands, so can America." "Fellow Americans," he concluded, "we are God's chosen people."[39] One of Beveridge's first acts upon taking his seat in the Senate was to make a personal inspection visit to the newly captured Philippines (he was one of the first American politicians to do so), in order better to involve the Senate in the organization of the territory.[40]

One important factor in the American organization of the Philippines—that is, the Americanization of the Philippines—was the establishment of an educational system for the territory based on the American model. Elmer Burritt Bryan, professor of education and psychology at Indiana University in Bloomington, became principal of the newly founded Philippines Normal School in 1901. In 1903 William Howard Taft, first United States governor of the Philippine Islands, appointed Bryan superintendent of education for the territory. One of Bryan's initial tasks was to hire approximately eight hundred American teachers, many of whom were Indiana University graduates, to work in elementary and secondary schools in all parts of the island territory.[41] Thus, from the beginning there was not only a strong American stamp to the Philippine educational system, but a Hoosier one as well.

Paul V. McNutt, governor of Indiana from 1933 to 1937 and a possible Democratic candidate for president in 1940, served as President Franklin D. Roosevelt's high commissioner in the Philippines from 1937 to 1939. McNutt again served as high commissioner from 1945 to 1946, appointed this time by President Harry Truman, and capably presided over the complex and difficult preparations for Philippine independence in 1946. It was McNutt, in fact, who lowered the American flag during the 4 July 1946 Philippine independence ceremonies in Manila. After independence McNutt then served as the first American ambassador to the Philippines from 1946 to 1947.[42] Because of his efforts to oppose a movement to postpone Philippine independence and also because of his efforts to get the United States government to adopt favorable trade and war rehabilitation policies toward the Philippines, McNutt came to be highly regarded by Philippine leaders. Manuel Roxas, who was about to become the first president of an independent Philippines, stated in a speech given in Indianapolis on 17 May 1946

that "[Paul V. McNutt] has been one of the greatest High Commissioners. . . . I am not merely being polite and generous to a friend. I am speaking the mind of the Filipino people."[43]

In the age-old tradition of Pacific peoples, Filipinos—even before independence, even before the islands became an American possession—were voyaging far from their island homes. Shortly after the establishment of Spanish rule in the Philippines in 1565, Filipinos were sailors on the Manila galleons that annually traveled across the Pacific between the Philippines and the Mexican port of Acapulco. Individual Filipinos soon settled permanently in Mexico. Antonio Miranda, for example, one of the founders of Los Angeles, California, in 1781 was probably of Filipino descent.[44] In the 1760s Filipinos from Mexico established a settlement in Louisiana, then a newly acquired part of the Spanish Empire.[45]

Since World War II tens of thousands of Filipinos have immigrated, on a permanent or temporary basis, to various parts of the world. A total of 129,615 Filipinos have immigrated to Canada, and the ethnic Filipino population of Toronto alone is now more than 28,000. Over 3,600 Filipinos immigrated to Australia between 1945 and 1972. In the mid-1970s there were approximately 6,000 Filipinos in Germany, 4,000 in Great Britain, and 1,300 in Italy, most of them temporary workers in the health or service industries. In the mid-1980s, before the Kuwait crisis and the Gulf War, there were over 340,000 Filipino workers in Saudi Arabia, Kuwait, and the other oil-producing states of the Persian Gulf region.[46]

Nevertheless, most Filipinos leaving their homeland in the twentieth century have immigrated to "Mother America."[47] Even though reliable records are not available for the years before 1946 (when the Philippine Islands strictly speaking were not a "foreign" country), more than one million Filipinos officially immigrated to the United States in the years from 1911 through 1991.[48] This immigration has passed through four distinct but overlapping stages. A first wave of immigrants, from 1903 through the 1920s, consisted mainly of Filipino students who came to the United States to enroll at various schools, colleges, and universities. A second wave of immigrants, from the 1920s into the 1930s, consisted almost entirely of male agricultural laborers to work in the vegetable fields of California or the sugarcane fields of Hawaii. Until the enactment of the Tydings-McDuffie Act in 1935, which created the Commonwealth of the Philippines and set a timetable for Philippine independence, Filipinos (as United States "nationals" exempted from the national quota system then in effect) were allowed virtually free access to the United States.

A third wave of Filipino immigrants, which lasted from the end of World War II to 1965, consisted in large part of Filipino military or war veterans and their families who enjoyed special rights to enter the United States apart from the national quota system then in use.[49] Finally, a fourth wave of Filipino immigrants entered the United States as a consequence of the immigration act of 1965, which ended national quotas and gave preference to family members of American citizens or residents and to individuals having skills deemed important for the United States. This stage has lasted from 1965 to the present.

During the first wave the rate of Filipino immigration was very low, approximately 20 individuals per year. During the second wave the rate rose to about 4,300 per year. During the third wave the rate was reduced significantly to about 2,000 per year. During the fourth wave, however, the rate of immigration has been averaging over 50,000 per year.[50] During 1991, in fact, 63,596 Filipinos immigrated to the United States.[51]

In recent decades the ethnic Filipino population of the United States has grown at a rate that is among the fastest of any ethnic group in the country. In 1910 there were only 160 Filipinos in the United States (excluding Hawaii). In 1920 there were 5,600, just under half of them in California. In the years 1923 to 1929 an average of 4,200 Filipinos arrived in California each year, and by 1930 there were 45,208 Filipinos in the United States, 94 percent of them males and 78 percent of them in California. By 1940 the Filipino population of the United States had reached 45,563, still heavily concentrated in California.[52] The 1950 census recorded 121,707 Filipinos, a figure that had grown to 176,310 by the time of the 1960 census.[53] The 1970 census counted 336,731 Filipinos (up 91 percent since 1960), while the 1980 census counted 781,894 (a phenomenal 132 percent increase since 1970). The 1990 census enumerated a total of 1,406,770 Filipinos in the United States (an 80 percent increase). By 1990, 52 percent of the Filipino-American population lived in California, while an additional 23 percent lived in Hawaii.[54]

The United States census first recorded a Filipino presence in Indiana in 1920: the census of that year noted that 7 Filipinos resided in the state. Seventy-seven Filipinos lived in Indiana by the time of the 1930 census. The 1960 census recorded 540 individuals of Filipino ancestry in Indiana. The 1980 census reported 4,174 Indiana residents of Filipino ancestry, including 3,507 who had been born in the Philippines. The 1990 census indicated that there were 4,754 Filipinos in Indiana, a growth of 14 percent over the decade.[55] Tagalog, the designated national language of the Philippines, was the principal language spoken in the homes of 2,367 Indiana residents in 1990.[56]

Indiana's Filipino population is currently growing at a much slower rate than the Filipino population of the United States as a whole, largely because of the greater attraction to Filipino immigrants of such states as California and Hawaii, with their more amenable climates and their already established concentrations of Filipino Americans. Immigration statistics for 1991 showed that, of the 63,596 Filipino immigrants entering the United States, only 232 (much less than half of 1 percent) stated that they intended to settle in Indiana.[57]

According to the 1990 census, however, Filipinos live in ninety of Indiana's ninety-two counties, making them one of the most widespread nonblack minority groups in Indiana. The greatest number of Filipinos live in Marion (1,157) and Lake (708) counties. Other concentrations occur in Allen (247), Porter (245), St. Joseph (234), Tippecanoe (216), and Monroe (168) counties.[58]

Probably the first Filipinos to reside in Indiana were the members of a small group of students who, after spending a year in California high schools, enrolled at Indiana University and Purdue University in September 1904. These students were part of the first wave of Filipinos to come to the United States and were stimulated by the efforts of Americans such as Hoosier Elmer Burritt Bryan to establish American standards and concepts of education in the Philippines.

Indiana University's four young *pensionados* (United States government-subsidized students from the Philippines) were law students Jorge Bocobo, Francisco Delgado, Mariano de Joya, and José Valdez. Three of these men later became prominent in the educational and political life of the Philippines. Jorge Bocobo, who won a number of prizes at Indiana University oratorical competitions—including one arguing passionately for Philippine independence—eventually became dean of the University of the Philippines College of Law, president of the University of the Philippines, associate justice of the Philippine Supreme Court, and Philippine secretary of public instruction.[59] Francisco Delgado served as resident commissioner of the Philippines in the United States Congress before World War II and later served as chief delegate to the United Nations and member of the International Court of Justice.[60] Mariano de Joya became a professor of law at the University of the Philippines, director of the Philippine Bar Association, and associate justice of the Philippine Supreme Court.[61]

In 1968, when Indiana University decided to honor former Indiana governor Paul V. McNutt by giving his name to a large new residence hall complex on the Bloomington campus, three wings were named in honor of Bocobo, Delgado, and de Joya. The three other wings were named after Elmer Burritt Bryan and two Indiana

*Paul V. McNutt Quadrangle on the campus of Indiana University in Bloomington (1995), honoring Indiana's long-established ties with the Philippines.*

University alumni, Frank Linden Crone and Harvey Albert Bordner, who helped develop the Philippine educational system.[62] McNutt Quadrangle thus stands as a monument to Indiana's long-standing and close ties to the Philippines.

In 1905 two other Filipino students enrolled at Indiana University.[63] One of these, Antonio de las Alas, became a successful Philippine businessman and minister of finance during the 1930s.[64] Other Filipino students enrolled at Indiana University in subsequent years.

In 1909 the presence of Filipino students on the Indiana University campus briefly became an issue in state politics. Alarmed by reports that Filipino students in Bloomington were being seen with white girls, state senator Cyrus E. Davis introduced a bill to amend Indiana's antimiscegenation law of 1852. Davis demanded that the phrase "or Filipino" be added to the clause in the law that prohibited whites from marrying an individual of "one-eighth or more of Negro blood." After much debate in the Senate and in the Indianapolis newspapers, Davis's bill failed to pass. During the fracas, one Filipino student published a daring and somewhat facetious letter in Indiana University's *Daily Student.* "If the Indiana Legislature in its unbounded wisdom, should see fit to pass a law requiring Filipino students not to marry American girls," he wrote, "we certainly, with sorrow, would have to violate that law."[65] Filipino students in Indiana and elsewhere in the country were not prepared for such blatant instances of racial prejudice. The writer, Carlos Bulosan, who originally came to America as a student, noted that "Western people are brought up to regard Orientals or colored people as inferior, but the mockery of it all is that Filipinos are taught [by their American teachers, many of whom were Hoosiers] to regard Americans as equals."[66]

Silverio Apostol came to Purdue University in September 1904. Apostol earned a B.S. degree in agriculture from Purdue in 1908 and later served the Philippines as undersecretary of agriculture and natural resources. By 1907 eleven Filipino students were enrolled at Purdue, second in number in the country only to the University of Illinois.[67] By 1917 there were fifty-three Filipino students at various Indiana colleges and universities. By 1929 the number of Filipino students in Indiana had dropped to seventeen: nine at Purdue, four at Tri-State College in Angola, three at Indiana University, and one at the University of Notre Dame.[68]

The number of Filipino students in Indiana declined dramatically during the 1920s, in large part because the United States government no longer subsidized their education. Most students were now being supported by their families back home and by their own efforts to find work. Many Filipino students, in Indiana and elsewhere in the Midwest, who could no longer afford the cost of an education or whose preparation for American college life was less than adequate, dropped out of school and moved to Chicago to find work. The Filipino population of Chicago, which had been 154 in 1920, grew to 1,796 by 1930.[69] Many Filipinos found work in the Chicago area with the United States Post Office, the Great Lakes Naval Training Station, or (in an effort by the company to check the growth of the black-led Brotherhood of Sleeping Car Porters) as attendants, cooks, and busboys on railroad cars operated out of Chicago by the Pullman Company.[70]

Indiana apparently did enjoy one "first" with respect to Filipino Americans during the 1930s. Ramon Ubaldo, who received a Ph.D. degree from Indiana University, was hired as professor of government and history at Huntington College in 1937. Ubaldo is considered to be the first Filipino appointed to a teaching position in an American college or university.[71]

The second wave of Filipino immigration, that of mainly unskilled agricultural laborers during the 1920s and 1930s, entirely bypassed Indiana. The third wave of Filipino immigration, however, resulted in a number of Filipinos who had served in the United States or Philippine military services during World War II and their families coming to Indiana. Among these immigrants was Rufo (Joe) Manawat, who had served as bodyguard to Paul V. McNutt during his tenure as Philippines high commissioner. Manawat came to Indianapolis in 1970, bringing with him eleven of his sixteen children.[72]

Most Filipinos in Indiana today are part of the fourth wave of Filipino immigration to the United States, the immigration of English-speaking, highly trained professional people and their families, most of whom arrived after United States immigration laws were liberalized in 1965. These immigrants have made their mark on Indiana most notably in the field of medicine.[73] As early as 1971 the Indiana-Philippine Medical Association (IPMA) listed 179 members in the state. At that time IPMA members were practicing medicine in seventy-two communities across Indiana, with the largest numbers in the Gary-Hammond-East Chicago area (46) and Indianapolis (24). In addition, Filipino physicians had settled in dozens of smaller communities across the state, such as Bedford, Connersville, English, Ferdinand, Martinsville, and Shelburn.[74] Most of these physicians received medical degrees in the Philippines and came to America for internships or residencies, with the intention of remaining in the country to practice. For example, a typical story is that of Manuel Z. Rosario, who received his medical degree from the University of Santo Tomas in Manila in 1952, immigrated to the United States in 1969, and worked for a year as a claims adjuster before being admitted to a residency at Methodist Hospital in Gary. By 1980 Rosario had his own medical practice in Gary.[75]

Filipino physicians in Indiana are frequently held in high regard by the local communities in which they practice. As one author has noted for the United States as a whole—and it seems to be true of Indiana as well—"Immigrant Filipino doctors have been less able to get the high-paying, comfortable positions attained by many American-born physicians and therefore have become an important medical resource for the poorer Americans who live in our inner cities and in rural areas."[76] Luis Advincula, for instance, practiced medicine for many years in the small Indiana city of Brazil. After his death in 1976, he was eulogized by the mayor of Brazil as a conscientious physician, a community-spirited citizen, and a true American. Advincula, the mayor declared, "became an American long before he came to the United States."[77]

In 1975 neurosurgeon Antonio B. Donesa of Fort Wayne was the leading organizer and first president of the American College of International Physicians, an organization of physicians practicing in the United States but trained overseas. Donesa is coeditor of a book that instructs foreign-trained physicians in the politics and sociology of American life and medicine.[78] Jesus C. Bacala, a family physician in Scottsburg, in addition to serving as president of the Optimist Club of Scottsburg, also has published two collections of his own poetry (one in the Philippines). He also edited a book of poems by members of the Bacala family, as well as a three-volume anthology of poetry by Indiana authors.[79]

In 1979, through the efforts of Patricio R. Mamot of Indianapolis, the Philippine Heritage Endowment Fund

*The Rice Bowl, a Filipino-American oriental restaurant located in Indianapolis's historic Union Station, 1995.*

was set up as part of the Indiana University Foundation. This fund, supported by financial contributions from a number of Filipino-American physicians and other donors, has as its purpose the "propagating [of] the cultural heritage of the Filipinos in the United States."[80] So far the fund's principal activity has been the sponsorship of the publication of four books dealing with Filipino heritage.[81]

Filipino-American organizations active in Indiana have included social clubs such as the Barangay Club of Indianapolis, founded in 1960 by Maria Lagadon (a Spanish teacher in the Indianapolis Public Schools), and the Indianapolis Chapter of the Philippine American National Association, founded in 1975. Also active in the state have been the IPMA and the Asian-American Medical Society of Merrillville. Prominent members of Indiana's Filipino-American community have included Father Ponciano Ramos, pastor of St. Rita's Roman Catholic Church in downtown Indianapolis, and Professor Rolando A. DeCastro of the Indiana University School of Dentistry, noted medical illustrator and artist as well as the coeditor of a well-known textbook on oral surgery.[82]

Filipino-owned businesses in Indiana vary from medical practices to quite a few "Oriental" restaurants, take-outs, and grocery stores. Many of these establishments, such as the Rice Bowl in Indianapolis's Union Station, support recent immigrants from the Philippines by giving them employment opportunities.[83] In 1987 there were 240 Filipino-owned businesses in the state, most of them small, but these businesses were responsible for adding $24,600,000 annually to the economy of Indiana.[84]

## Peoples of the Pacific in Indiana

Pacific immigrants, in large part because of their prior familiarity with American culture and the English

JAMES A. BALDWIN

*Rolando A. DeCastro's mural depicting the history of dentistry, located in the main lobby of the Indiana University School of Dentistry building in Indianapolis.*

language—a result of the long history of American imperialism in the Pacific—have tended to assimilate rather quickly and well into the fabric of Indiana life. Although Pacific peoples have never settled in Indiana in great numbers, their presence here has certainly added to the state's ethnic diversity and heritage. Australians, New Zealanders, Pacific Islanders, and especially Filipinos have all found homes in Indiana and continue to enrich the ethnic mosaic of the Hoosier state.

## Notes

1. For recent overviews of the migratory heritage of the peoples of the Pacific see Jim Allen, "When Did Humans First Colonize Australia?," *Search* 20 (Sept.–Oct. 1989): 149–54; James A. Baldwin, "Muruk, Dok, Pik, Kakaruk: Prehistoric Implications of Geographic Distributions in the Southwest Pacific," in *Pacific Production Systems: Approaches to Economic Prehistory,* ed. D. E. Yen and J. M. J. Mummery (Canberra: Department of Prehistory, Research School of Pacific Studies, Australian National University, 1990), 231–57; I. C.

Campbell, *A History of the Pacific Islands* (Berkeley: University of California Press, 1989); Douglas L. Oliver, *Oceania: The Native Cultures of Australia and the Pacific Islands,* 2 vols. (Honolulu: University of Hawaii Press, 1989).

2. Andrew Parkin, "Australians and New Zealanders," in *Harvard Encyclopedia of American Ethnic Groups,* ed. Stephan Thernstrom (Cambridge, Mass.: The Belknap Press of Harvard University Press, 1980), 163–64.

3. Approximately fifteen thousand Australian war brides settled in the United States during and after World War II, a figure that represented a significant portion of the adult unmarried female population of the country at the time. See John Hammond Moore, ed., *Australians in America, 1876–1976* (St. Lucia: University of Queensland Press, 1977), 234. For a general study of war brides see Elfrieda Berthiaume Shukert and Barbara Smith Scibetta, *War Brides of World War II* (Novato, Calif.: Presidio Press, 1988).

4. Moore, ed., *Australians in America,* 87, 234; Parkin, "Australians and New Zealanders," 163–64.

5. "1860 Census: Foreign Born for Indiana" (Unpublished manuscript, Indiana Historical Society, Education Division, 1991), 1–4; "1880 Census: Foreign Born for Indiana" (Unpublished manuscript, Indiana Historical Society, Education Division, 1991), 1–2; U.S. Census Office, *Compendium of the Eleventh Census, 1890,* 3 vols. (Washington, D.C.: Government Printing Office, 1892–97), 2: 622–23; U.S. Bureau

of the Census, *16th Census of the United States, 1940: Population, Second Series, Characteristics of the Population: Indiana* (Washington, D.C.: Government Printing Office, 1942), 26, 71–72.

6. U.S. Bureau of the Census, *Census of Population, 1960: The Eighteenth Decennial Census of the United States,* vol. 1, *Characteristics of the Population, Part 16: Indiana* (Washington, D.C.: U.S. Bureau of the Census, 1962), 330; U.S. Bureau of the Census, *1980 Census of Population, Characteristics of the Population, General Social and Economic Characteristics: Indiana* (Washington, D.C.: U.S. Bureau of the Census, 1984), Table A; U.S. Bureau of the Census, *Ancestry of the Population by State: 1980* (Washington, D.C.: U.S. Bureau of the Census, 1983), 73; U.S. Bureau of the Census, *1990 Census of Population: Social and Economic Characteristics: Indiana* (Washington, D.C.: U.S. Bureau of the Census, 1993), 56, 58.

7. Moore, ed., *Australians in America,* 218–20.

8. "1850 Census: Foreign Born for Indiana" (Unpublished manuscript, Indiana Historical Society, Education Division, 1991), 7; "1880 Census: Foreign Born for Indiana," 9–10, 15, 59; *Census of Population, 1960,* p. 330; *1980 Census of Population,* Table A; *1990 Census of Population,* 58.

9. Parkin, "Australians and New Zealanders," 164.

10. The term "East Indies" includes the Philippine Islands as well as Indonesia. Because of the divergent histories of these two island regions, particularly with regard to the United States, and because of contrasting patterns in the immigration of their peoples to the United States, this study regards the Philippines as a separate and distinct region.

11. The indigenous Maori people of New Zealand, currently about 8 percent of the population, are Polynesians in terms of their language and culture. It has been more convenient for this study, however, to group New Zealand with Australia since both countries now share a common British heritage.

12. *1980 Census of Population,* 440; *Ancestry of the Population by State: 1980,* p. 440.

13. Greta Kwik, *The Indos in Southern California* (New York: AMS Press, 1989), 1, 73. See also William Spencer Bernard, *Doubly Uprooted: Dutch Indonesian Refugees in the United States* (New York: Committee on Integration, American Immigration and Citizenship Conference, 1965).

14. Indiana had no ethnic Fijians recorded in 1980; since four individuals were listed as having been born in Fiji, those individuals were likely either of European or (Asian) Indian descent. See U.S. Bureau of the Census, *Asian and Pacific Islander Population by State: 1980* (Washington, D.C.: U.S. Bureau of the Census, 1983), 15; *1980 Census of Population,* Table A.

15. U.S. Bureau of the Census, *1990 Census of Population and Housing: Summary Tape File 1A: East North Central Division Computer File, Disk 1: Indiana, Ohio* (Washington, D.C.: Data User Services Division, U.S. Bureau of the Census, 1991), CD-ROM disk.

16. John Connell, "Paradise Left? Pacific Island Voyagers in the Modern World," in *Pacific Bridges: The New Immigration from Asia and the Pacific Islands,* ed. James T. Fawcett and Benjamin V. Cariño (Staten Island, N.Y.: Center for Migration Studies, 1987), 383.

17. *Asians in America: 1990 Census: Classification by State* (San Francisco: Asian Week, 1991), 6.

18. Faye F. Untalan, "Pacific Islanders in the U.S.: A Struggle against Anonymity," *Civil Rights Digest* 9 (Fall 1976): 43, and "Chamorros," in *Handbook of Social Services for Asians and Pacific Islanders,* ed. Noreen Mokuau (New York: Greenwood Press, 1991), 173; Bradd Shore, "Pacific Islanders," in Thernstrom, ed., *Harvard Encyclopedia of American Ethnic Groups,* 764; David Nelson Alloway,

"Guamanians," in *Dictionary of American Immigration History,* ed. Francesco Cordasco (Metuchen, N.J.: Scarecrow Press, 1990), 265–66.

19. *Ancestry of the Population by State: 1980,* p. 73; *1990 Census of Population and Housing,* CD-ROM disk.

20. "Frank J. Lujan," *Indiana Alumni* 55 (Sept.–Oct. 1992): 61.

21. *Census of Population, 1960,* p. 330; *Asian and Pacific Islander Population by State: 1980,* p. 15; *1990 Census of Population and Housing,* CD-ROM disk.

22. Susan B. Gall and Timothy L. Gall, eds., *Statistical Record of Asian Americans* (Detroit: Gale Research, 1993), 690–91.

23. Charles F. Urbanowicz, "Micronesians in Northeastern California: Some Ideas on Education for the Future," in *New Neighbors: Islanders in Adaptation,* eds. Cluny Macpherson, Bradd Shore, and Robert W. Franco (Santa Cruz: University of California at Santa Cruz, Center for South Pacific Studies, 1978), 195.

24. *1990 Census of Population and Housing,* CD-ROM disk.

25. Helen C. Chapin, "Hawaiians," in Cordasco, ed., *Dictionary of American Immigration History,* 289.

26. Gall and Gall, eds., *Statistical Record of Asian Americans,* 690–91.

27. *1990 Census of Population and Housing,* CD-ROM disk.

28. Ibid.

29. Geoffrey R. Hayes and Michael J. Levin, "How Many Samoans? An Evaluation of the 1980 Census Count of Samoans in the United States," *Asian and Pacific Census Forum* 10 (May 1984): 3.

30. Joan Ablon, "Samoans in Stateside Nursing," *Nursing Outlook* 18 (Dec. 1970): 33.

31. Gall and Gall, eds., *Statistical Record of Asian Americans,* 569; Connell, "Paradise Left?," 377–78.

32. For recent reviews of the Samoan diaspora see Dennis A. Ahlburg and Michael J. Levin, *The North East Passage: A Study of Pacific Islander Migration to American Samoa and the United States,* Pacific Research Monographs, no. 23 (Canberra: National Centre for Development Studies, Research School of Pacific Studies, Australian National University, 1990); John Connell, ed., *Migration and Development in the South Pacific,* Pacific Research Monographs, no. 24 (Canberra: National Centre for Development Studies, Research School of Pacific Studies, Australian National University, 1990); Futa Helu, "Diaspora of Pacific Islanders," *Pacific Islands Monthly* 61 (June 1991): 7–8; Frederic Koehler Sutter, *The Samoans: A Global Family* (Honolulu: University of Hawaii Press, 1989).

33. *Asian and Pacific Islander Population by State:* 1980, p. 9; *1980 Census of Population,* Table A; *1990 Census of Population and Housing,* CD-ROM disk.

34. *Asian and Pacific Islander Population by State: 1980,* p. 14; *1990 Census of Population and Housing,* CD-ROM disk.

35. Gall and Gall, eds., *Statistical Record of Asian Americans,* 690–91; Shore, "Pacific Islanders," 764–65.

36. *1990 Census of Population and Housing,* CD-ROM disk. The 1980 census indicated that there were sixteen "other Polynesians" in Indiana. *1980 Census of Population,* 330.

37. The preamble to the Jones Act (the Organic Act of the Philippine Islands), passed by Congress in 1916, states that "it has always been the purpose of the people of the United States to withdraw their sovereignty over the Philippine Islands and to recognize their independence as soon as a stable government can be established therein." Quoted in I. George Blake, *Paul V. McNutt: Portrait of a Hoosier Statesman* (Indianapolis: Central Publishing Co., 1966), 176–77.

38. Carlos P. Romulo, *Mother America: A Living Story of Democracy* (Garden City, N.Y.: Doubleday, 1943). For the other side of the often paternalistic U.S.-Philippine relationship see the chapter

entitled "The Little Brown Brother" in Carey McWilliams, *Brothers under the Skin,* rev. ed. (Boston: Little, Brown and Co., 1951), 229–49. See also Theodore Friend, "Goodby, Mother America: An Overview of Philippine-American Relations, 1899–1969," *Asia* 15 (1969): 1–12. The root of this paternalism was a commonly held racist attitude toward colonial people in general and Orientals in particular. For example, opposing the annexation of the Philippines in 1898, labor leader Samuel Gompers referred to the Filipinos—then and now the only Christian people in Asia—as "a semi-barbaric population, almost primitive in their habits and customs." McWilliams, *Brothers under the Skin,* 231.

39. Patricio R. Mamot, "Paul V. McNutt: His Role in the Birth of Philippine Independence" (Ph.D. diss., Ball State University, 1974), 29–30.

40. Bob Dole, *Historical Almanac of the United States Senate,* eds. Wendy Wolff and Richard A. Baker (Washington, D.C.: Government Printing Office, 1989), 165.

41. Thomas D. Clark, *In Mid-Passage,* vol. 2 of *Indiana University: Midwestern Pioneer* (Bloomington: Indiana University Press, 1973), 41; Romulo, *Mother America,* 42.

42. Blake, *Paul V. McNutt,* 365.

43. Mamot, "Paul V. McNutt," 168.

44. Jennifer Stern, *The Filipino Americans* (New York: Chelsea House, 1989), 37–38. For some possible Filipino effects on Mexican culture see Henry J. Bruman, "The Asiatic Origin of the Huichol Still," *Geographical Review* 34 (July 1944): 418–27.

45. Marina E. Espina, "Filipinos in New Orleans," *Proceedings of the Louisiana Academy of Sciences* 23 (1974)· 117–21.

46. Gall and Gall, eds., *Statistical Record of Asian Americans,* 464, 469; Eamonn Byrne, "Needs, Problems, and Aspirations of Filipinos Abroad," in *Proceedings of a Conference on International Migration from the Philippines, 10–14 June 1974* (Honolulu: East-West Population Institute, East-West Center, 1975), 44; Edward Roger John Owen, *Migrant Workers in the Gulf,* Minority Rights Group Report, no. 68 (London: Minority Rights Group, 1985), 18.

47. For general studies of Filipino (or "Pilipino" in Tagalog) immigration to the United States see Fred Cordova, ed., *Filipinos: Forgotten Asian Americans: A Pictorial Essay, 1763–circa 1963* (Dubuque, Iowa: Kendall/Hunt Pub. Co., 1983); Benjamin V. Cariño et al., *The New Filipino Immigrants to the United States: Increasing Diversity and Change,* Papers of the East-West Population Institute, no. 115 (Honolulu: East-West Center, 1990); Charles B. Keely, "Philippine Migration: Internal Movements and Emigration to the U.S.," *International Migration Review* 7 (Summer 1973): 177–87; Honorante Mariano, *The Filipino Immigrants in the United States* (San Francisco: R and E Research Associates, 1972); Antonio J. A. Pido, *The Pilipinos in America: Macro/Micro Dimensions of Immigration and Integration* (New York: Center for Migration Studies, 1986); Stern, *Filipino Americans.* For studies of Filipino immigration to specific states see Rubén Rúiz Alcántara, *Sakada: Filipino Adaptation in Hawaii* (Washington, D.C.: University Press of America, 1981); Valentin R. Aquino, *The Filipino Community in Los Angeles* (San Francisco: R and E Research Associates, 1974); Alvar W. Carlson, "Filipino and Indian Immigrants to Detroit and Suburbs, 1961–1974," *Philippine Geographical Journal* 19 (Dec. 1975): 199–209; Marina E. Espina, *Filipinos in Louisiana* (New Orleans: A. F. Laborde, 1988); Sarah R. Mason, "The Filipinos," in *They Chose Minnesota: A Survey of the State's Ethnic Groups,* ed. June Drenning Holmquist (St. Paul: Minnesota Historical Society Press, 1981). See also Shiro Saito, *Filipinos Overseas: A Bibliography* (Staten Island, N.Y.: Center for Migration Studies, 1977).

48. Gall and Gall, eds., *Statistical Record of Asian Americans,* 411.

49. 27,374 Filipinos were serving in the United States military in 1992, including 18,889 in the navy. Ibid., 556.

50. The idea of the four waves of Filipino immigration has been outlined by Juan L. Gonzales, Jr., *Racial and Ethnic Groups in America* (Dubuque, Iowa: Kendall/Hunt, 1990), 157–58.

51. U.S. Immigration and Naturalization Service, *Statistical Yearbook of the Immigration and Naturalization Service: 1991* (Washington, D.C.: Government Printing Office, 1992), 58.

52. Edwin B. Almirol, *Ethnic Identity and Social Negotiation: A Study of a Filipino Community in California,* Immigrant Communities & Ethnic Minorities in the United States & Canada, no. 10 (New York: AMS Press, 1985), 21–22; Gonzales, *Racial and Ethnic Groups in America,* 159.

53. Filipinos in Hawaii were counted in United States population totals for the first time in the 1960 census, following statehood in 1959. See Stern, *Filipino Americans,* 68.

54. *Asian and Pacific Islander Population by State: 1980,* p. 2; Gall and Gall, eds., *Statistical Record of Asian Americans,* 689.

55. Mariano, *Filipino Immigrants in the United States,* 18–19; *Census of Population, 1960,* p. 330; *Ancestry of the Population by State: 1980,* p. 72; *Asian and Pacific Islander Population by State: 1980,* p. 8; *1990 Census of Population and Housing,* CD-ROM disk.

56. Gall and Gall, eds., *Statistical Record of Asian Americans,* 127.

57. *Statistical Yearbook of the Immigration and Naturalization Service, 1991,* p. 58.

58. *1990 Census of Population and Housing,* CD-ROM disk.

59. *Filipinos in History,* 2 vols. (Manila: National Historical Institute, 1989–90), 1:119–22. See Bocobo's biography written by his daughter Celia Bocobo Olivar, *Aristocracy of the Mind: A Precious Heritage—A Biography of Jorge Bocobo,* ed. Norman Occena Yabut (Quezon City: New Day Publishers, 1981). Perhaps Bocobo's major contribution to Philippine jurisprudence was his revision of the code of family law to expand the rights of women. See Jorge Cleofas Bocobo, *Outlines of the Law of Persons and Family Relations,* 7th rev. ed. (Manila: Oriental Printing, 1935).

60. José Batungbakal, "Some Recollections about the 1903 Philippine Government Students in the United States," *Journal of History* 10 (1962): 293. See also the reprint of a speech Delgado delivered in the House of Representatives, in which he refers to having attended "some of the finest schools and colleges [in the United States]." Francisco Afau Delgado, *Governor General Frank Murphy* (Washington, D.C.: Government Printing Office, 1935). Delgado, like Bocobo, was interested in expanding women's rights in the Philippines. See Francisco Afau Delgado, *Las restricciones injustas sobre los derechos de la esposa en relación con sus bienes parafernales y la sociedad de gananciales deben desparecer del código civil* (Manila: Bureau of Printing, 1933).

61. Batungbakal, "Some Recollections about the 1903 Philippine Government Students in the United States," 293; Franz Z. Weissblatt, ed., *Who's Who in the Philippines: 1936–1937* (Manila: McCullough Printing Co., 1937), 102.

62. Clark, *In Mid-Passage,* 43; Mamot, "Paul V. McNutt," 35–36; Kathleen Van Nuys, *Indy International* (Indianapolis: Indianapolis News, 1977), 24.

63. *Indianapolis Morning Star,* 30 Sept. 1905.

64. Barbara M. Posadas and Roland L. Guyotte, "Aspiration and Reality: Occupational and Educational Choice among Filipino Migrants to Chicago, 1900–1935," *Illinois Historical Journal* 85 (Summer 1992): 97.

65. Quoted in Clark, *In Mid-Passage,* 41–42.

66. Carlos Bulosan, *Sound of Falling Light: Letters in Exile,* ed. Dolores S. Feria (Quezon City: n.p., 1960), 191.

67. H. Brett Melendy, *Asians in America: Filipinos, Koreans and East Indians* (New York: Hippocrene Books, 1981), 32.

68. Barbara M. Posadas and Roland L. Guyotte, "Unintentional Immigrants: Chicago's Filipino Students Become Settlers, 1900–1941," *Journal of American Ethnic History* 9 (Spring 1990): 30; Bruno Lasker, *Filipino Immigration* (New York: Arno Press, 1969), 370.

69. Barbara M. Posadas, "The Hierarchy of Color and Psychological Adjustment in an Industrial Environment: Filipinos, the Pullman Company, and the Brotherhood of Sleeping Car Porters," *Labor History* 23 (Summer 1982): 354 n. 14.

70. Melendy, *Asians in America,* 64; Posadas, "Hierarchy of Color and Psychological Adjustment in an Industrial Environment," 349–50.

71. Hyung-Chan Kim and Cynthia C. Mejia, eds., *The Filipinos in America, 1898–1974: A Chronology & Fact Book,* Ethnic Chronology Series, no. 23 (Dobbs Ferry, N.Y.: Oceana Publications, 1976), 30.

72. Van Nuys, *Indy International,* 23.

73. Indiana was one of the first states to allow physicians trained in the Philippines to obtain medical licenses. See Melendy, *Asians in America,* 48.

74. "List of Members," *Bulletin of the Indiana-Philippine Medical Association* 1 (June 1971): 3–6.

75. Patricio R. Mamot, *Filipino Physicians in America* (Indianapolis: Philippine Heritage Endowment Publications, 1981–83), 2:221–24.

76. Stern, *Filipino Americans,* 101–2.

77. Norval Pickett, Jr., "Eulogies Given Dec. 14 for Advincula," *Bulletin of the Indiana-Philippine Medical Association* 5 (Feb. 1976): 4.

78. Antonio B. Donesa and Patricio R. Mamot, eds., *The Dynamics of Political Participation: A Manual for International Physicians* (Fort Wayne, Ind.: American College of International Physicians, 1982).

79. Mamot, *Filipino Physicians in America,* 2:10–14; Jesus C. Bacala, *Lines to Prestina and Other Rhymes* (Manila: Jessepure, 1958); Jesus C. Bacala, *Poems on Loving, Living, and Believing,* 2d ed. (New York: Vantage Books, 1957); Jesus C. Bacala, ed., *The Blooming Years and Other Rhymes* (Scottsburg, Ind.: Bennett Printing Co., 1977); Jesus C. Bacala, ed., *Voices in the Wind: Poetry in Indiana,* 3 vols. (Scottsburg, Ind.: Southern Indiana Poetry Club, 1987–90).

80. Mamot, *Filipino Physicians in America,* 1:62.

81. The four books published (in Indianapolis) by the Philippine Heritage Endowment are: Dominador S. Gomez, *The 2-in-1 Milk Cosmetic: An Invention via Serendipity,* Filipinos in the United States Series, no. 2 (1982); José Maria S. Luengo and Patricio R. Mamot, *Lorenzo Ruiz, the Filipino Protomartyr in Nagasaki: The First Filipino Beatified by Pope John Paul II* (1984); Mamot, *Filipino Physicians in America;* and Juan M. Montero II, *Halfway Through: An Autobiography,* Filipinos in the United States Series, no. 1 (1982).

82. Donald E. Arens, William Ray Adams, and Rolando A. DeCastro, eds., *Endodontic Surgery* (Philadelphia: Harper and Row, 1981). A French translation has also appeared: Donald E. Arens, William Ray Adams, and Rolando A. DeCastro, eds., *Chirurgie endodontique* (Paris: Editions CdP, 1984).

83. *Indianapolis Star,* 2 Dec. 1989.

84. U.S. Bureau of the Census, *Survey of Minority-Owned Business Enterprises: Asian-Americans, American Indians, and Other Minorities* (Washington, D.C.: Government Printing Office, 1991), 29.

# POLES

PAULETTE POGORZELSKI BANNEC

*Male children were encouraged to follow an academic path only when they expressed an interest in the priesthood. Gradually, the working-class Pole saw the need for strong English language skills, especially in the workplace. The immigrant now recognized that his child had the right to be successful and to attain a better lifestyle, and school seemed to be the place to pursue this. This idea prompted the opening of St. Hedwig High School in South Bend in 1928.*

Although there are records documenting the presence of Poles in the first settlement at Jamestown in 1607, Polish immigrants did not constitute a sizable group in the United States until the end of the nineteenth century. A few individuals immigrated to the United States from 1608 to 1800 mainly for ideological or economic reasons, but at the turn of the nineteenth century most Poles came to escape the political turmoil that brewed in their homeland. By the 1850s economic and religious reasons pressed Poles to leave and search for a place where religious tolerance and economic opportunity could sustain them.[1]

The Poles originated as a separate Slavic group who banded together to form a strong political unit in the easternmost area of the European continent. Known as Polanie or dwellers of the plains, they converted to Christianity in the midtenth century when Mieszko I of the Piast dynasty married the Bohemian princess Dabrowska in 965. During the Piast dynasty and the Jagiello dynasty, Poland expanded and built a federation that included Lithuanians, Ruthenians, Poles, Tartars, and White Russians. Polish rulers during this time practiced religious tolerance; thus, few wars were fought and much cultural development occurred in the areas of literature, science, and the arts.

The next two centuries noted a political weakening attributed to the "Liberum Veto," which required that the laws enacted had to be unanimously passed. This mandate resulted in a decline of the economic, religious, monarchical, and military conditions of the country. Thus weakened, Polish territory became prey for Prussia, Russia, and Austria, which invaded and partitioned the conquered areas in 1772. A second partition occurred when the Poles incorporated a new constitution that frightened Russia and Prussia which quickly partitioned more of Poland in 1793. A final partition came when Thaddeus Kosciuszko attempted to free Poland from its neighbors in 1795. This third partition erased Poland from the map and forced these people to live in three different political, economic, and constitutional areas. Determined to remain faithful to their culture, language, Catholic faith, and native land, the Poles attempted to gain their independence. Failure to attain this goal, however, pushed many Poles out of the country as political exiles, making them realize an independent Poland would not materialize instantly.[2]

Along with the political deterioration of Poland came an economic deterioration, especially for the rural Pole who sought survival from the land. The 1848 emancipation of the peasant from serfdom gave the Polish peasant ownership of the land; however, because he lacked the funds not only to purchase land but also to modernize his existing landholdings and farming techniques, the peasant searched for another means of livelihood. Lack of industrialization caused further complications. Some industry existed in cities along the Baltic Sea and in Silesia and Bohemia, but most Poles lived in rural areas. Thus a

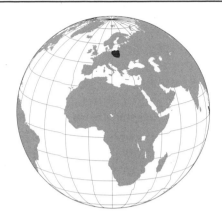

desire to buy land, or perhaps maintain property, forced the Pole to immigrate to other areas of eastern Europe, to western Europe, and to America.[3]

Around the midnineteenth century, the Polish population in the United States was negligible, with the 1860 census reporting 7,298 natives of Poland. In Indiana there were only 18 Poles listed for the six counties in the northern part of the state starting with St. Joseph County and going west. By 1870 the census showed 14,436 in the United States with 365 in the same six counties of Indiana, indicating the start of a flow that would not subside until World War I. From 1870 to 1880 Polish immigrants to the United States increased by more than 34,000 giving Indiana a 209 percent increase to 1,129 in the six counties. By 1910 Indiana could boast a total figure of 10,379 natives of Poland in the central northern and northwestern parts of the state. Over these forty years, which most historians consider as the major period of Slavic immigration to the United States, the number of Poles increased 96 percent. Of course, these numbers must be considered in light of the fact that domination of Poland by Prussia, Russia, and Austria not only contributed to the reasons many Poles immigrated, but it also posed problems for accurate census reporting. Instead of giving Poland as their place of birth, many Poles would report Prussia, Russia, or Austria-Hungary, depending on the country that was dominating their homeland. Fortunately, the census takers would further question the Pole so that he/she would finally state Poland as his/her birthplace, and the census taker would write Poland in parentheses next to the original response. However, this dilemma still casts some doubt about exact numbers.[4]

According to the federal manuscript censuses from 1860 to 1930, Polish-born persons living in Indiana were concentrated in a six-county area, consisting of St. Joseph, La Porte, Starke, Porter, Noble, and Lake counties. However, a few Poles resided in Indianapolis, Fort Wayne, and Evansville; in fact, thirty-seven Indiana counties recorded at least *one* Polish immigrant in the 1860 census.

In 1870 La Porte County had the highest concentration of Poles in these six Indiana counties with 60.8 percent of the total, pointing to the fact that Poles were mainly in the rural areas. The 1900 census shows that the Polish-born population shifted from a rural to an urban concentration because of the industrialization of South Bend, Hammond, Whiting, Michigan City, East Chicago, and Gary. By 1910 St. Joseph County had 31.6 percent of the Polish-born population and Lake County had 46.5 percent, leaving the remaining four counties (La Porte, Starke, Porter, and Noble) with only 21.9 percent. The 1930 census showed some Poles living in Madison, Marion, Vanderburgh, Vermillion, and Vigo counties, but the concentration of Polish immigrants still remained in the north central and northwest corner of the state.[5]

## Patterns of Settlement

The first Polish immigrants to Indiana came from Poznan, with most coming from the Keynia, Szubina, and Krolikowa districts, between 1855 and 1860.[6] They settled in La Porte County and the surrounding areas, living mainly along the line of the Lake Shore and Michigan Southern Railroad. Otis, the first village with Polish settlers, was located about ten miles west of La Porte; Terre Coupee hosted another settlement of Poles; and the village of Rolling Prairie had Poles in four of its townships. Later, Poles gravitated toward more industrialized Michigan City and South Bend and finally to Lake County, where large numbers of immigrants could be accommodated in the new cities of Hammond, East Chicago, Whiting, and Gary.[7]

Otis was an attractive place to Poles for several reasons. The main reason was that it offered Poles a means to obtain land and continue their agricultural traditions. Finding a means to support themselves and still save money to purchase land meant taking jobs that included general farm work, clearing land, ditching, wood splitting, and railroading. In fact, it was through the railroad that many of these early Poles made their way to Indiana. Fred Miller, a sawmill operator, railroad employee, and landowner living in Olive Township, boarded a train for New York, where he recruited Polish immigrants to work in his sawmills. Miller's kindness was so great that he gave tracts of land to these Poles in exchange for their work. Other Poles rented land and sometimes purchased it at a later date, helping them to acquire a reputation for paying their debts promptly, as well as for cultivating almost worthless land into productive soil. Because of the Poles' reliability for payment, many businessmen would approve loans for Poles before they would lend money to native-born Americans.[8]

Otis grew considerably because immigrants wrote to friends and relatives about the opportunities in the new country, particularly in farming. Consequently, by 1872 there were enough families to form a parish community. Up until that time a Jesuit from Chicago, Father Francis X. Szulak, ministered to the Poles in northern Indiana. Jacob Lewandowski, a pioneer in the area, promoted the organization of a Catholic church. With the permission of Bishop Joseph Dwenger, second bishop of the diocese of Fort Wayne, St. Mary's was founded in 1873 with Rev. Peter Koncz as its first resident pastor. Shortly thereafter a school was opened, and the Otis settlement provided for all the needs of the Polish immigrants.[9]

Only a few miles west of Otis, another Polish settlement, Terre Coupee, was following a similar course in its development. Poles in this area purchased land and began the difficult task of subsistence and survival. As in Otis, the Catholic church played an important role in stabilizing Terre Coupee's Polish community. Father Valentine Czyzewski visited Terre Coupee as well as Rolling Prairie from St. Hedwig, his parish in South Bend. The parishioners in Terre Coupee were grateful that Czyzewski so willingly gave of himself, but the group desired a church of their own. With the help of Fred Miller, who allowed the Poles to lumber his forest, St. Stanislaus Kostka Church was constructed in 1884. Beginning in 1885 the church served as a school, with the Holy Cross Brothers teaching the children of the parish.[10]

The third rural community of Poles began like Terre Coupee when many immigrants sought land because of a lack of work in Chicago. Eager to return to their agricultural roots, these immigrants worked to accumulate money for investment in farmland, taking timber and crop leases, a contract whereby the immigrants cleared land and grew crops, giving a certain amount of timber and crops to their landlords. The work was long and laborious, taking the immigrant from three to ten years of clearing and farming in the crop-lease system before a substantial amount of money was saved for the purchase of his own farm. Fighting against odds such as low marshlands, poor drainage, compact clay, pure muck, and bad roads, the Polish immigrant cultivated soil that topographers would not have believed possible.[11]

Although some of Indiana's early Polish immigrants geared their efforts to survive on the land, others sought a different means of providing for themselves and their families. South Bend's pioneers found the area appropriate for the development of an industrial center because of available transportation and other resources. James Oliver and others established the South Bend Iron Works in 1855, while the Studebaker brothers continued to expand the carriage factory that they began in 1852. The Singer Sewing Machine Company was the third largest employer of Polish immigrants. These three factories were firmly rooted in the economic mainstay of South Bend, and because of available immigrant labor their businesses expanded, serving as encouragement for others to bring their factories to the city. Consequently, cotton, woolen, and paper mills, machine and foundry shops, and watch and furniture factories employed what some major plant officials considered to be the better workers. The Polish laborer would work in the less skilled occupations and could be driven to do twice as much for the same pay.[12] This work ethic seemed to be characteristic of the Polish immigrant no matter where he settled in the state. Until the mid-1880s South Bend was one of the leading industrial cities in Indiana. It also had the largest share of Polish immigrants, even though it ranked fifth among the state's largest cities. However, South Bend was not the only place that could report a large portion of Polish immigrant laborers. The Poles settled in Lake County in an area of Indiana just south and east of Chicago called the Calumet Region. Here the cities of Hammond, Whiting, East Chicago, and Gary were built on land that was once covered by sand ridges, swamps, and sloughs. Because these cities share borders, they created a large megalopolis, each with its own industrial complex.[13]

In early 1869 George H. Hammond, Marcus M. Towle, and George W. Plumer established the State Line Slaughter House. Location of the plant was most important since the slaughtered beef would need to be transported to the East Coast in cooler cars. These cooler cars needed ice, and the most convenient place to obtain ice would be near a river which, in this instance, was the Calumet River. The birth of industrialized Hammond opened up an opportunity for Poles to secure employment. Poles came to the area for job opportunities in Hirsh, Stein and Company, a glue and fertilizer plant; W. B.

Conkey Company, a publishing company and the first to accommodate employees with a pleasant reading room; the Simplex Railway Appliance Company; and several others. The unskilled or semiskilled Polish immigrant relied heavily, though, on the meatpacking company for employment. The slaughterhouse burned in 1901, and by 1903 the company officials transferred the operation to the Chicago Stock Yards, so many Poles were out of work. Some followed the meatpacking company to Chicago; others returned to Poland. However, many joined new immigrants in the oil refinery of Whiting and the steel mills in East Chicago.[14]

Since the late 1880s and early 1890s immigrants from almost everywhere had been working in "The Twentieth Century Wonder," Indiana Harbor/East Chicago, also known as the "Twin City." Workers were recruited from the fields of Europe and Asia because opportunities for employment abounded. In addition to the Inland Steel Company in Indiana Harbor, Polish immigrants labored in the William Graver Tank Works, Grasselli Chemical Works, United States Reduction Company, Famous Manufacturing Company, Standard Forgings, and a host of others. While East Chicago could accommodate many immigrants, a large number of Poles gravitated to Whiting, where the oil refinery needed the commitment of Polish laborers for its plants.

From 1900 to 1910 the "Twin City" began bursting at the seams as trainloads of immigrants poured into the city. Mayor Edward DeBriae, elected in 1906, produced magical financing as he improved the city with miles of walks, brick streets, and sewers of vitrified material. The "City of the Century"—Gary, Indiana—had just begun its push to build a "state of the art" steel mill along Lake Michigan, extending its corporate limits to the Indiana Harbor line. The Gary steel mill, US Steel, literally changed the topography of the Calumet Region by moving the Grand Calumet River a half mile south and giving it a new channel. Then the tracks of the Lake Shore and Baltimore and Ohio Railroad were shifted more than twenty miles, the lakefront was filled in, and a harbor was dug from the lake to the river. Such maneuvers produced an unfriendly relationship between the two cities. However, the new steel mill provided boundless opportunities for the Polish immigrant whose desire to survive compensated for his lack of skills.[15]

Now that the immigrant had the means to support himself and, perhaps in a short time a family, where did he usually seek residency? In South Bend the Poles settled near the railroads and factories on the west side, where they lived with Germans and Irish. At first Poles lived in shanties or in tenements, which were tar paper shacks of one to three rooms with outside toilets, communal pumps, and no screens. After 1870 James Oliver and the Studebaker brothers built houses that the Poles rented. In a short time Oliver encouraged the Poles to buy homes, so that home ownership was more common ten to fifteen years later. In addition to owning homes, most immigrants owned pigs, chickens, rabbits, cows, or goats and grew a vegetable garden. The practice of keeping livestock was criticized by native-born Americans, but it enabled the Pole to increase his holdings. Living conditions for urban immigrant Poles in the Calumet Region and Michigan City area were similarly very poor at the initial stages of settlement. Even though different immigrant groups in South Bend were more dispersed and living among each other, this was not particularly true in the northwest corner of the state. Distinct ethnic neighborhoods defined the area where one could find only Poles, only Hungarians, or only Italians.[16]

In Indiana Harbor, for example, "Hunkeytown" was inhabited by the foreign born some distance away from the sandy beach front that sported the luxurious South Bay Hotel, a yacht club, and special breakwater for private boats. The structures along Cedar Street (now Main Street) and the flanking street were clapboard houses that were usually homes for an immigrant family as well as numerous boarders, who provided the immigrant wife with some means of contributing to the family income. Some of this income was sent to the Old Country to pay for passage of relatives to America. The charges for board varied, but in the 1900s two or three dollars a month, including laundry but not meals, was common. Despite the low charge, the thrifty immigrant family taking in boarders could save considerable amounts of money. One report stated that a Lake County man had fifty-five boarders and grossed seven thousand dollars in 1909. The boarding system (trzymanie bortnikow) was considered unsuitable for the landlord's wife and daughters. The moral standards of women living in or operating boardinghouses were questioned because the ratio of males to females changed dramatically from 1870 to 1900 in Lake County. In the early censuses the ratio varied only slightly from one male per female to 1.25 males per female. In 1900 the other five counties of Indiana with a heavy Polish population still maintained the same ratio; however, Lake County's ratio jumped to one female for every two males, and 82 percent of the males in the eighteen to twenty-five age range were single while 28 percent of the males in the twenty-six to thirty-five age range were single. After the age of twenty-five the young Polish immigrant usually found a suitable marriage partner but still lived in a boardinghouse to save money for his own home. Such arrangements gave the boarding family added income and status while improving questionable moral standards. Similar neighborhoods took form in East Chicago, Hammond, Whiting, Gary, and Michigan City, usually with the Catholic church as the central focus.[17]

## Religious Organizations

The Polish immigrant faced problems that he never had encountered in his homeland. Urban life, strange conditions in industries, and the language barrier often created bewilderment and sometimes suspicion. Hence, the immigrant found comfort with those who understood his language, shared his style of dress, enjoyed the same food, practiced the same customs, and celebrated the same holidays. All of these activities were brought together easily with the establishment of a church where the priest would serve as the leader for every activity including the formation of any religious or fraternal parish society, a parochial school, or parish welfare organization. The church was the substitute for the narrower but more coherent village group and the wider, more diffuse, and vaguely outlined *Okolica* (neighborhood or region). This was especially true in South Bend, where by 1910 there were four Polish neighborhoods each with its own Roman Catholic parish, its own business district, and its own distinct boundaries.[18]

Prior to 1877 the Polish Catholics of South Bend worshiped in St. Patrick's parish with the Irish immigrants. Although these two groups possessed the common bond of religion, the Poles were not comfortable in a church where Polish was not spoken. Signs of discouragement appeared because hearing a sermon in English, having no Polish-speaking priest to hear confessions, and mingling with persons with customs of other lands were not satisfying. Along with this, the Poles and the Irish have retained an animosity toward each other to the present day. Bishop Dwenger could not furnish a Polish-speaking priest until Father Valentine Czyzewski, a Polish immigrant, was ordained in December 1876 as a priest of the Congregation of the Holy Cross. Two days later he was assigned to begin the work of organizing a parish for South Bend's Poles. The St. Stanislaus Kostka Society, which had been organized approximately two years earlier as a mutual aid and benefit organization, worked with Father Czyzewski to attain its major goal: erecting a church. By June 1877 St. Hedwig's on the corner of Monroe Street was dedicated with an impressive procession and ceremonies.[19]

Now two Polish Roman Catholic churches in northern Indiana, one in Otis and the other in South Bend, had resident pastors, whereas Rolling Prairie and Terre Coupee were still served as missions, mainly from

St. Hedwig diamond jubilee celebration, Gary, 1983.

South Bend. Father Czyzewski felt compelled to travel to these areas instead of forcing the Poles to journey to South Bend. Thus he ministered to these immigrants under very trying circumstances. In 1889 St. Stanislaus Kostka Church in Terre Coupee relinquished its mission status when Father Wladyslaw Zborowski was assigned as first permanent pastor. Five years later St. John Kanty Church in Rolling Prairie received Father John Hosinski as its pastor.[20]

Although the Otis parish did not serve the missions of Rolling Prairie and Terre Coupee, Polish immigrants in the northwestern part of the state, particularly in Hammond and Michigan City, sought the service of a Polish priest. Father Urban Raszkiewicz from Otis ministered to the Poles in these vicinities until 1890 when St. Casimir parish was founded in Hammond and until 1892 when St. Stanislaus, Bishop and Martyr Church, was founded in Michigan City. This was the beginning of a network of parishes that evolved as more immigrants settled in a particular area with one parish serving as a parent to another and St. Mary's in Otis grandparenting them all. Consequently, St. Casimir's became the parent church to Poles who lived in the newly found town of East Chicago and who traveled to the northern part of Hammond on horseback, in horse-drawn carriage, and on foot to fulfill their spiritual obligations. Fathers Casimir Kobylinski and Peter Kahellek accommodated these worshipers until 1896 when Father Kobylinski received permission to locate a church on 150th and Baring Avenue in East Chicago. In 1900 Father John Kubacki became the first resident pastor of St. Michael parish, which later became St. Stanislaus Church of East Chicago.[21]

The church community worked hard to establish and maintain a congenial atmosphere within the parish; however, a disagreement about the use of funds raised by the St. Michael Men's Society, a mutual aid and benefit organization, prompted the pastor to suspend the children of its members from the parish school. Bitterness and disappointment ensued, so this group of Polish Catholics decided to organize a church under the Independent movement of Poles that was permeating the country at this time. This movement began among Polish immigrants who disliked some aspects of the Catholic Church in America. Poles were becoming divided because of altercations about parish property ownership, no bishop of Polish birth or descent in the American hierarchy, or internal disputes and dissatisfaction with local pastors. Thus, St. Michael the Archangel Polish National Catholic Church came into existence while the original St. Michael Church moved from Baring Avenue to Magoun Avenue and was renamed St. Stanislaus, Bishop and Martyr. Both groups of Catholics did not let this incident delay the expansion of their church buildings or their community life; both organized choirs, sodalities, mutual aid and benefit societies, and communities that would further enhance their parishes. And in the case of the Roman Catholic Church, St. Stanislaus served to expand further the network of immigrant churches in Lake County. By 1926 East Chicago had four Catholic churches that had mostly Polish parishioners; Hammond had two; Gary had three; and Whiting and Michigan City had one each.[22]

Poles had also settled in Fort Wayne, La Porte, and Ege. Fort Wayne's Polish population organized St. Hyacinth parish in the southeastern part of the city. La Porte and Ege, rural areas of Indiana, also witnessed Polish immigration into their areas; consequently, La Porte built Sacred Heart Church, which was dedicated by Bishop Paul Rhode, the first Polish-American bishop in the United States, while the Poles in Ege were persuaded by Father Dominic Duehmig to join the French Catholics in the Girard Settlement in 1871 instead of building an ethnic church in their village.[23] Although the 1920 and 1930 censuses reported a significant Polish population in Marion, Vanderburgh, and Vermillion counties, no church or other community organization outwardly reflected their presence.

South Bend's Polish community was also expanding— well beyond anyone's expectations. The 1890 figure for Polish immigrants and their descendants was six thousand; by 1900 that figure nearly doubled to almost twelve thousand; and by 1910 the number reached eighteen thousand. The Poles on the west side of the city accounted for one-third of the city's population and land area by 1913. Father Czyzewski played a vital role in guiding the spiritual needs of this ethnic community. He already served *Bogdarka,* meaning God's gift, as the neighborhood surrounding St. Hedwig's was called, and as the Golden

Hills section of the city was developing, he purchased land for a Polish group that immigrated from the German sector of Poland around Poznan. These Poles differed from St. Hedwig's Poles in their fidelity to Old Country characteristics. Consequently, the church was named St. Stanislaus, Bishop and Martyr, and the surrounding area was called *Poznaniem,* referring to the area in Poland from which the majority of its parishioners had emigrated. St. Stanislaus could not accommodate all the new immigrants, so a third Polish parish was formed at approximately the same time for a group of Poles from the Warsaw region of Poland. Thus its members were referred to as the people from *Warszawa* because their neighborhood took on the atmosphere of their village in Poland. By 1910 yet another church, St. Adalbert, was established for the Poles of South Bend and was called *Krakowa,* linking its neighborhood with Kraków, Poland. The *Goniec Polski* (Polish Messenger) dated 6 July 1910 describes the arrival and reception of the new pastor of St. Adalbert's, Father John Kubacki, who was greeted with a parade of cars at the Vandalia station. The committees of welcomers were invited to a dinner at the Oliver Hotel. From the hotel the cars proceeded to Division and Kosciuszko streets, where the St. Adalbert Society, marching with banners from Olive Street, met the parade. Father Kubacki was so touched by the warm welcome that he greeted his parishioners with tears in his eyes, saying: "I never expected such a wonderful reception and may God bless you for it."[24]

Ironically, Father Kubacki's ideas about management of church affairs, public criticism of parishioners' private lives, and his push to Americanize the people created a somewhat hostile environment. The Independent movement that had permeated American Catholicism a decade earlier seemed to be ignited by these disagreements. Consequently, by 1913 a faction of seventy-five Polish families from St. Adalbert parish organized St. Valentine Independent Catholic Church.[25]

In the meantime, the people of St. Casimir parish in the Warsaw district of South Bend became quite unhappy when Father Antoni Zubowicz was transferred to St. Hedwig Church, and Father Leon P. Szybowicz, a popular assistant, was not appointed pastor. The parishioners were calmed somewhat while Father Boniface Iwaszewski served as pastor, but his resignation due to ill health brought about petitions from parishioners to appoint Father Szybowicz pastor. Instead Father Szybowicz was sent to Portland, Oregon, on 6 November 1913, leaving the parish without a pastor for almost two months until Father Stanislaus A. Gruza received the appointment in January 1914. Father Gruza, wishing to fulfill his duties, tried to enter St. Casimir rectory on 25 January, but the people, especially a faction in the eighteen to thirty age range, would not permit him to do so. After several unsuccessful attempts to assume his position, Father Gruza sought legal advice. After such consultation, an ultimatum given to the parishioners explained that a quiet entry of Father Gruza to the church would be made or the rectory and school would be placed under police protection. But the ultimatum only incensed the people even more. On Sunday, 15 February 1914 Father Gruza was escorted by a cordon of police to his installation as pastor, but angry men, women, and children staved off his installation with chunks of ice, bricks, boards ripped from fences, and glass, causing some injury and destruction to the church property. Father Gruza, intensely upset by the whole chain of incidents that came to be known as Bloody Sunday, was further threatened by starvation and arson of the rectory.[26]

After much negotiation and some compromise with the bishop, lawyers, the police force, and the court, the dissidents permitted Father Gruza to take charge of St. Casimir's in late March. The rebels still expressed dissatisfaction by withholding support for the pastor and

by conducting religious meetings in Witucki Hall. Although most dissenters remained at St. Casimir, a small faction joined the Independent group from St. Adalbert, whose petition to remove Father Kubacki was ignored by Bishop Herman Joseph Alerding. This lack of response led the Independents from both parishes to incorporate as the Polish National Catholic Church of St. Mary.[27] Interestingly, the present-day parishioners of St. Casimir do not perceive the Polish National Catholic Church of St. Mary as a schismatic institution. Some St. Casimir parishioners attend Mass at St. Mary and have expressed the intention to join the Polish National Catholic Church if anything drastic happens at St. Casimir.[28]

Along with the churches, the Poles of Indiana established schools. Poles felt that the best way to develop and to maintain a strong faith and an awareness of Polish culture and customs in their children was through a Polish parochial school. This feeling was so strong that the parish school was promoted from the pulpit. At first the parish priest, a choir director, or a lay person provided the instruction. But more enrollment meant the need for more teachers who could teach in English as well as

*St. Hedwig's (Gary) first graduating class: (standing left to right) J. Malak, J. Siemion, J. Bartkowski, C. Goszczynski, J. Marzalek; (seated left to right) E. Jabczynska, M. Lello, Father Peter Kahellek, A. Golkowski, H. Sazastakowski, C. Rzeplinska.*

Polish. Thus nuns were sought to teach in these parochial schools partly because they worked for low wages. Also many nuns were available because religious congregations offered a woman a means to an education and improved living conditions. The first religious order of Polish-speaking nuns was the Felician Sisters who came to Otis in 1877. Besides the Felician Sisters, other orders who taught in the Polish immigrant schools of Indiana were the Sisters of St. Joseph, Third Order of St. Francis; the Sisters of the Holy Family of Nazareth; the Sisters of the Holy Cross; the Franciscan Sisters of the Blessed Kunegunda; the School Sisters of Notre Dame; the Sisters of Saint Francis; and the Sisters of the Resurrection.[29]

The curriculum included reading, writing, arithmetic, geography, and history in English, as well as reading, religion, and Poland's history in Polish. At times the Polish parochial school was looked down upon because of poor facilities, uneven student-teacher ratios, and a bilingual curriculum that limited time spent on English subjects. The mid-1920s and early 1930s witnessed a diminishing use of the Polish language in the curriculum. Students still said prayers and learned the catechism in Polish, but the use of the Polish language declined in other areas. Although most children remained in school until their reception of first Holy Communion, usually at the age of thirteen, a male child sometimes left school (some as early as age ten) to take a job in a factory to increase the family's income, which, in turn, would help the family financially and raise its social status. In actuality this hindered the advancement of the child who would now be surrounded by a working-class atmosphere instead of an academic one. Male children were encouraged to follow an academic path only when they expressed an interest in the priesthood. Gradually, the working-class Pole saw the need for strong English language skills, especially in the workplace. The immigrant now recognized that his child had the right to be successful and to attain a better lifestyle, and school seemed to be the place to pursue this. This idea prompted the opening of St. Hedwig High School in South Bend in 1928. The school operated on parish property until 1935 when the Polish Civic Committee leased the Laurel Public School and it became South Bend Catholic High School. By 1950 another change in administration occurred, and the school became known as St. Joseph High School, which it is to the present day. Until World War II, however, formal education did not usually advance beyond high school since most working-class families could not afford the opportunity for college-level studies.[30]

The church and the school were the primary vehicles for preserving the language, traditions, and faith of the immigrant, while at the same time according the children the opportunity to prepare for life in America. Along with a fervent religious behavior the immigrant followed his collective instincts so that he would not remain alone or isolated. The immigrant intertwined his religious and social behavior into a social web that became a fraternal and parish society network. Sister Mary Andrea in the journal *Polish American Studies* describes six types of religious fraternal organizations that were typical in Indiana's Polish Roman Catholic parishes. The original fraternal societies, such as the St. Stanislaus Kostka Society in South Bend and the St. Casimir Society in Hammond, organized for the primary goal of establishing a parish, although these groups also gave assistance to Poles as mutual aid and benefit societies. The second type of society, like the St. Vincent de Paul Society, carried out corporal works of mercy such as caring for the poor, visiting the sick, and burying the dead. The third type emphasized spiritual works by centering on a specific devotional practice or prayer such as adoration of the Blessed Sacrament or worship of the Blessed Virgin or a particular saint. Almost every parish had a Holy Name Society, a Rosary Sodality, a St. Cecilia Choir, and a St. Theresa Society that focused on maintaining reverence for the holy name of Jesus, praying the rosary, or singing at liturgies. A fourth type of society promoted humanitarian, educational, or charitable undertakings—for example the Young Ladies Sodality, the Temperance Society of the Immaculate Conception, the Citizens' Wartime Committee, or the School Safety and Patrol. Constituting the fifth type of society were groups formed to enhance the material welfare of the parish or organizations that defined their goals as dramatic or literary. The St. Joseph Society of St. Stanislaus parish in South Bend presented theatrical plays as early as 1906 to raise money for the parish treasury. St. Adalbert's Dramatic Circle staged plays such as *Perlo Celejskie* (Heavenly Pearl), *Ulicyzik Chicagoski* (Chicago Street Vendor), and *Zboj Madaj i Jego Cudowna Palka* (Thief Madaj and His Magic Wand) in La Porte, Michigan City, and other cities, and a youth group at St. Casimir parish presented the production of "*Gdzie Jestes Panie?*" ("Where Art Thou, Lord?") as late as 1939. According to Rita Trzop, theatrical productions were common until the 1950s, and she praised this kind of activity as a way of giving young members of the parish some experience in public speaking and acting. In addition to groups that presented dramatic productions, bands, choirs, orchestras, and glee clubs provided music for preserving folk songs as well as patriotic songs. Although the St. Cecilia Society was founded in 1879 for church purposes, its choir made many local public appearances alone and with the secular South Bend Orchestra and Mierzwinski Choir. The St. Stanislaus Kostka Society sponsored the first Polish band, which reorganized in 1898 as the St. Hedwig Marching Band, giving regular concerts at the municipal Howard Park. Literary activities centered around the first Polish library founded in 1881 by Father Czyzewski. Thirty years later three other libraries with a total of three thousand volumes were present in the city. While the original founding society of a parish still offered a mutual aid and benefit program, every parish had chapters of the sixth type of society, what William I. Thomas and Florian Znaniecki called the "supra-territorial" fraternals. The Polish Roman Catholic Union (PRCU), founded in 1873, remained a clerical stronghold, particularly under the influence of the priests of the Chicago province of the Congregation of the Resurrection, while the Polish National Alliance (PNA), founded in 1880, took a nationalist approach even though it recognized the preponderance of Catholicism among Polish immigrants. Both groups offered competitive insurance programs, publications, mortgage loans, and other services to its members. Polish immigrants in Indiana also organized chapters of the Polish Women's Alliance, the Polish White Eagles Association, and the Polish Falcons (Sokoly), a gymnastic group that was first formed in South Bend in 1894 and was the first chapter to build a Polish Falcons Hall (Sokolnia) in Indiana. These groups helped the immigrant to perpetuate his European culture while providing financial assistance for getting along in the American environment. These national fraternals interacted with parish societies and developed organizational leadership for individual parishes.[31]

While all the parish societies and men's, women's, and youth groups kept the immigrant active and the church vital, the most important function of the Polish Catholic Church was the promotion of religious devotions that followed the Old World liturgical calendar. Besides daily and Sunday Masses, there was always a devotion or celebration that paralleled spiritual aspects of the Pole's agricultural roots. In December Advent was the penitential season that preceded the Christmas Eve Supper (Wigilia), when traditional dishes, symbolizing religious beliefs, were served, and the custom of breaking the Christmas wafer (Oplatki), either dry or spread with honey, was carried out. The feasts of the Circumcision and the Epiphany in January brought the blessing of chalk, gold, and myrrh, representing the gifts of the Magi to the child Jesus. The chalk would be used to write K+M+B (the initials of the three kings) on all the doors when the priest blessed the houses of the immigrants each year. Candlemas in February signaled the feasts of the Purification and St. Blaise; candles and other sacramentals were blessed for use throughout the year, and throats were blessed to protect against illness. Lent had the same religious observances as in Poland as the

torments of the Crucifixion were contemplated in the Bitter Lamentations (Gorzkie Zale) and the Stations of the Cross. The feasts of St. Casimir and St. Joseph were also celebrated during Lent. In late March or early April, Palm Sunday initiated Holy Week services with special devotional rituals on Holy Thursday, Good Friday, and Holy Saturday that included the blessing of food baskets (Swiecone) and culminated with the celebration of the Mass of the Resurrection at sunrise on Easter Sunday. The month of May was dedicated to Mary, the Blessed Virgin and Mother of God, with ceremonies that usually focused on praying the rosary, processions, and crowning the statue of Mary by a member of the Rosary Sodality. The Sacred Heart of Jesus was honored in June as well as St. John the Baptist on whose feast day (24 June) the priest would bless swimming areas. In August numerous bouquets of flowers would be brought to the church to the altar of Mary for the feast of the Assumption, known in Poland as Matka Boska Zielna (Our Lady of the Herbs). The Blessed Mother was honored on her birthday in September, and many parishes honored the Blessed Sacrament with the Forty Hours devotion in October. All Saints Day and All Souls Day (Zaduszki) were set aside to pray for the dead. In whatever Polish parish community one chose to worship there were a multitude of religious practices that were basic to the immigrant's way of life, and most of these ceremonies were accompanied by religious songs that elicited deep emotional feelings. Serdeczna Matko (Beloved Mother) at Marian Devotions, Twoja Czesz Chala at Forty Hours, Witaj Krolowa (Hail Queen of Heaven), and Nieba at Requiem Masses were among the most popular and the most intense. These songs often brought a congregation to tears or to experience a magnificent force, uplifting their souls as though they were praying in unison.[32]

No matter how strong or intense the emotional reaction of a congregation was during a religious service, the immigrant pastor was the force who promoted the mystical connection between the individual parishioner and God. The immigrant revered the priest who was viewed as the wise one (Wiedzacy) with sacramental powers. In fact many Polish families felt that it was an obligation to give at least one son as a priest to the church. One such priest who stands out in Indiana's Polish history is the Reverend Valentine Czyzewski. During his thirty-six years as pastor of St. Hedwig's parish, he ministered to thousands of souls in South Bend, Terre Coupee, Rolling Prairie, and even Chicago. Although organizing new parishes and maintaining established ones were his foremost duties, he evidently had a talent for settling religious disputes as well as secular ones. Besides traveling to Chicago on numerous occasions to settle conflicts between a group of Lithuanian immigrants and the much larger Polish congregation at St. Stanislaus Kostka parish who wanted to incorporate the Lithuanians into their parish, Father Czyzewski negotiated a settlement in January 1885 between Polish strikers and James Oliver, owner of the factory that employed these immigrants. Although he was not able to prevent injuries and property damage, Father Czyzewski persuaded an uncontrollable mob to disperse peacefully, and he later helped these Poles to regain their jobs at the factory.[33]

Father Czyzewski realized, too, that if Polish immigrants were to make any progress in the American work force, they needed to improve their command of the English language. The Poles, especially women, fell behind other immigrant groups in learning English. In the early 1900s only about one-fourth of the foreign-born Polish women conversed in English. Some believe that since women were not present in the factories they had less opportunity to learn. Two-thirds of the Polish-born men, on the other hand, had mastery of the language. After World War I the illiteracy of the residents of Lake County, especially East Chicago, and St. Joseph County seemed to be more evident. In order to help the immigrant gain knowledge in English and, therefore, increase his possibility of procuring different or better jobs in the factory and to make the immigrant woman feel more comfortable in her American environment, night schools were established in both Lake and St. Joseph counties. William A. Wirt organized classes in the Gary Public Library, refusing to use the term "Americanization" to describe his program. Hammond had a night school in 1912 with 942 adults enrolled, while East Chicago enrolled 500 by 1915. Father Czyzewski recruited students for classes held in the Laurel Public School near St. Hedwig's in South Bend and the board of education paid the teachers.[34]

## Occupations and Businesses

Schooling did aid the immigrant in the Americanization process. In fact, it contributed to denationalization and some declining interest in the parish, even though it is doubtful as to how it raised the social and economic level of the group. Because the immigrant had his roots in the peasant class in Europe, he did not possess the academic or vocational skills that would permit him to seek jobs that required much training. Consequently, 60 percent of Polish immigrants in Indiana worked as common laborers on railroads; in scrap yards; in food, car, chemical, soap, bed, and shirt factories; in steel mills and concrete works; and in lumberyards and brickyards. Only 3.5 percent of them owned farms. Poles did not seem to aspire to major professions, particularly in their early years of settlement. There were a few lawyers, doctors, and dentists, but for the

most part immigrants could not afford the time or the money to invest in such ambitions unless, of course, a clerical path would be followed. If a man did have some ambition and savings, he very often would pursue a path into the business world, usually in the immediate neighborhood where he could rely on the support of his fellow immigrants.[35]

In 1877 a grocery store, the first Polish business undertaking in South Bend, opened. By 1912 food businesses were the most popular and were sometimes integrated with dry goods and liquor trades. These businesses dealt with the Northern Indiana Wholesale Grocery Corporation, a Polish stock company that supplied food to merchants after World War I. Other types of businesses included cigar factories, bakeries, pharmacies, movie theaters, department stores, photo studios, hardware stores, paint and wallpaper stores, barbershops, and poolrooms. One of the most popular businesses in a Polish-American settlement was the neighborhood saloon, even though it did not coincide directly with the life of the community as did the Old Country Polish village tavern that served as a gathering place for family and community members. Instead, the indirect influence of this Polish-American enterprise concerned the head of the household who would patronize the tavern so frequently that his wife had to plead with saloonkeepers at the "family entrance" to send her husband home. Prohibition helped to diminish this kind of activity; however, with the demise of Prohibition the liquor store enjoyed a resurgence of business since the immigrant found it more satisfactory to take his bottle home.[36]

At the beginning of Polish settlement in Indiana, saloonkeepers also served as bankers, job finders, and especially as liaisons for the new immigrant who was suspicious of the native-born American. With the saloonkeeper's help, the immigrant could make connections in seeking employment and at the same time have a place to keep his money safe, socialize with his own ethnic group, and still have someone to aid him in maintaining communications with the Old Country. Letter writing was a very important task for the Pole, who felt it was his duty to inform friends and family in Poland of the numerous job opportunities in America and of the wonderful lifestyle that he enjoyed (however inflated these claims were).[37]

Another type of business, the building and loan association, provided assistance for the immigrant who wished to own property. The first such association in South Bend was the Kosciuszko Building and Loan Association, which opened in 1882, and the second was the Sobieski Association, which opened in 1884. Both contributed to the expansion of Polish home ownership, but after a few years of maximum growth the Kosciuszko Building and Loan Association suffered some setbacks because of leadership changes and embezzlement charges brought against a secretary. Once the secretary was proven innocent, the association was successful until the Great Depression. The Sobieski Association, on the other hand, grew at a modest but steady pace, evolving into the Sobieski Bank, which is still operating on the west side of South Bend. Poles in East Chicago likewise followed a similar path. In 1913 Joseph Wleklinski and his brother Stanley established a savings and loan association, later named the East Chicago Building and Loan Association. The Wleklinski brothers' foremost goal was lending to potential home buyers, and by 1934 the Home Owner's Loan Corporation, an offshoot of the building association, was lending money to people with distressed mortgages. Finally, because of economic conditions the branch faded away, but it had the reputation of also serving people of other ethnic groups. Wleklinski's Savings and Loan Association remained in business through the hands of Wleklinski's sons, Chester and Joseph Paul, who in 1955 began an insurance business that is still in operation today. The Savings and Loan Association finally merged with Citizens Federal Bank in 1980.[38]

Along with building and loan associations, Polish real estate salesmen offered many services besides searching for appropriate residences for the immigrant. Loans, insurance, steamship tickets, remittances to the Old Country, money orders, and legal counsel were among the services provided. Leo M. Kucharski was the most promising real estate salesman in South Bend. After emigrating from Poznan in 1881 and working in the Studebaker factory, he began selling real estate in 1895. His career in real estate and in the Republican party was cut short by his death in 1905. Succeeding Kucharski was Joseph A. Werwinski, an American-born Pole, who received more education than the average working-class Polish descendant. After graduating from parochial elementary school and public high school, Werwinski attended South Bend Commercial College and Valparaiso Normal School, teaching for a while in Olive Township and acting as deputy trustee in Portage Township. Finally, he turned to real estate, becoming one of the most influential and successful agents in the city.[39]

Although Poles operated numerous businesses in the early part of the century, they did not see a need to form a general business association to protect their business interests. The only thing that these Poles did organize was a chapter of the Polish National Alliance for merchants in 1892. This disparity among the businessmen pointed to the divided conditions of the Poles, but this changed when the Poles protested against Jews who were selling merchandise in carts on the streets, complaining that the Jews were taking away business from Polish merchants. Thus in 1908 an association of delegates of Polish societies began meeting quarterly to consider questions that affected them, with Charles Valentine Korpal acting as the first president. Also, younger businessmen and priests were influencing attitudes and unifying institutions in Polonia.[40]

The Polish business districts struggled through the Great Depression of the 1930s but remained consistent during the 1940s and 1950s. By the 1960s urban development and population movement caused much deterioration in the ethnic business world except for a few establishments. Despite this occurrence and the supposed disinterest in moving up the social ladder, some Poles strived to be successful in professions, in industry, and in business. Poles were represented in religious communities as sisters, brothers, and priests. They were present in large industrial firms as corporate executives, insurance underwriters, accountants, and employees in major government offices. Poles were doctors, lawyers, county clerks, teachers, musicians, and scientists. After many years of accepting their low socioeconomic role in society because of their tendency to favor training in trades or in small business rather than to aspire to programs that could promise social or geographic mobility, Poles began to progress toward more prestigious walks of life.[41]

Poles tended to be satisfied with the menial jobs they had in factories or on the railroads, and for the most part they did not feel the need to organize a union to fight for job protection, higher wages, or better conditions, even after their bitter struggle for better wages in the Oliver factory in 1885. The labor movement did not urge unskilled industries to organize unions, and most Poles were reluctant to join a group involving non-Polish workers. However, one of the labor disputes that erupted in the United States between 1890 and 1900 involved Poles at the Singer factory in South Bend. The workers petitioned Leighton Price, the plant manager, for a wage increase, but the request was denied and the workers struck. Local businessmen and the public agreed with the aims of the strikers, but clergymen, preaching from the pulpit, urged strikers to avoid violence, ignore professional agitators, and go back to work. At first the Poles did not unite with the other employees in forming the Central Labor Union. In fact, the Poles were slow to join the strike in its early days, but when they finally did join they persisted despite criticism from clerical and business leaders. Irvin Cooper, the chairman of the strike committee, was offered a plan whereby workers would receive merit pay according to the amount of work produced, which

CALUMET REGIONAL ARCHIVES

*Program cover for the twenty-fifth anniversary of the Polish-American Democratic Club, Gary, 1956.*

plant owners promoted as resulting in greater pay for the workers than the general raise that the workers had asked for. The workers agreed to the offer without conditions, but within a week the unrest created by other factors such as a nonunion employment committee and changes in union leadership resulted in a continuation of the strike. Poles were willing to go along with the strike; however, accusations of violence attributed to them were unjust and false. No formal satisfactory resolution put an end to the strike, but the Poles, or ignorant foreigners as they were referred to, were looked down upon by the Central Labor Union, which claimed that unlimited immigration was the reason for its problems.[42]

The *Goniec Polski* (Polish Courier), South Bend's first and only Polish newspaper, expressed dislike of the Central Labor Union's criticism of Polish laborers. In fact, the *Goniec Polski* served as informer and instructor to the Polish immigrant on political affairs on the local, national, and international levels, especially when the news concerned Poland. George Kalczynski, founder, publisher,

and editor of the newspaper, contributed to the political awareness of Poles who were not wholeheartedly interested in politics. In fact, in the earliest stages of settlement the Poles in Indiana did very little to affect the political ongoings in their areas of the state. Reasons for the apparent early lack of political interest included the language barrier, the low rate of naturalization, and the concerns about getting property, building institutions, and supporting the church. Consequently political prominence was not a central focus. It was not until 1880 that a Pole named Charles Valentine Korpal became deputy street commissioner in South Bend. Thereafter, South Bend Poles consistently elected a Polish councilman in the predominantly Polish third ward. In 1898 Korpal made a serious bid for city treasurer; although he failed to win, the *Goniec Polski* wrote triumphantly: "The number of Polish votes in our city has reached such proportions that we are able to swing municipal elections. . . . Soon both parties will have to reckon with our political aspirations." A similar scenario ensued in Lake County where Polish councilmen were elected to office as early as 1898, but most of them were Poles living in East Chicago. In East Chicago a few police chiefs were of Polish descent; J. Sueski was elected city controller in 1918; Joseph Wleklinski became city treasurer in 1921; and in 1939 F. Migas was elected mayor, serving for three consecutive terms. Although Gary could not boast the same amount of Polish population as East Chicago, the Gary Poles were active in the city council and the board of works almost from the city's inception. John Siemniasko and Dominic Szymanski were on Gary's first city council. The Democrats, first in South Bend and later in Lake County, were eager to gain momentum in the political arena, and one way to do this was to increase party membership with new immigrants. Poles, on the other hand, knew little about the political system of their adopted country. The first Polish Democratic boss in South Bend was Nicodemus T. Tanski, an elementary teacher at the Polish Catholic school. He carried out the jobs of notary public, steamship passenger agent, collection agent, insurance and real estate dealer, mediator of small problems arising between Poles and the rest of the community, and close observer of the polls. Tanski was placed on the Democratic ticket for justice of the peace after the Republicans nominated their first Pole, Andrew Ginther, for constable. Both Poles won, but until as late as 1962 the office of justice of the peace was considered the most prestigious. Tanski became the organizational leader of the first political club in South Bend, a type of group usually formed only for the duration of campaigns. Poles also united in the Polish American Political Club, the Pulaski Democratic Club, and the Polish Voters' Club. By 1913 Jan T. Niezgodzki ran for mayor in South Bend, finishing third among six candidates in the primaries. Poles in Indiana were also aroused to political activity when Cong. Abraham L. Brick sponsored a bill in 1910 to erect a statue to Gen. Casimir Pulaski in Washington D.C. Seven years later at the statue's unveiling fourteen Poles, who had worked long and hard to obtain the necessary petitions that proved to be instrumental in getting President Theodore Roosevelt to approve the statue, represented South Bend.[43]

Americans of Polish descent became increasingly aware of the need to participate in the government. The Polish American had little desire to return to Poland, a place that he had never seen, and economically he and his family were comfortably situated in a somewhat idyllic heaven, surrounded by other Poles. So it seemed almost mandatory to create some means that would directly or indirectly benefit Polish immigrants and their children. Thus, the Polish-American Democratic Club, founded in 1931, served as an organization that would represent the Polish community in local government. The formation of the club signaled a Polish loyalty to the Democratic party that has prevailed very strongly, although not exclusively, to the present day. During the First World War, Polish Americans generally supported President Woodrow Wilson, whose efforts to finance Polish relief were rewarded with reelection in 1916. Indiana Poles proposed that the United States give moral and material support to end the war, reduce armaments, and establish an independent Poland that would be a buffer between European powers, abating future conflicts. However, not all Poles shared this idea, and many immigrants continued to organize a Polish militia, some through the training of South Bend's Polish Falcons.[44]

### Assimilation and Preservation in the Twentieth Century

After World War I, Poles were deeply rooted in their communities because the social and cultural character of their neighborhoods served as shock absorber for those who felt the pangs of being uprooted or unassimilated. Because this milieu possessed everything the immigrant needed—church, school, jobs, family organizational life—the Pole felt no inclination to move from his primary area of settlement. Immigration restrictions ended the large influx of native Poles into the United States after 1920, leaving the preservation of the Polish ethnic group to the children and the grandchildren of the immigrant.

One way Poles continued to strengthen ethnic bonds and to promote their culture and traditions was to form more Polish clubs and societies. Both Lake and St. Joseph counties had chapters of the Polish Roman Catholic Union, the Polish National Alliance, the Polish Falcons, and the Polish Women's Alliance. Poles wanted to expand

*Program for the fortieth anniversary banquet of the Polish Army Veterans, Gary, 1961.*

their activities and offer better facilities for these activities, so they organized the White Eagle Club in 1913. The Silver Bells Club, organized in 1925 as an extension of the Polish National Alliance, provided youths and adults the opportunity to compete in boxing, baseball, and basketball. Just two years prior to this, the Polish Home of Gary incorporated, giving Poles a place for social gatherings and lodge meetings. Even though the Polish Home had moved twice, the facility was still functioning in the late 1970s. Other groups included the Polish Army Veterans Association of America (1934), the Pulaski Citizens Club, the Sea League of America (1951), the Syrena Athletic Club (1952), and the Polish National Alliance Youth Camp, Inc., founded in 1958 to encourage third- and fourth-generation Poles to learn about Polish culture, history, songs, and traditions while participating in camping and conservation activities. Indiana Poles quickly combined the various Polish-American associations, societies, and clubs into a federation chapter of the Polish American Congress (PAC) six months after the national organization emerged in 1944. In the early years of this federation its aim was to unite Polish Americans in helping Poland regain statehood and self-determination. Through this united front, Poles lobbied Congress for the welfare of the war-torn Polish nation and were successful in making the public aware of the Katyn Forest massacre. After World War II, PAC emphasized Polish-American heritage with Pulaski Day observances, and by the 1960s activities centered on observing Poland's Millennium in 1966. The Indiana division of PAC is still active today, promoting the accomplishments of Polish Americans, lobbying Congress for greater aid to Polish army veterans, and placing a marker on federal highway I-65 in honor of Gen. Casimir Pulaski.[45]

During and particularly after World War II, a new wave of Polish immigrants entered the United States, leaving war-torn Europe and the ensuing political turmoil that made life difficult for many refugees and émigrés. The Displaced Persons Act allowed many more East Europeans to enter the United States than the restricted levels of the 1920 law. The postwar immigrants gravitated toward the Polish communities established by the turn-of-the-century immigrant who sympathized with the plight of his fellow countryman. In Gary, a group of Polish Americans wished to help the new Polish immigrant and did so by establishing the Klub Polski Nowej Imigracji (the Polish New Immigrant Club). The purpose of the club was to aid the immigrant in establishing himself in the city and in learning to speak, read, and write English. The club also contributed to organizations that helped displaced Poles in western Europe.[46]

There have been mixed feelings though about the melding of the same ethnic immigrant group from two different time eras. Some felt that this post–World War II immigration gave a boost to the Polish Roman Catholic Church, so that the national character of the church remained strong until the late 1950s. However, others felt that because the new immigration included many more people from the higher socioeconomic and intelligentsia classes in Poland rather than from the peasant stock that made up most of the 1860–1910 group of Polish immigrants, the two groups did not blend well. In fact, the newer immigrants found the ethnic culture of the earlier immigrant, which was based on the folk culture of the Polish peasant, to be "archaic" and low class. The brightest aspect of this situation was that the recent émigrés increased awareness of the conditions of present-day Poland, sparked interest in the Polish National Culture Society and the language in the Polish press, and shifted the content of status competition.[47]

The Roman Catholic Church in Indiana, particularly in the northwest corner, also benefited by this new wave

of immigration when the Salvatorian priests arrived in Merrillville in 1939 and the Carmelite fathers in Hammond in 1948. Both groups engaged in missionary work among Americans of Polish extraction by offering Mass, retreats, novenas, and other devotions and providing ample funds for the training of future priests and missionaries in the home province. The Carmelite fathers also conducted a Polish language school, particularly for adults, but offered classes for children and adolescents as well. The postwar years brought a new interest in learning the Polish language after many years of diminishing use.[48]

Although Polish organizations and the Carmelite fathers' Polish language school attempted to promote Polish culture and history, many second-, third-, and fourth-generation Poles did not speak Polish. Part of the reason stemmed from the decreasing use of the Polish language in the parochial school curriculum, but another factor was the experiences of Polish immigrant children who remembered that learning English in school was very difficult when only Polish was spoken at home. Consequently, these Poles did not wish to have their children confront the same pressures and did not force them to learn Polish. Other Poles felt that by speaking Polish, their children would develop an accent when speaking English, eliciting name-calling, such as "Hunkies," from other children. Evidence seems to confirm Andrew Piekarczyk's conclusion: "Now, there are American Poles five or six generations away from their immigrant grandparents. They don't speak Polish anymore."[49]

The decline in the use of the Polish language did not diminish the importance of the family to the Polish community, even though family patterns had undergone some variations. Previously, the husband was the head of the household and the primary source of income while the wife was the caretaker of domestic affairs. The children were subservient to their parents, but the entire family

*Gathering of the Polish National Alliance in Marquette Park, Gary, 1979.*

operated as a social and economic unit, especially when older children sought jobs or helped in the care and education of younger siblings. The immigrant's house symbolized economic success and many times provided shelter for the extended family as well. Having boarders to supplement the family's income was common, but sometimes economic necessity put pressure on Polish wives to find employment outside the home.[50]

As time went on other factors influenced, or, perhaps more accurately, weakened the strong ties of the family structure. More schooling or better education prompted Polish youths to attain jobs in other locations, causing some strain on the relationships of parents and children. Parents could not always comprehend a child's aspiration to a middle-class lifestyle since life as blue-collar workers had been satisfactory for them. Differences in the political concerns of Poland also caused disagreements between displaced Poles and their children. Sometimes differences within a community's organization brought about disillusions, disputes, or frustration to Polish youths who found assimilation more agreeable or desirable. Sociologist Milton Gordon theorized that "Anglo conformity" demanded that an immigrant group and its descendants completely give up their Old World traditions to take on the characteristics and habits of a society's dominant group. In a sense this meant that a particular ethnic group would have to shun any and every portion of ethnic identity—even institutions and organizations—to support the structures of American society. However, the immigrants' children and grandchildren did not divorce themselves entirely from Polish culture.[51]

Other factors pointed to changing values and perceptions of what it meant to belong to an ethnic group. Very early in their settlement of Indiana the Poles had little or no awareness of an ethnic consciousness that separated them into a special national group. This was due partly to the partitioning of their homeland, so that many Poles identified themselves from a certain region or locality rather than from Poland. As Poles lived and worked with other immigrants and native-born Americans, they became cognizant of a national identity. This cognizance brought about churches, schools, associations, and neighborhoods that evoked a spirit of Polish ethnicism and nationalism. Poles focused their community life around their church and school and were sometimes criticized for this by being called ethnocentric. But these institutions actually cultivated a strong and lasting attachment to American society and values. The elevation of Rev. Paul Rhode, a Pole, into the American Catholic hierarchy in 1908 and the advent of World War I deepened the allegiance that immigrant Poles had for both Poland and America. American Poles

supported the war militarily and financially without relinquishing their loyalty to either country. Some Poles returned to Poland at the war's end, but most knew and felt their home to be America.[52]

Poles were slowly following an assimilation process. American citizenship was urged for immigrants; English articles were being printed in Polish publications; and technological innovations such as movies, radios, and the automobile created a social mobility for the Pole that translated into the acquisition of American customs and abandonment of some ethnic traditions.[53]

The Great Depression slowed this process because Poles could not afford to leave their old working-class neighborhoods, but parents and children still experienced differences as the younger generation continued to adapt to the American values not promoted by their ethnic background. Despite these differences Poles did develop complete, stable, and satisfying communities around institutions that were ethnic by definition but at the same time inculcated respect for American values and traditions. What has survived is a group of people who not only identify themselves as Americans but also recognize their earlier beginnings and cultural roots as rooted in a Polish heritage. This is demonstrated in Polish neighborhoods and former Polish enclaves where more first-generation and fewer second-generation Poles live. Most Polish Roman Catholic churches have a Mass said in Polish every Sunday while others have a Polish Mass once a month, provided a Polish priest is available. If the pastor is not fluent in Polish some churches hire a Polish priest for Mass and particularly for hearing confessions in Polish. Forty Hours, Lenten, and May devotions are still practiced in these churches along with the blessing of homes shortly after the New Year, the blessing of throats on the feast of St. Blaise, and the blessing of Easter baskets. Besides these religious ceremonies the Polish parishes have festivals complete with ethnic food and polka dances, Dyngus Day celebrations, Oplatek dinner dances, and pre-Lenten festivities, many of which are fund-raisers, since the Polish congregations still support their chapters of the Polish National Alliance and the Polish Roman Catholic Union. In addition to the church-sponsored activities, radio stations broadcast Polish programs, usually on Sundays, with Polish songs and music, newscasts, and celebration and meeting reminders in Polish to Polish audiences that enjoy listening to programs that reflect their lives, interests, and likings. Many American Poles send money and packages of clothing, toiletries, and other goods to Poland to help their friends and relatives there.[54]

In more recent years there has been a reawakening of Polish ethnicity. In 1966 the Polish Millennium of

Christianity helped Poles and Polish Americans to focus on their ethnicity. Inspired by Stefan Cardinal Wyszynski of Poland, this event commemorated the conversion of Mieszko I, Poland's first historical ruler, to Roman Catholicism. Although this millenary was primarily a religious observance, Indiana Poles sponsored parades, banquets, cultural programs, and youth days. Monsignor Valerian Jasinski, professor of dogmatic theology at SS. Cyril and Methodius Seminary in Orchard Lake, Michigan, reflected on ethnicity in his remarks at the state millennium banquet at the Hotel Gary in May 1966. He said, "A person and a nation, in order to give, must have roots and must have identity. People without roots have no future and cannot survive. Combine the best of your Polish traditions, Catholic heritage, and American ideals for an adventure of grace." Other events that have renewed Polish awareness are the election of a Polish pope and Poland's Solidarity Union. Pope John Paul II has done much to diminish the idea that Poles are inferior, and the Solidarity movement has inspired American Poles to endorse the union's goals and to send financial aid while sparking interest in learning about what Poland is really like.[55]

The newest Polish immigrants, particularly the intelligentsia, have tried to redirect the folk culture identification of Polonia to a more middle-class ideology that emphasizes Polish literature, science, art, music, and a national culture, thus deemphasizing the food-dance-costume-religious items of the old immigration. The constant fluctuations in the composition of the ethnic community darkens predictions about the survival of any national or ethnic flavor that may exist. An ethnic identity seems to have changed; however, how much more change will occur depends on the willingness of the people to keep some level of involvement and financial support in the network of formal groups that promote Polish heritage. Because American Poles can live and work in the larger American society while still being involved in ethnic social relations, the binding ties of the past could continue in the future, at least through the celebration of special occasions and traditional customs.[56]

## Notes

1. Victor Greene, "Poles," in Stephan Thernstrom, ed., *Harvard Encyclopedia of American Ethnic Groups* (Cambridge, Mass.: The Belknap Press of Harvard University Press, 1980), 787–803; Polish American Congress, *Jamestown Pioneers from Poland* (Chicago: Alliance Printers and Publishers, 1958), 5–20; Frank A. Renkiewicz, comp. and ed., *The Poles in America, 1608–1972* (Dobbs Ferry, N.Y.: Oceana Publications, 1973).

2. Adam Zamoyski, *The Polish Way: A Thousand-Year History of Poles and Their Culture* (New York: F. Watts, 1988); Joseph Wytrwal, *America's Polish Heritage: A Social History of the Poles in America* (Detroit: Endurance Press, 1961).

3. *Encyclopaedia Britannica,* 15th ed., 30 vols. (Chicago: Encyclopaedia Britannica, 1983), 14:637–54; Wladyslaw Rusinski, "The Role of the Peasantry of Poznan (Wielkopolska) in the Formation of Non-agricultural Labor Market," *East European Quarterly* 3 (Jan. 1970): 509–24; Stefan Kieniewicz, *The Emancipation of the Polish Peasantry* (Chicago: University of Chicago Press, 1969); William I. Thomas and Florian Znaniecki, *The Polish Peasant in Europe and America,* 2 vols. (1918; reprint, New York: Dover Publications, 1958), 1:87–302.

4. U.S. Senate, *Reports of the Immigration Commission,* 61st Cong., 3d sess., vol. 11 (Washington, D.C.: Government Printing Office, 1911), 581–85.

5. Federal manuscript censuses, 1860–1930.

6. *Diamond Jubilee St. Mary's, Otis, Indiana, 1783–1948;* S. F. Lisewski, C.S.C., "The Poles in the Diocese of Fort Wayne," *Our Sunday Visitor,* 1 Oct. 1933, stated that Jacob Lewandowski and Valentine Kosmatka were the first Poles to settle near Otis. The Immigration Commission gives 1861, 1862, and another earlier unspecified date for the start of ongoing Polish settlement. *Reports of Immigration Commission,* 61st Cong., 2d sess., vol. 12, pp. 260, 270. The *Goniec Polski,* 15 Aug. 1928, states 1854 as the year. It seems that 1862 is the earliest date agreed on by all.

7. Jasper Packard, *History of La Porte County and Its Townships, Towns and Cities* (Evansville, Ind.: Unigraphic, 1976); Timothy Edward Howard, *A History of St. Joseph County, Indiana,* 2 vols. (Chicago/New York: Lewis Publishing Co., 1907); William Frederick Howat, *A Standard History of Lake County, Indiana, and the Calumet*

*Indiana Poles celebrate the Polish Millennium of Christianity, 1966.*

*Region,* 2 vols. (Chicago/New York: Lewis Publishing Co., 1915), 1:115–16, 360, 383, 417, 439.

8. W. C. Latta, *Outline History of Indiana Agriculture* (Lafayette, Ind.: Published by Alpha Lambda Chapter of Epsilon Sigma Phi in cooperation with Purdue University Agricultural Experiment Station and the Department of Agriculture Extension and the Indiana Agriculture Agents Assoc., 1938); John Joseph Delaney, "The Beginnings of Industrial South Bend" (M.A. thesis, University of Notre Dame, 1951), 1–10, 35–39; Marguerite McCord Watt and Kathlyn V. Wade, *New Carlisle: The Story of Our Town, 1835–1955* (La Porte, Ind.: Service Printing Co., 1956), 134–35.

9. *Diamond Jubilee St. Mary's, Goniec Polski,* 10 Sept. 1889, 13 Feb. 1909, 10 Aug. 1918, 23 June 1923; Lisewski, "Poles in the Diocese of Fort Wayne"; *Diamond Jubilee, St. Stanislaus Kostka Parish, Terre Coupee, Indiana, 1884–1959* (Terre Coupee, Ind., 1959), 9; *Westville Indicator,* 9 Jan. 1986; *Valparaiso Vidette-Messenger,* 16 Sept. 1985.

10. *Diamond Jubilee, St. Stanislaus Kostka,* 9–10; *St. Stanislaus Kostka Hundredth Anniversary, 1884–1984* (Terre Coupee, Ind., 1984), 17–22; Watt and Wade, *New Carlisle,* 136–37.

11. U.S. Senate, *Reports of Immigration Commission,* 61st Cong., 2d sess., vol. 12, pp. 158–60, 263–70; *Diamond Jubilee, St. Stanislaus Kostka,* 9–10; Howard, *History of St. Joseph County,* 1:223–24, 244–67.

12. U.S. Senate, *Reports of Immigration Commission,* 61st Cong., 2d sess., Sen. Doc. no. 633, p. 571; Frank A. Renkiewicz, "The Polish Settlement of St. Joseph County, Indiana: 1855–1935" (Ph.D. diss., University of Notre Dame, 1967), 35; DeWitt C. Goodrich and Charles R. Tuttle, *An Illustrated History of the State of Indiana* (Indianapolis: Richard S. Peale and Co., 1875), 434–40, 614–18.

13. Powell A. Moore, *The Calumet Region: Indiana's Last Frontier,* vol. 39 of *Indiana Historical Collections* (Indianapolis: Indiana Historical Bureau, 1959), 15; Howat, *Standard History of Lake County,* 1:360, 383, 417, 439.

14. Howat, *Standard History of Lake County,* 1:297–300; "A Brief History of Hammond," in Works Progress Administration Real Property Survey of Hammond, Indiana, 1936, pp. 14–16; Moore, *Calumet Region,* 141–66.

15. *Diamond Jubilee Historical Record Commemorating the 75th Anniversary of East Chicago, 1893–1968* (East Chicago, Ind.: East Chicago Historical Society, 1968), 8–13; Archibald McKinlay, *Twin City: A Pictorial History of East Chicago, Indiana* (Norfolk, Va.: Donning Co., 1988), 60–61, 92; Moore, *Calumet Region,* 226–36, 251–53; Howat, *Standard History of Lake County,* 1:304–10, 316.

16. Renkiewicz, "Polish Settlement of St. Joseph County," 37; Joseph Swastek, "The Poles in South Bend to 1914," *Polish American Studies* 2 (July–Dec. 1945): 79–88; John Aylward, "Immigrant Settlement Patterns in South Bend, 1865–1917" (Typewritten copy, Northern Indiana Historical Society, 1971), 13–14.

17. Moore, *Calumet Region,* 251–53, 369–70; McKinlay, *Twin City,* 82; Greene, "Poles," 797; Federal manuscript census, 1900.

18. Thomas and Znaniecki, *Polish Peasant,* 1:58–60; Joseph John Parot, *Polish Catholics in Chicago, 1850–1920: A Religious History* (De Kalb: Northern Illinois University Press, 1981), 225; Donald Stabrowski, C.S.C., "Rev. Valentine Czyzewski, C.S.C., Immigrant Pastor" (Paper presented at the 1985 Conference on the History of the Congregation of Holy Cross, 25–26 May, King's College, Wilkes-Barre, Pennsylvania), 1. Dr. Karl Wachtel, parishioner of St. Stanislaus Kostka, Chicago, Illinois, said, "Wherever there is a priest or church, wherever a parish is being created, there Polish life grows vigorously and numbers multiply, feeling better among their own kind, feeling more secure under the protective wings of the parish with their own pastor. . . . The priest is in every sense of the word a social and national worker."

19. St. Adalbert Parish, South Bend, *Fifty Years 1910–1960,* p. 20; Stabrowski, "Rev. Valentine Czyzewski," 8; St. Hedwig Parish, *One Hundredth Anniversary of St. Hedwig Parish, 1877–1977,* p. 20; Rita Trzop and Gertrude Wieczorek, interview with the author, South Bend, 14 Aug. 1990; Bertha Moskwinski, interview with the author, 16 Aug. 1990; Parot, *Polish Catholics in Chicago,* 21. In the Trzop/Wieczorek interview, Trzop mentioned that the Irish and Poles still demonstrate feelings of animosity from time to time. Just a few years back at a summertime outing the Irish had the water shut off so the Poles could not get a drink.

20. *Diamond Jubilee, St. Stanislaus Kostka,* 11; *St. Stanislaus Kostka Hundredth Anniversary,* 21; "Rolling Prairie Parish Celebrates 100th Anniversary," in *Northwest Indiana Catholic,* 3; Rev. Leonard Kronkowski, interview with the author, 7 Aug. 1990; Joseph Alvin, *The Light of Notre Dame* (Philadelphia: Derrance, 1978), 12; Stabrowski, "Rev. Valentine Czyzewski," 13. Father Kronkowski related that St. John Kanty parish was built on an open field several miles outside of the town proper. Two reasons for this were first, the land was donated by a Polish farmer and second, the immigrants wished to be away from the powerful force of the Ku Klux Klan.

21. St. Stanislaus Parish, East Chicago, Indiana, "The St. Stanislaus Story—Eight and One Half Decades of Excellence and the Pursuit Thereof" (Exhibition for celebration of Polish culture and heritage, June 1990, East Chicago Public Library); *Poland's Millennium of Christianity, 966–1966* (Munster, Ind.: Millennium Committee, 1966); St. Adalbert Parish, Whiting, Indiana, *Diamond Jubilee, 1902–1977,* p. 8; St. Stanislaus Kostka Parish, Michigan City, "History of the Polish People of Michigan City"; Moore, *Calumet Region,* 361; Rev. Emil Bloch, interview by author, Michigan City, 22 Aug. 1990; Howat, *Standard History of Lake County,* 1:368–69, 372, 431–32, 2:693–95.

22. St. Michael the Archangel Polish National Catholic Church, East Chicago, Indiana, "Historical Highlights of Our First Eighty Years" and "The St. Stanislaus Story" (Exhibitions displayed at the East Chicago Public Library for a celebration of Polish culture and heritage, June 1990).

23. St. Hyacinth Church, Fort Wayne, Indiana, *Souvenir of Dedication, December 5, 1954,* p. 15; Sacred Heart Church, Ege, Indiana, *Souvenir of Mass of Consecration* (14, 18 Nov. 1989) and in parish directory; *Golden Jubilee Booklet* of St. Mary's Church, Fort Wayne, Ind.; *The History of Noble County, Indiana* (Dallas, Tex.: Noble County History Book Committee, 1986), 367.

24. St. Adalbert Parish, *Fifty Years 1910–1960,* p. 26; Stabrowski, "Rev. Valentine Czyzewski," 17–18; *St. Adalbert Parish, South Bend, 1910–1985.*

25. Renkiewicz, "Polish Settlement of St. Joseph County," 179; *Goniec Polski,* 9 Aug., 7 Oct. 1911, 9 July 1913; *South Bend Tribune,* 30 June 1913.

26. St. Casimir Parish, South Bend, *Golden Jubilee Book, 1899–1949,* pp. 19–20; *South Bend Tribune,* 24, 31 Jan., 5, 7, 9, 13, 16, 21, 23, 25, 27 Feb., 4, 9, 11, 14, 16, 17, 23, 25, 30 Mar., 1, 17, 21 Apr. 1914; *Goniec Polski,* 31 Jan., 18–29 Feb., 7–25 Mar. 1914; Renkiewicz, "Polish Settlement of St. Joseph County," 203–5; Frank B. Roman Collection No. 77, Box 2, Indiana University Northwest, Calumet Regional Archives; Mary Benninghoff, "Bloody Sunday at St. Casimir's," *South Bend Tribune,* 11 Aug. 1974.

27. Renkiewicz, "Polish Settlement of St. Joseph County," 198–99, 206–9; *Goniec Polski,* 14, 18 Mar. 1914; *South Bend Tribune,* 20 Feb., 9 Mar., 17 Apr. 1914.

28. Trzop/Wieczorek interview.

29. Renkiewicz, "Polish Settlement of St. Joseph County," 23, 45; Thaddeus C. Radzialowski, "Reflections on the History of the Felicians in America," *Polish American Studies* (Spring 1975): 19–28; Waclaw X. Kruszka, *Historya Polska W. Ameryce,* 13 vols. (Milwaukee, Wis.: Drukien Spacoeki Wydawniczek Kuryea, 1905–8), 11:25, 27, 33, 35, 38, 39; Sister Ceciliann Broton, S.S.J.T.O.S.F., interview with the author, 11 July 1990.

30. Mary Borowiec, interview with the author, 12 June 1990; *One Hundredth Anniversary of St. Hedwig Parish,* 33; St. Casimir Parish, *Golden Jubilee Book,* 40–41; Sister M. Georgia Costin, C.S.C., "The Rise and Fall of St. Joseph Academy at South Bend" and "Tales of Schools at St. Hedwig, St. Mary, Sacred Heart and St. Stephen," *Today's Catholic,* 5, 26 May 1991; Emily Greene Balch, *Our Slavic Fellow Citizens, The American Immigrant Collection* (1910; reprint, New York: Arno Press, 1969), 477–78.

31. Thomas and Znaniecke, *Polish Peasant,* 2:1558–1623; Parot, *Polish Catholics in Chicago,* 223–25; *One Hundredth Anniversary of St. Hedwig Parish,* 39; St. Stanislaus Parish, South Bend, "History of Our Parish, 1900–1922," articles printed in church bulletins; St. Adalbert Parish, *Fifty Years, 1910–1960;* St. Casimir Parish, *Golden Jubilee Book;* Trzop/Wieczorek interview; Swastek, "Poles in South Bend to 1914," pp. 79–88; *Goniec Polski,* 25 Oct. 1911.

32. Parot, *Polish Catholics in Chicago,* 221–23; Trzop/Wieczorek interview; Borowiec interview; Moskwinski interview; Stella Dzieglowicz, interview with the author, 26 Dec. 1991; Helen Stankiewicz Zand, "Polish Folkways in the United States," *Polish American Studies* 7 (July–Dec. 1955): 65–72.

33. Thomas and Znaniecki, *Polish Peasant,* 1:48–50; Parot, *Polish Catholics in Chicago,* 225; Stabrowski, "Rev. Valentine Czyzewski," 11–14; *South Bend Tribune,* 13 Jan. 1885; Thomas J. McAvoy, C.S.C., *The History of the Catholic Church in South Bend* (South Bend, Ind., 1953), 23–24; Swastek, "Poles in South Bend to 1914," pp. 82, 83, 87; H. J. Alerding, *The Diocese of Fort Wayne, 1857–September 22, 1907: A Book of Historical Reference, 1669–1907* (Fort Wayne, Ind.: Archer Print. Co., 1907), 93.

34. Moore, *Calumet Region,* 374–76; Renkiewicz, "Polish Settlement of St. Joseph County," 121–23; *Goniec Polski,* 17 Nov. 1897, 23 Apr., 30 Aug. 1902, 1 June 1907; *Reports of the Immigration Commission,* Sen. Doc. no. 633, pp. 602–4; McKinlay, *Twin City,* 92; Howat, *Standard History of Lake County,* 1:354, 424; *Gary Weekly Tribune,* 1 Jan. 1909. Emily Greene Balch gives 31.6 percent as the figure for illiteracy among Polish immigrants fourteen years of age and over for the year ending 30 June 1900. Balch, *Our Slavic Fellow Citizens,* 479.

35. Renkiewicz, "Polish Settlement of St. Joseph County," 124; *Reports of the Immigration Commission,* Sen. Doc. no. 633, p. 600; Federal manuscript census, 1880 and 1900; *Goniec Polski,* 24 Oct. 1896, 23 Jan., 3 Feb., 10 Apr., 12 May, 1897, 15 Apr. 1899, 1 Aug. 1901, 13 Feb. 1907.

36. Renkiewicz, "Polish Settlement of St. Joseph County," 125–26; *Goniec Polski,* 3, 7 Oct. 1896, 27 Sept., 18 Oct., 22 Nov. 1919; Swastek, "Poles in South Bend," 81; Helen Stankiewicz Zand, "Polish American Leisure Ways," *Polish American Studies* 18 (Jan.–June 1961): 34–36; Bernard Pinkowski, *Memoir of a Sentimental Journey to Historic St. Hedwig's* (South Bend, Ind.: n.p., 1983).

37. Greene, "Poles," 792, 793; Balch, *Our Slavic Fellow Citizens,* 308, 309, 315.

38. Renkiewicz, "Polish Settlement of St. Joseph County," 126–28; Greene, "Poles," 794; Chester Wleklinski, interview with the author, 7 Aug. 1990; *Reports of the Immigration Commission,* Sen.

Doc. no. 633, p. 600; *Goniec Polski,* 11 Nov. 1903, 3 Apr. 1907, 27 Apr. 1910; *South Bend Tribune,* 14–19, 22 Oct. 1912.

39. Renkiewicz, "Polish Settlement of St. Joseph County," 129–30; Anderson and Cooley, comps. *South Bend and the Men Who Have Made It* (South Bend, Ind.: Tribune Printing Co., 1901), 325–26; *Goniec Polski,* 27 June, 18 July 1896, 1 May 1897, 22 Jan. 1898, 14 May 1902; *South Bend Tribune,* 24 Apr. 1900; Howard, *History of St. Joseph County,* 2:776–77.

40. Renkiewicz, "Polish Settlement of St. Joseph County," 131–32; *Goniec Polski,* 6 May, 14 Oct. 1908, 13 June 1909; St. Stanislaus Parish, "History of Our Parish, 1914," article printed in the church bulletin on the history of the parish; Moskwinski interview.

41. Pinkowski, *Sentimental Journey to Historic St. Hedwig's;* Polish American Congress, Indiana Division, Bicentennial Committee, *Indiana Poles in the Bicentennial Year of the United States, 1976* (Munster, Ind.: The Committee, 1976), 72–76.

42. Greene, "Poles," 795; Renkiewicz, "Polish Settlement of St. Joseph County," 134–53; *Goniec Polski,* 1 Apr. 1903; *South Bend Tribune,* 24 Oct. 1905.

43. Swastek, "Poles in South Bend to 1914," pp. 87–88; *Goniec Polski,* 12 Nov. 1898, 9 Aug. 1913; St. Stanislaus Parish, "History of Our Parish, 1910," article printed in the church bulletin on the history of the parish; *Diamond Jubilee Historical Record of East Chicago, 1893–1968,* pp. 30–31; Renkiewicz, "Polish Settlement of St. Joseph County," 60–61; Brother Maximus, C.S.C., *Album Zlatego Jubileuszu Parafji S.W. Jadwigi W. South Bend, Indiana, 1877–1927* (Chicago, 1927), 154; *South Bend Tribune,* 14, 20 May 1879, 1 Apr. 1880; *Gary Post-Tribune,* 10 June 1956, 17 Dec. 1965.

44. Renkiewicz, "Polish Settlement of St. Joseph County," 289–307; Polish-American Democratic Club, *Twenty-Fifth Anniversary Banquet,* 22 Apr. 1956, and *Thirty-Fifth Anniversary Banquet,* 16 Feb. 1966, Frank B. Roman Collection, No. 77, Box 2, Indiana University Northwest, Calumet Regional Archives.

45. *Indiana Poles in the Bicentennial Year,* 32–70; *Gary Post-Tribune,* 27 Mar. 1956, 17 Dec. 1965, 17 Mar. 1978; Polish American Congress, Indiana Division, Frank B. Roman Collection, No. 77, Box 2; Thomas I. Monzell, "The Polish National Alliance in History: Changing Priorities" (PAHA Convention, 28 Dec. 1973), ibid., Box 3; *Polish National Alliance 70th Anniversary Jubilee Banquet Book, 1907–1977* (Gary, Ind.); Indiana Polish National Alliance Youth Camp Incorporated, *Fifteenth Anniversary Banquet and Ball, 1958–1973* (Program booklet, Gary, Ind.).

46. *Poland's Millennium of Christianity.*

47. Parot, *Polish Catholics in Chicago,* 231; Helen Znaniecki Lopata, *Polish Americans: Status Competition in an Ethnic Community* (Englewood Cliffs, N.J.: Prentice-Hall, 1976), 67.

48. *Poland's Millennium of Christianity; Indiana Poles in the Bicentennial Year,* 17–21; Carmen Peter Pignatiello, *The Unshod—The Men of Carmel—We Would Walk with You: A Work of Love* (Munster, Ind.: Pignatiello Enterprises, 1981), 48–53.

49. Andrew Piekarczyk, quoted in Ernie Hernandez, *Ethnics in Northwest Indiana* (Gary, Ind.: Gary Post-Tribune, 1983), 51; Margaret Klekot Pogorzelski, interview with the author, 21 Aug. 1990; Moskwinski interview; Lorraine King, "Interviews with Gary Polish Immigrants," June/July 1970, Collection 242, Box 5, Calumet Regional Archives.

50. D. H. Avery and J. K. Fedorowicz, *The Poles in Canada,* booklet no. 4 (Ottawa: Canadian Historical Association, 1982), 18; King, "Interviews with Gary Polish Immigrants," 12, 23, 25.

51. Lopata, *Polish Americans,* 144–45; Catherine Sardo Weidner, "Building a Better Life," *Chicago History* 18 (Winter 1989–90): 25.

52. Greene, "Poles," 794, 801; William J. Galush, "Forming Polonia: A Study of Four Polish-American Communities, 1890–1940" (Ph.D. diss., University of Minnesota, 1975), 313–16; Lopata, *Polish Americans,* 144; Weidner, "Building a Better Life," 25.

53. Greene, "Poles," 801. The *Goniec Polski* was the only Polish newspaper printed in South Bend. In Gary, Indiana, there were two Polish newspapers prior to the depression years, *Glos Ludu* (Voice of the People) and *Glos Polonii* (The People's Voice). The Poles in the East Chicago/Hammond area depended on the Chicago publication, *Dziennik Chicagoski* and the *Zgoda* (Peace), a publication of the Polish National Alliance.

54. Walter Skibinski, interview with the author, June 1990; Trzop/ Wieczorek interview; Moskwinski interview; Broton interview; Kronkowski interview; Bloch interview; Dzieglowicz interview; Borowiec interview. A chapter of the United Polka Association, an outgrowth of the Chicago organization, was formed in 1984 in Hammond, Indiana. Its purpose is to promote polka music and dancing, but Polish ancestry is not a prerequisite for membership. There are approximately five hundred members from the areas of Lake and La Porte counties.

55. Betty Clark, et al., "Gary's Polish Americans" (Unpublished paper in Calumet Regional Archives, 1970), 20; Avery and Fedorowicz, *Poles in Canada,* 21.

56. Lopata, *Polish Americans,* 66, 67, 146, 148; Theresita Polzin, *The Polish Americans: Whence and Whither* (Pulaski, Wis.: Franciscan Publications, 1973); Victor Greene, *For God and Country: The Rise of Polish and Lithuanian Ethnic Consciousness in America, 1860–1910* (Madison: State Historical Society of Wisconsin, 1975).

# ROMANIANS

MARY LEUCA

*In 1913 a father with his sixteen-year-old son, who recently had joined him in Muncie, moved to Gary where better jobs could be found. They arrived by train in Gary in the evening and went in search of a Romanian boardinghouse. As they passed a large two-storied wooden structure they heard Romanian being spoken within. When the two of them entered they found to their amazement that "in about fifteen minutes . . . the whole saloon was filled with people from our village . . . all at one time in Gary there were 69 of us from Viisoara" (a small village in Transylvania).*

## Origins

Romanians came to America during the period of the new immigration between 1880 and 1914 to make a better living in a climate of religious and political liberty. Where is the area from which they came? Who were they and why did they come?

Romania is a country in southeastern Europe bounded by the Ukraine and Moldova, Hungary, Serbia, Bulgaria, and the Black Sea. Romania's history is deeply rooted in antiquity. Armies have fought for control of Romanian lands from its earliest Thracian beginnings. Thracians were ancient inhabitants of the eastern part of the Balkan peninsula. They fell before successive attacks by Persians, Macedonians, and Romans. The Roman legions in their march eastward and northward crossed the Danube and conquered the Dacians who peopled the area in the first century, completely subduing them in 106 A.D. under Roman Emperor Trajan.[1] Roman legions colonized virtually all the lands that make up Romania today. A Dacian-Roman ethnic element appeared, which soon became the dominant group of the region, and at the same time the Dacian language was supplanted with Latin. Most important, Christianity, with the conversion of Roman Emperor Constantine in 312 A.D., became a part of Romanian life.

Romania's location between East and West has been a blessing and a curse. Increasing pressure upon the Roman Empire by Germanic tribes and the Huns, as well as others, forced Rome to withdraw its forces from Romania. However, when the Roman Empire collapsed, Roman legionnaires remained in what is now Romania.

Romanians proved to be resilient and adaptive as Saxons, Teutonic knights, Jews, and Bulgars appeared in the area. In 864, after the conversion of Czar Boris of Bulgaria, the majority of Romania's population became Eastern Orthodox. In the late ninth century the Magyars drove out the Bulgars. Under the Magyars Romanians sought refuge in a pastoral village life, and many of them fled to the mountains. Romanians maintained their language and Eastern Orthodox religion—their way of life, but Romania's territory remained a pawn of Austria-Hungary, Poland, Russia, and Turkey until it achieved independence in 1881.

During the early 1900s a large number of Romanian immigrants from the province of Transylvania came to America to escape the oppression of the Magyars. They supplied what was needed to help build America—their labor.

## Immigration

Romanian immigration to the United States prior to 1880 was sporadic. Those Romanians who did immigrate

during this period were from the provinces of Walachia and Moldavia. With the period of new immigration in the 1880s to 1914 large numbers of Romanian immigrants left from Austria-Hungary, which included the province of Transylvania. The immigrants from Transylvania were not Austrians or Hungarians. More than 90 percent of them were Romanians. At Castle Gardens (New York City port) the Romanian immigrants who lived in the Hungarian-controlled area of Transylvania were listed as Hungarians, and the Romanians from the Austrian-ruled section of Bukovina were listed as Austrians. Thus, Romanians came to America with Hungarian or Austrian passports and were classified incorrectly.[2] As in the case of other nationality groups from Eastern Europe, where the people were ruled by a nation other than their own, United States immigration authorities listed such immigrants as nationals of the passport nations, producing errors that affected the immigrant quota laws passed by Congress during the 1920s.

Emigration authorities in Romania took account of the number of Romanians leaving from Transylvania and other provinces. For the period between 1899 and 1913, in conformity with the official statistics of the Hungarian authorities, the Hungarian Ministry published data showing that 222,977 persons immigrated to America from Transylvania. Figures from a number of sources show that the majority (over 95 percent) of the Romanian immigrants came from Transylvania. The Romanians who entered the United States originated from the districts of Sibiu, Făgăras, Sighişoara, Cluj, Alba Iulia, and other districts, including the areas known as the Banat and Bukovina.[3]

Romanian peasants from Transylvania had endured the oppressive rule of the Hungarians and Austrians for centuries. Less than 10 percent of the immigrants came from the area known as the "old kingdom" or Romania proper. The Romanian peasants from the old kingdom did not leave their homeland in any significant numbers.

Although their situation was not the best, their rulers at least were Romanians.

The conditions and reasons that motivate a people to seek a new country in which to live are many. The major causes of Romanian immigration were economic, political, and social problems that revolved around property rights. Landholdings were continually subdivided by the governing authorities, and for those with smaller plots this meant a decline in status, a decrease in an already precarious income, and an increase in debt and borrowing at excessive interest.

The programs of Magyarization instituted by the Hungarian regime in Budapest against the Romanian population in Transylvania were severe. The extensive, oppressive policies forced the teaching of the Hungarian language to Romanian children in the predominately Romanian populated province of Transylvania. The Romanians suffered agricultural exploitation and long-range policies of oppression in regard to civil services and commercial matters. Another serious concern was the efforts by Austrian-Hungarian authorities to subject people to Catholicism when more than 90 percent of the Romanian population were Eastern Orthodox.[4]

Romanian peasants from Transylvania had good reasons to come to America with such conditions in their homeland. They came to America and found their way to Indiana, attracted by high-paying jobs in the state's newly built mills and factories. Most of them came with the intention of helping families left in Romania by making money and sending back funds so that the others could survive, be better off, or come to America. Often this income from America meant the difference between poverty and a satisfactory living condition.[5]

Great numbers of immigrants were lured by representatives of companies and labor agencies seeking laborers for railroad gangs and industrial centers. Company agents

*Laborers in the Graver Tank Works, East Chicago, Indiana, ca.1888.*

*Two young men on their way to work with lunch buckets in hand, Gary, 1908.*

went to Romanian villages and offered jobs and passage to America. When newly arrived immigrants were asked, "How did you come?," a frequently heard response was "I came with Missler!" Missler referred to the travel and labor agency in Germany that brought many thousands of immigrants to America.

Letters from America reached Romanian villages, telling of high wages. Moreover, word came from the returning immigrants themselves, who told villagers about working for fifteen cents an hour—almost two dollars a day. In Romania the wages of a farm laborer totaled about twenty cents a day. The peasant realized he could make as much in one day in America as he did for ten days of work in the fields at home. Prosperous-looking immigrants who returned after a year or two in America, with money to pay family debts and buy bigger plots of land, livestock, and other necessities, influenced many to leave for the "golden land of opportunity."

The often heard expression of the time was *Mia si bani de drum!* (A thousand dollars and the passage home). The majority of these early immigrants intended to return to the Old Country, and many did return to their villages in Romania; many made several crossings. But many more stayed to make a new life and a new home in their new country.[6]

### Arrival and Settlement in Indiana

Although the majority of Romanians came to the Midwest directly from Ellis Island, it was not unusual for a newcomer to make three or four moves to cities in other states such as Ohio, Pennsylvania, or Michigan before settling to work in a particular community in Indiana. Romanians came to Garrett to work with the railroad companies, to Muncie and Fort Wayne to work in

factories, and to Indianapolis and Hammond to work in the meatpacking industries. They came to the Terre Haute and Clinton areas to work in the coal mines and to East Chicago (Indiana Harbor) to work in the steel mills and cement plant. Romanians also helped construct a new steel mill just a few miles east of East Chicago, and they stayed to help build a new city—Gary. Many more Romanians came to work in northwest Indiana, where they found immigrants from their own villages and where they formed their own colonies.

On their arrival they were naturally overwhelmed. The language was alien, the customs were confusing, and the cities were very different from their village life with age-old customs and traditions and the language of the Old Country. Nevertheless, the immigrant found that in these cities, which attracted other immigrant groups with equally foreign languages and ways, they had something in common—a desire to succeed and to make a new life in the New World.

The first wave of Romanian immigrants consisted of heads of households and older sons. Young men fifteen to twenty years old soon followed, hoping to make a new life for themselves in America. One of the young newcomers to Indiana Harbor described his arrival in these words:

> We were so poor in Romania . . . I was too young to think that far as to what I would become. I was young and I just wanted to do better. That was all there was to it. When I came here, it was a new life compared to what I had in the old country. That made me and millions like me—to try to do what we did. We found that here we could have a better life.[7]

The experiences of immigrant laborers in Muncie and Fort Wayne correspond to those in other Indiana cities in the early 1900s. The men who worked at Midland Iron and Steel in Muncie came to Fort Wayne in 1903 to work at the Fort Wayne Iron and Steel Company. These workers, including ten young Romanians, settled around the mill on a forty-acre site that became known as the Rolling Mill District. The District, as it was called, contained a mixture of immigrant groups along with a small black community whose residents the company also recruited. To outsiders the District was considered a "low-rent" district; to those who lived there it was Utopia! Most of them had emigrated from small villages without electricity, water, and other conveniences. It was as though a Romanian village had been transported to America. In the District they could find a Romanian grocery store, a Romanian bakery, several Romanian saloons, and by 1917 a Romanian Orthodox church. The only thing reminiscent of America in the District was the mill, for industry was nonexistent in Transylvania.[8]

Lake County was unknown to the industrial world in the early 1900s. In 1905 the total population of the entire county numbered about 12,800, and of this number 3,000 were listed as foreigners.[9] Cheap land and proximity to good markets attracted industrialists to northwest Indiana, located approximately twenty miles from Chicago. Ten great railroads crossed this narrow section, and excellent harbors on Lake Michigan could be built easily. A canal just west of Indiana Harbor connected Lake Michigan with inland waterways. Along the banks of this canal, mills and factories were constructed. Among the first workers attracted to northwest Indiana were Romanian immigrants.

In 1901 two Romanians, John Covach and Pete Cionta, and two Irishmen, Jim Doherty and John McGarth, left the Muncie plant of Midland Iron and Steel Company to come to Indiana Harbor where the new Inland Steel plant was to be built. R. J. Beatty, who operated the

Muncie firm and became the general manager of the Inland works, brought forty more men to the Inland site later that year. Covach worked first as a laborer during the construction of the plant and then as first helper in the No. 1 Open Hearth.[10]

The population figures show that Lake County grew rapidly from 12,800 in 1905 to 87,000 in 1916. The section of East Chicago known as Indiana Harbor grew so rapidly as a result of the building of the Inland Steel Company (1901) that East Chicago was considered the fastest-developing city in America at that time. Even more spectacular figures were recorded in the area that became Gary. Less than ten miles to the east of Indiana Harbor, the United States Steel Corporation, now known as USX, selected a site in 1906 for the world's largest steel mill and the city of Gary. By 1916 Gary had an estimated 50,000 residents.

Romanians were among the first laborers in Gary, living in tents or tar paper shacks until buildings were erected. Those who had come with the earliest groups by freight trains lived in boxcars and rowed in small boats from the train to the construction site of the new mill.[11] Romanian work gangs were common in early days in Gary. According to one of the workers in the Gary Works of United States Steel Corporation:

> There was a Romanian man . . . Prasca, at the Gary works who was a boss. He had a good education in Romania and had a good position in the mill. He had work gangs composed of Romanians—only Romanians. My father worked with him at the open hearth and I got a job working there, too.[12]

The early immigrants who were interviewed about their experiences were proud of the hard work and the contribution they made to the company. One was especially

*Romanian workers outside tar paper shack housing at the Gary Works, 1908.*

proud of the fact that he had worked for forty-seven years and had missed work on only six occasions.[13] Another made this comment about his work experience in 1905:

> I was 15 years old when my brother got a job for me in the cement plant in Indiana Harbor. I got 15 cents an hour. I worked 12 hours a day, seven days a week for 363 days a year. There were two holidays that the factory declared—Christmas and the 4th of July. If you were healthy, you worked 363 days a year; which I did![14]

The growth rate of East Chicago and Gary was phenomenal. Where there had been no cities as we know them—no buildings or streets—immigrants formed their own communities. As buildings were erected and homes constructed, little communities within the larger community developed providing protection, familiar surroundings, and social life.

## Social Structure

Very few women were among the early newcomers, and they came with their husbands or joined small groups departing from their villages. The few women who came with their husbands started boardinghouses; others found work as domestics. Later women found employment in the factories.[15]

The boardinghouse was an important part of the immigrant's life in America. Boardinghouses and saloons functioned as meeting places and served a purpose similar to the English inns and pubs as gathering places for talking, drinking, card playing, or billiards playing. The boardinghouses and saloons also held activities such as dances, weddings, and funerals.

If a Romanian immigrant did not join his family or other relatives in America he went to a city in America he knew about from letters received in his village. He journeyed to that place where others from his hometown had settled, and there he found a Romanian boardinghouse or saloon and others who had left before him.

In 1913 a father with his sixteen-year-old son, who recently had joined him in Muncie, moved to Gary where better jobs could be found. They arrived by train in Gary in the evening and went in search of a Romanian boardinghouse. As they passed a large two-storied wooden structure they heard Romanian being spoken within. When the two of them entered they found to their amazement that "in about fifteen minutes . . . the whole saloon was filled with people from our village . . . all at one time in Gary there were 69 of us from Viisoara" (a small village in Transylvania).[16]

## Boardinghouses

Early immigrants in those days had no means of transportation so they located as close to the factory as possible. In Indiana Harbor along Cedar Street, later renamed Main Street, boardinghouses, saloons, groceries, and other businesses were established. On the corner of Cedar Street and Broadway stood the Casa Romina (Romanian House), a prominent center with a large dormitory of forty beds. At Casa Romina a new Romanian settler could sleep and then go to work for his twelve-hour shift. While he was at work another from the second shift occupied his bed. This aspect of life in America was referred to by the Romanian immigrant as *bortul* (room and board).[17]

Romanian immigrants enjoyed simple entertainment and social activities when they gathered in a spacious room of one of the boardinghouses on Saturday nights and Sundays. They took turns entertaining each other with their favorite songs or sang together; they danced and challenged each other with a new step as is done in the *Caluserul* (Dance of the Horsemen); someone would play his flute or violin; or someone would read from one of the few Romanian books available. They also amused themselves by telling humorous or nostalgic stories that were often sentimental since their thoughts turned to the homeland on these occasions. They reserved solemn moments for the arrival of letters from the Old Country that someone read aloud while all listened. The more literate wrote letters for those who were less literate. Some would drink to forget their loneliness, but drinking was usually done in moderation in order to save money. Romanian immigrants valued frugality, and their hard-earned wages were saved to be sent back home. Yet they assisted one another whenever necessary:

> When money from America was sent home to those in Romania, it was like heaven. But, you know how they got together to send so much money home? What they did in the boarding house—is that a man would say "Next payday I am sending home money" and the others would loan him five or ten dollars and when he got it altogether . . . he had maybe 200 American dollars which was a huge sum in Romanian money. Back home [in Romania] they did not know this—they thought he earned it all in a short time. They thought America was paved with gold![18]

## Ballads and Immigrant Poetry

Romanian ballads are excellent sources of information about the Romanian character. Ballads and poems not only tell of immigrant dreams of what America might be but also homeland conditions, the reasons for immigration, farewells, the Atlantic crossing, and varied experiences—good and bad—in the New World.[19]

The Romanian *doina* is a ballad—a song of happiness or sorrow. Each Romanian had his favorite *doina,* his story. The immigrants' feelings of loneliness and longing for those back home in the Old Country are expressed in the poignant lyrics of their folk songs. "Doina din America" is a ballad written by an unknown composer in the Lake County area. A recording with a Columbia label was made in 1913 by several artists from Indiana Harbor; an English translation of the Romanian lyrics by Rev. George C. Muresan reveals the following:

> At home in my own village, my mother would take good care of me; my brothers were all around me. At home I owned no dollars; but I had my cart and oxen, and with them I made my living. The dollar may be mighty, if you toil for it . . . wretched thing that it is; but how many hundreds of stalwarts are lost among the mills because of it.[20]

The experiences of Romanians in America gave rise to the development of a popular poetry described by Nicolae Zamfirescu in 1912 as being "specifica a romanului american" (specifically belonging to the Romanian American). Immigrants composed and recited these poems, and since many of the authors could not write they memorized the verses they composed. They entertained each other reciting their verses, and in this manner the popular poetry of the immigrants spread from community to community. The poems reveal the sentiments of the immigrant about his new home far from the valleys and villages in Transylvania.

### Origin of Societies

Romanian immigrants who farmed in villages discovered a very different way of life in factories and mills. Their former work involved the oxen and plow, primitive farming methods, or work as a *cioban* (shepherd) tending sheep in the hills of Transylvania. Thus the factory was a strange place for them until they became adjusted to their new surroundings. In those

*Caluseri Group, dancers, pose in front of a saloon on Pennsylvania Avenue, Indiana Harbor, ca. 1915. Note wooden sidewalk and Inland Steel mills reflected in the storefront glass.*

*Casa Romina (Romanian House) boarders pose with the owner and his wife (far left in aprons), Indiana Harbor, early 1900s.*

early days accidents were not uncommon, and church records show that a significant number of workers were killed in factory accidents. The factory whistle, when used to signal a factory mishap, was a frightening sound heard too often in the era before strict plant safety rules were enforced.

The tragedies of factory work led to the formation of benevolent societies, as an early immigrant explains:

> We created the society; we had reasons for it because if someone had an accident, we had no old people among us . . . only young. We would have no place to go and get help and advice. We did not have any support. If someone got killed or injured in an accident, we would collect money—a quarter, dime or a dollar . . . that was rare—to help pay for a funeral. We did this among ourselves. That gave us the idea to start a society locally, with a quarter a month dues. And, when something happened among us, we were right there to help.[21]

In their homeland old customs and traditions in the villages governed people's lives. If the head of the household died the family was helped by relatives and their fellow villagers. In the United States immigrants were usually without family and among strangers so a new way had to be found to provide help during emergencies and need. The mutual or beneficial societies grew out of the need for Romanian immigrants to help each other financially in case of illness or death.

The first two Romanian societies in the United States were formed on the same day, 2 November 1902, in Cleveland, Ohio, and Homestead, Pennsylvania. The news spread quickly to other cities where Romanians lived and similar organizations were formed. In 1905 Indiana Harbor became the site of the third society formed in the United States.

In 1906 a national organization now known as the Union and League of Romanian Societies of America was established. In just a few years of immigrating, Romanian peasants, who had not been permitted to form any organizations in their own homeland, were able to organize local as well as state and national organizations in America.[22]

Many local societies and lodges were formed in Indiana. Those in existence today are:

Transilvaneana Society (Indiana Harbor) 1905
Treicolorul Roman Society (Gary) 1908
Lumina Romana Society (Indianapolis) 1908

Unirea Romana (East Chicago) 1913
Lodge #148, formerly known as Societatea Bihoriana
   Banatiana Abraham Lincoln (Gary) 1918

The following societies have dissolved:

Nicolae Iorga Club (Indiana Harbor) 1909
Ion O. Popaiov Society (Terre Haute) 1913
Independent Society Andrei Baron de Saguna
   (Terre Haute) 1915
Vasile Lucaciu Society (Clinton) 1915
Societatea Sentinela Romana (Fort Wayne) 1917

The history of the Romanian fraternal groups is an important part of the story of Romanians in America. Their work reflects a concern for the welfare of people, for tradition and cultural heritage, and for democratic processes.

On 10 December 1905 in the Casa Comunala (Community House) in Indiana Harbor, Societatea Transilvaneana (Transylvania Society) was the first fraternal society formed in Indiana. The society was named Societatea Transilvaneana since the majority of its members were from the province of Transylvania.[23] On 18 May 1913 an important and significant event in the history of the Transylvania Society took place. In the Orthodox church Rev. Simion Mihaltian blessed the American and the Romanian flags. Since Transylvania was under foreign control, it was unlawful and a serious offense for Transylvanians to have a Romanian flag or to wear the tricolors. This was a freedom not allowed until these Romanians came to America. In America they could buy a Romanian flag and display it.

Society records reveal that the privilege of purchasing flags and paying for the honor of being the sponsor for the American or Romanian flags that decorated their churches and meeting halls was given to the highest bidder. As much as two hundred dollars was paid for this honor, an amount of about one thousand dollars today.

*Family at Clinton, Indiana, picnic pose with the Romanian Beneficial Society flag, ca. 1910.*

Treicolorul Roman (Tricolor Romanian) Society was founded 15 April 1908 in Gary—just two years after the city's founding. There were 60 members in the founding organization, and before the end of the first year the ranks increased to 105 members. In 1910 the society became the twenty-fourth such group in the United States to join the national organization.[24]

The Tricolor Society took an active role in the founding of the Descent of the Holy Ghost Romanian Orthodox Church in Gary on 11 October 1908, just a few months after the society was formed. From its inception a very important part of the society's work was the building and support of the church. Since members of the society also held membership in the church this seemed quite natural and reasonable to them, even though the primary duty of the society was to care for members and their families in time of need or death.

As the society's role in the Romanian-American community expanded to include cultural, educational, political, and social activities, the organization made plans to build a society hall. In 1913 the group purchased two lots for two thousand dollars and contracted with Constantin Moga for the building of the hall for thirty thousand dollars. The hall was completed and the dedication ceremony was held on 27 May 1917.

The hall at 1208 Adams Street, along with the church that was a short block or two away from the hall, constituted the hub of activity for the Romanian community in Gary. For more than fifty years Tricolor Hall was the center for such events as meetings, banquets, dances, weddings, stage presentations, conventions, and political campaigns.

A fire in 1969 destroyed the society hall soon after the Urban Development Commission purchased and tore down the church at 12th and Madison streets. A new church complex in the nearby suburb of Merrillville serves the Romanian-American community. The society has not built another hall, and its meetings and activities now take place in the church hall.

A group of young Romanian immigrants from the East Chicago–Indiana Harbor area formed the Clubul Nicolae Iorga (Nicolae Iorga Club). Many societies and clubs selected their names from Romanian regions, events, or famous leaders. In the case of this group the name chosen was of a renowned historian, Nicolae Iorga, rector of the University of Bucharest, an associate professor at the Sorbonne in Paris, and in 1931 prime minister of Romania. Iorga actively advocated Romanian nationalism in Transylvania.[25]

In 1929 the club invited Iorga to America for the celebration of its twentieth anniversary. The group provided all the necessary funds for Professor and Mrs.

Iorga's trip to East Chicago and their travels throughout the United States. The club, under the direction of Nicolae Benchea, arranged a program of activities in cooperation with city, state, national, university, and diplomatic officials. Benchea received a bachelor of arts degree from Northwestern University in 1922, held a position in a bank, and headed the King Ferdinand Romanian School. He was regarded highly for his leadership and organizational skills. The Romanian community from all the churches, societies, auxiliaries, and other groups in Indiana took part.[26]

The Principesa Elena Romanian Ladies Association was one of the groups that played an active role in this important cultural event. The association's book of minutes shows that the local high school's band played at the welcoming ceremonies for Iorga. When the ladies discovered that the band uniforms were old and in terrible condition they took action. In a few months in 1929 the association, composed of members from the Eastern Orthodox, Catholic, and Baptist churches, raised money to purchase new uniforms for the East Chicago Washington High School Band.[27]

Iorga addressed the East Chicago club members as well as guests from the city, the state, the Romanian embassy, and other societies in the area at a festive banquet. Iorga also lectured in English at Harvard and Stanford universities during his tour in America.

After just two decades in America Romanian immigrants from villages in Transylvania hosted an internationally known historian in their American community, reflecting their growing cosmopolitanism.

## Churches

The preservation of customs and traditions is important to all immigrant groups. The Romanians as well as other ethnic groups created a subculture or community of their own; they organized churches, societies, and schools. This was an unprecedented phenomenon since Romanians did not participate in developing such institutions and organizations in their homeland. In Transylvania the churches were under state control and faced severe restrictions by foreign powers. No fraternal societies existed, and Romanian schools were either completely banned or controlled by a government not of their own choosing. In America, in spite of those impediments and their lack of experience, Romanians developed institutions in their traditional form but suitable to their life in America.

Romanian immigrants in Indiana were anxious to build churches where they could worship in the Romanian language according to their ancestral faith. The majority were Eastern Orthodox, but the faithful included

*Raising of the cross of the Descent of the Holy Ghost Romanian Orthodox Church, Gary, 1910.*

a large number of Catholics and Protestants. Today approximately 75 percent of the Romanian Americans are Eastern Orthodox, about 20 percent are Romanian Catholics, and the other 5 percent are Baptists, Adventists, and others.[28]

The two Romanian Orthodox parishes in northwest Indiana are the New Saint George Romanian Orthodox Church founded in 1906 in Indiana Harbor (now located in Lansing, Illinois, adjacent to the Indiana state line) and the Descent of the Holy Ghost Romanian Orthodox Church founded in 1908 in Gary (presently located in Merrillville).

The two historic Romanian Catholic parishes are the Saint Nicholas Romanian Catholic Church in East Chicago, founded in 1913, and the Saint Demetrius Romanian Catholic Church in Indiana Harbor, founded in 1914 and sold in 1985. The parishioners of Saint Demetrius are now members of Saint Nicholas. The Romanian Baptist Church, founded in Gary in 1914, is no longer in existence; its members have joined other Baptist churches in the area.

There were other Romanian churches in Indiana in the early 1900s: Saints Constantine and Helena in Indianapolis (1908) and still in existence; Saint Andrew Romanian Orthodox Church in Terre Haute; in Fort Wayne Saint Mary's Romanian Orthodox parish and Holy Archangels Michael and Gabriel are now united and known as the Romanian Orthodox Church.

## Saint George Romanian Orthodox Church

Saint George Church in Indiana Harbor was founded on 11 March 1906 under the leadership of Rev. Moise Balea. The church, completed and consecrated on 31 October 1906, was the first Romanian Orthodox church built in America. In 1914 a tornado destroyed several buildings in the city and caused irreparable damage to the church. The congregation purchased lots on Elm Street and a new church was constructed, consecrated in 1914, and renamed the New Saint George Romanian Orthodox Church.[29]

Rev. Ioan Tatu, the first parish priest, arrived on 23 June 1907 and remained only a few months. In 1908 Rev. Simion Mihaltian arrived from Romania and served as priest of the church for over fifty-five years. On 19 January 1964 the Very Rev. John Bugariu became the parish priest. After Bugariu's retirement in 1979, Rev. Ioan Ionita became the new priest. Ionita was trained in Romania and completed his master's degree in divinity at the McCormick Theological Seminary at the University of Chicago.

As part of an urban renewal program, in 1975 the church was razed to make way for the construction of a recreation center. The congregation purchased properties, which included a church complex and parish house, in Lansing, Illinois, a place accessible to the majority of the parish members who have moved to the suburbs of Lake County. The members of the parish combined their celebration of the seventieth anniversary of the founding of the New Saint George Romanian Orthodox Church and the bicentennial of the United States on 31 October 1976 in their new location.

The story of the Romanian Orthodox church in Indiana would not be complete unless mention is made of the fifty-five-year pastorate of the Very Rev. Simion Mihaltian. He came to Indiana Harbor on 20 June 1908 and served as the priest until his death on 31 December 1963. Between 1908 and 1914, with Indiana Harbor as his home parish, he traveled throughout the Midwest and helped establish parishes in Fort Wayne; Gary; Terre Haute; Indianapolis; Chicago; St. Paul, Minnesota; Omaha, Nebraska; and Cincinnati.[30]

In June 1958, at the celebration of his fiftieth anniversary as parish priest, the program listed the following statistics about his work: Mihaltian had married 462 couples, officiated at 1,332 funerals, and baptized 1,531 children. Mihaltian was an excellent violinist, took charge of choir rehearsals, and directed stage productions for the Romanian community. Before his ordination as a priest he had been a teacher in Romania; therefore, he did not lack experience when he initiated a Romanian school in 1915 in the church basement.

On the cold morning of 31 December 1963 Mihaltian was on his way to Fort Wayne, as was his practice every fifth Sunday for over forty years, to conduct religious services for the Romanian Orthodox community there. He collapsed and died before boarding the train. He was within two weeks of his eighty-third birthday.

He and his church became institutions to the Romanians of Indiana Harbor. During his years of service he was recognized for his dedication and devotion to the church and the Romanian community, and his leadership was acknowledged by Romanian communities throughout the United States.

## The Descent of the Holy Ghost Romanian Orthodox Church

The Romanian Orthodox church in Gary was founded on 11 October 1908. The first religious service of the Gary congregation took place on 25 December 1908 in an empty store at 1517 Washington Street. Rev. Simion Mihaltian officiated as priest and Vasile Magurean as cantor. Following the liturgy a general meeting was held and plans for building a church were made.[31]

Church construction began on 31 October 1909 when Mihaltian blessed the cornerstone donated by John Dobrea. The estimated cost for the church building was eight hundred dollars. When completed, the church cost amounted to eighteen hundred dollars. The location of the first church building was in the Tolleston area at the corner of 19th Avenue and Hayes Street. On 10 June 1910 the Descent of the Holy Ghost Church was completed and consecrated by Reverends Ioan Podea and Mihaltian. Rev. Teodosie Nica became the first parish priest although he remained only a short time.[32]

The donation of land and the belief that the center of Gary's activity would be in that area dictated the selection of the Tolleston section for the church. However, the business center of Gary developed along Broadway, the city's main thoroughfare. Also by this time a large number of Romanians had settled near Broadway and Harrison streets. In order that the church be closer to the center of the city and the Romanian community the parishioners decided to move the church to the corner of 12th and Madison streets. Two lots and a house, which would serve as the rectory, were purchased for twenty-five hundred dollars, and during the winter of 1915 the church was lifted off its old foundation and moved about twenty blocks. Several teams of large horses pulled the church down the street. This unusual event was heralded by a band and a parade that preceded it to the new site. The moving of the church cost eight hundred dollars.

*Consecration of the Descent of the Holy Ghost Romanian Orthodox Church in Gary, 1910.*

The original church and the rectory underwent modernization at a cost of $16,656.74 in 1924. In the 1930s additional improvements, including renovation of the interior, were made in preparation for the visit of a Romanian bishop. On 22 September 1935 the church was consecrated by the first Romanian Orthodox bishop of America, Bishop Policarp Morusca. Members underwrote the cost of building, repairing, and renovating the original church, and by 1939, in spite of difficult years, the church mortgage was paid.

Many changes took place with each passing year. Older members and early settlers in Gary passed away, while younger members moved to the suburbs or other parts of the country. In 1969 the church was sold and torn down as part of the urban renewal program in that section of the city. In 1963 property at 61st and Harrison streets in Merrillville (eight blocks south of the city of Gary) was purchased. The building program commenced and moved quickly. Within a few years the Descent of the Holy Ghost parish, comprising the church, hall, and parish house on 3.7 acres of land, was completed at a cost of approximately $500,000. More important, the mortgage loan for each phase of the program was paid much in advance of its due date at great savings in interest. The descendants of the church's early members had the same concern for economy as their forefathers.

The following priests have served the parishioners of the Descent of the Holy Ghost during the past eight decades: Rev. Teodosie Nica, 1911; Rev. George Hentea, 1912; Rev. Romul Doctor, 1912–15; Rev. Iuliu Holdar, 1915–20; Rev. Pavel Negovan, 1920–24; Rev. Ioan Trutza, 1924–28; Rev. Alexandru Borda, 1928–29; Rev. Aurel Reu, 1929–30; Rev. Andrei Moldovan, 1930–47; Rev. Eugene Lazar, 1948–63; Rev. Richard Grabowski, 1963–71; Rev. Mircea Marinescu, 1972–76; Rev. Theodore Gotis, 1976–83; Rev. George Gage, 1983–88; Rev. George Treff, 1988–95; Rev. Adrian Fetea, 1995–.

Two young men who were reared in the Gary area studied for the priesthood and have been ordained: Rev. Laurence Lazar (son of Rev. Eugene Lazar) and Rev. Romey Roscoe (grandson of Theodore Rosco, former president of the church council).

### Saint Nicholas Byzantine-Rite Catholic Church

Saint Nicholas Church was founded on 23 February 1913, and the cornerstone was laid the following October. The church is located at 4311 Olcott Avenue in East Chicago. Saint Nicholas has always had a resident pastor who, until 1957, also served Saint Demetrius Romanian Catholic Church in Indiana Harbor.[33] Pastors who have served both parishes were: Rev. Aurel Bungardean; Rev. Alexander Pop; Rev. Victor Crisan; Rev. Victor Vamos; Rev. Anton Dunca; Rev. George C. Muresan; and Rev. Aurel Pater.

## Saint Demetrius Byzantine-Rite Catholic Church

Saint Demetrius Byzantine Catholic Church was founded in Indiana Harbor on 10 September 1914. The church was built at 138th and Butternut streets and consecrated on 4 July 1915. Saint Demetrius was served by pastors from Saint Nicholas for over forty years. On 18 October 1957 its first pastor, Rev. John Popa, was installed. In the 1980s with a decline in membership and the death of Reverend Popa, Saint Demetrius Church was sold, and its members joined the Saint Nicholas congregation.

Rev. Aurel Bungardean was the first Romanian Catholic priest in the Lake County area. According to those who knew him, Bungardean was a tireless and energetic person and was dedicated to his parishioners in both of the churches that he founded in the East Chicago and Indiana Harbor areas. Bungardean was an excellent administrator and record keeper. His book *Din Pribegia Vietii Mele* (From My Travels through Life), published in 1919, provides much information about the Romanian Catholic churches in America. Names as well as villages of origin were listed of the founding members in those early days in the cities of East Chicago and Indiana Harbor.[34]

Rev. George C. Muresan, the pastor of Saint Nicholas Church in East Chicago, is a native son of the parish where he has served as priest since his ordination. His grandparents were immigrants to the area, and his parents lived in East Chicago. Muresan was born on 18 February 1916 and reared in close proximity of the Saint Nicholas Church. After his graduation from St. Joseph College in Rensselaer, Indiana, and St. Meinrad Seminary in southern Indiana, Muresan was ordained on 13 September 1942. He was appointed pastor of Saint Nicholas Church 4 May 1943. On 13 September 1992 Muresan celebrated the fiftieth anniversary of his ordination in the church.[35] Muresan died 22 March 1996.

Muresan was the national chaplain of the American Romanian Catholic Association, Youth Department (ARCAYD), which he founded. He was the editor of *Unirea* (The Union), the official publication of the Byzantine-Rite Catholic churches in America. Muresan also served as the director of the Publications Commission of the Romanian Catholic communities in the United States.

## The Romanian Baptist Church

In 1909 Ioan Groza, Sr., and Nicolae Buidos arrived in Gary to work in the factories, where they were joined later by other Romanian immigrants of the Baptist faith. Houses were rented at 10th and Jefferson, 1132 Adams Street, and 1628 Jefferson Street for their religious services.[36]

Ioan Vancu was ordained as pastor in 1914 and served as missionary for the Romanian Baptists in Indiana Harbor. His mission included Chicago, Lake Forest, Plano, and Aurora in Illinois. In 1919 Rev. Ilie Trutza became the pastor. Lots were purchased, and a Romanian Baptist church was built on the corner of 14th and Jefferson streets. The church was dedicated 4 December 1921.

On 1 January 1928 Rev. A. S. Lucaciu, who served as director of the Katherine House (a settlement house) in Indiana Harbor, became the pastor in Gary. Lucaciu organized a youth group, Bible school, and religious radio programs. During the summer groups of parishioners from the church held sidewalk services in Gary and Indiana Harbor.

After receiving his Doctor of Philosophy degree from the University of Chicago, Rev. Peter Trutza became the pastor. In 1952 Trutza left Gary to continue his mission in Hollywood, Florida, where he writes and broadcasts religious messages and programs for radio broadcasts.

The Gary Romanian Baptist Church continued to hold services until it was sold in 1964. Although the church is no longer in existence and members have joined other Baptist churches in the Lake County area, the older members still gather together from time to time. In an interview one of them reminisced:

> In the early days, our church started growing nicely. And then, it happened . . . since only the Romanian language was used in the services, some of the younger ones who married Americans wanted the service to be half in Romanian and half in English. The church committee and preacher did not want this. So, the church split. The youth left. In the beginning, the church was full—with lots of members. But little by little, they broke away. The youth left and only the older people were left. The older ones died and the church was gone.[37]

## Cultural Life

As later groups of Romanians arrived in Indiana's cities they were greeted warmly and welcomed by those immigrants who had come before them and established a permanent home. More women came, and families left in Romania came to join those who had come earlier. Wives came with children. It was not unusual for wives to join their husbands, followed by one or more children until the entire family was together. Grandparents and relatives in Romania cared for family members until homes were established and passage to America was sent.

Some of the single men sent letters asking their girlfriends to come to America so they could marry. Others wrote home to parents asking them to find a wife for them, and the necessary funds and ticket for the journey were transmitted.

Matches were often arranged by friends and relatives. A single girl did not remain single long. There were usually fifteen or twenty men for each woman. One of the men who was eighty-one years old when interviewed recalled:

> There were only two or three unmarried girls and about ten married women in the community when I arrived. When an unmarried girl came to town, she never got a moment's peace. Some of the young men would fight over the girls. . . . When there was a dance, she never got to sit down.[38]

## Weddings

Weddings were important social events, and the entire Romanian community took part at the religious services and the reception that followed. In most cases the parents, immediate family, and other relatives of the couple were in Romania. In America the couple's friends and *consateni* (townspeople—those from their village in Romania) took the place of family.

In Romanian wedding services the *nasi* (best man and matron of honor) play an important role. The *nasi* are usually a married couple, and it is their duty to sponsor and attend the bridal couple at the wedding ceremony. The honor of being *nasi* included an appropriate monetary donation at the reception to help the young couple get started. *Nasi* are regarded as spiritual parents and advise and counsel in the years that follow. Moreover, the *nasi* assume the role of godparents at christenings of the children.

The church services for the wedding were long but beautiful, symbolic of the rites of the church, and very well attended. A woman who was interviewed about those early days in Gary made the following comment about her wedding in 1915:

> People were very friendly then. They filled the church and hall. Even if they didn't know you, they would come. I had no relatives at my wedding. The people who came were acquaintances. A friend would come and bring others with him. But we got our expenses for the wedding out of donations.[39]

The donations were monetary gifts made to the bride and groom in lieu of presents. The sum that was collected paid for the wedding, and leftover funds helped the couple start their new life together.

During the 1920s and 1930s an average of about thirty or more weddings a year occurred in the Gary and East Chicago areas. The wedding banquet and dance that followed made it a festive and memorable occasion. Photographs of as many of the guests as possible were taken. These photographs were sent to Romania so that the family could share the event with the rest of the village. After years in America many of those who returned to visit their families in Romania were surprised to see their wedding photographs still prominently and proudly displayed in the old homestead.

## Funerals

Funerals were attended by virtually all the members of the Romanian community. The *saracusta* (wake) was held on the two evenings before the funeral service, and burial was on the third day. Funeral services and *saracuste* (wakes) were conducted by a priest with one or more cantors who assisted by singing the responses. In the early days funerals were held in boardinghouses, society halls, or the home of the deceased. Since the 1940s funerals have taken place in funeral homes with conventional customs, but the religious services have remained the same.

In the early 1900s men carried the casket from the deceased's home to the church for the funeral services. For short distances the casket was also carried from the church to the cemetery; otherwise, a horse and carriage were provided. The congregation walked or rode in horse-drawn buggies behind the casket in a procession to the cemetery. Early customs included a band (there were several Romanian bands in those days) to play dirges and funeral marches. One bandleader recalled that once he played for three funerals in one week during the influenza epidemic of 1918.

> I got $5.00 for each funeral . . . I was making $2.50 a day working in the mill . . . so I just took off work. Besides, my boss was Romanian and he had to attend the funeral, too.[40]

It is traditional to have a *pomana* (memorial lunch) following the burial services. On a Sunday (forty days after the burial) following a liturgy, a religious service (*parastas*) is held. After the *parastas* the congregation partakes of bread and wine with the words "Dumnezeu sa-l ierte" (May the Lord forgive him).

Today, American customs for funerals are observed; however, the religious services and traditions pertaining to the *pomana* and *parastas* continue.

## World War I

The immigration of Romanians to America was at its highest level just prior to the outbreak of the First World War. In that war Romania was a member of the allied forces. In America, as well as in Romania, the union of Transylvania with Romania was of special concern for Romanians and Romanian Americans. Those who had received American citizenship joined the army; several in northwest Indiana served with the Rainbow Division. On the home front in America, Romanian Americans raised funds for an ambulance and took part in the armed services, Liberty Bond drives, Red Cross work, and other such efforts.

The local fraternal societies and their national organization worked hard to promote the union of Transylvania with the rest of Romania. The idea of a united Romania free of Austrian-Hungarian control was uppermost in their minds. For this reason the Union and League of Romanian Societies of America organized a committee called the National League. Capt. Vasile Stoica, who had come from Romania to seek help for this cause, served as president of the committee, and John Sufana from Fort Wayne was the secretary. Cleveland hosted the meetings, and Sufana often traveled there. The committee's purpose was to inform the public about the situation in Romania and to assist in securing treaty agreements after the war that would include the union of Transylvania with Romania.[41]

The group's officers took petitions to President Woodrow Wilson with signatures of Romanians in America requesting recognition of Transylvania as a part of Romania. Sufana, with petitions from Indiana, was preparing to board a train from Fort Wayne to Washington, D.C., when a fire broke out in his place of business. Sufana phoned the fire department and got to the train station in time to take care of what he considered the more important business—Transylvania's freedom from Austrian-Hungarian control and Transylvania's union with the rest of Romania.[42]

The armistice in 1918 brought peace, and the postwar treaties afterward saw the creation of a united Romania. Although after the war large numbers of Romanians returned to their villages in Transylvania, now united with Romania, the majority preferred to remain in America, which had become their home.

## Early Business Ventures

Although most early immigrants worked in the mills and factories, some quit their jobs and ventured into their own businesses with the hope of earning more money.

They reasoned that many of their own nationality would become customers. Boardinghouses and saloons were the first businesses established by these immigrant entrepreneurs. The family grocery store was also a popular choice. For about five hundred dollars a grocery business could be acquired, and the wife and older children or relatives could help run the business. One businessman recalled when thinking back to his grocery in Gary in 1922:

> I started with $500 which I borrowed from a friend to open a business. I sold mostly ice cream and candy. Things went so well that in two or three months, I paid back the money I borrowed and decided to put in more groceries and meat. In those days, we didn't have machines to cut the meat, we did it by hand. When I needed more meat, I'd walk over to the Swift Company packers a few blocks from the store and carry the meat back on my shoulder. I stayed in that store at 10th and Jefferson until 1928 and then I moved to 11th Avenue and opened a bigger store.[43]

After World War I more Romanian Americans ventured into new businesses. The saloons expanded to include billiards or bowling. Buffets (restaurants), hotels for workers (previously called boardinghouses), barbershops, drugstores, tailor shops, bakeries, and other businesses were opened. Immigrants who had some education or training in Romania worked in banks or opened travel and exchange bureaus. Some became realtors, while others operated service stations. One person started a taxi and bus service, and another opened several motion picture houses. Two young immigrants started soda pop and beer distributorships.

## The Romanian Press

The Romanian-language newspaper played an important role in the lives of the immigrants in America. For those who had not learned to read, the newspaper was one means by which literacy could be developed so that the immigrant could learn about events taking place in America and in Romania.

Although the majority of these early immigrants were not formally educated, the fact remains that they were intelligent and capable of understanding the need and the importance of the press and of doing something about it. They often spent long hours as laborers working to improve themselves economically; nevertheless, many of them recognized that it was also imperative to read and to communicate—to publish newspapers and *calendari* (yearbooks).

In northwest Indiana there were several men who wrote articles for the larger Romanian-language newspapers in

MARY LEUCA

*A Romanian-American grocery in Indiana Harbor, ca. 1919.*

Cleveland and Chicago. Some of them traveled to various cities to take an active part on editorial boards of the newspapers. John Sufana served on the board of the *America* and was a staunch supporter from its inception. He mortgaged his home in Fort Wayne in order to keep the newspaper from bankruptcy.[44]

Others published local bulletins or leaflets, imparting community and national news. An example of this "newsy" form of publication was published monthly for several years in Gary by Olimpiu Clonta. His leaflet entitled *Tasala* (Bits and Pieces) was meant to be amusing as well as informative.[45]

The most prominent of the Romanian-language newspapers is the *America,* which is still published in Cleveland. Rev. Moise Balea, one of the early Romanian Orthodox priests, first published the *America* in 1906. He sold the newspaper to the Union of Romanian Societies of America in 1908. The *America* continues to be the publication of the national organization of the societies now known as the Union and League of Romanian Societies in

America and is published bimonthly. Since World War II more English has supplanted the Romanian language; approximately 80 percent of the *America* is printed in English.[46]

## The Romanian School

The Romanian school was an institution organized to teach the children of Romanian immigrants. Although religion was taught, these schools were not the traditional Sunday schools that meet primarily to give religious instruction at individual church centers. The Romanian schools were not substitutes for public schools, but supplementary schools meeting after public school hours to provide instruction in the Romanian language for children of immigrants. The schools became an integral part of the Romanian community surrounding the church and social societies, and they also served to maintain and perpetuate the culture and traditions of the people who immigrated to the United States.

*Romanian school class in Terre Haute, ca. 1930.*

The need for children to learn the Romanian language was important for a practical reason. Parents in most cases could more conveniently communicate with their children in Romanian. The youngsters quickly learned English in the American schools, but the parents worked long hours at laboring jobs that did not require much speaking knowledge of English. As a result the parents did not learn English as easily and therefore insisted that Romanian be spoken in the home. Also, many Romanian immigrants came to America during the 1900s with the intention of making money and returning to Romania. Therefore, it was important that their children acquire a knowledge of Romanian so they could take their place in the schools in Romania. And many did return in the 1920s after the restoration of Transylvania to Romania.

Romanian schools were organized in a number of Indiana communities: East Chicago, Gary, Fort Wayne, Muncie, Terre Haute, Indianapolis, and other settlements about the state. One of the earliest Romanian schools, Regele Ferdinand (King Ferdinand) in East Chicago, was organized in 1910 and directed by Nicolae Benchea.

Another Romanian school in East Chicago was organized in 1928 and conducted by the Principesa Elena Romanian Ladies Association. It was a unique undertaking by women from the Romanian Orthodox, Catholic, and Baptist faiths. The women joined together as an association with the purpose of caring for the education and cultural welfare of the children in the Romanian community. The activities of this association proved that there was a tendency toward a united Romanian colony rather than the maintenance of enclaves of Eastern Orthodox, Greek Catholics, Romanian Baptists, and others.[47]

Romanian schools were supported in several Indiana communities until the outbreak of World War II. Very few are in existence today. From time to time a few interested

second- and third-generation parents (many of whom were students in Romanian schools) have organized Romanian schools for their children. The last known Romanian school in East Chicago, however, was discontinued in 1958. When the need for organizing such schools ceased and the purposes for gathering children and young people together changed, new choral, dance, cultural classes, or English-speaking Sunday schools have taken the place of the traditional Romanian schools.

Young people now attend youth clubs such as MAROY (Merrillville American Romanian Orthodox Youth), RAYS (Romanian American Youth Society), or ARCAYD (American Romanian Catholic Association, Youth Department). As one of the elders explained: "Rather than lose the young ones because they don't know Romanian, we decided it is better to do it in English."

## The Romanian Language

Early Romanian immigrants sought to preserve their language and their culture through the establishment of a Romanian press, the organization of Romanian schools, and the promotion of Romanian cultural and social activities.

The immigrant's repeated references to his love of the Romanian language and the inculcations of this feeling to his children were expressed often. One is led to conclude that having been denied the right to use the Romanian language in his homeland because of political oppression by the Hungarians, and having suffered punishment for refusing to learn the Hungarian language, his language and his being as a person became one. The following stanzas selected from a popular Romanian poem *Limba Romaneasca* (The Romanian Language) illustrate the Romanians' deep feeling held for their language:[48]

> Beautiful and like a tonic
> Is the language we speak,
> You will find none more harmonic
> Try where you may seek.
> Every true Romanian loves it
> As his very soul.
> Speak the language, learn to write it,
> In God's name, be whole!

It was only after many years in the United States, and the realization that he would never return to live in the Old Country as he had intended, that the romanticization of his language ended.

Most of the younger generations in the United States do not speak Romanian, but youngsters have little difficulty learning Romanian from their elders since it is a phonetic language. Sunday schools, choral groups, and other organizational activities provide opportunities for learning Romanian lyrics to songs. Holidays such as Christmas and Easter within the Romanian-American community call upon those taking part to use the Romanian language during programs and festivals. In this fashion many of the younger generations use the language.

### World War II and the Postwar Period

With the outbreak of the Second World War the older generation renewed efforts for its adopted country—America. Again, as in World War I, the Romanian-American communities took part in war bond drives, Red Cross work, ambulance drives, as well as fuel, food, and rubber conservation. However, there was a difference. The younger generation of Romanian Americans, born in the United States, was actively involved in the war. Men and women on the home front worked long hours for the war effort.[49]

There was extraordinary concern about this particular conflict since nearly every household with sons of military age had members in the armed forces. Commemorative monuments for those young men and women who took part in World War II and those who gave their lives were erected near the entrances of churches. In Gary, the Descent of the Holy Ghost Romanian Orthodox Church's monument listed 133 parishioners. This is a sizable percentage when one considers that about 250 families or about 700 individual communicants made up the church's membership.

As in communities throughout the nation, Romanian Americans in Indiana can be listed among those who fought valiantly during World War II in the European as well as the Pacific theaters of conflict. Romanian-American communities shared the spirit of patriotism and pride for all young men and women who served their country and hailed them as heroes on their return home.

National attention was given East Chicagoan Alex Vraciu, who was the navy's leading flying ace in the South Pacific. After graduation from DePauw University in Greencastle, Vraciu enlisted in the navy and was trained as a pilot. He flew in the South Pacific theater under Edward "Butch" O'Hare, the Congressional Medal of Honor recipient for whom Chicago's O'Hare field is named. Vraciu served on six carriers in the South Pacific and shot down nineteen enemy planes, destroyed twenty more on the ground, and sank a Japanese ship. In 1944 Vraciu was shot down over Luzon in the Philippines and spent five weeks with guerrilla fighters in the jungle. Vraciu's impressive war record earned him the Navy Cross, the Distinguished Flying Cross with two gold stars, and the Air Medal with three gold stars. After the war he became a navy test pilot for the new jet plane technology.[50]

Many changes took place during the postwar period. The first fifty years of Romanian-American life (1895–1945) was quite different from the fifty years following the end of World War II. Significant numbers of young people entered universities under the GI Bill. Many entered the workforce or opened businesses of their own. Many marriages took place during the postwar period; more intermarriages with people of other nationalities occurred.

In this period English supplanted the use of the Romanian language in church and society activities. The size of the Romanian-American communities declined, as members of the older generation died. A movement away from the old ethnic neighborhoods to the suburbs occurred as urban redevelopment programs tore down homes. A number of the younger generation moved to other parts of the country seeking new employment opportunities.

### Conclusion

The *Noi-veniti* (the newly arrived) Romanians who have come to Indiana in recent years differ greatly from the first Romanian immigrants. They are well educated. Many have university degrees and are trained in the professions, know the English language, and are more able to adapt to the mainstream of life in the United States. For many acceptance in the workforce may take longer, but after a period of adjustment they tend to pursue a life of their own away from the organizations and societies that earlier generations of immigrants found necessary.

Many of the traditional institutions in Indiana continue, not for their own sake, as in Romania, but for the more utilitarian purposes of supporting the church and the building of new churches. The mutual benefit associations for fraternal insurance and cultural and charitable purposes, as well as ladies' auxiliaries, youth clubs, choral groups, dance groups, and political clubs have been maintained and modernized to keep pace with the changes in society as a whole.

The Romanian-American communities in Indiana adapted to these changes. Adjustments were made in their institutions and organizations so that their cultural and social life would accommodate both the older and younger generations. The older generation looked to the younger generation for new, enlightened leadership. Younger men and women took the places of their elders on church and society councils and as officers of various organizations.

Although most of the younger generation do not speak Romanian, their awareness of ethnic heritage is expressed by their participation in activities with the older generations. The important thing is that they want to know about their ethnic background—their Romanian heritage.

## Notable Romanians

Nick Angel (1920–1990) was a treasurer and a commissioner of Lake County. He served in the Indiana General Assembly from 1964 to 1968.

Mary Ban (1907–1976) became, on 1 September 1930, the first woman of Romanian descent to teach public school in Gary, Indiana.

John Chulay (Ciulei) (1923–1988), born in Indiana Harbor, was active in television and films. His television credits include *Rin-Tin-Tin, Captain Midnight, Ozzie and Harriet,* the *Dick Van Dyke Show,* and the *Mary Tyler Moore Show.*

Walter Jeorse (1909–1983) was elected mayor of East Chicago in 1951 and served in that position until 1963. He became the first Romanian American in an American city to hold that office.

Josef S. Kapitan (1927–1980), an official of Inland Steel in East Chicago, lent his name posthumously to a prestigious award established by the Iron and Steel Society of the American Institute of Mining, Metallurgical, and Petroleum Engineers to the author of the best research paper at the Institute's annual conference.

Walter Leuca (1922–1984) of Gary worked as a patent engineer for US Steel and was Indiana's first patent attorney of Romanian descent.

Dr. John Onila (1921–1996) was professor of industrial sociology at Purdue University and a consultant for several Midwest companies. Onila's research was in the field of industrial organizations, automation, and the worker.

Eli Popa (1912–1992) published the play *Give Us This Day* (1948) and a book *Romania Is a Song* (1966). In the 1930s this Indiana Harbor native wrote and produced Romanian dramas in his storefront theater in the heart of the Romanian community.

## Notes

1. Peter John Georgeoff, introduction to *Resource Guide,* in *Romanian Americans in Lake County, Indiana: An Ethnic Heritage Curriculum Project,* by Mary Leuca (West Lafayette, Ind.: Purdue University Department of Education, 1978).

2. Theodore Andrica, ethnic editor for the *Cleveland Press,* interview with the author, Cleveland, Ohio, 26 Sept. 1975; Vladimir Wertsman, ed., *The Romanians in America, 1784–1974: A Chronology & Fact Book* (Dobbs Ferry, N.Y.: Oceana Publication, Inc., 1974); Francis J. Brown and Joseph Slabey Roucek, eds., *One America: The History, Contributions, and Present Problems of Our Racial and National Minorities* (New York: Prentice-Hall, Inc., 1945), 223–32; Maldwyn Allen Jones, *American Immigration* (Chicago: University of Chicago Press, 1960).

3. Ion Josef Schiopul, *Romanii din America: O Calatoria de Studii in Statele Unite* (Romanians in America: A Study of My Travels in the United States) (Sibiu, Romania: W. Krafft Publisher, 1913), 11–12, table 1.

4. George Anagnostache, "Romanians in America," *New Pioneer* 2, no. 3 (July 1944): 13.

5. Andrica interview; Vasile C. Barsan, "The Historical Right of Romanians in Transylvania" (Paper submitted for publication in the *Congressional Record* of Aug.–Sept. 1976). "In spite of all the efforts of Magyarization and the mass emigration, the Romanians were and always remained the basic and predominant ethnical element in Transylvania, forming the absolute majority of the population. (53% according to Magyar statistics of 1910 and 58.3% Romanian statistics for 1940)" (13–14). Christine Avghi Galitzi, *A Study of Assimilation among the Roumanians in the United States* (New York: Columbia University Press, 1929). "The Hungarian Diet pursued a policy of strong Magyarization . . . [and] resorted to a series of intricate measures which created a great deal of dissatisfaction and suffering among the Transylvanians" (50). Vasile Stoica, *Suferintele din Ardeal* (Sufferings in Transylvania) (Chicago: Editura "Tribunei," 1917), lists over two hundred accounts of injustices and imprisonments of Romanians in Transylvania between June 1897 and April 1913 (339–84).

6. Andrica interview; Andrei Popovici to Andrei Simon, 20 Mar. 1933 (the letter contains a speech by Popovici entitled "Romanians in America"), 1–2; Anagnostache, "Romanians in America," 15.

7. Paul Tomy, interview with the author, Villa Park, Ill., 13 June 1976.

8. Steve Benecke, "Romanians in Fort Wayne, Indiana" (Research paper, Indiana University-Purdue University Fort Wayne, 1979), 14–15.

9. *The Foreign Problem in Northwest Indiana: In a Nut Shell* (New York and Indianapolis: American Baptist Home Mission Society Publishers and Indiana Baptist Convention, 1917), 2.

10. *Istoria Uniuii si Ligii Societatilor Romanesti din America, 1906–1956* (History of the Union and League of Romanian Societies of America, 1906–1956) (Cleveland: The Union, 1956), 230.

11. Zenobia Grusia, interview with the author, Merrillville, Ind., 1977.

12. Aron Suci, interview with the author, Gary, Ind., 1977.

13. Pete Magurean, interview with Pearl Mailath, Gary, Ind., 1977.

14. Tomy interview.

15. Mary Beu, interview with the author, East Chicago, Ind., 28 Sept. 1975. (Mary Beu celebrated her hundredth birthday in 1994.) Interviews of several women during 1976–77 by Mary Leuca, Mary Bogolia, and Pearl Mailath reveal that a number of Romanian women worked in the tin mills in East Chicago and Gary. The women worked twelve-hour days, sorting tin plates and pulling them apart with pliers. Virginia Adams and her sister Emilane Ardelean were among the first women to be promoted to the position of foremen.

16. Suci interview.

17. Mary Vintila and Rebecca Stanciu, interview with the author, Sept. 1975; *New Pioneer* 1–7 (Nov. 1942–Sept. 1948). These volumes contain many articles covering a wide range of information on Romanian-American life.

18. Tomy interview.

19. Marietta Cristia Baila, interview with the author, West Lafayette, Ind., Nov. 1975. Theodore Blegen quoted in Henry Steele Commager, ed., *Immigration and American History: Essays in Honor of Theodore C. Blegen* (Minneapolis: University of Minnesota Press, 1961), 140–41. "Among the many sources that offer research possibilities for the study of immigration are ballads and songs produced in great numbers and many languages by and about immigrants from the European countries to the United States." Mary Leuca, *Ballads of the Romanian Immigrant* (songbook, LP/Stereo recording, Bud Pressner Studios, Gary, Ind., 1977).

20. G. Stanculescu, "Viata Romanesca din America" (Romanian Life in America), in *Calendarul America* (America Yearbook) (Cleveland: Union and League of Romanian Societies of America, Inc., 1925), 36. Theodore Andrica has collected a large number of Romanian-immigrant poems and compiled a booklet *D'ale Noastre din America* (About Our Own in America). Andrica revealed that the immigrant to the Lake County area was known for his contribution to this poetry form. Eli Popa, *Romania Is a Song: A Sampler of Verse in Translation* (Cleveland: The America Publishing Co., 1966), 30–31.

21. Tomy interview.

22. Additional information about early Romanian societies in Indiana given by John and Mary Balas (Indianapolis), Steven Benecke (Fort Wayne), and Helen Balog (Terre Haute). No information was available from the Union and League of Romanian Societies of America concerning other societies in smaller communities in Indiana that no longer are in existence.

The following is from an article about Societatea Lumina Romana that appeared in the *Indianapolis Star*, 9 May 1913. "The Roumanian Light Society, a fraternal organization, with about 175 members, will celebrate its fifth anniversary Sunday. There will be a parade in the morning, led by the Roumanian band 'Doina' and a banquet in the evening to be followed by dancing. Dan Stansiulea is president of the society and Roumulus Jondrea is in charge of arrangements."

Helen Balog, interview with the author, Merrillville, Ind., Oct. 1994. Balog lived in the Terre Haute/Clinton area and recalls that the Romanians who worked in the Crown Hill coal mines referred to West Clinton as Centenary. The church and societies in that area were started about 1913 and ceased to function in the 1940s. "The size of the Romanian communities in that area were small in number and as the young people married and older folks passed away very few Romanians were left. Those who remained joined American churches. After our marriage my husband and I moved to northwest Indiana where we joined the Romanian Church in East Chicago."

23. A brief history of the Transilvaneana Society was written from information obtained from the officers of the society, record books, books of minutes, *America* yearbooks that are published by the national organization each year, and various program books commemorating anniversaries of the organization.

24. The records, minute books, and historical monographs about the Tricolor Romanian Society were very useful in preparing a history of this society in Gary, Indiana. Interviews with the authors of this group as well as access to various jubilee booklets and photographs provided valuable information.

25. Books of minutes for the Nicolae Iorga Club and the commemorative program books for its tenth and twentieth anniversaries were used to write the history of the club. Since the anniversary books were written by Nicolae Benchea, he was interviewed on several occasions and was very helpful in describing events during the early period in Indiana Harbor history. Nicolae Benchea, taped interviews with the author (ten sessions), Brasov, Romania, Oct. 1978.

26. Benchea, taped interviews. Benchea's interviews cover early Romanian-American life in Indiana Harbor, his first Romanian school, and other cultural and educational issues. Benchea left Indiana Harbor in 1930 and was personal secretary to Prof. Nicolae Iorga for several years. For about forty years Benchea conducted classes and tutored English in Romania, and each July, while his health permitted, he organized Fourth of July celebrations with Romanians who lived and worked in the United States in the early 1900s and had returned to the Old Country.

27. Principesa Elena Book of Minutes, in possession of author; Beu interview.

28. Andrica interview; *Calendarul America* (America Yearbook) (Cleveland: America Newspaper Press and *Calendarii Solia*, Romanian Orthodox Episcopate).

29. The New Saint George Romanian Orthodox Church record books, minute books, various program books, monographs, and yearbooks were very useful in writing a brief history of the church. Interviews with the Very Reverend John Bugariu, Rev. Ioan Ionita, Sorin Mihaltian, Joseph Ciovica, Mary Beu, and other members of the church were helpful.

30. Program book for fiftieth anniversary of Rev. Simion Mihaltian.

31. The Descent of the Holy Ghost Romanian Orthodox Church records, books of minutes, monographs, and ledgers. Anniversary and jubilee booklets, yearbooks, photographs, and interviews with members of the church were utilized in preparing a brief history of the Gary church.

32. Andrei Moldovan, *Monograph: Romanian Orthodox Parish of Gary, Indiana* (Gary: n.p., 1939).

33. Saint Nicholas Byzantine-Rite Catholic Church and Saint Demetrius Byzantine-Rite Catholic Church histories were provided by Father George Muresan from Saint Nicholas Church and Emil Breaz, president of Saint Demetrius Church Council.

34. Aurel Bungardean, *Din Pribegia Vietii Mele* (From My Travels through Life) (East Chicago, Ind., 1919). This rare book was made available for this essay by Father Muresan in 1977.

35. George C. Muresan, interview with Mary Breaz, Sept. 1977.

36. Ilie Trutza, interview with the author, Hallendale, Fla., 7 Jan. 1977. Trutza furnished the author with a copy of the *Istoria Baptistilor Romani din America* (The History of the Romanian Baptists in America), written by Vasile W. Jones, secretary general of the Romanian Baptist Association of America.

37. Mary Churdar Burtic, interview with Pearl Mailath, 19 Apr. 1977.

38. John Nicoara, interview with the author, 7 Aug. 1976.

39. Paraschiva Pantea, interview with Pearl Mailath, 19 Oct. 1976.

40. John Boldi, interview with the author, Phoenix, Ariz., 13 Aug. 1976.

41. Stoica, *Suferintele din Ardeal* (Sufferings in Transylvania). The author distributed copies of his book as he traveled to cities to lecture to Romanian societies.

42. John Simicin, interview with Pearl Mailath, Gary, Ind., 28 Apr. 1977. Mary Sufana and George Sufana verified information regarding their father's trip to Washington, D.C.

43. Nicoara interview.

44. Tomy interview.

45. Mrs. Olimpiu Clonta, interview with the author, Hobart, Ind., 7 Mar. 1977. Mrs. Clonta provided copies of *Tasala* and several yearbooks of Romanian organizations.

46. Andrica interview.

47. *Procesele Verbale Asociatiunü Doamnelor Romane* (Book of Minutes of the Romanian Ladies Association Princess Elena), 1; Galitzi, *Study of Assimilation among the Roumanians in the United States,* 116. "There is a tendency toward a united Romanian colony rather than a maintenance of neighborhoods of Transylvanians, Bukovinians, Romanian Baptists, or Greek Catholics. . . . Cooperation has become to the Romanian not only the keynote to their ethnic consciousness but also the condition *sine qua non* which would command the esteem of the Americans."

48. Popa's *Romania Is a Song* is subtitled *A Sampler of Verse in Translation.* Popa has done a number of translations for the *America,* Romanian yearbooks and periodicals, and individual writers. He was interviewed in Phoenix, Arizona, in December 1976 and provided information about his works. Eli Popa, *Give Us This Day: A Play in Three Acts* (New York: The Exposition Press, 1948) is the story of a young ethnic couple in an industrial steel town.

49. Benecke, "Romanians in Fort Wayne." "A group of Romanian-Americans were a part of the Manhattan Project . . . the production of the atom bomb. The men were told little about this secret project. The Joslyn Company's contribution was the manufacture of shafts that made up part of the weapon. The workers described the alloy as being so dense that if the shafts were lifted in the center, the shaft would bend due to the tremendous peripheral weight. . . . Also, one worker stated that the shafts were volatile if continually exposed to air . . . they were stored in special containers. The shafts were known to be radioactive and frequent Geiger-Mueller checks were done. The men received a diamond pin from the Joslyn Company and a certificate from the United States Government for their role. After the bombing of Hiroshima and Nagasaki, the response of the workers was one of sadness and disgust. They were proud to contribute to the war effort but viewed such wanton destruction with horror and sorrow. Few mentioned the project and very few knew where their award pins and certificates were" (28–30).

50. Theodore D. Mason, "Alex Vraciu," in *Stories from East Chicago's Century of People* in booklet titled *War Years* (East Chicago: East Chicago Public Library, 1993), 23.

# SCANDINAVIANS

ALAN H. WINQUIST

*The 1930 census data clearly showed that the Scandinavians in this state were overwhelmingly urban. Despite the fact that Norwegians were one of the most agriculturally oriented ethnic groups in the United States, in Indiana they were 82 percent urban. The Swedish born were 69 percent urban, and the Danish born were 67 percent urban.*

Geographically the term "Scandinavia" is generally used to describe Norway and Sweden, located on the Scandinavian Peninsula, as well as Denmark. Linguistically and culturally Iceland is also defined as Scandinavia with its Germanic language being closely akin to ancient Norse. Historically there are close ties with Finland. Swedish, one of Finland's two official languages, is spoken by the Swede-Finns concentrated along the western and southwestern coastal areas and on the Åland Islands. Finnish along with Estonian and Hungarian are Finno-Ugrian languages. "The Nordic countries" or "Norden" are more accurate terms to describe these five nations. However, since few people from Finland and Iceland settled in Indiana, "Scandinavia" will be frequently employed in this chapter.

## Emigration from the Nordic Lands

Between 1840 and 1930 over 2.5 million Nordic people immigrated to the United States, of whom the Swedes accounted for 45 percent, Norwegians 31 percent, and Danes and Finns 11.5 percent. Although Iceland's figures were generally counted with Danes and numerically were much smaller than the others, it is estimated that in the period from 1870 to 1900, 20 percent of the population of Iceland immigrated to North America. Almost nine hundred thousand Norwegians arrived in the United States between 1820 and 1975, approximating Norway's 1820 total population. Emigration from Norway began along the southwest coast in the Stavanger region, gradually spread northward, and then into the inner fjords and high mountains until every part of the nation was impacted. Swedish immigration between 1840 and 1930 amounted to about one-fourth of the country's total population of the late nineteenth century. By 1900 the provinces of Småland, consisting of the three counties (län) of Kalmar, Kronoberg, and Jönköping, along with Västergötland (including the city of Gothenburg), Skåne, and Värmland sent the largest numbers. But there were high percentages throughout Sweden, including the provinces of Östergötland, Halland, Dalsland, and Dalarna (Dalecarlia), and the island of Öland. Of all European countries, Iceland, Norway, Sweden, and Ireland lost the greatest percentage of their populations in the massive immigration across the North Atlantic. Although Danish and Finnish percentages were lower, a sizable portion of the population immigrated, especially from certain areas such as northern Jutland in Denmark and Vaasa and Oulu provinces of western and central Finland.[1]

There were numerous reasons for this vast emigration from the Nordic region. For the Norwegians and Swedes, prior to the American Civil War, the main cause was religious repression, and not until 1870 was a law enacted in Sweden guaranteeing religious toleration to dissenters. These early immigrants were generally better-off financially than later ones, and many came as families. After the Civil War and until 1930 economic factors were the chief motives. The rural population increased at a rapid rate. In Sweden there was insufficient arable land to subdivide, resulting in a large landless class that, beginning in the 1880s, sought alternatives of either moving to the cities or immigrating overseas. During the 1860s and 1870s there

were severe crop failures in both Norway and Sweden. At the same time in America the promise of land from the Homestead Act of 1862 became very attractive to Scandinavia's rural and landless poor.

While Norwegians and Swedes sought farmland in America before the 1880s, after that time the primary objective was to seek their fortunes in the cities. By the end of the century most of the Swedish immigrants were industrial workers. In the period 1900–13 the typical Swedish immigrant was a fortune-seeking, young, single adult attracted by American industry. Also at that time there was a significant pull factor from family members as demonstrated by the "letters from America." Other immigration motives for the Swedes included reading handbooks about America, avoiding military service (an unpopular 1901 law increased military service from three to eight months), reacting against the pretensions of the upper classes, responding favorably to state (e.g., Minnesota) and company (e.g., railway and steamship) recruiters, and desiring adventure.[2] In a limited survey taken among Swedes in Attica, Indiana, in 1948, five of the twelve Swedish immigrants queried responded that "they came to the United States to work since they thought America offered a better future for them. Five other foreign born informants came with their parents, who also came to America because they thought they could better themselves. One of the informants came to visit and just stayed. . . . The twelfth immigrant stated that he came to escape the draft."[3]

In addition, the Mormon faith had won a number of Danish converts, resulting in immigration to Utah. Also, Denmark's defeat by Prussia and Austria in the 1864 war and subsequent loss of Slesvig (Schleswig) prompted some Danes to immigrate. Many Danes received prepaid tickets from relatives in America. For Finns the increasingly repressive policies of the Russian czars in the late nineteenth and early twentieth centuries and the unstable Russian political situation caused some to consider immigration.

In the United States the early Nordic peoples seeking land to farm tended to settle in the upper Middle West. The Norwegians, having arrived first, initially settled in southern and central Wisconsin, then northern and southern Minnesota, and later the Dakotas. In addition, many chose to live in Chicago. The Swedes also concentrated in the homestead states of the upper Middle West, particularly Illinois and Minnesota, where land had not been fully taken by the Norwegians and Germans. In the late nineteenth century the shift to the cities occurred. At the turn of the century Chicago was the second most populous Swedish city in the world, outstripped only by Stockholm. In the period 1890–1930, one out of every ten Swedes in America lived in Chicago. By 1910 two-thirds of all Swedes in the United States lived in urban areas, Chicago and Minneapolis being the primary objectives for many Swedish immigrants. But Swedes were also attracted to some eastern cities, including New York City; Worcester, Massachusetts; and Jamestown, New York. Although Iowa's rolling farmlands interested many Danes, they tended to scatter to far-flung areas and thus assimilated more rapidly than other Scandinavians. Finns went to the mining areas of northern Minnesota and the forests of northern Michigan. By 1920 other states with sizable Nordic populations included California, Connecticut, Kansas, Nebraska, Pennsylvania, Utah, and Washington.

The number of foreign-born Scandinavians in Indiana began modestly. The 1850 national census figures noted some 3,600 Scandinavians had settled in the United States, nearly one-third of whom were residing in neighboring Illinois and less than 50 in Indiana. The general trend for Scandinavians in Indiana was to go first to Illinois (e.g., Chicago) and then make a second move to Indiana. Throughout the second half of the nineteenth and the first decade of the twentieth centuries, the Indiana figures gradually climbed until 1910, the peak year for total foreign-born Scandinavians, and particularly Swedes, in the Hoosier state. By that time over 6,500 Scandinavians had settled in the state, accounting for 4.1 percent of the total foreign born and seventh among white ethnic groups. (In 1890 Scandinavians had ranked fourth.) Among the Nordic immigrants, Swedes dominated every decade (except 1850) with over 80 percent of the Nordic foreign born total between 1860 and 1900, over 70 percent between 1900 and the 1950s, and dropping below 70 percent after 1960. Danes were the second largest Scandinavian group until 1980 when the Norwegians overtook them. The Danish-born totals peaked in 1920 at approximately 1,000, and the highest figures for Norwegians was around 600 in 1940. Very few Finns and Icelanders have settled in Indiana.[4]

During the period prior to 1860 the largest number of Norwegians and Swedes attracted to the last vacant farmland in the state (no Danes at that time) were in the west central counties of Tippecanoe, Fountain, Warren, Benton, Jasper, and Newton. By 1855 there were about five hundred Swedes in Tippecanoe and Fountain counties. Many came as families from the Gränna region of Jönköping län in northwest Småland. By 1860 Tippecanoe, Fountain, and Warren counties accounted for nearly one-half of the state's Swedes.

However, it was northwest Indiana (Lake, La Porte, and Porter counties) that would account for the largest number of Scandinavians in future decades. In 1860 there were only one hundred Swedes in Porter County and sixty-nine in neighboring La Porte County. However, by 1880 the three northwest counties had 50 percent of the state's Swedes (43 percent of the state's Scandinavian born), while the three west central counties had less than 20 percent. At 26 percent, Porter County had the largest share of the state's Swedish born, maintaining this leading position until the turn of the century. Swedes were attracted to Porter County by opportunities in the timber industry.

In the late 1860s a group of 40 young Danish men from the islands of Møn and Falster arrived in Indianapolis as construction workers. By 1880 there were 114 Danish born living in the city, the largest contingent of this ethnic group in the state. In 1872 the Danes organized their own church.[5]

By 1890 the three counties of the northwest region of Indiana comprised 53 percent of the state's Swedish born (47 percent of the state's Scandinavians), and the three west central counties a mere 13.3 percent. Lake and La Porte counties also had more Norwegians than any other counties of the state. In 1890 St. Joseph County, including the city of South Bend, accounted for 15 percent of the state's Swedish born. Studebaker Wagon Works and Oliver Chilled Plow Works, two of the three companies that dominated South Bend's economic life since the mid-1870s, were at the time actively recruiting Swedish workers.

Two decades later Lake County captured the largest share of Swedish born, nearly one out of every four in the state. A number of Scandinavian workers were attracted to Gary, Indiana's boomtown, and its economic opportunities, particularly when the Gary Works of the US Steel Corporation formally opened in 1908. Lake County's close proximity to Chicago was a significant factor in luring a number of workers away from the latter's large Swedish and Norwegian communities. In 1910 the three northwest counties together accounted for nearly one-half of Indiana's Swedish born. In percentages Porter County was decreasing rapidly as its 1910 figure was only one-half that of 1890, while St. Joseph County was holding its own. The year 1910 was the peak year for the number of Danish born in Marion County, where the census report noted that the Danish-born community had grown to 280, an increase of 73 from 1890.

By 1920 the Nordic region was well on its way to becoming a modern, prosperous economic region with increased political rights and opportunities for its citizens. This factor, coupled with restrictive American immigration laws in the mid-1920s, ended the large-scale emigration from Scandinavia by 1930. The Scandinavian born in the United States, like other European ethnic groups, continued to be drawn to the industries as well as building trade opportunities in the Calumet Region. In neighboring Chicago, Swedes dominated the construction business; by 1928 members of this ethnic group had constructed about 35 percent of all buildings. Together Porter and La Porte counties in 1930 comprised only 20 percent of the state's Swedish born. Elkhart County was holding its own at 4.6 percent and nearby St. Joseph County was at 13.5 percent. Swedes were continuing to be attracted to South Bend's economic opportunities, particularly to the Oliver plant, which had undergone a large physical expansion between 1917 and 1920. Another industrial entrepreneur to arrive in South Bend was Vincent Bendix. Established in 1929, the Bendix Aviation Corporation had a number of Swedish-born employees, one reason undoubtedly being that Bendix himself was of Swedish descent. By 1920 Swedes were also responding to business opportunities in Marion and Allen counties.

The 1930 census data clearly showed that the Scandinavians in this state were overwhelmingly urban. Despite the fact that Norwegians were one of the most agriculturally oriented ethnic groups in the United States, in Indiana they were 82 percent urban. The Swedish born were 69 percent urban, and the Danish born were 67 percent urban. In comparison to Indiana's other groups, such as the Germans, Poles, Czechs, and Italians, the

Swedes and Danes had a lower urban and a higher rural percentage. In 1930 for every 137.6 Swedish-born males in Indiana there were 100 Swedish-born females (this was very close to the figure for all foreign born in this state, namely 138 males to 100 females). The United States average in that year for Swedish born was 127.5 males for 100 females (for all foreign born it was 116.6 males for every 100 females).[6]

In 1940 the Swedish-born population had declined by nearly 25 percent from its 1930 total. Lake County still had one-third of the Swedish total. Although Porter and La Porte counties continued to decline, the three northwest counties still had one-half of the state's Swedish-born total. Lake County was also the leading county for Norwegian born in the state. Marion and Allen counties were increasing their share of the state's Swedes, while St. Joseph and Elkhart counties were holding their own.

By 1980 the Swedish- and Danish-born levels had dropped to what they had been between 1860 and 1880. No longer did Lake County have a dominant position among the Swedes. For the Norwegians their 1980 total had fallen off to the 1880s level. Clearly few additional Scandinavian born were migrating to Indiana. The few people who were coming were drawn to well-paid, white-collar jobs. Yet despite the end of Scandinavian immigration to this country and specifically to Indiana, a 1990 survey of total ancestries reported nearly 115,000 Hoosiers claimed some Scandinavian heritage, which ranked just behind the Italians.[7]

Why were not Nordic people drawn to Indiana in large numbers like the Germans, Irish, or eastern Europeans? One explanation is that in the early days most of the productive agricultural land had already been claimed and the price of land was expensive by the time the Scandinavians arrived. Therefore they moved on to the unoccupied areas of the upper Middle West. Secondly, there was a perception that Indiana was an unhealthy place and that the soil was not of very good quality. Eric Norelius, an early Swedish pastor, in an 1855 letter appearing in the leading Swedish newspaper in America made the following observations: "Indiana is one of the unhealthiest states of America. The soil is for the most part slack and swampy—an excellent breeding-place for ague and fever. And our countrymen know these illnesses only too well: I have met only few who have not had or have ague. Cholera has also time after time reaped its rich harvests in these regions."[8] Norelius had just visited a Swedish settlement in the Lafayette-Attica area of western Indiana. Thirdly, Scandinavians were drawn to nearby Chicago where they may have had a family member or had the perception of greater economic opportunities.

Fourthly, in contrast to states such as Minnesota, Indiana did not actively recruit Scandinavian immigrants.

Another factor was that Indiana lacked a significant number of advocates in the Nordic region in the late nineteenth and early twentieth centuries when mass immigration was occurring. Furthermore, some of the infrequent reports about Indiana were not always positive. In 1888 Baroness Alexandra Gripenberg, a Swede-Finn, author, and reformer in Finland, traveled widely in the United States. The narrative of her American experience was published in Helsinki in 1889, first in Swedish under the title *Ett halfår i Nya Verlden: Strödda resebilder från Förenta Staterna* (A Half Year in the New World: Miscellaneous Sketches of Travel in the United States), and then in Finnish (Uudesta maailmasta: Hajanaisia matkakuvia Ameriikasta). Her general impressions of America, including descriptions of Indiana and Indianapolis, were widely read in northern Europe. Although Gripenberg commented on Indiana's fertile land and on Indianapolis as a "well-furnished new city," she complained about the city's hot weather, an observation that Scandinavians would not be terribly enthusiastic to learn. "I arrived in the city [Indianapolis] at the beginning of the warm time of the year and experienced there a severe and continuing hot spell which lasted for two weeks without any abatement. . . . The hot bedrooms did not have time to cool off during the short cooler period which followed sunset and sleeping was hardly to be thought of. . . . The only time of day worth living was from half-past eight until eleven o'clock in the evening. Then every family sought its porch, with its children and its flowers." She also noted continued "race hatred" in Indiana. "Even though the laws no longer prohibit Negroes from entering schools or holding public offices, they experience race hatred and scorn in thousands of ways."[9] Nordic people in America in the nineteenth century were generally admirers of Abraham Lincoln, supported the Republican party, and were opposed to slavery. Undoubtedly these views were shared with family members back in the Mother Country. Gripenberg's observations would certainly have given her Nordic readers some apprehensions about Indiana.

## Scandinavians in the West Central Region

It is not certain when the first Scandinavian arrived in Indiana, but Ole Rynning, a Norwegian traveler and writer whose "America books" had considerable influence in Norway, noted in his *Underretninger om Amerika* (Information about America) that there were seven Norwegian settlements in the United States including Lafayette, Indiana, where a number of families from

Drammen, near Oslo, had acquired several hundred acres of land. Rynning's account was based on his 1837 journey.[10] Also, in the same year Niels Larsen Bilden (Nils Larssen Bilde), from Granvin, east of Bergen, Norway, with his wife and six children journeyed by boat for seven weeks from New York to Chicago. From there the family headed south to Brook, Indiana, in present-day Newton County, and purchased three hundred acres of land. Bilden died the following year. Svend, one of his sons, was killed in the Civil War. Eventually the family moved to Kendall County, Illinois. Lars Nielsen Bilden, another son, in an 1884 letter to relatives in Norway reminisced about Indiana and the "dangerous and not too desirable people living around us [in Brook]." The family apparently wished to join a Norwegian settlement in Illinois.[11]

Another Norwegian, Hans Erasmus Hjort (Hiorth), settled near Monticello, White County, before 1845. In his will Hjort instructed his executors "to lay out a village on my place to be called Mount Walleston in honor of the first ship that landed me in America and one street to be called Frances St.," honoring the ship's captain. Near Monticello is the small community of Norway, originally named Mount Walleston. Hjort's widow Bergetta married a clergyman from Denmark in 1847, and eventually they moved on to Iowa and Minnesota.[12]

In 1840 an Emigrant Society was organized in Stockholm, Sweden, with Carl Alex Adam von Schiele as its secretary. The following year he wrote an emigrant guide entitled *Några korta underrättelser om Amerika till upplyssning och nytta för dem som ämna dit utflytta* (Some Brief Information about America for Enlightenment and for the Purpose of Those Who Intend to Emigrate There). By 1843 the guide was translated into Norwegian. As a result of this and other guidebooks, the facts of emigration and the conditions in America were known in Scandinavia in the 1840s. Von Schiele advised settling in Illinois, Missouri, or Indiana because these states had been recommended earlier by Rynning. Von Schiele noted that the climate was like Sweden, though milder, and in 1841 land was cheap and fertile. There were very few taxes, no privileged class, and no quartering of troops. Canal and river transportation was considered good. Von Schiele gave instructions on how to reach these areas. To get to Illinois and Indiana required a steamer on the Great Lakes from Buffalo to Chicago and Milwaukee. It was noted that servant girls were in much demand and were treated with more respect than in Norway. The Norwegian edition also encouraged skilled artisans such as blacksmiths, tailors, shoemakers, and carpenters to immigrate; those who were lazy or who would not work with their hands should not go. "He who cannot, nor does not desire to work need never count on wealth nor well-being. No, in America a person does not attain it without work, but it is true that he can there, with industry and frugality, soon reach economic independence, and can meet old age without fear."[13]

Carl Peter Moberg, a tanner apprentice from Gränna, Jönköping län, Småland, may have been attracted to Indiana from Rynning's account. He had visited the United States in the early 1840s and had lived here for a few years. Moberg returned to Gränna in 1844, became a member of the city council, and spread information about America. Later Moberg returned to America with his family and came to Yorktown, a former community a couple miles south of Stockwell in southeast Tippecanoe County. Johannes Peterson, a peasant's son from Gränna, came to the United States in 1849, spent a couple of years in Greene County, New York, and in 1851 moved to Lafayette, Indiana. Peterson influenced his brother Peter to immigrate, and he appeared in 1852 with a large party.[14]

During the following two years other groups from Gränna and neighboring parishes arrived and settled in five locations in Tippecanoe and Fountain counties, namely Attica, Lafayette, Montmorency, West Point, and Yorktown. One party, led and financed by Nils Hokanson, a wealthy peasant, came to Lafayette via New Orleans and Evansville, Indiana, in 1853. When the party arrived in Evansville, "from there they did not know where to turn. None of them could speak a word of English, and no one in town understood what kind of people these were and where they wanted to go. Then an old devout woman, Mrs. Bjorklund, exclaimed, 'There is nothing else we can do than to pray to God, if we pray He will surely help us.' And they did pray.... On the second day of their predicament there appeared unexpectedly a Swede, the only one in the place, who had lived there a long time, married to a German lady, and almost altogether divorced from his native tongue. The preceding night he had experienced a peculiar restlessness and in the morning had a feeling that he should go down to the boat landing. When he got there he found a whole flock of his countrymen, to his great astonishment. He gladly served as an interpreter and assisted them to go on to Lafayette."[15] By 1855 there were about five hundred settlers in Lafayette, making it one of the largest Swedish communities in the United States.

Rev. Eric Norelius, one of the four pioneer Swedish Lutheran pastors, is perhaps the best source of information on the early Swedes in Indiana. Norelius, a native of Hälsingland in north central Sweden, arrived in New York in 1850 and proceeded to study at Capitol University, a newly organized Lutheran seminary in Columbus, Ohio. In 1860 he helped to found the Swedish American Lutheran Church, known as the Augustana Synod. During his lifetime Norelius traveled to many of the Swedish communities in the Middle West. His book *De Svenska Luterska Församlingarnas och Svenskarnes Historia i Amerika* (The Swedish Lutheran Congregations and the History of the Swedes in America), published in 1890, is an invaluable primary source for the early Swedish immigrants.

Norelius described the landscape of Tippecanoe County and the problems faced by the early Swedes. "The Wabash valley with its own prairies and wooded sections and fertile soil is a lush landscape. The Swedes who came here did not come to an empty wilderness, but to a rich land already well settled, where they could easily find work and earn a living. On the other hand the land was already expensive and therefore beyond the reach of our countrymen without means. During the first years sickness was rampant among the Swedes, especially in the cholera year 1854 when quite a few died. Many families were broken up, the children, becoming orphans, were placed in the American homes and brought up ignorant of their ancestry. Many succeeded economically, many had to endure much suffering."[16]

Norelius observed that a number of the early settlers were young single persons, "alert and willing to work." Although poor they found employment on the farms, but only a dozen acquired any real estate by 1855. Norelius also noted that "Father" Newman, a preacher from Chicago who attempted to convert the settlers to Methodism, visited the communities. Norelius observed that some were influenced, but he was reassured that most "wanted eagerly to hear a Lutheran pastor."[17] During the summer of 1854 Lutheran clergymen began to make regular visits. On 18 February 1855 Rev. Erland Carlsson of Chicago organized "The Swedish Evangelical Lutheran Congregation in Indiana" in West Point, the first Scandinavian church in the state. The congregation did not survive mainly because a number of parishioners moved on to Minnesota. During the summer of 1855 Norelius and Nils Hokanson journeyed to Minnesota to learn about settlement possibilities. At the end of 1855 Norelius accepted a pastoral call in Red Wing. Many in the Lafayette community followed Norelius to Minnesota, some of whom settled in Waseca County, where they established the Vista community.[18]

Despite the population loss, in 1858 another church was organized, this time in Attica, the second oldest permanent Swedish Lutheran congregation in Indiana.[19] Norelius became its pastor in 1859, serving for one year. A church sanctuary was erected the following year, which continues to serve the congregation of First Lutheran Church of Attica. Also in 1860, before a public school was created, the congregation organized a school in which

the minister served as instructor with teaching to be conducted in both English and Swedish. Other Swedish settlements in Indiana also launched schools before the public schools were created. A characteristic of Nordic immigrants was the emphasis placed on education. In Yorktown, dubbed "Swedetown," a Swedish Methodist church was built in 1873. Although neither the sanctuary nor the congregation exists today, a Swedish cemetery is near the church's former site. Several young men of the Yorktown community had fought in the Civil War on the Union side; two Swedish immigrants were killed, including Franz Nyberg who left a widow and five small children.[20]

Although a number of people departed from Attica for the Swedish settlement of Paxton, Illinois, between 1868 and 1871 additional immigrants from Sweden arrived in Tippecanoe, Fountain, Warren, Benton, Newton, and Jasper counties. The Scandinavians played a significant role in the area's farming. In the summer of 1918 plans were made in the Warren County home of Oscar N. Larm to organize what later would be called the Farm Bureau. An initial purpose of the organization was to seek military exemptions for farmers. By the fall of 1918 a state Farm Bureau was begun in Indianapolis, and later a national organization was formed.[21]

A number of Swedes were attracted to the stone quarries near Attica, others to a variety of jobs in the towns of west central Indiana. Attica's *Fountain-Warren Democrat* noted that Swedes were blacksmiths, musicians, grocers, carpenters, teachers, janitors, and hotel clerks, as well as farmers.[22] Many became businessmen. By 1891 the Attica Lutheran congregation stood at 185 members. Many of the Swedes came from the west coast around the city of Varberg in the province of Halland.[23] By 1890 a number of Danes had become successful farmers in Newton County. It was reported that the Scandinavians were members of both the Republican and Democratic parties, though the majority nationally at this time was more sympathetic to the former.

Thomas Leif was a successful Scandinavian businessman in Attica. He became general manager of the Leif Buggy Company, was president of the Attica Merchants Association, and served in the Indiana legislature. John A. Johnson was president of the Starr City Machine and Foundry Company of Lafayette. John Henry Grant came from Gränna, Jönköping län, with his parents in 1850, first settling in Illinois. At the age of twenty he enlisted in the Union army in the first call at Lafayette and subsequently was wounded. Following the war he was a farmer in Benton County and a member of a Methodist Episcopal church, as were many Swedes. One of Grant's daughters married and settled in Fowler. Her large home, the Ella Grant Lawson Hostess House, is the headquarters of the Benton County Historical Society. Monson Martin, born in Sweden in 1844, came to America with his mother after his father's death in 1853. In Tippecanoe County Martin was "bound" to a John Austin, who also was instrumental in sending the young Swede to school. Following service in the Civil War Martin purchased 160 acres of farmland in Bolivar Township, Benton County, where he developed "a very fine farm." His wife was a native of England. He was an active member of the Methodist Episcopal Church. In Warren County Charles Milburg, born in Sweden in 1853, was described as "the best assistant road superintendent Warren County ever had," at least up until the early 1900s. In Tippecanoe County Closson V. Peterson, son of Swedish immigrants, became principal of the high school in West Point in 1910 and then county superintendent of schools in 1917. Jonas A. Peterson, who emigrated from Sweden to the United States in 1859, reached Fountain County with two dollars. He was hired out to a farmer and after careful handling of his money was able to purchase 328 acres of land. He married an American woman in 1872, was a member of the Lutheran Church, and was affiliated with the Republican party.

Samuel and Marie Hanson were typical of the Danes who settled in Newton County. They had five children before leaving Denmark for Lake Village in the mid-1870s, and five more children were born in Indiana. Initially Hanson obtained 30 acres and planted fruit trees, rye, and wheat. He also worked for Lemuel Milk, an American who owned thousands of acres of land in the area. Christian Brandt, a Dane, also was associated with Milk. Eventually Brandt purchased a farm of 320 acres adjoining Milk's. John Lawson emigrated from Sweden with his mother in 1853 and settled in Benton County. Lawson formed a partnership with an attorney from Lafayette, and together they were involved in farming and banking. His son and grandson continued to be active in agriculture and were identified as "Swede." Grandson Robert D. "Swede" Lawson, farmer, grain elevator operator, and at one time president of the Farmers and Merchants Bank, was active in the Democratic party, and twice a delegate to the Democratic National Convention.[24]

## Scandinavians in the Northwest Region

Norelius noted that the first Swede in La Porte County was Capt. Edmund Johnson from northern Sweden, who had sailed on the Atlantic Ocean and Great Lakes for fifteen years and finally had settled in La Porte in the mid-1840s. Ten years later he was an established businessman. In the spring of 1853 Christina Westberg, a Swedish servant girl, arrived in La Porte with a Chicago family with whom she was working. Westberg's family then followed her to La Porte. That same spring the P. Palmblad family from Jönköping län settled in La Porte. They were followed by others, many from the same area in Sweden, who had come by way of Chicago. Two years later a group of thirty young, disgruntled Swedish men arrived from Plymouth, Marshall County. They had been employed as construction workers for the railroad but for seven months had not received their wages. In the fall of 1856 this Swedish community was enlarged by a group of servant girls from Lafayette and West Point.[25]

At the same time Tuve Nilsson Hasselquist, another pioneer Swedish Lutheran pastor, visited northwest Indiana following a trip to Attica. In *Hemlandet,* considered the oldest Swedish-language newspaper in America and widely read by the early Swedish immigrants, Hasselquist, in an article entitled "A Short Visit to Indiana," gave a description of La Porte:

> The town has an exceptionally attractive situation. There is a small lake with forest on one side and fruitful cultivated land on the other. It is expanding rapidly. Already several additions have been made by converting surrounding farm land into lots. . . . The owner said he would be willing to contribute a good site if the Swedes wanted to build a church for themselves. Many Americans expressed the desire to have Swedes move in—they considered them the best of the immigrants who had settled here. Opportunities for work are plentiful and will increase, but I believe the wages are not as high as in at least some other places. The persons I talked to were very contented with the place.[26]

By September 1857 there were sufficient Swedes in the area for a church to be organized. Today called Bethany Lutheran, it is the oldest permanent Swedish Lutheran congregation in the state. Three years later the first sanctuary was completed. Norelius noted that by 1859 there were ninety-seven Swedes in La Porte, most working in town as mechanics and manual laborers with only a few being farmers. Captain Johnson proved to be very helpful to the Swedes even though "he has forgotten his mother-tongue completely but he has remembered some Swedish songs which he learned as a child." Norelius observed that some Swedes, including Palmblad, became involved with "a new, peculiar sect" that is identified as the Seventh Day Adventists. He also bemoaned the fact that in later years some Swedes in the area had given themselves over to "ungodly conduct," including drunkenness and "low church discipline."[27]

A number of Swedes and some Norwegians were attracted to La Porte County's business opportunities.

An example was Emil Johnson, president of the La Porte Harness Company. He learned the harnessmaker's trade in Östergötland, where he was born in 1860. In the early 1880s he came to the United States, first locating in Chesterton, Indiana. His successful business was developed in La Porte in the mid-1890s. Charles O. Larson from Gränna, Småland, was a contractor and builder in La Porte at the turn of the century.[28]

Michigan City drew Swedes and Norwegians with its lumber and shipping opportunities. Samuel Webster Larsen, whose father was from Oslo (formerly Christiania), Norway, was the manager of the Greer-Wilkinson Lumber Company at the turn of the century. There was a "Swedeville" in town in the Franklin Street vicinity. The Zion Swedish Evangelical Lutheran Church was organized in 1887, and sermons were preached in both Swedish and English until 1925.[29]

Meanwhile, the community of Baillytown or Coffee Creek, Porter County, near Lake Michigan's sand dunes, was attracting Swedish settlers. According to Norelius the first Swedes in the area were probably "penniless workers who came from Chicago [in the late 1840s or early 1850s] and found work in the woods and in tree cutting around the sawmill in Baileytown."[30] The sawmill was established by the son-in-law of Joseph Bailly, a French-Canadian fur trader. In his 1856 visit Hasselquist described the area:

> About 40 miles east of Chicago . . . lies a small Swedish settlement which may prove the most enduring. As a rule the land is covered by a forest, in part, with large and old trees. The owners are well paid when selling to the network of railroads. The ground is probably low here and there, but where seeded it has shown itself highly fruitful. Almost a score of larger and smaller landowners live here, mainly from Östergötland. . . . Some of them own 100 or more acres, some 80 and 75 acres, and less down to $2^1/2$ acres of one couple. Their houses are yet of inferior quality, of the kind found among new-comers, but soon will be exchanged . . . for better and more convenient accommodations. Surprisingly one could find himself in a wild forest in America and there come upon Swedish families cultivating the earth around their small houses. They paid from $6 to $12 per acre, but prices have risen so that now one can demand $15 and over, even $50 per acre.[31]

Around 1855 Chicago's pioneer Swedish Lutheran minister, Erland Carlsson, and his assistant visited the Baillytown settlement and found "a good deal of apathy [regarding spiritual matters] about Baillytown's Swedes and not a small number loved the bottle."[32] However, conditions apparently improved because in 1857 Carlsson was able to organize a congregation with thirty-one communicant members, the Swedish Lutheran Church of Baillytown, today the Augsburg Evangelical Lutheran Church of Porter. Seven years later the congregation erected its first sanctuary, about a mile northeast of Baillytown. This log church was replaced by a second church in 1900, but it burned in 1933. The present handsome stone church, resting on the foundations of the second sanctuary, was completed in 1938.[33]

Matilda Swanson, the daughter of an original Swedish settler, recorded some childhood memories of her family and the area:

> Carl J. L. Swanson, my father, was born September 27, 1829, a member of a large family of Östergötland, Sweden. He came to America in 1854, accompanied by two sisters. . . . From New York, they came by train to Chicago. For a number of years, father worked for a farmer in Cook County, Illinois, until in 1859, he married Marie Monson, my mother [also an emigrant from Sweden]. . . . They bought a farm in . . . Cook County . . . and lived there until 1864. . . . Father was interested in cattle raising, and land was priced rather high so . . . they moved to Porter County, Indiana, where land was more reasonable and they could afford sufficient land for ranching. However, for about a year after moving to Indiana, they lived near Coffee Creek . . . where father worked at wood cutting [much of the wood was used by the railroad, particularly for track ties] in partnership with Peter Anderson, a brother-in-law.[34]

The Swedes wanted their children to have an education that included maintaining the Swedish language and customs. Matilda Swanson recalled that "the children of the settlers talked and understood Swedish but parents insisted that they should learn to read Swedish as well. We regularly attended the public school, but during summer vacations, the pastor of the church would conduct classes in Swedish." Frederick Burstrom, a member of the first Board of Deacons of the Augsburg Church, had a large toolshed on his farm that, after being moved across the road next to a Swedish cemetery and renovated, was used from 1880 to 1885 as the local school. From that time until 1912 Swedish-language classes were conducted during the summer months in this small $14^1/2 \times 20^1/2$-foot building, known as the Burstrom Chapel and Augsburg Svenska Skola (Swedish School).[35]

An example of a successful farmer in the area was Anders Ludwig Kjellberg, who came to the United States in 1863 from Västergötland with his wife, Johanna, their son, and Anders's two brothers. Kjellberg had been a

*Burstrom Chapel and Augsburg Svenska Skola (Swedish School), Porter, Indiana.*

*Chellberg Farm, Indiana Dunes National Lakeshore Park.*

farmer and tailor in Sweden. The group journeyed by railway from the East Coast to Chicago where another brother was living. In Chicago the Kjellbergs met the son-in-law of Joseph Bailly who needed farmers to clean out the brush and get the land ready for planting in Porter County. Anders and one brother went to Baillytown while the third brother moved to Michigan City. A small log house was provided for the Kjellbergs. Anders helped to establish the Augsburg Lutheran Church, was a lay preacher, and became the church school superintendent. In 1874 the Kjellbergs purchased eighty acres of Bailly property and developed a farm. At this time they became American citizens and changed the family name to Chellberg, presumably to make it look more "American." The Chellberg Farm grew grain until the nearby South Shore Railroad line was completed in 1908. At that time the Chellbergs began dairy farming, sending milk daily on the train to East Chicago. During summer months numerous people from Chicago came on the South Shore line to visit the nearby dunes, and often picnics were held at the Chellberg Farm. Three generations of Chellbergs made their living from the farm. Today the 1885 house and the various farm buildings are preserved

as part of the Indiana Dunes National Lakeshore. Not only is the Chellberg Farm a landmark commemorating an early Swedish pioneer family in Indiana, but it also serves as a laboratory for teaching environmental issues.[36]

Baillytown and nearby Chesterton are located in Westchester Township, which probably has had the heaviest concentration of Swedes in Indiana. In the 1880 census Swedes numbered nearly two-thirds of the 797 foreign born in the township. Although they were initially employed cutting timber for the railroad, Swedes pursued opportunities in farming and various business ventures. The Swedish population of Chesterton increased when Carl Oscar Hillstrom moved his organ factory from Chicago to Chesterton in 1880, making it the main industry in town. Hillstrom was born in Stockholm in 1846 and learned cabinetry and organ making before coming to America. From 1869 to 1880 the Hillstrom and Bredshall Organ Factory was located in Chicago. Hillstrom's friend P. A. Johnson, the owner of a dry goods store in Chesterton, persuaded him to relocate the organ business to Chesterton in 1880. In Chesterton Hillstrom built homes for many of his Swedish workers and their families. There were 125 men on the payroll in 1892 (the population of the town increased from 488 in 1880 to 931 in 1890). The workforce could make eighteen pump organs a week. The Hillstrom Organ Factory is said to have produced over thirty-five thousand organs before it closed in 1920. The company also manufactured organ and piano stools.[37]

In 1879 Chesterton's Swedes organized two churches, Bethlehem Evangelical Lutheran and Swedish Methodist. The latter congregation merged with First United Methodist.[38] Swedes were so dominant in Chesterton that in the 1880s the *Chesterton Tribune* occasionally ran front-page articles in the Swedish language. During that decade John D. Lindstrom Carpenter and Builder, Swanson & Son Merchant Tailors, and John B. Lundberg Furniture and Undertaker were regular front-page

*The Hillstrom organ factory workers, Chesterton, Indiana. Carl Oscar Hillstrom is in the center of the front row.*

advertisers. Lundberg was born in Sweden in 1840 and at the age of twelve came to Chicago with his father and stepmother. There he learned cabinetmaking and eventually began a furniture business. In 1866 he moved to Chesterton. Lundberg owned three horse-drawn hearses and at funerals wore a top hat and formal mourning attire. By the turn of the century nearly all the businesses in downtown Chesterton were owned by Swedes.[39]

One longtime Chesterton resident noted that in 1936 the Swedes dominated the grocery business. There were Peter Hokanson and Son, Pillman's, Smedman's, and Anderson's meat market. Shoes were purchased at L. P. Matson Shoes and Harness, and there was the Sundeen Barbershop. There were two funeral parlors, Flynn-Lundberg and Edmonds, both with Swedish connections.[40]

Brick making was also a significant local industry in nearby Porter in the late nineteenth century because of the considerable clay deposits in the region. The first brickyard was opened in 1872, and by 1883 three were in operation. Some Swedes were employed in the brickyards including

Peter M. Hokanson, a blacksmith from Sweden. In 1901 he and his son established a meat market in Porter known as P. Hokanson & Son. The Hokanson family was involved in a number of local business interests, including lumbering and finance.[41]

Another community in Porter County where Swedes settled was Portage. Initially they were agricultural people. Garyton Mission Covenant Church was founded in 1868 by parishioners of the Augustana Lutheran Church of Hobart and is the oldest Swedish Covenant Church in the state.

Nearby Marshall County attracted Swedes as early as 1854, initially to cut down trees for the Pennsylvania Railroad's track ties. The land was then cleared for farming. Although many of the county's first Swedes went on to La Porte, by the 1870s and 1880s more of their countrymen had moved to Donaldson. Originally called Donelson, the town was laid out in 1871 and settled largely by Swedish immigrants, who helped to transform the marshland of the northwestern part of the county into productive farmland.

*Johnson Brothers Department Store, Chesterton, Indiana, 1910.*

The Swedish Immanuel Lutheran Church of Donaldson was organized in 1876 and the Evangelical Covenant Church of Donaldson in 1897.[42]

Swedes were beginning to arrive in St. Joseph County and particularly South Bend in the 1870s. Germans and Irish were the first immigrant groups to come to South Bend, but as Studebaker Wagon Works and Oliver Chilled Plow Works expanded Swedes and others appeared. Through the use of a Swedish immigration agent Studebaker's executives actively sought and succeeded in recruiting Swedes to work in their plant. James D. Oliver then followed, inviting the agent to South Bend to look over his plow works. In Sweden word went out quickly for skilled workers. A number came from the cities of Borås and Kalmar, others from the provinces of Värmland and Småland. Apparently Oliver was particularly fond of the Swedes. He built homes for them and donated land and money for their Lutheran church, known as the Gloria Dei congregation. Most of the thirty-three charter members of the congregation organized in 1880 were employed by Oliver. A number of Swedish women worked as domestics for wealthy South Bend families including the Studebakers. The Swedish Lutherans' first small frame sanctuary was built on West Dunham Street in the heart of the Swedish settlement, and the Oliver family attended the dedicatory service in November 1881. In 1884 Oliver needed the church land for his expanding company, and he agreed to underwrite the total cost of moving the church building a few blocks to Chapin and Sample streets. In return for Oliver's kindnesses the Swedes became very loyal to him. When the Polish Labor League led a strike against Oliver in 1885 the Swedes refused to honor the picket line, resulting in strained relations between the two immigrant groups.[43]

In the mid-1920s Vincent Bendix became part of the economic life of South Bend. Bendix's father was from Småland and was a Swedish Methodist minister in Moline, Illinois. His mother was from Östergötland. As a young man Bendix held a variety of jobs in Chicago and New York

and took great delight in tinkering with bicycles and machines. In 1908, while in Chicago, Bendix designed and built his own car, the Bendix. He became famous for the Bendix drive, which was the beginning of the use of self-starters in automobiles. Bendix also improved the carburetor. In 1924 he introduced four-wheel brakes and established the Bendix Brake Company in South Bend. The following year he became interested in aviation and acquired a number of companies manufacturing aircraft instruments, resulting in the formation of the Bendix Aviation Corporation in 1929.[44] A number of Swedes came to South Bend to work for Bendix. Of the current members of the Gloria Dei Lutheran Church, approximately 60 percent are of Swedish ancestry, and most of these are descendants of employees of the Bendix company, who came from Chicago to South Bend.[45]

There were businesses in South Bend in the late 1800s founded by Scandinavians, including the Jacobson and Peterson Company, manufacturers of brooms and whisks. Ole Noisom from Tromsø, Norway, had a watchmaking and jewelry business in the city in the 1890s.[46] Nearby Elkhart also appealed to a number of Swedes. In 1873 the Augustana Lutheran Church was established, predating Gloria Dei of South Bend by seven years.

Lake County also attracted Swedes in the late nineteenth century. The oldest church in Miller is the Bethel Evangelical Lutheran Church founded by Swedish immigrants in 1874 in a one-room schoolhouse. Not until 1892, however, was a church sanctuary built. S. A. Nordstrom, one of the first settlers, was the lay preacher during the church's first thirty-one years. Since the congregation was not affluent, the church had frequent financial difficulties. The Swedes "hauled sand from pits, cut ice in winter, and kept the equipment of the Lake Shore and Michigan Southern Railroad in good repair for one dollar or less a day. The settlers also fished, picked berries, grew a few garden vegetables, and raised cows, pigs, and poultry."[47]

Swedes began arriving in Hobart in the 1860s. Farming was the most common occupation, followed by brick making. In 1862 Augustana Lutheran Church was organized and in the first year was conducting a Swedish school. In 1904 the church was still offering a six- to eight-week Swedish summer school. A sanctuary was completed in the early 1870s where the men sat on the right side upon entering the church and the women on the left. In 1868 the Garyton Mission Covenant Church in Portage was organized by a number of members of the Augustana congregation. Scandinavians, principally Swedes, continued to settle in Hobart Township through the 1880s and 1890s. For example, in 1882 a group of Swedish brick makers from Chesterton moved to Hobart and four years later organized the Swedish Methodist Church. In 1887 this congregation completed its own church sanctuary. In the early twentieth century many members worked for steel and construction companies in Lake County. The Hobart Swedes settled in two areas— near the brickyards and in an area along Michigan Avenue called "Swede" Avenue. One of the Swedish businessmen was Albert J. Swanson, who owned a hardware store and was a township trustee at the turn of the century. In nearby Whiting Charles A. Johnson had a funeral business, was president of the town board, and in 1904 was the Republican party's nominee for auditor of Lake County.[48]

With the founding of Gary in 1906 and the coming of the steel mills another group of Scandinavians arrived in Lake County, and many worked in the steel mills in a variety of positions. Albin G. Witting from Lund, Sweden, and a graduate of the Stockholm Institute of Technology, came to the United States in 1898. He began as a clerk in the Homestead Steel Works in Pittsburgh and eventually became chief engineer of one of Gary's major steel mills.[49]

Scandinavian contractors from Chicago were attracted to Lake County. Ingwald Moe, a Norwegian, was one of the first builders in Gary after US Steel commenced its operations. Moe became a successful builder, operating throughout northern Indiana. He obtained permission from the Gary Land Company in 1907 to construct a nickelodeon where patrons could see ten-minute silent movies. Moe's Broadway Theatre was the first motion picture house in Gary. He also built the "New Gary Theatre" shortly before World War I.[50]

One of the few Nordic place names in Indiana is Lake Dalecarlia south of Cedar Lake in Lake County. Some Swedish stockholders in a land development company named the lake for the central Swedish province of Dalarna (Dalecarlia in English), where many of them had originated.[51]

Chicago had more prominent businessmen of Swedish birth or parentage than any other city in the United States. Many of these individuals had an impact on neighboring Indiana, including Charles R. Walgreen, son of Swedish settlers in western Illinois. He began with one drugstore in Chicago, and eventually the chain extended throughout the United States. Some of the earliest Walgreen stores were in Indiana. Alfred Stromberg and Androv Carlson, two Swedish-born engineers living in Chicago, developed the "farmer's telephone," which significantly contributed to ending the isolation of many rural areas. The Stromberg-Carlson Company also developed telephone switchboards and after World War I began to make radio equipment.[52]

## Scandinavians in Indianapolis, Fort Wayne, and Hartford City

The only sizable Scandinavian community in Indiana not of Swedish origin was a Danish group that settled in Indianapolis in the late 1860s, attracted by building construction opportunities. The first Danes who came to Indianapolis in 1861 were Hans Peter Weis and Rasmus Svendsen, both from Fanefjord on the island of Møn. They lived in Cleveland, Ohio, but obtained work with an architect who had a contract to build St. Paul's German Lutheran Church in Indianapolis. Shortly, relatives and friends from Denmark came to join them. When Weis visited Denmark in 1865 he brought back a group of forty young men and women from Møn and the nearby island of Falster.[53]

Indianapolis Danes met in the spring of 1867 when it became apparent that the Danish community desired its own church. Weis and others were members of St. Paul's. Undoubtedly not all the Danes felt comfortable worshiping in a German church in light of Denmark's recent defeat by the Prussians and Austrians in the 1864 war. On Easter Sunday 1868 a young Danish student studying at

*Former Danish Evangelical Lutheran Trinity Church, Indianapolis.*

Concordia Seminary in St. Louis conducted the first Danish service in Indianapolis. Shortly thereafter the Dansk Evangelisk Lutherske Trefoldigheds Kirke (Danish Evangelical Lutheran Trinity Church) was organized. In 1872 a Gothic Revival church sanctuary was constructed at the corner of Noble and McCarty streets. The congregation experienced two significant splits in 1869 and the 1880s. In the late 1880s the congregation became embroiled in theological controversies, which was characteristic of many Danish churches at the time. In 1914 the congregation became affiliated with the newly organized United Danish Evangelical Lutheran Church of America, a merger of the Blair Synod and a faction of the Danish Lutheran Church in America, both with strong pietist leanings. The first services in English were conducted in 1919, but Danish-language services continued until 1956. Although not many Danes lived near Trinity, the church was such a strong magnet that Danes viewed it as the center of Danish life in Indianapolis. As late as 1938 the adjoining parsonage served as a meeting place for Danish societies. In 1905 Lodge No. 228 of the Danish Brotherhood in America was founded with eleven charter members. A lodge of the Danish Sisterhood of America was also established. The early Danes of Indianapolis were cabinetmakers, rolling mill workers, bricklayers, coopers, and bakers, and the community reached its peak in 1910 with 280 individuals in Marion County.

Scandinavians scattered throughout Indiana. The 1890 census reports indicate that of Indiana's ninety-two counties, only fourteen did not have Nordic-born residents. Olaf N. Guldlin of Oslo, Norway, came to Fort Wayne in 1885 to assume the post of engineer with a local manufacturing company. Three years later he formed a partnership with two other men, opening an office as consulting gas engineers known as Western Gas. Eventually Guldlin became the president and general manager of the Western Gas Construction Company. At the turn of the century Nestor Fries emigrated from Sweden to Fort Wayne and established the Nestor Fries Machine Tool Work Company. Other members of his family also traveled to Fort Wayne to become involved in the firm's operations.[54]

Olof Hedstrom from Norrköping, Sweden, was important in the economic life of Hartford City, Blackford County, in the early part of the twentieth century. He received a degree in civil engineering in Sweden and then went to Germany where he studied making greaseproof glassine paper. In 1905 Hedstrom immigrated to the United States and settled in Hartford City. The Hartford City Paper Company introduced this semitransparent and greaseproof glassine paper to the nation in 1907, and Hedstrom supervised its production.[55]

## Assimilation and Institutions

Generally Nordic people desired to become part of mainstream America as quickly as possible. They were eager to learn English, to become naturalized citizens, and to participate in the democratic process. Generally Scandinavians were Republican before the 1929 depression. In the 1930s a sizable number supported Franklin D. Roosevelt's New Deal program and the Democratic party. In areas where Scandinavians became widely dispersed, as was the case with Indiana, the Americanization process was rapid. Despite their relatively small number, by 1940 Scandinavian born were living in all but five of Indiana's ninety-two counties. Marriages frequently took place with "old stock" Americans or other ethnic groups, most often with fellow Scandinavians. Danes in particular were considered one of the most assimilable ethnic groups in America. Certainly factors contributing to this rapid assimilation were common values of democracy and individualism, a Protestant faith, a strong work ethic, and, with the exception of the Finns, some linguistic similarities.

However, in areas where Scandinavians settled as communities they were able to organize their own churches and secular groups that in turn reinforced traditions and slowed down the assimilation process, particularly in rural communities. On the other hand, churches and fraternal groups aided the Scandinavian in coping with difficulties stemming from homesickness and anxiety feelings about his/her new surroundings and helped the immigrant in adjusting and making a smoother transition to his/her adopted country.

The Swedes established four immigrant churches in the United States—the Lutheran Augustana Synod (organized in 1860) that initially included Norwegians until 1870, the Mission Friends that became known as the Swedish Mission Covenant Church, Swedish Methodists, and Swedish Baptists. Prior to 1917 the Norwegians had three main Lutheran groups—the Norwegian Evangelical Lutheran Church of America or Norwegian Synod, the United Norwegian Lutheran Church, and the Norwegian Evangelical Lutheran Synod in America, commonly called Hauge's Synod. In 1917 these three merged to form the Norwegian Lutheran Church of America, the largest Nordic religious organization in the country. Danish Lutherans were divided into the Danish Lutheran Church in America, the United Evangelical Lutheran Church in America or Blair Synod, and the Grundtvigian Danish Lutheran Church in America. Also there were Norwegian and Danish Baptists and Methodists. The Finns had three Lutheran groups—the Suomi Synod, the Apostolic Lutherans, and the National Lutherans. Today all the

*Servers, Bethlehem Lutheran Church bazaar, Chesterton, 1908.*

Scandinavian Lutheran groups have merged into the Evangelical Lutheran Church in America (ELCA). The Swedish Mission Covenant Church is the Evangelical Covenant Church of America, the Methodists are part of the United Methodist Church, and the Baptists have merged with larger groups (e.g., Swedish Baptists are now the Baptist General Conference).

In Indiana the Augustana Lutherans organized eleven congregations prior to World War I, all of which continue to exist as Bethany, La Porte (1857); First Lutheran, Attica (1858); Augsburg, Porter (1858); Augustana, Hobart (1862); Augustana, Elkhart (1873); Bethel, Gary (1874); Immanuel, Donaldson (1876); Bethlehem, Chesterton (1879); Gloria Dei, South Bend (1880); Zion, Michigan City (1887); and Bethlehem, Gary (1910). In addition, Calvary Lutheran, Gary (1947) is an outgrowth of Bethlehem Lutheran, Gary; Christ Lutheran, Hammond, was established in 1950; and Good Shepherd, South Bend, organized in 1955, is a daughter congregation of Gloria Dei.[56]

Lars Paul Esbjörn, Tuve Nilsson Hasselquist, Erland Carlsson, and Eric Norelius, the four early pastoral leaders of the Swedish Lutherans in America, were educated and gifted men. In one way or other they were all influenced by the religious revival that swept through large parts of Sweden in the midnineteenth century. They were dissatisfied with the state church in Sweden, particularly its perceived "coldness," but they were not prepared for the numerous sects that they quickly had to deal with in the United States. In addition, they were all temperance advocates. Esbjörn was the first of the group to arrive in America. He wrote letters to his homeland appealing for pastors to help guide the new Swedish communities in the United States, and Hasselquist and Carlsson responded to his call. Hasselquist became the leader, organizing the Augustana Synod in 1860 and becoming its first president. In 1855 Hasselquist started publishing the weekly *Det Gamla och det Nya Hemlandet,* known as *Hemlandet,* as a result of a deep concern about the lack of meaningful contact among the Swedish communities. It was an influential Swedish newspaper that defended the Lutheran faith against other proselytizing groups. With their Republican party, pro-Lincoln, and antislavery viewpoints, the editors of *Hemlandet* molded political opinion among the Swedes for decades. Norelius noted the paper was edited "with eminent tact and ability, used a dignified and

Christian language, and in a spirit in which the Christian peoples recognized themselves."[57]

The Swedish Covenant Church was the most significant dissenting group in Sweden. It focused on conversion and individual Christian lifestyle rather than on doctrine and institutions. In 1885 two rival synods in the United States following this tradition merged to form the Swedish Evangelical Mission Covenant Church, later to be called the Evangelical Covenant Church.[58] This denomination has eight congregations in Indiana: Garyton Mission Covenant Church of Portage, organized in 1873 (later the congregation split and a Swedish Free Church was organized); Church of Gary Covenant, Gary; Evangelical Mission Covenant Church of East Chicago; Evangelical Covenant Church of Donaldson; Evangelical Covenant Church of South Bend (originally Swedish Evangelical Lutheran Mission Church); Evangelical Covenant Church of Lafayette (earlier there were two Covenant congregations in the Lafayette area—the Wea Plains Church joined the Lafayette group in 1928); Christ the King Covenant, Crown Point; and Hope Evangelical Covenant, Indianapolis.[59]

Swedish Methodists formed their first congregations in New York City in 1845 and in Victoria, Illinois, the following year. They had congregations in Yorktown (Tippecanoe County), Chesterton, and Hobart. The Swedish Baptists have existed since 1852 when they were organized in Rock Island, Illinois. Their Indiana congregations were in La Porte and South Bend. None of the Methodist or Baptist groups currently exists as separate congregations in Indiana. The only Danish congregation in Indiana was Indianapolis's Danish Evangelical Lutheran Trinity Church, now known as First Trinity Evangelical Lutheran. There was a Norwegian Lutheran Church in Gary identified as the Central Lutheran Church of the Norwegian Synod, but by 1932 it had only twenty-four members and was merged with Bethlehem Lutheran in Gary.[60]

Generally the pastors had significant influence in trying to maintain the Nordic languages and traditions in the United States. In 1915 services in the Swedish language were conducted in about two thousand churches and chapels across the country. In that year the Augustana Synod had nearly 200,000 active members, and the various Norwegian Lutheran churches over 450,000.[61] It was at that time, however, that the churches began introducing English into the worship service. The First World War was certainly a major factor in stimulating this trend. Scandinavians were under pressure from intense American nationalism during the war to adopt English. Many Scandinavians wanted to make certain Americans did not confuse their languages with German. In addition,

the second generation was rapidly drifting away from the Swedish language and traditions. The Swedish-language Saturday schools set up by the churches were disappearing by 1915.

A brief survey of the Swedish churches in Indiana shows that this nationwide English language trend was here as well. In First Lutheran, Attica, an announcement was made in the 29 October 1896 issue of the *Fountain-Warren Democrat* that a funeral service for a parishioner would be conducted in both Swedish and English. At First Lutheran between 1905 and 1920 the English-language worship services gradually increased. In 1913 the congregation voted to have an English service the first Sunday morning and the third Sunday evening of each month. In 1922 Swedish was no longer spoken in the Young Peoples Endeavor Society, and three years later English was used in all Sunday morning services. In 1940 the congregation was renamed the First Evangelical Lutheran Church, "Swedish" being dropped from the title. One year earlier julotta, the traditional Swedish early Christmas morning service, was discontinued.[62]

Other congregations followed similar patterns. Augsburg Lutheran Church of Porter dropped the three-week Swedish summer school in 1912, and the last Swedish service was in 1924. Despite stiff resistance at the Augustana Lutheran Church of Hobart's congregational meeting of 1913, the members voted to have four services each year in English. By 1921 there was only one Swedish service per month, and English was used in all business meetings. In 1938 all worship services were conducted in English. The Willing Workers Society, composed of young married couples of the Augustana Lutheran Church of Elkhart, decided in 1911 that its meetings would be conducted in English. Many young people had married non-Swedes who spoke no Swedish. By 1933 the members of the entire congregation decided that the English service would be held at 10:45 A.M., Swedish at noon, and English again at 7:00 P.M. The Swedish service did not survive long.

In other congregations the Swedish language held on somewhat longer. In more rural Donaldson Immanuel Lutheran Church continued until 1938 to use Swedish in its morning worship service. Since South Bend continued to attract Swedish immigrants to its industries, Gloria Dei did not discontinue Swedish until 1941.[63] The Covenant churches generally followed the same pattern, although nationally they retained the Swedish language longer than the Lutherans. In contrast to the Lutherans many of the Covenant churches continued to have Swedish-American pastors. The last Scandinavian church in Indiana to discontinue the old language was Danish Evangelical Lutheran Trinity Church in

Indianapolis; the final Danish service was in 1956. Once the churches changed to English they were more willing to cooperate with American congregations. First Lutheran of Attica, for example, in 1924 began to participate with other congregations in occasional union services, and the following year it began to be represented by its pastor in commencement, baccalaureate, and Memorial Day services.[64]

Not all Scandinavians attended their ethnic churches. In fact, among Swedish-born settlers and their children, those who belonged to these congregations never made up more than one-fourth of the total number of Swedish immigrants (the figure was higher for the Norwegians, but lower for the Danes).[65] Undoubtedly many attended "American" churches, particularly Scandinavians who were isolated from their own ethnic communities. This was clearly the case in Indiana where they became members of various denominations, particularly Methodists and Presbyterians.

A number joined social and fraternal organizations, another important group of institutions that strengthened the ethnic bond by maintaining the language and cultural values. The first secular organizations were mutual benefit societies and/or charitable organizations and were generally founded by educated and economically prosperous urban people. Most of them were established in the three decades prior to World War I. For the Swedes, several were organized in Chicago, including the Independent Order of Vikings established in 1890. The most successful one was the Vasa Order of America (Vasa Orden av Amerika) founded in New Haven, Connecticut, six years later. Its purposes were "to establish and maintain funds for support for members who through sickness or accident were unable to work and support themselves; to establish and maintain funds for funeral benefits to deceased relatives. . . . To educate members in moral, social aspects and make them more valuable representatives of the Swedish nation."[66] Today the Vasa Order focuses on remembering Swedish heritage by sponsoring programs and celebrating special holidays.

The Sons of Norway (Sønner av Norge) was begun as a mutual insurance organization in the mid-1890s in Minneapolis. It is modeled after American fraternal lodges but focuses on developing and maintaining interest in Norwegian culture. The Danish Brotherhood (Det Danske Brodersamfund) is even older, having been founded in 1866 in Omaha, Nebraska, originally as an insurance plan for Danish war veterans. Sixteen years later it was reorganized to include the preservation of Danish culture.[67]

All these groups were or are represented in Indiana. Erik Lodge No. 48 of the Independent Order of Vikings was organized in La Porte in 1916 with forty charter members. Another Viking lodge was active in South Bend early in the twentieth century. The Vasa Order of America has three lodges in Indiana—Linne Lodge No. 153 of South Bend founded in 1909; Svea Lodge No. 253 established in Indianapolis in 1913 with forty-two charter members led by Gust Rosberg, an immigrant tailor; and Gary Lodge No. 484 dating from 1926. The Danish Brotherhood of America had lodges in South Bend and Indianapolis, the latter organized in 1905 with eleven charter members. The Danish Sisterhood of America also had lodges in these two cities. Four Sons of Norway lodges have recently been organized—in Chesterton (Scandiana Lodge) in 1985, in Carmel near Indianapolis (Circle City Lodge) in 1991, in Fort Wayne (Tre Elver or Three Rivers Lodge) in 1993, and in South Bend (Knute Rockne Lodge) in 1995.[68]

Nationally these organizations generally peaked in membership during the 1920s. The Vasa Order, for example, had seventy-two thousand members in over four hundred lodges by 1929. Because many of these societies steadfastly maintained the Scandinavian languages, they had less appeal to the second and third generations, resulting in steadily decreased memberships.

A third institution that tried to hold on to the languages and cultures of Scandinavia and to maintain contact among individuals and communities was the immigrant press. The Norwegian-American and Swedish-American presses were important links with the widely scattered immigrant population. In the period 1905–15 there were some 60 Swedish weekly newspapers and 230 biweekly or monthly publications. By 1915 the total circulation of the 72 more significant Swedish newspapers and other periodicals reached 650,000. For the Swedes the most significant newspapers were *Hemlandet* and *Svenska Amerikanaren*. The former reflected the attitudes of the Augustana Synod, the latter expressed a more liberal point of view. Johan Enander, a fiery Swedish patriot, became the editor and then owner of *Hemlandet*. He believed the Swedes should overcome any sense of inferiority, and he gave rousing speeches extolling Swedish culture and traditions. Two influential Norwegian newspapers, published in Chicago, were *Skandinaven* and *Scandia*.[69]

On the other hand, the immigrant press played a more limited role among second- and third-generation Scandinavian Americans. In a master's dissertation written in 1950 entitled "A Study of Assimilation among the Swedes at Attica, Indiana," Swedish-American Harry Linn commented on the significance of the immigrant press among the foreign born and the native (American) born. He discovered that eight of the twelve foreign-born

Swedes he interviewed subscribed to some Swedish newspaper or periodical, but only four of the twenty-four native-born informants of foreign-born parents subscribed at one time to a Swedish newspaper or magazine. Not one of the native born of mixed or native-born parents, who totaled forty-eight in his study, had subscribed to any Swedish publications. Linn found that the underlying reason for taking a publication was "because they wished to keep in touch with the Lutheran Church and/or probably secure news and gossip not available in the American press." Although the number of people involved in this study was small, it shows the importance of the immigrant press for the foreign born and its insignificance with the native born.[70]

Linn pointed out in his study that changes in food habits came very slowly. Linn found thirty-eight of the seventy-eight informants over twenty-one years old (both foreign and native born) maintained homes in which they occasionally served some Swedish food. Parenthetically, Swedish songs were seldom sung.[71] On the other hand, assimilation moved more rapidly with respect to naturalization, the Americanization of first and last names, and marriage with other ethnic groups. Linn discovered that fourteen of the fifteen foreign-born informants became naturalized citizens. Among the second-generation Swedes (native born of foreign-born parents), twelve of the thirteen males and four of the nine females married Americans. Of the native born of mixed parents, all five of the males and all six of the females married Americans. Although a small sampling, this study showed that in the Attica community there was considerable intermarriage among ethnic groups.[72]

Americans generally had positive opinions about the Nordic immigrants. Scandinavians became involved in most of a community's activities, including its political, economic, and social aspects. Linn found that Swedes in Attica were distributed throughout the community. He found Americans generally had friendly attitudes toward the Swedes. "Newspaper items show that the Attica Swedes and their descendants were, with very few exceptions, considered law abiding citizens and assets to the community."[73] Their Lutheran beliefs proved to be an asset in an overwhelmingly Protestant community such as Attica. The negative comments about the Swedes generally were complaints about the occasional drunken row. Eric Norelius bemoaned an incident in Buena Vista, Hamilton County, which was the home of some Swedes before 1857. He stated that "they enjoyed a good reputation until a young man from Gothenburg proved guilty of fraud in business matters and disappeared. This cast a pall of suspicion on all the Swedes in the place who suffered though innocent, and became anxious to leave."[74]

Far more serious was the story of Belle Gunness, born Brynhild Poulsdatter in Norway in 1859, who perhaps murdered as many as forty-two male suitors on her isolated farm outside La Porte in the first decade of this century.[75] But aside from this dreadful story, most Scandinavians were law abiding and were generally highly regarded by their American neighbors.

Scandinavians occasionally showed negative attitudes toward other ethnic groups, particularly those that were overwhelmingly Roman Catholic. Perhaps the most serious problem was the one between Swedes and Poles in South Bend, focusing on labor unrest in 1885. There were some isolated examples of sympathy with the Ku Klux Klan, but on the whole Scandinavians and other ethnic groups got along quite amicably.

## The Contemporary Era

Currently the Scandinavians of Indiana are few in number and generally affluent. Most people who display an active interest in Scandinavian culture are recent arrivals from other states (only a handful have arrived directly from Scandinavia), drawn to Indiana by business opportunities. Vasa lodges in Indianapolis, Gary, and South Bend continue to exist. In Carmel near Indianapolis is the Circle City Lodge of the Sons of Norway with some 100 members. Both the Indianapolis Vasa and Sons of Norway lodges participate in the city's annual International Festival.[76] The Scandiana Lodge of the Sons of Norway in Chesterton has a current membership of 130. Its activities include classes in rosemaling (richly colored floral folk painting) and participation in the annual Harvest Festival the third week in September at the nearby Chellberg Farm, where lefse, a Norwegian bread rolled thin and baked on a grill, is a featured food. Chellberg Farm also sponsors Walpurgis Night and St. Lucia festivals that are traditional Swedish events.[77]

The Fort Wayne Scandia Club, in existence for some seventy-five years, is an active 220-member organization including people of both Scandinavian and non-Scandinavian backgrounds. The majority of current members have come from other states and represent many career groups, including a number of engineers. The club meets four times a year to celebrate Danish Fastelavns (similar to Mardi Gras), Swedish Midsummer, Leif Ericsson Day, and St. Lucia's Day. Its members participate in Fort Wayne's Three Rivers Festival, held in mid-July, where a booth serves Scandinavian foods. A Scandinavian cookbook has been written by members of the Scandia Club.[78] In West Lafayette a group of Norwegian Americans annually celebrates Syttende Mai (17 May), Norway's Constitution Day, at the home of the city's five-term Democratic mayor Sonya Margerum. Margerum, whose grandparents were from the Stavanger region of southwestern Norway, hails from Minnesota and is a graduate of St. Olaf College. This group first began meeting in 1955, and its numbers have grown to approximately 100, mainly "transplants" from other states, many of whom are connected with Purdue University.[79] There is also a Norwegian association in Bloomington composed mostly of Indiana University personnel.

Scandinavian languages are seldom heard in today's Indiana churches. Julotta services, lutefisk dinners, and even genuine smorgasbords are events of the past. However, several churches still celebrate St. Lucia's Day (13 December), known for a charming ritual in which a young girl dressed in a white dress with a crown of lighted candles on her head appears and serves various Swedish foods. It is perhaps the only major Swedish cultural festival that has survived.[80]

Scandinavian heritage, however, appears in other ways in Indiana's past and present. There are at least three place names in Indiana associated with Scandinavians—Norway, north of Monticello in White County; Lake Dalecarlia in Lake County; and Lapland, a small village laid out in the 1880s in Montgomery County about eight miles south of Crawfordsville.[81] In La Porte there is a small Swedenborgian church in the Gothic Revival style built when the congregation was organized in 1859. The first public lecture of the Swedenborgian faith had been held in La Porte seventeen years earlier. Emanuel Swedenborg (1688–1772), Swedish scientist, religious teacher, and mystic, spent the last three decades of his life devoted to theological studies and writings filling some thirty volumes. "Eternal life he regarded as an inner condition, a continuation of personal existence on a spiritual plane." Probably Indiana's most prominent Swedenborgian was Johnny Appleseed (John Chapman), who spread this faith as well as apple seeds among settlers in Indiana, Ohio, and Michigan.[82]

A number of prominent Scandinavians or Scandinavian Americans have had connections with Indiana. On her famous singing tour of the United States, Jenny Lind, Sweden's famed soprano known as the "Swedish Nightingale," visited Madison in 1851.[83] John Sigvard "Ole" Olsen was born in Peru in 1892 to Norwegian immigrant parents. He and Harold Ogden "Chic" Johnson teamed up in 1914 to produce a memorable vaudeville comedy team. Olsen and Johnson appeared in two motion pictures and were stars on a half-hour prime-time television show in the late 1940s.[84] Col. Eli Lilly, founder of the giant Eli Lilly pharmaceutical company, claimed Swedish ancestry. His family tree was traced back to the 1200s to the province of Södermanland, west of Stockholm. In the mid-1450s Gregeer Mattson, one of his ancestors, adopted the name Lillja. Later generations of the family moved first to France, where the spelling was changed to Lilly, then to Holland and to England before immigrating to Maryland in 1789.[85]

Knute Rockne, the University of Notre Dame's famed head football coach from 1918 to 1931, was born in Voss, Norway, a town from which numerous Norwegian immigrants have come. The original spelling of his surname was "Rokne." In Voss his father Lars manufactured two-wheeled seated carts known as stolkjerre. In 1891 Lars displayed one of these carriages at the Chicago Columbian Exposition and decided to remain in that city. A year and a half later Lars sent for his wife and three children. The Rocknes lived in Chicago's Logan Square neighborhood where there were large numbers of Norwegians and Irish. Knute attended Notre Dame as a student and then was hired as a chemistry instructor and assistant football coach. He was frequently sought out as an after-dinner speaker, and in 1928, along with his head coaching position, became sales promotion manager for Studebaker. He was killed in an airplane crash in 1931, and some one hundred thousand people lined the route from the Notre Dame campus to Highland Cemetery to pay final tribute to their hero. A bronze bust of Rockne is in the Knute Rockne Memorial Building at the university. There also are exhibits of the coach at the Indiana Football Hall of Fame in Richmond. In Voss, Norway, a memorial plaque dedicated in 1962 commemorates this "Giant of American Football."[86]

Two recent presidents of Purdue University claimed Scandinavian ancestry. Frederick L. Hovde, president of Purdue for twenty-five years before his retirement in 1971, spent his boyhood at Devils Lake, North Dakota. He was the first son of a second-generation Scandinavian immigrant family. His paternal grandfather was from Romesdahlen near Oslo, and his maternal grandfather was from Vortofta, province of Skåne, Sweden. The Executive Building of the Purdue campus was renamed the Frederick L. Hovde Hall of Administration in 1975. Arthur G. Hansen succeeded Hovde as president and remained in that position until 1982. He was from Sturgeon Bay, Wisconsin, and his parents were of Scandinavian descent. His mother was the twelfth child of the Gilbert Andersens who had emigrated from Norway.[87]

Scandinavian Americans have been active in the struggle to preserve the Indiana Dunes. Chicago landscape architect Jens Jensen, of Danish ancestry, was described as "the most eloquent of those who first spoke out on behalf of the preservation of the Dunes."[88] He was responsible for landscaping Marquette Park in Gary.

Famed Swedish-American author Carl Sandburg also took an active interest in the Dunes. His home, "Chickaming Farm," was in nearby Harbert, Michigan. Sandburg was born in Galesburg, Illinois, in 1878, the son of Swedish immigrants.

There are several works of art by Scandinavian or Scandinavian-American sculptors in Indiana. Norwegian-born Sigvald Asbjornsen was commissioned the sculptor for the Soldiers and Sailors Monument (also known as the Middleton Monument) in Madison. It was designed in 1908 to honor the Jefferson County residents who fought in the Civil War. George Middleton, a veteran of the Civil War, was responsible for having the monument erected. Asbjornsen settled in Chicago after he immigrated in 1892, and he worked on some of the buildings at the Columbian Exposition. He was responsible for a number of Civil War monuments and other statues (e.g., Leif Ericsson statue in Humboldt Park, Chicago) throughout the United States.[89]

The Wendell Willkie bronze plaque in the Indiana State Capitol was by Norwegian-American sculptor Paul Fjelde. Lars Fletre from Voss, Norway, was the artist for "Lumberjack," a larger-than-life wood sculpture for Chester B. Stern, Inc., a wood veneer company in New Albany.[90] In Martin Luther King, Jr., Memorial Park in Anderson is an eight-foot bronze statue of the famed Civil Rights leader by Swedish-American artist-sculptor Ken Rydén of the Anderson University art faculty.[91] Other works by Rydén in Indiana include "The Beloved," a ten-foot bronze sculpture of John the Apostle designed for St. John's Hospital, Anderson; "The Crucible of Peace," City Building, Anderson, and some sculpture on the Anderson University campus; "Brothers," commemorating the five brothers who founded Ball Brothers Corporation, Muncie (the cast bronze sculpture is in the entry of Ball Brothers Corporation headquarters, Muncie); and the Samuel Morris sculpture on the Taylor University-Upland campus (Morris was a Liberian student who attended that school in the early 1890s, then known as Fort Wayne College).

Famed Finnish architects Eliel Saarinen and his son Eero were commissioned to design several buildings in Columbus and Fort Wayne. Both father and son designed the First Christian Church in Columbus, which was constructed in 1942. Eliel Saarinen's wife, Loja, directed the weaving of the altar tapestry, possibly the largest tapestry ever woven in the United States. The tapestry, depicting the Sermon on the Mount, was completed at the Cranbrook Academy of Art in Bloomfield Hills, Michigan, where the Saarinens were teachers. Also in Columbus, Eero Saarinen designed the glass-enclosed Irwin Union Bank and Trust Company (completed in 1954) and the hexagonal-shaped North Christian Church with its 192-

*St. Swithun's Viking Church, Marshfield, Indiana.*

foot-high spire, the last building to be designed by Eero before his death in 1961.[92]

In the 1950s Eero Saarinen was commissioned to be the architect for the campus of the current Concordia Theological Seminary in Fort Wayne. The campus resembles a northern European village with a centrally located college chapel. Architect Saarinen said of the campus design, "In giving visual expression to Lutheran traditions and objectives, the appropriate concept seemed to be one of common buildings intimately grouped around a central square with the chapel dominating the highest slope; the lesser buildings clustered around it; and the student housing radiating outward. Designing within this villagelike concept, we could achieve a tranquil, unified environment into which the students could withdraw to find a life complete and balanced and still related to the outside world. This villagelike plan also seemed suitable to the gently rolling prairie land—framed by protective forests."[93] Architect Jens Fredrick Larson, born in Boston in 1891 of Swedish-Danish parents, designed a number of college and university buildings in the United States and abroad, including the Wabash College chapel. It is in Georgian style.[94] Three buildings on the Taylor University-Upland campus are named in honor of Scandinavian Americans associated with the college—Grace Olson Hall, Smith-Hermanson Music Center, and Haakonsen Health Center.[95]

A half-scale copy of a thirteenth-century stave church in Oslo's Norsk Folkmuseum, an open air museum, is located on the farm of Reverends Grover and Mildred Williams of Marshfield, Warren County.[96] On their twenty-fifth wedding anniversary in 1984 the couple went to Norway to visit Stavanger, from which place many of Mildred's ancestors had come. Upon returning to Indiana, Mr. Williams personally constructed the church in honor of his wife's Norwegian and Swedish ancestors. The sanctuary, known as St. Swithun's Viking Church and named for Stavanger's patron saint, is used on special occasions such as weddings and baptisms. This lovely structure is a fine example of the underlying sense of pride and fascination that many Scandinavian Americans of Indiana continue to have for the lands of their ancestors.

## Notes

1. Articles about the Nordic groups are in Stephan Thernstrom, ed., *Harvard Encyclopedia of American Ethnic Groups* (Cambridge, Mass.: Belknap Press of Harvard University Press, 1980), Dorothy Burton Skårdal, "Danes," 273–82, A. William Hoglund, "Finns," 362–70, Valdimar Björnson, "Icelanders," 474–76, Peter A. Munch, "Norwegians," 750–61, and Ulf Beijbom, "Swedes," 971–81.

2. Partial list of significant sources on Scandinavian immigration to the United States includes Allan Kastrup, *The Swedish Heritage in America: The Swedish Element in America and American-Swedish Relations in Their Historical Perspective* (St. Paul, Minn.: Swedish Council of America, North Central Publishing Co., 1975); Florence E. Janson, *The Background of Swedish Immigration, 1840–1930* (Chicago: University of Chicago Press, 1931); Carlton C. Qualey, *Norwegian Settlement in the United States* (New York: Arno Press, 1970); Nils Hasselmo, *Swedish America: An Introduction* (New York: Swedish Information Service, 1976); George M. Stephenson, *The Religious Aspects of Swedish Immigration: A Study of Immigrant Churches* (Minneapolis: University of Minnesota Press, 1932); Helge Nelson, *The Swedes and the Swedish Settlements in North America* (New York: Arno Press, 1979); Harald Runblom and Hans Norman, eds., *From Sweden to America: A History of the Migration* (Minneapolis: University of Minnesota Press, 1976); Theodore C. Blegen, *Norwegian Migration to America, 1825–1860* (New York: Haskell House, 1969); June Drenning Holmquist, ed., *They Chose Minnesota: A Survey of the State's Ethnic Groups* (St. Paul: Minnesota Historical Society Press, 1981), 220–322; Kristian Hvidt, *Flight to America: The Social Background of 300,000 Danish Emigrants* (New York: Academic Press, 1975); John I. Kolehmainen, *The Finns in America: A Biographical Guide to Their History* (Hancock, Mich.: Finnish American Historical Library, 1947); Alan H. Winquist, *Swedish American Landmarks* (Minneapolis: Swedish Council of America, 1995). General histories of the Scandinavian countries include Franklin D. Scott, *Sweden: The Nation's History*

(Minneapolis: University of Minnesota Press, 1977); Karen Larsen, *A History of Norway* (Princeton, N.J.: Princeton University Press, 1948); W. Glyn Jones, *Denmark* (London: Benn, 1970); John H. Wuorinen, *A History of Finland* (New York: Published for American-Scandinavian Foundation by Columbia University Press, 1965).

3. Harry Linn, "A Study of Assimilation among the Swedes at Attica, Indiana" (M.A. thesis, Indiana University, 1950), 32.

4. United States Censuses, 1850, 1860, 1880, 1890, 1910, *Indiana's Foreign Born*; 1940, *Characteristics of the Population, Indiana*; 1970, *Social Characteristics for Counties*; 1980, *General Social and Economic Characteristics, Indiana's Foreign Born*; "1860 Census Foreign-Born for Indiana" (Education Division, Indiana Historical Society 1991); "Table A. Foreign-Born Persons by County of Birth for Indiana: 1980," Bureau of the Census, 1990, manuscript; Allen County Public Library-Genealogy Division, Indiana 1880, 1900 Soundex; Nelson, *Swedes and Swedish Settlements*, 52, 59, 121, 122, maps 16, 17.

5. First Trinity Evangelical Lutheran Church, Indianapolis, "Memories on the Occasion of the 40 Years Anniversary of the Organization of Trefoldigheds Dansk Evangeliske Lutherska Kirke, June 28, 1908, Indianapolis, Indiana," translated from the Danish by Elna Jensen.

6. The statistics for the male-female ratio in 1930 were based on United States census reports in Nelson, *Swedes and Swedish Settlements*, 52.

7. "Selected Social Characteristics: 1990." This date is based on a sample and subject to sampling variability.

8. Translation of a letter from Eric Norelius in *Hemlandet*, 2 June 1855, quoted in Nelson, *Swedes and Swedish Settlements*, 59.

9. Ibid.; Ernest J. Moyne, ed. and trans., *Alexandra Gripenberg's A Half Year in the New World: Miscellaneous Sketches of Travel in the United States (1888)* (Newark: University of Delaware Press, 1954), 81–88.

10. However, in the 1850 Indiana census, no Norwegians were listed in Tippecanoe and Fountain counties.

11. Information from Lawrence M. Nelson of Glenview, Illinois; Lawrence M. Nelson, "Two Pioneer Newark [Illinois] Area Families—Lars and Iver Nelson," brochure.

12. Information from Peter T. Harstad, executive director, Indiana Historical Society; Peter T. Harstad, "Ethnicity Is Sometimes Hard to See," Indiana Historical Society *News*, May–June 1992.

13. Quoted in Janson, *Background of Swedish Immigration*, 123, 124.

14. Eric Norelius, *De Svenska Luterska Församlingarnas och Svenskarnes Historia i Amerika*, translated by Conrad Bergendoff as *The Pioneer Swedish Settlements and Swedish Lutheran Churches in America, 1845–1860* (Rock Island, Ill.: Augustana Historical Society, 1984), 209–17.

15. Ibid., 34.

16. Ibid., 209.

17. Ibid., 210.

18. Ronald Johnson, *Vista '76: 120 Years of a Scandinavian-American Community* (New Richland, Minn.: 1976).

19. *Fifty Year Anniversary Book, First Lutheran Church, Attica, Indiana* (1908).

20. Harry Newburg, letter, Indianapolis, 12 Apr. 1992; information from Nancy Weirich, archivist, Tippecanoe County Historical Association, Lafayette; Teresa Sears, conversation with author.

21. *Rainsville Remembers* (Oxford, Ind., 1983), 115–16; Mrs. Edgar Hibbs, interview with the author.

22. Linn, "Study of Assimilation among the Swedes," 52.

23. Twenty Swedish Americans of Fountain, Tippecanoe, Benton, and Warren counties, interviews with the author, First Lutheran Church, Attica, 7 Mar. 1992; Karl J. Korbel, conversation with the author.

24. Information from *Counties of Warren, Benton, Jasper and Newton, Indiana: Historical and Biographical* (Chicago: F. A. Battey and Co., 1883); *Fowler Centennial, 1871–1971, Historical Review* (a historical record compiled by the Benton County Historical Society in cooperation with the Fowler Centennial Executive Committee); *Biographical History of Tippecanoe, White, Jasper, Newton, Benton, Warren, and Pulaski Counties, Indiana,* 2 vols. (Chicago: Lewis Publishing Co., 1899); H. W. Beckwith, *History of Fountain County* (Chicago: H. H. Hill and N. Iddings, Publishers, 1881); *History of Newton County, Indiana, 1985* (Rensselaer, Ind.: Jasper-Newton Counties Genealogical Society, 1985); information from Harold Furr, Fowler, and Benton County Historical Society; Thomas A. Clifton, ed., *Past and Present of Fountain and Warren Counties, Indiana* (Indianapolis: B. F. Bowen, 1913).

25. Norelius, *Svenska Luterska Historia,* 227, 228.

26. Ibid., 226.

27. Ibid., 229, 230.

28. E. D. Daniels, *A Twentieth Century History and Biographical Record of La Porte County, Indiana* (Chicago and New York: Lewis Publishing Co., 1904), 772–73, 782, 783.

29. Ibid., 744, 745.

30. Norelius, *Svenska Luterska Historia,* 232. Additional information on Porter County Swedes in Powell A. Moore, *The Calumet Region: Indiana's Last Frontier* (Indianapolis: Indiana Historical Bureau, 1959), 352–53.

31. Norelius, *Svenska Luterska Historia,* 227.

32. Ibid., 232.

33. *Augsburg Lutheran Church Anniversary Book.* On the front lawn of the Augsburg Lutheran Church is the bell of the second church with a Swedish inscription. The basement of the church contains a well-organized archival room and two old pump organs. A cemetery to the south of the sanctuary contains many Swedish graves. There is an interesting story about Dr. Erik Carlson, former pastor of the Augsburg Lutheran Church who, after retiring, built a planetarium on his farm near the church. Anna-Maud Tranberg, "The Carlson Planetarium in Porter, Indiana," *The Swedish Pioneer Historical Quarterly* 18 (July 1967): 123–27.

34. Matilda Swanson, "School and Early Days in Duneland," series of unpublished articles, vertical file, Westchester Public Library, Chesterton.

35. Anna-Maud Tranberg, "The Burstrom Chapel—An Indiana Swedish Landmark," *The Swedish Pioneer Historical Quarterly* 17 (Apr. 1966): 96–100; "Burstrom Chapel," vertical file, Westchester Public Library. This small structure referred to as the smallest church in Indiana actually was never used as a church except for midweek prayer meetings prior to 1912 and midweek vesper services during the 1930s. Gradually the building fell into disuse and deteriorated. Thanks to the efforts of local residents in the mid-1970s and early 1990s, today it is restored. The interior contains the original student desks as well as the pulpit from the second Augsburg Lutheran sanctuary and an old Hillstrom pump organ. Frederick Burstrom and Jonas Asp, who was one of the first to encourage his countrymen to settle in Porter County, are buried in the Swedish Cemetery. *Pictorial and Biographical Record of La Porte, Porter, Lake and Starke Counties, Indiana* (Chicago: Goodspeed Brothers, 1894), 339–41.

36. Martha Miller, *The Chellberg Family; The Chellberg Farm* (Chesterton, Ind.: Millar Publications, 1982); "Chellberg Farm," vertical file, Westchester Public Library.

37. "C. O. Hillstrom," vertical file, Westchester Public Library.

38. There is a well-organized archives in the Bethlehem Lutheran Church, Chesterton. A room identified as the Swedish Chapel is in the First United Methodist Church of Chesterton to commemorate the former Swedish Methodist congregation. "Churches," vertical file, Westchester Public Library; *The Seventy-fifth Anniversary, 1879–1954: The Bethlehem Evangelical Lutheran Church, Chesterton* (1954); Elmer C. Vedell, comp. and ed., *"The Beginnings," Feb. 12, 1879 to Jan. 1, 1924* (Chesterton, Ind.: Bethlehem Lutheran Church Archives Committee, 1970); Anna-Maud Tranberg, "John Torell and Old Baillytown, Indiana," *The Swedish Pioneer Historical Quarterly* 22 (July 1971): 153–61. There are references to Chesterton churches in *Counties of Porter and Lake, Indiana* (Chicago: F. A. Battey and Co., 1882), 160.

39. "Chesterton Downtown, 1900–1915" and "Chesterton Downtown, 1915–1925," vertical file, Westchester Public Library; *Chesterton Tribune,* 24 Jan. 1985; Westchester Township History, Westchester Public Library; *Chesterton Centennial 1852–1952,* Westchester Public Library.

40. Ed Gustafson, interview with the author; *Chesterton Tribune,* 10 Dec. 1987; *Pictorial and Biographical Record of La Porte, Porter, Lake and Starke Counties,* 214–16.

41. "Hokanson Family," vertical file, Westchester Public Library.

42. Information from the Marshall County Historical Society Museum, Plymouth; Mary Hawkins and Carla Smut Durnan, eds., *The History of Marshall County, Indiana* (Plymouth, Ind.: Marshall County Historical Society, 1986); *70th Anniversary, 1876–1946: Immanuel Lutheran Church of Donaldson;* Dorothy Hokanson, "Immanuel Lutheran Church, Donaldson, Indiana, 1968" (unpublished, Marshall County Historical Society Museum, Plymouth); *After 80 Years: Immanuel Lutheran Church, 1876–1956.*

43. *Gloria Dei Lutheran Church Centennial: 1880–1980* (South Bend, Ind.: Gloria Dei Lutheran Church, 1980); *South Bend Tribune Michiana,* 21 Sept. 1980; Joan Romine, *Copshaholm: The Oliver Story* (South Bend: Northern Indiana Historical Society, Inc., 1978), 33; John Aylward, "Immigrant Settlement Patterns in South Bend, 1865–1917" (unpublished manuscript, Northern Indiana Historical Society, South Bend, 1971), 7, 8; Timothy Edward Howard, *A History of St. Joseph County, Indiana,* 2 vols. (Chicago and New York: Lewis Publishing Co., 1907), 1:424; Helge Swanson and members of Linne Lodge #153 of the Vasa Order, interview with the author; Carol Bradley, conversation with the author; Rev. C. Marcus Engdahl, conversation with author.

44. "Vincent Bendix," vertical file, South Bend Public Library; Kastrup, *Swedish Heritage in America,* 392–93.

45. Engdahl conversation. Some of the Swedes had been employed by Ragnar Benson, a Swedish building contractor in Chicago.

46. *South Bend and the Men Who Have Made It: Historical, Descriptive, Biographical* (Evansville, Ind.: Unigraphic, Inc., 1973), 318, 333.

47. James B. Lane, *"City of the Century": A History of Gary, Indiana* (Bloomington: Indiana University Press, 1978), 16–20; James B. Lane and Ronald D. Cohen, *Gary, Indiana: A Pictorial History* (Norfolk, Va.: The Donning Co., 1983), 15; *Bethel Lutheran Church, 1874–1974; Gary Post-Tribune,* 20 May 1956; "Churches of Lake County," vertical file, Indiana Room, Gary Public Library; *Gary Post-Tribune,* 1931 and 1956 commemorative issues, Calumet Regional Archives, Indiana University Northwest-Gary Library.

48. Articles in Augustana Lutheran Church file, Calumet Regional Archives; Elin B. Christianson letter, 8 Mar. 1992; Edith Bood, "History of the Michigan Avenue United Methodist Church from November 10, 1886 to June 1, 1974"; Ann Weitgenant, *Lake County*

*Heritage* (Dallas, Tex.: Curtis Media Corp., 1990); T. H. Ball, ed., *Encyclopedia of Genealogy and Biography of Lake County, Indiana* (Chicago: Lewis Publishing Co., 1904), 304, 305, 433, 434.

49. Kastrup, *Swedish Heritage in America,* 442–43.

50. Lane, *"City of the Century,"* 44, 50–52, 121. Additional information on Scandinavians in northwest Indiana in Ernie Hernandez, *Ethnics in Northwest Indiana* (Gary, Ind.: Gary Post-Tribune, 1984), 86–88, 149–51.

51. Otto Robert Landelius, *Swedish Place-Names in North America* (Carbondale: Southern Illinois University Press, 1985); Robert M. Taylor, Jr., et al., *Indiana: A New Historical Guide* (Indianapolis: Indiana Historical Society, 1989), 599.

52. Kastrup, *Swedish Heritage in America,* 390–91, 394.

53. Sheryl Vanderstel, interview with the author; *First Trinity Evangelical Lutheran Church, Indianapolis, Indiana, 1868–1943*; Indianapolis Star, 20 Aug. 1911; Holy Rosary/Danish Church Historic District, National Register of Historic Places inventory, nomination form; First Trinity Evangelical Lutheran Church, "Memories."

54. Bert J. Griswold, *Builders of Greater Fort Wayne* (Fort Wayne: n.p., 1926), 216–17, 691–93, and *The Pictorial History of Fort Wayne, Indiana,* 2 vols. (Chicago: Robert O. Law Co., 1917), 2:243–48; Ingrid Swanson, conversation with the author.

55. Olof Hedstrom file, Blackford County Historical Museum, Hartford City; Benjamin G. Shinn, *Blackford and Grant Counties, Indiana,* 2 vols. (Chicago: Lewis Publishing Co., 1914), 1:257; Hartford City News-Times, 6 Nov. 1942.

56. Henry G. Waltmann, ed., *History of the Indiana-Kentucky Synod of the Lutheran Church in America: Its Development, Congregations, and Institutions* (Indianapolis: Central Publishing Co., 1971). West of La Porte, out in the country, is the delightful Carmel Chapel, constructed in 1896, to serve the farmers of the area. The sanctuary is still used occasionally and is maintained by Bethany Lutheran, La Porte. The congregation of Carmel Chapel was always considered part of Bethany Lutheran. There is a well-maintained Swedish cemetery next to Carmel Chapel. In Miller off Route 20 one-third of a mile east of Lake Street is a small cemetery; it is on a hillside to the west of a trailer park. Most of the gravestones have names of early Swedish settlers in Miller.

57. Quoted in Oscar N. Olson, *The Augustana Lutheran Church in America: Pioneer Period, 1846–1860* (Rock Island, Ill.: Augustana Book Concern, 1950), 350; Kastrup, *Swedish Heritage in America,* 233, 376, 377.

58. Information and history of the Evangelical Covenant Church in Karl A. Olsson, *By One Spirit* (Chicago: Covenant Press, 1962).

59. Information from the Evangelical Covenant Church headquarters, Chicago; *50th Anniversary Booklet: The Evangelical Covenant Church of South Bend* (1938); *85th Anniversary Booklet: The Evangelical Covenant Church of South Bend* (1973); *Evangelical Mission Covenant Church Lafayette, Indiana, Diamond Jubilee October 26–28, 1945.*

60. Kastrup, *Swedish Heritage in America,* 180–83 (Swedish Methodists), 239–42 (Swedish Baptists). References to the Norwegian church in Hernandez, *Ethnics in Northwest Indiana,* 151; additional information from Gary Public Library.

61. Linn, "Study of Assimilation among the Swedes," 88; Kastrup, *Swedish Heritage in America,* 637; Munch, "Norwegians," 754–56; Beijbom, "Swedes," 975, 976.

62. Linn, "Study of Assimilation among the Swedes," 89–99.

63. Waltmann, ed., *History of the Indiana-Kentucky Synod.*

64. Linn, "Study of Assimilation among the Swedes," 99, 100, 124, 125.

65. Skårdal, "Danes," 277, 278; Munch, "Norwegians," 754–56; Beijbom, "Swedes," 975, 976.

66. Sven G. Johansson, *Historical Review of Vasa Order of America, 1896–1971* (n.p., n.d.), 4.

67. Skårdal, "Danes," 278–79; Munch, "Norwegians," 758–59; Lawrence M. Nelson, ed., *From Fjord to Prairie: Norwegian-Americans in the Midwest, 1825–1975* (Chicago: Norwegian American Immigration Anniversary Commission, 1976), D2.

68. Swan Swanson, David Heighway, and members of Lodge No. 253, interview with the author, Indianapolis; Martha Clavey, conversation with the author, Gary Lodge No. 484; Helge Swanson, interview with the author, Linne Lodge No. 153, South Bend; Oleif Olsaker, conversation with the author, Sons of Norway Lodge, Chesterton; Nancy Tuznik, conversation with the author, La Porte.

69. Johansson, *Historical Review of Vasa Order of America, 1896–1971,* pp. 193, 199; Nelson, ed., *From Fjord to Prairie,* C22, C23; Kastrup, *Swedish Heritage in America,* 637, 638–39.

70. Linn, "Study of Assimilation among the Swedes," 43, 44, 84, 85.

71. Ibid., 110–14, 116.

72. Ibid., 44–46, 58, 59, 131, 132.

73. Ibid., 47–49, 63–65, 119–21.

74. Ibid., 82, 83; Norelius, *Svenska Luterska Historia,* 408.

75. Information from John Lauritz Larson, West Lafayette; Edward Baumann and John O'Brien, *Murder Next Door: How Police Tracked Down 18 Brutal Killers* (Chicago: Bonus Books, 1991).

76. Swanson and Heighway interview; *Indianapolis News,* 14 May 1991.

77. Dale Engquist and Jack Arnold, interview with the author, Indiana Dunes National Lakeshore; Nancy Tuznik, conversation with the author.

78. Patricia Urberg and Tim Holm, conversations with the author, Fort Wayne.

79. Sonya Margerum and John Lauritz Larson, conversations with the author, West Lafayette.

80. Gloria Dei Lutheran Church, South Bend, has a large and well-established annual St. Lucia Festival, reorganized in 1964 by Pastor C. Marcus Engdahl, that is modeled after festivals from various churches in the United States and Sweden.

81. Landelius, *Swedish Place-Names.*

82. Edith J. Backus, ed., *La Porte, Indiana: History of First Hundred Years, 1832–1932,* 4 vols. (La Porte, Ind., 1932), 2:813–16; Kastrup, *Swedish Heritage in America,* 58, 59; Taylor, et al., *Indiana: A New Historical Guide,* 606.

83. Kastrup, *Swedish Heritage in America,* 256–61.

84. *Indianapolis Star,* 2 June 1974; "Olsen and Johnson and Friends," *Indiana Business and Industry* (July/Aug. 1957): 38.

85. "The Name Lilly," series of articles by J. K. Lilly (son of Col. Eli Lilly), received from Anita Martin, archivist, Eli Lilly and Company, Indianapolis. A biography of Eli Lilly is James H. Madison, *Eli Lilly: A Life, 1885–1977* (Indianapolis: Indiana Historical Society, 1989).

86. Nelson, ed., *From Fjord to Prairie,* B24, B25; Jerry Brondfield, *Rockne: The Coach, the Man, the Legend* (New York: Random House, 1976), 33–37; Robert Quackenbush and Mike Bynum, eds., *Knute Rockne, His Life and Legend: Based on the Unfinished Autobiography of Knute Rockne* (Chicago: October Football Corp., 1988), 42–46.

87. Robert W. Topping, *The Hovde Years: A Biography of Frederick L. Hovde* (West Lafayette: Purdue University, 1980), 3–7, and *A Century and Beyond: The History of Purdue University* (West Lafayette: Purdue University Press, 1988), 246–378.

88. J. Ronald Engel, *Sacred Sands: The Struggle for Community in*

*the Indiana Dunes* (Middletown, Conn.: Wesleyan University Press, 1983), 23, 200–5.

89. The monument is located on the corner of Main and Walnut streets in Madison. Thomas Clemons, conversation with the author, West Lafayette, and John E. Galvin, Madison; Nelson, ed., *From Fjord to Prairie,* B10–11; *Madison Courier,* 28 Feb. 1991.

90. Clemons conversation; *Indianapolis Star Magazine,* 19 Feb. 1950; Nelson, ed., *From Fjord to Prairie,* B17.

91. Ken Rydēn, interviews with the author, Anderson and Upland; Taylor, et al., *Indiana: A New Historical Guide,* 455. The Martin Luther King, Jr., Memorial Park is located at 22nd Street and Pendleton and South Madison avenues.

92. Roger G. Kennedy, *American Churches* (New York: Stewart, Tabori & Chang Publishers, Inc., 1982), 42, 43, 245–47; Balthazar Korab, *Columbus, Indiana: An American Landmark* (Kalamazoo, Mich.: Documan Press, Ltd., 1989), 50–59, 70–81; Albert Christ-Janer, *Eliel Saarinen: Finnish-American Architect and Educator,* rev. ed. (Chicago: University of Chicago Press, 1979); Rupert Spade, *Eero Saarinen* (New York: Simon and Schuster, 1971); Taylor, et al., *Indiana: A New Historical Guide,* 21, 354, 359, 361, 366.

93. Excerpted from "A 'Village' Design for a College Campus," *Progressive Architecture* (Dec. 1958): 88–101; Jeff Oschwald, conversation with the author, Concordia Theological Seminary, 30 June 1992.

94. Kastrup, *Swedish Heritage in America,* 527, 566.

95. Grace D. Olson was a former history professor; Edward Hermanson, building contractor and musician; Lily Haakonsen, longtime campus nurse. William C. Ringenberg, *Taylor University: The First 125 Years* (Grand Rapids, Mich.: William B. Eerdmans Publishing Co., 1973), 149.

96. Reverends Grover and Mildred Williams, interview with the author, Marshfield.

# SCOTS

GORDON R. MORK

> McClelland and Galletly "often were together, both of them ardent admirers of Robert Burns, and I have spent many hours a delighted auditor, when a boy, in the company of those two old Scotchmen, listening to their tales of their beloved Scotland, and hearing them recite Burns' Poems hour after hour. They seemed to have committed to memory everything Burns had ever written."

A study of the Scots of Indiana presents one with an interesting paradox. Of the many ethnic groups that populate the state, the Scots are known for their colorfully visible and recognizable symbols. The lilt of the kilt, the skirl of the pipes, and the burr of the Scottish accent are well known. From Indiana's very beginnings there have been many citizens who trace their families' roots to Scotland, and there are currently over 225,000 of them.[1] Yet, paradoxically, the Scots of Indiana have often been an "invisible" minority.[2] This essay will describe the historical picture of the Scots of Indiana to demonstrate this thesis.

From the earliest days of European settlement in what is now the state of Indiana, Scots were present. Some had been born in Scotland, some were of Scottish ancestry and heritage but had been born in Ireland (the Scotch-Irish), and some had been born on the American continent, but identified themselves as being of Scottish ancestry and heritage. This essay will include all of these groups.[3]

In the 1740s George Croghan, a Pennsylvania trader of Scotch-Irish descent, began to compete with the French traders in the Ohio valley and as far north and west as the Wabash River.[4] Whether Croghan himself blazed the trail for the Indiana Scots who followed is unclear, but his trading enterprises certainly had an impact.

During the struggle for the Old Northwest during the era of the American Revolution, people of Scottish ancestry took a leading role. Both George Rogers Clark, the American hero, and Lt. Gen. Henry Hamilton, the British officer who was forced to capitulate to Clark at Vincennes in 1779, had Scottish ancestors.[5]

Early farmers also were often of Scottish descent. The Buchanan brothers, Wilson (or William), John, and George, arrived in Jefferson County from Pennsylvania about 1813. The brothers were the first white settlers in the area north of the village of Canaan, in Shelby Township, some dozen or so miles north of Madison. There they constructed "Buchanan's Station," a fortified settlement described as follows: "The fort was a square building of sixty feet front, built solid, and pierced with loop-holes for firing from. The upper story—rather the roof—projected over the wall of the main building, so as to overlook the sides. There were four block houses in a line, extending about 300 or 400 feet, in which the families of the country congregated and lived when danger of an Indian raid was feared. It was at this time the extreme frontier of the country in that direction, and was garrisoned the greater part of the time, for three or four years, by the rangers under Capt. Dunn and Capt. Hillis."[6]

Capt. Williamson Dunn, a settler of Scotch-Irish descent, had moved north across the Ohio River from Kentucky and bought a parcel of land in 1808, land on which Hanover College would eventually be built. His son William McKee Dunn, speaking at Hanover College in the late nineteenth century, remembered that the early settlers in the area "were mostly Scotch-Irish Presbyterians," along with a nearby settlement of "Presbyterians of a sterner sort, commonly called Seceders."[7] The area settlers soon set about establishing a school, which Dunn recalled with a mixture of nostalgia and proper critique. "All the benches were narrow, hard

and without backs, and those for little children, as I well remember, were a weariness to the flesh. The masters usually were Scotch or Irish, who believed in doing a good day's work every day themselves, and required the children to do the same. Good beech switches were always on hand back of the teacher's chair ready for use, and I can bear testimony that they *were* used."[8]

The local Presbyterians began a formal congregation in 1819 and erected a building in 1823. The first regular pastor was the Rev. John Finley Crowe. By 1827 he had formalized instruction in a school known as Hanover Academy and had a log cabin especially dedicated for this purpose. Hanover Academy was recognized by a state charter in 1829 and placed under the supervision of the Presbyterian Synod of Indiana the following year. Eventually the institution was recognized as Hanover College by a state charter in 1833.[9] The college remained true to its original religious orientation well into the twentieth century. Of 1,335 graduates in its first century, ending in 1926, 342 became ministers and ordained missionaries, just over 25 percent of the alumni.[10] Wabash College in Crawfordsville was also founded as a Presbyterian school, beginning in 1832.[11] Not all of these early educators and their patrons were Scots, but a large number of them were.

By the early nineteenth century many people with Scottish ancestors were active in Indiana. In 1822 William G. and George W. Ewing became active in the fur trade in the Fort Wayne area. The Ewings traced their heritage to Scotch-Irish forebears from Londonderry, Ireland, who left the British Isles in the mid-eighteenth century because of English repression and poor economic conditions. The family developed frontier trading and farming interests in Pennsylvania and upper New York State before coming to Indiana. Other traders of the 1820s bear the names Edward McCartney and Hugh B. McKeen.[12] John McCormack, a Scot, was said to be the first white settler in Marion County.[13]

Much of the extant information on nineteenth-century citizens comes from the biographical sections of commissioned county histories. The information, difficult to check, is generally highly laudatory of the individuals described, no doubt because the authors hoped to sell the books to the families being described. Yet some of the details are very useful in giving insight into the people of the time. For example, John Shaw and his wife Elizabeth were born in Scotland, in 1776 and 1779, respectively. In 1816 they and their eight children immigrated to the United States. They settled first in Philadelphia, "remaining there about five months, and then, coming to Pittsburgh in a butcher wagon, they proceeded down the Ohio River in a keel-boat to Vevay, and located upon a farm in Craig Township," Switzerland County. "He was a weaver by trade in the old country; here he followed farming exclusively." But they hardly arrived destitute. "Mr. S. left Scotland with moderate means, which was largely used in defraying the expenses of his large family to this country. He succeeded admirably after coming here and left his family comfortably well off." Two of their children also appear in the county history: Archibald Shaw, who came with his parents at the age of four, and James Shaw, also born in Scotland and an immigrant at the age of two. Both began their careers as farmers "inured to the hard labor of the farm in a new country," but James became a merchant and local postmaster. Archibald married Margaret Anderson, who was "a babe in her mother's arms when brought to America" from Scotland in 1817. All were described as devout Christians, members of Methodist and Baptist congregations rather than Presbyterians.[14]

In the 1820s a school was begun in Spencer, Owen County, and held in the log "meeting house" that also served as a church. Pioneers in the area remember the teacher, James Galletly, as a "sturdy old Scotchman. He was a man of varied attainments, and was a very useful member of the community—school teacher, Surveyor, architect, and a fine scholar, his services were largely in demand. Another Scotchman came at a later day, Alexander McClelland by name, a scholar and a gentleman." The narrator recalled that McClelland and Galletly "often were together, both of them ardent admirers of Robert Burns, and I have spent many hours a delighted auditor, when a boy, in the company of those two old Scotchmen, listening to their tales of their beloved Scotland, and hearing them recite Burns' Poems hour after hour. They seemed to have committed to memory everything Burns had ever written."[15]

Unlike some immigrants, the Scots did not settle in Indiana in large cohesive groups, nor did they retain a society separate from the general population. The fact that English, albeit of Scots variety, was their native tongue, that they were perceived as "racially" similar to

**SCOTLAND**
- City
— International
    Boundary
0              200
    Miles

Aberdeen

Glasgow
Edinburgh

N. IRELAND

IRELAND    Irish Sea

WALES    ENGLAND

ENGLISH CHANNEL

FRANCE

Among the early Scottish immigrants, not only were there craftsmen, weavers, miners, and farmers, but also educated professionals. Dr. Robert Gillespie was born in Scotland in 1793, a graduate of the University of Edinburgh (Master of Surgery) and an 1819 immigrant to America. He settled in Cass Township, Ohio County, and then in Dearborn County. In the words of the ethnocentric nineteenth-century chronicler, the good doctor "lived to see the wild woods of his early home converted into peaceful homes, and towns and villages of Christian people taking the place of wandering tribes of savages."[19]

Robert Stevenson of Shelby Township, Jefferson County, combined farming and preaching the gospel. Born in Ayrshire in 1815, he came to the United States at the age of thirteen with his family. Stevenson received his early education in Scotland, but on his American frontier farm he did not have "any advantages of schooling after he came to this country. They had only boards for slates and firecoals for pencils." Nevertheless, "in this way he became able to enter the ministry." He was a minister in the Baptist church and "may be called one of the pioneer preachers of this State." He was proud to point out to his biographer that he "once labored in the Long Run Mission" and "preached 342 days in one year."[20]

A colorful view of pioneer life is seen through the eyes of John Milton McBroom (1822–1892), as published in his reminiscences of early days in Fountain County. His father was among the first men to enter the land office at Crawfordsville in 1823 and to erect cabins in Cain Township, Fountain County. The family was proudly Scotch-Irish. John Milton McBroom's mother, Martha Snodgrass, was said to be "a fine scholar" and saw to the education of all the men of the family, including her husband.

Young McBroom received his early education in a log schoolhouse and from his mother, and "during his youth engaged in school-teaching" himself. He continued his studies on his own and eventually became a preacher in the Christian church and "one of the main up-builders and up-holders of the congregation." He continued to farm some three hundred acres.[21]

The family was not entirely pious. John Milton McBroom's brother, Ithamer Warner McBroom, wrote the following in the *Hillsboro (Ind.) Times,* 4 October 1907: "My grandfather was a hasty and passionate man, having the then national habit, drink; never accumulated much property, but worked himself and family hard to support life in a very poor style, going to the frontier of North Carolina, and then to east Tennessee, taking on other people's land. . . . At the end of a lease, he would sell off all the

most of their neighbors, and that their religious persuasions were not unlike those in the mainstream of early Hoosier society no doubt encouraged rapid assimilation. Nevertheless, identifiable groups are noted in the local histories. For example, in Pleasant Township, Switzerland County, "a colony from Scotland" settled around 1820. "Among them the Culbertsons, Scotts, Greys, Mortons, Glenns, and Makensies." According to the account, "they belonged to the more intelligent class, and as Scotchmen usually are, they were enterprising and industrious."[16] The village of Scotland, Indiana, in Greene County, was founded about the same time, allegedly because of a relatively large Scottish population in the area at the time. Among the early settlers were David and Jane Wallace, who arrived from Edinburgh and built a log cabin in Greene County. Other early settlers in the area were William and James Ferguson of Glasgow, who were active in establishing a school and a Presbyterian church.[17]

Another example is William Muir (1818–1888), a native of Ayrshire, Scotland. He learned the weaver's trade and immigrated to America at the age of twenty-two, joined his brother who had already settled in Wayne County, Indiana, worked for several years as a weaver and merchant, and finally acquired considerable land in Clay and Greene counties raising shorthorn cattle. Muir and his family were major figures in the local Presbyterian church at Howesville.[18]

stock for money, go to town and drink until all was spent, come home, move on and take another lease." McBroom's grandfather finally settled near Terre Haute, Indiana.

The next generation, however, had more discipline, or more luck, or both. John McBroom (1792–1857), father of John Milton and Ithamer, learned the carpentry trade, picked up enough education to read, write, and do arithmetic, and set off for Fountain County, Indiana. Ithamer tells the story of the family's arrival in Indiana in March 1824 as follows:

> His father and mother arrived very poor, with three children, having had a terrible time coming through the wilderness, with no tent cloth except a muslin wagon sheet. It was, as [his] mother and father told it, enough to kill anyone to endure, in such a season of the year to cut brush and pile down to put their beds on to hold them out of the mud and melted snow; then to throw down their beds, putting their driest clothes next to them and the wet ones over all; then to lie down with no roof but heaven and the starry canopy over you, with often two or three inches of snow on the covers; strike fire with a flint, catch it on dry rotten wood, or bark of some rotten log or stump or hollow tree, then to fire some fallen tree in two places, one for the kitchen and one of the parlor, and to dry the bedding of last night; this may be imagined with a weakly mother and three children [including John] Milton, one year and four months [old], all crying with colic and earache.[22]

John Milton McBroom, having survived the difficulties of the pioneer days to become a teacher, preacher, and farmer and prosper modestly, was anxious to pass along this heritage to his children. In February 1880 he wrote the following to his son Harvey, who was away at college at the Normal School then at Ladoga, Indiana. "Enclosed find the seven dollars you required. And again let me ask you that you spend none of it foolishly in tobacco or cigars & etc. . . . I am glad you are getting along so well & trying to make a man of yourself. Keep on trying & you will succeed. . . . Establish a good name among the students, your teachers, & the people generally and then you can meet them in after life with joy & gladness. And you will do credit to the McBroom name."[23]

John Milton McBroom may have lacked the literary greatness of his namesake, but he could tell a pretty good story, particularly when it could be used to warn men and women against the evils of alcohol. One of the best stories concerned a "Jim Mc," who neglected his family to drink and play cards with his cronies at a "still house" in Fountain County. Things got so bad that he "neglected his family and killed his wife by dissipation and was killing himself as fast as the whiskey of that day could kill." That was when the ghost intervened. One night he and his fellow revelers "heard at the further end of the distillery a dreadful, strange, mournful, weird noise with drumming on the head of a barrel. When they went, light in hand to see from whence the noise proceeded, they could find nothing, but heard the same sound in the opposite end of the room." Try as they might, they could not find the origin of the noise, which returned night after whiskey-filled night. "Finally a regular ghost catcher, a Donelson, interviewed the ghost, so he said, and it said she was the shade of Jim Mc's dead wife, and that she would have no rest until Mc would get good homes for her three little boys." The frightened Jim Mc complied, and the trouble ceased.[24]

Among the people who came to Indiana from Scotland were some of fame and fortune. Robert Owen, the entrepreneur and utopian socialist, came to Indiana with his family in the 1820s. Owen was born and raised in Wales but settled in Scotland, married a Scottish wife, Anne Caroline Dale, and his three children who came with him to Indiana were definitely Scottish. In 1825 he purchased the settlement of New Harmony from the Rappites, a German religious group, and he sought to create his perfect society along the Wabash. The venture was not a financial success, but its idealism was widely recognized. Three of Owen's sons accompanied him to Indiana: Robert Dale Owen, David Dale Owen, and Richard Owen, as well as one daughter, Jane Dale Owen Fauntleroy.[25]

Robert Dale was elected to Congress; David Dale became Indiana's first state geologist; and Richard was an officer in the Mexican and Civil wars. In 1864 Richard became professor of natural science at Indiana University and settled in Bloomington, one of seven professors there at the time.[26] He took an active role in the university, sought to bring an agricultural college to Bloomington under the Morrill Act of 1862, and in the community regularly taught Sunday school at the Presbyterian church. He accepted the position as the first president of Purdue University in 1872, while still holding his professorship at Indiana University. Owen immediately came into conflict with the Purdue trustees over precise plans to get the new institution off the ground, and after two years he resigned the presidency.[27] Eventually he retired to New Harmony.

Among the worthies who accompanied Robert Owen to New Harmony in his "Boatload of Knowledge" was William Maclure, who established the Workingmen's Institute in 1838 "to bring scientific and all other useful knowledge within the reach of Manual and Mechanical Laborers, without the aid of professional men as teachers."[28]

George Barr McCutcheon, author, and John T. McCutcheon, editorial cartoonist, descended from the

McCutchen family of Wigtownshire, Scotland, which found its way first to Virginia, then to Ohio, and then to Tippecanoe County in the 1830s. Though the family readily acknowledged its Scottish ancestry, Scottish ethnicity seems to have meant little to them. Both men had successful careers and traveled widely, but Scotland and things Scottish seemed to have no special attraction to them.[29]

The Meharry family established itself in Tippecanoe, Fountain, and Montgomery counties in the 1820s and 1830s. Family research and traditions traced their ancestry back to Lowlanders who left Scotland for northern Ireland, seeking religious freedom.[30] The family settled first in Ohio, but three of the sons sought better and cheaper land then opening in Indiana. They made a trip on horseback to Indiana in 1827, camping along the way and spading up the countryside as they went along to determine where they might find some good farmland. They selected some land near Crawfordsville at $1.25 per acre and returned to Ohio to find good wives and make the move west.

A Meharry family tradition illustrates the courting customs of the age and, perhaps, the proverbial penuriousness of the Scots. One of the three brothers, Thomas Meharry, came "a-sparking" to the home of the lady of his desires, one Eunity Patton in Brown County,

*Photograph of the Heshbon Bethel Church cornerstone.*

HISTORY OF THE MEHARRY FAMILY IN AMERICA... (LAFAYETTE, IND.: LAFAYETTE PRINTING CO., 1925)

Ohio. As a present he brought her a bag of apples. Shrewdly he watched how his potential bride treated the gift. "Would she pare the apples with a thick peeling? Would she waste a lot in quartering and coring the apples? Eunity, unconscious that a crucial test was being applied to her, ate seeds, core, rind and all, wasting nothing." Meharry had found the woman of his dreams. They were married 4 December 1827 and set off for the "wilds of Indiana" in May 1828.[31]

The Meharrys were Methodists, strongly opposed to the consumption of alcohol and fiercely critical of slavery. In 1837 the Meharrys and their neighbors near Shawnee Mound, Tippecanoe County, decided to erect a church building that they called "Heshbon Bethel." The little structure was to serve both as a church and a school. James Meharry's inscription on the cornerstone is a document that gives us important insights into the attitudes of these Scotch-Irish pioneers and deserves to be quoted in full:

Oct. A.D. 1837
or the
61st year of American Independence.
Fifteen years past in the prairies and groves
the red men of the wilderness
had their council fires and wigwams,
where their squaws lived and raised their papooses
and savage Indian and prowling wolf
had full possession of the plain,
but now those people are extinct
and schools and churches are growing up
for the instruction of the children
and the worship of God.
Wilderness rejoiced and the places are glad
by reason of vast change.
May God continue to send out his light and truth
into all the earth.[32]

The inscription implies much about the attitudes of these settlers. Their patriotism as Americans is evident, as is their concern for education and religion. The attitude shown toward the Native Americans is noteworthy, combining a grudging respect for those who had raised families in the region before them and an unhealthy condescension equating the "red men" with savage beasts. Indians were, of course, by no means "extinct" in Indiana in 1837. Indeed, the major Indian removal, which passed through the other end of Tippecanoe County, occurred just the next year.

Members of the Meharry family were generous in their support of education. In 1869 Jesse Meharry offered the state of Indiana his 394-acre farm at Shawnee Mound if it would establish its agricultural school there, but the state accepted the gift of John Purdue of Lafayette instead. The Meharrys donated significant amounts of money to DePauw University at Greencastle and were instrumental in establishing a medical college for African Americans in Nashville, Tennessee, in 1876.[33]

Not all of the Indiana Scots were of lowlander extraction. Andrew McCorkle traced his ancestors to the highlands, where they were known as the "Clan Nan Guinneath" or "Clan Gun," a "plaided clan" of "fierce warriors." The first McCorkles of the line came to America in 1730, and the family migrated from Philadelphia to Virginia, to Kentucky, and finally to a farm near Crawfordsville, Indiana. Andrew McCorkle and his wife Mary had thirteen children, the next to youngest of whom was a daughter, Margaret, born in 1843. The parents were strict Presbyterian Calvinists, and farmwork stopped at noon on Saturday to prepare for the Sabbath. "The boys would shave, shine their boots, and see that the 'carryall' and horses were in readiness. Mother and the girls were busy baking and roasting, for there would be no cooking, not even the preparation of hot coffee on the Sabbath day." Church services, with a noontide intermission, totally occupied the family on Sunday.

The family stories of the life of young Margaret during the Civil War give some insight into the social history of the period. Margaret was eighteen when the war began. It was her duty to till the fields, working "side by side with her aged father," while four brothers served at the front. During the war years "she became very proficient in the use of firearms." There was tension in Montgomery County, and the "pro-slavery people called her father 'the old abolitionist,'" so she felt it was necessary to be able to shoulder a musket to protect the family. In 1869 she married William Meharry and raised three children.[34]

Not all Indiana Scots became permanent settlers, of course. Some were sojourners who lived here for only a time and then moved on. One prominent example is John Muir, for whom Muir Woods in California was eventually named. Born in Scotland, he came to America with his parents at the age of nine. In 1866 Muir arrived in Indianapolis as a man of twenty-eight, with a background as a farm boy and student of mechanics and biology in Wisconsin. Merrill Moores recalled him as "a tall sturdy man with blue eyes and . . . a marked Scotch accent."

Muir stayed in Indiana less than two years, but they were crucial years in his life. He had a genius for invention and began a promising career as a woodworker and mechanic. In those boom years following the Civil War he might have become a wealthy industrialist. But while working in the shop he injured his eyes, and for a time was entirely blind. When he recovered he decided that his love of the outdoors beckoned him to become a naturalist, and he left Indiana "joyful and free," carrying a copy of Burns's poems and singing them along the way, first to the Gulf of Mexico, and then on to California.[35]

The development of coal mining in the Indiana countryside during the second half of the nineteenth century created the need for skilled miners. Many of these men came from Scotland, creating statistical bulges in Clay and Greene counties in the lists of the foreign born. Towns were named to encourage Scottish

*Andrew McCorkle and his wife Mary (Gooding) McCorkle.*

*William (left) and John R. Murdock, coal miners originally from Scotland, ca. 1912. The man in the middle is unidentified.*

population settlement, such as Perth in Clay County, founded by Michael McMillan in 1870.[36] The coal mines provided work that was rough, dirty, and dangerous, and many of the men who went into the mines, including the immigrants from the mines of Scotland, lived harsh lives. Some of these miners assumed positions of leadership. Samuel Anderson was born in Britain in 1843 and raised by his grandfather at Kinkintillock, Dumbartonshire, Scotland. His grandfather was a weaver, and he put the boy to work at the loom at the age of nine. At the age of eleven Anderson went to live with an uncle in Ayrshire, working with his uncle in the mines.[37] He married a Scottish lass, Isabella Wilson, in 1860, and she bore him fourteen children. He came to America in 1870, and his family came in 1871. They settled in Knightsville, Clay County, Indiana, where Anderson worked as a miner. In 1884 he represented local miners at the Knights of Labor assembly in Philadelphia, and in 1888 he was elected to the Indiana General Assembly. The author of the county history extolled him as "a good, conservative and worthy citizen" who had written articles on the state of his craft.[38]

John Andrew was even more successful. Born in Culochrig, Scotland, in 1827, he went into the mines at the age of nine, but was an entrepreneur before his marriage in his early twenties, leasing and operating small mines. In 1853 he came to America and was attracted to Indiana by companies that were beginning to prospect for coal around the Indiana towns of Terre Haute and Brazil. According to the Clay County history, Andrew was credited with being the last survivor of the party that put down the first shaft and hoisted the first block coal in the state, and eventually with putting down more coal shafts than anyone else in the history of Indiana.[39]

At least four Indiana governors were of Scottish ancestry. David Wallace, born in Pennsylvania of Scottish stock, served as quartermaster to William Henry Harrison in the War of 1812. He attended West Point, studied law, practiced in Brookville, Indiana, and was elected governor in 1837 as a Whig, serving until 1840.[40] Oliver Perry Morton, governor from 1861 to 1867, was of Scottish and English ancestry. In his early years he "seems to have received an overdose" of "Scotch Presbyterianism" in the home of two aunts with whom he lived. Warren Terry McCray, governor from 1921 to 1924, was of Scotch-Irish ancestry, tracing his lineage to William McCrae of Kintial, Rosshire, Scotland. Paul Vories McNutt, governor from 1933 to 1937, traced his ancestry to the MacNaughts of Kilguharity, Scotland, in the fifteenth century.[41]

Gen. Lew Wallace of Crawfordsville, the son of Governor Wallace, artist T. C. Steele, songwriter Hoagy Carmichael, and the Lockerbie family of Indianapolis all can claim Scottish ancestry. But Scottish heritage did not seem to manifest itself in their lives or works. Like a great many families of Scottish and Scotch-Irish ancestry, they had become thoroughly American, and even when traveling abroad or collecting objects from foreign lands they paid little attention to things Scottish.[42] It must be remembered, however, that much of the "distinctive national apparatus" of the Scots was developed only during the nineteenth century in Britain, from rather thin historical roots. Kilts, tartans, and highland regalia in general were largely the fruits of romantic imaginations, beginning with the visit of King George IV to Edinburgh in 1822, a visit staged with specially invented highland "traditions" managed by Sir Walter Scott.[43]

The Scottish Rite Cathedral, one major institution in Indianapolis that one might think is closely connected with things Scottish, really is quite unrelated to Scotland. The cathedral, a Neo-Gothic landmark in downtown Indianapolis, was constructed by the Ancient Accepted Scottish Rite in the Valley of Indianapolis, part of the Northern Masonic Jurisdiction of the United States, during the 1920s. The Scottish Rite started in Paris, France, in the 1750s, whence it found its way to Jamaica in the Caribbean, and then to Charleston, South Carolina, spreading throughout the United States. There were many men with Scottish names listed among the leaders of the Indiana lodge, but otherwise there was apparently little that was Scottish about it.[44]

Just how many Scots are there in Indiana, and what is known about them demographically? The 1990 census, using statistical sampling techniques, concluded that 225,103 persons in Indiana claimed Scottish ancestry, 113,568 of whom were Scotch-Irish, and 111,535 of whom were Scots. This makes the Scots the fourth most numerous European group in the state behind the Germans, the Irish, and the English.[45] According to the 1980 census, persons actually born in Scotland were widely distributed over the state, with concentrations in the major urban areas: Lake County (252), Marion County (256), and St. Joseph County (110).[46] Earlier census figures present some interesting results: numbers of the foreign born who gave Scotland as their country of origin showed relatively large numbers (in this context, several hundred individuals) in Jefferson County in 1850 and 1860, in Clay County in 1880 and 1890, in Lake County in 1930, 1940, and 1950, and in Vermillion and Vigo counties in 1930. Only once, in the Lake County census of 1930, did the number climb over 1,000 (it was 1,219).[47]

During the twentieth century, organizations that feature Scottish heritage have become popular in Indiana. The Scottish Society of Indianapolis Pipe Band was

*Roderick D. MacDonald and his father Roderick A. MacDonald of the Scottish Society of Indianapolis Pipe Band, 1990.*

founded in November 1980 under the leadership of Pipe Major Roderick A. MacDonald. The band selected as its name "Clan Na Gael" in honor of a clan that populated both Ireland and western Scotland, reflecting the fact that members of the band were of both Scottish and Irish descent. Since its founding in 1980 the band has sponsored "A Night wi' Burns," celebrating the traditions of the Scottish bard. The band has played for social events and in competition. In 1986 the founder's son, Roderick D. MacDonald, became pipe major. Father and son share a proud heritage, tracing their ancestry back genealogically to Roderick MacDonald of Coulags, Scotland, born in 1766.[48]

There is a separate Scottish Society of Indianapolis that publishes a newsletter, *The Thistle.* Also active in Indianapolis is the Indianapolis Scottish Festival, Inc., which sponsors competitions in Scottish folk dancing such as the Highland Fling and the Sword Dance, and the Cornelius Highland Dancers, Inc., led by Katherine A. Cornelius.

In Lafayette the 42d Royal Highlanders has been active under the leadership of Pipe Major Tom Griffin since 1975. The organization fields a pipe band that simulates eighteenth-century military dress and music using pipes, fifes, and rope tension drums, and has sponsored a Robert Burns dinner in the Lafayette community since 1982. When Pipe Major Griffin died in 1992, some thirty kilted and uniformed men gathered to form an honor guard at his funeral.

In Fort Wayne a Scottish Cultural Society was formed in 1986 and organized various gatherings including the first Indiana Highland Games in 1987 and a "Kirkin o' the Tartan" celebration at Trinity English Lutheran Church, where members of various clans show their colors as part of the church service. Columbus, Indiana, celebrates with a Scottish Festival each summer.

It is noteworthy that, although many of the people active in these events are recent arrivals from Scotland, they could by no means be successful if it were not for the widespread support of American-born persons of more or less Scottish ancestry. Just as a St. Patrick's Day parade attracts a great many honorary Irish, so do Scottish celebrations warmly welcome honorary Scots. No doubt there is something of a continuous tradition of commitment to things Scottish from the "old Scotchmen" quoting their Robert Burns in pioneer days to the present-day Burns dinners. The modern Burns dinner is a combination of culinary art, traditional music and dance, and witty toasts to the "lassies" and the "lads." It features the formal piping in of the haggis[49] and the toast to the "immortal memory" of the bard.

Isobel Stuart Miller's toast to "the immortal memory" of Burns, given at Lafayette in 1991, provides an excellent example. Born in Scotland, she came to Indiana as a young adult with her English-born husband David Miller. Isobel recalled her early exposure to the poems of Burns in Scotland but confessed that "the biggest problem non-Scots and Scots alike have with the poetry of Robert Burns is understanding just what he is trying to say." Even with the words of his poem "Address to the Haggis" in front of you, she went on, "I would guess you still wondered what it was all about. Just because I was born in Scotland does not mean it's any easier for me, as we don't talk that way."[50] So she used an English translation for her quotations from Burns's poems.

The Scots, I would suggest, have been easily accepted in Indiana and have never formed tightly knit organizations to preserve themselves from a real or perceived hostile environment. By "race," religion, language, and custom, they were part of the mainstream of Yankee or upland southern America. Thus they never had to circle their wagons into a defensive posture. Their ethnic uniqueness could, from the very first, be a festive ornament and an entertainment open to all. As such, they became part of the happy blend that some people call Hoosier.

## Notes

1. The Scots (including the Scotch-Irish) are the fourth largest ethnic group in the state, according to the census figures. See note 45 below.

2. For comparative purposes see Charlotte Erickson, "British Immigrants in the Old Northwest, 1815–1860," in *The Frontier in American Development: Essays in Honor of Paul Wallace Gates* (Ithaca and London: Cornell University Press, 1969), 323–56, particularly her evidence in the letters of thirty-four English and Scottish families who settled in Ohio, Michigan, Wisconsin, and Illinois (but not Indiana), 1820–50.

3. On the Scots and the Scotch-Irish see the novel by Nancy N. Baxter, *The Movers: A Saga of the Scotch-Irish* (Austin, Tex.: Guild Press, 1987). This adventure romance describes her ancestors: "The Scotch-Irish–Rough-tongued, hard-fighting, defiant, tens of thousands of them fled oppression and poverty in Northern Ireland in the 18th century to come to America and settle a frontier nation. . . . Pennsylvania, Kentucky, Indiana, and all the Midwest and South beckoned." The novel portrays much of the way of life of the Scotch-Irish, but shows them with little interest in Scottish culture as such.

4. James H. Madison, *The Indiana Way: A State History* (Bloomington and Indianapolis: Indiana University Press and Indiana Historical Society, 1986), 16.

5. William Hayden English, *Conquest of the Country Northwest of the River Ohio, 1778–1783,* 2 vols. (Indianapolis: Bowen-Merrill, 1896).

6. *Biographical and Historical Souvenir for the Counties of Clark, Crawford, Harrison, Floyd, Jefferson, Jennings, Scott and Washington, Indiana* (Chicago: John M. Gresham and Co., 1889), 171, 213. Thanks to my colleague Robert D. Buchanan, clan convener for Indiana, for information on the Buchanans.

7. *Early History of Hanover College: An Address by Hon. Wm. McKee Dunn, LL.D. Delivered at the Semi-Centennial Commencement of Hanover College, June 13, 1883* (Madison, Ind.: The Courier Co., 1883), 3.

8. Ibid., 7.

9. Ibid., 11–12; William Alfred Millis, *The History of Hanover College from 1827 to 1927* (Greenfield, Ind.: Wm. Mitchell Printing Co., 1927), 11–36.

10. Millis, *History of Hanover College,* 264.

11. James Insley Osborne and Theodore Gregory Gronert, *Wabash College: The First Hundred Years, 1832–1932* (Crawfordsville: R. E. Banta, 1932). For a discussion of George L. Mackintosh, longtime president of Wabash, see pp. 281 ff.

12. Robert A. Trennert, Jr., *Indian Traders on the Middle Border: The House of Ewing, 1827–54* (Lincoln: University of Nebraska Press, 1981), 9–11. The Ewings are also mentioned by Charles B. Lasselle, "The Old Indian Traders of Indiana," *Indiana Magazine of History* 2 (Mar. 1906): 9. Thanks to William F. Collins, Jr., an Indiana citizen of Scotch-Irish descent, for this information.

13. John H. B. Nowland, *Sketches of Prominent Citizens of 1876* (Indianapolis: Tilford and Carlon, 1877), 15.

14. *History of Dearborn, Ohio and Switzerland Counties, Indiana* (Chicago: Weakley, Harraman and Co., 1885), 904, 1267–68.

15. Charles Blanchard, ed., *Counties of Clay and Owen, Indiana: Historical and Biographical* (Chicago: F. A. Battey and Co., 1884), 571.

16. *History of Dearborn, Ohio and Switzerland Counties,* 1153.

17. Jack Baber, *The Early History of Greene County, Indiana* (Worthington, Ind.: N. B. Milleson, 1875), 73–75, 85.

18. William Travis, *A History of Clay County, Indiana* (New York: Lewis Pub. Co., 1909), 247.

19. *History of Dearborn, Ohio and Switzerland Counties,* 174, and *Biographical and Historical Souvenir for the Counties of Clark, Crawford, Harrison, Floyd, Jefferson, Jennings, Scott and Washington,* 228.

20. *Biographical and Historical Souvenir for the Counties of Clark, Crawford, Harrison, Floyd, Jefferson, Jennings, Scott and Washington,* 277.

21. H. W. Beckwith, *History of Fountain County, Indiana* (Chicago: H. H. Hill and N. Iddings, Publishers, 1881), 483–85. Thanks to his descendant, Eloise Joyce McBroom Truce, for this information.

22. *Hillsboro Times,* 4 Oct. 1907.

23. Typescript of letter, [Hillsboro, Indiana] 27 Feb. 1880, courtesy of Eloise Joyce McBroom Truce.

24. John Milton McBroom, "Early Settlement of Fountain County" (Typescript copy courtesy of Eloise Joyce McBroom Truce).

25. Victor Lincoln Albjerg, *Richard Owen: Scotland 1810-Indiana 1890* (West Lafayette, Ind.: Archives of Purdue University, 1946), 6, 10, 18.

26. Ibid., 20, 24, 46, 48.

27. For Owen's detailed report to the trustees on just how to go about the founding of Purdue, see ibid., 71–84, 89–91.

28. Robert M. Taylor, Jr., et al., *Indiana: A New Historical Guide* (Indianapolis: Indiana Historical Society, 1989), 251.

29. See A. L. Lazarus and Victor H. Jones, *Beyond Graustark: George Barr McCutcheon, Playwright Discovered* (Port Washington, N.Y.: Kennikat Press, 1981) and John T. McCutcheon, *Drawn from Memory* (Indianapolis: Bobbs-Merrill Co., Inc., 1950).

30. The substantial family chronicle, *History of the Meharry Family in America, Descendants of Alexander Meharry I, who fled during the reign of Mary Stuart, Queen of Scots, on account of Religious Persecution from near Ayr, Scotland, to Ballyjamesduff, Cavan County, Ireland; and whose descendant Alexander Meharry III emigrated to America in 1794* (Lafayette, Ind.: Lafayette Printing Co., 1925), is full of filiopicty and confuses Mary Queen of Scots with Bloody Mary Tudor of England, first daughter of Henry VIII. Still, it contains some fascinating information on a locally prominent Scotch-Irish family and its traditions.

31. Ibid., 61.

32. Ibid., 361.

33. Ibid., 306–7, 369–72.

34. Ibid., 96, 113–16.

35. Catherine E Forrest Weber, "'A Genius in the Best Sense': John Muir, Earth, and Indianapolis," *Traces of Indiana and Midwestern History* 5 (Winter 1993): 36–47.

36. Figures from 1871 list twenty-four mines in Clay County, which had a daily capacity of 2,450 tons of coal. Travis, *History of Clay County,* 623, 172.

37. According to family tradition, the grandfather of the author of this essay, Robert Gibb, worked in the Scottish mines as a boy with his father picking up lumps of coal that fell from the carts, before coming to America and settling in North Dakota. The author came to Indiana in 1970 with his wife, raising three children all well aware of their partially Scottish heritage.

38. Travis, *History of Clay County,* 272–73.

39. Ibid., 295.

40. Rebecca A. Shepherd et al., *A Biographical Directory of the Indiana General Assembly,* vol. 1, *1816–1899* (Indianapolis: Select Committee on the Centennial History of the Indiana General Assembly in cooperation with the Indiana Historical Bureau, 1980), 406.

41. I. George Blake, *Paul V. McNutt: Portrait of a Hoosier Statesman* (Indianapolis: Central Publishing Co., 1966), 2.

42. The Lew Wallace "study" in Crawfordsville, which is full of memorabilia, contains little if anything indicating an emphasis on Scottish heritage beyond a Wallace family crest.

43. Hugh Trevor-Roper, "The Invention of Tradition: The Highland Tradition of Scotland," in Eric Hobsbaum and Terence Ranger, *The Invention of Tradition* (Cambridge: Cambridge University

Press, 1983), 15–41, kindly called to my attention by two Indiana citizens of Scottish ancestry, Alan McKenzie and Monica Macaulay.

44. Charles E. Crawford, *History of the Ancient Accepted Scottish Rite in the Valley of Indianapolis, District of Indiana, 1863–1924, Northern Masonic Jurisdiction of the United States of America* (Indianapolis: Adoniram Grand Lodge of Perfection, 1924) and Mark C. Carnes, *Secret Ritual and Manhood in Victorian America* (New Haven, Conn.: Yale University Press, 1989), 134, who attributes the rite in its American form to Albert Pike, dating it from 1853. In spite of the many speculations about its original source, he says, "Scotland, oddly, is rarely suggested."

45. U.S. Census, 1990 CPH-L-80, Selected Social Characteristics (Education Division, Indiana Historical Society), Table 1. Similar statistics from 1980 (which did not distinguish between Scots and Scotch-Irish) reported 214,514 individuals. Ernie Hernandez, *Ethnics in Northwest Indiana* (Gary, Ind.: Gary Post-Tribune, 1984), 158, gives 1,362 as the number of Scots in Lake County in 1980.

46. Statistics from 1980 census (Education Division, Indiana Historical Society).

47. Statistics from census reports (Education Division, Indiana Historical Society).

48. Roderick A. MacDonald, letter and genealogical information to the author.

49. The haggis, to quote the program of the Burns dinner at Lafayette in 1993, "this unusual sausage, as some call it, is traditionally cooked in the stomach bag of a sheep. . . . Normally the contents are oatmeal, sheep's liver and heart, chopped onion, stock and suet."

50. Manuscript given to author by Isobel Stuart Miller.

# SLOVAKS

JOSEPH SEMANCIK

*Upon arrival, the Slovak immigrants, mostly young men, entered communities that were owned and managed by the immigrants who had preceded them. They brought only their strong bodies and a willingness to work. The supervisory positions in the refineries and mills were held by those who had already established themselves as Americans.*

This essay describes the history of the Slovak people in Indiana. That history is one hundred years old. It dates back to the 1890s. To understand this history it is necessary first of all to identify Slovaks, to locate them in Europe and in European history, and to note something of their characteristics such as language, religion, and economic and political experience.[1]

## Old Country Origins

The Slovaks in Indiana originated from what is now "Slovakia." Their country of origin is bounded on the north by Poland, on the east by Ukraine, on the south by Hungary, and on the west by Austria and the Czech Republic. During this century it was part of the Austrian-Hungarian Empire until the First World War when it became part of Czecho-Slovakia. From 1920 until the late 1930s the country was termed Czechoslovakia, without a hyphen. Following the Second World War, and during the Soviet occupation, it became the Czechoslovak Soviet Socialist Republic (CSSR).

Independence from the Soviets in 1989 resulted in the Czech and Slovak Federated Republic. Since 1 January 1993 the Czechs and Slovaks have separated into Slovakia and the Czech Republic, independent states.

Slovakia is a picturesque country with mountains resembling those of Pennsylvania, yet with the Tatra Mountains similar to the Rockies, though not as great in altitude. It is a country of valleys and rivers and farms and villages. There is some heavy industry, but relative to Czech lands Slovakia remains more rural and ecologically less damaged.

Although the history of the people now known as Slovaks has obscure origins dating to the fifth century, there are credible roots of Slovaks as part of the Great Moravian Empire of the ninth century.[2] During that period, beginning in 863, the work of brothers Cyril and Methodius brought the Christian faith and laid the groundwork for the written language, introducing the Cyrillic alphabet that is still used in the Russian language. The faith was that of the Byzantine Catholic (Eastern Rite).

After the destruction of the Great Moravian Empire in 907 by the Franks and Magyars, the Slovaks lived under Hungarian rule for a thousand years.[3]

During Hungarian rule Slovaks were forced to become Roman Catholics. However, Byzantine Catholicism gradually returned. Perhaps the greatest religious changes occurred in conjunction with the Protestant Reformation when Lutheranism became dominant, yet with the Counter-Reformation almost all the Slovaks returned to Catholicism, with 15 to 20 percent remaining Lutheran, and a few Calvinist. This influence carried over into the new country.[4]

Given the occupation of Slovak lands by Hungarians, many of whom were Magyars and spoke that tongue, it is astonishing that the language of the Slovaks endured, in spite of efforts to have everyone speak Hungarian.[5]

Slovak nationalism suffered a devastating setback as a result of the Ausgleich of 1867. This compromise

## The Slovak Language

Language is an identifying and distinguishing characteristic of a people. The Slovak language, in the absence of a political state, has served to identify for over a thousand years those people who live in what is now known as Slovakia. It is one of twelve Slavic languages, including Polish, Czech, Serbo-Croatian, Russian, and others.[8]

The language belongs to the Indo-European language family. In its early history it was not written and consequently has not been preserved in documents. Old Church Slavonic was the language in which the manuscripts were preserved, but it is not the same as Slovak. However, the Slovak language continued to be used for one thousand years in an oral form. From the tenth to the fourteenth century Latin was the language of administration and education. It was not until the seventeenth century that a literary Slovak emerged. The Slovak language was codified by Stur and incorporated into a grammar written by Hattala and published in 1852, which became the literary language of all the Slovaks, and it still provides the basis for modern Slovak.[9]

The language had not only to survive the pressures from without, i.e., the efforts of the Hungarians to have Magyar as the official language, but also from within. There were twenty-nine different dialects, generally classified into three regions (Eastern, Central, and Western), each with differences in words, accents, and pronunciations.[10]

These dialects were brought to the United States and to Indiana and served as an identifying characteristic along with the county of origin in a manner known principally to other Slovaks. For example, some considered persons from Saris County as hillbillies, while others would say that people from Orava spoke the "good Slovak." It was not until the time of the First and Second World Wars that the use of standard Slovak became more common, and dialects lost importance in the United States.

As the immigrants gradually learned to speak English, the question of conveying the language to the second generation became an issue. That generation mostly learned to speak Slovak at home and English at school. A very real problem was the absence of Slovak teaching nuns.

On one occasion the decision whether to teach Slovak in a parish school prompted controversy. Some say that the posture of the foreign-born parish priest at St. John in Whiting, Indiana, which stated that Slovak would not be taught in the school, was a very unpopular one, especially after the priest had taken the people's contributions to build the school.[11]

For the most part the churches were the institutions in which the language was preserved, at least until after the

agreement between Austria and Hungary, which elevated the status of Hungary in the Austro-Hungarian Empire, enabled the Magyars to enforce a policy of denationalization against the Slovaks. Instruction in the Slovak language was severely restricted.[6]

The occupation and domination of Slovaks as part of the Austro-Hungarian Empire lasted until World War I, after which the country of Czechoslovakia was created. It is interesting to note that the agreements to create Czechoslovakia were developed in the United States. The Cleveland Agreement (1916) and the Pittsburgh Agreement (1919) emerged from meetings between Czechs and Slovaks. Provisions in the agreements were not fulfilled by the Thomas Masaryk-led Czechs, and the Slovaks felt betrayed, with a good deal of the controversy occurring in the United States as well as in the Old Country.[7]

The reader may or may not be familiar with the history of Czechoslovakia since the time of the Second World War. For a brief period of time, during that war and the Hitler domination of Europe, the Slovaks had a separate state with Monsignor Joseph Tiso as president. With the end of World War II the Czechs and Slovaks were reunited. This period of history, with the hanging of Tiso, is complicated and controversial. Its history is still being reexamined.

The Communists took control in 1948, and the country found itself behind the Iron Curtain. During this time there was Russian dominance and Communist persecution of religion. In 1967 there was a reform movement begun by the Slovak Communist party with Alexander Dubcek, a Slovak, becoming the leader of Czechoslovakia. This period of reform was brief and ended when Russian tanks occupied the country in 1968. Czechoslovakia lived under Communist rule until the Velvet Revolution of 1989 when reform movements in Prague and Bratislava triumphed. On 1 January 1993 Slovakia became an independent state with joy in the streets of Bratislava. Slovakia is currently a country of about five million people working to establish its place in Central Europe economically and politically.

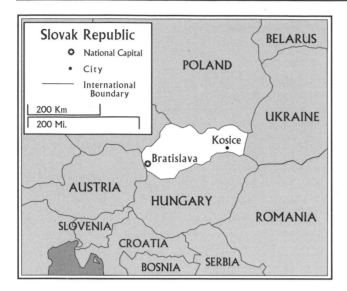

Second World War. Powell A. Moore notes that "most priests were farsighted men who, realizing their congregations were here to stay, encouraged the process of Americanization and the use of the English language."[12] The absence of first-generation immigrants has resulted in a minimal use of the Slovak language in church services in recent years.

As with other immigrant groups, some Slovak families chose not to speak or teach the Slovak language at home so that their children would speak unaccented English and become thoroughly American.

In northwest Indiana the Slovak language, as one of the Slavic tongues commonly used, enabled the immigrant to socialize and share existence with many other ethnic groups. Since there were similarities of language, the Poles, Croatians, Serbs, and Slovaks found it possible to converse among themselves. The Slovaks were also able to converse with the Hungarians since many of them had been compelled to learn Hungarian in the schools of Slovakia.

**Immigration**

Who were these Slovaks and why did they come to America? The immigration seems to have begun with young men from the eastern part of Slovakia. M. Mark Stolarik reports that fully three-quarters of the immigration to the United States from Slovakia came from four eastern counties of Slovakia—Saris, Zemplin, Abov, and Spis. These counties seem to have been where poverty was the greatest and where the growth in population made employment difficult.[13]

It is particularly difficult to identify and specify the exact number of Slovaks who came to the United States and to Indiana during these years (1890–1920) of heavy immigration. The census data for those years did not have a category for "Slovak," and oftentimes the respondents themselves did not have a clear answer to offer. As with other East European immigrants, their origin was lost in the political configurations of the time. Some answered Hungarian because they spoke Hungarian; some indicated Austria-Hungary as country of origin; and some may well have been considered Slovenes or other Slavic people.[14]

An examination of the church records of the early part of the century reveals that place of origin was often Austria-Hungary, or the county of origin in Slovakia. However, upon the creation of Czechoslovakia in 1918, the marriage and funeral records immediately began citing Czechoslovakia as place of birth or origin.

The reasons for immigrating were many. Poverty in Slovakia, the promise of employment, the political oppression by the Hungarians, the lack of opportunities, the threat of serving in the emperor's army, and the promise of riches in the new world all served to prompt the bold move to a new life. The cost of travel was comparatively low, though the steamship journey was long and tedious. Steamship companies advertised and gave special rates. For

*Slovak dancers in the production of "Europe in America," given at the YMCA in Gary, ca. 1915.*

the Slovaks this was a temporary situation. The intent for them was to make a great deal of money and then return home, which many did, some repeatedly. With the onset of World War I, however, the decision became permanent, and return immigration virtually ceased.

The immigration of Slovaks was stopped with the revision of the immigration law in 1924. The new formula discriminated in favor of Europeans from western and northern Europe and against those from southern and eastern Europe. Unlike some other ethnic groups that experienced large surges since that time, for example, the Hungarians in 1956, the Slovak entry into the United States since 1924 has been but a trickle.

The Slovak pattern of migration seems to have been to locate first in the East (Pennsylvania or New Jersey) and then to come to Indiana, usually because of word of mouth, to work in the oil refineries or the steel mills of Lake County or the coal mines of central Indiana. Such "chain migration" resembled that of other ethnic groups. The migrants' arrival coincided with the establishment of the oil and steel industries on the southern shore of Lake Michigan.

## Slovaks and the Census

The tracing of the number of Slovak immigrants into Indiana is difficult and confusing. The content and methodology of census data are changeable, and the origins of the Slovaks in the Old Country are at best confused because of the shifting political boundaries and their own perceptions of origin.

Even the most sophisticated data collection of the 1980 census does not do justice to Slovak enumeration, as is noted in *We the People: An Atlas of America's Ethnic Diversity*:

> The census data probably seriously underestimated the people of Slovak ancestry because the census incorporated all persons responding with the national origin Czechoslovakian into the Czech-ancestry total. Presumably ethnic Slovaks frequently reported their ancestry in terms of either the modern country of Czechoslovakia or Hungary, the old country of origin. Thus, the Slovak-ancestry population was probably somewhat larger than the totals reported, in comparison to the Czech-ancestry population and probably also the Hungarian-ancestry population.[15]

Tables offer little opportunity to describe the actual numbers involved because of the problems noted above and because of the changeability of the grounds for the collection of data. Perhaps a better way is to make some comments and provide some information regarding the available census data

from 1880 to 1990, thereby allowing the reader to make some judgment or estimation of the number of Slovaks in Indiana during the different decades.[16]

Prior to 1880 there is no reference to peoples who might be considered Slovaks.

In the 1880 census there were 267 persons listed from Bohemia (now the Czech Republic) and 68 from Hungary. Of those from Bohemia, 68 were located in Lake County and 56 in Starke County.

The 1890 census lists 288 from Bohemia, with 162 noted in Starke County and 47 in Lake County. This marks the beginning of what may be construed as the only Czech settlement in Indiana. The 1890 census lists 436 persons originating in Hungary, of whom 148 were in Lake County and 162 in St. Joseph County. The census of 1890 marks the beginning of the Slovak immigration since Hungary as place of origin would have included Slovaks who lived in the then existing Austria-Hungary.

The census of 1900 cites 268 persons from Bohemia, with 238 living in Starke County. It lists 1,379 from Hungary, 293 of whom were in Lake County, 743 in St. Joseph County, 38 in Vermillion County, and 47 in Clay County. The 1900 census figures account for the Slovaks who worked in the coal mines in central Indiana, for the large number of ethnic Hungarians who live in South Bend, and for the beginning of Slovak and Hungarian entry into the industrial northwest of Indiana.

Beginning with the census of 1910, Hungary is listed as a country of origin. Within that designation are contained Slovaks and perhaps other ethnic groups such as Romanians, Croatians, and others who would have come from what was then termed Austria-Hungary. The data indicate 18,622, of whom 14,370 were foreign born (this 1910 data also noted that the 1900 census showed 1,379) with Hungary as place of origin. Of these, 7,479 are located in Lake County. The data contain a breakdown by cities of over 10,000 population that lists 3,431 in East Chicago, 1,979 in Gary, and 920 in Hammond. One may presume that much of the remainder lived in Whiting, though as a small city it would not have had a listing.

One can only speculate as to how many of those listed as from Hungary were Slovaks. A very conservative estimate based on the shifting of questions and responses, which would have occurred in the 1920 census (after the creation of Czechoslovakia), would place at least 50 percent as Slovak.

In 1920 the census data specified Czechoslovakia as a country of birth. This resulted in 3,941 counted from Czechoslovakia and decreased the number from Hungary to 9,351, half of the 1910 total. The addition of Czechoslovakia to the census categories still leaves uncertainty regarding the total number of Slovaks, since many may still have listed Hungary as their place of origin. Also, Czechs and Moravians as well as Hungarians may well be included in the total from Czechoslovakia.

The 1930 census likely provided a more accurate accounting of Slovak presence in Indiana. It indicated native whites of foreign or mixed parentage with 13,173 from Czechoslovakia and 9,998 from Hungary. Of these, 8,325 were listed as foreign born from Czechoslovakia. Since 10,699 of the total are listed in Lake County, a somewhat better perspective can be gained concerning the actual number of persons of Slovak descent present in 1930, and the data can be used in an interpretive way on what the proportions actually were in previous decades.

With the 1940 census some of the foreign-born population has begun to diminish. Foreign-born whites from Czechoslovakia numbered 5,782, of whom 4,723 were in Lake County. Of those in Lake County, it is interesting that there were 930 in East Chicago, 980 in Hammond, and 949 in Whiting. It can be assumed that all of these were Slovaks.

The 1950 census lists 4,224 foreign born from Czechoslovakia living in Lake County, with 750 in East Chicago, 1,508 in Gary, and 1,051 in Hammond.

For 1960 the data collected information on foreign stock from Czechoslovakia, which recorded 15,823 from Czechoslovakia, with 3,773 being foreign born living in Lake County.

When the census for 1970 recorded people by nativity, parentage, or country of origin, there were 9,132 persons in Lake County of Czechoslovakian origin.

The 1980 census data show 1,773 persons of foreign birth from Czechoslovakia, of whom 1,163 lived in Lake County. The new inquiry of ancestry group resulted in 23,080 replying Slovak and 21,954 responding Czech or Czechoslovak. The figures, however, raise the issue of accuracy since persons replying Czechoslovak may have been either Czech or Slovak.

The preliminary data of the 1990 census indicate 44,412 persons of Slovak ancestry living in Indiana.

## Arrival and Settlement

Slovaks first came in substantial numbers to Lake County and located in Whiting to work in the newly created Standard Oil refinery that began in 1889.[17] The program books from the early history of St. John the Baptist parish in Whiting indicate that the people came from Illinois communities such as Streator to work at the refinery. Their Old Country origins indicate that they came primarily from Saris and Zemplin counties.[18]

There was an influx of Slovaks into central Indiana just prior to the turn of the century to work in the coal mines north of Terre Haute. They lived in Carbon, Clinton, and Diamond, Indiana. These Slovaks seem to have come from the coalfields of Pennsylvania, learning by word of mouth of the work available in Indiana.[19]

The establishment of the steel industry in East Chicago and in Gary brought Slovak laborers to these communities. The laborers came from the Old Country or from the steel and coalfields of Pennsylvania and the East. The origin of these Slovaks was something different. They came a little bit later, that is, after the turn of the century, and they came from other counties of Slovakia, particularly Orava and Liptov.

These immigrants came in what might be characterized as chain immigration. After one member of a village or family came, either he went back and told the good news, or he sent for his wife, brothers, or other family members. Although there were no hard or fast rules, there are clusters of people who came from the same villages of the same counties in Slovakia.

During the period preceding the First World War, there was a fair number of people who returned to Slovakia, but that has been difficult to determine with few references to such immigration. For the most part the immigrants settled and married and began to bring up their families.

Upon arrival, the Slovak immigrants, mostly young men, entered communities that were owned and managed by the immigrants who had preceded them. They brought only their strong bodies and a willingness to work. The supervisory positions in the refineries and mills were held by those who had already established themselves as Americans. In other parts of the United States, having had to indicate their country of origin as Hungary or Austria-Hungary, they were frequently referred to as "Hunkies."[20] Over the years the demeaning connotation of that phrase has diminished.

Slovaks in the communities of Lake County generally lived in the ethnic areas of the cities, for example, the Patch in Gary and the Harbor in East Chicago. Slovaks lived in proximity to their church, but did not form exclusive neighborhoods such as the Poles did. They also seemed to be able to associate amicably with other ethnic groups.

Slovaks have settled in substantial numbers in only two areas of Indiana, and this essay will focus on the four communities in which they settled, and near which their descendants still live. It will base this focus to a large extent on the churches and lodges that comprised the life of the people, especially in their immigrant years. Slovaks in Whiting, East Chicago, Gary, and central Indiana will comprise the principal sections of this essay.

## Slovaks in Whiting

Slovaks from Streator, Blue Island, and Chicago, Illinois, began to settle in Whiting in 1892 and 1893.[21] They came to work in the new refinery that Standard Oil of Indiana was building. Slovaks provided personnel for the unskilled jobs in the refinery and endured what was something of a life on the frontier. As the refinery increased its workforce, more eastern Europeans began to come to Whiting, mostly Slovaks. They lived in boardinghouses, but soon were joined by family through immigration or marriage and began living a new life. The need for individual assistance and social relationships resulted in the creation of lodges and churches. The life of both are intertwined.[22]

The National Slovak Society (NSS) was the first lodge created to attend to the needs of the Slovak people. The lodge was founded on 5 March 1893 when twelve Slovaks assembled and formed Lodge #111 "Slovak Brotherly Hand." The society, however, did not address itself to any religion; it was a fraternal association with insurance benefits and a sponsor of many social events. Jan Girman was the organizer and first president of the branch of the NSS.[23]

Lodges played an important part in the life of the immigrant. In addition to providing insurance that would somewhat compensate the widowed, lodges offered social opportunities for their members and their families. Lodge meetings in themselves were social occasions. They also sponsored picnics, dances, and socials of various kinds.

In April 1894 twelve Catholic Slovaks came together in the home of George Berdis to form a distinctively Catholic lodge, Branch #130 of the First Catholic Slovak Union, more commonly known as the Jednota. George Berdis was the organizer and guiding light of this Jednota Branch. It became an influential factor in the life of the people of Whiting, especially because it initiated the establishment of St. John the Baptist Church. Members of the Jednota were expected to practice faithfully the teachings and precepts of the church.[24]

Although the Slovak people of Whiting initially went to Mass at Sacred Heart, the Irish church, they grew in numbers and soon wanted a church of their own. The Jednota organized, planned, and helped to finance a church. A committee of the lodge presented a petition to Bishop Joseph Rademacher in Fort Wayne to establish a parish. Although the approval required a second petition, Bishop Rademacher sent for a priest from Slovakia, then known as Austria-Hungary, to minister to the Slovaks. In response to the bishop's summons, Father Benedict Rajcany arrived in Whiting and founded St. John the Baptist Church in 1897. Father Rajcany served the parish community for thirty years until his retirement in 1927.[25]

In the early years of settlement Father Rajcany not only filled the special spiritual needs of the Slovak community but also assumed some leadership roles in the community. He was one of the organizers of the "Slovak Home," was prominent in community events, and became an avid Chicago White Sox baseball fan. Legend has it that he had to return to the parish from Comiskey Park for a wedding he had forgotten about while the bridal party waited. He was responsible for founding Holy Trinity Hungarian Church in East Chicago and was instrumental in establishing Assumption parish in East Chicago. Many different nationalities were attracted to St. John in Whiting for spiritual services because of Father Rajcany's polyglot talent for languages that enabled him to speak Slovak, Hungarian, German, French, and English.[26] He was responsible for building the first church, school, and rectory for the parish. He seems to have been a good friend to the Reverend John Bradac, the Slovak Lutheran minister in Whiting. As this essay will indicate later, the early years of Slovak history were years in which the clergy played a prominent and responsible leadership role.

Although the Whiting community was predominantly Slovak as it grew, it was not exclusively Roman Catholic. In somewhat similar proportions to the religious distributions in Slovakia, there were numbers of Eastern Rite Catholics (Byzantine) and Lutherans who came to Whiting.

Paralleling the establishment of St. John the Baptist Roman Catholic Church, the Greek Catholic Lodge was instrumental in forming the congregation of St. Mary's Assumption Byzantine Church.[27] St. Mary's became the first Byzantine church in Indiana and, in fact, in the Midwest. It was established on 1 October 1899 and continues in existence to this day. After a series of priests who guided the parish for the first few years, Father George Thegze assumed a pastorship in 1929 that lasted until 1952. Father Thegze was one of the last priests, in communion with the Roman Pontiff, who was married with a family. Father Thegze had been married and ordained prior to the rescript that required celibacy of all priests in the United States, and he served the congregation in Whiting for those many years as a married priest. His son George Thegze became a medical doctor and practiced in Whiting for many years.

The religious divisions of Slovaks in the Old Country were carried into the new. Lutheran Slovaks settled in Whiting also and for a while went to Chicago for divine services. As immigration increased their numbers, they founded St. Paul Evangelical Lutheran Church in Whiting on 7 February 1904.[28] After organizing and holding services at St. John's Lutheran Church in South

Chicago they realized the need to build a church of their own, which they completed in 1908. It was not until 1933 that any of the services were held in English, Slovak being the language of both services and teaching. Most prominent among Slovak Lutherans was the Reverend John Bradac, pastor of this congregation. He was not only pastor of this parish but also served as president of the Slovak Evangelical Lutheran Synod of the United States, as a writer who frequently contributed to the Synod's publications, and as an active participant in community affairs. He was one of the founders of the Slovak Dom, the social and cultural building that Whiting Slovaks erected.[29]

In addition to the facilities that parishes offered to their members, the Slovaks of Whiting felt the need for a social and cultural center of their own. The *Whiting Call* on 28 July 1916 reported:

> Ground Broken for a Slovak Home. The Slovak people of Whiting are to have a "Home," in their language a "Slovensky Dom," a place where their lodges and societies can hold their regular meetings and a headquarters for all social and fraternal gatherings.[30]

The building cost $36,000, was three stories, and was able to accommodate six hundred people at banquets and social events. Shares of capital stock were sold for ten dollars to finance the building. It is of interest that the founding officers of the corporation were Rev. Benedict Rajcany, president, Rev. John Bradac, vice president, Joseph Matlon, treasurer, and Joseph Chilla, secretary. The text on the stock read:

> Shares of Capital Stock of Slovensky Dom (Slovak Home) of Whiting, Indiana fully paid and non-assessable, transferable only on the books of the Corporation by the holder thereof in person or by attorney, upon surrender of this certificate, properly endorsed, to a person or persons of Slavonic birth or descent or a Corporation or Corporations composed of individuals, of Slavonic birth or descent.[31]

The leadership of the clergy, the closeness of the Slovak community, and the ecumenical dimension resulted in ethnic origin transcending religious differences in this Slovak community effort.

Whiting Slovaks also established corresponding lodges for women. The First Catholic Slovak Ladies Union

*Founders of the First Catholic Slovak Ladies Union, Whiting.*

(Zenska Jednota) was organized at a meeting on 10 July 1899 in St. John Church. Father Benedict Rajcany called the meeting and wrote the minutes.[32] The formation of Branch #81 at St. John was followed by the creation of a Junior Order. The organizational work became the occupation of Helen Kocan. She not only was the heart and soul of the lodge community in Whiting, but also became a long-term national president of the First Catholic Slovak Ladies Union, one of the strongest and most securely established fraternal insurance organizations in the country. Kocan was the national president from 1933 to 1964. She needs to be recognized for her success in organizing and developing this association for women, which is so strong both socially and financially. The national "Zenska Jednota" has donated hundreds of thousands of dollars to charitable causes and has established junior branches with drill teams of girls who have competed nationally for honors.[33]

Although at first it may seem that the Slovaks were inward oriented, during the First World War a group of sixty-seven Slovak women met regularly, dressed in white uniforms with Red Cross symbols, to wrap bandages and perform other tasks for the war effort. Likewise, by way of example, the minutes of the Ladies Jednota for July 1926 show a donation of fifteen dollars for flood victims in Mississippi.[34]

*Parents of Sophie Gresko, Whiting, ca. 1900.*

In 1921 a major controversy arose with Father Rajcany at its center, which resulted in the formation of a second Slovak parish in Whiting. The controversy concerned the lack of financial accountability and grew to a point of no return. Some accused Rajcany of misappropriation, others supported him wholeheartedly. At the call of the bishop Rajcany returned from a Florida stay to resume his parochial responsibilities, but the formation of Immaculate Conception parish became a reality.[35]

For a while the Slovaks who separated themselves from St. John held services at SS. Peter and Paul, the Croatian church. Soon, however, they built their own church and dedicated it in 1926, at which time Father John Lach came to assume the pastorate. Father Lach proved to be a consummate promoter of Slovak leadership and Slovak causes.[36] He was pastor from 1926 until his death in 1958. His list of accomplishments includes helping to establish the Franciscan Seven Dolors Shrine and Calumet Park Cemetery, chairing the committee to raise money for the war effort in World War II, organizing Slovak Days, and, of special note, organizing Father Lach's Symphonic Band.[37]

During the decade of the depression this priest, who played the clarinet, organized a sixty-five-member band that toured the United States during the summer of 1931 and climaxed the tour with a concert at the White House for President Herbert Hoover. It was called Father Lach's Symphonic Band. Later in the decade an even more ambitious schedule had the band on a three-month tour of Europe, visiting nine countries. The band crossed the ocean on the *Ile de France,* accompanied by Adam Liscinsky, musical director. The tour was partially financed through a contest for the queen of the band that raised a large portion of the thirty thousand dollars necessary. One of the prizes for the nationwide contest to choose the queen for the band was a week's vacation in Whiting, Indiana.[38] Lach was an avid promoter of Slovaks as dedicated American citizens and of Slovak causes, some with international effects. In addition, he had literary interests, taking over the *Slovak v Amerike,* a Slovak weekly.

The vast majority of Slovaks in Whiting worked for the Standard Oil Company. Working first at the behest of the foremen and supervisors, the company gradually turned toward a paternalistic policy of dealing with its workers, with what basically was a company union.[39] Slovaks occupied the menial jobs at the refinery, first working twelve-hour days, seven days a week, later changing to five- and six-day weeks of eight hours a day. A characteristic sight in Whiting was men riding to work on bicycles, lunch pails hanging from their arms. There was little opportunity for real advancement in the company. Until the 1930s even the rules of the company union forbade foreign-born workers from holding office. Whether regular policy ever noted it or not, the Slovak worker, who was invariably Catholic, felt that without membership in the Masonic Order and without an Anglo-Saxon name, he would never attain a very high position at the refinery.

Not every Slovak worked at the Standard Oil Company. A class of businessmen and entrepreneurs arose from the beginning. Joseph Grenchik had a grocery store, Tomas Duraj had a saloon, Andrew Lipay had a clothing store, Joseph Kusbel and Andrew Smolen operated a dairy, and Joseph Semancik had a feed and grain business and later a coal yard. Joseph Chilla, Michael Kozacik, and Stephen Kovacik were in the banking and insurance business. During the Great Depression Joseph Grenchik put up his savings to preserve the American Trust and Savings Bank and ended up owning it. John Ciesar started as a blacksmith, became a car dealer, sent his sons through college, and organized an insurance company. One of his sons, William Ciesar, served as national vice president of the National Slovak Society for twenty years and a short time as its president, during which time he helped resolve some of the society's financial problems.[40]

In the late 1930s the Ciesars sponsored and owned a professional basketball franchise, called the Whiting, later the Hammond, Ciesars. Though the franchise was dissolved during the Second World War, the league later became the National Basketball Association (NBA).

The Slovak businessmen gave leadership to their community. They continuously fostered the notion that Slovaks were good citizens and patriotic Americans. The Slovak Days of the 1930s were promotions of Slovak identity and devotion to America. Hundreds of Slovaks would go to Wicker Park to engage in song, dance, games, and drinking and to hear congressmen speak of the greatness of the nation. The businessmen of the National Slovak Society brought speakers from the Chicago universities to speak on economic and social matters. The United States Marine Corps Band was sponsored to play for the community in 1956.[41]

It took a considerable amount of time before Slovaks found their way into political power. The Irish managed to hold on to the mayor's office in Whiting until after the Second World War. The political newsprint of the time proclaimed "Slovaks were for McNamara." In a city that

*Slovak lady volunteers, Whiting, during World War I.*

reputedly was 90 percent Slovak, an Irish mayor seemed an anomaly. George Kochis first broke the political ice by being elected to a county office. In Whiting, Andrew S. Kovacik, an attorney, managed in 1948 to succeed Mayor James McNamara, who resigned because of ill health. Most all mayors since then have been Slovaks, with William Bercik, Sr., being succeeded upon his death by his wife, and much later by his son, William, Jr. Joseph Grenchik, mayor on two different occasions, once ran for Congress as a Republican.

The Slovak language and much of the culture that accompanied it are almost gone. Sermons in church are almost always in English, and the language of the streets is English. The lodges meet infrequently, except for the ladies lodges that are still vibrant. The church school that taught Slovak is closed. The church school that did not teach Slovak still thrives. Yet the identity of Whiting as a Slovak community endures. Cardinals and bishops from Slovakia receive warm welcomes and draw good crowds for services and receptions. The first generation that spoke only Slovak is gone. The second generation that spoke Slovak fluently is meager in numbers. The third generation that

speaks halting, if any, Slovak will determine whether the culture and history of the old world will be remembered or just quietly lost in the American melting pot.

In the first half of the century the ethnic churches frequently sponsored plays and theater productions of various kinds. These amateur efforts provided both social events and an opportunity for developing the talents of the people. The most successful of these endeavors was the St. John Drama Club, originating in 1926 at St. John the Baptist Catholic Church in Whiting. Now known as the Marian Theater Guild, this theater group has taken on a life of its own and has become something of a cultural institution in Whiting. The guild continues to this day to produce and present plays and musicals of a high amateur quality that draw would-be thespians as well as theatergoers from surrounding communities as well as from the parish.[42]

## Slovaks in East Chicago

East Chicago was incorporated in 1893 with 3,411 inhabitants. When the Inland Steel Company began construction of its mill there in 1901 the population began to explode, and by 1910 there were over 19,000

*President Herbert Hoover at White House reception for Father John Lach's Band, 1931.*

people of whom 43 percent were foreign born. Among these were Slovaks in large numbers. The exact number of Slovaks is difficult to note because the census data for 1910 listed Austria 3,201 and Hungary 3,431. Slovaks were included but not identified among them. When the census for 1920 began to list Czechoslovakia as place of birth, there were 715 who noted this, with Austria having 1,706 and Hungary 2,154.[43]

East Chicago was a rough-and-tumble town. Work was hard and dangerous, but the abundance of jobs and the wages that surpassed the opportunities in the Old Country drew many immigrants. The immigration of Slovaks into East Chicago came largely from Orava and Liptov counties in what is now the central part of Slovakia. Many people came from the same village. The Letkos, Kurics, Ficko, and Palmy families came from Stankovany in Liptov County.[44]

Similar to the experience in Whiting, the Slovaks centered their lives on lodges and churches. Most were Roman Catholic and went to St. John in Whiting for religious services, some were Byzantine Eastern Rite Catholic and went to St. Mary's in Whiting, and others were Lutheran. Within a short period of time the East Chicago Slovaks were planning parishes of their own, and on 3 March 1914 they asked the bishop of Fort Wayne to start a parish. In 1915 Father Clement Mlinarovich was sent to them. He had spent a year in Whiting with Father Rajcany prior to coming.[45]

The Byzantine Rite Catholics likewise desired a church of their own and began planning for it in 1914. The pioneer committee raised the first nine dollars toward purchase of four lots on which it built Holy Ghost Church in 1920.[46]

The Holy Trinity Slovak Evangelical Lutheran Church was founded in 1906 and grew to ninety-seven families in 1934, with sixty students in a parish school that year.[47]

Concomitant with the formation of churches was the establishment of lodges. Some of the lodges established in East Chicago were: the First Catholic Slovak Union, Branch #525, dedicated to the Visitation of Our Lady; St. Michael's Sokol Lodge #239; Greek Catholic Union #361, St. Nicholas Lodge; Branch 409 of the First Catholic Slovak Ladies Union; Slovak Evangelical Union; and Branch 109 of the Pennsylvania Slovak Catholic Ladies Union. Most all the lodges had secondary names that bore a religious connotation. The religious names gradually lost usage as the religious requirements and duties of members diminished. Memberships in the lodges that were specifically religious carried obligations to attend Mass, to go to confession, and to marry within the church. Failure to meet these requirements canceled membership. The lodge members were often the strength of the parish.

Most of the men worked in the mills or the neighboring oil refineries. Some were businessmen: Peter Slamka operated a saloon, Anthony Suty a grocery store, and John Oleska a funeral home. One of the most prominent businessmen in the early days was John Tapajna who was in real estate. However, in the time of the Great Depression he lost all his holdings. Unlike the other communities, East Chicago was a community without a bank under Slovak auspices. Inland Steel was and is the principal employer in the city. The company encountered difficult times during the depression years, and men were given one- and two-day work weeks to survive. It was not an easy time to live in East Chicago. The highest rising Slovak in the management of Inland Steel was Joseph Matusek, a second-generation Slovak who became a general division manager.

Assumption parish comprised a large part of the life of the Slovak community in the Indiana Harbor section of East Chicago, mostly referred to as "The Harbor." To this day people in the suburbs of Lake County refer to themselves as being from "The Harbor." Assumption Church was dedicated in 1916 and began to baptize, confirm, and provide eucharistic services to the Slovaks in East Chicago. The rectory, convent, and school were built to accompany the work of the church. The school was opened in 1926 with nuns as teachers. For several decades the school prospered, with a new school and activity building constructed in 1955. The school graduated about thirty children a year. In the earlier days of the school, children were taught the Slovak language. The parish was vibrant and involved its members in a regular schedule of dinners, dances, and meetings of various kinds.[48]

The leadership of Assumption Church came from a small and at first unimposing man, Father Clement Mlinarovich. Never known for administrative prowess he nevertheless succeeded in building a church, convent, school, and rectory. His sermons were works of art, and he was considered to be the finest Slovak speaker in the United States. He possessed a closeness to people and was a particularly important person on the scene of national Slovak activities and organizations. He served many years as president of the Slovak Catholic Federation of America and as president of Slovak Catholic Higher Education in America. He was a prolific writer of novels and articles, but his literary stature is best determined by his poetry.[49]

Mlinarovich was voted the most popular Slovak in America in 1921 in a contest conducted by the *Daily Slovak American*. He was considered one of the most important Catholic authors in the 1940s because of his Slovak poetry. He was honored by two popes, as a Very Reverend Monsignor by Pope Pius XII and a Right Reverend Monsignor by Pope Paul VI. He was

*Indiana Harbor Slovaks, ca. 1932.*

instrumental in starting a mission of Assumption Church on the other side of town and later saw it become the independent Sacred Heart parish. He was continuously called upon to speak at Slovak gatherings of all kinds, especially throughout the Midwest. He spent his retirement years with the Franciscans at Valparaiso, having started his career as a Franciscan in 1913.

The radio voice for the Slovaks in Lake County was East Chicago resident John Babinec. At the urging of Father Mlinarovich, Babinec conducted a Sunday afternoon Slovak Hour on the radio over several decades. The American Slovak Hour began in 1931 and continued until 1957. It consisted of Slovak news, announcements of Slovak events, and Slovak music. The program was generally sponsored by Slovak businesses that advertised on the radio supporting the venture.

John Babinec was likewise instrumental in starting the American Slovak Civic Club of Indiana Harbor in 1939 and served as its president for twenty-five years. This club and its counterparts in Whiting and Gary represented a movement from the religious orientation of the lodges and an effort to further the interests of Slovaks in the community and often in the politics of that community.

The first Slovak to attain political office in East Chicago was John Fusek, a native of Nitra County in Slovakia who came to East Chicago in 1902. At first in the grocery and the real estate business, he was elected alderman in East Chicago in 1926 and was reelected to serve until 1935. He was an active member of the Slovak Evangelical Union (Lutheran), holding a number of national offices including the presidency of the supreme court of that organization in 1934.[50]

A 1959 study of the ethnic groups in East Chicago reported eight hundred Slovak families attending six Slovak churches—two Roman Catholic, three Greek Catholic, and one Lutheran.[51]

The last of the Slovak churches built in East Chicago was Sacred Heart. It originated as Assumption Mission, starting in 1926, and held services at St. Basil Byzantine Church and at St. Nicholas Romanian Catholic Church. In the later years of the depression its parishioners petitioned to have their own church and proceeded with the construction. Sacred Heart was dedicated on 11 May 1941.

Legend has it that the young Slovaks on the west side of town went to the pastor of the territorial parish and asked for time on Sundays for a Slovak Mass with a Slovak priest. The pastor's denial of this request prompted the Slovaks to purchase lots and petition the bishop for a new church. The correspondence between Father Mlinarovich and Bishop John Francis Noll is terse and reluctant, though eventually approving. The bishop's efforts to deter construction of another church in an area already geographically crowded with churches ended when he wrote: "I suppose that since you have already dug the foundation and have the bricks aside it, that I must give you permission."[52]

So started this small parish of some seventy families. Its first resident pastor was Father Andrew Grutka, who later became the first bishop of the diocese of Gary. For most of the last thirty-five years the parish has been cared for by Msgr. Joseph Semancik, director of Catholic Charities for the diocese of Gary. Semancik has attained a certain degree of prominence in Catholic social welfare, researching and writing about the directors of Catholic Charities, serving on various national committees, and acting as chairman of the directors of Catholic Charities. He has also given leadership to Indiana community programs on poverty, welfare, and planning.[53]

By far the most important personage of Slovak descent in East Chicago is Robert A. Pastrick. He has been mayor of East Chicago for over twenty years and chairman of the Democratic party in Lake County during that period. National publications have recently labeled him as the last of the old-time politicians and one of the most powerful in his time and place. Pastrick began working in the funeral home which his grandfather John Oleska began. He was born into the Byzantine Rite and in recent years has practiced Roman Rite Catholicism. He has received various honors as Young Democrat of Indiana and has run for state office for secretary of state and for county sheriff. He is considered one of the most influential Democratic politicians in the state apart from the governor himself. He has successfully governed a city that in recent years has become predominantly African American and Hispanic. During his administration the city has developed a marina on the lake (Robert A. Pastrick Marina), rebuilt the city's sanitation system, erected a new central high school and other schools, expanded its library system, and provided city services of a high quality. His Democratic pluralities have generally exceeded twenty to one over Republicans.

The early Slovaks in East Chicago worked in the steel mills with the promise of better things for their children. That seems to have taken place. Although some second-generation Slovaks have worked in the mill, many have also gone on into the professions. For two generations Dr. Albert Dainko and Dr. Frank Benchik gave medical services to the people of East Chicago. Assumption parish had seven men become priests. The Bajo family from

RON RYBARCZYK

*Robert A. Pastrick, mayor, East Chicago, 1995.*

"The Harbor" has its second-generation children as a doctor, a dentist, a priest, and a nurse. The third generation has several doctors and a hospital administrator. The Kuric family has second-generation members as accountants and nurses and third-generation members as neurosurgeon, psychiatrist, and microbiologist. These are illustrative of the upward mobility attained by many other second- and third-generation Slovaks.

What is occurring now, in the waning years of the twentieth century, is a transitional period in the Slovak history in East Chicago and in Lake County. The membership of Assumption Church has dwindled, Holy Ghost Church has been closed, and the Byzantine churches have relocated in the south suburbs. Holy Trinity Slovak Evangelical Lutheran Church closed at the end of 1994. Assumption School in East Chicago, Immaculate Conception School in Whiting, and Holy Trinity School in Gary have been closed. It is becoming increasingly more difficult for the church to provide priests to staff the parishes not only because priests are in short supply but also because there are few priests of Slovak ancestry. The language requirement is very minimal now, with few Slovak-speaking priests or professional persons. Whether the Slovak identity and culture can be preserved without language and a locus such as a church to sustain it will be demonstrated during the next generation.

## Slovaks in Gary

Some have termed Gary the "Steel City" or "City of the Century." It began in 1906 with the coming of the United States Steel Corporation and mushroomed to a city of over fifty-five thousand people in the next nine years. The period of its growth provided the setting for a polyglot invasion of people, especially from eastern Europe, with Slovaks among them.

The topography of Gary as it originated had an impact on the life that the early people experienced. The steel mill possessed and dominated the lakeshore. The strip of land north of the Wabash Railroad tracks at 10th Avenue was given to the early settlers and managers of the mill. The strip of territory near Broadway and south of the tracks became known in early history as the "Patch."[54] In Gary history the Patch was a place of numerous saloons, crowded quarters, gambling places, and houses of prostitution. It was in this area that the new immigrants lived. And to this area the first Slovaks came.

Slovaks, with other ethnic people, lived in this area, often in boardinghouses, and worked the long, difficult, and dangerous jobs at the steel mill. A somewhat paternalistic, but not labor friendly, steel corporation treated its workers with little deference and occasional generous gifts to community needs. The early years of life in Gary were not serene or luxurious for the immigrants.[55]

Slovaks in Gary soon formed branches of their lodges. These approximated the religious affiliation they held: the First Catholic Slovak Union Branch #581 (1908); St. Michael the Archangel Society; Branch #289 of the First Catholic Slovak Ladies Union; and St. John the Baptist Society Branch #348 of the Pennsylvania Men's Slovak Catholic Union. These lodges soon provided the nucleus through which Slovaks began their churches.

There were three Slovak churches formed in Gary— Holy Trinity for Roman Catholic Slovaks, St. Michael for Byzantine Catholics, and the Dr. Martin Luther Slovak Evangelical Lutheran Church.

In 1911 a formal effort was made to establish Holy Trinity Slovak Catholic Church in Gary. A committee of representatives from the lodges met and appointed a committee of three to petition the bishop of Fort Wayne to allow a parish. They were given permission and were commissioned to seek their own pastor who would be able to serve the needs of the Slovak people. The first ten years of existence were a time of real struggle. The people had been attending Masses at Holy Angels and at St.

Hedwig. They engaged Father Desiderius Major from Bridgeport, Connecticut, and held the first Mass in St. Emeric Hungarian Church on 29 October 1911.[56]

During these first years of struggle five priests were engaged as pastors. It was not until Father Ignatius Stepuncik became pastor in 1921 that some stability and true progress was made. It must have been a time of considerable sorrow in other ways also. Of the 166 funerals reported during these first ten years, 110 of them were of persons under the age of eighteen, with many infant deaths. During that same period of time, there were 103 marriages and an average of seventy-eight baptisms each year. Occasional notations with the deaths show that many were in childbirth and infancy, others were by accidents such as being struck by a horse and wagon, probably reflective of the health and living conditions of the time.[57]

St. Michael's Byzantine parish was formed and located on a site immediately south of Holy Trinity.[58]

The Slovak Lutherans of Gary began Dr. Martin Luther Slovak Evangelical Lutheran Church.[59]

## Business, Labor, Politics

As in the neighboring communities, there were some Slovaks who did not work in the mills or industries who became business people. Jan Molnar, Andrej Kmetz, and Bela Kellner had grocery stores. Jan Hunera, one of the founders of Holy Trinity parish, was an excavating contractor, later a saloon owner. John Oleska owned the only Slovak funeral home in Gary at that time. Joseph Tapajna had a paper company, and John Bosak began a car dealership that endures to this day.

The origins of one of the Slovak business ventures in northwest Indiana had its roots in the church. During the 1920s the people of St. Michael's Greek Catholic Church in Gary took up collections to provide for the needy, or those who needed to borrow for whatever reasons. Under the leadership of John Mulesa, Sr., the collection efforts became the First Federal Savings and Loan of Gary incorporated in 1934. When John Mulesa, Jr., married Justine Paunicka of Whiting, the families then carried on the ownership and direction of the corporation until the change in structure of savings and loan associations that occurred in the late 1980s. The Paunicka family business originated with four Paunicka brothers who owned grocery stores in Whiting at the same time early in the century.[60]

Although there were labor and management confrontations and difficulties in the other Indiana communities, they did not compare to the strife that labor encountered in Gary. The most significant confrontation produced the steel strike of 1919. The situation was such that United States Steel attempted to break the back of the strike by importing black laborers into Gary from the South. There was a good deal of violence that was put down by martial law and that in the end resulted in defeat for the establishment of a union. There seemed to be no hope for creation of a union or for collective bargaining until 1932 with the passage of the Wagner Act that allowed for the creation of unions. Prominent in efforts to establish a union, John M. Mayernik emerged as a leader of the steelworkers' efforts in dealing with the steel company. His leadership, which included a willingness to risk and sacrifice, eventually helped win the recognition of the union and progress toward better pay and working conditions. Mayernik remained as president of Local 1014 for fifteen years.[61]

James B. Lane, in *"City of the Century": A History of Gary, Indiana,* writes of Anna Rigovsky Yurin, a Slovak-American woman.[62] Yurin attended Holy Trinity School, lived amid the wildness of the central district of Gary, and married Henry Yurin, who secretly helped organize mill workers during the 1930s. Yurin's efforts to bring new life and organization to the Gary Slovak Club, through her work at creating an active Ladies Auxiliary, is characteristic of the role she played, one which may even be termed heroic.

In the political arena two Slovaks distinguished themselves. Betty Malinka held the office of city clerk under several mayoral administrations. John Visclosky, from the office of city controller, assumed the office of mayor during the 1960s.

Andrew Konrady, born in eastern Slovakia, came to Gary in 1909 and worked for the US Steel Company until 1919, when he began a prosperous coal business.[63]

Later, one of Konrady's sons played a controversial political role. In 1968 that son, Bernard W., ran in the race for mayor in such a way that Richard Gordon Hatcher was able to become the first black mayor of a major city in the United States. This spoiler role earned Konrady both praise and rebuke.[64]

The Slovak Club in Gary was organized both as a political force and as a social club without a religious orientation. For the most part the club seemed to be a bastion of male drinking, card playing, and socializing until 1948 when women became part of its activities, particularly assembling each Friday to make homemade pirohi which were sold to the public. The club erected a large building at the corner of 11th and Harrison only to have the changing neighborhood make it quite unusable in recent years.

In Gary, more than and differently from other cities, the movement of Slovaks from the central city following the Second World War was something that troubles them to this day. A large proportion of Slovaks had lived in the central district prior to World War II, and, after coming home from that war, marrying, and beginning families, they built homes in Merrillville and in the southern Glen Park section of Gary. Their move was partly caused by socioeconomic conditions. They were interested in homes with larger rooms, carports, and grassy areas, and they had good jobs that would enable them to build such homes. Since there was no room in the city, they moved out. At the same time African Americans from the South were moving into cities in the North, and many came to Gary. A continuous neighborhood takeover by these migrants from the South has irked the ethnic people, who have felt that their old neighborhood was taken from them.

Churches responded in different ways to this dislocation. The Byzantine church, St. Michael, relocated in Merrillville. Holy Trinity Roman Catholic Church remained at 12th and Madison and built a new church there, one that is now distant from the Slovak people who built it.

## Seven Dolors Shrine

To complement the work of the churches located in northwest Indiana, the Franciscan friars established the Seven Dolors Shrine in Valparaiso. Through the intercession and sponsorship of Monsignor Mlinarovich and Father Lach, John Fetteroff, a Whiting lawyer, donated one hundred acres of land to the project. The Slovak friars developed the plans and erected a pilgrimage center dedicated to Our Lady of Sorrows, patroness of the Slovak people. Records indicate that fifteen thousand people attended the dedication of the grotto by Bishop Noll in May 1931.[65]

The shrine became a place of pilgrimage for Slovaks and others. First surrounded only by farmland, it is now a suburban parish, still staffed by the Franciscan priests, but providing services to the community of South Haven as well as to its original Slovak constituency.

The Franciscans who established this shrine were of Slovak origin and most spoke Slovak. They became a resource for the Slovak Catholic parishes in Indiana, making priests available for missions, preaching, and teaching. Of special interest is that in 1944 Bishop Basil Takach, bishop of the Greek Catholic Byzantine Eparchy, asked the Franciscans to assist in staffing the Byzantine parishes since they were already familiar with the language. The Franciscans obtained the training and permissions necessary to become biritual priests and served many Byzantine parishes in the United States.[66]

This incident affirms the identification of the Greek Catholic churches as Slovak in origin, even though later that identification became more specifically Rusyn, as noted elsewhere in this essay.

## Slovaks in Central Indiana

There was a period of time, generally from 1890 to the First World War, when there was a flourishing Slovak community in the coal country north of Terre Haute. In little cities such as Carbon, Diamond, Clinton, Perth, Seelyville, Blanford, and Unionville, there were little communities of Slovaks, bound together in their fraternal lodges, working in the coal mines.

There was a proliferation of lodges in this area. The First Catholic Slovak Union had branches in Carbon, Diamond, Clinton, and Perth. The Sokol had a branch in Clinton. The First Catholic Slovak Ladies Union had branches in Terre Haute and Clinton. The National Slovak Society had branches in Clinton, Seelyville, and Blanford. According to Mary Zepi the lodges were a source of feasting and dancing up to the First World War, but now the lodges are all closed.[67]

These communities existed as long as the coal mines operated. There seems to have been only one Catholic church, St. Mary's, in Diamond. At the turn of the century the parish had forty families, and people came from all around to attend services there. Father Benedict Rajcany came from Whiting to preach and hear confessions. For a while the Diamond parish had its own priest, and the Ursuline nuns operated a parish school for five years after the Second World War. For the most part, however, the parish engaged different priests from time to time, who came and instructed the children in catechism and arranged for First Holy Communion. At St. Mary's the priests were baptizing thirty to fifty infants each year in the years 1900 and following, almost all of them of Slovak parentage. The parish closed in 1988.[68]

One of the lodge members, Jan Roskovinsky, wrote (in Slovak) to the *Jednota*:

> Diamond, Indiana. We built our church in 1899. Father Michal Siter came in 1904, before that it was Father Frantisek Sebik. We have no school, the parish is too small. We have 60 families.[69]

From Klement Murgac in Carbon:

> We do not have a Slovak priest, nor church or teacher. We go to confession and mass to the Irish church. Our children only learn English and we do not know how this will look. Just last month, for two weeks, Father Alex Sulak from Chicago taught the children for their First Communion. The last day he heard our confessions. We have 17 families.[70]

A 10 April 1910 *Jednota* article gives a glimpse of life in Carbon. The account not only tells about the church and the services in Carbon, but also relates some of the problems the miners had with the coal operators and how difficult it was to get even a five-cent raise. Nonetheless, the article encourages people to come to Carbon to work. The miners were paid with company scrip until the time of the First World War.[71]

According to Mary Zepi there are only three Slovaks in Diamond now. Everyone left when the mines closed after the First World War. Zepi's father died of black lung disease, and she did washing, ironing, and gardening and took care of her invalid mother.

Albert Klain, who frequently wrote about Slovak life in central Indiana to the *Jednota,* provided an interesting comment on life in Clinton, Indiana, in 1906. Klain noticed that some Slovaks in Illinois had formed political clubs. He wanted it known that for over seven years Clinton Slovaks had such a political club. In fact, he was pleased to note that the club had a license so that a person could get beer by the quart. And, he added, "we also have a good priest, even if he is Irish!"[72]

There are two cemeteries in Diamond, one for Roman Catholics and one for Greek Catholics. The tombstones seem to indicate that the Slovaks of the area were somewhat older than those who settled in other parts of Indiana. Many of them were born in the middle of the nineteenth century and were already forty or more years old when they worked in Diamond. Most originated from Zemplin County in Slovakia. After coming to Pennsylvania and then to Indiana, they called their compatriots to join them. Records of births, marriages, and deaths that reveal these origins are at Annunciation Church in Brazil.[73]

The National Slovak Society lists a lodge in New Albany, Indiana, that began in 1912 and was closed in 1915. It was founded by a man named Victor Vokolek. After sending in membership and dues for a number of people, Vokolek later sent in falsified death records and began receiving payment on their policies. When discovered, he was sentenced in federal court to five years in prison. There never was a lodge in New Albany.[74]

The chapter of Slovak history in central Indiana seems to be closed, though there are still some lodge members living in the Terre Haute area.

## Slovaks or Rusyns?

A substantial number of people emigrating from eastern Slovakia to the United States, many to Indiana,

*The Slovak family of Albert George Gajdos (upper right). His father George (center) came from Sol, Slovakia, in 1904 and married Mary Kucha, a native of Rudlov, Slovakia. Albert and his family lived in several Indiana cities including Richland, Evansville, Kokomo, and Indianapolis.*

considered themselves Greek Catholic Slovaks. Many maintain that identity today. They were also referred to as Rusnaks, as Ruthenians, and sometimes as Carpatho-Russians.[75] In recent years they identify as Byzantine Catholics for religious purposes and as Rusyns for ethnic purposes. Since their territory of origin was Slovakia, a large number simply continue to identify themselves as Slovaks.

In Indiana there are communities and churches comprised of people from Slovakia who are now being termed Rusyns. In the Old Country they lived in what is now the eastern part of Slovakia, the western part of Ukraine, and the extreme southeast portion of Poland known as Galicia. This generally is territory including and adjoining the eastern section of the Carpathian mountain range.[76]

In Whiting St. Mary's Church became the first Greek Catholic Church in Indiana. Later churches were formed in Indiana Harbor (Holy Ghost), in East Chicago (St. Basil), in Gary (St. Michael), and in Hammond (St. Nicholas). There was also a cluster of Greek Catholics in

central Indiana where a Greek Catholic cemetery still exists. In addition, there is a small mission church in Indianapolis, St. Anthony Byzantine Catholic Church, which has perhaps forty members.

These people formed lodges, for example, the Greek Catholic Union, started churches, and began acclimating to life in the United States. They came here for the same reasons as other immigrants—poverty and oppression in the Old Country. Different from other Slovak groups, the liturgies were in the Eastern Rite of the church, using the Old Church Slavonic language in that liturgy, and had a noncelibate clergy in the early years.

The history of these churches is steeped in a series of controversies, centering mainly around the ownership and administration of churches and with the Roman Church regarding membership and the celibacy of the clergy. These issues caused schisms that resulted in large numbers of people leaving the church to form or join Orthodox churches. The resulting confusion and disorientation created uncertainty among the churches. Many members were lost to the Roman Rite through marriage and legislation that favored the Roman Rite in the United States.

Three of the churches experienced schisms involving court cases and difficulties of many kinds. Schisms occurred in Gary, Hammond, and East Chicago, with the Catholic Eastern Rite churches having to begin again.

During this period similar difficulties were confronting the churches in the Old Country. The Ukrainian and Russian efforts to absorb and thereby eliminate the church were very strong.[77] Hungarian efforts to Romanize them were resented and resisted. Lacking a country of identity, the Greek Catholics received no support from the international community in their aspirations for independence. People from Carpatho-Russia, suffering from that same lack of identity, with country of origin often being noted as "Hungary" when they entered the United States, are only now able to make a statement as to their existence. The Carpatho-Russians are herein included as part of Slovaks in Indiana because that is the group with which they have most identified during the past one hundred years.

In spite of past difficulties, the Byzantine churches are doing quite well, surviving transition and even adding to the membership in recent years. The churches, having bought land and built new church structures in suburban areas, are in greater proximity to their constituents than had they remained in the inner-city locations. The more traditional liturgies have also attracted some Catholics who have eschewed the changes effected since the Second Vatican Council (1962–65).

The second generation has entered into the mainstream of American life. First District Congressman Peter Visclosky's and East Chicago Mayor Robert Pastrick's parentages are of Greek Catholic (Rusyn) origin.

To what extent these people who call themselves Slovaks will eventually accent their Carpatho-Russian origins by calling themselves Rusyns is unknown. It is likely that this will depend upon the leadership of the churches here in the United States and upon the success of the movement in Slovakia and the Carpathian region in attaining recognition as a distinct, if not separate, people.

## Old Country Customs and Issues in the New Land

### Slovak Customs

The immigrants not only brought their language, their willingness to work, and their religious practices to this new country, they also brought Slovak customs, some of which endure to this day.

One of the more beautiful customs surrounds the Christmas Eve supper, the *Stedry Vecer-Velija*. At this meal the Gospel is read and guests are greeted with the traditional *"Pochvalen Pan Jezis Kristus"* and the response

*"Na Veky Vekov, Amen."* (Praise be Jesus Christ, forever and ever, Amen.) Certain foods, depending upon availability, are traditional. They include mushroom soup, smoked fish, and bobalky (bread balls covered with poppyseed), in addition to fruits and nuts and kolače. The center of the meal is the serving of unleavened bread, symbolizing the Christian Eucharistic bread. It is broken and served by the mother with a dab of honey on the forehead, "That [you] will be sweet all year."[78]

Customs such as these were common in the first generation of immigrants and are now being revived by third-generation Slovaks, who say that their children are interested in it because they are interested in their Slovak roots.[79]

A custom that has virtually disappeared is the annual blessing of homes done in conjunction with the Feast of the Three Kings. This custom was one which the Slovaks shared with many other eastern Europeans. The priest would visit each home with an entourage of cantors and servers. It was a festive visit with singing, eating, and sharing good cheer, perhaps even taking up the annual collection at the time. In most churches this has become impossible because of the difficulty of visiting so many parishioners. Only one parish in Indiana still adheres to this custom.

Dear to the heart of older Slovaks is the custom of blessing the Paska, the Easter bread and food, which occurs on the Saturday before Easter. The sprinkling of girls with water on the Monday after Easter follows the custom of the Poles. These practices are losing place in the Slovak culture, both because the liturgical changes in the church make this blessing out of order and because the fertility rite connotation in our society is lost.

There have been certain foods that are indigenous to the Slovaks and other eastern Europeans that have become part of the culture in Lake County. The Greek and Roman Catholic ladies of the Slovak clubs make pirohi on Fridays and make them available to the general public, thus carrying on the old tradition and also making a profit for the church or club. These pirohi (dough stuffed with potatoes, sauerkraut, plum butter, or cheese) resemble Italian ravioli and are cooked in plenty of butter.

The many catering services and halls in the area have menus that include the distinctive holubky (stuffed cabbage or peppers) and klobasy (usually referred to as Polish sausage) as well as chicken and beef. It is not uncommon to find stuffed cabbage on restaurant menus in the area.

### Slovaks and the Old Country

In the early stages of their coming to the United States, Slovaks came and returned to their native land for many reasons—sometimes to bring back other members of their families, sometimes to show off their new wealth, and sometimes to take up their lives there again. Occasionally the repatriates intended to stay in Slovakia but soon realized how important freedom was to them and returned to the United States. So during the early days there was a direct and immediate contact, albeit a slow one, between the Old Country and the new.

Illustrative of the awareness and the concern that the immigrants had toward their compatriots in Slovakia was a meeting held on 2 June 1907 in Whiting. Representatives came from other cities to the Whiting Opera House, which was reported as filled with over one thousand Slovaks so that there was no more room, even to stand.

Father Benedict Rajcany opened the meeting asking why they assembled. "We stand before the American belief in justice to show that our brothers beneath the Tatra Mountains are being done wrong . . . since the uprising of the Magyars in 1848 was for freedom, why haven't they granted it to the Slovaks?" Michael Kozacik, then president of the local men's lodge, said, "Slovakia is like our Father, America our Mother."

A speaker from Chicago bemoaned the fact that the world was unaware of the Slovak people and that many Slovaks did not even know who they were themselves. He decried the actions of the Magyars in putting Slovaks in jail and excitedly (the report says that he was getting more and more excited, to the point of boiling over) shouting "we must protect our language and support our *Vlast,* our country."[80]

In addition to the collection that raised over a thousand dollars, a series of protest resolutions were passed. Two of particular import were:

> We protest against the Magyars for forcing their language on the Slovak people, we protest against the use of Magyar in the church services, we bind ourselves together to support our brothers in Europe so that they would have a life and freedom which we have here.[81]

It is easily seen that these people were well aware of their condition in the United States as being better than conditions in their homeland and committedly concerned in their desire to help those who had remained at home. The First World War changed the relationship. The Slovaks were now prevented from returning to Slovakia and, in fact, the Austria-Hungary from which they had emigrated no longer existed. The war closed the issue of return, and most Slovaks accepted their permanent presence in the United States. That, however, did not mean they had no relationship with the Old Country

and their relatives and friends there. The Slovaks believed that fighting as soldiers for the United States was a contribution toward their countrymen in Slovakia. They also saw that there was hope for Slovaks in the Old World to receive a new lease on life. They were supportive, and some of the Slovaks from Indiana were involved in the Cleveland and Pittsburgh accords, which created the nation of Czechoslovakia after the war. People like Rev. John Bradac were avid nationalists, who saw the possibility of Slovakia being free for the first time in its history. The Slovaks in the United States soon faced disappointment in this regard since they came to feel that Thomas Masaryk had not lived up to his previous agreements to give more autonomy to Slovakia.[82]

During the period between world wars the local Slovak community solidified its presence here and had no thought of returning to the homeland. It was through their lodges at the national level that they participated in movements and efforts to gain better recognition of the Slovak people. When Father Andrew Hlinka visited the United States in 1938 he was given a warm welcome in East Chicago and Whiting. Father Lach, Father Mlinarovich, and others formed the Catholic Slovak Federation that championed Slovak causes overseas as well as in the United States. During this same period Slovaks in Indiana found themselves both establishing their own identity and beginning to become more and more American.

During the 1920s the churches, lodges, and social clubs were active in sports, especially baseball and basketball. Sport had not yet become as commercialized and professionalized as it is today. These clubs played among themselves, formed leagues, and comprised a good portion of the recreational and social life of Slovaks. The Sokols made athletics a central part of their lodge activity. The Junior Jednota girls had drill teams that involved large numbers of young women.

Perhaps the Slovak Days of the 1930s are the best sign of the preservation of Slovak identity and the fulfillment of the process of Americanization. The First Catholic Slovak Day was held in Wicker Park, now Highland, in October 1933. The format for these celebrations was similar—the celebration of Mass, followed by dinner, games, speeches, music, and dancing. In 1933 everything was in Slovak; by 1944 almost everything was in English. In the early 1930s the speeches were really sermons along religious topics. By 1939 the Irish mayor of Whiting was on the program. In 1944 Sen. Samuel Jackson was the featured speaker.[83]

During the Second World War Slovaks in Lake County, along with Slovaks throughout the United States, were encouraged to buy war bonds. So great was the Slovak subscription rate that a Liberty Ship launched in May

1944 was named the *Rev. Stephen Furdek* for the priest who had organized the First Catholic Slovak Union and the Slovak League of America. Three other ships were named after Slovak-American leaders.[84]

Awareness of their own proper identity was still problematic in 1936 when the Slovak Day program found it necessary to address the question "Slovak, or Slavish?" "It is an offense to use the term 'Slavish' in reference to Slovak people. If you would establish a good feeling, always use the term SLOVAK and never 'Slavish.'"[85]

During the Second World War there were uncertain feelings toward what was happening in Europe. Though Slovakia was independent for the first time in its history, during the time of Monsignor Tiso as president it was still under the domination of Nazi Germany. There seemed to be no good ground to hold regarding the controversial status of Slovakia during that war.[86]

After the war the situation changed and Slovaks in the United States were rallied to help their countrymen recover from the war and the Communist occupation. Father John Lach led a campaign to help the Slovaks, selling seals and rallying others to the Slovak cause. "A faint cry is being heard from a distant land across the wide expanse of the Atlantic Ocean . . . we should pick up that faint call for help . . . so that all the world will be aware of the dangers and distress which have come to our fellow Slovaks."[87]

The Cold War made travel or commerce between Slovakia and the United States very difficult. A number of Slovaks escaped from Slovakia, and a few of them came to America as political refugees; however, their numbers were not great enough to influence the Slovak communities here.

In the late 1950s efforts were made to assist the people of Slovakia, especially with regard to the preservation and practice of their faith. Slovakia was dominated by the Communists and the practice of the faith severely curtailed. What transpired was the creation of the Institute of Sts. Cyril and Methodius in Rome, which became a center for Slovaks throughout the world.[88] Prayer books and religious literature were printed and sent to Slovakia. The institute also became a seminary for dispersed Slovaks and a training and education center for Slovaks who would eventually return to serve the church in Slovakia once it was free. What is important to note here is that Slovaks and Slovak organizations in America responded generously, giving millions of dollars toward the creation and support of the institute in Rome. Once alerted to the problems that the country of their ancestry was enduring, they were more than willing to assist. The national lodges, especially the men's and women's Jednotas, gave hundreds of thousands of dollars. The Slovak churches in Indiana

continue annually to contribute toward the work of the Slovak institute as well as other causes that assist the people of Slovakia.

Only during the twentieth century has the thousand-year existence of the Slovak people been brought to the attention of the world. The long submerged history and existence of this people has come to light largely through immigrant Slovaks, especially in the United States and Canada.

The creation of Slovakia as an independent nation in January 1993 is the culmination of this thousand-year yearning.

## Attainment and Service, Church and State

Occasionally someone may remark that there are two leadership positions in northwest Indiana that stand out because they virtually coincide in spanning municipal and county boundaries and because they serve constituencies larger than any others. These two positions are the bishop of the diocese of Gary and the congressman from the first district in Indiana. Both have constituencies that extend through Lake, Porter, and Starke counties.

In reflecting upon the past one hundred years, if Slovaks have achieved success and status, or have provided a high level of leadership and service, it is evidenced by these two positions and the two men of Slovak descent who have attained them, Andrew G. Grutka and Peter Visclosky.

### Andrew G. Grutka

Since 1957 the most prominent Slovak in the United States has been Bishop Andrew G. Grutka. The history of Slovaks in Indiana and, in fact, the United States would not be complete without recognizing the place that he held locally and nationally. Grutka came to northwest Indiana from Joliet, Illinois, after having studied in Rome. His first assignment in northwest Indiana was as pastor of Sacred Heart parish in East Chicago in 1942 and then as pastor of Holy Trinity in Gary from 1944 to 1957. At that time he was named as first bishop of Gary and commissioned to start the diocese. He functioned as bishop until the mandatory retirement age of seventy-five, retiring in 1984.

Grutka's pastorate at Holy Trinity comprised the golden years of that parish.[89] Young Slovaks were returning from the war, enjoying employment and educational opportunities, forming new families, and succeeding as Americans. In addition to the pastoral care he gave them, he added the dimension of his personal participation in race and labor issues, taking an enlightened position on both and actively collaborating with others in addressing and resolving such problems. That preceded and continued during his episcopacy. His leadership in northwest Indiana

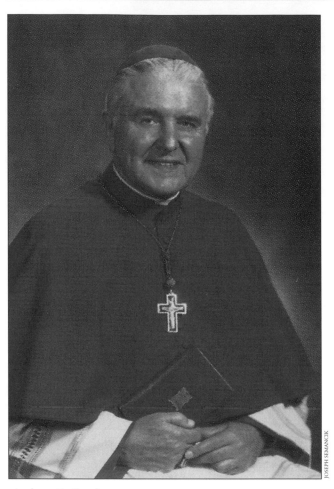

*Andrew G. Grutka.*

within and outside the church makes him worthy of a historical note as a person of eastern European ethnic ancestry who was able to transcend the boundaries of ethnic interest and serve the broader community.

In the early 1960s he acceded to the request of the Holy See to assume responsibility for the creation of the Sts. Cyril and Methodius Institute in Rome. This center for Slovak studies, publications, and education was created and financed because of his personal appeal throughout the United States to Slovaks and Slovak organizations. He literally raised millions to help keep the faith alive in Slovakia during a time of religious oppression. His talks on Radio Free Europe and Vatican Radio gained him a well-known name in Slovakia and regular refusal of visas to visit Slovakia by the Communist government.

The appointment of Grutka as a Slovak to the position of bishop of a diocese in the United States is of historic value given the long-standing policy of seeming to name predominantly priests of Irish descent. As a Slovak appointed as Ordinary of a diocese, Grutka was among the first ethnic or minority priests promoted to the episcopacy.

During his retirement years Grutka remained active in various community endeavors. He died on 11 November 1993. His achievements and place in the history of the region were noted in articles that accompanied his funeral. He was buried within Holy Angels Cathedral in Gary.

## Peter Visclosky

The election of Peter Visclosky to the congressional seat in the House of Representatives for the first district in Indiana can probably be seen as an attainment and acceptance of Slovaks as part of the American dream. He had been an administrative assistant to one of his congressional predecessors. A graduate of Indiana University Northwest, he attained a law degree from Notre Dame Law School and received a master's degree in international law from Georgetown University. Visclosky's father John had been mayor of Gary for a short time.

Peter Visclosky has served in Congress since 1984, holds a place on the Appropriations Committee, works for all the people of the district, and indentifies as a Slovak.

## The End of a Century

The history of the Slovaks in Indiana began with settlements in three cities on the shore of Lake Michigan and with a cluster of settlements in little cities in central Indiana. As has been indicated, the Slovaks in central Indiana have been dispersed in such a way that no Slovak community exists. However, some patterns are discernible regarding the current Slovak identity and direction.

The Slovaks of Whiting, East Chicago, and Gary have maintained an identity. In Whiting the community has remained somewhat intact. Although many have moved away, a sufficient number of the second and third generations have remained to form a community that generally identifies as Slovak. The Slovak communities of East Chicago and Gary are less favorably situated. Their neighborhoods have become inner-city areas, are occupied by other minorities, and consist of housing that the present generation would not find acceptable. Although some second- and third-generation Slovaks may remain, the majority have moved into the surrounding communities of Highland, Griffith, Hessville, Merrillville, and other towns and cities.

In these surrounding communities Slovaks have become integral participants in the life thereof. The Byzantine churches have relocated there and seem to be holding their own, if not experiencing something of a rebirth. The Roman Catholic churches that the Slovaks have joined are territorial parishes. The Slovaks have become persons of leadership and responsibility in those parishes, and they have helped to build the new schools and churches there during this past generation.

The future of Slovak life in Northwest Indiana essentially lies in the future of the Roman Catholic churches. St. John the Baptist parish in Whiting remains as the largest and most vibrant parish in that city. Its school flourishes, even drawing students from outside the city. It will celebrate the one hundredth anniversary of its founding in 1997 with joy of its Slovak heritage, even as that heritage wanes. Immaculate Conception parish in Whiting maintains a strong identification as Slovak, with the Slovak language still used more frequently than in the other churches.

Holy Trinity parish in central Gary has had its school closed and for the most part serves the African-American people of the area. Much of its formerly committed Slovak population has passed on. The remainder and the current generation have joined suburban parishes near their homes.

The two Slovak churches in East Chicago continue to serve people of Slovak ancestry. The Slovak speakers of Assumption have been joined by Lithuanians whose church has closed and by Hispanics from the neighborhood. Sacred Heart is now less than 40 percent Slovak, but it has grown somewhat in recent years with Hispanics and people from a closed neighboring parish.

The maintenance and renewal of Slovak culture has been assisted in recent years through an Annual Slovak Day, which has drawn a large attendance from Northwest Indiana and from adjacent areas in Illinois. The day is religious and cultural, with Mass, Slovak foods, music, and dancing. Its future success will depend upon its ability to attract the current and future generations of young people of Slovak ancestry.

Slovaks have become part of the broader community. They are no longer Slovak in their business. Whereas their parents may have owned a saloon that catered to Slovak immigrants, this generation may own a restaurant that has no ethnic connotation and that markets itself to the entire community. These Slovaks have joined and become officers in Rotary, Kiwanis, and Lions clubs. And instead of ethnic fraternal lodges they now join the Knights of Columbus and become officers and leaders of that organization, which cuts across ethnic boundaries but maintains its Catholic characteristics.

The reality of intermarriage has had its impact on Slovak identity as it has on other ethnic groups. Intermarriage has crossed both ethnic and religious lines. The influence of the other ethnic groups and other religions will assuredly affect the degree of ethnic identification and the notion of ethnic survival. How will children identify if they have an Irish surname and a Slovak mother, or vice versa? How does one interpret one's Slovak surname to in-laws who have no comprehension of ethnic meaning?

There are strengths that exist in the contemporary society that will make it possible for Slovaks and other ethnics to continue making progress. There is less of a stigma now connected with names that are clearly ethnic. Although eastern European names, Slovak among them, are not common in the upper echelon of management and boardrooms, they are less likely to need changing in order to get ahead in the future.

The language issue is more difficult. Louise B. Hammer has found that the first generation speaks fluent Slovak, understands it, and perhaps even can write it. The second generation can sometimes understand Slovak but is not really fluent. The third generation knows little of the language.[90] If language is necessary for the bearing of culture, then Slovaks and others have a clear task ahead—to find a way to communicate culture without language.

Some Slovaks have left Indiana entirely, usually for retirement purposes. Most remain within a reasonable distance of Gary, East Chicago, and Whiting. For those who have left the area, the attraction of a new lifestyle, sometimes more devoid of religious nomenclature and without support of customs and traditions, may well allow for further diminution of Slovak identification.

It remains to be seen what the next generation of Slovaks in America will do to maintain its identity and to preserve and enhance the traditions of its ancestors.

It may well be that the first hundred years of Slovak history in Indiana may also be the last.

## Notes

1. Emily Greene Balch, *Our Slavic Fellow Citizens* (New York: New York Charities Publications Committee, 1910), 86.

2. Joseph A. Mikus, "Slovakia: A Political and Constitutional History," *Slovak Studies* 24 (1984): 16.

3. M. Mark Stolarik, *The Slovak Americans* (New York: Chelsea House Publishers, 1988), 18.

4. Ibid.

5. Louise B. Hammer, "A Brief History of the Slovak Language," *Kalendar-Almanac* (Pittsburgh: National Slovak Society, 1988), 65–79.

6. Louise B. Hammer, "Early Slovak Communities in America," *Rocenka: Yearbook of the Czechoslovak Genealogical Society International* (winter 1992): 46.

7. Stolarik, *Slovak Americans,* 25.

8. Hammer, "Brief History of the Slovak Language," 65.

9. Ibid., 73–74.

10. Ibid., 69.

11. M. Mark Stolarik, "A Historical Perspective on the Declining Use of the Slovak Language over Three Generations in the United

States of America," *Kalendar-Almanac* (Pittsburgh: National Slovak Society, 1990), 66.

12. Powell A. Moore, *The Calumet Region: Indiana's Last Frontier,* vol. 39 of *Indiana Historical Collections* (Indianapolis: Indiana Historical Bureau, 1959), 373.

13. Stolarik, *Slovak Americans,* 33.

14. James Paul Allen and Eugene James Turner, *We the People: An Atlas of America's Ethnic Diversity* (New York: Macmillan, 1988), 3.

15. Ibid., 87.

16. U.S. census reports, 1880–1990.

17. *Pamatnik: Trytsat' Rocneho Jubilea, Osady Svateho Jana Krstitel'a vo Whiting, Indiana, 1897–1927* (Memorial Book, Thirtieth Anniversary, St. John the Baptist Church, Whiting, Indiana). The memorial books, published on anniversary celebrations, contain a variety of materials. The books have detailed histories; biographies of prominent families, including place of origin in the Old Country; pictures of officers, committees, and families; advertisements of businesses, political parties, and persons; and programs of the celebrations. The early books are totally in Slovak, with a gradual transition into almost everything in English. They provide an invaluable record.

18. *Menoslov,* First Catholic Slovak Ladies Union, Branch 81, Whiting, Indiana. These "lists of members" for lodges contain not only names but also often date of birth, county of origin in the Old Country, date of arrival in America, date of spouse's death, and other items. This particular book indicates the more common origins of members were Sarisska, Zemplinska, and Ungvar counties in Slovakia.

19. Records of St. Mary's Church, Diamond, Indiana. The church served the Roman Catholic needs of the Slovaks in several central Indiana towns. An examination of the records indicates thirty-five to forty-five baptisms per year in the early years of this century. The church was closed in 1988, though still maintained. The records are kept at Annunciation Church in Brazil, Indiana (visit to Diamond and Brazil, 18 Oct. 1990).

20. Stolarik, *Slovak Americans,* 35.

21. "History of St. John's Parish," in *Pamatnica: Oslavy 40-rocneho Jubilea Osady Sv. Jana Krstitel'a* (Whiting, Ind., 1937).

22. June Granatir Alexander, *The Immigrant Church and Community: Pittsburgh's Slovak Catholics and Lutherans, 1880–1915* (Pittsburgh: University of Pittsburgh Press, 1987).

23. R. Vladimir Baumgarten and Joseph Stefka, *The National Slovak Society, 100 Year History, 1890–1990* (Pittsburgh: The Society, 1990), 201.

24. *Pamatnik: Oslavu Zlateho Jubilea, Spolok Sv. Juraja, Cislo 130 I.K.S.J., Whiting, Indiana, April, 1944.* This history of the St. George Branch of the First Catholic Slovak Union was written on the occasion of its fiftieth anniversary celebration. It is available at the Whiting-Robertsdale Historical Society, Whiting, Indiana.

25. Edwin G. Kaiser, *History of St. John's Parish, Whiting, Indiana, 1897–1947: Fifty Years of Grace* (Whiting, Ind., 1948), 25. This book of 162 pages chronicles not only the history of St. John parish itself, but also posits that history within the history of northwest Indiana dating back to the French fur traders. Both St. John in Whiting and Holy Trinity in Gary showed a sense of history and farsightedness in engaging Edwin Kaiser, a historian from St. Joseph's College in Rensselaer, Indiana, to provide them with fifty-year histories.

26. Ibid., 31.

27. "Early History of St. Mary's Assumption Church," in *Anniversary Booklet of the Diamond Jubilee of St. Mary's Assumption Byzantine Catholic Church* (Whiting, Ind., 1974), 8.

28. "Brief History of St. Paul Evangelical Lutheran Church of Whiting, Indiana," contained in the booklet issued on the occasion of the dedication of the new church, 1957.

29. Ibid.

30. *Whiting Call,* 28 July 1916.

31. More than one elderly Whiting Slovak has copies of this stock certificate.

32. *Zapisnica, Zenskeho spolku vo Whiting, Ind vo roku 1899.* (Record Book of the First Catholic Slovak Ladies Union, Branch 81. Organized in 1899). This handwritten minute book contains names of charter members and minutes of meetings.

33. Sophie Gresko, interview with the author, Whiting, 11 Feb. 1992. Gresko, ninety when interviewed, is the current guardian of the early minute and roster books of the First Catholic Slovak Ladies Union.

34. *Zapisnica,* July 1926.

35. Kaiser, *History of St. John's Parish,* 41.

36. Edward Meador, ed., "John J. Lach," in *American Philosophy* (Boston: Meador Publishing Co., 1956), 111–33.

37. Anthony X. Sutherland, "Father Lach's Band," *Jednota,* 6 Mar. 1991. The *Jednota* is the newspaper of the First Catholic Slovak Union that has been published weekly for members since the beginning of the century. The early editions were exclusively in Slovak. Current issues are in English, with a Slovak section on the back pages.

38. *Jaro,* 26 June 1935 (a newspaper for young Slovaks).

39. Edward A. Zivich, *From Zadruga to Oil Refinery: Croatian Immigrants and Croatian-Americans in Whiting, Indiana, 1890–1950* (New York: Garland, 1990), 40, 44. In an interview with Zivich in Whiting on 30 Mar. 1990, he confirmed that his investigation of the situation of Croatian workers at the Standard Oil refinery clearly indicated that Slovaks shared the same working conditions.

40. Interviews with William Ciesar (2 Apr. 1992, Whiting), Joseph Grenchik (31 Mar. 1992, Whiting), and Lillian Semancik (16 Feb. 1992) along with others provided the information regarding Slovak business interests in Whiting. They and their parents were proprietors dating back into the early part of the century.

41. Baumgarten and Stefka, *National Slovak Society,* 201.

42. Kaiser, *History of St. John's Parish,* 50.

43. Floyd B. Bolton, et al., *East Chicago, A Historical Description* (East Chicago, Ind.: The Public Schools, 1947), 27.

44. Anthony Ficko, interview with the author, Whiting, 13 Feb. 1992. Ficko was familiar with ancestral origins of East Chicago Slovaks, his father was a personal friend of Andrew Hlinka, Slovak patriot, who visited Ficko in East Chicago in 1938.

45. John F. Noll, *The Diocese of Fort Wayne: Fragments of History* (Huntington, Ind.: Our Sunday Visitor, 1941), 359.

46. "The History of the Church of St. Basil the Great," in *Anniversary Booklet of the Golden Jubilee of the Church of St. Basil the Great, 1923–1973* (East Chicago, Ind., 1973), 22–28.

47. Daniel D. Droba, ed., *Czech and Slovak Leaders in Metropolitan Chicago: A Biographical Study of 300 Prominent Men and Women of Czech and Slovak Descent* (Chicago: Slavonic Club of the University of Chicago, 1934), 128.

48. "The Story of Our Parish," in *Fortieth Anniversary Book of Assumption Church, East Chicago, 1955.*

49. Droba, ed., *Czech and Slovak Leaders,* 105.

50. Ibid., 290.

51. Simon Miller, "Ethnic Minorities in the East Chicago Community" (East Chicago Public Library, 1959). Study prepared for the East Chicago Community Council.

52. Correspondence of Rev. Clement Mlinarovich and Bishop John Francis Noll regarding the erection of Sacred Heart Church, East Chicago, 1939–41.

53. Joseph Semancik, "Highlights of the History of Sacred Heart Parish," *Program and History Book, Sacred Heart Church, East Chicago, 1976.* Fiftieth anniversary booklet.

54. James B. Lane, *"City of the Century": A History of Gary, Indiana* (Bloomington: Indiana University Press, 1978), 34.

55. Ibid., 31.

56. Edwin G. Kaiser, *Fifty Golden Years: The Story of Holy Trinity Parish (Slovak), Gary, Indiana* (Gary, Ind., 1961), 30.

57. Baptismal and death records of Holy Trinity parish, Gary, 1911 to 1921.

58. "From 1911 to 1961," in *Souvenir Book of St. Michael's Byzantine Catholic Church, 50th Anniversary* (Gary, Ind., 1961).

59. Droba, ed., *Czech and Slovak Leaders,* 108.

60. Dolores Paunicka Callahan, interview with the author, Lowell, 27 June 1990.

61. Lane, *"City of the Century,"* 194.

62. Ibid., 224–27.

63. Droba, ed., *Czech and Slovak Leaders,* 78.

64. Lane, *"City of the Century,"* 286.

65. Richard Portasik, *Slovak Franciscans in America: History of Most Holy Savior Commissariat* (Pittsburgh: Franciscan Fathers, 1966).

66. Ibid., 85.

67. Mary Zepi, interview with the author, Brazil, 18 Oct. 1990. Now a resident of a Brazil nursing home, Mary Zepi, who was almost ninety years old and the self-appointed "Historian of Diamond, Indiana," spent her entire life in Diamond in the same house.

68. Records of St. Mary's Church, Diamond, Indiana (now kept at Annunciation parish, Brazil, Indiana).

69. *Kalendar, Jednota,* 1906, p. 46 (yearbook of the First Catholic Slovak Union).

70. Ibid., 52.

71. *Jednota,* 10 Apr. 1910.

72. Ibid., 5 Sept. 1906.

73. A visit to Diamond, Indiana, on 18 Oct. 1990 found the Church of St. Mary's closed insofar as services were concerned, but still maintained along with the grounds surrounding the church. The cemeteries were likewise well maintained, separated by about half a mile.

74. *Jednota* Archives, Middletown, Pennsylvania.

75. Paul Norbert Magosci, *Our People: Carpatho-Rusyns and Their Descendants in North America* (Toronto: Multicultural History Society of Ontario, 1984), 8.

76. Ibid., 5.

77. Ibid., 85.

78. *Hammond Times,* 12 Dec. 1987.

79. Stolarik, *Slovak Americans,* 103.

80. "Indignancna schodza vo Whiting, Ind.," *Jednota,* 26 June 1907 (protest meeting in Whiting, Ind.).

81. Ibid.

82. M. Mark Stolarik, "The Role of American Slovaks in the Creation of Czechoslovakia, 1914–1918," *Slovak Studies* 8 (1968): 7–82.

83. *Pamatnik a Program, Prveho Kat. Slov. Dna. 1933* (Memorial Book and Program, First Catholic Slovak Day, 1933); *Pamatnica, VII Kat. Slov. Dna v. Indiana, 1939* (Memorial Book, 7th Catholic Slovak Day in Indiana, 1939); *XII Catholic Slovak Day of Indiana, 1944.*

84. *XII Catholic Slovak Day.*

85. *Pamatnik a Program, Stvrteho Kat. Slov. Dna v Indiana, 1936* (Memorial Book and Program, Fourth Catholic Slovak Day in Indiana, 1936).

86. Stolarik, *Slovak Americans,* 28.

87. Meador, ed., "John J. Lach," 114.

88. Stefan Nahalka, "The Slovak Institute of Sts. Cyril and Methodius in Rome," *Slovak Studies* 13 (1973).

89. Kaiser, *Fifty Golden Years,* 75 ff.

90. Louise B. Hammer, "Cultural Change and Its Effect on Language Maintenance: The Slovak Language in America." Paper presented to the national meeting of the American Association for the Advancement of Slavic Studies, Chicago, November 1989.

# SOUTH SLAVS

## BULGARIANS/MACEDONIANS

## SERBS

## SLOVENES

# BULGARIANS/ MACEDONIANS

OPHELIA GEORGIEV ROOP AND LILIA GEORGIEV JUDSON

*Each immigrant Slav group lived in an ethnic enclave in which the structure of their home villages was replicated. Crystal Benton Fall noted in 1916 that "The neighborhood constitutes a unit within itself. It has all the attributes of the village life. . . . The trade of the foreigner is monopolized by the foreign merchant. . . . The saloons, the butcher-shops, the grocery stores, and the coffee houses, are all under local control. . . . The barber shop, the bakery shop, and the grocery are all operated by men born in the old country. . . . The saloons predominate in number over the other types of business but there are frequent combinations of coffee houses, pool-rooms and barber shops."*

## Bulgarian/Macedonian Immigration to the United States

There is evidence now that the story about the first Bulgarian/Macedonian to come to the Americas, a certain Drahan da Lihnida, or Dragan of Ohrid (Lihnida is the Greek name for the medieval Bulgarian city Ohrid, today in the Republic of Macedonia), is not an unsubstantiated myth. A world map in the naval museum in Madrid shows the two ships that Drahan da Lihnida took on an expedition to the Americas. One of the ships is flying the flag of medieval Bulgaria and carries the inscription, "This land was discovered in 1499 for Castile, and its discoverer was a Bulgarian."[1]

A few adventurous Bulgarians/Macedonians had made their way to the United States by the mid-1870s. A substantially larger group followed during the late 1870s until the end of the century. They were university students sponsored by Protestant missionaries in Bulgaria, who intended to return to the motherland upon completion of their studies. Many, however, chose to settle in the United States. There are no records indicating that any of the pre-1900 missionary-sponsored Bulgarians/Macedonians settled in Indiana. Nevertheless the American missionaries to Bulgaria have an Indiana connection. Dr. James F. Clarke, the preeminent Bulgarian studies scholar, one of the founders of the now renowned East European Institute at Indiana University and the institute's first president, was the son and grandson of American missionaries in Bulgaria and was born in Bitolja, then Monastir in the Turkish vilayet (province) of Monastir and today in the Republic of Macedonia.[2]

The first substantial immigrant wave of Bulgarians/ Macedonians appeared in Indiana during the first decade of the twentieth century. They constitute the smallest group of the South Slavs in America.[3] Figures about their early immigration are unreliable for a number of reasons. Until 1920 the Bulgarians, Serbians, and Montenegrins were listed together statistically.[4] Since an autonomous Macedonian state did not exist until 1991 when the Republic of Macedonia declared its independence from Yugoslavia following the demise of Communism in Eastern Europe, the emigrants coming from this geographic region were registered as nationals of the country whose passport they held. Macedonia was declared a nation by Marshal Tito after World War II when the Republic of Macedonia was established in Communist Yugoslavia. However, even after World War II emigrants

from Yugoslav Macedonia were not registered as Macedonian but as Yugoslavian, and studies of Yugoslav Americans exclude them altogether.[5] After 1920 Bulgarians were recorded separately, but Macedonians were not listed as a separate ethnic group.[6]

It is estimated that of the approximately 50,000 Bulgarians who immigrated to the United States between 1900 and 1909–10, 75 percent or more were Bulgarians from Macedonia.[7] In 1980 the *Harvard Encyclopedia of American Ethnic Groups* estimated that there were between 70,000 and 100,000 Bulgarians and their descendants living in the United States. These figures included Bulgarians from the geographic region of Macedonia who profess Bulgarian ethnicity. The same source calculated that between 25,000 to 30,000 Macedonian Americans, or individuals who identified with the Socialist Republic of Macedonia of former Yugoslavia, lived in the United States.[8] As an ethnic group the Bulgarians/Macedonians are invisible and have been successful in blending into American mainstream society. Those who come from the intelligentsia that emerged in post-Ottoman Bulgaria associate ethnic customs with the uneducated peasant class and with the Ottoman occupier. If these people do anything ethnic it might be to attend an Eastern Orthodox church, speak literary Bulgarian, be well informed about Bulgarian history, or identify closely with Russian Slavic culture. Bulgarians/Macedonians who have achieved national and international recognition—conceptual artist Christo, grandfather of computers John Atanasoff, Dow Chemical CEO Frank Popoff, writer and former Massachusetts senator Stoyan Christowe, former Chicago Bears star Boris (Babe) Dimancheff—are not distinguishable by particular ethnocentric feelings or behavior.

Bulgarians/Macedonians can be found in every strata of life and every profession. Often they are recognizable only by their Slavic last names ending in -off, -eff, -ov, -ev, -sky (-ski), and -ovsky (-ovski) or -evsky (-evski). Depending on the time and place of immigration, the same last name is spelled differently, i.e., Georgiev, or Georgieff, or Georgievsky/ki. Several reasons account for this discrepancy. Bulgarians/Macedonians use the Cyrillic alphabet as do the Russians and other Slavs. The -off/-eff endings do not exist within the Cyrillic, and all names with this ending are written with -ov/-ev in the Cyrillic. During the first part of the twentieth century Slavic names such as Romanoff (the Russian royal family) and Rachmaninoff (the Russian composer), as well as the majority of Bulgarian/Macedonian names, were written in English with the -off/-eff ending. Phoenetically the -ov/-ev had an -off/-eff sound. Transliteration (substituting a Roman letter for a Cyrillic one) was not practiced then as it is now. Today the correct spelling for Romanov is with a 'v,' whereas Rachmaninoff continues to be spelled with 'ff' because this was the composer's preference. Later emigrants arriving from kingdom Bulgaria spelled their names with the 'v' ending whereas emigrants from the geographic area Macedonia often, but not always, used the 'ff' ending. The reason for this was the higher level of education of the Bulgarians arriving from kingdom Bulgaria than that of those arriving from the region of Macedonia. The -sky/-ski is another genitive Slavic form, and the y/i is a personal preference. The -ovsky/ki, -evsky/ki ending is a double genitive, and Macedonians in Yugoslav Macedonia were encouraged to give their names this correct Macedonian ending, i.e., from Georgiev to Georgievsky/Georgievski.

## Historical Background and Its Effects on the Bulgarian/Macedonian Immigrants in the United States

The majority of the initial Bulgarian/Macedonian immigrants immigrated to the United States in order to escape political, cultural, and religious oppression. Since economic depression follows political oppression, they also came in search of economic opportunities. But the principal catalyst for immigration remains the historical and political events in the Balkans. Bulgarian/Macedonian immigration to the United States was and continues to be driven by history. Every aspect of the ethnic communities the Bulgarians/Macedonians established in the New World would be predicated on cultural and political factors in the motherland.

Bulgaria and the Republic of Macedonia are Balkan states. Geographically the Balkans are part of Europe, but historically, politically, and culturally they are outside the European experience. The Ottoman conquest deprived the various Balkan nationalities of the significant moments in European civilization—the Renaissance, the Reformation, the Age of Enlightenment.[9] Currently the geographic area Macedonia is divided into Vardar Macedonia—the recently recognized Republic of Macedonia (formerly southeastern Yugoslavia); Pirin Macedonia—southwestern Bulgaria;

Bulgaria/Macedonia
- Principal Cities
— International Boundaries
250 Km
250 Mi.

and Aegean Macedonia—northwestern Greece. The Bulgarians/Macedonians inhabit the ancient lands of Moesia, Macedonia, and parts of Thrace and Illyricum. The Bulgarian kingdom was the result of an assimilation of Proto-Bulgars and Slavs who challenged the power of Byzantium and wielded considerable military power and cultural influence in Europe until the Ottoman conquest.[10]

In 864 Bulgarian Tsar Boris I accepted Christianity from Constantinople and enforced mass conversion in the kingdom. He is a canonized saint of the Bulgarians/Macedonians and many of their American-born descendants are named after him. At the time of Boris's accession, the Slavic prince of Moravia (in former Czechoslovakia), asked the Byzantine Emperor Michael III to send him clerics who could preach Christianity in Slavonic. The emperor sent two scholars from Thessalonica—Constantine (Cyril) and Methodius. They invented the Glagolithic alphabet based on a Bulgarian dialect.[11] It was later revised and perfected into the Cyrillic alphabet most likely by Cyril and Methodius's Bulgarian student Clement.[12] Cyril and Methodius are canonized saints in both the Orthodox and Catholic churches and are perhaps the most beloved and revered saints of the Bulgarians/Macedonians. After their deaths several of their students continued their literary activity in Bulgaria. Clement set up the renowned Ohrid school to train scholars and clergy in Old Bulgarian. He is also a beloved saint of the Bulgarians/Macedonians and the patron saint of several immigrant churches in the United States. The alphabet Cyril and Methodius formulated made Old Bulgarian (Church Slavonic) the literary language of the Slavs and one of the three major literary languages of Europe during the Middle Ages.[13]

The reign of Tsar Samuel (997–1014) is of particular significance to the Macedonian Bulgarians. He relocated the Bulgarian capital to Ohrid and waged constant war with Byzantium. In 1014 Emperor Basil II defeated Samuel's army and captured and blinded fifteen thousand of his Bulgarian soldiers. Basil II has gone down in history as Bulgaroctonus (Bulgar-slayer).[14]

In 1393 the Turks captured the Bulgarian capital, and by the end of the fifteenth century they had conquered all of Europe east of Vienna. With the Ottoman conquest five centuries of dark ages commenced for Bulgaria. The Ottoman invader began a systematic destruction of Bulgarian cities, fortifications, churches, libraries, and schools. To prevent future armed resistance the Bulgarian aristocracy and leading citizenry were killed, imprisoned, or sent into slavery. Entire Bulgarian districts were forced to accept Islam or perish, and large groups of Turks were repatriated to conquered areas. Enormous taxes and social and legal restrictions were imposed on the Christian population. The Ottoman government eliminated the Bulgarian patriarchate and placed all the Christian churches in the Balkan peninsula under the Greek patriarchate. Liturgy in the Bulgarian churches began to be celebrated in Greek. Eventually Greek became the language of the Bulgarian upper classes.

The appearance in the mideighteenth century of the *Slav-Bulgarian History* written by the Macedonian monk Paisii Hilendarski precipitated the revival of nationalism and liberation movements that culminated in the 1876 April Uprising. It was crushed mercilessly. The massacres of Bulgarians were exposed by British prime minister William Gladstone.[15]

One year after the 1876 April Uprising (April 1877), Russia declared war on Turkey. The Russo-Turkish War of 1877–78 ended centuries of Turkish oppression for the Bulgarians. The Treaty of San Stefano (March 1878) granted Bulgaria its pre-Ottoman conquest borders that included Macedonia, but the rest of the Great Powers (England, Prussia, Austria-Hungary) refused to recognize it. The Treaty of Berlin (July 1878) annulled the Treaty of San Stefano and instead established the Principality of Bulgaria and the Turkish province of Eastern Rumelia. Macedonia was returned to Turkey, giving birth to the Macedonian Question. The Ottoman forces returned to Macedonia with a vengeance and subjected the Macedonian Bulgarians to violence and atrocities unfathomable to Westerners.[16]

Historically the Slavs living in the geographic area of Macedonia have professed Bulgarian ethnicity, and until the Treaty of Berlin no one disputed that. Ottoman census maps record them as Bulgarian. The Bulgarian immigrants prior to World War II came predominantly from Macedonia and identified with Bulgarian culture and ethnicity. They referred to themselves as Macedonian only to underscore a geographic identity, not a separate ethnicity. The majority had immigrated precisely because their Bulgarian ethnicity, culture, and church were being suppressed.

In 1885 the Principality of Bulgaria and Eastern Rumelia united, but Macedonia remained under Turkish rule. This precipitated the formation of the Macedonian Liberation Movement (MLM). The MLM operated in Macedonia for roughly fifty years, and many immigrants to America participated in the movement. In 1893 a group of Macedonian-Bulgarian intellectuals formed the Internal Macedono-Odrin (Adrianople/Edirne) Revolutionary Organization that became better known as the Internal Macedonian Revolutionary Organization (IMRO). The IMRO advocated an autonomous Macedonian state and possible unification with Bulgaria at some distant date.[17] It directed organized armed resistance against Turkish oppression and Greek religious and cultural domination through the formation of mountain-roaming brigades (*chetas*). The members of a *cheta* were *komitas* and were led by a *voevode* (warrior leader). By the early twentieth century the IMRO had become "in fact, a provisional system of government established by the Macedonian peasantry."[18] The IMRO is of enormous significance to twentieth-century Balkan affairs and to the Bulgarian/Macedonian Americans. The most powerful organization the Macedonian Bulgarians established in America, the Macedonian Political (since 1952 'Patriotic') Organization (MPO), was considered an extension of the IMRO and embraced its ideology.

In August 1903 on St. Elija's Day (Ilinden), the Macedonian Bulgarians rose against their Turkish oppressor. Dine G. Popcheff, one of the founders of the Bulgarian/Macedonian community in Indianapolis and a participant in the uprising, stated: "There was no hope for us. We wanted only to live our lives, to have peace, to have some privileges. . . . So we said, 'What if we die? It is better that we die than that we go on like this.'"[19]

The insurrection was crushed mercilessly—over 5,000 slain, nearly 120,000 homes destroyed, and 100,000 homeless. The Ilinden Uprising was the catalyst for the mass immigration of Macedonian Bulgarians to America that peaked in 1907. More than 30,000 fled to kingdom Bulgaria.

In the First Balkan War (1912) Greece, Serbia, and Bulgaria fought Turkey and successfully liberated Macedonia. In the Second Balkan War (1913) Bulgaria fought its allies over the division of Macedonia. The 1913 Treaty of Bucharest, signed at the end of the Second Balkan War, partitioned Macedonia between Greece, Serbia, and Bulgaria, a division that for the most part remains in effect today. As a result of this partition more than 70,000 Bulgarians from Aegean Macedonia sought refuge in Bulgaria,[20] and immigration to the United States and Indiana swelled.

The Bulgarians/Macedonians in America unanimously supported the Bulgarian war effort during both Balkan wars by sending money and returning to join the Bulgarian army.[21] During both wars a fifteen thousand-member regiment composed of volunteers from Macedonia fought under Bulgarian command. Many Balkan immigrants left America and returned to their homelands to fight in the Balkan wars. But there are no statistics indicating the number of Bulgarian/Macedonian Balkan wars returnees from Indiana. We only know of individuals who fought in these wars, but not whether as returnees from Indiana. Such is the case of Atanas (Tashe) Kitkoff, who emigrated from Voden (Edessa, Greece) to Indianapolis at an unknown date and served with a rank during both Balkan wars in the Macedonian volunteer regiment of the Bulgarian army.[22] This came as a surprise to his daughter, Mrs. William Christoff (Nadezhda Kitkoff). Since she does not know the exact date of her father's immigration, it is not possible to determine if he returned specifically to serve in the Balkan wars or immigrated afterwards.

After the 1913 division of Macedonia, the Greek and Serbian governments initiated campaigns to force the Macedonian Bulgarians to accept either Greek or Serbian nationality. The occupation forces closed almost two thousand Bulgarian schools and over one thousand Bulgarian churches and monasteries.[23]

During the two World Wars Bulgaria chose the side that would aid it in unification with Macedonia. However, the 1919 Treaty of Neuilly between Bulgaria and the victorious Allied Powers left most of Macedonia to Serbia and Greece again. According to George Prpic, "between 1918 and 1941 the Serbs and the Greeks treated Bulgarian-speaking Macedonians as enemies and mercilessly suppressed any signs of Bulgarian nationalism, forced the people to change their family names, abolished their schools . . . arrested men by the thousands . . . liquidated large numbers, and on the whole treated the Macedonians worse than the Turks had done."[24]

While the Bulgarians in Macedonia struggled for basic freedoms, kingdom Bulgaria was making great strides to join the twentieth century and the West. Whereas prior to liberation from Turkey, Macedonia had an advanced Bulgarian school system, now it was the Bulgarian kingdom that had universities and a modern education system. In an effort to accommodate the new century and to remove itself from Turkey, Turkish words were expunged from the Bulgarian language. The Bulgarian language of those in the conquered or unredeemed lands, as Vardar and Aegean Macedonia came to be called, remained simple, archaic, and riddled with Turkish, eventually becoming the language of the uneducated. Young Bulgarians from these lands yearned to escape to study in Bulgaria. Christo Nizamoff, who emigrated in 1921 from Vardar Macedonia and became a distinguished Indianapolis journalist and editor in chief of the Bulgarian language weekly *Macedonian Tribune* published in Indiana, describes this phenomenon in his autobiography.[25]

After the Balkan wars and World War I the IMRO directed its activities from Bulgaria against the Greeks and the Serbs. Occupied Macedonia became a war zone of constant arrests, tortures, and trials of clandestine revolutionary groups, shoot-outs, and assassinations. In the 1920s and 1930s the IMRO acquired an international reputation as a terrorist organization.[26] In addition it splintered with internal conflicts, and soon assassinations of opposing MLM members raged on the streets of Sofia, Bulgaria, as well. In 1934 a new Bulgarian government dissolved the IMRO and declared it illegal. The organization continued its activities underground until the establishment of Communism in Bulgaria and Yugoslavia, when the responsibility of maintaining the spirit of liberation of the Macedonian Bulgarians passed to the MPO in America. The MPO exposed Greek and Communist Serbian and Bulgarian atrocities against the population of Macedonia. Ivan Mihailov, the last leader and ideologue of IMRO, found an outlet for his revolutionary eloquence in the MPO's organ, the *Macedonian Tribune.*

After World War II Bulgaria and Yugoslavia became Communist republics, and Yugoslav Macedonia was declared a nation, that is a distinct ethnic group.[27] In 1945 a Communist commission created a new Macedonian language alphabet and orthography. "Literary Macedonian owes its existence largely to Tito," notes Dr. James F. Clarke.[28] The Bulgarian Communist government, under the directives of Stalin and in the interest of a Communist Balkan federation and proletarian internationalism, agreed to the creation of a new Macedonian nation. This was particularly compromising for the Bulgarian government. It now found itself in the uncomfortable position of having to renounce the Bulgarian nationality of many Bulgarian historical figures who were from the region Macedonia. The fact that "almost all of Bulgaria's great men have come from Macedonia" did not escape John Reed.[29] The Bulgarian Communists initiated mass arrests of those Macedonian Bulgarians who refused to accept Macedonian ethnicity and nationality.[30]

By the mid-1950s the idea of a Communist Balkan federation was dead, and the Bulgarian Communists now rejected the idea of a separate Macedonian ethnicity. By the early 1960s, however, the idea of a distinct Macedonian nation took root in Yugoslavia and in the United States, especially in industrial immigrant centers such as Gary and Detroit. In the forty-five years following World War II the primary objective of the MPO became to discredit the Marxist-Leninist theory of Macedonian ethnicity and language.

Since World War II Macedonia and Bulgaria have had separate identities. In 1991 the Republic of Macedonia declared its independence from Yugoslavia. Recognition by the United Nations and the United States was thwarted by Greece's objections to the name. Greece maintains that Macedonia is Greek, calls the Bulgarian-speaking Slavs in Aegean Macedonia Slavophone Greeks, and pursues a policy of reprisals toward those who refuse to change their Slavic names to Greek names or who desire to speak openly.

Bulgaria was first to recognize the Republic of Macedonia, supports an independent Macedonian state, and is currently the Republic's only ally in the Balkans. The Republic of Macedonia has declared Macedonian ethnicity, and during the recent census Bulgarian ethnicity was not a nationality option. The recently elected president of Macedonia is a former member of Tito's inner circle.

The Bulgarians/Macedonians came out of this vortex into the predominantly rational, pragmatic, Anglo-Protestant American society. In addition, Eastern Orthodox Christianity had a profound influence in shaping their communities in America. The canons of the Orthodox Church have changed little since Byzantine times. Because all the Holy Sees of the Orthodox Church except Moscow were in Islamic lands, all the Church's efforts went toward self-preservation. Orthodox Christianity remains spiritual, mystical, intuitive, and steeped in visions and miracles. The immigrants brought this intuitiveness and spirituality to the New World where it clashed with western empiricism.

The belief that the Slavic immigrants were inferior to the earlier American settlers was widespread. Edward Ross, a professor of sociology at the University of Wisconsin, noted, "without calling in question the worth of the Slavic race, one may note that the immigrant Slavs have small reputation for capacity," and "to the practiced eye, the physiognomy of certain groups unmistakably proclaims inferiority of type."[31]

## Bulgarian/Macedonian Immigration in Indiana

They came. They came against adversity, with their Balkan baggage, their indomitable spirit, and their Slavic capacity for infinite endurance. They settled in industrial areas that needed unskilled labor. Between 1904 and 1906 strong communities, which the immigrants called colonies, were established in Indianapolis, Fort Wayne, and Gary.

The prospect of a large infusion of Slavs into the fabric of the established white, Anglo-Saxon, Protestant American society alarmed many Indianans. Crystal Benton Fall introduces her 1916 thesis, "The Foreigner in Indianapolis," with the following comment:

> Indiana and Kansas are the two strongholds of the native stock and to them has been intrusted the task of experimenting with the possibilities of the real American. Edward A. Ross, in his book, *The Old World in the New*, points out that the physical attributes of the citizens of these two states are superior in quality due to non-intermarriage of races. No claims to mental superiority have been made, but the state of Indiana has an enviable reputation in educational and literary circles. Indianapolis, with which this study is alone connected, enjoys the unique distinction of being one of four cities with a population of 160,000 to have a majority of native white constituents.[32]

## Employment and Living Conditions

Initially only men came. Later they sent for families, wives, fiancées, and in many instances for mail brides. Violet Guleff of Indianapolis tells of her mother's arrival in Indianapolis in 1921 as part of a group of ten mail brides. According to Guleff's account these and other arranged marriages proved to be good and enduring. Women exercised great control over family and community matters.[33] Many had taken part in the Ilinden Uprising and in the Macedonian Liberation Movement. In an article in the *Indianapolis Star* Mrs. Popcheff, wife of Dine Popcheff of Indianapolis, talks about her own participation in the uprising as a sixteen-year-old scout and spy.[34]

In Indiana, as elsewhere in the United States, the single men lived in communal dormitories that they called *boorts,* presumably a derivation from boardinghouse. Called stag boardinghouses by Americans, the dormitories were organized by village and place in the Old Country. Often two men who worked different shifts shared one cot. The single-minded purpose of these men was to save money to send back home either as financial assistance or to pay passage to bring the rest of the family and a bride to the United States.

Taking advantage of the immigrants' ignorance of English and of American standards, American landlords charged exorbitantly high rents for small, dilapidated dwellings. Rent charged by landlords in the pocket around the Kingan and Company slaughterhouse in Indianapolis, which contained a large concentration of Bulgarian/Macedonian and other Slavic laborers, was at least 40 percent higher than the rent for similar dwellings in other parts of the city.[35] The *boorts* were overcrowded and unsanitary. The following description is from "The Foreigner in Indianapolis":

> The stag boarding houses are restricted in use to the Macedonians and Servians. Most . . . are housed in a row of three roomed tenements, which are without any paint and near the point of disintegration. Entrance to these homes is obtained by the rear door. The front door is locked and all the windows are nailed down. . . . The Macedonians have the reputation for living the cheapest of any of the foreigners, and hence under the most unsanitary conditions. Their weekly living expenses are less than $3.00. They are exceedingly parsimonious. Some Slovenians accuse them of being so stingy as to bury their dead in the cellars to avoid funeral expenses. Foreign-born citizens living under respectable conditions threatened to burn a house because the land-lord had rented it to Bulgarians.

(Throughout the work the author uses Bulgarian/Macedonian interchangeably.)[36] Often a single room without windows or ventilation and with bedding on the floor served as kitchen, sleeping, and recreation quarters for anywhere from ten to twenty or more men.[37]

In works detailing the living conditions of the Bulgarian/Macedonian immigrants, many references are made about the immigrants' ability, in fact desire, to live in seclusion behind walls and closed windows. Madame Deltchev in *Judgment on Deltchev* explains, "You will see such walls round most of our old houses. In Bulgaria and in Greece, in Yugoslavia, in all the countries of Europe that have lived under Turkish rule it is the same. To put a wall round your house then was not only to put up a barrier against the casual violence of foreign soldiers, it was in a way to deny their existence. Then our people lived behind their walls in small worlds of illusion that did not include an Ottoman Empire."[38]

Although the Bulgarian/Macedonian immigrants were predominantly peasant farmers in the Old Country, few became farmers in the New World. In Indiana they worked in steel mills, foundries, and on railroads. Accidents occurred at a high rate, and compensation, if any, was inadequate. As elsewhere in the United States, in Indiana the immigrants were exploited in the labor market. Bulgarian/Macedonian immigrants, partly because of ignorance and partly because of their unusual determination and endurance honed by living for centuries under oppression, worked for the lowest pay in deplorable, unsafe conditions, making them a target of hate for the American laborers.

The more enterprising individuals went into private business—usually a dry goods store, coffeehouse, saloon, barbershop, bakery, or luncheonette. The *kafené* or coffeehouse, an establishment transplanted from their Balkan environment, became the focal point of the social, political, and recreational activity of the community. Commonly the owner would be better educated and would provide assistance with legal matters, insurance, employment, translations, purchase of steamship tickets, international money orders, stamps, bonds, and the safekeeping of money. The *kafené* provided Bulgarian-language newspapers and other publications and a gathering place for passionate discussions of political news from the motherland. The proprietor often branched out into other businesses—a hotel or a *boort*, a bakery, a grocery, or a restaurant. The saloonkeeper also had great prestige in the community. He would be a person similar to the *kafené* owner and in many instances would own the saloon in addition to the *kafené* and other businesses. Many saloon/*kafené* proprietors acquired great affluence during Prohibition. Often the same individual owned an immigrant bank business, which was not a traditional bank but a purely immigrant phenomenon. The business was "a bureau for information and a clearing house of services necessary to the immigrant population, which had appeared to provide services to a specific immigrant group whose language, manner of life, customs, and requirements were unique."[39] The owner of the business helped newcomers find jobs and housing, arranged for travel and steamship tickets and for money to be sent home, and saw to all the other needs of the immigrants. Bakeries and barbershops also were very successful business ventures. By 1933 bakeries were the leading Bulgarian/Macedonian business ventures in the United States, with an estimated total capital of ten million dollars. Next came the grocery stores/butcher shops, restaurants and luncheonettes, confectioneries, and finally the wholesale businesses that in 1933 numbered an insignificant one hundred in the entire United States.[40]

Each immigrant Slav group lived in an ethnic enclave in which the structure of its home village was replicated. Crystal Benton Fall noted in 1916 that "The neighborhood constitutes a unit within itself. It has all the attributes of the village life. . . . The trade of the foreigner is monopolized by the foreign merchant. . . . The saloons,

*Bread loaf wrapper, Balkan Bakery, Gary, Indiana, ca. 1920s.*

the butcher-shops, the grocery stores, and the coffee houses, are all under local control. . . . The barber shop, the bakery shop, and the grocery are all operated by men born in the old country. . . . The saloons predominate in number over the other types of business but there are frequent combinations of coffee houses, pool-rooms and barber shops."[41]

## Religious Life

For the Bulgarians/Macedonians ethnic culture, religion, and political freedoms are inextricably bound. During the Ottoman occupation, and later during the Greek and Serbian occupations of Macedonia, the clergy of the Bulgarian Eastern Orthodox Church took a leadership position in the liberation and national revival movements. They were committed to national religion and culture. Thus the establishment of Bulgarian churches, Bulgarian language schools, and political/patriotic societies in the New World was an expression of the newly acquired freedoms.

From the very beginning of the establishment of the Bulgarian/Macedonian churches in the United States there was a shortage of clergy. Parishes remained without priests for long periods of time, and clergymen traveled a great deal to serve the needs of several congregations. Other parishes existed without church buildings, and occasionally Holy Liturgy was celebrated by visiting clergy in business establishments or in rented halls. All the churches in Indiana experienced this at one time or another. In most instances the initial intent of the Bulgarian/Macedonian clergy in America was not to remain in this country but to organize church parishes, Bulgarian schools, and patriotic societies. Their zeal was undaunted by the adverse conditions in the immigrant communities that were poor and unable to provide adequate compensation and were the object of ridicule by Americans. Elavina S. Stammel and Charles R. Parks in their 1930 thesis, "The Slavic Peoples in Indianapolis," describe the icons in the Bulgarian/Macedonian Church as "pictures of queer looking saints."[42]

The earliest Bulgarian/Macedonian parishes in America were under the direct jurisdiction of the Holy Synod of the Bulgarian Eastern Orthodox Church in Sofia, Bulgaria. The first administrator was Archimandrite Theophylact, a dynamic individual instrumental in the organization and building of the Bulgarian churches in the United States in the first two decades of the century, including the Bulgarian Church in Indianapolis. He was a theologian scholar, an intellectual, a Renaissance man, and a revolutionary who had taken part in the early Macedonian Liberation Movement. Eventually he left the Church, took back the truncated Americanized version of his lay name Malin (from Malinchev), received a medical degree, and spent the rest of his life practicing medicine.

In 1922 the Bulgarian Eastern Orthodox Church Mission for the United States and Canada was created. Doctor Christyo Tsenoff, its officially appointed administrator, had a tremendous effect on the Bulgarian/Macedonian communities in Indiana and in particular on the Indianapolis community. In 1931 he assumed the post of presbyter of St. Stephen's Bulgarian Eastern Orthodox Church in Indianapolis, thus making the city the administrative seat of the Bulgarian Orthodox Church in America. Tsenoff exercised tremendous religious and cultural influence on the Indianapolis immigrants in particular. His death in 1938 was a great cultural and spiritual loss for the Indianapolis community as well as for the entire Bulgarian/Macedonian community.

In 1938 the mission was elevated to a diocese with a bishopric of the Bulgarian Orthodox Church. The Holy Synod appointed as its head Bishop Andrei Velichki, a theologian scholar educated in imperial Russia. For the next twenty-five years the church history of the Bulgarians/Macedonians in America is convoluted and riddled with power struggles and political strife. The Indianapolis church became the battleground of tragic events and consequences. The Macedonian Political (Patriotic) Organization (MPO) that controlled the Bulgarian/Macedonian churches initially opposed the appointment of Bishop Andrei but later supported his 1947 election by the constituents of the American bishopric. After World War II Bishop Andrei was recalled by the Communist government of Bulgaria and sentenced to death when he did not return. In 1953 the Bulgarian patriarchate was restored, and Bishop Andrei found himself the head of a noncanonical diocese. To legitimize his churches with the Ecumenical Patriarchate of Constantinople he accepted a truce with the mother church in Bulgaria, which did not meet with MPO approval. This prompted fourteen Bulgarian churches in the United States and Canada to renounce his jurisdiction at a 1963 meeting convened at the suggestion of the Bulgarian/Macedonian Church in Fort Wayne. Since then the Bulgarian/Macedonian churches belong to two separate dioceses—one under the jurisdiction of the Holy Synod in Sofia with Bishop Andrei as its head (after his death in 1972 with other Sofia-appointed bishops) and the other as part of the Orthodox Church in America (OCA), with Bishop Kiril Yoncheff as its head. The Indianapolis church remained with the Holy Synod. The Fort Wayne church and a Gary church, recently relocated to Merrillville, are with OCA. Another Gary church, whose members profess separate Macedonian ethnicity, is under the jurisdiction of the Macedonian Church in Skopje, formerly in Yugoslavia.[43]

## Cultural Life

An overwhelming majority of the Bulgarian/Macedonian immigrants were peasants and laborers. Approximately 30 percent were illiterate or semiliterate.[44] Bulgarian language schools were set up in almost every immigrant community immediately upon arrival, and many immigrants acquired literacy in Bulgarian in the United States. A motivating factor in teaching Bulgarian to their American-born offspring was the immigrant parents' inability to communicate on the most basic level with their American-born and educated children. By 1933 fifty Bulgarian language schools, sponsored by church parishes and/or patriotic and philanthropic societies, operated in the United States.[45]

Luba Temcheff of Windsor, Canada, the American-born daughter of Dine Popcheff, one of the founders of the Indianapolis community, can reminisce in her fluent Bulgarian about the Bulgarian school of the 1920s and

1930s in Indianapolis, where she and her siblings learned literary Bulgarian.[46]

Bulgarian language publications began to appear in the United States as early as 1902, although many were short-lived. Two newspapers, *National Herald/Naroden Glas* and the *Macedonian Tribune/Makedonska Tribuna* had remarkable longevity and were of tremendous importance to all the Bulgarian/Macedonian immigrants. The publications were a unifying force, providing current information about the political situation at home, information about the immigrant communities in the United States and Canada, and an outlet for advertising Bulgarian/Macedonian businesses.

*National Herald/Naroden Glas* was published in Granite City, Illinois, from 1907 until 1950. Correspondents from Indianapolis, Fort Wayne, Gary, and East Chicago regularly sent news items to the paper.[47] The paper also published almanacs, which are the only documented historical records of the Bulgarian/Macedonian immigrant communities in America.

The *Macedonian Tribune/Makedonska Tribuna* was published in Indianapolis in 1927 as the organ of the Union of the Macedonian Political Organizations (today the Macedonian Patriotic Organization). In 1984 it relocated to Fort Wayne, where it is still published. It is the oldest Bulgarian-language newspaper still in existence in the United States. The Macedonian Tribune Company publishes Bulgarian language books, pamphlets, and papers on political, social, historical, and cultural topics. Most significant are the memoirs and other works of IMRO leader Ivan Mihailov. In 1940 the company published *Macedonian Almanac/Makedonski Almanah,* a remarkable historical document that was financed by business advertisements and by the family histories in it. By 1918 several Bulgarian bookstores in St. Louis and East Chicago supplied the Indiana communities with bilingual dictionaries and other books in Bulgarian.

Most immigrants picked up English in their workplace. Others, especially the women, spoke broken English for the rest of their lives. But there were many who learned proper English with speed and on their own or in night school. In 1916 in Indianapolis "the Bulgarians were setting the highest records in night school,"[48] and in 1930 they were "taking the lead amongst all the Slavs in Indianapolis in education."[49] American-born children attended regular public schools. From 1910 through the 1930s the Bulgarians of Gary were among the strongest immigrant supporters of public education.[50]

## Civic and Political Life

By 1913 there were thirty Bulgarian/Macedonian village brotherhoods and societies in America with many in Gary, several in Indianapolis, and a very solid one in Fort Wayne. The intent of these organizations was to provide moral and financial support to their members and funds for schools, churches, and the poor in the home village.

The Macedonian Liberation Movement remained a passion for many Bulgarian/Macedonian immigrants, and several efforts at organizing a liberation movement in exile were made from the early 1900s through the decades preceding World War II. A Bulgarian-Macedonian People's Union was organized in 1913 on the initiative of Archimandrite Theophylact, who also was instrumental in the establishment of the Indianapolis and other early immigrant churches. Chapters were organized in Indianapolis, Gary, Hammond, and Terre Haute. In 1917 the organization and its newspaper folded as the result of enormous financial difficulties, but the Indianapolis and Fort Wayne chapters remained active and became part of the founding chapters of the Macedonian Patriotic Organization (MPO).[51]

The founding congress of the Union of the Macedonian Political Organization, later the MPO, took place on 1 October 1922 in Fort Wayne. The mission of the MPO was to work legally for the creation of an autonomous Macedonia within Bulgarian cultural and linguistic frames. The majority of the elected officers and leaders of the organization were from Fort Wayne and Indianapolis. The 1924 MPO convention established a permanent central MPO office in Indianapolis, and Indiana became the center of national MPO activities. A number of key individuals in the MPO leadership continue to live in the state. Subsequently conventions were held in Indiana in 1923, 1925, 1937, 1947, and 1990 in Indianapolis; 1924, 1934, 1949, and 1986 in Fort Wayne; and 1931 and 1950 in Gary.[52]

The 1925 Indianapolis convention established a printing company, the Macedonian Tribune Company, and the first issue of the organ of the MPO, *Macedonian Tribune/Makedonska Tribuna,* was published on 10 February 1927. In 1952 the 'Political' of the MPO was dropped in favor of 'Patriotic.' The MPO is the single most significant national organization of the Bulgarians/Macedonians and has played a pivotal role in the Indiana communities. The MPO was, and perhaps still is, the most solid and well-funded Bulgarian/Macedonian immigrant national organization, with the majority of its membership coming from the affluent business class. During the 1929 convention the MPO formally elected to espouse the ideology of the IMRO branch led by Ivan Mihailov in Bulgaria. Until his death at the age of ninety-three in 1990 in Italy, where he had lived in exile since he had ordered the assassination of the Serbian king, Mihailov was the undisputed ideologue and leader of the MPO. His death, coinciding with the demise of Communism in the Balkans, created a vacuum and a dilemma for the organization. The MPO, facing a new political situation without a leader of Mihailov's stature and historical background, is foundering on the crucial issues of Macedonian ethnicity and language. The MPO strongly supports the newly independent Republic of Macedonia and has lobbied actively for its recognition. The MPO feels that the organization's mission for the establishment of an autonomous Macedonian state has been partially fulfilled.

The Macedonian Popular League was organized on the initiative of the Bulgarian Communist party, with the explicit purpose to counter the activities of the anti-Marxist MPO and IMRO. The League's most significant proponent was the leading Bulgarian Communist in America, George Zaikoff, better known by his nom de guerre, George Pirinski (as in "of Pirin Macedonia"). The organization's founding congress took place on 24 April 1931 in Gary, and it acquired a large following among the city's Bulgarian/Macedonian laborers. Its mission was the creation of a Communist Balkan federation in which the Macedonian Question would be resolved through the resolution of the class struggle in the Balkans.

At this point the political affiliations and movements of the Bulgarian/Macedonian immigrants became complex. The various subsequent all-Slav fronts in which the immigrants participated, which were organized to support the Soviet war effort and were banned after the war by the United States government as "subversive," were also directed by the Communists.[53] On 2 September 1941 a large number of American Slavs met in Gary under the leadership of Pirinski. Subsequent meetings of the same body in other locations established the American Slav Congress and the United Committee of South Slavic Americans, their goal being to support the Soviet war effort and to promote a Communist Balkan federation with Macedonia as one of the republics. Because of the wartime alliance between the United States and the Soviet

*Macedonian Political Organization convention, Indianapolis, 1937.*

Union, this was the appropriate affiliation for American Slavs. Those who supported the IMRO and MPO were denounced as traitors and fascists.

At the same time the Bulgarian Socialist Workers Union, which also supported a Communist Balkan federation with Macedonia as one of its republics, had active chapters in Fort Wayne, Indianapolis, and Gary.

## Social Life

Prior to World War II social life was based on religious, cultural, and political activities within the community. Traditionally Orthodox Christians did not celebrate birthdays but saints' days or name days. On saints' days there were open houses where ethnic fare was served, which included Turkish coffee along with a bowl of homemade preserves, *sladko,* to be eaten with a spoon. Virginia Nizamoff Surso of Fort Wayne wistfully recalls the days when every household served Turkish coffee and *sladko,* a tradition no longer maintained in the United States but only in the Bulgarian provinces.[54]

Plays and concerts were presented either in churches, patriotic societies' halls, or in coffeehouses. Luba Kazakoff of Indianapolis remembers attending a play as a child in Mr. Romanoff's coffeehouse. The coffeehouse was a popular gathering place. A *vecherinka*—an evening of music and dancing—was held in a church or social hall. The MPO conventions, banquets, and dances became the biggest marriage marts and social events of the year. Youth groups and ladies' auxiliaries attached to the churches and to the MPO also sponsored *vecherinkas,* picnics, and other social and recreational activities. After the Second World War social life began to include activities outside the ethnic community, such as high school proms and dances, movies, and eating out.

## Indianapolis

The Bulgarian/Macedonian community in Indianapolis dates to 1904. Two of the first immigrants to arrive were Dine (Constantine) Popcheff and Roman Romanoff from Ekshi-Su, Lerin region (Ksino Nero, Florina region,

*"Macedonian Bloody Wedding," presented by the Macedonian Political Organization, 17 May 1931, Indianapolis.*

Greece).[55] The majority of the first immigrants to Indianapolis were from Ekshi-Su, Ostrovo (Arnisa, Greece) and Putele (Pontokersia, Greece). *Boorts* were organized by village or region. There was a "Putele House," an "Ekshi-Su House," and an "Ostrovo House."[56] Many of the Bulgarian/Macedonian stag boardinghouses were on Ketcham Avenue and Washington Street.

East European Slav immigrants in Indianapolis were called "Hunyaks," presumably a derivation of Hungary. They worked for extremely low wages on the railroad, in factories and plants, at the National Malleable Castings Company, and the Kingan meat packing company. The "Hunyak quarter," where the Bulgarian/Macedonian immigrants lived with the rest of the Slav laborers, was around Kingan. In 1910 it covered an area approximately one-half a square mile, bordered on the north at Washington Street, on the south at the railroad yards, on the east at Missouri Street, and on the west at White River. Several hundred foreigners and their establishments were packed in this tiny area. Rents were abnormally high, and the housing was dilapidated and unsanitary.[57] Although by the late 1920s many Bulgarians/Macedonians had moved out of this area, newcomers continued to live and work there. Plumbing and utilities were nonexistent, garbage was collected infrequently, if at all, and altogether "a worse neighborhood in the living standards probably did not exist in the city."[58]

In 1918 Bulgarians operated five groceries, ten coffeehouses, five bakeries, and several restaurants. Dimitar Meditch's wholesale company was thriving as was the phonograph record store of Vangel Shishkoff. Mr. Vasil Stephanoff and Ivan Romanoff (graduating from Indiana University Law School in 1914) were practicing law.[59]

In 1930 there were five hundred Bulgarians living in Indianapolis, comprising the third largest Slavic group in the city.[60] At that time the Slavs in Indianapolis were still held in contempt: "He [the Slav] is disliked in the labor market since his lower or simpler standards allow him to work for a smaller wage. . . . He might be dirty and unwashed. He might smell of garlic. . . . Even his features and his strange language are accepted as those of a lower standard. . . . The American fears that increasing numbers of Slavs might lower American standards."[61]

However, by 1928 the "Bulgarians commanded more respect than many other Slavs [in Indianapolis]. . . . The Bulgar has risen from the level of meat packing and foundry work to a higher level of labor or has acquired a business of his own. . . . The Bulgarians also have the best record for the number who attempted independent business ventures for themselves. . . . The Bulgar is superior and he knows it. . . . The Bulgar has ambition, determination, dogged energy. He is not afraid to work. He often makes

*St. Stephen's Bulgarian Eastern Orthodox Church, Indianapolis, consecrated 14 October 1962.*

considerable money, and he does not hesitate to enter the professions that require much training. . . . He has the capacity for teamwork, as many Slavs have not . . . [and] shows more intellectual power."[62] In this study Bulgarian/Macedonian is used interchangeably.

By 1933 there were eighty families and one hundred bachelors in Indianapolis operating twenty restaurants, fifteen billiard halls, seven bakeries, seven barbershops, two fisheries, two shoe repair shops, three tailor shops, seven farms, two dry goods firms, one gasoline station, one large wholesale firm, three coffeehouses, and one printing press (the Macedonian Tribune Company). Indianapolis boasted several professionals, among them Dr. Theodore Petranoff, Dr. Stephen Pencheff, and Paul (Pando) Sirmin, a lawyer.[63]

The first Bulgarian church parish committee in Indianapolis was organized in 1907 but it was not until 1915 that an actual church building was purchased. At that time approximately one thousand Bulgarians from Macedonia and one hundred Bulgarians from the kingdom of Bulgaria lived in the city. Indianapolis had Greek and Romanian Orthodox churches, and the Bulgarians attended the Greek church because the majority of them were from Aegean Macedonia. An actual church building may not have been acquired for some time had it not been for an incident that inspired the Bulgarians to collect funds for a church as soon as possible. According to Eastern Orthodox tradition, on the evening of the first day of Easter the Gospel is read in several languages. The Bulgarians asked the Greek priest in advance to read it in Old Bulgarian (Church Slavonic), and he promised to do so. Their humiliation was immeasurable when this did not occur. On 30 May 1915 Archimandrite Theophylact, the administrator of the Bulgarian Eastern Orthodox

Church in America, presided over a general meeting at which the Indianapolis parish set committees for the collection of funds for the purchase of a church building. Some of the members of the various committees were Archimandrite Theophylact, Ivan Boshkoff, Basil Tersi, V. Shishkoff, Christ Guleff, Constantine Dumkoff, Dine Popcheff, and Roman Romanoff.[64] Within a short time the community purchased a house at 226 North Blackford Street, across from Military Park, where the majority of the Bulgarians lived. The house was remodeled, and St. Stephen's Bulgarian Eastern Orthodox Church opened its doors for worship on 10 October 1915.[65]

The icons adorning the sanctuary were painted in 1915 and 1916 by Stoicheff, a self-taught artist from Ekshi-Su, whose style combined traditional Byzantine iconography with Italian Renaissance. The icons were donated by parishioners and were later transferred to the current edifice. The sanctuary was on the first floor, and the second floor was used as an assembly hall and reading room. It seated 250 people and had a large stage and a collection of books and other publications in Bulgarian.[66] In the 1930s the second floor was converted into living quarters for Doctor Tsenoff.

The first clergyman was Rev. Nikola Pavloff who had been a priest in Macedonia, had participated in the 1903 Ilinden Uprising, and in both Balkan wars was a volunteer in the Macedonian regiment with the Bulgarian army. In 1920 Pavloff left for Shreveport, Louisiana, to try his hand at business.[67] The next priest was the Very Reverend V. Karadjoff, a theologian who had also studied law. He came from Macedonia in 1923, and in 1929, after serving the Indianapolis parish, became the priest of the newly established church in Gary.[68] Next Reverend Goreloff (in some Bulgarian language records he is listed as Gareloff) served the parish briefly. In 1931 Doctor Tsenoff, the highly regarded and beloved administrator of the Bulgarian Orthodox Mission in America, became presbyter of St. Stephen's Bulgarian Eastern Orthodox Church. Tsenoff had a doctorate from the university in Bern, Switzerland, had been on the faculty of the school of theology at the university in Sofia, Bulgaria, had written a number of theological tracts, and had edited the organ of the Bulgarian Holy Synod in Sofia before taking a post in the United States. After his death in 1938 the parish went into decline. On special occasions the community was served by the Very Rev. George Nickoloff from the Macedonian Bulgarian Orthodox Church in Detroit.

When Bishop Andrei Velichki visited Indianapolis in 1938 the dissatisfied MPO leaders, many of whom were also church board officers, banned him from entering the church by locking its portals. Also, by some accounts a fistfight ensued between parishioners. Later, members of the Bulgarian Macedonian Educational Club obtained a court order to open the church doors.[69]

Rev. Dimitri Bashenow, an émigré from Soviet Russia, became the priest in 1951. He was instrumental in attracting to the church the Russian and Ukrainian immigrants in the city. Bashenow contributed immensely to holding the parish together during a most difficult time.

After World War II the Bulgarian/Macedonian immigrants began to migrate even farther north and south of 16th Street, near Kessler Boulevard. A new church edifice with a Fellowship Hall was begun in December 1954 and completed in October 1955 at 1435 N. Medford Avenue. The mortgage was paid within seven years. At the time of the building of the new church a bitter quarrel between the MPO and the church board, presumably about money, created a split in the community that was deepened by the 1963 religious schism in the diocese. Since then the church and the MPO have existed separately and independently. A clause barring church members with political affiliations from the board of trustees was inserted into the church bylaws, thus assuring that the MPO would never gain control of this church.

Rev. Bashenow was advancing in age and looked to semiretirement. Briefly in 1959–60, Rev. Vasil Butchko, of Ukrainian background, served along with Rev. Bashenow, but once again the congregation started a search for a new priest. Some of the oldest members hoped to recapture the church's former golden years under Doctor Tsenoff. Through the efforts of Bishop Andrei, Very Rev. Boris Vangev Georgiev, a theologian educated at the theological seminary in Plovdiv and at the university in Sofia, Bulgaria, became the presbyter in August 1961. The elder parish members felt a particular kinship to Georgiev since his paternal family was from Vardar Macedonia and had taken an active part in the 1903 Ilinden Uprising, had participated in the Macedonian Liberation Movement, and had served in the volunteer Macedonian regiment of the Bulgarian army during both Balkan wars. In Indianapolis he reinstated the Bulgarian language school and enlarged and expanded the activities of the Sunday school, the church choir, the Sisterhood, and the Youth Organization. Georgiev also served the Bulgarian/Macedonian community in Cincinnati, retiring in 1985. Currently the parish is served by Rev. Dimitar Angelov, also born and educated in Bulgaria. By the request of the congregation, he celebrates Holy Liturgy and other feast days only in English.

In 1918 Indianapolis had the only Bulgarian-English school in the United States. It offered English correspondence courses and Bulgarian-English, English-Bulgarian translations. Its director was Dimitar Meditch (Meditchkoff).[70]

In 1924 Doctor Petranoff, Tashe Kitkoff, and five other Bulgarians/Macedonians in Indianapolis organized the Lion Club, which by 1930 had grown to one hundred members with capital of over one thousand dollars and had changed its name to the Bulgaro-Macedonian Educational Club. Besides mutual benefit activity, the club had an orchestra and presented cultural and educational programs.[71]

Although many descendants of the initial Bulgarian/ Macedonian immigrants are not familiar with the historical significance of the Ilinden Uprising and do not use Church Slavonic, the Indianapolis community continues to sponsor annually the Ilinden picnic and the SS. Cyril and Methodius spring *vecherinka* (dance).

In 1911 people from the village of Putele organized the Putele Mutual Benefit Brotherhood in Indianapolis, Granite City, Illinois, and Dayton, Ohio. Its mission was to provide financial and moral assistance to Putele immigrants and the village of Putele.

The Indianapolis MPO chapter, "Damian Grueff," was founded in 1922 and was the outgrowth of several

*Mr. and Mrs. Roman Romanoff, cofounders of the Indianapolis Bulgarian/Macedonian community.*

brotherhoods and associations. The MPO had sections for women and young people and a National Home at 774 Ketcham Avenue that accommodated three hundred people. Presumably part of the quarrel between the MPO and the church was due to a division of funds acquired from its sale.

Individuals and families rose to positions of leadership and prominence either in the church or in the MPO or in both simultaneously. Some names have vanished altogether, others appear in one of the two tracts. Several names remain a constant from the very beginning through the entire history of the community.

Dine Popcheff, one of the founders of the Indianapolis community, and the Popcheff family played an important role in the development of the MPO and the parish. Many direct and indirect Popcheff descendants still participate in the governance and social activities of the church. Dine Popcheff had participated in the 1903 Ilinden Uprising and fled to America in 1904. He worked briefly at Kingan and Company, but within a short time started a bakery business that eventually expanded into a grocery and a restaurant at 563 W. Washington Street. Popcheff traveled back home to bring his wife and daughter Vera to America. Vera graduated from Indiana University and Columbia's Graduate School of Library Science and became a librarian at the Indianapolis Public Library. Her career was cut short by her untimely death in 1934.[72] Dine Popcheff was also an active MPO member. Dine's brother Tashe Popcheff arrived in 1905, established a fish and poultry business, and became an active member of the church and the MPO Central Committee.[73]

In contrast Roman Romanoff, the other founder of the Indianapolis community from Ekshi-Su, was very much anti-MPO. He also arrived in 1904 and by 1906 had established the International Coffee House at 546–548 W. Washington Street, across the street from Dine Popcheff's business. Luba Popcheff Temcheff

*Orchestra of the Bulgaro-Macedonian Educational Club of Indianapolis, 1933.*

remembers that during her childhood her father and Romanoff did not speak to each other, presumably because of political disagreements.[74] Romanoff was also active in the governance of the church. He has no descendants living in Indianapolis.

The Shaneffs were and continue to be another prominent family. Pandil Shaneff arrived sometime in 1907 or 1908 and through his numerous business concerns rose to a position of prominence, leadership, and affluence. He was the general secretary of the MPO for fourteen years and was an active member of the church board. In 1912 he traveled to Sofia, Bulgaria, to marry. He returned with his bride on the *Lusitania*. His wife died in January 1995, ten days short of her one hundred and first birthday.

Today the story of the Shaneffs' lovely and elegant daughter Angeline dominates the lore of the community. She and Doctor Tsenoff's daughter Ivanka were indisputably the community's belles. Both received undergraduate degrees from Indiana University where they were roommates. While doing graduate work at Columbia, Angeline met Lambo Kiselincheff, the son of a wealthy Bulgarian family, significantly older, refined, educated, involved in the Macedonian Liberation Movement, and one of the key people in the MPO. Angeline died tragically of bone cancer at the age of forty, shortly before completing her dissertation on the Montessori method of education.[75] Other Shaneffs came later, and today many of their descendants command the respect of the community and are active participants in its affairs.

Kiril Chaleff arrived in 1909 from Ekshi-Su where he knew the legendary IMRO leader Dame Grueff. It is probably no accident that the Indianapolis MPO chapter, of which Chaleff was a founding member, bears the name "Damian Grueff." Currently Chaleff's American-born son Boris, a retired United States air force colonel, is the president of the central committee of the MPO.[76]

There were few individuals who became Americanized immediately. Dimitar Meditch (Meditchkoff) came in 1906, graduated from Valparaiso University, and in 1916 established a highly successful business, the National Wholesale Grocery. He was a member of the Indianapolis church and Indianapolis MPO chapter and numerous American cultural organizations. In 1940 he presided over the board of directors of the Macedonian Tribune Company.[77] Today his son Boris Meditch is an Indianapolis businessman and philanthropist.

Basil Stephanoff arrived in 1907, received embalmer's training, changed his name to Charles Stevens, and in 1920 opened the Charles Stevens Funeral Home at 2831 W. 10th Street. By 1933 it was still the only such Bulgarian/Macedonian enterprise in the country.[78] The funeral home funds the annual publication of the church calendar and supports a number of other church activities.

Dr. Theodore Petranoff, the son of a Congregational minister in Bulgaria, came to the United States to study for the ministry. He was probably sponsored by American missionaries. Instead he graduated from medical school and established a medical practice in Indianapolis.[79] Although he was not a member of the Bulgarian Eastern Orthodox parish, Petranoff participated in many social and cultural activities in the community and was a founding member of the Bulgaro-Macedonian Educational Club. Other prominent families in leadership positions either on the church board or the MPO, or simultaneously on both, were Adjieff, Alexoff, Boshkoff, Geleff, Gershanoff, and Guleff.

Christo Nizamoff, from Vardar Macedonia, came to Indianapolis in 1930 to work for the *Macedonian Tribune*. Along with his work for the MPO he acquired stature as an Indianapolis journalist and held memberships in the prestigious Literary Club and Indiana Journalism Hall of Fame. His son Nick Nizamoff is an Indianapolis attorney, and his daughter Virginia Nizamoff Surso is the MPO administrator. Not to be underestimated also is the cultural, educational, and literary influences exerted on the Indianapolis community by the Macedonian revolutionaries and intellectuals who came from Bulgaria for the leadership of the MPO and the editorship of the *Macedonian Tribune*. Until the first generation of American-born Bulgarians/Macedonians produced a crop of professionals, these men, along with the clergy and the few university-educated immigrants, constituted the cultural elite of the Indianapolis community.

Today church membership consists of approximately one hundred families, and there is a marked decline of ethnic cultural traditions and an indifference toward any knowledge of ethnic history. Minimal ethnic culture is maintained through social functions such as dances and Balkan foods served at picnics, weddings, and festivals. Whereas for the early immigrants the motivating factor in establishing the church was the ability to worship in their own language, their descendants prefer to worship only in English and they support the idea of American pan-orthodoxy. This would render the Bulgarian church obsolete were it not for the fact that the other Balkan ethnic churches in Indianapolis still worship in their own language.

The 1989 revolution in Eastern Europe has brought allegations against the Bulgarian Holy Synod of collaboration with the Communist government that once again has complicated the spiritual ties of the Indianapolis church with the mother church in Bulgaria.

## Fort Wayne

Immigrants from the villages of Visheni, Babchor, Chereshnitsa, Bulgarska Blaza, and Shestevo, of the Kostur (Kostoria, Greece) region settled in Fort Wayne.[80] In 1910 the Fort Wayne Bulgarian/Macedonian community numbered a mere twenty-five to thirty individuals. Most were employed by Bass Foundry and Machine Works and the Pennsylvania Roadhouse as cheap labor and lived in crowded and often unsanitary conditions. Argire Lebamoff, one of the community's founders, lived with his brother, sister-in-law, and three or four other immigrants in one small house. The sister-in-law kept house for all.[81]

By 1918 the community had grown to one thousand individuals who operated seven groceries, three bakeries, one storehouse, five coffeehouses, and two restaurants.[82] By 1933 the community had diminished to eighty families and two hundred single men operating fifteen restaurants, twelve groceries, one bakery, two barbershops, six shoe repair shops, three coffeehouses, three confectioneries, and a wholesale produce business. The community boasted a lawyer, an accountant, and several bank clerks and teachers. Over one hundred people and families owned their homes.[83]

Between 1918 and 1922 church services by visiting clergy were held in a hall above the grocery store of the Traycoff brothers. In the 1920s and 1930s the house of T. Dimitroff, the Ideal Grocery Store, and the Stolzaune Hall served the purpose. In 1946 in the Buether Sauter Hall, where occasional services were held from 1940 to 1948, the parish voted to start raising funds for a church building.[84] Services were held at the new edifice at 3506 Warsaw Street in November 1948. Initially the parish faced the usual problems of the shortage of clergy. The parish was served by the then Archimandrite Kiril Yoncheff (today Bishop Kiril), who came from Toledo, Ohio, on alternate Sundays. On 1 November 1956 the Very Rev. George Nedelkoff was appointed rector. He was born in Bulgaria, educated in the Sofia theological seminary and at the University of Nottingham, England, and was ordained in 1950 in New York by Bishop Andrei. Nedelkoff's ministry was marked by an active religious education school, a short-lived Bulgarian language school, and a number of other religious and cultural programs.[85] The parish also has an active women's guild that organizes traditional social events. Currently the membership of the congregation consists of approximately 313 adults and 60 children.[86]

In 1963 the Fort Wayne church, together with several other parishes, renounced the authority of Bishop Andrei and in 1977 joined the Orthodox Church of America. The first Divine Liturgy was celebrated in a new edifice at 3535 Crescent Avenue on 30 October 1983. In 1993 Very Reverend Nedelkoff retired. He currently writes and edits the Bulgarian language newsletter of the Bulgarian Orthodox Religious Education Society. The new rector, Rev. Brooks Ledford, does not have any Bulgarian/ Macedonian ethnic background. Divine Liturgy is celebrated in English, and the MPO chapter is separate from the church. During the first year of Ledford's ministry the Feast of SS. Cyril and Methodius was omitted from the church calendar by an oversight. Although officially the name of the church has not changed, the letterhead on its newsletter and other correspondence does not contain the Bulgarian-Macedonian part of it.

The Babchor Benevolent Brotherhood was established in 1912. Its mission was to assist all brotherhood members in need, to assist the poor of the motherland village, Babchor (Pimenikon, Greece), and to fund other village needs such as Bulgarian schools and churches. In 1918 it had 120 members. By 1933 the brotherhood had financed the planting of orchards and the installation of clean water pipes in the village and had planned the development of a modern village cemetery.[87]

A strong and active chapter of the Macedonian Political Organization was established in 1921. A ladies' section was organized in 1928 and a youth organization in 1929. The MPO chapter supported an active Bulgarian school.[88]

The Lebamoffs were prominent in their village of Visheni before immigrating and continue to be the leading Bulgarian/Macedonian family in Fort Wayne.[89] Atanas Lebamoff had worked as a courier for the IMRO in Constantinople and had taken an active part in the Ilinden Uprising in which the Lebamoffs lost family members. He came to America in 1905 and for a time worked in the coal mines in Pennsylvania. His brother Argire arrived in 1907 and after a stop in Philadelphia moved on to Fort Wayne where he started work at Bass Foundry making wheels for railroad cars.[90] Atanas Lebamoff returned to Macedonia, perhaps in 1908, married, built a home in Visheni, but fled again with his wife and child, this time from the Greeks right after the Balkan wars. In Fort Wayne he too worked at the foundry.[91] In 1925 Argire Lebamoff married in Sofia, Bulgaria, and returned to Fort Wayne with his bride.[92] Both brothers were established in private business before 1920. Atanas was proprietor of Weisser Park Grocery and Meat Market, and Argire operated the Liberty Grocery at 3239 Piqua Avenue. In 1924 Argire purchased property on the south side of town under the pseudonym John Silver because Jews, East Europeans, and blacks were prohibited from ownership of real estate in Fort Wayne. Both brothers were dedicated members of MPO.[93]

Today the children and grandchildren of the Lebamoff brothers participate in varying degrees in the MPO and are distinguished civic leaders and businessmen in Fort Wayne. Atanas's daughter Dita, who came here at age four, attended Indiana University and married Peter Atzeff, a leading MPO organizer, intellectual, and editor of the *Macedonian Tribune*. His granddaughter Doris Atzeff also edited the newspaper for a time. Argire's son George is a successful businessman and owner of the Cap n' Cork Company. Son Ivan is a lawyer who served as mayor of Fort Wayne. Both are active in the national governance of MPO, and Ivan was its president for several years.

Other leading families who still have descendants in Fort Wayne are the family of Mike Kosma, a participant in the Ilinden Uprising and proprietor of the Rainbow Grill, Vasil Ishkoff and Vasil Litchin who were partners in the proprietorship of Coney Island Weiner Stand on 131 W. Main Street, and Spiro Christ, proprietor of a bakery.[94]

T. Merle Kook (Konstantinov), born in the kingdom, graduated from law school and established a law practice in Fort Wayne. In spite of his rapid assimilation and changed name, he frequently defended without compensation Bulgarian prisoners.[95]

## Gary

Perhaps the most difficult story to unravel and document is that of the Bulgarian/Macedonian immigrants in Gary. They flocked to Gary as soon as it was founded in 1906 by the United States Steel Corporation. Many came from other United States cities where they had immigrated first. Gary was a fluid community with large numbers of Bulgarians/Macedonians coming for brief periods of time and then moving on to other places. The immigrants worked for low wages, suffered accidents without adequate workers' compensation, and, in order to economize, lived in crowded and unsanitary stag boardinghouses. A housing crisis had developed immediately upon Gary's founding. Cheap, shoddy dwellings were built for the lowest-paid, unskilled laborers and were soon filled with East European immigrants and became known as Hungary Row and Hunkyville. Although these were four-room houses intended for families, they were quickly turned into stag boardinghouses because the immigrant laborers were predominantly single men. In 1909 it was reported that 428 men slept in shifts in 142 rooms.[96]

In 1918 approximately 1,500 Bulgarians/Macedonians, employed mainly by US Steel, were living in Gary. Some also operated businesses: four bakeries, five groceries, six coffeehouses, six produce firms, two wholesale firms, one warehouse, four tailoring operations, two shoe repairs, two cafeterias, two hotels, one clothing store, and two cinemas. Mr. Iconomoff practiced law.[97] By 1933 the community numbered approximately 250 families and 500 single men. They operated ten restaurants, three coffeehouses, one hotel, one clothing store, eight groceries, ten cafés, five bakeries, one produce firm, one confectionery and tobacco shop, and two gas stations.[98]

Some of the leading businessmen were Christ Kusmanoff, who had immigrated in 1907 and established the International Fruit Company in 1910, Mr. Alabach, proprietor of the Broadway Food Company, and Christ Taseff, who established the Kostur Food Market in 1913. All were active MPO members.[99] Early professional men were Dr. Christo Stoykoff, a graduate of Loyola University, who established a medical practice in 1919 and Dr. Iliya Nickoloff from Dumbeni (Dendrohori, Greece), a graduate of Marquette University, who established a dental practice in 1926.[100]

Naum Krustanoff from the Ohrid region and the brothers Rokoff from the village of Dumbeni, Kostur region, are credited as the founders of the Gary Bulgarian/ Macedonian community.[101] In 1928 the ninth Bulgarian church in America, St. Clement Ohridski (of Ohrid), was established in Gary through the organizational efforts of Very Rev. V. Karadjoff (who also served the Indianapolis parish). The old Serbian Orthodox Church located at 39th and Washington Street was purchased for $5,500 as a temporary church, and services began on 7 January 1929. Later there was a question about the legal ownership of the property on which the church had been built. The building was abandoned and the community purchased three lots near Broadway and 15th Avenue. When Karadjoff relocated to Detroit, the Gary parish remained active in spite of the lack of a priest and a building.[102] Gary had a number of church-affiliated benevolent/mutual benefit societies and brotherhoods, which conducted various social and cultural events. The authors of *Steel City: Gary, Indiana, 1906–1950* comment, "For Gary's Orthodox immigrants, church and community were one and the same, and the social and cultural life of the ethnic group was centered on the parish church."[103] The schools of the Orthodox parishes were referred to as auxiliary folk schools and were open after public school hours and occasionally on Sundays, although they had no resemblance to Protestant Sunday schools. Establishing such a school took precedence over an actual church building. The curriculum focused on language, tradition, and religion. The Bulgarian parish sponsored classes in religion, the Bible, church history, catechism, Bulgarian language, history, geography, and music.[104] It is unclear when the church parish ceased to exist.

In 1962 approximately ninety Macedonian Americans from Gary organized the first Macedonian Orthodox Church in America. Initially church services were held in a rented building, and in 1963 SS. Peter and Paul Macedonian Orthodox Church relocated into its own church building. The present edifice at 9660 Broadway in Crown Point was built in 1988. SS. Peter and Paul Macedonian Orthodox Church is under the jurisdiction of the Macedonian Orthodox Church in Skopje (Republic of Macedonia), which was established in 1958 in Communist Yugoslavia. The founders of this Macedonian community in Gary are predominantly post–World War II immigrants who espouse a separate Macedonian identity and ethnicity. The community maintains Macedonian religious, cultural, and ethnic traditions. Members have formed two ethnic music groups that perform at Bulgarian, Macedonian, and Serbian weddings and festivals across Indiana. The church has a Sunday school and a Macedonian school in which the new Macedonian language and Macedonian cultural heritage are taught. Many Macedonian Americans born in the United States learn Macedonian in the church school. Divine Liturgy is in Church Slavonic, and the church board conducts its affairs in Macedonian. Very Rev. Tome Stamatov is the current priest. The parish has between 350 and 400 active members. An estimated 1,000 Macedonian families (identifying with separate Macedonian ethnicity) currently live in northwestern Indiana.[105]

In 1972–73 a number of families, together with the first priest to serve the church, Very Rev. Spiro Tanaskovski, left SS. Peter and Paul to form St. Clement of Ohrid (Ohridski) American Macedonian Church in Merrillville, under the jurisdiction of the Orthodox Church in America. Initially its membership consisted of 103 individuals but has diminished significantly since 1980. Tanaskovski retired in 1993 and passed away in April 1995. Rev. Topusliev, a dissident exiled by the former Communist government of Bulgaria for participating in the establishment of the Bulgarian Human Rights Committee, is temporarily attached to the church.[106] Although this church has the same patron saint as the Bulgarian church established in 1928, it is doubtful that they are in anyway connected.

Three benevolent/mutual benefit societies were formed in 1917. The Koratitza Benevolent Society's mission was to assist poor families and students in the home village of Koratitza (Republic of Macedonia) and to assist the village school and church and support a *chitalishte,* a nineteenth-century Bulgarian library/reading room/cultural center. The Velgosh Benevolent and

*Members of the ladies' section of the Macedonian Political Organization "Rodina" from Gary.*

Mutual Benefit Society "Progress" was formed to assist its members from the village Velgosh (Republic of Macedonia). The Bulgarian Mutual Benefit Society "Balkan Peace" (or "Balkan World") was formed on the initiative of Bulgarians from Macedonia. Its purpose was to assist its members during illness and work accidents.[107] One of its founders was Christo Sugareff of the remarkable Sugareff family from Bitolja (Republic of Macedonia). Following his brother Georgi's murder by the Turks in Macedonia, Christo and the rest of the family immigrated to different United States locations. Christo returned to Bulgaria in 1912 to join the Macedonian volunteer regiment of the Bulgarian army in the Balkan wars. Upon his return to the United States he lived in Indianapolis before moving to Gary, where he opened a produce business and became one of the leading Bulgarian/Macedonian businessmen and an active participant in the MPO. His brother Vangel Sugareff graduated from Harvard and became a professor.[108]

MPO chapter "Rodina" ("Motherland") was organized in 1930 by Asen Avramoff, secretary of the Central Committee of the MPO and an IMRO leader who returned to Bulgaria in 1932 and remained there practicing law. Gary hosted the 1931 MPO convention, and shortly thereafter a ladies' section was organized.[109]

If Indianapolis was the battleground of religious power struggles, Gary became the battleground of political strife. The founding congress of the MPO's adversary organization, the Macedonian Peoples League, whose mission was to work for the liberation of Macedonia through the creation of a Communist Balkan federation, also took place in Gary on 24 April 1931.[110] Christo Nizamoff says, "The deep depression of the 1930s created a fertile ground for many communist cells.... A few misguided Macedono-Bulgarians in industrial centers like Gary and Detroit had swallowed the communist bait. They invaded the coffee houses where unemployed immigrants spent their time and . . . boasted that the freedom, the salvation of Macedonia, lay in the victory of Communism. We had quite a few give-and-take sessions with them. We even had a few fist fights and bloody noses."[111] But it was more than mere fistfights and bloody noses. Their disruption of the 1931 MPO convention parade in Gary resulted in bloodshed and fourteen arrests. Other physical clashes followed.[112]

The Bulgarian Socialist Workers Union, whose mission was similar to the other Communist-based organizations, also had a strong chapter in Gary. Members from these organizations participated in the various Communist-led Slav World War II unions. According to Christo Nizamoff, "The American Communists 'in the name of democracy' formed something like a united front with the Serbians and the Greeks. Their venom was directed primarily against the MPO."[113] The 1940 Macedonian Almanac also mentioned that the efforts of the Serbian provocateurs in Gary had not been able to kill the Bulgarian spirit of the Gary MPO or to lead astray the Macedonian Bulgarians from their ideals.[114]

A number of Bulgarian/Macedonian communities existed in several other Indiana locations. In 1918 there were sixty to one hundred Bulgarians/Macedonians in Terre Haute, where most worked in factories and plants, one owned a bakery, and one owned a grocery. By 1933 there were only five families and ten single men left operating three restaurants, two tailor shops, and one farm.

In 1918 there were 100 immigrants in Logansport operating one grocery and one bakery; in Hammond 150 were employed in the factories and operating two coffeehouses, two bakeries, and one grocery. In 1933 Hammond had thirty-five families and fifty single men operating two groceries, one barbershop, one bakery, one hotel, one shoe repair shop, and one plumbing business. In 1918 Indiana Harbor had fifty immigrants operating one bakery, two coffeehouses, and one orchard, but by 1933 there were twenty families and fifty single men operating fifteen businesses—eight pastry cafés, three restaurants, two barbershops, one bakery, and one hotel.[115]

In 1933 there was one family in Elkhart; five families and ten single men in Elwood; three Bulgarian families, ten single men, and one barbershop in Kokomo; six Bulgarian families, ten single men, three restaurants, one grocery store, and one shoe repair in Mishawaka; a few families and one Bulgarian-owned restaurant in Montgomery; fifteen families and fifty single men operating fifteen restaurants, one farm, and four pastry cafés, one of which "Diana" was decorated in Art Deco style and was patronized by the "upper class" Americans in South Bend; and an occasional family in Plainfield, Lagrange, Bicknell, Somerville, East Chicago, and Straughn.[116] Today there are no Bulgarian/Macedonian ethnic communities in these locations. Presumably the depression caused many to move in search of employment, and the descendants of those few who stayed have become completely assimilated.

## Bulgarian/Macedonian Immigration Today

Since the 1989 revolution in Eastern Europe a new wave of Bulgarian/Macedonian immigrants has come to Indiana. The new Bulgarians are young and educated professionals. Although the ancestral roots of many are Bulgarian from Macedonia, they prefer western culture and immediate material gratification to the polarized views on Macedonian ethnicity. Many of those arriving from the newly established, autonomous Republic of Macedonia espouse a distinct Macedonian ethnicity. There are some who acknowledge Bulgarian ethnicity historically but consider themselves modern-day Macedonians.

The Bulgarian/Macedonian immigrants from Aegean Macedonia walk a tightrope. Those immigrants who have no families left in Greece to face reprisals call themselves Bulgarian freely. Some immigrate with the Greek names assigned to them under duress; thus, the only trace of their Slavic culture is the lovely, if archaic, Bulgarian language they speak.

It is not possible to gauge the actual beliefs of the Bulgarian/Macedonian Americans on the question of Macedonian ethnicity. There is a recent trend among the descendants of the initial immigrants, who by choice called themselves Bulgarian, to refer to themselves as Macedonian Americans. This attitude, however, does not reflect knowledge or understanding of the complex issues of culture, history, and theories on the subject. The majority are not curious about Balkan history or the controversies surrounding Macedonia. For them it is irrelevant what their ancestors called themselves. They feel Macedonian because the geographic area from which their ancestors came is Macedonia. However, it is reasonable to assume that those who are better educated and who support the *Macedonian Tribune* espouse views expressed in the newspaper such as:

> The Macedonian and Bulgarian people are a single entity. They are indelibly linked through a millennium of time and history. The fact that the people of Macedonia were separated by artificial boundaries in 1878 (Treaty of Berlin), 1913 (Treaty of Bucharest),

CALUMET REGIONAL ARCHIVES

*Macedonian Political Organization "Rodina," Gary, ca. 1960–65.*

and 1919 (Treaty of Neuilly) cannot change their heritage or their rights. Nor can the YCP (Yugoslav Communist party) simulate a new Macedonian race with its own language, culture and history.[117]

Indiana does not have a visible Bulgarian/Macedonian ethnic culture, which gives the impression that such an ethnic group does not exist. Yet the state is populated with numerous Bulgarian/Macedonian descendants who perhaps because of prejudice and discrimination have assimilated into Hoosier society without obvious traces of ethnicity. The heroic lives of the faceless and nameless Bulgarians/Macedonians or other Slav immigrant laborers are some of the foundation blocks upon which Indiana was built.

## Notes

1. *Macedonian Tribune,* 1 Nov. 1990; George J. Prpic, *South Slavic Immigration in America* (Boston: Twayne Publishers, 1978), 212.

2. Dennis P. Hupchick, ed., *The Pen and the Sword: Studies in Bulgarian History by James F. Clarke* (Boulder, Colo.: East European Monographs, distributed by Columbia University Press, 1988), ix–xiii.

3. Prpic, *South Slavic Immigration in America,* 212.

4. Emily Greene Balch, *Our Slavic Fellow Citizens* (New York: Charities Publications Committee, 1910), 462; Prpic, *South Slavic Immigration in America,* 213.

5. Nikolay G. Altankov, *The Bulgarian-Americans* (Palo Alto, Calif.: Ragusan Press, 1979), xi.

6. Prpic, *South Slavic Immigration in America,* 213.

7. *Makedonski Almanah* (Macedonian Almanac, in Bulgarian) (Indianapolis: Macedonian Tribune Co., 1940), 221; Balch, *Our Slavic Fellow Citizens,* 275; Prpic, *South Slavic Immigration in America,* 212–13.

8. Nikolay Altankov, "Bulgarians," in Stephan Thernstrom, ed., *Harvard Encyclopedia of American Ethnic Groups* (Cambridge, Mass.: The Belknap Press of Harvard University Press, 1980), 187; "Macedonians," in ibid., 691.

9. Dennis P. Hupchick, *Culture and History in Eastern Europe* (New York: St. Martin's Press, 1994).

10. David Marshall Lang, *The Bulgarians: From Pagan Times to the Ottoman Conquest* (London: Thames and Hudson, 1976).

11. Kenneth Katzner, *The Languages of the World* (New York: Funk and Wagnalls, 1975), 100.

12. Dimitri Obolensky, *Six Byzantine Portraits* (Oxford: Clarendon Press, 1988), 8–33; Lang, *Bulgarians,* 105.

13. Katzner, *Languages of the World,* 100; Obolensky, *Six Byzantine Portraits,* 19.

14. *Encyclopaedia Britannica,* 1967 ed., s.v. "Bulgaria."

15. William Gladstone, *The Bulgarian Horrors and the Question of the East* (London: J. Murray, 1876).

16. Robert D. Kaplan, *Balkan Ghosts: A Journey through History* (New York: Vintage Books, 1994), 55.

17. Christo Tatarchev, "Memoirs," (in Bulgarian), quoted in *Macedonian Tribune,* 17 June 1993; Todor Alexandrov, "Autonomy and Macedonism," quoted in Ivan Alexandrov, *Macedonia and Bulgarian National Nihilism* (Australia: Macedonian Patriotic Organization "TA" Australia, Inc., 1993), 32.

18. Albert Sonnichsen, *Confessions of a Macedonian Bandit* (New York: Duffield and Co., 1909), 108.

19. *Indianapolis Star,* 23 Aug. 1936.

20. *Makedonski Almanah,* 135.

21. *Jubileen sbornik na vestnik Naroden glas: 1907–1918* (Jubilee Almanac of Naroden Glas, in Bulgarian) (Granite City, Ill.: Naroden Glas, 1918), 28–29.

22. Nikola Pavloff, *Istoricheski Belezhki na Makedono-Odrinskoto Opulchenie vu Balkanskite Voini pres 1912–13: Iz Dnevnika na sauchastnika I chislyascht se vu Purva Brigada Sveshtenik Nikola Pavlov* (Historical Notes about the Macedono-Odrin Resistance in the Balkan Wars, 1912–1913: From the Diary of First Brigade Participant, Reverend Nikola Pavloff, in Bulgarian) (Granite City, Ill.: Naroden Glas, 1920), 12.

23. Dimitar G. Gotzev, *Mladezhkite natzionalno-osvoboditelni organizatzii na Makedonskite Bulgari, 1919–1941* (The Youth National-Liberation Organizations of the Macedonian Bulgarians, 1919–1941, summary in English) (Sofia, Bulgaria: Izd-vo na Bulgarska akademia na naukite, 1988), 6.

24. Prpic, *South Slavic Immigration in America,* 226.

25. Christo N. Nizamoff, *Struggle for Freedom: Reflections and Reminiscences* (Indianapolis: Hoosier Press, 1985).

26. Kaplan, *Balkan Ghosts,* 66; *The Wall Street Journal,* 6 Sept. 1991.

27. B. Brance, *Macedonia and Marxism* (Adelaide, Australia: MPOTAA, Inc., 1993); Alexandrov, *Macedonia and Bulgarian National Nihilism;* James F. Clarke, *Macedonia from S.S. Cyril and Methodius to Horace Lunt and Blazhe Koneski: Language and Nationality* (Indianapolis: Central Committee of the Macedonian Patriotic Organization of the United States and Canada, 1982).

28. Clarke, *Macedonia from S.S. Cyril and Methodius to Horace Lunt and Blazhe Koneski,* 4.

29. John Reed, *The War in Eastern Europe* (New York: Charles Scribner's Sons, 1919), 300–1.

30. Stoyan Vardarski, "Executorite na Bulgarskia dukh" ("The Executioners of the Bulgarian Spirit"), *Zora,* 24 July 1990, p. 8; Alexandrov, *Macedonia and Bulgarian National Nihilism,* 47–49.

31. Edward Alsworth Ross, *The Old World in the New: The Significance of Past and Present Immigration to the American People* (New York: The Century Co., 1914), 138, 286.

32. Crystal Benton Fall, "The Foreigner in Indianapolis" (M.A. thesis, Indiana University, 1916), no pagination.

33. Violet Guleff, conversation with the author.

34. *Indianapolis Star,* 23 Aug. 1936.

35. "Housing Conditions in Indianapolis," *Indiana University Bulletin* 8, no. 8 (Sept. 1910): 111–41.

36. Fall, "Foreigner in Indianapolis."

37. "Housing Conditions in Indianapolis," 111–41.

38. Eric Ambler, *Judgment on Deltchev* (New York: Alfred A. Knopf, 1951), 77.

39. Altankov, *Bulgarian-Americans,* 39.

40. *25- godishen ibileen almanah na vestnik Naroden glas, 1908–1933* (25th Anniversary Jubilee Almanac of Naroden Glas, 1908–1933) (Granite City, Ill.: Naroden Glas, 1933), 217–18.

41. Fall, "Foreigner in Indianapolis."

42. Elavina S. Stammel and Charles R. Parks, "The Slavic Peoples in Indianapolis" (M.A. thesis, Indiana University, 1930), 166.

43. Nick Nochevich, telephone conversation with the author; Altankov, "Bulgarians," 188; "Macedonians," 692.

44. *Naroden glas almanah* (1918), 6.

45. Ibid. (1933), 381.

46. Luba Popcheff Temcheff, conversations with the author.

47. *Naroden glas almanah* (1933), 164.

48. Fall, "Foreigner in Indianapolis."

49. Stammel and Parks, "Slavic Peoples in Indianapolis," 146.

50. Raymond A. Mohl and Neil Betten, *Steel City: Gary, Indiana, 1906–1950* (New York and London: Holmes and Meier, 1986), 148.

51. *Naroden glas almanah* (1933), 459; Altankov, *Bulgarian-Americans,* 57.

52. Annual Report and Convention Program: 69th Annual MPO Convention, Indianapolis, 1990.

53. Prpic, *South Slavic Immigration in America,* 234–44; Altankov, *Bulgarian-Americans,* 59–71.

54. Virginia Nizamoff Surso, conversations with the author.

55. *Naroden glas almanah* (1933), 292.

56. Boris Vangev Georgiev, "History of the Church," recorded oral history of St. Stephen's Bulgarian Eastern Orthodox Church (in Bulgarian), mid-1960s, private archive.

57. "Housing Conditions in Indianapolis," 127–28.

58. Stammel and Parks, "Slavic Peoples in Indianapolis," 105–6.

59. *Naroden glas almanah* (1918), 263.

60. Stammel and Parks, "Slavic Peoples in Indianapolis," 13 (table).

61. Ibid., 70.

62. Ibid., 35–36.

63. *Naroden glas almanah* (1933), 292.

64. *St. Stephen Bulgarian Eastern Orthodox Church Organizational Book, 30 May 1915–17 August 1919* (in Bulgarian), private archive. The publication contains meetings' agendas and discussion items, minutes of meetings, decisions, and signatures of board members and members of various other committees. *St. Stephen's Bulgarian Eastern Orthodox Church, Consecration Program, October 14, 1962,* no pagination; Georgiev, "History of the Church."

65. Georgiev, "History of the Church"; *St. Stephen Bulgarian Eastern Orthodox Church Organizational Book; Indianapolis Times,* 9 Oct. 1965.

66. *Naroden glas almanah* (1918), 97.

67. Pavloff, *Istoricheski Belezhki na Makedono-Odrinskoto Opulchenie vu Balkanskite Voini pres 1912–13; Naroden glas almanah* (1918) 96–97; (1933), 357.

68. *Naroden glas almanah* (1933), 74.

69. Nadezhda Kitkoff Christoff, conversations with the author.

70. *Naroden glas almanah* (1918), 69.

71. Ibid. (1933), 421–22.

72. Temcheff conversations.

73. *Makedonski Almanah,* 359.

74. Temcheff conversations.

75. Olga Alexoff Shaneff, conversations with the author.

76. Boris Chaleff, conversations with the author.

77. *Makedonski Almanah,* 234, 362.

78. *Naroden glas almanah* (1933), 137.

79. W. T. Petranoff, conversations with the author.

80. *Naroden glas almanah* (1933), 292.

81. Ivan Lebamoff, letter to O. G. Roop, 4 Jan. 1995.

82. *Naroden glas almanah* (1918), 263.

83. Ibid. (1933), 293–94.

84. Altankov, *Bulgarian-Americans,* 101.

85. Vita, Very Rev. George Nedelkoff.

86. Dita Atzeff, letter to O. G. Roop, 3 Aug. 1994.

87. *Naroden glas almanah* (1918), 79; (1933), 416.

88. *Makedonski Almanah,* 258.

89. A. J. Leikas, *The History of the Village Visheni* (Fort Wayne: George Lebamoff, 1991).

90. Lebamoff letter.

91. Ibid.

92. Leikas, *History of the Village Visheni,* 83.

93. *Makedonski Almanah,* 345; Lebamoff letter.

94. Lebamoff letter; *Makedonski Almanah,* 343, 345.

95. *Naroden glas almanah* (1933), 475.

96. Mohl and Betten, *Steel City,* 18–20.

97. *Naroden glas almanah* (1918), 263–64.

98. Ibid. (1933), 294.

99. *Makedonski Almanah,* 350–52.

100. *Naroden glas almanah* (1933), 488.

101. Ibid., 294.

102. Ibid., 358–59.

103. Mohl and Betten, *Steel City,* 170.

104. Ibid., 171.

105. Nochevich conversation.

106. Rev. Spiro Tanaskovski, conversation with the author.

107. *Naroden glas almanah* (1918), 76.

108. *Makedonski Almanah,* 352; Altankov, *Bulgarian-Americans,* 123.

109. *Makedonski Almanah,* 273.

110. *Naroden glas almanah* (1933), 465–66.

111. Nizamoff, *Struggle for Freedom,* 131.

112. Altankov, *Bulgarian-Americans,* 63.

113. Nizamoff, *Struggle for Freedom,* 133.

114. *Makedonski Almanah,* 273.

115. *Naroden glas almanah* (1918), 263; (1933), 294–95.

116. Ibid. (1933), 294–95.

117. *Macedonian Tribune,* 1 Nov. 1990.

# SERBS

NATALIE VUJOVICH

*There is little documentation for Serbian immigrants in Indiana prior to the turn of the century; however, one exception exists in Wabash County in a town known as New Madison, which was founded in 1835. When the railroad came through the town in 1881–82, a request was made to change the town's name to avoid confusion with a town with a similar name. The postmaster at the time was an immigrant from Serbia who used his influence to change the name of the town to "Servia" in 1883, which is its name today. In the nineteenth century Servia was a common spelling for Serbia. Possibly this is because in the Cyrillic alphabet "B" is the symbol for the "V" sound.*

Serbian immigrant family beside storyteller bard accompanied by his one-stringed instrument, the guslá, Blanford, Indiana, early 1920s. From left to right: Jovo Mandich, Andja Mirkovich, Bosko Mirkovich (guslar), and young Rose Mirkovich Kukich.

To understand Serbian immigrants in Indiana one must know something of their historical background since events in Europe have consistently affected their patterns of immigration and activities.

Serbs are descended from an Indo-European race of people, the Slavs, who began conquering and colonizing the Balkan Peninsula in the seventh century.[1] Serbs settled in the southern portion of the Balkans and are called South Slavs (Yugoslavs), along with Croatians, Montenegrins, and Slovenes. Serbs are extremely proud of their ancient democratic tradition that extended from the communal family (*zadruga*), led by the eldest male. His authority, however, was not absolute since other males and even females had a voice in decision making. The communal families joined together to form larger groups that were led by an elected leader (*župan*), whose authority was also limited by a representative assembly (*sabor*). This democratic tradition is reflected even today in the Serbian tendency toward individualism and resistance to any strong centralized authority.[2]

During the latter part of the ninth century Serbs were converted to Christianity by two Byzantine missionaries, Cyril and Methodius, who succeeded where missionaries from Rome had failed, largely because of their translation of the liturgy and religious texts into Old Slavonic.[3] The missionaries are credited with creating a phonetic system of writing that was the basis for the present-day Cyrillic alphabet still used by Serbs and Russians. The

*St. George Fraternal Lodge from Clinton, Indiana, in 1911.*

overwhelming majority of Serbs are Eastern Orthodox Christians who consider the Serbian Orthodox Church an integral part of their identity. The great schism that divided the Christian church in 1054 had a far-reaching effect in polarizing Slavs into those influenced by eastern and those influenced by western powers. So, too, did foreign occupations and ever-changing territorial boundaries.

The two most significant foreign occupations that directly relate to immigration and the present civil war in the former Yugoslavia were those of the Ottoman and Austrian-Hungarian empires. For two centuries prior to the Ottoman conquest, Serbia was a powerful medieval kingdom that extended from the Danube River to the Gulf of Corinth and the Aegean Sea all the way to the Adriatic Sea.[4] However, in 1389 the Ottoman Turks defeated the Serbs at the Battle of Kosovo and occupied their territories, except for the mountainous regions of Montenegro, for more than four centuries. The Serbian Orthodox Church was the only Serbian national institution to survive Turkish occupation, and it was the church that kept alive the faith and a sense of national identity.[5] It was during the Ottoman occupation that thousands of Serbs migrated into territories under Austrian-Hungarian control primarily along borders to create a military frontier (*krajina*) in defense against Turkish expansion. One such example was a mass exodus of nearly forty thousand Serbian families who left Serbia after having been promised religious freedom and some autonomous privileges by Leopold I of Hungary.[6]

After a series of uprisings that began in 1804 and continued through the nineteenth century, Serbia won independence from the Ottoman Empire. In 1878 the Congress of Berlin recognized Serbia as an independent nation but decreed that Bosnia and Herzegovina should be under Austrian-Hungarian control.[7] It is at this point in history that Serbs immigrated to America in significant numbers. Many came for economic reasons or to avoid conscription in the Austrian army and the possibility of being placed in opposition to troops from Serbia.

It is virtually impossible to ascertain Serbian immigration figures during this period since the United States census did not include Serbia or Montenegro as countries of birth. Those Serbs who came during this early period were chiefly from Bosnia, Herzegovina, Austria-Hungary, Bulgaria, Montenegro, and Dalmatia and were included in either Austrian or Bulgarian figures.[8] In the thirty years between 1880 and 1909 more than seventeen million immigrants came to America in contrast to less than ten million in the previous forty years. Slavs made up over one-fifth of the total immigrant number for the eleven years following 1899.[9] In 1907 Serbian presence was estimated at about 200,000 with about 20,000 in the "North Middle States."[10] It was common for immigrants to return to their homeland and reimmigrate. In the fiscal year 1908 there were 656 Serbs, Montenegrins, and Bulgarians who entered Indiana and 333 who left the state.[11]

There is little documentation for Serbian immigrants in Indiana prior to the turn of the century; however, one

Serbia
- Principal Cities
— International Boundaries

125 Km
125 Mi.

exception exists in Wabash County in a town known as New Madison, which was founded in 1835. When the railroad came through the town in 1881–82, a request was made to change the town's name to avoid confusion with a town with a similar name. The postmaster at the time was an immigrant from Serbia who used his influence to change the name of the town to "Servia" in 1883, which is its name today.[12] In the nineteenth century Servia was a common spelling for Serbia.[13] Possibly this is because in the Cyrillic alphabet "B" is the symbol for the "V" sound.

The first major wave of Serbian immigrants came to Indiana with the railroads to work in the mines of Vermillion and Vigo counties and in the newly expanding industrial areas of Lake County. The common denominator was work for the unskilled laborer who did not require fluency in English. The mining communities where Serbians worked included Clinton, Universal, Centenary, and Blanford, which was predominantly Serbian.[14] Three lodges or benevolent societies were formed in these communities for the protection of Serbian widows and orphans. These lodges also served a social purpose for ethnic groups to maintain their cultural heritage. Although there were no churches established by Serbs in these mining communities, their cultural heritage was transmitted orally by storytellers who sang of legendary or real heroes of the Serbian people, often accompanying themselves with a one-stringed guslá.[15] Baptisms, weddings, and funerals were performed by clergy from other nearby Eastern Orthodox churches. As the mining industry declined, many Serbs relocated to other areas.[16]

The opening of Inland Steel Company in 1901 in Lake County brought the first wave of Serbian immigrants to

East Chicago.[17] Many of these men had been in America for more than a decade working in eastern mines, factories, and railroads. By 1905 some of these laborers in the East Chicago and Hammond areas had opened their own businesses.[18] The saloon owned by a countryman was a social center for the single man, where his native language was spoken, familiar food was served, and folk songs cheered his heart. Single men often boarded with families. Eventually a few Serbs opened hotels near the mills.[19] The female population increased with mail-order brides sent upon request from an immigrant's native village. It is surprising to note how many of the immigrants were from the same villages in Lika (an area within the Croatian region of Austria-Hungary), Banat, Slavonija, and Bosnia.[20]

In 1906 one of the first educated, English-speaking Serbian immigrants to settle in East Chicago was Lazar Saric. Employed by the Citizens Trust and Savings Bank, he was responsible, along with fourteen other Serbs, for founding East Chicago's first Serbian benevolent society. Church life for the Serbs began in a storefront on Pennsylvania Avenue in 1911 when sixty-five families from East Chicago and Hammond formed the St. George Serbian Orthodox Church. A year later, on 5 May 1912, at a cost of $5,500 and scores of man hours, the church was dedicated at 140th and Elm streets in East Chicago. Elected officers were Lazar Saric, president, Paul Popovich, Nikola Popovich, Tode Stepanovich, Nikola Mayor, Miles Stokich, and Lako Bulatovich.[21] Plans were discussed for a future hall to be built next to the church, and numerous Serbian families purchased lots nearby to build their homes. As the city's industries expanded and the congregation grew, more lodges were formed and eventually were merged under the umbrella of the Serbian National Federation that had headquarters in Pittsburgh.[22]

Expanding industries, particularly the Studebaker plant, attracted the first Serbian immigrants to South Bend in 1902. Many of the first arrivals such as Vuksan Drca were from Lika. The first Serbian woman in South Bend arrived in 1905. By 1912 these early settlers had built St. Peter and St. Paul Church on Kendall Street. Rev. Jakov Odzich, a Serbian priest, along with a Russian bishop from New York and two Russian priests, performed the consecration. Officers of the congregation were Rade Medich, president, Stevan Petrovich, Danilo Obradovich, Jovan Polovina, Vuksan Medich, Danilo Voynovich, Gavro Gvozdenovich, Rade Tezich, Pavle Medich, and Ilija Medich.[23]

Work on the railroad and in the meatpacking plants brought Serbs in numbers to Indianapolis in 1904. Led by Jovan Perich, the majority were from Prizren in the Kosovo province. The Serbs organized two benevolent societies and attended services in the churches of other Eastern Orthodox immigrants. Plans to build a Serbian hall or National Home were not completed until after World War I.[24]

When Gary was founded in 1906 the US Steel Corporation offered employment opportunities to many Serbian immigrants.[25] A large number of Gary's Serbs were from Herzegovina, Lika, Bosnia, and Montenegro. A few chose to open businesses rather than to enter the labor market. One was John T. Marich, an immigrant from Herzegovina who arrived in Gary in 1907. In 1908 he opened a grocery store and later a travel agency. Marich was one of the original members of the Pioneer Society (later the Gary Historical Society), and in 1909 he was president of the newly formed Serbian Democratic Club.[26] In 1909 Mitchell Duchich, another Serb from Herzegovina, founded Gary's Cloverleaf Dairy. Other newly arrived Serbs opened boardinghouses, saloons, hotels, garages, and real estate businesses. Of those Serbs

who did not own businesses, many rose from unskilled to skilled and supervisory positions by working diligently for the railroads and in the mills.[27]

In 1910 the first Serbian Sokol (Falcon) group was organized in Gary for the purpose of educating its members "in patriotism and good citizenship" and "to elevate and maintain the consciousness of responsibility, morale education, national enlightenment, and physical development."[28] Sokol units were joined fraternally with other Slavic groups throughout America and met for athletic competitions and parades.

It was also in 1910 that a group of Gary Serbs met to discuss plans to build a church, school, and community hall. By 1912 they established a school board to attend to the education of their youth in the Serbian Orthodox faith. Board members included Superintendent Jovo Kladarin, Ljubomir Simich, John T. Marich, and Mitar Miskin. The board located a small building for the school at 14th Avenue and Massachusetts Street and secured a

*Serbian funeral shortly after the building of the St. George Serbian Orthodox Church, the first Serbian church in Indiana, in 1912 in East Chicago. Photos of the deceased were taken to be sent to relatives in Europe.*

*Gathering in Indianapolis in 1917 to honor the departure of 150 Serbian immigrant volunteers for World War I.*

teacher. In 1914 the school was in a rented hall at 13th and Connecticut and relocated in 1915 to 20th and Connecticut when property was purchased for a church school. Rev. Petar Stijacich served as priest and Steve Orlich was president.[29]

A crisis in the homeland caused all further building plans to be put aside in Indiana's Serbian communities. Despite a victory in the First Balkan War of 1912, the settlement of the Second Balkan War in 1913 created much unrest among Serbs in territories under Austrian-Hungarian control. Protest reached dire heights with the assassination of Archduke Francis Ferdinand in Sarajevo in 1914. As a result Austria declared war on Serbia, precipitating the onset of the First World War. Later Serbia was joined by France, Britain, Russia, Greece, and the United States as allies against Austria-Hungary, Germany, Bulgaria, and Turkey.[30] Before her allies entered the war, Serbia suffered severe losses and hardships. In 1917 a campaign to solicit aid for Serbia was waged throughout the United States and Canada. Not only were considerable funds contributed, but also thousands of Serbs in America and Canada joined the Serbian army, mainly at Salonica, an important base for Allied operations. President Woodrow Wilson wrote a letter approving the decision of these volunteers.[31] In Gary more than 450 young immigrants enlisted, including nine Vajagich brothers. Some were honored for bravery with the highest Serbian medals, such as Peter Demonja, Risto Vajagich, and Jovo Sever, who was decorated five times.[32] Two hundred volunteers enlisted from East Chicago,[33] while 153 from Indianapolis answered the

call.[34] Casualties were heavy. Of the 450 volunteers from Gary only 120 returned. More than half were killed, a few remained with their families, and the wounded were unable to return as long as medical treatment was needed.[35] Other Serbian immigrants across Indiana enlisted in the American army. John Mrmich from East Chicago was one. He was wounded at Verdun and decorated for valor.[36]

At the end of the war Serbs, Croats, and Slovenes in the Austrian-Hungarian territories were joined to form the Kingdom of Serbs, Croats, and Slovenes. In 1929 the new country was renamed Yugoslavia in an attempt to discourage separatist nationalism.[37] With the increase of United States immigration restrictions, Serbian immigration declined. Entry figures for Serbs are not distinguished from other ethnic Yugoslav census figures.

Serbian communities in Indiana were active during this period. In 1921 the Serbian Orthodox churches in America and Canada formed an American Serbian Diocese with approval from the mother church in Belgrade.[38] The seat of the new diocese was the St. Sava Monastery in Libertyville, Illinois, and many members of Indiana congregations played an active part in its consecration.

Also at this time church congregations in Indiana were busy expanding their own properties. In East Chicago in 1920 St. George Serbian Orthodox Church purchased a school building from the city for use as a social center and school on Elm Street. By 1923 additions to the property included quarters for the priest's family and a custodian.[39] In South Bend in 1927 a Serbian National Home was built for social gatherings beside the Kendall

Street church, and in 1940 a home for the priest's family was purchased.[40] In Indianapolis the two fraternal lodges combined efforts to build a hall for social gatherings at 3626 West 16th Street. Payment of the mortgage was facilitated through the efforts of a group of young men who had formed a tamburitza orchestra that played free of charge for all social events until the hall was debt free.[41] In Gary in 1938 a new St. Sava Church, school, library, and parish home were dedicated with great festivity at 13th and Connecticut. Building committee president Louis Christopher and parish president George Miljanovich hosted, among others, the Yugoslav ambassador. Inventor Nikola Tesla, himself the son of a Serbian priest and an immigrant, was a nominal sponsor (*kum*).[42]

Despite the economic depression that occurred, not only did physical facilities for Serbian immigrants expand during this period, but also opportunities for social interchange greatly increased. New organizations flourished, and one of the most important groups to emerge was the Circle of Serbian Sisters, established in East Chicago, Gary, South Bend, and Indianapolis. Still active today, this woman's auxiliary is a humanitarian group that serves whenever called upon by its churches or by those in need. A Serbian Singing Federation united the Karageorge Choir of Gary and the Aleksa Shantich Choir of South Bend with other Serbian choirs across America for concerts and social functions. Drama groups, particularly the group in Gary, traveled to various other Serbian communities to perform and to promote their cultural heritage. Social organizations such as the Yavor Club and the St. Sava Youth Club were formed to promote intermingling. Each colony had tamburitza groups to play for dances, weddings, and concerts several times a month. The Serbian National Federation instituted basketball and golf tournaments that were held in various cities across America to attract Serbian youth to meet others of the same background. Intermarriage was the norm, while mixed marriages were less common.

Also during the pre–World War II period, first- and second-generation Serbian Americans were actively entering the American mainstream in public service and in business. In 1932 the first captain of Gov. Paul V. McNutt's newly created Indiana State Police force was a former Gary policeman named Matt Leach, a Serbian immigrant born Matija Licanin. As captain of the state police, he was very instrumental in the capture of John Dillinger. Leach served in the United States army in both world wars, attaining the rank of major.[43] Other Serbs in Indiana also served as police officers. Nikola Ranich, former chief of detectives on the East Chicago force, had two sons, Charles Ranich and Steven Ranich, who were also police officers. In 1924 Paul Budich, another detective

Indianapolis tamburitza orchestra founded in 1920 that volunteered its services until the mortgage for the St. Nicholas Hall was paid in full. Seated left to right: Milos Tasich, Sam Jeftich, Mladen Tomich. Standing left to right: Marko Milatovich, George Savich, Ilija Alexich.

on the East Chicago police force, was killed in the line of duty and was honored as a fallen hero.[44]

With the outbreak of World War II hundreds of Indiana's Serbian-American men and women volunteered to serve in various branches of the armed services. Unlike World War I there was no recruitment among Serbs for service in a foreign army since both Yugoslavia and the United States entered the war in 1941. American Serbs were proud that their ancestral homeland, despite being occupied by Nazi invaders, had never completely surrendered but waged valiant guerrilla warfare against the Axis powers. Thousands of these resistance fighters made up the major wave of Serbian immigration to Indiana after World War II. Known as Chetniks, their commander, Gen. Draja Mihailovich, was awarded the Legion of Merit posthumously by President Harry Truman on 29 March 1948. The citation recognized his resistance efforts and the fact that the Chetniks rescued 432 American airmen who had been shot down over Yugoslavia during missions to bomb Hitler's oil supplies.[45] Hoosier airmen were among those rescued, and two of them, Frank Kincaid and Cecil Wink, were both from Evansville but had never met before being shot down over Yugoslavia and rescued by Mihailovich's men.[46] Some of those rescuers later immigrated to Indiana.

Of the Serbian Americans who entered the United States armed forces in World War II, there were more than four hundred from Lake County alone, and of these, twenty-one were killed in action.[47] Others served with distinction and were honored for their service. Col. Nick Stepanovich, a former East Chicago attorney, received

*Cast of drama group of St. Sava Serbian Church of Gary in a production staged in the 1920s. Note parents of actor Karl Malden, Petar Sekulovich (first row on left) and Minnie Sekulovich (first row, fourth from right).*

the Legion of Merit, the Order of the British Empire, and decorations from France, Italy, Greece, and Yugoslavia for his service as executive officer of Allied Counter Intelligence for the Mediterranean Theater of War.[48] After the war, on his return to Indiana and his law practice, Stepanovich took an active part in the Republican party on the state and national level. In 1954 Secretary of State John Foster Dulles appointed him as adviser to the American delegation in Geneva for the International Committee on European Migration.[49]

With the return of veterans after World War II, various Serbian colonies in Indiana again expanded. In 1948 St. George parish in East Chicago began plans to build a new hall as a memorial to its veterans. It was a joint effort with 150 members donating 6,800 hours of labor. The hall was dedicated on Memorial Day in 1950.[50] In South Bend twenty-two acres of land were purchased on Keria Trail where a new hall was completed in 1962.[51] In Indianapolis a committee was formed to organize the St. Nicholas Serbian Church and Parish School led by President Milo Cvetkovich, Bozidar Medich, Spaso Salatich, Chet Tasich, Stojilko Yovanovich, and Marko Milatovich, Sr. In 1951 a regular parish priest was hired to serve in the church's new chapel.[52] In 1956 in Gary, under the leadership of President Rudy Tuttle, the St. Sava congregation purchased forty-two acres of land in Hobart for a picnic ground and the site of a future community hall.[53]

The surge of building in Serbian-American communities after World War II was due largely to the mass influx of refugees and former prisoners of war who had fought the Nazis and/or Yugoslav Communists. These people had been in displaced persons camps scattered across Germany, Austria, and Italy because they refused to return to a Communist-controlled Yugoslavia. The passage of the Displaced Persons Act of 1948 and the Refugee Act of 1953 facilitated the immigration to America of 8,486 Yugoslavs from 1946 to 1950 and of another 26,706 from 1951 to 1955.[54] Although there is no exact breakdown specifying the number of Serbs involved in these figures, a vast number were sponsored by the Serbian Orthodox diocese in Libertyville, Illinois, the Serbian National Defense Council, the Serbian National Federation, the World Council of Churches, and individual congregations and families.[55]

At that time American industries were in full production and an unskilled labor force was still needed. The new arrivals were welcomed in their native tongue by Serbian Americans who found them jobs and homes. It was not uncommon for highly educated men to work as laborers until time and effort brought them advancement. Indiana Serbian communities doubled, and in the case of Indianapolis even tripled.[56] In Gary the International Institute of Northwest Indiana Social Service Agency was extremely helpful in assisting immigrants with their adjustment to American life. With the new arrivals came new cultural and political organizations. Also with them came numerous husbands for second-generation daughters of Serbian immigrants.

In 1963 an event occurred that sowed great discord in all Serbian-American communities and churches and which established two opposing factions. The basic issue that created the schism had to do with the extent of authority held by the Holy Council of Bishops and the Patriarch in Yugoslavia over the American diocese regarding administrative issues. One American faction was loyal to the church in Belgrade and supported Belgrade's decision to divide the American diocese into three separate dioceses and to suspend its bishop for various charges. The opposing American faction resolved to disregard the actions of the Council of Bishops in their belief that it had acted under the influence of the Communist commission of religious affairs, and that the bishop in America had not been given proper opportunity to answer the charges against him.[57] The conflict between the two factions resulted in much litigation, and in 1976 the United States Supreme Court ruled that the Patriarchal decision was not to be questioned.[58] The opposing American faction chartered a Serbian Eastern Orthodox Free Diocese of the United States and Canada and built a new monastery in Grayslake, Illinois, called Gracanica.[59]

As a result of this split, Indiana Serbian churches increased from four to six congregations as determined by votes in individual parishes. In South Bend the majority voted to remain under the auspices of the Patriarch.[60] The minority group attended churches of the autonomous new diocese and formed a new Circle of Serbian Sisters. In 1977 a fire destroyed the original St. Peter and St. Paul Church and a new one was completed in 1979 on the Keria Trail property.[61] In Indianapolis the congregation chose to be a part of the newly created American diocese.[62]

The voting in East Chicago and Gary resulted in the building of two new church complexes by those loyal to the Patriarchate. After failing to obtain the majority of votes at the Gary St. Sava Church, a group of parishioners, led by their founding president, Bronko Tarailo, purchased a church at 41st Avenue and Adams Street in Gary which became the St. Elijah congregation in 1964. By 1970 the congregation owned twenty acres of land on Taft Street in Merrillville, and in 1976 it dedicated a new Serbian American Bicentennial Hall with a seating capacity for one thousand. In 1983 a majestic new church, a replica of a fourteenth-century Byzantine Serbian church, was dedicated under the presidency of Zivan Pekovich.[63]

After a period of sharing the facilities of a Russian church, those members of East Chicago's St. George parish who were loyal to the Patriarchate formed a committee and purchased fifteen and a half acres in

REV. LAZAR KOSTUR

*St. Elijah Serbian Orthodox Church, Merrillville, Indiana.*

Schererville in June 1969. A hall was completed and dedicated in 1971, under the leadership of church president Nikola Puaca. Fund-raising efforts were aided by a catering service formed by the Circle of Serbian Sisters as well as events sponsored by the lodge and choir. Under the presidency of Dusan Grozdanich, a new parish home was built and a new St. George Church was dedicated. Father Dennis Pavichevich served the first liturgy in the new church on Serbian Christmas Eve in 1980.[64]

In 1978 a fire destroyed the St. Sava Church in Gary with the exception of the church's holy relics, which had miraculously been unharmed. That same year the membership voted to purchase 140 acres on Mississippi Street in Merrillville, and for a period of time services were held in a chapel on the congregation's Hobart property. By 1991 a new St. Sava Church was consecrated under the leadership of President Theodore Erceg and the Very Reverend John Todorovich.[65]

In 1991 a Serbian monastery was built near South Bend in New Carlisle. A dedicated sisterhood, whose members include immigrant and American-born Serbs, is on the premises. The monastery was chartered under the newly elected Patriarch Pavle of Yugoslavia, who was present at its consecration in 1994.[66] It was under this same patriarch that the schism in the American Serbian Orthodox churches came to an end in 1992 when the Free American Metropolitanate was officially recognized and returned to the synod.[67]

It has been almost a hundred years since the first Serbian immigrants established communities and began to build their churches and community centers in Indiana. Exact numbers of immigrants are impossible to determine as census figures do not distinguish between Yugoslav ethnic groups. In the 1980 census "about 200,000 Americans chose to identify their ancestry as Yugoslavian compared to a total of about 220,000 reporting the three ethnic ancestries" individually.[68] Figures for the 1990 census for Indiana are somewhat higher, listing 8,418 Indiana residents who claim Serbian ancestry. The largest representation remains near the church congregations in Lake County (5,246), Porter County (987), St. Joseph County (495), and Marion County (446). Lesser figures are scattered throughout the state.[69]

Serbian immigrants and their descendants have been active in all aspects of American life. Serbian Americans served their country in times of war with courage and pride, strove in times of peace to strengthen their country through strong family life, and realized the American dream. Many have won acclaim in various fields. Dr. Milomir Stanisic, a post–World War II immigrant, was a full professor in the School of Aeronautical Sciences and Engineering at Purdue University from 1961 until his retirement in 1985. He did valuable research on the mathematical theory of turbulence and supersonic motion and published numerous scientific studies in the fields of aviation and space.[70] Nick Trbovich, an electrical engineer from East Chicago, won recognition for his design for a power plant at Inland Steel Company. Trbovich bequeathed one million dollars to Purdue University in grateful acknowledgment of the education he received there.[71] A former Clinton resident, Dr. Eugene Knez, served from 1959 to 1979 as curator of anthropology at the National Museum of Natural History at the Smithsonian Institution.[72] A native of Gary, Dr. Danilo Orescanin was chancellor of Indiana University Northwest from 1975 to 1983 and was a vice president of Indiana University in Bloomington from 1983 to 1987. Scores of Serbian Americans serve as administrators and teachers in Indiana schools.

There are many examples of Indiana Serbs in public service. In 1955 Peter Mandich became the first mayor of Gary to win more than one consecutive term.[73] Former Indiana judges George Vann (Savanovich) and Peter Katic were natives of East Chicago. Michael Vinovich served as East Chicago chief of police from 1952 to 1960, and his son Robert was a state trooper. Steven Ranich was commander of the first state police post in Lake County and was one of the architects of the Indiana Law Enforcement Academy. After his retirement Ranich became chief of police in Highland from 1962 to 1969.

Entrepreneurs who realized success include Walter Milovich, founder of Ace Tool and Summit Engineering in South Bend; Alex Desancic, founder of Progress Pump in Schererville; Todor Stanjevic, Indianapolis owner of three furniture stores; and Dane Sever and Joe Buley, founders of Central Distributing in Gary.

In the arts two Serbian Americans from Lake County have won Academy Awards: Karl Malden (born Mladen Sekulovich), best supporting actor for his role in *A Streetcar Named Desire,* and Steve Tesich, best original screenplay for *Breaking Away,* which he based on his experiences at Indiana University.[74] A Pulitzer prize for specialized reporting was awarded in 1988 to Gary's Walter Bogdanich for his work with the *Wall Street Journal* on the subject of corruption in medical laboratory testing.[75]

A unique contributor to the arts is Schererville musician and tamburitza maker Milan Opacich, who participated in Smithsonian Festivals in 1976 and 1981 and whose instruments have been displayed at the Smithsonian's Renwick Gallery. He is the music columnist for the bimonthly periodical *Serb World U.S.A.,* a scholarly resource of Serbian cultural heritage and documentary of the achievements of immigrants and their descendants. Opacich was the subject of a documentary made by Indiana University featuring his art of constructing instruments and his performance with his tamburitza orchestra. He founded the St. Sava Tamburitza Orchestra in an attempt to propagate Serbian folk music and culture with young people.

Essential to an understanding of Serbian immigrants and their culture is a familiarity with their religious practices. Since the Serbian Orthodox Church adheres to the Julian calendar instead of the Gregorian calendar, used primarily throughout today's world, a difference of thirteen days exists for the dates of all holidays except Easter, which varies according to Jewish Passover.[76] Thus the Serbian Christmas falls on 7 January. The day before is a day of fasting with no meat or dairy products allowed. The evening of 6 January the faithful gather in church for vesper services and the burning of a yule log (*badnjak*), which is traditionally a young oak tree. The church is adorned with straw to symbolize the manger where Christ was born. Before the log is burned parishioners remove branches to take to their homes. On Christmas morning children miss school to attend church services with their families. The words "Christ Is Born!" are used instead of

*Original St. Sava Junior Tamburitzans, Gary, Indiana, 1963.*

other greetings. After church the family gathers for a festive meal of roast pork, stuffed cabbage, and other traditional foods that include a bread baked with coins to bring luck to those who find them.

A tradition that is unique to Serbs is Patron Saint's Day or "Slava." This holiday marks the day one's ancestors accepted Christianity. At the time of each clan's conversion more than a thousand years ago, it adopted a saint as family patron. In a Serbian marriage a woman accepts not only her husband's name but also his patron saint, which has been passed down from generation to generation. The day is marked by a special ceremony in which the priest blesses a special bread and a wheat dish called *zito* with wine and incense. The bread and wine symbolize Christ's sacrifice, and the wheat symbolizes resurrection. Prayers are said in honor of the saint and for all the family's deceased ancestors. A candle is kept burning all day to symbolize the presence of the Holy Spirit as family and friends gather to feast and celebrate.[77] Hospitality is almost a sacred obligation among Serbs. Even those families of humble means feel obliged to offer a guest refreshment not only on holidays but also on any visit to a Serbian home.

Another traditional celebration is held to honor St. Sava, the first archbishop of the autonomous medieval Serbian Orthodox Church and the founder of many churches and schools. On this occasion children learn poems and recitations for public declamation. It is not unusual to see children from as young as four years to teenagers stand in front of an audience of two hundred or more to recite their individual pieces in Serbian and then participate in folk dancing and singing.

Old Church Slavonic and Serbian prayers may be heard today in any of the six Serbian churches in Indiana and in the New Carlisle monastery. Church choirs sing responses in both Serbian and English, and sermons are delivered in either language, depending on whether those in attendance are fluent in Serbian. Baptisms, weddings, and funerals may be entirely in English as are some church services, although Serbian is used primarily. Sunday school classes are taught in English by volunteer teachers, while Serbian-language classes to teach Cyrillic reading and writing are the responsibility of the priest. Church choirs, always a cappella, serve to teach immigrants and American born church responses and secular music. These choirs are active in national singing federations that hold annual festivals in different cities across the United States and Canada to bring together hundreds of persons of the same ethnic background. They have performed in places as diverse as the World's Fair in Montreal and on the steps of the nation's Capitol. Age is no barrier. George Rapaich, a founder of the Gary Karageorge Choir, performed on stage at the age of one hundred.

Each congregation attracts its youth through dance groups that travel the country to other Serbian colonies and perform in full native dress. Dancers range in age from four to college age. There are summer camps held for children from ages six through sixteen sponsored by the dioceses and Circle of Serbian Sisters to teach children religious and cultural traditions. Indiana children have the option of attending any of these camps in Illinois, Ohio, Pennsylvania, or California to meet others of the same background. Often a large portion of the attendance fee is paid by church boards or parish organizations in order to encourage participation. Some educational scholarships are provided by the Serbian National Federation or by private endowments such as the Mitchell Duchich Educational Foundation.

For decades the Serbian National Federation and the churches have continued to sponsor basketball, bowling, tennis, and golf tournaments to bring young and old together. There one may see people dancing the *kolo* circle dances to native Serbian music. New immigrants are often surprised to see American youth so fervently dancing and maintaining cultural traditions that were almost lost during Yugoslavia's Communist rule, when youth tended to emulate western culture and music.

Despite increasing mixed marriages and assimilation into the American mainstream, there is still a strong desire among Serbian Americans to maintain their cultural identity. There are Serbian radio programs in Indiana, which air from Portage and go as far north as Wisconsin and as far south as Indianapolis. These programs broadcast news of interest to the Serbian-American community and play native music. Ethnic newspapers such as the *American Srbobran* and the *Observer* are printed bilingually. In recent years a Serbian American Bar Association and a Serbian American Medical Association were formed, which include numerous Indiana attorneys and medical professionals. Another organization called "SerbNet" was created after the onset of the civil war in Bosnia and other former republics of Yugoslavia. "SerbNet" was formed for the purpose of achieving unbiased reporting in the news media and preventing disinformation as was the case prior to the ending of World War II.[78]

Since the onset of the Bosnian War there has been another influx of political refugees. Serbian Americans have again been active in raising funds to aid those who have been displaced and have suffered the ravages of war. The Circle of Serbian Sisters groups in northern Indiana have joined together as "Mothers Against Hunger" to send food, medical supplies, and clothing abroad.

With the passing of time the face of the Serbian community has changed from one made up primarily of former peasants who became industrial workers to one of businessmen and professionals. One common philosophy that prevailed in immigrant homes was to work hard to provide children with an education so they could compete on an equal basis in this blessed new land of freedom and opportunity.

## Notes

1. *Encyclopedia Americana,* International ed., 30 vols. (Danbury, Conn.: Grolier Incorporated, 1992), 24:572.

2. Harold W. V. Temperley, *History of Serbia* (London: G. Bell and Sons, 1917), 82–83.

3. *Encyclopedia Americana,* 8:384.

4. Ibid., 24:572.

5. Ibid.

6. John P. Spielman, *Leopold I of Austria* (New Brunswick, N.J.: Rutgers University Press, 1977), 160.

7. *Encyclopedia Americana,* 24:572–73.

8. Emily Greene Balch, *Our Slavic Fellow Citizens* (New York: Charities Publication Committee, 1910; reprint, New York: Arno Press, 1969), 273.

9. Ibid., 4.

10. Ibid., 273–74.

11. *Indianapolis Star,* 17 Jan. 1909.

12. Richard Miller, curator of the Wabash County Historical Museum, telephone interview with the author, 24 Apr. 1995; Lonnie Lutz, "Servia Has a Rich Heritage," in *Wabash County History,* ed. Linda Robertson (Marceline, Mo.: Walsworth Pub. Co., 1976), 34.

13. *Oxford English Dictionary,* 20 vols. (Oxford: Clarendon Press, 1989), "Servian," 15:33, "Serbian," 15:4.

14. Louise Hitt Booth, *Clinton on the Wabash: A History of Clinton, Indiana from 1816 through 1912* (Villa Park, Calif.: D. R. Booth Assoc., 1994), 57.

15. Anthony Milanovich, "Serbian Tales from Blanford," *Indiana Folklore* 4, no. 1 (1971): 8.

16. Angie Mirkovich Devitt, interview with the author, Indianapolis, 25 Apr. 1995. Devitt's parents were early settlers in Blanford.

17. *St. George Serbian Orthodox Church 70th Anniversary Book* (East Chicago, Ind., 1981), 23.

18. Ibid.

19. Luka M. Pejovic, *Prikazi Nasih Iseljenika* (Akron: State Press, 1939), 109–10. This is a registry of Yugoslav immigrants in Illinois, Indiana, and Ohio that lists dates of immigration, places of birth, and occupations, printed in Serbo-Croatian.

20. Ibid., 103–12.

21. *St. George Serbian Orthodox Church of East Chicago 75th Anniversary Commemorative Book, 1911–1986,* p. 12.

22. *St. George Lodge 104 S.N.F. 50th Anniversary Booklet* (East Chicago, 1957), 31–33.

23. *St. Peter and St. Paul Serbian Orthodox Church Diamond Anniversary Book* (South Bend, 1986), 17.

24. *Gracanica Consecration* (Grayslake, Ill.: Serbian Orthodox Free Diocese of the United States and Canada, 1984), section on "Indianapolis Church History."

25. *St. Sava Serbian Orthodox Church 50th Anniversary Book: Our Religious Heritage in America* (Chicago: Palandech Press, 1964), hereafter cited as *Our Religious Heritage in America.*

26. *Gary Post-Tribune,* 17 Oct. 1965.

27. Pejovic, *Prikazi Nasih Iseljenika,* 77–103.

28. *Our Religious Heritage in America,* 84.

29. Ibid., 58–59, 60, 78.

30. *Encyclopedia Americana,* 3:96.

31. Theodore Erceg, interview with the author, 27 Oct. 1995, Hobart, Ind. Erceg's father was a World War I volunteer and the information is included in Theodore Erceg's *With Pious Gravity* (Valparaiso, Ind.: St. George Publishing Co., 1995).

32. *Our Religious Heritage in America,* 101, 106.

33. *St. George Serbian Orthodox Church of East Chicago 75th Anniversary Commemorative Book,* 14.

34. *Gracanica Consecration,* section on "Indianapolis Church History."

35. *St. Sava Serbian Orthodox Church 80th Anniversary Booklet, November 1994,* essay by Theodore Erceg.

36. Bessie Mrmich Ostoic, interview with the author, Schererville.

37. *The New Encyclopaedia Britannica: Micropaedia, Ready Reference and Index,* 15th ed., 10 vols. (Chicago: Encyclopaedia Britannica, 1990), 10:646.

38. *Gracanica Consecration,* 33.

39. *St. George Serbian Orthodox Church of East Chicago 75th Anniversary Commemorative Book,* 16.

40. *St. Peter and St. Paul Serbian Orthodox Church Diamond Anniversary Book,* 18.

41. *Gracanica Consecration,* section on "Indianapolis Church History."

42. *Our Religious Heritage in America,* 119.

43. Phillip D. Hart, "Captain Matt Leach: Dillinger's Nemesis," *Serb World U.S.A.* (May/June 1992): 47–54.

44. *The Calumet Day* (East Chicago/Whiting edition), 6 July 1983; *Calumet Globe* (East Chicago), 27 June 1984.

45. David Martin, *The Web of Disinformation: Churchill's Yugoslav Blunder* (New York: Harcourt Brace Jovanovich, 1990), 226, 239–40.

46. Frank Kincaid, telephone interview with the author, Evansville, Ind., 6 Apr. 1995; Richard Felman, president of the National Committee of American Airmen Rescued by General Mihailovich, Inc., telephone interviews with the author, 5 and 26 Apr. 1995, Tucson, Ariz.

47. *St. George Church 50th Anniversary Book,* 27; *St. Sava Serbian Orthodox Church 80th Anniversary Booklet,* essay by Theodore Erceg.

48. *Chicago Tribune,* 29 Dec. 1983.

49. Phillip D. Hart, "Nick Stepanovich," *Serb World U.S.A.* (Sept./Oct. 1991): 50–55.

50. *St. George Serbian Orthodox Church of East Chicago 75th Anniversary Commemorative Book,* 24.

51. *St. Peter and St. Paul Serbian Orthodox Church Diamond Anniversary Book,* 18.

52. *Gracanica Consecration,* section on "Indianapolis Church History."

53. *Our Religious Heritage in America,* 149.

54. U.S. Department of Commerce, Bureau of Census, *Statistical Abstract of the United States, 1951* (Washington, D.C.: Dept. of Commerce, 1951), 93; ibid., *1959,* p. 92.

55. *St. George Serbian Orthodox Church of East Chicago 75th Anniversary Commemorative Book,* 22.

56. *Gracanica Consecration,* section on "Indianapolis Church History."

57. Milan Karlo and Helen Karlo, *Early Days: Serbian Settlers in America* (Tucson, Ariz.: Privately printed, 1984), 226–27.

58. Ibid., 231.

59. Ibid., 247–48.

60. Ibid., 254.

61. *St. Peter and St. Paul Serbian Orthodox Church Diamond Anniversary Book*, 18.

62. Karlo and Karlo, *Early Days*, 254.

63. *A History of St. Elijah Serbian Orthodox Church: Dedication and Consecration, October 29–30, 1983* (Merrillville: St. Elijah Orthodox Church, 1983).

64. "Past and Present," in *St. George Serbian Orthodox Church of Schererville Dedication Book, July 26, 1980.*

65. *St. Sava Serbian Orthodox Church Consecration Book, Merrillville, May 1991*, pp. 30–31.

66. *Consecration Pamphlet, Nativity of the Mother of God Serbian Orthodox Patriarchal Monastery, New Carlisle, June 1994.*

67. *Path of Orthodoxy: The Liturgy of Reconciliation* (Skokie, Ill.: Great Lakes Graphics, 1992).

68. James Paul Allen and Eugene James Turner, *We the People: An Atlas of America's Ethnic Diversity* (New York: Macmillan, 1988), 12.

69. U.S. Department of Commerce, Bureau of Census, *1990 Census of Population: Social and Economic Characteristics, Indiana* (Washington, D.C.: Dept. of Commerce, 1993), Table 137.

70. Memorial Resolution, Milomir M. Stanisic, Office of the Dean of Engineering, Purdue University, West Lafayette, 9 Apr. 1991.

71. *State of the School, 1989* (Purdue University, School of Electrical Engineering), 9.

72. Dr. Eugene Knez, telephone interview with the author, 19 May 1995, Honolulu; Alan Knezevich (son of Dr. Eugene Knez), telephone interview with the author, 11 May 1995, Washington, D.C.

73. James B. Lane and Ronald D. Cohen, *Gary, Indiana: A Pictorial History* (Norfolk, Va.: Donning Co., 1983), 160.

74. Nancy Jacobson, *Indiana Awesome Almanac* (Fontana, Wis.: B. & B. Publishing, 1993), 65.

75. Michael D. Nicklanovich, "A Pulitzer for Bogdanich," *Serb World U.S.A.* (Nov./Dec. 1990): 40.

76. Stan W. Carlson and Leonid Scroka, *Faith of Our Fathers: The Eastern Orthodox Religion* (Minneapolis: Olympic Press, 1962), 152.

77. John Todorovich, *Serbian Patron Saint* (Merrillville, Ind.: Privately printed, 1978), 22.

78. Martin, *Web of Disinformation*, xvii.

# SLOVENES

JAMES J. DIVITA

*A Slovenian woman never patronized saloons and only when one opened an outdoor garden did she ever appear there. Her major responsibilities were housekeeping, meal preparation, tending the children, and looking after boarders. The boarders, unmarried young men, usually paid six dollars monthly for room, meals, and laundry service. She and the children shared leftovers and the drippings from boarders' suppers. Dried, stringy beef that she purchased for two cents per pound at Kingan and Company, meatpackers, supplemented the family diet. Preparing meals over a hot coal- or wood-burning stove and hand washing grimy work clothes occupied much of her time. During the day she relaxed only when chatting with neighbor ladies; at night she relaxed only when her chores were completed.*

Slovenes, a South Slavic people, are related ethnically and linguistically to the Croats, Serbs, Montenegrins, Bosnians, and Macedonians of Europe's Balkan Peninsula. Of these peoples, however, the Slovenes lived farthest north and west and were subject to strong German and Catholic influence. Except for a brief period in the early nineteenth century during which Napoleon governed them, the Slovenes lived under Hapsburg rule from 1277 to 1918. They populated the Austrian provinces of Carniola (Kranjsko), Styria (Štajersko), Carinthia (Koroško), and the Littoral (Primorsko), but only in Carniola were they a majority. Subsequent to the Hapsburg military defeat in World War I and the redrawing of international boundaries, most Slovenes joined with other South Slavs to form the Kingdom of the Serbs, Croats, and Slovenes (Yugoslavia).[1] Other Slovenes became residents of the Italian provinces of Trieste and Gorizia. With the modification of the Italo-Yugoslav border and the reorganization of Yugoslavia as a federal state after World War II, Slovenia became one of its six republics. In 1991 the nearly two million Slovenes quit Yugoslavia to form an independent state bordering on Italy, Austria, Hungary, and Croatia.

Among the first Slovenes to settle in America was Frederic Baraga (1797–1868), Catholic missionary to the Chippewa Indians and first bishop of Marquette, Michigan. In 1831 he arrived in Cincinnati and was sent to minister to the Catholics who recently settled in the southeastern corner of Indiana. In a letter to his sister Amalia back home, Baraga reported that in mid-April he preached the gospel to about twenty-five families in Dearborn County. He was pleased to find among them a Slovene, Peter Pohek (ca. 1784–1854), native of the parish of Crnomelj in the Metlika district of Carniola, a Napoleonic army veteran married to an Alsatian and the father of five children. Pohek had resided in America scarcely three years, but he already owned "a rather extensive plot of fertile land and a large herd of nice cattle." The priest, who had ministered in Metlika for two years, concluded that his meeting Pohek confirmed the old saying, "You find a Carniolan everywhere." Pohek is the first Slovene on record to reside in the state.[2]

Slovenes immigrated because of economic pressure. The Hapsburg government began to build railroads in its Slovenian provinces in 1846, and serfdom was abolished

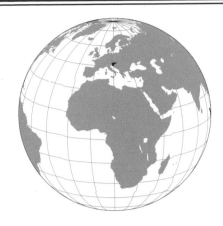

in 1848. The new transportation system and the new individual freedom were mixed blessings. Although Slovenian honey, dairy products, and hops could be profitably exported, iron, steel, and glass could now be easily imported to compete effectively with local manufacturers. Furthermore, viticulture was depressed with the spread of phylloxera (vine disease) in the 1880s, and workers' dissatisfaction is shown in the unsuccessful coal miners' strike in 1888. Rural and small-town dwellers relocated to Ljubljana in Carniola and other large cities while the more ambitious departed for Germany.[3]

Although Slovenes mined copper in Michigan's Upper Peninsula (1854) and farmed in central Minnesota as early as 1866, the high point of Slovenian immigration to the United States occurred in the two decades before World War I. American companies recruited labor in Europe, especially in Austria-Hungary. When relatives and friends wrote letters home describing economic opportunities in America, 8,000 immigrated annually between 1900 and 1910 out of a home population numbering 1,250,000. About 130,000 Slovenes entered the United States and found jobs as miners, meatpackers, and foundry or mill workers in the East, Midwest, and West by 1914. They congregated in Pittsburgh, Cleveland, Chicago, Joliet, Milwaukee, on the Iron Ranges of Minnesota, and in the mining towns of Colorado.

A small number of Slovenian immigrants found economic opportunity in the mills and mines of Indiana. Between 1906 and 1914 United States Steel Corporation recruited Croats, Hungarians, Slovaks, Lithuanians, and Poles to labor in its Gary Works. Slovenes (sometimes called Slavonians) accompanied these immigrants, but they were never numerous enough to follow the lead of other nationalities and organize their own church. They settled in Gary's Tolleston neighborhood in the area bound by 9th and 15th avenues and by Grant and Taft streets.[4] By 1924 Slovenes organized mutual aid societies in Gary, Clinton, Chesterton, and Elkhart.

The largest Slovenian community in the state developed in Indianapolis, a city of 105,000 in 1890. Most Slovenes came from Carniola, with small contingents originating in the Littoral and Styria. Jurij Lampert (1862–1925), known as George Lambert, brought many of them to the Hoosier capital. He crossed the Atlantic Ocean seven times between 1895 and 1907 to recruit workers for the National Malleable Castings Company. He was particularly successful in attracting young unmarried men from the economically depressed hill and farm towns around his native village of Besnica near Ljubljana. By 1920 about 1,200 Slovenes resided in Indianapolis, an estimate because when federal census takers asked for birthplace, Slovenes could respond "Austria," "Italy," or "Jugo-slavia."[5]

"Malleable," as the Slovenes always called the company, was organized in Cleveland, Ohio, in 1868. In 1882 it purchased the small Johnson Malleable Iron foundry at Michigan Street and Holmes Avenue west of White River in Haughville, then an unincorporated suburb that would be annexed to Indianapolis in 1897.[6] Malleable then employed over five hundred and manufactured castings for farm implements and machinery and subsequently made couplers for railroad cars and transmission housings for automobiles. Ewart Manufacturing Company, which produced detachable chain link, was a subsidiary. Later Ewart built a plant across the street from Malleable and in 1906 became the Link-Belt Company.[7] With few exceptions Slovenes worked for either Malleable or Link-Belt.

The normal workday for a Slovenian man began early in the morning. Although the Malleable whistle sounded at 7 A.M., sometimes he reported three hours earlier to prepare the furnaces. Starting time varied depending on whether he was a core maker, pattern maker, or molder and whether he worked the day or night shift. Foundry work was hard, hot, and tiring. Summer temperatures rose to 140 degrees. Winter temperatures often registered below freezing because cold air rushed in whenever doors were opened to admit coke or to ship the finished product. His only break was at lunchtime when a family member appeared at the foundry window and passed in a lunch basket. For all this he was paid ten to fifteen cents an hour in 1910, or he was paid by the piece and was docked if he produced too much scrap. His pay for a sixty-hour workweek, probably a five-dollar gold piece and a silver dollar, came in a small brown envelope bearing his name.

After work the Slovenian immigrant dragged himself home for supper, probably some combination of beef soup, homemade noodles, boiled cabbage, pork, or pigs' feet. During the evening he might play games with cronies

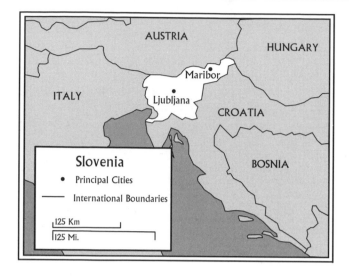

Slovenia
• Principal Cities
— International Boundaries
125 Km
125 Mi.

or relax with family members and boarders, enjoying a glass of wine or consuming a five-cent bucket of beer obtained at a nearby saloon.

A Slovenian woman never patronized saloons and only when one opened an outdoor garden did she ever appear there. Her major responsibilities were housekeeping, meal preparation, tending the children, and looking after boarders. The boarders, unmarried young men, usually paid six dollars monthly for room, meals, and laundry service. She and the children shared leftovers and the drippings from boarders' suppers. Dried, stringy beef that she purchased for two cents per pound at Kingan and Company, meatpackers, supplemented the family diet. Preparing meals over a hot coal- or wood-burning stove and hand washing grimy work clothes occupied much of her time. During the day she relaxed only when chatting with neighbor ladies; at night she relaxed only when her chores were completed.

A single woman might work outside the home to earn additional income for the family, but normally only a widow could take permanent employment. During the Great Depression a married woman might be forced to seek work because her husband was unemployed.[8]

Some Slovenes escaped foundry heat by seeking jobs at Kingan's. Butchering and other work there were monotonous and tiring, but at least the slaughterhouse was cooler. Others decided to return to farming and purchased land along the Morgan-Brown County line during and immediately after World War I. The land was marginal, however, and, in order to survive economically, the men were forced to return to Malleable during the winter months. Since the farms were too remote for a daily trip, the men lived apart from their families and boarded in Haughville. Others went into business, selling dry goods, hardware, or groceries or opening a tailor shop, bakery, or saloon.

The re-creation of village life characterized by strong ethnic and family loyalties moderated the dreariness created by the long workday and low wages. Malleable's recruits, crowded into boardinghouses along Michigan Street and into the small white frame houses along the unpaved streets (Holmes, Warman, and Haugh) north of the foundry, organized community life. They formed their first mutual aid society, St. Aloysius Lodge #52 KSKJ, in 1900. Some saved enough to return home rich while others married or brought their families from the Old Country. The appearance of women and children encouraged the emergence of a religious and social spirit centered on Holy Trinity Catholic Church founded in 1906, and the Slovenian National Home founded in 1918.

Holy Trinity Church, at Holmes Avenue and St. Clair Street, provided the usual spiritual services and sponsored community events ranging from parish suppers to annual street festivals. Rev. Joseph Lavric (1872–1915), a priest of the Ljubljana diocese, organized the parish. Franciscan Conventual priests, generally with eastern European backgrounds, ministered at Holy Trinity from 1910 to 1933. A parochial school was founded in 1911 and had an enrollment of 434 in 1923. Four years later the parish built a social hall containing bowling alleys, pool tables, and a large auditorium for plays and dances. After 1933 Indianapolis diocesan priests served parishioners. Several societies existed there—from the Living Rosary Society to the Young Ladies Sodality.[9]

The Slovenian National Home (Slovenski Narodni Dom), located in a frame structure at 729 North Holmes Avenue, provided a center for card playing, drinking, bowling, staging plays, and glee club singing. Its first president was Frank Jonta. The annual harvest festival, the Grape Arbor Dance, was held there. During the presidency of Valentine Stroj (1940) stockholders approved the construction of a larger, brick facility at 10th Street and Warman Avenue.[10] The hall was rented for wedding receptions and birthday and anniversary parties. The older generation continues to call this club "the Home" while the younger generation calls it "the Nash."

The two dozen corner saloons that existed in Haughville were major social institutions. Because of the heat on the job, Slovenes were noted for drinking beer to quench their almost overwhelming thirsts. When saloons were forced to close during Prohibition, like other immigrants Slovenes made beer and wine at home. Distinctive odors in the neighborhood always betrayed the location of these domestic vintners and brewers.

Athletics were an important recreational outlet, understandable because of the physical nature of foundry work. Kick the wicket, baseball, basketball, and bowling were the

*Slovenian National Home during World War II. Built in 1940, the clubroom with bar was one of the focal points of community life. Note two American flags, one flanked by a portrait of Gen. Douglas MacArthur.*

favorite sports. Former Marion County sheriff Robert A. O'Neal, a Haughville native, recalled: "There were a lot of good, solid, church-going families but it was a rough and tumble athletic crowd."[11] In 1936 the West Side Jugoslav eleven defeated a Fort Harrison football team 14-6 before fifteen hundred spectators in the Butler Bowl.[12]

Other diversions were dances, movies, and books. Gačnik's Hall at Ketcham and St. Clair was used for parties and dances. For five cents youngsters streamed into the Saturday and Sunday matinees at the Daisy or Princess theaters. Slovenes patronized the public library frequently. About 10 to 15 percent of the total circulation at the Haughville branch was in Slovenian and other foreign language books. Between 1926 and 1929 the number of books borrowed annually at the Haughville branch exceeded the number borrowed at any other branch in the city. Circulation reached its peak in 1933 when Haughville residents borrowed 182,733 books.[13]

Another aspect of village life was the important role that lodges played. Usually known by their national affiliations—the KSKJ (American Slovenian Catholic Union founded in 1894), the AFU (American Fraternal Union founded as the JSKJ in 1898), and the SNPJ (Slovene National Benefit Society founded in 1904)—they paralleled the Catholic Political party, National Progressive party (liberal), and Yugoslav Social Democratic party that emerged in the Slovenian provinces of the Hapsburg state between 1890 and 1896.[14] Organized as mutual aid societies between 1900 and 1905, the Indianapolis lodges provided sufficient insurance coverage to bury a member, with possibly a surplus to support the family of the deceased for a brief period. The lodges also provided sick benefits, usually one dollar, equal to a day's wage. Payment of the dollar was very strict and ordinarily meant that the recipient was bedridden. Since the membership at a lodge meeting approved the payment of sick benefits, if a

*On 23 November 1925 Anthony Petrich died at age forty-three. Here lodge members join with his family and friends before Holy Trinity Church to show solidarity with a deceased brother.*

member saw the applicant shopping or even sitting on his front porch on the day for which the dollar was to be paid the claim was denied.

As noted, the lodges reflected the ideological divisions among Indianapolis Slovenes. Although most Slovenes were practicing Catholics, about 20 percent were termed "socialists." Some had merely fallen away from Catholicism, others remembered that the Church favored the unpopular Hapsburg government in the Old Country, some were anticlerical and disliked the dictatorship of the "black capes" (the clergy), while others were ideologically committed to socialism. Slovenian socialists had much company in Indiana: the American Socialist party was organized in Indianapolis in 1901 and, when Eugene V. Debs of Terre Haute ran for president of the United States as the party's candidate in 1912, almost 37,000 Hoosiers voted for him.

Besides bringing European political attitudes to America, like all immigrants the Slovenes brought their cultural traditions. Merriment accompanied customs related to birth, baptism, confirmation, first communion, and marriage. These were times of gathering with family and friends.

One of the traditions transplanted to Haughville was shivaree. On the feast day of one's patron saint, family members, friends, and neighbors would play happy music on the harmonica or accordion before the namesake's house. To accompany the music, or if no instrument was available, noisemakers banged pans and lids until the honoree appeared at the door and invited them and the musicians in for something to eat and wine to drink.

Particularly striking were marriage customs. The day began with the actual wedding at Mass. Following the ceremony an accordionist would accompany the wedding

*On 24 November 1913 groom Tony Gorec (seated left) and bride Frances Luzar (seated center) posed with her extended family and the local musician. Among those present were her two brothers, a sister-in-law, an uncle by marriage, and a cousin and his wife.*

party from house to house inviting family and friends to the festivities that night. Conversation, dancing, and much food and drink were in evidence. Among the food items served was *potica,* a traditional nuts and honey rolled bread. All would participate in the pillow dance, a special polka for weddings. At midnight the bride and groom were seated with their parents beside them and were serenaded with Slovenian melodies and toasted to years of happiness. Then in a most solemn moment the bride's veil would be removed, signifying that her carefree girlhood days had ended and that she now was to shoulder family responsibilities.

Funerals were also a major community event. If the deceased was a lodge member, two lodge representatives wearing black badges maintained vigil while the corpse rested at home. While one lodge representative opened the door for mourners, the other remained in the room with the corpse and directed mourners to the room where the grieving family provided food and wine. The lodge representatives maintained six-hour shifts with four shifts per day so that the corpse was never left unattended. All

members were encouraged to attend the funeral service and to accompany the casket to its burial place. At the end of the funeral Mass the casket was carried outside of church, propped up, and opened. A formal photograph of the deceased, lodge members, and lodge banner was taken. A five- or six-piece band accompanied the cortege as far east as the Michigan Street bridge over White River on its way to the cemetery. These practices continued until the Malleable management complained that employees lost too many work hours attending funerals.

Slovenes were subject to the prejudices and rivalries only too common in the immigrant experience. When Slovenes arrived at Malleable other workers, fearful that wages would be lowered, threw rocks at them.[15] Some German residents of Haughville moved away. Conflict with the Irish-American pastor at nearby St. Anthony Catholic Church over the issue of temperance became so intense that the Slovenes purchased lots and offered them to the bishop if he would authorize a separate parish for them.[16] If an immigrant spoke Slovene on the Michigan Street trolley, someone was bound to say: "Who let those hunkies on here?" When asked if he had observed the building of the flood wall along White River in 1914, a Slovene born in Haughville responded: "Walk east of King Avenue? Once a group of us went down St. Clair Street to the river to see what was going on there. But usually we did not do that—especially by yourself. Those kids over there always wanted to beat us up." The Ku Klux Klan, however, was not particularly active in this part of Haughville. Although many of the residents were Catholic, foreign born, or offspring of a foreign-born parent, they generally kept to themselves in the "village" and did not appear to threaten the dominant culture.

On the other hand, a stranger walking through the Slovenian neighborhood also was at risk. "If you walked up Holmes Avenue to the Princess Theater," an Irish woman and former resident of Haughville recalled, "You heard a whistle, then another whistle, and then you'd be stopped and questioned by six guys. If they didn't like your answers or your looks they'd beat us up." "Aaw," responded her husband, a graduate of Holy Trinity school, "that happened because the kids outside of our neighborhood started it first. Hunkytown was our turf."

Elderly Slovenes in the 1980s vividly remembered life around Holy Trinity and the Slovenian National Home fifty years earlier. Everyone knew everyone else since they were coworkers, neighbors, or relatives. They could recite the names and addresses of neighbors more accurately than the list prepared for the city directory. Village life and its peculiar customs, however, disappeared with a new generation, the admission of Catholics of other ethnic backgrounds to Holy Trinity parish (1948), and neighborhood change.

The Slovenian neighborhood in the Hoosier capital began to disintegrate in the 1950s. Only a few Slovenes immigrated to Indianapolis after World War II. The causes of "the exodus" were many. Young, married Slovenian-American couples who could not find a home in Haughville in the early 1950s resided outside the neighborhood and sold the old family home when their parents died. Newcomers, displaced by the construction of Interstate highways 65 and 70 or the development of the campus of Indiana University-Purdue University at Indianapolis (IUPUI), purchased or rented these homes and brought unfamiliar faces and racial tension into the community. Malleable and Link-Belt, the economic stabilizers of Haughville, disappeared. Link-Belt closed its Michigan Street operation after it built a new plant in western Marion County in 1958 and Malleable abandoned its Indianapolis plant in 1962.[17] College-educated Slovene Americans trained in professional fields found Haughville unattractive and suburban life more

*On their way to participate in Slovenian Day, part of All Nationality Week at Keith's Theatre, downtown Indianapolis, on 11 April 1923, this costumed group assembled before the Slovenian National Home stage and on the trap door over the bar installed in the basement during Prohibition.*

appropriate to their new status. Symptomatic of the decline of old Haughville were the city of Indianapolis's construction of public housing in the area in 1966 and the merger of Holy Trinity school with three other parochial schools in 1976. Holy Trinity statistics show the seriousness of the exodus: membership declined from 2,250 in 1956 to 900 in 1981 and 647 in 1993.

From Haughville, descendants of Slovenian immigrants dispersed into the new residential areas north of 30th Street, into Speedway, along 10th Street into the Chapel Hill and Chapel Glen subdivisions, and into Hendricks County. In Haughville the Malleable site is an unimpressive vacant lot, and a Kroger supermarket has taken the place of Link-Belt.

Despite dispersal, the pillars of ethnic life remain Holy Trinity parish, the lodges, the Slovenian National Home, and the recently organized Slovenian Cultural Society.

Renovation and floodlighting of Holy Trinity give evidence that the old Slovenian parish with its African-American pastor seeks to retain a neighborhood presence and attract other constituencies. Yet periodically Holy Trinity Church reverberates with Slovenian hymns or a Polka Mass, and parishioners still present Easter baskets there for the priest's blessing. Parish bazaars feature ethnic crafts and foods. To fill hundreds of phone orders, both white and black women bake *potica* in the parish kitchen for the Thanksgiving, Christmas, and Easter holidays.

Earlier religious differences between the lodges have generally disappeared, and some members belong to more than one lodge. The lodges continue to provide insurance coverage, but they serve primarily as social outlets and sponsors of athletic events. Lodge basketball, bowling, and golf teams compete in annual tournaments with teams from other Slovenian-American communities and help maintain ethnic solidarity.

Besides hosting the monthly lodge meetings, the Slovenian National Home is also the site for gatherings of women (Slovene Women's Club) and men (Yaggers or Hunters). Thirsty bowlers and Grape Arbor Dance revelers still look forward to spending an evening there. The Home schedules an open house, an occasion for socializing and card playing, on the third Sunday of each month. Independence Day and Labor Day picnics are held on grounds the Home owns in western Marion County.

The Slovenian Cultural Society, founded in 1987, sponsors quarterly educational and cultural programs such as lectures or musical performances to help foster a sense of identity and community. It participates in Indianapolis's annual International Festival and maintains contact with other Slovenian-American communities. International recognition of an independent Slovenia (1992) has energized the community and helped to increase interest in society activities.[18]

In 1925 a Haughville branch librarian complained that most people in Indianapolis would say: "Oh yes, there are a few hunkies out in Haughville but we don't know anything about them."[19] Except for the Jews, the Slovenes were the largest group of eastern Europeans to settle in the city. Today, probably fifteen thousand Americans of Slovenian ancestry live in central Indiana. From pious ancestors have come many Catholics who contribute to the life of several westside parishes. From unlettered, tightfisted farmers and craftsmen have come skilled workers, businessmen, and professional people. From hard-drinking, exploited foreigners have come Philip L. Bayt, Jr., mayor of Indianapolis (1950–51, 1956–59) and Gerald S. Zore, Marion County Superior Court judge since 1974. To study the Slovenes is to study in microcosm the effects of urban, social, economic, and educational changes on an immigrant people and their descendants within American society.

## Notes

1. Three studies useful in understanding the political and social position of the Slovenes in the Hapsburg monarchy are Dragotin Loncar, *The Slovenes: A Social History* (Cleveland: American Jugoslav Printing and Publishing Co., 1939); Robert A. Kann, *The Habsburg Empire: A Study in Integration and Disintegration* (New York: Frederick A. Praeger, Inc., 1957); Oscar Jászi, *The Dissolution of the Habsburg Monarchy* (Chicago: The University of Chicago Press, 1929).

2. For the Baraga/Pohek meeting see Anthony A. Fette, *History of New Alsace, Indiana* (St. Meinrad, Ind.: Abbey Press, 1951), 72–76. Known to neighbors as Peter Buchert, Pohek's church cemetery marker at New Alsace, Dearborn County, reports his age as seventy at the time of his death.

3. Toussaint Hocevar, *The Structure of the Slovenian Economy, 1848–1963* (New York: Studia Slovenica, 1965), 56–57, 82–84. Also see John A. Arnez, *Slovenia in European Affairs: Reflections on Slovenian Political History*, Studia Slovenica 1 (New York: League of the CSA, 1958).

4. *Gary Post-Tribune*, 5 June 1983.

5. Estimate based on Holy Trinity Catholic Church's annual reports to Bishop Joseph Chartrand, Indianapolis Archdiocesan Archives; U.S. Department of Commerce and Labor, Bureau of the Census, *Thirteenth Census of the United States: Abstract of the Census* (Washington, D.C.: Government Printing Office, 1913), 624; U.S. Department of Commerce, Bureau of the Census, *Fourteenth Census of the United States Taken for the Year 1920* (Washington, D.C.: Government Printing Office, 1922), 2:743.

6. When Haughville was incorporated on 14 Feb. 1883, its boundaries were generally 10th Street on the north, Belmont Avenue on the east, Washington Street on the south, and Warman/Vermont/ Tibbs (to exclude Central State Hospital) on the west. Today residents apply the name to the area north of Michigan Street to 16th, and from White River to Tibbs. Sources on Haughville are Berry R. Sulgrove,

*History of Indianapolis and Marion County, Indiana* (Philadelphia: L. H. Evarts, 1884), 470–71; Jacob Piatt Dunn, *Greater Indianapolis,* 2 vols. (Chicago: The Lewis Publishing Co., 1910), 1:440.

7. For the early history of Malleable and Link-Belt see *Indianapolis Star,* 10 Feb. 1929; 31 Dec. 1948; 28 Dec. 1952.

8. The descriptions are composites based on interviews with several elderly Slovenes conducted during summer 1980. Interviews were especially valuable because of the paucity of written sources and the need to preserve the memories of the diminishing second generation of immigrants. The major written source is Elavina Sophia Stammel and Charles Roscoe Parks, "The Slavic Peoples in Indianapolis" (Master's thesis, Indiana University, 1930).

9. For parish history see the relevant sections of the Stammel-Parks thesis, the Silver (Velikan/Cvercko) and Golden Jubilee histories of Holy Trinity (1931 and 1956), and James J. Divita, *Slaves to No One: A History of the Holy Trinity Catholic Community in Indianapolis on the Diamond Jubilee of the Founding of Holy Trinity Parish* (Indianapolis: Holy Trinity Parish, 1981).

10. "Slovenian National Home Souvenir Journal and Dedication Program, October 1940."

11. *Indianapolis Times,* 24 Dec. 1961.

12. Ibid., 27 Nov. 1936.

13. "History of Haughville and the Haughville Branch Library," 2, clippings file "Haughville," Indiana Historical Society Library, Indianapolis.

14. Carol Rogel, *The Slovenes and Yugoslavism, 1890–1914* (New York: Columbia University Press, 1977), 28, 40, 51.

15. *Indianapolis News,* 10 Mar. 1978.

16. James J. Divita, *Rejoice and Remember: A Centennial History of the Catholic Community of St. Anthony of Padua, Indianapolis, Indiana* (Indianapolis: Centennial Committee, St. Anthony Parish, 1991), 30.

17. Link-Belt merged with FMC Corporation in 1967. Malleable became the National Castings Division of Midland-Ross Corporation in 1965. Forstmann Little and Company acquired Midland-Ross in 1986. See *Moody's Industrial Manual, 1981,* 2 vols. (New York: Moody's Investors Service, Inc.), 1:1184; 2:3893–94; ibid., 1993, 1:1159, "Additional Companies Formerly Included" section.

18. Interview of and written comments by Paul Barbarich of the Slovenian Cultural Society, Dec. 1992.

19. Vera Morgan, "Library Work with Foreigners," 1, clippings file "Haughville," Indiana Historical Society Library.

# SOUTHEAST ASIANS

CYRIAC K. PULLAPILLY

*What stunned this writer, more than any statistics, was the sight of a young woman in one South Bend high school begging a teacher to allow her to retake a chemistry test so that she could improve her grade from 98 percent to 100 percent. With a heavy accent but in grammatically correct English she explained that only a 100 percent grade would insure her admission to Harvard. The dismayed teacher allowed her to retake the test but wondered aloud to me, "She is in this country not even two years. She has decided to go to Harvard!" What instills in these immigrant students such desire for learning, such ambition for success? This question, asked of seventy-nine families picked at random in different parts of Indiana, received an almost identical answer, "Our people respect learning more than anything. The discipline and ambition come from the family."*

Southeast Asians are among the newest immigrants to the United States and Indiana. Asians as a whole were able to immigrate to the United States in significant numbers only after changes in the immigration regulations introduced in the 1960s. Even then the people from Cambodia, Laos, and Vietnam did not show much interest in immigration to the United States. By reasons of colonial connections and consequent cultural ties their interest was primarily in France. What made the difference was United States involvement in the Vietnam War. After the fall of Vietnam the United States opened its doors to many of its allies and refugees fleeing from Communist rule in South Vietnam and Laos. The United States also opened its doors to many Cambodians who fled their country during the Communist takeover and civil war that followed the fall of Vietnam.

There was, thus, a surge in the Southeast Asian population (here we narrowly define Southeast Asians as Cambodians, Laotians, and Vietnamese) in the United States since 1975. There were two large waves of refugees from Southeast Asia, the first in 1975 and the second in 1980–81, and many relatively smaller waves before and after these two landmarks. Most of these people were admitted to the United States on refugee status until 1986–87, but increasingly larger numbers of arrivals have been admitted since then under normal immigration rules. The number of refugees venturing out from each of these countries reflected internal political developments. United States withdrawal from Vietnam, for example, precipitated the first big wave of refugees from that country, but withdrawal did not impact Cambodia and Laos that drastically. On the other hand, the uniformly increasing grip of Communist rule in all three countries caused a high flow of refugees in 1980–81. Table 1 illustrates the annual immigration of Southeast Asians to the United States from 1975 through 1987.[1]

Table 2 shows the state by state distribution of Southeast Asian immigrants in percent of their total numbers in the United States in 1976, 1980, and 1984 and the

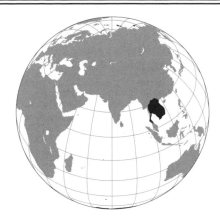

relative percentage of United States and Asian population in each state.[2]

Table 3 shows the demographic distribution of Southeast Asians in urban, suburban, and rural areas of the United States according to the 1980 census.[3]

Table 4 shows the relative strengths of male/female, native-born/foreign-born Southeast Asians in Indiana according to the 1980 census.[4]

Table 5 shows the demographic distribution of Cambodians, Hmong, Laotians, and Vietnamese in Indiana counties as per the 1990 census.[5]

In order to understand the dynamics of the immigrants from the Southeast Asian countries it is important to first gain some knowledge of their history and culture, starting with the physical locations and characteristics of the countries. Cambodians (Kampucheans) come from a subtropical, low-lying land of rain forests and mangroves, of which only 11 percent is under cultivation. Overwhelmingly agricultural and rural, the country also has limited industries—timber, tin, phosphate, and precious stones. Lake Tonle Sap, the source of the Mekong River, and the Mekong itself are the two

energizing features of the land around which most of the population resides.

Laotians, on the other hand, come from a mountainous country, of which 90 percent is at least six hundred feet above sea level. The Mekong River is the lifeline of the country, and the vast majority of its population resides around its drainage basin. Poorest of the three countries in this group, and one of the poorest in the world, Laos depends entirely on agriculture, forestry, and, more recently, the production of opium.

Vietnam is the narrow strip of land hugging the eastern coast of the Indochina Peninsula, stretching about one thousand miles from the Chinese border to the Gulf of Thailand. Mostly subtropical, Vietnam is made up of rugged mountain ranges to the west and coastal plains watered by the Yüan (Red) and the Mekong rivers. Seventy-five percent agrarian, Vietnam's economy depends mainly on rice and rubber cultivation and forestry.

The people who inhabit these lands belong to various ethnic groups. Of Cambodia's population 90 percent are Khmers who immigrated around 200 B.C. from southern China. There are also two large minorities of Vietnamese and Chinese. Most Vietnamese were killed or driven out during the Khmer Rouge regime, although some returned after the 1989 truce. There are also a small number of Cham-Malays and Khmer Loens, tribal people living in the upland forests. All these people, except possibly the upland tribes, were uprooted during the Khmer Rouge rule between 1975 and 1979, which left one million dead and made countless others refugees in Cambodia or Thailand. When the peace settlement was made in 1991 there were still four hundred thousand refugees within Cambodia and Thailand. The majority of the refugees, who sought and obtained asylum in the West and the

Table 1. The Annual Immigration of Southeast Asians to the United States from 1975 through 1987

| | Cambodia | | Laos | | Vietnam | |
|---|---|---|---|---|---|---|
| | Totals of Arrivals | Percentage of Total S.E. Asian Arrivals in U.S. | Totals of Arrivals | Percentage of Total S.E. Asian Arrivals in U.S. | Totals of Arrivals | Percentage of Total S.E. Asian Arrivals in U.S. |
| 1975 | 4,600 | 3.5 | 800 | .6 | 125,000 | 95.9 |
| 1976 | 1,100 | 7.6 | 10,200 | 70.3 | 3,200 | 22.1 |
| 1977 | 300 | 11.5 | 400 | 15.4 | 1,900 | 73.1 |
| 1978 | 1,300 | 6.4 | 8,000 | 39.2 | 11,100 | 54.4 |
| 1979 | 6,000 | 7.4 | 30,200 | 37.4 | 44,500 | 55.1 |
| 1980 | 16,000 | 9.6 | 55,500 | 33.3 | 95,200 | 57.1 |
| 1981 | 27,100 | 20.5 | 19,300 | 14.6 | 86,100 | 65.0 |
| 1982 | 20,100 | 27.8 | 9,400 | 13.0 | 42,600 | 59.1 |
| 1983 | 13,200 | 33.8 | 2,900 | 7.4 | 23,000 | 58.8 |
| 1984 | 19,900 | 38.2 | 7,200 | 13.8 | 24,900 | 47.9 |
| 1985 | 19,200 | 38.5 | 5,300 | 10.6 | 25,400 | 50.9 |
| 1986 | 10,100 | 22.2 | 12,900 | 28.4 | 22,400 | 49.3 |
| 1987 | 1,900 | 4.8 | 15,500 | 38.9 | 22,400 | 56.3 |

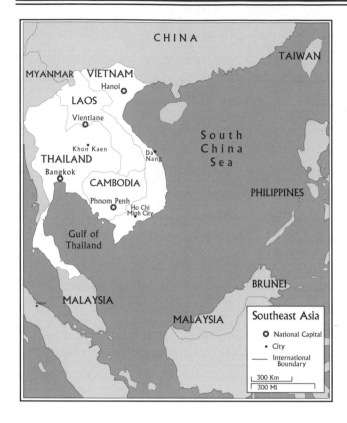

devices. Current population density is only 41 per square mile.

**Table 2. State by State Distribution of Southeast Asian Immigrants.**

| | Southeast Asian Immigrants | | | 1980 U.S. Population | |
|---|---|---|---|---|---|
| | 1976 | 1980 | 1984 | % of Total | % of Total Asian |
| Alabama | 1.0 | .5 | .4 | 1.7 | .3 |
| Alaska | .1 | .1 | — | .2 | .2 |
| Arizona | 1.0 | .6 | .3 | 1.2 | .7 |
| Arkansas | 1.5 | .7 | .6 | 1.0 | .2 |
| California | 21.6 | 32.6 | 40.1 | 10.4 | 35.2 |
| Colorado | 1.7 | 1.8 | 1.5 | 1.3 | .9 |
| Connecticut | .9 | .9 | .9 | 1.4 | .6 |
| Delaware | .1 | — | — | .3 | .1 |
| D.C. | .4 | .7 | .2 | .3 | .2 |
| Florida | 3.9 | 2.0 | 1.6 | 4.3 | 1.7 |
| Georgia | 1.1 | 1.0 | 1.2 | 2.4 | .7 |
| Hawaii | 1.5 | 1.4 | .9 | .4 | 15.9 |
| Idaho | .3 | .2 | .2 | .4 | .2 |
| Illinois | 3.1 | 3.7 | 3.3 | 5.0 | 4.6 |
| Indiana | 1.5 | .9 | .5 | 2.4 | .7 |
| Iowa | 2.0 | 1.6 | 1.2 | 1.3 | .4 |
| Kansas | 1.4 | 1.3 | 1.3 | 1.0 | .5 |
| Kentucky | .7 | .4 | .3 | 1.6 | .3 |
| Louisiana | 3.0 | 2.5 | 1.9 | 1.9 | .7 |
| Maine | .3 | .1 | .2 | .5 | .1 |
| Maryland | 2.1 | 1.1 | 1.2 | 1.9 | 1.8 |
| Massachusetts | 1.1 | 1.6 | 2.7 | 2.5 | 1.4 |
| Michigan | 2.1 | 1.8 | 1.4 | 4.1 | 1.7 |
| Minnesota | 3.0 | 3.4 | 3.2 | 1.8 | .9 |
| Mississippi | .4 | .3 | .2 | 1.1 | .2 |
| Missouri | 2.4 | 1.0 | .9 | 2.2 | .7 |
| Montana | .2 | .2 | .1 | .3 | .1 |
| Nebraska | 1.0 | .5 | .3 | .7 | .2 |
| Nevada | .4 | .4 | .3 | .4 | .4 |
| New Hampshire | .1 | — | — | .4 | .1 |
| New Jersey | 1.4 | 1.0 | .9 | 3.3 | 2.9 |
| New Mexico | .7 | .5 | .3 | .6 | .2 |
| New York | 3.3 | 2.9 | 3.5 | 7.8 | 8.9 |
| North Carolina | .9 | .9 | .7 | 2.6 | .6 |
| North Dakota | .3 | .1 | .1 | .3 | .1 |
| Ohio | 2.4 | 1.4 | 1.4 | 4.8 | 1.4 |
| Oklahoma | 2.7 | 1.5 | 1.2 | 1.3 | .5 |
| Oregon | 1.7 | 2.9 | 2.4 | 1.2 | 1.1 |
| Pennsylvania | 5.9 | 4.1 | 3.4 | 5.2 | 1.9 |
| Rhode Island | .2 | .5 | .7 | .4 | .2 |
| South Carolina | .7 | .4 | .3 | 1.4 | .4 |
| South Dakota | .4 | .2 | .1 | .3 | .1 |
| Tennessee | .8 | .8 | .6 | 2.0 | .4 |
| Texas | 7.9 | 8.7 | 7.2 | 6.3 | 3.6 |
| Utah | .6 | 1.3 | 1.1 | .6 | .5 |
| Vermont | .1 | — | — | .2 | — |
| Virginia | 4.1 | 2.8 | 3.0 | 2.4 | 1.9 |
| Washington | 3.7 | 4.4 | 4.6 | 1.8 | 3.0 |
| West Virginia | .2 | .1 | — | .9 | .2 |
| Wisconsin | 1.5 | 1.4 | 1.5 | 2.1 | .6 |
| Wyoming | .1 | — | — | .2 | .1 |
| Guam | .6 | .1 | — | | |
| Unknown | .3 | — | | | |
| Other | — | — | — | | |

United States since 1975, were Khmers who were able to cross over to camps in Thailand or near its border.

Laos has four ethnic groups. The Lao Lu, who speak Laotian, live in the lowlands, in cities, and beside the Mekong basin. The Lao Tai (Tai tribe), divided between the Black Tai and Red Tai—so-called because of their women's dresses—live mostly in the highlands, with a sprinkling throughout the plains. The Lao-Theng (Mountain Mon-Khmer), supposedly the oldest inhabitants of the region, live throughout Laos and neighboring countries. The Lao-Sonng (composed of the Meo or Hmong and the Man or Yao), probably eighteenth-century immigrants from southern China and contributing about 15 percent of the population, live throughout Laos, mostly in the highlands. There are small minorities of Chinese, Vietnamese, and European settlers also in Laos. Of these various groups the Meo and the Man are the relatively larger immigrants to the West and to the United States because they had the least-established roots in Laos, and they collaborated more readily with the United States in the Vietnam War. It is significant to note that Laotian immigration to China, Vietnam, and Thailand has been greater in scope, mainly due to political strife in the 1960s and 1970s. These immigrations, along with a high death rate (20 per 1,000), caused the population to decrease despite the high birthrate of 44 per 1,000. Because of the population decrease the government in 1976 banned all birth-control

Vietnam, by far the largest of the three countries, has a population of sixty-one million, 90 percent of whom are ethnic Vietnamese and are descendants of settlers from three thousand years ago who probably came from southern China. These original settlers spread from the Yüan Delta down to the Mekong Delta and farther south and created their own unique language (quite independent from the Indian or Chinese families of languages) and culture. There are, however, some minorities, the most important of whom are the Chinese who arrived in Vietnam as merchants and entrepreneurs in the seventeenth and eighteenth centuries. After the Communist takeover of the North, these Chinese moved to the South. In 1978 when the government of unified Vietnam planned to nationalize commerce and industry, they fled the country. Only about two million Chinese remain in Vietnam. The other minorities include the

*Three generations of Vietnamese women, all relatives of the Nguyen family, in their own generational dresses in South Bend.*

### Table 3. Demographic Distribution of Southeast Asians in the 1980 Census

|  | Vietnamese | Laotians | Hmong | Cambodian |
|---|---|---|---|---|
| Total in the United States | 245,025 | 47,683 | 5,204 | 16,044 |
| Female | 117,541 | 22,415 | 2,484 | 7,379 |
| Male | 127,484 | 25,268 | 2,720 | 8,665 |
| Living in metropolitan regions | 227,044 | 48,840 | 4,728 | 15,120 |
| Living in urban areas within metropolitan regions | 221,680 | 42,134 | 4,698 | 14,862 |
| Living in central cities | 126,510 | 29,907 | 3,749 | 9,821 |
| Living in suburbia within metropolitan regions | 95,170 | 12,227 | 949 | 5,041 |
| Living in rural areas within metropolitan regions | 5,364 | 706 | 30 | 258 |
| Living outside metropolitan regions | 17,981 | 4,843 | 476 | 924 |
| Urban areas outside metropolitan regions | 11,738 | 3,433 | 327 | 493 |
| Living in rural areas outside metropolitan regions | 6,243 | 1,430 | 149 | 431 |
| Native (born in the United States) | 23,376 | 2,994 | 494 | 982 |
| Foreign born | 221,649 | 44,689 | 4,710 | 15,062 |

### Table 4. The Relative Strengths of Male/Female, Native-Born/Foreign-Born Southeast Asians in Indiana According to the 1980 Census

|  | Total in Indiana | Female | Male | Native Born in U.S. | Foreign Born |
|---|---|---|---|---|---|
| Cambodians | 172 | 61 | 111 | 6 | 166 |
| Hmong | 0 | 0 | 0 | 0 | 0 |
| Laotians | 817 | 392 | 425 | 63 | 754 |
| Vietnamese | 2,137 | 1,032 | 1,105 | 285 | 1,852 |

Meo (Hmong) and the Montagnards, totaling about three million, and a few Khmers and Chams, all of whom have been pretty much absorbed into the Vietnamese culture. Those who fled the country seeking asylum abroad included Vietnamese from the South who collaborated with the Americans, some ethnic Chinese, and a smaller number of Meos and Montagnards.

Of the three nationalities the Cambodians have the most illustrious history. In the first century of the Christian era they established the kingdom of Funan and adopted an Indian-style royal court system and an alphabet and language patterned after Sanskrit. During the sixth and seventh centuries the kingdom of Chen-la was established by the Khmers and they created an empire comprising Laos, Vietnam, and Thailand. Later came the classical Angkor period, beginning in the midfifteenth century, when Cambodian artists displayed their genius in such monumental creations as the Angkor Thom and Angkor Wat. This period declined, and the Khmer empire collapsed. In 1863 Cambodia became a French protectorate and subsequently in 1887 it became a part of the French Indochinese Union. The Japanese invasion of 1945 was the next major event. After the Japanese withdrawal the nationalists pressed their king (Norodom Sihanouk, who had been installed by the French in 1941) to demand independence. It was granted in 1953. During the Communist upheaval in Indochina, Cambodia was used as a refuge by the rebels. The 1954 Geneva Agreement caused the Communists to leave Cambodia, and in 1955 Sihanouk gave his throne to his father and made himself a politician, prime minister, and eventually the elected head of state in 1960. The mercurial prince tried to keep his country out of the Vietnam conflict, but he was forced to let the North Vietnamese use Cambodian territory for transportation of goods and troops. In addition, native leftists under Pol Pot attempted to overthrow him. Sihanouk might have survived except in 1969 the United States bombed North Vietnamese sanctuaries in Cambodia. At this time one of Sihanouk's own ministers, Lon Nol, overthrew him. Cambodia thus became a bigger battleground. The 1973 peace accords did not stop the fighting in Cambodia. On 17 April 1975 the Khmer Rouge took Phnom Penh and began a so-called leveling and reeducation of the urban population, driving them into the country where over a million perished. Ensuing border disputes were then good justification for the newly victorious Communist government of Vietnam to send in troops. The Vietnamese set up a puppet government in 1979 under Heng Samrin, a defector from Khmer Rouge. The Khmer Rouge and other resistance groups led by the joint command of Sihanouk and Son Sann continued guerrilla war against the Vietnamese-backed government. These three factions also formed a coalition government in exile, which was recognized by the United Nations and held Cambodia's seat in the United Nations until 1990. In 1989 Vietnam withdrew its troops from Cambodia and China stopped sending arms to the Khmer Rouge. The United Nations prepared a comprehensive plan for peace to which all parties agreed in 1991. Sihanouk was made head of an interim government. The United Nations then oversaw key ministries, disarmed all factions, and prepared for free elections that took place in 1993.

The Laotians were the newest arrivals to the region, coming in the eighth century from China. Gradually they replaced tribal natives and by the twelfth and thirteenth centuries established their own principality of Luang Prabang. In the fourteenth century Fa Ngum established the first Laotian kingdom, Lan Yang, with the help of the powerful Cambodian rulers from Angkor. For a brief period (1574–1637) the Burmese took over Laos. Then in 1713 Laos was split into three kingdoms, Vientiane, Champassak, and Luang Prabang. In the eighteenth century all three kingdoms were brought under

the vassalage of the kingdom of Siam. During the late nineteenth century France gained control of the region, and in the early twentieth century Laos was made a protectorate of France. In 1945 the Japanese captured all of Indochina but in 1946, after the war, the French returned. The French then recognized the king of Luang Prabang as the king of all of Laos with some autonomy under the French Union. In the early 1950s the Pathet Lao (Communist) movement supported the Vietminh of Vietnam in their struggle against the French. At the Geneva Conference in 1954 Laos was given its independence, but the Pathet Lao continued its struggle against the government. At the second Geneva Conference in 1962 Laos was given a coalition government in which the Pathet Lao was included. In the 1960s Laos became involved in the Vietnam War, with the Pathet Lao supporting North Vietnam. The 1973 cease-fire established a coalition government in which the Pathet Lao was a partner, but in 1975 when the United States was

*After their Laotian-style wedding reception, Tao and Noi, according to tradition, changed into different costumes and entered their honeymoon quarters. Originally from Vientiane, they now live in South Bend.*

**Table 5. Demographic Distribution of Cambodians, Hmong, Laotians, and Vietnamese in Indiana Counties as per 1990 Census**

| | Vietnamese | Laotians | Hmong | Cambodians | | Vietnamese | Laotians | Hmong | Cambodians |
|---|---|---|---|---|---|---|---|---|---|
| **Indiana Total** | **2,467** | **674** | **57** | **412** | Lawrence | 5 | 0 | | 0 |
| Adams | 1 | 0 | | 4 | Madison | 17 | 2 | | 0 |
| Allen | 341 | 270 | | 44 | Marion | 600 | 76 | | 106 |
| Bartholomew | 49 | 6 | 57 | 0 | Marshall | 14 | 11 | | 0 |
| Benton | 0 | 0 | | 0 | Martin | 0 | 0 | | 0 |
| Blackford | 0 | 0 | | 0 | Miami | 1 | 0 | | 1 |
| Boone | 5 | 2 | | 0 | Monroe | 61 | 3 | | 6 |
| Brown | 0 | 0 | | 1 | Montgomery | 11 | 0 | | 0 |
| Carroll | 0 | 0 | | 0 | Morgan | 9 | 0 | | 0 |
| Cass | 6 | 0 | | 0 | Newton | 1 | 0 | | 0 |
| Clark | 20 | 0 | | 0 | Noble | 27 | 14 | | 0 |
| Clay | 0 | 0 | | 0 | Ohio | 0 | 0 | | 0 |
| Clinton | 2 | 0 | | 0 | Orange | 1 | 0 | | 0 |
| Crawford | 0 | 0 | | 0 | Owen | 1 | 0 | | 0 |
| Daviess | 0 | 0 | | 0 | Parke | 0 | 0 | | 0 |
| Dearborn | 6 | 0 | | 0 | Perry | 0 | 0 | | 0 |
| Decatur | 12 | 0 | | 0 | Pike | 0 | 0 | | 0 |
| De Kalb | 39 | 0 | | 5 | Porter | 47 | 12 | | 4 |
| Delaware | 32 | 3 | | 1 | Posey | 1 | 0 | | 0 |
| Dubois | 0 | 0 | | 0 | Pulaski | 0 | 0 | | 0 |
| Elkhart | 71 | 84 | | 75 | Putnam | 13 | 0 | | 0 |
| Fayette | 0 | 0 | | 4 | Randolph | 0 | 0 | | 0 |
| Floyd | 11 | 5 | | 3 | Ripley | 3 | 0 | | 0 |
| Fountain | 0 | 0 | | 0 | Rush | 0 | 0 | | 0 |
| Franklin | 8 | 0 | | 0 | St. Joseph | 201 | 47 | | 110 |
| Fulton | 0 | 4 | | 0 | Scott | 0 | 0 | | 0 |
| Gibson | 1 | 0 | | 0 | Shelby | 4 | 0 | | 0 |
| Grant | 19 | 0 | | 0 | Spencer | 7 | 0 | | 0 |
| Greene | 4 | 0 | | 0 | Starke | 0 | 0 | | 0 |
| Hamilton | 77 | 2 | | 0 | Steuben | 1 | 0 | | 2 |
| Hancock | 4 | 19 | | 0 | Sullivan | 0 | 0 | | 0 |
| Harrison | 6 | 0 | | 0 | Switzerland | 0 | 0 | | 0 |
| Hendricks | 34 | 0 | | 0 | Tippecanoe | 172 | 15 | | 2 |
| Henry | 6 | 0 | | 0 | Tipton | 2 | 0 | | 0 |
| Howard | 22 | 0 | | 0 | Union | 0 | 0 | | 0 |
| Huntington | 10 | 0 | | 0 | Vanderburgh | 138 | 0 | | 0 |
| Jackson | 32 | 0 | | 0 | Vermillion | 0 | 0 | | 0 |
| Jasper | 2 | 0 | | 0 | Vigo | 49 | 0 | | 3 |
| Jay | 8 | 0 | | 0 | Wabash | 13 | 25 | | 8 |
| Jefferson | 1 | 1 | | 0 | Warren | 0 | 0 | | 0 |
| Jennings | 7 | 0 | | 0 | Warrick | 3 | 0 | | 0 |
| Johnson | 15 | 0 | | 0 | Washington | 0 | 0 | | 0 |
| Knox | 5 | 1 | | 0 | Wayne | 16 | 19 | | 0 |
| Kosciusko | 33 | 18 | | 21 | Wells | 0 | 0 | | 0 |
| Lagrange | 11 | 0 | | 1 | White | 0 | 0 | | 0 |
| Lake | 101 | 33 | | 5 | Whitley | 2 | 0 | | 0 |
| La Porte | 46 | 2 | | 6 | | | | | |

defeated in Vietnam, the Pathet Lao grabbed control of the entire country. Laos thus became a partner in the Vietnamese-led Indochinese alliance of three leftist countries—Vietnam, Laos, and Cambodia (Kampuchea). Upon the Pathet Lao takeover of the country the leading rightists and supporters of the American war effort felt threatened, obviously, and they fled abroad for safety.

The Vietnamese also have a long and colorful history. Emigrants from southern China settled in the Yüan River delta about a thousand years before the Christian era, and they developed a civilization totally unique in the region. During the Han period China conquered Vietnam and kept it as a province for nearly a thousand years. In 939 the Vietnamese regained their independence and remained so for another nine hundred years. Then in the nineteenth century the French conquered them and made Vietnam part of their Indochinese Union. After the Japanese invasion of 1945 and the end of World War II the Vietminh pressed the French to withdraw from their country. In 1954 at the Geneva Conference the country was divided in two, the North controlled by the Communists and the South by Western-supported non-Communists. Armed conflict between North and South started immediately and lasted until the United States forces were withdrawn in 1975 and the Communist forces reunited the country.

Along with their legacy of a long and illustrious history Southeast Asian immigrants brought other cultural characteristics to America, especially religious traditions. By far the dominant religion of all three countries is Theravāda Buddhism—95 percent Cambodia, 90 percent Laos, and 85 percent Vietnam. Christian converts of the French colonial period form a small minority, more so in Vietnam, 5 percent, and less so in Laos, about 1.5 percent, and in Cambodia, about .5 percent. Other minorities include the Cao Dai (a mixture of Western and oriental religions), the Hoa Hao (a radical type of Buddhism) in Vietnam, and the animists among upland people in all three countries. There are no statistics about the religious affiliation of the immigrants, but it may be assumed that they reflect the complexion of society in their homelands.

The origin and growth of the religious traditions of Southeast Asia gave followers an approach and attitude toward religion that is nondogmatic, open, flexible, and extremely tolerant. The earliest known religious practice among all Southeast Asian peoples was a form of animism that still plays an important role in their lifestyles and rituals. The ever-present shrine inside or in the vicinity of Southeast Asian homes is the transformation of the ancient spirit house into ancestral abode, statuary, pagoda, and chapel, depending on the dominant religious persuasion of the inhabitants. For those who follow the traditions of Chinese ancestral worship it is the ancestral abode; for those who adhere to Buddhism/Hinduism, with greater emphasis on Hinduism, it is a statuary of gods; for typical Buddhists it is a pagoda; and for Christians it is a chapel. But the spirits still dwell in them all the same.

The move from animism to a somewhat more defined or organized religion occurred when itinerant Indian merchants and travelers introduced the gods, ideas, and rituals of Hinduism to the peoples of Southeast Asia in the first century of the Christian era and continued to influence the area for a thousand years. More than any

ethnic group of the region the Khmers welcomed the Indianization of their culture. According to legend, a Hindu immigrant named Kaudinya settled in Cambodia in the first century and established the first dynasty among the Khmers. With this, Brahminic Hinduism put its roots in Cambodia. Among Kaudinya's successors were some dynamic leaders, most notably Jayavarman VII and Suryavarman II who ruled approximately between 1112 and 1250 A.D. Jayavarman and Suryavarman brought the Hindu religion and Indian cultural influence to its height, the culmination of which was the building of the majestic and magnificent temple structures of Angkor Wat. The building of another magnificent temple complex, the Angkor Thom, in the 1180s added to the luster and Hindu character of the Cambodian capital.

Beginning in the late twelfth century, however, another Indian religion began to cast its spell on Cambodia. Theravāda monks from Ceylon brought their style of Buddhism to Cambodia and its neighboring countries. By the early sixteenth century Buddhism became so pervasive in Southeast Asia that it replaced Hinduism as the region's dominant religion. In Cambodia King Ang Chan, who ruled between 1516 and 1566, made Buddhism the nation's official religion.

The Indianization of Laos started between 1353 and 1431 when the Lao Tais attacked the Khmer empire and captured art treasures and artisans from Cambodia. In the fourteenth century when the Lao Tais established the kingdom of Lan Xang (later Laos), the rulers and aristocracy intermarried with the Cambodian royalty. The Laotians' Khmer relatives introduced them to Buddhist religion and rituals. Gradually Buddhism became the dominant religion of Laos.

Southeast Asian Buddhists venerate and make offerings to the statue of Baby Buddha on the occasion of the Buddha's birthday celebration.

*A couple venerating the Buddha image and requesting special blessings.*

Being in the shadow, and several times a province, of China, Vietnam was always in China's sphere of influence. Immigrants and monks from India or Ceylon did not penetrate that part of Southeast Asia. Mahayana Buddhism was introduced initially in Vietnam from China, but when China's political dominance diminished in the late Middle Ages Theravāda practices from Cambodia and Thailand spread to Vietnam, most notably the monastic tradition. Unlike the other countries of Southeast Asia, Vietnam did not experience the persistent Indian influence from the first century A.D. Therefore, the cultural characteristics of Vietnam are more similar to Chinese than Indian. The strong and visible presence of Confucian and Taoist ideals and concepts is a testimony to the Chinese roots of Vietnamese culture.

During the French colonial rule of Indochina Western Christianity was introduced to the region. Christianity's influence on Cambodia and Laos has been negligible, but in Vietnam, being the administrative center of the French empire, many Vietnamese had an opportunity to participate in the French bureaucracy. Closeness with the French and the advantages available in the colonial bureaucracy to those who followed the French culture induced many Vietnamese to adopt Western lifestyles and the Christian religion. At the time of the Geneva Agreement of 1954, which marked the end of French colonial rule, over two million of Vietnam's forty million or so people were Roman Catholics, adopting French as their language and Western culture as their lifestyle. Given the special opportunities open to them in the colonial bureaucracy, education, and the professions they gained more wealth, clout, and prominence in society. With the fall of Dien Bien Phu and the subsequent Geneva Agreement of 1954 that officially ended French colonial rule these Westernized Christians,

mostly Catholics, felt deeply threatened. Immediately after the division of Vietnam, the Catholics from the North made a mass exodus to the South, nearly doubling the Christian population in the South. The Catholic minority strenuously opposed the unification, fearing the worst under a Communist government controlled by a Buddhist majority. They thwarted the nationwide elections scheduled for 1956 in the Geneva Agreement, engineered the resignation of Bao Dai, emperor of the South, and advocated the election of Catholic Ngo Dinh Diem as president, thus precipitating war with the North. The Vietnamese Catholics, more than any other group, supported the war effort and collaborated with the South Vietnamese and United States military. For all these reasons the Vietnamese Catholics felt the most threatened when the United States pulled out of Vietnam. It is no surprise, then, that the majority of the first wave of Vietnamese refugees were from this Catholic minority.

Because Christianity's roots in the Southeast Asian culture were so shallow and the conversions to Christianity

*Offerings are made to ancestral spirits before the pictures of the deceased kept behind the main altar of the Buddhist temple.*

under colonial rule were more often for convenience or advancement rather than conviction, apart from occasional church attendance very little difference was visible in the religious lives of Southeast Asian Christians and their Buddhist compatriots. In a climate of Hindu/Buddhist culture that has no firm dogmas or rigid rituals but a multitude of interchangeable religious practices, the new religion of Christianity was welcomed as just another cult. The Christian converts of Southeast Asia did not feel any compulsion to separate themselves from their earlier religious practices either. In this climate, animism, Hinduism, Buddhism, and Christianity coexisted in the lives of many Southeast Asians. The ambiguity about religious affiliation that Americans perceive in the immigrants from Southeast Asia, therefore, is part of their culture, not affected for convenience. A random survey of seventy-five Southeast Asian families from South Bend, Elkhart, Gary, Fort Wayne, and Indianapolis in 1994 is shown below.

The same survey also revealed that of the eight marriages that took place in 1974 in the seventy-five families surveyed, four were interfaith (Buddhist and Christian) marriages and in the other four the couples belonged to either the Christian or Buddhist religion. Out of the eight only one was an interracial marriage, between a Vietnamese and a Caucasian American. Looking at this phenomenon positively, the openness, tolerance, and the sense of accommodation in religious matters that these immigrants brought to America is a refreshing contrast to the dogmatism and intolerance often seen among American Christians.

Just as there was a preponderance of Christians in the first wave of immigrants from Southeast Asia, mainly Vietnam, there was also a relatively higher percentage of well-educated and English-speaking men and women. The first preference in evacuation from Vietnam and admission to the United States was given to those who closely collaborated with the Americans in the military or civilian professions, and they were, of course, better educated and spoke English. The immigrants from Southeast Asia in the years subsequent to 1975 were mostly refugees fleeing from political persecution and with decreasing levels of education, ability to speak English, and financial means. The 1984 Office of Refugee Resettlement survey shows the following:[6]

*Yen (girl in center of picture) poses for picture with the other children who received their First Holy Communion at St. Matthew's Cathedral in South Bend, 1991.*

| Arrival Year of Refugees | Average Years of Education | Percent Speaking No English | Percent Speaking Good English |
|---|---|---|---|
| 1975 | 9.4 | 40.6 | 27.2 |
| 1976–77 | 7.5 | 49.3 | 10.9 |
| 1978 | 7.3 | 54.3 | 18.6 |
| 1979 | 7.4 | 67.8 | 6.2 |
| 1980 | 7.0 | 67.6 | 6.9 |
| 1981 | 6.7 | 61.9 | 7.0 |
| 1982 | 7.0 | 54.7 | 4.9 |
| 1983 | 6.5 | 48.9 | 8.6 |

The same survey also indicated that there was a marked difference between the literacy status of the

| | Have Spirit House or Shrine at Home | Keep Only Symbols of One Religion | Keep Symbols of More than One Religion | Practice Rituals of Only One Religion | Practice Rituals of Several Religions | Believe One Can Belong to More than One Religion at the Same Time | Believe One Can Belong to Only One Religion at a Time |
|---|---|---|---|---|---|---|---|
| Cambodian | 9 | 4 | 5 | 7 | 13 | 16 | 4 |
| Laotian | 6 | 2 | 3 | 4 | 6 | 5 | 5 |
| Vietnamese | 23 | 8 | 9 | 19 | 26 | 27 | 18 |

immigrants from the various Southeast Asian nations in the 1980s. While the literacy rate of immigrants of Cambodian origin was 41 percent and Laotians 35 percent, the Vietnamese registered an astounding 95 percent.

The changing political climate in Southeast Asian countries dictated the level of flow of emigrants from those countries to the United States and the West. The fall of Saigon precipitated the first big flow from Vietnam in 1975. The total number of Southeast Asian immigrants to the United States that year was approximately 130,000. Only trickles of insignificant numbers came in 1976 and 1977. Mounting pressures of purges and political persecutions caused the exodus to grow starting in 1978. That year the immigrant numbers were 20,000. It quadrupled in 1979 to 81,000 and doubled again in 1980 to 167,000, the highest number in any one year. The numbers began to fall in 1981 to 132,000, 72,000 in 1982, 39,000 in 1983, and since then remained an annual average of 40,000 to 50,000. The following table shows the number of arrivals from Cambodia, Laos, and Vietnam in each year from the years of 1975 to 1985 in percent of their total numbers in the United States.[7]

|      | Cambodians | Laotians | Vietnamese |
| --- | --- | --- | --- |
| 1975 | 3.6  | .5   | 25.9 |
| 1976 | .9   | 6.8  | .7   |
| 1977 | .2   | .3   | .4   |
| 1978 | 1.0  | 5.4  | 2.3  |
| 1979 | 4.7  | 20.2 | 9.2  |
| 1980 | 12.4 | 37.1 | 19.7 |
| 1981 | 21.0 | 12.9 | 17.8 |
| 1982 | 15.6 | 6.3  | 8.8  |
| 1983 | 10.2 | 1.9  | 4.8  |
| 1984 | 15.5 | 4.8  | 5.2  |
| 1985 | 14.9 | 3.6  | 5.3  |

Table 2 indicates the state by state distribution of Southeast Asian immigrants in the United States (see above, p. 580) and shows that Indiana absorbed 1.5 percent of the immigrants in 1976, .9 percent in 1980, and .5 percent in 1984. In 1980 Indiana had 2.4 percent of the total Southeast Asian population of the United States but that year, after these new immigrants were added, Indiana had only .7 percent of the total Asian population of the United States. When individual states are compared, Indiana ranks somewhere in the middle as a provider of homes for Southeast Asians. At the very top is California with 21.6 percent in 1976, 32.6 percent in 1980, and 40.1 percent in 1984. In 1980 California had 10.4 percent of the total United States population, while it had 35.2 percent of the United States Asian population.

Vermont and New Hampshire are at the bottom, absorbing only .1 percent each of the Southeast Asians in 1976 and none at all in 1980 and 1984. In 1980 New Hampshire had .4 percent of the United States population while it hosted .1 percent of the United States Asian population. Vermont in 1980 had .2 percent of the United States population with not enough Asian population to be registered on a numerical scale.

Two of the most significant values the Southeast Asian immigrants are noted for in this country are respect for education and respect for the integrity of the family. Although it is true that the first wave of immigrants from Vietnam were highly literate, the educational level of the majority of subsequent immigrants was not very high. Yearly statistics from 1975 to 1984[8] indicate that Vietnamese immigrants had an average of 9.5 to 6.8 years of schooling. The percentage of immigrants who could speak English well was highest in 1975, 32.1 percent, and the lowest in 1984, 9.2 percent. The percentage of people speaking no English at all was 40.6 percent in 1975, 67.8 percent in 1979, and 40.3 percent in 1984. Such a serious disadvantage on the part of the immigrants is a startling contrast to the outstanding educational achievements of their children. A 1985 survey of 529 Southeast Asian children in scattered middle schools and high schools in California revealed that 10 percent had a perfect GPA of 4.0 or straight-A grade, 27 percent held an A range GPA (3.6–4.0), and 46.7 percent had an A grade in mathematics. The survey further revealed that 52.1 percent had an overall GPA of B (2.6–3.5) and 32.3 percent had a B in mathematics; and that 17.2 percent held an overall GPA of C (1.6–2.5) and 14.7 percent had a C in mathematics. Only 3.7 percent held a D as an overall GPA and only 6.3 percent had a D in mathematics.

*Southeast Asian wedding—a blend of Eastern ceremonies and Western customs and dresses.*

Sixty-one percent of the Southeast Asian children were in the top 30 percent nationally in mathematics while they were slightly below average in reading and language skills.[9] A random survey of twenty-eight Indiana high schools in May 1994 produced similar statistics. What was most striking was that of the eighty-two students projected to be either valedictorians or salutatorians of these twenty-eight schools, nine were Vietnamese immigrants. What stunned this writer, more than any statistics, was the sight of a young woman in one South Bend high school begging a teacher to allow her to retake a chemistry test so that she could improve her grade from 98 percent to 100 percent. With a heavy accent but in grammatically correct English she explained that only a 100 percent grade would insure her admission to Harvard. The dismayed teacher allowed her to retake the test but wondered aloud to me, "She is in this country not even two years. She has decided to go to Harvard!" What instills in these immigrant students such desire for learning, such ambition for success? This question, asked of seventy-nine families picked at random in different parts of Indiana, received an almost identical answer, "Our people respect learning more than anything. The discipline and ambition come from the family."

There are no national statistics available concerning the stability of Southeast Asian families. But of the 330 different Southeast Asian families that the author contacted during the course of this study only 7 reported a marriage breakup or divorce. All 7 of the broken marriages were contracted in the United States and were less than ten years old. Of these, 4 were interracial marriages. Most parents prefer to arrange marriages for their children, although there is increasingly firm resistance on the part of the children, especially those who were brought up from infancy in the United States.

The majority of the Southeast Asians contacted did not hesitate to indicate the male-dominant nature of their families in answer to questions, delicately phrased, concerning the authority structure of their households. Heavy-handedness on the part of the fathers is almost expected, and there was little evidence of rebellion, even on the part of teenagers.

Another notable trait of the Southeast Asian immigrants is their work ethic and frugality. Legends about the hard work and dependability of Southeast Asians are supported by solid statistics. A study by John K. Whitmore, Marcella Trautmann, and Nathan Caplan shows how in a short period of time Southeast Asian refugees changed their status from unemployed to fully employed. According to this study the average percentage of unemployment for Southeast Asians at the 4-month point of their entry in the United States was 86 percent, but at the 44-month point

it declined to 19 percent. At the same time the percentage of refugee immigrants holding multiple jobs increased from 4 percent at the 4-month point to 47 percent at the 44-month point.[10] It is no surprise then that the household incomes of Southeast Asian immigrants tended to increase dramatically with the length of their stay in the United States. A study of Southeast Asian immigrants in Illinois between 1975 and 1979 by Young Yun Kim shows that after one year in the United States 85 percent of the households had an average monthly income of less than seven hundred dollars. After four or five years the number of households with less than seven hundred dollars monthly income decreased to 22.6 percent.[11] Although there is no comparable study on Indiana's Southeast Asian immigrants, the Illinois study is considered to be a reflection of the national pattern. It is more than likely that the Indiana immigrants experienced the same trend in employment and income growth. Southeast Asian immigrants' dependence on public assistance had, understandably, a reverse growth, although not as dramatic as the positive growth in employment and income levels. The annual survey by the Office of Refugee Resettlement showed that while in 1983 out of 984 households surveyed 598 (60.8 percent) were receiving assistance and 386 (39.2 percent) were not, in 1985 the number of immigrants dependent on assistance declined to 550 (55.9 percent) and those not receiving assistance increased to 434 (44.1 percent). This rate of decline in dependency continued in subsequent years.[12]

Initially, opportunities for employment and sponsorship dictated the locations of Southeast Asian immigrant settlements. Settlement around the major urban centers, almost inevitably, has become the national pattern since 1975. Even though circumstances often dictated this pattern of settlement, in time it became one of choice for most immigrants. The situation in Indiana was no different from the national pattern, and Southeast Asian immigrants settled around the major urban centers of the state. The 1980 census shows that there were 2,137 Vietnamese, 817 Laotians, and 172 Cambodians residing in Indiana. By 1990 numbers of the Vietnamese and Cambodians increased considerably—Vietnamese to 2,467 and Cambodians to 412—but the number of Laotians decreased to 674. Marion County hosted the highest number (600 Vietnamese, 106 Cambodians, and 76 Laotians) followed by Allen and St. Joseph counties. A highly disproportionate number of Laotians settled in Allen County—270 out of the total population of 674 in the state.

The settlement pattern of Southeast Asian immigrants is validated and justified by its correlation with the types of employment available only in the vicinities of urban

Table 6. National Sample Survey of 1983 by the Office of Refugee Resettlement

| | Ethnic Chinese | | Cambodian | | Laotian | | Ethnic Vietnamese | |
| --- | --- | --- | --- | --- | --- | --- | --- | --- |
| | Males | Females | Males | Females | Males | Females | Males | Females |
| Professional/Technical | 7.7% | 3.5% | 17.4% | 8.5% | 9.9% | 6.0% | 19.4% | 19.2% |
| Sales/Clerical | 46.7% | 60.7% | 38.0% | 36.5% | 29.6% | 39.4% | 34.3% | 60.8% |
| Craftsmen/Foremen | 17.5% | 15.9% | 3.6% | 3.1% | 20.8% | 5.4% | 16.7% | 5.2% |
| Operatives | 10.0% | 9.4% | 6.3% | 2.5% | 6.8% | 1.2% | 7.3% | 3.3% |
| Laborers | 3.2% | 3.3% | 1.1% | 1.5% | 3.5% | 1.8% | 2.5% | 0.4% |
| Service Workers | 6.0% | 3.6% | 9.6% | 5.1% | 10.3% | 9.5% | 6.0% | 3.1% |
| Farmers/Fishers | 8.9% | 3.6% | 24.2% | 42.8% | 19.1% | 36.7% | 13.7% | 7.9% |

Table 7. A Random Survey of Ninety-Eight Southeast Asian Families in Different Parts of Indiana

| Native Language at Home | Insist that Children Learn and Speak Native Language | Native Food at Main Meal at Home | Observe Native Holidays and Celebrate Native Feasts | Correspond Regularly with People Back Home | Eager to Go Home for a Visit as Soon as Conditions Allow | Support and Work for Normalization of Relations between Native Country and U.S. |
| --- | --- | --- | --- | --- | --- | --- |
| 90 | 87 | 85 | 76 | 84 | 78 | 71 |

centers. A national sample survey of 1983 by the Office of Refugee Resettlement indicated the employment distribution shown in Table 6.[13]

Statistics on the employment distribution of Indiana immigrants from Southeast Asia are not available, but their demographic distribution would indicate an

*Members of the South Bend Vietnamese Club carry the statue of the Blessed Virgin in procession during the Marian Festival in 1991.*

employment distribution similar to the national pattern shown in Table 6.

One important question that should be asked is how the Southeast Asian immigrants are adapting to American life. There is no national study, nor one specifically on Indiana, but there is a study about the Southeast Asian immigrants in Illinois who arrived between 1975 and 1979.[14] In 1979, the year the study was conducted, 54 percent of the immigrants surveyed reported feeling "awkward or out of place" in America. Exactly the same percentage of the immigrants said that they "found it easy to make friends" with Americans and an even larger percentage, 58 percent, said that they "felt they belong in America." Even more significant and revealing was that 93 percent believed it was important to understand "the ways that American people think and behave," 84 percent felt it was important to "make friends with American people," and 94 percent thought it was important to "learn about events and issues in American society." It is evident from this survey that Southeast Asian immigrants are strongly committed to the American way of life.

Adaptation to the culture and customs of their new homeland does not mean that the immigrants from Southeast Asia are abandoning their native roots. On the

REV. THICH MINH HANH, QUANG MINH TEMPLE, CHICAGO

*Lunar New Year is celebrated with many festivities such as dance and music and dragon races.*

contrary, they are equally committed to the cultivation of their native customs and traditions. A random survey of ninety-eight Southeast Asian families in different parts of Indiana is shown in Table 7.

Our Southeast Asian immigrants have enriched our cultural life by sharing their arts, cuisines, and festivals with their American neighbors. Statistics are not available, but it is hard for any Hoosier not to notice the Southeast Asian shops and restaurants dotting our towns or not to be enchanted by the colorful processions and dragon races conducted annually by our newest neighbors at their New Year, the Tet.

## Notes

1. Based on *Report to the Congress: Refugee Resettlement Program* (Washington, D.C.: Office of Refugee Resettlement, 1987a and 1987b). See also David W. Haines, ed., *Refugees as Immigrants: Cambodians, Laotians and Vietnamese in America* (Totowa, N.J.: Rowman and Littlefield, 1989), 3.

2. Taken from Haines, ed., *Refugees as Immigrants,* 4–5; HEW Refugee Task Force, *Report to Congress* (Washington, D.C., 1976); Office of Refugee Resettlement, *Report to the Congress: Refugee Resettlement Program* (Washington, D.C.: U.S. Department of Health and Human Services, 1981a, 1985a).

3. U.S. Department of Commerce, Bureau of the Census, *Census of Population,* 1980.

4. Ibid.

5. U.S. Department of Commerce, Bureau of the Census, *Census of Population,* 1990.

6. *Report to Congress: Refugee Resettlement Program* (Washington, D.C.: U.S. Department of Health and Human Services, 1984). See also Haines, ed., *Refugees as Immigrants,* 7.

7. Quoted in Haines, ed., *Refugees as Immigrants,* 11; *Report to the Congress: Refugee Resettlement Program* (1987a and 1987b).

8. Haines, ed., *Refugees as Immigrants,* 7.

9. John K. Whitmore, Marcella Trautmann, and Nathan Caplan, "The Socio-Cultural Basis for the Economic and Educational Success of Southeast Asian Refugees (1978–1982 Arrivals)," in Haines, ed., *Refugees as Immigrants,* 129–30.

10. Ibid., 126–27.

11. Young Yun Kim, "Personal, Social, and Economic Adaptation: 1975–1979 Arrivals," in ibid., 100.

12. Linda W. Gordon, "National Surveys of Southeast Asian Refugees: Methods, Findings, Issues," in ibid., 35. See also *Report to the Congress: Refugee Resettlement Program* (1983 and 1985).

13. Adopted from the table in Haines, ed., *Refugees as Immigrants,* 9–10; *Report to Congress: Refugee Resettlement Program* (1984), 101–12.

14. Young, "Personal, Social, and Economic Adaptation," 90–92.

# SWISS

LEO SCHELBERT

*If they were churchgoing people, most Swiss who settled in Indiana were either of the Reformed or the Catholic persuasion, reflecting the two dominant creeds of Switzerland. Once in the United States, however, Swiss newcomers often joined other religious denominations as circumstances or personal choice dictated. They participated in Indiana's religious life in general, just as they were involved in the state's economic, social, political, and educational pursuits. Yet some groups of Swiss newcomers helped shape Indiana's religious traditions in a special way by transplanting Swiss elements onto new soil.*

Newcomers from Switzerland belong to one of Indiana's smaller immigrant groups, yet the Swiss had an impact that transcends their numerical size. This profile of their presence in Indiana's past explores five dimensions: the general background of the newcomers from Switzerland; a numerical portrait of their settling in Indiana; the emergence of their secular presence; their religious involvements; and some biographical sketches that highlight the variety of their migratory experiences.

## Origins

Switzerland lies in the heart of western Europe and traces its national existence back to 1291 when the three districts called Uri, Schwyz, and Unterwalden renewed a mutual assistance covenant to safeguard internal order and, in case of need, to give assistance against external aggression.[1] The nation as it evolved by 1800 is surrounded by France to the west, Germany to the north, Liechtenstein and Austria to the east, and Italy to the south. The country's indigenous people belong to four language groups. About 70 percent speak German, 25 percent French, 4 percent Italian, and 1 percent Romansh. These language groups belong to a nation state claiming a seven-hundred-year history, yet they also are oriented culturally toward France, Germany, or Italy. In everyday life older forms of German, French, or Italian are spoken, which show numerous local variations as to pronunciation and word usage. Thus local and regional traditions of language and customs intersect with the general trends of the French, German, or Italian high culture and form in the Swiss multileveled attachments.[2]

The Swiss state covers at present some 15,943 square miles. One quarter of these miles consists of rocks, glaciers, lakes, and rivers; about eight million acres are suitable for farms, vineyards, and pastures.[3] Raw materials are sparse and need to be imported. The Swiss economy depends, therefore, on high quality, labor-intensive production of tools, machines, and textiles, the export of dairy products, and on tourism and international banking.[4] The economy derives much strength from stable democratic traditions that rest largely on the significant autonomy of over three thousand communes and twenty-six member states called cantons. Since 1848 the federal state has been governed by a bicameral, popularly elected legislature that in turn chooses the members of the seven-person executive. Each of the seven, called federal counselors (Bundesräte), heads a department, for instance of Justice or of Foreign Affairs, yet all decisions are made and reported collectively; the

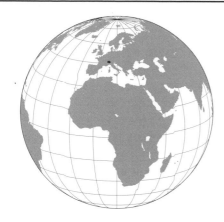

and 46.05 percent (107,780) resided in the Americas, 37.86 percent of whom had settled in the United States. The rest lived dispersed throughout Africa, Australia, and Asia.[8] Swiss immigration to the United States fluctuated widely as Table 1 shows.

These figures intimate five phases of Swiss immigration to the United States. On the one hand the five phases parallel the continental nineteenth-century expansion of the United States; on the other hand they reflect international events such as the two world wars, the post-1929 Great Depression, and the reemergence of an economically powerful Europe.

office of president, furthermore, rotates annually and is merely symbolic.[5]

Throughout the centuries Swiss political unity has been tested not only by linguistic and cultural diversity that is deeply rooted in ancient traditions, but also by the religious split of the early sixteenth century. Today the country's indigenous people are about 48 percent Roman Catholic, and 51 percent adhere to the Swiss Reformed persuasion that evolved from the theology of Huldreich Zwingli (1484–1531). He rejected Martin Luther's views of salvation and the church as well as those of medieval Christendom in favor of a biblical and humanist orientation that was welcome to the rising bourgeoisie of Swiss cities such as Zürich, Basel, and St. Gallen.[6] At the same time groups of Swiss Brethren and Sisters emerged. They rejected infant baptism, the oath, and the sword and advocated a total rejection of established churches and of the state, which they viewed as domains of Satan. They met with deep hostility from Catholic and Reformed groups after attempts at compromise had failed. The sects experienced sporadic persecutions, and some of their descendants were later to settle in Indiana where they are known as (Swiss) Mennonites, Amish, or Apostolic Christians, the latter a nineteenth-century form of the Anabaptist persuasion.[7]

### Emigration and Immigration

Since the formation of Switzerland as a separate political entity, Swiss went abroad and foreign born settled in Switzerland. From 1798 to about 1850 some 100,000 Swiss are estimated to have gone abroad at least temporarily and about 50,000 foreigners to have taken up residence in Switzerland. Between 1850 and 1914 about 410,000 Swiss left their homeland and about 409,000 foreign born entered it. These came mainly from neighboring regions of Germany, France, and Austria. Swiss immigrants settled permanently or for a time in many parts of the world. For the year 1880, for instance, 51.15 percent (119,707) lived in European countries,

Table 1. Emigration from Switzerland to the United States, 1820–1990.

| Decade | Number | Percentage of European Immigrants |
|---|---|---|
| 1820–1830[1] | 3,226 | 3.03 |
| 1830–1840[2] | 4,821 | 0.98 |
| 1841–1850 | 4,644 | 0.29 |
| Total | 12,691 | |
| Annual Mean | 423 | 1.43 |
| 1851–1860 | 25,011 | 1.01 |
| 1861–1870 | 23,286 | 1.13 |
| 1871–1880 | 28,293 | 1.24 |
| Total | 76,590 | |
| Annual Mean | 2,553 | 1.13 |
| 1881–1890 | 81,988 | |
| Annual Mean | 8,199 | 1.73 |
| 1891–1900 | 31,179 | 0.88 |
| 1901–1910 | 34,922 | 0.43 |
| 1911–1920 | 23,091 | 0.53 |
| 1921–1930 | 29,676 | 1.02 |
| Total | 118,868 | |
| Annual Mean | 2,972 | 0.76 |
| 1931–1940[3] | 5,500 | 1.58 |
| 1941–1950[3] | 10,500 | 1.69 |
| 1951–1960[3] | 17,700 | 1.33 |
| Total | 33,700 | |
| Annual Mean | 790 | 1.53 |
| 1961–1970[4] | 16,300 | 1.32 |
| 1971–1980[4] | 6,600 | 0.82 |
| 1981–1990[5] | 6,200 | 1.03 |
| Total | 29,100 | |
| Annual Mean | 970 | 1.05 |

[1]Oct. 1, 1820–Sept. 30, 1830   [4]Swiss born
[2]Oct. 1, 1830–Dec. 31, 1840   [5]Estimate; figure for 1981–1988: 5,400
[3]Switzerland as last residence

Sources: U. S. Bureau of the Census, *Statistical Abstract of the United States* (1920), 100; (1940), 101; (1955), 95; (1965), 93; (1991), 10.

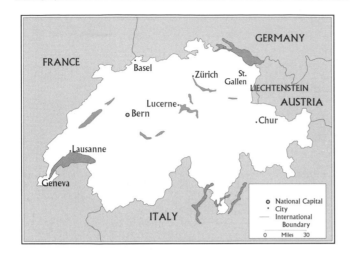

## Table 2. Swiss in Indiana, 1850–1990.

| Year | Number | Percent of Foreign Born |
|---|---|---|
| 1850 | 724 | 1.3 |
| 1860 | 3,813 | 3.2 |
| 1870 | 4,287 | 3.0 |
| 1880 | 3,695 | 2.5 |
| 1890 | 3,478 | 2.4 |
| 1900 | 3,472 | 2.4 |
| 1910 | 2,765 | 1.7 |
| 1920 | 2,334 | 1.5 |
| 1930 | 1,624 | 1.1 |
| 1940 | 1,083 | 1.0 |
| 1950 | 751 | 0.7 |
| 1960 | 436 | 0.4 |
| 1970 | 438 | 0.5 |
| 1980 | 280 | 0.3 |
| 1990 | 353 | 0.3 |

Sources: "1850 Census Foreign-Born for Indiana," unpublished manuscript, Education Division, Indiana Historical Society, 1991; for 1860 to 1950 see Table 24, U. S. Bureau of the Census, *Census of Population: 1950*, vol. 2: *Characteristics of the Population*, part 14: *Indiana* (Washington, D.C.: Government Printing Office, 1952), 43; ibid., *1960*, vol. 1: *Characteristics*, part 16 (1963), 330; *1970*, vol. 1: *Characteristics*, part 16 (1973), 235; *1980*, vol. 1, Chapter D: *Detailed Population Characteristics* (1983), Table 195; U. S. Dept. of Commerce, Bureau of the Census, Ethnic and Hispanic Branch, 1990 Census Special Tabulations, 16.

## Migratory Contexts

Answers to why Europeans in general and Swiss in particular emigrated vary, and consensus remains elusive.[9] In the eighteenth century some thirty thousand Swiss had settled in the British North American colonies, especially Pennsylvania and the Carolinas,[10] whose descendants joined the hundreds of thousands who took up lands in trans-Appalachian regions that had been wrested from the indigenous Indian peoples.[11] Newspapers, letters, and advertisements, as well as returners and entrepreneurs, spread the news also in Switzerland about the fertile lands available for settlement and ample work for artisans.[12]

Thus options widened for those longing for a wider world, for the land hungry, and for those whose skills were becoming obsolete by mechanized production, yet who rejected work in factories. Regions of the North American Midwest, Canada, Brazil, Argentina, and Russia offered varied settlement opportunities[13] not only for those displaced by industrialization, but also for those anxious to escape onerous parents, spouses, or the strictures of tightly knit village communities.[14] Thus the move of Swiss to what is now Indiana was on the one hand embedded in general historical developments such as Caucasian expansion and industrialization; on the other hand the immigration was a result of personal preference.

## Numerical Overview

As an important region of the American Midwest, Indiana attracted Swiss as soon as its lands became available to white settlement. The Swiss presence reached its numerical height in 1870 with 4,287 people who constituted 3 percent of Indiana's foreign born; the percentage of Swiss gradually diminished until it represented a mere 0.3 percent by 1980. Table 2 provides the decennial count based on figures of the United States census.

Yet Swiss newcomers dispersed quite unevenly over the state of Indiana. In 1850, for instance, they were concentrated in Allen and Wells counties in Indiana's northeastern region, in Jefferson and Switzerland counties, which border on the Ohio in the southeast, and in Greene and Jackson counties in the center of the southern third of the state. Table 3 presents the 1850 distribution of 575 Swiss for fourteen of the state's fifty-four counties.

According to the 1860 United States census Indiana counted 120,660 foreign born among its nearly 1.5 million people. With 3,541 persons or 2.93 percent, the newcomers from Switzerland occupied numerically fifth place after those from Germany (55.84 percent), Ireland (20.53 percent), England (7.76 percent), and France (4.89 percent).[15]

In 1870 the Indiana Swiss reached their highest number of 4,287; their presence was strongest in Perry, Adams, Allen, Marion, and Vanderburgh counties. Table 4 shows the distribution of Swiss for twenty-three of Indiana's ninety-two counties for selected United States census years as well as their gradual numerical decline by over 62 percent. The main Swiss concentration in some northeastern and southeastern counties and in greater Indianapolis remained pronounced throughout the 1870–1930 period. Within counties, however, Swiss tended to settle in particular townships.

### Table 3. Fourteen Indiana Counties with Fifteen or More Swiss in 1850.

| County | Swiss | Percent of For.-Born | Total For.-Born | Total Population |
|---|---|---|---|---|
| Allen | 95 | 2.49 | 3,822 | 16,919 |
| Jefferson | 89 | 2.89 | 3,082 | 23,916 |
| Wells | 76 | 25.94 | 293 | 6,152 |
| Greene | 50 | 11.60 | 431 | 12,313 |
| Vanderburgh | 43 | 0.98 | 4,366 | 11,414 |
| Switzerland | 42 | 9.52 | 441 | 12,932 |
| Jackson | 31 | 4.44 | 698 | 11,047 |
| Dearborn | 30 | 0.74 | 4,031 | 21,166 |
| Ripley | 26 | 1.39 | 1,873 | 14,820 |
| Floyd | 24 | 1.01 | 2,367 | 14,875 |
| Fountain | 20 | 6.51 | 307 | 13,253 |
| Kosciusko | 12 | 4.82 | 249 | 10,243 |
| Wabash | 11 | 2.76 | 399 | 12,138 |
| Steuben | 8 | 3.52 | 227 | 6,104 |
| Total | 557 | 2.47 | 22,586 | 187,292 |

Source: "1850 Census Foreign-Born for Indiana," unpublished manuscript, Education Division, Indiana Historical Society, 1991.

### Table 4. Swiss in Selected Indiana Counties, 1870–1930.

| Indiana Counties | 1870 | 1880 | 1890 | 1920 | 1930 |
|---|---|---|---|---|---|
| Perry (Tell City) | 474 | 245 | 229 | 62 | 28 |
| Adams (Berne) | 359 | 413 | 726 | 303 | 230 |
| Allen (Fort Wayne) | 311 | 306 | 281 | 274 | 189 |
| Marion (Indianapolis) | 243 | 284 | 269 | 267 | 187 |
| Vanderburgh | 157 | 238 | 122 | 105 | 54 |
| Wells | 151 | 142 | 131 | 76 | 50 |
| Floyd | 139 | 82 | 54 | 57 | 42 |
| Clark | 130 | 97 | 72 | 34 | 26 |
| Whitley | 124 | 88 | 66 | 22 | 13 |
| Elkhart | 109 | 100 | 116 | 89 | 75 |
| Spencer (St. Meinrad) | 103 | 72 | 55 | 14 | 10 |
| Marshall | 97 | 77 | 55 | 52 | 30 |
| Ripley | 80 | 54 | 46 | 22 | 9 |
| St. Joseph (South Bend) | 79 | 70 | 70 | 95 | 87 |
| La Porte | 78 | 62 | 57 | 45 | 49 |
| Huntington | 76 | 67 | 35 | 17 | 10 |
| De Kalb | 74 | 61 | 43 | 26 | 16 |
| Noble | 67 | 52 | 72 | 20 | 12 |
| Vigo | 64 | 68 | 56 | 50 | 35 |
| Switzerland (Vevay) | 55 | 29 | 20 | 0 | 0 |
| Tippecanoe | 45 | 41 | 51 | 33 | 18 |
| Wabash | 42 | 61 | 47 | 35 | 20 |
| Lake (Gary) | 27 | 27 | 111 | 127 | 101 |
| All Others | 1,203 | 959 | 694 | 509 | 333 |
| Total | 4,287 | 3,695 | 3,478 | 2,334 | 1,624 |

Sources: John Paul von Grueningen, ed., *The Swiss in the United States* (Madison, Wisc.: Swiss American Historical Society, 1940), 37; U. S. Census figures.

As to residence, the Indiana Swiss at first remained predominantly rural, but by 1930 their distribution was nearly even: 824 lived in urban areas, 800 in rural areas. Only four cities showed a relatively sizable number of Swiss, as Table 5 reveals:

### Table 5. Swiss in Four Cities of Indiana, 1880, 1930, 1970.

| City | 1880 | 1930 | 1970 | | | |
|---|---|---|---|---|---|---|
| | | | Swiss Born | Native Swiss or Mixed | Swiss Stock | Total Foreign Stock |
| Indianapolis | 220 | 153 | 56 | 278 | 334 | 42,757 |
| Evansville | 132 | 48 | 20 | 81 | 101 | 4,317 |
| Fort Wayne | 81 | 142 | 38 | 277 | 315 | 15,571 |
| South Bend | 32 | 41 | 15 | 101 | 116 | 24,177 |
| Totals (and | 465 | 384 | 129 | 737 | 866 | 86,822 |
| Percent of Indiana Swiss | (12.24) | (23.65) | (29.45) | (22.52) | (23.34) | |
| Totals of Indiana Swiss | 3,800 | 1,624 | 438 | 3,272 | 3,710 | |

Sources: "1880 Census Foreign-Born for Indiana," unpublished manuscript, Education Division, Indiana Historical Society, 1991; Table 18, U. S. Bureau of the Census, *Fifteenth Census of the United States: 1930. Population*, vol. 3, part 1, *Reports by States ... Alabama–Missouri* (Washington, D.C.: U.S. Government Printing Office, 1932), 721; Table 141, *Census of the Population: 1970*, vol. 1: *Characteristics of the Population*, part 16: *Indiana* (1973), 604-7.

By 1950, 437 of the 751 Swiss born of Indiana resided in urban areas, 197 were rural nonfarm, and 117 were rural farm people.[16] As to sexual distribution, the 1930 census counted 941 male and 683 female Swiss born. In 1940 the distribution was 612 males and 471 females. In 1960 the number of Indiana's Swiss born had shrunk to 436, yet 4,996, that is 1.3 percent of Indianans, were of Swiss stock, a number that by 1970 had decreased to 3,710. In 1980, 280 people, a mere 0.3 percent of Indiana's foreign born, were Swiss, but 39,994 persons reported at least one ancestor as Swiss. Of these, 11,515 declared exclusively Swiss origin, while 28,479 indicated multiple ancestry.[17]

In sum, statistical data indicate that newcomers from Switzerland were widely dispersed over Indiana's counties, yet tended to congregate in particular townships. Between 1860 and 1900 the numerical presence of the Swiss fluctuated between 3.2 and 2.4 percent, then decreased rapidly. In 1980 the Swiss stock was a mere 1 percent. Yet behind these figures hides a multidimensional secular and religious history that deserves to be sketched.

## Evolution of a Secular Presence

### Vevay

Some Swiss initiated two secular settlements in Indiana; others were involved in the state's history as individuals. The earliest settlement derived from the resolve of a

*Wine casks in the cellar of a Swiss home in Vevay.*

fourteen-year-old youth named Jean Jacques (John James) Dufour. He was born in 1767 as a citizen of the village of Châtelard in the parish of Montreux, located on Lake Geneva's northeastern shore. Reading newspapers in the late 1770s, Dufour explained that he found them "full of the American Revolutionary War" and containing letters of French officers "which complained of the scarcity of wine among them." A study of maps showed him, however, that "America was in the parallel of the best wine countries in the world." He then "made the culture of the grape," Dufour declared, "of its natural history, and of all that was connected with it my most serious study, to be better able to succeed there."[18]

J. J. Dufour set out for the United States on 20 March 1796. He had 736 pounds in cash and a bank draft of 1,400 pounds on him, and he purchased in Paris jewelry, clothing, and fifty-nine silver and gold watches. He took passage on the brig *Sally* bound for Philadelphia and paid customs at Wilmington, Delaware, in the amount of 59 pounds and 14 shillings. For the first two years Dufour was a traveling salesman and journeyed through Pennsylvania and the Ohio valley.[19] Although earning good money, he remained faithful to his youthful plan and kept looking for a suitable place for a vineyard. In the fall of 1796 Dufour met John Brown (1757–1837), a United States senator from Kentucky, who took a great interest in his plan.[20] Brown helped Dufour establish a joint stock company and select land on the Kentucky River. In 1799 Dufour began his vineyard and was delighted in its success. He sent news of his good fortune back to Montreux, where the following siblings and friends readied themselves to join him:

Daniel Dufour (1764–1854) and his wife Françoise (1779–1865)

Jeane Marie Dufour (1779–1861)

Antoinette [Antoinnette] Dufour (1781–1859)

Jean François [John Francis] Dufour (1783–1850)
Susanne Marguerite [Margrette] Dufour (1785–1860)
Jean David [John David] Dufour (1788–1845)
Peter Boralley [Barallay], his wife, their son Peter, and a daughter
Philip Bettens, Sr. (1774–1851), his wife Rose (1768–1846), and their daughter
François [Francis] Louis Siebenthal and son François [John Francis].[21]

They arrived at the "First Vineyard," as J. J. Dufour proudly called his place, on 6 July 1801 and were admitted into full and equal partnership. A "great many species of vines showed fruits, the third year; one vine of the sweet water was full of eminently good grapes" and was greatly admired. But then disaster struck: a "sickness took hold of all our vines," Dufour explained, "except the few stocks of Cape and Madeira grapes from each of which we made the fourth year [1802] some wine."[22] A small greenish insect native to North America that feeds on imported vines had infested the First Vineyard.[23] Yet the winegrowers were undaunted. In 1802 J. J. Dufour and associates petitioned Congress to be allowed to purchase a large tract of land on the north side of the Ohio River eight miles northeast of the mouth of the Kentucky River.[24] To strengthen their case, John Francis Dufour was sent in 1803 to Washington to present to Thomas Jefferson and a congressional committee "two kegs containing about Five gallons each" of wine made from the Cape grape. "It has a very thick skin and pulp, but the juice is very sweet . . . and has the taste of the strawberry, which gives a fine perfume to the wine; such as made President Jefferson say, that there was no other such tasted wine within his knowledge in the world."[25]

In 1803 the Swiss families of Samuel Mennet, Frederick L. Raymond, Frederick Deserens, Louis Gex, and Luc [Luke] Oboussier joined the winegrowers, who on 20 January 1803 had officially concluded "A Covenant of Association for the Settlement of the Lands of Switzerland on the Ohio River."[26] The act of Congress passed on 1 May 1802[27] empowered the Swiss to select twenty-five hundred acres for vineyards; they added about twelve hundred acres under outright purchase and called their colony "New Switzerland." They named Indian Creek, which ran through their purchase, "Venoge," after a Swiss river entering Lake Geneva.[28] They purchased some one hundred vines from a Mr. Legaux of Springhill near Philadelphia, who "certified having received them from the Cape of Good Hope." With them, J. J. Dufour explained:

We the Swissers have made our subsequent and prosperous plantation. . . . [They] must have now spread much through the country: for we have sent,

*Home of John Francis Siebenthal, Vevay.*

and now [in 1827] have to send abroad a great quantity of the scions every year.[29]

New Switzerland prospered. By 1813 each of the winegrower families had a dwelling surrounded by vineyards and pastures. Daniel Dufour's house, for instance, "stood in the midst of a wide tract of over two hundred acres, . . . the richest and most beautiful of all." Furthermore, his wife Françoise made straw hats that she marketed "even in faraway places." According to an 1813 report, Jean Daniel Morerod was the most successful proprietor. He had begun with eighty saplings that by 1812 had increased to twelve hundred vines. In that year he sold two hundred gallons of wine, while the following year his vineyard yielded over seven hundred gallons. Next came the properties of Bettens, Golay, the Siebenthals, and of Gex and Oboussier. The Oboussiers had "a very fine property, a good house, a barn and excellent land with vines," as did the Raymonds.[30] The homesteads "fronted the river about

four and a half miles," and their wine "was thought by good judges, to be superior to the claret of Bordeaux."[31] Wine production increased steadily until it reached more than twelve thousand gallons at the height of the grape cultivation.[32]

In 1806 John James Dufour went back to Europe to settle financial affairs and hopefully to induce his wife and son to join him in New Switzerland. He was to be absent for ten years, and the leadership passed to John Francis Dufour, his brother.[33] The latter successfully promoted the establishment of a United States post office in 1810 to be named Vevay, with J. F. Dufour as postmaster.[34] In the spring of 1813 the town of Vevay was laid out, and numerous lots were sold. The following year the first houses were built.[35] Thus a new compact settlement soon grew up beside the New Switzerland of the winegrowers. In 1817 Samuel Brown's emigrant directory found Vevay to be a "delightful village," forty miles "nearly equidistant from Cincinnati, Lexington, and Louisville" as the crow flies. It had "eighty-four dwelling houses, besides

*The Swiss Inn, Vevay, ca. 1920.*

thirty-four mechanics' shops . . . , [a] court house, jail, and school house of brick." A market house and a church were being built, and the town had "eight stores, three taverns, two lawyers, two physicians, and a printing office printing a weekly newspaper called the *Indiana Register.*" The library had three hundred volumes, and a literary society united "several persons of genius, science, and literature."[36]

John F. Dufour also was instrumental in inducing the territorial legislature to establish on 7 September 1814 "a new county out of counties Dearborn and Jefferson," to "be known and designated by the name and style of the county of Switzerland." In October he achieved the naming of Vevay as "Seat of Justice of Switzerland County" by offering "a Subscription . . . to the amount of upwards of Two thousand four hundred dollars." He was also appointed clerk of the circuit court and "empowered . . . to administer . . . oaths of office . . . to all officers civil and military."[37] Dufour also financed in part Vevay's public buildings, brought the printing press of William C. Keen from Cincinnati to Vevay, owned and edited the weekly *Indiana Register* from 1816 to 1820, donated a lot for the newly formed Baptist congregation, and served in the Indiana House of Representatives in 1828.

Among the other Swiss, Elisha Golay served as captain of the militia and in 1814 as county surveyor. John Siebenthal was sheriff from 1814 to 1817 and 1822 to 1826 and also held the office of tax collector. The Swiss winegrowers were of the Swiss Reformed persuasion and held their own Sunday services. Not until 1828 was a Presbyterian church built on land donated by Daniel Vincent Dufour, John James Dufour's only son.[38]

Among the first-generation Swiss were the following families:[39]

> Philip Bettens, Sr. (1774–1851) and his wife Rose (1768–1846), from Vevey, Switzerland, to the United States in 1801
>
> Abraham Chatelin (1796–1862) and his wife Louise (1793–1864)
>
> John Detraz (1789–1875), of Vevey, Switzerland, and his wife Charlotte (1798–1866)
>
> David L. Gex (1761–1845), to the United States in 1804, and his wife Lucille Oboussier (1770?–1806) to the United States in 1805
>
> Elisha Golay (1783–1866) and his wife Susanne (1785–1865).
>
> Frederick L. Grisard (1808–1881), from the Canton Bern to the United States in 1818; in 1828 married Zelia C. Simon (1807–1892), whose family had arrived in Vevay in 1823
>
> Rodolphe Morerod (1796–1826)
>
> John P. Schenck (1780?–1834?), his wife Mary (1788–1864), and their son Ulysses P. Schenck (1811–1884), born in the Canton Neuchâtel, to the United States in 1817; U. P. Schenck became a successful entrepreneur and was known as the "Hay King." His son Andrew J. Schenck was successful in commerce.[40]
>
> Henry Stucy (Stüssi) (1815–1893) and his wife Afra (1816–1894), both from the Canton Glarus
>
> Charles Aimée Thiebaud (1800–1871), born in the Canton Neuchâtel, and his wife Elisabeth (1805–1829) to the United States in 1817

Switzerland County grew rapidly in population. In 1812 the region had about 900 people, in 1816, 1,832. They were "emigrants from every part of the union, & as various in their customs and sentiments as in their persons."[41] Families tended to be large, and by midcentury the Dufours alone numbered more than 150 people.[42] With the passing of the first generation, however, the cultivation of the vine declined. Americans preferred hard liquor to wine, and the growing of corn and potatoes proved less labor intensive and more profitable. Few new immigrants arrived from Switzerland, and the Swiss became a minority in Switzerland County. In 1850 its population numbered among its 441 foreign born 143 from Ireland, 86 from Germany, 82 from Scotland, and only 42 from Switzerland.[43]

By the third generation the winegrower colony "New Switzerland" had nearly disappeared, and adjoining Vevay showed only a few traces of its Swiss origin. The county became a typical midwestern farming region with 85 percent of the land devoted to grains and livestock, with tobacco becoming a principal cash crop. Also culturally it became fully midwestern. The Schenck mansion, for instance, built by the wealthy "Hay King's" son, is Victorian in style. Yet in 1963 Vevay and Switzerland County celebrated a century and a half of existence as a town and county. The festivities' success led to the annual Swiss Wine Festival held in mid-August which attracts

*John Badollet.*

about seventy thousand people. Yet the elements of the Wine Festival are mixed: "Swiss Polkas" are performed by "Hank Haller's Lustige Schwaben"; "Stein Stossen," i.e., the tossing of "stones weighing upward of one hundred pounds," occurs beside "Hoedown and Western Square Dancing." The old Presbyterian church, built on Daniel V. Dufour's land in 1860, now serves as the Switzerland County Historical Museum.[44] At present, efforts are under consideration to renew viticulture and reintroduce cheese making on a larger scale as part of a much needed revitalization of the region.

## Badollet

In 1804, when the Dufours took up winegrowing in Switzerland County, John Badollet (1758–1837) moved to Vincennes, an important outpost of the Old Northwest, which in 1806 counted about a thousand inhabitants. Vincennes served as a meeting place of the territorial legislature, the general court, the site of the public land

office, and the supply depot for goods destined for Native American people.[45] Badollet had studied with Albert Gallatin (1761–1849) at the Geneva Academy. Gallatin had left for the United States in 1780 and by 1801 had risen to political prominence.[46] On Gallatin's invitation Badollet moved to Pennsylvania in 1786 and married Margaret Hannah the following year.[47]

As secretary of the treasury in the Jefferson administration, Gallatin recommended Badollet for the post of land register at Vincennes, which Badollet was to fill for thirty-two years.[48] Purchases at the land office were heavy, legal titles at times uncertain, and attempted dishonest deals quite common.[49] Badollet, who had held a minor office earlier in Greene County, Pennsylvania, also became involved in Indiana politics. In 1805 he was named the first chancellor of Indiana, an unsalaried office in charge of judicial appointments.[50] He also emerged soon as a leading opponent of the surreptitious introduction of slavery into the Indiana Territory. In 1809 he wrote "the petition against slavery and hastily the report of the committee of the House of representatives" of the territorial legislature. He unmasked the plan of the proslavery faction led by William Henry Harrison (1773–1841), then territorial governor and later the ninth president of the United States, by which African Americans brought into the territory were to be forced to sign indentures for life or be sold to people in a slave state. Badollet also demolished the claims of the proslavery people in four letters signed "A Farmer," which appeared in the *Vincennes Western Sun.*[51] In 1816 he was one of four delegates from Knox County to the Indiana Constitutional Convention, where again he worked for the formal prohibition of slavery in any legal guise. Badollet also wrote the major portion of the one unique article of the state constitution that made Indiana the first state of the Union explicitly to assume responsibility for educating its citizens by public schools, libraries, and the promotion of scholarship. In Section 4 of Article IX, Badollet declared that "it shall be the duty of the General assembly, as soon as circumstances permit, to form a penal Code, founded on the principles of reformation, not vindictive Justice." He also suggested the creation of "an asylum" for the unfortunate or indigent, where they could "find employment, and every reasonable comfort and lose, by their usefulness, the degrading sense of dependence." In 1812 Badollet also served on a committee appointed by the legislature to prepare a bill "for a general system of education."[52]

Yet Badollet was not only active in early Indiana politics. He also promoted the creation of Vincennes University and served as one of its trustees, convinced that "learning hath ever been found the ablest advocate of genuine liberty."[53] From 1806 to his death he was also instrumental in the creation and administration of a public library to which he bequeathed numerous titles, among them Voltaire's works in fifteen volumes.[54]

Margaret, born Hannah, and John Badollet had six children and by 1837 had twenty-eight grandchildren. The oldest son Albert was elected county treasurer in 1829, succeeded his father as land register in 1836, and in 1841 moved to Illinois.[55] John Badollet had gained, in Gallatin's words, a "respectable standing . . . in Indiana, by his virtues and talents"; he had shown "not simply strict integrity and morality, but a purity and disinterestedness rarely equaled, never within my knowledge surpassed by any human being."[56]

## Tell City

A second settlement initiated by the Swiss came to be known as Tell City. The settlement got its start on 21 April 1856 when a group of Swiss met in Cincinnati, Ohio, to establish the *Schweizer Ansiedlungsverein,* the Swiss Colonization Society.[57] The organization, initially Swiss, later "largely German . . . united for the purpose of encouraging and aiding the immigration of their countrymen to America."[58] The society also hoped "to furnish mutual aid in founding homes and business enterprises in what was then known as 'The West'"[59] and to enable newcomers to live in a linguistically and culturally homogeneous environment. Perhaps there was also a dose of ethnic-national conceit mixed in, as evident from an 1860 comment: Tell City's "inhabitants are no looting Americans, no whiskey-drinking Irish, but hard-working Germans looking for work."[60]

The actual incorporation of the Swiss Colonization Society occurred on 10 January 1857 in Hamilton County, Ohio, and was recorded on 15 January.[61] The officers of the new organization immediately went to work on two fronts. They actively sought to locate a suitable tract of land by writing to "land offices, to Swiss consuls in the United States, to the president of the Illinois Central Railroad and to prominent German Americans, such as Frederick Muench."[62] Branches were established in various cities of the United States via newspaper advertisements, and the society held its first convention from 19 to 21 April 1857 in Cincinnati, with fourteen of the fifteen branches represented and a treasury of $35,255 from receipts, yet with an expenditure of only $180.[63] The convention appointed a land selection commission consisting of J. J. Liver of Milwaukee, president; H. Eckhardt and J. J. Senn of Cincinnati; a Dr. Zwinger, treasurer, and S. Loew of Pittsburgh; A. Oehler of Dubuque, Iowa; and a Hösli of Illinoistown (in 1861 renamed East St. Louis).[64]

According to the instructions given by the convention, the members of the land selection commission were to locate a tract "not further north than 43 latitude" of "at least 10,000 acres" that was to allow for some six thousand town lots and one thousand garden shares. The commissioners were to "tour the States, Illinois, Missouri and Iowa, as well as the territories of Kansas and Nebraska." The site was to have a "healthful climate, fertile soil, good water, timber, stone, situation on a navigable river and if possible on a railroad." It should provide "a good landing place and must adjoin the river for at least two miles." The commission had "a cash capital of $70,000-$80,000 at its disposal" and hoped "to buy farmland for $20,000-$30,000 on credit."[65]

Sites in Missouri proved on inspection especially attractive, but they were located in "a slave holding state, and *none* of our colony would ever forget the sacred principles of Republicanism so far as to make use of such a privilege."[66] On 15 June 1857 the board decided to buy land on the Missouri River; however, the transaction did not occur. Instead, the Swiss Colonization Society, which had received an offer from A. G. Selman of Shelbyville on 30 May 1857, sent commissioners H. F. Oehlmann, Charles Rebstock, and Christian Tuffli in mid-July to Perry County to inspect the Selman site. After ten days they returned to Cincinnati with a favorable report, and in August the directorate offered Selman and his partner Ballard Smith a contract. After problems with land titles had been cleared up, the Colonization Society bought a total of 4,152 acres for $85,429 from twenty-two sellers.[67] Some branch societies, however, were unhappy with the purchase and withdrew from the society, as R. Henry Gay of Cannelton observed on 23 December 1857: "That Swiss Company had a devil of a time among themselves . . . three committees have been here within 10 days & most of them opposed . . . [yet] finally leave satisfied that this is the only suitable place to invest their money." Initially, the name chosen for the new town was "Helvetia," but it was changed to Tell City in the fall of 1857.[68]

On 4 January 1858 "the first meeting of the Executive Committee of the Swiss Colonization Society" was presided over by J. C. Appenzeller, a member of the board of directors.[69] The committee decided to send to Perry County engineer August Pfaefflin, who surveyed the land and laid out the town with "7,328 town lots and 974 garden lots."[70] The first roadway was "cut through the forest . . . in the exact centre of the plat and received the appropriate name of Tell Street."[71] On 18 January the committee decided that in order to attract industrial enterprises to the new town "(individuals or companies) which erect a factory before June 1, 1858, be granted the sites necessary . . . for the first five years free of all encumbrance and taxes, and for the next five years against a modest rent"; such enterprises were also granted "the privilege to acquire these sites, not to exceed 150 ft. fronts, by purchase at $1.00 per foot after the first five years."[72] On 28 January the committee also urged the purchase of several farms to ward off land speculators and permitted Messrs. Wolff and Stahl of Lexington to establish "a saw mill and possible a grinding mill as well."[73]

The executive committee met often, for instance, seven times in each of the months of February and March. Much detail had to be considered, often involving large sums of money, and it was done in a most meticulous, at times even querulous, manner. Often disagreements erupted, but were solved with the careful use of set procedures. The situation turned especially urgent after the first settlers arrived in March. To give them "a helping and supporting hand," the committee resolved to "put at their disposal until further decision by the Convention, possible available unoccupied dwellings." Within weeks "there were one hundred families in the town."[74]

On 22 February 1858 the shareholders who had actually settled at Tell City met "to establish themselves as a Branch of the above Society."[75] Louis Frey, a man who had been on the spot from the beginning, was chosen president and "occupied the precarious position of buffer between the worried settlers and the impatient directors."[76] Three days later the strict "Rules of Business and Rules of Order" were drawn up,[77] and the Tell City branch was soon to become the center of the society's activity.

The town grew quickly. In early June there were 620 inhabitants. By the end of the month 986, and by mid-July 1,230. The houses built numbered by early June 86, and by mid-July the town had 154 buildings. For the 4 July celebration numerous people visited the bustling new settlement; some 600 Swiss had come by boat from Cincinnati.[78] The second general convention of the Swiss Colonization Society was held in Tell City from 19–21 September 1858. The meeting decided to transfer the board of control, that is, the administrative body as opposed to the board of directors, from Cincinnati to Tell City.[79]

On 2 October 1858 the *Cannelton Reporter* declared Tell City "a marvel":

It has now over eleven miles of streets, cut seventy and eighty feet wide through the forests; it has 1,500 people and 300 houses. All this has been done since the middle of last April. The shareholders are coming in daily and as soon as they can find their lots, begin their improvements. . . . This union of German and Swiss, of industry and economy, of thrift and industry will accomplish wonders.[80]

Among the businesses established were two breweries, two lumberyards, a furniture factory, and stores. By the mid-1860s furniture making became a dominant industry. The list of exports only nine years after Tell City's founding included:

300,000 pounds of castings, exclusive of kettles, etc., from Kimbel and Zins' foundry; several hundred bedsteads, bureaus, tables, wardrobes, etc., from the Tell City Furniture Factory; 400 dozen chairs from the chair factories; 20 cotton presses and 2 hay presses from the Agricultural Machine Co.; 100 sacks of carded wool and cloth from Hanser, Becker and Spoerris' woolen factory; 220 barrels of flour from Steinauer and Co.'s mill; 50 half barrels of beer from F. Voelkers and C. Becker's breweries; 20,000 feet of flooring, doors, windows, etc., from M. Deckert's and J. Schoettlin and Co.'s Planing Mills; 500 new kegs; 20 fine marble gravestones from H. Ludwig; 25 pairs of bellows; 4 wagons; 12 spinning wheels; 2 spring wagons.[81]

Frederick Steiner, born 10 August 1830, from the Canton St. Gallen, became "a notable river man" and owned the three-story brick hotel, Steiner House, later called Hotel Moraweck.[82]

From the start the city's founders were concerned with the establishment of schools. The first school was opened only four months after the settlers had arrived, and instruction was exclusively in German. In the fall of 1858 the Swiss Colonization Society built a two-story frame house and employed two teachers. Although English was introduced, German remained a basic subject for the next forty years, until "relegated to the high school course, as an alternative with Latin for graduation."[83]

Tell City's first newspaper appeared 19 March 1859 under the name *Helvetia: Organ for Progress, Liberty, and Fatherland.* The paper had been founded in 1856 in Cincinnati, and then moved to Tell City where it was published by J. H. Walser and J. J. Schellenbaum until 1865. The paper was staunchly Republican and pro-Lincoln.[84] The press of Tell City was prochurch, but antitemperance, which it dismissed as *Kaltwasser-Muckerei*, as a "cold water spleen." Until about 1870 the press was also virulently against the Democratic party, a legacy of its antislavery stance.[85]

Culturally the community represented a fusion of elements as the chosen street names intimate: Tell, Winkelried, and Pestalozzi pointed to the Swiss; Mozart, Schiller, Gutenberg, and Humboldt to German; and Franklin, Washington, Jefferson, and Fulton to American traditions.[86] In 1887 the town had Catholic, Reformed, and Methodist churches, and numerous voluntary associations such as the Odd Fellows and Druids flourished. Two public schools employed nine teachers, and a parochial school was run by nuns.[87] Tell City did not reach the population size of 90,000 as its founders had envisioned. In 1950 it counted 5,768,[88] in 1990, 8,704 inhabitants, many of whom were of Swiss-German descent.[89] Although today a typical American town of southern Indiana, Tell City remains proudly conscious of its origins.

## Indianapolis

What a scholar observed for South Bend, Indiana, holds also for Indianapolis: "Swedes, Belgians, Swiss . . . faced the fewest restrictions upon their choice of residence or were least influenced by ethnic ties and . . . more easily assimilated into American society."[90] Indeed, Swiss settling in Indiana could pursue their goals as freely as other newcomers from the eastern or southern states of the Union. Sources allow, therefore, only occasional glimpses of a separate Swiss immigrant life in urban environments. A list of the "Indianapolis Schweizerbund" for 1915, for instance, lists sixty-seven members, fifty-four of whom were born in Switzerland, thirteen in Indianapolis.[91] The association was devoted to social cohesion and benevolence. Members met twice a month, held picnics, and annually celebrated the patriotic days of Switzerland. A men's choir enlivened festive occasions and increased revenue by giving performances.[92]

Although most Swiss blended in with the city's people in general and its German-speaking groups in particular, four personalities were involved in Indianapolis's past in a special way. One of them was Adolph Scherrer (1848–1925), who arrived in the city in 1872. He was the son of the architect Josef Anton Scherrer of Kirchberg, Canton St. Gallen, had studied architecture at the Academy of Fine Arts in Vienna, and had worked in the offices of several European architects.[93] About 1870 Scherrer left Switzerland, first for New York City, then Chicago, and settled finally in Indianapolis, where in 1873 he joined the architectural office of Edwin May (1824–1880), a recognized Indiana architect.[94] In 1878 when the Indiana legislature decided to erect a new statehouse, the jury selected the project labeled Lucidus Ordo. May's architectural firm had submitted the design, and May appointed Scherrer as chief engineer. On 20 February 1880 May died in Jacksonville, Florida, at age fifty-six, and Scherrer was appointed supervising architect.[95] For the next eight years Scherrer was busy implementing this monumental charge that included numerous changes in the original plans desired by the commissioners.[96]

*Adolph Scherrer.*

In 1888 Scherrer reported with quiet satisfaction that the capitol was "entirely completed, furnished and occupied by the State officials." Expenditures had been kept within the assigned limits, a fact "gratifying to every one connected with its management."[97] The building was, in one scholar's view, "probably the most notable architectural work of the decade" in Indianapolis.[98] A critical assessment of its merit, published in 1888 in the *Franklin Democrat,* declared that the design "selected was no doubt the best . . . [and] Mr. Adolph Scherrer was the designer." However, the writer thought that German architects were less than distinguished as a class, claiming that they betrayed "at times a studious mechanical hardness in its composition which affects one unpleasantly." The critic judged "the exterior of the building as a whole . . . the most satisfactory in design" and the "work of an educated architect." He found the dome's design "greatly improved," yet the interior's frescoes "atrocious," the "coloring . . . inharmonious, the [interior] design thoughtless, and the general result bad."[99] Whatever the building's merits, the sources show that Adolph Scherrer was the capitol's architect. Scherrer designed the project Lucidus Ordo, albeit in the office of the ailing Edwin May, made the numerous changes requested by the commissioners, served as chief engineer from the start, and was supervising architect for eight years. He justifiably, therefore, chose a lithograph of the capitol as his logo, the proudest achievement of his career.[100] Scherrer also designed other Indianapolis buildings such as the Maennerchor Hall, City Hospital, the Elks Club, and the Propylaeum.[101]

Another noted Indianapolis Swiss was Adolph Scherrer's son Anton. Born in 1878 and educated in Indianapolis, "he studied architecture in Switzerland," then practiced his craft in Indianapolis where he designed "Cathedral High School and the Antlers Hotel." But in 1929, at age fifty-one, Anton Scherrer "had finished with his career as an architect . . . [and] wove for himself an intricate reputation as an artist, musician, critic and, most of all, a skillful story teller."[102]

Scherrer's column "Our Town" in the *Indianapolis Times,* written between 1936 and 1949, was full of wit, keen observation, and a celebration of the lives of so-called common people.[103] He was also actively involved with the Indiana Historical Society,[104] served as president of the board of the Art Association of Indianapolis, and was a member of the Indiana Advisory Committee for the Historic American Buildings Survey (HABS) initiated by Harold Ickes.[105]

Two other names deserve to be mentioned. Louis Burckhardt (1865–1945) served Indianapolis for more than fifty years as a physician. Born 4 November 1865 in Basel, where the Burckhardts represent to this day one of the most ancient and distinguished families, Louis Burckhardt decided at age nine to study medicine. After completing his studies in Zurich, Paris, Vienna, and Leipzig, he moved in 1893 to Indianapolis and gradually became involved in the city's life as his obituary reveals:

> Dr. Burckhardt was associated with Dr. John Hurty in the latter's drive to provide pure milk for the children of Indianapolis. . . . Also was a former director of the Children's Summer Mission, a teacher in the old Central Medical College and a former professor of obstetrics at the Indiana University School of Medicine. He was a member of the Marion County Medical Society, the American Medical Association and member of the advisory committees of the Indiana University School of Medicine and the Public Health Nursing Association. . . . Other organizations of which he was a member include the Turnverein, Athenaeum, Maennerchor, the Contemporary Club, the University Club, the Meridian Hills Country Club and First Presbyterian Church.[106]

While Louis Burckhardt made his career in Indianapolis, Louis Chevrolet (1878–1941) spent only the years 1916 to 1928 in that city, yet is remembered by a special monument. He was born in La Chaux-de-Fonds,

*Anton Scherrer (right).*

Switzerland, and when he was six years old his family moved to Beaune, France. At age twenty he became involved with the Mors Auto Company in Beaune, then moved to the United States, where he successively entered different automaking firms. He also began car racing with great success; in 1917 he reached 106.5 miles per hour in the Chicago one hundred-mile derby. In 1911 Louis Chevrolet founded the Chevrolet Motor Company in Detroit, but sold it to William C. Durant in 1915. He then "perfected a Frontenac racer and for its manufacture organized the Frontenac Motor Co., Indianapolis," of which he remained president and manager until 1926. With the new racing car called the Monroe-Frontenac, Louis Chevrolet's brother Gaston won the Indianapolis 500 Mile Race in 1920, a feat repeated the following year with Louis Chevrolet's new eight-cylinder Frontenac. In 1925 Chevrolet became interested in speedboat racing and won a race that year in Miami, Florida. From 1926 to 1928 his firm made cylinder heads for the Ford Model T engine; he then joined the Indianapolis firm Stutz Motor Car Company, only to move after a few months to Baltimore in order to pursue airplane design.[107]

Although he was in Indianapolis for only twelve years, a memorial at the Indianapolis Motor Speedway acknowledges his achievement as an inventor and racer. On 14 June 1991, the Swiss ambassador to the United States deposited a wreath at the memorial—in the presence of dignitaries, Indianapolis residents of Swiss descent, members of the Chevrolet family, and representatives of the Chevrolet Motor Company—to commemorate "the 50th Anniversary of Chevrolet's death and the 80th Anniversary of the first Chevrolet automobile, the 1911 Classic Six."[108]

Swiss also settled in many other cities and towns in Indiana. Some, for instance, lived in Evansville where they had for some years a benevolent society called "Grütliverein." Joseph Frick (1821–1886) worked in Evansville as an architect and served in 1879 as superintendent of buildings. Respected and loved for her benevolence was Elisa Eberle Schwab (1814–1886), a resident of Evansville since 1852. Machinist Robert Blum (d. 1885) from Bilten, Canton Glarus, arrived in the town in 1858 and founded and directed the singing group Liederkranz.[109] The Farragut Post No. 27, founded 24 June 1881, listed among its "heroes" ten Swiss who had served a combined total of 321 months in the Civil War.[110] In Huntingburg, Dubois County, Ernst Pickhardt founded and edited the *Huntingburg*; in Fort Wayne Andreas Voegeli directed the Helvetia Maennerchor; and in Terre Haute H. Kafader owned the Hotel Cincinnati.[111] They all symbolize the general secular presence of the Swiss in Indiana's life; newcomers from Switzerland, however, also significantly coshaped the state's religious traditions.

### Emergence of a Religious Presence

If they were churchgoing people, most Swiss who settled in Indiana were either of the Reformed or the Catholic persuasion, reflecting the two dominant creeds of Switzerland. Once in the United States, however, Swiss newcomers often joined other religious denominations as circumstances or personal choice dictated. They participated in Indiana's religious life in general, just as they were involved in the state's economic, social, political, and educational pursuits. Yet some groups of Swiss newcomers helped shape Indiana's religious traditions in a special way by transplanting Swiss elements onto new soil.

### The Benedictines

In the 1840s and 1850s Catholic clergy viewed southern Indiana as a forlorn region and undesirable mission field, "the despised Indiana," and "the land of the poor."[112] Since 1838 Joseph Kundek (1810–1857), a priest from the Archdiocese of Agram in Croatia, had served Catholics in Jasper and its environs under the tutelage of the Leopoldine Society of Vienna. An energetic man, Kundek was determined to bring a Catholic religious order to the region. He first tried to interest the Redemptorists, but

failed. Then he approached the ancient Benedictine monastery of Einsiedeln in Switzerland, an institution dating back to the ninth century. The monastery had been rebuilt in the early eighteenth century in a magnificent Baroque style. Since about 1400 the church's "Chapel of Grace," a shrine adorned by the statue of a Black Madonna, has been a popular goal of pilgrims.[113]

Kundek's petition reached the monastery at an opportune time. Missionary endeavors were part of a centuries-old Benedictine tradition. A liberalism that was anticlerical and determined to do away with monasteries and convents and to make their possessions property of the state swept Switzerland.[114] "I should be happy," wrote Einsiedeln's Abbot Heinrich Schmid to the Catholic bishop of Vincennes, "if I with all my community could join you in the vast state of Indiana and help you cultivate a soil less ungrateful . . . but we have duties toward this country."[115] Thus, an ancient missionary orientation combined with concerns for Einsiedeln's future induced Abbot Schmid tentatively to explore Kundek's request by sending Ulrich Christen (1814–1871) and Bede O'Connor (1826–1875) to Vincennes.

Christen, an energetic and impulsive man, was given the parish of St. Ferdinand in Dubois County, where he also served the mission stations of Rockport and McLoughlin. Determined to establish a Benedictine monastery, he soon purchased in nearby Spencer County twenty-four hundred acres, but without authorization, in the name of the abbot of Einsiedeln and named the site St. Meinrad.[116] The purchase created much tension and unease during the next six years, and the very survival of the undertaking was in doubt. Yet the situation was clarified in 1860 after the arrival of Martin Marty (1834–1896) and Fintan Mundwiler (1835–1898). Both were men of moderation, had firm goals, and were wholly dedicated to their faith and the Benedictine tradition.[117] Within the following years several more monks arrived from Einsiedeln to promote Catholicism in southern Indiana.

In successive stages the monks built additions to the monastery, established an orchard and vineyard, cultivated fields, drained swamps, and cleared forests. By 1862 the monks served twelve parishes and several mission stations; they conducted spiritual exercises for the laity called missions, Forty Hour Devotions, and retreats. They opened parish schools and established a minor and major seminary for the education of the future clergy.[118] The monks built churches in places like New Boston (1859), Hawesville, Kentucky (1854), Huntingburg (1859), Mariah Hill (Maria Hilf) (1865), and, in the 1880s, in St. Anthony, Troy, and Jasper. Thus they secured Catholicism a firm place alongside southern Indiana's Methodist, Presbyterian, and Lutheran denominations.[119]

*St. Meinrad Benedictine Monastery, St. Meinrad, ca. 1930.*

In the fall of 1860 St. Meinrad's Benedictines decided to lay out a town nearby, also to be named St. Meinrad. The town lots were auctioned off on 28 January 1861 on the octave day of the millennium since the death of the hermit St. Meinrad. "The people of Mariah Hill came in procession; many other people from surrounding towns came also. . . . After holy Mass had been celebrated, the whole crowd, led by the Ferdinand brass band, marched to the new town site."[120] Initially the town grew slowly, but the construction of a new larger monastery announced in the spring of 1866 stimulated its further growth into an attractive, if small, village. In 1883, when the town was incorporated, Abbot Fintan Mundwiler was elected trustee and mayor, something unique in the annals of an American community.[121] The Ferdinand parish became also a domain of Swiss Benedictine activity. From 1853 to 1920 five Swiss-born monks served as pastors and influenced not only the spiritual but also the educational affairs of the town. Its people were largely of German extraction and hardworking farmers.

The influence of the Swiss Benedictines, however, reached beyond southern Indiana. In 1870 St. Meinrad monastery was elevated to an abbey, with Martin Marty its first abbot. He promoted missionary endeavors among the Sioux people and went with other St. Meinrad monks to the Standing Rock agency in 1873, learned the Sioux language, and in 1880 became a bishop active among the people of the Dakotas.[122] St. Meinrad's efforts inspired other Benedictines of Swiss monasteries to initiate foundations in the United States, which in 1881 were united into a Swiss-American Congregation, with St. Meinrad's abbot serving as its first president. In 1965 the congregation had about one thousand members and sixteen member institutions.[123] St. Meinrad represents, of course, the general Benedictine tradition within the Catholic faith. But the renamed "Benedictine Federation of the Americas," which St. Meinrad chairs,[124] preserves elements of the Swiss form of Benedictine monasticism by insisting on the autonomy of each member institution, perhaps a legacy of a general Swiss tradition.

### Swiss Mennonites and Amish

Whereas the Swiss Benedictines identified with the hierarchical and centralized ways of Catholic Christianity, Swiss Mennonites and Amish newcomers from Switzerland were of a radical congregational orientation. The terms Swiss Mennonite and also the often used term Anabaptist are actually misnomers. The latter name was a form of accusation since rebaptizing had been declared a capital offense by the Justinian Code of 529 A.D.[125] The term Mennonite implies a dependence of the Swiss Brethren on Menno Simons (ca. 1496–1561), the influential organizer and spiritual leader of the Brethren of the Netherlands.[126] In actuality a whole series of independent adult baptism-oriented groups had emerged within the so-called Radical

Reformation of the early sixteenth century. The groups may be divided into four main segments. The Münster group represented the "loud" Anabaptists, intent on overthrowing the given social and political order and on replacing it with a theocracy.[127] The "still" Anabaptists, in contrast, known as "Swiss Brethren and Sisters," "Hutterites," and "[Dutch] Mennonites," chose to withdraw from the given secular and religious domain, yet their claims too were inherently revolutionary. Their rejection of infant baptism, practiced in most of Christendom, implicitly declared all existent forms of Christianity as invalid and devilish perversions.

The earliest groups of "still" Anabaptists came to be called Swiss Brethren and Sisters, although their communities also emerged in the Tirol, the Alsace, and the Palatinate.[128] They formed autonomous congregations and after a generation viewed farming of a family-owned homestead and closely allied skills as the only God-ordained way of life. They also rejected the oath and the bearing of arms, an especially radical and threatening step in a state calling itself an Oath-Association, Eidgenossenschaft, which based its very existence on warring against a powerful nobility.[129] The second wing of "still" Anabaptists went a step further; in time they practiced congregational community of goods, inspired by the teaching of the Swiss Anabaptist minister Jacob Hutter, martyred in 1536, and were known as Hutterites or Hutterian Brethren.[130] The third wing of "still" Anabaptists formed in the Netherlands and neighboring northern regions and, after 1536, followed the leadership of Menno Simons. He had developed Anabaptist views independently from the Swiss Brethren, and his followers came to be known as Mennonites.[131]

In the 1690s the Swiss Brethren were split by the preaching of Jacob Ammann (1644–ca. 1730), a minister who viewed Swiss Brethren practices as too lax and insufficiently detached from the world around them. He insisted on strict avoidance not only of those not of the faith, but also of those disciplined for trespasses within the community. In time his followers, called Amish, added detailed congregationally enforced rules as to dress and appearance in order to safeguard homogeneity, separateness, and the daily practice of obedience to God's will as expressed by the decisions of a congregation's elders.[132] Anabaptists from both Swiss Brethren wings departed for North America, where the non-Amish group came to be known as Swiss Mennonites. From Pennsylvania, where they settled after 1710, they moved gradually westward in search of affordable, arable land and were joined by coreligionists directly from Swiss congregations.[133] Indiana became an important region of settlement for both Swiss Mennonite and Amish. Immigrants directly from

Switzerland built their congregations in Adams County, especially in the surroundings of present-day Berne, itself a town of Swiss Mennonite origin.

## Berne

In 1798 the old Swiss Confederacy had collapsed as a consequence of the French Revolution and Napoleon's rise to power. The new Helvetian Constitution granted the Swiss Brethren exemption from military service, recognized marriages performed by Mennonite preachers, and accepted a simple yes or no in place of an oath.[134] Yet good arable land that was needed for the grown sons of the often large Mennonite families was hard to come by. The opening of the trans-Appalachian regions, achieved by successful wars of the United States against the resisting indigenous peoples led by Tecumseh,[135] became known also among the Swiss Brethren of the Bernese Emmental and Jura regions, then under the jurisdiction of the Catholic bishop of Basel. Furthermore, crop failures, resulting from inclement weather between 1812 and 1819, also made survival difficult.[136] After 1817 some Swiss Brethren went to Ohio, and their reports praised the available lands and the absence of ecclesiastical or civil restrictions. In the following decades about twelve hundred Swiss Brethren of the non-Amish as well as Amish persuasions went to the American Midwest.[137]

The Swiss Mennonite newcomers began two settlements in Wayne County, Ohio, and a third on the border between Ohio's Putnam and Allen counties. The fourth settlement in Adams County, Indiana, was initiated in 1838, and the fifth was established in Morgan and Moniteau counties in Missouri between 1866 and 1870. Between 1838 and 1852 about twenty families had settled near present-day Vera Cruz in Wells County. The first arrivals were Christian and Peter Baumgartner, followed the next year by their father David Baumgartner, a preacher who became the spiritual guide of this "Baumgartner" congregation. In 1852 a group of Swiss Brethren and Sisters from the Münsterberg region of the Swiss Jura, of whom some eighty people settled about seven miles from the Baumgartner group, chartered a ship for the United States.[138] They formed the "Münsterberg" congregation that by 1854 counted some thirty families.

Both groups followed their accustomed Swiss Brethren tradition of Switzerland. They stressed biblical piety, were guided by preachers with no formal training, met in barns for religious services, kept aloof from secular society or public office, and insisted on a carefully regulated code of dress and appearance.[139] Non-Mennonites also moved into the area, many of whom hailed from German-speaking lands. The Swiss Mennonites gradually found American ways alluring; there, in contrast to Switzerland, denominational practice was a private not communal concern as long as it remained within the confines of Deism as shaped by the Enlightenment and American civil religion.[140] In 1856 the Swiss Mennonites built their first school and in 1858 their first house of worship. Gradually occupations other than farming, such as the selling of grain, lumber, hardware, and machinery, came to be tolerated. The acceptance of a position on school boards became permissible, Swiss German gradually gave way to English, and dress codes were first relaxed, then fully adjusted to general American practice.[141]

In August 1871 a town was platted in the midst of the Münsterberg congregation's land, and the Grand Rapids and Indiana Railroad was induced to establish a station there. When a name was to be chosen for the town, a committee settled on Berne "in honor of the Bernese settlers which made up the majority of the community." On 30 March 1887 the town was formally incorporated, with Daniel Welty, J. F. Lehman, and John C. Lehman as trustees, F. F. Mendenhall as clerk, David Bixler as treasurer, and J. F. Lachot as marshal.[142]

A major force in transforming the Swiss Mennonites of the Berne area into a regular American denomination was Samuel F. Sprunger (1850–1923). Chosen by lot in 1868 as one of the Münsterberg ministers, he decided to attend the Dutch Mennonite Seminary at Wadsworth, Ohio. On his return he remained pastor of the Berne congregations for thirty-three years. Sprunger united the Baumgartner and Münsterberg groups in 1878, and by 1890 he had allowed regular dress for men and women, the use of a song leader, the taking of photographs, and salaried pastors. He fostered the temperance movement, Sunday schools, midweek Bible study classes, and missionary work, all foreign to the original Swiss Mennonite tradition.[143]

These changes also conditioned a new perception of Berne's Swiss heritage, as tellingly formulated in an issue of Berne's newspaper *The Witness*:

> Berne! What a name to conjure up old pictures in the memory of the genuine "Bärner" or even his descendants! It is indeed a long and eventful story from 735 years ago when the Burgundian Duke Berchthold V of Zähringen founded mother "Bern" on the rocky promontory of the Aare river in the primeval wilds of Switzerland . . . up to the beautiful little daughter city of our own "Berne" here, nestled on the peaceful Hoosier plains, flourishing with the myriad sister towns of our glorious country.[144]

Switzerland had ceased to be perceived simply as a land of Swiss Brethren oppression. The new perception was one of a proud acknowledgment of Swiss roots combined with American civil religion as, for instance, expressed by the frontispiece of the *Berne Review* in 1935: "Franklin D. Roosevelt/By Divine Appointment President of the United States of America/The Best Country on Earth."[145]

Berne's development has been minutely documented in *The Berne Witness'* souvenir editions of 1906 and 1926 as well as in a centennial booklet of 1952.[146] By 1906 Berne had not only a Mennonite, but also a stately Evangelical and a German Reformed church. By 1950 Berne had the largest Mennonite congregation in the United States with a membership of 1,312.[147] Since about 1900 Berne has increasingly promoted its Swissness, until today its promotional pamphlet is titled "The Swiss City of Berne, Indiana." Although the use of Bernese German is gradually diminishing as a living, everyday means of communication, school courses try to keep its knowledge alive. There is a sense of being special, as the following comment made in 1979 intimates: "We Swiss do not drink like the Yankees; we work hard, therefore we have succeeded."[148]

In 1977 Berne celebrated its 125th anniversary with special fanfare. The governor of Indiana, the mayor of the city of Bern, Switzerland, and the consul general of Switzerland were guests of honor. A specially composed "Operetta 'In Grand Old Switzerland,'" featuring a love story between two young Swiss and resolved by an American visiting Switzerland, was performed with the Matterhorn scenery as background.[149] In recent decades buildings such as the public library, banks, and shops have adopted a modified chalet style in the hope of giving the town a genuine Swiss appearance.[150] Although such efforts reflect views of Switzerland that at best only marginally express its true culture, they are genuine attempts at creating a unique Swiss-American identity.

In the environs of Berne sixteen congregations of Bernese Amish also flourish with a total of about two thousand people. Although ethnically similar to the Swiss Mennonites, they keep strictly apart from them as well as the surrounding English-speaking world. Their Bernese German also sets them apart from other Amish groups of northern Indiana who are of Pennsylvanian or Alsatian origin. They hold on to the original forms of Swiss Brethren Christianity. To them religion is not a matter of individual experience, but of the abandonment of will in obedience to scripture, as interpreted by the sixteenth-century traditions of their faith and the preachers, who are chosen by lot. Life thus becomes a constant struggle against temptations to disobedience coming from within as well as from an ever encroaching outer world.[151]

## Apostolic Christians

*Indiana: A New Historical Guide* observes: "From Vera Cruz . . . continue north 1.1 *m.* to one of Indiana's most imposing rural churches. Apostolic Christians, a small denomination, built it in 1951. . . . [It] seats 1,400 worshipers in a breathtaking, fully-carpeted sanctuary. The congregation is largely of Swiss descent, and the soft sounds of Schwyzer Dütsch may still be heard in everyday conversation."[152] The denomination's founder was Samuel H. Fröhlich (1803–1857) of Brugg, Switzerland. He studied for the ministry in the Swiss Reformed faith but preached unorthodox views and was excluded from the Reformed Church in 1832. On missionary tours he gained converts among the Swiss Brethren of Langnau in the Bernese Emmental and formed the congregation "Gemeinschaft Evangelisch Taufgesinnter: Community of Evangelical Baptism-Minded." Since many of his converts were former Swiss Brethren and Sisters, his group came to be known as "Neutäufer," "New [Mennonite] Baptists."[153]

In the United States the denomination began in 1852 near Croghan, New York. On the invitation of the Amish Virkler family, Fröhlich sent Benedict Weyeneth to the United States. Weyeneth ordained Joseph Virkler and later gained converts among Amish in Illinois. Thus the group is at times also called "New Amish," although it represents an antithesis to the Swiss Brethren Amish tradition.[154] The denomination's doctrines include a strict biblicism in "that the King James version of the Holy Bible is the source of the spiritual truth and light." The *Zion's Harp* is the church's official hymnal. Baptism is administered by immersion, and women are veiled during prayer and "are to be silent in church." If drafted, the men serve only in noncombatant positions. In religious practice the emotional experience of a new birth is considered basic. At the same time "a free enterprise economy which fostered the precepts of incentive, ambition, ingenuity, and hard work . . . [has been] a real blessing to members of the church whose entire heritage was enshrouded in the work ethic."[155] In 1907 a branch split off from the main body and calls itself Apostolic Christian Church (Nazarene).

By 1984 thirteen Indiana congregations had been formed. The largest is in Bluffton and originated through the efforts of the Swiss Mennonite ministers Ulrich Ripfer and Matthias Strahm of the Baumgartner congregation near Berne. When still in Switzerland, these ministers had heard of Fröhlich. In 1858 they went to Sardis, Ohio, where they were converted by Isaac Gehring and formed the nucleus of the Bluffton congregation on their return.[156] By 1881 that congregation consisted of 485 families comprising about 1,100 persons.[157] From a cultural perspective the denomination may be viewed as a blending of evangelical experiential baptism-mindedness and biblical literalism of partly Swiss, partly United States origin, with American civil religion and conservative values.

Of the four religious groups in Indiana that derive directly from Switzerland, only the Amish of Swiss origin still represent original Swiss traditions. The Benedictines of St. Meinrad have been almost completely assimilated by American Benedictine forms of monastic life, and the Swiss Mennonites and the Apostolic Christians have become part of mainstream evangelical Protestantism. Berne, Indiana, developed in addition—influenced also by non-Mennonite Swiss immigrants—a vigorous folkloristic Swissness in stressing Bernese roots and an idealized Alpine origin. All four groups have been vitally involved in Indiana's religious history and remain active forces in its religious life today.

## "Ordinary" Lives

The above sketch of the coming of Swiss to Indiana has focused on the creation of settlements or on those individuals who have become noted for their activities. Most lives, however, although they are all worthy of note, leave only a few traces, a tombstone here, a notation in a parish or town register there, which give dates of birth, marriage, death, and, perhaps, the number of children born to a union. Biographical sketches, however, especially in nineteenth-century county histories, or autobiographical accounts, provide occasional glimpses beyond mere demographic data. Two randomly chosen examples may highlight the type of detail they offer, although one needs to remember that only rarely are the darker sides revealed.[158]

John Christen was born in 1812 on a farm in the Canton Bern, Switzerland. On 17 July 1835 he married Elizabeth Schaad, born in 1814. In 1850 the family moved with their eleven children born in Switzerland via New York to Root Township in Adams County, Indiana, where their twelfth child was born. For nine years they lived in a one-room cabin, family tradition claims, that was then expanded to three rooms and, in 1875, replaced by a stately brick house. As to religion, the family was Swiss Reformed. John Christen died in 1893, and Elizabeth Christen died in 1897. How did they view their immigration, the tasks of raising a large family, and local and national events? Perhaps some letters still hidden somewhere may someday give answers to such questions. Possibly, however, these immigrants, like thousands of others, took their knowledge with them to their graves.

One of their two sons who served in the Civil War under Nathaniel Banks (1816–1894) in the ill-fated Red

River expedition was Albright Christen, born in Switzerland in 1840. Initially a carpenter by trade, he eventually became a building contractor. In 1868 he married Mary O. Lord, born in 1843 of English stock; in 1874 the family moved to Decatur. Charles N., one of their five children, followed his father's occupation. When Charles Christen married Amelia Smith he converted to Catholicism and served as a second grand knight of the Knights of Columbus. In 1900 he went into partnership in the contracting firm Mann & Christen. In 1915 he established his own company and was also a partner of the plumbing firm of Christen & Smith. In 1913, after eight years of service on the city council, Charles Christen was elected mayor of Decatur on the Democratic ticket. The following year a cousin Edward S., also of Swiss origin, was elected superintendent of the county's public schools.[159]

A quite different story is that of Elizabeth Weidmann. Born in 1829 in Switzerland she met John C. Hirshbrunner about 1851. Hirshbrunner left for the United States in May 1851, alone, because the young woman he was dating refused to leave her native land. In contrast, Elizabeth Weidmann decided to join Hirshbrunner the next year. After fifty-six days on the Atlantic the boat landed at Nassau. While the passengers were on land, the boat was destroyed by fire. On the trip from Nassau to South Carolina cholera broke out on the boat and the passengers were quarantined for three weeks. Elizabeth finally reached New York around 20 January 1853 and married Hirshbrunner on 20 February. Elizabeth and her husband, a tanner by trade, then moved from New Jersey to Indianapolis.

On 19 January 1854 she gave birth there to her first child, Lena. Then the family moved to Terre Haute where her husband found better work, but fell ill with "brain fever." "Imagine what a trouble mother had without friends," Hirshbrunner commented, "nobody around that she could talk to, living upstairs with an Irish family below drunk every evening, making half the night hideous with their sports." The Hirshbrunners' physician alerted some German neighbors who selflessly helped Elizabeth manage. On 11 November 1856 another disaster struck; little Lena "fell into a vat and drowned. O, what a hard shock it was for us to lose the only child we had thus by our own neglect. . . . But God's will be done." On 17 April 1857 Elizabeth gave birth to a second child, also baptized as Lena in the German Reformed Church. Elizabeth died on 17 August 1892 at age sixty-three, survived by her husband, who lived until 1916, and their six children.[160]

Whether among those with ordinary or unusual lives, the Swiss in Indiana met no obstacles due to their origin or creed. They could pursue their calling as they pleased and as circumstances allowed. Their records reveal at least

partially that their lives included success and defeat, trials, and blessings. Although only a small group among Indiana's people, the Swiss helped shape the state's history in the secular as well as religious domains.

## Notes

1. An up-to-date, topically arranged guide to works on Swiss history and life, with concise summaries of each of the 974 titles is Heinz K. Meier and Regula A. Meier, comps., *Switzerland,* World Bibliographical Series, vol. 114 (Santa Barbara, Calif.: CLIO Press, 1990). Surveys of Swiss history are Christopher Hughes, *Switzerland* (London: Ernest Benn, [1975]); Dieter Fahrni, *An Outline of History of Switzerland: From the Origins to the Present Day,* 4th ed. (Zurich: Pro Helvetia, 1984); and J. Murray Luck, *A History of Switzerland* (Palo Alto, Calif.: Society for the Promotion of Science and Scholarship, 1985). Pages 37–127 cover the years 1300 to 1515.

2. See Kenneth D. McRae, *Conflict and Compromise in Multilingual Societies: Switzerland* (Waterloo, Ontario: Wilfrid Laurier University Press, 1983). A special aspect is explored in Robert H. Billigmeier, *A Crisis in Swiss Pluralism: The Romansh and Their Relations with German- and Italian-Swiss in the Perspective of a Millenium* (The Hague: Mouton Publisher, 1979). A comprehensive view is Jachen C. Arquint et al., *Die Viersprachige Schweiz* (Zurich: Benziger, 1982).

3. See Emil Egli, *Switzerland: A Survey of Its Land and People,* trans. Britta M. Charleston, Paul Swain, and Walter Sorell (Bern: Paul Haupt, 1978); Hans Weiss and Werner Kämpfen, *Focus on Switzerland: The Significance of the Landscape. Switzerland-Vacationland,* 2d ed. (Lausanne: Swiss Office for the Development of Trade, 1983).

4. See François Gross, *Focus on Switzerland: Economic Life and Export Industries,* trans. Roger Glémet, 2d ed. (Lausanne: Swiss Office for the Development of Trade, 1982).

5. A brief overview is Oswald Sigg, *Switzerland's Political Institutions,* trans. F. M. Blackwell, D. N. Roscoe, and M. Mettler, 2d ed. (Zurich: Pro Helvetia, 1987).

6. See G. R. Potter, *Zwingli* (Cambridge: Cambridge University Press, 1976). No overview in English exists on the Catholic tradition. Valuable is Johann B. Villiger, "Switzerland," in the *New Catholic Encyclopedia,* 18 vols. (New York: McGraw-Hill, [1967]–89), 13:845–53.

7. The complex issue of the rise of Anabaptism is explored in James M. Stayer, "The Swiss Brethren: An Exercise in Historical Definition," *Church History* 47 (June 1978): 174–95. The Amish split is discussed by Leo Schelbert, "Pietism Rejected: A Reinterpretation of Amish Origins," in *America and the Germans: An Assessment of a Three-Hundred-Year History,* eds. Frank Trommler and Joseph McVeigh, 2 vols. (Philadelphia: University of Pennsylvania Press, 1985), 1:118–27.

8. See Leo Schelbert, *Einführung in die schweizerische Auswanderungsgeschichte der Neuzeit* (Zurich: Leeman, 1976), 182–98.

9. For a useful set of interpretative essays see Rudolph J. Vecoli and Suzanne M. Sinke, eds., *A Century of European Migrations, 1830–1930* (Urbana: University of Illinois Press, 1991).

10. For brief overviews see Leo Schelbert, "Swiss," in Stephan Thernstrom, ed., *Harvard Encyclopedia of American Ethnic Groups* (Cambridge, Mass.: The Belknap Press of Harvard University Press, 1980), 983–84; "Swiss" in Francesco Cordasco, ed., *Dictionary of*

*American Immigration History* (Metuchen, N.J.: The Scarecrow Press, 1990), 698–700; and "Swiss Americans," in Judy Galens et al., eds., *Gale Encyclopedia of Multicultural America* (Detroit: Gale Research, 1995), 1298–1308.

11. For a statistical breakdown according to place of nativity see, for example, *Ninth Census of the United States,* vol. 1, *Population* (Washington, D.C.: Government Printing Office, 1872), Table 7, "State of Indiana," 352–53; *Tenth Census* (1883), Table 14, pp. 505–6. The Caucasian conquest of the midwestern regions is featured by Reginald Horsman, *The Frontier in the Formative Years, 1783–1815* (Albuquerque: University of New Mexico Press, 1975).

12. For a list of relevant titles see Schelbert, *Einführung,* 382–88. An analysis of an influential newspaper is given by Leo Schelbert, "Die Fünfte Schweiz in der Berichterstattung des 'Aufrichtigen und Wohlerfahrenen Schweizer-Boten,'" *Schweizerisches Archiv für Volkskunde* 57 (1971): 84–114.

13. See Schelbert, *Einführung,* for an attempt to place the migrations of Swiss to regions of the United States within their worldwide moves.

14. The transformation of the Swiss economy is discussed by Jonathan Steinberg, *Why Switzerland?* (Cambridge: Cambridge University Press, 1976), 131–39; and Luck, *History of Switzerland,* 425–41. Personal dimensions are explored in Leo Schelbert and Hedwig Rappolt, eds., *Alles ist ganz anders hier: Auswandererschicksale in Briefen aus zwei Jahrhunderten* (Olten, Switzerland: Walter Verlag, 1977). An English version is Leo Schelbert, ed., *America Remembered. Eighteenth and Nineteenth Century Accounts of Swiss Immigrants.* Documents translated by Hedwig Rappolt (Camden, Maine: Picton Press, 1996).

15. Based on "1860 Census Foreign-Born for Indiana" (unpublished manuscript, Education Division, Indiana Historical Society, 1991).

16. U.S. Bureau of the Census, *U.S. Census of Population: 1950,* vol. 2, *Characteristics of the Population,* part 14: *Indiana* (Washington, D.C.: Government Printing Office, 1952), 43, Table 24.

17. 1930 and 1940 figures in U.S. Bureau of the Census, *U.S. Census of Population: 1940* (Washington, D.C.: Government Printing Office, 1943), 2:692, Table 14; ibid., *1960,* vol. 1, *Characteristics,* Part 16: *Indiana* (Washington, D.C.: Government Printing Office, 1983), 8, Table 195; ibid., *1980 Census of Population: Ancestry of Population by State: 1980, Supplementary Report,* "Ancestry of the Population, Indiana: 1980" (Washington, D.C.: Government Printing Office, 1983).

18. *The American Vine-Dresser's Guide: Being a Treatise on the Cultivation of the Vine, and the Process of Wine Making, Adapted to the Soil and Climate of the United States by John James Dufour* (Cincinnati: Printed by J. S. Browne, 1826), 7.

19. See French and English translation of "Broillard de Voyage pour Jean Jacques Dufour de Sales a Montreux, au Bailliage de Vevey," in Perret Dufour, *The Swiss Settlement of Switzerland County, Indiana,* vol. 13 of *Indiana Historical Collections* (Indianapolis: Indiana Historical Commission, 1925), 234–347, quotations, 235, 247. The first entry is dated 20 Mar. 1796, the last 23 June 1816.

20. On John Brown see *Dictionary of American Biography,* 11 vols. (New York: Charles Scribner's Sons, 1928–58), 2:130–31. "A constant supporter of Jefferson . . . he was widely acquainted and . . . on intimate terms of friendship with the first five presidents of the United States," 2:131.

21. Dufour, *Swiss Settlement of Switzerland County,* 11; Wanda L. Morford, *Switzerland County, Indiana: Cemetery Inscriptions, 1817–1985* (Cincinnati: W. L. Morford, 1986), 119, 129, 134.

22. *American Vine-Dresser's Guide,* 9.

23. See V. B. Wigglesworth, *The Principles of Insect Physiology* (London: Chapman and Hall, 1974), 500. The Vine Phylloxera (*Viteus vitifolii*) secretes a damaging viscous saliva; its reproductive cycle occurs in different stages and forms, and at one stage the insect feasts on the roots.

24. See *Debates and Proceedings in the Congress of the United States, Seventh Congress* (Washington, D.C.: Gales and Seaton, 1851), 188, 199, 200 for the Senate's actions; 1018, 1025, 1126–27, 1253 for those in the House; 1355–56 for final passage.

25. Dufour, *Swiss Settlement of Switzerland County,* 19; *American Vine-Dresser's Guide,* 26.

26. Text in Dufour, *Swiss Settlement of Switzerland County,* 19–21; on families, 16.

27. *Debates and Proceedings in the Congress of the United States, Seventh Congress,* 1355–56.

28. Dufour, *Swiss Settlement of Switzerland County,* map following 16. Indian Creek is crossed out and replaced by Venoge.

29. *American Vine-Dresser's Guide,* 24.

30. Report from *Schweizerische Monathschronik* (1816), ed. J. J. Hottinger, Jr. (Zurich: J. J. Ulrich, 1817), 1:30–32, 46–48; Dufour, *Swiss Settlement of Switzerland County,* 16.

31. Samuel R. Brown, *The Western Gazetteer, or Emigrant Directory* (Auburn, N.Y.: Robert Taylor, 1817), quoted in Harlow Lindley, ed., *Indiana as Seen by Early Travelers,* vol. 3 of *Indiana Historical Collections* (Indianapolis: Indiana Historical Commission, 1916), 154–56. Some of the material underlying this description of New Switzerland's evolution follows Leo Schelbert, "Vevay, Indiana, and Chabag Bessarabia: The Making of Two Winegrower Settlements," *Yearbook of German-American Studies* 25 (1990): 109–29.

32. Dufour, *Swiss Settlement of Switzerland County,* 34.

33. Ibid., 15.

34. Ibid., 27, letter of B. Thurston.

35. Ibid., 34–35.

36. Brown, *Western Gazetteer,* 155. See also John Scott, *The Indiana Gazetteer or Topographical Dictionary* (1826; reprint, Indianapolis: Indiana Historical Society, 1954), 117. For photographs of buildings see Janet Miller et al., eds., *An Architectural and Historical Survey of Switzerland County* (Vevay, Ind.: Switzerland County Junior Historical Society, 1969), esp. 6–10.

37. Dufour, *Swiss Settlement of Switzerland County,* 35, 39–42 passim.

38. Ibid. There are numerous references in the index to Daniel V. Dufour, John F. Dufour, Elisha Golay, and Francis L. Siebenthal.

39. Based on Morford, *Cemetery Inscriptions,* 118, 129, 137, 138, 145, 150, 152, 154, 256.

40. Biographical sketches in *History of Dearborn, Ohio and Switzerland Counties* (Chicago: Weakley, Harraman and Co., Publishers, 1885), 1262–63; also L. Gex Oboussier Papers, SC-620, Indiana Historical Society Library, Indianapolis. Oboussier had entered the service of Jean Mennet, an Antwerp merchant who had purchased one thousand acres in West Virginia and which Oboussier was to cultivate or sell. The land was not on the Ohio River as presented by the seller, and it was inaccessible and hilly. Oboussier thus went to Switzerland County, Indiana; in 1826 he moved to New Harmony.

41. Charles Kettleborough, *Constitution Making in Indiana,* 3 vols. (Indianapolis: Indiana Historical Commission, 1930), 1:69, 72.

42. Dufour, *Swiss Settlement of Switzerland County,* 63.

43. "1850 Census Foreign-Born for Indiana" (unpublished manuscript, Education Division, Indiana Historical Society, 1991).

44. 1974 Swiss Wine Festival (pamphlet), page 8 (Swiss costume contest), 12 (stone tossing), 18 (the Schenck mansion), 14–15 (activities), 43 (the county museum), 46 (U. P. Schenck mansion built in 1844).

45. For a description of Vincennes and environs by John Badollet see Gayle Thornbrough, ed., *The Correspondence of John Badollet and Albert Gallatin, 1804–1836,* Indiana Historical Society *Publications,* vol. 22 (Indianapolis: Indiana Historical Society, 1963), 54–60. This outstandingly edited work is basic to the Badollet story.

46. An authoritative biography of Gallatin is Raymond Walters, Jr., *Albert Gallatin: Jeffersonian Financier and Diplomat* (New York: Macmillan, 1957).

47. Thornbrough, ed., *Correspondence of John Badollet and Albert Gallatin,* 10–11.

48. Ibid., 25–26, letter of appointment, with valuable critical commentary.

49. For a description of the business of land receiver see Paul William Miller, "John Badollet: Indiana Land Receiver, Slavery Opponent, and Political Commentator, 1804–1837" (unpublished research paper, Southern Illinois University at Carbondale, 1981), 12–18. See also Stephen Frederick Strausberg, "The Administration and Sale of Public Land in Indiana, 1800–1860" (Ph.D. diss., Cornell University, 1970), 51–58.

50. Thornbrough, ed., *Correspondence of John Badollet and Albert Gallatin,* 49–50 n. 9.

51. Ibid., 20, 40, 64–65, 91–93; (text of petition), 333–55; (letter to the *Western Sun*), 335–47.

52. Ibid., 262 n. 9; Donald F. Carmony, ed., "Journal of the Convention of the Indiana Territory, 1816," *Indiana Magazine of History* 61 (June 1965): 77–85. Text of the constitution in ibid., [87]–[155], reproduced from pages 1–69 of the *Journal of the Convention of the Indiana Territory* (Louisville: Printed by Butler and Wood, 1816).

53. See J. Robert Constantine, ed., "Minutes of the Board of Trustees for Vincennes University," *Indiana Magazine of History* 54 (Dec. 1958): 313–63.

54. J. Robert Constantine, "The Vincennes Library Company: A Cultural Institution in Pioneer Indiana," ibid. 61 (Dec. 1965): 305–20, 321–89; "Minutes of First Library Board."

55. Thornbrough, ed., *Correspondence of John Badollet and Albert Gallatin,* 330; ibid., passim for numerous comments on his children.

56. Albert Gallatin to John B. Caldwell of Shawneetown, Illinois, 3 June 1841, Manuscript Collection, SC-168, Indiana Historical Society Library.

57. Adelrich Steinach, *Geschichte und Leben der Schweizer Kolonien in den Vereinigten Staaten von Nord-Amerika: unter Mitwirkung des Nord-Amerikanischen Grütli-Bundes* (New York: Druck von T. Bryner, 1889), 224–31 (Tell City). A new edition with extensive indexes by Urspeter Schelbert is *Swiss Colonists* (Camden, Maine: Picton Press, 1995).

58. Will Maurer, "A Historical Sketch of Tell City, Indiana," *Indiana Magazine of History* 14 (June 1918): 108.

59. Thomas James De la Hunt, *Perry County: A History* (Indianapolis: The W. K. Stewart Co., 1916), 185.

60. *Helvetia: Tell City Volksblatt,* 25 Apr. 1860, p. 3, quoted in Rainer Baumgartner, "The Immigrant Press and Americanization: A Comparative Study of the German Communities in Tell City and Indianapolis, 1856–1882" (M.A. thesis, Indiana University, 1987), 24.

61. De la Hunt, *Perry County,* 185–86, English version of Minutes.

62. Maurer, "Historical Sketch of Tell City," 108. On Frederick Muench (1799–1881) see Steven Rowan, ed. and trans., *Germans for a Free Missouri: Translations from the St. Louis Radical Press, 1857–1862* (Columbia: University of Missouri Press, 1983), 71 n; photograph, 33.

63. De la Hunt, *Perry County,* 186–87.

64. Steinach, *Schweizer Kolonien,* 224.

65. Quoted in Maurer, "Historical Sketch of Tell City," 109.

66. Ibid.

67. Ibid., 110–11, list of sellers.

68. R. H. Gay of Cannelton to S. M. Allen, Manuscript Collection, SC-617, Indiana Historical Society Library. On 9 Jan. 1858 Gay wrote that 2,700 acres had been bought. On the name choice see De la Hunt, *Perry County,* 198.

69. *Swiss Colonization Society Records in German: A Translation Project,* trans. Marga Meier (Tell City, Ind.: Tell City Historical Society, 1990). The publication contains as "First Book" the "Minutes of the Executive Committee," 4 Jan. 1858–10 Mar. 1859; the "Second Book" contains the "Minutes of the Board of Directors"; the "Third Book" the "Minutes of the Tell City Branch"; each "Book" is paginated separately (hereafter cited as *Records,* One, Two, or Three). *Records,* One, pp. 1, 2 (two meetings were held the same day).

70. Maurer, "Historical Sketch of Tell City," 112.

71. De la Hunt, *Perry County,* 188.

72. *Records,* One, p. 7.

73. Ibid., 11.

74. Ibid., 21; Maurer, "Historical Sketch of Tell City," 113.

75. *Records,* Three, p. 1.

76. Maurer, "Historical Sketch of Tell City," 114.

77. *Records,* Three, pp. 3–5a, 5b–5e, list of 354 members.

78. De la Hunt, *Perry County,* 193.

79. *Records,* One, p. 108; on Steinauer see De la Hunt, *Perry County,* 190.

80. De la Hunt, *Perry County,* 196.

81. Maurer, "Historical Sketch of Tell City," 120–21, list on 121.

82. De la Hunt, *Perry County,* 195.

83. Ibid., 195–96.

84. Baumgartner, "Immigrant Press and Americanization," 132–33.

85. Ibid., 11, 30.

86. Maurer, "Historical Sketch of Tell City," 127.

87. Steinach, *Schweizer Kolonien,* 225–31. He gives numerous biographical details.

88. *Tell City, Indiana . . . City Directory* (1954), 5.

89. *Commercial Atlas and Marketing Guide 1992* (Skokie, Ill.: Rand McNally, 1992), 382.

90. Dean R. Esslinger, *Immigrants and the City: Ethnicity and Mobility in a Nineteenth-Century Midwestern Community* (Port Washington, N.Y.: Kennikat Press, 1975), 50.

91. [S. Meier, ed.], *Nord-Amerikanischer Schweizer-Bund 1865–1915* (Union Hill, N.J.: Druck von Michel und Rank, [1915]), 135–36, 67–68. On the national society see Leo Schelbert and Urspeter Schelbert, "Portrait of an Immigrant Society: The North American Grütli-Bund, 1865–1915," in *Yearbook of German-American Studies* 18 (1983): 233–54.

92. Steinach, *Schweizer Kolonien,* 232.

93. The Adolph Scherrer Collection, BV 1722-1723, M245, Indiana Historical Society Library.

94. See *Who Was Who in America: Historical Volume 1607–1896,* rev. ed. (Chicago: A. N. Marquis Co., 1967), 410; Lee Burns, *Early Architects and Builders of Indiana,* Indiana Historical Society

*Publications,* vol. 11, no. 3 (Indianapolis: Indiana Historical Society, 1937), 198–99. May had designed the courthouses of Brookville, Greensburg, Sullivan, Vincennes, and Fort Wayne and one of the buildings for the Hospital for the Insane in Indianapolis.

95. On May see *Who Was Who in America,* 410. For Scherrer's appointment see Board of State House Commissioners, *Report of Proceedings of the Board of State House Commissioners, from January 1, 1879, to December 31, 1880, to the Governor,* no. 14 (Indianapolis: Carlon and Hollenbeck, Printers and Binders, 1880), 16–17.

96. Board of Commissioners, *Final Report of the Board of State House Commissioners Containing a Synopsis of Proceedings from Commencement May 24, 1877, to Completion of Building, October 2, 1888, to the Governor,* no. 46 (Indianapolis: Wm. B. Burford, Contractor for Printing and Binding, 1888), 27.

97. Ibid., 45.

98. Eva Draegert, "The Fine Arts in Indianapolis, 1880–1890," *Indiana Magazine of History* 50 (Dec. 1954): 346.

99. "State House Scrap Book," 130 (the text is signed "An Architect"), Indiana Division, Indiana State Library, Indianapolis.

100. Copy of a letter dated 14 Aug. 1899, Scherrer Collection.

101. Draegert, "Fine Arts in Indianapolis," 345; George Theodore Probst, *The Germans in Indianapolis, 1840–1918,* rev. ed. by Eberhard Reichmann (Indianapolis: German-American Center and Indiana German Heritage Society, 1989), 131 (picture of Maennerchor Hall), 105 (picture of Scherrer and state capitol).

102. *Indianapolis Times,* 9 Jan. 1960. Scherrer died on 8 Jan. 1960 at Methodist Hospital. Details about his mother are still unknown.

103. Ibid., 30 Mar. 1945.

104. The obituary claims that A. Scherrer "served for a time as president," ibid., 9 Jan. 1960. Lana Ruegamer, *A History of the Indiana Historical Society, 1830–1980* (Indianapolis: Indiana Historical Society, 1980), 137, states: "though not an officer of the Society until 1945, [he] was a member from 1932."

105. "Comment," *Indiana Magazine of History* 30 (Mar. 1934): 112. See Anton Scherrer, "Charles Major," ibid., 45 (Sept. 1949): 265–67, for Scherrer's delightfully mischievous toast to Charles Major, an Indiana writer, at a dinner commemorating the publication of Indiana authors and their books.

106. *Indianapolis Star,* 21 Mar. 1945, Louis Burckhardt obituary. A report on a dinner honoring Burckhardt's fifty years in the medical profession mentions that when Burckhardt found only one microscope for medical usage, he brought back from his next visit to Switzerland "50 microscopes as a starter." Ibid., 14 Apr. 1940.

107. The above is based on *The National Cyclopedia of American Biography,* 53 vols. (New York: James T. White and Co., 1971), 53:315–16; picture, 314.

108. *Swiss American Review* 123 (14 Aug. 1991): 10.

109. Steinach, *Schweizer Kolonien,* 232–33.

110. Joseph P. Elliott, *A History of Evansville and Vanderburgh County, Indiana* (Evansville, Ind.: Keller Printing Co., 1897), 323–37. The following Swiss born are listed: F. Brandenberger, Jacob Dietrich, Fred Frank, Nicholas Gostelli, Jacob Laubscher, Henry Merz, Christian Schweitzer, Francis Schuler, Christian Strucker, and John Ulrich.

111. Steinach, *Schweizer Kolonien,* 233–35, with further data on individuals.

112. Albert Kleber, *Ferdinand, Indiana, 1840–1940: A Bit of Cultural History* (St. Meinrad, Ind.: [A. Kleber], 1940), 100, quotations from a letter by U. Christen.

113. *New Catholic Encyclopedia,* 5:232–34. The "Gnaden-Kapelle" was replicated at St. Meinrad, Indiana. See Albert Kleber, *History of St. Meinrad Archabbey, 1854–1954* (St. Meinrad, Ind.: A

Grail Publication, 1954), 437.

114. Kleber, *History of St. Meinrad Archabbey,* 16; Luck, *History of Switzerland,* 356–78.

115. Luck, *History of Switzerland,* 84.

116. Ibid., 33–34, for Christen's traits; 49–55 on purchase; 93–94 rebuke by Abbot Schmid. O'Connor was born in London, of Irish parents. He became a Benedictine at Einsiedeln and, later, vicar general of the diocese of Vincennes. Ibid., 34, 163–67.

117. *New Catholic Encyclopedia,* 9:311–12; 10:72; Kleber, *History of St. Meinrad Archabbey,* passim.

118. Kleber, *History of St. Meinrad Archabbey,* 140. Among the Swiss-born Benedictines were Jerome Bachmann, Chrysostom Foffa, Isidor Hobi, Wolfgang Schlumpf, Eugen Schwerzmann, Eberhard Stadler, Athanasius Tschopp, and Isidor Zarnx.

119. For a general portrait of the religious situation, see Elfrieda Lang, "German Influence in the Churches and Schools of Dubois County, Indiana," *Indiana Magazine of History* 42 (June 1946): 151–72; Kleber, *History of St. Meinrad Archabbey,* 197.

120. See Peter Behrman, comp., *Centennial of St. Meinrad, Town and Parish, St. Meinrad, Indiana: A Historical Sketch from 1861 to 1961* ([St. Meinrad, Ind.]: St. Meinrad Church, 1961), 17.

121. Ibid., 19.

122. On Martin Marty see *Dictionary of American Biography,* 6:352.

123. *New Catholic Encyclopedia,* 2:301–2. A listing of all members: St. Meinrad founded New Subiaco, Arkansas, in 1878; St. Joseph, Louisiana, in 1890; Marmion in Aurora, Illinois, in 1933; Blue Cloud in Marmion, South Dakota, in 1952; St. Charles Priory in Oceanside, California, in 1958; and the Priorato de San Benito in Huaraz, Peru, in 1964.

124. Paul K. Meagher, Thomas C. O'Brien, and Consuelo M. Aherne, eds., *Encyclopedic Dictionary of Religion,* 3 vols. (Washington, D.C.: Corpus Publications, 1979), 1:419.

125. *Twentieth Century Encyclopedia of Religious Knowledge,* 2 vols. (Grand Rapids, Mich.: Baker Book House, 1955), 1:35.

126. *The Encyclopedia of Religion,* 16 vols. (New York: Macmillan, 1987), 13:324–25; *The Mennonite Encyclopedia,* 4 vols. (Hillsboro, Kans.: Mennonite Brethren Pub. House, 1955–59), 3:577–84.

127. *The New Schaff-Herzog Encyclopedia of Religious Knowledge,* 13 vols. (Grand Rapids, Mich.: Baker Book House, 1949–50), 8:43–46.

128. *Mennonite Encyclopedia,* 4:669–71.

129. For an early summary of Swiss Brethren views see John C. Wenger, "The Schleitheim Confession of Faith," *The Mennonite Quarterly Review* 19 (Oct. 1945): 243–53. A critical edition of the German text is Beatrice Jenny, *Das Schleitheimer Täuferbekenntnis 1527* (Thayngen, Switzerland: Karl Augstin, 1951).

130. For an overview see *Encyclopedia of Religion,* 6:542. A monographic study is John A. Hostetler, *Hutterite Society* (Baltimore: The Johns Hopkins University Press, 1974).

131. See *Twentieth Century Encyclopedia of Religious Knowledge,* 1:37.

132. Documentary evidence in Milton Gascho, "The Amish Division of 1693–1697 in Switzerland and Alsace," *The Mennonite Quarterly Review* 11 (Oct. 1937): 235–66. A monograph is John A. Hostetler, *Amish Society,* 3d rev. ed. (Baltimore: The Johns Hopkins University Press, 1980). A different view about the nature of the schism is in Schelbert, "Pietism Rejected," 118–27.

133. A survey from a denominational perspective is Delbert L. Gratz, *Bernese Anabaptists and Their American Descendants* (Scottdale, Pa.: Herald Press, 1953). The migrations of the non-Amish Swiss

Brethren are sketched in Leo Schelbert, *Swiss Migration to America: The Swiss Mennonites* (New York: Arno Press, 1980), 143–261.

134. See Luck, *History of Switzerland,* 305–8, for a description of general events.

135. See, for instance, R. David Edmunds, *Tecumseh and the Quest for Indian Leadership* (Boston: Little, Brown, 1984).

136. See Leo Schelbert, "On Becoming an Emigrant: A Structural View of Eighteenth and Twentieth Century Swiss Data," in *Perspectives in American History* 7 (1974): 473–74, 454 n. 29 for bibliographic references.

137. See S. F. Pannabecker, "The Nineteenth Century Swiss Mennonite Immigrants and Their Adherence to the General Conference Mennonite Church," *The Mennonite Quarterly Review* 21 (Apr. 1947): 64–102, data, 69–70.

138. See *Eine Kurze Chronik der Famillie Lehmann, berichtet von Peter S. Lehmann und Peter Gilliom. Sowie ein Bericht der Reise von der Schweiz nach Amerika von Abraham Zurfluh* (n.p.: Lehmann[?], 1914[?]).

139. Pannabecker, "Nineteenth Century Swiss Mennonite Immigrants and Their Adherence to the General Conference Mennonite Church," 76–77. In the author's view Pannabecker misjudges their religiosity as "externalistic and devoid of substance." The author favors a pietistic, experientially fervent form of Christianity, rejected as alien by the original Swiss tradition. See Schelbert, "Pietism Rejected," 123–24.

140. Catherine Albanese, *America, Religions and Religion* (Belmont, Calif.: Wadsworth, 1981), 283–302.

141. See Pannabecker, "Nineteenth Century Swiss Mennonite Immigrants and Their Adherence to the General Conference Mennonite Church," 99. The table neatly details these shifts.

142. See Edward Liechty, "The Story of Berne," in *1852–1952 Berne Centennial* (Berne, Ind.: Historical Souvenir and Centennial Program, 1952), 5–35; quotation, 13. The booklet is richly illustrated with historically valuable material.

143. Pannabecker, "Nineteenth Century Swiss Mennonite Immigrants and Their Adherence to the General Conference Mennonite Church," 82–87; Gratz, *Bernese Anabaptists and Their American Descendants,* 154–56. Pannabecker views Sprunger's efforts as "revitalizing activities." In actuality he replaced the forms of a vital Swiss Brethren tradition, still powerfully shaping Amish life, with the forms of American Evangelical Protestantism.

144. *Thirtieth Anniversary Souvenir Edition of the Witness: Berne, Ind., Sept. 3, 1926* ([Berne, Ind.: Berne Witness, 1926]), 8.

145. *Berne Review,* 7 Nov. 1935, p. 11.

146. *Tenth Anniversary Souvenir Edition: The Berne Witness, Sept. 4, 1906* ([Berne, Ind.: Berne Witness, 1906]), has seventy-six pages (unpaginated). It gives a brief history, then covers such topics as the fire company, the post office, schools, churches, banks, and stores.

147. Ibid., 13–16; Gratz, *Bernese Anabaptists and Their American Descendants,* 155.

148. Reported by Walter Haas, a linguist, in the article, "Berndeutsch in Berne, Indiana," *Bericht uber das Jahr 1979. Schweizerdeutsches Worterbuch* (Zurich, 1979), 13–14.

149. See *1977 Program for Swiss Days,* unpaginated.

150. See promotional booklet *The Swiss City of Berne, Indiana* (Berne, Ind.: Berne Chamber of Commerce, [1991?]), for numerous illustrations.

151. See S. L. Yoder, "Berne, Ind., Old Order Amish Settlement," *Mennonite Encyclopedia,* 4 vols. plus supplement (1990), 5:71; Schelbert, "Pietism Rejected," 122–24. Brigitte and Eugen Bachmann-Geiser, *Amische-Die Lebensweise der Amischen in Berne, Indiana* (Bern: Benteli Verlag, 1988), is a sympathetic scholarly monograph, based on extensive fieldwork, and uniquely illustrated by watercolors and drawings done on the spot by the noted artist Eugen Bachmann.

152. Robert M. Taylor, Jr. et al., eds., *Indiana: A New Historical Guide* (Indianapolis: Indiana Historical Society, 1989), 41.

153. For his teachings see Samuel Heinrich Fröhlich, *The Mystery of Godliness and the Mystery of Ungodliness: Their Essence and the Contrast between Them Viewed in the Light of the Word of God* (St. Gallen: S. H. Fröhlich, 1838) and "Individual Letters and Meditations" (Syracuse, N.Y.: Apostolic Christian Publishing Co., 1926), typescript letters from between 1836 and 1856.

154. See Perry A. Klopfenstein, *Marching to Zion: A History of the Apostolic Christian Church of America, 1847–1982* (Fort Scott, Kans.: Sekan Printing Co., 1984), 8–151, for a historical sketch of the denomination's origins and early development in the United States.

155. Ibid., 540, 478, 1.

156. Ibid., 90–91; Gratz, *Bernese Anabaptists and Their American Descendants,* 153–54.

157. On the Bluffton congregation see Klopfenstein, *Marching to Zion,* 146–51. His "Index of Congregations" lists the following in Indiana: Bluffton, Bluffton North, Bremen, Francesville, Fort Wayne, Indianapolis, La Crosse, Leo, Milford, Remington, South Bend, Valparaiso, and Wolcott. Swiss family names such as Bächtold, Bolliger, Gerber, Haab, Hauptli, Kaiser, Rudin, Siebenthal, Wüthrich, and Zimmermann are common in the group.

158. The Indiana Historical Society Library has a comprehensive collection of county histories mainly of the later nineteenth and early twentieth centuries that also contain numerous biographical sketches of Swiss.

159. John W. Tyndall and O. E. Lesh, *Standard History of Adams and Wells Counties, Indiana,* 2 vols. in 1 (Chicago: The Lewis Publishing Co., 1918), 757–59, 958–60. Charles Christen's brother William was mayor of Rockford, Ohio. Ibid., 759.

160. See John Caspar Hirshbrunner, Manuscript Collection, SC-1666, Indiana Historical Society Library. The set contains biographical data, the marriage record, and the "Autobiography of John Caspar Hirshbrunner," xi, xiv. Pages i–vii cover Hirshbrunner's extensive travels in Switzerland as a tanner, xi–xii Elizabeth's letter to her brother Leonard Weidmann, xiv the first child's death.

# APPENDIX 1

# Indiana's Ethnicity in the Context of Ethnicity in the Old Northwest in 1850

Gregory S. Rose

Relying upon his knowledge and impressions, Gov. Joseph A. Wright in 1851 claimed, "There is less known abroad, this day, of Indiana, in her great elements of wealth, than of any other State in the Union of her age and position."[1] Nativity data from the 1850 census provide statistical support for Governor Wright's intuitive statement. Indiana was the least ethnically diverse among the five Old Northwest states, having a small portion of the total immigrant population born in foreign countries and a limited number of countries contributing the majority of foreign immigrants. By 1850 the total immigrant stream flowing to the United States was neither as diverse nor as large as it would become in the late nineteenth and early twentieth centuries, since only 11.1 percent of the total population had foreign birthplaces and the vast majority came from western and northern Europe.[2] Slightly more of the total Old Northwest population (12.1 percent) had foreign birthplaces, but the impact of the foreign born within the Old Northwest and within the immigrant stream and among the region's counties varied considerably. Nearly 35 percent of Wisconsin's total population was foreign born; Michigan possessed the next highest proportion with 13.8 percent; Illinois had 13.0 percent and Ohio 11.0 percent. Only 5.5 percent of Indiana's population was foreign born. Comparing Indiana's ethnicity in 1850 to ethnicity in the surrounding Old Northwest states clearly reveals Indiana's small foreign immigrant population (numerically and proportionally least in the region) and the dominance of United States-born immigrants, especially those from the South.[3]

Yet Indiana had an ethnic presence in 1850. Indiana received significant infusions of immigrant settlers from within and beyond the United States, displacing an ethnically diverse Native American population that itself contained recent immigrants. Indiana also held the second largest black population in the Old Northwest.[4] While foreign-born immigrants seem the most obviously ethnic, migrants to Indiana from within the United States reflected the cultural diversity of their birthplaces in nearly every state or territory and of their own particular ethnic ancestry and heritage.[5] Even if "ethnic" is reserved for the foreign born, Indiana's early history is peppered with distinctive and well-known ethnic settlements—French at Vincennes, Swiss at Vevay, and Germans at New Harmony.[6] After 1850 the intensity and diversity of immigration to the United States increased and opportunities in Indiana's expanding urban areas grew, bringing more and different foreign-born immigrants to the state, somewhat enlarging Indiana's ethnic base from its low level in 1850 and leaving a new imprint on many aspects of the state's social, economic, and political history.[7]

The ethnic character of the Old Northwest during and shortly after the settlement period has been examined by a number of authors, mainly relying upon published totals for states in the 1850 and 1860 censuses or on some published totals for counties from the 1870 and subsequent federal censuses.[8] This study, however, draws upon county-based nativity data to analyze ethnicity in the Old Northwest in 1850. That year, following the example of the 1841 British census, the United States census canvassers asked each inhabitant to identify his or her state or country of birth, making the 1850 census the first statistically complete determination of population origins in the United States.[9] Indicators of origins also appear in sources ranging from land settlement records, biographical sketches, and ship passenger lists to analyses of surnames in the 1790 census, but no source can offer the comprehensiveness and representativeness of the 1850 and subsequent censuses.[10] Because it postdates the pioneer period, 1850 is too late for assessing original ethnicity in much of the southern Old Northwest. Where white settlement was oldest, as in Ohio's Gallia County (including Gallipolis), most birthplaces were within the United States and particularly within the state in question. Approximately five hundred French immigrants, duped by unscrupulous agents of the Scioto Company, settled Gallipolis in 1790, yet by 1850 only twenty-three natives of France lived in Gallipolis Township and only thirty-one lived throughout the county. Most French settlers were deceased by 1850 or had moved elsewhere years before.[11] This is not to say that French ethnicity and culture were gone. While the ethnic origins of the population may be obscured by the passage of decades between the initial settlement and 1850, subsequent generations retained at least some of their ancestors' ethnicity, and architecture, churches, place-names, and settlement patterns reflected the original settlers' imprints.[12] In much of the northern Old Northwest, 1850 preceded a great tide of post-Civil War immigration that transformed recently and long settled places. While no single date can be ideal for a region as large as the Old Northwest, 1850 provides the first benchmark against which to compare ethnicity in subsequent years.

In 1850 the foreign-born portion of the Old Northwest population was 12.1 percent; the foreign-born portion of the immigrant population (defined as those born outside the state or region being considered) was 24.7 percent (Table 1). The latter measure permits the taking of a standardized perspective concerning the ethnic impact on each Old Northwest state and the entire region. Examining the foreign-born portion of the immigrant rather than of the total population is superior because the number and percentage of immigrants varied considerably from state to state. Wisconsin had the largest percentage (81.6) of its total population comprised of immigrants from other states and countries; Ohio had the lowest at 32.5 percent; and Indiana's 47 percent was the next lowest. Differences among states basically reflected the duration of non-Native American settlement. Ohio, the "oldest" state according to length of settlement, date of statehood, overall population density, and other measures had the lowest immigrant percentage. Wisconsin, the "youngest" state, had the largest immigrant percentage. Over time, as the pioneer era in the Old Northwest receded, the percentage of immigrants within each state's total population declined.[13] Foreign-born immigrant percentages varied greatly from state to state (from a low of 12.3 percent in Indiana to a high of 44 percent in Wisconsin), and the sources of immigration differed significantly. Table 1 lists the fourteeen countries or groups of associated countries supplying the most foreign-born immigrants. Germany provided the largest percentage in the Old Northwest (10.4 percent) and in each state except Michigan, where Canadians ranked first. But the German percentage ranged from as much as 15.7 percent in Wisconsin and 15.0 percent in Ohio to 6.6 percent in Indiana and to as little as 4.0 percent in Michigan. The Irish formed the second largest foreign immigrant group at 5.7 percent, with Wisconsin having the largest percentage (8.8) and Indiana having the lowest (3.0).

The English were the next largest group, accounting for 3.6 percent of immigrants. Other foreign-born immigrants accounted for significant percentages in some states but not in others. Canadian natives comprised 5.5 percent of Michigan's immigrants but only 0.5 percent in Indiana. The Welsh born were 1.6 percent of Wisconsin's immigrants, 0.8 percent in Ohio, and barely over or less than 0.1 percent in the other three states. Natives of the Netherlands formed a notable portion of the ethnic immigrants in Michigan (1.2 percent) and Wisconsin (0.7 percent) but were rare in Illinois, Indiana, and Ohio. Scandinavians accounted for 3.5 percent of the immigrant population in Wisconsin but hardly any in Indiana and Ohio. Blacks were another component of the Old Northwest's ethnic diversity. Only Ohio had more blacks than Indiana (25,279 compared to 11,296) and only in Ohio did they form a larger portion of the population (1.3 percent compared to 1.1 percent). Together, Ohio and Indiana contained over three quarters of the region's blacks. In years to come, particularly during the twentieth century, blacks would significantly increase their presence in the Old Northwest, yet they were among the first immigrants.

The number or percentage of foreign immigrants also varied among counties within each state, but these locationally specific data must be taken from the manuscript census schedules.[14] The author has collected nativity data by county from the manuscript schedules of the 1850 census for Illinois, Indiana, Michigan, and Wisconsin; the Ohio data were collected and published by H. G. H. Wilhelm with additional counting by this researcher.[15] Beginning with the 1850 manuscript schedules, the nativity of inhabitants in each United States county can be analyzed. County data for each ethnic group were transformed into percentages by comparing the number of natives from each country to the county's total immigrant population, revealing significant variations in foreign immigrant percentages from county to county within and among states. For example, only 0.3 percent of the immigrants in Johnson County, Illinois, and 0.6 percent in Johnson County, Indiana, had foreign birthplaces (no foreigners lived in Midland County, Michigan). As many as 77.2 percent of the immigrants in Washington County, Wisconsin, and 88.3 percent in Houghton County, Michigan, had foreign birthplaces. Also revealed were significant county to county variations in specific immigrant groups. For example, Germans among the immigrants ranged from only 0.1 percent in Clay County, Illinois (no Germans lived in Johnson, Piatt, and Williamson counties) and Branch County, Michigan (no Germans lived in Midland, Montcalm, and Schoolcraft counties) to as much as 54.1 percent in St. Clair County, Illinois, 56.6

**Table 1. Number and Percent of Natives of Foreign Countries Living in the Old Northwest in 1850**

| | | Ger | Swi | Ire | Wal | Eng | Sco | Fra | Den |
|---|---|---|---|---|---|---|---|---|---|
| Illinois | # | 39,681 | 1,665 | 27,920 | 573 | 18,305 | 4,773 | 3,453 | 72 |
| | % | 7.7 | 0.3 | 5.4 | 0.1 | 3.6 | 0.9 | 0.7 | .01 |
| Indiana | # | 30,398 | 735 | 13,667 | 156 | 5,542 | 1,371 | 2,414 | 8 |
| | % | 6.6 | 0.2 | 3.0 | .03 | 1.2 | 0.3 | 0.5 | .002 |
| Michigan | # | 10,248 | 114 | 13,290 | 130 | 10,633 | 2,321 | 953 | 11 |
| | % | 4.0 | 0.04 | 5.1 | 0.1 | 4.1 | 0.9 | 0.4 | .004 |
| Ohio | # | 112,990 | 3,208 | 51,874 | 5,876 | 26,214 | 4,110 | 7,388 | 38 |
| | % | 15.0 | 0.4 | 6.9 | 0.8 | 3.5 | 0.7 | 1.0 | .005 |
| Wisconsin | # | 39,030 | 1,281 | 21,829 | 4,040 | 19,245 | 3,611 | 788 | 161 |
| | % | 15.7 | 0.5 | 8.8 | 1.6 | 7.7 | 1.5 | 0.3 | .06 |
| **ONW Total** | # | 232,247 | 7,003 | 128,580 | 10,775 | 79,939 | 17,186 | 14,996 | 290 |
| | % | 10.4 | 0.3 | 5.7 | 0.5 | 3.6 | 0.8 | 0.7 | .01 |

| | | Net | Bel | Nor | Swe | Can | Car | Bla | For |
|---|---|---|---|---|---|---|---|---|---|
| Illinois | # | 346 | 37 | 2,335 | 1,115 | 11,104 | 85 | 5,418 | 112,429 |
| | % | 0.1 | .01 | 0.5 | 0.1 | 2.2 | .02 | 0.6 | 21.8 |
| Indiana | # | 85 | 95 | 18 | 21 | 2,075 | 16 | 11,296 | 56,932 |
| | % | .02 | .02 | .004 | .01 | 0.5 | .003 | 1.1 | 12.3 |
| Michigan | # | 3,174 | 111 | 104 | 23 | 14,202 | 38 | 2,357 | 55,571 |
| | % | 1.2 | .04 | .04 | .01 | 5.5 | .01 | 0.6 | 21.4 |
| Ohio | # | 406 | 70 | 25 | 45 | 5,816 | 105 | 25,279 | 219,763 |
| | % | .05 | .01 | .002 | .006 | 0.8 | .01 | 1.3 | 29.1 |
| Wisconsin | # | 1,623 | 47 | 8,635 | 87 | 8,641 | 30 | 637 | 109,766 |
| | % | 0.7 | .02 | 3.4 | .03 | 3.5 | .01 | 0.2 | 44.0 |
| **ONW Total** | # | 5,634 | 360 | 11,117 | 1,291 | 41,838 | 274 | 44,987 | 554,461 |
| | % | 0.3 | .02 | 0.5 | .06 | 1.9 | .01 | 1.0 | 24.7 |

Abbreviations:

| | | | | | | | |
|---|---|---|---|---|---|---|---|
| Ger | = Germany | Eng | = England | Net | = Netherlands | Can | = Canada |
| Swi | = Switzerland | Sco | = Scotland | Bel | = Belgium | Car | = Caribbean |
| Ire | = Ireland | Fra | = France | Nor | = Norway | Bla | = Black |
| Wal | = Wales | Den | = Denmark | Swe | = Sweden | ONW | = Old Northwest |

*The number is a count of the natives of each country or countries living in the Old Northwest according to manuscript schedules of the 1850 census. The percentage is of the total immigrant population, defined as those not native to the state in question. Black population percentages are of the total population.*

percent in Auglaize County, Ohio, 57.9 percent in Washington County, Wisconsin, and 58.1 percent in Dubois County, Indiana.

Maps displaying these data show areas of concentration and relative absence and present a snapshot of the distribution of foreign immigrants, but two caveats must be observed when comparing percentages and examining maps. First, the immigrant and the total population varied considerably from county to county. Over 76,000 immigrants resided in Hamilton County, Ohio, but only 16 in Schoolcraft County, Michigan. If, for example, 50 percent of the immigrants in both counties were foreign, they would number over 38,000 or just 8, respectively. And a county below the Old Northwest average could contain more foreign natives than an above average county. For example, in LaPointe County,

Wisconsin, 36 foreign natives comprised 52.2 percent of all the immigrants (well over twice the Old Northwest average), while in Muskingum County, Ohio, 3,891 foreign natives comprised 24.0 percent of all the immigrants, slightly below the Old Northwest average. Second, county area varied considerably: Ohio County, Indiana, included 87 square miles, while Mackinac County, Michigan, included approximately 14,100 square miles. Most northern, less populated counties were larger than the older, southern counties in 1850, but as population increased the northern counties were subdivided: the Michilimackinac County of 1850 yielded twenty-three complete counties and parts of five others by 1920.[16] County area did not necessarily correspond to county population: huge Michilimackinac County held 3,598 inhabitants at a population density of 0.3 persons per square mile, while Ohio County's 5,308 inhabitants were more tightly packed at 61 persons per square mile. The enormous size of Michilimackinac County causes the shaded pattern indicating an above average foreign presence to make a far greater visual impact than it would for Ohio County.

## Foreign Natives

In 1850, 24.7 percent of the Old Northwest's immigrant population had been born in foreign countries (Table 1). The foreign immigrant percentage in Ohio (29.1 percent), Illinois (21.8 percent), and Michigan (21.4 percent) approximated the Old Northwest average, while in Wisconsin 44.0 percent of the immigrant population was native to foreign countries. Only Indiana fell considerably below average at 12.3 percent. The distribution of counties having foreign immigrants in greater percentage than Old Northwest average percentage is shown in Figure 1. Even a quick glance at this map reveals a characteristic "clustering" of the foreign immigrants into certain counties, with settlement concentrations often in particular townships. Foreigners with languages, religions, or customs different from the host society regularly clustered together since they often arrived in groups or selected new homes in locations already settled by persons from their Old Country.[17] Associating with relatives, friends, neighbors, or fellow ethnics offered advantages to newly arrived immigrants. The compatriots shared their culture and assisted the immigrants by providing shelter, food, clothing, and funds, and they benefited from the experiences of established immigrants as they "learned the ropes" and sought land and opportunities in America. The chain migration of relatives, friends, and neighbors lured to the new settlement by earlier immigrants' glowing descriptions reinforced clustering. Sometimes a few pioneers made arrangements for new arrivals and then returned to the homeland to lead others to the promised land. Other times money and instructions sent to the homeland assisted the next wave of immigrants. Sometimes the next wave simply came alone, guided by the presumed destinations of earlier immigrants. Less geographically extensive but no less homogeneous, clusters of immigrants appeared in some urban centers. While county-level analysis is too broad to permit outlines of urban ethnic clusters or ghettos to be distinguished, counties containing large and moderately sized urban centers in 1850 tended to hold foreign-born immigrants in greater than average percentages. For example, counties surrounding Cincinnati, Detroit, Chicago, and Milwaukee, and counties across the Mississippi River

from St. Louis, all had above average percentages of foreign immigrants. In Indiana, counties including New Albany, Madison, Fort Wayne, and Evansville also held above average foreign percentages, but those including Indianapolis and Jeffersonville did not.

Nearly every Wisconsin and northern Michigan county had greater than average foreign immigrant percentages, but farther south their settlement concentrations clearly reflect the importance of access to waterways, for in the interior of Indiana, the southern Lower Peninsula of Michigan, and central Illinois, foreign immigrant percentages regularly fell below the Old Northwest average. Wisconsin's largest foreign immigrant percentages, up to 77.2 percent in Washington County, occurred close to Lake Michigan. Large percentages also appeared in the southwest near the Mississippi River, including Iowa County (63.5 percent). Ohio's foreign immigrant percentage (29.1) was the next largest, with above average percentages scattered in counties around the state. In Auglaize County in the west center, 61.5 percent of the immigrants were foreign born; in the north close to Lake Erie and westward along the Maumee River, 45.5 percent of the immigrants in Lucas, 43.8 percent in Putnam, and 51.6 percent in Cuyahoga counties were foreign. Counties in southwest Ohio near the Ohio River included many foreign natives among the immigrants, such as the 68.0 percent in Hamilton County (Cincinnati). Two major concentrations of counties in Illinois held many foreign natives. In the southwest, 66.5 percent of the immigrants (the largest percentage) were foreign in St. Clair County across the Mississippi River from St. Louis, while 63.5 percent of immigrants in the northeast's Cook County (Chicago) were foreign. Jo Daviess County in the northwest, with 52.3 percent foreign immigrants, did not fit the generalization but was part of the lead mining district that attracted many foreign laborers. Foreign natives comprised 82.3 percent of Houghton County's immigrants in Michigan's Upper Peninsula. In the west central Lower Peninsula along Lake Michigan, large percentages appeared in Ottawa (59.1 percent) and Oceana (46.8 percent) counties, while in the eastern and southeastern Lower Peninsula, foreign immigrants formed significant percentages in Sanilac (65.3) and Wayne (53.0) counties.

Nearly all Indiana counties holding foreign immigrants in greater than average percentages fell within the southern third of the state. The largest value, 65.0 percent, appeared in Vanderburgh (Evansville) and Dubois (58.7 percent) counties in the southwest. In the southeast, 41.5 percent of immigrants in Dearborn County (Lawrenceburg) had foreign birthplaces and in Floyd County (New Albany), in the south center on the Ohio River, 34.5 percent had foreign birthplaces. The two above average counties in

# Figure 1

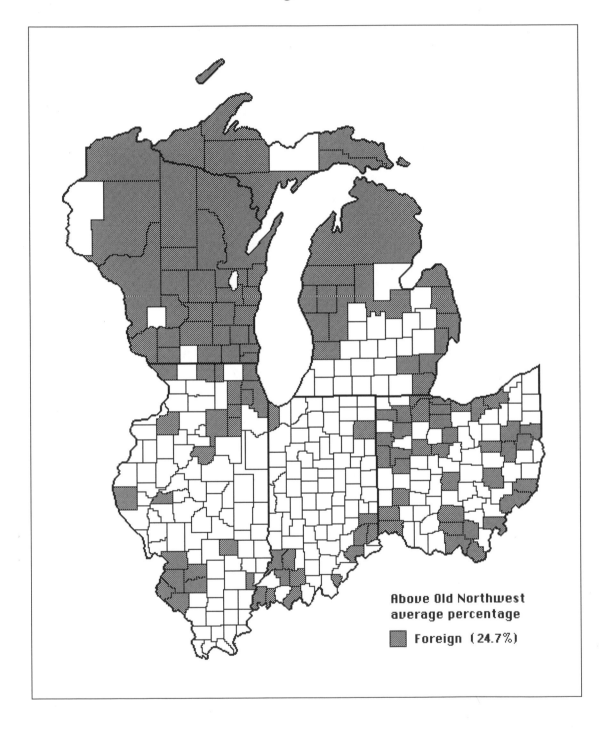

Above Old Northwest
average percentage

Foreign (24.7%)

northern Indiana were Allen (Fort Wayne) in the northeast with 33.7 percent and Lake in the extreme northwest with 30.4 percent. Foreign immigrant percentages fell below the Old Northwest average throughout the remainder of Indiana, giving it the fewest number (14 of 91) and least percentage (15.4) of counties with above average foreign immigrant concentrations in the Old Northwest. The smallest foreign immigrant percentages generally appeared in central counties, where Johnson had the lowest percentage at 0.6 (30 individuals) and Boone, a little to the north, was next at 1 percent.

### Natives of Germany and Switzerland

Germans always formed one of the largest immigrant groups, especially during the century before and the century after the American Revolution.[18] Their immigration was motivated primarily by economic opportunities, although religious freedom for Amish, Mennonites, and others and political freedom for those fleeing upheavals such as the 1848 Revolution encouraged immigration.[19] Although occasional German immigrants arrived during most of the seventeenth century, often in the company of Dutch colonists, large-scale immigration began when William Penn invited German Protestants to join his Quaker colony of Pennsylvania where they established Germantown in 1683. Another major influx of German settlers resulted from the exodus of thousands of Palatinates to England in 1709. Eventually, nearly three thousand were sent to England's New York colony, from where many moved to Pennsylvania. Economic opportunity, religious tolerance, and political freedom experienced by Germans in America, coupled with inducements by agents for colonial proprietors and shipping companies, drew additional immigrants. They settled along the seaboard but also moved into the back country, beginning to penetrate the Shenandoah and other valleys after 1760. Estimates drawn from the first United States census in 1790 indicate that nearly 9 percent of the population was ethnically German and that Pennsylvania, which continued to be their primary focus, was as much as one-third German.[20]

Between 1820 and 1850 Germans typically were the second largest group among newly arriving immigrants, and only Irish natives comprised a larger portion of the foreign-born population in the United States in 1850.[21] German immigrants usually avoided "New England and the South in favor of the middle Atlantic, east north-central, and west north-central states" and in particular "perceived greater opportunity in the newly opened farmland and frontier cities of the Midwest."[22] Germans comprised 10.4 percent of the Old Northwest immigrants with

232,347, were nearly twice as numerous as any other foreign group, and appeared in nationally significant numbers. Only New York had more German natives than Ohio in 1850 (120,609 compared to 112,990), and Illinois, Wisconsin, and Indiana ranked fifth, sixth, and seventh, respectively, in number of Germans (Table 1). Within the Old Northwest Germans formed as much as 15.7 percent of the immigrant population in Wisconsin (and 15.0 percent in Ohio) and as little as 4.0 percent in Michigan. Their county distribution also varied, reflecting in particular the importance of accessibility (Figure 2). Counties along the Great Lakes, the Ohio and Mississippi rivers, or connecting rivers and canals tended to house larger percentages of Germans. They also found the urban centers of Cincinnati (and neighboring Dearborn County, Indiana), Milwaukee, Chicago, and St. Louis, reflected in the large German population across the river in southwestern Illinois. Smaller cities such as Columbus, Ohio, and Evansville and New Albany, Indiana, had large German populations by 1850, as did many predominantly rural counties.

Germans comprised by far the largest portion of the immigrant population in Wisconsin, especially in the eastern third of the state closest to Lake Michigan. Here were the state's highest German immigrant percentages, ranging from 57.9 percent in Washington County to 27.9 percent in Sheboygan County. Yet counties in south central, central, and northwestern parts of the state had low German percentages. Ohio had the second largest German portion (15.0 percent) among the immigrants. Some of the strong German presence may be associated with the large number of Pennsylvania Dutch or Pennsylvania Germans found especially across central Ohio.[23] The highest German percentages appeared in Auglaize County (56.6 percent) in the west center. Putnam County (34.8 percent) in the northwest contained many Germans. In southwestern Ohio, Cincinnati's Hamilton (41.5 percent) and Pike (31.6 percent) counties were heavily populated by Germans, whose immigrants also made a significant impact on Tuscarawas County in the east center (30.3 percent) (the location of the German settlements of Schoenbrunn, Zoar, and Gnadenhutten) and neighboring Stark (22.3 percent) and Holmes (18.4 percent) containing many Amish and Mennonites. Illinois had 7.7 percent of its immigrants native to Germany. The highest percentages were found in St. Clair (54.1) and Monroe (50.0) counties in southwest Illinois across from St. Louis, while counties in the northeast, especially Cook (Chicago) at 28.3 percent and Du Page (19.1 percent), held large German percentages. Germans comprised less than 1 percent of immigrants in most interior counties of Illinois, especially in the east center. Saginaw

# Figure 2

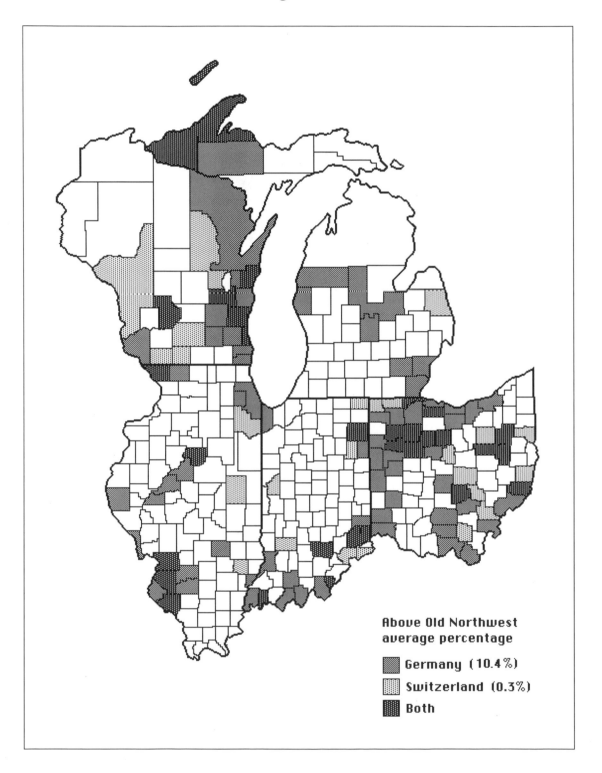

Above Old Northwest
average percentage

Germany (10.4%)

Switzerland (0.3%)

Both

County in the central Lower Peninsula of Michigan, containing the settlement of Frankenmuth, had 31.0 percent of its immigrants born in Germany. Three counties in the southeastern Lower Peninsula, including Wayne (14.2 percent), held greater than average German immigrant percentages as did western Upper Peninsula counties, especially Houghton (23.1 percent). German immigrant percentages of less than 1 percent appeared in the southwestern Lower Peninsula.

Germans accounted for 6.6 percent of Indiana's immigrants, below the Old Northwest average of 10.4 percent, although many counties had considerably above average percentages.[24] German concentrations commonly appeared in the southern quarter of Indiana, particularly along the Ohio River. Extraordinarily high percentages occurred in two southwestern counties: Dubois (at 58.1 percent having the largest German immigrant proportion in the Old Northwest) and Vanderburgh (44.9 percent). In the former county German settlers were almost exclusively rural, while in the latter many lived in Evansville on the Ohio River. Two other southwestern counties, Posey (18.5 percent), which contained the German social experiment of New Harmony, and Knox (20.7 percent) also held many German settlers. In southeastern Indiana German immigrant percentages were high in Dearborn County (26.2 percent) adjacent to the large German population in Cincinnati, and in Ripley (21.4 percent) and Franklin (20.1 percent) counties. In the south center along or near the Ohio River, counties including Spencer (22 percent), Jackson (17.1 percent), Floyd (16.9 percent), and Harrison (16.7 percent) held German immigrants in above average percentages. Germans comprised 21.1 percent of the immigrants in Allen (Fort Wayne) and 17.8 percent in Adams counties in the northeast while in the northwest 19.9 percent of Lake County's immigrants were German.

An estimated forty-five to fifty-five thousand Swiss immigrants had arrived in the United States by 1850. The multilingual nature of Switzerland compounded the difficulty of estimating since it caused confusion between German-speaking Swiss and Germans, French-speaking Swiss and French, and Italian-speaking Swiss and Italians, although the recording of self-reported birthplaces should have eliminated this problem in the 1850 census.[25] The religious freedom America offered drew many Swiss members of Brethren, Amish, or Mennonite congregations. While a few came before 1700, larger numbers followed, often settling first in association with Germans in Pennsylvania and then spreading westward with America's expansion. Many chose the Old Northwest and established some well known settlements. Although Swiss natives accounted for just 0.3 percent of the Old

Northwest's immigrant population in 1850, the region held a large portion of those residing in the United States. Well over half of the 13,358 Swiss natives lived in the Old Northwest and nearly one quarter resided in Ohio (Table 1).[26] Differences in Swiss immigrant proportions within the Old Northwest were narrow—0.5 percent in Wisconsin, 0.4 percent in Ohio, 0.3 percent in Illinois, 0.2 percent in Indiana—except Michigan had only 0.04 percent.

Because of the relatively small Swiss presence in the Old Northwest, counties having above average Swiss immigrant percentages scattered around the region (Figure 2). Two counties in southwestern Wisconsin, Sauk (8.8 percent) and Green (5.3 percent, including New Glarus), held high concentrations of Swiss immigrants. In every other county Swiss immigrant percentages were below 1.0 percent, and few or no Swiss lived in central and northwestern Wisconsin. Two areas of Ohio contained most of the counties with above average concentrations of Swiss immigrants. In the east-southeast the largest percentage of Swiss immigrants occurred in Monroe County (6.1), and nearby Tuscarawas County had 5.4 percent of its immigrants native to Switzerland. Northwest Ohio included Fulton County with 3.4 percent Swiss immigrants and Hardin County with 3.3 percent. Only nine Illinois counties contained Swiss immigrants in above average percentages, including Madison (8.5 percent) and Bond (2.0 percent) counties in southwest Illinois across from St. Louis, while forty-one counties held no Swiss natives. Just three Michigan counties, two in the western Upper Peninsula and one in the Thumb region of the Lower Peninsula, had slightly above average Swiss immigrant percentages.

Only 0.2 percent of Indiana's immigrants had Swiss birthplaces in 1850, although the Swiss were early and conspicuous settlers. The largest group of counties with above average Swiss immigrant percentages were in the southeast—Switzerland County had 1.1 percent of its immigrants born in its namesake. The settlement's core consisted of Swiss natives who arrived in 1802 from the Vevay District to establish vineyards for wine making.[27] In 1850 the settlement was nearly half a century old, and most of the original settlers were deceased (only fifty-one Swiss natives lived in the county). However, descendants continued their ethnic influence. Neighboring or nearby counties housing greater than average percentages of Swiss immigrants included Jackson (0.9 percent), Jefferson (0.8 percent), Ripley (0.4 percent), and Dearborn and Floyd (0.3 percent each). A small group of northeastern counties held above average percentages, especially Wells County which, with 2.1 percent Swiss immigrants, contained the state's largest percentage. Neighboring Allen County's percentage was 0.8 and Steuben County, in the northeastern corner, had 0.3 percent. Additional counties with Swiss immigrants in above average percentages scattered around the state were Vanderburgh County in the southwest with 0.4 percent of its immigrants born in Switzerland, to the north Greene County had 1.0 percent, in west central Indiana Swiss natives comprised 0.3 percent of the immigrants in Fountain County, and in the northwest Pulaski County had 0.3 percent Swiss. Few Swiss lived elsewhere, and none lived in thirty-nine of Indiana's counties.

### Natives of Ireland and Wales

Irish were among the first Europeans to settle in America, arriving in significant numbers in Virginia as early as the 1620s.[28] Some were Ulster Protestants, or Scotch-Irish, while many were Roman Catholics from throughout the island. Roman Catholics hoped, as did the Protestants, to benefit from the chronic labor shortage in the New World and its economic opportunities but the Catholics also sought, and often failed to find, religious toleration. Many Irish did not possess the funds necessary for the ocean voyage and so indentured themselves or became redemptioners. Combined, Roman Catholic and Protestant Irish formed the largest non-English ethnic group in the United States before the Revolution, and by 1790 approximately "400,000 people of Irish birth or descent" lived in the United States, "about half from an Ulster background."[29] From 1820 to 1850 the Irish failed to form the largest group of registered arrivals only in 1846, and by 1850 Irish natives in the United States vastly outnumbered the second-ranking Germans, 961,719 to 583,774.[30] However, in the Old Northwest the Irish comprised the second largest group of immigrants, with 128,580 natives compared to Germans, or 5.7 percent of the region's immigrants (Table 1). Irish percentages varied from state to state less than other ethnic groups, reaching 8.8 percent of the immigrants in Wisconsin, 6.9 percent in Ohio, 5.4 percent in Illinois, 5.1 percent in Michigan, and 3.0 percent in Indiana. Not only did Indiana have the smallest percentage, but also only eleven of its ninety-one counties had Irish immigrant percentages greater than the Old Northwest average.

The distribution of Irish natives coincided with the location of waterways that not only made reaching their destinations easier but also provided employment (Figure 3). Irish laborers helped build canals and railroads across the Old Northwest states to link the Great Lakes with the Ohio and Mississippi rivers and the East with the West.[31] Wisconsin had the largest Irish immigrant percentage,

with below average Irish percentages in only five counties, less than 2 percent in only one county, and no Irish natives in only one county. Southeastern counties including Milwaukee (17.2 percent) held especially high percentages of Irish natives as did the southwestern lead mining district, where Lafayette County's immigrants were 21.1 percent Irish. Ohio had many counties with above average percentages of Irish and only five counties in which Irish natives comprised less than 1 percent of the immigrants. In the east and east center, counties such as Carroll (12.9 percent), Perry (12.3 percent), and Jefferson (12.1 percent) held many Irish; in the northwest Lucas County had 15.2 percent Irish immigrants; in the southwest Hamilton County (Cincinnati) had 17.6 percent of its immigrants native to Ireland.

The largest group of Illinois counties with above average Irish percentages occurred in the northeast, including Cook County (Chicago) with 21.0 percent. Jo Daviess County in the northwestern lead mining district had 18.4 percent of its immigrants native to Ireland. Southwestern counties across from St. Louis, including Randolph (11.4 percent) and Monroe (9.4 percent), also held high proportions of Irish immigrants. Every county in Michigan's Upper Peninsula contained Irish in greater than average percentages (the largest percent, 19.5, occurred in Ontonagon County), and strongly above average percentages appeared adjacent to Canada in the eastern and southeastern Lower Peninsula, particularly in Wayne County (Detroit) with 15.3 percent and Huron County with 13.3 percent. Irish and other British immigrants commonly took advantage of cheaper trans-atlantic fares to the British colony of Canada, reaching their ultimate goal by crossing into a border state such as Michigan.[32]

Indiana had the smallest Irish immigrant percentage of any Old Northwest state and the fewest counties, mostly in the southern third of the state, with above average percentages of Irish.[33] The greatest Irish immigrant percentages were in neighboring Pike (24.1 percent) and Daviess (21.1 percent) counties in the southwest. In nearby Vanderburgh County (Evansville) 7.3 percent of the immigrants were native to Ireland. Southeastern Indiana counties held large percentages, including 11.8 in Jefferson (Madison), 8.5 in Dearborn (Lawrenceburg), 8.3 in Jennings, and 6.4 in Ohio. Lawrence County in south central Indiana had 6.8 percent Irish immigrants, and in Floyd County (New Albany) on the Ohio River the percentage was 6.7. In northern Indiana only Tippecanoe County (8.6 percent) contained an above average percentage of Irish, although they were present throughout the region. Forty counties had Irish immigrant percentages below 1 percent.

# Figure 3

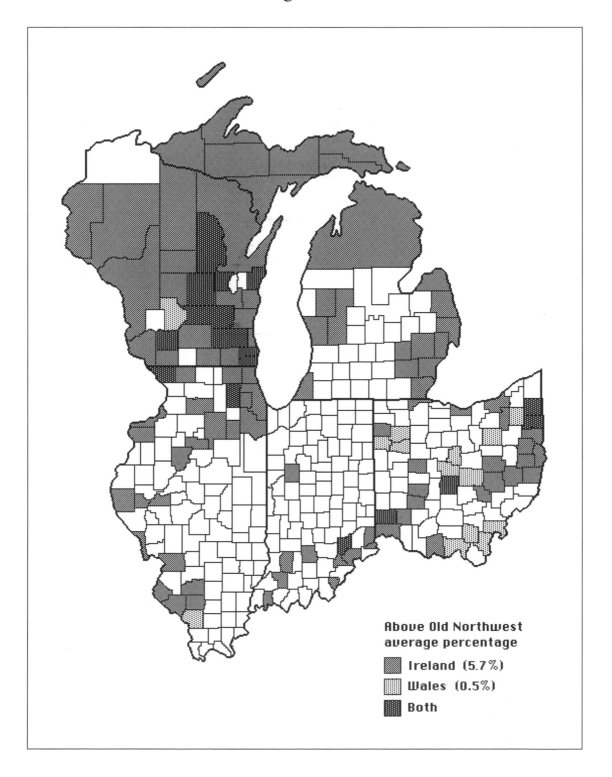

Above Old Northwest
average percentage
Ireland (5.7%)
Wales (0.5%)
Both

In 1667 Rhode Island received the first recorded settlement of Welsh in the United States.[34] Some early Welsh immigrants came to form colonies of religious separatists: the Rhode Island colony and another in the late 1790s in Pennsylvania were led by Baptists, while Welsh Quakers tried to build a Pennsylvania colony in the 1680s. A changing rural economic system, a rapidly growing population, and an economic depression following poor harvests in the 1790s supported a significant increase in Welsh immigration after the War of 1812. Welsh appeared in many locations throughout the northern United States, first in Pennsylvania and then, as frontiers opened and new opportunities emerged, they settled in Ohio, Wisconsin, and beyond the Mississippi River. Employment in stone quarries, mines, and metal smelting attracted some Welsh natives. By 1850 they numbered 29,868 with about 90 percent of them living, in descending order, in Pennsylvania, New York, Ohio, and Wisconsin.[35] Although fewer than eleven thousand natives of Wales, or 0.5 percent of the immigrants, lived in the Old Northwest, the region contained one-third of the nation's Welsh (Table 1). Their relatively low number and percentage explain their scattered distribution in the Old Northwest (Figure 3).

Wisconsin had a smaller number of Welsh natives than Ohio but a greater percentage of Welsh inhabitants of any other Old Northwest state. Counties in the center including Columbia (8.7 percent) and in the southwestern lead mining district including Iowa (8.1 percent) held natives of Wales above the Old Northwest average. Most Ohio counties had at least some Welsh natives among their immigrants. Central counties such as Licking (5.6 percent) and Delaware (5.2 percent) held many Welsh natives, while in the extreme south center near the Ohio River counties such as Meigs (4.7 percent), Gallia (8.9 percent), and especially Jackson (24.1 percent), the focus of early mining and smelting, attracted Welsh settlers. Only three Illinois counties had Welsh natives in slightly above average percentages, including Jo Daviess County (0.9 percent) in the northwestern lead mining district. No Michigan county had an above average percentage of immigrants native to Wales. In Indiana only Jennings County in the southeast (0.7 percent and thirty-three Welsh natives) had Welsh in excess of the Old Northwest average. Only Jennings and neighboring Jefferson County contained more than ten Welsh natives, and more than half of Indiana's counties had no Welsh residents in 1850.

### Natives of England and Scotland

Although the English were not the first European settlers in North America, their social and political culture became dominant, making assimilation of subsequent English immigrants relatively easy.[36] Their immigration was motivated by economic opportunity, the chance to establish large proprietary holdings and, for some, the desire to escape persecution. In 1607 the English established a foothold at Jamestown, Virginia, and during the rest of the century additional English immigrants arrived, initially establishing settlements around Chesapeake Bay and in New England. By 1700 approximately 90 percent of the colonial population in what became the United States was of English ethnicity. English immigration to the American colonies continued during the 1700s, while increasing emigration from other places, especially Germany, Ireland, and Africa (an involuntary emigration, to be sure), changed America's ethnic mix. As a result, by the time of the American Revolution only an estimated half of the population had English ethnicity, and after independence, countries other than England, at first Ireland and Germany, supplied the largest number of immigrants. But before 1850, in the absence of nativity data, it often is difficult to separate English natives from natives of other areas having much English ethnicity such as Scotland, Wales, and Canada.

English natives were scattered around the United States in 1850.[37] The three most populous states in 1850—New York, Pennsylvania, and Ohio—also contained the largest numbers of English natives. The fourth largest number of persons born in England resided in Wisconsin; the fifth largest number lived in Illinois. English natives accounted for 3.6 percent of the Old Northwest's immigrants, making them the third largest foreign-born group (Table 1). In Wisconsin, English natives comprised 7.7 percent of the immigrants, and in Michigan they comprised 4.1 percent; in Illinois they formed 3.6 percent, and in Ohio they formed 3.5 percent. Indiana's English immigrant percentage of 1.2 was the least among Old Northwest states. The distribution of counties with above average concentrations of English natives in 1850 reveals an apparent avoidance of Indiana and for the most part of neighboring west central Ohio and east central and central Illinois (Figure 4). Cornish men and women from the mining district of southwestern England, including Cornwall County, dominated among the English immigrants in areas of the Old Northwest.[38] Large-scale immigration began in the 1830s and, at the urging of compatriots already in America, most new arrivals settled first in the southwestern Wisconsin and northwestern Illinois lead mining districts, later moving on to copper and iron mining areas in the Lake Superior region. Replicating their life in Cornwall, many miners purchased land and became part-time farmers.

Wisconsin was the most "English" state in percentage, with every county having at least one immigrant from

# Figure 4

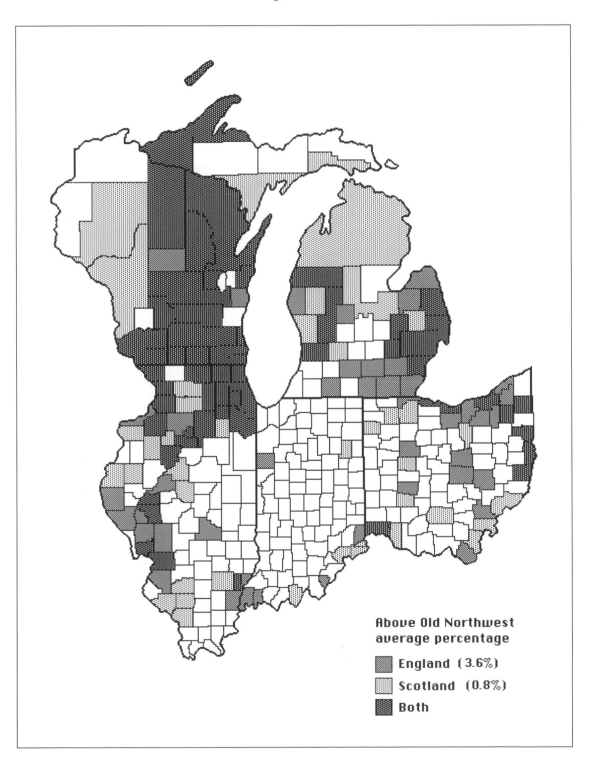

**Above Old Northwest
average percentage**

England ( 3.6% )

Scotland ( 0.8% )

Both

England and some having fifteen hundred or more. In the southwestern lead mining district, Iowa (37.2 percent English immigrants), Lafayette (23.0 percent), and Grant (16.7 percent) counties contained so many miners from England that one author claims by "1850 some 6,000 Cornish immigrants and their children were living in Grant, Iowa, and Lafayette" counties.[39] Significant percentages also occurred in some central and southeastern counties. Most Upper Peninsula counties in Michigan had very large English immigrant percentages (Houghton County's was 42.9) but small overall populations. A few west central Lower Peninsula counties had above average percentages of English natives as did most counties in the southeastern Lower Peninsula closest to Canada. English immigrant concentrations were common in northern Illinois counties. Significantly above average percentages appeared in the northeastern county of Cook (7.9 percent) and in the northwestern county of Jo Daviess (15.2 percent) in the lead mining district. In 1850, according to one author, Jo Daviess County, Illinois, and Dubuque, Iowa, shared as many as three thousand Cornish natives and descendants.[40] By far the greatest English immigrant concentration, 31.2 percent, occurred in the southeast in Edwards County, Illinois, home of Morris Birkbeck and George Flower's English Prairie settlement at Albion.[41] Few English lived in east central Illinois and in the extreme southern region known as "Egypt." The highest English immigrant percentages in Ohio appeared around its northern, eastern, and southeastern margins and in some central counties. Counties along or close to Lake Erie, such as Cuyahoga (13.9 percent) in the northeast and Lucas (8.2 percent) in the northwest, housed many English immigrants. In the southwest, Hamilton County (Cincinnati) on the Ohio River had 5.2 percent of its immigrants native to England. The lowest English percentages generally were found in the west center.

Few Indiana counties, mostly those scattered along the Ohio River, displayed above average English immigrant percentages. In the southwest, Vanderburgh County (Evansville) had 11.0 percent of its immigrants born in England; in neighboring Posey County the percentage was 3.8. Floyd (4.1 percent, including New Albany) and Perry (3.6 percent) counties in south central Indiana held many English immigrants, as did Dearborn County (Lawrenceburg) in the southeast with 3.9 percent. In northwestern Indiana Benton County had 3.7 percent of its immigrants born in England. Immigrants in over sixty Indiana counties were less than 1 percent English, although at least two English natives resided in every county.

The political association between England and Scotland began at the same time as English colonial settlement in North America, and Scottish immigrants were among the first arrivals in the American colonies. The Highlands region supplied many Scottish immigrants as did Ulster, an initial colonization locale for many Scots who as Scotch-Irish later continued their immigration to America.[42] All varieties of Scots merged quickly into the colonial population, commonly settling in Pennsylvania, Virginia, and North Carolina, although a few unsuccessful colonies of dissenters and others began during the 1680s in New Jersey and South Carolina. By 1790 an estimated 260,000 Scottish natives and descendants lived in the United States. Early on they moved westward into the interior, appearing in Kentucky by 1773, Ohio by 1779, and beyond the Mississippi River within the first decades of the 1800s. In 1850, 70,550 natives of Scotland resided in the United States, almost one-third of them residing in New York.[43] Pennsylvania ranked second among the states, with Ohio third, Illinois fourth, and Wisconsin sixth. In the Old Northwest natives of Scotland comprised 0.8 percent of the immigrants and were distributed in a pattern largely similar to that of English natives (Table 1; Figure 4). Only in Wisconsin (1.5 percent) did they exceed 1 percent of the immigrants, although in Illinois and Michigan they reached 0.9 percent.

All but seven Wisconsin counties exceeded the average Scottish immigrant percentage in the Old Northwest. Percentages were highest in the central portion of the state where Columbia County had 4.1 percent; in Waukesha County in the southeast their numbers were largest (456) and their percentage also above average (3.0 percent). Counties heavily populated by Scottish natives were the rule in the northern third of Illinois, with additional counties appearing in the west center and southwest. Northeastern Illinois's Kane (3.1 percent), Cook (2.4 percent), and Lake (2.2 percent) counties had Scots immigrants above average, although the largest percentage appeared in the southwest in Randolph County (5.5 percent), across the Mississippi from St. Louis. Some immigrants native to Scotland lived in most Michigan counties. Counties with the highest percentages extended from the southeast corner of the Lower Peninsula (2.3 percent in Wayne County) northward to the Thumb (3.1 percent in St. Clair County) and then westward (reaching a maximum of 3.7 percent of the immigrants in Saginaw County) to Lake Michigan. While only two Ohio counties had no Scottish residents in 1850, counties with above average percentages were distributed around the margins of the state. In east central Ohio they formed 3.3 percent of the immigrants in Columbiana County; in southeastern Ohio they formed 2.9 percent in Washington County. Hamilton County (Cincinnati) in the southwest had 1.0 percent

Scottish immigrants, and in the northwest they comprised 3.1 percent in Wood County.

Only five Indiana counties had Scottish-born immigrants in above average percentages, and forty-two of the state's counties were populated by five or fewer Scots natives. Four above average counties were along the Ohio River, including the largest Scottish immigrant percentage (2.9) in Jefferson County (Madison) in the southeast and above average percentages in nearby Switzerland (1.8) and Ohio (1.4) counties. Downstream, Perry County had 1.0 percent of its immigrants native to Scotland, and Wells County in northeastern Indiana (1.1 percent) had an above average Scottish immigrant percentage.

### Natives of France and Denmark

Emigration from France to North America began in the first days of colonization, although the French impact became greater in what became Canada.[44] Among the earliest French immigrants were Roman Catholic priests who served as missionaries to the native population in the interior and established the church in seaboard areas. Many Protestants, or Huguenots, joined the immigrant stream during the late 1600s, escaping persecution in predominantly Roman Catholic France and finding welcome in all colonies, particularly Massachusetts. The French Revolution encouraged at least ten thousand refugees, some of whom lived temporarily in the French Caribbean, to enter the United States, and another small influx came following the defeat of Napoleon in 1815. Other French settlers came for less dramatic reasons, simply desiring to find work and success in America. The French and their French Canadian descendants explored the waterways and portages, established a commercial system, and developed trading posts, forts, and missions (often from existing villages) into the first permanent European settlements in the Old Northwest.[45] Because both French and French Canadians were involved in the Old Northwest, the influence of French ethnicity cannot be considered without including the French Canadians, yet nativity data from the 1850 census do not permit reliable separation of Canadians into French, English, or other subgroups. Furthermore, the distribution of French and Canadian natives in the Old Northwest typically does not coincide (compare Figures 5 and 8).

By 1850, 54,069 natives of France lived in the United States, with about 12,500 residing in New York and about 11,500 in Louisiana.[46] Ohio had the third largest number of French natives, while Illinois ranked fifth and Indiana sixth. Only 0.7 percent of the Old Northwest's immigrants in 1850 were natives of France,

although a century earlier natives of France and French Canada would have comprised nearly all of the nonnative American population (Table 1). Even as late as 1850 remnants of French ethnicity in the Old Northwest could be discerned, more from names for natural features and places (Vincennes, La Porte, Prairie du Chien, Sault Saint Marie, Des Plaines) and in isolated long lot land survey remnants than from the distribution of the French ethnic population scattered around the Old Northwest[47] (Figure 5). Some locations reflect the history of French settlement: Sault Saint Marie and the Raisin River (Monroe County) in Michigan, Vincennes (Knox County) in Indiana, Illinois counties across from St. Louis, and northwest Wisconsin. Some locations reflect the use by the French of waterways such as the Ohio, Maumee, Wabash, Chicago, Illinois, and Fox rivers, but along other important waterways such as the Straits of Mackinac or the Wisconsin River, low percentages appeared. French immigrant concentrations indicate more recent pre–1850 settlement, not remnants of the French presence in the Old Northwest during the voyageur era of the seventeenth and eighteenth centuries. The 1850 pattern may mimic the historical pattern in that areas initially settled by the French might be considered hospitable by subsequent French settlers, but to a greater degree it reveals the location of economic opportunities.

Ohio's French immigrant percentage was 1.0, and nearly half of its counties held French settlers in percentages greater than the Old Northwest average. The largest percentage, 8.1, occurred in the northeast in Stark County, and northwestern counties such as Fulton (5.3 percent) and Williams (4.4 percent), and west central counties such as Shelby (4.4 percent) and Darke (4.0 percent) also held many French immigrants. Along the Ohio River, Clermont (3.0 percent) and Brown (3.7 percent) counties contained many French natives among the immigrants. Despite Gallia County's French origins with Gallipolis the French formed only 0.5 percent of its immigrants in 1850, below the Old Northwest average. The French accounted for 2.4 percent of the immigrants slightly downriver in Scioto County, where the French Grant from Congress provided the Gallipolis settlers with something missing from their original settlement: clear title to the land.[48] Woodford County in north central Illinois had the state's largest French percentage at 7.4, with the next largest value (6.3 percent) in Jasper County in the southeast. St. Clair County, in the southwest across from St. Louis, had 5.3 percent of its immigrants native to France, while fairly high proportions occurred in northeastern counties such as Du Page (4.4 percent). Forty Illinois counties had 0.1 percent or less of their immigrant population native to France. In the

# Figure 5

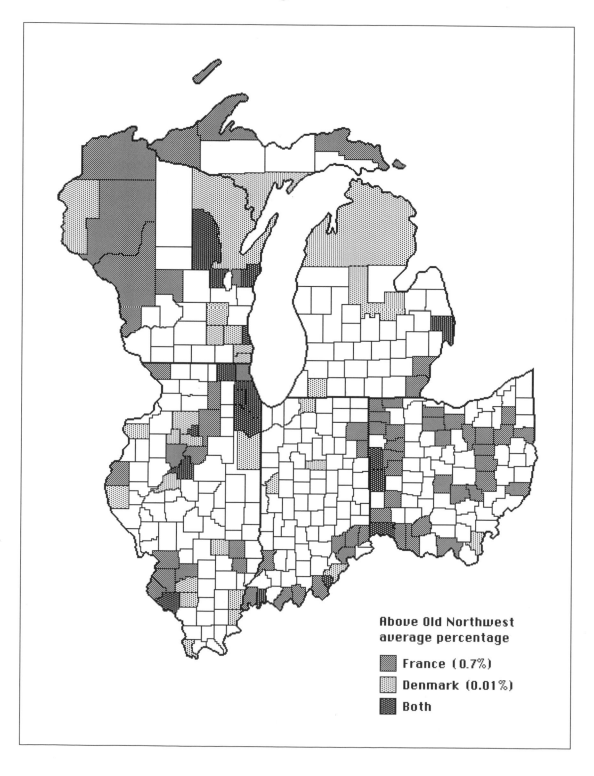

**Above Old Northwest average percentage**

France ( 0.7% )

Denmark ( 0.01% )

Both

southeastern Lower Peninsula of Michigan, Wayne County (Detroit) held 2.4 percent French immigrants. The French comprised 0.6 percent of the immigrants in Monroe County, home of early French settlements along the Raisin River, and 1.0 percent in St. Clair County at the southern tip of Lake Huron. Chippewa County in the Upper Peninsula, which contained the old French settlement of Sault Saint Marie, had a less than average French percentage of 0.5, with just three French natives in residence. Eight Wisconsin counties rose above the Old Northwest average. In the north central-northwest, used by the French as a connector between Lake Superior and the Mississippi River, 1.5 percent of the immigrants in Crawford (La Crosse) and La Pointe counties and 1.4 percent in Chippewa County were French. In Milwaukee County, 203 French natives comprised 0.8 percent of the immigrants.

Only thirteen Indiana counties had French natives above the Old Northwest average.[49] Most counties along the Ohio River fell into this category: 4.9 percent in Floyd (New Albany), 3.5 percent in Harrison, 1.1 percent in Posey, 0.7 percent in Vanderburgh (Evansville), 0.8 percent in Jefferson (Madison), and 2.0 percent in Dearborn (Lawrenceburg). In the southeastern interior, Ripley and Jennings counties held 2.1 percent and 1.2 percent, respectively. Knox County in the southwest, including the old French settlement of Vincennes, had seventy-five immigrants (or 2.2 percent) native to France. Although fourteen natives of Canada lived in the county in 1850, it cannot be discerned from the census if any were French Canadians. By 1850, given the passage of time, most inhabitants of French or French Canadian ethnicity had been born in Indiana, but the French influence in Vincennes continued. Allen County in northeastern Indiana, the site of Fort Wayne and earlier of the French Fort Miamis, also had a high French immigrant presence at 4.8 percent; adjoining Adams County's percentage was 1.2.

Some Danish immigrants arrived in America during the 1600s, settling mainly among the Dutch in New York. During the 1700s Danish Moravians fleeing religious repression immigrated to Pennsylvania and merged into German communities.[50] Later, religious persecution by the Lutheran state church drove recently converted Danish Baptists to seek tolerance and opportunity in the United States, with some arriving as early as the 1840s. But for the most part conditions in Denmark were not sufficiently difficult to encourage significant immigration until after the Civil War, and only 1,838 Danish natives lived in the United States in 1850. Nearly one-quarter resided in New York, many others appeared in Louisiana and Massachusetts, and the fourth largest number chose Wisconsin. Fewer than 300 Danish natives had settled in

the Old Northwest by 1850, forming 0.01 percent of the immigrant population (Table 1). In only two states was their presence notable: Wisconsin had 161 (0.06 percent of the immigrants) and Illinois had 72 (0.01 percent). Generally Danes were few enough to make their impact local rather than regional, and the presence of just one or two Danes in a county with a moderately sized immigrant population could raise the Danish immigrant percentage above the Old Northwest average (Figure 5).

Most Wisconsin counties contained no more than one native of Denmark, although forty-one lived in Racine County in the southeast, and eighteen in Brown and twenty-one in Winnebago counties, both in the northeast. In the latter county Danes comprised 0.4 percent of the immigrants. In Illinois the largest percentage of Danish immigrants appeared in Alexander County (0.4 percent) in the extreme southwest, with Stark (north center), Randolph (southwest), and McHenry, Cook, and Will (all in the northeast) counties each having 0.1 percent Danish immigrants. Every Michigan, Ohio, and Indiana county had less than 0.1 percent of its immigrants born in Denmark. Eleven Danes lived in Michigan, with the two natives in Wayne County in the southeast representing more than in any other county. Only ten Ohio counties held any Danes, and only four had Danish natives above the Old Northwest average. Hamilton County (Cincinnati) had the largest number (23) and an above average percentage (0.2). In Indiana eight natives of Denmark were spread among six counties, giving each county a percentage above the Old Northwest average. Two counties were in the southeast, including Floyd where three Danes formed 0.04 percent of the immigrants, with the others scattered around the state.

## Natives of the Netherlands and Belgium

Dutch involvement in North America has a long history, beginning with the explorations by Henry Hudson in 1609, the establishment of a fort on the Hudson River near Albany in 1614, and the colonization of Manhattan Island in 1626.[51] Early Dutch activity focused on the Hudson and Delaware river valleys, but for nearly two hundred years following the 1664 capture by the English of the Dutch New Netherlands colony, no large-scale or organized immigration of Dutch settlers occurred. Then, during the 1830s and especially by the mid-1840s, Dutch immigration dramatically increased, spurred on by group immigration of congregations, extended families, and neighborhoods to places where land was available and a new or re-created life could be established. By 1850, 9,848 Dutch natives lived in the United States, with Michigan housing the largest number, New York second, and Wisconsin third. The 5,634 natives of Holland in the Old Northwest formed 0.3 percent of the immigrants, concentrated mostly around Lake Michigan where two of the leading Dutch settlements in the United States appeared in the west central Lower Peninsula of Michigan and in eastern Wisconsin (Figure 6).

Although the 3,174 Dutch in Michigan comprised 1.2 percent of the immigrant population, thirty of the state's forty-three counties had no more than one Dutch native.[52] The vast majority lived in west central Michigan near the intentionally named settlement of Holland, where in surrounding Ottawa County 1,987 Dutch natives formed 43.4 percent of the immigrants. Nearby, 544 Dutch natives accounted for 14.9 percent of the immigrants in Allegan County, 355 accounted for 4.2 percent in Kent County, and 157 natives accounted for 1.7 percent in Kalamazoo County. In Wisconsin, with half the number and percentage of Dutch as Michigan, natives of Holland settled primarily in the east along the Lake Michigan shore. At 7.7 percent, Brown County in the northeast had the largest percentage of Dutch immigrants; Milwaukee County in the southeast had the largest number (518 compared to Brown County's 345) but a smaller percentage (2.0). Sheboygan County in the east center had both a large percentage (6.2) and number (447) of Dutch among its immigrants. Holland natives accounted for just 0.1 percent of the immigrants in Illinois, and they lived in only one-third of the counties. Two hundred seventy-five of the 346 Dutch in Illinois lived in the northeastern county of Cook (Chicago) and comprised 0.8 percent of the immigrants. In Ohio, Dutch formed 0.05 percent of the immigrants, and only twenty-four counties had more than one native. Two counties in the northwest, Putnam (1.8 percent) and Van Wert (1.1 percent), had the largest Dutch-born immigrant proportions, in the northeast in Cuyahoga County (Cleveland) the percentage was 0.6. Indiana's 85 Dutch-born settlers comprised 0.02 percent of the immigrants. Only Tippecanoe County in the northwest had an above average Dutch nativity percentage: 27 natives of Holland formed 0.3 percent of its immigrants.

Belgians arrived early in North America—Belgian Catholics served with French and Spanish Catholics as frontier missionaries and Belgian Protestants settled with the Dutch in New Amsterdam—but by 1850 only 1,313 Belgian natives lived in the United States.[53] Since the country of Belgium had existed for less than twenty years by 1850, nativity totals probably underrepresent the true Belgian population for many may have attributed their birthplaces to Holland, Germany, or France. Belgium contains two major ethnic groups, Flemings in the north and Walloons in the south, but the 1850 census canvassers rarely made that distinction, recording ten Flanders birthplaces in just three counties and no Walloonia birthplaces. Although French-influenced Walloons dominated nineteenth-century Belgium, the northern and western regions of Flanders provided most Belgian immigrants well into the 1900s. Belgians formed a mere 0.02 percent of immigrants in the Old Northwest in 1850, but the 360 inhabitants represented one-quarter of all Belgian natives in the United States (Table 1). At such a low percentage minor differences in the number of natives affect whether a county had above or below average immigrant percentages. Belgians were scattered about the region in 1850, with some more urban counties receiving greater than average percentages (Figure 6).

Michigan had the largest number and percentage of Belgian immigrants in the Old Northwest in 1850. Above average percentages appeared in the southeastern counties, including Wayne (Detroit) whose 79 natives (0.3 percent) were the most in any other Old Northwest county. Forty-seven natives of Belgium forming 0.02 percent of the immigrant population, resided in Wisconsin in 1850, with above average percentages (in each case, 0.1 percent) found especially in east central (Manitowoc, Washington, and Fond du Lac) and southeastern (Jefferson) counties. Only fourteen Ohio counties held any Belgian natives in 1850 and the largest concentration was in the southwest. Here 35 of Ohio's 70 Belgians lived in Brown County, where they formed 0.5 percent of the immigrants, 17 (0.2 percent) lived in Hamilton County, 10 (0.1 percent) in Clermont County, and another 6 (0.1 percent) resided in Clinton County. Just a handful of Illinois counties had Belgian natives. The largest number, 11 (0.03 percent of the immigrants), appeared in the northeastern county of Cook (Chicago), two nearby counties, De Kalb and Du Page, had 0.1 percent and four each, while Monroe, Randolph, and St. Clair counties across the Mississippi River from St. Louis contained Belgians in above average percentages. Indiana had the Old Northwest's second largest number and tied with Wisconsin for second largest percentage of Belgians, primarily on the strength of the 51 natives (1.7 percent of the immigrants) living in Perry County along the Ohio River. They concentrated in Leopold Township as part of the larger, primarily German, Catholic community.[54] Upriver in Floyd County (New Albany), 27 Belgians formed 0.4 percent of the immigrants; above average percentages also were found in Clark (Jeffersonville) and Jefferson (Madison) counties. In the northeast Huntington County contained 0.1 percent Belgian immigrants.

# Figure 6

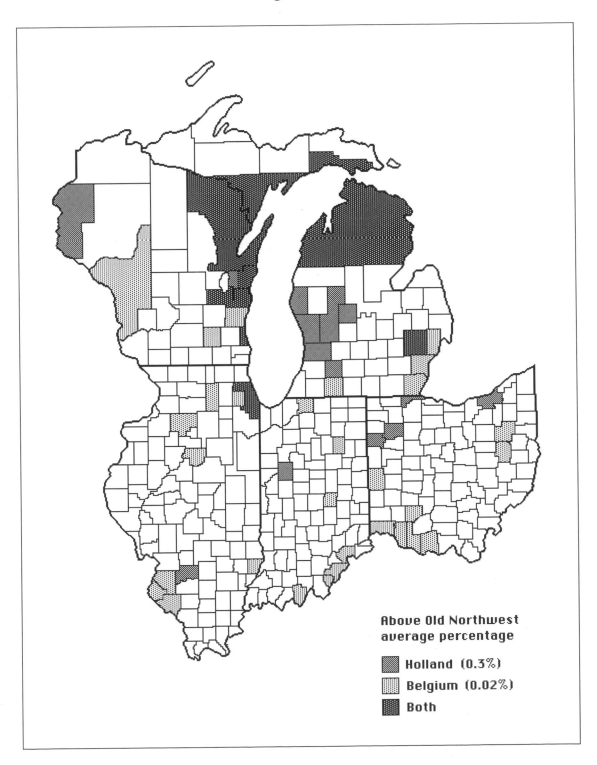

Above Old Northwest
average percentage

Holland (0.3%)
Belgium (0.02%)
Both

## Natives of Norway and Sweden

Some Norwegian immigration to the United States occurred as early as the seventeenth century, but most followed the Civil War.[55] By 1850, 12,678 Norwegian natives lived in the United States, with over two-thirds residing in Wisconsin and almost one-fifth living in Illinois. During the first half of the 1800s some Norwegian religious separatists and communal utopians established colonies in the Old Northwest to escape persecution, while other Norwegian extended families or neighborhood groups arrived in search of economic opportunity. The immigrants tended to settle together in clusters and, if the group was large enough, they geographically subdivided themselves into smaller clusters of people from the same location in Norway. Norwegians comprised 0.5 percent of the Old Northwest immigrants in 1850, with a northward orientation highlighting their clustering (Figure 7).

Wisconsin had the largest Norwegian immigrant percentage (3.4) and number (8,635) in the Old Northwest (Table 1). Their heaviest concentration occurred in the south central counties of Dane (2,689 natives or 19.5 percent of the immigrants) and Rock (1,252 natives or 7.1 percent). Percentages well above average appeared in the southeast, including Racine County (5.6 percent), and across the state from east (8 percent in Manitowoc County) to north (8.5 percent in Marathon County) to west (8.2 percent in Crawford County). Illinois housed the next largest number of Norwegian immigrants, much smaller in percentage (0.5 percent) and number (2,335) than in Wisconsin, and most counties had no Norwegians. Grundy County in the northeast contained the largest percentage (7.2) but scattered counties in the north, including Boone (6.3 percent) and La Salle (5.2 percent), also had many Norwegians. Only fifteen of Michigan's forty-three counties held any Norwegians, mostly in the northern Lower Peninsula. In Oceana County 7.5 percent of immigrants had been born in Norway, in Mason County they comprised 3.4 percent of the immigrants, in Michilimackinac County 1.2 percent, and in Newaygo County 1.1 percent. Ohio had no counties with above average Norwegian immigrant percentages. Just six counties housed natives of Norway; fourteen of the state's twenty-five Norwegians lived in Hamilton County in the southwest, and another five lived in Ashtabula County in the northeast. Indiana's situation was similar. Only fourteen counties contained any Norwegian natives, and Marshall County in the north center had the largest number—three.

In 1638 the colony of New Sweden was established along the lower Delaware River.[56] It failed to attract continuing immigration from Sweden (indeed, Dutch and Finns comprised many of its inhabitants), coming under Dutch control in 1655 and then English control in 1665. Swedish immigration to America lagged until the 1840s, when difficult times at home combined with economic opportunities in America to lure increasing numbers. According to the 1850 census, 3,559 natives of Sweden lived in the United States. Nearly one-third of them, more than in any other state, resided in Illinois, but elsewhere in the Old Northwest they were few and unevenly distributed (Table 1; Figure 7).

The 1,115 Swedes in Illinois accounted for almost 90 percent of Swedes in the Old Northwest, yet they formed only 0.1 percent of Illinois's immigrants and only twenty-five counties housed any Swedes in 1850. Some northwestern Illinois counties had high Swedish immigrant percentages, including Knox (2.8), and Rock Island and Stark counties (1.2 each). In the northeast Cook County (including Chicago, a major Swedish urban settlement) held 182 natives (0.5 percent of the immigrants), but by far the largest percentage of Swedes anywhere in the Old Northwest appeared in Henry County, where 493 natives (18.5 percent of the immigrants), mostly religious dissenters, concentrated in the Bishop Hill settlement.[57] Wisconsin had the next largest percentage (0.03) and number (87) of Swedes. St. Croix County in the northwest had 1.1 percent Swedish immigrants (only 6 persons), while three southeastern counties, Jefferson, Waukesha, and Washington, had slightly above average percentages and larger numbers. Only six Michigan counties held any Swedish natives. The largest proportion (1.2 percent), occurred in Oceana County in the west central Lower Peninsula, Berrien County in the southwest had 0.1 percent, and Mackinac County straddling the two peninsulas held 0.2 percent. Seven Ohio counties housed Swedish natives in 1850. Hamilton County (Cincinnati) in the southwest had 29 Swedes (but only .03 percent of the immigrants); every other county had 5 or fewer. Of the six Indiana counties with Swedish natives, three in the southwest and south center had percentages above the Old Northwest average. The largest percentage occurred in Jennings County in the southeast, where 6 Swedes comprised 0.1 percent of the immigrants.

## Natives of Canada and the Caribbean

Some of the Old Northwest's immigrants by 1850 originated in two "American" locations. Canadians formed the largest group.[58] Census canvassers largely failed to distinguish between Upper Canadian and Lower Canadian birthplaces, identifying most as being in Canada, so census data cannot reveal geographic and ethnic

# Figure 7

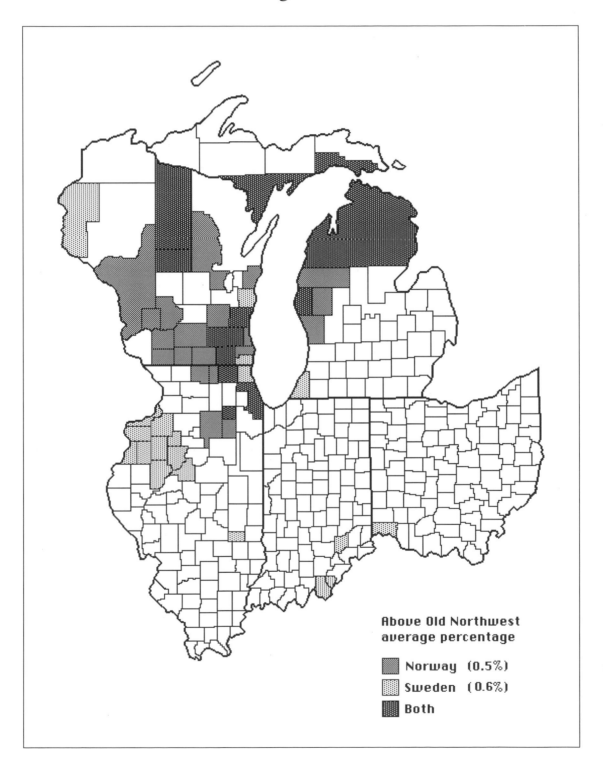

**Above Old Northwest average percentage**

◼ Norway (0.5%)

▨ Sweden (0.6%)

◼ Both

distinctions between French and British Canadians or their settlement patterns.[59] Published tables of nativity data from the 1850 census include all Canadians under the heading "British Americans," although on the manuscript schedules the canvassers recorded "Canada" as the most common birthplace. Irregularly and without any apparent methodology, census takers identified a separate part of British America (such as Nova Scotia) or a province within Canada (such as Upper Canada). The earliest Canadian immigrants to the Old Northwest consisted mainly of French Canadian trappers, traders, missionaries, and associated settlers. Redeveloping in the 1840s following a long lull, immigration from French Canada brought laborers to New England factories and lumbering camps in the northern Midwest. British Canadian immigration to the Old Northwest increased significantly after the War of 1812, when opportunities across the border lured many to escape difficult conditions at home.[60] Some were children of British natives who took advantage of cheaper Atlantic Ocean passage fares to Canada and remained there for a time before moving to the United States. Some were children of Loyalists who fled during or after the American Revolution and who now found limited opportunities and political difficulties in Canada. Since British Canadians shared most of their cultural characteristics with Americans, they assimilated easily into American society.

Nearly one-third of the 147,711 Canadian natives in the United States in 1850 lived in New York, while Michigan contained the fifth largest number of Canadians, Illinois the sixth, and Wisconsin the seventh.[61] On average in the Old Northwest they formed 1.9 percent of the immigrant population and concentrated in northern areas (Table 1; Figure 8). Michigan had the largest Canadian immigrant presence (5.5 percent) in the Old Northwest, and only three of its counties were below the Old Northwest average. In Sanilac County, close to Canada in the east central Lower Peninsula, 52.5 percent of the immigrants were Canadian, and in Wayne County (Detroit) in the southeast the immigrants were 10.5 percent Canadian. Many Canadians lived in west central Lower Peninsula counties such as Oceana (23.0 percent) and Newaygo (18.4 percent), while proportions as large as 37.8 percent occurred in Upper and northern Lower peninsula counties. Illinois counties with above average Canadian immigrants formed a solid mass in the northern third of the state, with the largest percentage, 16.3, appearing in Will County in the northeast. Every Wisconsin county except Richland in the southwest had Canadians in above average concentrations, with the greatest percentage (47.8) appearing in the northwestern county of La Pointe. Canadian percentages tended to

decline but still exceeded the Old Northwest average toward southern Wisconsin. Most extreme northern Ohio counties held above average percentages of Canadians, especially the northwestern counties of Ottawa (5.6 percent) and Lucas (4.6 percent), but also Cuyahoga (Cleveland) in the northeast with 3.4 percent. Statewide they were only 0.8 percent of the immigrant population.

Canadians formed 0.5 percent of Indiana's immigrants and, although they lived in all but three counties, only four northern counties had them in above average concentrations.[62] All four counties bordered Michigan or Lake Michigan. Canadians appeared in largest percentages in the northwestern counties of Porter (6.7) and Lake (6.2), while 2.2 percent of the immigrants in both La Porte and Elkhart counties to the east were native to Canada.

"Caribbean" natives are defined as immigrants born on the islands within or near that region, including Bermuda. Only 274 natives of the Caribbean resided in the Old Northwest in 1850, forming 0.01 percent of the immigrants, yet they represent the second largest Western Hemisphere group (Table 1). The vast majority of these native Caribbeans indicated a birthplace in the West Indies, although Jamaica, Bermuda, Cuba, and other islands were mentioned specifically; by 1850, 5,772 West Indian natives lived in the United States, primarily in Louisiana, New York, Pennsylvania, and Florida.[63] The history of Caribbean natives in the United States before 1850 has not been researched fully. Most studies of West Indian immigrants focus on blacks who immigrated to the United States primarily after the Civil War, although "more than 50,000 white planters, free blacks, and slaves left for the United States" during the Haitian Revolution of 1791–1803.[64] The majority of Caribbean immigrants to the Old Northwest were not "Black" or "Mulatto" according to the 1850 census. Some may have been white planters fleeing political turmoil; others may have been traders or processors of Caribbean products. Some may have been descendants of the English, French, Dutch, or others who established and built Caribbean colonies.

Counties with concentrations of Caribbean natives, while scattered around the Old Northwest in 1850, were found particularly near water access and in some urban areas (Figure 8). Illinois had the largest percentage of Caribbean natives (0.02), especially in the southeast in Edwards County (including the English Settlement at Albion) where they formed 0.5 percent of the immigrants. In Michigan, Caribbean natives scattered among southern counties, especially in Berrien (southwest) and Hillsdale (south center). Caribbean natives in Ohio resided in twenty counties. The largest number (28) appeared in Hamilton (Cincinnati) County in the southwest and the largest percentage (0.3) occurred in Clark County in the

# Figure 8

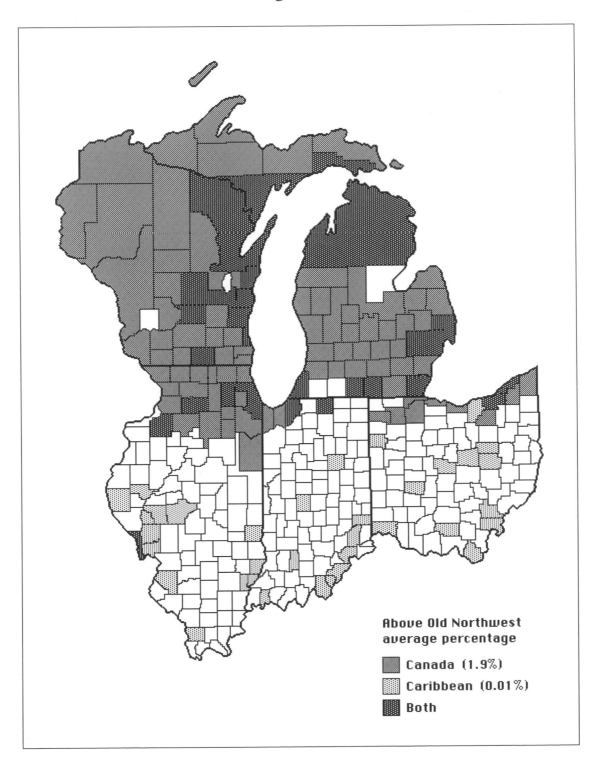

Above Old Northwest
average percentage

■ Canada (1.9%)
▨ Caribbean (0.01%)
■ Both

west center; an above average percentage was found in Cuyahoga County (Cleveland) in the northeast (.06 percent with 19 natives). In Wisconsin, Caribbean natives reached 0.2 percent of the immigrants in Brown County (northeast), while the counties of Manitowoc (east center), Marquette (center), Milwaukee (southeast), and Rock (south) all had above average percentages. In Indiana, sixteen Caribbean natives comprised 0.003 percent of the immigrants. Thirteen counties contained all the natives; in twelve counties they achieved above average immigrant percentages. Eight counties were along or close to the Ohio River, including Clark (Jeffersonville), Floyd (New Albany), and Jefferson (Madison). In the southwest Vanderburgh County (Evansville) had one Caribbean native (0.01 percent), while another native in Martin County formed 0.1 percent of its immigrants. Grant and Hendricks counties in the center each had one Caribbean native, or 0.02 percent, while one native each in La Porte and Elkhart counties along the northern border formed 0.01 percent of the immigrant population in each county.

### Natives of Other Foreign Countries

Many other ethnic groups were represented in the Old Northwest by handfuls of immigrants. Austrians, Hungarians, Italians, Mexicans, Poles, Spaniards, and Russians lived in all five states; natives of Africa, Bohemia, India, Portugal, and South America lived in four. A great variety of places, such as Greece, the Sandwich Islands (Hawaii), Australia, the East Indies, Armenia, the Azores, Gibraltar, Persia, and Singapore provided settlers to three or fewer states. In Indiana the unusual birthplaces included Africa, the Cape Verde Islands, India, New Zealand, and South America. Given that counties surrounding both smaller and larger cities such as Cincinnati, Chicago, Detroit, and Milwaukee held more people and more economic opportunities, it is not surprising that urban counties displayed a greater variety of birthplaces. In Indiana, Clark County (Jeffersonville) contained settlers born in Hungary, Italy, and Poland; Floyd County (New Albany) held natives of Hungary, Poland, and Portugal; Jefferson County (Madison) had Austrian, Italian, and Russian immigrants; and Vanderburgh County (Evansville) included natives of Mexico, Poland, and Portugal.

### Blacks

In 1850 blacks accounted for 1.0 of the total (not just immigrant) Old Northwest population.[65] Their largest percentages occurred in Ohio (1.3) and Indiana (1.1); their largest number by far occurred in Ohio (25,279) with Indiana second (11,296) (Table 1). In the published census blacks were listed as "Free Colored," legally accurate since slavery was not permitted in the Old Northwest but realistically inaccurate in many parts of the Old Northwest with restrictive "Black Codes."[66] Furthermore, as late as 1840, according to the census, 348 slaves actually lived in the Old Northwest, with 331 found in Illinois especially in the northwestern lead mining district and three in Indiana.[67] Only Michigan had no slaves in 1840; by 1850 there were none in any Old Northwest state. These slaves typically had migrated into Old Northwest states with their masters who were not forced to free them by legal challenges or social pressures.[68]

Most Old Northwest counties contained at least one black inhabitant in 1850. There numbers were highest in the southern areas where southern migrants and their descendants dominated, and particularly high in southwestern Ohio and southeastern Indiana (Figure 9).[69] Only two Ohio counties had no black residents. Blacks were found in largest percentages in Gallia County (7.0) on the Ohio River and in Ross (5.9), Pike (5.6), and Jackson (3.1) counties in the south center. Between 2.5 and 5.2 percent of the residents were black in west central and southwestern counties such as Mercer, Highland, Brown, Clinton, and Greene, while in the southwest in Hamilton County (Cincinnati) the percentage was 2.3 and in Franklin County (Columbus) in the center of the state it was 3.8 percent. Southeastern and southwestern Illinois contained the most counties with above average percentages of blacks in the state. In the southeast Gallatin County had the largest percentage at 6.9, while Lawrence County's figure was 4.5 percent. In the southwest across from St. Louis, blacks accounted for 3.5 percent of the inhabitants in Randolph County and 2.2 to 2.9 percent in neighboring St. Clair, Clinton, and Madison counties. Michigan's largest black percentage (6.3) occurred in Oceana County in the west central Lower Peninsula; in the southwest corner where southerners and Quakers had settled, 3.6 percent of the population in Cass County and 2.1 percent in Berrien County were black.[70] Just two Wisconsin counties had above average black population percentages, east central Calumet (7.1 percent) and northwestern La Pointe (1.2 percent).

Only four Indiana counties had no black inhabitants in 1850.[71] Blacks formed 4.9 percent of the population in Knox County (Vincennes) in the southwest and in nearby Vigo County (Terre Haute). In the east central part of the state, an area heavily settled by southern Quakers, 4.5 percent of the inhabitants were black in Randolph, 4.1 percent in Wayne, and 2.6 percent in Rush counties. Blacks comprised 3.6 percent of the population in Clark,

# Figure 9

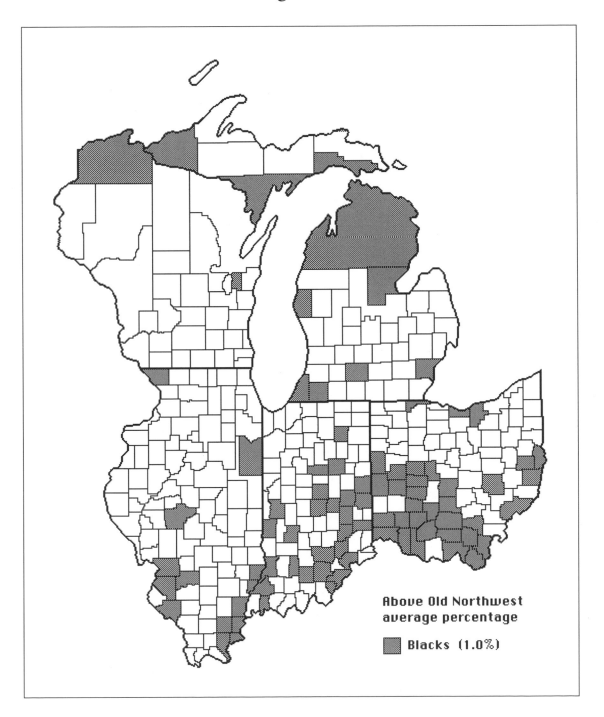

Above Old Northwest
average percentage

Blacks (1.0%)

2.8 percent in Jefferson (Madison), and 2.7 percent in Jennings counties in the southeast near the Ohio River. Downstream, their percentage was 3.8 in Floyd County (New Albany), while in the south center blacks accounted for 2.5 percent in Orange County and 2.7 percent in the central county of Marion (Indianapolis).

Because the 1850 census separated only blacks, mulattoes, and whites by "Color," it is impossible to determine exactly which other racial groups lived in the Old Northwest. Native Americans, a few indicated improperly by an "R" (for "Red") in the "Color" column, resided in the Old Northwest. The Indiana counties of Miami and Wabash contained some Native Americans and others lived in northern Michigan and Wisconsin. The 1850 census, however, reveals far fewer than the actual number probably residing in the Old Northwest: in Indiana alone 290 were counted ten years later.[72] Surely Hispanics and Asians were present in the Old Northwest, but means such as analyzing surnames must be used to tease suggestions of their numbers from the manuscript schedules. Sources other than the census must be consulted to gain a more accurate sense of all racial groups in the Old Northwest.

## Concluding Remarks

Why did Indiana lack the ethnic diversity of other Old Northwest states in 1850? Indiana indeed was poorly known abroad, as Governor Wright lamented, since no concerted effort had been made to publicize the state's attractions. By 1850 Old Northwest states had just begun official advertising campaigns intended to lure immigrants.[73] Traditionally information about states had been spread by word of mouth, personal letter, the press, published guidebooks, or promotional activities by private entrepreneurs, but relying upon this unmanaged flow of information risked the dissemination of inaccurate, incomplete, or even damaging information. Not everyone viewed Indiana positively: the state reputedly was swampy, disease ridden, backward, and populated by easygoing, lower class, and nativist settlers.[74] Whether its sullied reputation deflected foreign-born settlers away from Indiana cannot be determined, but the comparatively more alluring reputations of other Old Northwest states surely did not dissuade potential immigrants from settling there.

Indiana was at a competitive disadvantage compared to other states, particularly Ohio, because it lacked an efficient internal waterway system and good access to markets.[75] Easy access to a potentially productive interior was crucially important in encouraging interior development and growth of commercial and trade centers that collected products from the interior for export. The best future

was predicted for cities on the Great Lakes, on major rivers like the Ohio and Mississippi, or on rivers or canals linking the lakes and rivers. After the Erie Canal opened, the focus of east-west transportation increasingly shifted toward the Great Lakes, which provided direct access to the East Coast. However, northern Indiana failed to benefit from its proximity to Lake Michigan because interior access was limited by its swampy or dune-blocked shoreline. The sequence and timing of settlement also may have contributed to Indiana's failure to acquire a large foreign-born population. After 1790 settlement in the Old Northwest basically expanded from the southeast to the northwest.[76] Indiana's lands were never the only ones available since parts of surrounding states were sold and settled at approximately the same time: much of Ohio and southern and central Illinois contemporaneously with southern and central Indiana; southern Michigan, southern Wisconsin, and northern Illinois contemporaneously with northern Indiana. Given its poorer accessibility and tarnished reputation, Indiana may have been avoided by many foreign immigrants who were more attracted by real or perceived opportunities elsewhere in the Old Northwest.

Economic opportunities may have been fewer in Indiana than in other states by 1850. An established agricultural economy existed across much of Ohio and was emerging in the most environmentally favored areas of southern Indiana, Illinois, Michigan, and Wisconsin, while lumbering in northern Michigan and Wisconsin and mining in parts of Illinois, Ohio, Michigan, and Wisconsin was expanding. Immigrants not only purchased new land or partially cleared farms but also sought employment in the cities, where opportunities as laborers or artisans, or in commerce, education, and other spheres awaited. However, Indiana lacked major urban centers such as Cincinnati or St. Louis, the latter affecting parts of southwestern Illinois across the Mississippi River, and lacked other urban areas with eventual regional or national importance such as Chicago, Milwaukee, Cleveland, and Detroit. In this era access to waterways with external connections, such as the Ohio River or the Great Lakes, and to a productive interior via river, canal, road, and increasingly railroad was necessary for urban expansion. Certainly the Ohio River towns and cities in southern Indiana fit part of the profile, but the dominance of nearby Cincinnati and the growth of Louisville, coupled with the more rugged terrain and lower agricultural potential of southern compared to central and northern Indiana, may have stymied the potential for urban centers such as Madison, Jeffersonville, and Evansville.

The 1850 census provides the first statistical picture of Indiana's ethnicity. It reveals that the state was much less affected by foreign immigrants than other states in the Old

Northwest, although Hoosier blacks did represent a larger portion of the population than in any other Old Northwest state except Ohio. Years of ethnic arrivals preceded 1850, ranging from Native Americans to French and French Canadian voyageurs to American and European immigrants who arrived during the heyday of settlement after 1800. Despite their relatively small presence in 1850, Indiana's ethnic minorities comprise an important and valuable part of the state's settlement history and cultural fabric, and their impact endures in many places and within many people.

## NOTES

1. Quotation in Richard Lyle Power, "Wet Lands and the Hoosier Stereotype," *Mississippi Valley Historical Review* 22 (June 1935): 34.

2. J. D. B. De Bow, *Statistical View of the United States . . . Being a Compendium of the Seventh Census, 1850* (Washington, D.C.: A. O. P. Nicholson, Public Printer, 1854), Table cxx, 117–18. General studies of immigration to the United States include Thomas J. Archdeacon, *Becoming American: An Ethnic History* (New York: Free Press, 1983); John Bodnar, *The Transplanted: A History of Immigrants in Urban America* (Bloomington: Indiana University Press, 1985); Leonard Dinnerstein, Roger L. Nichols, and David M. Reimers, *Natives and Strangers: Blacks, Indians, and Immigrants in America,* 2d ed. (New York: Oxford University Press, 1990); Marcus Lee Hansen, *The Immigrant in American History* (New York: Harper and Row, 1964); Maldwyn A. Jones, *American Immigration* (Chicago: University of Chicago Press, 1960); Philip Taylor, *A Distant Magnet: European Emigration to the U. S. A.* (London: Eyre and Spottiswood, 1971); Carl Wittke, *We Who Built America: The Saga of the Immigrant* (Cleveland: Press of Western Reserve University, 1964); Virginia Yans-McLaughlin, ed., *Immigration Reconsidered: History, Sociology, and Politics* (New York: Oxford University Press, 1990).

3. Gregory S. Rose, "Hoosier Origins: The Nativity of Indiana's United States-Born Population in 1850," *Indiana Magazine of History* 81 (Sept. 1985): 201–32, and "The Distribution of Indiana's Ethnic and Racial Minorities in 1850," ibid. 87 (Sept. 1991): 224–60.

4. Rose, "Distribution of Indiana's Ethnic and Racial Minorities in 1850."

5. Rose, "Hoosier Origins," 206–9.

6. Harlow Lindley, ed., *Indiana as Seen by Early Travelers: A Collection of Reprints from Books of Travel, Letters, and Diaries Prior to 1830,* vol. 3 of *Indiana Historical Collections* (Indianapolis: Indiana Historical Bureau, 1916), 184, 194, 451–52, 154–55, 441, 448–49, 286–90, 328–36.

7. Robert L. LaFollette, "Foreigners and Their Influence on Indiana," *Indiana Magazine of History* 25 (Mar. 1929): 14–27; Stephen S. Visher, "Distribution of the Birthplaces of Indianians in 1870," ibid. 26 (June 1930): 126–42.

8. Andrew R. L. Cayton and Peter S. Onuf, "The Peopling of the Old Northwest," in *The Midwest and the Nation: Rethinking the History of an American Region* (Bloomington: Indiana University Press, 1990), 25–42; John C. Hudson, "The American Origins of Middlewestern Frontier Populations," *Annals of the Association of American Geographers* 78 (Sept. 1988): 395–413; Malcolm J. Rohrbough, "Diversity and Unity in the Old Northwest, 1790–1850:

Several Peoples Fashion a Single Region," in *Pathways to the Old Northwest: An Observance of the Bicentennial of the Northwest Ordinance* (Indianapolis: Indiana Historical Society, 1988), 71–85; Joseph Schafer, "Peopling the Middle West," *Wisconsin Magazine of History* 21 (Sept. 1937): 85–106; Robert P. Swierenga, "The Settlement of the Old Northwest: Ethnic Pluralism in a Featureless Plain," *Journal of the Early Republic* 9 (spring 1989): 73–105; Richard K. Vedder and Lowell E. Gallaway, "Migration and the Old Northwest," in *Essays in Nineteenth Century Economic History: The Old Northwest,* eds. Richard K. Vedder and David C. Klingaman (Athens: Ohio University Press, 1975), 159–76; De Bow, *Statistical View of the United States,* 116–18; United States Bureau of the Census, *The Statistics of the Population of the United States . . . Ninth Census, June 1, 1870* (Washington, D.C.: Government Printing Office, 1872), Table VII, 351–53, 359, 367–68, 376–77.

9. Margo J. Anderson, *The American Census: A Social History* (New Haven, Conn.: Yale University Press, 1988), 35–37, 45; De Bow, *Statistical View of the United States,* 12–13, 21–22, 61, 116–18. For an interesting review of the accuracy of nativity information in the 1850 census see ibid., *Statistical View of the United States,* 119–23.

10. Gregory S. Rose, "Information Sources for Nineteenth Century Midwestern Migration," *The Professional Geographer* 37 (Feb. 1985): 66–72; Everett S. Lee and Anne S. Lee, "Internal Migration Statistics for the United States," *Journal of the American Statistical Association* 55 (Dec. 1960): 677–79; Hudson, "American Origins of Middlewestern Frontier Populations"; Robert P. Swierenga, "List Upon List: The Ship Passenger Records and Immigration Research," *Journal of American Ethnic History* 10 (spring 1991): 42–53.

11. William G. Sibley, *The French Five Hundred and Other Papers* (Gallipolis, Ohio: The Tribune Press, 1933); Hubert G. H. Wilhelm, *The Origin and Distribution of Settlement Groups: Ohio, 1850* (Athens, Ohio: H. G. H. Wilhelm, 1982), 90, Appendix B; Ray Allen Billington, *Westward Expansion: A History of the American Frontier,* 4th ed. (New York: Macmillan Co., 1949), 209–10, 214–15, 219–20.

12. Raymond D. Gastil, *Cultural Regions of the United States* (Seattle: University of Washington Press, 1975); Henry Glassie, *Pattern in the Material Folk Culture of the Eastern United States* (Philadelphia: University of Pennsylvania Press, 1968); John Fraser Hart, *The Look of the Land* (Englewood Cliffs, N.J.: Prentice-Hall, 1975); John A. Jakle, Robert W. Bastian, and Douglas K. Meyer, *Common Houses in America's Small Towns: The Atlantic Seaboard to the Mississippi Valley* (Athens: University of Georgia Press, 1989); Terry G. Jordan and Matti Kaups, *The American Backwoods Frontier: An Ethnic and Ecological Interpretation* (Baltimore: Johns Hopkins University Press, 1989); Fred Kniffen, "Folk Housing: Key to Diffusion," *Annals of the Association of American Geographers* 55 (Dec. 1965): 549–77; Edward T. Price, "The Central Courthouse Square in the American County Seat," *Geographical Review* 58 (Jan. 1968): 29–60; Glenn T. Trewartha, "Some Regional Characteristics of American Farmsteads," *Annals of the Association of American Geographers* 38 (Sept. 1948), 169–225; Wilbur Zelinsky, *The Cultural Geography of the United States* (Englewood Cliffs, N.J.: Prentice-Hall, 1973), and "Some Problems in the Distribution of Generic Terms in the Place-Names of the Northeastern United States," *Annals of the Association of American Geographers* 45 (Dec. 1955): 319–49.

13. Vedder and Gallaway, "Migration and the Old Northwest," 162–64.

14. National Archives and Records Service, *Federal Population Censuses, 1790–1890: A Catalog of Microfilm Copies of the Schedules* (Washington, D.C.: The Service, 1979).

15. Data for counties in Illinois, Indiana, Michigan, and Wisconsin were collected from a hand tally by the author from the

microfilms of the 1850 manuscript census schedules. Some supplemental counting of manuscript schedules for Ohio was done by the author, but the basic county data were collected by Hubert G. H. Wilhelm (Wilhelm, *Origin and Distribution of Settlement Groups*). Totals do not necessarily agree with those in the published census tables, or with the Indiana data collected by the Indiana Historical Society staff for other chapters in this book. Discrepancies in totals should not be unexpected given the large number of individuals to be counted and the problems of faded inks, occasionally illegible writing, and skipped or duplicated pages on the microfilms. Discrepancies in totals among various tables in the published census also are not uncommon. See Lee and Lee, "Internal Migration Statistics for the United States."

16. William Thorndale and William Dollarhide, *Map Guide to the U. S. Federal Censuses, 1790–1920* (Baltimore: Genealogical Pub. Co., Inc., 1987), 163–68.

17. Kathleen Neils Conzen, *Immigrant Milwaukee, 1836–1860: Accommodation and Community in a Frontier City* (Cambridge, Mass.: Harvard University Press, 1976); Leonard Dinnerstein and David M. Reimers, *Ethnic Americans: A History of Immigration and Assimilation*, 3d ed. (New York: Harper and Row, 1988), 27–41; Swierenga, "Settlement of the Old Northwest," 76–77; Taylor, *Distant Magnet*, 210–12; Zelinsky, *Cultural Geography of the United States*, 28–33.

18. In this essay Germany is defined as all principalities, kingdoms, and independent states (including Prussia) that formed the German Confederation. See William Carr, *A History of Germany, 1815–1945* (London: E. Arnold, 1979), 1–124; John E. Rodes, *The Quest for Unity: Modern Germany, 1848–1970* (New York: Holt, Rinehart and Winston, 1971), 14, 17–86. Although the entities would not be forged into Germany for another twenty years, the published 1850 census listed only Prussia as a separate unit and lumped the balance of the units into a category headed "Rest of Germany." De Bow, *Statistical View of the United States*, 117.

19. Kathleen Neils Conzen, "Germans," in Stephan Thernstrom, ed., *Harvard Encyclopedia of American Ethnic Groups* (Cambridge, Mass.: The Belknap Press of Harvard University Press, 1980), 406–7, 410–11; Don Yoder, "Pennsylvania Germans," in ibid., 770–72; Mack Walker, *Germany and the Emigration, 1816–1885* (Cambridge, Mass.: Harvard University Press, 1964); Carl Wittke, *Refugees of Revolution: The German Forty-Eighters in America* (Westport, Conn.: Greenwood Press, 1970).

20. Conzen, "Germans," 407.

21. United States Bureau of the Census, *Historical Statistics of the United States, Colonial Times to 1957* (Washington, D.C.: Government Printing Office, 1960), 57; De Bow, *Statistical View of the United States*, 117.

22. Conzen, "Germans," 412.

23. Wilhelm, *Origin and Distribution of Settlement Groups*, 35–39; Yoder, "Pennsylvania Germans," 770–72.

24. Descriptions of German settlements in Indiana appear in *Indiana: A Guide to the Hoosier State* (New York: Oxford University Press, 1941), 187, 236–44, 274–75, 355, 388–89, 399, 411, 430–31, 455–56, 459, 479; Robert M. Taylor, Jr., et al., *Indiana: A New Historical Guide* (Indianapolis: Indiana Historical Society, 1989), 2, 39, 82, 101, 108–10, 112, 154–55, 172, 188, 209, 232–33, 236–37, 247–53, 289–90, 396, 598, 600, 608; Elfrieda Lang, "German Immigration to Dubois County, Indiana, during the Nineteenth Century," *Indiana Magazine of History* 41 (June 1945): 131–51; Rose, "Distribution of Indiana's Ethnic and Racial Minorities in 1850," 231–38; William A. Fritsch, *German Settlers and German Settlements in Indiana: A Memorial for the State Centennial* (Evansville, Ind.: By the Author, 1915).

25. Leo Schelbert, "Swiss," in Thernstrom, ed., *Harvard Encyclopedia of American Ethnic Groups*, 981, 983–86.

26. De Bow, *Statistical View of the United States*, 118.

27. John D. Barnhart and Dorothy L. Riker, *Indiana to 1816: The Colonial Period*, vol. 1 of the *History of Indiana* (Indianapolis: Indiana Historical Society and Indiana Historical Bureau, 1971), 364; Ralph H. Brown, *Historical Geography of the United States* (New York: Harcourt, Brace and Co., 1948), 239–40; Schelbert, "Swiss," 984–85; *Indiana*, 376, 377, 410, 431; Taylor et al., *New Historical Guide*, 148–52, 41.

28. Patrick J. Blessing, "Irish," in Thernstrom, ed., *Harvard Encyclopedia of American Ethnic Groups*, 524–45; Maldwyn A. Jones, "Scotch-Irish," in ibid., 895–908; Dennis Clark, *Hibernia America: The Irish and Regional Cultures* (New York: Greenwood Press, 1986); Carl Wittke, *The Irish in America* (Baton Rouge: Louisiana State University Press, 1956).

29. Blessing, "Irish," 528.

30. Ibid.; De Bow, *Statistical View of the United States*, 117; *Historical Statistics of the United States*, 57.

31. Ronald E. Shaw, "The Canal Era in the Old Northwest," in *Transportation and the Early Nation* (Indianapolis: Indiana Historical Society, 1982), 93–95, 103–4.

32. Alan A. Brookes, "Canadians, British," in Thernstrom, ed., *Harvard Encyclopedia of American Ethnic Groups*, 192.

33. Descriptions of Irish settlements in Indiana appear in *Indiana*, 372, 455–56; Taylor et al., *New Historical Guide*, 2, 82, 118, 154–55, 396; Elfrieda Lang, "Irishmen in Northern Indiana before 1850," *Mid-America* 36 [new series, 25] (July 1954): 190–98.

34. Rowland Berthoff, "Welsh," in Thernstrom, ed., *Harvard Encyclopedia of American Ethnic Groups*, 1011–17.

35. De Bow, *Statistical View of the United States*, 117.

36. Charlotte J. Erickson, "English," in Thernstrom, ed., *Harvard Encyclopedia of American Ethnic Groups*, 319–36; Zelinsky, *Cultural Geography of the United States*, 13–14, 23. Because the English were the first effective settlers, United States culture developed basically from English culture. Assimilation into American society by immigrants from England and other ethnically related places, including British Canada, occurred quickly, especially compared to ethnic groups having greater degrees of dissimilarity, and the presence and settlements of British natives often were overlooked. See Charlotte Erickson, *Invisible Immigrants: The Adaptation of English and Scottish Immigrants in Nineteenth-Century America* (Coral Gables, Fla.: University of Miami Press, 1972).

37. De Bow, *Statistical View of the United States*, 117.

38. John Rowe, "Cornish," in Thernstrom, ed., *Harvard Encyclopedia of American Ethnic Groups*, 243–45.

39. Ibid., 244.

40. Ibid.

41. Robert P. Howard, *Illinois: A History of the Prairie State* (Grand Rapids, Mich.: William B. Eerdmans Pub. Co., 1972), 125–28; Brown, *Historical Geography of the United States*, 250–52, 242; *Illinois: A Descriptive and Historical Guide* (Chicago: A. C. McClurg and Co., 1947), 428–29; Morris Birkbeck, *Letters from Illinois* (London: Printed for Taylor and Hessey, 1818).

42. Gordon Donaldson, "Scots," in Thernstrom, ed., *Harvard Encyclopedia of American Ethnic Groups*, 909, 911–12; Jones, "Scotch-Irish," 895–908.

43. De Bow, *Statistical View of the United States*, 117.

44. Patrice Louis René Higonnet, "French," in Thernstrom, ed., *Harvard Encyclopedia of American Ethnic Groups*, 379–88.

45. Billington, *Westward Expansion,* 110–31; Elliott Robert Barkan, "French Canadians," in Thernstrom, ed., *Harvard Encyclopedia of American Ethnic Groups,* 388–401.

46. De Bow, *Statistical View of the United States,* 118.

47. Brown, *Historical Geography of the United States,* 45–48, 252–54, 277–79; R. Louis Gentilcore, "Vincennes and French Settlement in the Old Northwest," *Annals of the Association of American Geographers* 47 (Sept. 1957): 285–97; Hart, *Look of the Land,* 48–49.

48. Billington, *Westward Expansion,* 210, 215, 219–20; Sibley, *French Five Hundred and Other Papers.*

49. Descriptions of French settlements in Indiana appear in *Indiana,* 194, 195–96, 251–52, 256, 261, 270, 272–74, 275, 288, 305, 386, 443, 455; Taylor et al., *New Historical Guide,* 1, 16, 137, 140, 254–55, 257, 523, 604, 622; Ronald L. Baker, *French Folklife in Old Vincennes* (Terre Haute, Ind.: Indiana Council of Teachers of English and Hoosier Folklore Society, 1989); Gentilcore, "Vincennes and French Settlement in the Old Northwest."

50. Dorothy Burton Skårdal, "Danes," in Thernstrom, ed., *Harvard Encyclopedia of American Ethnic Groups,* 273–82; De Bow, *Statistical View of the United States,* 118.

51. Robert P. Swierenga, "Dutch," in Thernstrom, ed., *Harvard Encyclopedia of American Ethnic Groups,* 284–95, and *The Dutch Transplanting in Michigan and the Midwest* (Ann Arbor: Historical Society of Michigan, 1986), and "Dutch Immigration Patterns in the Nineteenth and Twentieth Centuries," in *The Dutch in America: Immigration, Settlement, and Cultural Change,* ed. Robert P. Swierenga (New Brunswick, N.J.: Rutgers University Press, 1985), 15–42; Yda Saueressig-Schreuder, "Dutch Catholic Immigrant Settlement in Wisconsin," in ibid., 105–24; De Bow, *Statistical View of the United States,* 117.

52. *Michigan: A Guide to the Wolverine State* (New York, 1941), 105–6; *Wisconsin: A Guide to the Badger State* (New York: Duell, Sloan and Pearce, 1941), 49.

53. Pierre-Henri Laurent, "Belgians," in Thernstrom, ed., *Harvard Encyclopedia of American Ethnic Groups,* 179–81; De Bow, *Statistical View of the United States,* 118.

54. Descriptions of Belgian settlements in Indiana appear in *Indiana,* 397–99; Taylor et al., *New Historical Guide,* 236–37.

55. Peter A. Munch, "Norwegians," in Thernstrom, ed., *Harvard Encyclopedia of American Ethnic Groups,* 750–61; De Bow, *Statistical View of the United States,* 118.

56. Ulf Beijbom, "Swedes," in Thernstrom, ed., *Harvard Encyclopedia of American Ethnic Groups,* 971; De Bow, *Statistical View of the United States,* 118.

57. Beijbom, "Swedes," 973–75; *Illinois,* 5, 33, 196, 99–100, 548–50.

58. Settlers who indicated a birthplace anywhere in the country now called Canada are considered to be Canadians in this essay. As then defined, "Canada" was the administratively merged "Province of Canada" consisting only of Upper Canada (today's Ontario) and Lower Canada (today's Quebec), without the rest of the provinces. See J. M. S. Careless, *The Union of the Canadas: The Growth of Canadian Institutions, 1841–1857* (Toronto: McClelland and Stewart, 1967), 1–36; Reginald George Trotter, *Canadian Federation: Its Origins and Achievements, A Study in Nation Building* (Toronto and London: J. M. Dent and Sons, Limited, 1924), 5, 132–37; Walter L. White et al., *Canadian Confederation: A Decision-Making Analysis* (Toronto: Macmillan of Canada, 1979), 19–43. On the census schedules birthplaces were most commonly recorded as being in Canada rather than in another portion of the British North American empire such as Nova Scotia, Newfoundland, or Upper or Lower Canada. In the published 1850 census those born in what today is Canada were listed as natives of "British America." See De Bow, *Statistical View of the United States,* 119.

59. Brookes, "Canadians, British," 191–97; Barkan, "French Canadians," 392.

60. Brookes, "Canadians, British," 191–93; Ronald J. Eady, "Anti-American Sentiment in Essex County in the Wake of the Rebellions of 1837," *Ontario History* 61 (Mar. 1969): 1–8; Lillian F. Gates, *Land Policies of Upper Canada* (Toronto: University of Toronto Press, 1968), 19–22, 66–67, 145–95, 257, 261–67; Marcus Lee Hansen and John Bartlet Brebner, *The Mingling of the Canadian and American Peoples* (New Haven, Conn.: Yale University Press, 1940), 12, 46–65, 81–82, 95, 103, 105, 115–18; Fred Landon, *Western Ontario and the American Frontier* (Toronto: The Ryerson Press, 1941), 13–19, 21, 46, 195; R. S. Longley, "Emigration and the Crisis of 1837 in Upper Canada," *Canadian Historical Review* 17 (Mar. 1936): 29–40; A. R. M. Lower, "Immigration and Settlement in Canada, 1812–1820," *ibid.* 3 (Mar. 1922): 37–47; J. Howard Richards, "Lands and Policies: Attitudes and Controls in the Alienation of Lands during the First Century of Settlement," *Ontario History* 50 (autumn 1958): 193–209.

61. De Bow, *Statistical View of the United States,* 119.

62. Descriptions of Canadian settlements in Indiana appear in Taylor et al., *New Historical Guide,* 254, 257, 616.

63. De Bow, *Statistical View of the United States,* 118.

64. Ueda Reed, "West Indians," in Thernstrom, ed., *Harvard Encyclopedia of American Ethnic Groups,* 1020–27; Michel S. Laguerre, "Haitians," in ibid., 446–47.

65. "Black" is used in this essay to indicate persons identified in the manuscript schedules as black or mulatto. A column in the schedules was provided for the canvasser to indicate each inhabitant's "color"; the choices were "white, black, or mulatto." See Barnes F. Lathrop, "History from the Census Returns," *Southwestern Historical Quarterly* 51 (Apr. 1948): 296. The definition and application of these descriptions appear to have been at the canvasser's discretion since no official guidelines were provided. See United States Bureau of the Census, *Negro Population, 1790–1915* (Washington, D.C.: Government Printing Office, 1918), 207.

66. Gwendolyn J. Crenshaw, *"Bury Me in a Free Land": The Abolitionist Movement in Indiana* (Indianapolis: Indiana Historical Bureau, 1986), 5–12; Paul Finkelman, "Slavery and the Northwest Ordinance: A Study in Ambiguity," *Journal of the Early Republic* 6 (winter 1986): 343–70; Leon F. Litwack, *North of Slavery: The Negro in the Free States, 1790–1860* (Chicago: University of Chicago Press, 1961), 66–72; Emma Lou Thornbrough, *The Negro in Indiana: A Study of a Minority,* vol. 38 of *Indiana Historical Collections* (Indianapolis: Indiana Historical Bureau, 1957), 1–30, 55–70.

67. *Negro Population,* 57.

68. Merrily Pierce, "Luke Decker and Slavery: His Cases with Bob and Anthony, 1817–1822," *Indiana Magazine of History* 85 (Mar. 1989): 31–49.

69. Thomas C. Holt, "Afro-Americans," in Thernstrom, ed., *Harvard Encyclopedia of American Ethnic Groups,* 5–23; Douglas K. Meyer, "Native-Born Immigrant Clusters on the Illinois Frontier," *Proceedings of the Association of American Geographers* 8 (1976): 41–44, and "Southern Illinois Migration Fields: The Shawnee Hills in 1850," *Professional Geographer* 28 (May 1976): 151–60; Rose, "Hoosier Origins"; Wilhelm, *Origin and Distribution of Settlement Groups.*

70. Everett S. Claspy, *The Negro in Southwestern Michigan: Negroes in the North in a Rural Environment* (Dowagiac, Mich.: n.p., 1967); Gregory S. Rose, "The County Origins of Southern Michigan's Settlers: 1800–1850," *East Lakes Geographer* 22 (1987): 75–76.

71. Descriptions of black settlements in Indiana appear in *Indiana,* 273, 338–39, 418–19; Taylor et al., *New Historical Guide,* 88–90, 93, 98–99, 117, 119–20, 137, 154, 155, 188–89, 275, 339, 399, 407–8, 470–71. See Gregory S. Rose, "Quakers, North Carolinians, and Blacks in Indiana's Settlement Pattern," *Journal of Cultural Geography* 7 (fall/winter 1986): 35–48.

72. Rose, "Distribution of Indiana's Ethnic and Racial Minorities in 1850," 257–59.

73. Maurice G. Baxter, "Encouragement of Immigration to the Middle West during the Era of the Civil War," *Indiana Magazine of History* 46 (Mar. 1950): 34–36.

74. Richard Lyle Power, "The Hoosier as an American Folk-Type," *Indiana Magazine of History* 38 (June 1942): 107–22, and *Planting Corn Belt Culture: The Impress of the Upland Southerner and Yankee in the Old Northwest,* vol. 17 of Indiana Historical Society *Publications* (Indianapolis: Indiana Historical Society, 1953), 72–74, 81–86, and "Wet Lands and the Hoosier Stereotype," 33–48.

75. Lindley, ed., *Indiana as Seen by Early Travelers,* 523–24.

76. John Fraser Hart, "The Spread of the Frontier and the Growth of Population," *Geoscience and Man* 5 (June 1974): 77–79; Thorndale and Dollarhide, *Map Guide to the U. S. Federal Censuses,* 163–68; United States Bureau of the Census, *Statistical Atlas of the United States, Based Upon Results of the Eleventh Census* (Washington, D.C.: Government Printing Office, 1898), Plates 3 and 4.

# APPENDIX 2

The data contained in the following tables were obtained primarily from the U.S. Bureau of the Census published census reports. The data pertaining to 1860 were derived from the computerized 1860 Indiana census data base. In 1988 the Indiana Historical Society completed a four-year project to computerize the 1860 census for Indiana. Indiana University-Purdue University at Indianapolis (IUPUI) developed the software that allowed all the data to be entered into searchable fields. A team of transcribers entered the information for over eighteen million census reponses from the microfilm of the original records. A document at the end of this appendix gives more specific information on the sources of the data contained within each table.

The editors would like to alert the reader to the possibility of errors in the following tables. The actual census data for any particular year may be incorrect. The census has always relied on the honesty of the individual reporting the information. In many cases, and for a variety of reasons, individuals gave inaccurate information. More recently, the Bureau of the Census has used sampling techniques to determine the quantity and characteristics of the population. A margin of error occurs with any sampling. In addition, the reported population differed between censuses. For example, early census figures reflected all foreign born, while in 1910 the numbers referred to foreign born white. Thus comparing censuses is fraught with problems. Moreover, the possibility exists that the tables embody figures incorrectly transferred by transcribers from either the published data or the microfilm records. With the above in mind, the reader should surmise that the data used in the essays may not be the same as is found in one of these tables in the appendix, although the authors for the most part shared a common set of census numbers and other sources for population counts. In short, the editors

recommend the reader employ these figures as a general reference, and, if desired, verify the given information by checking the original census table for accuracy and for an explanation of how the actual figures were derived by the Census Bureau.

For more information about the difficulties involved in using the U.S. federal census data we suggest:

Appendix I, "Methods of Estimating the Size of Groups," by Charles A. Price in the *Harvard Encyclopedia of American Ethnic Groups*, Stephan Thernstrom, editor, Belknap Press of Harvard University, Cambridge, 1980, pp. 1033-44.

A series of reports on the federal census appearing in the *Indiana Magazine of History* authored by Robert G. Barrows:

> "The Manuscript Federal Census: Source for a 'New' Local History," *Indiana Magazine of History* 69 (Sept. 1973): 181-92.

> "The Ninth Federal Census of Indianapolis: A Case Study in Civic Chauvinism," *Indiana Magazine of History* 73 (Mar. 1977): 1-16.

> "The 1900 Federal Census: A Note on Availability and Potential Uses," *Indiana Magazine of History* 74 (June 1978): 146-52.

> "The 1900 Federal Census: A Note," *Indiana Magazine of History* 78 (Dec. 1982): 341-45.

> "The 1920 Federal Census: A Note," *Indiana Magazine of History* 88 (Mar. 1992): 320-23.

Jon A. Gjerde, "Appendix on Statistics," *They Chose Minnesota*, Minnesota Historical Society Press, St. Paul, 1981, pp. 593-95.

TABLE 1. FOREIGN BORN IN INDIANA BY ETHNIC GROUP, 1850–1990

| Birthplace | 1850 | 1860 | 1870 | 1880 | 1890 | 1900 | 1910 | 1920 | 1930 | 1940 | 1950 | 1960 | 1970 | 1980 | 1990 |
|---|---|---|---|---|---|---|---|---|---|---|---|---|---|---|---|
| **Europe** | | | | | | | | | | | | | | | |
| Austria | 12 | 286 | | 430 | 544 | 2,086 | 11,830 | 16,876 | 2,709 | 4,405 | 3,677 | 2,579 | 1,941 | 1,415 | 1,042 |
| Belgium | 103 | 334 | 452 | 486 | 733 | 2,575 | 2,298 | 2,523 | 3,254 | 2,600 | | 1,645 | 1,231 | 855 | 634 |
| Czechoslovakia | | | 18 | | | | | | 8,325 | 5,782 | 5,343 | 3,773 | 2,666 | 1,773 | 1,101 |
| Denmark | 7 | 67 | | 554 | 718 | 783 | 990 | 975 | 964 | 768 | 614 | 411 | 340 | 249 | 164 |
| Estonia | | | | | | | | | | | | 160 | 116 | 132 | 50 |
| Finland | | 1 | | 10 | 109 | | | 231 | 265 | 195 | 217 | 187 | 176 | 91 | 215 |
| France | 2,335 | 6,254 | 6,283 | 4,293 | 3,297 | | 2,388 | 2,571 | 2,160 | 1,459 | 1,397 | 1,215 | 1,204 | 1,065 | 1,544 |
| Germany | 29,990 | 67,315 | 77,658 | 72,133 | 84,900 | 73,302 | 62,177 | 46,000 | 28,152 | 18,784 | 13,780 | 13,474 | 11,050 | 11,895 | 16,461 |
| Greece | | 39 | | 2 | | 82 | 1,370 | 3,511 | 4,087 | 3,747 | 4,032 | 3,517 | 3,321 | 2,861 | 2,489 |
| Holland | 60 | 513 | 872 | 1,338 | | 1,731 | 2,131 | | | | | | | | |
| Hungary | 5 | 33 | | 68 | 436 | 1,379 | 14,370 | 13,812 | 7,674 | 7,733 | 6,703 | 5,816 | 3,470 | 2,151 | 1,494 |
| Ireland | 13,208 | 24,772 | 28,549 | 24,823 | 20,819 | | 11,266 | 8,300 | 3,931 | 2,657 | 2,351 | 1,673 | 1,152 | 825 | 789 |
| Italy | 8 | 100 | | 195 | 468 | | 6,911 | 6,631 | 6,873 | 6,309 | 5,501 | 4,756 | 3,868 | 2,510 | 2,566 |
| Latvia | | | | | | | | | 116 | 98 | | 1,173 | 1,002 | 785 | 604 |
| Lithuania | | | | | | | | | 2,109 | 2,078 | 2,003 | 1,410 | 1,125 | 596 | 423 |
| Luxembourg | | | | 138 | | | | 112 | 56 | 60 | | 40 | 63 | | |
| Netherlands | 4 | 52 | 17 | 1,182 | | | | 2,035 | 1,992 | 1,617 | 1,525 | 1,729 | 1,530 | 1,344 | 1,591 |
| Norway | 26 | 35 | | 177 | 285 | | | 517 | 730 | 599 | 552 | 440 | 379 | 311 | 177 |
| Poland | 29 | 92 | 523 | 870 | 3,114 | | | | 17,482 | 14,257 | 11,877 | 9,600 | 5,944 | 4,136 | 3,129 |
| Portugal | 6 | 5 | | 5 | | | | 13 | 88 | 27 | | 25 | 12 | 95 | 130 |
| Romania | 1 | | | 2 | | | 709 | 2,561 | 3,292 | 2,456 | 1,804 | 1,587 | 929 | 650 | 547 |
| Spain | 2 | 14 | | 94 | | | | 475 | 619 | 499 | | 382 | 527 | 541 | 683 |
| Sweden | 15 | 729 | 2,296 | 3,015 | 4,512 | | 5,031 | 4,979 | 4,666 | 3,565 | 2,736 | 1,710 | 945 | 724 | 427 |
| Switzerland | 718 | 3,461 | | 3,800 | 3,478 | | 9,766 | 2,301 | 1,624 | 1,083 | | 436 | 438 | 280 | 353 |
| United Kingdom | | | 560 | 68 | 15,032 | | | | | | | | | | 8,274 |
| (England) | 5,490 | 9,363 | 10,449 | 10,873 | | 10,844 | 9,780 | 8,658 | 7,465 | 5,562 | 6,343 | 5,866 | 5,067 | 5,008 | |
| (Northern Ireland) | | | | | | | | | 1,045 | 541 | 58 | 499 | 328 | 147 | |
| (Scotland) | 1,368 | 2,105 | 2,503 | 2,612 | | | 3,419 | 4,114 | 3,898 | 3,063 | 2,715 | 2,188 | 1,837 | 1,385 | |
| (Wales) | 142 | 232 | | 914 | | | 1,498 | 1,081 | 934 | 596 | | 411 | 201 | 191 | |
| Yugoslavia | | | | | | | | | 6,646 | 5,342 | 5,011 | 5,531 | 5,154 | 4,272 | 3,751 |
| Other Europe | 86 | 303 | | 1,287 | 541 | | | 1,528 | 778 | 708 | 4,781 | 332 | 510 | 302 | 325 |
| **Soviet Union** | 5 | 46 | | 192 | 576 | | 9,599 | 15,077 | 4,749 | 4,126 | 3,582 | 3,115 | 2,384 | 2,143 | 1,697 |
| **Asia** | | | | | | | | 134 | | | | | | | |
| Afghanistan | | | | | | | | | | | | | | 70 | 105 |
| Burma | | | | 2 | | | | | | | | | | 62 | 102 |
| Cambodia | | | | | | | | | | | | | | | 283 |
| China | | 6 | | 27 | 91 | | | | | | | 596 | 1,121 | 1,260 | 2,525 |
| Hong Kong | | | | | | | | | | | | | | 571 | 650 |
| India | 5 | 6 | | | | | | | | | | 220 | 811 | 2,510 | 4,979 |
| Indonesia | | | | | | | | | | | | | | 210 | 573 |
| Iran | | | | | | | | | | | | | | 1,123 | 931 |
| Iraq | | | | | | | | | | | | | | 160 | 71 |
| Israel | | | | | | | | | | | | 85 | 147 | 301 | 436 |
| Japan | | | | 4 | | | | | | | | 601 | 732 | 1,536 | 4,942 |
| Jordan | | | | | | | | | | | | | | 166 | 171 |
| Korea | | | | | | | | | | | | 199 | 380 | 3,208 | 4,598 |
| Laos | | | | | | | | | | | | | | 839 | 631 |
| Lebanon | | | | | | | | | | | | 260 | 230 | 365 | 367 |
| Malaysia | | | | | | | | | | | | | | 497 | 526 |
| Pakistan | | | | | | | | | | | | 39 | | 390 | 856 |
| Philippines | | | | | | | | | | | | 283 | 876 | 2,572 | 3,349 |
| Saudi Arabia | | | | | | | | | | | | | | 468 | 324 |
| Syria | | | | | | | | | 783 | 738 | | 334 | 230 | 184 | 309 |
| Taiwan | | | | | | | | | | | | | | 843 | 1,617 |
| Thailand | | | | | | | | | | | | | | 580 | 767 |
| Turkey | | | | 3 | | | 2,577 | 1,815 | 308 | 462 | | 348 | 353 | 269 | 433 |
| Vietnam | | | | | | | | | | | | | | 1,957 | 1,961 |
| Other Asia | | 4 | | 13 | | | | | 415 | 363 | 1,677 | 1,023 | 1,517 | 603 | 1,181 |
| **North America** | | | | | | | | | | | | | | | |
| Canada | 1,865 | 3,191 | 4,754 | 5,069 | 4,954 | 5,842 | 5,784 | 3,170 | 6,203 | 5,588 | 6,138 | 6,533 | 5,597 | 6,467 | 7,088 |
| Other North America | 3 | 15 | | 120 | | | | 46 | 69 | 56 | | | | 63 | 160 |
| **Central America** | | | | | | | | | | | | | | | |
| Bahamas | | | | | | | | | | | | | | 29 | 93 |
| Barbados | | | | | | | | | | | | | | 76 | 81 |
| Cuba | | 3 | | 6 | 32 | | | | | | | 149 | 1,178 | 856 | 877 |
| Dominican Republic | | | | | | | | | | | | 21 | 67 | 73 | 170 |
| Haiti | | | | | | | | | | | | 27 | 106 | 80 | 134 |
| Jamaica | 2 | | | 4 | | | | | | | | 63 | 155 | 478 | 643 |
| Trinidad/Tobago | | | | | | | | | | | | | 50 | 130 | 268 |
| Other Caribbean | 16 | 16 | | 18 | | | | 34 | | | | | 103 | 94 | 131 |
| Belize | | | | | | | | | | | | | | 52 | 79 |
| Costa Rica | | | | | | | | | | | | 24 | 82 | 142 | 192 |
| El Salvador | | | | | | | | | | | | 24 | 12 | 112 | 154 |

TABLE 1.  FOREIGN BORN IN INDIANA BY ETHNIC GROUP, 1850–1990 (*continued*)

| Birthplace | 1850 | 1860 | 1870 | 1880 | 1890 | 1900 | 1910 | 1920 | 1930 | 1940 | 1950 | 1960 | 1970 | 1980 | 1990 |
|---|---|---|---|---|---|---|---|---|---|---|---|---|---|---|---|
| Guatemala | | | | | | | | | | | | 31 | 40 | 128 | 255 |
| Honduras | | | | | | | | | | | | 44 | 32 | 84 | 191 |
| Mexico | 19 | 22 | | 26 | 39 | | | 650 | 7,601 | 2,160 | 3,232 | 5,058 | 5,060 | 9,460 | 10,805 |
| Nicaragua | | | | | | | | | | | | 18 | 23 | 48 | 110 |
| Panama | | | | 7 | | | | | | | | 53 | 134 | 282 | 799 |
| Other Central America | | | | 4 | | | | | 53 | 97 | | 156 | | | 21 |
| **South America** | 3 | | | | | | | | | | | | | | |
| Argentina | | | | | | | | | | | | 149 | 229 | 212 | 347 |
| Bolivia | | | | | | | | | | | | 34 | 26 | 85 | 203 |
| Brazil | | 6 | | 9 | | | | | | | | 178 | 162 | 458 | 589 |
| Chile | | | | 1 | | | | | | | | 76 | 150 | 178 | 258 |
| Colombia | | | | | | | | | | | | 87 | 243 | 393 | 463 |
| Ecuador | | | | | | | | | | | | 26 | 46 | 174 | 209 |
| Guyana | | | | | | | | | | | | | | 102 | 152 |
| Peru | | | | | | | | | | | | 83 | 120 | 227 | 243 |
| Uruguay | | | | | | | | | | | | | 27 | 38 | 51 |
| Venezuela | | | | | | | | | | | | 81 | 75 | 357 | 219 |
| Other South America | | 4 | | 6 | | | | 40 | 150 | 171 | | 113 | 149 | 18 | 169 |
| **Africa** | | | | | | | | | | | | | | | |
| Egypt | | 1 | | 1 | | | | | | | | | 112 | 296 | 388 |
| Ethiopia | | | | | | | | | | | | | | 88 | 221 |
| Ghana | | | | | | | | | | | | | | 67 | 118 |
| Kenya | | | | | | | | | | | | | | 87 | 117 |
| Morocco | | | | | | | | | | | | | | 65 | 162 |
| Nigeria | | | | | | | | | | | | | | 236 | 503 |
| South Africa | | | | 3 | | | | | | | | 35 | 117 | 165 | 211 |
| Other Africa | 2 | 4 | | 4 | | | | | | | | 126 | 379 | 474 | 1,201 |
| **Oceania** | | | | | | | | | | | | | | | |
| Australia | | 7 | | 22 | 61 | | | | 98 | 104 | | 277 | 292 | 317 | 616 |
| Fiji | | | | | | | | | | | | | | 4 | 20 |
| New Zealand | 1 | | | 7 | | | | | | | | 44 | 109 | 105 | 162 |
| Tonga | | | | | | | | | | | | | | 2 | 12 |
| Western Samoa | | | | | | | | | | | | | | 19 | 60 |
| Other Oceania | | | | | | | | | 3 | 4 | | 52 | 122 | 11 | 35 |
| **Not Reported** | 10 | 1,039 | 1,566 | 129 | 393 | | 1,964 | 98 | 179 | 172 | 2,816 | 310 | 2,894 | 7,760 | 3,894 |
| **Total Foreign Born** | 55,546 | 120,493 | 136,465 | 133,881 | 146,205 | 98,733 | 165,858 | 150,868 | 142,545 | 110,631 | 100,465 | 93,540 | 83,198 | 100,068 | 116,221 |

## TABLE 2. FOREIGN BORN BY COUNTY AS PERCENTAGE OF TOTAL INDIANA POPULATION, 1850–1990

| | 1850 | | | 1860 | | | 1870 | | | 1880 | | | 1890 | | |
|---|---|---|---|---|---|---|---|---|---|---|---|---|---|---|---|
| | Total Population | Foreign Born | Percentage For. Born | Total Population | Foreign Born | Percentage For. Born | Total Population | Foreign Born | Percentage For. Born | Total Population | Foreign Born | Percentage For. Born | Total Population | Foreign Born | Percentage For. Born |
| Indiana | 988,416 | 61,788 | 6.25% | 1,350,428 | 53,165 | 3.94% | 1,680,637 | 140,628 | 8.37% | 1,978,301 | 144,178 | 7.29% | 2,192,404 | 141,996 | 6.48% |
| Adams | 5,797 | 834 | 14.39% | 9,252 | 634 | 6.85% | 11,382 | 1,321 | 11.61% | 15,385 | 1,401 | 9.11% | 20,181 | 1,808 | 8.96% |
| Allen | 16,919 | 3,954 | 23.37% | 29,328 | 2,723 | 9.28% | 43,491 | 8,759 | 20.14% | 54,763 | 9,187 | 16.78% | 66,689 | 10,388 | 15.58% |
| Bartholomew | 12,428 | 449 | 3.61% | 17,865 | 415 | 2.32% | 21,133 | 1,433 | 6.78% | 22,777 | 1,282 | 5.63% | 23,867 | 1,113 | 4.66% |
| Benton | 1,144 | 68 | 5.94% | 2,809 | 210 | 7.48% | 5,615 | 686 | 12.22% | 11,108 | 1,466 | 13.20% | 11,903 | 1,264 | 10.62% |
| Blackford | 2,860 | 68 | 2.38% | 4,122 | 51 | 1.24% | 6,272 | 191 | 3.05% | 8,620 | 194 | 2.25% | 10,461 | 195 | 1.86% |
| Boone | 11,631 | 62 | 0.53% | 16,753 | 157 | 0.94% | 22,593 | 405 | 1.79% | 25,922 | 416 | 1.60% | 26,572 | 294 | 1.11% |
| Brown | 4,846 | 87 | 1.80% | 6,507 | 77 | 1.18% | 8,681 | 152 | 1.75% | 10,264 | 121 | 1.18% | 10,308 | 81 | 0.79% |
| Carroll | 11,015 | 281 | 2.55% | 13,489 | 472 | 3.50% | 16,152 | 747 | 4.62% | 18,345 | 639 | 3.48% | 20,021 | 551 | 2.75% |
| Cass | 11,021 | 729 | 6.61% | 16,843 | 1,090 | 6.47% | 24,193 | 2,620 | 10.83% | 27,611 | 2,402 | 8.70% | 31,152 | 2,349 | 7.54% |
| Clark | 15,828 | 1,137 | 7.18% | 20,502 | 1,014 | 4.95% | 24,770 | 2,695 | 10.88% | 28,610 | 2,465 | 8.62% | 30,259 | 1,871 | 6.18% |
| Clay | 7,944 | 153 | 1.93% | 12,161 | 190 | 1.56% | 19,084 | 1,786 | 9.36% | 25,854 | 2,655 | 10.27% | 30,536 | 3,276 | 10.73% |
| Clinton | 11,869 | 116 | 0.98% | 14,505 | 151 | 1.04% | 17,330 | 203 | 1.17% | 23,472 | 327 | 1.39% | 27,370 | 324 | 1.18% |
| Crawford | 6,524 | 63 | 0.97% | 8,226 | 127 | 1.54% | 9,851 | 242 | 2.46% | 12,356 | 214 | 1.73% | 13,370 | 181 | 1.35% |
| Daviess | 10,352 | 986 | 9.52% | 13,323 | 736 | 5.52% | 16,747 | 907 | 5.42% | 21,552 | 1,024 | 4.75% | 26,227 | 926 | 3.53% |
| Dearborn | 20,166 | 4,058 | 20.12% | 24,406 | 2,048 | 8.39% | 24,116 | 4,596 | 19.06% | 26,671 | 4,127 | 15.47% | 23,364 | 2,870 | 12.28% |
| Decatur | 15,107 | 435 | 2.88% | 17,294 | 497 | 2.87% | 19,053 | 1,233 | 6.47% | 19,779 | 995 | 5.03% | 19,277 | 797 | 4.13% |
| De Kalb | 8,251 | 289 | 3.50% | 13,880 | 250 | 1.80% | 17,167 | 964 | 5.62% | 20,225 | 1,199 | 5.93% | 24,307 | 1,340 | 5.51% |
| Delaware | 10,843 | 171 | 1.58% | 15,753 | 283 | 1.80% | 19,030 | 501 | 2.63% | 22,926 | 470 | 2.05% | 30,131 | 748 | 2.48% |
| Dubois | 6,321 | 1,617 | 25.58% | 10,394 | 197 | 1.90% | 12,597 | 2,461 | 19.54% | 15,992 | 2,120 | 13.26% | 20,253 | 1,769 | 8.73% |
| Elkhart | 12,690 | 613 | 4.83% | 20,986 | 868 | 4.14% | 26,026 | 1,777 | 6.83% | 33,454 | 2,122 | 6.34% | 39,201 | 2,625 | 6.70% |
| Fayette | 10,217 | 338 | 3.31% | 10,225 | 464 | 4.54% | 10,476 | 764 | 7.29% | 11,394 | 681 | 5.98% | 12,630 | 651 | 5.15% |
| Floyd | 14,875 | 2,401 | 16.14% | 20,183 | 1,971 | 9.77% | 23,390 | 3,695 | 15.80% | 24,590 | 3,296 | 13.40% | 29,458 | 2,985 | 10.13% |
| Fountain | 13,253 | 411 | 3.10% | 15,566 | 539 | 3.46% | 16,389 | 948 | 5.78% | 20,228 | 1,193 | 5.90% | 19,558 | 669 | 3.42% |
| Franklin | 17,968 | 2,321 | 12.92% | 19,549 | 762 | 3.90% | 20,223 | 2,928 | 14.48% | 20,092 | 2,416 | 12.02% | 18,366 | 1,534 | 8.35% |
| Fulton | 5,982 | 214 | 3.58% | 9,422 | 234 | 2.48% | 12,726 | 514 | 4.04% | 14,301 | 506 | 3.54% | 16,746 | 468 | 2.79% |
| Gibson | 10,771 | 621 | 5.77% | 14,532 | 510 | 3.51% | 17,371 | 1,193 | 6.87% | 22,742 | 1,143 | 5.03% | 24,920 | 986 | 3.96% |
| Grant | 11,092 | 91 | 0.82% | 15,797 | 200 | 1.27% | 18,487 | 314 | 1.70% | 23,618 | 413 | 1.75% | 31,493 | 681 | 2.16% |
| Greene | 12,313 | 509 | 4.13% | 16,041 | 220 | 1.37% | 19,514 | 296 | 1.52% | 22,996 | 280 | 1.22% | 24,379 | 339 | 1.39% |
| Hamilton | 12,684 | 264 | 2.08% | 17,310 | 176 | 1.02% | 20,882 | 391 | 1.87% | 24,801 | 324 | 1.31% | 26,123 | 303 | 1.16% |
| Hancock | 9,698 | 275 | 2.84% | 12,802 | 196 | 1.53% | 15,123 | 543 | 3.59% | 17,123 | 510 | 2.98% | 17,829 | 416 | 2.33% |
| Harrison | 15,286 | 1,203 | 7.87% | 18,521 | 477 | 2.58% | 19,913 | 1,255 | 6.30% | 21,326 | 1,052 | 4.93% | 20,786 | 769 | 3.70% |
| Hendricks | 14,083 | 370 | 2.63% | 16,953 | 271 | 1.60% | 20,277 | 515 | 2.54% | 22,981 | 490 | 2.13% | 21,498 | 332 | 1.54% |
| Henry | 17,605 | 207 | 1.18% | 20,119 | 300 | 1.49% | 22,986 | 454 | 1.98% | 24,016 | 357 | 1.49% | 23,879 | 258 | 1.08% |
| Howard | 6,657 | 103 | 1.55% | 12,524 | 141 | 1.13% | 15,847 | 305 | 1.92% | 19,584 | 343 | 1.75% | 26,186 | 768 | 2.93% |
| Huntington | 7,850 | 459 | 5.85% | 14,867 | 522 | 3.51% | 19,036 | 1,290 | 6.78% | 21,805 | 1,158 | 5.31% | 27,644 | 1,344 | 4.86% |
| Jackson | 11,047 | 728 | 6.59% | 16,286 | 325 | 2.00% | 18,974 | 1,595 | 8.41% | 23,050 | 1,508 | 6.54% | 24,139 | 1,219 | 5.05% |
| Jasper | 3,540 | 74 | 2.09% | 4,291 | 96 | 2.24% | 6,354 | 340 | 5.35% | 9,464 | 813 | 8.59% | 11,185 | 873 | 7.81% |
| Jay | 7,047 | 131 | 1.86% | 11,399 | 173 | 1.52% | 15,000 | 508 | 3.39% | 19,282 | 558 | 2.89% | 23,478 | 567 | 2.42% |
| Jefferson | 23,916 | 3,238 | 13.54% | 25,036 | 2,073 | 8.28% | 297,741 | 3,583 | 1.20% | 25,977 | 2,457 | 9.46% | 24,507 | 1,624 | 6.63% |
| Jennings | 12,096 | 1,003 | 8.29% | 14,749 | 929 | 6.30% | 16,218 | 1,574 | 9.71% | 16,453 | 1,202 | 7.31% | 14,608 | 885 | 6.06% |
| Johnson | 12,101 | 30 | 0.25% | 14,854 | 244 | 1.64% | 18,366 | 484 | 2.64% | 19,537 | 354 | 1.81% | 19,561 | 223 | 1.14% |
| Knox | 11,084 | 1,007 | 9.09% | 16,056 | 815 | 5.08% | 21,562 | 2,114 | 9.80% | 26,324 | 2,095 | 7.96% | 28,044 | 1,738 | 6.20% |
| Kosciusko | 10,243 | 290 | 2.83% | 17,418 | 354 | 2.03% | 23,531 | 728 | 3.09% | 26,494 | 673 | 2.54% | 28,645 | 577 | 2.01% |
| Lagrange | 8,387 | 417 | 4.97% | 11,366 | 438 | 3.85% | 14,148 | 693 | 4.90% | 15,630 | 634 | 4.06% | 15,615 | 513 | 3.29% |
| Lake | 3,991 | 894 | 22.40% | 9,145 | 766 | 8.38% | 12,339 | 3,597 | 29.15% | 15,091 | 4,010 | 26.57% | 23,886 | 6,876 | 28.79% |
| La Porte | 12,145 | 846 | 6.97% | 22,919 | 2,160 | 9.42% | 27,062 | 6,642 | 24.54% | 30,985 | 7,177 | 23.16% | 34,445 | 7,730 | 22.44% |
| Lawrence | 12,097 | 346 | 2.86% | 13,692 | 261 | 1.91% | 14,628 | 237 | 1.62% | 18,543 | 333 | 1.80% | 19,792 | 416 | 2.10% |
| Madison | 12,375 | 152 | 1.23% | 16,518 | 287 | 1.74% | 22,770 | 633 | 2.78% | 27,527 | 653 | 2.37% | 36,487 | 998 | 2.74% |
| Marion | 24,103 | 1,949 | 8.09% | 39,855 | 2,803 | 7.03% | 71,939 | 12,647 | 17.58% | 102,782 | 14,743 | 14.34% | 141,156 | 17,615 | 12.48% |
| Marshall | 5,348 | 293 | 5.48% | 12,722 | 536 | 4.21% | 20,211 | 1,375 | 6.80% | 23,414 | 1,301 | 5.56% | 23,818 | 1,245 | 5.23% |
| Martin | 5,941 | 107 | 1.80% | 8,975 | 240 | 2.67% | 11,103 | 257 | 2.31% | 13,475 | 240 | 1.78% | 13,973 | 185 | 1.32% |
| Miami | 11,304 | 401 | 3.55% | 16,851 | 447 | 2.65% | 21,052 | 1,103 | 5.24% | 24,083 | 1,239 | 5.14% | 25,823 | 1,287 | 4.98% |
| Monroe | 11,286 | 185 | 1.64% | 12,847 | 347 | 2.70% | 14,168 | 375 | 2.65% | 15,875 | 304 | 1.91% | 17,673 | 246 | 1.39% |
| Montgomery | 18,084 | 216 | 1.19% | 20,888 | 515 | 2.47% | 23,765 | 887 | 3.73% | 27,316 | 783 | 2.87% | 28,025 | 630 | 2.25% |
| Morgan | 14,576 | 360 | 2.47% | 16,110 | 190 | 1.18% | 17,528 | 328 | 1.87% | 18,900 | 300 | 1.59% | 18,643 | 211 | 1.13% |
| Newton | | | | 2,360 | 87 | 3.69% | 5,829 | 440 | 7.55% | 8,167 | 839 | 10.27% | 8,803 | 830 | 9.43% |
| Noble | 7,946 | 310 | 3.90% | 14,915 | 339 | 2.27% | 20,389 | 1,500 | 7.36% | 22,956 | 1,520 | 6.62% | 23,359 | 1,383 | 5.92% |
| Ohio | 5,308 | 343 | 6.46% | 5,462 | 130 | 2.38% | 5,837 | 453 | 7.76% | 5,563 | 324 | 5.82% | 4,955 | 246 | 4.96% |
| Orange | 10,809 | 94 | 0.87% | 12,076 | 97 | 0.80% | 13,497 | 99 | 0.73% | 14,363 | 54 | 0.38% | 14,678 | 43 | 0.29% |
| Owen | 12,106 | 179 | 1.48% | 14,376 | 118 | 0.82% | 16,137 | 379 | 2.35% | 15,901 | 306 | 1.92% | 15,040 | 310 | 2.06% |
| Parke | 14,968 | 181 | 1.21% | 15,538 | 268 | 1.72% | 18,166 | 271 | 1.49% | 19,460 | 408 | 2.10% | 20,296 | 755 | 3.72% |
| Perry | 7,268 | 734 | 10.10% | 11,847 | 1,326 | 11.19% | 14,801 | 2,736 | 18.49% | 16,997 | 2,329 | 13.70% | 18,240 | 1,859 | 10.19% |
| Pike | 7,720 | 827 | 10.71% | 10,078 | 127 | 1.26% | 13,779 | 369 | 2.68% | 16,383 | 371 | 2.26% | 18,544 | 383 | 2.07% |
| Porter | 5,234 | 417 | 7.97% | 10,313 | 1,299 | 12.60% | 13,942 | 2,839 | 20.36% | 17,227 | 3,477 | 20.18% | 18,052 | 3,764 | 20.85% |
| Posey | 12,549 | 2,630 | 20.96% | 16,167 | 476 | 2.94% | 19,185 | 2,254 | 11.75% | 20,857 | 1,896 | 9.09% | 21,529 | 1,376 | 6.39% |
| Pulaski | 2,595 | 117 | 4.51% | 5,711 | 225 | 3.94% | 7,801 | 948 | 12.15% | 9,851 | 1,122 | 11.39% | 11,233 | 1,153 | 10.26% |
| Putnam | 18,615 | 305 | 1.64% | 20,681 | 430 | 2.08% | 21,514 | 790 | 3.67% | 22,501 | 589 | 2.62% | 22,335 | 398 | 1.78% |
| Randolph | 14,725 | 188 | 1.28% | 18,997 | 260 | 1.37% | 22,862 | 560 | 2.45% | 26,435 | 549 | 2.08% | 28,085 | 453 | 1.61% |
| Ripley | 14,820 | 1,922 | 12.97% | 19,054 | 733 | 3.85% | 20,977 | 3,404 | 16.23% | 21,627 | 2,926 | 13.53% | 19,350 | 2,261 | 11.68% |
| Rush | 16,445 | 191 | 1.16% | 16,193 | 334 | 2.06% | 17,626 | 530 | 3.01% | 19,238 | 504 | 2.62% | 19,034 | 467 | 2.45% |
| St. Joseph | 10,954 | 839 | 7.66% | 18,455 | 1,054 | 5.71% | 25,322 | 227 | 0.90% | 33,178 | 5,518 | 16.63% | 42,457 | 8,539 | 20.11% |
| Scott | 5,885 | 125 | 2.12% | 7,303 | 152 | 2.08% | 7,873 | 812 | 10.31% | 8,343 | 156 | 1.87% | 7,833 | 105 | 1.34% |
| Shelby | 15,502 | 393 | 2.54% | 19,569 | 392 | 2.00% | 21,892 | 1,856 | 8.48% | 25,257 | 778 | 3.08% | 25,454 | 681 | 2.68% |
| Spencer | 8,616 | 987 | 11.46% | 14,556 | 305 | 2.10% | 17,998 | 342 | 1.90% | 22,122 | 1,762 | 7.96% | 22,060 | 1,330 | 6.03% |
| Starke | 557 | 9 | 1.62% | 2,195 | 137 | 6.24% | 3,888 | 447 | 11.50% | 5,105 | 556 | 10.89% | 7,339 | 967 | 13.18% |
| Steuben | 6,104 | 242 | 3.96% | 10,374 | 288 | 2.78% | 12,854 | 3,572 | 27.79% | 14,645 | 377 | 2.57% | 14,478 | 322 | 2.22% |
| Sullivan | 10,141 | 113 | 1.11% | 15,064 | 159 | 1.06% | 18,453 | 269 | 1.46% | 20,336 | 425 | 2.09% | 21,877 | 389 | 1.78% |
| Switzerland | 12,932 | 510 | 3.94% | 12,698 | 409 | 3.22% | 12,134 | 415 | 3.42% | 13,336 | 388 | 2.91% | 12,514 | 316 | 2.53% |
| Tippecanoe | 19,377 | 2,379 | 12.28% | 25,726 | 2,654 | 10.32% | 33,515 | 5,374 | 16.03% | 35,966 | 4,496 | 12.50% | 35,078 | 4,206 | 11.99% |
| Tipton | 3,532 | 42 | 1.19% | 8,170 | 71 | 0.87% | 11,953 | 222 | 1.86% | 14,407 | 297 | 2.06% | 18,157 | 331 | 1.82% |
| Union | 6,944 | 177 | 2.55% | 7,169 | 381 | 5.31% | 6,311 | 291 | 4.61% | 7,673 | 292 | 3.81% | 7,006 | 223 | 3.18% |
| Vanderburgh | 11,414 | 4,534 | 39.72% | 20,552 | 2,301 | 11.20% | 33,145 | 9,323 | 28.13% | 42,193 | 8,528 | 20.21% | 59,809 | 8,448 | 14.12% |
| Vermillion | 8,661 | 122 | 1.41% | 9,422 | 145 | 1.54% | 10,840 | 236 | 2.18% | 12,025 | 204 | 1.70% | 13,154 | 347 | 2.64% |
| Vigo | 15,289 | 863 | 5.64% | 22,517 | 1,384 | 6.15% | 33,549 | 3,707 | 11.05% | 45,658 | 4,799 | 10.51% | 50,195 | 4,411 | 8.79% |
| Wabash | 12,138 | 449 | 3.70% | 17,547 | 517 | 2.95% | 21,305 | 906 | 4.25% | 25,241 | 982 | 3.89% | 27,126 | 823 | 3.03% |
| Warren | 7,387 | 130 | 1.76% | 10,057 | 451 | 4.48% | 10,204 | 460 | 4.51% | 11,497 | 450 | 3.91% | 10,955 | 352 | 3.21% |
| Warrick | 8,811 | 437 | 4.96% | 13,261 | 417 | 3.14% | 17,653 | 1,388 | 7.86% | 20,162 | 1,274 | 6.32% | 21,161 | 1,024 | 4.84% |
| Washington | 17,040 | 518 | 3.04% | 17,909 | 287 | 1.60% | 18,495 | 352 | 1.90% | 18,955 | 269 | 1.42% | 18,619 | 195 | 1.05% |
| Wayne | 25,320 | 1,166 | 4.61% | 29,558 | 1,273 | 4.31% | 34,048 | 2,949 | 8.66% | 38,613 | 2,888 | 7.48% | 37,628 | 2,592 | 6.89% |
| Wells | 6,152 | 305 | 4.96% | 10,844 | 312 | 2.88% | 13,585 | 556 | 4.09% | 18,422 | 591 | 3.21% | 21,514 | 564 | 2.62% |
| White | 4,761 | 131 | 2.75% | 8,258 | 320 | 3.88% | 10,554 | 568 | 5.38% | 13,795 | 830 | 6.02% | 15,671 | 803 | 5.12% |
| Whitley | 5,190 | 254 | 4.89% | 10,730 | 335 | 3.12% | 14,399 | 846 | 5.88% | 16,941 | 739 | 4.36% | 17,768 | 625 | 3.52% |

## TABLE 2. FOREIGN BORN BY COUNTY AS PERCENTAGE OF TOTAL INDIANA POPULATION, 1850–1990 (continued)

| | 1900 Total Population | 1900 Foreign Born | 1900 Percentage For. Born | 1910 Total Population | 1910 Foreign Born | 1910 Percentage For. Born | 1920 Total Population | 1920 Foreign Born | 1920 Percentage For. Born | 1930 Total Population | 1930 Foreign Born | 1930 Percentage For. Born | 1940 Total Population | 1940 Foreign Born | 1940 Percentage For. Born |
|---|---|---|---|---|---|---|---|---|---|---|---|---|---|---|---|
| Indiana | 2,516,462 | 142,094 | 5.65% | 2,700,876 | 159,493 | 5.91% | 2,930,390 | 150,868 | 5.15% | 3,238,503 | 142,545 | 4.40% | 3,427,796 | 110,631 | 3.23% |
| Adams | 22,232 | 1,449 | 6.52% | 21,840 | 958 | 4.39% | 20,503 | 672 | 3.28% | 19,957 | 468 | 2.35% | 21,254 | 345 | 1.62% |
| Allen | 77,270 | 9,330 | 12.07% | 93,386 | 9,251 | 9.91% | 114,303 | 7,741 | 6.77% | 146,743 | 6,570 | 4.48% | 155,084 | 5,108 | 3.29% |
| Bartholomew | 24,594 | 822 | 3.34% | 24,813 | 561 | 2.26% | 23,887 | 335 | 1.40% | 24,864 | 210 | 0.84% | 27,289 | 135 | 0.49% |
| Benton | 13,123 | 999 | 7.61% | 12,688 | 695 | 5.48% | 12,206 | 412 | 3.38% | 11,886 | 252 | 2.12% | 11,117 | 153 | 1.38% |
| Blackford | 17,213 | 929 | 5.40% | 15,820 | 629 | 3.98% | 14,584 | 270 | 1.92% | 13,617 | 193 | 1.42% | 13,783 | 115 | 0.83% |
| Boone | 26,321 | 214 | 0.81% | 24,673 | 131 | 0.53% | 23,575 | 136 | 0.58% | 22,290 | 198 | 0.89% | 22,081 | 70 | 0.32% |
| Brown | 9,727 | 41 | 0.42% | 7,975 | 45 | 0.56% | 7,019 | 45 | 0.64% | 5,168 | 41 | 0.79% | 6,189 | 47 | 0.76% |
| Carroll | 19,953 | 427 | 2.14% | 17,970 | 263 | 1.46% | 16,315 | 140 | 0.86% | 15,049 | 86 | 0.57% | 15,410 | 65 | 0.42% |
| Cass | 34,545 | 2,138 | 6.19% | 36,368 | 2,031 | 5.58% | 38,333 | 1,610 | 4.20% | 34,518 | 1,173 | 3.40% | 36,908 | 1,046 | 2.83% |
| Clark | 31,835 | 1,353 | 4.25% | 30,260 | 883 | 2.92% | 29,381 | 518 | 1.76% | 30,764 | 309 | 1.00% | 31,020 | 145 | 0.47% |
| Clay | 34,285 | 2,638 | 7.69% | 32,535 | 1,869 | 5.74% | 29,447 | 885 | 3.01% | 26,479 | 522 | 1.97% | 25,365 | 315 | 1.24% |
| Clinton | 28,202 | 283 | 1.00% | 26,674 | 186 | 0.70% | 27,737 | 179 | 0.65% | 27,329 | 159 | 0.58% | 28,411 | 80 | 0.28% |
| Crawford | 13,476 | 117 | 0.87% | 12,057 | 69 | 0.57% | 11,201 | 48 | 0.43% | 10,160 | 30 | 0.30% | 10,171 | 11 | 0.11% |
| Daviess | 29,914 | 689 | 2.30% | 27,747 | 389 | 1.40% | 26,556 | 246 | 0.93% | 25,832 | 153 | 0.59% | 26,163 | 85 | 0.32% |
| Dearborn | 22,194 | 1,924 | 8.67% | 21,396 | 1,163 | 5.44% | 25,600 | 812 | 3.17% | 21,056 | 312 | 1.48% | 23,053 | 190 | 0.82% |
| Decatur | 19,518 | 606 | 3.10% | 18,793 | 370 | 1.97% | 20,033 | 594 | 2.97% | 31,508 | 135 | 0.43% | 17,722 | 93 | 0.52% |
| De Kalb | 25,711 | 1,156 | 4.50% | 25,054 | 1,060 | 4.23% | 17,813 | 219 | 1.23% | 24,911 | 519 | 2.08% | 24,756 | 342 | 1.38% |
| Delaware | 49,624 | 2,025 | 4.08% | 51,414 | 1,199 | 2.33% | 56,377 | 959 | 1.70% | 67,270 | 706 | 1.05% | 74,963 | 559 | 0.75% |
| Dubois | 20,357 | 1,173 | 5.76% | 19,843 | 699 | 3.52% | 19,215 | 374 | 1.95% | 20,553 | 222 | 1.08% | 22,579 | 109 | 0.48% |
| Elkhart | 45,052 | 2,396 | 5.32% | 49,008 | 2,521 | 5.14% | 56,384 | 2,224 | 3.94% | 68,875 | 2,329 | 3.38% | 72,634 | 1,895 | 2.61% |
| Fayette | 18,495 | 494 | 2.67% | 14,415 | 363 | 2.52% | 17,142 | 261 | 1.52% | 19,243 | 185 | 0.96% | 19,411 | 126 | 0.65% |
| Floyd | 30,118 | 1,960 | 6.51% | 30,283 | 1,233 | 4.07% | 30,661 | 748 | 2.44% | 34,655 | 454 | 1.31% | 35,061 | 285 | 0.81% |
| Fountain | 21,446 | 546 | 2.55% | 20,439 | 412 | 2.02% | 18,823 | 283 | 1.50% | 17,971 | 218 | 1.21% | 18,299 | 138 | 0.75% |
| Franklin | 16,388 | 1,184 | 7.22% | 15,335 | 681 | 4.44% | 14,806 | 340 | 2.30% | 14,498 | 149 | 1.03% | 14,412 | 80 | 0.56% |
| Fulton | 17,453 | 350 | 2.01% | 16,879 | 251 | 1.49% | 16,478 | 172 | 1.04% | 15,038 | 146 | 0.97% | 15,577 | 141 | 0.91% |
| Gibson | 30,099 | 806 | 2.68% | 30,137 | 518 | 1.72% | 29,201 | 296 | 1.01% | 29,202 | 193 | 0.66% | 30,709 | 125 | 0.41% |
| Grant | 54,693 | 2,611 | 4.77% | 51,426 | 1,722 | 3.35% | 51,353 | 1,054 | 2.05% | 51,066 | 831 | 1.63% | 55,813 | 701 | 1.26% |
| Greene | 28,530 | 473 | 1.66% | 36,873 | 1,647 | 4.47% | 36,770 | 1,207 | 3.28% | 31,481 | 692 | 2.20% | 31,330 | 498 | 1.59% |
| Hamilton | 29,914 | 632 | 2.11% | 27,026 | 235 | 0.87% | 24,222 | 166 | 0.69% | 23,444 | 97 | 0.41% | 24,614 | 86 | 0.35% |
| Hancock | 19,189 | 367 | 1.91% | 19,030 | 402 | 2.11% | 17,210 | 137 | 0.80% | 16,605 | 100 | 0.60% | 17,302 | 69 | 0.40% |
| Harrison | 21,702 | 562 | 2.59% | 20,232 | 312 | 1.54% | 18,656 | 156 | 0.84% | 16,728 | 75 | 0.45% | 17,106 | 36 | 0.21% |
| Hendricks | 21,292 | 252 | 1.18% | 20,840 | 172 | 0.83% | 20,291 | 126 | 0.62% | 19,725 | 128 | 0.65% | 20,151 | 131 | 0.65% |
| Henry | 25,088 | 359 | 1.43% | 29,758 | 465 | 1.56% | 34,682 | 299 | 0.86% | 35,238 | 223 | 0.63% | 40,208 | 184 | 0.46% |
| Howard | 28,575 | 703 | 2.46% | 33,177 | 993 | 2.99% | 43,965 | 1,258 | 2.86% | 46,696 | 1,043 | 2.23% | 47,752 | 731 | 1.53% |
| Huntington | 28,901 | 1,061 | 3.67% | 28,982 | 735 | 2.54% | 31,671 | 648 | 2.05% | 29,073 | 352 | 1.21% | 29,931 | 284 | 0.95% |
| Jackson | 26,633 | 888 | 3.33% | 24,727 | 570 | 2.31% | 24,228 | 348 | 1.44% | 23,731 | 182 | 0.77% | 26,612 | 145 | 0.54% |
| Jasper | 14,292 | 1,036 | 7.25% | 13,044 | 843 | 6.46% | 13,961 | 763 | 5.47% | 13,388 | 596 | 4.45% | 14,397 | 562 | 3.90% |
| Jay | 26,818 | 609 | 2.27% | 24,961 | 407 | 1.63% | 23,218 | 223 | 0.96% | 20,846 | 133 | 0.64% | 22,601 | 92 | 0.41% |
| Jefferson | 22,913 | 986 | 4.30% | 20,483 | 471 | 2.30% | 20,709 | 311 | 1.50% | 19,182 | 170 | 0.89% | 19,912 | 108 | 0.54% |
| Jennings | 15,757 | 663 | 4.21% | 14,203 | 358 | 2.52% | 13,280 | 214 | 1.61% | 11,800 | 101 | 0.86% | 13,680 | 65 | 0.48% |
| Johnson | 20,223 | 192 | 0.95% | 20,394 | 140 | 0.69% | 20,739 | 94 | 0.45% | 21,706 | 91 | 0.42% | 22,493 | 86 | 0.38% |
| Knox | 32,746 | 1,382 | 4.22% | 39,183 | 1,398 | 3.57% | 46,195 | 2,079 | 4.50% | 43,813 | 1,177 | 2.69% | 43,973 | 833 | 1.89% |
| Kosciusko | 29,109 | 444 | 1.53% | 27,936 | 555 | 1.99% | 27,120 | 365 | 1.35% | 27,488 | 275 | 1.00% | 29,561 | 225 | 0.76% |
| Lagrange | 15,284 | 390 | 2.55% | 15,148 | 336 | 2.22% | 14,009 | 198 | 1.41% | 13,780 | 119 | 0.86% | 14,352 | 100 | 0.70% |
| Lake | 37,892 | 9,425 | 24.87% | 82,864 | 30,434 | 36.73% | 159,957 | 46,046 | 28.79% | 261,310 | 48,921 | 18.72% | 293,195 | 43,862 | 14.96% |
| La Porte | 38,386 | 7,696 | 20.05% | 46,797 | 8,847 | 18.91% | 50,443 | 7,264 | 14.40% | 60,490 | 6,375 | 10.54% | 63,660 | 4,942 | 7.76% |
| Lawrence | 25,729 | 449 | 1.75% | 30,625 | 813 | 2.65% | 28,228 | 406 | 1.44% | 34,788 | 430 | 1.24% | 35,045 | 277 | 0.79% |
| Madison | 70,470 | 4,397 | 6.24% | 65,224 | 2,704 | 4.15% | 69,151 | 1,868 | 2.70% | 82,888 | 1,501 | 1.81% | 86,646 | 1,147 | 1.32% |
| Marion | 197,227 | 18,724 | 9.49% | 263,661 | 21,210 | 8.04% | 348,061 | 18,185 | 5.22% | 422,666 | 15,258 | 3.61% | 460,926 | 12,075 | 2.62% |
| Marshall | 25,119 | 929 | 3.70% | 24,175 | 828 | 3.43% | 23,744 | 718 | 3.02% | 25,077 | 589 | 2.35% | 25,935 | 536 | 2.07% |
| Martin | 14,711 | 144 | 0.98% | 12,950 | 105 | 0.81% | 11,865 | 47 | 0.40% | 8,370 | 20 | 0.24% | 9,529 | 16 | 0.17% |
| Miami | 28,344 | 1,260 | 4.45% | 29,350 | 1,245 | 4.24% | 28,668 | 700 | 2.44% | 29,032 | 481 | 1.66% | 27,926 | 343 | 1.23% |
| Monroe | 20,873 | 217 | 1.04% | 23,426 | 273 | 1.17% | 24,519 | 227 | 0.93% | 35,756 | 288 | 0.81% | 36,364 | 241 | 0.66% |
| Montgomery | 29,388 | 465 | 1.58% | 29,296 | 253 | 0.86% | 28,490 | 209 | 0.73% | 26,980 | 135 | 0.50% | 27,231 | 94 | 0.35% |
| Morgan | 20,457 | 167 | 0.82% | 21,182 | 178 | 0.84% | 20,010 | 128 | 0.64% | 19,424 | 84 | 0.43% | 19,801 | 58 | 0.29% |
| Newton | 10,448 | 821 | 7.86% | 10,504 | 597 | 5.68% | 10,144 | 430 | 4.24% | 9,841 | 350 | 3.56% | 10,775 | 350 | 3.25% |
| Noble | 23,533 | 1,128 | 4.79% | 24,009 | 942 | 3.92% | 224,710 | 594 | 0.26% | 22,404 | 397 | 1.77% | 22,776 | 317 | 1.39% |
| Ohio | 4,724 | 151 | 3.20% | 4,329 | 119 | 2.75% | 4,024 | 71 | 1.76% | 3,747 | 41 | 1.09% | 3,782 | 19 | 0.50% |
| Orange | 16,854 | 42 | 0.25% | 17,192 | 70 | 0.41% | 16,974 | 88 | 0.52% | 17,459 | 69 | 0.40% | 17,311 | 36 | 0.21% |
| Owen | 15,149 | 147 | 0.97% | 14,053 | 136 | 0.97% | 12,760 | 55 | 0.43% | 11,351 | 39 | 0.34% | 12,090 | 29 | 0.24% |
| Parke | 23,000 | 1,047 | 4.55% | 22,214 | 856 | 3.85% | 18,875 | 300 | 1.59% | 16,561 | 181 | 1.09% | 17,358 | 141 | 0.81% |
| Perry | 18,778 | 1,258 | 6.70% | 18,078 | 753 | 4.17% | 16,692 | 368 | 2.20% | 16,625 | 171 | 1.03% | 16,670 | 76 | 0.46% |
| Pike | 20,486 | 228 | 1.11% | 19,684 | 164 | 0.83% | 18,684 | 106 | 0.57% | 16,361 | 53 | 0.32% | 17,045 | 39 | 0.23% |
| Porter | 19,175 | 2,871 | 14.97% | 20,540 | 2,939 | 14.31% | 20,256 | 2,243 | 11.07% | 22,821 | 1,979 | 8.67% | 27,836 | 1,817 | 6.53% |
| Posey | 22,333 | 971 | 4.35% | 21,670 | 710 | 3.28% | 19,334 | 292 | 1.51% | 17,853 | 151 | 0.85% | 19,183 | 68 | 0.35% |
| Pulaski | 14,033 | 1,047 | 7.46% | 13,312 | 825 | 6.20% | 12,385 | 572 | 4.62% | 11,195 | 393 | 3.51% | 12,056 | 387 | 3.21% |
| Putnam | 21,478 | 236 | 1.10% | 20,520 | 201 | 0.98% | 19,850 | 131 | 0.66% | 20,448 | 146 | 0.71% | 20,839 | 107 | 0.51% |
| Randolph | 28,653 | 395 | 1.38% | 29,013 | 555 | 1.91% | 26,484 | 232 | 0.88% | 24,859 | 127 | 0.51% | 26,766 | 133 | 0.50% |
| Ripley | 19,881 | 1,639 | 8.24% | 19,452 | 1,019 | 5.24% | 18,694 | 579 | 3.10% | 18,078 | 294 | 1.63% | 18,898 | 161 | 0.85% |
| Rush | 20,148 | 331 | 1.64% | 19,349 | 214 | 1.11% | 19,241 | 127 | 0.66% | 19,412 | 68 | 0.35% | 18,927 | 55 | 0.29% |
| St. Joseph | 58,881 | 10,995 | 18.67% | 84,312 | 16,866 | 20.00% | 103,304 | 17,174 | 16.62% | 160,033 | 19,343 | 12.09% | 161,823 | 15,467 | 9.56% |
| Scott | 8,307 | 75 | 0.90% | 8,323 | 53 | 0.64% | 7,424 | 25 | 0.34% | 6,664 | 18 | 0.27% | 8,978 | 20 | 0.22% |
| Shelby | 26,491 | 578 | 2.18% | 26,802 | 401 | 1.50% | 25,982 | 276 | 1.06% | 26,552 | 157 | 0.59% | 25,953 | 119 | 0.46% |
| Spencer | 22,407 | 913 | 4.07% | 20,676 | 527 | 2.55% | 18,400 | 260 | 1.41% | 16,713 | 156 | 0.93% | 16,211 | 78 | 0.48% |
| Starke | 10,431 | 1,402 | 13.44% | 10,567 | 1,484 | 14.04% | 10,278 | 1,375 | 13.38% | 10,620 | 1,256 | 11.83% | 12,258 | 1,261 | 10.29% |
| Steuben | 15,219 | 261 | 1.71% | 14,274 | 195 | 1.37% | 13,360 | 139 | 1.04% | 13,386 | 164 | 1.23% | 13,740 | 185 | 1.35% |
| Sullivan | 26,005 | 399 | 1.53% | 32,439 | 1,474 | 4.54% | 31,630 | 911 | 2.88% | 28,133 | 540 | 1.92% | 27,014 | 398 | 1.47% |
| Switzerland | 11,840 | 217 | 1.83% | 9,914 | 123 | 1.24% | 9,311 | 72 | 0.77% | 8,432 | 26 | 0.31% | 8,167 | 11 | 0.13% |
| Tippecanoe | 38,659 | 3,622 | 9.37% | 40,063 | 3,111 | 7.77% | 42,813 | 2,115 | 4.94% | 47,535 | 1,698 | 3.57% | 51,020 | 1,201 | 2.35% |
| Tipton | 19,116 | 306 | 1.60% | 17,459 | 206 | 1.18% | 16,152 | 125 | 0.77% | 15,208 | 107 | 0.70% | 15,135 | 82 | 0.54% |
| Union | 6,748 | 170 | 2.52% | 6,260 | 105 | 1.68% | 6,021 | 45 | 0.75% | 5,880 | 28 | 0.48% | 6,017 | 23 | 0.38% |
| Vanderburgh | 71,769 | 6,788 | 9.46% | 77,438 | 4,944 | 6.38% | 92,293 | 3,361 | 3.64% | 113,320 | 2,234 | 1.97% | 130,783 | 1,494 | 1.14% |
| Vermillion | 15,252 | 696 | 4.56% | 18,865 | 2,334 | 12.37% | 27,625 | 4,027 | 14.58% | 23,238 | 2,254 | 9.70% | 21,787 | 1,695 | 7.78% |
| Vigo | 62,035 | 4,092 | 6.60% | 87,930 | 5,574 | 6.34% | 100,212 | 5,676 | 5.66% | 98,861 | 4,060 | 4.11% | 99,709 | 2,865 | 2.87% |
| Wabash | 28,235 | 781 | 2.77% | 26,926 | 629 | 2.34% | 27,231 | 415 | 1.52% | 25,170 | 285 | 1.13% | 26,601 | 198 | 0.74% |
| Warren | 11,371 | 252 | 2.22% | 10,899 | 210 | 1.93% | 9,699 | 126 | 1.30% | 9,167 | 80 | 0.87% | 9,055 | 49 | 0.54% |
| Warrick | 22,329 | 770 | 3.45% | 21,911 | 508 | 2.32% | 19,862 | 258 | 1.30% | 18,230 | 149 | 0.82% | 19,435 | 80 | 0.41% |
| Washington | 19,409 | 105 | 0.54% | 17,445 | 56 | 0.32% | 16,645 | 42 | 0.25% | 16,285 | 33 | 0.20% | 17,008 | 33 | 0.19% |
| Wayne | 38,970 | 2,077 | 5.33% | 43,757 | 2,044 | 4.67% | 48,136 | 1,424 | 2.96% | 54,809 | 1,103 | 2.01% | 59,229 | 855 | 1.44% |
| Wells | 23,449 | 498 | 2.12% | 22,418 | 330 | 1.47% | 20,509 | 282 | 1.38% | 18,411 | 191 | 1.04% | 19,099 | 140 | 0.73% |
| White | 19,138 | 803 | 4.20% | 17,602 | 589 | 3.35% | 17,351 | 416 | 2.40% | 15,831 | 257 | 1.62% | 17,037 | 201 | 1.18% |
| Whitley | 17,328 | 450 | 2.60% | 16,892 | 298 | 1.76% | 15,660 | 173 | 1.10% | 15,931 | 137 | 0.86% | 17,001 | 111 | 0.65% |

TABLE 2. FOREIGN BORN BY COUNTY AS PERCENTAGE OF TOTAL INDIANA POPULATION, 1850–1990 *(continued)*

| | 1950 | | | 1960 | | | 1970 | | | 1980 | | | 1990 | | |
|---|---|---|---|---|---|---|---|---|---|---|---|---|---|---|---|
| | Total Population | Foreign Born | Percentage For. Born | Total Population | Foreign Born | Percentage For. Born | Total Population | Foreign Born | Percentage For. Born | Total Population | Foreign Born | Percentage For. Born | Total Population | Foreign Born | Percentage For. Born |
| Indiana | 3,934,224 | 100,630 | 2.56% | 4,662,498 | 93,202 | 2.00% | 5,193,669 | 83,198 | 1.60% | 5,480,224 | 101,802 | 1.86% | 5,544,159 | 94,263 | 1.70% |
| Adams | 22,393 | 227 | 1.01% | 24,643 | 192 | 0.78% | 26,871 | 164 | 0.61% | 29,619 | 313 | 1.06% | 31,095 | 222 | 0.71% |
| Allen | 183,722 | 4,391 | 2.39% | 232,196 | 5,185 | 2.23% | 280,452 | 4,782 | 1.71% | 294,335 | 6,389 | 2.17% | 300,836 | 5,882 | 1.96% |
| Bartholomew | 36,108 | 194 | 0.54% | 48,198 | 273 | 0.57% | 57,022 | 470 | 0.82% | 65,088 | 649 | 1.00% | 63,657 | 987 | 1.55% |
| Benton | 11,462 | 113 | 0.99% | 11,912 | 110 | 0.92% | 11,262 | 51 | 0.45% | 10,218 | 64 | 0.63% | 9,441 | 44 | 0.47% |
| Blackford | 14,026 | 105 | 0.75% | 14,792 | 89 | 0.60% | 15,888 | 28 | 0.18% | 15,570 | 75 | 0.48% | 14,067 | 41 | 0.29% |
| Boone | 23,993 | 101 | 0.42% | 27,543 | 175 | 0.64% | 30,870 | 152 | 0.49% | 36,446 | 518 | 1.42% | 38,147 | 310 | 0.81% |
| Brown | 6,209 | 40 | 0.64% | 7,024 | 70 | 1.00% | 9,057 | 83 | 0.92% | 12,377 | 103 | 0.83% | 14,080 | 98 | 0.70% |
| Carroll | 16,100 | 82 | 0.51% | 16,934 | 52 | 0.31% | 17,734 | 73 | 0.41% | 19,722 | 89 | 0.45% | 18,809 | 112 | 0.60% |
| Cass | 38,793 | 949 | 2.45% | 40,931 | 358 | 0.87% | 40,456 | 344 | 0.85% | 40,936 | 389 | 0.95% | 38,413 | 246 | 0.64% |
| Clark | 48,330 | 244 | 0.50% | 62,795 | 235 | 0.37% | 75,876 | 322 | 0.42% | 88,838 | 808 | 0.91% | 87,777 | 742 | 0.85% |
| Clay | 23,918 | 241 | 1.01% | 24,207 | 186 | 0.77% | 23,933 | 86 | 0.36% | 24,862 | 147 | 0.59% | 24,705 | 127 | 0.51% |
| Clinton | 29,734 | 131 | 0.44% | 30,765 | 92 | 0.30% | 30,547 | 73 | 0.24% | 31,545 | 314 | 1.00% | 30,974 | 142 | 0.46% |
| Crawford | 9,289 | 20 | 0.22% | 8,379 | 12 | 0.14% | 8,033 | 6 | 0.07% | 9,820 | 55 | 0.56% | 9,914 | 17 | 0.17% |
| Daviess | 26,762 | 90 | 0.34% | 26,636 | 59 | 0.22% | 26,602 | 71 | 0.27% | 27,836 | 69 | 0.25% | 27,533 | 66 | 0.24% |
| Dearborn | 25,141 | 166 | 0.66% | 28,674 | 128 | 0.45% | 29,430 | 130 | 0.44% | 34,291 | 295 | 0.86% | 38,835 | 240 | 0.62% |
| Decatur | 18,218 | 67 | 0.37% | 20,019 | 61 | 0.30% | 22,738 | 152 | 0.67% | 23,841 | 113 | 0.47% | 23,645 | 212 | 0.90% |
| De Kalb | 26,023 | 330 | 1.27% | 28,271 | 266 | 0.94% | 30,837 | 255 | 0.83% | 33,606 | 243 | 0.72% | 35,324 | 261 | 0.74% |
| Delaware | 90,252 | 622 | 0.69% | 110,938 | 632 | 0.57% | 129,219 | 783 | 0.61% | 128,587 | 1,262 | 0.98% | 119,659 | 1,355 | 1.13% |
| Dubois | 23,785 | 116 | 0.49% | 27,463 | 116 | 0.42% | 30,934 | 166 | 0.54% | 34,238 | 173 | 0.51% | 36,616 | 207 | 0.57% |
| Elkhart | 84,512 | 1,770 | 2.09% | 106,790 | 2,222 | 2.08% | 126,529 | 2,288 | 1.81% | 137,330 | 3,033 | 2.21% | 156,198 | 3,314 | 2.12% |
| Fayette | 23,391 | 155 | 0.66% | 24,454 | 116 | 0.47% | 26,216 | 85 | 0.32% | 28,272 | 135 | 0.48% | 26,015 | 152 | 0.58% |
| Floyd | 43,955 | 258 | 0.59% | 51,397 | 153 | 0.30% | 55,622 | 247 | 0.44% | 61,169 | 440 | 0.72% | 64,404 | 596 | 0.93% |
| Fountain | 17,836 | 106 | 0.59% | 18,706 | 62 | 0.33% | 18,257 | 85 | 0.47% | 19,033 | 97 | 0.51% | 17,808 | 67 | 0.38% |
| Franklin | 16,034 | 73 | 0.46% | 17,015 | 74 | 0.43% | 16,943 | 13 | 0.08% | 19,612 | 120 | 0.61% | 19,580 | 70 | 0.36% |
| Fulton | 16,565 | 186 | 1.12% | 16,957 | 127 | 0.75% | 16,984 | 130 | 0.77% | 19,335 | 170 | 0.88% | 18,840 | 69 | 0.37% |
| Gibson | 30,720 | 104 | 0.34% | 29,949 | 104 | 0.35% | 30,444 | 147 | 0.48% | 33,156 | 226 | 0.68% | 31,913 | 88 | 0.28% |
| Grant | 62,156 | 720 | 1.16% | 75,741 | 816 | 1.08% | 83,955 | 538 | 0.64% | 80,934 | 796 | 0.98% | 74,169 | 579 | 0.78% |
| Greene | 27,886 | 416 | 1.49% | 26,327 | 239 | 0.91% | 26,894 | 134 | 0.50% | 30,416 | 136 | 0.45% | 30,410 | 113 | 0.37% |
| Hamilton | 28,491 | 162 | 0.57% | 40,132 | 276 | 0.69% | 54,532 | 411 | 0.75% | 82,027 | 1,200 | 1.46% | 108,936 | 2,363 | 2.17% |
| Hancock | 20,332 | 96 | 0.47% | 26,665 | 117 | 0.44% | 25,096 | 201 | 0.80% | 43,939 | 510 | 1.16% | 45,527 | 501 | 1.10% |
| Harrison | 17,858 | 64 | 0.36% | 19,207 | 32 | 0.17% | 20,423 | 48 | 0.24% | 27,276 | 156 | 0.57% | 29,890 | 201 | 0.67% |
| Hendricks | 24,594 | 165 | 0.67% | 40,896 | 234 | 0.57% | 53,974 | 328 | 0.61% | 69,804 | 618 | 0.89% | 75,717 | 461 | 0.61% |
| Henry | 45,505 | 233 | 0.51% | 48,899 | 167 | 0.34% | 52,603 | 184 | 0.35% | 53,336 | 247 | 0.46% | 48,139 | 169 | 0.35% |
| Howard | 54,498 | 707 | 1.30% | 69,509 | 855 | 1.23% | 83,198 | 741 | 0.89% | 86,896 | 1,173 | 1.35% | 80,827 | 971 | 1.20% |
| Huntington | 31,400 | 247 | 0.79% | 33,814 | 263 | 0.78% | 34,970 | 183 | 0.52% | 35,596 | 353 | 0.99% | 35,427 | 288 | 0.81% |
| Jackson | 28,237 | 104 | 0.37% | 30,556 | 78 | 0.26% | 33,187 | 76 | 0.23% | 36,523 | 228 | 0.62% | 37,730 | 285 | 0.76% |
| Jasper | 16,538 | 658 | 3.98% | 18,842 | 379 | 2.01% | 20,429 | 302 | 1.48% | 26,138 | 480 | 1.84% | 24,960 | 250 | 1.00% |
| Jay | 23,157 | 125 | 0.54% | 22,572 | 42 | 0.19% | 23,575 | 68 | 0.29% | 23,239 | 138 | 0.59% | 21,512 | 78 | 0.36% |
| Jefferson | 21,613 | 115 | 0.53% | 24,061 | 120 | 0.50% | 27,006 | 97 | 0.36% | 30,419 | 198 | 0.65% | 29,797 | 297 | 1.00% |
| Jennings | 15,250 | 52 | 0.34% | 17,267 | 80 | 0.46% | 19,454 | 65 | 0.33% | 22,854 | 124 | 0.54% | 23,661 | 81 | 0.34% |
| Johnson | 26,183 | 127 | 0.49% | 43,704 | 262 | 0.60% | 61,138 | 351 | 0.57% | 77,240 | 633 | 0.82% | 88,109 | 1,128 | 1.28% |
| Knox | 43,415 | 677 | 1.56% | 41,561 | 313 | 0.75% | 41,546 | 218 | 0.52% | 41,838 | 464 | 1.11% | 39,884 | 286 | 0.72% |
| Kosciusko | 33,002 | 322 | 0.98% | 40,737 | 423 | 1.04% | 48,127 | 347 | 0.72% | 59,555 | 781 | 1.31% | 65,294 | 798 | 1.22% |
| Lagrange | 15,347 | 110 | 0.72% | 17,380 | 68 | 0.39% | 20,890 | 64 | 0.31% | 25,550 | 148 | 0.58% | 29,477 | 247 | 0.84% |
| Lake | 368,152 | 39,247 | 10.66% | 513,269 | 36,436 | 7.10% | 546,253 | 28,962 | 5.30% | 522,965 | 27,435 | 5.25% | 475,594 | 19,461 | 4.09% |
| La Porte | 76,808 | 4,057 | 5.28% | 95,111 | 3,276 | 3.44% | 105,342 | 2,607 | 2.47% | 108,632 | 2,571 | 2.37% | 107,066 | 1,917 | 1.79% |
| Lawrence | 34,346 | 266 | 0.77% | 36,564 | 152 | 0.42% | 38,038 | 121 | 0.32% | 42,472 | 283 | 0.67% | 42,836 | 171 | 0.40% |
| Madison | 103,911 | 1,057 | 1.02% | 125,819 | 869 | 0.69% | 138,451 | 765 | 0.55% | 139,336 | 1,335 | 0.96% | 130,669 | 914 | 0.70% |
| Marion | 551,777 | 10,897 | 1.97% | 697,567 | 11,552 | 1.66% | 792,299 | 11,547 | 1.46% | 765,233 | 14,845 | 1.94% | 797,159 | 15,291 | 1.92% |
| Marshall | 29,468 | 548 | 1.86% | 32,443 | 451 | 1.39% | 34,986 | 394 | 1.13% | 39,155 | 540 | 1.38% | 42,182 | 487 | 1.15% |
| Martin | 10,678 | 51 | 0.48% | 10,608 | 43 | 0.41% | 10,969 | 80 | 0.73% | 11,001 | 135 | 1.23% | 10,369 | 47 | 0.45% |
| Miami | 28,201 | 263 | 0.93% | 38,000 | 601 | 1.58% | 39,246 | 517 | 1.32% | 39,820 | 642 | 1.61% | 36,897 | 420 | 1.14% |
| Monroe | 50,080 | 591 | 1.18% | 59,225 | 1,001 | 1.69% | 84,849 | 2,357 | 2.78% | 98,785 | 4,147 | 4.20% | 108,978 | 4,736 | 4.35% |
| Montgomery | 29,122 | 177 | 0.61% | 32,089 | 147 | 0.46% | 33,930 | 158 | 0.47% | 35,501 | 223 | 0.63% | 34,436 | 223 | 0.65% |
| Morgan | 23,726 | 118 | 0.50% | 33,875 | 175 | 0.52% | 44,176 | 207 | 0.47% | 51,999 | 358 | 0.69% | 55,920 | 377 | 0.67% |
| Newton | 11,006 | 300 | 2.73% | 11,502 | 180 | 1.56% | 11,606 | 199 | 1.71% | 14,844 | 163 | 1.10% | 13,551 | 209 | 1.54% |
| Noble | 25,075 | 303 | 1.21% | 28,162 | 235 | 0.83% | 31,382 | 241 | 0.77% | 35,443 | 256 | 0.72% | 37,877 | 339 | 0.90% |
| Ohio | 4,223 | 22 | 0.52% | 4,165 | 8 | 0.19% | 4,289 | 0 | 0.00% | 5,114 | 17 | 0.33% | 5,315 | 8 | 0.15% |
| Orange | 16,879 | 75 | 0.44% | 16,877 | 55 | 0.33% | 16,968 | 47 | 0.28% | 18,677 | 205 | 1.10% | 18,409 | 80 | 0.43% |
| Owen | 11,763 | 34 | 0.29% | 11,400 | 20 | 0.18% | 12,163 | 38 | 0.31% | 15,841 | 79 | 0.50% | 17,281 | 89 | 0.52% |
| Parke | 15,674 | 123 | 0.78% | 14,804 | 97 | 0.66% | 14,600 | 37 | 0.25% | 16,372 | 89 | 0.54% | 15,410 | 103 | 0.67% |
| Perry | 17,367 | 75 | 0.43% | 17,232 | 38 | 0.22% | 19,075 | 47 | 0.25% | 19,346 | 38 | 0.20% | 19,107 | 61 | 0.32% |
| Pike | 14,995 | 39 | 0.26% | 12,797 | 36 | 0.28% | 12,281 | 36 | 0.29% | 13,465 | 69 | 0.51% | 12,509 | 40 | 0.32% |
| Porter | 39,779 | 1,860 | 4.68% | 60,279 | 1,661 | 2.76% | 87,114 | 1,964 | 2.25% | 119,816 | 3,186 | 2.66% | 128,932 | 2,964 | 2.30% |
| Posey | 19,818 | 87 | 0.44% | 19,214 | 40 | 0.21% | 21,740 | 81 | 0.37% | 26,414 | 144 | 0.55% | 25,968 | 69 | 0.27% |
| Pulaski | 12,493 | 383 | 3.07% | 12,837 | 233 | 1.82% | 12,534 | 127 | 1.01% | 13,258 | 150 | 1.13% | 12,643 | 83 | 0.66% |
| Putnam | 22,950 | 141 | 0.61% | 24,927 | 134 | 0.54% | 26,932 | 92 | 0.34% | 29,163 | 170 | 0.58% | 30,315 | 243 | 0.80% |
| Randolph | 27,141 | 128 | 0.47% | 28,434 | 97 | 0.34% | 28,915 | 96 | 0.33% | 29,997 | 135 | 0.45% | 27,148 | 126 | 0.46% |
| Ripley | 18,763 | 106 | 0.56% | 20,641 | 79 | 0.38% | 21,138 | 52 | 0.25% | 24,398 | 134 | 0.55% | 24,616 | 61 | 0.25% |
| Rush | 19,799 | 55 | 0.28% | 20,393 | 57 | 0.28% | 20,352 | 72 | 0.35% | 19,604 | 66 | 0.34% | 18,129 | 42 | 0.23% |
| St. Joseph | 205,058 | 13,699 | 6.68% | 238,614 | 11,620 | 4.87% | 245,044 | 9,039 | 3.69% | 241,617 | 7,658 | 3.17% | 247,052 | 7,424 | 3.01% |
| Scott | 11,519 | 31 | 0.27% | 14,643 | 9 | 0.06% | 17,144 | 58 | 0.34% | 20,422 | 213 | 1.04% | 20,991 | 40 | 0.19% |
| Shelby | 28,026 | 121 | 0.43% | 34,093 | 149 | 0.44% | 37,797 | 135 | 0.36% | 39,887 | 223 | 0.56% | 40,307 | 252 | 0.63% |
| Spencer | 16,174 | 82 | 0.51% | 16,074 | 45 | 0.28% | 17,134 | 13 | 0.08% | 19,361 | 101 | 0.52% | 19,490 | 114 | 0.58% |
| Starke | 15,282 | 1,195 | 7.82% | 17,911 | 929 | 5.19% | 19,280 | 613 | 3.18% | 21,997 | 603 | 2.74% | 22,747 | 433 | 1.90% |
| Steuben | 17,087 | 220 | 1.29% | 17,184 | 226 | 1.32% | 20,159 | 332 | 1.65% | 24,694 | 410 | 1.66% | 27,446 | 254 | 0.93% |
| Sullivan | 23,667 | 332 | 1.40% | 21,721 | 166 | 0.76% | 19,889 | 123 | 0.62% | 21,107 | 151 | 0.72% | 18,993 | 22 | 0.12% |
| Switzerland | 7,599 | 29 | 0.38% | 7,092 | 7 | 0.10% | 6,306 | 18 | 0.29% | 7,153 | 33 | 0.46% | 7,738 | 29 | 0.37% |
| Tippecanoe | 74,473 | 1,388 | 1.86% | 89,122 | 1,866 | 2.09% | 109,378 | 2,705 | 2.47% | 121,702 | 3,792 | 3.12% | 130,598 | 6,680 | 5.11% |
| Tipton | 15,566 | 97 | 0.62% | 15,856 | 85 | 0.54% | 16,650 | 83 | 0.50% | 16,819 | 145 | 0.86% | 16,119 | 66 | 0.41% |
| Union | 6,412 | 21 | 0.33% | 6,457 | 23 | 0.36% | 6,582 | 14 | 0.21% | 6,860 | 17 | 0.25% | 6,976 | 20 | 0.29% |
| Vanderburgh | 160,422 | 1,323 | 0.82% | 165,794 | 891 | 0.54% | 168,772 | 772 | 0.46% | 167,515 | 1,606 | 0.96% | 165,058 | 1,532 | 0.93% |
| Vermillion | 19,723 | 1,169 | 5.93% | 17,683 | 782 | 4.42% | 16,793 | 442 | 2.63% | 18,229 | 319 | 1.75% | 16,773 | 152 | 0.91% |
| Vigo | 105,160 | 2,300 | 2.19% | 108,458 | 1,553 | 1.43% | 114,528 | 1,251 | 1.09% | 112,385 | 2,227 | 1.98% | 106,107 | 2,333 | 2.20% |
| Wabash | 29,047 | 197 | 0.68% | 32,605 | 219 | 0.67% | 35,553 | 174 | 0.49% | 26,640 | 442 | 1.66% | 35,069 | 284 | 0.81% |
| Warren | 8,535 | 53 | 0.62% | 8,545 | 23 | 0.27% | 8,705 | 6 | 0.07% | 8,976 | 51 | 0.57% | 8,176 | 31 | 0.38% |
| Warrick | 21,527 | 90 | 0.42% | 23,577 | 73 | 0.31% | 27,972 | 58 | 0.21% | 41,474 | 303 | 0.73% | 44,920 | 361 | 0.80% |
| Washington | 16,520 | 42 | 0.25% | 17,819 | 12 | 0.07% | 19,278 | 31 | 0.16% | 21,932 | 66 | 0.30% | 23,717 | 91 | 0.38% |
| Wayne | 68,566 | 797 | 1.16% | 74,039 | 630 | 0.85% | 79,109 | 522 | 0.66% | 76,058 | 696 | 0.92% | 71,951 | 450 | 0.63% |
| Wells | 19,564 | 143 | 0.73% | 21,220 | 78 | 0.37% | 23,821 | 95 | 0.40% | 25,401 | 218 | 0.86% | 25,948 | 80 | 0.31% |
| White | 18,042 | 186 | 1.03% | 19,709 | 129 | 0.65% | 20,995 | 134 | 0.64% | 23,867 | 249 | 1.04% | 23,265 | 156 | 0.67% |
| Whitley | 18,828 | 131 | 0.70% | 20,954 | 101 | 0.48% | 23,395 | 194 | 0.83% | 26,215 | 192 | 0.73% | 27,651 | 135 | 0.49% |

TABLE 3.  FOREIGN BORN IN SELECTED CITIES, 1860–1990

| | 1860 | 1870 | 1880 | 1900 | 1910 | 1920 | 1930 | 1940 | 1950 | 1960* | 1970 | 1980 | 1990 |
|---|---|---|---|---|---|---|---|---|---|---|---|---|---|
| Anderson | 122 | 339 | 321 | | 977 | 940 | 804 | 630 | 558 | 869 | 412 | | 517 |
| Bloomington | | | | | | 120 | 226 | 200 | 439 | 1,001 | | | 4,115 |
| East Chicago | | | | | 10,295 | 14,663 | 13,793 | 12,338 | 10,092 | | 6,222 | | 3,917 |
| Elkhart | 16 | 355 | 731 | | 1,636 | 1,526 | 1,665 | 1,296 | 1,096 | 2,222 | | | 1,159 |
| Evansville | 4,933 | 6,276 | 6,103 | 5,621 | 4,462 | 3,145 | 2,082 | 1,179 | 1,085 | | 670 | 2,581 | 1,173 |
| Fort Wayne | | 5,041 | 5,852 | 6,775 | 7,204 | 6,634 | 5,729 | 4,409 | 3,597 | 5,185 | 3,760 | 7,163 | 3,829 |
| Gary | | | | | 8,242 | 16,460 | 19,345 | 17,270 | 14,960 | 36,436 | 10,194 | | 1,660 |
| Indianapolis | 5,677 | 10,657 | 12,610 | 17,070 | 19,767 | 16,958 | 13,740 | 10,555 | 8,919 | 11,552 | 10,873 | 18,905 | 13,963 |
| Lafayette | 2,986 | 3,639 | 2,813 | | 2,019 | 1,372 | 1,128 | 771 | 650 | 1,866 | 1,651 | | 1,083 |
| La Porte | 1,494 | 2,635 | 1,565 | | 1,954 | 2,216 | 1,643 | 1,223 | 1,047 | 3,276 | | | 413 |
| Michigan City | 1,444 | 1,585 | 2,223 | | 1,528 | 3,500 | 3,285 | 2,329 | 1,705 | | | | 674 |
| Muncie | 157 | 240 | 268 | | 840 | 820 | 551 | 457 | 462 | 632 | 595 | | 1,023 |
| South Bend | 670 | 1,365 | 3,426 | 8,583 | 13,420 | 13,391 | 14,202 | 10,877 | 9,128 | 11,620 | 5,750 | 8,198 | 3,546 |
| Terre Haute | 1,881 | 3,101 | 3,992 | 2,945 | 3,796 | 3,667 | 2,665 | 1,887 | 1,451 | 1,553 | 876 | | 1,439 |

*Figures provided by the U.S. Census for 1960 were for foreign stock, not foreign born for selected cities.

For comparison purposes, we used the county figures for 1960.

Lake county was entered under Gary but includes Hammond and East Chicago; La Porte County was entered under La Porte but includes Michigan City.

TABLE 4.  NATIVE AMERICAN POPULATION IN INDIANA, 1850–1990

| | 1850 | 1860 | 1870 | 1880 | 1890 | 1900 | 1910 | 1920 | 1930 | 1940 | 1950 | 1960 | 1970 | 1980 | 1990 |
|---|---|---|---|---|---|---|---|---|---|---|---|---|---|---|---|
| Indiana | 290 | 240 | 246 | 343 | 243 | 279 | 125 | 285 | 223 | | 438 | 948 | 3,887 | 18,990 | 12,503 |
| Adams | | | | 1 | | | | | | | | 2 | 9 | 118 | 42 |
| Allen | 22 | 24 | 34 | 26 | 5 | 9 | | | | | 29 | 90 | 297 | 1,166 | 880 |
| Bartholomew | | | | | | | | | | | | 3 | 14 | 114 | 95 |
| Benton | | | | | | | | | | | | | 4 | 18 | 16 |
| Blackford | | | | | | | | | | | | 6 | 9 | 44 | 44 |
| Boone | | | | 1 | | | | | | | | 6 | 27 | 100 | 88 |
| Brown | | 4 | | | | | | | | | | | 6 | | 47 |
| Carroll | | | | 1 | | | | | | | | 2 | 6 | 60 | 22 |
| Cass | 8 | | 1 | 4 | | | | | | | 13 | 4 | 20 | 82 | 135 |
| Clark | | | 1 | 1 | | | | | | | | 12 | 46 | 298 | 183 |
| Clay | | 4 | | 1 | | | | | | | | 2 | 7 | 10 | 36 |
| Clinton | | | | 4 | | 2 | | | | | | 7 | 18 | 128 | 51 |
| Crawford | | | | | | | | | | | | 1 | 11 | 76 | 25 |
| Daviess | | | | 1 | | | | | | | | 1 | 9 | 100 | 26 |
| Dearborn | | | | 1 | | | | | | | | | 20 | 124 | 47 |
| Decatur | | | | 1 | | | | | | | | | 3 | 22 | 18 |
| De Kalb | | | | | | | | | | | | 1 | 25 | 102 | 91 |
| Delaware | | 1 | 7 | 6 | | | 1 | 1 | 1 | | 18 | 41 | 102 | 454 | 268 |
| Dubois | | | | | | | | | | | | 1 | 12 | 50 | 30 |
| Elkhart | | | | 1 | | | | 1 | | | | 36 | 117 | 746 | 440 |
| Fayette | | | | | | | | | | | | | 5 | 154 | 36 |
| Floyd | | | 9 | 10 | | | | | | | | 2 | 10 | 54 | 92 |
| Fountain | | | | | | | | | | | | 1 | 19 | 20 | 25 |
| Franklin | | | | | | | | | | | | | 9 | 16 | 34 |
| Fulton | | | | | | | | | | | | 1 | 3 | 142 | 47 |
| Gibson | | | 3 | 1 | | | | | | | | | 14 | 60 | 38 |
| Grant | | 1 | | 48 | 47 | 19 | 22 | | | | 14 | 18 | 108 | 526 | 295 |
| Greene | | | 7 | | | | | | | | | 2 | 19 | 52 | 47 |
| Hamilton | | | | 3 | | | 3 | | | | | 6 | 46 | 102 | 160 |
| Hancock | | | | | | | | | | | | 6 | 13 | 78 | 58 |
| Harrison | | | | | | | | | | | | 4 | 8 | 38 | 57 |
| Hendricks | | | 2 | | | | | | | | | 6 | 29 | 62 | 150 |
| Henry | | | 5 | 10 | 4 | 1 | | | | | | 5 | 19 | 126 | 78 |
| Howard | | | | | | | | | | | | 10 | 70 | 474 | 223 |
| Huntington | | | 3 | 10 | 1 | 1 | 9 | 9 | | | | 23 | 54 | 242 | 154 |
| Jackson | | | | | | | | | | | | 3 | 16 | 36 | 62 |
| Jasper | | | | | | | | | | | | 8 | 6 | 20 | 60 |
| Jay | | | | | | | | | | | | | 12 | 32 | 32 |
| Jefferson | | | 3 | 2 | 1 | | | | | | | 1 | 18 | 100 | 55 |
| Jennings | | | | 1 | 6 | | | 9 | | | | | 7 | 74 | 31 |
| Johnson | | | | | | | | | | | | 3 | 37 | 228 | 138 |
| Knox | | | | 1 | | | | | | | | 6 | 21 | 104 | 69 |
| Kosciusko | | | | | | | | | | | 1 | 8 | 9 | 212 | 110 |
| Lagrange | | | | | | | | | | | | 4 | 2 | 38 | 57 |
| Lake | | | | | | 1 | 11 | 9 | | 66 | 43 | 164 | 441 | 1,602 | 845 |
| La Porte | | | 5 | | | | 19 | 7 | | | 13 | 31 | 120 | 434 | 252 |
| Lawrence | | | | 1 | | | | | | | | 6 | 19 | 88 | 88 |
| Madison | | | | | | | | 2 | | | 19 | 12 | 89 | 442 | 284 |
| Marion | | 4 | 1 | 10 | | | | 13 | 28 | 6 | 58 | 133 | 572 | 2,874 | 1,690 |
| Marshall | 173 | 145 | 109 | | | | | | | | | 1 | 12 | 78 | 71 |
| Martin | | | | | | | | | | | | 3 | | 40 | 14 |
| Miami | | | 3 | 97 | 130 | 119 | 18 | 81 | 28 | | 14 | 58 | 155 | 658 | 567 |
| Monroe | | | | | | | | | | | 10 | 15 | 62 | 220 | 212 |
| Montgomery | | | | 3 | | | | | | | | | 10 | 98 | 67 |
| Morgan | | | | | | | | | | | | | 38 | 82 | 137 |
| Newton | | | | | | | | | | | | | 6 | 74 | 39 |
| Noble | | | | 1 | | | | | | | | 1 | 6 | 98 | 79 |
| Ohio | | | | | | | | | | | | | 2 | 10 | 8 |
| Orange | | | 4 | | | | | | | | | 1 | 8 | 50 | 38 |
| Owen | | | | | | | | | | | | | 8 | 98 | 46 |
| Parke | | | 2 | | | | | | | | | 1 | 4 | 94 | 42 |
| Perry | | | | | | | | | | | | 2 | 9 | 98 | 25 |
| Pike | | | | | | | | | | | | 1 | 1 | 106 | 16 |
| Porter | | | | | | 2 | 1 | 1 | | | 2 | 5 | 63 | 432 | 237 |
| Posey | | | | | | | | | | | | 7 | 4 | 212 | 38 |
| Pulaski | | | | | | | | | | | | | 6 | 10 | 21 |
| Putnam | | | | | | | | | | | | 3 | 7 | 70 | 77 |
| Randolph | | | 1 | 4 | | | | | | | | 1 | 20 | 86 | 49 |
| Ripley | | | | | | | | | | | | 4 | 4 | 48 | 44 |
| Rush | | | 1 | | 2 | | 11 | | | | | 2 | 16 | 52 | 15 |
| St. Joseph | 29 | 7 | 10 | 1 | 9 | 39 | | 8 | | 34 | 32 | 49 | 289 | 930 | 840 |
| Scott | | | | | | | | | | | | | 6 | 16 | 23 |
| Shelby | | | | | | | | | | | | 3 | 5 | 96 | 64 |
| Spencer | | | | | | | | | | | | 5 | 5 | 74 | 37 |
| Starke | | | | | | | | | | 1 | | | 8 | 138 | 86 |
| Steuben | | | | | | | | | | | 3 | 2 | 38 | 100 | 64 |
| Sullivan | | | | | | | | 1 | | | | | 6 | 78 | 39 |
| Switzerland | | | | | | | | | | | | 1 | | 30 | 16 |
| Tippecanoe | 1 | | | | | 3 | | 2 | 1 | | 9 | 11 | 94 | 302 | 311 |
| Tipton | | | 3 | | | | | | 1 | | | 3 | 3 | 46 | 20 |
| Union | | 6 | | | | | | | | | | 3 | 2 | 32 | 15 |
| Vanderburgh | | | 2 | 2 | | | | | | | 9 | 22 | 105 | 512 | 279 |
| Vermillion | | | | | | | | | | | | 3 | 11 | 30 | 32 |
| Vigo | | 3 | 1 | | | | | | | | 16 | 19 | 68 | 570 | 289 |
| Wabash | 45 | 47 | 16 | 94 | 26 | 14 | 12 | 21 | 16 | | 4 | 12 | 97 | 250 | 258 |
| Warren | | | 1 | | 6 | | | | | | | 1 | 2 | 18 | 16 |
| Warrick | | | | | | | | 1 | | | | 5 | 15 | 206 | 82 |
| Washington | | | | 1 | | | | | | | | 1 | 13 | 56 | 28 |
| Wayne | | | 1 | 1 | | | | 1 | | | | 13 | 63 | 302 | 149 |
| Wells | | | | | | | | | | | | 11 | 31 | 36 | 40 |
| White | | | | | | | | | | | | | 16 | 16 | 50 |
| Whitley | 1 | | | | | | 19 | 12 | | | | 1 | 12 | 196 | 72 |
| Other counties | | | | | | 9 | 17 | | 135 | 71 | 130 | | | | |

## TABLE 5. African-American Population in Indiana, 1850–1990

| | 1850 | 1860 | 1870 | 1880 | 1890 | 1900 | 1910 | 1920 | 1930 | 1940 | 1950 | 1960 | 1970 | 1980 | 1990 |
|---|---|---|---|---|---|---|---|---|---|---|---|---|---|---|---|
| Indiana | 11,262 | 11,428 | 24,560 | 39,228 | 45,215 | 57,478 | 60,320 | 80,810 | 111,932 | 121,916 | 174,168 | 269,275 | 357,464 | 414,489 | 432,092 |
| Adams | 8 | 6 | | 2 | | 2 | | | 5 | 6 | 8 | 1 | 7 | 3 | 36 |
| Allen | 102 | 63 | 42 | 169 | 248 | 300 | 601 | 1,471 | 2,379 | 2,553 | 5,269 | 11,702 | 19,298 | 25,997 | 30,314 |
| Bartholomew | 82 | 7 | 11 | 138 | 314 | 385 | 319 | 229 | 191 | 181 | 241 | 315 | 513 | 1,025 | 1,005 |
| Benton | | | | 6 | 46 | 72 | 71 | 44 | 20 | 18 | 12 | 11 | 9 | 4 | 6 |
| Blackford | 11 | | 14 | 17 | 3 | 23 | 40 | 9 | 10 | 3 | 2 | 2 | | 2 | 7 |
| Boone | 20 | 90 | 240 | 238 | 168 | 119 | 123 | 110 | 116 | 86 | 61 | 41 | 28 | 43 | 83 |
| Brown | 19 | | 1 | | 7 | 1 | 1 | 1 | | 6 | 12 | 3 | 20 | 31 | 13 |
| Carroll | 33 | 13 | 24 | 42 | 17 | 27 | 7 | 5 | 8 | 7 | 9 | 16 | 1 | 17 | 19 |
| Cass | 61 | 65 | 111 | 197 | 143 | 243 | 240 | 306 | 288 | 353 | 372 | 318 | 284 | 345 | 330 |
| Clark | 582 | 520 | 1,970 | 2,536 | 2,859 | 3,182 | 2,745 | 2,298 | 1,965 | 1,803 | 2,199 | 2,821 | 3,388 | 4,289 | 4,703 |
| Clay | 18 | 22 | 26 | 298 | 412 | 412 | 227 | 291 | 323 | 318 | 218 | 189 | 129 | 133 | 113 |
| Clinton | 24 | 20 | 7 | 65 | 105 | 99 | 84 | 81 | 96 | 72 | 53 | 38 | 24 | 24 | 36 |
| Crawford | 1 | | 3 | 2 | 14 | 2 | | 3 | 4 | 3 | 3 | | | 17 | 9 |
| Daviess | 44 | 74 | 129 | 307 | 271 | 379 | 210 | 196 | 174 | 142 | 134 | 109 | 123 | 41 | 99 |
| Dearborn | 147 | 74 | 58 | 57 | 87 | 149 | 180 | 110 | 168 | 204 | 189 | 236 | 202 | 210 | 252 |
| Decatur | 156 | 24 | 87 | 235 | 164 | 133 | 89 | 122 | 10 | 9 | 5 | 3 | 4 | | 39 |
| De Kalb | 10 | 15 | 4 | 5 | 20 | 11 | 21 | 51 | 129 | 62 | 177 | 38 | 31 | 54 | 37 |
| Delaware | 4 | 16 | 53 | 213 | 451 | 994 | 1,460 | 2,103 | 2,678 | 3,035 | 4,460 | 5,762 | 6,959 | 7,709 | 7,167 |
| Dubois | 21 | 12 | 35 | 58 | 98 | 19 | 9 | 7 | 3 | 1 | 2 | | 12 | 22 | 33 |
| Elkhart | 16 | 20 | 35 | 28 | 57 | 51 | 91 | 383 | 551 | 562 | 1,093 | 2,219 | 4,395 | 5,632 | 7,106 |
| Fayette | 72 | 87 | 92 | 242 | 346 | 433 | 440 | 504 | 449 | 542 | 526 | 486 | 490 | 473 | 435 |
| Floyd | 574 | 757 | 1,462 | 1,552 | 2,167 | 2,107 | 1,749 | 1,535 | 1,399 | 1,325 | 1,446 | 2,010 | 2,105 | 2,288 | 2,642 |
| Fountain | 52 | 73 | 47 | 108 | 31 | 29 | 30 | 20 | 4 | 1 | 11 | 5 | 3 | | 4 |
| Franklin | 209 | 103 | 24 | 12 | 6 | 7 | 6 | 4 | | 1 | 6 | 3 | 4 | 2 | 10 |
| Fulton | 2 | 6 | 16 | 23 | 21 | 26 | 6 | 15 | 34 | 41 | 9 | 39 | 106 | 124 | 151 |
| Gibson | 217 | 274 | 437 | 1,027 | 1,239 | 1,481 | 1,445 | 965 | 789 | 739 | 644 | 657 | 653 | 572 | 596 |
| Grant | 147 | 384 | 737 | 867 | 866 | 1,366 | 1,528 | 1,605 | 1,408 | 1,543 | 2,139 | 3,199 | 4,512 | 5,228 | 5,047 |
| Greene | 75 | 79 | 21 | 250 | 169 | 133 | 85 | 48 | 13 | 9 | 9 | 5 | 16 | 11 | 10 |
| Hamilton | 182 | 350 | 515 | 762 | 560 | 524 | 555 | 464 | 369 | 361 | 343 | 319 | 272 | 294 | 676 |
| Hancock | 104 | 93 | 54 | 101 | 92 | 114 | 125 | 47 | 28 | 49 | 40 | 41 | 42 | 33 | 44 |
| Harrison | 91 | 114 | 349 | 350 | 330 | 358 | 293 | 201 | 130 | 98 | 95 | 117 | 119 | 157 | 124 |
| Hendricks | 36 | 45 | 182 | 402 | 398 | 364 | 301 | 221 | 162 | 175 | 155 | 253 | 348 | 353 | 685 |
| Henry | 287 | 283 | 441 | 679 | 544 | 472 | 415 | 456 | 485 | 423 | 429 | 421 | 468 | 530 | 474 |
| Howard | 105 | 165 | 304 | 404 | 506 | 546 | 490 | 913 | 1,329 | 1,241 | 1,536 | 2,598 | 3,577 | 4,257 | 4,398 |
| Huntington | 3 | 2 | 5 | 7 | 21 | 12 | 16 | 6 | 5 | 1 | 39 | 3 | 24 | 64 | 52 |
| Jackson | 214 | 179 | 164 | 344 | 270 | 228 | 136 | 74 | 67 | 118 | 126 | 149 | 147 | 136 | 138 |
| Jasper | 1 | 5 | 3 | | 3 | 6 | 6 | 11 | 3 | 4 | 4 | 8 | 24 | 56 | 111 |
| Jay | 30 | 21 | 21 | 155 | 120 | 145 | 171 | 132 | 135 | 109 | 65 | 85 | 63 | 57 | 30 |
| Jefferson | 568 | 512 | 1,105 | 944 | 999 | 868 | 604 | 490 | 420 | 411 | 399 | 392 | 388 | 470 | 363 |
| Jennings | 323 | 151 | 422 | 408 | 294 | 374 | 295 | 247 | 257 | 220 | 249 | 286 | 230 | 110 | 209 |
| Johnson | 15 | 19 | 115 | 355 | 342 | 418 | 360 | 402 | 311 | 294 | 301 | 370 | 1,834 | 868 | 845 |
| Knox | 530 | 449 | 380 | 629 | 588 | 612 | 572 | 355 | 337 | 259 | 236 | 250 | 350 | 321 | 486 |
| Kosciusko | 1 | 2 | 10 | 49 | 62 | 30 | 28 | 40 | 42 | 38 | 60 | 84 | 123 | 225 | 309 |
| Lagrange | 18 | 16 | 25 | 15 | 8 | 9 | 10 | 4 | 2 | 12 | 5 | 9 | 11 | 16 | 44 |
| Lake | 1 | 5 | 3 | 2 | 23 | 41 | 493 | 6,918 | 23,748 | 27,253 | 50,726 | 87,109 | 112,014 | 126,066 | 116,688 |
| La Porte | 78 | 135 | 228 | 249 | 217 | 269 | 338 | 469 | 1,284 | 1,148 | 2,453 | 4,890 | 7,037 | 8,656 | 9,580 |
| Lawrence | 94 | 118 | 250 | 335 | 377 | 435 | 345 | 188 | 244 | 174 | 134 | 109 | 102 | 41 | 109 |
| Madison | 14 | 60 | 88 | 126 | 226 | 1,179 | 690 | 1,026 | 1,699 | 1,645 | 2,774 | 4,976 | 8,026 | 9,670 | 9,870 |
| Marion | 650 | 825 | 3,938 | 8,038 | 11,118 | 17,536 | 23,256 | 35,634 | 44,722 | 51,949 | 65,010 | 99,912 | 134,486 | 155,455 | 169,654 |
| Marshall | 2 | 3 | | 9 | 5 | 15 | 71 | 106 | 123 | 103 | 119 | 65 | 65 | 53 | 76 |
| Martin | 96 | 52 | 36 | 22 | 23 | 217 | 18 | 4 | 3 | 3 | 18 | 29 | 24 | | 12 |
| Miami | 11 | 47 | 51 | 135 | 112 | 80 | 109 | 173 | 281 | 161 | 127 | 630 | 991 | 998 | 1,115 |
| Monroe | 27 | 25 | 259 | 345 | 408 | 428 | 438 | 508 | 541 | 441 | 711 | 704 | 1,437 | 2,641 | 2,835 |
| Montgomery | 143 | 150 | 167 | 427 | 357 | 282 | 246 | 270 | 227 | 219 | 177 | 200 | 181 | 53 | 201 |
| Morgan | 75 | 107 | 74 | 150 | 114 | 106 | 94 | 51 | 8 | 14 | 23 | 8 | 7 | 13 | 9 |
| Newton | | | 33 | 86 | 44 | 40 | 20 | 9 | 9 | 9 | 5 | 11 | 9 | 10 | 9 |
| Noble | 6 | 8 | 13 | 47 | 10 | 6 | 26 | 6 | 4 | 7 | 14 | 12 | 11 | 30 | 58 |
| Ohio | 37 | 23 | 189 | 205 | 154 | 143 | 144 | 103 | 87 | 60 | 56 | 52 | 58 | 54 | 41 |
| Orange | 251 | 260 | 159 | 149 | 70 | 194 | 363 | 264 | 482 | 217 | 157 | 144 | 126 | 214 | 127 |
| Owen | 156 | 85 | 59 | 127 | 83 | 108 | 89 | 57 | 42 | 16 | 23 | 15 | 21 | 38 | 44 |
| Parke | 228 | 196 | 152 | 288 | 356 | 321 | 160 | 101 | 74 | 41 | 29 | 36 | 28 | 43 | 118 |
| Perry | 9 | 3 | 150 | 208 | 253 | 252 | 193 | 91 | 64 | 19 | 20 | 17 | 84 | 15 | 210 |
| Pike | 10 | 14 | 14 | 27 | 56 | 146 | 133 | 137 | 51 | 35 | 18 | 15 | 14 | 34 | 3 |
| Porter | 5 | 17 | 39 | 33 | 11 | 11 | 8 | 2 | 17 | 24 | 32 | 69 | 160 | 295 | 454 |
| Posey | 98 | 136 | 564 | 955 | 1,193 | 1,226 | 963 | 518 | 496 | 368 | 326 | 278 | 297 | 266 | 283 |
| Pulaski | | | | 4 | 9 | 6 | 2 | 9 | 5 | 8 | 8 | 42 | 60 | 40 | 65 |
| Putnam | 34 | 19 | 105 | 576 | 357 | 258 | 221 | 228 | 550 | 355 | 454 | 409 | 490 | 492 | 826 |
| Randolph | 662 | 825 | 617 | 591 | 606 | 396 | 235 | 214 | 136 | 99 | 123 | 90 | 81 | 42 | 56 |
| Ripley | 96 | 87 | 103 | 157 | 74 | 32 | 31 | 7 | 10 | 3 | 4 | 8 | 4 | 6 | 16 |
| Rush | 427 | 419 | 463 | 550 | 534 | 577 | 418 | 416 | 270 | 252 | 241 | 235 | 183 | 108 | 142 |
| St. Joseph | 29 | 88 | 120 | 279 | 340 | 627 | 722 | 1,304 | 3,525 | 3,702 | 8,665 | 14,022 | 18,587 | 21,888 | 24,190 |
| Scott | 15 | 2 | 5 | 10 | 1 | 1 | 1 | | | | 2 | 3 | 6 | 8 | 16 |
| Shelby | 19 | 21 | 128 | 287 | 313 | 383 | 483 | 420 | 413 | 365 | 328 | 379 | 318 | 279 | 330 |
| Spencer | 14 | 2 | 949 | 1,492 | 1,388 | 1,321 | 837 | 562 | 438 | 333 | 241 | 189 | 168 | 135 | 111 |
| Starke | | 1 | | | 3 | 4 | 14 | 22 | 19 | 13 | 6 | 19 | 44 | 56 | 73 |
| Steuben | 2 | 2 | 5 | 8 | 6 | 8 | 22 | 10 | 21 | 8 | 12 | 25 | 37 | 81 | 51 |
| Sullivan | 38 | 120 | 105 | 146 | 182 | 169 | 120 | 105 | 91 | 55 | 47 | 44 | 37 | 10 | 15 |
| Switzerland | 66 | 42 | 121 | 214 | 135 | 81 | 48 | 38 | 23 | 25 | 18 | 11 | 1 | 7 | 15 |
| Tippecanoe | 161 | 143 | 172 | 304 | 352 | 386 | 387 | 397 | 455 | 388 | 392 | 632 | 1,035 | 1,921 | 2,660 |
| Tipton | 7 | 35 | 61 | 58 | 19 | 7 | 7 | 4 | | 1 | 5 | 1 | 8 | | 10 |
| Union | 38 | 40 | 112 | 144 | 161 | 120 | 101 | 143 | 98 | 87 | 39 | 64 | 30 | 8 | 20 |
| Vanderburgh | 227 | 127 | 2,151 | 3,843 | 6,080 | 8,059 | 6,548 | 6,568 | 7,228 | 7,560 | 9,167 | 9,547 | 10,279 | 12,089 | 12,410 |
| Vermillion | 18 | 30 | 48 | 74 | 47 | 120 | 121 | 235 | 69 | 53 | 23 | 18 | 11 | 11 | 15 |
| Vigo | 748 | 706 | 1,099 | 1,506 | 1,720 | 2,253 | 3,323 | 4,478 | 4,116 | 4,049 | 4,415 | 4,802 | 5,378 | 6,047 | 5,916 |
| Wabash | 14 | 33 | 84 | 254 | 141 | 151 | 167 | 174 | 128 | 87 | 53 | 67 | 119 | 157 | 138 |
| Warren | 9 | 17 | 22 | 19 | 15 | 24 | 18 | 15 | 17 | 24 | | | | 2 | 1 |
| Warrick | 29 | 19 | 487 | 619 | 614 | 715 | 456 | 366 | 382 | 362 | 274 | 251 | 186 | 293 | 371 |
| Washington | 252 | 187 | 18 | 3 | 9 | 5 | 8 | 1 | | 1 | | | | 9 | 23 |
| Wayne | 1,036 | 870 | 1,238 | 1,710 | 1,370 | 1,402 | 1,591 | 1,871 | 2,416 | 2,735 | 3,298 | 3,522 | 3,835 | 3,896 | 3,795 |
| Wells | 11 | 1 | | 5 | 3 | 3 | 3 | 3 | 2 | 7 | 2 | 1 | 42 | | 10 |
| White | 9 | 21 | 3 | 6 | 9 | 11 | 11 | 2 | | | | 5 | | 4 | 2 |
| Whitley | 95 | 92 | 97 | 108 | 51 | 61 | 40 | 4 | 12 | | | 2 | | 16 | 29 |

## TABLE 6. FOREIGN BORN IN INDIANA BY COUNTY, 1860

| | Africa | At Sea | Asia | Australia | Austria | British Channel | Belgium | Brazil | Canada | China | Cuba | Czechoslovakia | Denmark | Egypt | East Indies | England | Europe | France | Finland | Germany | Greece | Holland | Hungary | India |
|---|---|---|---|---|---|---|---|---|---|---|---|---|---|---|---|---|---|---|---|---|---|---|---|---|
| Indiana | 4 | 107 | 1 | 7 | 286 | 8 | 334 | 6 | 3,191 | 6 | 3 | 18 | 67 | 1 | 1 | 9,363 | 262 | 6,254 | 1 | 67,315 | 39 | 513 | 33 | 6 |
| Adams | | 5 | | | | | | | 16 | | | | | | | 21 | | 183 | | 777 | | | | |
| Allen | 9 | | | | 2 | | | | 116 | | | | 1 | | | 327 | | 1,132 | | 4,150 | 4 | | | 1 |
| Bartholomew | 1 | | | | | | | | 7 | | | | | | | 52 | | 7 | | 846 | | | | 1 |
| Benton | | 1 | | | | | | | 18 | | | | | | | 70 | | | 1 | 33 | | 2 | | |
| Blackford | | | | | | | | | | | | | | | | 12 | | | | 50 | | | | |
| Boone | 1 | | | | | | | | 9 | | | | 1 | | | 31 | | 6 | | 46 | | | | |
| Brown | | | | 1 | | | | | 3 | | 1 | | | | | 22 | | 7 | | 120 | | | | |
| Carroll | | | | | | | | 1 | 30 | | | | | | | 53 | | 15 | | 237 | | | | |
| Cass | | 2 | | | 4 | | | | 82 | | | | 1 | | | 166 | | 29 | | 701 | | | | |
| Clark | 1 | | | | 2 | | 1 | | 37 | 1 | | | | | | 168 | | 79 | | 1,484 | 36 | 2 | 2 | |
| Clay | | 4 | | | | | 1 | | 7 | | | | | | | 30 | | 2 | | 374 | 1 | 1 | 1 | |
| Clinton | 1 | | | | | | | | 15 | | | | | | | 41 | | 7 | | 76 | | 2 | | |
| Crawford | | | | | | | 1 | 1 | 10 | | | | | | | 62 | | 25 | | 87 | | 1 | | |
| Daviess | | | | | | | | | 10 | | | | | | | 68 | | 23 | | 97 | | 2 | | |
| Dearborn | | 5 | | | 24 | | 2 | | 46 | | | | 5 | | | 368 | | 475 | | 3,730 | | 17 | | |
| Decatur | 4 | | | | | | | | 11 | | | | | | | 89 | 16 | 33 | | 560 | | 3 | | |
| De Kalb | | | | | | | | | 37 | | | | 1 | | | 101 | 2 | 12 | | 397 | | | | |
| Delaware | | | | | 5 | | | | 7 | | | | 1 | | | 44 | | 27 | | 86 | | | | |
| Dubois | 1 | | | | 2 | | 1 | | | | | | | | | 18 | | 111 | | 2,569 | | 6 | | |
| Elkhart | | | | | 10 | | 1 | | 384 | | | | 1 | | | 114 | | 47 | | 615 | | 36 | | |
| Fayette | 1 | | | | | | | | 6 | | | | | | | 55 | | 22 | | 249 | | 2 | | |
| Floyd | 6 | | | 3 | 2 | 21 | | | 43 | 1 | | | 6 | | | 389 | 8 | 435 | | 2,045 | 2 | 3 | 1 | |
| Fountain | | 2 | | | 1 | | | | 19 | | | | 1 | | | 65 | | 13 | | 280 | | 3 | | |
| Franklin | | 2 | | | 6 | | | | 25 | | | | | | | 247 | | 114 | | 2,399 | | 4 | | |
| Fulton | | | | | 1 | | | | 28 | | | | 1 | | | 26 | | 25 | | 346 | | 4 | | |
| Gibson | 3 | | | | | | | | 13 | | | | | | | 127 | | 37 | | 628 | | 1 | 1 | |
| Grant | | | | | | | | | 4 | | | | | | | 67 | | 5 | | 31 | | | | |
| Greene | | | | | | | 1 | | 7 | | | | | | | 63 | | 16 | | 146 | | 1 | | |
| Hamilton | | 1 | | 1 | 1 | | | | 4 | | | | | | | 22 | | 36 | | 248 | | | | |
| Hancock | 1 | | | | | | | | 2 | | | | | | | 20 | | 19 | | 296 | | | | |
| Harrison | | 4 | | | 4 | | 23 | | 5 | | | | | | | 62 | 2 | 275 | | 1,285 | | 1 | 1 | |
| Hendricks | 2 | | | | | | | | 1 | | | | | | | 27 | | 14 | | 45 | | | | |
| Henry | | 2 | | | | | | | 3 | | | | | | | 58 | | 6 | | 100 | | | | |
| Howard | | | | | | | | | 3 | | | | 2 | | | 24 | | 5 | | 64 | | | | |
| Huntington | | 1 | | | 1 | | | | 23 | 1 | | | | | | 54 | | 69 | | 704 | | | | |
| Jackson | | 5 | | | | | | | 15 | | | | | | | 30 | | 30 | | 1,208 | | 14 | | |
| Jasper | | | | | | | | | 5 | | | | | | | 23 | | 2 | | 76 | | | | |
| Jay | | | | | | | | | 5 | | | | | | | 34 | | 60 | | 236 | | | | |
| Jefferson | 1 | | | | 1 | | 1 | | 19 | 2 | | | 1 | | | 243 | 218 | 186 | | 1,552 | | 2 | | |
| Jennings | 1 | | | | 6 | | | | 9 | | | | | | | 102 | | 183 | | 701 | | | | |
| Johnson | 1 | | | | 1 | | | | 10 | | | | | | | 41 | | 8 | | 170 | | 1 | | |
| Knox | 2 | | | | 8 | | 1 | | 19 | 2 | | | 1 | | | 96 | | 282 | | 1,239 | | 9 | | |
| Kosciusko | 1 | | | | | | | | 41 | 1 | 1 | | | | | 102 | | 13 | | 272 | | | | |
| Lagrange | | | | | | | | | 89 | | | | | | | 205 | | 13 | | 116 | | 1 | | 2 |
| Lake | | 1 | 3 | 1 | | | 4 | | 209 | | | | 1 | | | 154 | | 69 | | 1,870 | | 28 | 9 | |
| La Porte | 1 | 3 | | | 123 | | 9 | 1 | 275 | | | | 5 | | | 454 | | 57 | | 2,941 | | 38 | 3 | |
| Lawrence | | | | | | | | | 4 | | | | | | | 21 | 5 | 44 | | 150 | | | | |
| Madison | | | | | | | | | 8 | | | | | | | 21 | | 4 | | 106 | | 1 | | |
| Marion | 1 | 2 | 1 | | 6 | | | | 83 | | 4 | | 4 | | | 359 | | 211 | | 3,913 | | 13 | 3 | |
| Marshall | | | | | 7 | | | | 37 | | | | 1 | | | 48 | | 86 | | 507 | | 7 | | |
| Martin | | | | | | | | | 13 | | | | | | | 32 | | 10 | | 50 | | | | |
| Miami | | | | | 1 | | | | 42 | | | | | | | 59 | | 29 | | 589 | | | | |
| Monroe | | 2 | | | | | | | 11 | | | | 4 | | | 35 | | 27 | | 64 | | | | |
| Montgomery | 2 | | | | | | 1 | | 17 | | | | | | | 57 | | 4 | | 119 | | | | 1 |
| Morgan | | | | | | | | | 4 | | | | | | | 21 | | 6 | | 164 | | | | |
| Newton | | | | | | | | | 27 | | | | 3 | | | 33 | | 1 | | 14 | | | 1 | |
| Noble | | | | | 1 | | | | 37 | | | | | | | 94 | 1 | 31 | | 589 | | 1 | | |
| Ohio | | | | | | | | | 8 | | | | | | | 23 | 5 | 2 | | 300 | | | | 3 |
| Orange | | | | | | | | | 1 | | | | | | | 28 | | 4 | | 35 | | 1 | 1 | |
| Owen | | 1 | | | | | | | 12 | | | | | | | 26 | 1 | | | 204 | | | | |
| Parke | | | | | | | | | 21 | | | | | | | 67 | | 5 | | 66 | | | | |
| Perry | | 2 | | | 10 | | 243 | | 8 | | | | 7 | | | 249 | 1 | 157 | | 1,542 | | 11 | 1 | |
| Pike | | | | | | | | | 6 | | | | | | | 57 | | 22 | | 151 | | 1 | | |
| Porter | | | | | | | | | 372 | 1 | | | 6 | | | 139 | | 24 | | 526 | | | | |
| Posey | 1 | | | 1 | 1 | | | | 4 | | | | | | | 258 | | 77 | | 1,846 | | | 1 | |
| Pulaski | | | | | | | | | 14 | | | | | | | 26 | | 24 | | 380 | | 1 | | |
| Putnam | 1 | | | | | | | | 20 | | | | | | | 41 | | 6 | | 117 | | 1 | | |
| Randolph | 1 | | | | | | | | 9 | | | | | | | 60 | | 9 | | 197 | | | | |
| Ripley | | 4 | | | 1 | | | 3 | 12 | | | | | | | 85 | | 231 | | 2,693 | | 2 | | |
| Rush | | | | | | | 1 | | 6 | | | | 1 | | | 39 | | 10 | | 103 | | 1 | | |
| St. Joseph | | | | | 27 | | 20 | | 212 | 1 | | | 1 | | | 120 | | 172 | | 1,337 | | 8 | 1 | |
| Scott | | | | | | | | | 5 | | | | | | | 18 | | 1 | | 32 | | | | |
| Shelby | | | | | | | | | 6 | | | | | | | 81 | | 26 | | 408 | | 2 | | |
| Spencer | | 1 | | | 2 | | | | 11 | | | | | | | 52 | | 148 | | 1,630 | | | 1 | |
| Starke | | | | | | | | | 23 | | | 12 | | | | 5 | | 13 | | 98 | | 5 | | |
| Steuben | | | | 1 | | | | | 61 | | | | | | | 130 | | 11 | | 103 | | 2 | | |
| Sullivan | | | | | | | | | 17 | | | | | | | 59 | | 6 | | 65 | | 1 | 1 | |
| Switzerland | | | | | | | | | 6 | 1 | | | 2 | | | 58 | | 16 | | 260 | | | | |
| Tippecanoe | | 4 | | | 1 | | 2 | | 116 | | | | 1 | | 1 | 313 | | 84 | | 1,713 | | 148 | | |
| Tipton | | | | | | | | | 8 | | | | | | | 5 | | 3 | | 105 | | 1 | | |
| Union | | | | | | 1 | | | 3 | | | | | | | 16 | | 2 | | 86 | | | | |
| Vanderburgh | 6 | | 1 | | 14 | | | | 28 | | | | 2 | | | 856 | | 347 | | 6,076 | | 81 | 2 | |
| Vermillion | 1 | | | | | 1 | | | 10 | | | | | | | 24 | | 1 | | 91 | | | | |
| Vigo | | | | | 4 | | 1 | | 34 | | | | | | | 226 | 2 | 65 | | 1,047 | | 24 | 1 | |
| Wabash | | | | | 2 | | | | 23 | | | | 1 | | | 67 | | 8 | | 451 | | | | |
| Warren | | | | | | | | | 35 | | | | | | | 62 | | 2 | | 130 | | 3 | | |
| Warrick | | | | | 2 | | | | 13 | | | | | | | 221 | | 16 | | 848 | | | | |
| Washington | 1 | | | | | | 1 | | 5 | | | | 1 | | | 129 | | 9 | | 134 | | 1 | | |
| Wayne | 3 | | | | | | 1 | | 21 | 2 | | | | | | 241 | 1 | 20 | | 1,292 | | 5 | | |
| Wells | | | | | | | | | 5 | | | | | | | 46 | | 17 | | 176 | | 1 | | |
| White | 1 | | | | | | | | 34 | | | | 1 | | | 70 | | 5 | | 156 | | 3 | | 1 |
| Whitley | | 1 | | | | | | 1 | 12 | | | | | | | 39 | | 44 | | 370 | | | | |

## TABLE 6. FOREIGN BORN IN INDIANA BY COUNTY, 1860 (*continued*)

| COUNTY | Ireland | Isle of Man | Italy | Luxembourg | Malta | Mexico | Newfoundland | Norway | Palestine | Persia | Poland | Portugal | Russia | South America | Scotland | Spain | Switzerland | Sweden | Unknown | Wales | West Indies | Total |
|---|---|---|---|---|---|---|---|---|---|---|---|---|---|---|---|---|---|---|---|---|---|---|
| Totals | 24,722 | 32 | 100 | 52 | 1 | 22 | 15 | 35 | 1 | 1 | 92 | 5 | 46 | 4 | 2,105 | 14 | 3,461 | 729 | 932 | 232 | 16 | 120,493 |
| Adams | 44 | | | | | | | | | | 1 | | | | 1 | | 360 | | 4 | 2 | | 1,414 |
| Allen | 697 | | 2 | | | 1 | | 2 | | | 5 | | | | 131 | 1 | 264 | 3 | 19 | 6 | | 6,873 |
| Bartholomew | 291 | | | | | | 5 | | | | | | 12 | | 22 | | 8 | | 9 | | | 1,261 |
| Benton | 100 | | | | | | | | | | | | | | 1 | | | 6 | 9 | 1 | 1 | 243 |
| Blackford | 38 | | | | | | | | | | | | | | 1 | | | | | | | 101 |
| Boone | 97 | | | | | | | | | | | | | | 4 | | 2 | 1 | 5 | | | 203 |
| Brown | 32 | 1 | | | | | | 1 | | | | | | | 2 | | 3 | | | 4 | | 197 |
| Carroll | 330 | | 3 | | | | | | | | | | | | 10 | | 12 | 11 | 5 | 2 | | 709 |
| Cass | 667 | | | | | | 1 | | | | 7 | | | | 17 | | 4 | | 108 | 2 | | 1,791 |
| Clark | 572 | 1 | | | | | | | | | 4 | | | | 32 | 1 | 77 | 1 | 27 | 5 | | 2,533 |
| Clay | 65 | | | | | | | | | | | | | | 23 | | 43 | | 6 | 6 | | 564 |
| Clinton | 69 | | 1 | | | | | | | | | | 1 | | 9 | | | | 1 | 4 | | 227 |
| Crawford | 15 | | | | | | | | | | | | | | 11 | | 1 | | | | | 214 |
| Daviess | 609 | 7 | | | | | | | | | 2 | | | | 7 | | 2 | | 3 | 4 | | 834 |
| Dearborn | 866 | | | | | | | | | | | | | | 33 | | 169 | 18 | 10 | 10 | | 5,778 |
| Decatur | 315 | | | | | | | | | | | | | | 13 | 1 | 7 | | 4 | 1 | | 1,057 |
| De Kalb | 52 | | | | | | | | | | | | | | 6 | | 33 | | 6 | | | 647 |
| Delaware | 172 | | | | | | | | | | | | | | 9 | | 4 | | 11 | 3 | | 369 |
| Dubois | 7 | | | | | | | | | | | | | | 2 | | 49 | | | | | 2,766 |
| Elkhart | 126 | | 1 | 1 | | | | | | | | | | | 13 | | 128 | 2 | 4 | 1 | | 1,484 |
| Fayette | 356 | | | | | | | 1 | | | 1 | | | | 17 | | 2 | 1 | | | | 713 |
| Floyd | 835 | | 1 | 1 | | 1 | | | | | 2 | 1 | | | 49 | 1 | 132 | 1 | 21 | 5 | | 4,014 |
| Fountain | 223 | | | | | | | 1 | | | | | | | 24 | | 41 | 138 | 5 | 3 | | 819 |
| Franklin | 281 | | 4 | 7 | | | | | | | | | | | 20 | | 22 | 3 | 24 | 2 | 1 | 3,161 |
| Fulton | 87 | 2 | | | | | | | | | | | | | 22 | | 36 | 1 | 1 | | | 580 |
| Gibson | 267 | | | | | | 1 | 2 | | | | | | | 41 | | 3 | 2 | 5 | 6 | 1 | 1,138 |
| Grant | 113 | | | | | | | | | | | | | | 3 | | 2 | | 3 | 2 | 1 | 231 |
| Greene | 56 | | | 1 | | | | | | | | | | | 11 | | 58 | | 3 | 3 | | 366 |
| Hamilton | 78 | | | | | | | | | | | | | | 4 | | 15 | 12 | 2 | | | 424 |
| Hancock | 130 | | | | | | | | | | | | | | 14 | | 10 | | | | | 492 |
| Harrison | 57 | | | | | 1 | | 1 | | | | | 3 | | 3 | | 28 | | 6 | | 1 | 1,762 |
| Hendricks | 206 | | | | | | | | | | | | | | 7 | | 5 | | 6 | 2 | 1 | 316 |
| Henry | 211 | | | | | | | | | | | | | | 11 | | 6 | | 2 | 1 | | 400 |
| Howard | 77 | | | | | | | | | | | | | | 5 | | 9 | 2 | 13 | | 1 | 205 |
| Huntington | 146 | 1 | | | | | | 1 | | | 1 | | | | 29 | 2 | 187 | | 6 | | | 1,226 |
| Jackson | 155 | | 1 | | | | 2 | | | | 1 | | 1 | | 4 | | 45 | | 19 | 3 | | 1,533 |
| Jasper | 62 | | | | | | | | | | | | | | 2 | | | | | 2 | | 172 |
| Jay | 48 | | | | | | | | | | | | | | 1 | | 24 | | 1 | | | 409 |
| Jefferson | 970 | | 1 | 1 | | 4 | 4 | 4 | | | | | 2 | | 312 | | 71 | 11 | 6 | 12 | 1 | 3,625 |
| Jennings | 557 | | 3 | | | | | | | | 1 | | | | 24 | | 14 | 3 | | 26 | | 1,630 |
| Johnson | 149 | | | 1 | | | 1 | | | | 2 | | 1 | | 23 | | 3 | | 2 | | | 414 |
| Knox | 339 | | 1 | | | | | | | | 3 | | | | 28 | | 12 | | 4 | 8 | | 2,054 |
| Kosciusko | 114 | 1 | | | | | | | | | | | | | 19 | | 24 | 1 | 35 | 1 | | 626 |
| Lagrange | 64 | | | | | | | | | | | | | | 24 | | 21 | | 15 | 4 | | 554 |
| Lake | 219 | | | | | 1 | | 2 | | | | | 1 | | 13 | | 20 | 30 | 1 | | | 2,636 |
| La Porte | 877 | 3 | 4 | 6 | | | 4 | 11 | | | 11 | | 5 | | 88 | 1 | 100 | 69 | 3 | 7 | 1 | 5,101 |
| Lawrence | 164 | | | | | | | 1 | | | | | | | 1 | 1 | 19 | | 1 | | | 411 |
| Madison | 222 | | | | | | | | | | | | | | 8 | | 5 | | 14 | 3 | | 392 |
| Marion | 1,748 | 2 | 19 | 8 | | 3 | 1 | | | | 1 | | | 1 | 185 | 1 | 88 | 7 | 30 | 18 | 1 | 6,713 |
| Marshall | 186 | | | | | | 3 | | | | 3 | | 1 | | 4 | | 95 | 6 | 50 | 1 | | 1,043 |
| Martin | 164 | | | | | | | 1 | | | | | | | 5 | | 4 | 1 | 10 | | | 290 |
| Miami | 197 | | | | | | | | | | | | | | 9 | | 63 | | 47 | | | 1,036 |
| Monroe | 237 | | | | | | | | | | | | | | 12 | | 1 | | 18 | | | 411 |
| Montgomery | 406 | | | | | | | | | | | | | | 20 | | 3 | 2 | | 2 | | 634 |
| Morgan | 131 | | | | | | | 1 | | | | | | | 17 | | 4 | | 4 | 2 | | 354 |
| Newton | 12 | | | | | | | | | | | | | | 2 | | 1 | 3 | 3 | 1 | | 101 |
| Noble | 116 | 9 | | | | | 2 | | 1 | | 1 | | | | 17 | | 25 | | 2 | 1 | | 928 |
| Ohio | 74 | | | | | | | | | | | | | | 9 | | 3 | | 2 | 1 | | 430 |
| Orange | 42 | | | | | | | | | | | | | | 3 | | 3 | 1 | 12 | 1 | | 132 |
| Owen | 43 | | | | | | | | | | | | | | 14 | | 20 | | | 1 | | 322 |
| Parke | 122 | | | 1 | | | | | | | | | | 1 | 17 | | 9 | 2 | 21 | 2 | | 334 |
| Perry | 261 | | 13 | | | | 1 | 1 | | | 3 | | | | 20 | | 331 | 2 | 5 | 1 | | 2,868 |
| Pike | 35 | | | | | | | | | | | | | | 4 | | 1 | | 1 | | | 278 |
| Porter | 586 | 3 | 3 | | | | 6 | | | | 2 | | | | 15 | | 4 | 100 | 30 | 8 | | 1,825 |
| Posey | 106 | | 1 | | | 1 | | | | | 2 | | | | 15 | | 5 | | 3 | | | 2,322 |
| Pulaski | 131 | | 1 | | | | | | | | | | | | 8 | | | | 20 | | | 605 |
| Putnam | 348 | | | | | | | | | | | | | | 6 | | 2 | | 4 | 1 | | 547 |
| Randolph | 161 | | | | | | | | | | | | | | 4 | | 7 | | 7 | 2 | | 457 |
| Ripley | 240 | | 11 | 2 | 1 | | | | | | 3 | | | | 19 | | 102 | 4 | 9 | 2 | 2 | 3,426 |
| Rush | 267 | | 1 | 1 | | | | | | | | | | | 7 | | | | | | | 437 |
| St. Joseph | 395 | | 2 | 1 | | 1 | | | | | 1 | | | | 30 | 1 | 57 | | | 2 | | 2,389 |
| Scott | 106 | 1 | | | | | | | | | | | | | 10 | | 5 | | | 5 | | 184 |
| Shelby | 221 | | | | | | | | | | | | | | 19 | | 7 | | 26 | 4 | | 800 |
| Spencer | 50 | | 5 | | | 1 | | | | | | | | | 13 | | 10 | 1 | 5 | 5 | | 1,935 |
| Starke | 65 | | | | | | | | | | | | | | | | | | | | | 221 |
| Steuben | 37 | | | | | | | | | | | | 1 | | 12 | | 18 | 6 | 9 | | | 391 |
| Sullivan | 62 | | | | | | | 1 | | | | | | | 8 | | 2 | | | 1 | 1 | 224 |
| Switzerland | 137 | | 1 | | | | | | | | 1 | | | | 92 | 1 | | 79 | 15 | | | 669 |
| Tippecanoe | 1,645 | | 10 | | | | | 9 | | | | | 9 | | 66 | 1 | 63 | 117 | 55 | 2 | 2 | 4,362 |
| Tipton | 30 | | | | | | | | | | | | | | 6 | | 4 | 14 | | | | 176 |
| Union | 344 | | | | | | | | | | | | | | 10 | | 3 | 1 | | 1 | | 467 |
| Vanderburgh | 730 | | 19 | | | 7 | | 1 | | | 4 | 2 | 4 | 1 | 75 | 1 | 114 | 2 | 2 | 1 | 1 | 8,377 |
| Vermillion | 79 | | | | | | | 1 | | | | | 1 | | 4 | | 3 | | 14 | 6 | | 236 |
| Vigo | 949 | | 3 | 3 | | | 1 | | | | | | | 1 | 39 | | 18 | 2 | 7 | 4 | | 2,431 |
| Wabash | 341 | | | | | | | | | | | | 4 | | 7 | | 51 | | 8 | 5 | | 968 |
| Warren | 274 | 2 | | | | | 1 | | | | 1 | | | | 5 | | 1 | 53 | 11 | 1 | | 581 |
| Warrick | 91 | | 1 | 1 | | | | | | | | | | | 21 | | 8 | 1 | 40 | 2 | | 1,265 |
| Washington | 114 | | 2 | | | | | | | | 1 | | | | 16 | | 3 | | 1 | 2 | | 421 |
| Wayne | 884 | | 1 | 2 | | 1 | | | 1 | | | | | | 41 | | 15 | | 31 | 3 | | 2,565 |
| Wells | 77 | | | | | | | | | | 1 | | | | 32 | | 132 | | 1 | | | 488 |
| White | 155 | | | | | | 1 | | | | | | | | 31 | | 8 | 9 | | | 1 | 476 |
| Whitley | 146 | | | | | | | | | | | | | | 2 | | 88 | | | 2 | | 705 |

## TABLE 7.  FOREIGN BORN IN INDIANA BY COUNTY, 1910

| | Austria | Belgium | Canada-French | Canada | Denmark | England | France | Germany | Greece | Holland | Hungary | Ireland | Italy | Romania | Russia | Scotland | Sweden | Switz | Turkey-Asia | Turkey-Europe | Wales | Other | Total |
|---|---|---|---|---|---|---|---|---|---|---|---|---|---|---|---|---|---|---|---|---|---|---|---|
| Indiana | 11,830 | 2,298 | 789 | 4,995 | 900 | 9,780 | 2,388 | 62,177 | 1,370 | 2,131 | 14,370 | 11,266 | 6,911 | 709 | 9,599 | 3,419 | 5,081 | 2,765 | 808 | 2,274 | 1,498 | 1,969 | 156,451 |
| Adams | | | | 17 | | 9 | 17 | 455 | 1 | 2 | | 38 | 4 | | 3 | 1 | 2 | 404 | | | 1 | 4 | 958 |
| Allen | 99 | 12 | 40 | 292 | 11 | 415 | 321 | 5,599 | 24 | 40 | 359 | 449 | 109 | 14 | 398 | 99 | 66 | 326 | 62 | 402 | 24 | 90 | 9,161 |
| Bartholomew | 1 | 3 | 1 | 15 | 3 | 29 | 6 | 404 | 14 | 3 | | 58 | 3 | | 8 | 5 | | 6 | | | | 2 | 559 |
| Benton | | 2 | 76 | 25 | 32 | 58 | 9 | 211 | | 9 | 1 | 99 | 14 | | 8 | 29 | 105 | 11 | | | 1 | 5 | 690 |
| Blackford | 5 | 146 | 2 | 37 | 1 | 30 | 19 | 83 | 1 | | | 54 | 146 | 1 | 18 | 10 | 9 | 12 | 1 | 38 | 2 | 14 | 615 |
| Boone | | | 1 | 12 | | 14 | 2 | 51 | | | | 41 | 1 | | | 5 | | 1 | | | | 3 | 128 |
| Brown | | | | 1 | 3 | 10 | | 19 | | 1 | | 3 | | | | 7 | | | | | 1 | | 45 |
| Carroll | | | 4 | 20 | 1 | 29 | | 104 | | 5 | 3 | 63 | 10 | | 3 | 2 | 9 | 3 | | | 5 | 2 | 261 |
| Cass | 16 | 4 | 22 | 59 | 25 | 136 | 27 | 793 | 11 | 2 | 5 | 298 | 479 | | 12 | 8 | 33 | 10 | 7 | 68 | 6 | 10 | 2,021 |
| Clark | 7 | 2 | 5 | 23 | 4 | 60 | 17 | 506 | 1 | | 2 | 168 | 9 | 1 | 19 | 11 | 2 | 36 | | | 2 | 8 | 875 |
| Clay | 80 | 55 | 4 | 37 | 2 | 452 | 90 | 348 | | 2 | 29 | 106 | 75 | | 22 | 334 | 10 | 16 | 5 | | 193 | 9 | 1,860 |
| Clinton | 1 | | | 19 | | 35 | 2 | 69 | | 2 | 1 | 35 | 1 | | 6 | 11 | | | | | 1 | 3 | 183 |
| Crawford | 1 | 1 | | 3 | | 9 | 6 | 28 | | | | 10 | | | | 2 | 1 | 8 | | | | | 69 |
| Daviess | 1 | | 8 | 10 | 1 | 48 | 45 | 154 | | 3 | | 90 | 7 | | 5 | 2 | 6 | | | | 5 | 4 | 385 |
| Dearborn | 6 | | 1 | 17 | 3 | 41 | 24 | 902 | | 2 | 1 | 95 | 9 | 1 | 7 | 5 | 1 | 13 | 1 | 32 | | 2 | 1,161 |
| Decatur | | | | 8 | | 20 | 6 | 265 | 4 | 2 | | 43 | | | 4 | 4 | 1 | 9 | | | 1 | 3 | 367 |
| De Kalb | 17 | 3 | 9 | 51 | 1 | 71 | 13 | 642 | | 3 | 104 | 27 | 5 | 2 | 43 | 16 | 8 | 29 | | | | 16 | 1,044 |
| Delaware | 29 | 25 | 15 | 74 | 5 | 195 | 35 | 267 | 12 | 35 | 34 | 183 | 22 | 75 | 57 | 37 | 9 | 16 | 9 | 6 | 33 | 26 | 1,173 |
| Dubois | 7 | | | 1 | | 4 | 11 | 629 | | 4 | | 6 | 1 | 1 | | 1 | 2 | 25 | | | | 7 | 692 |
| Elkhart | 48 | 3 | 24 | 250 | 9 | 186 | 15 | 881 | 13 | 104 | 97 | 86 | 316 | | 68 | 34 | 241 | 101 | | | 5 | 40 | 2,481 |
| Fayette | 5 | | 1 | 8 | | 36 | 4 | 164 | 4 | 6 | | 74 | 31 | | 8 | 2 | 8 | 9 | | | 1 | 2 | 361 |
| Floyd | 6 | 3 | 3 | 10 | 9 | 149 | 79 | 734 | | 3 | | 114 | 9 | | 27 | 4 | 2 | 60 | | | 12 | 9 | 1,224 |
| Fountain | 1 | 5 | 4 | 14 | 1 | 41 | 2 | 101 | | 74 | 1 | 41 | 8 | | 10 | 5 | 85 | 12 | | | 5 | 2 | 410 |
| Franklin | 7 | | | 8 | | 30 | 7 | 592 | | | 1 | 18 | | | 2 | | 11 | | | 2 | | 3 | 678 |
| Fulton | 2 | | | 12 | | 41 | 8 | 125 | 7 | | | 24 | | | 1 | 19 | 10 | | | | | 2 | 249 |
| Gibson | 1 | | | 14 | | 67 | 7 | 285 | | 5 | | 92 | 4 | | 6 | 21 | 2 | 3 | | | 5 | 6 | 512 |
| Grant | 61 | 34 | 9 | 96 | 10 | 253 | 48 | 345 | 60 | 6 | 3 | 200 | 115 | 1 | 118 | 35 | 22 | 15 | 37 | 5 | 120 | 129 | 1,593 |
| Greene | 83 | 41 | 1 | 6 | | 251 | 397 | 241 | 2 | | 27 | 54 | 28 | | 47 | 361 | 3 | 13 | 6 | 1 | 58 | 27 | 1,620 |
| Hamilton | 1 | 3 | 1 | 16 | 6 | 28 | 3 | 110 | | | | 23 | 3 | | 12 | 4 | 10 | 7 | | | 5 | 3 | 232 |
| Hancock | 20 | 12 | | 12 | | 9 | 2 | 134 | 49 | | 1 | 60 | 80 | | 14 | 3 | 1 | 1 | | | 2 | 2 | 400 |
| Harrison | 1 | 4 | | 4 | | 26 | 26 | 230 | | 1 | | 7 | | | 6 | | 2 | 3 | | | | 2 | 310 |
| Hendricks | 4 | | | 3 | 2 | 36 | | 33 | | 4 | | 70 | 4 | 4 | 1 | 2 | 4 | 1 | | | | 3 | 169 |
| Henry | 1 | 3 | 4 | 57 | 1 | 74 | 3 | 89 | 1 | 14 | 1 | 64 | 47 | 27 | 26 | 15 | 20 | 4 | | | 2 | 12 | 453 |
| Howard | 36 | 12 | 3 | 45 | 6 | 292 | 33 | 210 | 9 | 3 | 85 | 105 | 32 | 16 | 22 | 23 | 29 | 10 | | 4 | 7 | 11 | 982 |
| Huntington | 4 | 6 | 6 | 63 | 1 | 45 | 11 | 469 | 3 | 5 | | 48 | 2 | 2 | 15 | 12 | 6 | 27 | 1 | | | 9 | 726 |
| Jackson | 1 | | 2 | 11 | 1 | 10 | 10 | 462 | 1 | 6 | | 37 | 11 | | 7 | 3 | 1 | 6 | | | | 1 | 569 |
| Jasper | 14 | 3 | 11 | 23 | 13 | 46 | 22 | 415 | | 156 | 8 | 48 | | | 18 | 14 | 19 | 17 | | | 1 | 15 | 828 |
| Jay | 9 | 9 | 1 | 22 | | 34 | 11 | 199 | | 2 | | 33 | 26 | | 15 | 12 | | 20 | | 8 | 3 | 3 | 404 |
| Jefferson | | | 1 | 12 | 1 | 30 | 10 | 310 | | 5 | | 67 | 2 | | | 24 | | 7 | | | 1 | 1 | 470 |
| Jennings | | 1 | | 11 | 1 | 23 | 8 | 237 | | | 1 | 47 | | | 7 | 4 | 1 | 9 | | | 4 | 4 | 354 |
| Johnson | | | | 11 | 1 | 24 | 1 | 51 | 3 | 8 | | 25 | 2 | | 5 | 5 | 1 | | | | | 3 | 137 |
| Knox | 19 | 166 | 1 | 22 | | 66 | 54 | 801 | 7 | 2 | 14 | 80 | 26 | 6 | 8 | 63 | 7 | 10 | | | 35 | 11 | 1,387 |
| Kosciusko | 1 | 2 | 8 | 38 | 4 | 50 | 4 | 189 | | 22 | 3 | 36 | 9 | 28 | 6 | 1 | 11 | 40 | | 86 | | 17 | 538 |
| Lagrange | | | 6 | 29 | | 63 | 4 | 119 | | | | 11 | 34 | | 1 | 21 | 34 | | 1 | | 4 | 4 | 332 |
| Lake | 7,193 | 35 | 70 | 615 | 103 | 686 | 46 | 4,982 | 338 | 477 | 7,479 | 729 | 1,279 | 231 | 3,610 | 278 | 1,185 | 112 | 43 | 304 | 186 | 453 | 29,981 |
| La Porte | 459 | 4 | 26 | 199 | 35 | 202 | 18 | 5,250 | 212 | 17 | 46 | 174 | 471 | | 580 | 43 | 629 | 51 | 343 | 15 | 1 | 68 | 8,779 |
| Lawrence | 45 | | 6 | 13 | | 62 | 9 | 182 | | 1 | 80 | 43 | 242 | | 7 | 57 | 13 | 4 | 2 | 12 | 6 | 29 | 784 |
| Madison | 87 | 38 | 9 | 147 | 9 | 522 | 75 | 606 | 21 | 12 | 77 | 259 | 50 | 43 | 225 | 48 | 39 | 32 | 16 | 3 | 360 | 26 | 2,678 |
| Marion | 1,254 | 25 | 84 | 802 | 280 | 1,291 | 232 | 8,304 | 290 | 220 | 861 | 3,383 | 663 | 132 | 1,260 | 429 | 166 | 300 | 88 | 908 | 51 | 187 | 21,023 |
| Marshall | 46 | 2 | 3 | 52 | 5 | 31 | 15 | 364 | | 7 | 15 | 21 | 4 | | 27 | 3 | 149 | 44 | 18 | 14 | | 8 | 820 |
| Martin | | 1 | | 2 | | 17 | | 34 | 9 | | | 20 | | | | 3 | 3 | 3 | | 12 | 1 | | 105 |
| Miami | 13 | 1 | | 67 | 3 | 55 | 20 | 572 | 47 | 3 | 1 | 113 | 183 | 1 | 19 | 9 | 16 | 13 | | 99 | 2 | 8 | 1,237 |
| Monroe | 2 | 2 | | 14 | 1 | 43 | 2 | 61 | 5 | 4 | 6 | 48 | 40 | | 8 | 25 | 5 | | | | | 7 | 266 |
| Montgomery | 2 | | 2 | 42 | 1 | 47 | 1 | 61 | | 2 | | 133 | 4 | | 10 | 12 | 8 | 1 | | | 2 | 4 | 329 |
| Morgan | | | 1 | 10 | 1 | 11 | 3 | 76 | | | | 20 | 9 | | 11 | 5 | 2 | 2 | | 24 | 1 | 2 | 176 |
| Newton | 11 | 4 | 32 | 36 | 38 | 88 | 11 | 131 | 2 | 94 | 1 | 55 | 9 | | 8 | 28 | 40 | 6 | | | 1 | | 595 |
| Noble | 14 | 1 | 11 | 44 | 2 | 47 | 11 | 574 | | 6 | | 38 | 88 | 2 | 21 | 8 | 26 | 37 | 2 | 3 | 3 | 4 | 938 |
| Ohio | | | | 1 | | 2 | | 113 | | | | 3 | | | | | | | | | | | 119 |
| Orange | | | | 2 | 1 | 11 | 1 | 25 | | | | 7 | | | 5 | 4 | 9 | 1 | 1 | | | 3 | 67 |
| Owen | 1 | | | 4 | | 10 | | 50 | | | | 5 | 12 | | 12 | 3 | 1 | | | 35 | | 3 | 133 |
| Parke | 176 | 8 | 3 | 10 | 2 | 149 | 21 | 32 | | 1 | 46 | 35 | 163 | | 32 | 103 | 8 | 5 | 1 | 16 | 28 | 17 | 839 |
| Perry | 4 | 97 | | 3 | | 25 | 29 | 435 | | 4 | | 49 | | | 4 | 1 | 1 | 99 | | | 1 | 1 | 751 |
| Pike | | | | 6 | | 24 | 3 | 113 | | | | 8 | | | 1 | 4 | 3 | | | | 1 | 1 | 163 |
| Porter | 54 | 2 | 45 | 159 | 35 | 95 | 8 | 1,236 | 1 | 14 | 30 | 113 | 194 | 7 | 168 | 24 | 636 | 11 | 1 | 3 | 9 | 94 | 2,845 |
| Posey | 84 | 21 | | 3 | | 40 | 7 | 516 | | 3 | 6 | 14 | | | 1 | 2 | 2 | 8 | 1 | | | 12 | 708 |
| Pulaski | 50 | | 5 | 12 | 3 | 31 | 6 | 578 | | | 27 | 45 | | | 8 | 3 | 27 | 17 | | | 1 | 12 | 813 |
| Putnam | 1 | 1 | | 8 | 1 | 29 | 8 | 51 | 2 | | | 35 | 18 | 8 | 4 | 8 | | 3 | | 13 | 6 | 5 | 196 |
| Randolph | 2 | 12 | 3 | 25 | 2 | 29 | 1 | 146 | 1 | | | 58 | 133 | | 3 | 15 | 1 | | | 73 | 1 | 49 | 506 |
| Ripley | 3 | | 1 | 4 | 1 | 27 | 9 | 887 | | 2 | | 28 | 6 | | 16 | 2 | | 29 | | | 1 | 8 | 1,016 |
| Rush | | | | 13 | 1 | 19 | 3 | 66 | 3 | 3 | | 95 | | | 6 | 4 | | 1 | | | | | 214 |
| St. Joseph | 591 | 1,386 | 138 | 574 | 104 | 337 | 76 | 6,573 | 44 | 112 | 4,046 | 466 | 176 | 36 | 1,201 | 101 | 618 | 109 | 41 | 4 | 1 | 132 | 16,734 |
| Scott | | 4 | | 3 | 4 | 5 | | 16 | | | | 12 | | | 7 | | | | | | 1 | | 52 |
| Shelby | 3 | | 1 | 15 | 3 | 28 | 6 | 214 | 2 | 1 | | 50 | 27 | 1 | 24 | 9 | | 13 | | | 1 | 3 | 398 |
| Spencer | 7 | 1 | | 2 | 1 | 13 | 9 | 443 | | | 2 | 8 | 3 | | 4 | 5 | | 24 | | | 2 | 1 | 526 |
| Starke | 296 | 1 | 9 | 25 | 16 | 40 | 5 | 649 | | 24 | 20 | 34 | 26 | 3 | 84 | 8 | 197 | 6 | | 4 | 4 | 33 | 1,451 |
| Steuben | | | 6 | 19 | 3 | 46 | 3 | 59 | | | | 11 | 4 | | | 8 | 2 | 8 | 19 | | | 7 | 188 |
| Sullivan | 45 | 55 | 4 | 11 | | 524 | 93 | 112 | | 1 | 118 | 44 | 4 | | 109 | 290 | 17 | 5 | 1 | | 40 | 1 | 1,473 |
| Switzerland | | | | 2 | | 1 | 3 | 101 | | 1 | | 6 | | | | 6 | | 3 | | | | | 123 |
| Tippecanoe | 6 | 6 | 10 | 102 | 4 | 119 | 35 | 1,418 | 52 | 437 | 13 | 395 | 12 | 1 | 149 | 51 | 235 | 47 | 5 | | 4 | 10 | 3,101 |
| Tipton | 1 | | 2 | 9 | 1 | 20 | 3 | 97 | | | | 47 | 2 | | 1 | 2 | 11 | | | 4 | | 5 | 201 |
| Union | | | 1 | | | 7 | | 24 | | | 2 | 57 | 5 | | 3 | 2 | 2 | | | | | 2 | 103 |
| Vanderburgh | 76 | 2 | | 69 | 10 | 327 | 74 | 3,738 | 32 | 19 | 6 | 165 | 44 | 3 | 150 | 62 | 16 | 105 | | 8 | 4 | 32 | 4,912 |
| Vermillion | 342 | 5 | 1 | 10 | 36 | 90 | 2 | 178 | | 2 | 230 | 22 | 811 | 27 | 210 | 179 | 16 | 1 | 1 | 16 | 61 | 94 | 2,240 |
| Vigo | 208 | 9 | 18 | 193 | 6 | 717 | 56 | 1,714 | 38 | 57 | 452 | 624 | 164 | 16 | 503 | 258 | 128 | 63 | 90 | 39 | 156 | 65 | 5,509 |
| Wabash | 32 | 7 | 3 | 36 | 3 | 47 | 12 | 335 | 5 | 4 | 3 | 54 | | | 8 | 15 | 7 | 4 | 44 | | 2 | 8 | 621 |
| Warren | | 5 | 2 | 16 | 5 | 13 | 2 | 56 | 10 | 20 | | 27 | | | 3 | 43 | | | | 2 | 2 | 4 | 206 |
| Warrick | 19 | | | 2 | | 52 | 3 | 394 | | 1 | | 16 | | | 1 | 17 | | 1 | | | | 2 | 506 |
| Washington | | 1 | | | | 17 | 2 | 21 | | | | 8 | | | 2 | 1 | 1 | | | | | | 55 |
| Wayne | 103 | 1 | 1 | 44 | 6 | 119 | 23 | 969 | 19 | 1 | 15 | 247 | 375 | 6 | 11 | 14 | 13 | 23 | 3 | 10 | 4 | 37 | 2,007 |
| Wells | 2 | | 4 | 7 | | 33 | 2 | 120 | 9 | | | 32 | | | 19 | 12 | 1 | 88 | | | | 1 | 329 |
| White | 2 | | 10 | 31 | 16 | 39 | 7 | 304 | | 40 | | 56 | 5 | | 5 | 13 | 26 | 21 | | | 10 | 3 | 586 |
| Whitley | 1 | 1 | 2 | 14 | | 18 | 14 | 142 | 1 | 1 | 3 | 24 | 1 | | 15 | 2 | 8 | 46 | | | 1 | 4 | 294 |

## TABLE 8. FOREIGN BORN IN INDIANA BY COUNTY, 1940

| County | Australia | Austria | Azores | Belgium | Bulgaria | Canada-French | Canada | Central & S. America | Cuba/ W. Indies | Czecho-slovakia | Denmark | England | Finland | France | Germany | Greece | Hungary | Irish Free State | Italy | Latvia | Lithuania | Luxembourg |
|---|---|---|---|---|---|---|---|---|---|---|---|---|---|---|---|---|---|---|---|---|---|---|
| Indiana | 104 | 4,405 | 4 | 2,619 | 393 | 563 | 5,025 | 171 | 97 | 5,782 | 768 | 5,562 | 195 | 1,459 | 18,784 | 3,747 | 7,733 | 2,657 | 6,309 | 98 | 2,078 | 60 |
| Adams | | 2 | | 8 | | 2 | 14 | | | 1 | 1 | 7 | | 1 | 103 | | | | | | | 1 |
| Allen | 4 | 86 | | 56 | 24 | 29 | 312 | 7 | 8 | 15 | 32 | 309 | 5 | 93 | 2,311 | 273 | 54 | 97 | 284 | 4 | 23 | 1 |
| Bartholomew | 1 | 4 | | 3 | 2 | | 12 | | 2 | | 2 | 8 | | 1 | 70 | 5 | 1 | 2 | 2 | 1 | 1 | |
| Benton | | 1 | | | | 9 | 5 | | | | 10 | 5 | | 6 | 46 | 2 | | 14 | 4 | | | |
| Blackford | | 1 | | 49 | 1 | | 7 | 1 | | | | 7 | 7 | | 16 | | 1 | 1 | 7 | | 1 | |
| Boone | | 1 | | 1 | | 1 | 11 | | | | | 11 | | | 20 | 1 | 1 | 5 | 4 | | | |
| Brown | | 5 | | 2 | | | 1 | 1 | | | | 4 | 1 | 4 | 11 | 1 | | 1 | 3 | | | |
| Carroll | | | | | | 1 | 18 | | | 2 | | 3 | | | 16 | 2 | | 4 | | | | |
| Cass | | 65 | | 8 | 1 | 2 | 42 | | | 29 | 11 | 42 | 1 | 16 | 226 | 19 | 62 | 44 | 217 | | 6 | |
| Clark | | 2 | | | | 1 | 6 | | | 2 | | 11 | | 3 | 65 | 1 | 3 | 13 | 4 | | | |
| Clay | 1 | 13 | | 16 | | | 9 | | | 3 | 1 | 84 | | 13 | 59 | | 10 | 1 | 17 | | 2 | |
| Clinton | | 1 | | 1 | | | 6 | | 1 | 2 | | 13 | | 4 | 16 | 5 | | 5 | 3 | | | |
| Crawford | | | | | | | | | | | | 1 | | 2 | 3 | | | 2 | | | | |
| Daviess | 1 | 1 | | 1 | | | 3 | | | 2 | | 12 | 1 | 13 | 22 | 3 | | 4 | 1 | | | |
| Dearborn | | 5 | | 1 | | | 16 | 3 | 2 | | | 8 | | 10 | 92 | 3 | 3 | 10 | 5 | | 2 | |
| Decatur | | 1 | | | | 1 | 4 | | | 2 | | 3 | | 3 | 55 | 1 | | 6 | 4 | | | |
| De Kalb | | 2 | | 3 | 8 | | 33 | 1 | | 1 | 1 | 12 | | 11 | 153 | 3 | 10 | 4 | 24 | | | |
| Delaware | | 5 | | 18 | 2 | 13 | 60 | 2 | 1 | 1 | 9 | 88 | 9 | 16 | 98 | 31 | 5 | 26 | 15 | | 7 | |
| Dubois | 1 | 2 | | | | 1 | 5 | | | 1 | | 2 | | 1 | 79 | 1 | | 1 | 2 | | | |
| Elkhart | | 67 | | 17 | 5 | 12 | 217 | 4 | 3 | 26 | 19 | 103 | | 26 | 379 | 46 | 71 | 13 | 323 | 1 | 12 | 1 |
| Fayette | | 4 | | 3 | | 2 | 11 | 1 | | | | 3 | | 3 | 37 | 8 | 3 | 3 | 6 | | | |
| Floyd | | 7 | | 2 | | 1 | 9 | 1 | 1 | 2 | 9 | 27 | 1 | 15 | 119 | 2 | 1 | 5 | 16 | | 2 | |
| Fountain | | 3 | | | 1 | 2 | | | | 3 | 2 | 9 | | 8 | 22 | 5 | 1 | 3 | 1 | | | |
| Franklin | | 2 | | | | 1 | 4 | | | | | 2 | | 3 | 59 | | | 2 | | | | |
| Fulton | | 2 | | 1 | | | 10 | | | 9 | 1 | 15 | | 1 | 39 | 6 | | 4 | 9 | | 7 | |
| Gibson | | 2 | | 4 | | 1 | 8 | | | 2 | 2 | 16 | | 12 | 31 | 14 | 2 | 9 | 1 | | | |
| Grant | 1 | 12 | | 28 | 1 | 6 | 76 | 1 | | 5 | 3 | 82 | 1 | 9 | 99 | 28 | 4 | 12 | 47 | | 30 | |
| Greene | | 20 | | 18 | | | 6 | | | 6 | 3 | 102 | | 120 | 81 | 3 | 3 | 1 | 9 | | 3 | |
| Hamilton | 5 | 2 | | 3 | | | 11 | 1 | | 1 | 3 | 10 | | 2 | 23 | 2 | 2 | 1 | 2 | | | |
| Hancock | | 1 | | 1 | | 2 | 4 | | 1 | | 1 | 8 | | | 30 | 1 | | | 2 | 2 | | |
| Harrison | | 1 | | | | 1 | 3 | | | | 2 | 5 | | 1 | 15 | 1 | | 1 | | | | |
| Hendricks | 2 | 4 | | 2 | | 2 | 12 | | | 1 | 2 | 22 | | 3 | 22 | | 7 | 7 | 5 | | | |
| Henry | | 3 | | 3 | | 3 | 29 | | | 3 | 7 | 40 | 1 | 1 | 28 | 3 | 2 | 5 | | | 6 | |
| Howard | 1 | 15 | | 11 | 5 | 3 | 47 | 2 | 3 | 13 | 3 | 194 | 4 | 20 | 96 | 24 | 5 | 24 | 81 | 4 | 4 | 1 |
| Huntington | | 17 | 1 | 7 | | 4 | 32 | | | 2 | 1 | 19 | | 5 | 99 | 12 | 4 | 11 | 20 | | 1 | |
| Jackson | | 6 | | | | | 9 | | | 2 | 1 | 2 | | | 65 | 4 | | 11 | 9 | | 2 | |
| Jasper | 1 | 14 | | | | 2 | 11 | | | 21 | 5 | 20 | | 11 | 135 | 5 | 24 | 7 | 8 | | 17 | 2 |
| Jay | | 4 | | 3 | | | 5 | | | 2 | | 10 | | 7 | 19 | 4 | 1 | 7 | 2 | | | |
| Jefferson | 1 | 3 | | 1 | | 1 | 8 | 1 | | | 2 | 12 | | 5 | 38 | 3 | 4 | 5 | 5 | | | |
| Jennings | | | | 1 | | | 2 | | | 2 | | 8 | | | 27 | | 3 | 4 | 4 | | 1 | |
| Johnson | | | | | | 2 | 11 | 1 | | 2 | 4 | 11 | | 2 | 15 | 2 | | 4 | | | | |
| Knox | 2 | 9 | | 86 | 3 | | 17 | 1 | | 2 | 2 | 89 | | 153 | 151 | 13 | 26 | 10 | 31 | | 15 | |
| Kosciusko | | 3 | | 1 | 2 | 4 | 32 | | 1 | 2 | 2 | 16 | 1 | 6 | 63 | 20 | 4 | 7 | 3 | 1 | | |
| Lagrange | | | | 2 | | 2 | 16 | | | | | 2 | | | 24 | | | 2 | | | | 5 |
| Lake | 41 | 2,098 | | 39 | 183 | 201 | 1,458 | 36 | 15 | 4,743 | 149 | 1,155 | 113 | 138 | 2,829 | 2,117 | 3,625 | 474 | 2,094 | 26 | 1,217 | 15 |
| La Porte | 3 | 115 | | 33 | 4 | 13 | 202 | 3 | 1 | 104 | 30 | 152 | 2 | 16 | 1,646 | 56 | 85 | 49 | 130 | 5 | 108 | 4 |
| Lawrence | | 1 | | 5 | | 1 | 20 | | | | 5 | 21 | | 2 | 49 | 11 | 9 | 7 | 57 | 1 | | |
| Madison | 1 | 17 | | 24 | 8 | 5 | 113 | 4 | 3 | 20 | 12 | 176 | | 22 | 220 | 86 | 7 | 55 | 37 | | 7 | 1 |
| Marion | 18 | 506 | | 19 | 79 | 58 | 634 | 24 | 26 | 75 | 158 | 867 | 22 | 184 | 3,117 | 461 | 250 | 1,086 | 658 | 10 | 129 | 4 |
| Marshall | | 12 | | 9 | | 3 | 21 | 5 | 4 | 6 | 6 | 24 | 1 | 6 | 156 | 5 | 23 | 11 | 10 | 3 | 8 | 2 |
| Martin | | 1 | | 1 | | | | | | 1 | | 3 | | 1 | 5 | | | 1 | | | | |
| Miami | | 10 | | 5 | | 3 | 25 | | | 1 | 2 | 20 | 1 | 13 | 159 | 9 | 4 | 13 | 33 | | 1 | |
| Monroe | 1 | 11 | | 1 | | | 24 | 2 | | 1 | 2 | 29 | 1 | 7 | 25 | 21 | 5 | 6 | 29 | | | |
| Montgomery | | | | | | 1 | 11 | 1 | | 1 | | 10 | | 2 | 12 | 9 | 2 | 13 | 2 | | 1 | |
| Morgan | 1 | 2 | | | | | 7 | | | | 3 | 3 | 1 | 2 | 15 | 1 | | 4 | 4 | | | |
| Newton | 1 | 9 | | 1 | | 3 | 16 | | 1 | 42 | 16 | 29 | | 2 | 44 | 9 | 6 | 6 | 5 | | 39 | 2 |
| Noble | | 7 | | 2 | 2 | 7 | 12 | 5 | 1 | 2 | 3 | 24 | | 3 | 159 | 7 | 8 | 7 | 3 | 2 | | |
| Ohio | | | | | | | | | | | | | | | 18 | | | | | | | |
| Orange | | 3 | | | | | 6 | | | | 1 | 5 | | 1 | 10 | | 1 | 1 | 1 | | | |
| Owen | | 3 | | 1 | | | 1 | | | 1 | 2 | 4 | | 2 | 5 | | 1 | 1 | 1 | | | |
| Parke | | 15 | | | | 1 | 4 | 3 | | 8 | | 33 | | 2 | 13 | 4 | 1 | 5 | 24 | | | 1 |
| Perry | | 1 | | 7 | | | 4 | | | | | | | 4 | 45 | | | 3 | 1 | | | |
| Pike | | | | | | | 5 | | | | | 9 | | 3 | 10 | 3 | | 1 | | 1 | 1 | |
| Porter | 2 | 75 | | 4 | 3 | 20 | 127 | 2 | | 55 | 49 | 77 | 1 | 5 | 421 | 30 | 57 | 20 | 30 | 1 | 45 | |
| Posey | | | | | | | 3 | | | | | | | 2 | 48 | 3 | | | 2 | | | |
| Pulaski | | 13 | | 1 | 4 | | 9 | | | 24 | 5 | 18 | | 7 | 115 | 1 | 18 | 9 | 5 | | 21 | |
| Putnam | | 7 | | 1 | | 1 | 13 | | 1 | 2 | 1 | 10 | | 1 | 20 | 1 | 1 | 3 | 12 | | | |
| Randolph | | 1 | | 1 | | | 28 | 2 | | 4 | 4 | 8 | | 1 | 39 | 2 | 2 | 5 | 1 | | | |
| Ripley | | 3 | | | | 1 | 6 | 1 | | 2 | | 4 | | 7 | 109 | 2 | | 6 | 1 | | | |
| Rush | | | | | | 1 | 8 | | | | | 3 | | | 11 | | | 3 | 16 | | | |
| St. Joseph | 5 | 772 | 3 | 2,000 | 36 | 72 | 600 | 11 | 6 | 133 | 93 | 346 | 11 | 105 | 1,547 | 207 | 2,957 | 198 | 728 | 7 | 115 | 10 |
| Scott | | | | | | 1 | 2 | | | | | 1 | | | 6 | | | | 1 | | | |
| Shelby | | 1 | | | | | 11 | | 1 | | 3 | 12 | 1 | 2 | 50 | | | 6 | 2 | | 3 | |
| Spencer | | 2 | | | | 1 | 3 | | | | 1 | | | | 67 | | 1 | | 1 | | | |
| Starke | 1 | 46 | | 3 | 1 | 3 | 29 | | 1 | 236 | 14 | 28 | 1 | 10 | 232 | 3 | 57 | 8 | 67 | | 39 | 6 |
| Steuben | | 1 | | 2 | | 3 | 56 | 14 | 1 | 8 | 5 | 12 | | 1 | 29 | 7 | 14 | 1 | | | 3 | |
| Sullivan | | 2 | | 10 | | | 10 | | | 3 | 1 | 147 | | 10 | 13 | 1 | 22 | 6 | 4 | | 3 | |
| Switzerland | | | | | | | 2 | | | | | | | | 9 | | | | | | | |
| Tippecanoe | 1 | 12 | | 7 | 1 | 14 | 96 | 7 | 2 | 7 | 8 | 64 | 1 | 24 | 424 | 22 | 7 | 44 | 14 | | 9 | |
| Tipton | | 1 | | 2 | | | 16 | 1 | | 3 | 1 | 6 | | 3 | 16 | 5 | | 18 | | | 1 | |
| Union | | | | | | | 3 | | | | | | | 2 | 9 | | | 3 | 1 | | 1 | |
| Vanderburgh | 1 | 29 | | 6 | | 6 | 78 | 6 | 1 | 7 | 7 | 98 | 2 | 38 | 800 | 14 | 15 | 29 | 39 | 19 | 11 | |
| Vermillion | 1 | 102 | | 16 | 4 | | 5 | 1 | | 52 | | 95 | 11 | 22 | 66 | 2 | 68 | 6 | 742 | | 72 | |
| Vigo | 3 | 91 | | 34 | 16 | 10 | 98 | 7 | 2 | 74 | 6 | 439 | | 169 | 461 | 39 | 124 | 95 | 170 | 4 | 90 | 4 |
| Wabash | | 7 | | 4 | | 2 | 22 | 2 | | 1 | 1 | 11 | | 2 | 87 | 4 | | 4 | 7 | 3 | | |
| Warren | | 1 | | 1 | | | 3 | 1 | | | | 10 | | | 14 | | | 1 | 1 | | 1 | |
| Warrick | | | | | | | 5 | | 1 | | 3 | 11 | | | 43 | 2 | | 1 | 1 | | | |
| Washington | | 1 | | 2 | | | 1 | | | 1 | | | | 2 | 10 | 4 | | | | | | |
| Wayne | 1 | 21 | | 21 | 5 | 4 | 34 | 3 | 3 | 2 | 4 | 61 | 1 | 13 | 273 | 37 | 35 | 28 | 207 | 2 | 5 | |
| Wells | | 2 | | 2 | | | 8 | | 1 | 1 | 3 | 18 | | 2 | 36 | 3 | | | 2 | | | |
| White | | | | 1 | | 2 | 14 | | 1 | 1 | | 5 | | 17 | 89 | | 2 | | 5 | | 3 | |
| Whitley | | 5 | | | | 1 | 16 | 1 | | | 5 | 11 | | 3 | 26 | | | 1 | 3 | | | |

TABLE 8.  FOREIGN BORN IN INDIANA BY COUNTY, 1940 (*continued*)

| County | Mexico | Netherlands | Newfoundland | N. Ireland | Norway | Other | Other Asia | Other Europe | Palestine/Syria | Poland | Portugal | Romania | Russia | Scotland | Spain | Sweden | Switzerland | Turkey/Asia | Turkey/Europe | Wales | Yugoslavia | Total |
|---|---|---|---|---|---|---|---|---|---|---|---|---|---|---|---|---|---|---|---|---|---|---|
| Indiana | 2,160 | 1,617 | 56 | 541 | 599 | 172 | 363 | 315 | 738 | 14,257 | 27 | 2,456 | 4,126 | 3,063 | 499 | 3,565 | 1,083 | 440 | 22 | 596 | 5,342 | 110,650 |
| Adams | 58 | | | | | | | | | 1 | 2 | | 4 | | | 1 | 136 | | | | 2 | 345 |
| Allen | 6 | 35 | 1 | 16 | 26 | 5 | 9 | 6 | 72 | 255 | 2 | 138 | 155 | 61 | 1 | 90 | 134 | 9 | | 23 | 37 | 5,108 |
| Bartholomew | 2 | | | 1 | 1 | | | | | 2 | | | 4 | 3 | | 3 | 1 | | | | 1 | 135 |
| Benton | | 4 | | 1 | 3 | | | | 1 | 2 | | | 2 | 4 | | 30 | 4 | | | | | 153 |
| Blackford | | | | | | | | | | 5 | | | 2 | 1 | | 4 | 3 | | | 1 | | 115 |
| Boone | 1 | 1 | | 1 | | | 1 | | | | | | | 6 | | 2 | 2 | | | | | 70 |
| Brown | | 1 | | | | 1 | | | | 6 | | 2 | 1 | | | | 1 | | | | 1 | 47 |
| Carroll | | 3 | | 1 | 1 | | | | | 4 | | | | | 1 | 3 | | | 1 | | | 65 |
| Cass | 9 | 8 | 1 | 7 | 5 | 4 | 5 | | 1 | 93 | | 9 | 33 | 9 | | 22 | 5 | 1 | 1 | 2 | 39 | 1,046 |
| Clark | | | | 3 | 1 | 2 | | | 1 | 1 | | | 5 | 6 | 1 | 2 | 12 | | | | | 145 |
| Clay | | | | 1 | 1 | 4 | | 1 | 5 | | | 3 | 40 | 2 | 4 | 2 | | | | 23 | | 315 |
| Clinton | | 5 | 1 | | 2 | | 2 | | | 2 | | | 4 | 1 | | 4 | | | | 1 | | 80 |
| Crawford | | | | | | | | | | | | | | | | 2 | 1 | | | | | 11 |
| Daviess | | | | 4 | | | | | | 1 | | | 4 | 8 | | 1 | 1 | | | 2 | | 85 |
| Dearborn | | 1 | | | 1 | | 2 | | | 4 | | 1 | 10 | 3 | | | 5 | | | 1 | 1 | 190 |
| Decatur | | | | 1 | | 1 | | | | 1 | | | 4 | 1 | | 1 | 4 | | | | | 93 |
| De Kalb | | | | | 1 | 1 | | | | 2 | 25 | | 21 | 2 | 7 | | 5 | 11 | | | | | 342 |
| Delaware | 2 | 19 | | 2 | 6 | 4 | 4 | | 6 | 18 | | 11 | 25 | 23 | | 12 | 15 | 1 | | 5 | | 559 |
| Dubois | | 1 | | | 1 | | | | | 3 | | | | 2 | | 2 | 4 | | | | | 109 |
| Elkhart | | 90 | 1 | 3 | 24 | 5 | 7 | 2 | 1 | 62 | | 14 | 61 | 26 | 1 | 163 | 57 | 2 | | 9 | 22 | 1,895 |
| Fayette | 3 | | | 2 | 1 | | 3 | | | 2 | | 3 | 3 | 6 | | 4 | 3 | | | | 1 | 126 |
| Floyd | | 2 | | | 3 | 1 | | | 2 | 9 | | | 9 | 2 | | | 32 | 2 | | 2 | 1 | 285 |
| Fountain | | 36 | | | 1 | | 1 | | | 3 | | 1 | 10 | 4 | | 17 | 1 | 1 | | | 3 | 138 |
| Franklin | 1 | 1 | | | | | | | | 2 | | | | | | 2 | | | | | 1 | 80 |
| Fulton | | | | 1 | | | | 1 | | 2 | | 2 | | 3 | | 20 | 7 | | | | 1 | 141 |
| Gibson | | 2 | | 4 | | | 1 | | | | | | | 10 | | | | | | 2 | 1 | 125 |
| Grant | 30 | 12 | 1 | 7 | 5 | | 1 | 1 | 2 | 49 | | 3 | 56 | 28 | | 15 | 6 | 3 | | 34 | 3 | 701 |
| Greene | | | | 7 | | | | | | 10 | | 1 | 5 | 72 | | 1 | 3 | | | 15 | 9 | 498 |
| Hamilton | 1 | 1 | | 1 | | | | | 1 | 2 | | | 3 | 3 | | 4 | 1 | | | 1 | | 86 |
| Hancock | | | | | | 5 | | | | 1 | | | 2 | 4 | | 4 | | | | | | 69 |
| Harrison | | | | | | | | | | | | | 2 | 1 | | 1 | 2 | | | | | 36 |
| Hendricks | | 19 | | 2 | 2 | | | | | 1 | | 4 | 2 | 3 | | 3 | | | | 3 | | 131 |
| Henry | | 1 | | | 3 | 1 | | | 1 | 5 | | 1 | 9 | 11 | | 15 | 2 | | | | 1 | 184 |
| Howard | | 1 | | 5 | 4 | 1 | 1 | 12 | 4 | 16 | | 32 | 13 | 13 | | 42 | 12 | 4 | | 2 | 9 | 731 |
| Huntington | 3 | 2 | | | 4 | | 2 | | | 21 | 1 | | 2 | 3 | | 4 | 5 | | | 1 | 1 | 284 |
| Jackson | 1 | | | 2 | 1 | | 1 | | | 7 | | | 5 | 4 | | 8 | 1 | | | | | 145 |
| Jasper | | 174 | | | 5 | | 1 | 13 | | 32 | | 5 | 10 | 1 | | 19 | 10 | 1 | | | 8 | 562 |
| Jay | 1 | | | 2 | 1 | | | | | 5 | | 2 | 3 | 2 | | 5 | 2 | | 1 | 1 | | 92 |
| Jefferson | | 2 | | | | 5 | | | | 2 | | | 5 | 4 | | 1 | | | | | | 108 |
| Jennings | | | | | | 1 | | | | 2 | | | | 1 | | 6 | 3 | | | | | 65 |
| Johnson | | 13 | | | 1 | | 2 | | | 4 | | | 1 | 5 | 3 | | 5 | | | 2 | 1 | 86 |
| Knox | | | | 2 | 1 | 1 | | | | 24 | | | 19 | 163 | | 1 | 1 | | | 10 | 1 | 833 |
| Kosciusko | | 5 | | 2 | 1 | 1 | | 1 | | 5 | | | 5 | 9 | | 9 | 14 | 1 | | | 4 | 225 |
| Lagrange | | | | 1 | | 2 | | 1 | | | | 1 | 1 | 3 | | 6 | 8 | | | | | 100 |
| Lake | 1,919 | 344 | 24 | 157 | 191 | 38 | 195 | 156 | 56 | 7,602 | 4 | 1,489 | 1,689 | 987 | 467 | 1,156 | 74 | 238 | | 184 | 4,126 | 43,862 |
| La Porte | 19 | 37 | | 11 | 49 | 7 | 2 | 8 | 185 | 1,317 | | 12 | 118 | 59 | 1 | 278 | 33 | 3 | | 5 | 37 | 4,942 |
| Lawrence | | 1 | | 2 | 1 | | 1 | | | 4 | | 1 | 10 | 42 | | 10 | 2 | | 3 | 3 | 4 | 277 |
| Madison | 3 | 6 | 2 | 6 | 7 | 1 | 6 | 2 | 2 | 85 | | 23 | 30 | 27 | | 28 | 10 | 5 | | 80 | 5 | 1,147 |
| Marion | 33 | 188 | 5 | 197 | 67 | 35 | 37 | 31 | 217 | 414 | 4 | 414 | 791 | 426 | 10 | 183 | 131 | 112 | 1 | 31 | 363 | 12,075 |
| Marshall | 4 | 10 | 1 | 2 | 8 | 1 | | | 3 | 22 | | 15 | 11 | 12 | | 102 | 16 | | | 3 | 11 | 536 |
| Martin | | | | | | | 1 | | | | | | | | 1 | | 1 | | | | | 16 |
| Miami | 2 | 5 | | 1 | 4 | | | | 2 | 4 | | | 1 | 2 | | 10 | 6 | 1 | | 2 | 4 | 343 |
| Monroe | 2 | 2 | | | 2 | 2 | 3 | | | 4 | | 4 | 8 | 41 | | 6 | | 1 | | | 1 | 241 |
| Montgomery | | 2 | 1 | | 2 | | 1 | | 1 | 1 | | 1 | 8 | 2 | | 8 | 1 | | | | | 94 |
| Morgan | 1 | 1 | | 1 | 1 | 1 | | | | | 1 | | 6 | | | 1 | | | | | 2 | 58 |
| Newton | 1 | 44 | | | 4 | | 1 | | | 25 | | 4 | 8 | 6 | | 23 | 2 | | | | | 350 |
| Noble | 1 | 8 | | 1 | 3 | | | 3 | | 14 | | 1 | 4 | 3 | | 17 | 6 | | | | 2 | 317 |
| Ohio | | | | | 1 | | | | | | | | | | | | | | | | | 19 |
| Orange | | | | | | 1 | | | | 1 | | | 1 | 1 | | 1 | 1 | | | | | 36 |
| Owen | | | | | | | | | | 3 | | | 1 | 3 | | | | | | | | 29 |
| Parke | | | | | 1 | | | | 1 | 1 | | | | 18 | | 1 | 2 | 1 | | | 2 | 141 |
| Perry | | | | | | | | | | 1 | | | | 1 | | 1 | 7 | | | | | 76 |
| Pike | | 1 | | | | | | | | | | 1 | 3 | | | | | | | 1 | | 39 |
| Porter | 13 | 23 | | 8 | 24 | 4 | 1 | | 1 | 152 | | 20 | 48 | 53 | 5 | 382 | 12 | | | 8 | 39 | 1,817 |
| Posey | | | | 1 | | 1 | | | | | | | | 2 | | | | | | | | 68 |
| Pulaski | | 1 | | 1 | 8 | 3 | 2 | | | 57 | | 4 | 6 | 2 | | 21 | 9 | 1 | | | 22 | 387 |
| Putnam | 2 | 2 | | 3 | 2 | 1 | | | 1 | 5 | | 1 | 1 | 3 | 1 | 1 | 2 | 2 | 2 | 4 | | 107 |
| Randolph | 7 | | 1 | | 1 | 1 | | | | | | | 5 | 11 | 1 | | 2 | | | 1 | 1 | 133 |
| Ripley | 1 | | | 1 | | | | | | 4 | | 1 | 7 | 1 | | | 2 | | | 1 | | 161 |
| Rush | 1 | | | | 1 | | | | | | | | | 4 | | | | | | 2 | | 55 |
| St. Joseph | 11 | 190 | 13 | 29 | 58 | 19 | 16 | 60 | 49 | 3,412 | 15 | 56 | 528 | 133 | 3 | 480 | 67 | 22 | 6 | 5 | 333 | 15,467 |
| Scott | | | | | 1 | | 2 | | | 1 | | | | | | | 3 | | 1 | | | 20 |
| Shelby | | 3 | | 1 | | 1 | 1 | | | 6 | | 1 | 6 | | | 1 | 6 | | | | | 119 |
| Spencer | | | | | | | | | | | | | | | | | 2 | | | | | 78 |
| Starke | | 9 | | 4 | 15 | 6 | 35 | 2 | 5 | 195 | | 18 | 23 | 5 | | 121 | 3 | 11 | | 1 | 23 | 1,261 |
| Steuben | 1 | | 1 | | 4 | | 4 | | | 1 | | | 1 | 1 | 2 | 3 | 2 | | 2 | 6 | | 185 |
| Sullivan | | 1 | 1 | | 1 | | | | | 29 | | 1 | 4 | 107 | | 13 | | | | 9 | | 398 |
| Switzerland | | | | | | | | | | | | | | | | | | | | | | 11 |
| Tippecanoe | 3 | 228 | | 10 | 6 | 3 | 1 | | 3 | 24 | | 3 | 58 | 18 | 2 | 58 | 11 | 2 | | 2 | 5 | 1,201 |
| Tipton | | | | | 2 | | | | | | | | | 1 | | | 6 | | | | | 82 |
| Union | | 1 | | | | 1 | | | | 1 | | | | | | | 1 | | | | | 23 |
| Vanderburgh | 7 | 8 | | 2 | 6 | 3 | 2 | 3 | 5 | 27 | | 5 | 124 | 36 | 2 | 16 | 31 | 1 | 1 | 6 | 3 | 1,494 |
| Vermillion | | 1 | | 2 | 2 | | | | | 44 | | 18 | 8 | 178 | | 2 | | 1 | 1 | 13 | 160 | 1,695 |
| Vigo | 1 | 29 | 2 | 13 | 15 | 4 | 1 | 1 | 100 | 89 | | 77 | 119 | 270 | 1 | 47 | 30 | 10 | | 89 | 31 | 2,865 |
| Wabash | | 4 | | | 2 | | | 2 | | 2 | | 1 | 5 | 6 | | 3 | 10 | | | | 6 | 198 |
| Warren | | 3 | | | | | | | | | | | | | | 13 | | | | | | 49 |
| Warrick | | 4 | | | 1 | | 1 | | | | | 1 | | 4 | | | 2 | | | | | 80 |
| Washington | | | | | | | 2 | | | 1 | | | | | | | 2 | 2 | | | | 33 |
| Wayne | | 4 | | 5 | 5 | | | | 1 | 10 | | 33 | 3 | 22 | | 10 | 13 | 5 | | 1 | 2 | 855 |
| Wells | 12 | 1 | | 1 | 1 | | | | | 4 | | | | | | 9 | 33 | | | 1 | | 140 |
| White | | 13 | | 3 | | | | | | 3 | | | | 8 | | 20 | 12 | | | 1 | 1 | 201 |
| Whitley | 1 | | | 2 | 1 | | 2 | | | 2 | | | 7 | 7 | | 3 | 10 | | | 2 | | 111 |

## TABLE 9.  FOREIGN BORN IN INDIANA BY COUNTY, 1980

| | Total Population | Foreign Born | Africa | Asia | Austria | Canada | China | Cuba | Czechoslovakia | Dominican Republic | England | Europe | France | Germany | Greece | Hungary | India | Ireland | Northern Ireland | Italy |
|---|---|---|---|---|---|---|---|---|---|---|---|---|---|---|---|---|---|---|---|---|
| Indiana | 5,490,224 | 101,629 | 1,922 | 7,706 | 1,415 | 6,462 | 1,260 | 839 | 1,773 | 73 | 4,990 | 4,970 | 1,065 | 11,870 | 2,861 | 2,151 | 2,510 | 837 | 147 | 2,484 |
| Adams | 29,619 | 313 | 18 | | | 57 | | | | | 18 | 28 | 7 | 42 | 2 | | | | | |
| Allen | 294,335 | 6,389 | 146 | 900 | 56 | 518 | 52 | 43 | 25 | | 379 | 177 | 69 | 996 | 317 | 70 | 263 | 44 | 7 | 121 |
| Bartholomew | 65,088 | 649 | | 1 | 10 | 46 | | | | | 67 | 29 | 8 | 172 | | 27 | 28 | | | 2 |
| Benton | 10,218 | 64 | | | | | | | 3 | | 6 | 2 | 2 | 17 | | 2 | | | | |
| Blackford | 15,570 | 75 | 1 | 2 | 8 | 32 | | | | | | | 2 | 1 | | | | 2 | | |
| Boone | 36,446 | 518 | | 2 | 7 | 44 | 21 | | 3 | | 73 | 42 | 24 | 84 | 9 | | | 7 | 7 | 6 |
| Brown | 12,377 | 103 | | | 4 | 5 | | | | | | 15 | | 48 | | | | | | 3 |
| Carroll | 19,722 | 89 | 2 | 3 | 2 | 5 | | | | | 3 | 2 | | 19 | | | | 6 | | 3 |
| Cass | 40,936 | 389 | | 14 | 2 | 19 | 12 | 2 | | | 27 | 7 | 13 | 88 | 8 | 10 | 5 | 13 | 5 | 32 |
| Clark | 88,838 | 808 | 19 | 59 | | 70 | | 3 | 4 | | 85 | 29 | 12 | 115 | | 5 | 45 | | | 8 |
| Clay | 24,862 | 147 | 2 | 1 | 5 | 4 | 2 | 6 | | | 6 | | | 11 | | | | | | 22 |
| Clinton | 31,545 | 314 | | 9 | | 16 | | | 2 | | 14 | 13 | 3 | 23 | | | 29 | 9 | | 9 |
| Crawford | 9,820 | 55 | 3 | | | | | | | | 8 | | 4 | 18 | | | | | | |
| Daviess | 27,836 | 63 | | | | 8 | 5 | | | | 11 | | 8 | 7 | | | | | | 2 |
| Dearborn | 34,291 | 295 | | 18 | 5 | 12 | | | 3 | | 25 | 14 | 12 | 59 | | 4 | 24 | 2 | | 11 |
| Decatur | 23,841 | 113 | | | | 18 | | 2 | | | 15 | | | 37 | | | | 9 | | |
| De Kalb | 33,606 | 243 | | 16 | | 25 | | | 4 | | 24 | 9 | 3 | 52 | | | 7 | | | |
| Delaware | 128,587 | 1,262 | 59 | 192 | 13 | 113 | 56 | 5 | 25 | | 96 | 16 | 18 | 144 | 9 | | 86 | 6 | | 9 |
| Dubois | 34,238 | 173 | | | 2 | 8 | | | | | 14 | 15 | 2 | 31 | | 2 | 3 | | | 2 |
| Elkhart | 137,330 | 3,033 | 48 | 160 | 37 | 529 | 8 | 24 | 13 | | 119 | 105 | 25 | 357 | 37 | 30 | 63 | | | 84 |
| Fayette | 28,272 | 135 | | 9 | 5 | 13 | 6 | | | | 11 | | | 11 | | | | | | |
| Floyd | 61,169 | 440 | 7 | 67 | | 18 | 17 | | 6 | | 18 | 12 | 5 | 95 | | | 6 | 11 | | 17 |
| Fountain | 19,033 | 97 | | 9 | | 3 | | | | | 2 | | | 26 | | | | | | 6 |
| Franklin | 19,612 | 120 | | 6 | | 4 | | | | 6 | 17 | 4 | | 26 | | 2 | | 2 | | |
| Fulton | 19,335 | 170 | | 25 | 3 | 9 | | | 2 | | 12 | 7 | | 30 | 3 | 6 | | | | 2 |
| Gibson | 33,156 | 226 | | 14 | 6 | 11 | | 7 | | | 53 | 4 | | 33 | | 5 | 22 | | | 2 |
| Grant | 80,934 | 796 | 23 | 38 | 6 | 111 | 13 | 32 | 13 | | 58 | 42 | | 82 | 17 | | 52 | 7 | | 3 |
| Greene | 30,416 | 136 | | | 3 | 7 | | | | | 11 | 2 | 18 | 35 | | | 2 | | | 2 |
| Hamilton | 82,027 | 1,200 | 18 | 80 | 6 | 126 | 43 | 17 | 13 | | 119 | 140 | 18 | 204 | 23 | 9 | 30 | 7 | | 16 |
| Hancock | 43,939 | 510 | 32 | 93 | 6 | 48 | | 13 | | | 30 | 12 | 12 | 94 | | | 8 | 8 | | 12 |
| Harrison | 27,276 | 156 | | | 2 | 5 | | | | | 9 | 5 | 2 | 54 | | | 2 | 5 | | |
| Hendricks | 69,804 | 468 | 10 | 41 | | 25 | | 7 | | | 16 | 23 | 12 | 42 | | 2 | 4 | 2 | | 3 |
| Henry | 53,336 | 247 | 5 | | | 27 | | 6 | | | 18 | 15 | | 58 | | | | | | |
| Howard | 86,896 | 1,173 | 18 | 54 | 23 | 69 | 39 | 28 | 19 | | 171 | 35 | 15 | 165 | 10 | 9 | 39 | | | 65 |
| Huntington | 35,596 | 353 | 28 | 16 | 2 | 53 | | | | | 27 | 14 | 4 | 28 | 3 | 7 | 25 | | | |
| Jackson | 36,523 | 228 | | | | 23 | | | 7 | | 13 | 3 | | 65 | | | | 11 | | |
| Jasper | 26,138 | 480 | 8 | 15 | 9 | 44 | 6 | | 5 | | 9 | 32 | | 62 | 10 | 13 | | 2 | | 6 |
| Jay | 23,239 | 138 | | 10 | | 13 | | | | | | 2 | 2 | 31 | | 12 | | | | 12 |
| Jefferson | 30,419 | 198 | | 44 | | 12 | | 3 | | | 23 | 18 | | 20 | | | 7 | | | |
| Jennings | 22,584 | 124 | | | | 4 | | | | | 8 | | 3 | 11 | | | | | | 19 |
| Johnson | 77,240 | 633 | | 17 | 8 | 67 | 23 | 5 | 6 | | 52 | 31 | 1 | 84 | 6 | 12 | 26 | 6 | | 7 |
| Knox | 41,838 | 464 | 25 | 129 | 6 | 34 | 6 | | | | 56 | 2 | 26 | 65 | | | 3 | | | |
| Kosciusko | 59,555 | 781 | | 38 | 5 | 85 | 9 | | 3 | | 53 | 26 | 20 | 103 | 15 | 2 | 55 | 5 | | 4 |
| Lagrange | 25,550 | 148 | | | | 17 | | 4 | 4 | | 23 | 17 | | 19 | 2 | | | 3 | | 3 |
| Lake | 522,965 | 27,435 | 221 | 561 | 375 | 788 | 123 | 186 | 1,163 | 23 | 552 | 1,121 | 97 | 1,633 | 1,843 | 645 | 196 | 144 | 13 | 786 |
| La Porte | 108,632 | 2,571 | 23 | 140 | 67 | 211 | 3 | 6 | 55 | | 134 | 104 | 42 | 461 | 29 | 15 | 40 | 41 | 2 | 39 |
| Lawrence | 42,472 | 283 | | | 13 | 18 | | 19 | | | 12 | 9 | | 38 | 6 | | 30 | | | 17 |
| Madison | 139,336 | 1,335 | 45 | 43 | 6 | 75 | 15 | 34 | 14 | | 106 | 56 | 26 | 270 | 16 | 7 | 65 | 22 | | 5 |
| Marion | 765,233 | 14,845 | 319 | 1,007 | 182 | 910 | 283 | 228 | 61 | 15 | 866 | 1,023 | 185 | 1,940 | 206 | 183 | 544 | 227 | 65 | 252 |
| Marshall | 39,155 | 540 | | 7 | | 36 | | | | | 7 | 42 | 13 | 97 | 15 | 23 | 2 | 13 | | 6 |
| Martin | 11,001 | 135 | | 6 | 2 | | | | 8 | | 9 | | 2 | 15 | | | | | | |
| Miami | 39,820 | 651 | 15 | 52 | 2 | 31 | | 2 | | | 93 | 46 | 15 | 37 | 2 | 18 | 11 | 4 | | 2 |
| Monroe | 98,785 | 4,147 | 415 | 1,378 | 33 | 181 | 61 | 7 | | | 118 | 180 | 64 | 333 | 32 | 22 | 105 | 6 | 7 | 37 |
| Montgomery | 35,501 | 223 | | | | 38 | 12 | | 9 | | 30 | | 8 | 51 | 7 | | | | | 5 |
| Morgan | 51,999 | 358 | 5 | 33 | 3 | 34 | 36 | 2 | 7 | | 38 | 24 | 5 | 68 | | | 10 | | 3 | 4 |
| Newton | 14,844 | 163 | | 4 | 2 | 8 | 2 | | 7 | | 5 | 6 | 5 | 23 | | | | 4 | | |
| Noble | 35,443 | 256 | | 6 | | 17 | 4 | | | | 22 | 21 | 6 | 41 | | | | | | |
| Ohio | 5,114 | 17 | | | | 2 | | | 2 | | 4 | | | 7 | | | | | | |
| Orange | 18,677 | 205 | 4 | | | 23 | | | | | 27 | 2 | | 28 | | | 4 | | | |
| Owen | 15,841 | 79 | 2 | 2 | | 6 | 4 | | | | 11 | 7 | | 15 | | 3 | | | | |
| Parke | 16,372 | 89 | | | 8 | 2 | | | | | 10 | 5 | 2 | 25 | | | | 2 | | |
| Perry | 19,346 | 38 | | | | | 6 | | | | | | | 26 | | | | | | |
| Pike | 13,465 | 69 | | 12 | | 5 | | | | | 7 | 6 | | 4 | | | | | | |
| Porter | 119,816 | 3,160 | 55 | 119 | 48 | 328 | 41 | 20 | 106 | 17 | 183 | 254 | 28 | 478 | 37 | 60 | 81 | 25 | 12 | 104 |
| Posey | 26,414 | 144 | | 10 | | 4 | | 4 | | | 20 | | 6 | 37 | | | 9 | | 5 | |
| Pulaski | 13,258 | 150 | | 16 | 3 | 8 | | | 5 | | 7 | 5 | | 23 | 7 | | 3 | | | |
| Putnam | 29,163 | 170 | 3 | 8 | | 21 | | | 6 | | 9 | 11 | | 9 | | | 2 | 2 | | |
| Randolph | 29,997 | 135 | | | | 15 | | 4 | | | 2 | | 8 | 35 | | | | | | |
| Ripley | 24,398 | 134 | 16 | 2 | | 15 | 3 | | | | 2 | 14 | 2 | 23 | | | | | | 3 |
| Rush | 19,604 | 66 | | | | 6 | | | 3 | | 5 | | | 15 | 7 | | | | | |
| St. Joseph | 241,617 | 7,658 | 47 | 394 | 344 | 498 | 80 | 19 | 49 | | 249 | 710 | 44 | 898 | 110 | 794 | 124 | 55 | 8 | 406 |
| Scott | 20,422 | 213 | | | 2 | 17 | | | | | 2 | 2 | | 17 | 2 | | | | | |
| Shelby | 39,887 | 223 | | 28 | | 3 | | | 11 | | 13 | 6 | 13 | 29 | | 4 | 5 | | | |
| Spencer | 19,361 | 101 | | | | 28 | | | | | 4 | | | 20 | | 3 | | | 2 | |
| Starke | 21,997 | 603 | 2 | 6 | 14 | 20 | | | 52 | | 17 | 34 | 7 | 103 | 8 | 24 | 2 | 11 | | 29 |
| Steuben | 24,694 | 410 | | 166 | | 26 | 7 | | 7 | | 20 | 14 | 5 | 46 | 5 | 5 | 24 | | | 15 |
| Sullivan | 21,107 | 151 | | | | 12 | | | | | 10 | 2 | 6 | 40 | | | 2 | | | 9 |
| Switzerland | 7,153 | 33 | | 8 | | | | | | | 6 | | | | | | | | | |
| Tippecanoe | 121,702 | 3,792 | 148 | 712 | 22 | 190 | 156 | 35 | 22 | | 160 | 142 | 32 | 358 | 40 | 12 | 222 | 48 | | 79 |
| Tipton | 16,819 | 145 | | | | 34 | | 12 | 6 | | 21 | 10 | 2 | 2 | | | 7 | | | |
| Union | 6,860 | 17 | | | | | | | | | 4 | | | 4 | | | | | | |
| Vanderburgh | 167,515 | 1,606 | 21 | 261 | 16 | 122 | 64 | 18 | | | 76 | 60 | 19 | 209 | 6 | 6 | 8 | 17 | | 35 |
| Vermillion | 18,229 | 319 | | 2 | | 30 | | | | | 42 | 5 | 7 | 2 | | 11 | | | | 67 |
| Vigo | 112,385 | 2,227 | 63 | 494 | | 123 | 24 | 8 | 8 | 6 | 113 | 36 | 35 | 193 | | 31 | 147 | 25 | | 26 |
| Wabash | 36,640 | 442 | 29 | 104 | | 24 | 6 | 10 | | | 10 | 8 | | 71 | 5 | 5 | | 1 | | 8 |
| Warren | 8,976 | 51 | | 5 | | 6 | | | | | 2 | | | 6 | | | | | | |
| Warrick | 41,474 | 303 | 4 | | | 53 | 5 | | | | 28 | 5 | | 47 | | 7 | 32 | 2 | | |
| Washington | 21,932 | 66 | | | | 5 | | | 6 | | 1 | | | 18 | | 2 | | | | |
| Wayne | 76,058 | 696 | | 12 | 23 | 53 | 5 | | | | 60 | 12 | 24 | 148 | 6 | 14 | 25 | 2 | | 74 |
| Wells | 25,401 | 218 | | | | 5 | | | 7 | | 38 | 6 | | 45 | 1 | | | 3 | | |
| White | 23,867 | 249 | | 18 | 3 | 34 | 6 | | 2 | | 7 | 9 | 6 | 44 | | 9 | | | | |
| Whitley | 26,215 | 192 | | | 6 | 16 | | | 3 | | 1 | 10 | | 42 | | 2 | | 5 | | 3 |

TABLE 9. FOREIGN BORN IN INDIANA BY COUNTY, 1980 (*continued*)

| County | Jamaica | Japan | Korea | Mexico | Netherlands | Other North, Central Am. | Other British | All Other Countries | Philippines | Poland | Portugal | USSR | South America | Scotland | Sweden | Not Reported | Vietnam | Wales | West Indies | Yugoslavia |
|---|---|---|---|---|---|---|---|---|---|---|---|---|---|---|---|---|---|---|---|---|
| Indiana | 478 | 1,536 | 3,208 | 9,460 | 1,333 | 913 | 116 | 533 | 395 | 2,572 | 4,136 | 2,133 | 2,325 | 1,385 | 713 | 7,702 | 1,909 | 191 | 512 | 4,672 |
| Adams | | 2 | 15 | 75 | 7 | 5 | | | | | | | | | 2 | 30 | 5 | | | |
| Allen | 17 | 46 | 148 | 302 | 145 | 26 | 28 | 36 | 187 | 134 | 5 | 124 | 211 | 90 | 50 | 287 | 139 | 13 | 97 | 121 |
| Bartholomew | | 40 | 40 | 39 | 2 | 14 | | 11 | 12 | 9 | | 6 | 26 | 5 | | 44 | | 6 | 5 | |
| Benton | | | | 6 | | | | | | | | | | | 2 | 24 | | | | |
| Blackford | | 2 | | | | | | | | | | | | | | 25 | | | | |
| Boone | | 2 | | 2 | 2 | | | | 5 | | | 49 | 36 | 5 | | 17 | 65 | 6 | | |
| Brown | | 13 | 5 | | | | | | 2 | 3 | | | | 2 | | 3 | | | | |
| Carroll | | | | 5 | | | | | | | | | 2 | | 2 | 35 | | | | |
| Cass | | 8 | | 3 | | | | 4 | 3 | 6 | | 3 | 14 | 2 | | 72 | 2 | | | 15 |
| Clark | 32 | 31 | 16 | 7 | | 7 | 2 | | 43 | 16 | | 24 | 6 | 7 | | 127 | 25 | | | 11 |
| Clay | | 10 | | 2 | | | | | | | | | 18 | | | 58 | | | | |
| Clinton | | | 7 | 66 | | 4 | 7 | 9 | 12 | | | 9 | | 6 | | 61 | | | | 6 |
| Crawford | | 3 | 2 | | | | | | | | | | | | | 17 | | | | |
| Daviess | | 12 | 2 | | | | | | | | | | | | | 7 | | | | 7 |
| Dearborn | | 3 | 29 | 2 | 3 | 3 | 18 | | 11 | 2 | | | 5 | | | 18 | 5 | 2 | | 5 |
| Decatur | | 4 | 10 | | | | 3 | | | | | | | 2 | | 7 | | 4 | | |
| De Kalb | | | 5 | 6 | 7 | 9 | | 2 | 5 | | | 2 | 14 | 9 | | 2 | 39 | | | 3 |
| Delaware | | 25 | 45 | 24 | 5 | 33 | | | 43 | 20 | | 7 | 25 | 12 | 8 | 151 | 12 | | | 5 |
| Dubois | | | 7 | 14 | 5 | 17 | | | | 12 | | | | 7 | | 32 | | | | |
| Elkhart | 12 | 16 | 123 | 225 | 169 | 21 | 16 | 13 | 20 | 56 | 24 | 220 | 72 | 45 | 47 | 172 | 79 | 11 | 12 | 39 |
| Fayette | | 9 | 2 | | | | 14 | 14 | 9 | | | | | | | 15 | 17 | | | |
| Floyd | 2 | 22 | 14 | 16 | 3 | 6 | | | 19 | | | | | 5 | 18 | 39 | | | 6 | 11 |
| Fountain | | 9 | 6 | | | | 2 | | 2 | | | | | 2 | | 30 | | | | |
| Franklin | | | | 9 | | | | | 11 | | | | | | | 3 | 30 | | | |
| Fulton | | | 6 | 6 | | 2 | | | 22 | | | 5 | 8 | | | 12 | | | | 10 |
| Gibson | | 2 | | 3 | 3 | 2 | | 2 | 24 | | | 2 | | | 11 | 13 | | | | 7 |
| Grant | 7 | 27 | 18 | 68 | 6 | | | 2 | 26 | 26 | | 16 | 16 | 23 | 13 | 38 | 2 | | 9 | 2 |
| Greene | | 2 | 6 | 3 | 5 | | | | 8 | 10 | | 4 | 4 | 3 | | 3 | 4 | 4 | | |
| Hamilton | 12 | 61 | 10 | 25 | 13 | | 2 | 6 | 13 | | | 19 | 34 | 7 | 8 | 63 | 52 | | | 6 |
| Hancock | | 4 | 38 | 11 | | | | | 5 | 11 | | 2 | 2 | | | 52 | | 13 | | 4 |
| Harrison | | 13 | 11 | 5 | 2 | 6 | 2 | 2 | | | | | | 3 | | 28 | | | | |
| Hendricks | 2 | | 6 | | | 8 | | 14 | 2 | | | 6 | 2 | 12 | | 10 | | | | 7 |
| Henry | | 24 | 16 | 8 | 5 | 3 | 6 | | | 7 | | 2 | | 8 | | 39 | | | | |
| Howard | 19 | 30 | 42 | 87 | | 22 | | 12 | 15 | 21 | | 6 | 6 | 17 | 6 | 43 | 57 | | 24 | 7 |
| Huntington | | 7 | 34 | | | | | | | 12 | | 33 | 12 | | 2 | 21 | 25 | | | |
| Jackson | | | 41 | 8 | 17 | 5 | | 2 | 1 | | | | | 4 | | 15 | 13 | | | |
| Jasper | | 34 | 4 | 17 | 49 | 3 | | 1 | | 24 | | 16 | | 2 | 11 | 56 | 8 | | 6 | 28 |
| Jay | 4 | | 15 | | | | | | | | | | | | 9 | 28 | | | | |
| Jefferson | | 10 | | | | | | | 17 | 2 | | | 13 | 18 | 2 | 9 | | | | |
| Jennings | | 9 | 14 | 2 | | 1 | | | 27 | 12 | | | | | | 6 | 8 | | | |
| Johnson | | 2 | 53 | 4 | 22 | 14 | | 2 | 19 | | | 5 | 32 | | 13 | 97 | | | 7 | 12 |
| Knox | | 6 | 12 | | | 6 | | | | | | 18 | 7 | 41 | | 22 | | | | |
| Kosciusko | | 14 | 70 | 118 | 19 | 15 | | | | 7 | | | 11 | | 2 | 39 | 31 | | 6 | 14 |
| Lagrange | | | 9 | 10 | 2 | 4 | | | | | | 2 | | 3 | 3 | 11 | 11 | | | |
| Lake | 160 | 85 | 335 | 6,767 | 143 | 96 | 21 | 67 | 537 | 2,099 | 15 | 492 | 217 | 252 | 115 | 1,631 | 182 | 8 | 63 | 3,680 |
| La Porte | 1 | 21 | 71 | 245 | 49 | 5 | | 10 | 55 | 229 | | 67 | 3 | 10 | 95 | 261 | 12 | | 19 | 6 |
| Lawrence | | 17 | 9 | 2 | 3 | | 4 | | 26 | | | 14 | | 17 | | 29 | | | | |
| Madison | 15 | 82 | 93 | 52 | 9 | 15 | 14 | 13 | 27 | 6 | | 2 | 45 | 19 | 2 | 85 | | | 51 | |
| Marion | 69 | 299 | 749 | 417 | 203 | 243 | 86 | 156 | 697 | 231 | | 458 | 417 | 256 | 71 | 1,259 | 435 | 37 | 139 | 127 |
| Marshall | | 4 | 10 | 87 | 26 | | | 6 | 19 | 14 | | 2 | 6 | 11 | 11 | 49 | 11 | 10 | | 5 |
| Martin | | 9 | 5 | | | | | 6 | 25 | 5 | | 15 | | | | 14 | 22 | | | |
| Miami | | 16 | 55 | 4 | | 35 | 20 | | 53 | 6 | | 51 | 20 | 7 | 3 | 32 | 8 | | 2 | |
| Monroe | 5 | 106 | 183 | 97 | 22 | 31 | 36 | 26 | 80 | 48 | | 56 | 238 | 74 | 26 | 53 | 52 | 21 | 7 | 5 |
| Montgomery | | 2 | 4 | 6 | | 5 | | 15 | | | 5 | 7 | | | 6 | 18 | | | | |
| Morgan | | 12 | | 7 | | | | 5 | 2 | | | | 2 | 2 | | 50 | | | 2 | 9 |
| Newton | | 3 | 5 | 8 | 17 | | 2 | | 5 | 5 | | 7 | | | 3 | 31 | | 4 | | 12 |
| Noble | | 2 | 4 | 50 | 2 | | | | 5 | | | | 4 | 40 | 7 | 14 | 6 | | 5 | 2 |
| Ohio | | 2 | 2 | | | | | | | | | | | | | | | | | |
| Orange | 81 | | 2 | | | 3 | | | | | | | | 7 | 6 | 18 | | | | |
| Owen | | 2 | 4 | | 3 | 4 | | | 2 | | | | | 3 | | | 14 | | | 1 |
| Parke | | 2 | | 3 | | | | | | | | | | | 10 | 20 | | | | |
| Perry | 3 | | 1 | | | | | | | | | | | | | 2 | | | | |
| Pike | | | | 1 | | 2 | | | 25 | | | 2 | 5 | | | | | | | |
| Porter | 7 | 14 | 44 | 124 | 33 | 15 | 2 | 8 | 78 | 129 | 9 | 30 | 74 | 80 | 57 | 231 | 48 | 21 | 2 | 184 |
| Posey | 1 | | 7 | | | | | 2 | 2 | 2 | | 2 | | | 12 | 21 | | | | |
| Pulaski | 2 | | 4 | 3 | | | | | 2 | 18 | | | | | 4 | 20 | 2 | | | 16 |
| Putnam | | 9 | 13 | | 2 | | | | 8 | | | | | 2 | | 55 | 2 | 8 | | |
| Randolph | | 16 | | | 3 | 3 | | | 27 | | | | | | | 11 | 4 | 7 | | |
| Ripley | | 4 | 13 | | | | | | 5 | 2 | | | | 9 | | 19 | 2 | | | |
| Rush | | 2 | 5 | | | | | | 2 | | | 6 | | | | 18 | | | | |
| St. Joseph | 14 | 80 | 257 | 226 | 168 | 30 | 23 | 42 | 36 | 679 | 6 | 179 | 95 | 110 | 65 | 506 | 101 | | 26 | 186 |
| Scott | | 2 | 13 | 10 | | | | | 36 | | | | 6 | | | 104 | | | | |
| Shelby | | 15 | 8 | 7 | | | | | 5 | 17 | | | 6 | 2 | | 48 | | | | 3 |
| Spencer | 7 | | 3 | | | | | | 18 | 2 | | | | | | 7 | 7 | | | |
| Starke | | | 2 | 4 | 6 | 4 | 2 | | | 110 | | 50 | 2 | 29 | 6 | 49 | | | | 10 |
| Steuben | | 8 | 7 | 4 | 13 | | | 7 | | 5 | | | 2 | | | 14 | 4 | | 6 | |
| Sullivan | | | 2 | | | | | | | | | | 3 | | 24 | 41 | | | | |
| Switzerland | | 2 | | | | | | | | | | | | | | 17 | | | | |
| Tippecanoe | 3 | 195 | 171 | 50 | 43 | 56 | 74 | 8 | 28 | 36 | | 24 | 259 | 29 | 20 | 267 | 77 | 6 | 7 | 61 |
| Tipton | | | 2 | 2 | | | 11 | | | | | 5 | 7 | | | 20 | 44 | | | |
| Union | | | | | | | | | 5 | | | | | | | 4 | | | | |
| Vanderburgh | | 18 | 67 | 37 | 5 | 13 | 23 | 7 | 40 | 55 | 6 | 51 | 49 | 22 | 5 | 138 | 83 | | | 20 |
| Vermillion | | 9 | 10 | 2 | | | | | | | | | 13 | 20 | | 89 | | | | 10 |
| Vigo | 7 | 14 | 17 | 21 | 8 | 98 | 16 | | 64 | 32 | | 21 | 140 | 22 | 19 | 308 | 102 | 6 | | |
| Wabash | | 2 | 37 | 19 | 5 | 13 | | | | | | 5 | 9 | 2 | | 54 | 15 | | | |
| Warren | | 4 | 2 | 9 | | | 6 | | 2 | 2 | | | | 1 | 4 | 2 | | | | |
| Warrick | | 5 | 41 | | | | | 9 | 26 | | | | 9 | 5 | | 25 | | | | |
| Washington | | | 2 | | | 5 | | | 4 | | | | | | | 15 | | | | 2 |
| Wayne | | 13 | 7 | 22 | 28 | 10 | 1 | 9 | 18 | | | 2 | 34 | 8 | | 36 | 42 | 8 | | |
| Wells | 3 | | 3 | 7 | | | | 8 | 20 | 2 | | | 12 | 2 | | 56 | | | | |
| White | | | | 4 | 3 | | | 5 | 6 | | | | 5 | 9 | | 28 | 51 | | | |
| Whitley | | 4 | 11 | 4 | 3 | | 15 | | 21 | 2 | | | | | | 40 | | | | |

## TABLE 10. FOREIGN BORN IN INDIANA BY COUNTY, 1990

| COUNTY | TOTAL | Foreign-Born | Europe | Austria | Belgium | Czech | Denmark | Estonia | Finland | France | Germany | Greece | Hungary | Ireland | Italy |
|---|---|---|---|---|---|---|---|---|---|---|---|---|---|---|---|
| Adams | 31,095 | 222 | 84 | 6 | | 5 | | | | | 33 | | | | 7 |
| Allen | 300,836 | 5,882 | 2,085 | 82 | 6 | 8 | 17 | | | 8 | 592 | 298 | 60 | 31 | 120 |
| Bartholomew | 63,657 | 987 | 369 | 17 | | | | | | | 79 | | 17 | | 6 |
| Benton | 9,441 | 44 | 27 | | | | | | | | 8 | | | | |
| Blackford | 14,067 | 41 | 10 | | | | | | | | 2 | | | | |
| Boone | 38,147 | 310 | 191 | 5 | | | | | | | 74 | 9 | | | 17 |
| Brown | 14,080 | 98 | 78 | 9 | | | | | | 4 | 38 | | | | |
| Carroll | 18,809 | 112 | 78 | | 7 | | | | | | 36 | | | | |
| Cass | 38,413 | 246 | 125 | | | 10 | | 7 | | | 33 | | 6 | 3 | 31 |
| Clark | 87,777 | 742 | 298 | 14 | | 8 | | | 3 | 6 | 106 | | | | 38 |
| Clay | 24,705 | 127 | 88 | | | | | | | | 34 | | | 8 | 17 |
| Clinton | 30,974 | 142 | 47 | | | | | | | 7 | 12 | | 8 | | |
| Crawford | 9,914 | 17 | 9 | | | | | | | | 5 | | | | |
| Daviess | 27,533 | 66 | 36 | | | | 2 | | | 8 | 6 | | | | |
| Dearborn | 38,835 | 240 | 164 | | | | | | | | 43 | | 9 | | |
| Decatur | 23,645 | 212 | 67 | | | | | | | | 25 | | | | |
| De Kalb | 35,324 | 261 | 123 | | | | | | | | 51 | | 9 | | |
| Delaware | 119,659 | 1,355 | 400 | 22 | 14 | 4 | | | 9 | 19 | 110 | | | 14 | 19 |
| Dubois | 36,616 | 207 | 64 | | 6 | | | | | | 30 | | 2 | 9 | |
| Elkhart | 156,198 | 3,314 | 937 | 35 | 7 | | 13 | 9 | | 34 | 324 | 22 | 8 | | 73 |
| Fayette | 26,015 | 152 | 67 | | 7 | | | | | | 24 | | 6 | | |
| Floyd | 64,404 | 596 | 200 | 17 | | | | | | 8 | 53 | | | 6 | 7 |
| Fountain | 17,808 | 67 | 47 | | | | | | | 13 | 10 | | | | |
| Franklin | 19,580 | 70 | 39 | | | | | | | | 13 | | 7 | | |
| Fulton | 18,840 | 69 | 15 | | | | | | | | 4 | | | | |
| Gibson | 31,913 | 88 | 19 | | | | | | | | 17 | | | | |
| Grant | 74,169 | 579 | 203 | 9 | | | | | | 10 | 84 | | 5 | 4 | |
| Greene | 30,410 | 113 | 63 | 17 | | | | | | 6 | 6 | 7 | | | |
| Hamilton | 108,936 | 2,363 | 968 | 6 | 6 | 4 | 6 | | | 24 | 270 | 90 | 19 | 39 | 63 |
| Hancock | 45,527 | 501 | 239 | 2 | | 2 | | | | | 99 | 10 | | | 15 |
| Harrison | 29,890 | 201 | 122 | | | | 2 | | | | 58 | | | | |
| Hendricks | 75,717 | 461 | 276 | 4 | 11 | | | | | | 62 | 26 | 13 | | 15 |
| Henry | 48,139 | 169 | 53 | | | 5 | | | | 7 | 26 | | 10 | | |
| Howard | 80,827 | 971 | 391 | | | 34 | | | | 24 | 139 | 22 | | | 19 |
| Huntington | 35,427 | 288 | 122 | 10 | * | | | | | | 21 | 9 | | 7 | 7 |
| Jackson | 37,730 | 285 | 81 | | | | | | | | 38 | | 2 | 6 | 8 |
| Jasper | 24,960 | 250 | 193 | 16 | | | | | | | 19 | 13 | | 19 | 1 |
| Jay | 21,512 | 78 | 37 | | | | | | | | 37 | | | | |
| Jefferson | 29,797 | 297 | 113 | | 10 | | 8 | | 9 | 12 | 7 | | 10 | | |
| Jennings | 23,661 | 81 | 38 | | | | | | | | 17 | | | 15 | |
| Johnson | 88,109 | 1,128 | 364 | | 7 | 6 | 8 | | 13 | 29 | 136 | | 13 | 8 | 6 |
| Knox | 39,884 | 286 | 79 | | | | | | | 7 | 31 | | | 2 | |
| Kosciusko | 65,294 | 798 | 223 | | | | | | | 5 | 51 | 28 | 9 | 6 | 8 |
| Lagrange | 29,477 | 247 | 68 | | | | 2 | | | | 16 | | 7 | | |
| Lake | 475,594 | 19,461 | 9,611 | 175 | 38 | 594 | | | 21 | 72 | 1,185 | 1,265 | 300 | 122 | 513 |
| La Porte | 107,066 | 1,917 | 1,071 | 43 | | 15 | 8 | | | 7 | 289 | 21 | 43 | 29 | 58 |
| Lawrence | 42,836 | 171 | 78 | 6 | | 7 | | | | | 24 | | | | 4 |
| Madison | 130,669 | 914 | 383 | 6 | | 6 | 7 | | 13 | 6 | 117 | 5 | | 11 | |
| Marion | 797,159 | 15,291 | 5,096 | 134 | 14 | 98 | 15 | 21 | 30 | 188 | 1,555 | 175 | 107 | 150 | 277 |
| Marshall | 42,182 | 487 | 193 | 5 | 11 | | | | | 10 | 53 | 6 | 10 | 6 | |
| Martin | 10,369 | 47 | 28 | | | | | | | | 13 | | | | |
| Miami | 36,897 | 420 | 187 | | | 12 | | | | 6 | 77 | | 8 | 7 | 18 |
| Monroe | 108,978 | 4,736 | 1,138 | 14 | 7 | 23 | 30 | | | 93 | 267 | 30 | 67 | 31 | 28 |
| Montgomery | 34,436 | 223 | 79 | | | | | | | 2 | 40 | 2 | | | |
| Morgan | 55,920 | 377 | 228 | | | | | | | | 33 | | | | 12 |
| Newton | 13,551 | 209 | 127 | | | 6 | | | | | 56 | 10 | | | 6 |
| Noble | 37,877 | 339 | 73 | | | | | | | 4 | 13 | 7 | 2 | | 10 |
| Ohio | 5,315 | 8 | 8 | | | | | | | | | | | | |
| Orange | 18,409 | 80 | 12 | | | | | | | | 6 | | 3 | 1 | |
| Owen | 17,281 | 89 | 56 | | | | | | | | 13 | | | | |
| Parke | 15,410 | 103 | 71 | | 3 | | | | | 6 | 21 | | 10 | | |
| Perry | 19,107 | 61 | 43 | | | | | | | | 23 | 2 | | | |
| Pike | 12,509 | 40 | 10 | | | 5 | | | | | | 5 | | | |
| Porter | 128,932 | 2,964 | 1,645 | 8 | 16 | 72 | | | 22 | 77 | 305 | 134 | 68 | 24 | 41 |
| Posey | 25,968 | 69 | 52 | | | | | | | | 21 | | | | 2 |
| Pulaski | 12,643 | 83 | 66 | 10 | | | | | | 2 | 19 | 7 | | | |
| Putnam | 30,315 | 243 | 75 | 3 | | | | | | | 32 | | 11 | 2 | |
| Randolph | 27,148 | 126 | 48 | | | | | | | | 24 | | | | |
| Ripley | 24,616 | 61 | 27 | | | | | | | | 16 | | | | |
| Rush | 18,129 | 42 | 28 | | | | | | | | 19 | | | | |
| St. Joseph | 247,052 | 7,424 | 3,494 | 199 | 355 | 29 | 13 | | | 57 | 636 | 116 | 513 | 71 | 319 |
| Scott | 20,991 | 40 | 23 | | | | | | | | 15 | | | | |
| Shelby | 40,307 | 252 | 72 | | 7 | | | | | | 25 | | | | |
| Spencer | 19,490 | 114 | 41 | | | | | | | | 15 | | 8 | 5 | 2 |
| Starke | 22,747 | 433 | 348 | | | 13 | | | | 3 | 91 | 4 | 17 | 12 | 13 |
| Steuben | 27,446 | 254 | 81 | | | | | | | | 32 | | | | |
| Sullivan | 18,993 | 22 | 21 | | | | | | | | 17 | | | | |
| Switzerland | 7,738 | 29 | 27 | | | 2 | | | | | 10 | | | | |
| Tippecanoe | 130,598 | 6,680 | 1,279 | 41 | 5 | 14 | 5 | | 71 | 53 | 278 | 88 | 30 | 24 | 47 |
| Tipton | 16,119 | 66 | 30 | | | | | | | | 5 | 7 | | 6 | |
| Union | 6,976 | 20 | 12 | | | | | | | | 9 | | | | |
| Vanderburgh | 165,058 | 1,532 | 475 | 11 | 7 | | | | | 34 | 205 | | 8 | 12 | 15 |
| Vermillion | 16,773 | 152 | 68 | | | | | | | | 2 | 3 | 2 | 3 | 29 |
| Vigo | 106,107 | 2,333 | 562 | | 7 | 7 | | | 8 | 18 | 158 | 5 | 52 | 27 | 38 |
| Wabash | 35,069 | 284 | 83 | | | | 7 | | | | 55 | | | | 6 |
| Warren | 8,176 | 31 | 9 | | | | | | | | 2 | | | | |
| Warrick | 44,920 | 361 | 104 | 8 | | 5 | | | | | 42 | | 6 | 6 | 6 |
| Washington | 23,717 | 91 | 49 | 7 | | 7 | | | | | 31 | | | | |
| Wayne | 71,951 | 450 | 233 | | | 11 | | | | 33 | 55 | | | | 27 |
| Wells | 25,948 | 80 | 62 | 7 | | | | | | | 19 | | | | 7 |
| White | 23,265 | 156 | 74 | | | | | | | | 19 | | 2 | | |
| Whitley | 27,651 | 135 | 71 | | | | | | | | 42 | | | | 5 |

TABLE 10.  FOREIGN BORN IN INDIANA BY COUNTY, 1990 (*continued*)

| COUNTY | Latvia | Lithuania | Netherlands | Norway | Poland | Portugal | Romania | Spain | Sweden | Switzerland | United Kingdom | Yugoslavia | Soviet Union |
|---|---|---|---|---|---|---|---|---|---|---|---|---|---|
| Adams | | | 6 | | | | | 3 | | 5 | 19 | | 21 |
| Allen | 6 | 127 | | | 108 | 16 | | 20 | 30 | 20 | 327 | 153 | 109 |
| Bartholomew | | | 29 | | 20 | | | | | | 187 | | 8 |
| Benton | | | | | 9 | | | | | | 4 | | |
| Blackford | | | | | | | | | | | 8 | | |
| Boone | 2 | | 10 | | 13 | | | | | | 61 | | |
| Brown | 2 | | | | 9 | | | | | | 16 | | |
| Carroll | | | 6 | | | | | | | | 19 | | |
| Cass | | | 8 | | | | | | | | 17 | 10 | |
| Clark | | 6 | | 7 | | | | 12 | | 6 | 92 | | 6 |
| Clay | | | | | | | | | | | 29 | | |
| Clinton | | | | 2 | | | | | | | 18 | | |
| Crawford | | | | | | | | | | | 4 | | |
| Daviess | | | | | | | 7 | 2 | | | 11 | | |
| Dearborn | | | | | 2 | | | 5 | | | 94 | | |
| Decatur | 7 | | | | | | | | 5 | | 30 | | |
| De Kalb | | | | | | | | 36 | 6 | | 21 | | |
| Delaware | | 15 | | 6 | 10 | | | 17 | 7 | | 113 | 15 | 11 |
| Dubois | | | | | | | | | 6 | | 2 | | |
| Elkhart | 2 | 133 | | 15 | 70 | | | 12 | 7 | 38 | 102 | 26 | 127 |
| Fayette | | | | | | | | | 4 | | 26 | | |
| Floyd | | 9 | | | | | | 2 | 8 | 10 | 60 | 12 | |
| Fountain | 11 | | | | | | | | | | 13 | | |
| Franklin | 5 | | | | | | | | | | 14 | | |
| Fulton | | | 5 | | | | | | | | 6 | | |
| Gibson | | | | | | | | | | | 2 | | |
| Grant | | | 22 | | 22 | | | | | | 24 | 15 | 10 |
| Greene | | | | | | | | | | 5 | 22 | | |
| Hamilton | 90 | | 45 | | 18 | | | 9 | 16 | | 258 | 5 | 61 |
| Hancock | 15 | | 23 | | 5 | | | 11 | | 6 | 51 | | |
| Harrison | | | | | | | | 9 | | | 47 | 6 | |
| Hendricks | 27 | | 7 | | 4 | | | 9 | 7 | | 82 | 9 | |
| Henry | | | 5 | | | | | | | | | | |
| Howard | 18 | | 5 | 9 | 15 | | | 4 | 7 | | 82 | | 25 |
| Huntington | | | | | 15 | | | | 8 | 7 | 38 | | |
| Jackson | | | 9 | | | | | | | | 10 | | |
| Jasper | | | 29 | 8 | 34 | | | | 8 | | 25 | 21 | |
| Jay | | | | | | | | | | | | | |
| Jefferson | 10 | | | 7 | | | | | | 28 | 12 | | |
| Jennings | | | | | | | | | | | 6 | | |
| Johnson | 7 | | 28 | | | | | | | 10 | 80 | 13 | |
| Knox | | 8 | | | 6 | | | | | | 17 | 8 | |
| Kosciusko | | 3 | 11 | 5 | 52 | | | | | 2 | 43 | | 22 |
| Lagrange | | 3 | 2 | | | | | | 10 | 2 | 15 | 11 | |
| Lake | 33 | 116 | 188 | 17 | 1,171 | | 139 | 122 | 54 | 8 | 633 | 2,815 | 264 |
| La Porte | | 42 | 107 | 6 | 132 | | 9 | 10 | 22 | 6 | 156 | 10 | 38 |
| Lawrence | | | | | | | 11 | | | | 26 | | |
| Madison | 7 | 5 | 6 | | 17 | | | 12 | 7 | 8 | 144 | 6 | 2 |
| Marion | 305 | 64 | 227 | 20 | 294 | 16 | 110 | 27 | 45 | 19 | 1,072 | 111 | 542 |
| Marshall | | 12 | 16 | | 7 | 7 | | | | | 36 | 14 | |
| Martin | | | | | | | | | | | 15 | | |
| Miami | | | | | 10 | | | 5 | | | 44 | | 17 |
| Monroe | 15 | | 106 | | 57 | | 30 | 46 | 13 | 29 | 227 | 25 | 73 |
| Montgomery | 5 | | | | | | | | | | 30 | | 4 |
| Morgan | 9 | | 8 | | 6 | | | 6 | | 8 | 122 | 6 | |
| Newton | | | 8 | | | | | | 3 | 4 | 14 | 20 | |
| Noble | | | | | 7 | | | 3 | | | 27 | | |
| Ohio | | | | | | | | | | | 8 | | |
| Orange | | | | | 2 | | | | | | | | 6 |
| Owen | | | | | | | | 5 | | 12 | 24 | 2 | |
| Parke | | | | | | | | 2 | | | 29 | | |
| Perry | | | | | 12 | | | | | | 6 | | |
| Pike | | | | | | | | | | | | | 3 |
| Porter | | 115 | 37 | 33 | 117 | | 18 | 24 | 41 | 12 | 356 | 123 | 24 |
| Posey | | | | | | | | 3 | | | 26 | | |
| Pulaski | | 7 | | 5 | 9 | | | | | | | 7 | |
| Putnam | | | | | | | | | | | 27 | | |
| Randolph | | | | | | | | | 15 | | 9 | | 6 |
| Ripley | | | | | 2 | | | | | | 9 | | |
| Rush | | | | | | | | | | | 7 | 2 | |
| St. Joseph | 8 | 4 | 101 | | 429 | | 38 | 44 | 31 | 30 | 410 | 76 | 84 |
| Scott | | | | | | | | | | | 8 | | |
| Shelby | | | 7 | | | | | | | | 33 | | |
| Spencer | | | | | | | | | | | 10 | 1 | |
| Starke | | 6 | 6 | | 98 | | 37 | | 8 | 6 | 21 | 13 | 18 |
| Steuben | 8 | | 5 | | | | | | | | 36 | | |
| Sullivan | | | | | | | | | | | 4 | | |
| Switzerland | | | | | | | | | | | 15 | | |
| Tippecanoe | 7 | 13 | 29 | 25 | 74 | 17 | | 14 | | 40 | 345 | 26 | 50 |
| Tipton | | | | | 8 | | | | | | 4 | | |
| Union | | | | | | | | | | | 3 | | |
| Vanderburgh | 5 | | | | 64 | | | | | 6 | 108 | | 22 |
| Vermillion | | 17 | | | | | | | | | 12 | | |
| Vigo | | | 16 | | 17 | | | | | 8 | 153 | 33 | 14 |
| Wabash | | | | | | | | | 6 | | 9 | | 5 |
| Warren | | | | | | | | | | | 7 | | |
| Warrick | | | 6 | | | 6 | | 12 | | | 7 | | 27 |
| Washington | | 8 | 3 | | | | | | | | | | |
| Wayne | | | 19 | | | | | 3 | 8 | | 85 | | 10 |
| Wells | | 2 | | | 5 | | | | | | 15 | | |
| White | | | | | | | | | | | 42 | | |
| Whitley | | | | | | | | | | 7 | 17 | | |

TABLE 10. FOREIGN BORN IN INDIANA BY COUNTY, 1990 (*continued*)

| COUNTY | Asia | Afghanistan | Burma | Cambodia | China | Hong Kong | India | Indonesia | Iran | Iraq | Israel | Japan | Jordan | Korea | Laos | Lebanon | Malaysia | Pakistan | Philippines | Saudi Arabia | Syria | Taiwan | Thailand | Turkey | Vietnam |
|---|---|---|---|---|---|---|---|---|---|---|---|---|---|---|---|---|---|---|---|---|---|---|---|---|---|
| Adams | 21 | | | | 6 | | | | | | | | | 15 | | | | | | | | | | | |
| Allen | 1,839 | | 5 | 38 | 35 | 18 | 228 | 54 | 121 | 28 | 9 | 105 | 14 | 179 | 164 | 22 | 33 | 68 | 176 | | 49 | 46 | 48 | 33 | 301 |
| Bartholomew | 394 | | | | | | 83 | 13 | | | | 222 | | 22 | | | 5 | 4 | 15 | | | | | 8 | 22 |
| Benton | 2 | | | | | | | | | | | | | | | | | | | | | | | 2 | |
| Blackford | 7 | | | | | | | | | | | | | 7 | | | | | | | | | | | |
| Boone | 49 | | | | 10 | | 2 | 10 | | | 6 | | | 2 | | | | | 19 | | | | | | |
| Brown | 18 | | | | | | | | | | | | | 18 | | | | | | | | | | | |
| Carroll | | | | | | | | | | | | | | | | | | | | | | | | | |
| Cass | 85 | | | | 13 | 7 | 2 | | | | | 17 | | 2 | | | | 5 | 24 | | | 2 | | | 13 |
| Clark | 238 | | | | 28 | 2 | 17 | | 7 | | | 21 | | 49 | | | | 37 | 31 | | | 19 | 9 | | 18 |
| Clay | 7 | | | | | | | | | | | | | 5 | | | | | 2 | | | | | | |
| Clinton | 36 | | | | | | 1 | | | | | 22 | | | | | | | 8 | | | | | 5 | |
| Crawford | 6 | | | | | | | | | | | 6 | | | | | | | | | | | | | |
| Daviess | 3 | | | | | | | | | | | | | 3 | | | | | | | | | | | |
| Dearborn | 46 | | | | | | 9 | | | | | 15 | | 5 | | | | | 7 | | | 2 | | | |
| Decatur | 113 | | | | | | | | | | | 77 | | 12 | | | | | 24 | | | | | | |
| De Kalb | 42 | | | 11 | | | 2 | | | | | | | 8 | | | | | 5 | | | | | | 16 |
| Delaware | 582 | | | | 65 | 15 | 180 | 9 | 24 | | | 39 | 7 | 71 | 11 | 13 | 51 | 9 | 18 | | 5 | 29 | 18 | | 7 |
| Dubois | 47 | | | | | | 32 | | | | | 6 | | | | | | | | | | 2 | | | |
| Elkhart | 728 | | | 41 | 67 | 5 | 91 | 40 | | | 6 | 17 | | 124 | 186 | | | 11 | 32 | | 15 | 27 | 17 | 8 | 41 |
| Fayette | 60 | | | | | | 49 | | | | | | | 6 | | | | | 5 | | | | | | |
| Floyd | 249 | | | | | | | 8 | 12 | | 32 | 65 | | 17 | 7 | | | | 69 | | | 8 | 9 | | 17 |
| Fountain | 1 | | | | | | 1 | | | | | | | | | | | | | | | | | | |
| Franklin | 11 | | | | | | | | | | | | | | | | | | | | | | | | 11 |
| Fulton | 11 | | | | | | | | | | | 11 | | | | | | | | | | | | | |
| Gibson | 54 | | | | | | | 7 | | | | 39 | | 8 | | | | | | | | | | | |
| Grant | 218 | | | | 21 | | 50 | | | | 10 | 29 | | 8 | 5 | | | 2 | 55 | | | | | | 27 |
| Greene | 19 | | | | | | 5 | | | | | 3 | | | | | | | | | 4 | 7 | | | |
| Hamilton | 1,031 | | | | 53 | 33 | 226 | 21 | 82 | | 11 | 206 | 7 | 46 | 33 | | 35 | 47 | 44 | | 6 | 89 | 16 | | 40 |
| Hancock | 160 | | | | | | | 6 | | | | 9 | | 88 | 44 | | | | 6 | | | | | | 7 |
| Harrison | 60 | | | | | | 7 | | | | | 31 | | 12 | | | | 10 | | | | | | | |
| Hendricks | 96 | | | | | | 29 | 8 | | | | 25 | | 7 | | | 11 | | 13 | | | 3 | | | |
| Henry | 28 | | | | 6 | | | | | | | 7 | | 9 | | | | | | | | | | | 6 |
| Howard | 325 | | | | 18 | 30 | 75 | 9 | 7 | | | 30 | 11 | 31 | | | 16 | | 31 | | | 17 | 17 | 12 | 13 |
| Huntington | 76 | | | | | 1 | 40 | | | 6 | | | | 6 | 9 | | | | 7 | | | | | | |
| Jackson | 98 | | | | | | | | | | 8 | 70 | | | | | | | | | | | | | 20 |
| Jasper | 24 | | | | | | 12 | | | | | | | 12 | | | | | | | | | | | |
| Jay | 30 | | | | | | 8 | | | | | 21 | | | | | | | 1 | | | | | | |
| Jefferson | 91 | | | | | | 22 | | | | 7 | 48 | | | | | | | 7 | | | | | | |
| Jennings | 39 | | | | | | 3 | 6 | | | | 10 | | | | | 6 | | | | | | | | 14 |
| Johnson | 520 | | | 15 | 28 | 6 | | 5 | 27 | | 25 | 218 | | 90 | 7 | | 12 | 13 | 42 | | | 10 | | 5 | 7 |
| Knox | 94 | | | | | | | 14 | 6 | | | 35 | | 25 | | | | 8 | 6 | | | | | | |
| Kosciusko | 207 | | | | 55 | 11 | 12 | | | | | 11 | | 27 | 7 | | | | 46 | | | | | 4 | 26 |
| Lagrange | 62 | | | | 8 | 27 | | | | | | 5 | | | | | | | | | | | | | 22 |
| Lake | 1,756 | | 28 | | 45 | 11 | 556 | 8 | 42 | 13 | 58 | 77 | 22 | 246 | 42 | 13 | | 68 | 236 | 9 | 12 | 53 | 66 | | 45 |
| La Porte | 304 | | 6 | 12 | 9 | 6 | 65 | | | | 2 | 4 | | 17 | 8 | | 34 | 5 | 76 | | | 9 | | | 43 |
| Lawrence | 44 | | | | | | | | | | | 15 | | 7 | | | | | 22 | | | | | | |
| Madison | 245 | 7 | | | 14 | 2 | 50 | 6 | | | | 31 | | 26 | | | 39 | | 33 | | | | | | 37 |
| Marion | 5,601 | 18 | 8 | 44 | 504 | 162 | 993 | 47 | 216 | | 34 | 519 | 32 | 821 | | 35 | 45 | 348 | 780 | 118 | 72 | 145 | 74 | 29 | 401 |
| Marshall | 47 | | | | | | 2 | | | | | 9 | | 6 | | | | | 23 | | | 2 | 5 | | |
| Martin | 14 | | | | | | | | | | | 9 | | | | | | | | | | | | | |
| Miami | 137 | | | | 28 | | 2 | | | | | 32 | | 29 | | | | | 25 | | | | 15 | | |
| Monroe | 2,430 | 17 | | 14 | 256 | 124 | 213 | 155 | 114 | | 44 | 267 | 22 | 445 | | 58 | 53 | 47 | 82 | 96 | 8 | 194 | 39 | 60 | 45 |
| Montgomery | 97 | | | | | | 25 | | | | | 22 | | 13 | | | 12 | | 7 | | | 7 | | | 4 |
| Morgan | 69 | | | | 6 | | 7 | 19 | | | | 7 | | 5 | | | | | 18 | | | | | | |
| Newton | 8 | | | | | | | | | | | | | | | | | 2 | 6 | | | | | | |
| Noble | 52 | | | | | | | 13 | | | | | | 11 | | | | | 12 | | | | | 4 | 12 |
| Ohio | | | | | | | | | | | | | | | | | | | | | | | | | |
| Orange | 26 | | | | | | 11 | | | | | | | 2 | | | | | 11 | | | 2 | | | |
| Owen | 27 | | | | | | 6 | | | | | 10 | | 11 | | | | | | | | | | | |
| Parke | 2 | | | | | | | | | | | | | 2 | | | | | | | | | | | |
| Perry | 7 | | | | | | | | | | | 2 | | | | | | | | | | | | 5 | |
| Pike | 14 | | | | | | | | | | | | | 6 | | | | | 8 | | | | | | |
| Porter | 623 | | | | 78 | 12 | 170 | | 19 | | 17 | 37 | 11 | 46 | | | 12 | 3 | 80 | | 8 | 6 | | | 69 |
| Posey | 10 | | | | | | | | | | | | | 2 | | | | | | | | | | | |
| Pulaski | 2 | | | | | | | | | | | | | | | | 2 | | | | | | | | |
| Putnam | 79 | | | | 17 | | | | 9 | | | 37 | | 5 | | | 5 | | 4 | | | | | | 2 |
| Randolph | 24 | | | | 5 | | | | | | | 4 | | | | | | 3 | 8 | | | 4 | | | |
| Ripley | 10 | | | | 2 | | | | | | | 2 | | | | | | | | | | 6 | | | |
| Rush | 13 | | | | | | 6 | | | | | | | 7 | | | | | | | | | | | |
| St. Joseph | 1,744 | | | 89 | 297 | 26 | 395 | 27 | 23 | 8 | 34 | 136 | 7 | 186 | 16 | 17 | 11 | 23 | 164 | | 11 | 30 | 37 | 34 | 75 |
| Scott | | | | | | | | | | | | | | | | | | | | | | | | | |
| Shelby | 85 | | | | | | 9 | | | | 8 | 52 | | 9 | | | | | | | | | | | |
| Spencer | 47 | | | | | | | | | 7 | 7 | 24 | | | | | | | 9 | | | | | | |
| Starke | 20 | | | | | | 13 | | | | | 7 | | | | | | | | | | | | | |
| Steuben | 113 | | | | | | 17 | | | | | 5 | | | | | 9 | | | | | 9 | 9 | 10 | |
| Sullivan | 1 | | | | | | | | | | | | | 1 | | | | | | | | | | | |
| Switzerland | | | | | | | | | | | | | | | | | | | | | | | | | |
| Tippecanoe | 4,171 | 56 | | 6 | 592 | 86 | 583 | 37 | 121 | | 65 | 546 | 6 | 452 | 18 | 37 | 46 | 42 | 92 | 36 | 7 | 735 | 45 | 50 | 253 |
| Tipton | 17 | | | | | | 7 | | | | | 10 | | | | | | | | | | | | | |
| Union | 8 | | | 4 | | | 2 | | | | | | | | | | | | 2 | | | | | | |
| Vanderburgh | 719 | 7 | 7 | | 96 | 8 | 44 | | 29 | | | 47 | 14 | 35 | | | 6 | 111 | 42 | | | 113 | 35 | 10 | 98 |
| Vermillion | 9 | | | | | | | | | | | 5 | | 4 | | | | | | | | | | | |
| Vigo | 1,021 | | 48 | | 85 | 12 | 155 | 24 | 18 | | | 143 | | 68 | | | 122 | | 73 | 32 | 79 | 61 | 15 | 13 | 26 |
| Wabash | 113 | | | | 13 | 7 | | | | | | | | | 76 | | | | 5 | | | | | | 6 |
| Warren | 8 | | | | | | | | | | | | | | | | | | 2 | | | | | 6 | |
| Warrick | 140 | | | | | | 37 | | 9 | | 5 | 12 | | 7 | | | | 7 | 58 | | | | | | |
| Washington | 15 | | | | | | | | | | | | | 6 | | | | | 9 | | | | | | |
| Wayne | 86 | | | | | | 14 | | | | | | | 21 | 5 | | | | 19 | | | | | 13 | 14 |
| Wells | 2 | | | | | | | | | | | | | 2 | | | | | | | | | | | |
| White | 58 | | | | | | 8 | 20 | | | | 7 | | 14 | | | | | 9 | | | | | | |
| Whitley | | | | | | | | | | | | | | | | | | | | | | | | | |

TABLE 10.  FOREIGN BORN IN INDIANA BY COUNTY, 1990 (*continued*)

| COUNTY | North America | Canada | Mexico | Caribbean | Bahamas | Barbados | Cuba | Dominican Republic | Grenada | Haiti | Jamaica | Trinidad/Tobago | Central America | Belize | Costa Rica | El Salvador | Guatemala | Honduras | Nicaragua | Panama |
|---|---|---|---|---|---|---|---|---|---|---|---|---|---|---|---|---|---|---|---|---|
| Adams | 83 | 19 | 57 | | | | | | | | | | 7 | | | | | 7 | | |
| Allen | 1,286 | 426 | 503 | 221 | 6 | 32 | 123 | | | | 42 | 18 | 136 | | 14 | | 35 | 18 | | 69 |
| Bartholomew | 65 | 41 | 19 | | | | | | | | | | 5 | | | 5 | | | | |
| Benton | 9 | 5 | 4 | | | | | | | | | | | | | | | | | |
| Blackford | 18 | 13 | 5 | | | | | | | | | | | | | | | | | |
| Boone | 53 | 29 | 21 | 3 | | | 3 | | | | | | | | | | | | | |
| Brown | 2 | 2 | | | | | | | | | | | | | | | | | | |
| Carroll | 15 | 13 | 2 | | | | | | | | | | | | | | | | | |
| Cass | 25 | | 16 | 2 | | | 2 | | | | | | | | | | | | | 7 |
| Clark | 109 | 82 | 7 | 20 | | | | | | | 7 | 13 | | | | | | | | |
| Clay | 17 | 10 | 7 | | | | | | | | | | 7 | | | | | | | |
| Clinton | 48 | 19 | 29 | | | | | | | | | | | | | | | | | |
| Crawford | 2 | 2 | | | | | | | | | | | | | | | | | | |
| Daviess | 12 | 12 | | | | | | | | | | | | | | | | | | |
| Dearborn | 10 | 10 | | | | | | | | | | | | | | | | | | |
| Decatur | 25 | 8 | 1 | 16 | | | | | | 16 | | | | | | | | | | |
| De Kalb | 57 | 57 | | | | | | | | | | | | | | | | | | |
| Delaware | 129 | 85 | 17 | | | | | | | | | | 27 | | | | | 11 | 16 | |
| Dubois | 83 | 12 | 71 | | | | | | | | | | | | | | | | | |
| Elkhart | 1,349 | 459 | 717 | 70 | | | 6 | | | 14 | 42 | 8 | 103 | | | | 47 | 40 | 9 | 7 |
| Fayette | | | | | | | | | | | | | | | | | | | | |
| Floyd | 101 | 40 | | | | | | | | | 7 | | | | | | | | | |
| Fountain | 7 | | | | | | | | | | | | | | | | | | | |
| Franklin | 20 | 14 | | | | | | | | | | | | | | | | | | |
| Fulton | 43 | 3 | | | | | | | | | | | 2 | | | | 2 | | | |
| Gibson | 8 | 8 | | | | | | | | | | | | | | | | | | |
| Grant | 135 | 39 | | | | | | | | | | | 11 | | | 5 | | 6 | | |
| Greene | 12 | | | | | | | | | | | | 7 | | 5 | | | | | 2 |
| Hamilton | 194 | 136 | | | | | | 8 | | | | | 18 | | | | | | | 18 |
| Hancock | 76 | 25 | | | | | | | | | | | 3 | | | 3 | | | | |
| Harrison | 11 | 11 | | | | | | | | | | | | | | | | | | |
| Hendricks | 62 | 47 | 2 | 13 | | | 7 | | | | 6 | | | | | | | | | 5 |
| Henry | 51 | 38 | | 10 | | | 10 | | | | | | 3 | | 3 | | | | | 8 |
| Howard | 203 | 119 | 32 | 47 | | | 31 | 10 | | | 6 | | 5 | | | 5 | | | | 10 |
| Huntington | 48 | 20 | 22 | | | | | | | | | | 6 | | | | | 6 | | 17 |
| Jackson | 55 | 19 | 22 | 8 | | | 8 | | | | | | 6 | | | | | | 6 | |
| Jasper | 27 | 13 | 14 | | | | | | | | | | | | | | | | | |
| Jay | 11 | | 11 | | | | | | | | | | | | | | | | | |
| Jefferson | 41 | 21 | | 15 | | | 15 | | | | | | | | | | | | | 15 |
| Jennings | | | | | | | | | | | | | | | | | | | | 4 |
| Johnson | 152 | 86 | 40 | 21 | | | 21 | | | | | | 5 | | | | | | | 5 |
| Knox | 22 | 22 | | | | | | | | | | | | | | | | | | |
| Kosciusko | 236 | 90 | 118 | 11 | | | | | | | 6 | | 17 | | 7 | 3 | | | | 7 |
| Lagrange | 114 | 17 | 91 | | | | | | | | | | 6 | | | | | | | 6 |
| Lake | 6,756 | 640 | 5,568 | 361 | 12 | | 130 | 36 | | 51 | 81 | 41 | 175 | 14 | 6 | 6 | | 83 | 11 | 50 |
| La Porte | 332 | 138 | 160 | 22 | | | 16 | | | | | 6 | 12 | | | | 12 | | | |
| Lawrence | 35 | 35 | | | | | | | | | | | | | | | | | | |
| Madison | 150 | 65 | 25 | 60 | | 11 | 11 | | | | 38 | | | | | | | | | |
| Marion | 2,676 | 893 | 728 | 734 | 29 | 17 | 172 | 12 | | 7 | 303 | 136 | 275 | 15 | 20 | 29 | 23 | 14 | 59 | 105 |
| Marshall | 207 | 26 | 171 | | | | | | | | | | 10 | | | | | 5 | | 5 |
| Martin | 5 | | 5 | | | | | | | | | | | | | | | | | |
| Miami | 51 | 7 | 31 | 13 | | | | | | | | | | | | | | | | |
| Monroe | 431 | 291 | 27 | 8 | | | 8 | | | | 6 | 7 | | | | | | | | |
| Montgomery | 19 | 10 | 9 | | | | | | | | | | 105 | | 27 | 13 | 18 | | 11 | 36 |
| Morgan | 45 | 15 | 21 | | | | | | | | | | | | | | | | | |
| Newton | 48 | 30 | 18 | | | | | | | | | | 9 | | | | | | | 9 |
| Noble | 147 | 9 | 138 | | | | | | | | | | | | | | | | | |
| Ohio | | | | | | | | | | | | | | | | | | | | |
| Orange | 29 | 23 | | 6 | | | | | | | 6 | | | | | | | | | |
| Owen | | | | | | | | | | | | | | | | | | | | |
| Parke | 18 | 3 | 3 | 7 | | | | | | | 7 | | 5 | | | | 5 | | | |
| Perry | 1 | 1 | | | | | | | | | | | | | | | | | | |
| Pike | 11 | | | | | | | | | | | | 11 | | | | 11 | | | |
| Porter | 371 | 169 | 185 | 17 | | | | | | | | 17 | | | | | | | | |
| Posey | | | | | | | | | | | | | | | | | | | | |
| Pulaski | 13 | 2 | 3 | 8 | | | 8 | | | | | | | | | | | | | |
| Putnam | 28 | 20 | 1 | 5 | | | | | | | | | 2 | | | 2 | | | | |
| Randolph | 48 | 8 | 35 | 5 | | | | | | | 5 | | | | | | | | | |
| Ripley | 24 | 14 | 10 | | | | | | | | | | | | | | | | | |
| Rush | 1 | | | | | | | | | | | | 1 | | | | | | | 1 |
| St. Joseph | 1,449 | 595 | 727 | 75 | | | 23 | 34 | | | 13 | | 52 | | 4 | 4 | | 13 | | 31 |
| Scott | 17 | 5 | 12 | | | | | | | | | | | | | | | | | |
| Shelby | 68 | 68 | | | | | | | | | | | | | | | | | | |
| Spencer | 18 | 9 | | 9 | 9 | | | | | | | | | | | | | | | |
| Starke | 44 | 15 | 24 | | | | | | | | | | 5 | | | | | | | 5 |
| Steuben | 44 | 37 | 7 | | | | | | | | | | | | | | | | | |
| Sullivan | | | | | | | | | | | | | | | | | | | | |
| Switzerland | | | | | | | | | | | | | | | | | | | | |
| Tippecanoe | 526 | 139 | 268 | 44 | | | 6 | 21 | | | 10 | | 75 | 8 | 18 | 15 | 7 | | 9 | 18 |
| Tipton | 13 | 13 | | | | | | | | | | | | | | | | | | |
| Union | | | | | | | | | | | | | | | | | | | | |
| Vanderburgh | 144 | 65 | 11 | 55 | | | 25 | 13 | | | 5 | 7 | 13 | 6 | 7 | | | | | |
| Vermillion | 7 | 7 | | | | | | | | | | | | | | | | | | |
| Vigo | 358 | 151 | 50 | 136 | | | 90 | 14 | | | 23 | 9 | 21 | | | | 7 | | | 14 |
| Wabash | 45 | 13 | 12 | 13 | | | 13 | | | | | | 7 | | | 7 | | | | |
| Warren | 7 | | 7 | | | | | | | | | | | | | | | | | |
| Warrick | 74 | 57 | 6 | 11 | | | 11 | | | | | | | | | | | | | |
| Washington | 20 | 10 | 2 | | | | | | | | | | 8 | 8 | | | | | | |
| Wayne | 66 | 36 | 20 | 5 | | | | | | | 5 | | 5 | | | 5 | | | | |
| Wells | 16 | 6 | 10 | | | | | | | | | | | | | | | | | |
| White | 18 | 7 | 1 | | | | | | | | | | 10 | | | | | | | 10 |
| Whitley | 13 | 11 | 2 | | | | | | | | | | | | | | | | | |

## TABLE 10. FOREIGN BORN IN INDIANA BY COUNTY, 1990

| COUNTY | South America | Argentina | Bolivia | Brazil | Chile | Colombia | Ecuador | Guyana | Peru | Uraguay | Venezuela | Africa | Cape Verde | Egypt | Ethiopia | Ghana | Morocco | Nigeria | South Africa | Oceania | Autralia | New Zealand | Not Reported |
|---|---|---|---|---|---|---|---|---|---|---|---|---|---|---|---|---|---|---|---|---|---|---|---|
| Adams | 9 | | | | | | | | | | | | | | | | | | | | | | 4 |
| Allen | 158 | 6 | | 58 | | 26 | 49 | | 9 | | 10 | 187 | 32 | 42 | | | | | 24 | 76 | 69 | 7 | 142 |
| Bartholomew | 42 | | 2 | | | | | 33 | | | 7 | 20 | 3 | | | | | | 6 | 10 | 6 | 2 | 79 |
| Benton | 2 | | | 2 | | | | | | | | | | | | | | | | | | | 4 |
| Blackford | | | | | | | | | | | | | | | | | | | | | | | 6 |
| Boone | 1 | | | | | 1 | | | | | | 2 | | | | | | | | 12 | 12 | | 2 |
| Brown | | | | | | | | | | | | | | | | | | | | | | | |
| Carrol | | | | | | | | | | | | | | | | | | | | | | | |
| Cass | | | | | | | | | | | | | | | | | | | | | | | 11 |
| Clark | 12 | | | 12 | | | | | | | | 5 | | | | | 5 | | | 36 | | | 38 |
| Clay | 10 | | | | | 10 | | | | | | | | | | | | | | | | | 5 |
| Clinton | | | | | | | | | | | | | | | | | | | | 5 | 5 | | 6 |
| Crawford | | | | | | | | | | | | | | | | | | | | | | | |
| Daviess | | | | | | | | | | | | | | | | | | | | 13 | | 6 | 2 |
| Dearborn | | | | | | | | | | | | | | | | | | | | 12 | 12 | | 8 |
| Decatur | 7 | | | 7 | | | | | 7 | | | | | | | | | | | | | | |
| De Kalb | 7 | | | | | | | | | | | 22 | | | | | | | | 7 | 7 | | 3 |
| Delaware | 60 | 44 | | | | | | | | | 8 | 96 | | 5 | | | | 20 | 8 | 5 | | | 72 |
| Dubois | 5 | | | | | | 5 | | | | | | | | | | | | | 5 | 5 | | 3 |
| Elkhart | 54 | | | 7 | 3 | | 8 | | | | 19 | 24 | | 8 | | | | 7 | | 56 | 50 | 6 | 39 |
| Fayette | 9 | | | | | | 9 | | | | | 7 | | | | | | | | | | | 9 |
| Floyd | 11 | | | 2 | 9 | | | | | | | 17 | | | | | | | 10 | 9 | 2 | | 9 |
| Fountain | 6 | | | | | | | 6 | | | | | | 7 | | | | | | | | | 6 |
| Franklin | | | | | | | | | | | | | | | | | | | | | | | |
| Fulton | | | | | | | | | | | | | | | | | | | | | | | |
| Gibson | | | | | | | | | | | | | | | | | | | | 7 | | 7 | |
| Grant | 7 | | | 2 | | | | | | | 5 | 6 | | | | | | | | | | | 8 |
| Greene | | | | | | | | | | | | 11 | | | | 5 | | | | | | | 8 |
| Hamilton | 37 | | | 16 | | 15 | | | 6 | | | 44 | | | | | | | 7 | | | | 28 |
| Hancock | 13 | | | | | | 13 | | | | | | | | | | | | | 9 | | 9 | 4 |
| Harrison | | | | | | | | | | | | | | | | | | | | | | | 8 |
| Hendricks | | | | | | | | | | | | 15 | | 7 | | | | | | 7 | 7 | | |
| Henry | | | | | | | 8 | | | | | | | | | | | | | 7 | 7 | | 22 |
| Howard | | 10 | | | | | | | | | | 5 | | 5 | | | | | | 6 | | 6 | 6 |
| Huntington | | | 10 | 7 | | | | | | | | 18 | | | | | | | | 5 | 5 | | 2 |
| Jackson | | | | | | | | | | | | 34 | | | | | | | | | | | 17 |
| Jasper | | | | | | | | | | | | | | | | | | | | | | | 6 |
| Jay | | | | | | | | | | | | | | | | | | | | | | | |
| Jefferson | | | | 15 | | | | | | | | | | | | | | | | 18 | 11 | 7 | 19 |
| Jennings | | | 4 | | | | | | | | | | | | | | | | | | | | |
| Johnson | 42 | | | 10 | | 7 | | | 17 | | 8 | | | | | | | | | | | | 50 |
| Knox | | | | | | | | | | | | 51 | | | | | | 33 | | | | | 40 |
| Kosciusko | 19 | | 5 | 7 | | 7 | | | | | | 30 | | | | 17 | | 7 | | 10 | | | 51 |
| Lagrange | | | | | | | | | | | | 3 | | | | | | | 3 | | | | |
| Lake | 235 | 38 | 19 | 52 | 17 | 32 | 10 | | 60 | | 7 | 188 | | 69 | | | 11 | 85 | | 37 | 14 | 19 | 614 |
| La Porte | 17 | | | 2 | 5 | | | 8 | | | 2 | 2 | | | | | | 2 | | 11 | | 2 | 142 |
| Lawrence | | | | | | | | | | | | | | | | | | | | 9 | 9 | | 5 |
| Madison | 42 | | | 26 | 11 | | | | | | | 29 | | 8 | | | | 6 | 7 | 9 | 9 | | 54 |
| Marion | 449 | 38 | 8 | 61 | 36 | 98 | 29 | 39 | 81 | | 44 | 599 | | 112 | 89 | 29 | 18 | 98 | 14 | 31 | 25 | 6 | 297 |
| Marshall | | | | | | | | | | | | | | | | | | | | 6 | 6 | | 26 |
| Martin | | | | | | | | | | | | | | | | | | | | | | | |
| Miami | 5 | | | | | | | | 5 | | | | | | | | | | | | | | 23 |
| Monroe | 75 | 9 | | 8 | 24 | | 14 | | 9 | | 11 | 195 | | 24 | | 10 | 9 | 38 | 27 | 47 | 47 | | 347 |
| Montgomery | 16 | | | 16 | | | | | | | | 9 | | | | | | | | | | | 8 |
| Morgan | 6 | 6 | | | | | | | | | | 9 | | | | | | | 7 | 10 | 10 | | 10 |
| Newton | 14 | | | 12 | | | | | | | 2 | 4 | | | | | | | | | | | 8 |
| Noble | 7 | | | 7 | | | | | | | | | | | | | | | | 8 | 8 | | 52 |
| Ohio | | | | | | | | | | | | | | | | | | | | | | | |
| Orange | 2 | | 2 | | | | | | | | | | | | | | | | | 5 | 5 | | |
| Owen | 6 | | | | | 6 | | | | | | | | | | | | | | | | | |
| Parke | | | | | | | | | | | | | | | | | | | | | | | 12 |
| Perry | | | | | | | | | | | | | | | | | | | | | | | 10 |
| Pike | | | | | | | | | | | | | | | | | | | | 2 | | 2 | |
| Porter | 56 | 22 | | 5 | 8 | | | | | | | 43 | | 35 | | | | 8 | | 28 | 22 | | 174 |
| Posey | | | | | | | | | | | | 7 | | | | | 7 | | | | | | |
| Pulaski | | | | | | | | | | | | | | | | | | | | 2 | 2 | | |
| Putnam | 28 | 10 | | 7 | | | | | 11 | | | 15 | | | | | | | | 18 | 8 | 10 | |
| Randolph | | | | | | | | | | | | | | | | | | | | | | | |
| Ripley | | | | | | | | | | | | | | | | | | | | | | | |
| Rush | | | | | | | | | | | | | | | | | | | | | | | |
| St. Joseph | 326 | 12 | 17 | 30 | 101 | 21 | 46 | 43 | 3 | 14 | 24 | 191 | | 14 | 20 | 5 | | 103 | 8 | 25 | 23 | 2 | 111 |
| Scott | | | | | | | | | | | | | | | | | | | | | | | |
| Shelby | 21 | | 7 | 8 | | 6 | | | | | | | | | | | | | | | | | 6 |
| Spencer | | | | | | | | | | | | | | | | | | | | | | | 8 |
| Starke | 3 | | | | | 3 | | | | | | | | | | | | | | | | | |
| Steuben | 2 | | | 2 | | | | | | | | | | | | | | | | | | | 14 |
| Sullivan | | | | | | | | | | | | | | | | | | | | | | | |
| Switzerland | | | | | | | | | | | | 2 | | | 2 | | | | | | | | |
| Tippecanoe | 259 | 114 | 34 | 80 | | 19 | | | 7 | 5 | | 209 | | 13 | 10 | 31 | 10 | 21 | 8 | 54 | 27 | 13 | 132 |
| Tipton | 2 | 2 | | | | | | | | | | | | | | | | | | | | | 4 |
| Union | | | | | | | | | | | | | | | | | | | | | | | |
| Vanderburgh | 37 | 7 | 10 | | | 7 | | | 7 | 6 | | 81 | | 31 | 17 | | | 5 | | 14 | 4 | 10 | 40 |
| Vermillion | 6 | | | | | | 6 | | | | | 5 | | | | | | | | | | | 57 |
| Vigo | 77 | 8 | | 13 | | 56 | | | | | | 124 | | 13 | | 19 | | 25 | 23 | 23 | 14 | 9 | 154 |
| Wabash | | | | | | | | | | | | 7 | | | | | | | | 9 | | 9 | 22 |
| Warren | | | | | | | | | | | | | | | | | | | | 3 | 3 | | 4 |
| Warrick | 8 | | | | | 8 | | | | | | | | | | | | | | | | | 8 |
| Washington | | | | | | | | | | | | | | | | | | | | | | | 7 |
| Wayne | 38 | | | 14 | | 17 | | | 7 | | | 11 | | | | | | 11 | | | | | 6 |
| Wells | | | | | | | | | | | | | | | | | | | | | | | |
| White | | | | | | | | | | | | | | | | | | | | | | | 6 |
| Whitley | 12 | | | 12 | | | | | | | | | | | | | | | | 2 | | 2 | 37 |

## TABLE 11.  SELF-IDENTIFICATION GROUPS FOR INDIANA, 1990

| Ancestry Group Total Population | United States 248,709,873 | Percent 100.00 | Indiana 5,544,159 | Percent 100.00 |
|---|---|---|---|---|
| **European** | | | | |
| *(excluding Hispanic Groups)* | | | | |
| Alsatian | 16,465 | 0.00 | 286 | 0.00 |
| Austrian | 870,631 | 0.40 | 8,358 | 0.20 |
| Basque | 47,956 | 0.00 | 190 | 0.00 |
| Belgian | 394,655 | 0.20 | 14,942 | 0.30 |
| British | 1,119,154 | 0.40 | 24,749 | 0.40 |
| Cypriot | 4,897 | 0.00 | 68 | 0.00 |
| Celtic | 29,652 | 0.00 | 470 | 0.00 |
| Danish | 1,634,669 | 0.70 | 14,918 | 0.30 |
| Dutch | 6,227,089 | 2.50 | 196,589 | 3.60 |
| English | 32,655,779 | 13.10 | 767,098 | 13.80 |
| Finnish | 658,870 | 0.30 | 4,470 | 0.10 |
| French | 10,320,935 | 4.10 | 209,181 | 3.80 |
| German | 57,985,595 | 23.30 | 2,085,487 | 37.60 |
| Greek | 1,110,373 | 0.40 | 18,978 | 0.30 |
| Icelander | 40,529 | 0.00 | 224 | 0.00 |
| Irish | 38,739,548 | 15.60 | 965,132 | 17.40 |
| Italian | 14,714,939 | 5.90 | 125,297 | 2.30 |
| Luxembourger | 49,061 | 0.00 | 685 | 0.00 |
| Maltese | 39,600 | 0.00 | 121 | 0.00 |
| Manx | 6,317 | 0.00 | 78 | 0.00 |
| Norwegian | 3,869,395 | 1.60 | 25,978 | 0.50 |
| Portuguese | 1,153,351 | 0.50 | 2,476 | 0.00 |
| Scandinavian | 678,880 | 0.30 | 6,528 | 0.10 |
| Scotch-Irish | 5,617,773 | 2.30 | 113,568 | 2.00 |
| Scottish | 5,393,581 | 2.20 | 111,535 | 2.00 |
| Swedish | 4,680,863 | 1.90 | 69,619 | 1.30 |
| Swiss | 1,045,495 | 0.40 | 44,511 | 0.80 |
| Welsh | 2,033,893 | 0.80 | 42,004 | 0.80 |
| Albanian | 47,710 | 0.00 | 255 | 0.00 |
| Bulgarian | 29,595 | 0.00 | 944 | 0.00 |
| Carpath Russian | 7,602 | 0.00 | 78 | 0.00 |
| Croatian | 544,270 | 0.20 | 18,633 | 0.30 |
| Czech | 1,300,192 | 0.50 | 11,603 | 0.20 |
| Czechoslovakian | 315,285 | 0.10 | 3,458 | 0.10 |
| Estonian | 26,762 | 0.00 | 315 | 0.00 |
| European | 466,718 | 0.20 | 7,263 | 0.10 |
| German Russian | 10,153 | 0.00 | 167 | 0.00 |
| Hungarian | 1,582,302 | 0.60 | 40,828 | 0.70 |
| Latvian | 100,331 | 0.00 | 1,622 | 0.00 |
| Lithuanian | 811,865 | 0.30 | 11,098 | 0.20 |
| Macedonian | 20,365 | 0.00 | 3,210 | 0.10 |
| Polish | 9,366,106 | 3.80 | 179,501 | 3.20 |
| Rom | 5,693 | 0.00 | 147 | 0.00 |
| Romanian | 365,544 | 0.10 | 7,725 | 0.10 |
| Russian | 2,952,987 | 1.20 | 18,288 | 0.30 |
| Serbian | 116,795 | 0.00 | 8,418 | 0.20 |
| Slavic | 76,931 | 0.00 | 1,252 | 0.00 |
| Slovak | 1,882,897 | 0.80 | 44,412 | 0.80 |
| Slovene | 124,437 | 0.10 | 1,495 | 0.00 |
| Soviet Union | 7,729 | 0.00 | 91 | 0.00 |
| Ukrainian | 740,803 | 0.30 | 6,379 | 0.10 |
| Yugoslavian | 257,994 | 0.10 | 4,214 | 0.10 |
| Other European | 259,585 | 0.10 | 2,537 | 0.00 |
| **West Indian** | | | | |
| *(excluding Hispanic Groups)* | | | | |
| Bahamian | 21,081 | 0.00 | 64 | 0.00 |
| Barbadian | 35,455 | 0.00 | 62 | 0.00 |
| Belizean | 22,922 | 0.00 | 129 | 0.00 |
| Bermudan | 4,941 | 0.00 | 22 | 0.00 |
| British West Indies | 37,819 | 0.00 | 11 | 0.00 |
| Dutch West Indies | 61,530 | 0.00 | 256 | 0.00 |
| Haitian | 289,521 | 0.10 | 316 | 0.00 |
| Jamaican | 435,024 | 0.20 | 1,368 | 0.00 |
| Trinidad/Tobagoan | 76,270 | 0.00 | 157 | 0.00 |
| US Virgin Islander | 7,621 | 0.00 | 63 | 0.00 |
| West Indian | 159,167 | 0.10 | 494 | 0.00 |
| Other West Indian | 4,139 | 0.00 | 17 | 0.00 |
| **Central and South America** | | | | |
| *(excluding Hispanic Groups)* | | | | |
| Brazilian | 65,875 | 0.00 | 419 | 0.00 |
| Guyanese | 81,665 | 0.00 | 81 | 0.00 |
| Other Cen. & S. America | 1,217 | 0.00 | 0 | 0.00 |
| **North Africa and Southwest Asia** | | | | |
| Algerian | 3,215 | 0.00 | 10 | 0.00 |
| Arab | 127,364 | 0.10 | 1,513 | 0.00 |
| Armenian | 308,096 | 0.10 | 1,052 | 0.00 |
| Assyrian | 51,765 | 0.00 | 398 | 0.00 |
| Egyptian | 78,574 | 0.00 | 571 | 0.00 |
| Iranian | 235,521 | 0.10 | 1,230 | 0.00 |
| Iraqi | 23,212 | 0.00 | 47 | 0.00 |
| Isreali | 81,677 | 0.00 | 521 | 0.00 |
| Jordanian | 20,656 | 0.00 | 170 | 0.00 |
| Lebanese | 394,180 | 0.20 | 3,610 | 0.10 |
| Middle Eastern | 7,656 | 0.00 | 23 | 0.00 |
| Moroccan | 19,089 | 0.00 | 138 | 0.00 |
| Palestinian | 48,019 | 0.00 | 471 | 0.00 |
| Saudi Arabian | 4,486 | 0.00 | 49 | 0.00 |
| Syrian | 129,606 | 0.10 | 1,773 | 0.00 |
| Turkish | 83,850 | 0.00 | 742 | 0.00 |
| Yemeni | 4,011 | 0.00 | 0 | 0.00 |
| Other N. African/ SW Asian | 10,670 | 0.00 | 117 | 0.00 |
| **Subsaharan Africa** | | | | |
| African | 245,845 | 0.10 | 3,108 | 0.10 |
| Cape Verdean | 50,772 | 0.00 | 53 | 0.00 |
| Ethiopian | 34,851 | 0.00 | 196 | 0.00 |
| Ghanian | 20,066 | 0.00 | 111 | 0.00 |
| Kenyan | 4,639 | 0.00 | 12 | 0.00 |
| Liberian | 8,797 | 0.00 | 39 | 0.00 |
| Nigerian | 91,688 | 0.00 | 720 | 0.00 |
| Sierra Leon | 4,627 | 0.00 | 19 | 0.00 |
| South African | 17,992 | 0.00 | 109 | 0.00 |
| Sudanese | 3,623 | 0.00 | 9 | 0.00 |
| Ugandan | 2,681 | 0.00 | 20 | 0.00 |
| African | 20,607 | 0.00 | 201 | 0.00 |
| **Pacific** | | | | |
| Australian | 52,133 | 0.00 | 826 | 0.00 |
| New Zealander | 7,742 | 0.00 | 65 | 0.00 |
| **North America** | | | | |
| Acadian | 668,271 | 0.30 | 1,860 | 0.00 |
| American | 12,396,057 | 5.00 | 373,498 | 6.70 |
| Canadian | 560,891 | 0.20 | 6,501 | 0.10 |
| French Canadian | 2,167,127 | 0.90 | 20,094 | 0.40 |
| Pennsylvania German | 305,841 | 0.10 | 9,684 | 0.20 |
| United States | 643,602 | 0.30 | 21,625 | 0.40 |
| Other N. American | 12,927 | 0.00 | 392 | 0.00 |
| **Other** | | | | |
| Other groups | 63,562,346 | 25.60 | 795,095 | 14.30 |
| Unclassified/ Not reported | 26,101,616 | 10.50 | 790,121 | 14.30 |

**Note:**

In the 1980 and 1990 censuses, individuals were allowed to identify their ethnic origin with no prelisted categories. Some respondents reported a single ancestry group, while others reported more than one ancestry group. Since persons who reported multiple ancestries were included in more than one group, the sum of the persons reporting the ancestry group is greater than the total. For example, a person reporting "English-French" was tabulated in both the "English" and "French" categories. Some respondents reported "American" or "United States" as their ancestry group. Others reported a religious or unclassifiable response. The data for this table are based on a sample and are subject to sampling variability.

MAP.  DENSITY OF FOREIGN BORN IN INDIANA, 1860, 1900, 1950, 1990

# Percent of Foreign Born in Total Population

## 1860

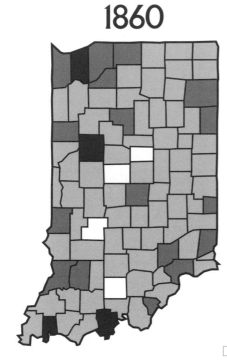

## 1900

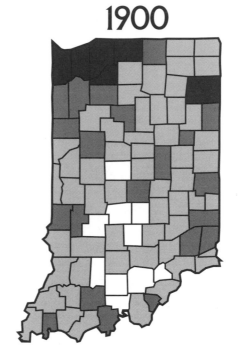

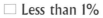

☐ Less than 1%
▨ 1% to 4.9%
▨ 5% to 9.9%
■ 10% to 25%

## 1950

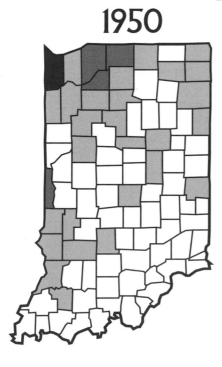

## 1990

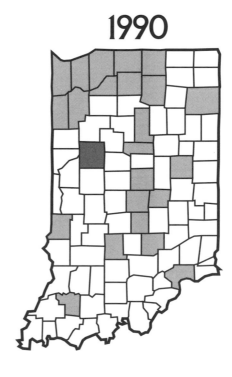

# SOURCES FOR CENSUS DATA TABLES

**Table 1. Foreign Born in Indiana by Ethnic Group, 1850–1990**

Note: Figures given for 1900 through 1950 are for the foreign-born white population. The rest are for the total foreign-born population.

1850: Indiana Historical Society, Education Division, *1850 Indiana Foreign-Born by Township*, 1991.

1860: Indiana Historical Society computerized Indiana federal census for 1860.

1870: Table VII.-pp. 352–53. *Ninth Census of the United States. Statistics of Population*. Washington: Government Printing Office, 1872. [The figures for England and Wales are combined, as are the figures for Sweden and Norway.]

1880: Indiana Historical Society, Education Division, *1880 Indiana Foreign-Born by Township*, 1991.

1890: Table 3. Foreign Born Population, Distributed According to Country of Birth, by Counties: 1890. *Compendium of the Eleventh Census: 1890*, pp. 625–27.

1900: Table 34. Foreign Born Population, Distributed According to Country of Birth, by Counties: 1900. *12th Census of the United States, Taken in the Year 1900. Population. Part I.* Washington: U.S. Census Office, 1901, pp. 747–48.

1910: Table I. Composition and Characteristics of the Population for Counties: 1910. *13th Census of the United States.* Volume II: *Composition and Characteristics. Population - Indiana.* U.S. Department of Commerce, Bureau of the Census, 1913, pp. 548–64.

1920: Table 23. Country of Origin and Mother Tongue of the Foreign White Stock, for the State: 1920. *14th Census of the United States. State Compendium. Indiana.* U.S. Department of Commerce, Bureau of the Census, 1924, p. 62.

1930, 1940: Table 14. Foreign-Born White, by Country of Birth, by Sex, for the State, Urban and Rural: 1940 and 1930. *16th Census of the United States. Population. Characteristics of the Population.* U.S. Department of Commerce, Bureau of the Census,

1941, p. 26. [Figures for Syria include individuals from Palestine.]

1950: Table 42a. Country of Birth of the Foreign-Born White Population, for Counties: 1950. *United States Census of Population: 1950. General Characteristics. Indiana. 1950 Population Census Report P-B14*, 1952, pp. 110–11. [Figures for England include individuals from Wales.]

1960: Table 28. Characteristics of the Population, for Counties: 1960. *Census of the Population: 1960.* Volume I: *Characteristics of the Population.* Part 16: *Indiana.* U.S. Department of Commerce, Bureau of the Census, 1961, pp. 129–35. [Figures for Canada include individuals from Newfoundland.]

1970: Table 119. Social Characteristics for Counties: 1970. *1970 Census of the Population.* Volume I: *Characteristics of the Population.* Part 16: *Indiana.* U.S. Department of Commerce, Bureau of the Census, 1972, pp. 479–86.

1980: Table 195. Citizenship and Year of Immigration for Foreign-Born Persons by Country of Birth: 1980. *1980 Census of Population. Detailed Population Characteristics. Indiana.* U.S. Department of Commerce, Bureau of the Census, 1983, p. 14.

1990: Table 139. Place of Birth of Foreign-Born Persons: 1990. *1990 Census of the Population, Social and Economic Characteristics, Indiana.* U.S. Department of Commerce, Bureau of the Census, September 1993, pp. 214–23.


**Table 2. Foreign Born by County as Percentage of Total Indiana Population, 1850–1990**

Note: Figures given for 1900 through 1950 are for the foreign-born white population. The rest are for the total foreign-born population.

1850, 1860, 1870, 1880: General population figures are from Table II. State of Indiana. Population by Counties: 1790–1880. *Tenth Census of the United*

*States. Statistics of Population.* Washington: Government Printing Office, 1883.

1850: Indiana Historical Society, Education Division, *1850 Indiana Foreign-Born by Township,* 1991.

1860: Indiana Historical Society computerized Indiana federal census for 1860.

1870: Foreign-born figures are from Table V. Nativity (General) 1870. *Ninth Census of the United States. Statistics of Population.* Washington: Government Printing Office, 1872.

1880: Table XIV. Native and Foreign-Born Population, by Counties, etc.: 1880. *Statistics of the Population of the United States at the Tenth Census (June 1, 1880).* U.S. Department of the Interior, Census Office, 1883, pp. 505–6.

1890: Table 3. Foreign Born Population, Distributed According to Country of Birth, by Counties: 1890. *Compendium of the Eleventh Census: 1890,* pp. 625–27.

1900, 1910: Table I. Composition and Characteristics of the Population for Counties: 1910. *13th Census of the United States.* Volume II: *Composition and Characteristics. Population - Indiana.* U.S. Department of Commerce, Bureau of the Census, 1913, pp. 548–64.

1920, 1930: Table 13. Composition of the Population, by Counties: 1930. *15th Census of the United States. Population. Characteristics of the Population.* U.S. Department of Commerce, Bureau of the Census, 1931–33, pp. 25–30.

1940: Foreign-born figures are from Table 24. Foreign-Born White, by Country of Birth, by Counties, and for Cities of 10,000 to 100,000: 1940. *16th Census of the United States. Population. Characteristics of the Population.* U.S. Department of Commerce, Bureau of the Census, 1941, pp. 71–73.

1950: Table 42. General Characteristics of the Population, for Counties: 1950. *United States Census of Population: 1950. General Characteristics. Indiana. 1950 Population Census Report P-B14,* 1952, pp. 104–9.

1960: Table 82. Social Characteristics of the Population, for Counties: 1960. *Census of the Population: 1960.* Volume I: *Characteristics of the Population.* Part 16: *Indiana.* U.S. Department of Commerce, Bureau of the Census, 1961, pp. 247–54.

1970: Table 119. Social Characteristics for Counties: 1970. *1970 Census of the Population.* Volume I: *Characteristics of the Population.* Part 16: *Indiana.* U.S. Department of Commerce, Bureau of the Census, 1972, pp. 479–86.

1980: Table 172. Nativity and Language for Counties: 1980. *1980 Census of Population, General Social and Economic Characteristics, Indiana.* U.S. Department of Commerce, Bureau of the Census, 1983, pp. 432–40.

1990: Table 138. Nativity, Citizenship, Year of Entry, Area of Birth, and Language Spoken at Home: 1990. *1990 Census of Population and Housing. Summary Social, Economic, and Housing Characteristics, Indiana.* U.S. Department of Commerce, Bureau of the Census, May 1992, pp. 204–13.

**Table 3. Foreign Born in Selected Cities, 1860–1990**

Note: Figures given for 1900 through 1950 are for the foreign-born white population. The rest are for the total foreign-born population.

1860: Indiana Historical Society computerized Indiana federal census for 1860.

1870, 1880: Table IX. Population, as Native and Foreign-Born, of Cities, etc.: 1880 and 1870. *Statistics of the Population of the United States at the Tenth Census (June 1, 1880).* U.S. Department of the Interior, Census Office, 1883, p. 449.

1890: Figures were not included in the table for 1890.

1900: Table II. Compostion and Characteristics of the Population for Cities of 25,000 or More. *13th Census of the United States.* Volume II: *Composition and Characteristics. Population - Indiana.* U.S. Department of Commerce, Bureau of the Census, 1913, p. 566. [This table from the 1910 federal census included figures for the 1900 census.]

1910: Table III. Compostition and Characteristics of the Population for Cities of 10,000 to 25,000. *13th Census of the United States.* Volume II: *Composition and Characteristics. Population - Indiana.* U.S. Department of Commerce, Bureau of the Census, 1913, p. 568.

1920: Table 12. Country of Birth of the Foreign-Born White, for Counties and for Cities of 10,000 or More: 1920. *14th Census of the United States. State Compendium. Indiana.* U.S. Department of Commerce, Bureau of the Census, 1924, pp. 54–55.

1930: Table 18. Foreign-Born White by Country of Birth, for Counties and for Cities of 10,000 or More: 1930. *15th Census of the United States. Population. Characteristics of the Population.* U.S. Department of Commerce, Bureau of the Census, 1931–33, pp. 720–21.

1940: Table 24. Foreign-Born White, by Country of Birth, by Counties, and for Cities of 10,000 to 100,000: 1940. *16th Census of the United States. Population. Characteristics of the Population.* U.S. Department of Commerce, Bureau of the Census, 1941, p. 74.

1950: Table 34a. Country of Birth of Foreign-Born White Population, for Standard Metropolitan Areas, Urbanized Areas, and Urban Places of 10,000 or More: 1950. *United States Census of Population: 1950. General Characteristics. Indiana. 1950 Population Census Report P-B14.* U.S. Department of Commerce, Bureau of the Census, 1952, p. 64. [Figures used are those for urban places.]

1960: Table 82. Social Characteristics of the Population, for Counties: 1960. *Census of the Population: 1960.* Volume I: *Characteristics of the Population.* Part 16: *Indiana.* U.S. Department of Commerce, Bureau of the Census, 1961, pp. 247–54. [Figures used are for the foreign born for the county. The published census figures for urbanized areas were for foreign stock, which includes persons with foreign parents.]

1970: Table 81. Ethnic Characteristics for Areas and Places: 1970. *1970 Census of the Population.* Volume I: *Characteristics of the Population.* Part 16: *Indiana.* U.S. Department of Commerce, Bureau of the Census, 1972, pp. 277–83. [The figures for Lafayette include the city of West Lafayette.]

1980: Table 195. Citizenship and Year of Immigration for Foreign-Born Persons by Country of Birth: 1980. *1980 Census of Population. Detailed Population Characteristics. Indiana.* U.S. Department of Commerce, Bureau of the Census, 1983, pp. 9–15.

1990: Table 172. Geographic Mobility, Commuting and Veteran Status: 1990. *1990 Census of Population, Social and Economic Characteristics, Indiana.* U.S. Department of Commerce, Bureau of the Census, September 1993, pp. 469–75.

### Table 4. Native American Population in Indiana, 1850–1990

1850, 1860, 1870: Table II. State of Indiana. Population by Counties: 1790–1870. *Ninth Census of the United States. Statistics of Population.* Washington: Government Printing Office, 1872, p. 27.

1860, 1870, 1880: Table V. Population, by Race and by Counties: 1880, 1870, 1860. *Statistics of the Population of the United States at the Tenth Census (June 1, 1880).* Washington: Government Printing Office, 1883, pp. 88–89.

1890: Table 19. White, Negro, and Indian Population, by Counties: 1880 to 1900. *Twelfth Census of the United States, Taken in the Year 1900. Population. Part I.* Washington: U.S. Census Office, 1901, pp. 536–37.

1900, 1910, 1920: Table 7. Indians, Chinese, and Japanese, for Counties and for Cities of 25,000 or More: 1920, 1910, and 1900. *14th Census of the United States. State Compendium. Indiana.* U.S. Department of Commerce, Bureau of the Census, 1924.

1930, 1940: Table 25. Indians, Chinese, and Japanese, by Sex, for Counties, and for Cities of 10,000 to 100,000: 1940 and 1930. *16th Census of the United States. Population. Characteristics of the Population.* U.S. Department of Commerce, Bureau of the Census, 1941, p. 74.

1950: Table 47. Indians, Japanese, and Chinese, by Sex, for Selected Counties and Cities: 1950. ["Figures shown for counties and for cities of 10,000 inhabitants or more with 10 or more Indians, Japanese, or Chinese in 1950."] *Census of Population: 1950.* Volume II: *Characteristics of the Population.* Part 14: *Indiana.* U.S. Department of Commerce, Bureau of the Census, 1952, p. 129.

1960: Table 28. Characteristics of the Population, for Counties: 1960. *Census of the Population: 1960.* Volume I: *Characteristics of the Population.* Part 16: *Indiana.* U.S. Department of Commerce, Bureau of the Census, 1961, pp. 129–35. ["Indians living in Indian territory or on reservations were not included in the official population count for the United States until 1890."]

1970: Table 34. Race by Sex, for Counties: 1970. *1970 Census of the Population.* Volume I: *Characteristics of the Population.* Part 16: *Indiana.* U.S. Department of Commerce, Bureau of the Census, 1972, pp. 156–58.

1980: U.S. Bureau of the Census "1980 Census Summary Tape File 4." Indiana Business Research Center, Graduate School of Business, Indiana University.

1990: 1990 Census Summary Tape File 1A, File 0, Geography and Tables P1 to P10. Information received via the State Data Center, Indiana State Library.

### Table 5. African-American Population in Indiana, 1850–1990

1850, 1860, 1870: Table II. State of Indiana. Population by Counties: 1790–1870. *Ninth Census of the United States. Statistics of Population.* Washington: Government Printing Office, 1872, pp. 26–27.

1880: Table V. Population, by Race and by Counties: 1880, 1870, 1860. *Statistics of the Population of the United States at the Tenth Census (June 1, 1880).* U.S. Department of the Interior, Census Office, 1883, pp. 88–89.

1890, 1900, 1910: Table I. Composition and Characteristics of the Population, for Counties: 1910. *13th Census of the United States.* Volume II: *Composition and Characteristics. Population - Indiana.* U.S. Department of Commerce, Bureau of the Census, 1913, pp. 548–64.

1910: *Negro Population, 1790–1915.* U.S. Department of Commerce, Bureau of the Census, 1918, pp. 806–7.

1920: Table 9. Composition and Characteristics of the Population, for Counties: 1920. *14th Census of the United States. Population - Indiana. Composition and Characteristics.* U.S. Department of Commerce, Bureau of the Census, pp. 288–96.

1930: *Negroes in the United States, 1920–1930.* U.S. Department of Commerce, Bureau of the Census, pp. 718–23.

1940: Population. Sex, Race, Age, & Rural-Farm Residence for Counties: 1940. *16th Census of the United States,* Series P-7, No. 27. U.S. Department of Commerce, Bureau of the Census, 1941.

1950: *Census of the Population: 1950.* Volume II: *Characteristics of the Population.* Part 14: *Indiana.* U.S. Department of Commerce, Bureau of the Census, 1952, pp. 104–9.

1960: *Census of the Population: 1960.* Volume I: *Characteristics of the Population.* Part 16: *Indiana.* U.S. Department of Commerce, Bureau of the Census, 1961, pp. 129–35.

1970: Table 34. Race by Sex, for Counties: 1970. *1970 Census of the Population.* Volume I: *Characteristics of the Population.* Part 16: *Indiana.* U.S. Department of Commerce, Bureau of the Census, 1972, pp. 156–58.

1980: U.S. Bureau of the Census "1980 Census Summary Tape File 4." Indiana Business Research Center, Graduate School of Business, Indiana University.

1990: 1990 Census Summary Tape File 1A, File 0, Geography and Tables P1 to P10. Information received via the State Data Center, Indiana State Library.

## Table 6. Foreign Born in Indiana by County, 1860

Indiana Historical Society computerized Indiana federal census for 1860.

## Table 7. Foreign Born in Indiana by County, 1910

Table I. Composition and Characteristics of the Population, for Counties: 1910. *13th Census of the United States.* Volume II: *Composition and Characteristics. Population - Indiana.* U.S. Department of Commerce, Bureau of the Census, 1913, pp. 548–64.

## Table 8. Foreign Born in Indiana by County, 1940

Table 24. Foreign-Born White, by Country of Birth, by Counties, and for Cities of 10,000 to 100,000: 1940. *16th Census of the United States. Population. Characteristics of the Population.* U.S. Department of Commerce, Bureau of the Census, 1941, pp. 71–73.

## Table 9. Foreign Born in Indiana by County, 1980

U.S. Bureau of the Census "1980 Census Summary Tape File 4." Indiana Business Research Center, Graduate School of Business, Indiana University.

## Table 10. Foreign Born in Indiana by County, 1990

Table 139. Place of Birth of Foreign-Born Persons: 1990. *1990 Census of Population, Social and Economic Characteristics, Indiana.* U.S. Department of Commerce, Bureau of the Census, September 1993, pp. 214–23.

## Table 11. Self-Identification Groups for Indiana, 1990

Table 137. Ancestry: 1990. *1990 Census of Population, Social and Economic Characteristics, Indiana.* U.S. Department of Commerce, Bureau of the Census, September 1993, pp. 194–203.

## Map. Density of Foreign Born in Indiana, 1860, 1900, 1950, 1990

This map was generated from the figures given in Table 2: Foreign Born by County as Percentage of Total Indiana Population, 1850–1990.

# INDEX

Woman's Improvement Club
    (Indianapolis), 19
WACs: blacks in, 24
WAVES: blacks in, 24
Women's Club (Richmond), 327
Wong Ah Mae, 91
Wong, David, 97
Wong, Hank, 97
Wong Kai Kah, 89, 91
Wood, Gen. Leonard, 200
Woodman (Knox County), 79
Woodward, William, 115
Workingmen's Institute
    (New Harmony), 501
Workingmen's Institute Library
    (New Harmony), 120
Workmen's Circle (Indianapolis), 329
Works Progress Administration: and blacks, 24
World Council of Churches, 562
World Federation of Hungarians, 242 n. 43
World War I: blacks, 20–21; Belgians, 363;
    German Americans, 147, 171–72;
    Greeks, 188, 190; Hungarian
    immigration, 228, 239; Italians, 290;
    Jews, 324; Mexican Americans,
    199–200, 208–9; Middle Easterners,
    382; Polish Americans, 448;
    Romanians, 467; Serbs, 560;
    Slovakians, 526; and American
    nationalism, 488
World War II: blacks, 24–25; effects of on
    English immigration, 120; German
    Americans, 173–74; Greeks, 196–97;
    Hungarians, 235, 238; Italian
    Americans, 291, 292; relocation of
    Japanese Americans, 299, 301, 302;

Japanese Americans, 305; Jews flee Nazi
    persecution, 316; Koreans, 339;
    adoption of war orphans, 341; Latvians,
    54; Mexican Americans 209–10; Polish
    immigration after, 447; Romanians,
    470; Serbs, 561; Slovaks, 526–27; and
    steel industry boom, 208–10
World War Memorial (Indianapolis), 290
World Zionist Organization of America, 331
World's Parliament of Religions, Women's
    Committee, 327
Wright, George, 112
Wüthrich family, 613 n. 157
Wyneken, Friedrich Konrad Dietrich, 154, 155
Wyszynski, Cardinal Stefan, 449

Xenia (Jefferson County), 364

Yamamoto, Catherine, 305
Yaney, Silvester, 289
Yavor Club, 561
Yee, Clifford, 97
Yee, Kathleen, 97
Yen, Terrence, 97
Ying, Rev. Peter, 100
Yoncheff, Bishop Kiril, 541, 549
York Township (Dearborn County):
    Dutch in, 365
Yorktown (Tippecanoe County), 478, 488
Young, Eusebio, 97
Young Men's Hibernian Society
    (Lafayette), 261
Young Peoples Endeavor Society (Attica), 488
Yovanovich, Stojilko, 562

Yu, Josephine, 97, 98, 99
Yune, Dr. Heun, 346, 350
Yung, Lee, 89
Yurin, Anna Rigovsky, 522
Yurin, Henry, 522
Yzaguirre, Raul, 216

Zactecas, Mexican baseball team
    (Calumet Region), 204
Zai, Dr. Baqi, 384–85
Zamfirescu, Nicolae, 459
Zandstra, Bartel H., 371, 372
Zandstra, Rev. Jack, 372
Zappia, Joseph, 292
Zarick, Dr. Waheeb, 382
Zarnx, Isidor, 612 n. 118
Zavatta, Rev. Octavius, 203
Zazas, John, 185, 189
Zborowski, Rev. Wladyslaw, 438
Zepi, Mary, 523
Zhou, Feng C., 97
Ziakoff, George, 543
Zimmermann family, 613 n. 157
Zinzendorf, Count Nikolaus Ludwig von,
    178 n. 39
Znaniecki, Florian, 442
Zondervan family, 367
Zore, Gerald S., 575
Zsigrai, Joe, 232
Zubowicz, Antoni, 439
Zur Oeveste, J. Heinrich Kessens, 157–58
Zwingli, Huldreich, 593
Zylman family, 376 n. 68

*Designer:* Dean Johnson Design, Inc., Indianapolis, Indiana
*Typeface:* AGaramond
*Typographer:* Douglas & Gayle Ltd., Indianapolis, Indiana
*Paper:* 60-pound Cougar Opaque Natural Vellum
*Printer:* BookCrafters, Chelsea, Michigan